PRACTICE AND PROCEDURE OF THE COMPANIES COURT

LLOYD'S COMMERCIAL LAW LIBRARY

Interests in Goods
by Norman Palmer and
Ewan McKendrick
(1993)

The Law of Insurance Contracts
second edition
by Malcolm A. Clarke
(1994)

EC Banking Law
second edition
by Marc Dassesse, Stuart Isaacs QC
and Graham Penn
(1994)

The Law and Practice
Relating to
Appeals from Arbitration Awards
by D. Rhidian Thomas
(1994)

Force Majeure and Frustration
of Contract
second edition
Edited by Ewan McKendrick
(1995)

The Practice and Procedure
of the Commercial Court
fourth edition
by The Hon. Sir Anthony Colman
and Victor Lyon
(1995)

Arbitration Law
by Robert Merkin
(looseleaf)

Professional Liability:
Law and Insurance
by Ray Hodgin
(1996)

Practice and Procedure
of the Companies Court
Edited by Alan Boyle QC
and Philip Marshall
(1997)

PRACTICE AND PROCEDURE OF THE COMPANIES COURT

GENERAL EDITORS

ALAN BOYLE QC
of Thirteen Old Square, Lincoln's Inn

AND

PHILIP MARSHALL
of Thirteen Old Square, Lincoln's Inn
Sometime fellow of Queen's College, Cambridge

CONTRIBUTORS

LESLIE KOSMIN QC, DAVID RICHARDS QC

DAVID CHIVERS, PHILIP GILLYON, JAMES POTTS
all of Erskine Chambers

AND

PHILIP JONES, DAVID DRAKE
of Thirteen Old Square, Lincoln's Inn

FOREWORD BY

THE HONOURABLE MR JUSTICE LIGHTMAN

|L|L|P|

LONDON HONG KONG
1997

LLP Limited
Legal & Business Publishing Division
69–77 Paul Street
London EC2A 4LQ

SOUTH EAST ASIA
LLP Asia Limited
Room 1101, Hollywood Centre
233 Hollywood Road
Hong Kong

British Library Cataloguing in Publication Data
A catalogue record for this book is
available from the British Library

ISBN 1–85044–502–8

Text set in 10/12 Times by
Interactive Sciences Ltd
Gloucester
Printed in Great Britain by
Hartnolls Ltd
Bodmin, Cornwall

FOREWORD

The need for an authoritative textbook on the practice and procedure of the Companies Court has long been recognised by judges and practitioners alike. The need has now been handsomely filled by this impressive work under the general editorship of a leading silk in this field, Mr Alan Boyle QC, assisted by a first-class team of experienced practitioners.

The alternative vehicles for commercial enterprise are the individual trader, the partnership and the limited company. Of these the limited company is for most businessmen the first choice. This fact is reflected in the increasing recognition of the critical importance of company law as a core subject for lawyers and law students. No legal practitioner can with confidence or competence give advice in a matter involving a limited company without some knowledge of company law and practice.[1] For company law can create traps for the unwary, and such knowledge is essential if the practitioner is to be alert to the hazards. To understand company law it is necessary, at the same time, to have some understanding of the role and functioning of the Companies Court.

Each of the year's four legal terms is broken up into consecutive fortnightly slots. In each slot one judge of the Chancery Division is assigned the duties of "Companies Judge". These duties are wide-reaching. The most widely known is to wind-up, and appoint administrators of, companies. But they extend far beyond, from sanctioning reductions of capital to resolving disputes between shareholders, from validating company charges to directing the examination of officers and disqualifying directors of companies. As a result of its specialist role the Companies Court has its own practices and procedures distinct from those of the Chancery Division. This work considers in turn each occasion when an application can or should be made to the Companies Court, and in the case of each such application sets out the relevant practice and procedure and a succinct commentary on the applicable rules of substantive law. The procedural guidance is sure and the commentary reliable, indeed authoritative.

Company law specialist practitioners can be expected to keep this book at hand at all times as a *vade-mecum* and indispensable resource. But practitioners in other fields of law also would be well advised to keep this book on their shelves. For it is user-friendly and affords the necessary help and guidance to those unfamiliar with the Companies Court and

1. In the same way he cannot advise in respect of any transaction without some knowledge of tax law. See, for example, *Hurlingham Estates* v. *Wilde* [1997] 1 Lloyd's Rep. 525.

its working. It enables both the experienced and the novice alike to proceed with confidence. It will always be near at hand when I am sitting as Companies Judge.

July 1997 THE HONOURABLE MR JUSTICE LIGHTMAN

Royal Courts of Justice

PREFACE

This book is intended to provide a practical and succinct guide to the practice and procedure of the Companies Court. Our aim has been to enable practitioners, whether they are regular users of the Companies Court, or inexperienced novices, and whether barristers or solicitors or other court users, to find the answer to any procedural question quickly and easily. We have sought to be comprehensive, and to cover not only the frequently used procedures such as the winding-up of insolvent companies, but all applications which might need to be made, whether in respect of a solvent or an insolvent company.

The task has turned out to be much harder, and to require a much larger book (as well as a much longer period of writing, for which we can only apologise to those we have kept waiting), than we anticipated when it was conceived. Court procedure ought to be clear and simple and as such to enable expeditious and economical access to justice. However, the nature of the court's jurisdiction over companies, the large number of applicable statutes, and the variety and extent of the different ways in which a company's affairs may be regulated by the court, necessarily mean that there is a multitude of different types of application, the procedure for which has been specifically tailored to meet particular requirements.

To make the book useful to practitioners, we therefore decided that all of this heterogeneous material had to be covered not only by reference to the underlying subject-matter of the application in question, but that we should also include general guidance on the main types of procedure in use for both solvent and insolvent companies.

The scheme of the book is as follows:

Part I contains two introductory chapters. Chapter 1 (by Philip Marshall) deals with the origin and jurisdiction of the Companies Court. Chapter 2 (also by Philip Marshall) contains a general guide to the practice and procedure relating to applications under the Companies Act 1985.

Part II deals with those proceedings and applications which affect solvent companies. Chapter 3 (by David Richards QC) deals with schemes of arrangement, and Chapter 4 (also by David Richards QC) with proceedings relating to capital. Chapter 5 (by Philip Gillyon) is a compendious guide to a large number of other miscellaneous applications which may need to be made in relation to the affairs of a solvent company under the Companies Act 1985.

There follow two chapters which deal with the most common forms of contentious proceedings affecting solvent companies: petitions for relief in respect of unfair prejudice under the Companies Act 1985, s. 459 (Chapter 6, by Leslie Kosmin QC), and petitions for winding-up a company on the "just and equitable" ground (Chapter 7, also by Leslie Kosmin QC).

These are followed by a Chapter (by Philip Marshall) dealing with the important topic of investigations into the affairs of a company, and the related court applications to which this can give rise.

Part III deals with insolvent companies. The most obvious and important jurisdiction here is for winding-up. Detailed and comprehensive guidance to the procedure in this important area is contained in Chapter 9 (by Philip Gillyon). Chapter 10 (by Philip Jones) contains a general guide to the procedures, by way of originating and ordinary application, introduced by part 7 of the Insolvency Rules 1986. This is followed by a chapter (also by Philip Jones) examining the specific procedures applicable to the many applications which may need to be made in connection with the carrying out of the liquidation of a company. Chapter 12 (by myself) is devoted to the procedures relating to the making and carrying out of administration orders. Chapter 13 (by James Potts) deals with the applications which may need to be made in connection with the receivership of a company, and Chapter 14 (by David Drake) covers applications in voluntary arrangements. Finally in part III, there is a chapter (by Philip Marshall) devoted to the various ways in which the affairs of an insolvent company may be investigated, and the applications to the court which may need to be made by the liquidator or others in this connection.

Part IV contains a single chapter (Chapter 16, by David Chivers) dealing with a topic which is *sui generis* but without which the book would be incomplete, namely, the practice and procedure governing the disqualification of directors of companies under the Company Directors Disqualification Act 1986.

I would like to thank all of the contributors for their efforts, and all of the staff at LLP for their patience and assitance.

It has been our aim to make this book as useful as possible to practitioners. However, we are acutely aware that it may contain errors and omissions, and that we may not have made it as user-friendly as it should be. I would greatly appreciate it if any reader who detects any errors or omissions or who has any suggestions for improvements, amendments or additional material would contact me, so that these may be considered for inclusion in any later edition.

This is a book about practice and procedure, not substantive law. For the latter, reference should be made to the standard texts on company law.

The law and practice are stated as at 1 July 1997

20 July 1997 ALAN BOYLE QC

Thirteen Old square.
Lincoln's Inn,
London WC2A 3UA

CONTRIBUTORS

ALAN BOYLE QC was called to the Bar by Lincoln's Inn in 1972 and was appointed a Queen's Counsel in 1991. He is a member of the chambers at Thirteen Old Square, and his practice encompasses general chancery and commercial litigation, including company law and corporate insolvency. He is a member of the Supreme Court Rules Committee.

PHILIP MARSHALL was called to the Bar by Lincoln's Inn in 1986. He is a member of the chambers at Thirteen Old Square, and his practice includes company and insolvency litigation including asset recovery and fraud claims arising out of corporate insolvency. He has acted in several of the major insolvency investigations in recent years including those arising out of the collapse of the Maxwell empire. He was formerly a Fellow of Queens' College, Cambridge.

DAVID CHIVERS is a barrister specialising in company law and corporate insolvency. He attended Downing College, Cambridge, was called to the Bar in 1983 and has practised from his present Chambers since 1984. He has contributed to *Co-operatives that Work* (spokesman) and *Gore-Browne on Companies* (Jordans, 44th edn).

DAVID DRAKE is a former scholar of Worcester College, Oxford, who was called to the Bar in 1994. He is a member of the Inner Temple, but practises at Thirteen Old Square in Lincoln's Inn. His areas of specialism include corporate insolvency, commercial and private international law.

PHILIP GILLYON was called to the Bar by the Middle Temple in 1988. He joined Erskine Chambers in 1989 and has practised since that date, specialising in company and corporate insolvency law.

PHILIP JONES was called to the Bar in 1985. Since then he has specialised in commercial litigation but with a particular emphasis on disputes relating to companies, insolvency and financial services, and practises at Thirteen Old Square, Lincoln's Inn. In 1994 he was appointed Junior Counsel to the Crown, Chancery. In that capacity he often acts for, and advises, the DTI, the Insolvency Service and HM Treasury in respect of regulatory matters affecting companies and the financial services industry.

LESLIE KOSMIN QC was called to the Bar by the Middle Temple in 1976 and was appointed a Queen's Counsel in 1994. He is a member of Erskine Chambers, and his practice encompasses company law and corporate insolvency, especially litigation in the field of shareholder disputes, minority rights, directors duties, takeovers and share transactions. He was a member of the Law Commission Working Party on Shareholder Remedies and is a former college lecturer and Supernumerary Fellow of Gonville and Caius College, Cambridge.

JAMES POTTS was called to the Bar by Gray's Inn in 1994 and is a tenant at Erskine Chambers. His practice includes all aspects of company law, corporate insolvency and the law of partnerships, especially litigation and advisory work involving shareholder disputes, the conduct of meetings, minority rights, directors' duties, disqualification proceedings and professional negligence.

DAVID RICHARDS QC has been in practice at the Bar since 1975, specialising in company and insolvency law, and is a member of Erskine Chambers. He was appointed a QC in 1992 and had previously been Junior Counsel to the DTI from 1989 to 1992. He is a contributor to *Buckley on the Companies Acts.*

OUTLINE CONTENTS

DETAILED CONTENTS

TABLE OF CASES

TABLE OF LEGISLATION, RULES AND CONVENTIONS

TABLE OF STATUTORY INSTRUMENTS

TABLE OF PRACTICE DIRECTIONS

ABBREVIATIONS

CA 1862	Companies Act 1862
CA 1867	Companies Act 1867
CA 1879	Companies Act 1879
CA 1900	Companies Act 1900
CA 1907	Companies Act 1907
CA 1928	Companies Act 1928
CA 1929	Companies Act 1929
CA 1948	Companies Act 1948
CA 1980	Companies Act 1980
CA 1983	Companies Act 1983
CA 1985	Companies Act 1985
CA 1989	Companies Act 1989
CDDA 1986	Company Directors Disqualification Act 1986
FSA 1986	Financial Services Act 1986
IA 1985	Insolvency Act 1985
IA 1986	Insolvency Act 1986
ICA 1982	Insurance Companies Act 1982
IR 1986	Insolvency Rules 1986
RSC	Rules of the Supreme Court

PART 1

INTRODUCTION

CHAPTER 1

ORIGIN AND JURISDICTION OF THE COMPANIES COURT

1.1 Nature and origin

The term "Companies Court" is one which is adopted within the Chancery Division of the High Court of Justice. Despite the fact that county courts have jurisdiction to, and do frequently deal with business, such as winding-up, which is generally listed in the High Court as Companies Court business, the phrase "Companies Court" has no currency in county courts.[1]

Whether through frequent usage or the separate procedural requirements associated with it, the title "Companies Court" is often mentioned in a way which suggests that a distinct sub-division exists as a part of the Chancery Division of the High Court of Justice which has exclusive jurisdiction in relation to company matters. In fact these impressions, both as to the nature as well as the jurisdiction of the Companies Court, are false.

The Companies Court does not operate as a distinct entity within the High Court in the same way as the Patents, Admiralty or Commercial Courts which have their own statutory foundation and jurisdiction.[2] The term "Companies Court" is instead merely a descriptive one. The position was explained in this way by Brightman J. in *Re Shilena Hosiery Co. Ltd*[3]:

"The Companies Court is not a court separate and distinct from the High Court, with its own peculiar jurisdiction. The jurisdiction to wind up a company is conferred on the High Court, not the Companies Court . . . nor is the companies judge invested with a special jurisdiction not possessed by a High Court judge sitting elsewhere. The Companies Court is a way of describing the High Court when dealing with matters originating in the chambers of the Bankruptcy Registrar when dealing with company matters, and the companies judge is a way of describing a High Court judge when trying such matters . . . "

1.1.1 Given its purely descriptive function one might expect the adoption of the title "Companies Court" at an early stage resulting from practitioners, judges and court staff using it as a convenient rubric for the Chancery Division when operating in the particular

1. For details of county court jurisdiction in the winding-up of companies see IA 1986, s. 117. Generally, where the amount of a company's paid up share capital does not exceed £120,000, the county court of the district in which the company's registered office is situated has concurrent jurisdiction with the High Court to wind up the company.

2. See ss. 6 and 62 of the Supreme Court Act 1981.

3. [1980] Ch. 219, at 220; approved by the Court of Appeal in *Fabric Sales Ltd* v. *Eratex Ltd* [1984] 1 WLR 863 (in which what appeared to be contrasting dicta of Buckley J. in *Eastern Holdings Establishment of Vaduz* v. *Singer and Friedlander Ltd* [1967] 1 WLR 1017 were explained). See also *Re Rolls Razor (No. 2)* [1970] Ch. 576, at 588 *et seq.*; *Re Wool Textile Employers Mutual Insurance Co. Ltd* [1955] 1 WLR 862, at 867; *Re Tasbian Ltd (No. 2)* [1990] BCC 322 and *Re Probe Data Systems Ltd (No. 3)* [1992] BCC 110.

manner to which Brightman J. referred. In fact the phrase "Companies Court" is a relatively modern one dating back to no earlier than the Companies Act 1929. Furthermore, although as presently used the term does have the advantage of convenience, in origin it appears instead to have resulted from a change in court forms designed largely to assuage sensibilities. Thus under pre-1929 companies legislation forms were prescribed in which the term "Companies Winding-up" was adopted. This was disliked by those who desired to apply to the court for relief under the Act in relation to companies which were entirely solvent, such as for example, for confirmation of a reduction of capital. Accordingly with the new 1929 Act came forms with a fresh heading, "Companies Court", a title which quickly gained wide currency.[4]

1.1.2 Yet the current adoption of the term "Companies Court" is not merely a matter of usage. It has been given legitimacy in a number of ways. Matters are listed separately in the Chancery Division under the heading of "Companies Court"[5] with the judge sitting being described as the Companies Court Judge. Similarly, the Companies Court Judge is assisted by Companies Court Registrars defined in the Rules of Court[6] as officers of the High Court who are registrars under any rules for the time being in force relating to the winding-up of companies.[7] The court office dealing with the issue of applications relating to the Companies Court is referred to in the Rules of Court as the office of the Companies Court Registrar.[8] Many Practice Directions issued for the Chancery Division also adopt the term "Companies Court".[9]

1.2 Jurisdiction

The caseload of the High Court when dealing with matters under the description Companies Court arises as follows. Under s. 61(1) and sch. 1 of the Supreme Court Act 1981, the business of the High Court in relation to all causes and matters involving the exercise of the High Court's jurisdiction under the enactments relating to companies is assigned to the Chancery Division. This statutory provision is augmented by the rules of court contained in RSC O. 102, r. 5(1) whereby all proceedings to which that Order relates are assigned to the Chancery Division. Order 102 relates to all applications to the High Court under the statutory jurisdiction conferred by the Companies Act 1985 other than proceedings under s. 459 of that Act.[10] Each of the above general heads of business assigned to the Chancery Division is customarily dealt with by the Companies Court. The consequent practical effect is that the Companies Court deals with matters falling within the following categories:

(1) Applications and proceedings commenced in the High Court under the statutory

4. See *Re Wool Textile Employers Mutual Insurance Co. Ltd*, *supra*, and *Re Rolls Razor (No. 2)*, *supra*.
5. See Chancery Division Practice Direction No. 12, para. (iii) (*Supreme Court Practice 1997*, Vol. 2, p. 189, para. 849).
6. RSC O. 102, r. 1.
7. The present provision is contained in the IR 1986 (S.I. 1986 No. 1925), r. 13.2 (defining a registrar for the purposes of High Court proceedings as a Registrar in Bankruptcy of the High Court).
8. RSC O. 102, rr. 2(4), 3(2), 4(2), 7(1), 11.
9. See the recent *Chancery Guide*, p. 1, para. 1.3 and pp. 49–50, para. 12.2 brought into force by the Practice Direction (Chancery Division: Procedure and Case Management) [1995] 1 WLR 785.
10. These relate to protection of a company's members against unfair prejudice and are governed by the Companies (Unfair Prejudice Applications) Proceedings Rules 1986 (S.I. 1986 No. 2000).

jurisdiction conferred by the Companies Act 1985 (as amended by the Companies Act 1989) and for which provision is made under Order 102.[11]

(2) Applications and proceedings under s. 459 of the Companies Act 1985 (applications relating to conduct of the affairs of a company in a manner which is unfairly prejudicial to the interests of members).[12]

(3) Certain proceedings under the Company Directors Disqualification Act 1986.[13]

(4) Certain applications and proceedings under the Insurance Companies Act 1982 (as amended by the Insurance Companies (Third Insurance Directive) Regulations 1994[14] and the Insurance Companies (Amendment) Regulations 1994)[15] relating to schemes for the transfer of long term business carried on by insurance companies.

(5) Applications and proceedings under the Insolvency Act 1986 relating to companies.[16]

(6) Actions by a debenture holder against a company which has been the subject of an order for its winding-up.[17]

1.2.1 As mentioned above, the fact that as a matter of practice the Companies Court deals with the above matters does not operate as a jurisdictional bar upon another court

11. The jurisdiction of the High Court under the CA 1985 to which Order 102 refers in assigning business to the Chancery Division arises in the following manner: under s. 744 of the CA 1985, the court having jurisdiction to deal with applications and proceedings under the Act is defined as the court having jurisdiction to wind up the company concerned. By virtue of IA 1986, s. 117(1) the High Court has jurisdiction to wind up any company registered in England and Wales and also by virtue of s. 221(1) and (3) and s. 225 of the 1986 Act it also has jurisdiction to wind up unregistered companies and overseas companies which have carried on business in Great Britain.

12. These proceedings are not regulated by RSC O. 102 but by the Companies (Unfair Prejudice Applications) Proceedings Rules 1986, *supra*.

13. The jurisdiction of the High Court on the basis of which this business arises, flows from the following provisions of the 1986 Act: s. 2(2) (disqualification on conviction of an indictable offence may be ordered by the court having jurisdiction to wind up the company in relation to which the offence was committed); s. 3(4) (disqualification for persistent breaches of companies legislation may be ordered by the court having jurisdiction to wind up a company in relation to which an offence or default referred to in the section has been or is alleged to have been committed); s. 4(2) (disqualification for fraud and other matters in the context of winding-up may be ordered by a court having jurisdiction to wind up any company in relation to which an offence or other default referred to in the section has been or is alleged to have been committed); s. 6(3) (in the context of disqualification of unfit directors of insolvent companies the court which is required to make a disqualification order is as follows: (a) in the case of a person who is or has been a director of a company which is being wound up by the court, the court by which the company is being wound up; (b) in the case of a person who is or has been a director of a company which is being wound up voluntarily, any court having jurisdiction to wind up the company; (c) in the case of a person who is or has been a director of a company in relation to which an administration order is in force, the court by which that order was made; and (d) in any other case the High Court); s. 8(3) (disqualification following investigation of a company may be ordered by the High Court). Additionally rr. 1(2)(c) and 7 of the Insolvent Companies (Disqualification of Unfit Directors) Proceedings Rules 1987 (S.I. 1986 No. 2023), which apply to applications under ss. 7(1) and 8 of the 1986 Act, provide for hearings of applications before a registrar defined as having the same meaning as provided for in IR 1986, rr. 13.2(4) and (5). As a result of the operation of RSC O. 102 and r. 13.2 of the Insolvency Rules, in the High Court, this in practice is a reference to the Companies Court Registrar.

14. S.I. 1994 No. 1696.

15. S.I. 1994 No. 3132.

16. By s. 117(1) of the 1986 Act the High Court has jurisdiction to wind up any company registered in England and Wales. It also has jurisdiction to wind up an unregistered company under s. 221(1) and (3) and also an overseas company which has carried on business in Great Britain under s. 225 of the Act.

17. RSC O. 4, r. 2 whereby it is provided that hearings in chambers in relation to any such action are to be dealt with by the officer of the High Court who is a registrar within the meaning of any rules for the time being in force relating to the winding-up of companies. In practice this is the Companies Court Registrars.

within the Chancery Division dealing with a matter coming within the above categories.[18] Where it is for some special reason convenient to do so, such a court might well be prepared to deal with the matter.[19] An example of a case in which it might be more appropriate for a matter normally dealt with by the Companies Court to be heard in another court in the Chancery Division is where the matter is more appropriate to be dealt with by writ. This might be the case with proceedings arising out of the winding-up of a company normally commenced by a misfeasance summons under s. 212 of the Insolvency Act 1986 where third party proceedings are likely. Given that under a misfeasance summons third party proceedings are unavailable, a writ action in the Chancery Division may be considered more appropriate.[20]

1.2.2 Absent particular circumstances, however, another court within the Chancery Division could be expected to decline to hear the matter and to remit it to the Companies Court.[21] Remitting the matter to the Companies Court has the obvious advantage of the case being dealt with, at least for most interlocutory matters, by court officers greatly experienced in companies matters, namely the Companies Court Registrars.

1.2.3 Furthermore, by virtue of the provisions of ss. 4(3), 5(5) and 61(6) of the Supreme Court Act 1981,[22] it is permissible for a judge of a Division of the High Court other than the Chancery Division to hear a matter coming within the normal province of the Companies Court, a position which accords with the general approach prior to the 1981 Act whereby the High Court was treated as a single integrated court despite the existence of divisions.[23] In considering dealing with such a matter, however, the relevant judge of another division would normally determine whether the cause or matter required to be transferred.[24] Given that one of the intentions behind the assignment of company business to the Chancery Division and the existence of the Companies Court within that Division is to ensure that companies matters are dealt with efficiently in the High Court by those having particular experience, it will usually be convenient to transfer.[25] Irrespective of transfer, however, the judge hearing the matter in another Division may simply refuse to exercise any jurisdiction which he may have.[26] If the judge does order the matter to be transferred or refuses to exercise jurisdiction, the party bringing the matter before a judge in the wrong Division may be required to pay for any wasted costs incurred thereby.[27]

18. Conversely the Companies Court might also deal with matters outside its normal caseload where to do so avoids multiplicity of proceedings and saves costs (see *Re Therm-a-Stor* [1996] 3 All ER 228).

19. Compare *Re Therm-a-Stor, supra*.

20. See *Re Shilena Hosiery, supra*, at 227, *Re Singer and Co. (Hat Manufacturers) Ltd* [1943] Ch. 121 and *Re Land Securities Co.* 2 Mans. 127.

21. See the approach taken in *Eastern Holdings Establishment of Vaduz* v. *Singer and Friedlander Ltd* [1967] 1 WLR 1017.

22. See also Practice Direction (High Court: Division) [1973] 1 WLR 627. This provides that any division of the High Court to which a cause or matter is assigned has jurisdiction to grant any remedy or relief arising out of or related to or connected with any claim made in that cause or matter notwithstanding that proceedings for such remedy or relief are assigned to another division of the court. It was applied by Donaldson J. in *Midland Bank Ltd* v. *Stamps* [1978] 1 WLR 635 where the judge exercised jurisdiction in the Commercial Court to deal with a mortgage action which was assigned to the Chancery Division under RSC O. 88, r. 2.

23. See *Re Hastings (No. 3)* [1959] Ch. 368 at 379 (per Vaisey J.).

24. S. 65 of the 1981 Act.

25. See *Pinney* v. *Hunt* (1877) 6 Ch.D. 98.

26. See *Pinney* v. *Hunt* (1877), *supra*; *Bradford* v. *Young* [1884] 26 Ch.D 656.

27. See *Re Pollard* [1888] 20 QBD 656.

CHAPTER 2

PROCEEDINGS UNDER THE COMPANIES ACT 1985: GENERAL PRACTICE AND PROCEDURE

2.1 Commencing proceedings

Proceedings in the Companies Court under the jurisdiction conferred by the Companies Act 1985 are commenced in one of three ways, namely, originating summons, originating motion, and petition. These are the three permissible forms of commencing proceedings in the context of matters governed by RSC O. 102.[1] Proceedings under the 1985 Act which are not governed by O. 102,[2] namely, those under s. 459 of the 1985 Act,[3] are required to be commenced by petition.[4]

Certain procedural requirements are common to each method of commencing proceedings. Thus all proceedings under Order 102 are required to be entitled in the matter of the company in question and in the matter of the Companies Act 1985.[5] The same applies in the context of petitions under s. 459.[6] As a matter of practice, a summons, motion or petition will also be entitled in the Chancery Division and, in the case of proceedings governed by Order 102, will state the section of the Act and the rule and paragraph of Order 102 under which the application is made.[7] Additionally, all documents presented, issued or filed in the Companies Court must meet the prescribed requirements as to format.[8]

I. APPLICATIONS BY ORIGINATING SUMMONS

2.2 Applications by originating summons

Except where otherwise specifically provided, proceedings under the Act must be commenced by originating summons.[9] This is in accordance with the general rule that all

1. See RSC O. 102, rr. 2–4.
2. All proceedings under the Act are governed by RSC O. 102 save for those under s. 459. See Chapter 1, para. 1.2, *supra*.
3. Broadly covering applications relating to the conduct of the affairs of a company in a manner which is unfairly prejudicial to the interests of members.
4. See s. 459(1) of the 1985 Act and the Companies (Unfair Prejudice Applications) Proceedings Rules 1986 (S.I. 1986 No. 2000).
5. RSC O. 102, r. 5(2). The company name is always given before the reference to the Act (*Supreme Court Practice 1995*, Vol. 1, p. 1506, para. 102/1/6).
6. This would appear to be the effect of the Companies (Unfair Prejudice Applications) Proceedings Rules 1986 r. 2(1) which applies the Rules of the Supreme Court and practice of the High Court to proceedings under s. 459 in the High Court save where inconsistent with the Act and 1986 Rules.
7. *Supreme Court Practice 1997*, Vol. 1, p. 1533, para. 102/1/6.
8. See RSC O. 66, r. 1(1).
9. See RSC O. 102, r. 2(1).

proceedings under a statute are to be begun by originating summons unless specifically required to be begun by other means.[10]

As a result of this rule, most types of application under the Act are required to be commenced by the originating summons procedure. A detailed treatment of the applications coming within this category is contained in Part II of this book but a brief description of those which it includes are discussed below.

2.2.1 Applications pursuant to s. 6(2) (Alteration of Objects)

These applications relate to circumstances in which a company has passed a resolution altering its objects and an application has been made to the court to have the alteration cancelled.[11] If such an application is made, a prescribed notice is required forthwith to be delivered to the registrar of companies followed by an office copy of the court order made on the application within 15 days from the date of that order.[12] S. 6(2) allows applications for an extension of time for delivery of such documents. If the hearing relating to the application for cancellation is yet to be concluded and the need for an extension is anticipated, the matter can be raised before the court at that stage without the need for a new set of proceedings. Alternatively, if liberty to apply has been granted in the court's order in the cancellation proceedings, the application for extension of time can be made in the form of an ordinary interlocutory summons rather than an originating summons. Only if neither of these routes is available will an originating summons prove necessary.

2.2.2 Applications pursuant to s. 169(8) (Company Purchase of Own Shares)

Proceedings of this type arise in the context of off-market purchases by a company of its own shares.[13] In the case of such purchases the contract must be approved in advance[14] and a copy of the contract, if in writing, or if not in writing a memorandum of its terms, must be kept at its registered office, from the conclusion of the contract for a period of 10 years.[15] The copy contract and memorandum are to be open to inspection by members in the case of private companies, and by anyone in the case of public companies, without charge.[16] If inspection is refused, application may be made to compel immediate inspection under s. 169(8).

2.2.3 Applications under s. 185(6) (Delivery of Certificates for Shares etc.)

Applications under this provision relate to the completion and delivery of certificates for shares, debentures and certificates for debenture stock allotted or transferred. Unless the conditions of such shares, debentures and debenture stock otherwise provide, this must be

10. RSC O. 5, r. 3.
11. S. 5.
12. S. 6(1).
13. Chapter VII of part V of the Act.
14. Ss. 164 and 165.
15. S. 169(4). By this provision the period of 10 years is calculated as beginning with the date on which the purchase of all the shares in pursuance of the contract is completed or (as the case may be) the date on which the contract otherwise determines.
16. S. 169(5).

done within two months of their allotment or within two months of the date on which a transfer is lodged with the company (as the case may be).[17] If this is not done and 10 days elapse after a notice is served requiring the default to be made good, application may be made under s. 185(6) by the person entitled to have the certificates or debentures issued to him, for an order directing the company and any officer of it to make good the default.[18]

2.2.4 Applications under s. 191(5) (Register of Debenture Holders)

The register of debenture holders of a company is to be open to inspection by the registered holder of any debentures, or any shareholder, without a fee, and to any other person on payment of a fee.[19] A copy of the register may also be required by such persons on payment of a fee.[20] If inspection is refused or copies refused or not forwarded, application may be made for immediate inspection or for copies to be provided under s. 191(5).

2.2.5 Applications under s. 192(4) (Relief of Trustees of Deed Securing Issue of Debentures)

These proceedings relate to trustees of a deed for securing an issue of debentures. A meeting of debenture holders may pass a resolution carried by a majority of not less than three-quarters in value for the relief of trustees' liability.[21] The method of summoning a meeting for this purpose may be provided for in the deed. If it is not, approval must be sought from the court for the manner of summoning the meeting under s. 192(4).

2.2.6 Applications under s. 216(1) (Failure to Provide Information regarding Interests in Shares)

Proceedings of this type relate to notices issued by a public company under s. 212 requiring the provision of information regarding interests in issued share capital carrying voting rights. Where a notice is served on a person who is or was (within the previous three years) interested in shares in the company and the person fails to provide the information within the time specified in the notice, then the company may apply under s. 216(1) for an order directing that the shares in question be subject to the restrictions imposed by part XV of the Act (among other things preventing transfers of the shares and removing voting rights applying in respect of them[22]).

2.2.7 Applications under s. 219(4) (Register of Interests in Shares)

These applications arise in relation to the register of interests in shares maintained by a public company[23] and to reports prepared by a public company following an investigation

17. S. 185(1).
18. See also s. 185(7).
19. S. 191(1).
20. S. 191(2).
21. S. 192(4).
22. S. 454(1).
23. As to which see ss. 211 and 220.

into interests in shares under s. 212 where the investigation was instituted on the basis of a requisition by members.[24] The register of interests in shares and any such report is to be open to inspection by any member or any other person without charge. Also any member or other person may require a copy of the register or report or any part of it on payment of a fee and on being so required the company must send a copy to the person requesting it within 10 days beginning with the day next following that of receipt of the request.[25] If inspection is refused or a copy which is required is not sent within the proper period, application may be made under s. 219(4) for an order to compel an immediate inspection and for directions that the copy required be sent to the person requiring it.

2.2.8 Applications under s. 242(3) (Delivery of Annual Accounts etc.)

The directors of a company are required in respect of each financial year to deliver to the registrar a copy of its annual accounts and reports.[26] If these requirements are not complied with and if the directors of the company fail to make good their default within 14 days after the service of a notice on them requiring their compliance, application may be made to the court under s. 242(3) by any member or creditor of the company concerned, or by the registrar of companies, for an order directing the directors (or any of them) to make good the default within a specified time period.

2.2.9 Applications under s. 288(5) (Register of Directors and Secretaries)

Every company is required to keep at its registered office a register of its directors and secretaries.[27] Such register is required to be open to the inspection of any member of the company without charge and also to any other person on payment of a fee.[28] If inspection of the register is refused, application may be made to the court under s. 288(5) for an order compelling an immediate inspection.

2.2.10 Applications under s. 304(4) (Directors' Representations)

A company may by ordinary resolution remove a director before the expiration of his period of office, notwithstanding anything in its Articles or in any agreement between it and him, but special notice is required of such a resolution.[29] On receipt of a notice of an intended resolution to remove a director under s. 303, the company is required to send a copy of that notice to the director concerned.[30] The director concerned may then make representations in writing to the company concerning the intended resolution and may request their notification to members of the company. The company is then required, unless the representations are received by it too late for it to do so, in any notice of the resolution given to members of the company to state the fact that the representations have been made and to send a copy of them to each member of the company to whom the notice

24. Ss. 214 and 215.
25. S. 219(1) and (2).
26. S. 242(1).
27. S. 288(1).
28. S. 288(3).
29. S. 303(1) and (2).
30. S. 304(1).

of the meeting is sent.[31] Application may be made, however, under s. 304(4) by the company or by any other person who claims to be aggrieved, for a direction that copies of the representations need not be sent out and that the representations need not be read out at the meeting on the basis that the rights conferred by s. 304 are being abused to secure needless publicity for defamatory matter.

2.2.11 Applications under s. 318(9) (Directors' Service Contracts)

A company is required, subject to certain limited exceptions,[32] to keep at an appropriate place[33] a copy of each of its director's contracts of service which is in writing or if not in writing, a written memorandum of their terms. Similarly, it is required to keep a copy of any written contract or a memorandum of terms of employment of each director employed with a subsidiary of the company.[34] Every copy contract and memorandum required to be kept by the company is to be open to inspection by any member of the company without charge.[35] If inspection is refused, application may be made under s. 318(9) for an order compelling immediate inspection.

2.2.12 Applications under s. 326(6) (Register of Directors' Interests)

A director is required to give notice to the company in writing, among other things, of the existence of any interest which he has in shares in or debentures of the company.[36] The company is required to maintain a register for the purposes of entering against each director's name any information received pursuant to these obligations, together with the date on which it was entered.[37] The register is to be open to the inspection of any member without charge and of any other person on payment of a fee.[38] Also any member or any other person may require a copy of the register or any part of it to be provided on payment of a fee.[39] If inspection is refused or a copy is not sent within a period of 10 days after the date on which a requirement for a copy has been received by the company, application may be made under s. 326(6) for an order compelling immediate inspection of the register and/or directing that a copy be sent to the person requiring it.

31. S. 304(2).
32. A company is not required to keep a copy of a director's contract of service with it or with a subsidiary company if the contract requires him to work wholly or mainly outside the United Kingdom but a memorandum giving specified details is required to be maintained (s. 318(5)). Additionally, a company is not required to keep a copy of a contract nor a memorandum setting out the terms of a contract with a director at a time when the unexpired portion of the term for which the contract is to be in force is less than 12 months or where the contract can, within the ensuing 12 months, be terminated by the company without payment of compensation (s. 318(11)).
33. Defined in s. 318(3) as the company's registered office, a place where its register of members is kept or its place of business (provided that it is situated in that part of Great Britain in which the company is registered) (s. 318(3)).
34. S. 318(1).
35. S. 318(7).
36. S. 324(1).
37. S. 325(1) and (2).
38. S. 325(5) and sch. 13, para. 25.
39. S. 325(5) and sch. 13, para. 26.

2.2.13 Applications under s. 356(6) (Register of Members)

Every company is required to keep a register of its members.[40] A company may also be required to maintain an index of members if it has more than 50 in total.[41] Save in particular circumstances provided for under the Act, the register and any index are to be open to the inspection of any member without charge and any other person on payment of a fee.[42] Any member and any other person may require a copy of the register or any part of it on payment of a fee. The copy must be sent within 10 days of the date from which the requirement is received by the company.[43] If inspection is refused or a copy is not sent within the proper period, application may be made to the court under s. 356(6) for an order compelling immediate inspection or directing that the copies required be sent to the persons requiring them.

2.2.14 Applications under s. 371(1) (Company Meetings)

If it proves impracticable to call a meeting of the company in any manner in which meetings of that company may be called, or to conduct a meeting in a manner prescribed by the company's articles or by the Act, application may be made to the court under s. 371(1) by any director of the company or any member who would be entitled to vote at the meeting, for an order that a meeting be called, held and conducted as directed by the court.[44]

2.2.15 Applications under s. 377(3) (Circulation of Members' Resolutions)

It is the duty of a company, on the requisition in writing of the required number of members,[45] to give notice of any resolution which can properly be moved and is intended to be moved at the next annual general meeting to all members of the company that are entitled to receive notice of the meeting. The company is also required, on the requisition of the same number of members, to circulate to members entitled to notice of the next annual general meeting, any statement of not more than 1000 words with respect to the matter referred to in any proposed resolution or business to be dealt with at that meeting.[46] Application can be made, however, under s. 377(3) to the court by the company or by any person who claims to be aggrieved, for an order excusing the company from circulating a statement which is submitted on the basis that the rights conferred on the requisitionists are being abused to secure needless publicity for defamatory matter.

2.2.16 Applications under s. 383(5) (Inspection of Minute Books)

A company is required to cause minutes of all proceedings at general meetings, or proceedings at meetings of its directors and, where there are managers, all proceedings at

40. S. 352(1).
41. S. 354(1).
42. S. 356(1).
43. S. 356(3).
44. The court may also make such an order of its own motion.
45. Defined as members representing not less than a 20th of total voting rights or 100 members holding shares on which there has been paid up an average sum, per member, of not less than £100 (s. 376(2)).
46. S. 376(1).

meetings of its managers, to be entered in books kept for that purpose.[47] The books containing minutes of proceedings of any general meeting of the company are to be open to the inspection of any member without charge.[48] In addition a member is entitled within seven days after so requesting the company, to have a copy of any such minutes on payment of a fee.[49] If inspection is refused or a copy is not sent within the proper time, application may be made under s. 383(5) for an order compelling immediate inspection or directing the copies required to be sent to the persons requiring them.

2.2.17 Applications under ss. 391A(6), 392A(7) and 394(6) (Representations of Auditors)

Applications under these provisions relate to the rights of auditors who are removed, resigning or ceasing to hold office. Special notice is required to be given of a resolution to remove an auditor before the expiration of his term of office or appointing as auditor a person other than a retiring auditor.[50] The auditor proposed to be removed or the retiring auditor may make representations in writing to the company and request their notification to members.[51] Subject to considerations of timing a company is required to notify members of the fact that representations have been made in the notice of the resolution and to send a copy of the representations to every member of the company to whom notice of the meeting is or has been sent.[52] Application, however, can be made under s. 391A(6) to the court by the company or by any other person claiming to be aggrieved for an order that the representations need not be sent out and read out at the meeting on the basis that the rights conferred on the auditor concerned are being abused to secure needless publicity for defamatory matter.

Additionally, an auditor may resign his office by depositing a notice in writing to that effect at the company's office and may also deposit with it a signed requisition calling on the directors of the company to convene an extraordinary general meeting for the purpose of receiving and considering an explanation of the circumstances connected with the resignation.[53] The auditor may request the company to circulate to its members a statement in writing of the circumstances connected with his resignation.[54] The company is required in any notice given of the requisitioned meeting to state the fact that a statement has been made and to send a copy of the statement to every member of the company to whom notice of the meeting is or has been sent.[55] As in the case of removal, however, application can be made under s. 392A(7) by either the company or by any person who claims to be aggrieved, for an order that copies of the statement need not be sent out and the statement need not be read out at the meeting on the basis that the rights conferred upon the auditor are being abused to secure needless publicity for defamatory matter.

47. S. 382(1).
48. S. 383(1).
49. S. 383(3).
50. S. 391A(1).
51. S. 391A(3).
52. S. 391A(4).
53. Ss. 392(1) and 392A(2).
54. S. 392A(3).
55. S. 392A(4).

Finally, when an auditor ceases to hold office for any reason he must deposit at the company's registered office a statement of any circumstances connected with his ceasing to hold office which he considers should be brought to the attention of members or creditors of the company.[56] This is in addition to any representations and statements of the kind mentioned above which may be made on removal or resignation.[57] The statement of the auditor which he considers should be brought to members' or creditors' attention must be sent by the company to those persons entitled to be sent copies of the company's accounts or else an application must be made to court.[58] Under s. 394(6), if on such application the court is satisfied that the auditor is using the statement to secure needless publicity for defamatory matter, it will direct that copies of the statement need not be sent out.

2.2.18 Applications under s. 404 (Validation of Charges)

Most charges created by a company are void as against a liquidator or administrator and any creditor of the company unless prescribed particulars of the charge, together with any instrument creating or evidencing it, are delivered to the registrar of companies within 21 days of the creation of the charge.[59] If a charge is not registered within the required time or any particular is omitted or mis-stated in relation to it,[60] application may be made by the company or by a person interested for an extension of time for registration or for an order that the omission or mis-statement be rectified.[61] The application may be made on the basis that the failure to comply with the requirements as to time or particulars was accidental; due to inadvertence; due to some other sufficient cause; not of such a nature as to prejudice creditors or shareholders; or that on other grounds it is just and equitable to grant relief.[62]

The above provisions are proposed to be replaced by others introduced by the Companies Act 1989 but which are not yet in force and which are the subject of consultation.[63] In particular under s. 97 of the 1989 Act it is proposed to insert a new s. 402 into the 1985 Act. This would provide that, where a charge created by a company is required to be registered and the particulars which are registered are not complete and accurate, the charge will be void to the extent that rights are not disclosed by the registered particulars which would be disclosed if they were complete and accurate.[64] Application, however, could be made by the chargee, under the new s. 402(4), for an order that the charge is effective as against an administrator or liquidator of the company, where the omission or error is not likely to have misled materially to his prejudice any unsecured creditor of the company or induced a person to become an unsecured creditor of the company at a time when the registered particulars of the charge were incomplete or inaccurate in a relevant

56. S. 394(1). If there are no such circumstances he is required to state there are none.
57. See s. 394(2).
58. S. 394(3).
59. S. 395(1).
60. Or a memorandum of satisfaction recording, for example, payment or satisfaction of the debt to which the charge relates (see s. 403).
61. S. 404(2).
62. S. 404(1).
63. CA 1989, ss. 92–104. In November 1994 the DTI issued a consultative document entitled "Company Law Reform: Proposals for Reform of Part XII of the CA 1985".
64. S. 97 of the 1989 Act, inserting a new s. 402(1).

respect. Additionally, under a new s. 402(5), the chargee might apply to court for an order that the charge is effective as against a person acquiring an interest or right over property subject to the charge on the basis that that person did not rely, in connection with the acquisition, on registered particulars which were incomplete or inaccurate in a relevant respect.

2.2.19 Applications under s. 408(4) (Register of Charges)

Every company is required to keep at its registered office a register of charges and to enter in it all charges specifically affecting property of the company and all floating charges on the company's undertaking or any of its property.[65] Copies of instruments creating any charge requiring registration with the registrar of companies and the register of charges itself are to be open to the inspection of any creditor or member without fee.[66] The register of charges is also to be open to the inspection of any other person on payment of a fee.[67] If inspection is refused, application may be made under s. 408(4) for an order compelling immediate inspection of the copies or register.

2.2.20 Applications under new s. 417 (Signature relating to Charge Details)

The Companies Act 1989, s. 103 introduces an amendment to the 1985 Act relating to dispensing with a signature in connection with details regarding charges over a company's property. The amendment is not yet in force and is the subject-matter of consultation.[68] If the amending provisions were to be introduced they would insert a new s. 417 into the 1985 Act. This would provide that, where it is proposed to deliver further particulars of a charge or to deliver a memorandum of a charge ceasing to affect a company's property and the chargee refuses to sign or authorise a person to sign on his behalf or cannot be found, or alternatively the company refuses to authorise a person to sign on its behalf, application might be made under a new s. 417(1), by the company or the chargee or by any other person having a sufficient interest in the matter, for an order authorising the delivery of the particulars or memorandum without that signature to the registrar of companies.

2.2.21 Applications under s. 425(1) (Compromises or Arrangements proposed between a Company and its Creditors or its Members)

Where a compromise or arrangement is proposed between a company and its creditors or members or any class of them, application may be made to the court by the company or by any creditor or member or, in the case of a company being wound up or in administration, by the liquidator or administrator, pursuant to s. 425(1), for an order that a meeting

65. S. 407(1).
66. S. 408(1).
67. S. 408(2).
68. It forms part of the provisions considered in the DTI consultative document "Company Law Reform: Proposals for Reform of Part XII of the CA 1985".

of the creditors or members (as the case may be), be summoned to consider the proposal.

2.2.22 *Applications under s. 427(1) (Reconstructions and Amalgamations)*

Applications of this type relate to the making of provisions facilitating a company reconstruction or amalgamation. Where an order is made under s. 425(1) and, at the subsequent meeting, three-quarters in value of the creditors or members (as the case may be) agree to a compromise or arrangement, sanction for it may be sought from the court.[69] Once sanctioned, the compromise or arrangement will be binding on all creditors or members (as the case may be).[70] Where application is made for the sanctioning of a compromise or arrangement in this manner and it is shown that (a) the compromise or arrangement has been proposed for the purposes of or in connection with a scheme for the reconstruction of any company or companies or the amalgamation of two or more companies, and (b) under the scheme the whole or any part of the undertaking or property of any company concerned in the scheme is to be transferred to another company, the court may make provision for various matters.[71] An example of the matters for which the court may make provision is the transfer to the transferee company of the whole or any part of the undertaking and of the property or liabilities of any transferor company.[72]

These provisions may be made by the order sanctioning the compromise or arrangement or by subsequent order for which separate application has been made.[73] Thus, if the need for provisions of this type is anticipated in good time, then the application can be made at the hearing of the sanction proceedings. Alternatively, if there is liberty to apply in the order containing the court's sanction, application can be made by an ordinary interlocutory summons. Only if neither of these routes is available will an originating summons prove necessary.

2.2.23 *Applications under s. 430C (Acquisitions of Shares)*

Proceedings of this kind arise in the context of preventing or settling the terms of the acquisition of shares of dissenting shareholders in connection with a takeover offer. Where, in the course of a takeover offer the offeror has acquired at least nine-tenths in value of the shares to which the offer relates, he may give notice to any relevant shareholder whose shares he has not acquired or contracted to acquire that he desires to acquire his shares.[74] Additionally, where a takeover offer relates to all the shares in the company and within the period allowed for acceptance the offeror has acquired or contracted to acquire at least nine-tenths in value of those shares, a shareholder who has not accepted the offer may make a written communication to the offeror requiring the purchase of his shares by the offeror.[75]

69. S. 425(2).
70. In the case of a company being wound up it will be binding on the liquidator and contributories of the company (s. 425(2)).
71. S. 427(2).
72. S. 427(3)(a).
73. S. 427(2).
74. S. 429(1).
75. S. 430A.

Where a notice has been given by an offeror to a shareholder as described above for the acquisition of outstanding shares, the relevant shareholder may apply under s. 430C(1), within six weeks from the date on which the notice was given, for an order that the offeror will not be entitled and bound to acquire his shares or specifying terms of acquisition different from those of the offer. Moreover, if a shareholder exercises his right as described above to require an offeror to acquire his shares, an application may be made by the shareholder or the offeror pursuant to s. 430C(3) for an order that the terms on which the offeror is entitled and bound to acquire the shares is to be such as the court prescribes.

Finally, where a takeover offer has not been accepted by nine-tenths in value of shareholders to which the offer relates, the offeror may apply under s. 430C(5) for an order authorising him to give notice to those shareholders who have not accepted the offer that he desires to acquire their shares. This may be done on the basis that first, the offeror has, after reasonable enquiry, been unable to trace one or more shareholders, secondly, that the shares which the offeror has acquired together with the shares held by such persons amount to nine-tenths of the shares to which the offer relates, and thirdly, that the consideration offered is fair and reasonable. The court on such an application may only make an order if it considers it just and equitable to do so having regard, in particular, to the number of shareholders who have been traced but who have not accepted the offer.

2.2.24 Applications under s. 653(2) (Restoration to the Register)

Where a company's name has been struck off the register of companies, application may be made by the company or a member or creditor[76] pursuant to s. 653(2), for an order that the company's name be restored on the basis that the company was at the time of the striking-off carrying on business or in operation or otherwise that it is just that the company be restored to the register. If the application is made in conjunction with winding-up proceedings it should be made by petition.[77]

2.2.25 Applications under s. 690(2) (Constitution of Companies not formed under Companies Legislation)

This relates to those companies which have not been formed under the companies legislation but which are authorised to be registered as an unlimited company, a company limited by shares or as a company limited by guarantee. Such companies may by special resolution alter the form of their constitution by substituting a memorandum and articles for a deed of settlement.[78] Application may be made for cancellation of any alterations of the objects to the company in the same manner as provided for in ss. 5–6 of the Act, subject to changed terminology.[79] Thus, the same procedures are available as under s. 6(2) for an extension of time for the delivery of the relevant documents to the registrar where any application has been made for an alteration to be cancelled. The same observations as

76. This must be commenced before the expiration of 20 years from the publication in the *Gazette* of a notice that the company will be struck off the register and the company dissolved (as to which see s. 652).

77. See para. 2.24.12, *infra*.

78. S. 690(1).

79. S. 690(2). There is substituted for the printed copy of the altered memorandum required to be delivered to the registrar of companies a printed copy of the substituted memorandum and articles.

made earlier regarding such applications being made by ordinary as opposed to originating summons apply here.

2.2.26 Applications under s. 713 (Enforcement of a Company's Duty to make Returns)

Where a company makes default in complying with any provisions of the Act requiring it to deliver to the registrar of companies any document or to give notice to him of any matter, and fails to make good that default within 14 days after the service of a notice requiring it to do so, application may be made under s. 713(1) by any member or creditor of the company or by the registrar of companies for an order directing the company and any officer of it to make good the default within such time as may be specified in the order.

2.2.27 Applications under s. 721(1) (Production and Inspection of Books of a Company where an offence is suspected)

Application may be made to a judge of the High Court by the Director of Public Prosecutions, the Secretary of State or the Chief Officer of Police on the basis that there is shown to be reasonable cause to believe that a person has, while an officer of the company, committed an offence in connection with the management of the company's affairs and that evidence of the commission of the offence is to be found in any books or papers of or under the control of the company. The application is for an order authorising inspection of the books or papers in question for the purposes of investigating and obtaining evidence of the offence or requiring the secretary of the company or another officer of it to produce the books or papers to a person named in the order.[80] A similar application may be made in relation to any books or papers of a person carrying on the business of banking insofar as they relate to a company's affairs as it applies to any books or papers of or under the control of the company, save that requirement may not be made of the secretary of the banker to produce the books or papers to a person named in the order.[81]

2.2.28 Applications under s. 651 (Declaration that Dissolution of Company Void)

Where a company has been dissolved, an application may be made under s. 651(1) by the liquidator of the company or by any other person appearing to the court to be interested, for an order declaring that the dissolution is void. Following such an order, proceedings may be taken in the same way as they might have been taken if the company had not been dissolved.[82]

This form of application should now be made by originating summons, whether or not the company has been wound up.[83]

80. S. 721(1) and (2).
81. S. 721(3).
82. S. 651(2).
83. RSC O. 102, r. 3(1)(f) (providing for such applications to be by originating motion in cases where the company had been wound up) has now been revoked by S.I. 1995 No. 2206, r. 46.

All of the different types of application described above, save for certain specific exceptions, are to be commenced by an originating summons in the expedited form[84] provided for in the Rules of Court.[85] Four exceptions to this standard procedure are applications under ss. 242(3),[86] 216,[87] 427[88] and 713.[89] Any applications coming within these four categories will be in the general form of originating summons which is prescribed.[90] The difference in effect is that in the four exceptions specified no fixed hearing date is given so that a notice of appointment has to be issued and signifies that speed is not considered to be essential in such cases. In every other case a fixed date is provided for. Additionally in the case of applications under s. 721 of the Act,[91] proceedings may be commenced by *ex parte* originating summons.[92] Such a summons will be in a prescribed form different from the other two forms of originating summons provided for under RSC O. 102.[93] As a matter of practice four further types of application commonly take this *ex parte* form, namely those under ss. 6,[94] 425,[95] 690(2)[96] and 192(4).[97] Finally, as noted previously, in the case of applications under ss. 6(2), 427(1) and 690(1), the issue of an ordinary summons in the interlocutory form[98] may be appropriate given the existence of other pending proceedings to which those applications are ancillary.

2.3 Content of the summons

The forms of originating summons which are prescribed under Order 102 (other than that in *ex parte* form[99]) refer to "plaintiff" and "defendant".[100] Given that the majority of applications under the Companies Act are in fact non-contentious, such expressions have been considered to be inappropriate. As a result, the terms "applicant" and "respondent" tend to be substituted.[101] If the originating summons is to be heard by a judge, as opposed to registrar, it need not refer to the name of the judge of the Companies Court by whom it is due to be heard.[102]

84. If the wrong form is used, the proceedings are not a nullity but the court may, as a matter of discretion, set the proceedings aside (see RSC O. 2, rr. 1–2).
85. See RSC O. 102, r. 2(2) and Form No. 10 in RSC, Appendix A.
86. Described at para. 2.2.8, *supra*.
87. Described at para. 2.2.6, *supra*.
88. Described at para. 2.2.22, *supra*.
89. Described at para. 2.2.26, *supra*.
90. See Form No. 8 in RSC, Appendix A. This is the combined effect of RSC O. 102, r. 2(2) and O. 7, r. 2(1).
91. Described at para. 2.2.27, *supra*.
92. RSC O. 102, r. 2(3).
93. See Form No. 11 in RSC, Appendix A.
94. Described at para. 2.2.1, *supra*.
95. Described at para. 2.2.21, *supra*.
96. Described at para. 2.2.25, *supra*.
97. Described at para. 2.2.5, *supra*.
98. See RSC O. 32, rr. 1–2.
99. Where the term "applicant" is generally used.
100. This follows from RSC O. 7, r. 2(2) which prescribes such terms for all originating summonses other than those in the *ex parte* form.
101. This practice appears to derive from one of the other primary areas of work within the Companies Court, namely that deriving from the High Court's jurisdiction to wind up companies, where under the IR 1986 the terms "applicant" and "respondent" are adopted.
102. It is sufficient just to refer to "the Companies Court Judge" (see Practice Direction (Chancery Division: Forms) (No. 2 of 1992) [1992] 1 WLR 791).

2.3.1 Each originating summons must include a statement of the questions on which the applicant seeks the determination or direction of the court or, as the case might be, a concise statement of the relief or remedy claimed in the proceedings begun by the originating summons, with sufficient particulars to identify the cause or causes of action in respect of which the applicant claims that relief or remedy.[103] An originating summons is not a pleading[104] but nevertheless it is still correct practice in each originating summons to make use of convenient paragraphs, to express dates, sums and other numbers in figures and not in words and to state facts and not evidence. Additionally, it is convenient that points of law be raised and that full particulars, insofar as they are not inserted in the summons itself, be contained in the supporting affidavit evidence in order to identify the points in issue. Notwithstanding that an originating summons is not a pleading, it may nevertheless be struck out as if it were a pleading under RSC O. 18, r. 19.[105]

An originating summons of any type may be amended with leave of the court under RSC O. 20, r. 5.[106] Amendment of originating summonses is generally permitted with considerable freedom before a final order has been made. After such an order is made, the summons will not be live unless the order specifically so provides. One example of keeping an originating summons alive following the making of an order is by standing it over with liberty to restore some question or relief raised by the summons. But once an originating summons has been exhausted any fresh question, although arising between the same parties or concerning the same subject-matter, must be raised by a fresh originating summons.[107]

2.4 Issue

Originating summonses under RSC O. 102, r. 2 may be issued[108] out of the office of the Companies Court Registrar.[109] Issue of an originating summons is obtained by preparing a summons in duplicate. One copy will be stamped with the appropriate fee and both copies taken to the office of the Registrar of the Companies Court for sealing and for a distinctive number to be assigned.[110] The stamped copy will be retained for filing and the other copy returned to the applicant.[111] Additionally, before the originating summons is issued it must be endorsed where the applicant sues in a representative capacity, with a statement of the capacity in which he sues, or where the respondent is sued in a representative capacity, with a statement of the capacity in which he is sued.[112] The required endorsements in the context of writs on matters relating to address are applied to originating summonses.[113] Thus, in the context of a company which is an applicant, the endorsement must state the company's registered office. If it is a foreign company

103. See RSC O. 7, r. 3(1).
104. See RSC O. 1, r. 4 and *Lewis* v. *Packer* [1960] 1 WLR 452.
105. See RSC O. 18, r. 19(3).
106. See RSC O. 20, r. 7.
107. See *Re Pattman's Will Trusts* [1965] 1 WLR 728.
108. The process of issue can be conducted by post in accordance with Practice Direction (Chancery No. 6(c)), *Supreme Court Practice 1997*, Vol. 2, p. 173, para. 814.
109. The office of the Companies Court Registrar which deals with the issue of summonses is presently located in room TM209 in the Thomas More Building of the Royal Courts of Justice.
110. See RSC O. 6, r. 7 (except sub-rule (2) applied to originating summonses by RSC O. 7, r. 5(3)).
111. See RSC O. 7, r. 5(3) and RSC O. 6, r. 7.
112. See RSC O. 6, r. 3 applied by RSC O. 7, r. 3(2).
113. RSC O. 6, r. 5 applied by RSC O. 7, r. 3(2) (which relate to the address of a solicitor on the record or litigant in person to be contained in the originating summonses).

registered in England its English address must be stated. If a foreign address is given, the endorsement must state that the applicant is a corporate body according to the law of a foreign country and naming it.[114]

2.4.1 Concurrent originating summonses can be issued in the same way as a concurrent writ.[115] Thus, in the same way as a concurrent writ may be issued, one or more concurrent originating summonses may also be issued at the request of an applicant at the time at which the original originating summons is issued or at any time thereafter before the original originating summons ceases to be valid. The concurrent originating summons will be a true copy of the original with only such differences as may be necessary having regard to the purpose for which it has been issued.[116]

The duration of an originating summons is governed by the same rules as apply to a writ.[117] Accordingly, save in cases where leave to serve the originating summons out of the jurisdiction is required under RSC O. 11, the originating summons will be valid in the first instance for a period of four months, beginning with the date of its issue. Where service abroad is required under RSC O. 11, a period of six months is allowed. Extensions may be granted.[118]

2.5 Service

Originating summonses, other than those in the *ex parte* form, must be served and this must be done in the same manner as required for a writ, with any necessary modifications.[119] Accordingly, personal and postal service will be required in accordance with the rules applying generally to writs.[120] In the case of a company registered in England, service should be effected by leaving it at, or sending it by post to, its registered office in accordance with s. 725 of the Act. In the case of an overseas company with a place of business within the jurisdiction, service can normally be effected on the person notified to the registrar of companies as the person authorised to accept service on its behalf or, failing this, by leaving the document at, or posting it to, any place of business established by the company in Great Britain.[121]

In the case of the originating summons in expedited form, the applicant must ensure that it is served four clear days before the date fixed for hearing, unless the respondents have already been served with the summons prior to the hearing being fixed, in which case he must serve notice of the day fixed for the hearing.[122]

2.6 Service out of the jurisdiction

Service of originating summonses in the Companies Court may be effected out of the jurisdiction without leave or with leave in the manner prescribed in RSC O. 11, r. 1.[123]

114. RSC O. 6, r. 5 and *Supreme Court Practice 1997*, Vol. 1, p. 48, para. 6/5/4.
115. RSC O. 6, r. 6 as applied by RSC O. 7, r. 4.
116. RSC O. 6, r. 6(3).
117. See RSC O. 7, r. 6 and RSC O. 6, r. 8(1).
118. RSC O. 6, rr. 8(2) and (2A).
119. RSC O. 10, r. 5.
120. See generally RSC O. 10 and O. 65.
121. See ss. 691–695 of the Act and *Supreme Court Practice 1997*, Vol. 1, p. 1195, paras 65/3/10 and 65/3/11.
122. RSC O. 28, r. 3(2).
123. RSC O. 11, r. 9.

This provision takes into account the Civil Jurisdiction and Judgments Act 1982 which implements the Brussels[124] and other European Conventions on jurisdiction and enforcement of judgments.[125] Service can accordingly be effected without leave, provided that each claim made in the originating summons is one which the court has power to determine under the 1982 Act where[126]:

(a) no proceedings between the parties regarding the same cause of action are pending in another part of the United Kingdom or of any other Convention territory[127]; and, among other things,
(b) either the defendant is domiciled[128] in any part of the United Kingdom or the proceedings are ones to which Article 16 of Schedule 1 of the Act refers.[129]

2.6.1 For these purposes it is significant that art. 16(2) of sch. 1 to the Civil Jurisdiction and Judgments Act 1982 provides for the courts of the Contracting State in which a company has its seat to have exclusive jurisdiction in certain proceedings, namely those which have as their object the validity of the constitution, or the nullity or the dissolution of the decisions of the organs of that company. The provision is intended to avoid conflicting decisions in this area. It is envisaged that in the country in which a company has its seat, information about the company will have been notified and made public, so making proceedings in that jurisdiction more convenient in this context.[130]

In art. 16(2) the "object" of the proceedings does not refer to their purpose but to their subject-matter.[131] Additionally the words "validity of" govern not only the constitution of a company but also the decisions of its organs.[132]

2.6.2 According to s. 43(2) of the 1982 Act a company has its seat in the United Kingdom for the purposes of art. 16(2) if, and only if, (a) it was incorporated or formed under the law of a part of the United Kingdom or (b) its central management and control is exercised in the United Kingdom. Under s. 43(6), a company has its seat in a contracting state other than the United Kingdom if, and only if, (a) it was incorporated or formed under the law of that state; or (b) its central management and control is exercised in that state. Under s. 43(7), however, a company will not be regarded as having its seat in a contracting state other than the United Kingdom if, either it has its seat in the United Kingdom because it was incorporated or formed in a part of the United Kingdom, or if it is shown that the courts of that other state would not regard it as having its seat in that state. Ss. 43(3)–(5) go on to define a company's seat for the purposes of determining where it lies within the United Kingdom.

124. Convention on Jurisdiction and the Enforcement of Judgments in Civil and Commercial Matters, signed at Brussels on 23 September 1968.

125. For the various conventions and their effect on jurisdictional issues see Dicey & Morris, *The Conflict of Laws* (12th Edn), Vol. I, Chap. 11 and O'Malley & Layton, *European Civil Practice* (1989).

126. RSC O. 11, r. 1(2)(a).

127. Meaning the territory of a contracting state (as defined in s. 1(3) of the 1982 Act) to which the Conventions defined in s. 1(1) of the 1982 Act apply (RSC O. 11, r. 1(4)).

128. Defined in ss. 41–42 of the 1982 Act.

129. This is not the only case provided for. The others are set out in RSC O. 11, r. 1(2)(a)(ii).

130. See P. Jenard, "Report on the Convention of 27 September 1968 on jurisdiction and the enforcement of judgments in civil and commercial matters", *Official Journal of the European Communities*, 1979, C59, p. 1, at p. 35.

131. *Newtherapeutics Ltd* v. *Katz* [1991] Ch. 226 and *Re Fagin's Bookshop plc* [1992] BCLC 118.

132. *Ibid.*

The effect of the provisions appears to be that if a company has been formed in the United Kingdom it will be treated as having its seat exclusively in the United Kingdom even if its management and control is located in another contracting state. If, however, its management and control is located in the United Kingdom but the company was formed in another contracting state (whose courts treat it as having its seat there) then the seat of the company will be both in the United Kingdom and that other Contracting State.[133]

2.6.3 Thus it is possible, because of the definition of the seat of a company in the 1982 Act, that the seat in some cases is located in two jurisdictions. In such circumstances the English court if not the court first seised must decline jurisdiction in favour of the courts of the other contracting state which are first seised of the matter.[134]

In cases, other than those within art. 16, which involve an alternative jurisdiction which is not a contracting state the *forum non conveniens* doctrine will apply.[135]

2.7 Acknowledgement of service

Both the originating summons in expedited form and in general form require an acknowledgement of service to be filed. The acknowledgement should be filed with the office of the Companies Court Registrar in the same manner and within the same time limits as an acknowledgement of service of a writ, namely 14 days after service by the applicant of his originating summons.[136] Unsurprisingly, in the context of an *ex parte* originating summons no acknowledgement of service is required.[137]

2.8 Evidence

Evidence in support of originating summonses in any form in the Companies Court is normally by way of affidavit.[138] Technically no affidavit should be sworn until after the summons to which it relates has been issued and, if an affidavit is sworn previously, it should be re-sworn. In practice, the court does not generally require affidavits which predate issue to be re-sworn but will do so if the affidavit seeks to prove facts which have to be shown to be existing as at the date of the commencement of proceedings and if the cause of action would not otherwise be established.[139]

2.8.1 The affidavit evidence sworn in support of and in opposition to an originating summons must comply with the requirements as to form and content which apply to such evidence generally in proceedings in the High Court.[140] In particular, the rules contained

133. See s. 43(2), (3) and (7) of the 1982 Act, *supra*.

134. Sch. 1, art. 23 of the 1982 Act. Cf.:*Gubisch Maschinenfabrik KG* v. *Palumbo* [1987] ECR 4861; *Zelger* v. *Salinitri (No. 2)* [1984] ECR 2397; and *Dresser (UK) Ltd* v. *Falcongate Freight Management Ltd* [1992] QB 502; and *The Sargasso* [1994] 3 All ER 180.

135. *Re Harrods (Buenos Aires) Ltd* [1992] Ch. 72. As to the *forum non conveniens* doctrine generally see Dicey & Morris, *supra*, Vol. I, Chap. 12. On the *forum non conveniens* doctrine in the context of the European Conventions implemented by the 1982 Act see Fentiman, 26 Cornell Int'l L.J. 201 (1993).

136. RSC O. 12, rr. 1–5 applied in the context of originating summonses by RSC O. 12, r. 9.

137. RSC O. 12, r. 9(1) and (3).

138. RSC O. 38, r. 2(3) and O. 28, r. 1A. Under these rules the use of affidavit evidence is permissive rather than mandatory and the court retains the power to direct evidence to be given otherwise than by affidavit (cf. *Leiserach* v. *Schalit* [1934] 2 KB 353).

139. Chancery Practice Direction No. 8A(iii) printed in *Supreme Court Practice 1997*, Vol. 2, p. 175, para. 820.

140. See RSC O. 41 and *Chancery Guide*, p. 19, para. 3.14.

in RSC O. 41, r. 5 regarding hearsay evidence should be complied with.[141] The notice procedures contained in the Civil Evidence Act 1995 and RSC O. 38, rr. 20–25 regarding hearsay evidence[142] do not apply to statements contained in affidavit evidence,[143] unless the court specifically directs evidence to be given at trial by statement on oath of information or belief.[144]

If the affidavits are to be used for the purposes of an interlocutory application in the course of proceedings on an originating summons, evidence in the form of statements of information or belief may be given, so long as the source and grounds thereof are provided.[145]

2.8.2 The contents of any affidavit may not contain matter which is scandalous, irrelevant or otherwise oppressive.[146] If it does contain such matters, the affidavit may be required to be taken off the court file or the scandalous matter may be expunged. The court, however, is not bound to strike out such matters and it retains a discretion not to do so.[147] In addition, evidence which is simply inadmissible, for example, on the basis that it contains privileged material, may be struck out.[148] The court also has an inherent power to remove an affidavit from the court file for prolixity, and may disallow costs occasioned by prolixity in affidavits.[149]

2.8.3 In hearings on an originating summons and in interlocutory applications arising in the course of the hearing of an originating summons, application may be made for cross-examination of the person making an affidavit with the result that, if the person does not attend for such cross-examination, his affidavit is not to be used in evidence without the leave of the court.[150] On an originating summons commenced under Order 102, such an application is unlikely to be made in relation to the affidavits which were filed in support of or in opposition to the originating summons itself prior to the return date before the registrar. At that hearing the registrar has power to give directions as to the further hearing of the matter and may include provision for deponents of affidavits to attend for cross-examination.[151]

Cross-examination may be readily permitted where there are important disputes as to factual issues and particularly where there is a question of motive or of good faith of the deponent.[152] This might apply in respect of applications under ss. 304(4), 377(3), 391A(6), 392(A)(7) and 394(6) of the Companies Act 1985 which all relate to the exclusion of statements to be used at meetings of a company or intended to be brought to the attention of members or creditors on the basis that rights conferred by the Act are being abused to secure needless publicity for defamatory matter. In such cases the motive

141. RSC O. 41, r. 5 has not been altered as a result of the Civil Evidence Act 1995 (which came into force with effect from 31 January 1997).

142. The notice procedures have altered substantially in the light of the Civil Evidence Act 1995.

143. RSC O. 38, r. 21.

144. RSC O. 38, r. 3 and RSC O. 41, r. 5(1)(e).

145. RSC O. 41, r. 5(2).

146. RSC O. 41, r. 6.

147. See *Rossage* v. *Rossage* [1960] 1 WLR 249 and *Re J.* [1960] 1 WLR 253. Examples of matters which are treated as irrelevant or oppressive include references to the report of inspectors investigating the affairs of a company under the CA 1985, ss. 432(2), 442 and 443 (*Savings and Investment Bank Ltd* v. *Gasco Investments (Netherlands) B.V.* [1984] 1 WLR 271).

148. *Chocolade-Fabriken Lindt and Sprungli AG* v. *Nestlé Co. Ltd* [1978] RPC 287.

149. *Supreme Court Practice 1997*, Vol. 1, p. 705, para. 41/6/1.

150. RSC O. 38, r. 2(3). See *Re Dominion Group plc* [1995] 1 WLR 849.

151. RSC O. 28, r. 4(3).

152. *Re Smith and Fawcett* [1942] Ch. 304.

or the good faith of the persons preparing the statement in issue may be central to the proceedings. An application for cross-examination might also be readily allowed where the court is required to determine issues arising between expert witnesses.[153] Cross-examination on affidavits used for interlocutory proceedings on an originating summons, however, will be highly exceptional.[154] Otherwise such interlocutory applications might become lengthy trials within trials.

2.8.4 The timing for the filing of evidence is provided for under Order 28. In the case of any originating summons other than an *ex parte* summons, the applicant must, within 14 days after the respondent has acknowledged service (or if there are two respondents at least one of them has acknowledged service), file with the office of the Companies Court Registrar the affidavit evidence on which he intends to rely.[155] Where the application is by way of an *ex parte* originating summons, the applicant must file any evidence on which he intends to rely not less than four clear days before the date fixed for the hearing.[156] For originating summonses other than in the *ex parte* form, copies of the affidavits filed must be served on all respondents within 14 days after service has been acknowledged by each of them.[157] If a respondent has acknowledged service and wishes to adduce affidavit evidence in response to an originating summons, he must file such evidence with the court and serve it on the applicant within 28 days after service of the applicant's evidence upon him. He is also required to serve a copy of the evidence on any other respondent affected.[158] Provision is made for an applicant to file and serve affidavit evidence in reply within 14 days after service of the respondent's evidence.[159] After this, no further affidavits will be received in evidence without leave of the court.[160] The court, however, retains the power to direct different timetables from those set out above.[161]

2.9 Interlocutory applications

Interlocutory applications in relation to originating summonses under Order 102 can be made most conveniently simply by restoring the originating summons itself for a further hearing before the registrar. This is possible by reason of the provisions of Order 28 which allow the hearing of a summons to be adjourned by the court, as necessary, from time to time, either generally or with a particular date. If adjourned, generally any party may restore the hearing of the summons to the list on 14 days notice to all other parties.[162] Where interlocutory matters cannot be dealt with by means of a restored hearing of the originating summons itself, applications can be made in the same way as in a writ action in the Chancery Division, namely by an ordinary summons which in the first instance will come before the registrar, or by motion direct to the judge. Only applications which need

153. *Re Lifecare International* [1990] BCLC 222, at 225.
154. See, for example, *Re Manlon Trading Ltd* [1996] Ch. 136 at 159C and 170C. Cf. *Berkeley Hotel Co. Ltd v. Berkeley International (Mayfair) Ltd* [1971] FSR 300.
155. RSC O. 28, r. 1A(1).
156. RSC O. 28, r. 1A(2).
157. RSC O. 28, r. 1A(3).
158. RSC O. 28, r. 1A(4).
159. RSC O. 28, r. 1A(5).
160. RSC O. 28, r. 1A(6).
161. RSC O. 28, r. 1A(8).
162. RSC O. 28, r. 5.

to be heard by a judge, however, should be made by motion. Unless exceptional circumstances arise,[163] any procedural application, such as one for directions, should be made to the registrar. Otherwise the applicant runs the risk of the motion being dismissed with costs.[164]

On interlocutory applications, the general Chancery Division requirements as to preparation of bundles, skeleton arguments, reading lists and authorities will apply.[165] Additionally, the Companies Court requires any evidence which any party intends to adduce, together with exhibits, to be filed at least two days prior to the date of hearing, unless the time available is too short in which case it must be filed as soon as possible. If this requirement is not complied with and the hearing has to be adjourned because it has not been possible to read the evidence, the court may make an appropriate order for the costs thrown away.[166]

2.10 Hearing

In the case of a general form originating summons, the applicant is required, within one month of the deadline for service of his affidavit evidence, to obtain an appointment for a hearing of the summons. Once a date and time for the hearing is obtained, a notice in prescribed form[167] must be served on every other party not less than 14 days before the date fixed for the hearing.[168] The notice which is served in this prescribed form will specify what orders or directions the party serving the notice intends to seek at the hearing, and any party who is served with the notice who wishes to seek different orders or directions must, not less than seven days before the hearing, serve on every other party to the summons a notice specifying the different orders or directions which he intends to seek.[169] In the case of a notice specifying different directions or orders, the respondent is required to serve it not only on the applicant but on every other respondent affected.[170]

The first hearing of the originating summons in general form is in many ways similar to a summons for directions hearing in a writ action. Accordingly, it will be good practice for the parties to prepare a list of essential issues in the case and for the information sheet applicable for directions summonses in writ actions to be filled in.[171] If such a form is not filled in and court time is wasted, the party at fault may be required to pay the costs. Additionally, where a party has a legal representative present at the hearing for directions, that person should be someone familiar with the case.[172] If the company concerned is a party (or indeed if any other party is a corporate body) then it will have to be represented

163. Exceptional circumstances will include situations in which it is not possible to obtain an appointment before the registrar in sufficient time before the final hearing of the originating summons (*Chancery Guide*, p. 17, para. 3.12).
164. *Chancery Guide*, p. 21, para. 4.6.
165. *Chancery Guide*, pp. 26–29, paras 5.3–5.6.
166. *Supreme Court Practice 1997*, Vol. 1, p. 1533, para. 102/1/7.
167. RSC Appendix A, Form No. 12.
168. RSC O. 28, rr. 2(1) and 3(1).
169. RSC O. 28, r. 3(3).
170. See RSC O. 28, r. 3(5)(b).
171. *Chancery Guide*, pp. 12–13, paras 3.6(1)–(2).
172. *Chancery Guide*, p. 13, para. 3.6(3).

by a solicitor or counsel as it cannot be represented by a director or any other person without leave of the court.[173]

2.10.1 In the case of an originating summons in expedited form and an *ex parte* originating summons, a date and time for the hearing is fixed on the application of the applicant. For the expedited originating summons, the time limited for acknowledging service will be abridged where appropriate so as to expire on the next day but one before the day fixed for the hearing. The time limits for lodging the applicant's affidavits under the automatic provisions contained in Order 28 will also be abridged where appropriate. The applicant under the expedited form will be required to file his evidence by the fifth day before, and the *ex parte* applicant on the next day but one before, the day so fixed.[174]

2.10.2 If an applicant fails to apply for an appointment for the hearing of an originating summons in general form any respondent may, with leave of the court, obtain an appointment in accordance with the provisions applying to an applicant, providing that he has acknowledged service of the originating summons first.[175] If a hearing of an originating summons in expedited or general form is adjourned and any party to the proceedings wishes to apply at a resumed hearing for an order or direction not previously asked for, he is required, not less than seven days before the resumed hearing of the summons, to serve on every other party a notice specifying the orders and directions which he seeks.[176]

Save for applications under s. 721 of the 1985 Act, which will be made to a judge, an originating summons will come on for hearing in the first instance before the registrar. For all hearings of the originating summons the general practice of the Chancery Division as to bundles, skeleton arguments, authorities and reading lists will apply, as will the Companies Court practice as to filing of evidence.[177]

2.10.3 On the hearing of an originating summons, other than in *ex parte* form, the court has various options as to how to deal with the matter:

(1) The court may, if it considers the liability of the respondent in respect of any claim made by the applicant to be established, make such order in favour of the applicant as the nature of the case requires. If the court takes this course against a respondent who does not appear at the hearing, the order may nevertheless be varied or revoked by a subsequent order of the court on such terms as it thinks just. This in effect permits the respondent to apply to have the order varied or revoked at any subsequent hearing.[178] The relevant principles in relation to any such application will be similar to those applied in the case of judgments in

173. RSC O. 5, r. 6(2). See also *Frinton and Walton UDC* v. *Walton and District Sand and Mineral Co. Ltd* [1938] 1 All ER 649; *Radford* v. *Samuel* (1993) BCC 870; *Arbuthnot Leasing International Ltd* v. *Havelet Leasing Ltd* [1991] 1 All ER 591; and *Radford* v. *Freeway Classics Ltd* [1994] 1 BCLC 445. Leave may be granted for a director to represent the company only in exceptional circumstances such as where its assets are frozen pursuant to a Mareva injunction so that it cannot instruct solicitors, or where the director is also a party and the purposes of the director's appearance coincide with those of the company (see *Arbuthnot Leasing International* v. *Havelet Leasing, supra*).

174. RSC O. 28, r. 2(2).

175. RSC O. 28, r. 2(3).

176. RSC O. 28, r. 3(4).

177. *Chancery Guide*, pp. 26–29, paras 5.3–5.6 and *Supreme Court Practice 1997*, Vol. 1, p. 1533, para. 102/1/7.

178. RSC O. 28, r. 4(1).

default in writ actions.[179] Where the order or judgment has been granted irregularly, the respondent is entitled *ex debito justitiae* to have the judgment or order set aside although, given the terms of Order 28, the court always has the power to vary a judgment in an appropriate case so as to correct any irregularity which has taken place. In the case of an order or judgment obtained regularly, the court may in its discretion nevertheless set aside the judgment or order where the respondent can establish a defence on the merits after having regard to any explanation for the failure to oppose the claim at the previous hearing.[180]

(2) If the court does not dispose of the originating summons summarily in the manner described above, or at least does not dispose of it in its totality in that manner, then further directions may be given as to the conduct of the proceedings.[181] In giving directions the guiding principle is that the steps required should be those best adapted to secure the just, expeditious and economical disposal of the proceedings.[182] In giving directions, two basic options are available:

(a) The court may conclude that the proceedings ought to be continued as if they had been begun as a writ action.[183] In these circumstances the court has a discretion as to how it deals with the continuation of the proceedings and it is specifically provided that it might order that affidavits are to stand as pleadings which will of course hasten matters. This may or may not be with liberty to any of the parties to add to those affidavits or to apply for particulars of them.[184] When the court decides to take this course it will conduct the hearing largely as if it was a summons for directions in a writ action.[185] This can all be done despite the requirements under Order 102 for proceedings under the Companies Act to be commenced in a manner other than by way of writ.[186]

(b) If the court does not order the proceedings to be continued as if they had been begun by writ, the court may nevertheless give any directions which it might give on hearing a summons for directions in a writ action.[187] In doing so, the court may at any stage provide for pleadings by ordering that any affidavit or any particulars of any claim, defence or other matters stated in the affidavits are to stand as a pleading. Alternatively, an order may be made for points of claim, defence or a reply to be delivered.[188] Pleadings will of course be more appropriate where the issues are of a more complex

179. See RSC O. 13, r. 9, O. 14, r. 11 and O. 19, r. 9.

180. Compare *The Saudi Eagle* [1986] 2 Lloyd's Rep. 221.

181. RSC O. 28, r. 4(2). This can include a transfer of the matter to some other court.

182. *Ibid.*

183. This might be because of the number of issues of fact which require to be determined or the nature of the issues, an example being that an allegation of fraud has arisen in the course of the proceedings (see *Re Deadman* [1971] 1 WLR 426).

184. RSC O. 28, r. 8(1). Generally, however, particulars will not be ordered unless justice cannot be done without them (*Chancery Guide*, p. 10, para. 3.3(3)).

185. RSC O. 28, r. 8(2) applies RSC O. 25, rr. 2–7 with the omission of r. 7(1) insofar as it requires parties to serve a notice specifying the orders and directions which they require.

186. RSC O. 28, r. 8(3).

187. RSC O. 28, r. 4(4).

188. RSC O. 28, r. 4(5).

nature or for allegations which normally require particularity in the context of writ actions. Discovery may also be ordered[189] and will be ordered on the application of a party unless the court is satisfied that it is not necessary.[190] Additionally, Order 28 provides that further directions may be given for the filing of evidence and attendance of deponents for cross-examination.[191]

(3) In deciding which procedure to adopt, the court will consider, at as early a stage as is practicable, whether there is or may be a dispute as to fact and whether the just, expeditious and economical disposal of the proceedings can accordingly be best secured by hearing the summons on oral evidence or mainly on oral evidence. As a result, it may order that no further evidence will be filed and that the summons will be heard on oral evidence or partly on oral evidence and partly on affidavit evidence with or without the cross-examination of any deponents.[192]

2.10.4 As indicated earlier in the context of interlocutory applications the Court may adjourn the summons before it, from time to time, as it thinks fit. In the same way that, in the case of a summons for directions in a writ action, adjournment may occur and commonly does occur because the court does not consider it possible to deal with all of the matters relating to the procedure to be adopted at the stage at which a particular hearing takes place, the court may conclude that it is expedient to adjourn the hearing of the originating summons.[193]

If, on the hearing of an originating summons, application is made for an order affecting a party who has not acknowledged service, then the application can proceed but the court will require to be satisfied that the relevant party has in fact failed to acknowledge service. This in practice means that the applicant must file an affidavit of service in relation to the party from whom an acknowledgement has not been received.[194]

2.10.5 Where the application has not been disposed of summarily and the evidence is complete and all the directions as to discovery or other matters have been complied with, the registrar will make a further order as to the hearing of the matter as may be appropriate.[195] If there are serious disputes of law or fact then the registrar may consider the matter is more appropriate to be dealt with by a judge and transfer the matter so that it can be heard in that manner. The matter will then be heard by a Companies Court Judge who himself may conduct a pre-trial review, as in a writ action, if the circumstances warrant it.[196] Directions may also be given as to whether the matter is to be heard in open court or in chambers. Once directions have been given, the applicant is required to lodge documents basically in the same manner as in an action begun by writ.[197] Preparations for

189. Where a party applies for a discovery direction it will be helpful to draw up and, if possible, agree a list of the essential issues in the case with the other side. This will assist the court in deciding to which issues discovery should relate (*Chancery Guide*, p. 11, para. 3.4(d)).

190. *Re Lifecare International*, *supra* at 225 and *Coni* v. *Robertson* [1969] 2 All ER 609. Compare *Re Press Caps* [1948] 2 All ER 638 which predated the present RSC O. 24, rr. 3 and 8.

191. RSC O. 28, r. 4(4).

192. RSC O. 28, r. 4(3).

193. RSC O. 28, r. 5. Cf. RSC O. 25, r. 2(1).

194. RSC O. 28, r. 6.

195. RSC O. 28, r. 9.

196. See *Chancery Guide*, pp. 16–17, para. 3.10.

197. RSC O. 28, r. 9(2) and (3).

a final hearing will involve the completion of a pre-trial checklist and the submission of bundles, skeleton arguments, reading lists and lists of authorities in accordance with standard Chancery Division practice.[198] Any order made by the registrar as to the manner in which the hearing is to take place and the mode of hearing, may be varied by a subsequent order of the court made either at or before the final hearing of the matter.[199]

Of course, in the case of an *ex parte* originating summons, all parties affected will not have had an opportunity to be heard. Any order made *ex parte*, however, can be set aside.[200] In appropriate circumstances it is even possible that an order obtained on an *ex parte* originating summons could be set aside *ex parte* where sufficiently clear grounds appear for doing so.[201] No specific provision is made in the rules for circumstances arising in which an *ex parte* originating summons effectively becomes *inter partes*. The rules as to the giving of directions for the further hearing of an originating summons, however, are for general application and, accordingly, appropriate further directions for the hearing of the matter may be given on that basis.

2.10.6 As a general rule in relation to any originating summons, if any party makes default in complying with the rules contained in RSC O. 28 or any order or direction of the court as to the conduct of the proceedings, then the court may make an order for the cause or matter to be dismissed or that the defendant be debarred from adducing such evidence as the court may specify or that the defence be struck out and judgment be entered.[202]

No order for dismissal of the proceedings for want of prosecution, however, will be made unless, in the exercise of its discretion, the court comes to the conclusion that if the proceedings were in the form of a writ action they would warrant dismissal on this basis.[203] Additionally, the normal rules as to abatement apply to originating summonses so that if a matter has been set down for a hearing and the application becomes abated, or the interest or liability of any party to the action is assigned or transmitted to or devolves on some other person, then the party having the conduct of the action is under a duty, as soon as is practicable after becoming aware of it, to certify the abatement or change of interest or liability and to send the certificate to the proper officer who will make an appropriate entry in the list of matters to be set down for hearing. After the matter has stood for one year marked as abated or under order to stand over, generally in the light of such an entry the action will be struck out unless, where the matter has been stood over generally, the order otherwise provides.[204]

2.10.7 Finally, provision is made in Order 28 for a respondent, who has acknowledged service of the summons and who alleges that he has any claim or is entitled to any relief or remedy as against the applicant in respect of any matter, to make a counterclaim instead of bringing separate proceedings. Such a respondent must, at the first or any resumed hearing of the originating summons, but in any event as early as practicable, inform the court of the nature of this claim. Upon doing so the court may determine or give directions

198. *Chancery Guide*, p. 16, para. 3.9 and pp. 26–29, paras 5.3–5.6.
199. RSC O. 28, r. 9(3).
200. This fundamental rule of practice is embodied in RSC O. 32, r. 6.
201. Cf. *London City Agency (JCD)* v. *Lee* [1970] Ch. 597.
202. RSC O. 28, r. 10.
203. *Halls* v. *O'Dell* [1992] QB 393.
204. RSC O. 28, r. 11 applying RSC O. 34, r. 9.

for the further hearing of the claim in the same way as provided for in relation to the originating summons itself.[205] No specific procedure is laid down as to how the respondent is to notify the court as to the nature of his claim but it has been suggested that he should serve on the applicant and also lodge in the office of the Companies Court Registrar proposed points of counterclaim, before the hearing of the application, so that the court is then in the position to give directions as appropriate.[206] It is open to a plaintiff against whom a counterclaim is made to apply for the counterclaim to be struck out, or for an order that it be dealt with separately, or for other directions, as are expedient on the basis that the subject-matter of the counterclaim ought to be disposed of by separate proceedings.[207]

2.11 Appeals

The Companies Act 1985 and Order 102 provide no specific procedure for appeals from orders made by Companies Court Registrars. In the absence of any guidance in statute or statutory instrument, the Court of Appeal has stated that the matter is an internal matter for arrangement between the judge of the Companies Court and the registrar.[208]

The current arrangement or practice is one established early in this century.[209] There is a right of appeal in respect of any order of the registrar. The appeal from the registrar takes the form of a motion to vary or discharge the registrar's order. At the hearing before the judge, the matter will be gone into afresh and any discretion to be exercised will be that of the judge, unfettered in any way by the decision of the registrar.[210]

2.11.1 The time within which a motion to vary or discharge the registrar's order must be brought is 28 days from the date on which the order is sealed. This is in accordance with a practice established over a century ago, whereby the time limit for appealing to the Court of Appeal from interlocutory orders was adopted by analogy for appeals from the registrar.[211]

Appeals from the judge are to the Court of Appeal[212] although it should be noted that orders of the judge on *ex parte* originating summonses issued under s. 721 of the 1985 Act are not appealable.[213] On the appeal, the usual procedures relating to appeals to the Court of Appeal contained in Order 59 will apply.

Where an appeal is sought from the judge on an interlocutory matter, the normal rules as to leave to appeal and other matters relating to such appeals will apply as they apply in the context of writ actions.[214] The consequence of this is that, although new evidence may be adduced relatively freely before the judge, important restrictions are imposed in the case of appeals from the judge to the Court of Appeal.[215]

205. RSC O. 28, r. 7(1) and (2).
206. See *Supreme Court Practice 1997*, Vol. 1, p. 499, para. 28/7/1.
207. RSC O. 28, r. 7(3).
208. *Re Tasbian Ltd (No. 2)* [1990] BCC 322, at 325 (per Dillon L.J.). See also *Re Probe Data Systems (No. 3)* [1992] BCC 110.
209. *Re Bryndu and Port Talbot Collieries Ltd* [1904] WN 136.
210. *Re Rolls Razor Ltd (No. 2)* [1970] Ch. 576.
211. *Re Lifecare International* [1990] BCLC 222, at 224.
212. Supreme Court Act 1981, s. 16.
213. *Re Racal Communications Ltd* [1981] AC 374.
214. See RSC O. 59.
215. See *Supreme Court Practice 1997*, Vol. 1, pp. 1001–1004, paras 59/10/7–59/10/14.

2.12 Costs

Generally, costs, as in other proceedings in the Chancery Division of the High Court, will be at the discretion of the court.[216] In specific instances, however, the discretion may be limited. For example, in applications under s. 430C (concerning the acquisition of shares in a takeover) no order for costs can be made against a shareholder making an application, unless the court considers the application was unnecessary, improper or vexatious or that there was unreasonable delay in making it or unreasonable conduct on the shareholder's part in conducting the proceedings.[217]

In certain instances of proceedings to be commenced by originating summons, the Act indicates that a person who is not a party to the proceedings may be held liable for costs. Thus, in an application under s. 304(4) (for an order that a company may not circulate or read out at a meeting representations by a director who is sought to be removed) it is provided that the court may order the company's costs in such an application to be paid in whole or in part by the director concerned, notwithstanding that he is not a party to the application.[218] Similar provisions apply in applications under s. 377(3) (where the court may order the company's costs to be paid in full or in part by the requisitionists, notwithstanding that they are not parties) and ss. 391A(6), 392A(7) and 394(6) (where the company's costs on the application may be ordered to be paid in whole or in part by the auditor, notwithstanding that he is not a party).

II. APPLICATIONS BY ORIGINATING MOTION

2.13 Applications by originating motion

Order 102 provides specifically for certain proceedings under the Act to be commenced by originating motion.[219] The various types of proceeding which are required to be commenced in this manner are considered in detail elsewhere in this book[220] but a summary follows.

2.13.1 Applications under s. 88(6) (Extension of Time for Delivery of Documents to the Registrar of Companies)

Where a company which is limited by shares or limited by guarantee has made an allotment of shares it is required, within one month after the allotment, to deliver to the registrar of companies for registration a return of the allotments in a prescribed form.[221] Additional specific requirements apply for returns in the case of shares allotted as fully or partly paid up otherwise than in cash.[222]

If default is made in complying with the above requirements, every officer of the company who is in default is liable to a fine. This, however, is subject to the provisions

216. See generally RSC O. 62.
217. See s. 430C(4) and *Re Lifecare International* [1990] BCLC 222, at 226.
218. S. 304(5).
219. O. 102, r. 3(1).
220. See Part II, *infra*.
221. S. 88(2)(a).
222. S. 88(2)(b).

in s. 88(6). This section permits the company or any officer liable for default to apply to the court for relief. The court, if satisfied that the omission to deliver the document was accidental or due to inadvertence, or that it is just and equitable to grant relief, may make an order extending the time for the delivery of the document for such period as the court thinks proper.

2.13.2 Applications under s. 432(1) (Company Investigations)

There are various provisions in the Act for investigations into the affairs of a company to be instigated by the Secretary of State by his appointment of one or more inspectors.[223] Application may also be made to the court under s. 432(1) for a declaration that the affairs of the company ought to be investigated. If the court makes such an order, the Secretary of State is required to appoint one or more competent inspectors to investigate the affairs of the company and report on them in such manner as he directs.

2.13.3 Applications under s. 436 (Enquiry into Obstruction of Inspectors)

Inspectors appointed by the Secretary of State may certify in writing to the court that a person has failed to co-operate with them in various prescribed ways, for example, by refusing to answer any question put to him by the inspectors for the purposes of the investigation.[224] Following such certification, under s. 436(3), the court may inquire into the case. After hearing any witnesses who may be produced against or on behalf of the alleged offender, and after hearing any statement which may be offered in defence, the court may punish the offender as if he had been guilty of contempt of court.

2.13.4 Applications under s. 456(1) (Relaxation and Removal of Restrictions on Shares)

Shares of a company may be the subject of a restriction in various circumstances. One example is where there has been a failure to provide information regarding interests in shares in a public company. As discussed above[225] this may result in the court imposing restrictions under s. 216. A further example arises where, under s. 442(1) the Secretary of State has appointed inspectors to investigate and report on a company so as to determine the true identity of the persons who are or have been financially interested in the success or failure of the company or able to control or materially influence its policy. If, in connection with such an investigation, the Secretary of State considers there is difficulty in finding out the relevant facts about any shares, he may direct that the shares shall be subject to restrictions.[226]

The restrictions referred to are contained in part XV of the Act and include a provision that any transfer of the relevant shares is void.[227] Section 456(1) provides that, where shares in a company are made subject to restrictions of this type, application may be made to the court for an order removing them. Additionally, the court, if satisfied that an order

223. See ss. 431(1) and 432(2).
224. S. 436(1).
225. See para. 2.2.6, *supra*.
226. S. 445(1).
227. S. 454(1).

subjecting the shares to restrictions unfairly affects the rights of third parties, may protect such rights but subject to such terms as it thinks fit.[228]

The court will only make an order directing the removal of restrictions if satisfied that the relevant facts about the shares have been disclosed to the company and no unfair advantage has accrued to any person as a result of the earlier failure to make disclosure, or if the shares are to be transferred for valuable consideration and the court approves the transfer.[229] These conditions for the court to make an order do not, however, apply where the court is making provision for the protection of the rights of third parties in relation to any restrictions applying to shares as described above.[230]

2.13.5 Applications pursuant to s. 456(4) (Directions that Shares or Debentures shall on sale cease to be subject to Restrictions)

These applications also arise in the context of an order imposing restrictions on shares. Under s. 456(4) application may be made to the court for shares which are the subject of restrictions to be sold, subject to the court's approval as to the sale, and for directions that the shares shall cease to be subject to restrictions. Application to the court under this provision may be made by the Secretary of State unless the restrictions were imposed by the court itself under s. 216 of the Act or alternatively the application may be made by the company.[231]

After an order has been made in this form, the court may make such further order relating to the sale or transfer of shares as it thinks fit. Application for this to be done may be made by the Secretary of State (unless the restrictions were imposed by the court under s. 216), by the company, by the person appointed by or in pursuance of the order to effect the sale, or by any person interested in the shares.[232]

2.13.6 Applications pursuant to s. 359(1) (Rectification of the Register of Members)

Under s. 359(1), if the name of any person is, without sufficient cause, entered or omitted from a company's register of members, any person aggrieved or any member of the company or the company itself may apply to the court for rectification of the register. The same applies if default is made or unnecessary delay takes place in entering on the register the fact of any person having ceased to be a member. The court may either refuse the application or may order rectification of the register and payment by the company of any damages sustained by any party aggrieved.[233] On this type of application the court may deal with questions which it considers "necessary and expedient" to decide, including questions relating to title.[234]

228. S. 456(1A).
229. S. 456(3).
230. S. 456(1A).
231. S. 456(4).
232. S. 456(5).
233. S. 359(2).
234. S. 359(3).

2.13.7 Applications pursuant to s. 217(5) (Amendment of the Register of Interests in Shares)

These applications concern the register of interests in shares which is required to be maintained by a public company to record information which persons are required to disclose regarding their interest in certain share capital of the company.[235]

Amendment to such a register may arise in various ways. For example, where a person in fulfilment of an obligation gives to the company the name and address of another person as being interested in shares of the company, the company is required, within 15 days of the date from which it was given that information, to notify that other person that he has been so named. The company must include in the notification certain particulars, including a statement informing him of his right to apply to have the entry removed.[236] The person concerned may then apply in writing to the company for the removal of that entry and the company is then required to remove the entry if satisfied that the information in pursuance of which the entry was made was incorrect.[237]

Under s. 217(5), where an application is made to the company to alter the register and it is refused, an application may be made to the court for an order directing that the company remove the entry in question from the register or include the information in question in the register as appropriate.

2.13.8 Applications pursuant to s. 245B(1) (Annual Accounts not complying with Requirements)

These proceedings relate to defective accounts. Where, for example, a copy of the company's annual accounts has been laid before the company in a general meeting or delivered to the registrar of companies, and the Secretary of State considers that there is a question as to whether the accounts comply with the requirements of the Act, he may notify the directors of the company indicating the respects in which it appears to him that such a question arises.[238] The notice must specify a period of not less than one month for an explanation to be given. If, at the end of that period, the Secretary of State considers that no satisfactory explanation of the accounts has been given, and that the accounts have not been revised so as to comply with the requirements of the Act, the Secretary of State may apply to the court.[239]

Under s. 245B such an application may be made to the court by the Secretary of State or by a person authorised by him for the purpose, for a declaration that the annual accounts of the company do not comply with the requirements of the Act and for an order requiring the directors of the company to prepare revised accounts. If the court finds that the accounts do not comply with the requirements of the Act, an order may be made for all or part of the costs of and incidental to the application, and any reasonable expenses incurred by the company in connection with or as a consequence of the preparation of revised accounts, to be borne by such of the directors as were party to the approval of the defective accounts.[240]

235. S. 211.
236. S. 217(2).
237. S. 217(3).
238. S. 245A(1).
239. S. 245A(2) and (3).
240. S. 245B(4).

The only person currently authorised by the Secretary of State to apply to the court for these purposes is the Financial Reporting Review Panel Limited.[241]

2.13.9 Each form of application described above will normally be made *inter partes*. It is possible, however, that an application in an appropriate case might be made *ex parte*. This will be so if the court is satisfied that the delay caused in proceeding in the ordinary way would or might entail irreparable or serious mischief.[242] If an application is made *ex parte* and an order is made by the court, any party affected by the order may apply to the court to set it aside.[243] In a sufficiently clear case it would appear that the application to set the order aside might also be made *ex parte*.[244] One basis on which such an application might be made to set aside an *ex parte* order is on the ground that all the facts were not laid before the court before the order was made or that certain material facts were suppressed. In such circumstances the order which has been made may be set aside without regard to the merits.[245] Instead of a fully *ex parte* application it may be that an applicant may wish to adopt the practice which has recently developed in the Chancery Division and in the Court of Appeal of applying "*ex parte* on notice". This results in an *ex parte* hearing at which the respondent is present and takes part in order to assist the court.[246] This may well give the applicant some protection against a later application being made to set aside the order on the basis of all the facts not being before the court or material facts being suppressed. If the application fails, however, and the respondent is present at the express or tacit invitation of the applicant, the court has jurisdiction to award the respondent his costs.[247]

Not all of the applications which are listed in Order 102 need necessarily be made by instituting new proceedings in the form of an originating notice of motion. Thus, in the case of proceedings under s. 456(1), where the order imposing the restrictions was made by the court rather than by the Secretary of State, and under such order there is liberty to apply for a direction that the shares cease to be subject to the restrictions, the motion can be in an interlocutory form and need not be originating. The application will be made in the existing proceedings which led to the imposition of restrictions.

2.14 Contents of the originating notice of motion

Where notice of the originating motion is to be given, the form of the notice of motion must comply with Form No. 13 contained in the Appendix to the Rules of the Supreme Court.[248] In the notice of motion there must be a concise statement of the nature of the claim made or the relief or remedy required.[249] Also, where an abridgement of time has been made for service of the notice of motion, this fact must be stated in the notice.[250]

241. The Companies (Defective Accounts Authorised Person) Order 1991, S.I. 1991 No. 13.
242. RSC O. 8, r. 2(1).
243. *Ibid.*
244. Cf. *London City Agency (JCD) Ltd* v. *Lee, supra.*
245. See, for example, *R.* v. *Kensington Income Tax Commissioners* [1917] 1 KB 486, at 504. See also *Chancery Guide*, p. 22, para. 4.7(2).
246. See *Chancery Guide*, p. 23, para. 4.9.
247. *Pickwick International Inc. (GB) Ltd* v. *Multiple Sound Distributors Ltd* [1972] 1 WLR 1213.
248. RSC O. 8, r. 3(1) and Appendix A.
249. RSC O. 8, r. 3(2).
250. RSC O. 8, r. 3(1).

The notice of motion is required to be addressed to the correct parties. If a name is omitted, the notice will have to be amended.[251] It need not refer to the name of the judge of the Companies Court by whom it is to be heard.[252]

The provisions of RSC O. 6, r. 5 (concerning endorsements of address) apply with necessary modifications to originating notices of motion[253] in the same way as in the case of originating summonses.[254]

2.14.1 Application may be made for amendment of a notice of motion in the same way as in relation to a writ.[255] Given the short period of time normally arising between service of the notice of motion and the first hearing, applications to amend are normally sought or consented to at that hearing rather than before it.

The provisions contained in the Rules of the Supreme Court regarding striking out do not specifically refer to originating notices of motion[256] but no doubt an application could be made for the contents of an originating notice of motion to be struck out under the inherent jurisdiction of the court where the proceedings are obviously frivolous or vexatious or an abuse of the process of the court.[257]

2.15 Issue

The issue of an originating notice of motion coming within Order 102 may be obtained from the office of the Companies Court Registrar.[258] The process of issuing is carried out in the same way as a writ of summons with a copy for filing being required. The actual issue of the notice of originating motion takes place upon its being sealed by an officer of the office from which it is issued.[259]

The process of issue can be conducted by post in accordance with the current Chancery practice.[260]

2.16 Service

A notice of originating motion must be served at least two clear days before the day named in the notice for hearing of the motion unless the court gives leave to the contrary.[261] An order granting leave to give short notice may be obtained *ex parte* by application to the judge but will only be made when the circumstances of the case make it appropriate. Any such application must be made to the judge because this leave cannot be granted by a Master in the Chancery Division and, by analogy, a Registrar of the Companies Court, even during vacation periods.[262] If leave to serve short notice of motion is given, copies

251. *Pollard* v. *Doyle* [1854] 2 WR 509.
252. It is sufficient to refer to "the Companies Court Judge", see Practice Direction (Chancery Division: Forms) (No. 2 of 1992), *supra*.
253. RSC O. 8, r. 3(3).
254. See para. 2.4, *supra*.
255. RSC O. 20, r. 7 applying O. 20, r. 5.
256. RSC O. 18, r. 19.
257. See *Reichel* v. *Magrath* [1889] 14 App. Cas. 665 and *Supreme Court Practice 1997*, Vol. 1, p. 334, para. 18/19/18).
258. RSC O. 102, r. 3(2).
259. RSC O. 8, r. 3(6).
260. See Practice Direction (Chancery No. 6), *supra*.
261. RSC O. 8, r. 2(2).
262. *Conacher* v. *Conacher* [1881] 29 WR 230.

of all affidavits intended to be used at the hearing in support of the notice of motion should be served with it, in the interests of fairness and in order to save delay.[263]

Service of the originating notice of motion will be effected in the same way as a writ of summons. Accordingly, personal or postal service will be required in accordance with the rules applying generally to writs, and the comments made above in this context in relation to originating summonses will also apply here.[264]

2.17 Service out of the jurisdiction

Service of an originating notice of motion out of the jurisdiction is effected in the same way as service out of the jurisdiction of an originating summons. The comments made above in relation to originating summonses therefore apply in this context.[265]

2.18 Acknowledgment of service

Acknowledgement of service to an originating notice of motion is not required.

2.19 Evidence

As in the case of originating summonses in the Companies Court, the evidence filed in support of and in opposition to an originating motion is normally in the form of affidavits.[266] This is subject to any direction of the court to the contrary and, in an appropriate case, the court may require oral evidence to be adduced instead of or as a supplement to affidavit evidence filed. An example of a case in which oral evidence may be required rather than affidavits is in proceedings under s. 436 concerning obstruction of inspectors.[267] In any event, in relation to any affidavits which are filed, application may be made for an order for the attendance of the deponents for cross-examination and, if an order is made for that purpose and a deponent does not attend, his affidavit may not be used in evidence without leave of the court.[268]

The comments made earlier regarding the contents of affidavits in the context of originating summonses are also applicable here.[269]

2.20 Interlocutory applications

Interlocutory applications may be made in proceedings begun by originating motion in the same way as in actions commenced by writ.[270] Thus for example, discovery may be applied for and ordered where it is considered by the court to be necessary for the purpose

263. *Paravichini Del Succri* v. *Lewis CR Gunner* [1919] WN 173.
264. See para. 2.5, *supra* and RSC O. 10 and O. 65.
265. See para. 2.6 *et seq.*, *supra.*
266. RSC O. 38, r. 2(3).
267. S. 436 itself refers to the hearing of witnesses.
268. *Ibid.* See also *Re Dominion International*, *supra.*
269. See para. 2.8 *et seq.*, *supra.*
270. This reflects the fact that proceedings commenced by originating motion are as much substantive proceedings as an action commenced by writ. See Supreme Court Act 1981, s. 151(1).

of disposing fairly with the matter, or to save costs.[271] Similarly, an application may be made for the provision of answers to interrogatories where appropriate.[272]

Rather than issuing an ordinary interlocutory summons or interlocutory motion for the purpose of seeking orders of this kind, it may be easier and more convenient to deal with interlocutory issues either at the first hearing of the originating motion before the judge or, alternatively, at an adjourned hearing if the matter is stood over, for example, for evidence to be filed. If the matter is adjourned, there will often be a liberty to restore or liberty to apply provision contained in the order, with the result that either party can raise interlocutory matters before the court. In most cases, even with such a provision, it will be appropriate to set out the interlocutory relief sought, in the form of a notice of motion or otherwise in writing, so that appropriate preparation for the interlocutory application can take place and so that the parties are clear as to the precise relief sought.

On interlocutory applications, the general Chancery Division requirements as to preparation of bundles, skeleton arguments, reading lists and authorities will apply,[273] as will the usual Companies Court requirements for evidence to be filed at least two days prior to the date of hearing or as soon as possible if the time available is too short.[274]

2.21 Hearing

The nature of a motion is an oral application made to the judge in open court unlike the originating summons procedure which is usually commenced in chambers. Motions in the Companies Court are not as a rule set down but are heard in court before the Companies Court Judge on the usual motion day which is presently a Monday.[275] If the matter is a heavy one such that it is estimated as being likely to exceed two hours duration, then it will be liable to be stood over for a date to be fixed by the Chancery Clerk of the Lists. If the application is adjourned with a time estimate of at least three days, it will be listed in the same way as an action set down in the Witness List Part I.[276] In any event, the court has power to adjourn the hearing of the motion for the filing of evidence, on such terms, if any, as it thinks fit.[277]

The form of the evidence for the final hearing of the motion will depend upon the manner in which the court directs it is to be given. Normally the matter will proceed by affidavits being filed in support of the application, the respondent filing affidavits in response and with the applicant having the right to reply on affidavit to that evidence.[278] The court, as explained above, has power, however, to order discovery, to order evidence to be given orally either in substitution for or in addition to any affidavit evidence filed, and may order cross-examination on affidavits.[279]

271. RSC O. 24, rr. 3(1) and 8. Such an application should be accompanied by a list of essential issues in the case in accordance with the *Chancery Guide*, p. 11, para. 3.4(d).

272. See RSC O. 26, r. 1. Interrogatories will not be appropriate unless necessary for disposing fairly of the cause or matter, or for saving costs. If the interrogatories do not satisfy this test they will be disallowed (see *Chancery Guide*, p. 12, para. 3.4(2)).

273. *Chancery Guide*, pp. 26–29, paras 5.3–5.6.

274. See *Supreme Court Practice 1997*, Vol. 1, p. 1533, para. 102/1/7.

275. Chancery Division Practice Direction, No. 12 (B)(iii) printed in *Supreme Court Practice 1997*, Vol. 2, p. 189, para. 849. See also *Chancery Guide*, p. 49, para. 12.2(3).

276. *Ibid.*

277. RSC O. 8, r. 5.

278. RSC O. 38, r. 2(3).

279. See para. 2.19, *supra*.

For all hearings of the motion, the Chancery Division standard requirements concerning bundles, skeleton arguments, reading lists and lists of authorities will apply.[280] In some cases, for example, where the hearing is expected to exceed 10 days in length and preparatory steps such as discovery have occurred, a pre-trial review may be appropriate.[281]

2.22 Appeals

An originating motion will be heard by a judge and all consequent appeals will be to the Court of Appeal. The procedure governing such appeals is that set out in RSC O. 59 and will mirror that applying in the context of writ actions where there is an appeal from the judge. In the case of an *ex parte* application where the application is "on notice", the hearing is treated as effectively *inter partes* for the purposes of any appeal. It is, however, considered unsatisfactory for the Court of Appeal to be asked to adjudicate on such an appeal when only one side's evidence has been heard. It is accordingly preferable that the motion is stood over to a subsequent *inter partes* hearing when all the evidence is before the court so that thereafter the aggrieved party can appeal to the Court of Appeal with all the evidence having been filed.[282]

2.23 Costs

Costs of originating motions referred to in Order 102 will be dealt with in the same way as other proceedings coming before the Chancery Division of the High Court. Consequently, costs are at the discretion of the court.[283] In some cases, specific provision is made under the Act regarding the court's discretion. Thus, in proceedings under s. 245B (applications in respect of defective accounts) the court, on finding that the accounts which were the subject of the application do not comply with the requirements of the Act, has power to order that the costs of and incidental to the application are to be borne by such of the directors as were party to the approval of the defective accounts.[284]

III. PETITIONS

2.24 Petitions

Proceedings under the Act which are required to be started by way of petition fall into three categories:

(1) petitions under s. 459, which broadly arise where allegations have been made that the affairs of a company have been conducted in a manner which is unfairly prejudicial to the interests of members;
(2) petitions concerning schemes for the transfer of long term business under the Insurance Companies Act 1982; and

280. *Chancery Guide*, pp. 26–29, paras 5.3–5.6.
281. *Ibid.*, pp. 16–17, para. 3.10.
282. *Hunter and Partners* v. *Wellings and Partners* [1987] FSR 83.
283. See generally RSC O. 62.
284. S. 245B(4).

(3) a residual category of other applications under the Act which are specifically required to be commenced by way of petition.

Petitions under s. 459 have their own special form of procedure provided for under the Companies (Unfair Prejudice Applications) Proceedings Rules 1986.[285] Petitions under the Insurance Companies Act 1982 also have their own special procedure provided for in part I of sch. 2C of the 1982 Act. The procedural and evidential requirements arising under these particular rules are dealt with in detail elsewhere in this book.[286] Other proceedings under the Act which are required to be commenced by way of petition, although in some cases having certain special requirements which are considered in detail later,[287] also have common procedural features by reason of the fact that they are all governed by the provisions of Order 102. It is these common procedural aspects which are considered here.

There follows a brief summary of the residual class of petitions coming within category (3) above.

2.24.1 Applications under s. 5(1) (Cancellation of the Alteration of a Company's Objects)

Petitions of this type arise where a special resolution has been passed so as to alter the statement of the company's objects contained in its memorandum.[288] Where this has occurred, an application may be made under s. 5(1) for that alteration to the memorandum to be cancelled. There are provisions as to the entitlement of persons to make such an application and specified time limits within which it must be made.[289] On hearing the application, the court may, among other things, make an order confirming the alteration, whether wholly or in part, or on such terms and conditions as it thinks fit, or it may make an order adjourning the proceedings so that an arrangement can be made to its satisfaction for the purchase of the interests of dissentient members.[290]

2.24.2 Applications under s. 17(1) (Cancellation of the Alteration of a Condition in the Memorandum)

This form of application arises where the conditions of the memorandum cover matters which might have been dealt with in the articles of association of a company. This is often so, for example, in the case of special class rights attaching to preferred shares.[291] Where a condition of this type has been included in the memorandum rather than in the articles of association, it may be altered by special resolution. If this occurs, however, application may be made under s. 17(1) for such alteration to be cancelled and, in these circumstances, the alteration will not have effect except insofar as it is confirmed by the court. Section 17(1) operates subject to part XVII of the Act (which protects members against unfair

285. S.I. 1986 No. 2000.
286. See Chapter 5, *infra*.
287. See Part II, *infra*.
288. See s. 4(1).
289. S. 5(2) and (3).
290. S. 5(4).
291. See *Gore-Browne on Companies* (44th Edn), Vol. 1, para. 2.6, p. 2.014.

prejudice) and also subject to certain other requirements. For example, it does not authorise any variation or abrogation of the special rights of any class of members.[292]

2.24.3 Applications under ss. 130(3) and 136(1) (Confirmation of Reductions of Share Premium Account and Share Capital)

A special resolution may be passed in certain circumstances in order to reduce the share capital or share premium account of a company.[293] Where a resolution of this type has been passed, the company may apply to the court under ss. 130(3) and 136(1) for an order confirming the reduction. Certain specific safeguards exist for the protection of creditors if such an application is made. Thus, if the proposed reduction involves either a diminution of liability in respect of unpaid share capital or the payment to a shareholder of any paid up share capital, every creditor of the company who would be permitted to prove in a winding-up will be entitled to object to the reduction of capital.[294] Provisions are also made for the settlement of a list of creditors entitled to object and for the securing or payment of a debt or claim of a dissenting creditor so as to allow the application to proceed.[295] Where the court is satisfied that every creditor entitled to object has either consented to the reduction or had his debt or claim discharged or determined or secured, it may make an order confirming the reduction on such terms and conditions as it thinks fit.[296]

2.24.4 Applications under s. 127(2) (Cancellation of Variation of Class Rights)

A memorandum or articles may authorise the variation of the rights attached to a class of shares, subject to the consent of a specified proportion of the shareholders of that class or the sanction of a resolution passed in a separate meeting of those shareholders.[297] If rights attach to a class of shares otherwise than by the memorandum, and the articles do not provide for variation, statutory procedures exist for the class rights to be altered.[298]

If, by any of the above procedures, the rights attached to any class of shares are varied, then under s. 127(2) shareholders with not less than 15% in the aggregate of the issued shares of the class in question may apply to have the variation cancelled. If this is done then the variation will have no effect unless and until it is confirmed by the court. Provisions are made for the time limits within which the application must be made and as to representation in relation to the proceedings.[299] On hearing the application, the court may if satisfied, having regard to all the circumstances of the case, that the variation would unfairly prejudice the shareholders of the class represented by the applicant, disallow the variation and must if not so satisfied, confirm it. In either event the decision of the court is final.[300]

292. S. 17(2).
293. See generally ss. 130 and 135.
294. S. 136(2) and (3).
295. S. 136(4) and (5).
296. S. 137(1).
297. S. 127(1)(a).
298. See s. 125(2).
299. S. 127(3).
300. S. 127(4).

2.24.5 Applications under s. 425(2) (Sanction of a Compromise or Arrangement)

This form of petition arises where a compromise or arrangement is proposed between a company and its creditors or members and has been proposed and considered at a meeting of the creditors or members.[301] Under s. 425(2), where a majority, representing three-quarters in value of the creditors or members present and voting, agree to the compromise or arrangement, then the compromise or arrangement will be binding on all creditors or members and also on the company.[302] The section states, however, that this is subject to the sanction of the court. Accordingly an application is necessary for this purpose.

2.24.6 Applications under s. 690(2) (Cancellation of Alterations to Company's Constitution)

Applications of this type arise in connection with companies which are not formed under the Companies Act 1985 but which are permitted to register under that Act.[303] A company so registered may, by special resolution, alter the form of its constitution by substituting a memorandum and articles for a deed of settlement.[304] In these circumstances the same type of provisions as those outlined above in relation to ss. 5(1) and 17(1), concerning the alteration of objects and conditions of a memorandum, apply in this context under s. 690(2). That section simply adds certain modifications as to the documents to be delivered to the registrar of companies in this case.[305]

2.24.7 Applications under s. 727(1) (Relief from Liability of Officer or Auditor)

Where any proceedings for negligence, default, breach of duty or breach of trust are brought against an officer of a company or its auditor, and that person appears to be liable but has acted honestly and reasonably, and the court concludes that, having regard to all the circumstances of the case (including those connected with his appointment) he ought fairly to be excused, the court may relieve him from his liability on such terms as it thinks fit.[306] Before proceedings actually commence, however, an officer or an auditor may have reason to apprehend that a claim will or might be brought against him of this type. In these circumstances he may apply to the court for relief under s. 727(2) and on this application the court will have the same power to relieve him from liability as it would where proceedings had already been started.

2.24.8 Applications under s. 54(1) (Cancellation of Resolution for Re-registration as Private Company)

These applications arise where a public company has passed a resolution for its re-registration as a private company.[307] Where such a special resolution has been passed,

301. S. 425(1).
302. If the company is in the course of being wound up it will also be binding on the liquidator and contributories of the company.
303. See part XXII of the Act and in particular ss. 680 to 689.
304. S. 690(1).
305. S. 690(2)(b).
306. S. 727(1).
307. See s. 53(1).

an application may be made under s. 54(1) for its cancellation. Various requirements exist governing who is entitled to make the application and the time within which it must be commenced.[308] On hearing the application, the court is required to make an order either cancelling or confirming the resolution. The court may also adjourn the proceedings so that an arrangement may be made to the satisfaction of the court for the purchase of the interests of dissenting members, and it may also give directions and make orders as it thinks expedient for facilitating or carrying into effect any such arrangement.[309]

2.24.9 Applications under s. 157(2) (Cancellation of Resolution Permitting Company to give Financial Assistance)

These petitions arise in the context of the prohibition on a company or any of its subsidiaries giving financial assistance directly or indirectly for the purposes of the acquisition of its own shares.[310] Under s. 155 there is no prohibition on a private company giving financial assistance where the acquisition of shares is in another company of which it is a subsidiary, subject to satisfaction of certain conditions. One such condition is that, unless the company which is proposing to give the financial assistance is a wholly owned subsidiary, the giving of assistance must be approved by special resolution of the company in a general meeting.[311] Where such a resolution has been passed, an application may be made under s. 157(2) for cancellation of that resolution. The application may be made by shareholders holding not less than 10% in aggregate of the nominal value of the company's issued share capital, or if the company is not limited by shares, by not less than 10% of the company's members. The application cannot be made, however, by a person who has consented to or voted in favour of the resolution. On hearing the application, the court must make an order, cancelling or confirming the resolution, and has power to make additional orders of an equivalent type to those described above in connection with petitions under s. 54(1).[312]

2.24.10 Applications under s. 170(4) (Confirmation of Reduction of Capital Redemption Reserve)

This type of petition arises in connection with the capital redemption reserve of a company. A company may, in certain circumstances, redeem or purchase its own shares.[313] Where it does so wholly out of profits, the amount by which the company's issued share capital is diminished by cancellation of the shares redeemed or purchased is to be transferred to a reserve, called "the capital redemption reserve".[314] Under s. 170(4), the provisions of the Act described earlier, relating to the reduction of a company's share capital, apply as if the capital redemption reserve were paid up share capital of the company. The only exception is that the reserve may be applied by the company in paying

308. S. 54(2) and (3).
309. S. 54(5).
310. See generally ss. 151 to 154.
311. S. 155(4).
312. S. 157(3).
313. See generally ss. 159 to 169.
314. S. 170(1).

up its unissued shares to be allotted to members of the company as fully paid bonus shares.

2.24.11 Applications under s. 176(1) (Cancellation of Resolution Approving Redemption or Purchase of Shares)

These applications arise in connection with a private company where that company seeks to make a payment in respect of the redemption or purchase of its own shares otherwise than out of its distributable profits or the proceeds of a fresh issue of shares. For such a payment out of capital to be lawful it must, among other things, be approved by a special resolution of the company.[315] Under s. 176(1), where a private company passes such a special resolution, any member of the company, other than one who consented to or voted in favour of the resolution, and any creditor of the company may, within five weeks of the date on which the resolution was passed, apply to the court for the cancellation of that resolution. On hearing the application, the court may adjourn the proceedings in order that an arrangement can be made to the court's satisfaction for the purchase of the interests of dissentient members or for the protection of dissentient creditors.[316] In any event, the court must make an order, on such terms and conditions as it thinks fit, either confirming or cancelling the resolution.[317]

2.24.12 Applications under s. 653 (Restoration of Name of Company to Register in Conjunction with Winding-Up)

Applications under s. 653 have already been discussed above in the context of originating summonses.[318] Where such applications are made in conjunction with a petition for the winding-up of a company, however, it is appropriate that the application for restoration of the name of the company to the register should also be disposed of by way of petition.[319]

2.25 Contents of the petition

Petitions presented to the Companies Court must comply with the requirements as to the contents of petitions generally in the High Court. Thus, they must include a concise statement of the nature of the claim made or the relief or remedy required.[320] Each petition must also include, at the end, a statement of the names of the persons, if any, required to be served with it or, if no person is required to be served, a statement to that effect.[321] As in the case of originating summonses and originating notices of motion, the provisions of RSC O. 6, r. 5 (concerning endorsement of address) apply, with any necessary modifications to petitions.[322]

315. S. 173(2).
316. S. 177(1).
317. S. 177(2).
318. See para. 2.2.24, *supra*.
319. O. 102, r. 4(1)(g).
320. RSC O. 9, r. 2(1).
321. RSC O. 9, r. 2(2).
322. RSC O. 9, r. 2(3). See also para. 2.4, *supra*.

As in the case of a notice of originating motion, amendment of a petition can be applied for in the same way as an amendment to a writ.[323] Also, although a petition is excluded from the definition of a pleading under the Rules of the Supreme Court,[324] application may be made to have a petition struck out in the same way as if it were a pleading.[325]

2.26 Issue

The petitions governed by Order 102 may be presented in the office of the Companies Court Registrar.[326] In presenting the petition, two copies should be prepared, together with any necessary additional copies where it is required that they be served. The petitioner should have one of the copies stamped and then deliver all of the copies to the office of the registrar where they will be sealed and a distinctive number assigned.[327]

If a summons for directions is not required to be taken out,[328] a time and place will be fixed for the hearing of the petition. If a summons for directions is to be taken out, this will not occur. Notice of any fixture will be inserted in each copy of the petition.

One copy of the petition will be retained by the court for the use of the judge, and the original petition, the stamped copy, will be returned to the petitioner to be exhibited to the affidavit verifying the petition.

2.27 Service of a petition

Where a petition is required to be served then this must be done not less than seven days before the date fixed for the hearing unless the court otherwise directs.[329] Service is to be effected in the same way as a writ.[330] Thus personal and postal service will be required in accordance with the rules which apply to writs and the discussion in this connection under the heading of originating summonses is also applicable here.[331]

2.28 Service out of the jurisdiction

A petition may be served out of the jurisdiction in the same way as an originating summons. The discussion in relation to originating summonses on this point is therefore also relevant here.[332]

2.29 Acknowledgement of service

Acknowledgement of service is not required and indeed there is no obligation on any person who wishes to oppose a petition to give notice of his position to the petitioner. It

323. RSC O. 20, r. 7 applying O. 20, r. 5.
324. RSC O. 1, r. 4(1).
325. RSC O. 18, r. 19(3).
326. O. 102, r. 4(2).
327. Attendance in person at the offices of the registrar of the Companies Court is not required. Presentation can be carried out by post in accordance with Practice Direction (Chancery No. 6 (C)), *supra*.
328. As to which see para. 2.31 *et seq.*, *infra*.
329. RSC O. 9, r. 4(2).
330. See *Supreme Court Practice 1997*, Vol. 1, p. 70, para. 9/4/1.
331. See para. 2.5, *supra* and RSC O. 10 and O. 65.
332. See para. 2.6, *supra*.

is, however, advisable and convenient so as to avoid delay resulting from an adjournment, that every person intending to oppose the petition should give notice of his intention to do so to the petitioner or the petitioner's solicitors. For the same purpose, it is advisable to furnish them with copies of the evidence filed in opposition to the petition as long as possible before the hearing, so that the petition can if possible be disposed of on the first occasion on which it comes before the court.

2.30 Evidence

Evidence in support of and in opposition to a petition is normally by way of affidavit.[333] Where an affidavit has been sworn shortly before the presentation of a petition, it may nevertheless be received in evidence.[334] This is subject to any direction of the court to the contrary, and with certain petitions the court may require oral evidence to be adduced instead of, or as a supplement to, the evidence which has been filed by way of affidavit. In addition, the court may make an order for the cross-examination of deponents to affidavits. If such an order is made and the deponent does not attend for cross-examination, his affidavit may not be used in evidence without leave of the court.[335]

The earlier discussion, in the context of originating summonses, regarding the contents of affidavits is also relevant here.[336]

2.31 Summons for directions

After the presentation of certain petitions, the petitioner is normally required to take out a summons for directions.[337] Such a summons for directions is not required in the case of the following types of petition, namely those under s. 54(1) (cancellation of resolution for public company to be re-registered as a private company); under s. 157(2) (financial assistance); under s. 176(1) (cancellation of resolution for redemption or purchase of shares out of capital); under s. 425 (sanction of a compromise or arrangement), unless there is also included in the petition an application for provision for a company reconstruction or amalgamation under s. 427 of the Act; and under s. 653 (restoration to the register).[338]

Where a summons for directions is required, it should be prepared in duplicate. The date for the hearing of the summons will then be fixed by the office of the Companies Court Registrar and marked in the body or in the margin of the summons, and a copy will be retained for filing, with the other copy being returned to the applicant.

For the hearing of the summons, as a matter of good practice, the parties should prepare (and if possible agree) a list of the essential issues in the case.[339] Moreover, to assist the court, the parties must deliver to the court, not later than two clear days before the day on which the summons for directions is to be heard, a signed information sheet.[340] If this is

333. RSC O. 38, r. 2(3).
334. Practice Direction (Chancery No. 8(A)(iii)), *Supreme Court Practice 1997*, Vol. 2, p. 175, para. 820.
335. RSC O. 38, r. 2(3).
336. See para. 2.8 *et seq.*, *supra*.
337. O. 102, r. 6(1).
338. O. 102, r. 6(2).
339. *Chancery Guide*, p. 12, para. 3.6(1).
340. A form is contained in Appendix 5 to the *Chancery Guide*.

not done and time is wasted as a result, the court may order the party responsible to pay the costs.[341]

Where a party has a legal representative at the hearing of the summons for directions, that representative should be a person who is familiar with the case.[342]

2.31.1 On the hearing of the summons for directions, the court will give such directions as it thinks fit for the hearing of the petition. In the case of petitions for the confirmation of a reduction of share capital, share premium account or capital redemption reserve, the court may give directions for an inquiry as to the debts or claims against the company or any class or classes of such debts or claims and as to the proceedings to be taken for settling the list of creditors entitled to object to the reduction. Directions may also be given for the fixing of the date by reference to which such a list is to be made.[343] Where the proposed reduction of share capital involves either the diminution of any liability in respect of unpaid share capital or the payment to any shareholder of any paid up share capital, the court has the power under s. 136(6) to direct that ss. 136(3) to (5) will not apply to any class or classes of creditors, if having regard to any special circumstances of the case it thinks it proper to do so. Ss. 136(3) to (5) provide for the entitlement of certain creditors to object, for the settling of a list of such creditors, and for the dispensing of their consent on terms. Exercise of the court's powers under s. 136(6) may be carried out on the hearing of a summons for directions.[344]

It is open to the court in an appropriate case to direct that pleadings be served and that other procedural steps, such as discovery, which form a standard feature of a writ action, should be followed.[345]

2.31.2 Directions will normally require steps to be taken within a specified period from the date of the hearing of the summons rather than within a specified date prior to the hearing of the petition.[346]

As in the case of other proceedings the hearing of which is estimated to exceed 10 days in length, a pre-trial review may occur.[347]

When appropriate directions have been given, and all the evidence required to be filed has been checked by the appropriate official in the office of the Companies Court Registrar, a date and place will be appointed for the hearing of the petition.

2.32 Interlocutory applications

Where a summons for directions is required to be issued, it may be more convenient to deal with interlocutory applications either at the first hearing of that summons or at a restored hearing. If a summons for directions is not required, or if for any reason it is not appropriate that the application be made under the summons for directions, then an application might either be made on a hearing of the petition itself or, alternatively, in the

341. *Chancery Guide*, p. 13, para. 3.6(b).
342. *Ibid.*, p. 13, para. 3.6(3).
343. O. 102, r. 6(4).
344. O. 102, r. 6(4).
345. RSC O.102, r. 6(3), which provides that the court may give such directions as to the proceedings to be taken before the hearing of the petition as it thinks fit. Cf. Companies (Unfair Prejudice Applications) Proceedings Rules 1986 (S.I. 1986 No. 2000), concerning petitions presented under s. 459, r. 5 of which expressly contemplates pleadings as a possible subject of directions.
346. *Chancery Guide*, p. 13, para. 3.6(4).
347. *Ibid.*, pp. 16–17, para. 3.10.

same way as an interlocutory application in a writ action in the Chancery Division. This may be by way of an ordinary summons which will come before the registrar in the first instance in the normal way, or by way of a motion direct to the judge. The comments made above, in the context of originating summonses concerning such applications also apply here.[348]

Applications to the registrar in chambers for orders convening meetings to consider schemes and for directions on reduction applications can be heard in the long vacation. So long as notice is given to the court before the long vacation begins, a timetable will be fixed which will enable the necessary documents to be settled in chambers and enable the registrar to hear the application.[349]

As in the case of interlocutory applications in proceedings by originating summons and motion, the general Chancery Division requirements as to preparation of bundles, skeleton arguments, reading lists and authorities will apply[350] as will the usual Companies Court requirements for evidence to be filed at least two days prior to the date of hearing or as soon as possible if the time available is too short.[351]

2.33 Hearing

The hearing of a petition will be fixed in the manner described above, under the headings of Issue and Summons for Directions. Petitions for approval of a scheme of arrangement are heard by the Companies Court Judge and petitions for confirmation of a reduction of capital are heard by the registrar unless otherwise ordered.[352] Hearings before the judge take place on Mondays. Hearings before the registrar occur on Wednesdays, in open court, after completion of the list of winding-up petitions.

In some cases, the petition can come on for hearing during the long vacation.[353] Applications which can be made in the long vacation in this way are those coming under ss. 130, 136 and 170 (confirmation of the reduction of share premium account, share capital and capital redemption reserve respectively) and under s. 425 (sanctioning a compromise or arrangement). To be heard in the long vacation, the application must not only come within one of the specified sections, but financial, commercial or economic reasons must make it desirable that the application is heard before the end of the long vacation (this category will include cases of mergers and takeovers which arise in the summer and are likely to be affected by market fluctuations). The application must be one which could not be made and prosecuted with reasonable diligence before the beginning of the long vacation. When these conditions are fulfilled, an informal application in Chambers must be made as soon as possible to the court manager, accompanied by an advocate's certificate that these conditions have been satisfied, whereupon a timetable will be settled including a date for the hearing. Other reduction applications not within the above categories will be heard by the registrar, provided there is an urgent need for a hearing, or there is sufficient time available after the disposal of urgent applications.[354]

348. See para. 2.9, *supra*.
349. Practice Direction (Companies Court: Schemes and Reductions) [1997] 1 WLR 1.
350. *Chancery Guide*, pp. 26–29, paras 5.3–5.6.
351. See *Supreme Court Practice 1997*, Vol. 1, p. 1533, para. 102/1/7.
352. Practice Direction (Companies Court: Schemes and Reductions) [1997] 1 WLR 1.
353. RSC O. 64, r. 3 and *Re Showerings, Vine Products and Whiteways Ltd* [1968] 1 WLR 1381.
354. Practice Direction (Companies Court: Schemes and Reductions), *supra*.

The vacation judge will hear petitions to sanction schemes and such petitions to confirm reductions as are adjourned to him, on one Wednesday in August and on two Wednesdays in September, of which notice is given in the Long Vacation Notice printed in the daily case list. The vacation judge may hear such petitions on other days if he thinks fit.[355]

2.33.1 At the hearing of the petition, the court may hear not only the petitioner and respondents but also, in some cases, any other persons who applied to the court to be heard and appear to the court to be interested in the application. This can happen, for example, in applications to cancel a variation of class rights of shareholders under s. 127(2).[356] In any event, if, on hearing a petition, it appears to the court that a person has not been given notice of the hearing of the petition and ought to have been given such notice, the petition may be either dismissed or adjourned to a different date so that notice may be given.[357]

The court may in any event adjourn the hearing of the petition, from time to time, on such terms, if any as it thinks fit.[358] In some cases, the petition may be adjourned with leave to present it afresh. In these circumstances it would technically be a different petition although using the same documents.[359]

When the petition comes on for hearing before the judge, he may at any stage adjourn any matter arising for determination, to be heard by the registrar in chambers, on the basis that it can be more conveniently dealt with there.[360] Following this, an appointment will be fixed before the registrar when the matter can be dealt with and any necessary directions given. After disposal of the matters required to be dealt with in chambers, the petition can be restored for hearing in court, with notice of restoration being given to all parties.

2.33.2 For all hearings of the petition, the Chancery Division standard requirements concerning bundles, skeleton arguments, reading lists and lists of authorities will apply.[361] In some cases, for example, where the hearing is expected to exceed 10 days in length and preparatory steps such as discovery have occurred, a pre-trial review may be appropriate.[362]

2.34 Appeals

Appeals from orders made on a petition in the Companies Court are brought on in the same way as appeals from orders on petitions in other cases. Thus, a notice of appeal will be served in the normal way on all parties to the proceedings in the court below, who are directly affected by the appeal, within four weeks from the date on which the judgment or order of the court below was sealed or otherwise perfected.[363] It should be noted that, in

355. *Ibid.*

356. S. 127(4).

357. This practice originates from the specific provisions of the former RSC O. LII6 which applied in 1883.

358. See *Hinckley and South Leicestershire Permanent Benefit Building Society* v. *Freeman* [1941] Ch. 32 and *Birmingham Citizens Permanent Building Society* v. *Caunt* [1962] Ch. 883. See also *Re Heyl ex parte DP Morgan* [1918] 1 KB 452.

359. See *Re Knox's Trusts* [1895] 1 Ch. 538, at 543 (per Kekewich J.).

360. RSC O. 32, r. 19. See *Re Judkins' Trusts* [1880] WN 198; *Re Moates Trust* (1883) 22 Ch.D. 635 and *Re Tweedy* (1885) Ch.D. 529.

361. *Chancery Guide*, pp. 26–29, paras 5.3–5.6.

362. *Ibid.*, pp. 16–17, para. 3.10.

363. RSC O. 59, rr. 3(1), (5) and 4(1).

relation to petitions under s. 127(2), there is no appeal from the decision of the court.[364]

2.35 Costs

As in the case of proceedings in the Companies Court by way of originating summons and originating notice of motion, costs will be at the discretion of the court.[365] Where a creditor in an application to reduce capital comes to prove his title, debt or claim in relation to the company, he will, if his claim succeeds, be entitled to his costs incurred in establishing it and, if his claim or any part of it fails, he may be ordered to pay the costs incurred by any person in opposing it.[366] Parties who attend at the hearing of the petition and have no interest in the subject-matter of the petition, may not be allowed their costs. Where a person has been served but has no interest, his proper course is not to appear but to notify the petitioner that he has no interest. Also, a person who is served with a petition solely as a result of his own unwarranted claims will not be allowed his costs.[367]

Where there are two petitions having the same object, the costs of both may still be allowed, provided they have been presented in good faith. Where the second petition, however, is presented with knowledge of the first one, the costs of it will not generally be allowed.[368] If the second petition is abandoned as soon as the existence of the first is known, the costs up to the time of abandonment may be allowed.[369] If the second petition is more complete in the form of relief which it seeks, and the court accedes to that wider form of relief, then the costs of it may correspondingly be allowed.[370]

364. S. 127(4).
365. See generally RSC O. 62.
366. RSC O. 62, r. 6(3)(b) and O. 102, r. 12.
367. See for example *Re Shrewsbury School* (1849) 1 Mac. & G. 85.
368. *Re Chaplin's Trusts* (1863) 3 New Rep. 192.
369. *Re Saville's Trusts* (1886) 14 WR 603.
370. *Re Pring's Trusts* (1873) 42 LJ Ch. 473.

PART 2

PARTICULAR PROCEEDINGS UNDER THE COMPANIES ACT 1985

CHAPTER 3

SCHEMES OF ARRANGEMENT

3.1 Introduction

Section 425 of the Companies Act 1985 provides a mechanism whereby a compromise or arrangement between a company[1] and its members or creditors, or a class or classes of its members or creditors, can be made binding without the separate agreement of all the members or creditors affected by it. In order to achieve this result, the section requires:

(i) an order of the court to convene a meeting of the members or the creditors or of each class involved in the scheme;
(ii) approval of the scheme at the meeting or meetings by a majority in number representing three-fourths in value of those present and voting in person or by proxy at the meeting; and
(iii) the sanction of the court to the scheme of arrangement.

3.1.1 There is no statutory limitation on the compromises or arrangements which can be promoted under the section. The only limitation is that it must be a compromise or arrangement. In *Re NFU Development Trust Ltd*,[2] Brightman J. held that those words implied some accommodation on both sides and could not apply to a scheme whereby members' rights were totally surrendered without compensation. Schemes of arrangement have been sanctioned for a very wide range of purposes. Examples involving members include:

(i) Schemes for the reconstruction of a company, involving the interposition of a new holding company by the transfer of the issued share capital of the company to the new holding company in exchange for an issue of its shares to the members of the company. Alternatively, this may be achieved by a cancellation of the issued share capital of the company and the capitalisation of the reserve arising from such cancellation and its application in paying up new shares to be issued to the new holding company, with the new holding company issuing shares to the members of the company.
(ii) Schemes whereby an existing company acquires the issued share capital (other than any shares already owned by it) of another company, for consideration in such form as the scheme provides.[3]

1. "Company" is widely defined to mean any company liable to be wound up under the Insolvency Act 1986 (Companies Act 1985, ss. 425(6)(a) and 735A(1)). A scheme of arrangement can therefore be proposed in relation to a foreign company: for example, see *Re Heron International NV* [1994] 1 BCLC 667; *Re RMCA Reinsurance Ltd* [1994] BCC 378.
2. [1972] 1 WLR 1548.
3. *Re National Bank Ltd* [1966] 1 WLR 819; *Re Savoy Hotel Ltd* [1981] Ch. 351.

(iii) Schemes for the reorganisation of the share capital of a company including the alteration of rights attached to shares.[4] Section 425(6)(b) specifically provides that "arrangement" includes the consolidation of shares of different classes or the division of shares into shares of different classes.

(iv) Schemes whereby assets or part of the business of the company are directly or indirectly distributed to shareholders, sometimes in conjunction with a sale or other disposal of the relevant assets or business to a third party. In this way a scheme can facilitate a disposal in such a way that the consideration is provided by the third party acquirer directly to shareholders.

Schemes involving creditors may provide for a moratorium on payment, a composition, or the replacement of the whole or part of debts with shares or other securities of the debtor company or of some other company or companies; as with members' schemes, there is no limitation on the proposals which can be embodied in a scheme. While schemes involving creditors will usually result from the actual or prospective insolvency of the company concerned,[5] this need not be the case. In particular, a solvent company might propose a scheme with the holders of bonds or loan stocks.

As with applications to confirm a reduction of capital,[6] the court might refuse to sanction the scheme, or to convene meetings for the purpose of considering a scheme, where the proposal can, without difficulty, be achieved by the unanimous agreement of the members or creditors involved, so that the application to invoke the court's powers under the Act constitutes an abuse of its process.

3.2 Application to convene meetings

3.2.1 Timetable

As with applications to confirm reductions of capital, the company's solicitors should be in contact with the Companies Court office in good time before the issue of the originating summons to agree a draft timetable. This will aim to cover all steps from the issue of the summons to the hearing of the petition to sanction the scheme.

3.2.2 Originating summons

The first procedural step in relation to a scheme of arrangement is the application to the court for an order pursuant to s. 425(1) to convene the meeting or meetings of members or creditors. The application is usually made by the company concerned, but may be made by a member or creditor of the company or, in the case of a company being wound up or a company in administration, by the liquidator or administrator.[7] The application is made by originating summons,[8] entitled in the matter of the company and in the matter of the Companies Act 1985. It is made *ex parte* unless the applicant is a member or creditor in

4. See CA 1985, s. 126.
5. See for example *Re British and Commonwealth Holdings plc* [1992] 1 WLR 672; *Re Maxwell Communication Corp. plc* [1993] 1 WLR 1402; *Re Heron International NV* [1904] 1 BCLC 667.
6. *Re Rylands Whitecross Ltd*, 21 December 1973, Brightman J., unreported.
7. CA 1985, s. 425(1).
8. RSC O. 102, r. 2(1).

which case the company should be joined as respondent. Although the Rules of the Supreme Court[9] provide that the originating summons should be in Form No. 10 in Appendix A, this form is appropriate only to an application by a member or creditor with the company as respondent.[10] In the normal case of an application by the company, or by a liquidator or administrator, the summons should be in the *ex parte* form set out in Form 11 in Appendix A.

The summons should specify the class or classes of members or creditors of which meetings are required, seek directions as to the method of convening the meetings and an order appointing a named individual and one or two alternates to be the chairmen of the meetings (or, if appropriate, different chairmen for different meetings, although this is rarely necessary). In the case of a scheme involving members or creditors of different companies, it is possible to seek the required orders in a single summons entitled in the matter of all the companies, but it is more usual to issue a separate summons for each company. Two copies should be taken to the general office of the Companies Court where one will be retained on the court file and the other will be returned, stamped, to the person issuing the summons. A return date for the hearing of the summons, which will be before the registrar, is given at the time of issue.

3.2.3 Affidavit

An affidavit should be sworn in support of the application. Where the company is the applicant, the affidavit is usually sworn by the chairman of its board of directors or by another director. If the company is in liquidation or in administration, the deponent would usually be the liquidator or the administrator. After giving details of the incorporation, registered office, objects and current authorised and issued share capital of the company, and exhibiting its certificate(s) of incorporation and current memorandum and articles of association, the affidavit should give sufficient information to explain the background to the proposed scheme and the reasons for it, as well as a summary of its terms and effects. It should specify the proposed class or classes of members or creditors and give the information necessary to enable the court to give directions as to the method of convening and holding the meetings. In addition to these matters and the matters dealt with below, the affidavit should give a brief summary of any general or other meetings being held in connection with the scheme and the latest audited accounts of the company should be exhibited to it. The affidavit must be filed at the general office.[11]

3.2.4 Classes of members and creditors

Although the meetings of members or creditors are convened in accordance with the directions of the court, the responsibility for determining the appropriate classes of members or creditors lies with the applicant.[12] Any issue as to the correct composition of the classes will generally be determined on the hearing of the petition to sanction the scheme. Unless the classes are correctly constituted, the court will not have jurisdiction to

9. RSC O. 102, r. 2(2).
10. As to service, see Chapter 2, *supra*.
11. As to the service of evidence if the application is not made *ex parte*, see Chapter 2, *supra*.
12. Practice Note [1934] WN 142.

sanction the scheme[13] and it will be no answer for the applicant to say that meetings of those classes were convened pursuant to the directions of the court. In principle it might be open to an applicant to raise an issue on the composition of classes at the stage of the originating summons, but the determination would not be binding on members or creditors unless representatives were joined as respondents and appropriate representation orders were made. Recently, where difficult issues have arisen as to the composition of classes for schemes to be proposed by companies in administration, the administrators have used the power under s. 14(3) of the Insolvency Act 1986 to seek directions determining the issues,[14] thereby avoiding the expense of a scheme only to find at the last stage that the court could not sanction it.

In the case of members, the classes for the purposes of the scheme will usually be defined by reference to the existing classes of shares or members involved. Each separate class of shares should be treated as a separate class for the purposes of the scheme and where the terms of the scheme treat members of the same class differently, each group of members will constitute separate classes for the purposes of the scheme. In addition, there can be cases in which the differences between members of the same class of shares are so great that they must be divided into separate classes for the purposes of the scheme.[15] Similarly, where some shares in a class are partly paid and others are fully paid, it may be necessary to treat their respective holders as constituting separate classes, depending on the terms of the scheme.[16]

In the context of a scheme involving creditors, it has been said that the reason for dividing creditors into different classes is that:

"the creditors composing the different classes have different interests; and, therefore, if we find a different state of facts existing among different creditors which may differently affect their minds and their judgment, they must be divided into different classes"

and that the term "class"

"must be confined to those persons whose rights are not so dissimilar as to make it impossible for them to consult together with a view to their common interest".[17]

It was held in that case, involving an insurance company, that the holders of matured policies on which a definite sum was due and payable, constituted a separate class from the holders of unmatured policies.

Where some members or creditors have other interests or rights in relation to the company, they may be included in the same class as members or creditors without those interests or rights where there is a sufficient community of interest between them, and in

13. *Re United Provident Assurance Co. Ltd* [1910] 2 Ch. 477; *Re Hellenic and General Trust Ltd* [1976] 1 WLR 123, [1976] 3 All ER 382.

14. *Re British & Commonwealth Holdings plc (No. 3)* [1992] 1 WLR 672; *Re Maxwell Communication Corp. plc* [1993] 1 WLR 1402, [1994] 1 All ER 737.

15. *Re Hellenic and General Trust Ltd, supra* (where the scheme involved the acquisition of the shares of the company and it was held that a wholly-owned subsidiary of the acquirer which owned shares in the company constituted a separate class).

16. *Re United Provident Assurance Co. Ltd, supra.*

17. *Sovereign Life Assurance Co.* v. *Dodd* [1892] 2 QB 573 at 580 per Lord Esher M.R. and at 583 per Bowen L.J.

the last resort it is a question of degree whether a sufficient community of interest exists.[18]

The consent of a class of members or creditors is not required where their rights are not affected by the scheme or where it can be shown that they have no interest in the matter because, for example, on a distribution of assets there would be no assets available for that class.[19]

3.3 Directions as to meetings

3.3.1 Directions as to notice

As regards notice of a meeting, it used to be the case that the court would require both a newspaper advertisement of the meeting and notice to be sent to each member or creditor concerned whose address was known. In the case of bearer shares, a newspaper advertisement will still be required, usually in accordance with the provisions of the company's articles for giving notice of meetings to bearer shareholders. The shares in the vast majority of companies are in registered form, and the practice of the court has changed so that a newspaper advertisement is required only where a notice sent to their registered address is unlikely to be received by a material number of shareholders. As a rule of thumb, the holders of 5% or less of the shares of the relevant class will not be regarded as material. Evidence must therefore be given of the number (if any) of shareholders, and the total size of their holdings, who are known by the company not to receive documents sent to their registered addresses (e.g. because they are returned or dividend warrants are regularly not encashed). The affidavit should also state whether the company maintains a branch register or has any bearer shares in issue, and if so should give details. If the articles provide that, in the case of joint holdings of shares, notice need be sent only to the first-named joint holder appearing in the register of members, the court will make a similar order in respect of the meetings convened by the court. This should be specifically mentioned in the affidavit.

3.3.2 Shares in the CREST system

The shares of many listed companies are now held in uncertificated form in the CREST system which is governed by The Uncertificated Securities Regulations 1995 (S.I. 1995 No. 3272). Regulation 34(3) empowers a company to determine the members entitled to receive notice of a meeting by reference to the register of members at the close of business on a record date, which must not be more than 21 days before the day on which notice of the meeting is sent. This provision does not apply to meetings convened by order of the court for the purposes of a scheme. However, as the directions for convening such meetings are a matter of discretion for the court, it is open to the court to permit the use of a record date. In practice the court has been willing to do so, provided that the record date is as close as practicable to the date of despatch of the notice of the meeting.

18. *Re Heron International NV* [1994] 1 BCLC 667.

19. *Re Tea Corp. Ltd* [1904] 1 Ch. 12; *Re Oceanic Steam Navigation Co. Ltd* [1939] Ch. 41; *Re British & Commonwealth Holdings plc (No. 3)* 1 WLR 672.

3.3.3 Directions as to place and chairman

The affidavit should also state the city or other place in which it is proposed to hold the meeting[20] and the proposed chairman. The court may order meetings to be held abroad.[21] It is sensible to make provision for one or two alternate chairmen, to avoid a further application to the court for the appointment of a new chairman in the event that the chairman appointed by the order is unable to chair the meeting.

3.3.4 Directions as to proxy voting

Section 425(2) expressly provides for voting by proxy, as well as voting in person, at meetings convened under the section. The order convening the meeting will provide for forms of proxy to be settled by the court in chambers and to be sent to members and creditors with notice of the meeting. In practice, the form of proxy is usually settled by the registrar at the hearing of the originating summons. It will be a two-way voting form, making express provision for members or creditors to vote for or against the scheme. Members and creditors are not confined to using that form of proxy but may use any form, at any rate if the company is not in liquidation.[22] The order will normally direct that forms of proxy should either be delivered to a specified address not later than 48 hours before the time fixed for the meeting, or handed to the chairman at the meeting. If forms of proxy are returned pursuant to the court's order, appointing the chairman of the meeting, or a director as proxy, they are bound to use them. Where resolutions are proposed at the meeting to modify a scheme or to defer consideration of it, a proxy may, under the usual form of proxy, vote on the proposal although he may not have direct instructions from the appointor, using his own judgement in the light of the appointor's instruction to vote in favour of or against the scheme.[23] Where the circumstances require it, for example if creditors are resident in another country, the court may give directions for lodging proxies at a place in that country and for details of the proxies to be communicated to the chairman of the meeting.[24]

3.3.5 Size of class

Where a particular class comprises only one person, or a small number of persons all of whom are willing to consent to the scheme, it is usual not to hold a meeting of that class but to rely on their individual consents and on an undertaking by them to the court to be bound by the scheme given at the hearing of the petition. However, the court has jurisdiction to convene a meeting of a particular class, even though there can only be one person comprised in the class.[25]

20. The exact venue need not be stated.
21. *Re RMCA Reinsurance Ltd* [1994] BCC 378.
22. *Re Dorman, Long and Co. Ltd* [1934] Ch. 635.
23. *Re Dorman Long & Co. Ltd, supra*, at p. 662; *Re Waxed Papers Ltd* [1937] 2 All ER 481.
24. *Re English Scottish and Australian Chartered Bank* [1893] 3 Ch. 385.
25. *Re RMCA Reinsurance Ltd, supra*.

3.4 Explanatory statement

Section 426 requires an explanatory statement to be sent with every notice summoning the meetings.[26] If a meeting is convened by advertisement, the statement must be included in the advertisement or copies must be available at a place and in a manner stated in the advertisement,[27] although in practice the latter course is usually adopted. The statement must explain the effect of the compromise or arrangement. No particular form is prescribed as this will inevitably depend on the circumstances of the particular case.[28] In the case of a listed company, it will not differ essentially from the sort of circular which would usually be sent to shareholders in connection with a proposal being put forward for their approval. Commonly, the statement will be made by the merchant bank or other financial adviser of the company or, where more than one company is involved, jointly by their advisers. In such a case there is also likely to be included in the document to be sent to shareholders, a shorter letter from the chairman dealing with the proposal in a more general way. Any further information considered necessary or desirable, together with the text of the scheme itself and the notice of the meeting or meetings, will usually be included in the same document.

A copy or print of the latest draft of the document available at the time of swearing the affidavit should be exhibited to it. If a further draft is available by the time of the hearing of the originating summons, it should be given to the registrar at the hearing. At the hearing, the registrar will approve the form of explanatory statement and the form of scheme,[29] subject to the completion of any blanks (such as latest share prices) and such minor modifications as may be approved by counsel or, where counsel will be unavailable, by the applicant's solicitors. This approval does not indicate anything more than that the scheme and statement are fit to be sent to members or creditors. If, following the hearing, changes need to be made which are not minor, an application must be made to the registrar to approve them.

There are two matters which s. 426 specifically requires to be stated in the explanatory statement. First, it must state any material interests of the directors of the company to which the scheme relates (whether as directors or as members or as creditors of the company or otherwise) and the effect on those interests of the scheme, in so far as it is different from the effect on the like interests of other persons.[30] Where the effect is not different, it is usual to include a statement to that effect. Secondly, where the scheme affects the rights of debenture holders, a similar statement as to the interests of the trustees of any deed for securing the issue of the debentures and the effects of the scheme on those interests must be included.[31]

A wide meaning is to be given to "material interests". It includes anything which may affect the interest of the director or trustee in recommending acceptance or rejection of the

26. CA 1985, s. 426(2).
27. CA 1985, s. 426(3).
28. See para. 3.6.6, *infra*.
29. The registrar is not directly concerned with any other parts of the circular to be sent to members or creditors, such as any letter from the chairman, unless they are expressly made part of the explanatory statement.
30. CA 1985, s. 426(2). If the directors have an interest as trustees, this must be disclosed: *Second Scottish Investment Trust Co. Ltd*, 1962 SLT (Notes) 78.
31. CA 1985, s. 426(4).

scheme[32] or which might, in a business sense, be regarded as influencing his judgment.[33] It will include not only interests with respect to the company to which the scheme relates, but all material interests including those with respect to other companies involved in the scheme. If, for example, the scheme provides for the acquisition of the share capital of one company by another company, the interests of directors in relation to both companies should be disclosed. Interests in shares should always be stated, as should details of any service contracts if they could be material. Obviously any arrangements with directors which are contingent on the success or failure of the scheme or which might be affected by its success or failure should be disclosed.

If, between the despatch of the statement and the meeting(s) of members or creditors, the disclosed interests are altered in a way which may affect the attitude of members or creditors, the directors must communicate the alteration to them. Where it is not communicated to them, the court will not sanction the scheme if the alteration in interests is likely to have affected the decision of a reasonable members or creditors as to how to vote on the scheme or as to whether to vote or abstain. It is for the petitioner to satisfy the court that the alteration would not have affected the members or creditors.[34]

3.5 Hearing of the application to convene meetings

The summons is heard by the registrar in chambers. It is an *ex parte* application except in the case of applications by a member or a creditor and, save with the leave of the court, no person other than the applicant will be heard on the application. Where the application is made by a member or a creditor, the company is respondent and is entitled to be heard. In *Re Savoy Hotel Ltd*[35] an application by a member was opposed by the company and was adjourned by the registrar to the judge.

In the usual *ex parte* or unopposed case the registrar will give all necessary directions in relation to the meeting(s). There should be handed to the registrar the latest proof of the explanatory statement and scheme, a final proof of the form or forms of proxy (a separate form for each meeting) and a draft order. If satisfied with those documents, the registrar will initial them. By prior informal arrangement with the officer of the Companies Court assigned to the case, the applicant's solicitor can take those documents and the court file immediately to that officer, who will stamp the order and, if newspaper advertisement has been directed, settle the form of advertisement.

3.6 Application for sanction of scheme

3.6.1 Petition

If the scheme has been approved by the requisite majorities prescribed by s. 425(2) at the meeting or meetings convened by the court,[36] application is made to the court for its sanction of the scheme. The application is made by petition.[37] The petitioner will normally

32. *Rankin & Blackmore Ltd* [1950] SC 218.
33. *Coltness Iron Co. Ltd* [1951] SC 476.
34. *Re Jessel Trust Ltd* [1985] BCLC 119; *Re Minster Assets plc* [1985] BCLC 200.
35. [1981] Ch. 351.
36. The scheme may provide that it is capable of becoming effective as regards those classes which approved it at their meetings, even though it has not been approved by all classes.
37. RSC O. 102, r. 4.

be the applicant on the originating summons. If the petitioner is the company or liquidator or administrator, there will be no respondent named in the petition, which accordingly will not need to be served. If the petitioner is a member or creditor, the company will be named as respondent and the petition will need to be served on it. The court will not sanction a scheme without the consent of the company or, if it is in liquidation, the liquidator.[38]

3.6.2 Contents of petition

The petition should be entitled in the same manner as the originating summons and should start by setting out, in separate paragraphs, details of the incorporation of the company and any changes of name or re-registration as a public or private company, its registered office, a brief summary of its objects and its present authorised and issued share capital. It should then set out a summary statement of the background to, and reasons for, the scheme, and a similar statement of its principal terms and effects. The petition should refer to the order made on the originating summons to convene meetings and state that the meetings were convened and held in accordance with the order, giving the date, place and chairman. Details should be given of the numbers of members or creditors attending the meeting and the amounts of their shares or claims. It should also give the same information with respect to the members or creditors voting for, and those voting against, the scheme (distinguishing in each case between those who attended in person and those who attended by proxy). If any amendments have been made to the scheme at the meetings, details should be stated.

3.6.3 Evidence

The evidence in support of the petition will normally comprise an affidavit by the chairman of the company or other senior officer (or liquidator if the company is in liquidation) and affidavits to prove service of the notices convening the meetings. It is convenient if the principal affidavit is made by the person who chaired the meetings. If not, a separate affidavit will be required from him, exhibiting his report to the court, of the proceedings at and results of the meetings. A report to the court by the chairman of each meeting is required even if the scheme was rejected. A sealed copy of the petition is exhibited to the principal affidavit and verified by it. Much of the detail in the petition will have been dealt with in the affidavit in support of the originating summons and relevant documents exhibited to it. This need not be repeated in the affidavit verifying the petition and it is sufficient to refer to the earlier affidavit. The circular to shareholders or creditors, comprising the explanatory statement, scheme, notices of meetings and any other material, should be exhibited and verified. The evidence as to giving notice of the meetings is similar to that required for a petition to confirm a reduction of capital: see para. 4.6.4, *infra*.

3.6.4 Advertisement

If the court has ordered that notice of the meetings should be advertised, a copy of the newspaper containing the advertisement must be lodged with the evidence in support of the petition.

38. *Re International Contract Co.* (*Hankey's Case*) 26 LT 358; *Re Savoy Hotel Ltd, supra.*

3.6.5 *Reduction of capital*

Schemes of arrangement involving members commonly include a reduction of share capital. In this event, the petition will also seek the confirmation of the court to the reduction, and will include the additional material necessary for a reduction of capital, viz. the history of the company's authorised share capital, the relevant articles conferring authority for a reduction, any relevant class rights, the special resolution, and the proposed minute: see para. 4.5, *infra*. Likewise, the principal affidavit in support of the petition should give details of the general meeting at which the special resolution was passed, the purpose of the reduction, the liabilities of the company and how it is proposed to safeguard the interests of creditors,[39] and should exhibit earlier sets of articles of association if relevant to the capital history, the minute book containing minutes of the general meetings, and any documents relevant to creditors: see para. 4.6.3, *infra*. It will also be necessary to issue a summons for directions to deal with the position of creditors and advertisement of the hearing of the petition: see paras 4.8–4.9.13, *infra*. No summons for directions is required if there is no reduction of capital involved in the scheme.

3.6.6 *Hearing*

The petition is heard in open court by the judge, usually on a Monday in term.[40] Neither the Act nor the Rules of the Supreme Court specify those who may oppose a petition. However, any member or creditor affected by the scheme will be entitled to be heard. The procedure adopted is similar to the procedure on the hearing of petitions to sanction reductions of capital. The judge will hear the petition immediately if there is no opposition. If there is opposition, he may nonetheless hear the petition immediately or he will give any directions needed for the further conduct of the petition, such as directions relating to any further evidence. The opponents may wish to file evidence if they have not already done so or to supplement it, and the petitioner may wish to file evidence in reply. All such evidence will be by way of affidavit and the judge will direct a timetable for such further evidence as he may permit. However, it has been held that an opposing member or creditor is not entitled to any order for discovery against the petitioner on the grounds of not being a "party" to the petition within the meaning of s. 151(1) of the Supreme Court Act 1981 and RSC Order 24, rule 10,[41] although the court may order the petitioner to produce documents at the hearing of the petition.[42]

In relation to the merits of the scheme, whether or not there is opposition, the court will be concerned to see that the requirements of ss. 425 and 426 have been complied with. First, the classes of members or creditors must have been properly constituted: see para. 3.2.4, *supra*. Secondly, the court will need to be satisfied by the evidence that the meetings were duly convened in accordance with the directions given by the court on the hearing of the originating summons. The detailed evidence on this will have been scrutinised by the court's officers, and the judge will have been alerted to any possible problems

39. Schemes, such as those to effect the takeover of one company by another, will often provide for the cancellation of all or some of the issued shares, to be followed immediately by the capitalisation of the reserve resulting from the cancellation. In such a case, the capitalisation fully safeguards the interests of creditors and no further protection will be required.

40. Practice Direction (Companies Court: Schemes and Reductions) [1997] 1 WLR 1.

41. *Re Heron International NV* 21 July 1993, Harman J., unreported.

42. *Re Heron International NV* [1994] 1 BCLC 667 at 674.

which may have come to the court's notice. Unlike ordinary company meetings which will generally be invalidated by a failure to comply with the requirements of the articles of association in giving notice, a failure to comply with the court's directions for convening a meeting will not *ipso facto* invalidate the proceedings at the meeting, as the court may waive a non-compliance with its directions. Thus, where notice of the meetings was not advertised in newspapers as directed, but it was proved that out of the 31 shareholders, 30 holding between them the vast majority of the shares had received the notices sent to them, the court waived the defect and sanctioned the scheme.[43]

Thirdly, the court must be satisfied that members or creditors have been given a sufficient explanation of the scheme and its effects, and sufficient information to enable them to make a reasonable judgment as to how to vote at the meeting.[44] The extent and quality of the information required to be supplied depends on the facts of each particular case.[45] If relevant information is not made available, the court will not treat it as a bar to sanctioning the scheme if it is unlikely to have caused assenting members or creditors to change their view, or abstaining members or creditors to have voted against the scheme.[46] The need to supply material information to members or creditors extends to any changes in circumstances which are material, occurring between the date of the explanatory statement and the date of the meeting. This requirement was underlined in respect of the disclosure of directors' interests in *Re Jessel Trust Ltd*[47] and *Re Minster Assets plc*.[48] In *Re MB Group plc*[49] Harman J. made clear that this requirement extended to all information and said that a change in circumstances was material if "a reasonable shareholder would be likely to be affected in his voting by the new fact". If material changes have occurred, either before or after the meeting, one course open to the court is to order a new meeting so that the members or creditors can be apprised of the new information.[50]

Fourthly, the court must be satisfied that the requisite majority, a simple majority in number representing three-quarters in value of those present and voting in person or by proxy at the meeting, has voted in favour of the scheme at the meeting of each class sought to be bound by the scheme. A scheme may contain express provision that, notwithstanding that the scheme has not been approved by the requisite majority at one or more of the meetings or is not sanctioned by the court as regards one or more classes, the scheme can still be sanctioned so as to be binding on the remaining class or classes. As a matter of discretion, the court may refuse to sanction a scheme as regards a particular class, if the majority was reached only with the votes of members or creditors who have conflicting interests which, while not excluding them from the class as a matter of jurisdiction, are material. It will not do so, however, if the conflict is not such as to destroy the necessary

43. *Re Anglo Spanish Tartar Refineries Ltd* [1924] WN 222.
44. *Re Dorman Long and Co. Ltd* [1934] Ch. 635.
45. *Re Heron International NV* [1994] 1 BCLC 667. See *Re National Bank Ltd* [1966] 1 WLR 819 for a case where the omission of information which might be regarded as material was not fatal to the scheme. The information concerned assets and liabilities of a bank which, under the relevant legislation in force at that time, did not for reasons of public policy have to be disclosed in a bank's published accounts. Plowman J. held that where the scheme was expressly based on withholding such information, the court could properly sanction the scheme, provided it was satisfied, on the evidence, that the scheme was fair.
46. *Ibid.*
47. [1985] BCLC 119.
48. [1985] BCLC 200.
49. [1989] BCLC 672.
50. *Ibid.* at 681–682.

degree of community of interest among the members of the class concerned, such community of interest being a question of degree in each case.[51]

Finally, the court must consider whether, overall, the scheme is one which should be sanctioned. The court is not, of course, bound to sanction the scheme simply because it has been approved by the necessary majority at each class meeting. Equally, however, the court does not approach this question without regard to the fact that the scheme has been approved by that majority. Where differences arise as a matter of commercial judgement as to what is in the best interests of the relevant class, the court will not substitute its view for the reasonable decision of the majority.[52] The court's function is to determine whether the scheme is such that, as an intelligent and honest man, a member of the class concerned and acting in respect of his interest might reasonably approve of it.[53]

3.6.7 Order

The procedure so far as the court is concerned is the same as for an order confirming a reduction of capital.[54] At the hearing a draft form of order should be handed to the registrar who will initial it if the scheme is sanctioned, subject to any necessary changes in the form of order. The order will direct that it be delivered for registration to the registrar of companies. The scheme becomes effective only once it is lodged with the registrar of companies.[55] If, therefore, circumstances arise following the hearing but before delivery of the order to the registrar of companies which make it inexpedient to bring the scheme into effect, the company or other petitioner should restore the matter to the court for a further order to release it from the obligation to file the order.

3.6.8 Costs

The court has a discretion to order that an unsuccessful opposing creditor or member should pay the costs of the applicant, although such an order could properly relate only to the extent to which the applicant's costs have been increased by the opposition. Although exceptionally the court has made orders for costs against opposing creditors or members, where their grounds of opposition have lacked all substance, the tendency of the court has been to make no order as to the costs[56] or to order their costs to be paid by the applicant where their argument has been helpful to the court.[57]

3.6.9 Long vacation

The arrangements for dealing with schemes during the long vacation are those for petitions to confirm reductions of capital and are considered together below.[58]

51. *Re Heron International NV* [1994] 1 BCLC 667.
52. *Ibid.*
53. *Re Dorman Long and Co. Ltd, supra*; *Re National Bank Ltd* [1966] 1 WLR 819 at 829, citing with approval *Buckley on the Companies Acts* (13th Edn) 1957 p. 409.
54. See para. 4.12, *infra.*
55. CA 1985, s. 425(3).
56. *Re Imperial Tobacco Group Ltd* 11 February 1969, Plowman J., unreported.
57. *Re National Bank Ltd* [1966] 1 WLR 819 at 830.
58. See para. 4.14, *infra.*

3.7 Reconstructions and amalgamations

Additional powers are conferred on the court by s. 427 Companies Act 1985 in cases where an application is made to the court to sanction a compromise or arrangement under s. 425 and the following conditions are satisfied[59]:

(a) the compromise or arrangement has been proposed for the purposes of, or in connection with, a scheme for the reconstruction of any company or companies or the amalgamation of any two or more companies,[60] and
(b) under the scheme the whole or any part of the undertaking or the property of any company concerned in the scheme is to be transferred to another company.[61]

In such cases, the court is empowered to make provision for all or any of the matters listed in s. 427(3), which are designed to facilitate the scheme of reconstruction or amalgamation. They include matters which could not otherwise be achieved simply by agreement between the transferor and transferee companies: the transfer (i.e. novation) of liabilities, the continuation by or against the transferee company of any legal proceedings and the dissolution, without winding up, of any transferor company. The court may also make provision for any persons who, within such time and in such manner as the court directs, dissent from the compromise or arrangement: in this way, the court can mirror the provisions for the purchase of dissenters' interests contained in s. 111 Insolvency Act 1986 and thereby ensure that the effect of those provisions is not side-stepped by a company using the machinery of ss. 425–427 Companies Act 1985 rather than carrying out a reconstruction under s. 110 Insolvency Act.[62]

Procedurally there are two alternative means whereby orders under s. 427 may be sought. Normally the orders will be sought at the same time as the sanction of the court to the scheme of arrangement under s. 425. In that case the application for the necessary orders should be included in the petition.[63] Alternatively, application may be made by originating summons after the scheme of arrangement has been sanctioned.[64]

Whichever procedure is adopted, it is necessary to issue a summons for directions.[65] The principal purposes of the summons for directions are to make such provision, if any, as may be appropriate for the protection of creditors of the transferor company and to direct appropriate newspaper advertisement(s). The court approaches these questions in the same way as on a summons for directions where confirmation of a reduction of capital is being sought.

59. CA 1985, s. 427(2).

60. The terms "reconstruction" and "amalgamation" are not defined but have been the subject of a number of decisions arising in various contexts: see, for example *Re South African Supply and Cold Storage Co.* [1904] 2 Ch. 268 and *Brooklands Selangor Ltd* v. *IRC* [1970] 1 WLR 429.

61. The definition of "company" is restricted to companies formed and registered under the Companies Acts, ss. 427(6) and 735(1). The powers under s. 427 are therefore exercisable in relation to a narrower range of companies than the powers under s. 425 and do not, for example, apply to foreign companies.

62. See *Re General Motor Cab Co.* [1913] 1 Ch. 377 and *Re Anglo-Continental Supply Co.* [1922] 2 Ch. 723.

63. Express provision for this is not made in RSC O. 102, r. 4 which deals with applications to be made by petition, but it is recognised by RSC O. 102, r. 6(2)(a).

64. RSC O. 102, rr. 2(1) and 2(2)(a).

65. The rules provide expressly for this step where the orders are sought in the petition for sanction of the scheme: RSC O. 102, r. 6(1). Although there is no equivalent provision in the rules where the application is made subsequently by originating summons, it is the practice of the court to require a summons for directions.

The evidence in support of the application for orders under s. 427 will be by affidavit, and should address the same issues as regards creditors as the evidence in support of a petition for confirmation of a reduction of capital.

Where a scheme of arrangement under s. 425 is proposed between a public company and members or creditors for the purposes of, or in connection with, a scheme for the reconstruction or amalgamation of any two or more companies, involving certain categories of transfer of the undertaking, property and liabilities of the public company, ss. 425–427 take effect subject to certain additional provisions contained in s. 427A and sch. 15B. To date, there have been few, if any, transfers to which these provisions relate.

3.8 Schemes for the transfer of long term business under the Insurance Companies Act 1982

3.8.1 Introduction

The Insurance Companies Act 1982 (the Act) makes provision for the transfer of insurance business, including a novation of liabilities, without a requirement for the consent of policyholders. General business (as defined in sch. 2 part 1 of the Act) can be transferred with the consent of the Secretary of State and does not involve court approval. Long term business, which is defined in sch. 1 and includes life assurance, permanent health and pension policies and annuities,[66] can be transferred in accordance with the Act but it requires the sanction of the court.

The origins and purpose of the provisions relating to the transfer of long term business were summarised by Hoffmann J. in *Re London Life Association Ltd*[67] as follows:

"The need for court approval to a transfer of life insurance business dates back to the Life Assurance Companies Act 1870. Until then, life assurance business in this country had been virtually unregulated. One company could transfer its entire business to another without the knowledge or consent of its policyholders provided only that it had the necessary powers under its deed of settlement or articles of association and the small print of the policy made it subject to such powers. The Act of 1870 was passed in the aftermath of the spectacular failure in 1869 of the Albert Life Assurance Company, which had been highly acquisitive and taken over the businesses of more than twenty other societies. The main purpose of the Act of 1870 was to give regulatory powers to the Board of Trade, but section 14 provided that no life insurance company should amalgamate with another or transfer its business to another unless such amalgamation or transfer was confirmed by the court. Before such an application could be made, a statement of the nature of the arrangements and copies of the actuarial reports on which it was founded had to be sent to all policyholders. The court was given power, after hearing the directors and any 'other persons whom it considers entitled to be heard', to confirm the arrangement if it was satisfied that 'no sufficient objection to the arrangement' had been established. This power was however subject to a proviso that the arrangement should not be confirmed if it appeared that more than a tenth by value of the policyholders of the transferor company objected.

The Assurance Companies Act 1909 added a requirement that the material to be made available to the policyholders and the court should include the report of an independent actuary, but in all other respects the provisions of the 1870 Act remained substantially unchanged until the Insurance Companies Amendment Act 1973 replaced them with what are now sections 49 and 50 of the Insurance Companies Act 1982. For present purposes, the following changes are relevant. First, the veto exercisable by one-tenth or more of the transferor's policyholders disappeared. Secondly,

66. This includes reinsurance as well as insurance: *Re NRG Victory Reinsurance Ltd* [1995] 1 WLR 239.
67. 21 February 1989, unreported.

the persons entitled to be heard on the petition (in addition to the applicant) were specified as the Secretary of State and –

> any person (including any employee of the transferor company or the transferee company) who alleges that he would be adversely effected by the carrying out of the scheme.

Thirdly, the power of the court to sanction the transfer is no longer expressly conditional on it being satisfied that "no sufficient objection" has been established. It is expressed as a completely unfettered discretion. I doubt whether this change of language makes any difference except to make it clear that even in the absence of objection the court is not obliged to sanction a scheme.

Although the statutory discretion is unfettered, it must be exercised according to principles which give due recognition to the commercial judgment entrusted by the company's constitution to its board. The court in my judgment is concerned in the first place with whether a policyholder, employee or other person would be "adversely affected" by the scheme in the sense that it appears likely to leave him worse off than if there had been no scheme. It does not however follow that any scheme which leaves someone adversely affected must be rejected. For example, as we shall see, one scheme which might have been adopted in this case would have adversely affected many of London Life's employees because they would have become redundant. But such a scheme might nevertheless have been confirmed by the court. In the end the question is whether the scheme as a whole is fair as between the interests of the different classes of persons affected. But the court does not have to be satisfied that no better scheme could have been devised. A board might have a choice of several possible schemes, none of which, taken as a whole, could be regarded as unfair. Some policyholders might prefer one such scheme and some might think they would be better off with another. But the choice is in my judgment a matter for the board. Of course one could imagine an extreme case in which the choice made by the board was so irrational that a court could only conclude that it had been actuated by some improper motive and had therefore abused its fiduciary powers (*Howard Smith Ltd* v. *Ampol Petroleum Ltd* [1974] A.C. 821, 835). In such a case a member would be entitled to restrain the board from proceeding. But that would be an exercise of the court's ordinary jurisdiction to restrain breaches of fiduciary duty; not an exercise of the statutory jurisdiction under section 49 of the Insurance Companies Act 1982.

What is true of choices as between different schemes is also true of the details within a scheme. There are no doubt few schemes which could not in some respect be improved. But the terms of a scheme are a matter of negotiation between transferor and transferee companies and will, to a greater or lesser extent depending upon their respective bargaining strengths, involve concessions on both sides. Under the 1982 Act the court cannot, any more than under the Act of 1870, sanction the scheme subject to the making of amendments (*Re Argus Life Assurance Company* (1888) 39 Ch.D. 571, 580). It must be either confirmed or rejected, although no doubt the court in rejecting a scheme could indicate that it thought the vice lay in some particular term and that a fresh scheme without that term was likely to be acceptable. I am therefore not concerned with whether, by further negotiation, the scheme might be improved, but with whether, taken as a whole, the scheme before the court is unfair to any person or class of persons affected.

In providing the court with material upon which to decide this question, the Act assigns important roles to the independent actuary and the Secretary of State. A report from the former is expressly required and the latter is given a right to be heard on the petition. The question of whether policyholders would be adversely affected by the scheme is largely actuarial and involves a comparison of their security and reasonable expectations without the scheme with what it would be if the scheme were implemented. I do not say that these are the only considerations but they are obviously very important. The Secretary of State, by virtue of his regulatory powers, can also be expected to have the necessary material to express an informed opinion on whether policyholders are likely to be adversely affected."

3.8.2 Jurisdiction

The provisions which were then contained in ss. 49–50 of the Insurance Companies Act 1982 have been replaced by part 1 of sch. 2C thereto, introduced by the Insurance

Companies (Third Insurance Directive) Regulations 1994[68] and applicable to all applications made on or after 1 July 1994.[69] The provisions contained in sch. 2C reproduce many of the provisions previously contained in ss. 49–50 but additional provisions are included to give effect to the requirements of Council Directive 92/96/EEC.

Schedule 2C, part 1 applies where it is proposed to carry out a scheme for the transfer of the whole or part of the long term business carried on by an insurance company ("the transferor company") to another body, whether incorporated or not ("the transferee company") and:

(a) where the transferor company is a UK company, the business to be transferred is business carried on in one or more member states; and
(b) where the transferor company is not a UK company, the business to be transferred is business carried on in the United Kingdom.

Under these provisions the court has no jurisdiction to sanction a scheme for the transfer of long term business carried on outside the member states under (a), or outside the United Kingdom under (b).[70]

The transferor company must be an insurance company to which part II of the Insurance Companies Act 1982 applies, as to which see s. 15. Any such transfer requires the sanction of the court.[71] Such a transfer is not to be made under ss. 425–427(1) of the Companies Act 1985, unless it involves a compromise or arrangement falling within s. 427A(1) of the Companies Act 1985 in which case the provisions of both ss. 425–427A of that Act and part I of sch. 2C apply.[72]

3.8.3 Procedural requirements under ICA 1982, sch. 2C

The application to the court for its sanction must be made by petition[73] and sch. 2C provides that certain requirements must be satisfied before the court can sanction the scheme of transfer. The requirements are:

(i) The petition must be accompanied by a report on the terms of the scheme by an independent actuary.[74] This is a requirement of the greatest significance, both because of the technical and complex nature of much long term business and because, in contrast with s. 425, there is no requirement for approval to be given by policyholders at meetings or otherwise. If the actuary concluded that the effect of the proposed scheme was to worsen materially the security or prospects of policyholders of either the transferor company or the transferee company, it is highly unlikely that the court would sanction the transfer. The evidence in support of the petition frequently also includes reports prepared by the actuaries to the transferor company and to the transferee company, giving details of the

68. S.I. 1994 No. 1696.
69. Reg. 28(3).
70. *Re Eagle Star Insurance Co. Ltd*, 23 November 1990, Morritt J., unreported, a decision on s. 49(1) Insurance Companies Act 1982.
71. Sch. 2C, para. 1(3).
72. Sch. 2C, paras 1(2), (3).
73. Sch. 2C, para. 1(1).
74. Sch. 2C, para. 2(1).

classes of business written by the companies and dealing with the scheme, although this is not a requirement.

(ii) Notices must be published stating that the application has been made and giving the addresses of the offices at which, and the period for which, copies of the petition and independent actuary's report will be available for inspection.[75] The notices must be published in the London, Edinburgh and Belfast *Gazettes* and, except where the court has otherwise directed, in two national newspapers. In addition, where the transferor company is a UK or non-EC company[76] and the proposed transfer includes any policy which evidences a contract of direct insurance and the "State of the commitment" as regards the policy is a member state other than the United Kingdom, the notice must be published in two national newspapers in that member state.[77] The definition of the "State of the commitment" was added to s. 96(1) of the Insurance Companies Act 1982 by the 1994 Regulations and refers, in the case of a policyholder who is an individual, to the state in which he had his habitual residence at the date he took out the policy. A similar provision[78] applies where the transfer includes any EFTA policy[79] as regards which an EEA State[80] other than the United Kingdom is the state of the commitment. It is therefore necessary for the evidence to give details of any policies to which these provisions apply, to enable the court to be satisfied that the advertisement requirements have been complied with. The evidence should also give details of the countries in which, so far as known to the companies, policyholders live. If there are a material number in any countries outside the United Kingdom, the court will usually direct advertisement in an appropriate newspaper or newspapers circulating in each of those countries.

(iii) Unless the court otherwise directs, a statement setting out the terms of the scheme and containing a summary of the independent actuary's report must be sent to each long term policyholder and each member of the transferor and transferee companies.[81] It is usual to seek a direction from the court dispensing with at least strict compliance with this requirement. The reasons are, first, the addresses of many policyholders may not be known to the company and, secondly, the definition of "policyholder" in s. 96(1) as the person who for the time being is the legal holder of the policy includes legal assignees holding the policy as security, and the task of identification may be very onerous. The company may send a statement to original or other readily identifiable policyholders or, on the basis of the independent actuary's report, the company may suggest that it should not be required to send out a statement at all.

75. Sch. 2C, para. 2(2)(a).
76. These terms are defined in ICA 1982, s. 5(4) (added by the 1994 Regulations).
77. Sch. 2C, para. 2(2)(a)(ii).
78. Sch. 2C, para. 2(2)(a)(iii).
79. See sch. 2C, para. 2(5) for definition, although it appears that the effect of ICA 1982, s. 2(7), which deems Iceland and Norway to be member states for the purposes of ICA 1982 is that there can at present be no EFTA policies (as defined).
80. See ICA 1982, s. 96(1) (as amended by the 1994 Regulations) for definition.
81. Sch. 2C, para. 2(2)(a).

(iv) A copy of the petition, the independent actuary's report and the statement, if any, sent to policyholders must be served on the Secretary of State for Trade and Industry not less than 21 days before the hearing of the petition.[82]

(v) Copies of the petition and the independent actuary's report must be open for inspection at the offices specified in the newspaper and *Gazette* notices, for not less than 21 days beginning with the first date of publication of the notice.[83]

(vi) The detailed regulatory requirements set out in sch. 2C, para. 3, dealing with authorisation of the transferee company, its margin of solvency after the transfer and, where applicable, consultation with the supervisory authorities in other Member States and EEA States, must be satisfied.

3.8.4 Petition

The petition seeking the sanction of the court may be presented by the transferor company or the transferee company or, presumably, both companies.[84] It will be entitled in the matters of the companies concerned and in the matter of the Insurance Companies Act 1982. It will not have any named respondents. It should give the formal details relating to the incorporation, registered office, objects and share capital of the companies, as in the case of other petitions and it should state the power of the transferor company to transfer its business and the power of the transferee company to acquire the business.[85] It should state that the transferor company is an insurance company to which part II of the Insurance Companies Act 1982 applies, and it should detail the actual or prospective authority of the transferee company to carry on the business to be transferred. It should give brief particulars of the size and classes of the long term business to be transferred and of the long term business, if any, already carried on by the transferee company. A brief statement of the reasons for the transfer should be included and reference made to the independent actuary's report and to any report by the companies' own actuaries. The petition should expressly seek an order sanctioning the scheme and the consequential orders sought under sch. 2C, para. 5, such as the transfer of property or liabilities and the continuation by or against the transferee company of any legal proceedings pending against the transferor company. The scheme of transfer should be annexed to the petition.

3.8.5 Evidence

The principal evidence in support of the petition will usually be an affidavit sworn by the chairman or another senior officer of the transferor, exhibiting and verifying the petition. It should also exhibit the certificate of incorporation and memorandum and articles of association, or equivalent documents of the transferor and transferee companies and their latest audited accounts and Insurance Companies Act return. The report of the independent actuary and any other actuarial reports should be exhibited. If it is proposed to seek an order dispensing with a statement to members or policyholders, the reasons and relevant circumstances should be explained. Information relating to the whereabouts of

82. Sch. 2C, para. 2(2)(c).

83. Sch. 2C, para. 2(2)(d) which also contains requirements for inspection at places within relevant member states and EEA States as directed by the court.

84. Sch. 2C, para. 1(1).

85. See *Re Sovereign Life Assurance Co.* 42 Ch.D. 540.

policyholders should be included to enable the court to order the appropriate newspaper advertisements in accordance with sch. 2C, para. 2(2)(a) and to enable the court to make orders for the petition and independent actuary's report to be available for inspection in accordance with sch. 2C, para. 2(2)(d).

3.8.6 Preliminary procedure

The procedure for presenting the petition and filing the evidence is the same as for petitions for the confirmation of a reduction of capital. Similarly, steps should be taken before presentation of the petition, to agree a provisional timetable with the court. At the same time as the petition is presented, a summons for directions is issued.

3.8.7 Summons for directions

The summons for directions will be heard by the registrar in chambers. He will give directions as to newspaper advertisements, the offices and other places at which copies of the petition and the independent actuary's report are to be open to inspection and, if appropriate, dispensing with a statement to members or policyholders of the transferor and transferee companies. The registrar will normally initial a draft order at the hearing. By prior informal arrangement with the court officer assigned to the case, the company's solicitor can immediately take the initialled order, draft advertisements and the court file to the court officer who will stamp the order and settle the forms of advertisement.

The advertisements required by the Act and directed by the court are then placed, and copies of the petition and the independent actuary's report are made available for inspection in accordance with sch. 2C, para. 2(2)(d) for a period of not less than 21 days from the first publication of the advertisement.

3.8.8 Service

Not less than 21 days before the date fixed for the hearing of the petition, copies of the petition, the independent actuary's report and the statement, if any, must be served on the Secretary of State and, if the transferee company is an incorporated friendly society or registered friendly society authorised under part IV of the Friendly Societies Act 1992, the Friendly Societies Commission.[86] In practice, the Insurance Division of the Department of Trade and Industry and, where appropriate, the Friendly Societies Commission will have been consulted about the proposals at an early stage and kept abreast of developments.

3.8.9 Further procedural steps

Copies of the newspapers and *Gazettes* containing the advertisement must be lodged in court, as must an affidavit or affidavits proving that the necessary documents were made available for inspection at the requisite offices, that the advertisements were duly published, and that the petition and other documents were duly served on the Secretary of State and, where appropriate, the Friendly Societies Commission, and detailing any objections to the transfer which have been received.

86. Sch. 2C, para. 2(6).

3.8.10 Hearing of petition

The petition is heard by a judge in open court. If it is opposed, he may give directions for further evidence and generally for the conduct of the petition. As well as the Secretary of State and, where appropriate, the Friendly Societies Commission, any person who alleges that he would be adversely affected by the carrying out of the scheme is entitled to be heard.[87] This includes employees of the transferor or transferee companies.[88]

Two office copies of the order on the petition must be lodged with the Secretary of State[89] and, in certain cases, the court must direct publication of notice of the making of the order to enable rights of cancellation of policies to be exercised.[90]

87. Sch. 2C, para. 2(4).
88. Hoffmann J. so held in *Re London Life Association* (*supra*) and it is now expressly provided in sch. 2C, para. 2(4)(b).
89. Sch. 2C, para. 5(5).
90. Sch. 2C, para. 4.

CHAPTER 4

PROCEEDINGS RELATING TO CAPITAL

4.1 Introduction

It is a fundamental feature of the law governing companies limited by shares, which account for the vast majority of limited liability companies, that they must not return paid-up share capital to members, or otherwise reduce their issued share capital except as the law permits. The importance of this principle derives from the basic characteristic of such companies that the liability of members to the company is limited to the amount which they agree to pay on the shares issued to them. It is not to say that the capital raised by a company may not be expended in its business or otherwise in furtherance of its objects; the restriction is on returning capital to members,[1] or in other ways reducing issued share capital.

It is a striking feature of successive Companies Acts that so important a rule was never stated as such in the legislation, until the Companies Act 1980 enacted an express prohibition on the acquisition by a company of its own shares, now contained in s. 143 of the Companies Act 1985. For some years after the enactment of the Companies Act 1862, it was considered that a company limited by shares was permitted to purchase shares from its members and thereby return capital to them. However, in *Trevor* v. *Whitworth*,[2] the House of Lords overruled a series of earlier decisions and held that such returns of capital were unlawful unless carried out in accordance with the procedures laid down in the statute. It was the presence of the statutory forerunner of s. 135 of the Companies Act 1985, with its requirements for approval by special resolution and confirmation by the court, which showed that a reduction of capital was not permitted unless those requirements were satisfied.

More recent reforms have enabled companies to repay capital by other means. The Companies Act 1929 for the first time permitted companies to issue preference shares on terms that they were redeemable.[3] This was extended by the Companies Act 1981 to enable any shares, not merely preference shares, to be issued as redeemable and to permit redemption to be at the option of the shareholder as well as the company.[4] The Companies

1. For these purposes, members will include those persons so closely connected with the registered members that the distinction should be ignored: see *Aveling Barford Ltd* v. *Perion Ltd* [1989] BCLC 626. For further discussion of the principles referred to in this paragraph see *Re Halt Garage (1964) Ltd* [1982] 3 All ER 1016; *Re Horsley & Weight Ltd* [1982] Ch. 442; *Barclays Bank plc* v. *British & Commonwealth Holdings plc* [1996] 1 BCLC 1.

2. (1887) 12 App.Cas. 409.

3. This permitted only the issue of redeemable shares, not the conversion of issued shares into redeemable shares: *Re St James' Court Estate Ltd* [1944] Ch. 6.

4. See now CA 1985, ss. 159–160.

Act 1981 also permitted, for the first time, a company to purchase its own shares without an application to court. The relevant provisions, now contained in ss. 162–181 of the Companies Act 1985, include provisions for the protection of members and creditors. They have proved, in practice, to be a useful addition to the powers of companies, but there remain many circumstances in which a reduction of capital must or is more appropriately undertaken by the conventional procedure involving application to the court.

4.2 Jurisdiction

The power of a company to reduce its capital, and the jurisdiction of the court to confirm a reduction of capital, are conferred and governed by ss. 135–141, which re-enact provisions which, with minor variations, have been contained in the Companies legislation since 1867.[5] The sections apply to companies limited by shares and to companies limited by guarantee and having a share capital.[6] They do not apply to other companies limited by guarantee or to unlimited companies, even though the latter may have a share capital.[7]

4.2.1 Section 135(1)

Section 135(1) sets out the principal requirements for a lawful reduction of capital:

(a) the company must be authorised by its articles to reduce its share capital;
(b) the proposed reduction of share capital must be approved by a special resolution of the company (subject as discussed in para. 4.3 below);
(c) the proposed reduction of share capital must be confirmed by the court.

4.2.2 Form of reduction

There is no statutory restriction on the form which the reduction may take or on its purpose. Section 135(1) provides expressly that a company may reduce its share capital "in any way" and the three examples given in s. 135(2) are expressed to be "in particular, and without prejudice to subsection (1)". Early decisions to the effect that it was an exhaustive list were overruled by the House of Lords in *Poole* v. *National Bank of China*.[8] Reductions of share capital will frequently take one of the forms set out in s. 135(2), particularly the cancellation of share capital which has been lost, or the repayment of share capital which is in excess of the wants of the company. However, there are many other purposes for which reductions are proposed, including the elimination of deficits on

5. CA 1867, ss. 9–19 (amended by CA 1879, ss. 4 and 9, s. 27(1) CA 1900 and CA 1907, s. 50 and sch. III), ss. 46–56 Companies (Consolidation) Act 1908, CA 1929, s. 19 and sch. 2 (incorporating amendments to the 1908 Act made by CA 1928, s. 19 and sch. II), CA 1948, ss. 66–71.

6. Its application to companies limited by guarantee and having a share capital is of little practical significance. Not only are such companies very uncommon but also, since 22 December 1980, it has not been permissible to form such companies: CA 1985, s. 1(4).

7. Unlimited companies are permitted to return capital or repurchase shares without any requirement for court sanction: *Re Borough Commercial and Building Society* [1893] 2 Ch. 279.

8. [1907] AC 229.

distributable reserves where they are not the result of permanent losses of capital,[9] the creation of reserves to write off goodwill in the company's accounts or in consolidated accounts,[10] to enable the issued share capital to be re-denominated in a different currency,[11] to reduce the nominal value of listed shares so as not to exceed prevailing market prices, or to facilitate the acquisition of companies as part of a scheme of arrangement.[12] This is by no means an exhaustive list of the circumstances in which reductions of capital have been proposed by companies and approved by the court, and it follows from s. 135(1) and (2) and the decision in *Poole* v. *National Bank of China* that there cannot be a closed list of appropriate cases. The court has refused to confirm a reduction where the company had only three members and the entire substance of the proposal could have been achieved by their unanimous agreement.[13]

4.2.3 Protection of members

Both the statutory provisions and case law provide measures to protect the members of a company against an unfair or inappropriate reduction of capital. As mentioned above, s. 135(1) requires the reduction to be approved by a special resolution. If the share capital of the company is divided into more than one class of shares, the court requires that the proposed reduction should be in accordance with the special rights attached to the different classes, or that the class consents of the affected classes have been obtained. The statutory requirement for sanction by the court enables shareholders opposed to the reduction to raise their objections with the court and, in any event, means that the court must be satisfied that it is an appropriate proposal for confirmation. These aspects are discussed in paras 4.4.4–4.4.6 and 4.11.2–4.11.4, *infra*.

4.2.4 Protection of creditors

As the rules governing the raising and maintenance of capital are designed primarily for the benefit of those dealing with a company as creditors, the Act contains some detailed provisions for the protection of creditors and requires the court to apply those provisions as part of the process whereby the confirmation of the court is sought. Section 136 makes provision for the settlement by the court of a list of creditors and for securing payment of the company's debts and liabilities by appropriating either their full amount or, in the case of debts and liabilities which are not admitted or are contingent or prospective, an amount fixed by the court. These apply where the proposed reduction of share capital involves either a diminution of liability in respect of unpaid share capital or the payment to a shareholder of any paid-up share capital and in any other case if the court so directs.[14] However, the court is empowered to direct that the relevant provisions for an enquiry as to creditors shall not apply if, having regard to any special circumstances of the case, it thinks proper to do so.[15] In practice, companies applying for confirmation of a reduction

9. *Re Grosvenor Press plc* [1985] 1 WLR 980.
10. *Re Thorn EMI plc* [1989] BCLC 612, although this is normally effected by a reduction or cancellation of share premium account.
11. *Re Scandinavian Bank Group plc* [1988] Ch. 87.
12. *Re National Bank Ltd* [1966] 1 WLR 819.
13. *Re Rylands Whitecross Ltd*, 21 December 1973, Brightman J., unreported.
14. CA 1985, s. 136(2).
15. CA 1985, s. 136(6).

always put forward proposals for safeguarding the interests of creditors which will avoid the need for an enquiry. There is further discussion of the protection of creditors in paras 4.9.1–4.9.13, *infra*. Like shareholders, creditors are entitled to be represented and heard at the hearing of the application[16] for confirmation of the proposed reduction.

4.2.5 Publicity

The hearing of the application to the court is advertised in such newspaper(s) as the court may direct, so as to give notice to shareholders and creditors.[17] If the reduction is confirmed, the order is delivered to the registrar of companies who must register it.[18] Notice of the registration must be published by the company in such manner as the court may direct.[19] In practice, the court invariably directs advertisement in the same newspaper(s) as contained the notice of the hearing. The court is empowered by s. 137(2) to make additional orders: (a) that the words "and reduced" be added to the name of the company for such period as the court specifies; and (b) that the company publish the reasons for the reduction or such other information in regard to it as the court thinks expedient, with a view to giving proper information to the public and (if the court thinks fit) the causes which led to the reduction. It is many years since the court made any order under s. 137(2).

4.2.6 Public companies

There is no difference in the application of the provisions relating to reductions of capital to public companies and private companies, except as provided by s. 139. Under the rules governing public companies, introduced by the Companies Act 1980 to give effect to the Second EC Directive on Company Law[20] and now contained in ss. 1(3), 11, 25, 43–48 and 117–118 of the Companies Act 1985, a public company is prohibited from doing business or exercising any borrowing power unless (*inter alia*) the nominal value of its allotted share capital is not less than the "authorised minimum" which is currently £50,000.[21] If a reduction of capital has the effect of bringing the nominal value of the allotted share capital of the company below the authorised minimum, the registrar of companies must not register the order unless the court otherwise directs, or the company is first re-registered as a private company.[22] The practical effect is that public companies applying for confirmation of a reduction of capital must remember to seek a direction under s. 139 on the hearing of the petition. It most commonly arises when, as part of a scheme of arrangement involving the acquisition of a company, its issued capital is momentarily reduced to nil before being increased by an issue of shares to the new owner. It should be noted that, unless the new owner is already a member of the company and shares held by it are not cancelled, it appears that a valuation of the consideration for the allotment of the

16. Which is by petition, see para. 4.5.1, *infra*.
17. O. 102, r. 6(3).
18. CA 1985, s. 138(1).
19. CA 1985, s. 138(3).
20. OJ 77/91/EEC.
21. CA 1985, s. 118(6).
22. CA 1985, s. 139(1) and (2).

new shares will be required pursuant to s. 103(1), in view of the terms of s. 103(2), which exempts capitalisation issues but only if they are made to members.

4.3 RSC Order 102

Order 102 contains additional procedural provisions governing applications for confirmation of a reduction of capital. Rule 4(1)(d) requires that the application should be made by petition. Rule 6(1) requires that the petitioner must take out a summons for directions. On the hearing of the summons, the court may by order give such directions as to the proceedings to be taken before the hearing of the petition as it thinks fit, including directions for the publication of notices and the making of any inquiry (r. 4(3)). Without prejudice to the generality of r. 4(3), r. 4(4) makes specific provision for the court to give directions for an inquiry as to creditors, and for the settlement of a list of creditors, and for the exercise of the power conferred by s. 136(6) to direct that there shall not be an inquiry as to creditors. Rules 7–13 contain detailed provisions for the conduct of an inquiry as to creditors. Proceedings on the hearing of the summons for directions are considered further at paras 4.8–4.9.13, *infra*.

4.4 Steps before the commencement of court proceedings

4.4.1 Authority in articles

As noted in para. 4.2.1, *supra*, a company cannot reduce its share capital unless it is authorised to do so by its articles. The authority must exist before the special resolution for the reduction is passed. It has been held that a single resolution to insert the requisite authority in the company's articles and to reduce the capital is ineffective.[23] A company should therefore check its articles to ensure that they contain the authority required for a reduction of the type that is proposed. If they do not contain the necessary power, a special resolution should be proposed to alter the articles accordingly. That resolution can be proposed at the same meeting as the resolution for the reduction,[24] but it must be passed before the latter resolution.

4.4.2 Special resolution

Section 135(1) provides that a reduction is to be approved by a special resolution. It is therefore important to ensure that all the requirements for a valid special resolution are observed. Following presentation of the petition, the court will scrutinise the petition and the evidence, to satisfy itself that the resolution has been validly passed as a special resolution. The relevant requirements appear in the definition of "special resolution" in s. 378(2) of the Companies Act 1985. Three points in particular must be observed:

(1) The meeting at which the resolution is to be proposed must be convened on not less than 21 days notice, unless shorter notice is agreed by the majorities prescribed by s. 378(3). This means 21 clear days notice, i.e. exclusive of the

23. *Re West India and Pacific SS Co.* (1868) 9 Ch.App. 11r, 23; *Re Patent Invert Sugar Co.* (1885) 31 Ch.D. 166.

24. *Re John Crossley & Sons* [1892] WN 55.

date on which notice is deemed to be received and of the date of the meeting.[25] For this purpose, the provisions in a company's articles dealing with notice need to be examined to ascertain the date on which notice of a meeting is deemed to be received by members.[26]

(2) The resolution as passed at the meeting must be in the form set out in the notice, subject only to such changes as involve no departure whatever from the substance. In determining the substance, the actual notice of the meeting and any accompanying circular should be read as one.[27] Although changes in the text of a resolution may be made strictly in accordance with these principles and it may be possible to overcome errors by a process of construction,[28] best practice is to finalise the correct text of the resolution before the meeting is convened and insert that text into the notice of the meeting. The court will scrutinise any variation from the resolution set out in the notice.

(3) The memorandum and articles and any other documents conferring rights on shareholders should be examined to ensure that notice is given to all those persons entitled to it. Where there is more than one class of shares, it is frequently the case that a class or classes will not generally carry the right to notice of general meetings, but will do so in specified circumstances. It is also often the case that such circumstances include a meeting at which a resolution for a reduction of capital is to be proposed. Alternatively, there may be some other business at the meeting (e.g. a change in borrowing powers) which means that notice must be given to a particular class not generally entitled to it. Failure to give notice in these circumstances will invalidate the proceedings at the meeting.

4.4.3 Alternatives to special resolution

Although s. 135(1) of the Companies Act 1985 specifies a special resolution as the means by which the shareholders must approve a reduction of capital, there are alternatives. By s. 381A (inserted by the Companies Act 1989 and amended by Deregulation (Resolutions of Private Companies) Order 1996 as from 19 June 1996) a private company may do anything which would otherwise require a resolution of the company in general meeting, including a special resolution, by a resolution in writing signed by or on behalf of all the members of the company who at the date of the resolution would be entitled to attend and vote at such meeting. Such a written resolution requires neither a meeting nor any previous notice.[29] The signatures need not be on a single document provided each is on a document which accurately states the terms of the resolution, and the date of the resolution is taken to be the time when the resolution is signed by or on behalf of the last member to sign.[30] Section 381B (as amended) requires that a copy of the resolution is sent

25. *Re Hector Whaling Ltd* [1936] Ch. 208.
26. E.g. Reg. 115, Table A in The Companies (Tables A to F) Regulations 1985 (S.I. 1985 No. 805) as amended by S.I. 1985 No. 1052.
27. *Re Moorgate Mercantile Holdings Ltd* [1980] 1 WLR 227.
28. *Re Willaire Systems plc* [1987] BCLC 67.
29. CA 1985, s. 381A(1).
30. CA 1985, s. 381A(2), (3).

to the company's auditors, or that they are otherwise notified of its contents, at or before the time the resolution is supplied to a member for signature.

Even before the introduction of s. 381A it had been held that the unanimous consent of members could override otherwise fatal defects in a purported special resolution.[31] It had also been held in *Re Barry Artist Ltd*[32] that a reduction of capital could be approved by a unanimous written resolution. While this decision would apply equally to public companies and to private companies, it was stated that it was not the practice of the Companies Court to confirm a reduction which had been approved in this way and that, although the court confirmed the reduction in that case, it would not generally do so. Any such practice must now give way to the express terms of s. 381A in relation to private companies.

4.4.4 Class consents

The court will not confirm a reduction of capital unless all necessary class consents have been obtained. This is of relevance only where the capital of the company is divided into different classes of shares. The requirement for class consents may arise in two principal ways. First, the terms attached to a class of shares by the memorandum or articles or otherwise, may provide that the company shall not reduce its capital, or reduce its capital in particular ways, without the consent of that class.[33]

Secondly, irrespective of whether an express requirement for a class consent exists, the courts have developed a requirement that a reduction of capital should be carried out in accordance with the capital rights attached to the various classes, unless the classes in question agree otherwise. Accordingly, where a company proposes to return capital to shareholders, it must do so by first repaying capital to those classes which carry a right of priority to capital in a winding-up. If it does not do so, it must obtain the consent of those classes whose capital rights are not being satisfied.[34] Similarly, where a company is proposing to cancel capital which has been lost, it should first cancel the shares of those classes which rank last on a repayment of capital. If the company wishes to cancel or reduce the nominal value of shares in any other order, it must obtain the consent of those classes which are adversely affected.[35] A reduction which takes neither of these forms but involves a transfer from capital to distributable reserves or to reserves which may in time become distributable, should also, it is suggested, require the consent of those classes which would enjoy priority if the sums so transferred had been repaid as capital. Alternatively, the position of such classes would be sufficiently protected by an undertaking to the court or an alteration to the articles preventing the use of the reserve to pay dividends without first obtaining the consent of the classes concerned.

If a reduction is consistent with class rights as to capital and there is no express provision for a class consent, shareholders of that class cannot object on the grounds that

31. *Re Pearce Duff & Co. Ltd* [1960] 1 WLR 1014; but see *Cane* v. *Jones* [1980] 1 WLR 1451 at 1458–59.

32. [1985] 1 WLR 1305, applying *Cane* v. *Jones* (*supra*).

33. See, for example, *Re Northern Engineering Industries plc* [1994] 2 BCLC 704.

34. *Re Chatterley–Whitfield Collieries Ltd* [1948] 2 All ER 593 (CA) (affirmed [1949] AC 512).

35. *Re Floating Dock Co. of St Thomas Ltd* [1895] 1 Ch. 691; *Re London and New York Investment Corp. Ltd* [1895] 2 Ch. 860.

the cancellation of their shares will deprive them of other rights (e.g. the payment of dividends in the future) without their consent.[36]

4.4.5 Form of class consent

The articles will generally make provision for the means by which class consents are to be given, and there will commonly be an extraordinary resolution passed at a separate meeting of the class, or a resolution in writing signed by or on behalf of either all the members of the class or the holders of three-quarters of the shares of the class. In addition, s. 125(2) and (3) of the Companies Act 1985 require that, where a variation of rights is connected with a reduction of share capital, there must be either the written consent of the holders of three-quarters of the shares of the class, or an extraordinary resolution passed at a separate class meeting, as well as compliance with any further requirement of the memorandum or articles.

4.4.6 Different treatment of shares of the same class

The court has jurisdiction under s. 135 to confirm a reduction which treats shares of the same class in different ways.[37] However, the practice of the court is to require such a reduction to be carried out by means of a scheme of arrangement under s. 425 of the Companies Act 1985, on account of the greater protection given by that section.[38]

4.4.7 Circular

There is no statutory requirement for a circular to shareholders explaining the proposed reduction.[39] Unless the company is a wholly-owned subsidiary or all the members can be shown in some other way to understand the proposal, an explanatory circular should be sent to shareholders so that the shareholders can exercise a properly informed judgment on the proposal.[40] The court will refuse to confirm a reduction if the circular gives an inadequate or misleading account of the proposal.[41] In the case of a company with shares listed on the Stock Exchange, such a circular is a requirement of the Listing Rules.[42]

4.4.8 Other consents

The company should ensure that it obtains such other consents as it is obliged to obtain.[43] For example, the terms attached to an issue of loan stock, particularly if it is convertible into shares, may require the company to obtain consent of the stockholders or the trustee of the stock (if any) to the reduction.

36. *House of Fraser plc* v. *ACGE Investments Ltd* [1987] AC 387, approving *Re Saltdean Estate Co. Ltd* [1968] 1 WLR 1844.
37. *British and American Trustee and Finance Corp.* v. *Couper* [1894] AC 399.
38. *Re Robert Stephens Holdings Ltd* [1968] 1 WLR 522.
39. Contrast CA 1985, s. 426.
40. *Re Ratners Group plc* [1988] BCLC 685, (1988) 4 BCC 293; *Re Thorn EMI plc* [1989] BCLC 612, (1988) 4 BCC 698.
41. *Re European Home Products plc* [1988] BCLC 690, (1988) 4 BCC 779.
42. Chapter 14 of the Listing Rules.
43. See *Re MB Group plc* [1989] BCLC 672, (1989) 5 BCC 684.

4.4.9 Draft timetable

The officials of the Companies Court are always willing to discuss a timetable for the various stages in the court proceedings, before the petition is presented. For listed companies in particular this can be important, as there may be other matters, such as the admission of new shares to listing, which will depend on the timetable of the court proceedings. However, it is a useful facility for all companies and the Companies Court welcomes the opportunity to fix a provisional timetable. It is best done by an informal approach by the company's solicitors to the chief clerk or other senior officials of the court.

4.5 The form and contents of the petition

4.5.1 The originating process

This is a petition presented to the court.[44] The steps involved in presentation are the same as for any petition.[45] Its basic format is also the same as for other petitions. Its contents are described below. There are no respondents to the petition and there are therefore no requirements as to service.

4.5.2 Name and date of incorporation

Paragraph 1 should state the date of incorporation of the company, the Companies Act or Acts under which it was incorporated, and the type of company (e.g. limited by shares) on incorporation. Any previous names and the dates of change should be stated, as should any changes in its status such as the re-registration of a private company as a public company or vice versa.

4.5.3 Registered office

This should be stated in para. 2.

4.5.4 Objects

A brief statement of the present principal objects of the company as stated in its memorandum of association should be given in paragraph 3.

4.5.5 Capital history

Paragraph 4 should set out the history of the authorised share capital of the company. This starts with its capital on incorporation, unless the company has already had a reduction of capital confirmed by the court. In that case the history starts with the reduction or, if there has been more than one, with the most recent reduction, stating the date of the court order, the date of the registrar of companies' certificate under s. 138(4), and the text of the minute registered pursuant to s. 138(1). Each subsequent change in the authorised share

44. RSC O. 102, r. 4(1)(d).
45. See Chapter 2, *supra*.

capital should be stated, with its date and a very brief description of the change. This paragraph should end with a statement of the present authorised share capital, stating also the number of shares in each class in issue and whether fully or partly paid; if partly paid up, the amount paid up should be given. A history of the issued share capital is not required.

4.5.6 *Share premium account*

If confirmation of a reduction of share premium account is also sought, paragraph 5 should state the present amount standing to its credit. This also applies to the capital redemption reserve if a reduction of that reserve is to be confirmed. It is not necessary to state the history of either reserve. If the petition does not seek confirmation of a reduction of share capital, the petition should not set out the capital history.

4.5.7 *Articles*

The relevant provisions in the articles of association should be set out. In all cases this will include the articles authorising the company to reduce its capital and to make any further capital changes conditional on the proposed reduction. Additionally, if there is more than one class of share, the capital rights attached to each class and any provision expressly deeming a reduction to be a variation of class rights should be stated. If the class consent of any class has been obtained, the article(s) dealing with the giving of such consent should be set out or summarised.

4.5.8 *Resolution*

The special resolution for the reduction and any other relevant resolutions passed by the shareholders, such as one authorising an increase or other change in the share capital, conditional on the reduction taking effect, should be set out. The same applies to any class resolution.

4.5.9 *Purpose*

There should be a statement of the purpose of the proposed reduction of capital. In many cases, such as a return of excess capital, or the cancellation of lost capital, or a reduction to establish a reserve for writing off goodwill, a single sentence will be sufficient.

If the reduction does not involve either the diminution of any liability in respect of unpaid capital or the payment to any shareholder of any paid-up capital, there should be a statement to this effect, tracking the wording of s. 136(2). In the case of a company with more than one class of share, and a reduction which does not involve any variation of class rights, there should also be a statement to that effect.

4.5.10 *Minute*

Following confirmation by the court, the reduction takes effect only when the registrar of companies has registered both the order of the court and a minute.[46] The minute must be

46. CA 1985, s. 138(2).

approved by the court and must state with respect to the company's share capital as altered by the order:

(a) the amount of the share capital;
(b) the number of shares into which it is to be divided, and the amount of each share; and
(c) the amount (if any) at the date of registration deemed to be paid up on each share.[47]

In addition to these statutory requirements, the court will normally require the minute to state the amount of the authorised share capital immediately before the reduction, and its division into shares and their nominal amount, and a reference to the authority for the reduction (e.g. special resolution). The minute should also refer to any capital changes which are to occur contingently on the reduction taking effect, such as the creation of further shares or the consolidation or subdivision of shares.[48]

The proposed form of minute, which the court will be asked to approve, should be set out in the petition.

4.6 Evidence in support of the petition

4.6.1 General

The company must file affidavit evidence to verify the statements in the petition, to explain, where necessary, the nature of and grounds for the proposed reduction, and to provide the court with the material to enable it to give such directions as to creditors as are appropriate. The application to the court is *ex parte* and it is incumbent on the company to place all relevant material before the court.

4.6.2 Principal affidavit

It is conventional for a senior officer of the company, usually the chairman of the board of directors, to swear the principal affidavit in support of the petition. It is usually the chairman who makes this affidavit, both because of his overall knowledge of the company's affairs and because he will usually have chaired the meeting of shareholders at which the special resolution for the reduction was passed. If he did not chair the meeting, it may be convenient for the director who took the chair to swear this affidavit, provided that he has the necessary overall knowledge of the company. Alternatively, the chairman of the meeting can swear an affidavit dealing with the meeting, while another officer such as the managing director deals with the other matters in a separate affidavit.

4.6.3 Contents of the principal affidavit

The deponent will state his position with the company and the period that he has held it and, if different, the period that he has been a director. He will also state that he is authorised by the company to make the affidavit on its behalf.

47. CA 1985, s. 138(1).
48. *Re Castiglione, Erskine & Co. Ltd* [1958] 1 WLR 688, [1958] 2 All ER 455; *Re Anglo American Insurance Co. Ltd* [1991] BCLC 564.

The petition should be exhibited to the affidavit, as should the company's certificate of original incorporation and any subsequent certificates showing changes of name or re-registrations. If the certificates cannot be found, the registrar of companies will issue a composite certificate showing the date of original incorporation and subsequent changes. There must also be exhibited the memorandum and present articles of association. Where any changes to the authorised share capital were made at a time when the company had other articles of association, these articles must also be exhibited so that the court can be satisfied that the changes were made with due authority.

The affidavit must deal with the meeting at which the special resolution for the reduction was passed, and any separate meetings of classes of shareholders. The notice covering each such meeting should be exhibited, together with any circular to shareholders which was sent in connection with the meeting. It is sensible for the deponent expressly to verify the contents of any circulars, as they thereby formally become part of the evidence on which the company can rely in support of its application. The deponent should state that the special resolution, and any extraordinary resolutions passed at separate class meetings, were duly passed in the form set out in the petition, and that a quorum was present. The minute book, containing duly signed minutes of the meeting or meetings, should be exhibited.[49]

The affidavit should contain a description of the proposed reduction, the background facts relevant to it and an explanation of the grounds for the proposal. Although it has been held that an affidavit in general terms was sufficient,[50] this is not the course adopted in practice and, where the petition is based on a loss of capital, the court requires evidence to this effect.[51] The extent of the description and explanation must inevitably depend on the particular proposal. If a full explanation is contained in a circular to shareholders, it will not be necessary to repeat it in the affidavit, provided that the circular is exhibited and verified.

If the reduction is proposed in order to write off losses, the nature of the evidence will depend on the nature of the losses. Trading or revenue losses can usually be proved by reference to the audited accounts of the company. If the company is a holding company and its losses stem from a reduction in the value of its investment in subsidiaries as a result of the trading results of those subsidiaries, the loss can generally be proved by reference to the accounts of the subsidiaries and the directors' assessment of the value of the subsidiaries.

Alternatively, the losses may stem from the realisation or revaluation of assets. If an asset has been sold at a loss, the loss is established by evidence of the sale. If the asset is still owned by the company but there has been a reduction in its value, the court will require evidence of the loss of value from a deponent qualified to give such evidence. If the asset in question is a freehold or leasehold interest in land, evidence should be given by a valuer qualified to value the land in question. In relation to other assets, the appropriate deponent will of course depend on the asset concerned. If it is an asset for which a recognised body of expert valuers exists, the deponent will normally be a member of that body. Where reliance is placed on a valuation, an affidavit by the valuer himself

49. Such minutes are themselves evidence of the proceedings at the meeting: CA 1985, s. 382.
50. *Re Mains Manufacturing Co. Ltd* [1884] WN 171.
51. *Caldwell* v. *Caldwell* [1916] WN 70 per Lord Parker.

should, as a rule, be filed, in which he deposes to the effect that the value shown by the valuation, which should be exhibited, is in his opinion fair and proper.[52]

4.6.4 Evidence as to convening the meeting(s)

Strict proof is required that the general meeting at which the special resolution for the reduction is passed, and any class meetings, have been duly convened. In the case of a company with a small number of members, a single affidavit from the secretary deposing that he maintains the register of members and that he gave the requisite notice to each member will normally be sufficient. In the case of a company with a large number of shareholders, it can be an elaborate exercise. Evidence is required from the registrars or others who maintain the register, that they have kept it up to date and that they supplied the names and registered addresses of all members entitled to notice of the meeting. Commonly, these will have been supplied to the printers producing the circular to shareholders. A representative of the printers with personal knowledge of the steps taken to address the circular, notice and proxy card to shareholders should swear an affidavit. If a different representative personally effected or supervised the posting of those documents, an affidavit will be required from him. Care must also be taken to ensure that notice is sent to all members on the register of members entitled to notice. The shares of many listed companies are held in uncertificated form in the CREST system which is governed by The Uncertificated Securities Regulations 1995 (S.I. 1995 No. 3272). Those companies are empowered by Regulation 34(3) to determine the members entitled to notice of a meeting by reference to the register of members at the close of business on a record date, which must not be more than 21 days before the day on which notice of the meeting is sent. In the case of other companies, notice will under the terms of most articles of association need to be given to the members as at the date of despatch of the notice. Frequently the registrars will supply the names and addresses of members to the printers a few days before despatch and this should be updated to include any new members subsequently added to the register, before the record date or the date of despatch, whichever is applicable. Under most forms of articles an accidental omission to give notice to a member will not invalidate the meeting.[53]

4.7 Preliminary steps in the court proceedings

4.7.1 Presentation of petition

The petition is presented by filing it at the office of the Companies Court Registrar. Two copies are required, both of which will be stamped by the court. One copy is retained by the court and the other is given back and should be exhibited to the principal affidavit in support of the petition. It is common practice for the evidence to be sworn shortly before presentation of the petition and for the exhibited copy of the petition to be stamped by the court. At the same time, the summons for directions is issued. Again two copies are needed, one of which is retained by the court and placed in the file and the other is returned to the person attending the office of the Companies Court Registrar on behalf of

52. Practice Direction [1947] WN 116.
53. See reg. 39 of the 1985 Table A Regulations and *Re West Canadian Collieries Ltd* [1962] Ch. 370.

the company. The company's solicitors should take the copy of the summons for directions, the affidavits and the exhibits to the court officer to whom the petition has been assigned.

4.7.2 Checking evidence

The court undertakes an exercise of checking the evidence in support of the petition, primarily with a view to ensuring that the capital history is correct so that the minute, when approved by the court, will be accurate and to ensuring that the general meeting at which the special resolution for the reduction was passed and any class meetings were properly convened in accordance with the Act. The company's solicitor may have a meeting at court with the court officer to go through any points arising from the evidence. More commonly now, the court officer will simply deal with the matter over the telephone. Any further evidence required should be filed, if possible before the hearing of the summons for directions.

4.8 Summons for directions

The hearing of the summons for directions[54] takes place before the registrar in chambers. It is *ex parte* and, accordingly, even if opposition to the petition has materialised at this stage, the opposing members or creditors are not entitled to be present or heard at this hearing, without the leave of the court. Their opportunity to oppose the petition will arise at the hearing in open court of the petition itself. The petitioning company is normally represented by counsel at the hearing of the summons for directions.

The main purposes of the summons for directions are to ensure that the petition is ready for hearing and to deal with the position of creditors.[55] Any matters arising from the checking of evidence and remaining unresolved should be dealt with and, where necessary, leave to amend the petition will be given. Directions will also be given for advertising the hearing of the petition. The purpose is to give notice to all persons who might be interested. If there is a concentration of creditors and members in a particular area, advertisement may be directed in a local newspaper circulating in that area. Normally, advertisement is directed in one national newspaper which is named in the order.

4.9 Protection of creditors

4.9.1 General

The protection of the interests of creditors is one of the most important functions of the court in relation to a reduction of capital. As already noted, the principle underlying the rules for the maintenance of capital is that creditors deal with the company in the knowledge that capital will not be returned to shareholders except as permitted by the Companies Acts. It follows that, in this context, the court acts to protect those persons who

54. See RSC O. 102, r. 6.

55. Other matters, such as fairness between members, will be dealt with at the subsequent hearing of the petition in open court. If any creditors are dissatisfied with the proposal as it affects their interests, they too can raise their objections at the hearing of the petition.

already have claims against the company but is not specifically concerned with those who may in the future have dealings with the company.[56] Future dealings will be on the basis of a share capital reduced in accordance with the Act and, as a consequence of the registration of the order of the court confirming the reduction, those dealing with the company in the future will have the means of knowing its issued share capital.

4.9.2 Inquiry as to creditors

Section 136 of the Companies Act 1985 makes provision for an inquiry as to creditors and, by virtue of RSC O. 102, r. 6(3) and (4), any order for such an inquiry is to be made at the hearing of the summons for directions. Section 136(2) provides that, where the proposed reduction of capital involves either diminution of liability in respect of unpaid share capital or the payment to a shareholder of any paid-up share capital, an inquiry as to creditors in accordance with ss. 136(3)–(5) is to take place, unless the court, having regard to any special circumstances of the case, thinks it proper to order otherwise that those provisions shall not apply as regards any class or classes of creditors.[57] Additionally, the court may order such an inquiry in any other case.[58]

In practice, nowadays an inquiry as to creditors is never ordered.[59] It is a complex and onerous procedure for which elaborate provision is made in the Rules.[60] Companies petitioning for the confirmation of a reduction of capital will put forward some means, appropriate to the particular circumstances of the case, for dealing with creditors in a way which will satisfy the court that an inquiry is unnecessary.

4.9.3 Meaning of "creditors"

The statutory provisions define the persons who are treated as creditors for these purposes. They comprise "every creditor of the company who at the date fixed by the court is entitled to any debt or claim which, if that date were the commencement of the winding up of the company, would be admissible in proof against the company" (s. 136(3)). It is thus not confined to creditors with presently payable debts but includes those whose debts are payable at a future date, contingent creditors (such as those with the benefit of a guarantee given by the company), and persons with claims (such as for liquidated or unliquidated damages for breach of contract or in tort) against the company, whether or not those claims have in fact been advanced against the company at the relevant date.

The discretions conferred on the court by s. 136(3) and (6) are not subject to any express limitations save that, in cases to which s. 136(6) applies, the court should direct that there be no inquiry only if it thinks it proper to do so "having regard to any special circumstances of the case". The court must therefore decide in the circumstances of each case whether the safeguards proposed by the company sufficiently protect the interests of creditors.

The court is not limited to accepting only certain means of providing appropriate protection. Nevertheless, there has developed over the years a variety of methods of

56. *Re Grosvenor Press plc* [1985] 1 WLR 980.
57. CA 1985, s. 136(6).
58. CA 1985, s. 136(2).
59. It is believed that the last inquiry as to creditors was ordered in 1949.
60. RSC O. 102, rr. 7–14.

providing protection which will usually be regarded by the court as acceptable. The suitability of different methods depends on the particular type of reduction. In unusual cases, the registrar may be willing to discuss with counsel or with the company's solicitors, in advance of the summons for directions or presentation of the petition, whether a particular approach may be acceptable. In this way, unnecessary expense in pursuing an unsatisfactory method may be avoided.

4.9.4 Loss reductions

Where capital has been lost in the business of the company, creditors are not *prima facie* entitled to any form of protection. Since capital is properly employed in the pursuit of the company's objects, creditors must accept the risk that it may thereby be lost. For these purposes a loss must be permanent, although not necessarily irretrievable. In many cases, such as trading losses, there is no distinction. However, in the case of an unrealised loss, such as a decline in the value of property as a result of market conditions, the loss will be regarded as permanent even though market conditions in the future may change so that the property rises again in value.[61]

The court will therefore require evidence that the loss is indeed permanent, as opposed to either temporary or balanced in whole or in part by gains on other assets. The company may have assets which quite properly do not appear as such in its balance sheet. For example, it may have a litigation claim which, if successful, will increase the assets of the company and may recoup the loss already suffered by the company. Alternatively, certain assets may have increased in value over the value at which they are carried in the company's books. If realised, the profit resulting from such increase in value would reduce or extinguish the loss suffered by the company. Another possibility is that, while the accounts show realised losses resulting from the company's trading activities or fixed asset sales, they may also show a revaluation reserve to which have been credited increases in the value of fixed assets retained by the company. Alternatively, the loss may result in whole or in part from writing down the value of an asset, not because there has been a permanent decline in its value but because, due to uncertainties, it is considered prudent to write down its value.[62] Or the loss may result from provisions against liabilities which are not certain to occur.

In all these cases the company has actual or potential profits at the date on which the petition is before the court. The writing-off of its realised losses will enable the company to distribute those actual or potential profits, if and when they become realised. This could involve prejudice to the interests of creditors entitled under s. 136 to object to the reduction. Accordingly, the court will require those interests to be safeguarded. Since the reduction does not involve any outflow of funds from the company, it is not necessary to show that the company has sufficient liquid assets to meet its liabilities or to provide a bank guarantee or similar protection (see paras 4.9.8–4.9.13, *infra*).

4.9.5 Undertaking to the court

In the circumstances outlined above, the court will generally regard as appropriate an undertaking given to the court by the company that any such profit, as and when realised,

61. *Re Jupiter House Investments (Cambridge) Ltd* [1985] 1 WLR 975.
62. *Re Grosvenor Press plc* [1985] 1 WLR 980.

will be credited to a non-distributable reserve. Since the court is concerned to protect the interests of existing creditors, not persons who may become creditors in the future, it is not necessary that the reserve should be permanent.[63] The profit must remain credited to the non-distributable reserve for as long as any debt or claim which would be admissible in a winding-up of the company commencing on a date specified by the court (normally, the date on which the reduction of capital takes effect) remains outstanding. The undertaking will provide that, with the consent of all the relevant creditors, it can cease to apply at an earlier date. It will also provide that—to the extent that the paid-up share capital is subsequently increased by an issue of shares for new consideration, or paid up by a capitalisation of distributable profits—the amount to be carried to, or standing to the credit of, the undistributable reserve pursuant to the undertaking, can be reduced. The basis for this proviso is that the existing creditors are protected if and to the extent that the paid up capital is increased to its previous amount.

4.9.6 Reductions in order to create reserves

A reduction of capital may be proposed, not to write off losses nor to return capital to shareholders, but to create a reserve of an amount equal to the cancelled capital. Most commonly in recent years, such reductions have been put forward so as to create reserves against which goodwill in the company's own accounts or goodwill arising on consolidation can be written off.[64] In such cases, the interests of creditors are met by an undertaking relating to the reserve along the lines discussed in para. 4.9.5, *supra*. Whereas the undertaking can be applied in a simple way to a reserve which will be used in the consolidated accounts, the position is more complex where the point of creating the reserve is to write off goodwill in the company's own accounts. In that case, the undertaking will permit the reserve to be used for that purpose but will also provide that any amount subsequently realised in respect of the goodwill will be credited to the reserve, subject to the provisions discussed in para. 4.9.5, *supra*.

4.9.7 Return of capital

So far, in dealing with creditors, the discussion has centred on cases where the reduction involves no return of capital (or diminution of liability in respect of unpaid share capital[65]). This is an important distinction as regards creditors, because reductions not involving a return of capital do not of themselves deplete the assets of the company available for payment of their debts or claims. The distinction is drawn by s. 136 which provides that s. 136(3)–(5) apply to such reductions only if the court so directs, whereas, in the case of a reduction involving a return of capital, those subsections apply unless the court directs that they shall not apply as regards any class or classes of creditors, "if having regard to any special circumstances of the case it thinks proper to do so".

63. *Re Grosvenor Press plc* [1985] 1 WLR 980. *Re Jupiter House Investments (Cambridge) Ltd* [1985] 1 WLR 975 is not a decision to the contrary effect, since in that case the company offered an undertaking to establish a permanent reserve.

64. For example, *Re Ratners Group plc* [1988] BCLC 685, (1988) 4 BCC 293; *Re Thorn EMI plc* [1989] BCLC 612, (1988) 4 BCC 698.

65. Reductions involving a diminution of liability in respect of unpaid share capital are now very rare, as partly or nil paid shares are themselves rare. References in the text will be to reductions involving a return of capital but the same principles apply where there is a diminution of liability.

4.9.8 Special circumstances

There is clearly no limit imposed on the circumstances which the court may consider to be special in this context. However, a number of methods of safeguarding the interests of creditors have, over the years, come to be recognised as justifying a direction that s. 136(3)–(5) is not to apply to any class of creditors. First, and most obviously, the consent of all creditors to the proposed reduction will obviate the need for an inquiry. Secondly, evidence that the company has cash and other liquid assets sufficient to meet all its liabilities will be accepted: see paras 4.9.9–4.9.11, *infra*. Thirdly, a guarantee of all non-consenting creditors will suffice: see para. 4.9.12, *infra*.

4.9.9 Cash

The court will direct that there be no inquiry as to creditors if the company shows, by evidence, that it has cash and other liquid assets sufficient to make the proposed return of capital, pay all its liabilities and leave a margin equal to, say, 10% of its liabilities. Other liquid assets for these purposes will include certificates of deposit, government securities and other listed securities. Narrower-range trustee investments, as defined in the Trustee Investments Act 1961, will be accepted at their full current market value, while wider-range trustee investments will be taken into account at half their current market value. Evidence will be required, in the form of certificates from the banks at which the company has accounts, showing the balances on those accounts at the latest available date and, in the case of securities, a valuation by brokers as at the latest available date before the hearing of the summons for directions. Evidence must also be given of the liabilities of the company, including all debts payable at a future date, contingent liabilities, and claims (such as unliquidated claims for damages) against the company. Again these must be given as at the latest practicable date. In the case of a large company, this may be a major exercise and, while it is a matter for the court in each particular case, the court will normally require the liabilities to be shown as at a date not more than about six weeks before the hearing of the summons for directions.

4.9.10 Long term and other special liabilities

Particular problems may arise with certain categories of liability, particularly long term liabilities and claims for damages. Where the company is lessee of premises, the company *prima facie* must show sufficient cash and liquid assets to cover all liabilities arising under the lease for the entirety of its term. In the case of a lease with rent review clauses, the rent will usually be calculated for these purposes at the current rate. However, if by evidence from an appropriately experienced valuer, the company can show that the terms of the lease as to rent and other matters are not onerous in comparison with terms generally available in the market for properties of that type, and the lease has an unexpired term in excess of 10 years, the court will limit the amount of cash required to be shown to match the liability under the lease to 10 years' rent.[66] Claims for damages present considerable problems. The court cannot assume that the claim is not well founded and will probably, in most cases, require it to be fully provided for. To the extent that the claim is covered

66. *Re Lucania Temperance Billiard Halls (London) Ltd* [1966] Ch. 98.

by insurance from reputable insurers, the court is likely to regard that as a sufficient safeguard of the claimant's interests.[67]

4.9.11 Consenting creditors

Cash cover need not be shown for creditors who consent to the proposed reduction. Their consents must be in writing and put in evidence. They must also agree to subordinate their claims to the debts and claims of all other creditors, who have not consented as at the relevant date.

4.9.12 Guarantee

The most common alternative to the cash method of dealing with creditors is to obtain a bank guarantee for all relevant liabilities. It used to be the case that the court would accept only guarantees given by one of the UK clearing banks. More recently, the court has accepted guarantees from major merchant banks and major foreign banks with a substantial presence in the United Kingdom. The amount of the guarantee should be the aggregate amount of the debts of and claims against the company, excluding the debts and claims of consenting creditors, or the amount of the reduction of capital, whichever is less. Such consents should be in evidence, but they need not include a subordination to the debts and claims of non-consenting creditors. The duration of the guarantee is determined by the period during which the liabilities are likely to be discharged. If there are no long term debts or claims subject to litigation, the usual period is three to 12 months, depending on the circumstances. A longer period may be required for particular debts and claims or categories of debts and claims, and there is no reason why the same guarantee should not provide for different periods for different debts, thereby reducing the overall amount, and therefore cost, of the guarantee. The amount of the guarantee may also be reduced to the extent of any subsequent increase in share capital or share premium account resulting from an issue of shares for new consideration or paid up by a capitalisation of distributable profits. The rules for determining the liabilities and for dealing with long leases, discussed in para. 4.9.10, *supra*, apply for the purpose of a guarantee.

4.9.13 Other methods

As already observed, there is no limit to the special circumstances justifying a direction that s. 136(3)–(5) shall not apply. In some cases it may be possible to pay all creditors. Alternatively, money can be paid into a trust account to meet the claims of relevant creditors. If the company has distributable profits which it is prepared to apply for these purposes, it can apply, by analogy, the provisions of part V, chapter VII of the Companies Act 1985 relating to the redemption and purchase by a company of its own shares. This involves the amount of the repayment being debited to distributable profits, and the creation of a reserve of an amount equal to the nominal amount of the cancelled capital. An undertaking would be given to the court, on the hearing of the summons for directions, to debit the repayment in this way and to create the appropriate non-distributable reserve

67. Contrast the position in a winding-up: see *Re R-R Realisations Ltd* [1980] 1 WLR 805, [1980] 1 All ER 1019.

in terms similar to those discussed in para. 4.9.5, *supra*. Although the statutory provisions in part V, chapter VII require the reserve arising on a redemption or purchase of shares to be treated as a permanent capital reserve,[68] there seems no reason why the undertaking in respect of the reserve should not be limited in time to their debts and claims as at the date of the petition, in accordance with the principles on which the court acts on a reduction of capital of safeguarding the interests of existing creditors only. If, as part of the arrangements involving the reduction, the issued share capital is to be increased by the receipt of new consideration or the capitalisation of distributable profits in an amount at least equal to the reduction, that, too, would justify a direction that s. 136(3)–(5) is not to apply.

4.10 Steps following the summons for directions

Following the hearing of the summons for directions, two copies of a draft order for directions and a draft advertisement should be lodged with the court. This should be lodged with the court officer who is dealing with the petition, and arrangements can often be made to see the officer immediately after the hearing so that the drafts can be approved then and steps taken immediately to arrange for the advertisement to appear in the newspaper as identified in the order. If a draft order is given to the registrar at the hearing, he will initial it with such amendments if any as are necessary and this will again speed up the process. The court file, the initialled draft order and two forms of order should be taken to the officer concerned, if arrangements have been made to see him immediately after the hearing. The forms of order will be stamped, and one form will be retained on the court file and the other copy returned to the company's solicitors. The order will state the date fixed for the hearing of the petition which will appear in the newspaper advertisement. A copy of the newspaper containing the advertisement should be lodged with the court.

4.11 Hearing of petition

4.11.1 General

The petition will be listed for hearing before the registrar sitting in open court on a Wednesday during term.[69] The registrar will have the court file containing the petition, orders already made, and the affidavits filed. The exhibits will have been returned to the company's solicitors and should be brought to the hearing. If there is no opposition, the registrar will immediately hear the petition.

4.11.2 Opposition

If any member or creditor of the company appears to oppose the petition, the registrar may either proceed to hear the petition or give directions for its future conduct. If he considers that there is little substance to the opposition, he may hear the petition immediately. Otherwise, he will not hear it then but will give directions. The opposing member or

68. S. 170.

69. Practice Direction (Companies Court: Schemes and Deductions) [1997] 1 WLR 1. For hearings during vacations, see para. 4.14, *infra*.

creditor may seek an adjournment to file evidence or to supplement evidence already filed, and the company may seek directions with a view to filing evidence in reply to any evidence that has been or will be filed in opposition to the petition. It has been held that a creditor or member opposing a petition for the sanction of a scheme of arrangement is not a "party" within s. 151(1) of the Supreme Court Act 1981 and RSC Order 24, rule 10 and therefore not entitled to seek an order for discovery.[70] It was subsequently held that the court may order the petitioner to produce documents at the hearing of the petition.[71] In practice, orders for cross-examination are rarely if ever made; the court could order cross-examination where it was necessary for a proper determination of the matter.[72] The registrar will also adjourn the petition to come before the judge dealing with Companies Court business, who sits in open court each Monday during term, with a view to an effective hearing as soon as possible.

4.11.3 Principal considerations of the court

On the hearing of the petition, the court will be concerned to see that the jurisdictional requirements are satisfied, that the reduction is in accordance with class rights, or that the requisite class consents have been obtained, that it has been properly explained to shareholders, and that it is a reduction which ought to be confirmed.[73] The onus as regards these matters will rest on the company, whether or not there is opposition. However, in considering whether the reduction should be confirmed, the court will not substitute its view for that of the shareholders who have voted in favour of it. Rather, the function of the court is to decide whether it is a proposal that shareholders, having regard to their interests as shareholders, could reasonably approve. The existence of reasonable grounds for opposing the reduction is not of itself a sufficient basis for a refusal to sanction the reduction.

4.11.4 Conditional reductions

Resolutions for the reduction of share capital or share premium account may be conditional on the creation of the shares or share premium account to be reduced or cancelled. This is legitimate, and a petition to confirm the reduction may be presented before the shares or share premium account have been issued or created. However, the shares must be issued or the share premium account created by the time of the hearing of the petition.[74]

4.11.5 Costs

In practice, the company will in any event be responsible for its own costs, at least to the extent that they are not increased by opposition. As regards the further costs of the

70. *Re Heron International NV* 21 July 1993, Harman J., unreported.
71. *Re Heron International NV* [1994] 1 BCLC 667 at 674.
72. Cf. *Re Lifecare International plc* [1990] BCLC 222.
73. *Ex parte Westburn Sugar Refineries Ltd* [1951] AC 625; *Re Ratners Group plc* [1988] BCLC 685, (1988) 4 BCC 293; *Re Thorn EMI plc* [1989] BCLC 612, (1988) 4 BCC 698.
74. *Re Transfesa Terminals Ltd* (1987) 3 BCC 647; *Re TIP-Europe Ltd* [1988] BCLC 231, (1987) 3 BCC 647.

company and the costs of opposing members or creditors, the company will usually bear those costs if the opposition is successful. It does not, however, follow that an unsuccessful opponent will be ordered to pay costs. The court will tend to adopt the same approach to costs as it does in relation to schemes of arrangement, as to which see para. 3.6.8, *supra*.

4.12 Order

The usual order made by the court if it confirms the reduction is: (i) to confirm the reduction; (ii) to approve the minute as set out in the petition (as amended, if necessary); and (iii) to direct advertisement of the registration of the order in the same newspaper as that in which the hearing was advertised.[75] Section 137(1) enables the court to confirm the reduction "on such terms and conditions as it thinks fit" but, in practice, terms or conditions are rarely, if ever, attached. Section 137(2) enables the court to direct that the company should add the words "and reduced" as the last words of its name for such period as it specifies, and that the company should publish the reasons for the reduction or information with regard to it. These powers have not been exercised for many years. If the company is a public company and its allotted share capital as reduced will be less than the "authorised minimum" set in accordance with s. 118(1) of the Companies Act 1985, the company must obtain a direction from the court before the registrar of companies can register the order, unless the company first re-registers as a private company.[76]

At the hearing of the petition, the registrar or judge will initial a draft order. The office copy of the order should then be delivered to Companies House for registration. Arrangements exist for the order to be lodged at the London office of the registrar of companies. The registrar of companies issues a certificate of registration which is conclusive evidence that all the requirements of the Act with respect to the reduction have been complied with and that the share capital is as stated in the minute.[77] The order of the court will usually provide that notice of the registration by the registrar of companies be published within 21 days after registration. In accordance with s. 138(2), the reduction takes effect on the registration of the order and minute, and in practice the date of registration may be a day or two after delivery of the order to the registrar of companies.

4.13 Reduction of share premium amount or capital redemption reserve

The provisions in ss. 135 *et seq.* relating to the reduction of share capital, apply to these reserves as if they were part of the paid up share capital.[78] Accordingly, the procedure set out above applies to the reduction of either reserve. There are only a few differences. First, if no reduction of share capital is involved, the capital history of the company should not be set out in the petition, nor is it necessary to set out the history of the share premium account or capital redemption reserve. It is enough to state the present authorised and

75. CA 1985, s. 138(3).
76. CA 1985, s. 139.
77. CA 1985, s. 138(4). The effect of the certificate as "conclusive evidence" is that no challenge can thereafter be made to the matters to which it relates, except by the Attorney-General: see *R* v. *Registrar of Companies, ex parte Esal (Commodities) Ltd* [1986] QB 1114, [1986] 1 All ER 105.
78. CA 1985, ss. 130(4) and 170(4).

issued share capital and the amount presently standing to the credit of the relevant reserve. Secondly, there is no minute for a reduction of share premium account or capital redemption reserve.[79]

4.14 Long vacation

In response to the commercial and financial needs of companies, arrangements were made in 1977[80] to enable petitions for the confirmation of reductions of capital and for the sanction of schemes of arrangements to be heard in the long vacation, even though they might not satisfy the strict requirements for vacation business. Under these arrangements, now set out in Practice Direction (Chancery No. 6E) as amended by Practice Direction (Companies Court: Schemes and Deductions),[81] the petition must be one in which, for financial, commercial or economic reasons a hearing before the end of the long vacation is desirable; this category includes mergers and takeovers which arise in the summer and are likely to be affected by market fluctuations. It must also be an application which could not, with reasonable diligence, have been made and prosecuted in time to be heard before the long vacation. An informal application in chambers, to the court manager, accompanied by an advocate's certificate that these requirements are satisfied, must be made as soon as possible so that a suitable timetable may be settled, including a date for hearing.

A judge is available to hear petitions to schemes of arrangement and schemes under sch. 2C to the Insurance Companies Act 1982 and any petitions to confirm reductions of capital which require to be heard by a judge on one Wednesday in August and two Wednesdays in September. The vacation judge may also hear petitions on other days if he thinks fit. In the case of reduction petitions to be heard by the registrar which do not fall within the above categories, they will be heard provided that either there is an urgent need for a hearing or there is sufficient time available after the registrar has disposed of urgent applications. Applications to the registrar in chambers for orders convening scheme meetings and for directions in reduction petitions are heard during the long vacation. Notice of such applications should be given before the start of the long vacation so that a suitable timetable can be fixed.

79. *Re Paringa Mining and Exploration Co. Ltd* [1957] 1 WLR 1143, [1957] 3 All ER 424.

80. Practice Direction (Companies Court: Long Vacation) [1977] 1 WLR 317 subsequently amended and replaced.

81. [1997] 1 WLR 1, replacing Chancery No. 6E set out in *Supreme Court Practice 1997*, Vol. 2 para. 816.

CHAPTER 5

MISCELLANEOUS APPLICATIONS UNDER THE COMPANIES ACT 1985

5.0 This Chapter draws together a number of miscellaneous applications under the Companies Act 1985, which are not dealt with elsewhere in this book. The first four parts of the Chapter deal with applications which are frequently encountered; the remaining parts deal with applications which are less common.

I. RECTIFICATION OF THE REGISTER OF MEMBERS

5.1 Jurisdiction

Where a company wrongly fails to register a transfer of shares in it, the transferee may bring an action by writ for a declaration that the directors are bound to register the transferee as the holder of shares transferred[1]; but it will usually be quicker and more convenient for the transferee to apply by motion for rectification of the company's register of members under s. 359 of the Companies Act 1985.[2] The court[3] has power to order that the register of members maintained by a company pursuant to s. 352 should be rectified if: (i) the name of any person is, without sufficient cause, entered in or omitted from the register; or (ii) the company fails to enter or unnecessarily delays in entering on the register the fact that a person has ceased to be a member.[4] The court's power to order rectification under s. 359 is discretionary.[5] The wording of s. 359 has been liberally interpreted, and the court will exercise its power of rectification in a wide variety of circumstances.[6] The English court has exclusive jurisdiction in respect of an application under s. 359 for the rectification of the register of a company incorporated under the Companies Acts.[7]

1. *Tett* v. *Phoenix Property and Investments Co. Ltd* [1984] BCLC 599; on appeal at [1986] BCLC 149.
2. All references in the text are to sections of the CA 1985 unless otherwise stated.
3. "The court" means the court having jurisdiction to wind up the company (s. 744), which is further defined by IA 1986, s. 117. Applications are usually made in the Chancery Division of the High Court.
4. S. 359(1)
5. S. 359(2). For a case where rectification was refused in the exercise of the court's discretion, see *Re Piccadilly Radio plc* [1989] BCLC 683.
6. See paras 5.8 and 5.9, *infra*.
7. *Re Fagin's Bookshop plc* [1992] BCLC 118 at 123h–i (where rectification was sought by motion); and *International Credit and Investment Co. (Overseas) Ltd* v. *Adham* [1994] 1 BCLC 66 at 78b–f (where rectification was sought by writ).

5.2 Form of application

Save in exceptional cases[8] the application should be by notice of originating motion[9] supported by affidavit.[10] The notice of originating motion need not state the name of the Companies Court Judge before whom the motion will be moved on the return date—it is sufficient if the notice is stated to be returnable before "the Companies Court Judge".[11] The notice must name a motion day on which the motion is to be heard: in term time, Companies Court motions will normally be listed for hearing in the first instance on the first available Monday at 10.30am. The notice of originating motion should be issued at the chambers of the Companies Court Registrar,[12] or by post[13] or at any Chancery district registry.[14] Three copies of the notice of motion will be required for issue, one copy of which should be stamped with the appropriate fee and will be retained for filing: one copy will be retained for use by the judge and one copy will be returned to the applicant. The application should be issued promptly, once the grounds for rectification arise.[15]

5.3 Application by writ

There may exceptionally be cases where the issues to be determined in the application for rectification are unsuitable for determination in a summary manner (i.e. on motion supported by affidavit), but require a full trial with pleadings, discovery, inspection and cross-examination of witnesses. Summary determination may be inappropriate where, for example, the case is particularly complex, or where the applicant relies on allegations of fraud which ought to be clearly set out in pleadings, or where the applicant seeks other relief in addition to rectification (e.g. an injunction to restrain further wrongful purported transfers of shares).[16] Where the applicant proceeds by way of motion and the case is not suitable for summary determination, the court may refuse to exercise its discretionary power under s. 359 to order rectification, leaving the applicant to bring an action for rectification by writ of summons.[17] However, the mere fact that the application for rectification involves determination of disputed questions of title or fact is not in itself a bar to proceeding by motion—the court has power on an application for rectification by

8. See paragraph 5.3, *infra*.

9. RSC O. 102, r. 3(1)(g): *Supreme Court Practice 1997*, Vol. 1, paras 102/3/8–102/3/10, pp. 1548–1549. For the form of the notice of originating motion, see Form No. 13 in Appendix A to the RSC: *Supreme Court Practice 1997*, Vol. 2, para. 8, p. 8.

10. See para. 5.7, *infra*.

11. Practice Direction (Chancery Division: Forms) [1992] 1 WLR 791.

12. Room 2.09, Second Floor, Thomas More Building, Royal Courts of Justice.

13. See Chancery Division Practice Direction No. 6(C): *Supreme Court Practice 1997*, Vol. 2, para. 814, p. 173.

14. RSC O. 102, r. 3(2). At the time of writing, there are Chancery District registries in Birmingham, Bristol, Cardiff, Leeds, Liverpool, Manchester, Newcastle-upon-Tyne and Preston: see the definition in RSC O. 1, r. 4(1).

15. *Re New Zealand Banking Corp. (Sewell's Case)* (1868) 3 Ch.App. 131 at 138 and *Re Scottish Petroleum Co.* (1882) 23 Ch.D. 413 at 436–437 (both of which were concerned with the question of whether certain names were properly placed on the list of contributories in a winding-up).

16. When ordering rectification, the court has power under s. 359(2) to order the company to pay damages. The power to order damages may be exercised whether the application for rectification is brought by Writ or notice of originating motion, but not where rectification is refused: *Re Ottos Kopje Diamond Mines Ltd* [1893] 1 Ch. 618 at 624–625.

17. *Re Greater Britain Products Development Corp. Ltd* (1924) 40 TLR 488 at 489; *Re British Sugar Refining Co.* (1857) 26 LJ Ch. 369 at 372–373; *Re National and Provincial Marine Insurance Company, ex parte Parker* (1867) 2 Ch.App. 685 at 690.

motion to determine questions of fact and of title,[18] and contested applications by motion will often require disputed issues of fact to be resolved.

5.4 Conversion to writ action

Where the applicant proceeds by way of notice of originating motion, and objection is taken to the form of the application as being inappropriate, given the complexity of the case or the nature of the allegations, the court hearing the motion may dismiss the motion or it may effectively "convert" the motion into a writ action by giving directions for pleadings (i.e. points of claim, points of defence, and points of reply) discovery, inspection, possibly exchange of witness statements,[19] and cross-examination of any deponents or makers of witness statements.[20] Alternatively, the court may simply direct that the deponents should be cross-examined on their affidavits.[21] If the judge gives detailed directions, it may be convenient for the proceedings to be adjourned to the registrar in chambers so that he can oversee the interlocutory stages and give further directions as and when necessary. Once all the interlocutory stages have been completed, the proceedings may then be adjourned back to the judge for final determination.

5.5 Parties

The applicant may be the company itself, any member[22] of the company or a person aggrieved.[23] In most cases, the applicant will be the person who claims to have been wrongfully excluded from, or wrongfully entered on, the register of members of the company. Where the applicant claims to be entitled to be entered on the register and complains about his omission therefrom, the respondents should be the company and the person (if any) presently shown as the registered holder of the shares in question, unless that person is a co-applicant.[24] Where the applicant complains of a failure or delay in removing his name from the register, the respondents should be the company[25] and the person who ought to be shown as the registered holder of the shares in question, unless that person is a co-applicant. Since the company is able to represent the interests of any other shareholders, they need not be joined as parties.[26] The directors of the company

18. S. 359(3).

19. I.e. pursuant to RSC O. 38, r. 2A.

20. See *Re The Diamond Rock Boring Co. Ltd, ex parte Shaw* (1876–77) 2 QBD 463 at 480 per Lord Coleridge C.J.; the *Supreme Court Practice 1997*, Vol. 1, p. 1548, para. 102/3/9; and *Re Vestal Hosiery Co. Ltd* (1922) 91 LJ Ch. 627 at 629–630 (a misfeasance summons on which pleadings, discovery and inspection were ordered).

21. See *Re New Zealand Banking Corp. (Sewell's Case), supra*, at 136–137.

22. For the definition of "member", see s. 22.

23. S. 359(1). A person "aggrieved" is someone who has suffered a legal grievance, or against whom a decision has been given which has wrongfully deprived him of something, or has wrongfully refused him something to which he is entitled or has wrongfully affected his title to something: *Re Sidebotham, ex parte Sidebotham* (1880) 14 Ch. 458 at 465 per James L.J.; *Re Reed Bowen & Co., ex parte Official Receiver* (1887) 19 QBD 174 at 177. See also *Attorney-General of the Gambia* v. *N'Jie* [1961] AC 617 at 634–635 and *Re ACLI Metals (London) Ltd (AML Holdings Inc.* v. *Auger)* (1989) 5 BCC 749 at 754D–G.

24. *Morgan* v. *Morgan Insurance Brokers Ltd* [1993] BCLC 676 at 678a–c.

25. *Re The Denver United Breweries Ltd* (1893) 63 LT 96.

26. *Morgan* v. *Morgan Insurance Brokers Ltd, supra*, at 678b–c.

should not be joined as respondents even if they are alleged to be guilty of wrongdoing, unless they request to be joined[27] or an order for costs is sought against them.[28]

5.6 Service

The notice of originating motion should be served on any respondents in the usual way described previously[29]—i.e. at least two clear days before the date fixed for the hearing stated in the notice of motion, unless leave for short service is given by the court.[30] In calculating the period of two clear days, the day of service and the day of the hearing are not counted, nor are weekends or bank holidays.[31] Where the respondent is a company, the notice of motion should be served by leaving it at or posting it to the company's registered office[32]; where the respondent is an individual, the notice of motion should be left at or posted first class to the respondent's usual or last known address.[33]

5.7 Affidavit in support

The affidavit should set out all material facts relied upon by the applicant in support of his claim to be entitled to rectification. Where the applicant claims to have been wrongly excluded from the register of members, the evidence should establish the applicant's title to the shares in question and should show that the applicant has complied with all procedural requirements for registration imposed by the company's articles of association[34]: for example, the affidavit should identify the contract or stock transfer form by which the applicant acquired the shares (which should be exhibited), the procedural requirements for registration imposed by the articles, and the applicant's compliance with requirements (such as the tender of a duly completed transfer form[35] and the lodging of the relevant share certificates[36]), the request for registration, the refusal of registration, any grounds for refusing registration cited by the company, and an explanation as to why those grounds are unfounded. Where the applicant claims to be entitled to have his name removed from the register, the affidavit and exhibits should show that the applicant never acquired shares in the company or that he has disposed of his shareholding and has duly complied with all requirements to have the transferee entered on the register as the holder of the shares in question.

27. *Re Keith Prowse & Co. Ltd* [1918] 1 Ch. 487; *Re Copal Varnish Co. Ltd* [1917] 2 Ch. 349.
28. See *Morgan* v. *Morgan Insurance Brokers Ltd*, *supra*, at 678c–h per Millett J. To the extent that *Keith Prowse* and *Copal Varnish*, *supra*, suggest that it is never appropriate to join the directors against their wishes merely to obtain a punitive costs order against them, those decisions are no longer good law following *Morgan Insurance*.
29. See para. 2.13 *et seq.*, *supra*.
30. RSC O. 8, r. 2(2).
31. RSC O. 3, r. 2(4), (5). Therefore, a notice of motion for a hearing before the Companies Court Judge on a Monday must be served before close of business on the preceding Wednesday.
32. S. 725(1).
33. RSC O. 10, rr. 5(2) and 1(2).
34. See, for example, regs 23–28 inclusive of the 1985 Table A: the Companies (Tables A to F) Regulations 1985, S.I. 1985 No. 805, as amended by S.I. 1985 No. 1052.
35. *Ibid.*, reg. 23.
36. *Ibid.*, reg. 24(a).

5.8 When will the court order rectification?

The court's power to order rectification is discretionary.[37] The power to remove a name entered on the register of members "without sufficient cause" under s. 359(1)(a) has been widely construed. The jurisdiction to order rectification is not restricted to cases where a person has been entered on the register improperly, but extends to all cases where the entry was without sufficient cause.[38] In other words, under s. 359(1)(a) it is not necessary for the applicant to show any deliberate wrongful act or fault by the company—it is sufficient to show that the register of members is incorrect because an entry has been omitted or made in error.[39] In deciding whether to order rectification, the court will go into all relevant circumstances[40] and should have regard to the "justice of the case".[41] Rectification has been ordered, for example: where an overseas company had been entered on the register of members of an English company but the issue of shares was void as it contravened the Exchange Control Act 1947 without the permission of the Treasury[42]; where rectification was necessary to enable the members of the company to have a fair and reasonable exercise of their rights (for example, where joint holders of shares wished to have their joint holding split between them and the register rectified accordingly, so that the second-named joint holder could vote at a general meeting notwithstanding the absence or illness of the first-named joint holder)[43]; where there had been an irregular issue of bonus shares because the directors and the company acted under the common mistake of fact that there were profits available for distribution capable of being capitalised for the bonus issue, when in fact there were none[44]; where there had been an allotment of shares to two members when a third member did not have actual notice of the allotment, despite a provision in the articles deeming notice to have been given to the third member[45]; where an allotment of shares was invalid as a consequence of its approval at an inquorate board meeting[46]; where a member's name was wrongly deleted from the register by the company following receipt by the company of a forged stock transfer form[47]; where a person subscribed for shares in reliance upon a misleading prospectus[48]; and where the company wrongly re-registered a transferee's shares back into the name of the transferor (who was indebted to the company) in order to create a lien over the shares.[49] The court's power to rectify may also be invoked where the company's register of members has been lost or destroyed and the directors wish to create a replacement register, in effect by rectifying a

37. S. 359(2); *Re The Diamond Rock Boring Co. Ltd, ex parte Shaw* (1876–77) 2 QBD 463 at 479.
38. *Re Imperial Chemical Industries Ltd* [1936] 2 All ER 463 at 469.
39. *Re Fagin's Bookshop plc* [1992] BCLC 118 at 123a–h; *Re The Diamond Rock Boring Co. Ltd, ex parte Shaw, supra*, at 482–483.
40. *Re Russian (Vyksounsky) Iron Works Co. (Stewart's Case)* (1866) 1 Ch.App. 574 at 586.
41. *Trevor* v. *Whitworth* (1888) 12 AC 409 at 440 (a case on CA 1862, s. 35 which, unlike s. 359 of the 1985 Act, expressly required the court to be "satisfied of the justice of the case" before it could order rectification).
42. *Re Transatlantic Life Assurance Co. Ltd* [1980] 1 WLR 79 at 84C–E.
43. *Burns* v. *Siemens Bros Dynamo Works* [1919] 1 Ch. 225 at 231–232; *Re Stranton Iron and Steel Co. Ltd* (1873) LR 16 Eq 559 at 562–563.
44. *Re Cleveland Trust plc* [1991] BCC 33.
45. *Re Thundercrest Ltd* [1994] BCC 857.
46. *Re Portuguese Consolidated Copper Mines Ltd* (1889) 42 Ch.D. 160.
47. *Re the Bahia and San Francisco Railway Co. Ltd* (1868) LR 3 QB 584.
48. *Re Russian (Vyksounsky) Iron Works Co., Stewart's Case* (1866) 1 Ch.App. 574; *Re Scottish Petroleum Co. (Anderson's Case)* (1881) 17 Ch.D. 373.
49. *Re Ystalyfera Gas Co.* [1887] WN 30.

blank register to show the names of the present members.[50] An order for rectification under s. 359 may be made in relation to some rather than all of a registered shareholder's shares.[51]

5.9 Directors' failure to register transfers

The court may also order rectification where the directors fail to place a valid transfer before the board for consideration and approval, or unreasonably delay in doing so, even where the articles empower the directors to refuse to register a transfer. Whether there has been unnecessary delay depends upon all the facts of the case: a delay of two months would usually be unreasonable,[52] but exceptional circumstances may oblige the directors to register a transfer within a much shorter period.[53] Where the directors do consider a valid transfer within a reasonable time but refuse to register the transfer, relying on a wide and unqualified power contained in the company's articles, the court may in its discretion refuse to order rectification of the register unless the applicant proves that the directors acted outside their powers or were not acting *bona fide* in the best interests of the company.[54] The court may order rectification where the company is in compulsory liquidation[55]; but where the transfer occurred after the making of a compulsory winding-up order, the transferee does not have an absolute right to be entered on the register of members and the applicant must establish strong grounds for rectification.[56]

5.10 Refusal of rectification

The court has refused to order rectification in the following situations: where a statement filed in lieu of a prospectus pursuant to which shares were subscribed, contained a mistake[57]; where a director assented to become a member on receipt of an allotment of shares at a discount, mistakenly believing the allotment to be valid[58]; where the shares to which the applicant claimed to be entitled were not in issue or had been issued and properly allotted to a third party[59]; and where the directors had refused to register a valid transfer relying on a wide and unfettered power to refuse registration contained in the

50. *Re Data Express Ltd*, *Times*, 27 April 1987.
51. *Re Transatlantic Life Assurance Co. Ltd*, *supra*, at 84F.
52. *Tett* v. *Phoenix Property and Investment Co. Ltd* [1984] BCLC 599 at 620d–g; *Re Zinotty Properties Ltd* [1984] 1 WLR 1249 at 1261B–E; *Re Swaledale Cleaners Ltd* [1968] 1 WLR 1710 at 1715C (where reliance was placed on clause 19 of Table A of the Companies Act 1929—see now ss. 183(5) and 185(1), and reg. 25 of the 1985 Table A); *Popely* v. *Planarrive Ltd*, [1997] 1 BCLC 8 at 15a–b.
53. See *Re Stranton Iron and Steel Co. Ltd*, *supra*, where the facts justified an order for rectification only three days after the application for registration of the transfer to enable the transferees to vote at an imminent extraordinary general meeting; and *Re Joint Stock Discount Co. (Shipman's Case)* (1868) LR 5 Eq 219 (where rectification would have been ordered after a delay of six weeks but for the fact that the transferee was an "irresponsible person", entitling the directors under the articles to refuse to register the transfer).
54. *Popely* v. *Planarrive Ltd*, *supra* at 15f–16h and 18i–19a.
55. IA 1986, s. 148.
56. *Re Onward Building Society* [1891] 2 QB 463 at 474–475 and 483.
57. *Re Blair Open Hearth Furnace Co. Ltd* [1914] 1 Ch. 390 (CA).
58. *Re James Pitkin & Co. Ltd* [1916] WN 112; cf *Re Derham and Allen Ltd* [1946] Ch. 31.
59. *Re BTR plc* (1988) 4 BCC 45 at 49. See also *Re Willaire Systems plc* (1986) 2 BCC 99,054 and 99,311; *Re Piccadilly Radio plc* [1989] BCLC 683; *Dempsey* v. *Celtic Football and Athletic Co. Ltd* [1993] BCC 514 at 516E–517G; *Re Welsh Highland Railway Light Railway Co.* [1993] BCLC 338 at 351e–352c.

company's articles, there being no evidence that the directors were acting outside their powers or that they were not acting *bona fide* in the best interests of the company.[60]

5.11 The hearing

The hearing of the motion is before the Companies Court Judge sitting in open court. The court has a discretion[61] to refuse the application for rectification and, if rectification is ordered, the court may order the company to pay damages to the applicant.[62] The court may generally decide any question necessary or expedient to be decided for rectification of the register and, in particular, may determine questions of fact or of title arising on the application.[63]

5.12 Order for rectification and costs

Where the court orders rectification of the register of members of a company which is obliged to send a list of its members to the registrar of companies,[64] the court will at the same time direct that notice of the rectification be given to the registrar of companies by the delivery to him of an office copy of the order.[65] In an appropriate case, the order for rectification may be retrospective, taking effect at the date when the directors ought to have registered the transfer[66]: an order for retrospective rectification may be appropriate, for example, where there has been a transfer of partly paid shares which has not been registered, and a subsequent call is made, liability for which, but for an ante-dated rectification, would fall on the transferor rather than the transferee.[67] Where the application for rectification succeeds, the company (if the respondent) will usually be ordered to pay the applicant's costs; where the company is the applicant, a respondent who unsuccessfully opposes rectification will usually be ordered to pay the costs.[68] The directors of the company responsible for a refusal to register a member may be joined as respondents and ordered to pay the successful applicant's costs where they acted beyond their powers, even if their refusal was based on legal advice and thought by them to be in the best interests of the company.[69] An order for costs against the directors personally may be appropriate where it is proved that they have been guilty of wrongdoing or have refused to register a member by reason of an ulterior motive or for their own personal benefit.[70] The rationale for making the directors liable for the costs is that, where it is clearly

60. *Popely* v. *Planarrive Ltd, supra.*
61. S. 359(2).
62. *Ibid.* The court may not award damages on a motion under s. 359(2) if it does not order rectification: *Re Ottos Kopje Diamond Mines Ltd* [1893] 1 Ch. 618 at 624–625; cf. *The Balkis Consolidated Co. Ltd* v. *Tomkinson* [1893] AC 396.
63. S. 359(3).
64. I.e. a company having a share capital: s. 364A(4).
65. S. 359(4).
66. The directors may have up to two months in which to consider a transfer: *Re Zinotty Properties Ltd* [1984] 1 WLR 1249 at 1261B–E; see also Notes 52 and 53, *supra*.
67. *Re Cawley & Co.* (1889) 42 Ch.D. 209; *Re Sussex Brick Co.* [1904] 1 Ch. 598 at 605; *Re Joint Stock Discount Co. (Nation's Case)* (1866) LR 3 Eq 77 at 83. A retrospective order is referred to in the authorities as an order *nunc pro tunc*.
68. *Re Indo-China Steam Navigation Co.* [1917] 2 Ch. 100.
69. See *Morgan* v. *Morgan Insurance Brokers Ltd* [1993] BCLC 676 at 678h–i.
70. See *Re Keith Prowse & Co.* [1912] 1 Ch. 487; *Re Copal Varnish Co.* [1917] 2 Ch. 349; and Note 28, *supra*.

established that the directors acted unreasonably in refusing registration, it is objectionable for the company to pay any costs since part of those costs would effectively fall on the applicant who successfully applies to be added to the register.[71] Although the court has power to make an order for costs against the directors even where they are not joined as respondents,[72] the better practice is to join the directors as respondents if the applicant intends to seek an order for costs against them.

5.13 Method of rectification

Where rectification involves the removal of a name from the register or the substitution of a name, the original entry should not be completely erased. A line should be drawn through the original entry and the new name (if any) added. A copy of any order for rectification signed by the company secretary should be attached to the register (or at the very least an annotation should be made giving details of the order for rectification).[73] The register should not be rectified by a director or secretary without an order from the court.[74] If the company no longer has any officer to effect the rectification of the register, the court may provide in the order for rectification that the rectification be made by the applicant or some other person.[75] The court may, however, in the first instance direct the company to effect the rectification, giving the applicant liberty to apply in the event of default.[76] Where it is clear that an order against the company is certain to be ineffective, an immediate order should be sought under O. 45, r. 8 of the Rules of the Supreme Court giving the applicant liberty to effect the rectification at the cost of the company.

II. APPLICATION TO EXTEND TIME FOR REGISTRATION OF A CHARGE/ TO RECTIFY THE REGISTER OF CHARGES

5.14 The relevant statutory provisions

Part XII of the Companies Act 1985 contains provisions governing the registration of charges created by companies registered in Great Britain[77] and by overseas companies,[78] including provisions enabling an application to be made to the court for an order extending time for registration and rectifying errors in the register of charges.[79] These provisions were prospectively repealed and replaced by a new regime inserted by part IV of the

71. See *Morgan* v. *Morgan Insurance Brokers Ltd*, *supra*, at 678h–i.
72. Supreme Court Act 1981, s. 51(1); *Aiden Shipping Co. Ltd* v. *Interbulk Ltd* [1986] AC 965; *Re Land & Property Trust Co. plc (No. 3)* [1991] BCLC 856 at 862i–863e.
73. *Re Iron Shipbuilding Co.* (1865) 34 Beav. 597; 55 ER 766.
74. *Re Derham and Allen Ltd* [1946] Ch. 31 at 36; but cf *First National Reinsurance Co. Ltd* v. *Greenfield* [1921] 2 KB 260 at 279–280 and the cases there cited.
75. Pursuant to RSC O.45, r. 8.
76. *Re LL Syndicate* (1901) 17 TLR 711; and see *Re Manihot Rubber Plantations Ltd* (1919) 63 SJ 827.
77. Ss. 395–408.
78. Ss. 409 and 424.
79. S. 404.

Companies Act 1989.[80] However, the new provisions have not been and will not be brought into force. On 17 November 1994 the Department of Trade and Industry published a consultation document on the registration of company charges[81] as part of a continuing move towards deregulation of private companies. The consultation document put forward three main options: (i) retention of the present legislation[82]; (ii) retention of the core procedural provisions of the present legislation with certain improvements; or (iii) the introduction of a "notice filing" system (i.e. a system requiring delivery to the registrar of companies of a notice that a charge has been created giving certain particulars, but not requiring delivery of the charging instrument itself). Following a lengthy period of consultation the Department of Trade and Industry announced that the second of the above options for reform was most favoured and that part IV of the Companies Act 1989 would be repealed accordingly.[83] No new amendments to part XII of the Companies Act 1985 have been formulated at the time of writing. The following paragraphs therefore deal only with the existing regime under the Companies Act 1985.

5.15 When is an order of the court required?

The need for an order of the court to extend time for registration of a charge or to rectify the register of charges generally arises in one of three circumstances: (1) where a company creates a registrable charge[84] over some or all of its assets, but fails to deliver the charge and the prescribed particulars of the charge to the registrar of companies for registration within 21 days of its creation[85]; (2) where a company acquires real or personal property which is subject to a charge which, had it been created by the company, would have been registrable[86] but the company acquiring the asset fails to register the charge within 21 days of the completion of the acquisition[87]; or (3) where a mistake is made in the registered particulars of the charge[88] or in a memorandum of satisfaction[89]—for example, a memorandum of satisfaction is filed in error, showing that the debt secured by the charge has been repaid in full when in fact the debt remains outstanding or only part has been repaid; or the memorandum mistakenly refers to the wrong item of property having been released from a charge which included several different assets. Where there is a mistake in the prescribed particulars delivered to the registrar of companies, who nevertheless issues his certificate under s. 401(2), the certificate is conclusive evidence that the requirements of the Act have been complied with. The charge will therefore be valid and there would usually be no need for the chargee to apply to rectify the register.[90]

80. CA 1989, ss. 92–104.
81. "Company Law Reform: Proposals for Reform of Part XII of the CA 1985".
82. I.e. the provisions contained in part XII (ss. 395–408) of the CA 1985.
83. See [1996] 12 Current Law, para. 80.
84. S. 396(1) defines the charges which must be registered. S. 409 extends the registration requirement to overseas companies where the property charged is in England and Wales and the company has a place of business in England and Wales: see *Re Oriel Ltd* (1985) 1 BCC 99,444.
85. As required by s. 395(1).
86. I.e. would have fallen within s. 396(1).
87. As required by s. 400(2).
88. Filed pursuant to ss. 395(1) and 399(1). Minor clerical or typographical errors in the prescribed particulars which are apparent from the charge itself may be corrected by the registrar of companies without any order of the court if the person effecting registration so requests: see (1985) 129 Sol J 623.
89. Filed pursuant to s. 403.
90. *National Provincial and Union Bank of England* v. *Charnley* [1924] 1 KB 431 at 448.

5.16 Jurisdiction

In the above cases, the court has jurisdiction to order that the time for registration of the charge be extended or that an omission or mis-statement in the particulars of the charge or in a memorandum of satisfaction be rectified.[91] The statutory power to extend time or order rectification is discretionary,[92] and the court has no inherent power of rectification.[93] The court may only make an order under s. 404 if it is satisfied that the failure to register the charge within the prescribed time[94] or the omission or mis-statement in the particulars of the charge or in the memorandum of satisfaction, was accidental or due to inadvertence or to some other sufficient cause,[95] or is not of a nature to prejudice the position of creditors or shareholders, or that on other grounds it is just and equitable to grant relief.[96] The "just and equitable" ground confers on the court the widest possible discretion.[97] In deciding whether to grant an extension of time under s. 404, the overriding principle guiding the court is whether, for any reason, it would be just and equitable to grant the extension.[98] The court is concerned to protect persons who have acquired rights in the assets of the company prior to the application to extend time for registration, but is not concerned to protect the rights of unsecured creditors generally.[99] In giving relief, the court may impose such terms and conditions as it thinks just and expedient.[100] The court generally will not grant relief where the company is in liquidation.[101] The court may grant an extension of time for registration where the validity of the charge is in issue, or where there is doubt as to whether it is registrable, and the court will not determine those issues on an application for registration.[102] The court cannot grant interim relief (such as a temporary or interim registration).[103] Under s. 404, the court cannot direct the deletion of the registration of a charge in its entirety,[104] but the court will cancel the entry of a memorandum of satisfaction in its entirety.[105] Where the charge and the prescribed particulars were delivered to the registrar of companies in accordance with s. 395(1), but were rejected because the company had been struck off the register and dissolved under

91. S. 404(2). See *Supreme Court Practice 1997*, Vol 1, paras 102/2/14–102/2/17, pp 1538–1540.
92. *Re Kris Cruisers Ltd* [1949] Ch. 138 at 140.
93. *Exeter Trust Ltd* v. *Screenways Ltd* [1991] BCLC 888 at 895b–d.
94. I.e. within 21 days after the date of creation of the charge: s. 395(1).
95. For example, because incorrect legal advice was obtained that the charge was not registrable: *Re S Abrahams & Sons* [1902] 1 Ch. 695 at 699.
96. S. 404(1).
97. *Re Braemar Investments Ltd* [1989] Ch. 54 at 60H–61B.
98. *Re Fablehill Ltd* [1991] BCLC 830 at 841d–f; *Re Braemar Investments Ltd, supra*, at 61B.
99. *Re Kris Cruisers Ltd* [1949] Ch. 138 at 140–142; *Re MIG Trust Ltd* [1933] Ch. 542 at 570; *Re Ashpurton Estates Ltd* [1983] Ch. 110 at 123B–F; *Re Ehrmann Brothers Ltd* [1906] 2 Ch. 697.
100. S. 404(2). See *Re Chantry House Developments plc* [1990] BCLC 813 at 822h–823i for an example of a case where detailed terms were imposed; and *Re Herts and Essex Waterworks Co. Ltd* [1909] WN 48 (where time was extended subject to the applicant company obtaining the written consent of its principal creditor).
101. See para. 5.24, *infra*.
102. *Re Cunard Steamship Co.* [1908] WN 160; *Re Heathstar Properties Ltd* [1966] 1 WLR 993 at 1000E–1002E.
103. *Re Heathstar Properties Ltd, supra*, at 998D–999B; but see *Re Chantry House Developments plc* [1990] BCLC 813 at 823f–j where relief was granted on terms which required notice to be given to creditors and which could lead to the subsequent setting aside of the order on the application of a creditor.
104. *Re CL Nye Ltd* [1971] Ch. 442 at 474G–H and 477D; *Exeter Trust Ltd* v. *Screenways Ltd* [1991] BCLC 888 at 894j.
105. See s. 404(2) and *Re C Light & Co. Ltd* [1917] WN 77.

s. 652, an application to extend time under s. 404 is not appropriate: an application to restore the company to the register of companies under s. 653[106] should be made and, on restoration, the documents will be deemed to have been duly delivered for registration.[107]

5.17 Form of application

The application is by way of originating summons[108] in the expedited form,[109] returnable before the Companies Court Registrar in chambers[110] (although in exceptional cases of urgency, the use of an originating motion returnable before the Companies Court Judge may be appropriate[111]). The summons should be issued promptly once the failure to register the charge, or the defect in registration, is discovered—a delay in applying may result in the court dismissing the summons in the exercise of its discretion.[112] The summons should state one or more of the grounds for an extension of time or for rectification mentioned in s. 404(1).[113] Where the application is for an extension of time to register a charge, the summons should usually seek an extension of 21 days from the date of the order in which to register the charge and the prescribed particulars; where the application is for rectification of the register or of a memorandum of satisfaction, the summons should state clearly the rectification required. The summons should be issued at the chambers of the registrar of the Companies Court[114] or in any Chancery district registry.[115] Two copies of the summons will be required on issue, one of which should be stamped with the appropriate fee.[116] The court office will insert in the summons a time and date for a hearing before the registrar in chambers, both copies will be sealed, one will be retained by the court for filing and the other will be returned to the applicant.

5.18 The parties

The applicant may be the company[117] or "a person interested"[118]—typically the chargee. Where the company is the applicant, the application may be made *ex parte*. Where the applicant is a person interested, the company should be joined as the respondent.

106. See para. 5.29 *et seq.*
107. *Re Boxco Ltd* [1970] Ch. 442.
108. RSC O. 102, r. 2(1).
109. RSC O. 102, r. 2(2). See Form No. 10 in Appendix A to the RSC: *Supreme Court Practice 1997*, Vol. 2, para. 4, p. 6.
110. I.e. in Room 4.12, fourth floor, Thomas More Building, Royal Courts of Justice.
111. *Re Chantry House Developments plc, supra*, at 817g–818g.
112. *Re Telomatic Ltd* [1994] 1 BCLC 90 at 96h–97b; *Re Ashpurton Estates Ltd* [1983] Ch. 110 at 132A–C; *Re Resinoid & Mica Products Ltd* [1983] Ch. 132 at 134A.
113. See para. 5.16, *supra.*
114. I.e. Room 2.09, second floor, Thomas More Building, Royal Courts of Justice.
115. RSC O. 102, r. 2(4).
116. £120 at the time of writing: see Supreme Court Fees Order 1980 (S.I. 1980 No. 821), r. 3, Sch., s. 1, para. A1(b) (as amended by S.I. 1982 No. 1707, S.I. 1983 No. 1680, S.I. 1986 No. 637, S.I. 1986 No. 2144, S.I. 1988 No. 510, S.I. 1990 No. 1460, S.I. 1993 No. 3191 and S.I. 1995 No. 2629).
117. Whose duty it is to register the charge: s. 399(1).
118. S. 404(2).

5.19 Service

Where the company is joined as the respondent, the originating summons should be served on the company at least four clear days before the date fixed for the hearing[119] by leaving it at or posting it to the company's registered office.[120] It should, in practice, be possible to serve the summons much earlier than four clear days before the date fixed for the hearing. If the summons is served on the company as respondent, it should be accompanied by a form of acknowledgement of service.[121]

5.20 Affidavit in support

The application for extension of time for registration or for rectification of the register of charges must be supported by an affidavit,[122] which should be filed in court not less than four clear days before the day fixed for the hearing where there is a respondent to the summons and not less than one clear day before the day fixed for the hearing where the application is made *ex parte*.[123] The affidavit must establish one (or more) of the grounds for an extension or rectification mentioned in s. 404(1)—i.e. that the failure to register the charge in time, or the omission or mis-statement in the register, was accidental or due to inadvertence or to some other sufficient cause, or is not of a nature to prejudice the position of creditors or shareholders of the company, or that on other grounds it is just and equitable to grant relief.[124]

5.21 The affidavit should give a full history of events in relation to the charge—for example, how and why the charge came to be executed; the transaction in which it was created; details of the underlying loan (if any); what happened to the charge on creation; who (if anyone) was agreed to be responsible for registration; why registration was not effected; the circumstances of the preparation of any memorandum of satisfaction (including the repayment of the loan or the release of property from the charge, if any); who was to be responsible for the preparation and filing of the memorandum; why the memorandum was not filed (when it should have been) or was filed (when it should not have been) or was filed containing errors; and generally how the defaults came to light and what was then done to remedy them, including a full explanation of any delay in applying for rectification. The exhibits should contain copies of any relevant documents, including a copy of the charge,[125] any memorandum of satisfaction, and any relevant documentation or correspondence (for example, correspondence showing that the applicant believed that some other person was responsible for registration).

5.22 Particulars of inadvertence

It is not sufficient for the affidavit merely to state that the failure to register the charge in time, or the error or omission sought to be rectified, occurred through "inadvertence". The

119. RSC O. 28, r. 3(2).
120. S. 725(1). On an application in relation to an overseas company (see s. 409), service should be at the principal place of business of the company.
121. RSC O. 10, rr. 5(1) and 1(6). See Form No. 15 in Appendix A to the RSC: *Supreme Court Practice 1997*, Vol. 2, para. 10, p. 14.
122. RSC O. 28. r. 1A.
123. RSC O. 28, r. 2(2).
124. See *Re Telomatic Ltd* [1994] 1 BCLC 90 at 95c–j, where the court refused to extend time for the registration of a charge because the evidence did not establish one of the grounds in s. 404.
125. The original charge may need to be produced at the hearing: see para. 5.27, *infra*.

court has to be "satisfied" that one or more of the grounds set out in s. 404(1) apply, and that the default was not motivated by any fraudulent purpose. The affidavit should therefore give full particulars of the inadvertence[126]: for example, that the parties were ignorant of the requirement of registration under the Act[127]; or that, owing to pressure of work, the need for registration was overlooked or errors were made in the documents delivered to the registrar of companies or instructions were misunderstood; or it was thought that someone else had registered or would register the charge. The inadvertence relied upon will frequently be that the requirement of registration was simply overlooked. Where the evidence shows that the person responsible for registration mistakenly believed that the charge was not registrable owing to its nature,[128] or received advice to that effect, the failure to register cannot be said to be "accidental" or "due to inadvertence"; but the court will regard the failure as being "due to some other sufficient cause" within s. 404(1) because of the mistake made.[129]

5.23 Affidavit regarding winding-up

Where an application is made to extend time for registration of a charge, or where the application is for a rectification of the register which could prejudice creditors (for example, the applicant wishes to amend the particulars of the charge to show that the charge secures a larger debt of the company or to delete a memorandum of satisfaction), an affidavit is required confirming (*inter alia*) that winding-up proceedings are not pending against the company. Such an affidavit is not required where the application is to extend time for registration following the acquisition by a company of property subject to a charge registrable under s. 400, nor where the application is for rectification of a sort which could not prejudice creditors (for example, to reduce the amount of the secured debt as stated in the particulars). The affidavit must be sworn by an officer (i.e. a director or the secretary) of the company: indirect evidence sworn by the chargee who is not an officer of the company is not adequate.[130]

5.23.1 Although the affidavit is commonly described as an "affidavit of solvency", it does not usually describe the company's financial position in any great detail (for example, it will not usually explain whether the company's assets exceed its liabilities or whether it is trading profitably). The affidavit will usually state[131]: (1) the office which the deponent holds in the company and the period during which he has held that office; (2) that no winding-up order has been made against the company, no winding-up petition is pending against the company, no resolution for a voluntary winding-up has been passed, no notice of a resolution for voluntary liquidation has been given, and none is contemplated; (3) where appropriate, that the company continues to carry on business, that no

126. Practice Note [1948] WN 179; *Re Kris Cruisers Ltd* [1949] Ch. 138 at 140 and 142; *Re Telomatic Ltd, supra.*

127. *Re Jackson & Co. Ltd* [1899] 1 Ch. 348 at 351.

128. I.e. did not fall within s. 396(1).

129. *Re S Abrahams & Sons* [1902] 1 Ch. 695 at 699; cf *Re E&F Beattie Ltd* [1901] WN 152.

130. The Civil Evidence Act 1995, which came into force (save for ss. 10 and 16(5)) on 31 January 1997 (see Civil Evidence Act 1995 (Commencement No. 1 Order) S.I. 1996 No. 3217), abolished the rule against the admission of hearsay in civil proceedings. It may now, therefore, be possible for hearsay evidence as to the company's solvency to be given (for example by the solicitor for the company), but the affidavit should still be based on information provided by an officer of the company.

131. See *Re Bootle Cold Storage Co.* [1901] WN 54.

creditor has entered judgment against the company which remains unsatisfied or is in a position to enter judgment; and (4) that no other charges over the property in question have been created by the company subsequent to the charge which is the subject of the application. If subsequent charges have been created, particulars should be given.[132] It may also be convenient to record in the affidavit the consent of the company to the application for rectification. If the application is made by the chargee, and the company and its officers will not co-operate in swearing the affidavit, the chargee will not be able to obtain an unqualified order for rectification or for extending time for registration.[133]

5.24 Company in liquidation or insolvent

Once the company is in liquidation (i.e. the liquidation has commenced because a resolution has been passed or a compulsory winding-up order has been made on a winding-up petition), unless there are very exceptional circumstances, the court will not, in the exercise of its discretion, extend time for registration of a charge or remove a memorandum of satisfaction from the company's file maintained by the registrar of companies.[134] Since the commencement of a compulsory liquidation dates back to the date of presentation of the winding-up petition,[135] the court will also refuse to extend time for registration of a charge whilst a winding-up petition is pending in respect of the company: if the petition is undisputed and will result in a winding-up order, the court will dismiss the application under s. 404; if the petition is disputed, the court may either dismiss the application under s. 404, leaving the applicant to apply again if the petition is dismissed, or it may adjourn the application for rectification pending the outcome of the petition. It would be possible in such a case for the court to make an order for rectification under s. 404, subject to a *Re Charles* proviso (described below), although this is unlikely. Where the company is in administration and an insolvent liquidation will inevitably follow, the court will also refuse to grant an order extending time for registration.[136] The court may make an order for the rectification of a memorandum of satisfaction notwithstanding the fact that the company is in liquidation, but the court will only do so in highly exceptional circumstances[137] where the rectification does not prejudice creditors of the company. Where the company is not in liquidation but a liquidation is imminent, it is now settled[138] that this is a factor which the court takes into account in the exercise of its discretion in deciding whether to extend time for registration[139]: the imminence of liquidation will often lead the court to refuse to extend time for registration, but it is not an absolute bar to such an order.[140] If time is extended notwithstanding the imminence of

132. As to the effect of subsequent charges, see para. 5.26, *infra*.

133. See para. 5.25, *infra*.

134. *Re Resinoid and Mica Products Ltd* [1983] Ch. 132 at 133G–H; *Re Ashpurton Estates Ltd* [1983] 110 at 123F–124B and 129H; *Re John Bateson & Co. Ltd* [1985] BCLC 259 at 260h–j; *Re RM Arnold & Co. Ltd* [1984] BCLC 535 at 537a–c; *Re S Abrahams & Sons* [1902] 1 Ch. 695; *Re Eric Holmes (Property) Ltd* [1965] Ch. 1052 at 1072B–D; and *Re Mechanisations (Eaglescliffe) Ltd* [1966] Ch. 20 at 36G–37A.

135. IA 1986, s. 129.

136. *Re Barrow Borough Transport Ltd* [1990] Ch. 227 at 232G–H.

137. See, by way of analogy, the cases cited in Note 134, *supra*.

138. Despite suggestions to the contrary in *Re Kris Cruisers Ltd* [1949] Ch. 138 and *Re MIG Trust Ltd* [1933] Ch. 542.

139. *Re Ashpurton Estates Ltd* [1983] Ch. 110 at 131G–H.

140. See *Re Braemar Investments Ltd, supra*, at 62A–F; *Re LH Charles & Co. Ltd* [1935] WN 15 (where time was extended despite an imminent liquidation); and *Re Kris Cruisers Ltd, supra* (where time was extended despite indications that the company was insolvent).

liquidation, the order should usually include a *Re Charles* proviso,[141] discussed in para. 5.25, *infra*.

5.25 Re Charles order

In certain circumstances, the court, when ordering an extension of time for registration or rectification of the register, inserts a proviso in its order designed to enable any liquidator appointed to the company or any creditor, to apply within a reasonable time of the order to challenge the order for an extension or rectification. The proviso is usually inserted where the court, in its discretion, makes an order under s. 404 despite the fact that a liquidation may be imminent,[142] or where the applicant is the chargee and he cannot procure evidence from an officer of the company that a liquidation is *not* imminent. The proviso usually inserted in such a case is known as a "*Re Charles* order"[143]—i.e. an order extending time for registration or an order for rectification, subject to the proviso that the company, acting by any liquidator or administrator of it, or any unsecured creditor of the company,[144] has liberty to apply to discharge the order within a certain period: for example, within 56 days after: (a) the commencement of a voluntary winding-up of the company becoming effective on or before a date, say, 28 days from the date of the order for rectification under s. 404; or (b) an order for the winding-up of the company, or an administration order in relation to the company, made on a petition presented on or before a date, say, 28 days from the date of the order for rectification under s. 404.[145] Where the proviso is included in the order, the registrar of companies will delay the issue of his certificate of registration under s. 401(2) until the time for challenge has expired because, once the certificate has been issued, it is conclusive as to the validity of the registration and no subsequent challenge to the order under s. 404 is possible.[146] The rationale for the *Re Charles* proviso is that once the company has gone into liquidation, existing unsecured creditors are interested in all the assets of the company, since the liquidator is bound to distribute net proceeds (after payment of preferential debts) *pari passu* amongst unsecured creditors; consequently, the assets of the company are then vested in the company for the benefit of its creditors generally.[147] An order under s. 404, on the eve of liquidation or administration, derogates from the principle of *pari passu* distribution, because it allows the chargee to have first recourse against the assets comprised in the unregistered security which would otherwise be available for all unsecured creditors on a *pari passu* basis (subject to preferential debts). The *Re Charles* proviso enables the court, on the application of a liquidator, administrator or unsecured creditor, to set aside the order under s. 404, thereby re-establishing the principle of *pari passu* distribution, but only within a limited

141. See *Exeter Trust Ltd* v. *Screenways Ltd* [1991] BCLC 888 at 895j–896c.

142. But see *Re RM Arnold & Co. Ltd, supra*, where special factors justified an order under s. 404 without a *Re Charles* proviso despite the imminence of liquidation.

143. So-called because the proviso derives from the order made in *Re LH Charles & Co. Ltd* [1935] WN 15.

144. See the comments of Harman J. in *Re RM Arnold & Co. Ltd, supra*, at 541j–542b as to those persons who should be protected by the *Re Charles* proviso.

145. This was the form of the registrar's order in *Re Braemar Investments Ltd*: see [1989] Ch. 54 at 57E–F.

146. See *Exeter Trust Ltd* v. *Screenways Ltd, supra*, at 896b–d.

147. See *Re Ashpurton Estates Ltd* [1983] Ch. 110 at 123D–G.

period, giving certainty of the charge-holder's rights thereafter. If a liquidator, administrator or creditor does challenge the order for rectification, such challenge is not bound to succeed.[148]

5.26 Subsequent charges

Where a charge is not registered within 21 days, and therefore becomes void as against any liquidator or creditor of the company,[149] a duly registered subsequent charge over the same property created after the earlier charge has become void (i.e. after the expiry of the 21 days[150]) has priority to the earlier unregistered charge. This is the case, even where the subsequent chargee took his charge with notice of the earlier charge.[151] Where the court grants an extension of time for registration under s. 404, the order will normally expressly provide that it is without prejudice to the rights of any person acquired between the date of creation of the charge[152] and the date of its actual registration.[153] However, where it would plainly be inequitable to allow the subsequent chargee to have priority (for example, where the subsequent charge is made in favour of the company's directors who have taken advantage of the company's failure to register the earlier charge by procuring a charge in their favour), the order extending time for registration of the earlier charge may not include such a proviso, so as not to make the earlier charge subject to the later charge.[154] The earlier charge when registered would then have priority.

5.27 The hearing

The summons will be heard by the Companies Court Registrar sitting in chambers, unless the matter is disputed, in which case the registrar may adjourn the summons into court for determination by the Companies Court Judge. Where the application is for an extension of time to register a charge, or for rectification of the particulars of the charge, (but not where the application is for an extension of time in relation to property acquired subject to a charge or for rectification in relation to a memorandum of satisfaction), the original charge must be produced in court: if the original charge is not produced, the registrar will adjourn the hearing to enable the original to be produced.

5.28 The order

Where the court extends time for registration of a charge,[155] the extension will usually be for 21 days from the date of the order, in which period the applicant must deliver the

148. See *Re Braemar Investments Ltd*, *supra*, where the liquidator's subsequent challenge was dismissed: Hoffmann J. held that the chargee bank acted reasonably in delegating registration to its solicitor, that it acted as speedily as possible on discovery of the fact of non-registration, and that it was therefore just and equitable to grant relief under s. 404 (see p. 61A–D); the fact that liquidation was imminent was a factor to be taken into account in the exercise of discretion but was not an absolute bar to an extension of time (at 62A–F).

149. S. 395(1).

150. See *Watson* v. *Duff, Morgan & Vermont (Holdings) Ltd* [1974] 1 WLR 450.

151. *Re Monolithic Building Co.* [1915] 1 Ch. 643 at 662–663.

152. I.e. the date of its execution, not necessarily the date which it bears: *Esberger & Son Ltd* v. *Capital and Counties Bank* [1913] 2 Ch. 366 at 372.

153. *Re Joplin Brewery Co. Ltd* [1902] 1 Ch. 79. For the effect of such a provision, contrast *Re Monolithic Building Co.*, *supra*, and *Watson* v. *Duff, Morgan & Vermont (Holdings) Ltd*, *supra*, at 454C–455E.

154. *Re Fablehill Ltd* [1991] BCLC 830 at 841e–f.

155. Whether registrable under s. 395(1) or s. 400.

charge and the prescribed particulars thereof to the registrar of companies. If the applicant fails to register the charge in that period, he will have to apply again to the court for a further extension of time, explaining the reason for the further default. Where the application is for rectification of the particulars of the charge, or of the memorandum of satisfaction, no time limit will ordinarily be imposed, but the rectification will not be effective until an office copy of the order under s. 404, is delivered to the registrar of companies. The order may also impose terms for the protection of creditors of the chargor and will usually include protection for those who have acquired rights in relation to the charged property whilst the charge was invalid against them.[156] In all cases, the court will order the applicant to deliver an office copy of the order to the registrar of companies. Once the registrar of companies has issued his certificate of registration under s. 401(2), no challenge to the order under s. 404 is possible.[157]

III. RESTORATION TO THE REGISTER

5.29 Introduction

This sub-chapter deals with the procedure for restoring the name of a company to the register of companies[158] where it has been struck off the register and dissolved under s. 652 of the Companies Act 1985.[159] It does not deal with applications for restoration to the register coupled with an application for the winding-up of the company, which must be made by petition[160] and are discussed in Chapter 9, *infra*.

5.30 Sections 651 and 653

Where a company has been struck off the register and dissolved, the court will often have jurisdiction either to declare the dissolution of the company void under s. 651(1)[161] or to restore the name of the company to the register of companies under s. 653(2). A member or creditor (who was a member or creditor at the date of dissolution) will often have *locus standi* under both sections and may choose between them.[162] In most cases, an application for restoration to the register under s. 653 offers advantages and an applicant is likely to apply for an order under that section:

(1) section 653 provides for a limitation period of 20 years from the date of dissolution,[163] whereas the limitation period under s. 651 is usually only two

156. S. 404(2); see paras 5.25 and 5.26, *supra*; and see *Re Chantry House Developments plc* [1990] BCLC 813 where detailed terms were imposed for the protection of creditors); *Re Herts and Essex Waterworks Co. Ltd* [1909] WN 48 (where time was extended subject to the applicant company obtaining the written consent of its principal creditor); and *Re IC Johnson & Co. Ltd* [1902] 2 Ch. 101 at 109–111.

157. *Exeter Trust Ltd* v. *Screenways Ltd*, *supra*, at 896b–d.

158. Maintained by the registrar of companies under CA 1985, s. 714.

159. All references hereafter are to the CA 1985 unless otherwise stated.

160. RSC O. 102, r. 4(1)(g).

161. This procedure is dealt with in para. 5.51 *et seq.*, of this Chapter.

162. *Re Test Holdings (Clifton) Ltd* [1970] Ch. 285 at 287G–H, 288B–C, 291H–292A; *Re M Belmont & Co. Ltd* [1952] Ch. 10 at 15.

163. S. 653(2).

years from the date of dissolution[164] (unless the purpose of the application is to bring an action for personal injuries or in respect of a fatal accident[165]).

(2) Following restoration to the register under s. 653, the company is deemed always to have continued in existence as if its name had not been struck off[166] and anything done whilst the company was dissolved is valid and effective, but there is no such deeming provision under s. 651.[167] Although a practice recently developed (without any opposition from the registrar of companies or the Treasury Solicitor) whereby applicants for an order declaring a dissolution void under s. 651 have sought orders on terms that the company should be deemed to have continued in existence as if its name had not been struck off,[168] the practice should not be followed: it appears to be contrary to the speeches of the House of Lords in *Morris* v. *Harris*[169] and disregards the exclusion from s. 651(1) of any express deeming provision as set out in s. 653(3).

(3) Under s. 653, the court has an unfettered power to direct that the period between the company's dissolution and its restoration should not count for the purpose of any limitation period,[170] whereas under s. 651 the power[171] may be more limited, arising only where the application is made under s. 651(5), with a view to bringing proceedings for personal injuries or a fatal accident.[172]

5.30.1 It has been suggested that the procedure under s. 651(1) will be preferred to that under s. 653(2) because its conditions are less stringent.[173] It is submitted that, where a company has been dissolved as a result of being struck off under s. 652, the requirements for revival are no less onerous under s. 651 than they are under s. 653, and an application under s. 653 is to be preferred:

(1) the application under s. 653 has the advantages identified above;

(2) although s. 653(2) lays down criteria which have to be satisfied before the court will order restoration, whereas s. 651(1) stipulates no criteria for applying to have a dissolution declared void, the generality of the criteria in s. 653(2)[174] enables the jurisdiction to be invoked in a wide variety of circumstances. The difference in the wording of the sections is not a compelling reason to apply under s. 651 rather than s. 653;

(3) where the dissolution results from a striking-off for failing to file returns, the court is likely to require the filing of all outstanding returns[175] and protection for

164. S. 651(4). See para. 5.52, *infra*.
165. See s. 651(5).
166. S. 653(3).
167. Contrast s. 653(3) with s. 651(2); and see *Morris* v. *Harris* [1927] AC 252 and *Re Philip Powis Ltd*, New Law Digest, 28 April 1997.
168. See *Re Workvale Ltd* [1991] 1 WLR 294 at 302E.
169. *Re Mixhurst Ltd* [1994] 2 BCLC 19 at 24g–28h per Evans-Lombe J. and see *Re Philip Powis Ltd, supra*; but contrast *Re Townreach Ltd* [1995] Ch. 28 at 38F–45B which appears to support the practice.
170. See s. 653(3) and para. 5.49, *infra*.
171. See s. 651(6) and para. 5.63, *infra*.
172. *Re Mixhurst Ltd* [1994] 2 BCLC 19 at 28g–29b; contrast *Townreach Ltd* [1995] Ch. 28 at 44H–45A (which suggests that the power under s. 651 is as wide as the power under s. 653).
173. See, for example, *Palmer's Company Law* (25th Edn) para. 15.487, p. 15237; but contrast *Re Test Holdings (Clifton) Ltd, supra* at 292F–G.
174. I.e. restoration if it is "just that the company be restored to the register".
175. See paras 5.47 (s. 653) and 5.60 (s. 651), *infra*.

those who subsequently deal with the company where it appears to be insolvent,[176] before making an order, whether the application is made under s. 651 or 653.

5.31 Jurisdiction to strike companies off the register

Where the registrar of companies has reason to believe that a company is not carrying on business or in operation, he may write to the company to enquire whether it is carrying on business or remains in operation.[177] In practice, he will do so where a company fails to file accounts or annual returns. If the registrar of companies does not receive a response from the company within one month, he must send a second letter to the company within the next 14 days (this time by registered post) referring to the first letter and the lack of any response thereto, and giving the company notice of his intention to strike the name of the company off the register if no response is received to the second letter within one month of its date.[178] If the registrar is informed that the company is not carrying on business or in operation, or receives no response to his second letter within one month after it was sent, he may publish a notice in the *Gazette* and send a copy of the notice to the company: the notice will state that unless cause is shown to the contrary, after three months from the date of the notice the name of the company will be struck off the register and the company will be dissolved.[179] At the expiration of the three month period, unless cause to the contrary has been shown by the company, the name of the company may be struck off the register of companies; the registrar must then publish notice of the striking-off in the *Gazette*, at which point the company is dissolved.[180] Any liability of the members, directors or managing officers of the company survives dissolution,[181] and the company may still be wound up by the court.[182]

5.32 The registrar of companies is entitled to assume that a company is not carrying on business or in operation where it has failed to file accounts or returns at Companies House. It will usually be no bar to striking the name of the company off the register that the company is in fact carrying on business, if it is in default of its filing obligations. If the company responds to the letters or notice sent to it under s. 652(1)–(3) stating that it is carrying on business, the registrar of companies will require the company to file its outstanding accounts or returns.

5.33 Voluntary striking-off

The Deregulation and Contracting Out Act 1994 which came into force on 1 July 1995[183] introduced a new statutory procedure for striking the name of a non-trading private company off the register at the request of its directors[184]: although the registrar of

176. See paras 5.44 (s. 653) and 5.61 (s. 651), *infra*.
177. S. 652(1).
178. S. 652(2).
179. S. 652(3).
180. S. 652(5).
181. S. 652(6)(a).
182. S. 652(6)(b).
183. By virtue of the Deregulation and Contracting Out Act 1994 (Commencement No. 3) Order 1995 (S.I. 1995 No. 1433).
184. See the CA 1985, ss. 652A–652F, introduced by s. 13 of and Sch. 5 to the 1994 Act. All references in this section hereafter are to the CA 1985 as amended by the 1994 Act unless otherwise stated.

companies has, in the past, been prepared to strike the name of a company off the register following an informal request from the directors, the new statutory scheme contains restrictions and safeguards against abuse by the directors.[185] It is unlikely that the registrar of companies will in future strike off a company following an informal request from its directors but will require the directors to use the new statutory procedure.

5.34 Jurisdiction to restore companies to the register

The court may make an order to restore to the register of companies the name of a company which has been struck off the register, if the court is satisfied that the company was, at the time of the striking-off, carrying on business or in operation, or otherwise that it is just that the company be restored to the register.[186] Whilst the application is not a formality nor is success a foregone conclusion; the court's practice is to make an order for restoration if a real advantage would accrue to the contributories or creditors of the company from its revival, provided that all filing defaults are remedied, the costs of the registrar of companies are provided for, and the Treasury Solicitor expresses no objection on behalf of the Crown in respect of *bona vacantia*.[187] Where the striking-off was at the request of the directors under the new statutory regime,[188] the court has jurisdiction to order restoration if it is satisfied that any duty imposed by s. 652B or 652C was not performed,[189] or that the making of the application for striking-off involved a breach of duty under s. 652B(1) or (3),[190] or that it is otherwise just to order restoration.[191] In all cases, the application for restoration must be made within 20 years of the publication of the notice in the *Gazette* for striking the name of the company off the register[192]; but provided that the application for restoration is issued within the 20-year period, the court may make an order on such an application, notwithstanding that the 20-year period has expired by the date of the hearing.[193] A person seeking restoration of the name of the company to the register of companies should issue a summons as soon as possible after becoming aware of the striking-off and dissolution.[194] If the need for restoration arises because the company is a party to ongoing litigation, that litigation should be stayed pending an application for restoration under s. 653.[195] It is no bar to restoration that an order for restoration might expose a third party to a substantial liability.[196]

185. See, in particular, ss. 652A(3) and 652B–F.

186. S. 653(2). See *Supreme Court Practice 1997*, Vol. 1, paras 102/2/29–102/2/31, pp. 1543–1544. For a case where the company was not carrying on business or in operation, but the court was satisfied that it was just to order restoration; see *Re Priceland Ltd* [1997] BCC 207 (restoration ordered, despite the fact it would expose a third party to a significant liability).

187. *Steans Fashions Ltd* v. *Legal and General Assurance Society Ltd* [1995] 1 BCLC 332 at 335i–336b per Nourse L.J.; and see *Re Priceland Ltd, supra*.

188. I.e. ss. 652A–652F.

189. E.g. the obligation to notify members, employees, and creditors of the company, and other prescribed persons, of the making of the application: see s. 652(B)(6).

190. I.e. the application was made at a time when the company's circumstances prohibited an application, because, for example, the company had carried on business within the last three months: s. 652B(1)(b).

191. S. 653(2B).

192. S. 653(2), (2B) and (2D).

193. See *Re Scad Ltd* [1941] Ch. 386.

194. *Re Thompson & Riches Ltd* [1981] 1 WLR 682 at 689C–E.

195. *Steans Fashions Ltd* v. *Legal and General Assurance Society Ltd, supra*, at 336d.

196. *Re Priceland Ltd, supra*, at 214D–F and 215A–B.

5.35 Form of application

The application is made by originating summons[197] in the expedited form,[198] supported by affidavit returnable before the Companies Court Registrar in chambers.[199] The summons should be issued at the chambers of the Companies Court Registrar[200] or any Chancery district registry.[201] Two copies of the summons will be required on issue, one of which should be stamped with the appropriate fee. The court office will insert in the margin of the summons a time and date for the hearing before the registrar in chambers, both copies will be sealed and numbered, the stamped copy will be retained by the court for filing, and the other will be returned to the applicant. The hearing date will normally be fixed for several weeks after the date of issue (say six weeks later), to enable all outstanding returns to be filed with the registrar of companies in the period between the issue of the summons and the hearing. If the need for restoration is particularly urgent (for example, the company to be restored is to be party to a contract of which completion is imminent), an *ex parte* application may be made to the registrar for a speedier hearing: if satisfied of the urgency of the application the court may abridge the time between the issue and the hearing of the summons, but the filing of all outstanding returns is still likely to be required before the registrar of companies will consent to an order for restoration.[202]

5.36 Parties: the applicant

Where the company has been struck off the register under s. 652, the application for restoration to the register may be made by the company itself (although for all other purposes the company is then non-existent[203]), or by any member or creditor of the company who feels aggrieved by the company having been struck off the register.[204] For a member to be "aggrieved" by the striking-off he will usually have to show that the company is solvent and therefore that he has an interest in its assets[205]; a creditor will usually be aggrieved by the striking-off irrespective of the company's solvency, because the fact of striking-off in effect precludes him from taking any steps to recover his debt. "Member" includes the personal representatives of a deceased member, even if not entered on the register of members.[206] The section is directed at those who would be legally prejudiced by the striking-off of the company and, accordingly, "creditor" should be construed widely. The status of "creditor" in this context does not require a vested cause of action as at the date of striking-off and, thus, includes a contingent or prospective creditor.[207] The company should not be the sole applicant: a member or creditor (whether

197. RSC O. 102, r. 2(1).
198. See Form No. 10 in Appendix A to the RSC: *Supreme Court Practice 1997*, Vol. 2, para. 4, p. 6.
199. I.e. in Room 4.12, fourth floor, Thomas More Building, Royal Courts of Justice.
200. Room 2.09, second floor, Thomas More Building, Royal Courts of Justice.
201. RSC O. 102, r. 2(4).
202. See para. 5.47, *infra*.
203. On restoration, the company is deemed to always have continued in existence as if its name had never been struck off: s. 653(3).
204. S. 653(1)(2). For the meaning of "aggrieved", see para. 5.5, Note 23, *supra*.
205. *Re Lindsay Bowman Ltd* [1969] 1 WLR 1443 at 1448B–C.
206. *Re Bayswater Trading Co. Ltd* [1970] 1 WLR 343 at 345F–346A; and see *Roberts* v. *Letter "T" Estates* [1961] AC 795. A person who acquires shares in the company after dissolution can only apply under s. 651 as a "person . . . interested".
207. *Re Harvest Lane Motor Bodies Ltd* [1969] 1 Ch. 457 at 462C–G; *City of Westminster Assurance Co. Ltd* v. *Registrar of Companies*, 28 June 1996, Millett, Phillips and Ward L.L.J. (CA) unreported.

a present, contingent or prospective creditor) who was a member or such a creditor at the date of striking-off,[208] should be joined as co-applicant so as to be able to give any necessary undertakings[209] and to be responsible for the costs of the registrar of companies. If the application were to fail, the company would not exist, its former assets would remain vested in the Crown as *bona vacantia*,[210] and the other applicant would be ordered to pay the costs of the application. If a member (but not the company) is named as the applicant, the court may order the summons to be amended to include the company as co-applicant.[211] In the vast majority of cases, the joint applicants will be the company and a person who was a member at the date of striking-off: a creditor wishing to revive a dissolved company will usually petition for an order firstly for the restoration and then for the compulsory winding-up of the company.[212] A person who is neither a member nor creditor of a dissolved company but who claims to have an interest in its revival has no standing to apply for restoration under s. 653: unless he can persuade someone with standing (i.e. a member or creditor of the company who feels aggrieved at the striking-off) to apply, in which case the third party may be joined as a respondent,[213] the third party can only apply under s. 651(1) for an order declaring the dissolution void.

5.37 Applicant after voluntary striking-off

Where a private company has been struck off, at its own request, under the new statutory procedure for voluntary striking off,[214] an application for restoration may be made by a "notifiable person"—i.e. a person to whom notice of the application for striking-off should have been given under s. 652B or 652C[215]: such persons include the company's members, its employees, creditors, directors (if they were not party to the application for striking-off), and managers or trustees of any employee pension fund.[216] A member who has consented to the voluntary striking-off should nevertheless be able to seek restoration under s. 653(2) where there has been a change of circumstances or for other good reasons he does not wish the company to remain dissolved. In that event, the affidavit sworn in support of the application should explain the change of circumstances or explain why the applicant agreed to the voluntary striking-off but now seeks to reverse that decision. Provision is also made for the Secretary of State to apply for the restoration of a company which has been voluntarily struck off, if he is satisfied that it is in the public interest to do so.[217]

208. *Re New Timbiqui Gold Mines Ltd* [1961] Ch. 319 (an application by a person claiming to be a member); *Re Aga Estate Agencies Ltd* [1986] BCLC 346 (an application by a person claiming to be a creditor).

209. See para. 5.44, *infra*.

210. S. 654(1). See para. 5.45, *infra*.

211. *Re Walter Wright Ltd* [1923] WN 128 (although joinder of the company was ordered in that case for the company to give undertakings to file outstanding returns, a practice which is no longer acceptable to the registrar of companies: see para. 5.47, *infra*).

212. I.e. under RSC O. 102, r. 4(1)(g); see *Re Cambridge Coffee Room Association Ltd* [1951] WN 621 at 623 and *Supreme Court Practice 1997*, Vol. 1, paras 102/4/33–102/4/35, p. 1652.

213. See para. 5.39, *infra*.

214. S. 652A–F.

215. S. 653(2B) and (2C).

216. S. 652B(6). As to the grounds on which such persons can challenge a voluntary striking-off, see para. 5.34, *supra*.

217. S. 653(2D).

5.38 Respondent

The registrar of companies should be named as respondent.[218] Where the company is not the applicant (for example, where the application is made by a creditor), the company should not be named as a respondent because it does not exist: s. 653(2) gives the company an existence only for the purposes of being an applicant for restoration, not a respondent.[219] Consequently, the company cannot be heard on an application under s. 653 unless it is an applicant, and cannot oppose an application for restoration. A fully paid-up member cannot oppose the application.[220] If the Crown (as the person entitled to the dissolved company's assets as "*bona vacantia*" under s. 654[221]) does not consent to the application, it will be necessary to join the Attorney-General as a respondent to represent the Crown,[222] but in practice the Crown will seldom refuse to consent to an application under s. 651 or 653.

5.39 Joinder of third parties

An interested third party who is not a creditor or member of the company but whose rights might be directly affected by an order for restoration may not be joined as an applicant,[223] but he may be joined as a respondent.[224] If such a third party is not named as a respondent when the summons is issued, he may subsequently be joined as a respondent on his own application[225] or on the application of the person seeking restoration. An application for joinder should be made to the Companies Court Registrar in chambers, by summons supported by an affidavit[226] setting out the grounds on which joinder is sought. For joinder, it is essential to show that an order for restoration would directly affect the rights of the third party; he should not be joined as a respondent if he merely wishes to argue that the applicant has no claim against the company or that the proceedings which the revived company might bring against the third party would be bound to fail.[227]

5.40 Service

The Rules of the Supreme Court provide that the summons and affidavit in support (which may be sworn shortly before the issue of the summons[228]) should be served on the registrar of companies at least four clear days before the date fixed for the hearing,[229] by posting it to him at Companies House, Crown Way, Maindy, Cardiff. The summons and affidavit in support should be served as soon as possible after issue to give sufficient time

218. *Re Test Holdings (Clifton) Ltd* [1970] Ch. 285 at 287G–H.
219. *Re Workvale Ltd* [1991] 1 WLR 294 at 299B–C; *Re H Clarkson (Overseas) Ltd* [1987] 3 BCC 606 at 607.
220. *Re Clarkson (Overseas) Ltd, supra.*
221. See para. 5.45, *infra.*
222. *Re Belmont & Co.* [1952] 1 Ch. 10 at 15.
223. S. 653(2).
224. *Re Workvale Ltd* [1991] BCLC 528; *Re Forte's (Manufacturing) Ltd* [1994] BCC 84 at 90C–F.
225. I.e. under RSC O. 15, r. 6; see *Re Forte's (Manufacturing) Ltd, supra*, at 86E–F.
226. RSC O. 15, r. 6(3); and see *Supreme Court Practice 1997*, Vol. 1, para. 15/6/14, p. 213.
227. *Re Forte's (Manufacturing) Ltd, supra*, at 90C–F; *Re Jayham Ltd* [1995] 2 BCLC 455. To the extent that *Re Portrafram Ltd* [1986] BCLC 533 suggests that there is no jurisdiction to order joinder, it should be taken to have been overruled.
228. *Chancery Practice Direction No. (8)A(iii): Supreme Court Practice 1997*, Vol. 2, para. 820, p. 175.
229. RSC O. 102, r. 2(2) and O. 28, r. 3(2).

for the registrar of companies to identify any outstanding returns which need to be filed and for the applicants to prepare those documents. If service is delayed until the last moment allowed under the Rules, an adjournment may be necessary and the applicant may be penalised in costs. The summons should be accompanied by a form of acknowledgement of service.[230] Where the company is not one of the applicants, it has no existence and therefore the summons and affidavit cannot be served on it.[231] Copies of the summons and affidavit in support should also be sent by post to the Treasury Solicitor[232] at Queen Anne's Chambers, 28 Broadway, London SW1H 9JS, who conducts the restoration proceedings on behalf of the registrar of companies. Once the summons has been served on him, the registrar of companies will accept any outstanding documents for filing (including any documents which were received and rejected after the striking-off but before the summons was served), and all such documents should promptly be sent to him. All other correspondence and communication regarding the application should be with the Treasury Solicitor. An affidavit will be required proving service of the summons and supporting evidence on the registrar of companies and the posting of copies to the Treasury Solicitor.[233]

5.41 Affidavit in support

An affidavit in support of the summons is required, which should be filed at the chambers of the Companies Court Registrar, served on the registrar of companies, and sent to the Treasury Solicitor, at the same time as or very shortly after service of the summons. The affidavit may be sworn prior to the issue of the summons.[234] Where the application is made by a member, the affidavit should state the following:

(i) the capacity of the deponent and his status in relation to the company at the time of its striking-off (i.e. that he was then a member of the company);
(ii) details of the company's incorporation (exhibiting the certificate of incorporation and a print of its memorandum and articles of association);
(iii) the company's registered office address, and its principal objects;
(iv) details of the company's authorised and issued capital (including the number of shares and their denomination, the number of shares which have been issued, whether they are credited as fully paid-up or are partly paid, the number of shares held by the deponent and the holder(s) of the remainder (if any);
(v) when the company commenced business and whether it has continued to carry on business ever since (if the company has not carried on or now does not carry on business, an explanation should be given of the reason why restoration is sought);
(vi) details of any failures to file accounts or returns with the registrar of companies which led to the striking-off and an explanation as to why those defaults occurred;

230. RSC O. 10, rr. 5(1) and 1(6). For the form of acknowledgement of service, see Form No. 15 in Appendix A to the RSC: *Supreme Court Practice 1997*, Vol. 2, para. 10, p. 14.
231. See para. 5.38, *supra*.
232. Practice Note [1928] WN 218.
233. Practice Note [1931] WN 199; and see para. 5.46, *infra*.
234. Chancery Practice Direction No. (8)A(iii): *Supreme Court Practice 1997*, Vol. 2, para. 820, p. 175.

(vii) details of the various letters and notices sent by the registrar of companies to the company, pursuant to ss. 651(1)–(3) prior to striking-off, and an explanation why those letters and notice were not received (for example, because the company moved offices without giving notice to the registrar of companies) or were not responded to, or why the response did not reach the registrar of companies[235]; and

(viii) in the majority of cases, evidence of the solvency of the company must be given.[236]

Where the application is made by a creditor, the affidavit should contain as much of the above information as is known to the creditor and should explain why the creditor is seeking restoration. Where undertakings are required and their terms are obvious,[237] the evidence may set out the undertakings offered and the identity of the person who will give them, although this will often not be possible because the form of undertaking remains to be agreed with the Treasury Solicitor.

5.42 Evidence of solvency

It will generally be necessary for the affidavit in support of the application for restoration to describe the company's financial position and show that it is solvent: the most recent audited accounts of the company should be exhibited together with any more recent management accounts. Where the application for restoration is made by a member of the company, evidence of solvency is essential to the applicant's standing—unless the company is solvent, a member is unlikely to be "aggrieved" by the striking-off as required by s. 653(1). In exceptional cases, the court may be prepared to order restoration in the absence of evidence of solvency, or where the evidence suggests insolvency—for example, where restoration is sought by a company which has disposed of real property after the date of striking-off and needs to execute the formal documentation for the disposition to the purchaser. However, in such cases the court may require the applicants to give certain undertakings for the protection of third parties owing to the company's insolvency.[238]

5.43 Insolvent company

The court is reluctant to order the restoration to the register of a company which is or appears to be insolvent, because this would enable the company to continuing trading with limited liability, at a potential risk to creditors. Where a creditor seeks restoration of a company which is or appears to be insolvent, in most cases he should proceed by petition seeking an order for restoration and a winding-up order.[239] Where a member seeks restoration of a company which is or appears to be insolvent, the affidavit in support should explain why the member feels aggrieved at the striking-off, notwithstanding the insolvency: for example, the insolvency may be attributable to start-up costs which will

235. Practice Direction [1974] 1 WLR 1459 at C–F.
236. See paras 5.42–5.44, *infra*.
237. See para. 5.44, *infra*.
238. See the next two paras.
239. RSC O. 102, r. 4(1)(g). For the procedure on such a petition, see *Supreme Court Practice 1997*, Vol. 1, paras 102/4/33–102/4/35, p. 1562, and Chapter 9, *infra*.

be eradicated by anticipated profitable trading; or a previously unprofitable business will be profitable when restored to the register, because of a new product or lucrative contract; or the member has agreed to dispose of the company or its assets at a price which the evidence shows to be favourable.

5.44 Undertakings

If a member of a company which is or appears to be insolvent can satisfy the court that he is aggrieved by the striking-off and that the company ought to be restored to the register, or a creditor applies for restoration of such a company without petitioning for winding-up, the court is likely to refuse restoration unless some protection is provided for any third parties who might deal with the insolvent company following restoration. In such cases, the court will generally require undertakings to be given for the protection of third parties as follows:

(1) Where a member seeks the restoration of an insolvent company which he hopes will thereafter trade profitably, the court may require the member to inject sufficient funds into the company to make it solvent or to undertake personally to satisfy any new liabilities incurred by the company from the date of restoration until such date as it is solvent.

(2) Where a member seeks the restoration of an insolvent company to complete a transaction but does not wish to carry on business thereafter, the court may require the member to undertake steps to put the company into voluntary liquidation forthwith upon restoration and to undertake not to dispose of any of the company's assets until the appointment of a liquidator.

(3) Where a creditor seeks the restoration of an insolvent company without winding-up—for example, because it is a necessary party to pending litigation—the court may require the creditor to undertake to notify the registrar of companies when the need for restoration is at an end (for example, at the conclusion of the litigation): the registrar of companies will then be able to recommence the striking-off proceedings. Less commonly, the court may require the creditor to undertake to commence compulsory winding-up proceedings when the need for the company's existence is at an end.

5.44.1 Where the evidence in support of the application for restoration does not show the company to be solvent, the Treasury Solicitor will usually write to the applicant following receipt of the evidence in support, and will identify the undertakings which are required before the registrar of companies will consent to the application. Where the applicant agrees to those undertakings, they can be given at the hearing by reference to the Treasury Solicitor's letter. If the parties cannot agree on the appropriate undertakings, the Companies Court Registrar will decide what undertakings should be given.

5.45 *Bona vacantia* waiver letter

Once the Treasury Solicitor has considered the evidence and is satisfied that it is an appropriate case for restoration, he will formally write to the applicant on behalf of the Crown stating that, insofar as the Crown is interested in the company's assets as *bona vacantia*, the Crown does not oppose the making of the order for restoration: this is known as "the *bona vacantia* waiver letter". The letter is required by the court before it will make an order for restoration because, on dissolution, all of the property and assets of the company became vested in the Crown as *bona vacantia*.[240] The Treasury Solicitor's practice now is to make a charge for providing the *bona vacantia* waiver letter.[241]

5.46 Affidavit of service

In all cases, an affidavit of service is required, proving service of the summons and supporting affidavit on the Treasury Solicitor by post. The affidavit of service should state that the Treasury Solicitor does not object to the order sought[242] and must exhibit the *bona vacantia* waiver letter. Where the *bona vacantia* waiver letter is received only shortly before the hearing, and the affidavit of service is sworn but not filed owing to the shortness of time, the Companies Court Registrar will usually be prepared to accept the affidavit at the hearing. Where there is insufficient time to swear an affidavit of service prior to the hearing, if the Treasury Solicitor is present at the hearing and does not oppose an order for restoration, the registrar may be prepared to make such an order on an undertaking to swear and file an affidavit of service forthwith: in such a case the applicant ought to produce a copy of the *bona vacantia* waiver letter at the hearing in order that the registrar can note its date in the court file.

5.47 Filing of returns

It was formerly the practice of the registrar of companies to consent to an order for the restoration of a company which had been struck off owing to defaults in filing accounts or returns, on the undertaking of the applicant to ensure that all outstanding accounts and returns were promptly filed with the registrar of companies. That practice no longer applies. A member applying for restoration will now usually have to ensure that all outstanding accounts and returns are filed before the court will order restoration: this may involve the payment of significant late filing fees. The court may be persuaded to dispense with the requirement of filing outstanding returns where the applicant member intends to put the company into voluntary liquidation immediately following restoration and gives appropriate undertakings in that regard.[243] A creditor who applies for restoration of the company without seeking a winding-up order[244] will obviously not be required to ensure that the company's outstanding returns are filed, but may be required to give undertakings to notify the registrar of companies when the need for the company's restoration is at an end, to enable the registrar of companies to retake steps to strike the company off the register.[245] Where it is not possible for the applicant member to prepare and file all outstanding accounts and returns by the date fixed for the hearing, an adjournment will be necessary to enable that to be done. Where virtually all of the outstanding returns have been filed, but the applicant has overlooked the need to file a minor return (for example, a notice of change in the particulars of the directors), the court may exceptionally be

240. S. 654(1).
241. £25 at the time of writing.
242. Practice Note [1931] WN 199.
243. See para. 5.44, *supra*.
244. For example, where the company is a necessary party to pending litigation.
245. See para. 5.44, *supra*.

persuaded to order restoration without an adjournment, on an undertaking to file the missing return forthwith. The court would not, however, accept such an undertaking where there are several returns outstanding or the missing return is of a more important character (such as audited accounts or an annual return). The registrar of companies may conduct a search to ascertain whether the applicant is a director of other companies which are in default of their filing obligations. If so, the registrar of companies may require the applicant to undertake to the court to bring those companies' files up to date before he will consent to an order for restoration.[246] A failure to honour an undertaking may be a contempt of court.[247]

5.48 The hearing

The hearing is before the Companies Court Registrar in chambers.[248] The registrar hears applications for restoration at 2.00pm each Friday during court term and on certain weekdays in the vacation. The registrar of companies is represented at the hearing by the Treasury Solicitor. Where undertakings are required to be given,[249] the applicant will give the undertakings set out in the relevant letter from the Treasury Solicitor, or the registrar will adjudicate on the proper form of the undertakings to be given. If an adjournment is necessary to complete the filing of returns, this should be agreed in advance of the hearing with the Treasury Solicitor, who will usually be prepared to request the adjournment on behalf of the applicant, without the need for the applicant's attendance or representation.[250] It is rarely the case that an application for restoration is opposed by the registrar of companies, provided that all outstanding returns are filed and the company is solvent, or appropriate undertakings are given. If an application is opposed, the Companies Court Registrar is likely to give directions for evidence, at the conclusion of which he may adjourn the application to the Companies Court Judge for determination.

5.49 The order

If the Companies Court Registrar orders the restoration of the name of the company to the register of companies, he will direct the applicant to deliver an office copy of the order to the registrar of companies for registration, and direct the registrar of companies to advertise the order in the *Gazette*. It is important for the applicant to send the office copy of the order to the registrar of companies as soon as the applicant receives a copy of the order from the court, because the restoration does not take effect until the office copy of the order is delivered to the registrar of companies for registration.[251] The order will also provide for the costs of the application. When ordering restoration, the court has power under the Act to give such directions or make such provisions as it thinks just, to place the company and all other persons in the same position (or as nearly as possible in the same

246. But note that, when ordering restoration under s. 653, the court does not have power to impose a penalty on those who were responsible for the defaults which led to the striking-off: see *Re Moses and Cohen Ltd* [1957] 1 WLR 1007 at 1010–1011.

247. See generally, *Supreme Court Practice 1997*, Vol. 1, para. 52/1/4, p. 831.

248. Room 4.12, fourth floor, Thomas More Building, Royal Courts of Justice.

249. See para. 5.44, *supra*.

250. As to costs of an adjournment, see para. 5.50, *infra*.

251. S. 653(3).

position) as if the name of the company had not been struck off the register[252]; but the court does not have power under s. 653(3) to impose terms or conditions designed to protect a third party from any adverse consequences resulting from restoration—i.e. the court may not make direction on restoration to put the parties in the same position as if the company had remained struck off.[253] In practice, directions under s. 653(3) to put the parties into the same position as if the company had not been struck off are rarely necessary because, on restoration, the company is deemed always to have continued in existence as if never struck off, and the order for restoration effectively validates any purported acts of the company done whilst it was dissolved. However, the power to make directions has been exercised to ensure that claims against the company which were valid at the date of dissolution are not statute-barred at the date of restoration, by the court directing that the period during which the company was dissolved should not count for any relevant statute of limitation. Thus, in a case where monies became available to the company long after dissolution, the court directed that the period between dissolution and restoration should not count for the purposes of limitation, in order that creditors whose debts were not time-barred on dissolution could still enforce their claims against the company.[254]

5.50 Costs

The applicants for restoration will usually be ordered to pay the costs of the registrar of companies. It is usual to agree the amount of the registrar of companies' costs with the Treasury Solicitor in advance of the hearing: the applicants will then be ordered to pay that sum to the registrar of companies, which avoids the need for a taxation of the registrar of companies' costs.[255] If the costs are paid in advance of the hearing, no order for costs will be made. Where the costs are not agreed and the company was struck off following a failure to file accounts or returns with the registrar of companies, the applicants may be ordered to pay the costs of the registrar of companies in relation to the application on the indemnity basis[256]; but the more onerous basis of taxation will not be appropriate where the striking-off occurred without any default on the part of the company or the applicants. In recent years, the Treasury Solicitor has adopted the practice of charging a fee[257] for providing the *bona vacantia* waiver letter, although this does not form part of the order for costs made by the Companies Court Registrar. If the application for restoration is dismissed, the order for costs will be made against the individual applicant alone and not against the company (which does not exist).

252. S. 653(3). See *Shire Court Residents Ltd* v. *Registrar of Companies* [1995] BCC 821 for an example of a case in which the court ordered restoration to the register on terms.

253. *Re Priceland Ltd, supra*, at 212g–213c.

254. *Re Donald Kenyon Ltd* [1956] 1 WLR 1397 at 1401–1402; contrast *Re Huntingdon Poultry Ltd* [1969] 1 WLR 204 at 207A–E. A third party adversely affected by such a direction may apply to set it aside, provided that he was not party to the earlier application under s. 653 and applies promptly on learning of the direction; if he was party to the earlier application, he should challenge any such direction by appeal: *Re Regent Insulation Ltd*, *Times*, 5 November 1981; *Re Advance Insulation Ltd* (1989) 5 BCC 55; *Re Workvale Ltd* [1992] 1 WLR 416.

255. At the time of writing, the registrar of companies' costs are usually £250 in a straightforward case, together with a further £10 for each adjournment if the application is not determined at its first hearing.

256. See *Re Court Lodge Development Co. Ltd* [1973] 1 WLR 1097 at 1101G–1102B.

257. £25 at the time of writing.

IV. APPLICATIONS TO HAVE A DISSOLUTION DECLARED VOID

5.51 Introduction

A company may be dissolved either as a result of its liquidation being concluded[258] or because it is struck off the register of companies.[259] In either case, an application may be made for the dissolution to be declared void.[260] The purpose of an application to have a dissolution declared void under s. 651 is commonly to enable a liquidator to distribute an overlooked asset or a creditor to make a claim which he has not previously made.[261] Where the company has been dissolved following the striking-off the register of its name, an applicant who was a member or creditor of the company at the date of dissolution will usually be able to choose between applying to have the dissolution declared void under s. 651 of the Act or to have the name of the company restored to the register under s. 653: the fact that the name of the company has been struck off the register does not require the applicant to apply for a restoration order under s. 653.[262] In most cases, an applicant with *locus standi* under s. 651 and s. 653 is likely to seek an order for the restoration of the company's name to the register under s. 653[263] (unless, for example, the application is made with a view to bringing proceedings for personal injuries or a fatal accident, and the applicant wishes to take advantage of the extended limitation period under s. 651(5)[264]).

5.52 Jurisdiction to declare a dissolution void

The court's power to declare a dissolution void is discretionary, and s. 651 does not stipulate any criteria which must be satisfied for the court to exercise its power, other than that the company must have been dissolved.[265] The court's discretion is unfettered. Provided that an application falls within the general legislative purpose of s. 651—namely, to enable a liquidator to distribute an overlooked asset or to enable a creditor to make a claim which he has not otherwise made—the court will generally make an order under s. 651 declaring the dissolution void; the court will not attempt to determine whether or not the revival of the company will ultimately benefit any person, but will leave that question to be determined in another forum.[266] Except where the application for dissolution is made under s. 651(5), to enable the applicant to bring an action for damages for personal injury or under the Fatal Accidents Act 1976, the application for dissolution may not be made more than two years after the date of dissolution.[267] Provided that the originating summons is issued within the two-year period,

258. I.e. under IA 1986, ss. 201–205.

259. I.e. under CA 1985, s. 652(3). All references hereafter are to CA 1985 unless otherwise stated. The procedure for restoration under s. 653 is dealt with in Part III of this Chapter, para. 5.29 *et seq.*

260. S. 651(1).

261. Per Hoffmann L.J. in *Re Forte's (Manufacturing) Ltd* [1994] BCC 84 at 87D–E; and per Robert Walker J. in *Re Oakleague Ltd* [1995] 2 BCLC 624 at 628a–e.

262. *Re Test Holdings (Clifton) Ltd* [1970] Ch. 285 at 291G; *Re Townreach Ltd* [1995] Ch. 28 at 36E–38F.

263. For the reasons given in para 5.30, *supra.*

264. See next para.

265. Contrast the criteria for a restoration to the register stipulated in s. 653(1) and (2).

266. *Re Oakleague Ltd* [1995] 2 BCLC 624 at 628i–629a.

267. S. 651(4).

the court may make an order on the summons, notwithstanding that, by the date of the hearing, more than two years have expired since the date of dissolution.[268] Where the application to have the dissolution declared void is brought under s. 651(5) in order to enable the applicant to bring an action for damages against the company for personal injury or under the Fatal Accidents Act 1976, there is no time limit for bringing the application; but the court will refuse to make a declaration under s. 651(1) if it appears to the court that the action for damages against the company is bound to fail because it is time-barred under the relevant statute of limitation.[269] Where the applicant's claim was not time-barred at the date of dissolution, the court has power to direct that the period between dissolution and the order under s. 651(5) should not count for the purpose of any statute of limitation.[270] Such a direction would enable the applicant to pursue his personal injury claim without having to make an application in the Queen's Bench Division under s. 33 of the Limitation Act 1980 to extend the primary limitation period. It is unclear whether the power to make such a direction is limited to applications under s. 651(5) to have a dissolution declared void for the purposes of bringing personal injury or fatal accident proceedings,[271] or extends to any application under s. 651.[272] An application made under s. 651(5) with a view to bringing a personal injury action may be made at any time: it can be made where the company was dissolved prior to s. 651(5) coming into force and, notwithstanding that the time limit then applicable to such an application (i.e. two years) had by that date expired; but no application may be made where the company was dissolved more than 20 years before the commencement of s. 651(5)[273] (i.e. where the company was dissolved before 16 November 1969). In all cases, the application to have the dissolution declared void should be issued as soon as possible after the applicant becomes aware of the dissolution.[274]

5.53 Form of application

Prior to 1 October 1995, the form of an application to have a dissolution declared void depended on whether the dissolution resulted from the completion of a liquidation of the company or from the company being struck off the register under s. 652(3) of the Act: in the former case, the application had to be made by originating summons,[275] whereas in the latter, the application had to be by notice of originating motion.[276] That distinction was anomalous. There was no good reason why applications for restoration to the register under s. 653 and applications to have a dissolution declared void under s. 651, where the dissolution resulted from a liquidation rather than a striking-off, had to be made by originating summons to the Companies Court Registrar in chambers, yet an application to have a dissolution declared void where the dissolution resulted from a striking-off had to be made by motion to the Companies Court Judge in open court. Happily, the anomaly has

268. See *Re Scad Ltd* [1941] Ch. 386.
269. S. 651(5) (as inserted by CA 1989, s. 141(3)), which came into force on 16 November 1989. See further para. 5.56, *infra* as to joinder of third parties.
270. S. 651(6); and see *Re Workvale Ltd (No. 2)* [1992] 1 WLR 416 at 424H–425C.
271. As suggested in *Re Mixhurst Ltd* [1994] 2 BCLC 19 at 28i–29j.
272. As suggested in *Re Townreach Ltd, supra*, at 44H–45A.
273. CA 1989, s. 141(4).
274. *Re Thompson & Riches Ltd* [1981] 1 WLR 682 at 689C–D.
275. Under RSC O. 102, r. 2(1); *Re Scicon Consultancy International Ltd* [1992] BCC 385.
276. Under RSC O. 102, r. 3(1)(f), in force until 30 September 1995.

been removed with effect from 1 October 1995, by the Rules of the Supreme Court (Amendment) Order 1995[277] which revoked the requirement in O. 102, r. 3(1)(f) of the Rules of the Supreme Court that an application to have a dissolution declared void should be made by motion where the company has not been wound up.

5.53.1 Accordingly, since 1 October 1995, *any* application to have a dissolution declared void must be made by originating summons[278] in the expedited form[279] returnable before the Companies Court Registrar in chambers,[280] even if the dissolution occurred before that date. The summons may be issued in London out of the chambers of the Companies Court Registrar,[281] or out of any Chancery district registry.[282] Two copies of the summons will be required on issue, one of which should be stamped with the appropriate fee: an action number and hearing date will be marked on both copies, the stamped copy will be retained for filing, and the other copy will be returned to the applicant. If the applicant seeks any further orders or directions in addition to the declaration that the dissolution be void, he should set them out in the originating summons.[283]

5.54 Parties: the applicant

The applicant may be the liquidator of the company (where the company has been wound up prior to dissolution), or any other person who appears to the court to be interested.[284] The applicant need not have been a member or creditor of the company at the date of dissolution.[285] A person who has a proprietary or pecuniary interest in the revival of the company is a "person ... interested" within s. 651(1),[286] but the section is not limited to such persons[287]: a person may be "interested" within the meaning of s. 651(1), even where he has no proprietary or pecuniary interest in the revival of the company (although such persons will not frequently be encountered). Hence, an order under s. 651 may be sought to enable the Secretary of State to exercise his statutory powers in relation to the company (for example, the appointment of inspectors to investigate the company or the bringing of disqualification proceedings), and the Secretary of State is a "person ... interested", with standing to apply under s. 651.[288] The applicant's interest does not have to be firmly established or highly likely to prevail, but must not be "merely shadowy".[289]

277. S.I. 1995 No. 2206, r. 46.

278. RSC O. 102, r. 2(1). See generally, *Supreme Court Practice 1997*, Vol. 1, para. 102/2/32, p. 1544.

279. RSC O. 102, r. 2(2). The relevant form is at Form No. 10 in Appendix A to the RSC: see *Supreme Court Practice 1997*, Vol. 2, para. 4, p. 6.

280. I.e. in Room 4.12, fourth floor, Thomas More Building, Royal Courts of Justice.

281. I.e. in Room 2.09, second floor, Thomas More Building, Royal Courts of Justice.

282. RSC O. 102, r. 2(4).

283. The supplemental orders and directions which may be sought are considered in para. 5.63, *infra*.

284. S. 651(1).

285. Hence, the class of applicants under s. 651(1) is wider than under s. 653(2): see para. 5.36, *supra*.

286. See *Re Roehampton Swimming Pool Ltd* [1968] 1 WLR 1693 at 1698E; *Re Wood and Martin (Bricklaying Contractors) Ltd* [1971] 1 WLR 293 at 247E–G (where a company which had been struck off the register and dissolved under s. 652 purported to appoint a liquidator who realised its assets: the appointee could not apply as a liquidator to have the dissolution declared void under s. 651 because his appointment was invalid, but he could apply as a "person . . . interested").

287. Despite the suggestion to that effect in *Re Roehampton Swimming Pool Ltd, supra*, per Megarry J.

288. *Re Townreach Ltd, supra*, at 36D.

289. *Re Wood and Martin (Bricklaying Contractors) Ltd, supra*, at 197F–G; *Re Forte's (Manufacturing) Ltd* [1994] BCC 84 at 90A–B; *Re Mixhurst Ltd* [1994] 2 BCLC 19 at 22g.

Unlike s. 653(2) which permits the company to apply for its own restoration to the register, s. 651(1) does not give the company a notional existence for the purposes of applying to have its dissolution declared void. Accordingly, the company may not be named as an applicant or heard on the application.

5.55 The respondent

Where the company has not been wound up, the respondent should be the registrar of companies,[290] who will be represented throughout the application by the Treasury Solicitor. Although it has been said that joinder of the registrar of companies will usually be unnecessary where the company was wound up prior to its dissolution,[291] the registrar is nevertheless commonly joined as a respondent.[292] Where the liquidator who acted prior to dissolution can be located and is willing and still able to act as liquidator of the company, he may be joined as a respondent (if he is not an applicant) so that the court may order his re-appointment as liquidator.[293] If the person who acted as liquidator cannot be located or is unwilling to act or is not entitled to be re-appointed as liquidator (for example, because he is not a licensed insolvency practitioner), a licensed insolvency practitioner who is willing and able to act may be joined as a respondent, to be appointed liquidator when the dissolution is declared void. Since the company ceased to exist on dissolution, it may not be joined as a respondent.[294] If the Crown, which is entitled to the dissolved company's assets as *bona vacantia* under s. 654, does not consent to the application, it will be necessary to join the Attorney-General as a respondent to represent the Crown[295]; but in practice the Crown will seldom refuse to consent to an application under s. 651 or 653.

5.56 Joinder of third parties

Where the rights of a third party would be directly affected by an order declaring the dissolution of the company void, that third party may be joined as a respondent.[296] If the third party is not joined as a respondent when the originating summons is issued, he may subsequently be joined as a respondent on the application of the third party himself, or on the application of the person seeking to have the dissolution declared void.[297] An application for joinder should be made by summons supported by affidavit to the Companies Court Registrar sitting in chambers.[298] The affidavit should explain the grounds on which joinder is sought. Where the application for joinder is opposed, the registrar may give directions for further evidence, at the completion of which he may adjourn the summons to the Companies Court Judge for determination. Applications for joinder typically arise where a person seeks to have a dissolution declared void in order to bring

290. *Re Test Holdings (Clifton) Ltd* [1970] Ch 285 at 292G–H.
291. *Re Thompson and Riches Ltd* [1981] 1 WLR 682 at 688E–F.
292. See, for example, *Re Forte's (Manufacturing) Ltd, supra*, at 86E; and *Re Workvale Ltd* [1991] BCLC 528i–j.
293. Under the IA 1986, s. 108(1).
294. *Re Workvale Ltd* [1991] BCLC 528g–h; *Re H Clarkson (Overseas) Ltd* [1987] 3 BCC 606.
295. See *Re Belmont & Co.* [1952] Ch. 10 at 15.
296. *Re Workvale Ltd, supra*; *Re Forte's (Manufacturing) Ltd, supra*, at 90C–F.
297. Under RSC O. 15, r. 6; see *Re Forte's (Manufacturing) Ltd, supra*, at 86E–G and 90E.
298. RSC O. 15, r. 6(3); see *Supreme Court Practice 1997*, Vol. 1, para. 15/6/14, p. 213.

an action for damages against the company for personal injuries or under the Fatal Accidents Act 1976, in respect of which claims the company was insured.[299] In such cases, the insurer may seek to be joined as respondent to the application and to be heard thereon. However, the court will not permit joinder where the third party merely intends to assert that the applicant has no claim against the company or that any proceedings against the third party would have no prospect of success: the third party seeking joinder must show that an order under s. 651(1) would directly affect his rights.[300] A third party who has been joined as a respondent may oppose the application for an order under s. 651 declaring the dissolution of the company void on the grounds, for example, that the applicant's claim against the company for damages for personal injury or under the Fatal Accidents Act 1976 is time-barred and therefore bound to fail.[301] The court will refuse to declare the dissolution void on this ground only if it is clear beyond doubt that the applicant's claim would be time-barred: if the applicant has an arguable case that the proceedings contemplated against the company would not be time-barred, the court will declare the dissolution to be void, leaving the question of limitation to be determined in the subsequent proceedings.[302] The burden of establishing an arguable case is on the applicant.[303]

5.57 Service

Where the registrar of companies is the respondent, the originating summons and the affidavit in support should be served on him by post, addressed to Companies House, Crown Way, Maindy, Cardiff. Where a licensed insolvency practitioner is named as a respondent with a view to his appointment as liquidator of the company, the originating summons and affidavit in support should be served on him personally, or by first class post at his usual or last known address.[304] In all cases, copies of the application and evidence in support should also be sent to the Treasury Solicitor, who will represent the Crown in relation to the Crown's interest in the former assets of the dissolved company as *bona vacantia*.[305]

5.58 Affidavit in support

In all cases, an affidavit in support of the application should be sworn and filed in the chambers of the Companies Court Registrar,[306] and served on each respondent. The affidavit should set out the grounds for seeking to have the dissolution declared void: it should explain how the company came to be dissolved (i.e. whether as a consequence of being struck off the register under s. 652(3) or at the conclusion of a liquidation[307]) and should identify the benefit which the applicant would derive from the dissolution being

299. I.e. where the applicant intends to rely on the Third Parties (Rights Against Insurers) Act 1930.
300. *Re Forte's (Manufacturing) Ltd*, *supra*, at 90C–E; and see *Re Jayham Ltd* [1995] 2 BCLC 455 (a case on s. 653).
301. See the proviso to s. 651(5).
302. *Re Workvale Ltd (No. 2)* [1992] 1 WLR 416 at 421H–422E.
303. *Ibid.* at 422D.
304. RSC O. 10, rr. 5(1) and 1(2).
305. S. 654(1).
306. I.e. Room 2.09, second floor, Thomas More Building, Royal Courts of Justice.
307. Under the IA 1986, ss. 201–205.

declared void—for example, where the application is by a member or creditor of a company which has been dissolved following a liquidation, the affidavit may identify an asset of the company which was overlooked in the liquidation or to which the company has subsequently become entitled, and which the applicant wishes to have realised for the benefit of the company's members or creditors.[308] Where the application is made with a view to enabling the applicant to bring an action against the company for damages for personal injuries or under the Fatal Accidents Act 1976, the affidavit should briefly describe the nature of the injury and of the intended proceedings, and should exhibit a draft statement of claim; the affidavit should also deal with the question of limitation and, where the primary period of limitation expired prior to dissolution, the affidavit should set out all facts relied on for contending that an extended period of limitation[309] should apply. Where the dissolution resulted from a concluded winding-up, the affidavit should also identify the person who is to become liquidator if an order under s. 651 is made, and should exhibit evidence of that person's consent and qualification to act as liquidator. In some cases, evidence of the solvency of the dissolved company (if revived) may be necessary.[310]

5.59 Affidavit of service

In all cases, an affidavit of service is required, proving service of the originating summons and supporting evidence by post on the Treasury Solicitor. The affidavit should exhibit a copy of the *bona vacantia* waiver letter.[311] The affidavit should state that the Treasury Solicitor does not object to the order sought[312] (which will be confirmed in the *bona vacantia* waiver letter). Where the *bona vacantia* waiver letter is received by the applicant only shortly before the hearing, the Companies Court Registrar will usually be prepared to accept the affidavit at the hearing. If, owing to the shortness of time, it has not been possible to prepare an affidavit of service but the *bona vacantia* waiver letter is produced in court, the court may be prepared to declare the dissolution void on an undertaking by the applicant forthwith to swear an affidavit of service exhibiting the *bona vacantia* waiver letter.

5.60 Filing of returns and undertakings

Where the dissolution of the company was as a result of its being struck off the register under s. 652 as a defunct company for failing to file accounts or returns with the registrar of companies, and the company has not been wound up, the registrar of companies is unlikely to consent to an application to have the dissolution declared void made by a member of the company[313] unless (i) all outstanding returns have been filed by the date of the hearing, or (ii) undertakings are given to put the company into voluntary liquidation as soon as possible upon the dissolution being declared void and not to dispose of any

308. *Re Servers of the Blind League* [1960] 1 WLR 564 at 565; *Re Forte's (Manufacturing) Ltd, supra*, at 87D–E; *Re Oakleague Ltd, supra*, at 628a–e.

309. For example, under s. 11 or 33 of the Limitation Act 1980.

310. See para. 5.61, *infra*.

311. For an explanation of the *bona vacantia* waiver letter, see para. 5.45, *supra*.

312. Practice Note [1928] WN 218; Practice Note [1931] WN 199.

313. I.e. where the member is using the procedure under s. 651(1) as an alternative to an application under s. 653(2).

assets pending the appointment of such a liquidator. Where the applicant is a person who is not in a position to complete the company's outstanding returns (for example, a creditor of the company), the applicant may be required to give undertakings to notify the registrar of companies when the need for the revival of the company is at end (for example, when any litigation involving the company is concluded): at that stage the registrar of companies will be able to recommence the striking-off procedure under s. 652 of the Act, which will result in the company once again being dissolved.[314] These requirements apply equally to applications under s. 653 for restoration to the register, and where a member or creditor can apply for restoration under that section, there is no real advantage in applying to have the dissolution declared void under s. 651(1).

5.61 Evidence of solvency and undertakings

Similarly, where dissolution resulted from the company being struck off the register under s. 652(3), and the dissolved company has not been wound up, a member who applies to have the dissolution declared void should provide evidence of the company's solvency in the affidavit sworn in support of the application.[315] Where the applicant is unable to adduce evidence of solvency (for example, because the applicant is a creditor of the company, or the applicant is a member of the company but the company is in fact insolvent), the registrar of companies is unlikely to consent to the application and the court will not declare the dissolution void, unless undertakings are given for the protection of the third parties who might otherwise deal with the company following its revival. The undertakings which may be required are discussed in para. 5.44, *supra*.

5.62 The hearing

The hearing will be before the Companies Court Registrar sitting in chambers. The registrar of companies will be represented at the hearing by the Treasury Solicitor. Where the summons is opposed, the Companies Court Registrar may adjourn the application to the Companies Court Judge for determination, once the evidence is complete. If the Crown, which is entitled to the company's assets as *bona vacantia*, opposes the application, the Attorney-General may be represented at the hearing on behalf of the Crown. This will seldom occur in practice.

5.63 The order

The order declaring the dissolution of the company void will set out any necessary undertakings which are given by the applicant. In making an order declaring the dissolution void, the court may impose such terms as it thinks fit.[316] The court will normally order the applicant to deliver an office copy of the order to the registrar of companies within seven days for registration (although the applicant is obliged to do so by the Act,[317] and

314. S. 652(3). See further para. 5.44, *supra*.

315. See further the discussion in para. 5.42, *supra*, in respect of applications under s. 653(2).

316. S. 651(1). For examples of cases where the court made an order subject to terms, see *Foster Yates and Thom Ltd* v. *HW Edgehill Equipment Ltd* (1978) 122 Sol J 860; *Re Townreach Ltd* [1995] Ch. 28 at 44H–45F; but cf *Re Mixhurst Ltd* [1994] 2 BCLC 19 at 28g–h.

317. S. 651(3).

such an order is not, strictly speaking, necessary unless the court requires the office copy of the order to be delivered within a period other than seven days). Where an order is sought under s. 651(5) to enable an applicant to bring an action against the company for damages for personal injury or under the Fatal Accidents Act 1976, the court, when declaring the dissolution void, may direct that the period between the dissolution of the company and the making of the order under s. 651 should not be counted when calculating the limitation period for such an action.[318] If such a direction is to be sought, it should be expressly referred to in the summons. It is unclear whether the power to make such a direction is confined to applications under s. 651(5),[319] or extends to any application under s. 651[320]: if the former, the power is more limited than under s. 653.[321] Where the company has been wound up prior to dissolution, the terms of the order ought to provide for the appointment of a named licensed insolvency practitioner as liquidator,[322] and such an order ought to be sought in the originating summons. Where the company, prior to dissolution, had been wound up voluntarily and no order has been made giving a general liberty to apply to the court, it is usual for the order declaring the dissolution void to grant (and the originating summons should seek) a general liberty to the applicant, the liquidator or any creditor or contributory, to apply to the court for directions in relation to the winding-up.

5.64 Effect of the order

Once the dissolution of a company is declared void, such proceedings may thereafter be taken as if the company had not been dissolved.[323] However, unlike an order under s. 653 restoring a company to the register, which has the effect that the company is deemed always to have been in existence,[324] on an order declaring the dissolution void there is no deemed continuity of the company's existence. The order results in the former property of the company which had passed to the Crown on dissolution as *bona vacantia*[325] being automatically re-vested in the company without the need for an express vesting order,[326] but any purported activity of the company in the period between the dissolution and the order declaring the dissolution void is not thereby validated.[327] Any proceedings brought by or against the company which were pending at the date of dissolution of are brought permanently to an end by the dissolution and are not revived by an order declaring the dissolution void.[328] Proceedings which could have been brought prior to the date of dissolution may (subject to the question of limitation) be commenced once the dissolution is declared void.[329]

318. S. 651(6); *Re Workvale Ltd* [1992] 1 WLR 416 at 424G–425C.
319. As suggested in *Re Mixhurst Ltd* [1994] 2 BCLC 19 at 28i–29a.
320. As suggested in *Re Townreach Ltd, supra*, at 44H–45A.
321. See para. 5.49, *supra*.
322. Under IA 1986, s. 108(1).
323. S. 651(2).
324. S. 653(3).
325. Under s. 654(1).
326. *Re CW Dixon Ltd* [1947] Ch. 251.
327. See *Morris* v. *Harris* [1927] AC 252 and *Re Mixhurst Ltd* [1994] 2 BCLC 19; but contrast *Re Townreach Ltd* [1995] Ch. 28 (where the court made an order under s. 651 and by consequential directions validated a purported resolution for voluntary winding-up passed after the date of striking-off the register and dissolution).
328. *Foster Yates and Thom Ltd* v. *HW Edgehill Equipment Ltd* (1978) 122 Sol J 860.
329. S. 651(2).

5.65 Where, in the period between the date of dissolution of the company and the order declaring the dissolution void under s. 651(1), another company is incorporated with (or changes its name to) the name by which the dissolved company was known prior to dissolution, when reviving the dissolved company the court cannot direct that its name be changed to avoid there being two companies on the register with the same name.[330] The court may, however, under its inherent jurisdiction make a direction on the application of the registrar of companies that the name of the revived company should appear with its company number in any records maintained by the registrar of companies and in any correspondence with him.[331]

5.66 Costs

Where an application to have a dissolution declared void is made in relation to a company which has not been wound up, the applicant will usually be ordered to pay the costs of the registrar of companies (including the costs incurred by the Treasury Solicitor when acting on the registrar of companies' behalf). Where an application is made in relation to a company which has been wound up, the court is likely to direct that the costs of the summons be payable as a cost of the winding-up. Where a third party is joined as a respondent and opposes the application to have the dissolution declared void,[332] the third party will usually be ordered to pay the costs of the contested hearing where the opposition fails and an order under s. 651(1) is made; where the opposition succeeds and the court refuses to make an order declaring the dissolution void, the applicant will ordinarily be ordered to pay the successful respondent's costs. In all cases, the Treasury Solicitor will make a charge for providing the *bona vacantia* waiver letter.[333]

V. OTHER MISCELLANEOUS COMPANIES ACT APPLICATIONS

5.67 Introduction

The Companies Act 1985 contains a miscellany of provisions governing the administration of a company which may give rise to applications to the court: certain sections of the Act provide for applications by the company itself (for example, applications for an extension of time in which to file documents with the registrar of companies[334]); other sections make provision for applications by a minority of shareholders to challenge and cancel special resolutions passed by a majority in specified circumstances (for example, to challenge an alteration to the company's memorandum of association[335]); yet others provide for applications by persons under a liability to be released from that liability (for example, a liability incurred in relation to a share purchase in contravention of the Act[336]). In contrast to the first four applications discussed in this Chapter, these applications are less common in practice. It is beyond the scope of this book to examine each individual

330. *Re Selectclass Ltd*, 13 December 1994, Arden J., unreported.
331. *Re Selectclass Ltd*, 3 February 1995, Arden J., unreported.
332. See para. 5.56, *supra*.
333. £25 at the time of writing.
334. CA 1985, s. 6(2). (All references hereafter are to the CA 1985, unless otherwise stated).
335. S. 5.
336. S. 113(1).

application in detail, but it is possible to identify distinct categories of applications which share common features. In the following paragraphs, the common features of each category are considered before identifying specific procedural requirements of particular applications.

1. CHALLENGES TO THE PASSING OF SPECIAL RESOLUTIONS

5.68 The resolutions which may be challenged

The 1985 Act enables a minority of shareholders to seek the cancellation of special resolutions passed by the majority of shareholders in the following six circumstances:

(i) Where the majority have resolved by special resolution to alter the company's principal objects clause in its memorandum of association,[337] a minority may apply to the court for an order cancelling the alteration.[338]

(ii) Where the majority have resolved by special resolution to alter a provision of the company's articles of association which could lawfully have been contained in its memorandum of association,[339] a minority may apply to the court for an order cancelling the alteration.[340]

(iii) Where the majority have resolved by special resolution that a public company should be re-registered as a private company,[341] a minority may apply to the court for an order cancelling the resolution.[342]

(iv) Where the requisite majority of a class of members has consented to a variation of the rights attaching to their class of shares,[343] a minority of that class may apply to the court for an order cancelling the variation of class rights.[344]

(v) Where the majority in a private company have approved by special resolution the giving of financial assistance for the purpose of an acquisition of shares in that company or its holding company,[345] a minority may apply to the court for an order cancelling the resolution.[346]

(vi) Where the majority in a private company have approved by special resolution a payment out of capital by the company for the redemption or purchase of its own shares,[347] a minority may apply to the court for an order cancelling the resolution.[348]

337. I.e. under s. 4(1).
338. S. 5(1). A member of a company not formed under, but registered under, the Companies Legislation may also apply under s. 5(1) to challenge a special resolution altering the form of that company's constitution: s. 690(1) and (2).
339. I.e. under s. 17(1).
340. S. 17(1), (3), and s. 5.
341. I.e. under s. 53(1)(a).
342. S. 54(1).
343. I.e. under s. 125(2).
344. S. 127(2).
345. I.e. under s. 155(4).
346. S. 157(2).
347. I.e. under s. 173(2).
348. S. 176(1).

5.69 Form of application

In each of the above cases, the application to cancel the special resolution, or to cancel the alteration effected by the special resolution, is made by petition.[349] The petition should be presented at the chambers of the registrar of the Companies Court[350] or in any Chancery district registry.[351] Two copies of the petition (together with a further copy for each respondent on whom the petition is to be served) are required on presentation, one of which should be stamped with the appropriate fee. One copy of the petition will be retained on the court file, the others will be sealed and returned to the petitioner.

5.70 Contents of petition

The petition should contain the following information in numbered paragraphs: details of the incorporation of the company; its registered office address; its principal objects; its authorised and issued capital; the circumstances of the passing of the special resolution sought to be cancelled, including the date of the meeting at which the resolution was passed and the text of the resolution set out verbatim; details of the shareholding qualification of the petitioner(s) required by the Act, the conduct of the petitioner(s) in relation to the resolution (i.e. whether they attended the meeting in question and whether they abstained or voted against the resolution); and the grounds for the challenge to the resolution.

5.71 Grounds for challenging the resolution

Although shareholders frequently delegate day-to-day management decisions to the board of directors,[352] the Act provides for certain decisions to be binding on the company only if approved by a resolution of a specified majority of members. The power of a minority of shareholders to challenge a special resolution duly passed by the requisite majority derogates from the principle of majority rule. It is therefore necessary for the dissentient minority member(s) to show cogent reasons why the majority's resolution should be cancelled. In order to succeed in a challenge to a special resolution, the dissentient member(s) will generally have to show that the special resolution passed is prejudicial to them in some way which does affect the majority shareholders, or unduly benefits the majority shareholders at the expense of the dissentient minority. The petition should also identify any procedural irregularities in the passing of the resolution which, although not invalidating the resolution, have prejudiced the minority shareholders.

In the following paragraphs, the special procedural rules applicable to each application to challenge a special resolution are considered separately.

(a) Challenges to alterations in the company's constitution

5.72 The procedure whereby a minority shareholder may challenge an alteration in the company's constitution by special resolution is virtually identical whether the challenge is

349. RSC O. 102, r. 4(1)(a), (b), (e), (h), (j), (k), (l).

350. I.e. Room 2.09, second floor, Thomas More Building, Royal Courts of Justice.

351. RSC O. 102, r. 4(2). For the location of the Chancery district registries, see para. 5.2, Note 14, *supra*.

352. For example, under reg. 70 of the 1985 Table A.

to an alteration of the company's objects clause,[353] or to an alteration of a provision in the articles of association which could have been contained in the memorandum of association,[354] or to an alteration in the constitution of a company registered (but not formed) under the Companies Legislation.[355] Where an application is made to cancel the alteration in a company's constitution, the alteration does not have effect unless, and only to the extent that, it is subsequently confirmed by the court.[356]

5.73 Jurisdiction: shareholding requirements

A challenge to an alteration of the company's constitution by special resolution may only be made where: (a) the applicants have the minimum shareholding qualification required by the Act; (b) they did not consent to or vote in favour of the special resolution[357]; and (c) the petition to cancel the alteration is presented within the strict time limit imposed by the Act. The petitioners[358] must hold not less in aggregate than 15 per cent in nominal value of the company's issued share capital or any class of share capital; where the company is not limited by shares, the petitioners must be not less than 15 per cent in number of the company's members.[359] Where the petition seeks to challenge an alteration to the company's objects clause[360] or an alteration to the constitution of a company registered (but not formed) under the Companies Legislation,[361] the petition may be presented by the holders of not less than 15 per cent of the company's debentures, if those debentures entitle the holders to object to alterations to the company's objects.[362] The Act does not permit debenture holders to challenge an alteration to a condition contained in the company's articles of association which could have been contained in its memorandum of association.[363] The court, hearing a petition to cancel an alteration to a company's constitution made by special resolution, has a wide discretion as to the relief which it may grant,[364] and the petition should clearly state the relief which the petitioner seeks.

5.74 Timing

The petition must be presented within 21 days after the date on which the special resolution objected to was passed.[365]

5.75 Parties: the petitioners

The petitioners will be members of the company (or, in the case of challenges to an alteration to the company's objects clause under s. 4(1) or to a company's constitution

353. Under ss. 4 and 5. See generally, *Supreme Court Practice 1997*, Vol. 1, paras 102/4/2–102/4/6, pp. 1550–1551.

354. Under ss. 5 and 17(3). See generally, *Supreme Court Practice 1997*, Vol. 1, para. 102/4/7, p. 1552.

355. Under ss. 5 and 690(2).

356. See ss. 4(2), 17(1) and 690(2).

357. Ss. 5(2), 17(3) and 690(2).

358. See para. 5.75, *infra*, as to representative petitioners.

359. Ss. 5(2)(a), 17(3) and 690(2).

360. I.e. under s. 5(1).

361. I.e. under s. 690(2).

362. Ss. 5(2)(b) and 690(2)—i.e. debentures which are secured by a floating charge issued or first issued before 1 December 1947 or forming part of a series of debentures so issued: s. 5(8).

363. S. 17(3).

364. S. 5(4)–(7). See para. 5.83, *infra*.

365. Ss. 5(3), 17(3) and 690(2).

under s. 690(2), debenture holders) holding the requisite proportion of the company's issued capital (or relevant debentures) who did not consent to or vote in favour of the special resolution. Where the minimum shareholding (or debenture-holding) requirement is achieved by the aggregation of the holdings of a number of different persons, each such person may be named as a petitioner; alternatively, the persons entitled to present a petition may nominate in writing one of their number to petition on their behalf[366] as sole representative petitioner. The nomination of a representative petitioner should be recited in the petition, identifying the names of his appointors and stating that they have, in aggregate, the necessary qualification to petition. If the persons entitled to petition wish to appoint a representative petitioner, they must do so in writing *before* the petition is presented: a petition presented by a person who does not have the requisite shareholding (or debenture-holding) qualification and does not have the *prior* written authority of those other persons who together in aggregate have that qualification, is defective. The defect will not be cured by obtaining appropriate authority from other members in the period between presentation of the petition and the hearing, and a petition presented without the prior written authority of the requisite proportion of shareholders or debenture-holders will be struck out.[367] Members or debenture-holders who are not named as petitioners and have not joined in the appointment of a representative petitioner, may appear at the hearing of the petition to support or oppose it. Where the company's share capital is divided into different classes of shares and the petitioner(s) hold or represent at least 15 per cent in nominal value of a particular class, a member who holds shares of a different class not amounting to 15 per cent of that other class may not be joined as a petitioner; and although he may be heard on the petition in support of the complaints advanced by the petitioner(s), he may not put forward other or additional grounds of complaint.[368]

5.76 The respondent

The company should be the respondent to the petition.

5.77 Settling a timetable

Prior to the presentation of the petition, the intended petitioner(s) should attend the chambers of the Companies Court Registrar[369] (or the relevant Chancery district registry) to settle a timetable for the progress of the petition. The timetable will typically fix dates for the filing and checking of evidence in relation to the petition, the hearing of a summons for directions, the settling of the order for directions and the advertisement thereof, the hearing of the petition, and the settling of the order made on the petition. The timetable operates as a guide for the parties and may be varied on the hearing of the summons for directions.[370]

366. S. 5(3).
367. *Re Suburban and Provincial Stores Ltd* [1943] Ch. 156 at 160–161; *Re Sound City (Films) Ltd* [1947] Ch. 169 at 176–177.
368. *Re Hampstead Garden Suburb Ltd* [1962] Ch. 806 at 819–820.
369. I.e. Room 2.09, second floor, Thomas More Building, Royal Courts of Justice.
370. See para. 5.80, *infra*.

5.78 Service and notice of petition

Once the petition has been presented, it should be served on the company by leaving it at, or posting it to, the company's registered office.[371] Notice of the presentation of the petition in the prescribed form[372] should forthwith be given to the registrar of companies.[373] The court has power to extend time for giving notice of the petition to the registrar of companies[374]: an application for an extension of time should be made to the Companies Court Registrar in chambers by summons supported by affidavit, explaining why an extension of time is required.

5.79 Affidavit in support of petition

The petitioner(s) should swear and file an affidavit in support of the petition (and lodge the exhibits thereto) in the chambers of the Companies Court Registrar[375] or in the Chancery district registry in which the petition was presented.[376] Where the applicant is a representative petitioner authorised in writing to present the petition on behalf of other members or debenture-holders,[377] the affidavit should explain the authorisation of the petitioner as the representative applicant and should exhibit his written appointment. In all cases, the affidavit should exhibit a copy of the petition and verify its contents as being true. The affidavit should also usually describe the events leading to the passing of the special resolution to which objection is taken; set out verbatim the wording of the resolution passed; explain whether the petitioner(s) attended the meeting at which the resolution was passed, and (if so) whether they voted against the resolution or abstained[378]; identify any procedural irregularity in the convening or conduct of the meeting; and explain why the alteration is prejudicial to the petitioners or unduly benefits the majority who voted in favour of the resolution at the expense of the minority. Relevant supporting documents should be exhibited. In most cases, the exhibits will include a print of the company's memorandum and articles of association, a copy of the notice convening the general meeting, and the copy of the resolution sent to the registrar of companies for registration[379] (if in the possession of the petitioner(s)). The affidavit should confirm that the print of the company's memorandum and articles of association contains copies of all special resolutions altering the same (except the resolution objected to) or that there have been no such alterations.

5.80 Summons for directions

Following presentation of the petition, the petitioner(s) must issue a summons for directions[380] returnable before the Companies Court Registrar in chambers. The respondent to

371. S. 725(1).
372. See Form No. 6 in the Companies (Forms) Regulations 1985, S.I. 1985 No. 854 (as amended by, *inter alia*, S.I. 1995 No. 736).
373. S. 6(1)(b)(i).
374. S. 6(2).
375. I.e. in Room 2.09, second floor, Thomas More Building, Royal Courts of Justice.
376. RSC O. 102, rr. 4(2) and 16.
377. S. 5(3). See para. 5.75, *supra*.
378. See s. 5(2).
379. Under s. 380(1).
380. RSC O. 102, r. 6(1).

the summons should be the company. The summons should be served on the company by leaving it at, or posting it to, its registered office.[381] At the hearing of the summons for directions, the court will make whatever directions it considers appropriate to ensure that proceedings are made ready for final determination.[382] Typically, on the hearing of the summons for directions, the court will make directions for filing any further evidence which appears to be necessary and for giving notice of the presentation of the petition to members or debenture-holders, will fix a hearing date, and will direct the advertisement of that date.

5.81 Directions and advertisement

In most cases, the court will require the petition to be advertised in a national newspaper prior to its hearing, thereby giving third parties notice that a cancellation is sought of an alteration made by special resolution. Whether the petition is to be advertised will be determined at the summons for directions. Following the hearing of the summons for directions, the court will produce a draft advertisement (where the petition is to be advertised) and a draft of the order for directions which it will send to the petitioner(s) and the company for consideration. At the same time the court will give notice of an appointment at the chambers of the Companies Court Registrar to be attended by the parties to check the evidence and to settle the form of the advertisement and draft order. Once the evidence has been checked and the form of advertisement and order settled at that appointment, the petitioner(s) will carry out the directions given—i.e. the petitioner(s) will: (i) set the petition down for hearing on the date fixed; (ii) lodge the settled draft of the advertisement and an engrossment thereof in the chambers of the registrar (whereupon the court will send a copy of the sealed order for directions to the petitioner(s)' solicitors); (iii) advertise the petition as directed; (iv) lodge in the chambers of the registrar a copy of the newspaper containing the advertisement; (v) give notice of the hearing of the petition to any member or debenture-holder required by the order for directions to be notified; and (vi) where notices are required, swear and file an affidavit proving service of the necessary notices.

5.82 The hearing

The hearing will be before the Companies Court Judge sitting in open court. Members or debenture-holders who are not parties to the petition may appear at the hearing of the petition to support or oppose it, but a member of a class who does not himself hold a sufficient proportion of the nominal value of that class to petition, may not support the petition on grounds other than those relied upon by the petitioner(s).

5.83 The order

The Act gives the court a wide discretion in deciding what relief (if any) should be granted on the application to cancel the alteration. The court may:

381. S. 725(1).
382. RSC O. 102, r. 6(3).

(1) refuse to confirm the alteration, in which case the alteration does not take effect[383];
(2) confirm the alteration in whole or in part, imposing such terms and conditions as the court thinks fit[384];
(3) adjourn the petition in order to enable arrangements to be made for buying out the dissentient members[385] and perhaps make directions to facilitate a buy-out[386];
(4) order that the company should buy out the dissentient members, and reduce the company's capital, or alter its memorandum or articles of association as necessary[387] (in which case, the alteration of the memorandum or articles of association is valid and effective as if made by a resolution of the company[388]);
(5) prohibit the company from making any subsequent alteration to its memorandum or articles of association, or prohibit particular alterations by the company—in either case, a purported alteration without the leave of the court in contravention of the order is ineffective.[389]

5.84 Costs

The usual practice of the High Court as to the incidence of costs[390] applies in relation to challenges to alterations to a company's constitution made by special resolution: in particular, the principle that costs should generally follow the event will apply. Where the challenge succeeds (i.e. the court refuses to confirm the alteration), the company is likely to be ordered to pay the costs occasioned by the application; where the challenge fails (i.e. the court confirms the alteration), the dissentient shareholders are likely to be ordered to pay the costs. Where the unsuccessful petitioner is a representative petitioner who has been authorised to petition on behalf of a number of other dissentient members or debenture-holders,[391] the proper order would be for the company's costs to be paid by all the dissentient members or debenture-holders, not just by the petitioner.[392] Aside from the above, it is difficult to state with certainty what order for costs the court will make in a particular situation, given that the Act gives the court a wide discretion in granting relief on a petition[393] and costs are generally at the discretion of the court.[394] The following points are made as a guide only.

5.84.1 Where the court confirms the alteration only in part, or makes some other order (for example, an order to buy out the dissentients), the incidence of costs will generally depend on the extent to which it can be said that the dissentients have succeeded in their challenge to the alteration, and apportionment of the costs may be necessary. Where

383. Ss. 4(2), 17(1) and 690(2).
384. S. 5(4).
385. S. 5(4)(a).
386. S. 5(4)(b).
387. S. 5(5).
388. S. 5(7).
389. S. 5(6).
390. See generally RSC O. 62.
391. Under s. 5(3).
392. Relying, if necessary, on the court's power to order costs to be borne by a non-party: see the Supreme Court Act 1981, s. 51; *Aiden Shipping Ltd* v. *Interbulk Ltd* [1986] AC 965.
393. See s. 5(4)(5) and para. 5.83, *supra*.
394. See RSC O. 62, r. 3.

members or debenture-holders (who are not petitioners and have not authorised the petitioner to bring the proceedings) appear on the hearing of the petition to support or oppose it, the incidence of their costs is also likely to follow the event: where their support or opposition is unsuccessful, they are likely to bear their own costs of supporting or opposing the petition; where their support or opposition is successful, their costs of supporting or opposing the petition are likely to be payable by the company or the petitioner(s) (including their appointors) respectively. However, the court may disallow the costs or part of the costs of supporters or opposers where, for example, there is unnecessary duplication of legal representation by them, or a supporter was entitled and able to join in the authorisation of a representative petitioner but failed to do so.

5.85 Registration of the order

The company should obtain from the court an office copy of the order and deliver it to the registrar of companies within 15 days of the order being made.[395] Where the order confirms the alteration objected to, the company must also, within 15 days of the making of the order, deliver a copy of the memorandum or articles of association, as amended pursuant to s. 4(1) or 17(1) respectively, or a copy of the memorandum or articles of association substituted for the deed of settlement under s. 690(1).[396] The court has power to extend the 15-day limit for such period as it thinks proper at any time (i.e. both before and after the expiry of the period).[397] If difficulty in complying with the 15-day limit is anticipated by the company at the hearing of the petition, an application for an extension of time should be made to the judge hearing the petition (who may require affidavit evidence explaining the difficulty in complying with the usual 15-day period for delivery of the documents). If the difficulty is appreciated only after the hearing of the petition is concluded, the application by the company for an extension of time should be made by *ex parte* summons to the Companies Court Registrar in chambers. The summons should be supported by an affidavit explaining why it is not possible to comply with the usual 15-day time limit.

(b) Petition to cancel a variation of a shareholder's class rights

5.86 Jurisdiction

Where a company's share capital is divided into different classes of shares[398] which have attached to them differing rights and obligations (i.e. where there are "class rights"), such rights may be varied in one of two ways: (i) the memorandum or articles of association of the company may permit the variation of the rights attaching to a class of shares with the consent of a specified constituency of that class or by a resolution of a separate meeting of that class of shareholders[399]; or (ii) where rights are attached to a company's shares in its articles of association and the articles do not provide for the variation of those rights, they may be varied pursuant to a statutory power of variation if the holders of three-

395. S. 6(1)(b)(ii).
396. Ss. 6(1)(b)(ii), 17(3) and 690(2).
397. S. 6(2).
398. Most commonly, ordinary shares and preference shares.
399. See s. 127(1)(a).

quarters in nominal value of the issued shares of that class of shares consent in writing to the variation or an extraordinary resolution approving the variation is duly passed at a properly convened separate meeting of that class by three-quarters of the members of the class present (i.e. a class extraordinary resolution).[400] Where class rights are so varied[401] (whether pursuant to a power contained in the memorandum or articles of association or pursuant to the statutory power), the Act permits dissentient members of the class in question to seek the cancellation of the variation.[402]

5.87 The court's powers

The court's powers on an application for the cancellation of a variation of class rights under s. 127(2) are discretionary.[403] Those powers differ in two important respects from the court's powers on an application for the cancellation of an alteration to a company's constitution under ss. 5(1), 17(3) and 690(2) discussed above.[404] First, the court may only interfere with a variation of class rights where it is satisfied that the variation would unfairly prejudice the shareholders of the class represented by the petitioner,[405] whereas the Act does not stipulate any criteria for the exercise of the court's discretion under s. 5 to confirm or refuse to confirm an alteration to the company's constitution. Secondly, where a variation of class rights is challenged, the court's powers are considerably more limited than on a petition to challenge an alteration to the company's constitution under s. 5: the court *may* disallow the variation of class rights where it is satisfied, having regard to all the circumstances of the case, that it would unfairly prejudice the class to which the applicants belong, and the court *must* confirm the variation if it is not so satisfied.[406] The petition should accordingly contain an averment that the variation would unfairly prejudice the class of shareholders represented by the petitioner(s), and the affidavit in support should establish the unfair prejudice alleged. The Act does not give the court the wide discretion to make consequential orders and directions which it enjoys on an application under s. 5[407] to cancel an alteration to a company's constitution. Moreover, the court's decision on a petition under s. 127(2) challenging a variation of class rights is final[408] and may not be appealed.

5.88 Procedure

The procedure whereby a member of a class may challenge a variation of his class rights is the same as the procedure for challenging an alteration in the company's constitution under ss. 5, 17(1) and 690(2) of the Act discussed above.[409] The application is made by

400. S. 125(2).
401. A "variation" of class rights in this context includes an abrogation of such rights: s. 127(6).
402. See s. 127(2). See generally, *Supreme Court Practice 1997*, Vol. 1, paras 102/4/26–102/4/28, pp. 1559–1560.
403. See s. 127(4).
404. See paras 5.72–5.85, *supra*.
405. S. 127(4): this appears to require that the variation be prejudicial to the class as a whole, not merely to the petitioner(s), in order for the court to intervene.
406. *Ibid.*
407. S. 5(4)–(7): see para. 5.83, *supra*.
408. S. 127(4).
409. See paras 5.69–5.85, *supra*.

petition,[410] which must be presented within 21 days of the date on which the requisite majority of the class consented to the variation of class rights or passed a resolution sanctioning the variation.[411] The Act does not permit any extension of the 21-day period. Once a petition has been presented, the variation does not take effect unless and until it is confirmed by the court.[412]

5.89 Parties: the petitioners

The petitioners must hold not less in aggregate than 15% of the issued shares of the class in question, and must not have consented to or voted in favour of the resolution for the variation.[413] Each of the dissentient members of the class whose shareholdings comprise the 15% shareholding qualification may be named as petitioners, or they may all appoint in writing one of their number as a representative petitioner to bring the proceedings on their behalf.[414] Any such appointment must be made before the petition is presented, to be effective.[415] Section 127 permits a variation of class rights to be challenged only by members of the class in question,[416] and does not permit debenture-holders to petition.[417] The Act expressly permits a person who claims to be interested in the application to apply to the court to be heard on the petition; and if it appears to the court that the person is interested in the application, the court will permit that person to be heard.[418] An interested third party who wishes to be heard on the petition should preferably apply in advance of the hearing of the petition for leave to be heard on the petition: the application should be by originating summons[419] (or by ordinary summons in the existing petition proceedings if a general liberty to apply has already been granted, say, at the summons for directions), returnable before the Companies Court Registrar in chambers. The summons should be supported by an affidavit setting out the nature of the third party's interest and explaining why it is desirable or necessary for him to be heard on the petition: for example, he may represent a class of persons who are affected by the variation of class rights sought to be cancelled, but whose interests are not conveniently represented by the petitioner(s) or the respondent (i.e. the company). Where the application for leave to be heard on the petition is opposed, the registrar may adjourn the summons to the Companies Court Judge for determination in advance of the hearing of the petition. Alternatively, the registrar may leave the question to be determined by the judge who hears the petition and, in that event, the interested third party will make his application to be heard at the hearing of the petition. It is preferable, however, for the identity of the parties who will be heard on the petition to be decided at an early stage if possible. This will enable the third party to participate in the filing of evidence if he so wishes. At the hearing of the summons for

410. RSC O. 102, r. 4(1)(e) and see *Supreme Court Practice 1997*, Vol. 1, paras 102/4/26–102/4/28, pp. 1559–1560.
411. S. 127(3).
412. S. 127(2).
413. *Ibid.*
414. S. 127(3).
415. See para 5.75, *supra* and the cases there cited.
416. S. 127(2).
417. Contrast challenges to alterations in the company's constitution under ss. 5(2)(b) and 690(2): para. 5.75, *supra*.
418. S. 127(4).
419. RSC O. 102, r. 2(1).

directions,[420] the Companies Court Registrar may direct that the advertisement[421] should state that any person who appears to be interested and wishes to apply to be heard on the petition should attend the hearing in person or by counsel. It may also be convenient to direct that any person intending to appear at the hearing of the petition should give notice of that fact to the petitioner(s) in order that any consequential directions (for example, as to evidence) can be sought.

5.90 The order

As mentioned above,[422] the range of orders which a court may make on a petition under s. 127 for the cancellation of a variation of class rights is considerably more limited than where the challenge is to an alteration in the company's constitution under s. 5[423]: the court can only confirm or disallow the variation.[424] The company must send a copy of the order to the registrar of companies within 15 days after the making of the order,[425] and the Act does not permit the court to extend that time limit.[426]

(c) Petition to cancel the re-registration of a public company as private

5.91 Jurisdiction

A public company may be re-registered as a private company if: (i) a special resolution that the company should be re-registered as a private company is duly passed,[427] which amends the company's memorandum so that it no longer states that the company is a public company and amends any other provisions in the company's memorandum or articles of association which are inappropriate for a private company[428]; (ii) an application for re-registration as a private company in the prescribed form,[429] signed by a director or the secretary of the company is duly delivered to the registrar of companies, together with a copy of the amended memorandum and articles of association[430]; and (iii) there has been no application under s. 54 for the cancellation of the special resolution for re-registration, or the application has failed.[431]

5.92 Jurisdiction to challenge re-registration

Where a public company duly passes a special resolution for its re-registration as a private company, the Act permits members who object to the re-registration to apply to the court

420. See para. 5.80, *supra*.
421. See para. 5.81, *supra*.
422. See para. 5.87, *supra*.
423. See para. 5.83, *supra*.
424. S. 127(4).
425. S. 127(5).
426. Contrast s. 6(2).
427. S. 53(1)(a).
428. S. 53(2).
429. I.e. Form No. 53 of the Companies (Forms) Regulations 1985, S.I. 1985 No. 854, as amended (*inter alia*) by S.I. 1995 No. 736.
430. S. 53(1)(b).
431. S. 53(1)(c), (d).

for the cancellation of the special resolution.[432] The application must be made: (a) by the holders of not less in aggregate than 5% in nominal value of the company's issued share capital or any class thereof; or (b) where the company is not limited by shares, by not less than 5% of its members in number; or (c) by not less than 50 of the company's members.[433] The dissentient applicants must not have consented to or voted in favour of the resolution for re-registration as a private company.[434]

5.93 Procedure for challenging re-registration

The procedure for seeking the cancellation of a special resolution for re-registration as a private company is virtually identical to the procedure under s. 5 of the Act for challenging a special resolution altering a company's constitution, discussed above.[435] The following paragraphs summarise the salient features of an application seeking the cancellation of a special resolution for re-registration as a private company and identify the respects in which it differs from an application seeking the cancellation of an alteration to the company's constitution.

5.94 Form of application

The application for the cancellation of a special resolution for re-registration as a private company is made by petition[436] supported by affidavit. The petition and affidavit in support should show that the petitioners have the requisite standing to petition[437] and should explain why they object to the re-registration of the company as a private company. This will usually involve an allegation that the petitioners would be prejudiced by the re-registration.

5.95 Parties

The petitioners will be the member or members who object to the re-registration and who hold the requisite proportion of the company's nominal share capital or constitute the requisite proportion of the company's members in number.[438] Where more than one member objects to the resolution for re-registration, those entitled to petition may appoint one of their number in writing as a sole representative petitioner to conduct the proceedings on their behalf.[439] Any such appointment must be made before the petition is presented and will not be effective if made after presentation but before the hearing of the petition.[440] The company should be the respondent to the petition.

432. S. 54(1).
433. S. 54 (2).
434. *Ibid.*
435. See paras 5.69–5.85, *supra*.
436. RSC O. 102, r. 4(1)(j). See generally, *Supreme Court Practice 1997*, Vol. 1, para. 102/4/7, p. 1552.
437. See s. 54(2) and para. 5.92, *supra*.
438. *Ibid.*
439. S. 54(3).
440. See para. 5.75, *supra* and the cases there cited.

5.96 Timing

The petition must be presented within 28 days after the date on which the resolution for re-registration as a private company was passed.[441] The company must forthwith give notice of the presentation of the petition to the registrar of companies.[442]

5.97 No summons for directions

Where dissentient members apply under s. 54 for the cancellation of a special resolution for re-registration as a private company, they are not required to issue a summons for directions.[443] The company may file evidence in answer to the petition prior to its first hearing but, in most cases, directions for the filing of further evidence will be given by the Companies Court Registrar at the first hearing of the petition. The registrar might also direct the cross-examination of deponents. Once the evidence is complete, the registrar is likely to adjourn the petition to the Companies Court Judge for determination.

5.98 The order

On the hearing of the petition, the court must either cancel or confirm the resolution for re-registration as a private company.[444] In addition, the Act gives the court a wide discretion by its order to impose such terms and conditions as it thinks fit[445]: these may include directions for the purchase of the dissentient members' shares by the majority shareholders,[446] or for the purchase of those shares by the company itself and a reduction of capital accordingly[447]; or the order may prohibit any future alterations, or specified alterations, in the company's memorandum or articles of association without the leave of the court.[448] An office copy of the court's order must be sent to the registrar of companies within 15 days of the order being made, unless the court extends time for the delivery of the office copy.[449]

(d) Petition to cancel a resolution approving the giving of financial assistance by a private company for the acquisition of shares

5.99 Introduction

The statutory prohibition on a company giving financial assistance, directly or indirectly, for the purpose of an acquisition of shares in that company or its holding company,[450] may be disapplied in relation to a private company if, *inter alia*, the giving of the financial

441. S. 54(3).
442. S. 54(4).
443. RSC O. 102, r. 6(2)(c). Contrast the requirement where the challenge is to an alteration in a company's constitution: see para. 5.80, *supra*.
444. S. 54(5).
445. *Ibid.*
446. S. 54(5)(a).
447. S. 54(6).
448. S. 54(8).
449. S. 54(7). The procedure for applying for an extension of time is discussed in para. 5.85, *supra*.
450. I.e. s. 151.

assistance is approved by a special resolution of the company in general meeting.[451] Where the giving of the financial assistance is approved by special resolution, the Act permits dissentient members to apply to the court for an order cancelling the special resolution.[452]

5.100 Procedure

An application for the cancellation of a special resolution approving the giving of financial assistance by a private company is made by petition[453] supported by affidavit. The petition must be presented by or on behalf of the holders of not less in aggregate than 10% in nominal value of the company's issued share capital or any class of it, or where the company is not limited by shares, by not less than 10% of the company's members in number.[454] Where more than one member is entitled to petition, those entitled to petition may appoint one of their number, in writing, as a sole representative petitioner to conduct the proceedings on their behalf.[455] Any such appointment must be made before the petition is presented, to be effective.[456] The petitioner(s) and those who authorise the petition must not have consented to or voted in favour of the resolution.[457] The company should be the respondent to the petition. In all other respects, the procedure on such a petition is identical to the procedure on a petition to challenge a special resolution for the re-registration of a public company as a private company,[458] discussed above.[459]

(e) Petition to cancel a resolution approving a payment out of capital by a private company for the redemption or purchase of its own shares

5.101 Introduction

Where a private company proposes to redeem or purchase its own shares, it may do so out of its capital rather than out of distributable profits[460] if, *inter alia*, it is authorised to do so by its articles, and the payment out of capital is approved by a special resolution of the company in general meeting.[461] Where such a resolution is passed, the Act enables any dissentient member who did not vote in favour of the resolution, or any dissentient creditor, to apply to the court for an order cancelling the resolution.[462]

5.102 Procedure

The procedure for challenging a special resolution approving a payment out of capital by a private company for the redemption or purchase of its own shares is identical to the

451. Ss. 155(4) and 157.
452. S. 157(2).
453. RSC O. 102, r. 4(1)(k). See generally, *Supreme Court Practice 1997*, Vol. 1, para. 102/4/7, p. 1552.
454. S. 157(2).
455. Ss. 157(3) and 54(3).
456. See para. 5.75, *supra* and the case there cited.
457. S. 157(2).
458. S. 157(3).
459. See paras 5.91–5.98, *supra*.
460. Ss. 171–177.
461. S. 173(2).
462. S. 176(1).

procedure under s. 54 of the Act for challenging a special resolution for the re-registration of a public company as a private company, discussed above.[463] The following paragraphs summarise the salient features of an application under s. 176 to challenge a special resolution approving a payment out of capital.

5.103 Form of application

The application is made by petition supported by affidavit.[464] The petition and affidavit should explain why the payment out of capital is opposed: this will usually involve detailed evidence as to the company's solvency and future trading prospects, in order to establish that the directors' belief as to solvency and the company's ability safely to make a payment out of capital[465] is unsound or unduly optimistic.

5.104 Parties

The application to cancel the special resolution approving a payment out of capital may be made by any member of the company who did not consent to vote in favour of the resolution or by any creditor of the company.[466] Where the application is made by a member or members of the company, there is no minimum shareholding requirement nor minimum number of petitioners imposed by the Act. Where the special resolution is objected to by more than one member and/or creditor of the company, they may all be named as petitioners. Alternatively, those who object to the special resolution may appoint one or more of their number in writing to conduct the petition on their behalf as a representative petitioner.[467] To be effective, the appointment should be made prior to the presentation of the petition.[468] The company should be the respondent to the application.

5.105 Timing

The petition seeking the cancellation of the resolution must be presented within five weeks of the date on which the resolution was passed.[469] Once a petition is presented, the company must forthwith give the registrar of companies notice of its presentation[470] in the prescribed form.[471]

5.106 The court's powers

The Act gives the court a wide discretion in the orders which it may make on hearing a petition under s. 176 to challenge a special resolution for the redemption or purchase of

463. See paras 5.91–5.98, *supra*.
464. RSC O. 102, r. 4(1)(k). See generally, *Supreme Court Practice 1997*, Vol. 1, para. 102/4/7, p. 1552.
465. See s. 173(3).
466. S. 176(1).
467. S. 176(2).
468. See para 5.75, *supra* and the cases there cited.
469. S. 176(1).
470. S. 176(3)(a).
471. Form No. 176 of the Companies (Forms) Regulations 1985, S.I. 1986 No. 854, as amended.

shares out of capital[472]: (i) the court may adjourn the petition to enable arrangements to be made for the purchase of dissentient members' shareholdings in the company or for the protection of the interests of dissentient creditors, and in either case, the court may make such supplemental directions or orders as it thinks fit, to facilitate the arrangements[473]; (ii) if the court does not adjourn the petition under s. 177(1), it must either confirm or cancel the special resolution and, in so doing, may impose whatever terms it thinks fit[474]; (iii) if the court confirms the special resolution, it may vary or extend any time-limit for the redemption or purchase of the shares in the company (whether imposed by the resolution itself or by the Act)[475]; (iv) the court may order that the company should purchase the shares of any member of the company, that the company's capital be reduced accordingly, and that any necessary alterations be made to the company's memorandum and articles of association[476]; and (v) the court may prohibit the company from making any, or any specified, alterations in its memorandum or articles of association without the leave of the court, and any subsequent purported alteration without such leave will be void.[477]

2. APPLICATIONS TO OBTAIN ACCESS TO COMPANY DOCUMENTS

5.107 Introduction

The Act contains a number of provisions which require a company to maintain various registers, indices and records, and to make those documents available for inspection.[478] Where the company refuses to allow inspection of documents which the Act requires the company to make available, a person entitled to inspection may apply to the court for an order directing the company: (i) to make the documents available for immediate inspection by the applicant(s); or (ii) in certain cases to supply a copy of the document to the applicant(s). Depending on the category of documents, the Act requires the company to allow inspection by its members,[479] its debenture-holders,[480] its creditors,[481] or any other person,[482] and in the latter case may require that inspection should only be available on payment of the appropriate fee.[483] The manner in which inspection should be allowed and the fee payable for inspection is regulated by statutory instrument.[484] Where the company refuses to permit inspection, or permits inspection only on unduly restrictive terms which do not comply with the regulations laid down in the statutory instrument, a person entitled to inspection may apply to the court for an order directing the company to permit inspection in accordance with those regulations. The procedure whereby an aggrieved

472. S. 177.
473. S. 177(1).
474. S. 177(2).
475. *Ibid.*
476. S. 177(3), (5).
477. S. 177(4).
478. See, for example, ss. 169(5), 175(6), 191(1), 219(1), 288(3), 318(7), 325(5) (and part IV of sch. 13), 356(1), 383(1), and 408(1).
479. See ss. 169(5), 175(6), 191(1)(a), 219(1), 288(3), 318(7), 325(5), 356(1), 383(1) and 408(1).
480. See s. 191(1)(a).
481. See ss. 175(6)(b) and 408(1).
482. See ss. 191(1)(b) and 219(1).
483. See ss. 191(1)(b), 288(3), 325(5) and 356(1).
484. Companies (Inspection and Copying of Registers, Indices and Documents) Regulations 1991, S.I. 1991 No. 1998.

person may compel inspection of a document which the company has refused to make available is the same whether the applicant is a member, debenture-holder, creditor or other person. The following paragraphs set out the documents which must be made available for inspection before describing the common procedure for compelling inspection.

5.108 Documents available for inspection

A company must make available the following documents to the following persons:

Documents	***Persons entitled to inspection***
(i) A contract for the purchase by a company of its own shares.	*Any member of the company, or in the case of a public company, any person, in each case without charge.*[485]
(ii) The directors' statutory declaration and the auditors' report for a company's redemption or purchase of its own shares out of capital.	*Any member or creditor of the company, without charge.*[486]
(iii) A company's register of debenture-holders.	*Any such debenture-holder or any member without payment of any fee; and any other person on payment of the prescribed fee.*[487]
(iv) A report by a public company to its members of the results of an investigation into interests in its shares under s. 212 of the Act.	*Any member of the company or any other person, without charge.*[488]
(v) The register of a company's directors and secretaries.	*Any member of the company, without charge; and any other person on payment of the prescribed fee.*[489]
(vi) A director's service contract, or a memorandum of its terms.	*Any member of the company, without charge.*[490]
(vii) The register of directors' interests in their company's share capital.	*Any member of the company, without charge; and any other person on payment of the prescribed fee.*[491]

485. S. 169(5).
486. S. 175(6)(b).
487. S. 191(1).
488. S. 219(1).
489. S. 288(3).
490. S. 318(7).
491. S. 325(5) and sch. 13, para. 25.

(viii) The company's register of members and index of members' names.	*Any member of the company, without charge, and any other person on payment of the prescribed fee.*[492]
(ix) The company's minute book.	*Any member of the company, without charge.*[493]
(x) Any instrument creating a charge by a company, registrable under s. 396.	*Any member or creditor of the company without charge.*[494]

5.109 Form of application to compel inspection

In each of the above cases, the Act provides that the court may order inspection in the event of a default by the company.[495] The application to compel the company to permit inspection is made by originating summons[496] in the expedited form[497] supported by affidavit. Two copies of the summons will be required on issue, one of which should be stamped with the appropriate fee. The date and time fixed for the hearing will be inserted on both copies, the stamped copy will be retained for filing and the other copy will be returned to the applicant. The summons should be issued at the chambers of the Companies Court Registrar[498] or at any Chancery district registry.[499] Where the applicant is not acting in person, a certificate signed by his solicitor or counsel estimating the time needed for the hearing will be required. A draft order should also be submitted.

5.110 Parties and service

The applicant will be the person(s) entitled to inspection of the document in question under the relevant statutory provision.[500] The company should be named as the respondent to the summons. The summons and affidavit in support should be served on the company by leaving them at, or posting them to, the company's registered office.[501] The Rules of the Supreme Court provide that the summons should be served on the company not less than four clear days before the day fixed for the hearing,[502] and that the affidavit in support should be filed in court and exhibits lodged not less than four clear days before the day

492. S. 356(1).
493. S. 383(1).
494. S. 408(1). This section is prospectively replaced by CA 1989, ss. 92–104, although the amendment will not be brought into force: see para. 5.14, *supra*. If the new provisions were to be brought into force, a new s. 412(1), inserted in the 1985 Act, by the 1989 Act would permit inspection of the register of charges by any member or creditor of the company without charge and by any other person on payment of the prescribed fee; the court would have power to order inspection in the event of default: s. 412(4)(b).
495. See ss. 169(8), 175(8), 191(5), 219(4), 288(5), 318(9), 326(6), 356(6), 383(5) and 408(4).
496. RSC O. 102, r. 2(1). See generally, *Supreme Court Practice 1997*, Vol. 1, paras 102/2/2 and 102/2/27, pp. 1535 and 1543.
497. See Form No. 10 in Appendix A to the RSC: *Supreme Court Practice 1997*, Vol. 2, para. 4, p. 6.
498. Room 2.09, second floor, Thomas More Building, Royal Courts of Justice.
499. RSC O. 102, r. 2(4). For the location of the Chancery district registries, see para. 5.2, Note 14, *supra*.
500. See the table in para. 5.108, *supra*.
501. S. 725.
502. RSC O. 28, r. 3(2).

fixed for the hearing.[503] In practice, it will usually be possible to serve the summons and supporting affidavit at an earlier date than required by the Rules, and it is good practice to do so. If service is delayed until shortly before the day fixed for the hearing, as permitted by the Rules, the company may be unable to prepare evidence in answer by the date of the hearing, an adjournment may be necessary, and the applicant may be penalised in costs.

5.111 Affidavit in support

The supporting affidavit should: establish that the applicant falls within the category of persons to whom the Act gives a right of inspection in relation to the document in question[504]; identify the document sought to be inspected; state briefly the circumstances leading up to the applicant's request to inspect the document; describe the applicant's request for inspection, proving that the request was made at a proper time as permitted by the Act[505]; describe the company's refusal or failure to permit inspection, or the company's imposition of unreasonable terms when permitting inspection; and counter any reasons which have been relied upon by the company for refusing inspection—for example, where the company contends that the register sought to be inspected is closed as permitted by the Act,[506] the applicant should explain why the company was not entitled to close its register at that time. The exhibits should contain copies of the applicant's request(s) for inspection (if made in writing), any written refusal by the company, and any other relevant documents. Where the applicant is entitled to inspection of the document in question only on payment of the prescribed fee,[507] the affidavit should describe the applicant's tender of or offer to pay that sum to the company and should assert the applicant's continued willingness to pay the prescribed fee. Where the application is to compel inspection of the company's register of charges or instruments creating a charge,[508] the affidavit must state that the company is registered in England and Wales, as the Act gives no right of inspection in relation to overseas companies.[509] Where the Act entitles the applicant to obtain a copy of a document from the company, the affidavit should similarly identify the copies sought and explain the request and refusal of copies, the tender of the prescribed fee and the applicant's continued willingness to pay that fee.

5.112 Production of copy documents

In respect of the following documents, a person who has a right to inspect the document under the Act also has a right to obtain copies of the document or extracts therefrom: the register of debenture-holders[510]; the register of interests and report under s. 215[511]; the

503. RSC O. 28, r. 2(2).
504. See the table in para. 5.108, *supra*.
505. See ss. 169(4), (5), 175(6) and 408(1).
506. See ss. 191(1) and 356(1).
507. See the table in para. 5.108, *supra*.
508. I.e. under s. 408(1).
509. See s. 408(4).
510. S. 191(2).
511. S. 219(2).

register of directors' interests in the company's shares[512]; the register of members[513]; and the minute book.[514] In each case, the person requesting copies must pay the prescribed fee.[515] Where the company refuses to supply the applicant with the copies to which he is entitled, or imposes unreasonable terms for the production of the copies sought, the court may direct the company to send the copies to the applicant.[516] Where an application is made to compel the company to provide the copies to which the applicant is entitled, the affidavit in support should assert the applicant's willingness to pay the prescribed fee.

5.113 The hearing

In the first instance, the hearing is before the Companies Court Registrar sitting in chambers.[517] Where the evidence is not yet complete, the registrar will give directions for further evidence and adjourn the summons. Once the evidence is complete, the registrar will either determine the application himself, or will adjourn the originating summons to the Companies Court Judge to be heard in open court: the registrar is likely to adjourn the summons to the judge where the application is contested and the hearing would take some time. In cases of real urgency, the registrar may be persuaded to adjourn the summons directly to the judge on the *ex parte* application of the applicant made shortly after the issue of the summons.

5.114 The order

Where the court is satisfied that the applicant is entitled to inspection of the document in question, has duly requested inspection and tendered the prescribed fee (if any), and the company has refused inspection or imposed unreasonable terms for inspection, the court may order the company to give immediate inspection of the document.[518] Where copies of the document have been duly requested by the applicant and production is wrongly refused, or production is only offered on unreasonable terms, the court may order the company to provide the applicant with copies,[519] on payment of the prescribed fee. Where the court orders inspection or the delivery of a copy document, the company will usually be ordered to pay the applicant's costs.

3. APPLICATIONS TO CONVENE COMPANY MEETINGS

5.115 Introduction

From time to time, circumstances may arise within a company which prevent a general meeting being held as required by the company's articles of association or by the Act. Where it is impracticable for whatever reason to convene *or* conduct a general meeting of

512. S. 325(5) and sch. 13, para. 26.
513. S. 356(3).
514. S. 383(3).
515. See the Companies (Inspection and Copying of Registers, Indices and Documents) Regulations 1991 (S.I. 1991 No. 1998), reg. 5 and sch. 2.
516. See ss. 191(5), 219(4), 326(6), 356(6) and 383(5).
517. Room 4.12, fourth floor, Thomas More Building, Royal Courts of Justice.
518. Ss. 169(8), 175(8), 191(5), 219(4), 288(5), 318(9), 326(6), 356(6), 383(5) and 408(4).
519. Ss. 191(5), 219(4), 326(6), 356(6) and 383(5).

a company in accordance with the requirements of its articles or of the Act, the court has power to direct that a meeting be convened, held and conducted in whatever manner the court thinks fit.[520] The court has power to impose any ancillary or consequential directions which it considers to be expedient,[521] and may direct that one member present in person or by proxy should constitute a valid quorate meeting.[522] The order may be made by the court of its own motion, or may be made on the application of any director of the company, or any member of the company who would be entitled to vote at the meeting.[523]

5.116 Form of application

An application for an order of the court convening a meeting of a company, is made by originating summons[524] in the expedited form[525] supported by affidavit. The summons should state precisely the order which the court is asked to make under s. 371, including any ancillary or consequential directions to be made under s. 371(2). It will usually be convenient to set out in a schedule to the summons the resolutions intended to be proposed at the meeting convened by order of the court. The procedure for the issue of the summons is described in Chapter 2 and para. 5.109, *supra*. Where the applicant is not acting in person, a certificate signed by his solicitor or counsel estimating the time required for the hearing will be needed. A draft order should also be submitted.

5.117 Parties and service

The applicant may be a director of the company or a member of the company who would be entitled to vote at the meeting of the company.[526] The company should usually be the respondent to the summons. Where the conduct of one member is preventing the holding of a valid meeting, it may be appropriate to join that member as a respondent[527] who may be ordered to pay the costs of the summons if it is successful, since a costs order against the company would indirectly penalise the applicant if he is a member of the company. The summons and affidavit in support should be served on an individual respondent at his usual or last known address,[528] and should be served on the company by leaving them at, or posting them to, the company's registered office[529]; in either case the summons should be accompanied by a form for acknowledgment of service.[530] The Rules of the Supreme Court provide that the summons should be served on the respondent not less than four clear days before the day fixed for the hearing, and that the affidavit in support should be

520. S. 371(1).
521. See, for example, *Re Sticky Fingers Restaurant Ltd* [1992] BCLC 84 at 90b–d, and the unusual directions given in *Re British Union for the Abolition of Vivisection* [1995] 2 BCLC 1 at 15g–16c.
522. S. 371(2).
523. S. 371(a), (b).
524. RSC O. 102, r. 2(1). See generally, *Supreme Court Practice 1997*, Vol. 1, para. 102/2/3, p. 1535.
525. Form No. 10 in Appendix A to the RSC: *Supreme Court Practice 1997*, Vol. 2, para. 4, p. 6.
526. S. 371(1).
527. See *Re Opera Photographic Ltd* [1989] BCLC 762–763; *Re Sticky Fingers Restaurant Ltd*, *supra*, at 85e; and para. 5.118, *infra*.
528. RSC O. 10, rr. 5(1) and 1(2).
529. S. 725.
530. RSC O. 10, rr. 5(1) and 1(6). For the form of acknowledgment of service, see Form No. 15 in Appendix A to the RSC: *Supreme Court Practice 1997*, Vol. 2, para. 10, p. 14.

filed in court not less than four clear days before the day fixed for the hearing.[531] As explained in para. 5.110, *supra*, it will usually be possible and is good practice to serve the summons earlier than required by the Rules.

5.118 Grounds for the order

The court has a discretion under s. 371 to order a meeting of a company to be convened and conducted in whatever manner the court directs, whenever it is not practicable for any reason to convene or conduct a meeting in accordance with the company's articles or the Act.[532] The jurisdiction under s. 371 can be invoked in a wide range of factual situations: the applicant need not show that it is impossible to call or conduct the meeting, but that it is "impracticable" to do so, which is to be assessed on the particular circumstances of the case.[533] Examples of circumstances in which the court's power under s. 371 has been invoked are: where a company had two members who were also the only directors of the company, and the majority shareholder wished to remove the minority shareholder as a director[534] and appoint a replacement, but the minority shareholder had refused to attend any board meeting or general meeting which required a quorum of two, with the consequence that he could not be removed, a replacement could not be appointed and a transfer of shares by the majority shareholder could not be approved[535]; where a company which required a quorum of two in general meetings had had two members, one of whom had been the sole director and had died, but the articles did not entitle a personal representative to be counted in a quorum until registered as a member, with the consequence that no quorate general meeting could be held and no share registration could be approved by the board; and where a meeting attended by all members was likely to be violently disrupted to the extent that it was impracticable to hold the meeting, the court ordered that a meeting be convened which only member directors or particular shareholders should be entitled to attend, with all other members being entitled to vote only by postal ballot and their right of personal attendance under the articles being dispensed with.[536] Where the court is asked to convene a meeting of a company to consider a resolution for the removal from office of a director under s. 303 of the Act at a time when unfair prejudice proceedings under s. 459 of the Act are pending, the court retains a discretion whether to make the order sought under s. 371[537]: the court may order a meeting to be convened or it may refuse to make an order, leaving any deadlock to be resolved in the unfair prejudice proceedings. Alternatively, the court may, in its discretion, convene a meeting to allow relatively non-contentious but essential business (such as the consideration of accounts and VAT returns) to be conducted, but direct that contentious business which is objected to in the unfair prejudice proceedings (such as the removal of the

531. RSC O. 28, rr. 2(2) and 3(2).
532. S. 371(1).
533. *Re British Union for the Abolition of Vivisection*, *supra*, at 13a–h; *Re El Sombrero Ltd* [1958] Ch. 900 at 904.
534. I.e. under s. 303.
535. *Re Opera Photographic Ltd* [1989] BCLC 763; *Re HR Paul & Son Ltd* (1973) 118 Sol J 166; *Re El Sombrero Ltd* [1958] Ch. 900.
536. *Re British Union for the Abolition of Vivisection*, *supra*, at 14g–15g.
537. *Re Whitchurch Insurance Consultants Ltd* [1993] BCLC 1359 at 1362e–f; *Harman* v. *BML Group Ltd* [1994] 1 WLR 893 at 897e–f.

petitioner from office) should not be dealt with until resolved in the unfair prejudice proceedings.[538]

5.119 Grounds for refusing an order

The court will not order a meeting of a company to be convened under s. 371 where to do so would override the class rights of some of the company's members.[539] Where a company requires its two members to be present either in person or by proxy to form a quorum, and one member believes that the other would not attend a general meeting, the former should not seek an order under s. 371 unless the other member has actually failed to attend a meeting or has clearly indicated that he will not attend: if the application is issued merely on an apprehension that the other will not attend a meeting without any evidence of the other's intention, the court may not be able to conclude that it is impracticable to hold the meeting and may dismiss the application as premature.[540] S.371 is a procedural section which does not enable the court to vary substantive voting rights or to override a potential deadlock by allowing one 50% shareholder to overthrow another 50% shareholder.[541]

5.120 Affidavit in support

The affidavit in support of the summons should describe the company's date of incorporation, its authorised and issued capital, the division of its issued shares and the constitution of its board (if relevant to the application). The affidavit should explain the requirements for validly convening and conducting a meeting of the company under the articles of association, and exhibit a print of the company's memorandum and articles of association. The affidavit should also state why it is impracticable to convene or conduct a meeting in accordance with such requirements. Where the application is based on an abuse of the company's quorum provisions,[542] the affidavit should show that the convening of a meeting has proved to be impracticable or would clearly be impracticable, rather than merely stating a belief that it would be impracticable.[543]

5.121 The hearing

In the first instance, the hearing is before the Companies Court Registrar in chambers.[544] If the evidence is not then complete, the registrar will adjourn the summons to allow the evidence to be completed. Once the evidence is complete, the registrar may either determine the application himself or adjourn the summons to the Companies Court Judge sitting in open court for determination. Where the hearing of the application will take some time or is contested, the registrar is likely to adjourn the summons to the judge. In

538. *Re Sticky Fingers Restaurant Ltd*, *supra*, at 88f–g and 90b–d.
539. *Harman* v. *BML Group Ltd*, *supra*, 898f–h.
540. *Re Jeda Holdings Pty Ltd* (1977) ACLR 438 at 441–442 (Supreme Court of New South Wales).
541. *Ross* v. *Telford*, New Law Digest, 25 June 1997; *The Times*, 4 July 1997.
542. See, for example, *Re Opera Photographic Ltd*, *supra*.
543. See *Re Jeda Holdings Pty Ltd*, *supra*.
544. Room 4.12, fourth floor, Thomas More Building, Royal Courts of Justice.

cases of real urgency, the registrar may be prepared to adjourn the summons directly to the judge at the request of the applicant, made shortly after the issue of the summons.

5.122 The order

The Act gives the court a wide discretion to make whatever order it thinks fit for the calling, holding or conducting of a meeting which would otherwise be impracticable.[545] The order may be made to cure a difficulty in convening the meeting (for example, when a quorum cannot be achieved[546]), or in holding the meeting (for example, because of the probable violent disruption of any meeting[547]). The court also has a wide power to make ancillary or consequential directions, and may direct that a meeting may be validly held with a lesser quorum than is required by the company's articles, including a quorum of one.[548] The order convening a meeting under s. 371 may limit the business to be conducted at the meeting—for example, to the consideration of a resolution for the appointment of directors or for voluntary winding-up. Where the company has directors in office who are able to call a meeting, the order will usually direct those directors to convene the meeting, and the court will give directions for the applicant to serve the order on those directors. Where there are no directors in office who are able to convene the meeting, the order may direct the applicants to convene the meeting, and the court may give directions as to the manner in which notice of the meeting is to be given. Alternatively, (although less commonly) the order may itself contain a notice convening the meeting and, in such a case, the court would give directions for service of the order on all persons entitled to receive notice of the meeting. The order should include a liberty to apply, under which the applicant(s) may seek further directions if it transpires that the court's original order cannot be given effect to, or is ineffective in convening a meeting. The costs of the application will normally follow the event: where the application fails, the court will usually order the applicant to pay the respondent's costs; but where the court orders a meeting under s. 371, the respondent will generally be ordered to pay the applicant's costs. Where one member has refused to attend a meeting to prevent there being a quorum, an order for costs against the company would indirectly penalise the member applicant who is prepared to attend the meeting. In those circumstances, the individual respondent may be ordered to pay the costs of the applicant.[549]

Convening meetings of debenture holders

5.123 Introduction

It is convenient to mention here the power of the court in certain circumstances to summon a meeting of a company's debenture holders to consider a resolution to extend the benefit of a provision which exempts a trustee of a trust deed for securing an issue of debentures from liability for breach of trust.[550] This arises where the trust deed validly contains an

545. See s. 371(1).
546. *Re Opera Photographic Ltd, supra*, at 765d–h.
547. *Re British Union for the Abolition of Vivisection, supra.*
548. S. 371(2).
549. See, for example, the order made in *Re Opera Photographic Ltd, supra*, at 765h.
550. S. 192(4).

exemption provision (which was in force on 1 July 1948) in favour of one trustee[551] but makes no provision for summoning meetings to extend the benefit to other trustees. In such a case, a meeting of debenture holders may be summoned in any manner approved by the court.[552] Such applications are very rarely encountered in practice, and the relevant procedure is described below only in outline.

5.124 Procedure

The applicant may be the company, the trustees or any debenture holder. The application is made by *ex parte* originating summons,[553] returnable before the Companies Court Registrar in chambers. The procedure for the issue of the summons is as described in para. 5.109, *supra*.

5.125 Affidavit in support

The summons should be supported by an affidavit proving that the requirements of s. 192 of the Act are satisfied. The affidavit should identify (and exhibit) the trust deed or contract containing the provision which exempts a trustee from liability or indemnifies him and which was in force on 1 July 1948[554]; prove that there is presently at least one trustee who enjoys the benefit of that provision[555]; explain why it is thought appropriate to extend the benefit of that provision to other trustees by a resolution passed at a meeting of debenture holders,[556] but that the deed or contract does not provide for the convening of such a meeting; and describe when and where the proposed meeting would be held and how it would be conducted.

4. APPLICATIONS TO COMPEL PERFORMANCE OF OBLIGATIONS OF THE COMPANY OR ITS DIRECTORS

5.126 Introduction

The Companies Act 1985 contains a number of provisions which enable an application to be made to the court for an order compelling the company and/or its directors to perform obligations imposed on them by the Act or by the company's articles where they are in default of such obligations.[557] In each case, the court's power is discretionary. It is convenient to consider these applications together, although the form of application[558] differs, depending on the obligation sought to be enforced.

551. S. 192(1)–(3).
552. S. 192(4).
553. RSC O. 102, r. 2(1). See generally, *Supreme Court Practice 1997*, Vol. 1, paras 102/2/22–102/2/23, pp. 1541–1542. For the form of the summons, see Form No. 11 in Appendix A to the RSC: *Supreme Court Practice 1997*, Vol. 2, para. 5, p. 7.
554. S. 192(3)(a).
555. *Ibid.*
556. S. 192(4).
557. The procedure to compel access to documents maintained by a company is described in paras 5.107–5.114, *supra*. The procedure on applications to be released from obligations under the Act is described in paras 5.134–5.141, *infra*.
558. See para. 5.127, *infra*.

5.126.1 Delivery up of share certificates, debentures and debenture stock certificates

Where shares, debentures and debenture stock in a company are allotted or transferred, and the company fails to have the relevant certificates or debentures ready for delivery within two months as required by s. 185(1) of the Act, the person entitled to receive the certificates or debentures may serve a notice on the company requiring it to make good the default within 10 days; and if the company remains in default after the expiry of the 10-day period, the person entitled to delivery of the certificates or debentures may apply to the court for an order directing the company, and any officer of the company, to make good the default.[559] The company should be the respondent to the application. It may be appropriate to join as respondent any officer of the company alleged to have been responsible for the default, especially if an order for costs is to be sought against him under s. 185(7), discussed below.

5.126.2 Amendment of the register of interests in shares

Where a person is incorrectly shown in a public company's register of interests in its shares[560] as being interested in shares in that company, he may apply to the company in writing for the amendment of the register, and the company must amend its register if it is satisfied that the applicant should not be shown as being interested in shares in the company.[561] If the company refuses to amend its register, the applicant may apply to the court for an order directing the company to amend its register.[562] The company should be the respondent to the application.

5.126.3 Delivery of accounts to the registrar of companies

Where the directors of a company fail to deliver to the registrar of companies copies of the company's accounts, directors' report and auditors' report for a financial year, within the time required by the Act,[563] any member or creditor of the company, or the registrar of companies, may serve a notice on the directors requiring them to make good the default; if the default continues for a further 14 days, any member or creditor of the company, or the registrar of companies, may apply to the court for an order directing the directors (or some of the directors) to make good the default.[564] The directors should be the respondents to the application.

5.126.4 Delivery of revised accounts

Where the directors of a company deliver accounts to the registrar of companies which, in the opinion of the Secretary of State, do not or may not comply with the requirements of the Act, the Secretary of State may give notice of that fact to the directors, inviting the directors to give an explanation or prepare revised accounts within a stated period of not

559. S. 185(6). See generally, *Supreme Court Practice 1997*, Vol. 1, para. 102/2/11, p. 1538.
560. Maintained under s. 211.
561. S. 217(3), (4).
562. S. 217(5). See generally, *Supreme Court Practice 1997*, Vol. 1, para. 102/3/11, p. 1549.
563. See ss. 242(1) and 244.
564. S. 242(3). See generally, *Supreme Court Practice 1997*, Vol. 1, para. 102/2/28, p. 1543.

less than one month.[565] Thereafter, if the Secretary of State remains dissatisfied with the explanation (if any) given, and no satisfactory revised accounts have been prepared, he or a person authorised by him[566] may apply to the court for a declaration that the accounts of the company do not comply with the requirements of the Act, and for an order requiring the directors to prepare revised accounts.[567] The company and the directors should be named as respondents to the application, notice of which should be given to the registrar of companies, together with a general statement of the matters at issue in the proceedings.[568]

5.126.5 Delivery of returns to the registrar of companies

Where the Act requires a company to deliver any document or return to the registrar of companies, or to give him notice of any matter, and the company is in default of that obligation without having sought an extension of time for compliance (where such an application can be made),[569] any member or creditor of the company or the registrar of companies may serve a notice on the company requiring the company to make good the default; and if the default continues for a further 14 days, any member or creditor of the company or the registrar of companies may apply to the court for an order requiring the company or any officer of the company to make good the default.[570] The company should be the respondent to the application. It may also be appropriate to join as respondent any officer of the company alleged to have been responsible for the default, particularly if an order for costs is sought against him.[571]

5.127 Form of application

Applications to compel delivery of share certificates, debenture stock certificates or debentures, under s. 185(6) of the Act, are made by originating summons[572] in the expedited form[573] returnable before the Companies Court Registrar in chambers.[574] Applications to compel directors to deliver accounts to the registrar of companies under s. 242(3) of the Act, or to compel the company or its officers to make returns to the registrar of companies under s. 713(1) of the Act, are made by originating summons[575] in the general form[576] returnable before the Companies Court Registrar in chambers. Applications to compel a company to amend its register of interests in its shares under s. 217(5)

565. S. 245A(1), (2).
566. Ss. 245B(1)(b) and 245C. The Secretary of State has authorised the Financial Reporting Review Panel Ltd for the purposes of applying to the court under s. 245B: see the Companies (Defective Accounts) (Authorised Person) Order 1991, S.I. 1991 No. 13.
567. Ss. 245A(3) and 245B(1). See generally, *Supreme Court Practice 1997*, Vol. 1, para. 102/3/12, pp. 1549–1550.
568. S. 245B(2).
569. See paras 5.142–5.151, *infra* for the procedure on applications to extend time for making returns to the registrar of companies under ss. 6(2) and 88(6).
570. S. 713(1). See generally, *Supreme Court Practice 1997*, Vol. 1, para. 102/2/12, p. 1538.
571. See s. 713(2).
572. RSC O. 102, r. 2(1).
573. RSC O. 102, r. 2(2). See Form No.10 in Appendix A to the RSC: *Supreme Court Practice 1997*, Vol. 2, para. 4, p. 6.
574. Room 4.12, fourth floor, Thomas More Building, Royal Courts of Justice.
575. RSC O. 102, r. 2(1), (2).
576. Form No. 8 in Appendix A to the RSC: *Supreme Court Practice 1997*, Vol. 2, para. 3, p. 5.

or to compel directors of a company to prepare revised accounts under s. 245B(1), are made by originating motion[577] returnable before the Companies Court Judge. The application should clearly state the obligation which the application wishes the court to order the respondent(s) to perform and, where the applicant seeks to make certain directors responsible for the costs of the application,[578] that relief should also be set out in application. The originating summons or notice of originating motion may be issued at the chambers of the Companies Court Registrar[579] or at any Chancery district registry.[580] Where an originating summons is required, the procedure for its issue is as described in para. 5.109, *supra*. Where a notice of originating motion is required, the procedure for its issue is as described in para. 5.2, *supra*. An affidavit in support of the application is required in all cases, whether the application is by originating summons or notice of originating motion. In an application to compel the delivery of revised accounts under s. 245B(1), the applicant[581] must give the registrar of companies a general statement of the matters in issue in the application, for registration (s. 245B(2)). It is unclear whether the applicant may rely on this statement in court in place of affidavit evidence: neither the Act nor the Rules of the Supreme Court contain any provision permitting its use in court in place of an affidavit, and sworn affidavit evidence is preferable.

5.128 Parties

The persons entitled to apply to the court to compel the performance by a company or its directors of their obligations under the Act or under the company's articles, and the appropriate respondents, are discussed in para. 5.126, *supra*.

5.129 Service and acknowledgement of service

The originating summons or originating motion and evidence in support should be served on the respondents in the usual way: where the company is a respondent, the application and evidence in support should be posted to or left at the company's registered office[582]; where the directors are respondents, the application and evidence in support may be served by leaving them at or sending them by first class post to each of the directors' usual or last known addresses.[583] The relevant time limits for service are as follows:

(i) Where the application is to compel delivery of share or debenture stock certificates or debentures under s. 185(6) (i.e. an originating summons in the expedited form), the summons must be served on the respondent(s) not less than four clear days before the day fixed for the hearing,[584] together with a form for acknowledgement of service[585]; the affidavit in support must be filed in court

577. RSC O. 102, r. 3(1)(h), (i). See Form No. 13 in Appendix A to the RSC: *Supreme Court Practice 1997*, Vol. 2, para. 8, p. 8.
578. See the powers contained in ss. 185(7), 242(3), 245B(4) and 713(2).
579. Room 2.09, second floor, Thomas More Building, Royal Courts of Justice.
580. RSC O. 102, rr. 2(4) and 3(2). For the location of the Chancery district registries, see para. 5.2, Note 14, *supra*.
581. I.e. the Secretary of State or the Financial Reporting Review Panel Ltd.
582. S. 725(1).
583. See RSC O. 10, rr. 1 and 5.
584. RSC O. 28, r. 3(2).
585. RSC O. 10, rr. 5(1) and 1(6). For the form of acknowledgement of service see Form No. 15 in Appendix A to the RSC: *Supreme Court Practice 1997*, Vol. 2, para. 10, p. 14.

and the exhibits lodged not less than four clear days before the day fixed for the hearing[586]; and the respondent(s) must acknowledge service not less than two clear days before the day fixed for the hearing.[587] In practice, it should be possible (and is desirable) to serve the summons and affidavit in support, well before the final day for service under the Rules.

(ii) Where the application is to compel directors to deliver accounts to the registrar of companies under s. 242(3) or to compel the company or its officers to make returns to the registrar of companies under s. 713(1) (i.e. an originating summons in the general form), the respondent must acknowledge service within 14 days of service[588]; within 14 days thereafter the applicant must file in court the affidavit evidence in support of the summons[589] and serve the evidence on the respondent.[590] Any evidence to be relied upon by the respondent should be filed in court and served on the applicant within 28 days of service of the applicant's evidence,[591] and the applicant should file in court and serve on the respondent any evidence in reply within 14 days thereafter.[592] No other affidavit evidence may be filed without the leave of the court,[593] and the court may vary any of the time limits mentioned above.[594] Within one month of the expiry of the time permitted for the completion of evidence, the applicant must obtain a date for the hearing of the originating summons and issue a notice of appointment to hear the originating summons at the chambers of the Companies Court Registrar,[595] which must be served on every respondent at least 14 days before the day fixed for the hearing.[596]

(iii) Where the application is to compel an amendment to a public company's register of interests in its shares under s. 217(5) or to compel directors to prepare revised accounts under s. 245B(1) (i.e. a notice of originating motion), the notice of originating motion and affidavit in support should be served on every respondent at least two clear days before the day fixed for the hearing.[597] The respondent may serve evidence in answer in advance of the hearing, although in many cases there will be insufficient time for evidence to be prepared, and directions for further evidence will be given at the first hearing of the motion.

5.130 Affidavit in support

In all cases an affidavit in support of the application is required, identifying the respects in which the respondent is said to be in breach of its obligations under the Act or under

586. RSC O. 28, rr. 1A(1) and 2(2).
587. RSC O. 28, r. 2(2).
588. RSC O. 12, rr. 5(a) and 9(1).
589. RSC O. 28, r. 1A(1).
590. RSC O. 28, r. 1A(3).
591. RSC O. 28, r. 1A(4).
592. RSC O. 28, r. 1A(5).
593. RSC O. 28, r. 1A(6).
594. RSC O. 28, r. 1A(8).
595. RSC O. 28, r. 2(1). For the form of the Notice of Appointment to hear the originating summons, see Form No. 12 in Appendix A to the RSC: *Supreme Court Practice 1997*, Vol. 2, para. 7, p. 7.
596. RSC O. 28, r. 3(1).
597. RSC O. 8, r. 2(2).

the company's articles of association, and setting out the grounds upon which the applicant claims to be entitled to an order compelling the respondent to remedy that default. The following paragraphs take each application in turn.

5.130.1 Delivery up of share certificates or debentures

The affidavit in support of an application under s. 185(6) should describe: the allotment or transfer of the shares, debenture stock or debentures and the lodgement of a duly stamped and valid transfer (where applicable); the company's failure to deliver up the relevant certificates or debentures within two months[598]; the applicant's requests for delivery up of the relevant certificates or debentures, including details of the notice to remedy the default served on the company under s. 185(6) (which should be exhibited); and the company's continuing default. The relevant articles of association should be referred to, and a print of the memorandum and articles of association should be exhibited. The affidavit should also deal with the reasons (if any) relied on by the company for not issuing the relevant certificates or debentures. Where the applicant seeks an order[599] that the costs of the application should be paid by a particular officer of the company rather than by the company itself, the affidavit should fully explain that person's role in the default in issuing the certificates or debentures.

5.130.2 Amendment of the register of interests in shares

The affidavit in support of an application under s. 217(5) should describe: briefly the history of the applicant's dealing with the company; the circumstances in which the applicant came to be entered in the company's register of interests in its shares (if known); how the applicant became aware of the contents of the register; why the register is inaccurate and the precise respects in which the register requires amendment; the applicant's requests to the company that the register be amended under subs. 217(3) or (4); the company's refusal or failure to make the amendment requested; and why any reasons relied upon by the company for not making the amendment are unfounded.

5.130.3 Delivery of accounts

The affidavit in support of an application under s. 242(3) should describe: the applicant's standing in relation to the company (i.e. where the applicant is not the registrar of companies, the affidavit should prove that the applicant is a member or creditor of the company); when the accounts were due for delivery to the registrar of companies; the directors' failure to lay and deliver accounts as required by s. 244 of the Act; the applicant's requests to the directors that they should remedy their default, including the service on them of the notice required by s. 242(3); the directors' continuing default for 14 days or more thereafter; and why any reasons relied on by the directors for not delivering accounts are unfounded. Where the applicant seeks to make particular directors liable for the costs occasioned by the application,[600] the affidavit should fully describe the role and responsibility of those directors in allowing the default to occur.

598. S. 185(1).
599. Under s. 185(7).
600. Under s. 242(3).

5.130.4 Delivery of revised accounts

The affidavit in support of an application under s. 245B(1) should describe: the respects in which the applicant considers that the accounts delivered by the company to the registrar of companies do not comply with the Act and require revision; the notice sent to the directors of the company under s. 245A(1) in respect of the accounts; the directors' response thereto (if any); and the reasons why the directors' explanation of the accounts, or any attempted revision of the accounts, is inadequate. The affidavit should also identify which (if any) of the directors the applicant seeks to be made liable for the costs of the application,[601] and the affidavit should fully describe their role and responsibility in the preparation of the defective accounts.

5.130.5 Delivery of returns to the registrar of companies

The affidavit in support of an application under s. 713(1) should describe: the applicant's standing in relation to the company (i.e. where the applicant is not the registrar of companies, the affidavit should prove that the applicant is a member or creditor of the company); the failure of the company to deliver the return(s) in question to the registrar of companies; the applicant's requests that the company should remedy the default(s), including the notice to remedy the default(s) served on the company under s. 713(1) (which should be exhibited); the company's continuing default for 14 days thereafter; and why any reasons relied on by the company for the failure to file the return(s) in question are unfounded. Where the applicant seeks to make particular directors liable for the costs of the application,[602] the affidavit should fully describe the role and responsibility of those directors in allowing the default to occur.

5.131 Respondent's evidence in answer

Where the respondent denies that there has been any breach of obligations imposed by the Act or by the company's articles, the respondent's evidence in answer should explain why—for example, because the applicant has miscalculated the time limit for performing the obligation in question and time for compliance has not yet expired; or because the time for delivery of the return in question has been extended,[603] or because the articles permit the company to act as it did. Where there has been a breach of an obligation imposed by the Act or by the articles, the respondent's affidavit should explain how the default arose and why it was not possible or practicable to comply with the obligation in question. On each of the applications discussed above, the court retains a discretion not to direct that the default be remedied, although it is to be assumed that the court will require compelling reasons before it will refuse to direct that a breach of a statutory obligation or a breach of the articles be remedied. Where the default is one in respect of which the court has power to extend time,[604] the respondent(s) may issue a cross-application seeking an extension of time.[605] In such a case the respondent's evidence should set out all matters relied upon in

601. Under s. 245B(4).
602. Under s. 713(2).
603. See ss. 6(2), 88(6) and 244(5).
604. See ss. 6(2) and 88(6).
605. For the procedure on such an application, see paras 5.142–5.151, *infra*.

support of that application, including the grounds for the extension sought and its duration.

5.132 The hearing

Where the application is to compel delivery of share or debenture stock certificates or debentures under s. 185(6), to compel directors to deliver accounts to the registrar of companies under s. 242(3), or to compel a company or its officers to make returns to the registrar of companies under s. 713(1) (i.e. an application by originating summons), the application will in the first instance be heard by the Companies Court Registrar in chambers.[606] The registrar will initially give directions for any further evidence required. Once the evidence is complete, the registrar will either determine the case himself or adjourn the matter to the Companies Court Judge in open court for determination: an adjournment to the judge is likely where the application is opposed and the hearing would take some time. Applications to compel the amendment of a public company's register of interests under s. 217(5) or to compel the preparation of revised accounts under s. 245B(1) (i.e. applications by originating motion), are heard by the Companies Court Judge, usually sitting in open court.

5.133 The order

On each of the applications discussed above, the court's power to direct that the default in complying with the statutory obligation or the obligation under the articles be remedied, is discretionary. Where the application is to compel the delivery of share certificates or debentures, or the delivery of accounts or other returns to the registrar of companies, the court may order the directors responsible for the default to pay the costs of the application.[607] Where the application is to compel directors to prepare revised accounts, the court has power to order some or all of the directors to pay the costs occasioned by the application and the preparation of revised accounts, having regard to their responsibility for the preparation of the earlier defective accounts.[608] The court may also make directions as to the way in which the revised accounts are to be prepared and publicity for the revision.[609]

5. APPLICATIONS TO BE RELEASED FROM OBLIGATIONS UNDER THE COMPANIES ACT 1985

5.134 Introduction

The Companies Act 1985 contains a number of provisions which, in certain circumstances, entitle a person to deposit with a company written statements or representations which the company is then obliged to circulate to its members. Where those representations contain defamatory material for which the depositor is seeking needless publicity, an application may be made to the court for an order that the representations need not be

606. Room 4.12, fourth floor, Thomas More Building, Royal Courts of Justice.
607. See ss. 185(7), 242(3) and 713(2).
608. S. 245B(4), (5).
609. S. 245B(3).

circulated by the company as required by the Act. These applications may conveniently be considered together. It should be noted that such applications are comparatively rare, and there are no reported cases offering guidance as to when an application may appropriately be made.

5.135 Obligation to circulate representations

The obligation of the company to circulate representations deposited with it, and the court's power to dispense with that obligation, may arise in five situations:

5.135.1 Removal of a director

Where a company receives special notice[610] of an intention to move an ordinary resolution for the removal from office of one of its directors under s. 303 of the Act, the company must forthwith send a copy of the notice to the director concerned.[611] Thereafter, the director may send written representations to the company regarding his proposed removal. Provided that the representations are received in good time and are not too lengthy, the company must send a copy of the representations to every member who receives notice of the meeting[612]; and if the representations are not circulated to the members in advance of the meeting (for example, because they are received too late, or the company breaches its obligation under s. 304(2)), the director may require that the representations be read out at the meeting.[613] However, where the director's representations contain statements which are defamatory of any person, the company or any person aggrieved by the representations may apply to the court for an order that the representations need not be circulated or read out; and if the court is satisfied that the right to make representations is being abused to give needless publicity to the defamatory statement, the court may release the company from its obligations to circulate or read out the statement.[614]

5.135.2 Requisitionists' representations

Where a company is obliged to give its members notice of a resolution intended to be moved at its next annual general meeting on the requisition of a sufficient proportion of its members[615] the company must also serve on every member of the company entitled to have notice of any general meeting any statement made by or on behalf of the requisitionists (not exceeding 1000 words) concerning the proposed members' resolution or the business to be conducted at that meeting.[616] Notice of the resolution must be given and the statement circulated at the same time as, and in the same manner as notice of the annual general meeting is given, or as soon as is practicable thereafter.[617] The company need not

610. See s. 379.
611. S. 304(1).
612. S. 304(2).
613. S. 304(3).
614. S. 304(4). See generally, *Supreme Court Practice 1997*, Vol. 1, paras 102/2/25–102/2/26, pp. 1542–1543.
615. S. 376(1), (2).
616. S. 376(1)(b), (3).
617. S. 376(3)–(5).

give notice of the resolution or circulate the statement to its members unless the requisition is duly signed and lodged in time, and payment of the company's reasonable expenses in complying with the requisition is tendered or deposited.[618] However, where the requisitionists' statement contains defamatory material, the company, or any person aggrieved by the statement, may apply to the court for an order that the statement need not be circulated; and where the court is satisfied that the requisitionists' rights under s. 376(1) are being abused to secure needless publicity for the defamatory statement, the court may release the company from its obligation to circulate the statement to its members.[619]

5.135.3 Representations of removed auditors

Where a company receives special notice[620] of an ordinary resolution intended to be moved at a general meeting of the company for the removal of the company's auditor from office,[621] or for the appointment of a different auditor in place of a retiring auditor, the company must forthwith send a copy of the notice to the auditor proposed to be removed, or (as the case may be) to the proposed appointee and the retiring auditor.[622] The auditor proposed to be removed, or (as the case may be) the retiring auditor, may then make written representations to the company of a reasonable length regarding the proposed resolution, and request that the representations be notified to the members of the company.[623] Unless the company receives the representations too late, it must refer to the representations in any notice of the proposed resolution sent to its members and send a copy of the representations to every member of whom notice of the meeting is or has been given.[624] If the company receives the representations too late to circulate them, or simply fails to do so, the auditor may require that the representations be read out at the meeting.[625] However, where the auditor's representations contain defamatory material, the company or any person aggrieved by the representations may apply to the court for an order that the representations need not be circulated or read at the meeting; and if the court is satisfied that the auditor's rights under s. 391A(3) are being abused to secure needless publicity for a defamatory statement, the court may release the company from its obligation to circulate the representations or read them at the meeting.[626]

5.135.4 Representations of resigning auditors

Where an auditor resigns his office by the deposit of a notice in writing to that effect at the company's registered office,[627] he may also deposit a statement of circumstances which he considers should be brought to the attention of members or creditors of the company.[628] The resigning auditor may at the same time deposit a signed requisition that

618. S. 377(1).
619. S. 377(3). See generally, *Supreme Court Practice 1997*, Vol. 1, para. 102/2/24, p. 1542.
620. Ss. 391A(1) and 379.
621. S. 391(1).
622. S. 391A(2).
623. S. 391A(3). See also s. 394, discussed *infra*.
624. S. 391A(4).
625. S. 391A(5).
626. S. 391A(6). See generally, *Supreme Court Practice 1997*, Vol. 1, paras 102/2/25–102/2/26, pp. 1542–1543.
627. S. 392(1).
628. S. 392A(1).

the directors of the company should forthwith convene an extraordinary general meeting of the company to enable the members to receive and consider the resigning auditor's explanation of his resignation and the circumstances leading to it.[629] The resigning auditor may also require the company to circulate to its members a written statement made by him (which is not unreasonable in length) of the circumstances leading to his resignation.[630] Unless the statement is received by the company too late, the company must circulate the statement to its members.[631] Where the statement is not so circulated, either owing to the company's default or because it was received too late, the resigning auditor may require the statement to be read out at the meeting.[632] However, where the statement contains defamatory material, the company or any person aggrieved by the representations may apply to the court for an order that the statement need not be circulated or read out at the meeting; and if the court is satisfied that the resigning auditor's rights under s. 392A are being abused to secure needless publicity for a defamatory statement, the court may release the company from its obligation to circulate the statement or read it out at the meeting.[633]

5.135.5 Statement by former auditor

Where an auditor ceases to hold office for any reason, he must deposit at the company's registered office (within the time prescribed by s. 394(2)) a statement of any circumstances connected with his ceasing to hold office which he considers ought to be brought to the attention of the company's members or creditors[634]; if there are no such circumstances, the statement should say so.[635] Where the statement identifies circumstances which ought to be brought to the attention of the company's members or creditors, the company must, within 14 days of the deposit of the statement, send a copy of it to every person who is entitled to receive copies of the company's accounts under s. 238 of the Act[636] (i.e. members, debenture holders and those entitled to receive notice of general meetings). However, the company need not circulate a copy of the statement if the statement contains defamatory material and the company applies to the court for an order that the statement need not be circulated.[637] Notice of the application must be given to the auditor.[638] If the court is satisfied that the auditor is using his right under s. 394 to secure needless publicity for a defamatory statement, the court will direct that the statement need not be circulated[639]; if the court is not so satisfied, the statement must be duly circulated within 14 days of the court's order.[640]

629. S. 392A(2).
630. S. 392A(3).
631. S. 392A(4).
632. S. 392A(6).
633. S. 392A(7). See generally, *Supreme Court Practice 1997*, Vol. 1, paras 102/2/25–102/2/26, pp. 1542–1543.
634. S. 394(1).
635. *Ibid.*
636. S. 394(3)(a).
637. S. 394(3)(b) and (6).
638. S. 394(4).
639. S. 394(6). See generally, *Supreme Court Practice 1997*, Vol. 1, paras 102/2/25–102/2/26, pp. 1542–1543.
640. S. 394(7).

5.136 Form of application

In each case, the application for an order that the defamatory statement need not be circulated or (where applicable) read out at a meeting, is made by originating summons[641] in the expedited form[642] supported by affidavit. The summons is returnable before the Companies Court Registrar in chambers. The summons should seek a direction that the company is not bound to circulate the document in question (which should be clearly identified), or (where applicable) to read it at a meeting, on the grounds that the document is intended to secure needless publicity for a defamatory matter. The summons should also identify the person whom the applicant contends should be ordered to pay the costs of the summons, who should preferably be made a respondent to the summons, although joinder is not a prerequisite of liability for the costs of the application.[643] The procedure for issuing the summons is as described in para. 5.109, *supra*.

5.137 Parties

Where the application is to avoid circulation of a former auditor's statement under s. 394, the application may be made only by the company.[644] In all other cases, the applicant may either be the company or any person who claims to be aggrieved by the defamatory statement[645] (usually the person defamed). In any case, where the company is not the applicant, it should be joined as a respondent. In addition, where the application is made under s. 304(4) to avoid the circulation or reading of representations by a director sought to be removed, the director should be joined as a respondent. Where the application is made under s. 377(3) to avoid the circulation of the statement of requisitionists, all requisitionists should be joined as respondents (particularly where an order for costs is sought against them). Where the application is made under s. 391A(6), s. 392A(7) or s. 394(3) to avoid the circulation or reading of a statement made by an outgoing auditor, the auditor should be joined as a respondent.[646] Although the Act permits the court to make an order for costs against the maker of a defamatory statement (whether a director, requisitionist or outgoing auditor) even where he is not a party to the summons,[647] the better practice is to joint the maker of the statement as a respondent. If the joinder of all requisitionists as respondents to an application under s. 377 is inconvenient owing to the large number of requisitionists, the applicant may seek an order to proceed against representative requisitionists.[648]

5.138 Service

The summons and affidavit in support should be served on the respondents in the usual way: where a company is the respondent, the summons and affidavit in support should be

641. RSC O. 102, r. 2(1),(2); see *Supreme Court Practice 1997*, Vol. 1, para. 102/2/1(q), (r), pp. 1534–1535.
642. Form No. 10 in Appendix A to the RSC: *Supreme Court Practice 1997*, Vol. 2, para. 4, p. 6.
643. See the powers contained in ss. 304(5), 377(3), 391A(6), 392A(7) and 394(6)(b).
644. S. 394(3).
645. See ss. 304(4), 377(3), 391A(6) and 392A(7).
646. Note that s. 394(4) requires the company merely to give notice of the application to a former auditor.
647. Ss. 304(5), 377(3), 391A(6), 392A(7) and 394(6)(b).
648. See RSC O. 15, r. 12.

left at or posted to the company's registered office[649]; where an individual is the respondent, the application and evidence in support should be served by leaving them at, or by sending them by first class post to, his usual or last known address.[650] The Rules of the Supreme Court provide that the summons should be served on the respondent, and the affidavit in support filed in court, not less than four clear days before the day fixed for the hearing.[651] However, as discussed in para. 5.110, *supra*, the better practice is to serve the summons and evidence in support earlier than the last day permitted under the Rules.

5.139 Affidavit in support

In all cases, an affidavit in support of the application is required, setting out the grounds on which the applicant contends that the company should not be required to circulate, or (where applicable) have read out, the statement or representations alleged to be defamatory. Where the company is the applicant, a duly authorised officer of the company should be the deponent. Where the applicant is a person who claims to be aggrieved by the defamatory statement,[652] that person should be the deponent. The affidavit should describe the events giving rise to the delivery to the company of the defamatory statement or representations: for example, the receipt of special notice to remove a director under s. 303 and the giving of notice to the director; or the receipt of a requisition under s. 377; or the resignation, removal or other cessation of office of an auditor under s. 391A, 392A or 394, and the reasons therefor. The affidavit should identify the words or parts of the statement or representations alleged to be defamatory and the person allegedly defamed, and should set out all matters relied upon in support of the allegations of defamation. The affidavit should also explain the potential harm which is likely to be caused to the company or other person if the company were to circulate the defamatory statement (for example, the possible liability of the company for damages for defamation). Where the applicant seeks an order for costs against a maker of a defamatory statement who is not a party to the summons,[653] or against only some of the requisitionists under s. 377, the affidavit should fully explain their role and why an order for costs against them is justified.

5.140 The hearing

The hearing is in the first instance before the Companies Court Registrar sitting in chambers. If the evidence is not complete, the registrar will adjourn the summons to allow the evidence to be completed. The registrar will also deal with any procedural issues (for example, an order that certain requisitionists under s. 377 should represent all requisitionists[654]). Once the evidence is complete and any procedural issues resolved, the registrar may either determine the application himself or may adjourn the matter to the Companies Court Judge, usually sitting in open court, for determination. Where the hearing is contested or will take some time to hear, the registrar is likely to adjourn

649. S. 725(1).
650. RSC O. 10, rr. 1 and 5.
651. RSC O. 28, rr. 2(2) and 3(2).
652. I.e. an application under ss. 304(4), 377(3) 391A(6) or 392A(4).
653. Under ss. 304(5), 377(3), 391A(6), 392A(7) and 394(6)(b).
654. See RSC O. 15, r. 12.

the summons to the judge. Where the summons is adjourned to the judge, it may be appropriate for the applicant to apply to the judge at the start of the hearing for an order that the summons be heard in chambers[655] rather than in open court (i.e. in private rather than in public) to prevent publicity for the allegedly defamatory matter whilst the case is argued.

5.141 The order

Where the court is satisfied that the statement or representations objected to are defamatory and that their maker is abusing his rights under the Act in order to secure needless publicity for the defamatory matter, the court will direct that the statement or representations need not be circulated by the company and (where applicable) need not be read out at a general meeting. It is clear from the wording of s. 394(6) that the court has no discretion to permit the circulation of a statement made by a former auditor on ceasing to hold office if it is being used to secure needless publicity for a defamatory matter,[656] and it is to be inferred that the same is true of other defamatory statements: the Act envisages that the company will be excused from its obligation to circulate a statement where the court is satisfied that its purpose is to secure needless publicity for a defamatory matter.[657] In the event that the court directs that a statement need not be circulated, the maker(s) of the statement will usually be ordered to pay the applicant's costs of the summons, and the court has power to make such order even where the maker of the statement is not joined as a respondent.[658] Where the court is not satisfied that the statement or representations are defamatory, the court will dismiss the summons and the applicant will usually be ordered to pay the respondent's costs of the summons. Where the summons is dismissed, it appears that the company will thereafter have to circulate the statement or representations as required by the Act: this is expressly provided for in s. 394(7)(a) in respect of a statement made by an auditor ceasing to hold office and, it is to be inferred, must also be the case on an application under ss. 304(4), 377(3), 391A(6) and 392A(7).

6. EXTENSION OF TIME FOR FILING RETURNS

5.142 Introduction

The Act does not contain any general power enabling a company or its directors to apply to the court for an extension of time for making returns to the registrar of companies. The Act does, however, contain specific provisions permitting an application to be made for an extension of time in which to file the following documents: (i) office copies of orders of the court (and related documents) made at the conclusion of various applications under the Act[659]—for example, an office copy of the court's order made on a petition under s. 5 for the cancellation of an alteration to a company's constitution made by special resolution,[660] and where the court's order confirms the alteration made by special resolution, a printed

655. Under RSC O. 32, r. 19.
656. See s. 394(6)(a).
657. See ss. 303(4), 377(3), 391A(6) and 392(A)(7).
658. Ss. 304(5), 377(3), 391A(6), 392A(7) and 394(6)(b).
659. See, for example, ss. 6(2), 54(7) and 157(3).
660. Under ss. 4, 17 or 690: see s. 6(2).

copy of any amended document[661]; and (ii) a company's return as to allotments and the related contract or particulars of the contract.[662] The procedure for seeking an extension of time in each of the above categories is different, and they are dealt with separately in the following paragraphs.

(a) Applications for an extension of time for the delivery of orders of the court and related documents

5.143 Introduction

In respect of many of the applications to the court discussed in this Chapter (referred to in the following paragraphs as "the principal application"), the Act requires the applicant to deliver to the registrar of companies an office copy of the order made by the court at the conclusion of the application,[663] together with related documents (such as an amended memorandum of association where the court's order confirms the amendment[664]). In some cases, the Act does not expressly impose any time limit for the delivery of the office copy of the order[665] (although the order itself may impose a time limit); in some cases, the Act stipulates a period within which the office copy of the order must be delivered to the registrar of companies, which cannot be extended by order of the court[666]; and in others, the Act stipulates a period for delivery of the office copy of the order which can be extended by the court.[667] The following paragraphs describe the procedure for seeking such an extension of time.

5.144 Form of application

The form of application for an extension of time for the delivery of an office copy of the court's order depends on the stage at which the application for an extension of time is made.

(i) If it is clear at the time when the court hearing the principal application makes its order that there will be difficulty in delivering the appropriate documents to the registrar of companies in the period as required by the Act,[668] an application for an extension of time may be made orally to the court hearing the principal application: the reasons for the difficulty in complying with the Act and the duration of the extension of time sought should be explained, and the court may require those facts to be confirmed by affidavit.

(ii) In all other cases, the application for an extension of time should be made by *ex parte* summons supported by affidavit. The summons will be returnable before the Companies Court Registrar sitting in chambers.

661. S. 6(1)(b).
662. S. 88(2), (3).
663. See, for example, ss. 6(1)(b), 54(7), 127(5), 157(3), 176(3), 359(4), 651(3) and 653(3).
664. See s. 6(1)(b)(ii).
665. See, for example, s. 653(3).
666. See, for example, s. 127(5).
667. See, for example, ss. 6(2), 54(7), 157(3), 176(3)(b) and 651(3). See generally, *Supreme Court Practice 1997*, Vol. 1, para. 102/2/13, p. 1538.
668. The period under ss. 6(2), 54(7), 157(3) and 176(3) is 15 days from the date of the order; the period under s. 651(3) is seven days.

In all cases, the applicant will be the person required by the Act to deliver an office copy of the order to the registrar of companies.

5.145 Affidavit in support

An affidavit in support of the application for an extension of time should be sworn by a duly authorised officer or agent of the company. The affidavit should set out all facts relied upon in support of the application for an extension of time, including: why it has not been (or will not be) possible to comply with the timescale for filing documents as required by s. 6(1)(b)(ii); where the difficulty in filing the documents was not raised at the hearing of the petition, why the difficulty was not then appreciated; and the duration of the extension required for filing the documents.

5.146 The hearing

The hearing is before the Companies Court Registrar sitting in chambers.

(b) Applications for an extension of time under section 88(6)

5.147 Jurisdiction

When a company which is limited by shares, or a company which is limited by guarantee and has a share capital,[669] allots shares, the company must, within one month thereafter, deliver to the registrar of companies a return of allotments in the prescribed form.[670] The return must state: the number and nominal amount of the shares allotted; the names and addresses of the allottees; any amount paid, or due and payable, on each share (whether as nominal amount or premium).[671] Where shares are allotted as fully or partly paid-up otherwise than in cash, the company must also deliver to the registrar of companies within one month of the allotment: a written contract constituting the allottee's title to the shares in question, any contract of sale or contract for services or other consideration for the allotment,[672] and a return detailing the terms of the allotment[673]; where the contract is not in writing, the company must deliver the prescribed particulars of the contract.[674] Where there is a breach of the obligations imposed by s. 88, every officer of the company who is in default is liable to a fine,[675] but the company or such officer may apply to the court for relief.[676] If the court is satisfied that the failure to deliver the relevant document to the registrar of companies was accidental, or due to inadvertence, or that it is just and equitable to grant relief, the court may extend the time for delivery of documents for such period as it thinks proper.[677]

669. S. 88(1).
670. S. 88(2).
671. S. 88(2)(a).
672. S. 88(2)(b)(i).
673. S. 88(2)(b)(ii).
674. S. 88(3).
675. S. 88(5).
676. S. 88(6).
677. *Ibid.* See generally, *Supreme Court Practice 1997*, Vol. 1, para. 102/3/2, p. 1546.

5.148 Form of application

The application should be made by notice of originating motion[678] returnable before the Companies Court Judge in open court supported by affidavit. The notice of originating motion should state which of the three grounds set out in s. 88(6) is relied upon, and the ground(s) should be fully explained in the affidavit in support. The notice of originating motion should also identify the duration of the extension of time sought. The procedure for the issue of the notice of originating motion is as described in para. 5.2, *supra*.

5.149 Parties

The application may be made by the company or by any officer who is liable for the default.[679] Where the company is the applicant, the application is made *ex parte*. Where the applicant is an officer liable for the default, the company should be joined as a respondent. If the company is joined as a respondent, the notice of originating motion and evidence in support should be served on the company by leaving them at, or posting them to, the company's registered office,[680] at least two clear days before the day fixed for the hearing.[681]

5.150 Affidavit in support

The affidavit in support of the notice of originating motion should explain all the circumstances leading to the failure to deliver the relevant documents to the registrar of companies, including details of the allotments, and (where applicable) why it was impractical or impossible to deliver the documents. Where the default is alleged to have been due to "inadvertence", full particulars of the inadvertence or oversight should be given: for example, that there was a misunderstanding between two people, each believing the other to have delivered the relevant document to the registrar of companies, which resulted in the default; or that the applicant was ignorant of the obligation to make the return, or overlooked the requirement owing to pressure of work. By analogy with the similarly worded provision for extending time for the registration of a charge[682] and the cases decided thereunder, it will not be sufficient merely to state that the omission occurred through "inadvertence", because the court has to be satisfied that one or more of the grounds stated in s. 88(6) exists.[683] Copies of the documents mentioned in s. 88(2) and (3) (where applicable) may be exhibited to the affidavit.

5.151 The hearing and order

The hearing is before the Companies Court Judge sitting in open court. Where the court is satisfied that the default was caused by one of the reasons stated in s. 88(6), the court

678. RSC O. 102, r. 3(1)(a). See Form No. 13 in Appendix A to the RSC: *Supreme Court Practice 1997*, Vol. 2, para. 8, p. 8.
679. S. 88(6). "Officer" includes any director, manager or secretary: s. 744.
680. S. 725(1).
681. See RSC O. 8, r. 2(2).
682. S. 404(1).
683. See para. 5.22, *supra*; Practice Note [1948] WN 179; *Re Kris Cruisers Ltd* [1949] Ch. 138 at 140 and 142.

retains a discretion[684] whether to extend time for delivery of the returns, thereby relieving from liability the company and any officer in default.

7. APPLICATIONS TO BE RELEASED FROM LIABILITIES

5.152 Introduction

Certain of the applications discussed in the earlier parts of this Chapter may result (if successful) in the applicant avoiding a liability which he would otherwise incur for a breach of his obligations under the Act—for example, an application for an extension of time in which to deliver certain documents to the registrar of companies.[685] In addition, the Act contains two provisions which enable a person to apply to the court for an order relieving him from a liability: namely, (i) an application by an officer of, or an auditor employed by, a company to be relieved of a liability for a breach of duty[686]; and (ii) an application by an allottee or subsequent holder of shares allotted in contravention of ss. 99–112 of the Act.[687] These are considered separately below.

(a) Relief from liability for breach of duty

5.153 Jurisdiction

If proceedings are brought against an officer[688] of a company or a person employed by a company as auditor (whether or not he is an officer), alleging negligence, default,[689] breach of duty (whether imposed by statute or common law) or breach of trust, the court may relieve that person from his liability (either in whole or in part) on such terms as the court thinks fit, if it appears to the court hearing the case that: (i) the officer/employee auditor is or may be liable in respect of the negligence, default, breach of duty or breach of trust; (ii) he has acted (a) honestly and (b) reasonably; and (iii) that having regard to all the circumstances of the case (including the circumstances of his appointment) he ought fairly to be excused for the negligence, default, breach of duty or breach of trust.[690] The criteria are cumulative—i.e. the applicant has to establish each of (i) to (iii) above. The test is essentially subjective.[691] Further, where an officer or employee auditor apprehends that a claim for negligence, default, breach of duty or breach of trust will or might be made against him, he may apply to the court to be relieved from that liability; and in such a case the court has the same power to grant relief as if proceedings had actually been brought against the officer/employee auditor[692] (i.e. the powers conferred by s. 727(1)).

684. S. 88(6).
685. See ss. 6(2) and 88(6); and paras 5.142–5.151, *supra*.
686. S. 727.
687. S. 113.
688. "Officer" includes a director, manager or secretary (s. 744), an administrator (*Re Home Treat Ltd* [1991] BCLC 705 at 711c–e) and a liquidator (*Re X Co. Ltd* [1907] 2 Ch. 92 at 96).
689. "Default" includes any liability under CA 1985 to the company of which the defendant is a director (for example, under s. 322(3)): *Re Duckwari plc* [1997] 2 WLR 48 at 56F (*obiter*).
690. S. 727(1). For the effect on a jury trial, see s. 727(3).
691. See *Re Produce Marketing Consortium Ltd* [1989] 1 WLR 745 at 750F–G.
692. S. 727(2). See generally, *Supreme Court Practice 1997*, Vol. 1, paras 102/4/37–102/4/38, pp. 1562–1563.

Section 727 thus gives the court a wide and general power[693] to relieve an officer or employee auditor from liability for a range of defaults, which may be invoked either before or after litigation is commenced against him in respect of the default. The burden of satisfying the court that it should grant relief from liability is upon the person invoking s. 727.[694]

5.154 Form of application

Where an officer or employee auditor seeks to be relieved from liability for a breach of duty in advance of the commencement of any proceedings against him (i.e. a *quia timet* application for relief from liability), the application should be made by petition[695] supported by affidavit. Where proceedings have been brought against an officer or employee auditor alleging a breach of duty or other default, the officer or employee auditor may seek relief under s. 727 at the hearing of the proceedings, without issuing a petition for such relief or including a prayer for such relief in his pleading—the question of s. 727 relief may be raised by the defendant for the first time at trial.[696] However, the better practice is for a defendant intending to rely on s. 727 to include in his pleading a request for relief from any liability proven against him. If an officer or employee auditor who intends to rely on s. 727 makes no such reference in his pleading and gives no notice of his intended reliance on s. 727 until trial, with the result that further evidence needs to be adduced on those issues and an adjournment of the trial is ordered, the director/employee auditor may be ordered to pay the costs thrown away by the adjournment. In addition, if the court has ordered the parties to exchange written statements of the oral evidence which they intend to adduce on any issues of fact to be decided at trial[697] without limiting the issues to be covered in the statements, the officer/employee auditor requires the consent of the other parties or the leave of the court to adduce evidence on other issues of fact not covered in his original witness statements.[698] Once proceedings have been commenced against a director or employee auditor for breach of duty, it is doubted whether the defendant can issue a cross-petition seeking relief under s. 727 to be heard concurrently with those proceedings.[699] Once proceedings for breach of duty have been commenced, only the court hearing those proceedings can grant relief from liability under s. 727(1).[700] It has been suggested that a *quia timet* application for relief under s. 727 by

693. *Re Claridge's Patent Asphalte Co. Ltd* [1921] 1 Ch. 543 at 548; *Customs and Excise Comrs* v. *Hendon Alpha Ltd* [1981] QB 818 at 822–824. See also *Re Barry and Staines Linoleum Ltd* [1934] 1 Ch. 227 at 233 in which Maugham J. stated that the power "ought to be exercised with great care". See also *Re Duckwari plc, supra*, in which it was held (*obiter*): (i) that s. 727 can be relied upon to relieve liability for a breach of s. 320 and its operation is not impliedly excluded by s. 322(5) or (6); but (ii) where a director has a direct or indirect interest in an arrangement or transaction entered into without shareholder approval contrary to s. 320, and intends to profit it from it, he should not be excused from liability for loss or damage resulting from it.

694. *Re Kirby's Coaches Ltd* [1991] BCLC 414 at 415f. For a case where directors failed to discharge the burden, see *Dorchester Finance Co. Ltd* v. *Stebbing* [1989] BCLC 498 at 505h–506c; *Bishopsgate Investment Management Ltd* v. *Maxwell (No. 2)* [1994] 1 All ER 261 at 265j; and *Guinness plc* v. *Saunders* [1990] AC 663.

695. RSC O. 102, r. 4(1)(i).

696. *Re Kirby's Coaches Ltd, supra*, at 416e.

697. I.e. pursuant to RSC O. 38, r. 2A(2).

698. RSC O. 38, r. 2A (7)(b).

699. See *Supreme Court Practice 1997*, Vol. 1, para. 102/4/37, p. 1562. In such a case, the defendant should plead a claim for relief under s. 727 in his defence.

700. *Re Gilt Edge Safety Glass Ltd* [1940] 1 Ch. 495 at 501.

an officer or employee auditor of a company in liquidation, where proceedings have not been commenced against him, may be made by an originating or ordinary application under the Insolvency Act 1986 (the choice of application depending on whether any other proceedings in the liquidation have yet been before the court).[701] There are difficulties with that suggestion: originating or ordinary applications must be used for applications under the Insolvency Act 1986 (unless a petition is stipulated by the relevant rules),[702] but the application for relief under s. 727 is made under the Companies Act 1985; moreover, O. 102, r. 4(1) of the Rules of the Supreme Court states that an application under s. 727 "must be made by petition"; and there is nothing in that rule or the commentary thereon which suggests any relaxation of the requirement where the company in question is in liquidation. It should be noted, however, that the court has relieved administrators of a company from liability on the hearing of an ordinary application for directions under s. 43 of the Insolvency Act 1986.[703]

5.155 Issue of petition

Where the officer or employee auditor seeks relief under s. 727 by petition, two copies of the petition (together with a further copy for each respondent on whom the petition is to be served) will be required on presentation: one copy should be stamped with the appropriate fee. The action number will be entered on all copies, which will be sealed. One copy will be retained by the court for filing, the stamped copy will be returned to the applicant to be exhibited to the affidavit supporting the petition, and any additional copies will be returned to the applicant for service on the respondent. No date for the hearing of the petition will be given on presentation. The petition may be presented at the chambers of the Companies Court Registrar[704] or at any Chancery district registry.[705] The petition should conclude with a concise statement of the nature of the claim or the relief sought,[706] and a statement of the persons to be served with the petition[707]: usually the company will be named as the respondent to the petition. The petition should be served on the company by leaving it at, or posting it to, the company's registered office.[708] Where the breach of duty or default sought to be relieved is one which could be the subject of a prosecution by the Secretary of State for Trade and Industry (for example, breaches of statutory duties under the Act to deliver documents to the registrar of companies), notice of the petition should be given to the Department of Trade and Industry.

5.156 The affidavit in support

The petitioner should file in court and serve on the respondent (usually the company) an affidavit which verifies the petition, a copy of which should be exhibited to the affidavit. The affidavit should set out all facts relied upon by the petitioner and, in particular, should satisfy the criteria stipulated in s. 727(1)—i.e. it should establish: (a) that the petitioner is

701. See, for example, *Atkin's Court Forms*, Vol. 9 (1995 Edn), para. 22, p. 31.
702. See IA 1986, rr. 7.1 and 7.2.
703. *Re Home Treat Ltd*, *supra*.
704. I.e. Room 2.09, second floor, Thomas More Building, Royal Courts of Justice.
705. RSC O. 102, r. 4(2).
706. RSC O. 9, r. 2(1).
707. RSC O. 9, r. 2(2).
708. S. 725(1).

or may be liable for a breach of duty or other default; (b) that he has acted honestly and reasonably; and (c) that in all the circumstances (including the circumstances of his appointment), he ought fairly to be excused from liability.

5.157 The summons for directions

Following presentation of the petition, the petitioner should take out a summons for directions.[709] Two copies of the summons will be required for issue at the chambers of the Companies Court Registrar, together with a time estimate for the hearing of the summons signed by his solicitor or counsel. A time for the hearing of the summons for directions by the Companies Court Registrar will be inserted on both copies of the summons, one copy will be retained for filing, and the other copy will be returned to the applicant for service on the respondent (i.e. the company). At the hearing of the summons for directions, the Companies Court Registrar may make any directions he thinks fit for bringing the petition to a hearing, including directions for completion of outstanding evidence and for the advertisement of the petition.[710] Advertisement may exceptionally be necessary where the application for release from liability raises issues on which the members or creditors of the company can be expected to have views—for example, where the applicant seeks to be relieved from an obligation to make a payment to the company or its liquidator.[711] However, in most cases (for example, where the application seeks relief for a breach of an obligation to make returns to the registrar of companies) advertisement will be unnecessary and, after the completion of evidence, the registrar will simply give directions for fixing the hearing of the petition. In most cases, the registrar will adjourn the petition to the Companies Court Judge for hearing in open court on a date to be fixed.

5.158 The hearing of the petition and order

The court's power to grant relief under s. 727(1) or (2) is discretionary. If the court is satisfied that the criteria set out in s. 727(1) are met, it may order relief from liability either in whole or in part, and may impose such terms as it thinks fit.[712] Where proceedings are taken against an officer or employee auditor in a court of summary jurisdiction,[713] that court alone has jurisdiction to grant relief in respect of those defaults, but a petition may nevertheless be issued under s. 727(2) seeking relief against other anticipated claims.[714] Where, by the date of the hearing of the petition, other proceedings are pending against the petitioner in a court of summary jurisdiction, the High Court, if satisfied that relief should be granted, would generally grant relief against liability except in relation to the potential liability under the summary proceedings, leaving it to the court of summary jurisdiction to make whatever order it thinks fit having regard to the order made by the High Court on the petition. The court will not make an order under s. 727 to relieve an officer from liability for wrongful trading under s. 214 of the Insolvency Act 1986,[715]

709. RSC O. 102, r. 6(1).
710. RSC O. 102, r. 6(3).
711. See *Re Barry and Staines Linoleum Ltd* [1934] Ch. 227 at 234.
712. S. 727(1). For a case where liability in negligence was relieved in part, see *Re D'Jan of London Ltd* [1994] 1 BCLC 561 at 564c–h.
713. E.g. a prosecution in a Magistrates Court to impose a fine or penalty.
714. *Re Gilt Edge Safety Glass Ltd, supra*, at 501–502.
715. *Re Produce Marketing Consortium Ltd* [1989] 1 WLR 745 at 750H–751H.

although it may grant relief under s. 727 on a misfeasance application issued by a liquidator under s. 212 of the Insolvency Act 1986.[716] Some guidance as to when the court will be prepared to grant relief from liability may be obtained from cases concerning applications to relieve trustees from liability under the analogous power contained in s. 61 of the Trustee Act 1925 and its predecessors.

(b) Relief from liability following an irregular allotment of shares

5.159 Jurisdiction

Where shares are allotted by a company in contravention of the various restrictions on allotment imposed by ss. 99 and 102–105 of the Act—for example, where a public company accepts, in payment for the shares allotted, an undertaking by the allottee to perform future services for the company,[717] or where a public company allots shares for non-cash consideration which has not been independently valued[718]—the allottee or subsequent holder of the shares may be liable to recompense the company, usually by the payment of the nominal value of the shares allotted, together with the whole of any premium thereon and interest.[719] In such cases, the person liable to the company as a result of the irregular allotment may apply to the court to be the exempted in whole or in part from the liability.[720] The Act distinguishes between two differing classes of liability and imposes different criteria to be established in each case before the court will grant relief from liability.

5.159.1 Where the liability of the applicant arises in relation to a payment in respect of any shares, under s. 113(1), the court may exempt the applicant from that liability only (a) if and to the extent that it appears to the court just and equitable to grant an exemption *in relation to the payment* (taking into account the matters stated in s. 113(3)), and (b) if and to the extent that it appears to the court just and equitable to do so *in relation to any interest payable by the applicant to the company under the relevant sections.*[721]

The matters required by s. 113(3) to be taken into account by the court in deciding whether to grant an exemption against the liability to pay up the shares (but not the liability to pay interest), include:

- (a) whether the applicant has paid or is liable to pay any amount in respect of any other liability in relation to the shares under the relevant sections or by virtue of any undertaking given in connection with payment for the shares;
- (b) whether any person other than the applicant has paid or is likely to pay that amount; and
- (c) whether any person has or is likely to perform any undertaking (in whole or in part) or do any other thing in payment or part payment for the shares.

The clear purpose of these provisions is to enable the court to grant relief from a liability which, if enforced, would result in a double penalty for the shareholder or would result in an over-compensation of the company.

716. See *Re Welfab Engineers Ltd* [1990] BCLC 833 at 838C; *Re D'Jan of London Ltd, supra.*
717. Contrary to s. 99(2).
718. Contrary to s. 103(1)(a).
719. See ss. 99(3), 102(2), 103(6), 105(3), 112(1), 112(2) and 112(5).
720. S. 113(1).
721. S. 113(2).

5.159.2 Where the liability of the applicant arises by virtue of an undertaking given to the company in connection with payment for shares in it,[722] the court may exempt the applicant under s. 113(1) from that liability only if and to the extent that it appears to the court just and equitable to do so.[723] In deciding whether it is just and equitable, the court will have regard to:

(a) whether the applicant has paid or is liable to pay any amount under any liability in relation to the shares under any of the statutory provisions mentioned in s. 113(1); and
(b) whether any person other than the applicant has paid or is likely to pay that amount.[724]

Again, these factors are designed to enable the court to grant relief from a liability which would otherwise over-penalise the shareholder or over-compensate the company.

5.159.3 In either of the above cases (i.e. whether the application is to be exempted under s. 113(2) from a liability in respect of a payment for shares, or under s. 113(4) from a liability by virtue of an undertaking given in connection with payment for shares), the court must have regard to two "overriding principles"—namely:

(a) the principle that a company which allots shares should receive money or money's worth at least equal in value to the total of the nominal value of the shares allotted plus the whole of any premium thereon (or so much thereof as is treated as paid up); and
(b) the principle that (subject to (a) above), where but for the court's exemption the company would have more than one remedy against a person, it should be for the company to decide which remedy it should remain entitled to pursue.[725]

Where the person under the liability has performed his part of the bargain with the company which was in breach of the Act, and the transaction has benefited the company, the first of the overriding principles may be a matter of little weight.[726]

5.159.4 The Act also empowers the court to grant a person an exemption[727] from liability[728] arising out of the transfer contrary to s. 104 of a non-cash asset to a public company within the first two years of it being entitled to do business,[729] if and to the extent that it appears to the court just and equitable to do so having regard to any benefit accruing to the company by virtue of the agreement. Finally, where proceedings are bought by one person (such as a subsequent holder of shares), against another (such as the original allottee thereof)—the latter being referred to in the Act as "the contributor"—for a contribution in respect of a liability to the company arising out of the earlier irregular allotment, and it appears to the court that the contributor is liable to make such a

722. E.g. liability under ss. 99(3) or 102(2).
723. S. 113(4).
724. *Ibid.*
725. S. 113(5).
726. See *Re Ossory Estates plc* [1988] BCLC 213 (where an exemption under s. 113(1) was granted); but contrast *Re Bradford Investments plc (No. 2)* [1991] BCLC 688 at 703h, where the court refused to grant relief because the applicant had not discharged the burden of showing that the company had received value for its shares.
727. Under s. 113(8).
728. Under s. 105.
729. See s. 117.

contribution,[730] the court may extinguish, reduce or increase the liability which the contributor would otherwise have to make under the Act, if it appears to the court just and equitable to do so having regard to their respective culpability in relation to the company.[731]

5.160 Form of application

In any of the cases mentioned in para. 5.159, *supra*, the application to the court to be exempted from liability for an irregular allotment is made by originating summons[732] in the expedited form[733] supported by affidavit. The application should state clearly the liability in respect of which exemption is sought, identifying any section of the Act under which the liability arises and stating whether the applicant seeks exemption from the whole or from part of that liability. The summons is returnable before the Companies Court Registrar sitting in chambers. The summons may be issued at the chambers of the Companies Court Registrar[734] or out of any Chancery district registry.[735] The procedure for the issue of the summons is as described in para. 5.109, *supra*. Where proceedings are brought by writ seeking a contribution in respect of a liability for an irregular allotment,[736] it may be possible for the defendant to seek an exemption from liability in his pleaded defence.[737] However, the better course is to issue an originating summons seeking an exemption from liability, which should be heard at the same time as the action for a contribution.[738]

5.161 Parties and service

In all cases, the applicant will be the person under a liability to pay up shares following the irregular allotment, who seeks to be exempted from liability.[739] In most cases, the respondent will be the company. Where the application for an exemption is made under s. 113(6) (i.e. where a subsequent holder of shares which were initially allotted irregularly brings proceedings against the original allottee seeking a contribution in respect of the subsequent holder's liability to the company for the irregular allotment), the person bringing the proceedings for a contribution should also be joined as a respondent to the originating summons seeking exemption. Where the respondent is a company, the summons and affidavit in support should be served on it by leaving them at or posting them to the company's registered office.[740] Where the respondent is an individual, the summons and evidence in answer should be served by posting them first class to, or leaving them

730. S. 113(6).
731. S. 113(7).
732. RSC O. 102, r. 2(1).
733. RSC O. 102, r. 2(2). See Form No. 10 in Appendix A to the RSC: *Supreme Court Practice 1997*, Vol. 2, para. 4, p. 6.
734. I.e. Room 2.09, second floor, Thomas More Building, Royal Courts of Justice.
735. RSC O. 102, r. 2(4).
736. E.g. under s. 113(6).
737. By analogy with the procedure on an application for relief under s. 727; see para. 5.154, *supra*. Note that there is no authority approving that practice in the context of s. 113.
738. See, for example, the cross-action and application in *Re Bradford Investments plc (No. 2)*, *supra*, at 689c–d.
739. S. 113(1).
740. S. 725(1).

at, the respondent's usual or last known address.[741] The originating summons should be served on the respondent(s) at least four days before the date fixed for the hearing,[742] although in practice it will usually be possible to effect service at an earlier date: if service of the summons is delayed until shortly before the hearing as permitted by the Rules, an adjournment may be required to enable the respondent(s) to consider the application and prepare evidence in answer, in which case the applicant could be penalised for the costs thrown away by the adjournment. The summons should be accompanied by a form of acknowledgement of service.[743]

5.162 Affidavit in support

The originating summons should be supported by an affidavit setting out the grounds on which the applicant relies in claiming that it is just and equitable[744] for the court to grant an exemption from liability in respect of the irregular allotment. The affidavit should describe in detail the events giving rise to the allotment and the breach of the Act; identifying the relevant section contravened; and where the applicant is not the original allottee, it should describe how the applicant became the holder of the shares in question. The affidavit should also deal with all facts or matters relevant to the statutory criteria which the court must take into account,[745] and the "overriding principles"[746] which the court applies in deciding whether to grant an exemption (for example, whether the applicant has paid or is liable to pay any amount in respect of any other liability in relation to the shares; whether any person other than the applicant has paid or is likely to pay such amount; and whether the applicant has performed any undertaking or done anything in payment for the shares). Where the application for an exemption is made under s. 113(6) in response to proceedings by a subsequent holder of the irregularly allotted shares seeking a contribution for the liability to the company in respect of the irregular allotment, the applicant's affidavit should deal with the parties' respective culpability.[747] The affidavit should be filed in court not less than four clear days before the day fixed for the hearing.[748]

5.163 The hearing and order

The hearing will, in the first instance, be before the Companies Court Registrar sitting in chambers. The registrar will initially make directions for the completion of any further evidence required and any other procedural matters, adjourning the summons where necessary. Once the evidence is complete, the registrar will usually adjourn the summons to the Companies Court Judge sitting in open court for determination. The court may exempt the applicant in whole or in part in respect of his liability for the irregular

741. RSC O. 10, rr. 1 and 5.
742. RSC O. 28, r. 3(2).
743. RSC O. 10, rr. 5(1) and 1(6). See Form No. 15 in Appendix A to the RSC: *Supreme Court Practice 1997*, Vol. 2, para. 10, p. 14.
744. See s. 113(2), (4), (7) and (8).
745. I.e. the criteria laid down in s. 113(3), (4).
746. S. 113(5).
747. See s. 113(7).
748. RSC O. 28, r. 2(2).

allotment[749]; and where the application is made under s. 113(6) to be exempted from a liability to make a contribution in respect of the irregular allotment, the court may order the applicant to make a larger contribution than he would otherwise have had to make under the Act.[750]

8. APPLICATIONS RELATING TO RESTRICTIONS ON SHARES

(a) Applications to impose restrictions

5.164 Jurisdiction

Where a public company knows or has reasonable cause to believe that a person has, or in the previous three years had, an interest in that company's relevant share capital,[751] the company may, by notice in writing, require the person to confirm his interest or to indicate whether or not he has or had an interest, and where he has or had an interest, to give further information prescribed by the Act.[752] The further information which may be sought is set out in s. 212(2). Where a public company serves a notice under s. 212 on a person who appears to be or to have been interested in its relevant share capital, and that person fails to give the company any information required by the notice within the time specified in it,[753] the company may apply to the court for an order that the shares in question be subject to the restrictions set out in s. 454 of the Act.[754] The restrictions may be imposed where there is no response to the notice under s. 212 or where the response is incomplete or untruthful.[755] The restrictions are draconian and effectively disenfranchise a person who wrongly fails to comply with a notice served under s. 212.

5.164.1 The restrictions are as follows:

(a) any transfer or right to transfer the shares, or any right to be issued with the shares in the case of unissued shares, is void[756];
(b) no voting rights are exercisable in respect of the shares[757];
(c) no further shares are to be issued in right of the shares in question or in pursuance of any offer made to their holder[758];
(d) no payment may be made by the company of any sums due from it in respect of the shares, whether in respect of capital or otherwise, except in a liquidation.[759]

749. See s. 113(7), (8).
750. S. 113(7)(b).
751. As defined by s. 198(2).
752. S. 212(1).
753. Provided that the time allowed for compliance is reasonable: see s. 212(4) and *Re Lonrho plc (No. 2)* [1989] BCLC 309 at 316c–d.
754. S. 216(1). See generally, *Supreme Court Practice 1997*, Vol. 1, paras 102/2/33–102/2/35, pp. 1544–1545.
755. *Re TR Technology Investment Trust plc* [1988] BCLC 256.
756. S. 454(1)(a), (2).
757. S. 454(1)(b).
758. S. 454(1)(c), (2).
759. S. 454(1)(d), (2).

The same restrictions may also be imposed by order of the Secretary of State following an investigation by inspectors appointed by the Secretary of State[760] into a company's ownership.[761]

5.164.2 A public company may apply for an order imposing restrictions on shares under s. 216(1), and the court may impose such restrictions, whether or not the company's memorandum or articles of association include a power enabling it to require information about the beneficial ownership of its shares and to impose similar restrictions on the shares in the event of default.[762] The court's powers on an application under s. 216 are discretionary, and the court may make an interim order, either unconditionally or on such terms as the court thinks fit.[763] An order imposing restrictions may be made, notwithstanding that the person who has the beneficial interest in the shares is a foreign national.[764]

5.165 Limits on the court's jurisdiction and discretion

Although the court's powers to impose restrictions under s. 216 are discretionary, an order will usually be made where a valid notice served under s. 212 has not been complied with, since the clear purpose of the procedure "is to give a public company, and ultimately the public at large, a *prima facie* unqualified right to know who are the real owners of its voting shares".[765] It was formerly the case that where an order was made imposing restrictions on shares under s. 216, the court would impose all four of the restrictions set out in s. 454 and would not tailor the order in a way which would meet the concerns of the applicant but avoid hardship to innocent third parties.[766] The potential prejudice to innocent third parties of the draconian sanction of imposing restrictions on shares under s. 216 has been alleviated by the Companies (Disclosure of Interests in Shares) (Orders imposing restrictions on shares) Regulations 1991 (S.I. 1991 No. 1646).[767] Those regulations introduce new sections in the Companies Act 1985 enabling the court: (i) to make interim orders (either unconditionally or on such terms as it thinks fit)[768]; (ii) for the purpose of protecting rights of third parties who would be unfairly affected by the imposition of restrictions, to direct (on such terms as it thinks fit) that certain acts by such persons should not constitute a breach of the statutory restrictions set out in s. 454[769]; and (iii) to make such a direction subsequent to the imposition of restrictions on an application for the relaxation or removal of the restrictions.[770] The court may refuse to impose restrictions on shares following non-compliance with a notice served under s. 216 if the recipient of the notice satisfies the court that service of the notice was frivolous or

760. Under ss. 442 or 444.
761. S. 445(1).
762. S. 216(2).
763. S. 216(1A), inserted by the Companies (Disclosure of Interests in Shares) (Orders imposing restrictions on shares) Regulations 1991, S.I. 1991 No. 1646, reg. 4(a).
764. *Re FH Lloyd Holdings plc* [1985] BCLC 293.
765. *Re FH Lloyd Holdings plc, supra*, at 300h per Nourse J, followed in *Re Geers Gross plc* [1987] BCLC 140 at 143a–d and 144d–h and *Re Lonrho plc (No. 2)* [1990] Ch. 695 (a different decision to that cited above). For a case where the court refused to maintain restrictions in the exercise of its discretion, see *Re Ricardo Group plc (No. 3)* [1989] BCLC 771 at 773c–h.
766. *Re Lonrho plc (No. 4)* [1990] BCLC 151; see the criticism of the inflexibility of the court's powers by Peter Gibson J. at p. 161b.
767. Made pursuant to the power contained in the CA 1989, s. 135.
768. S. 216(1A).
769. S. 216(1B).
770. S. 456(1A).

vexatious,[771] or the recipient is at the time exempted by the Secretary of State from compliance with s. 212,[772] or the initial default has been remedied by the disclosure of full and correct information.[773]

5.166 Form of application

An application for an order imposing restrictions on shares under ss. 216 and 454 is made by originating summons[774] in the general form[775] supported by affidavit. An *ex parte* application should not be made unless the company making the application has reason to believe that the respondent is deliberately withholding information and would dispose of the shares if given prior warning of the application.[776] The originating summons should clearly identify the shares which the applicant seeks to be made subject to restrictions under s. 454 of the Act.[777] The summons may be issued out of the chambers of the Companies Court Registrar[778] or any Chancery district registry. The originating summons should not be issued until the recipient of the notice served under s. 212 has failed to comply with the notice within the time stated therein, which must not be an unreasonably short period for compliance. The procedure for issuing the summons is as described in para. 5.109 above, save that a date for the hearing of the summons will not be inserted in the summons on issue, but will be fixed after acknowledgement of service by the respondent.

5.167 Parties, service and evidence

The company which served the notice under s. 212 will be the applicant. The respondents should be the persons who were served with notices under s. 212 and who have failed to give the information requested. Usually, the respondents will be the person believed to be beneficially interested in the shares in question and the registered holder or former holder of those shares. It may also be appropriate to join as a respondent any person who might be directly affected by the imposition of restrictions, such as a person making a takeover bid for the company. Where that person is not named as a respondent, he may apply to be joined as a respondent pursuant to O. 15, r. 6 of the Rules of the Supreme Court.[779] The originating summons should be served on the respondents accompanied by a form for acknowledgment of service.[780] Where the respondent is a company, service of the originating summons may be effected by leaving it at, or posting it to, the company's registered office[781]; where the respondent is an individual, service may be effected by

771. See s. 216(4).
772. S. 216(5).
773. See *Re Lonrho plc (No. 3)* [1989] BCLC 480 at 483a–d; *Re Ricardo Group plc* [1989] BCLC 566 at 572f.
774. RSC O. 102, r. 2(1).
775. RSC O. 102, r. 2(2)(d). See Form No. 8 in Appendix A to the RSC: *Supreme Court Practice 1997*, Vol. 2, para. 3, p. 5.
776. *Re Ricardo Group plc, supra*, at 577j–578a.
777. *Ibid.* at 578d.
778. I.e. Room 2.09, second floor, Thomas More Building, Royal Courts of Justice.
779. See *Re Ricardo Group plc (No. 3)* [1989] BCLC 771 at 772d–e.
780. RSC O. 10, rr. 5(1) and 1(6). For the form of acknowledgment of service, see Form No. 15 in Appendix A to the RSC: *Supreme Court Practice 1997*, Vol. 2, para. 10, p. 14.
781. S. 725(1).

leaving the originating summons at, or posting it first class to, the respondent's usual or last known address.[782] The respondent(s) must acknowledge service within 14 days.[783] The applicant should file in court any evidence intended to be relied upon in support of the summons within 14 days of the first acknowledgment of service[784]; and the evidence must be served on each respondent within 14 days of that respondent's acknowledgment of service.[785] If the respondents fail to acknowledge service, the applicant should produce a certificate to that effect and proceed to fix the hearing. Where a respondent who has acknowledged service wishes to rely on evidence in opposition to the application, he must file in court his evidence in opposition within 28 days of service of the applicant's evidence on him, and serve copies of his evidence on the applicant and any other respondent affected thereby.[786] The applicant may serve evidence in reply within 14 days of service on him of the respondent's evidence.[787] After that date, no further affidavit evidence may be adduced without the leave of the court.[788] The court may extend any of the above periods.[789]

5.168 Fixing a hearing date

Within one month of the time permitted for the completion of evidence, the applicant must obtain a date for the hearing of the originating summons[790] by issuing a notice of an appointment for the attendance of the parties from the chambers of the Companies Court Registrar[791]: two copies of the notice[792] will be required on issue, together with a time estimate signed by the applicant's solicitor or counsel. The notice of the date fixed for the hearing must be served on each respondent not less than 14 days before that date.[793] The notice must state what orders or directions the applicant intends to seek at the hearing, and if the respondent intends to seek different directions or orders, he must serve a counter-notice specifying them, not less than seven days before the hearing.[794] If the summons is adjourned and any party proposes at the resumed hearing to seek directions or orders not previously notified, a notice specifying the same must be served on every other party, not less than seven days before the resumed hearing.[795]

5.169 Affidavit in support

The originating summons should be supported by an affidavit setting out the facts on which the applicant relies in seeking to have restrictions imposed on the shares in

782. RSC O. 10, rr. 5(1) and 1(2).
783. RSC O. 12, rr. 5 and 9.
784. RSC O. 28, r. 1A(1).
785. RSC O. 28, r. 1A(3).
786. RSC O. 28, r. 1A(4).
787. RSC O. 28, r. 1A(5).
788. RSC O. 28, r. 1A(6).
789. RSC O. 28, r. 1A(8).
790. RSC O. 28, r. 2(1).
791. I.e. Room 2.09, second floor, Thomas More Building, Royal Courts of Justice.
792. For the form of the notice, see Form No. 12 in Appendix A to the RSC: *Supreme Court Practice 1997*, Vol. 2, para. 7, p. 7.
793. RSC O. 28, r. 3(1).
794. RSC O. 28, r. 3(3).
795. RSC O. 28, r. 3(4).

question. The affidavit should contain the usual preliminary information regarding the company's incorporation, its registered office location, its objects, and its capital; the affidavit should also explain how the company knows or why the company has good reason to believe that a person has become interested in its shares, and should identify the registered holder of those shares. The affidavit should describe the proper service of notices under s. 212 and explain why the responses (if any) were inadequate, and should exhibit the notices and any responses received. Where it is anticipated that the imposition of the statutory restrictions on shares is likely to have an adverse effect on third parties, the affidavit ought to explain why the restrictions should nevertheless be imposed (although this may not be possible unless and until a third party has explained its opposition to the application).

5.170 The hearing, order and costs

The hearing will, in the first instance, be before the Companies Court Registrar sitting in chambers.[796] The registrar will give directions for the completion of any further evidence required and any procedural matter arising. Once the evidence is complete, the registrar will usually adjourn the originating summons to the Companies Court Judge sitting in open court for determination. The court's powers on hearing the summons are dealt with in paras 5.164 and 5.165, *supra*. Where the court imposes restrictions on shares as a result of a failure to comply with a s. 212 notice, the order will usually require the company's costs to be paid by the person on whom the s. 212 notice was served, who failed to provide full information and whose default caused or contributed to the costs incurred; and he will also pay the costs of an application to remove the restrictions once full information has been given.[797] Where the court refuses to impose restrictions, the costs of the summons may be payable by the company—for example, where the s. 212 notice was invalid because it gave insufficient time for acceptance.[798] Where the originating summons is dismissed because the person served with the s. 212 notice provides the information sought at a late stage after the issue of the summons, the recipient of the notice is likely to be ordered to pay the company's costs. Where the company discontinues proceedings under s. 216 against an intermediary shareholder where the information sought has been obtained from some other source, the costs may be payable by the company to the intermediary on the indemnity or standard basis, or there may be no order as to costs, depending on the extent (if any) to which the intermediary can be said to have brought the application upon himself.[799]

(b) Relaxation and removal of restrictions

5.171 Jurisdiction

Where an order has been made by the court under s. 216 (or by the Secretary of State under s. 445) directing that shares in a company should be subject to the restrictions set out in s. 454, the court has power to relax or remove the restrictions on the application of

796. I.e. Room 4.12, fourth floor, Thomas More Buildings, Royal Courts of Justice.
797. *Re Bestwood plc* [1989] BCLC 606.
798. *Re Lonrho plc (No. 2)* [1989] BCLC 309 at 317a.
799. *Re Ricardo Group plc (No. 2)* [1989] BCLC 766 at 768f–h.

any person aggrieved,[800] and also on the application of the company where the restrictions were imposed by order of the court under s. 216.[801] However, the restrictions may only be removed by order of the court if: (a) the court is satisfied that the relevant facts about the shares have been disclosed to the company and no unfair advantage has been obtained by any person as a result of the earlier default in making disclosure; or (b) the shares are to be transferred for valuable consideration and the court approves the transfer.[802] The reference to a transfer "for valuable consideration" in s. 456(3)(b) enables the restrictions to be removed where the shares are to be exchanged (say, in a takeover) rather than simply sold—this remedies an unfortunate limitation on the court's powers which existed under the former provision in s. 174 of the 1948 Act.[803] Where the court is satisfied that the restrictions which have been imposed affect the rights of third parties unfairly, the court may direct that certain acts of the third parties should not constitute a breach of the restrictions imposed.[804] The court may also direct, on the application of the Secretary of State (where the restrictions were imposed under s. 445) or of the company, that the shares which are subject to the restrictions should be sold and cease to be subject to the restrictions.[805] Where the court has made an order for the sale of shares, the court may then make any further orders which it thinks fit,[806] on the application (*inter alios*) of the company, a person appointed to effect the sale or any person interested in the shares.[807] Where the court directs that the shares should cease to be subject to the restrictions with a view to their sale, the court may continue the restrictions set out in s. 454(1)(c) and (d) (i.e. excluding the shares from entitlement by way of rights issues or distributions otherwise than on a liquidation).

5.172 Form of application

Where the order of the court imposing restrictions on an originating summons under s. 216 granted a general liberty to apply, an application for the relaxation or removal of the restrictions may be made by ordinary summons in the originating summons proceedings. In all other cases, the application will usually be by originating summons[808] in the expedited form[809] supported by affidavit. In cases of urgency, the application may be made by motion directly to the Companies Court Judge.[810] The summons (or notice of motion) should set out the precise form of order sought, identifying the shares in respect of which the application is made and the restrictions sought to be relaxed. It is helpful for the

800. For the meaning of a "person aggrieved", see para 5.5, Note 23, *supra*.
801. S. 456(2).
802. S. 456(3). See also *Re Ricardo Group plc (No. 3)* [1989] BCLC 771 at 773b where the court in its discretion lifted the restrictions even though the relevant s. 212 notice had not been fully answered.
803. See *Re Westminster Property Group plc* [1985] BCLC 188 at 196b–197c.
804. S. 456(1A).
805. S. 456(4) (although this power is unlikely to be exercised where the shares are already subject to a binding agreement for sale: *Re Westminster Property Group plc, supra*, at 199a–c, construing s. 174 of the 1948 Act).
806. S. 456(5).
807. *Ibid.*
808. RSC O. 102, r. 2(1) (although the application for the removal of the restrictions in *Re Westminster Property Group plc, supra*, under the predecessor of s. 456(3), was made by motion: see [1984] BCLC 459 at 460b).
809. RSC O. 102, r. 2(2). See Form No. 10 in Appendix A to the RSC: *Supreme Court Practice 1997*, Vol. 2, para. 4, p. 6.
810. See *Re Ricardo Group plc (No. 3)* [1989] BCLC 771 at 772b.

summons to state the section under which the application is made. The procedure for issuing such a summons is described in para. 5.109, *supra*.

5.173 Parties and service

Where the application to the court is made to relax or remove restrictions imposed by the Secretary of State who has refused to relax or remove them, the applicant may be any person aggrieved[811] (for example, the registered holder of the shares, the person alleged to have a beneficial interest in the shares, or a third party adversely affected by the restrictions imposed); where any of the foregoing persons are not the applicant, they should be joined as respondents. Where the application is to relax or remove restrictions imposed by the court under s. 216, the applicant may be a person aggrieved or the company.[812] Where an interested party is not named as a respondent, he may apply to be joined as a respondent pursuant to O. 15, r. 6 of the Rules of the Supreme Court.[813] Where the restrictions were imposed by order of the Secretary of State who refuses to remove them, he should be joined as a respondent. Where the application is made under s. 456(4) for an order that the shares be sold and cease to be subject to the restrictions, only the Secretary of State (if the restrictions were imposed by the Secretary of State under s. 445, and not by the court under s. 216) or the company may be an applicant, and any person affected by the sale should be joined as a respondent (for example, the registered holder of the shares or any person thought to have a beneficial interest in the shares). Where the application is made under s. 456(5) for an order consequent upon an order for sale, the application may be made by the Secretary of State (if the restrictions were imposed by him under s. 445, and not by the court under s. 216), by the company, by the person appointed to effect the sale, or by any person interested in the shares[814]; and where any of the foregoing are not the applicant, they may be joined as a respondent.

5.174 Affidavit in support

The application for a relaxation or removal of the restrictions imposed by the court should be supported by an affidavit setting out the grounds relied upon in making the application. This will often involve an explanation as to why the circumstances which originally justified the imposition of the restrictions no longer apply—particularly where the application is made by the company which originally sought the restrictions. Where there has not been a change of circumstances but the imposition of the restrictions is adversely affecting the rights of a third party, the affidavit should explain that person's interest and the way in which his rights are adversely affected.

5.175 The hearing, order and costs

Where the application is made by summons or originating summons, the hearing will, in the first instance, be before the Companies Court Registrar in chambers. Once the evidence is complete and any procedural issues resolved, the registrar is likely to adjourn

811. S. 456(2).
812. *Ibid.*
813. *Re Ricardo Group plc (No. 3)*, *supra*, at 772d–e.
814. S. 456(5)(a)–(d).

the summons to the Companies Court Judge for determination. Where the person served with the s. 212 notice was initially in default but has belatedly complied with the notice and has given the information sought, the court should discharge the order imposing restrictions rather than adjourn the summons to allow the company to investigate further possible defaults of which there is no *prima facie* evidence before the court.[815] Where the application to remove the restrictions fails (for example, where the court finds that the person served with the s. 212 notice is still in default of giving the required information), he will usually be ordered to pay the costs of the application. Where the application to have the restrictions lifted succeeds because the applicant has supplied the necessary information belatedly (i.e. after the restrictions were imposed) he will usually be ordered to pay the company's costs of the application.[816] Where the restrictions are lifted owing to some default by the company (for example, the restrictions were exceptionally imposed on an *ex parte* application and the court, having heard the recipient of the s. 212 notice, is satisfied that there was no default in supplying information), the company is likely to be ordered to pay the costs of the person served with the s. 212 notice.

VI. COMPULSORY ACQUISITION OF SHARES

5.176 Introduction

Where a takeover offer is made for a company[817] and the offer is accepted by the holders of nine-tenths in value of the shares to which it relates, the offeror is entitled to give notice to shareholders who have not accepted the offer that it proposes to acquire their shares. The giving of the notice will set in motion a procedure which will lead to the compulsory acquisition of the relevant shares, subject to the right of the shareholder to apply to the court. The right to give such a notice arises only if certain preconditions have been met. These conditions, together with the procedure for acquisition and special provisions relating to such matters as joint offers and convertible securities, are contained in ss. 428–430F Companies Act 1985.[818]

The right of a dissenting shareholder to apply to the court is conferred by s. 430C(1). On any such application, the court may order that the offeror shall not acquire the dissenter's shares or may specify terms of acquisition different from those of the offer,[819] or it may, of course, dismiss the application. The application must be made within six weeks from the date on which the offeror gave notice to the applicant to acquire his shares,[819] and the compulsory acquisition procedure in respect of the applicant's shares is suspended until the application has been disposed of.[820]

A separate right of application to the court arises where a minority shareholder has exercised his right under s. 430A to give notice to an offeror to acquire his shares. Such a notice may be given where (a) a takeover offer is made for all the shares in a company or all the shares of one or more classes, and the offeror has, by virtue of acceptances of

815. *Re Ricardo Group plc* [1989] BCLC 566 at 577d–f.
816. See *Re Bestwood plc* [1989] BCLC 606.
817. I.e. a company formed and registered under the Companies Acts: s. 735. It includes private as well as public companies.
818. As amended by s. 172(1) and sch. 12, Financial Services Act 1986.
819. S. 430C(1).
820. S. 430C(2).

the offer, acquired or contracted to acquire some but not all of the shares to which the offer relates and (b) those shares, with or without any other shares which the offeror has acquired or contracted to acquire, amount to not less than nine-tenths in value of all the shares in the company or the particular class concerned. Where a shareholder has given such a notice, either he or the offeror may apply to the court under s. 430C(3) for an order that the terms on which the offeror is entitled and bound to acquire the shares should be such as the court thinks fit.

5.177 Application

All such applications should be made by originating summons[821] in the expedited form set out in Form No. 10 in Appendix A to the Rules of the Supreme Court.[822] The originating summons should be entitled in the matter of the company whose shares are the subject of the relevant offer and in the matter of the Companies Act 1985. The respondent will be the offeror, save for an application under ss. 430C(3) by the offeror, when the shareholder who has given notice under s. 430A will be the respondent. Unless directed by the court, the company should not be made a respondent.[823]

5.178 Evidence

The application should be supported by affidavit evidence setting out details of the share capital of the company, the offer, the level of acceptances, the notice under s. 429 or 430A and the grounds of the application, including any evidence which the applicant wishes to adduce in support of those grounds.

5.179 Directions

The originating summons will come before the registrar in chambers in the first instance and he may give directions as to the future conduct of the proceedings, including a timetable for any further affidavits, expert evidence, discovery and cross-examination of deponents. Although the court has power to direct pleadings and oral evidence in place of affidavit evidence,[824] the power will rarely, if ever, be exercised on an application under s. 430C. Discovery will be ordered where necessary, for example, where an important issue is whether professional financial advice given to the board of the target company on which the board based its recommendation to shareholders to accept the offer was good advice.[825] *Prima facie* deponents are liable to be cross-examined on their affidavits in proceedings which are of a final rather than an interlocutory nature. The court will order deponents to attend for cross-examination where it will be advantageous for the proper resolution of the issues raised in the proceedings, for example where there is a conflict of expert evidence.[825]

821. RSC O. 102, r. 2(1).
822. RSC O. 102, r. 2(2). For Form No. 10 in Appendix A, see *Supreme Court Practice 1997*, Vol. 2, para. 4.
823. *Supreme Court Practice 1997*, Vol. 1, para. 102/2/19.
824. RSC O. 28, r. 4(3) and (5).
825. *Re Lifecare International plc* [1990] BCLC 222.

5.180 Hearing

The full hearing of the application will usually be before a judge in open court, following adjournment by the registrar. There will be a significant burden on the applicant to show that the terms or circumstances of the offer are such either that his shares should not be acquired at all or that his shares should be acquired only on terms which differ from those accepted by other shareholders. The weight of the burden derives from the high level of acceptances (90%) imposed by the legislation as a precondition to the exercise by the offeror of the statutory power of compulsory acquisition. In matters of commercial judgment, the court is very slow to substitute its own view for the view of those directly involved. This has been emphasised in the reported decisions on applications under this section and its predecessors.[826] However, the court will be ready to intervene where the powers of compulsory acquisition are being abused,[827] or where the offeree shareholders are deprived of material information which was available to the offeror and should have been provided to the offerees,[828] or where there have been breaches of statutory or other provisions designed to protect the position of the offerees.[828]

5.181 Costs

The usual practice as to costs in contested litigation does not apply. Section 430C(4) provides that no order for costs or expenses shall be made against a shareholder making an application under s. 430(C)(1) or (3) unless the court considers either that the application was unnecessary, improper or vexatious, or that there has been unreasonable delay in making the application or unreasonable conduct on his part in conducting the proceedings or the application. The operation of this provision was considered by the Court of Appeal in *Re Britoil plc*,[829] in which its general purpose was described as being "not to discourage [dissentient shareholders] from applying except in cases which ought not properly to engage the attention of the court. If there is something which it is proper for the court to consider, the applicant, even though unsuccessful, ought not to pay the offeror's costs."[830]

826. See *Re Hoare & Co. Ltd* (1933) 150 LT 374; *Re Evertite Locknuts Ltd* [1945] Ch. 220; *Re Press Caps Ltd* [1949] Ch. 434; *Re Sussex Brick Co. Ltd* [1961] Ch. 289n; *Re Grievson, Oldham & Adams Ltd* [1968] Ch. 17.

827. *Re Bugle Press Ltd* [1961] Ch. 270.

828. *Re Chez Nico (Restaurants) Ltd* [1992] BCLC 192.

829. [1990] BCC 70.

830. *Ibid.* at p. 74 per Nourse L.J.

CHAPTER 6

PROCEEDINGS UNDER SECTION 459, COMPANIES ACT 1985

6.1 Section 459

This section forms a key element in part XVII of the Companies Act 1985 which contains provisions for the protection of a company's members against unfair prejudice. The section provides shareholders with a procedural remedy for their grievances and a ready means of inviting the assistance of the Companies Court. The section is in the following terms:

"(1) A member of a company may apply to the court by petition for an order under this Part on the ground that the company's affairs are being or have been conducted in a manner which is [unfairly prejudicial to the interests of its members generally or of some part of its members][1] (including at least himself) or that any actual or proposed act or omission of the company (including an act or omission on its behalf) is or would be so prejudicial.
(2) The provisions of this Part apply to a person who is not a member of a company but to whom shares in the company have been transferred or transmitted by operation of law, as those provisions apply to a member of the company; and references to a member or members are to be construed accordingly.
[(3) In this section (and so far as applicable for the purposes of this section, in section 461(2) 'company' means any company within the meaning of this Act or any company which is not such a company but is a statutory water company within the meaning of the Water Act 1989.][2]"

6.2 History

Section 459 is a re-enactment of s. 75 of the Companies Act 1980, which first introduced a remedy for shareholders on the grounds of unfair prejudice. Prior to the enactment of that provision, the statutory remedy available to a shareholder (who did not wish to seek the winding-up of his company) was contained in s. 210 of the Companies Act 1948, which was based on the concept of "oppression". Owing to the restrictive interpretation given to s. 210 by the courts, Parliament decided to intervene in 1980 in order to introduce a wider and more liberal remedy, requiring the proof by the complainant merely of "unfair prejudice" in the conduct of his company's affairs. This is now contained in s. 459 which is one of the most useful procedural devices available to a shareholder.

1. Subs. (1): words in square brackets substituted by CA 1989, sch. 19, para. 11, as from 4 February 1991.
2. Subs. (3): inserted by the Water Act 1989, s. 190(1), sch. 25, para. 71(3), words in square brackets substituted by Water Consolidation (Consequential Provisions) Act 1991, s. 2(1), sch. 1, para. 40(2).

6.3 The concept of unfair prejudice

To invoke the jurisdiction of the court, the applicant must show that the company's affairs are being (where the petition is based upon present conduct) or have been *conducted* (where it is based upon past conduct) in a manner which is unfairly prejudicial to the interests of its members generally or some part of its members, including at least himself, or that any actual or proposed act or omission of the company (including an act or omission on its behalf) is or would be so prejudicial. The Companies Act gives little or no guidance as to the meaning of the term "unfair prejudice". Accordingly, reference must be made to the decisions of the Companies Court and to practitioners' textbooks for guidance in this area. It is hoped that the following summary may be of assistance:

(1) The conduct complained of must relate to the affairs of the company of which the petitioners are members and be the conduct of the company's affairs.[3] Similarly, the act or proposed act or omission must be an act or omission of the company, or on its behalf. In the absence of any act or proposed act or omission, the court has no jurisdiction to make any order.[4]

(2) The conduct must be both prejudicial (in the sense of causing prejudice or harm) to the relevant interests and also unfairly so. The conduct must be objectively unfair.[5]

(3) In construing "unfairly", account has to be taken of the petitioner's legal rights and any equitable considerations, such as the petitioner's legitimate expectations. To establish unfairness it is not enough to show that some managerial decision might have prejudiced the petitioner's interest.[6]

(4) The test is of unfair prejudice, not of unlawfulness, and conduct may be lawful but unfairly prejudicial.

(5) The relevant interests are the interests of the members (including the petitioners) as members, but such interests are not necessarily limited to strict legal rights under the company's memorandum and articles of association. The court will take into account wider equitable considerations such as any legitimate expectations which a member has which go beyond his legal rights.[7]

(6) The conduct complained of must affect the petitioner in his capacity as a member of the company (i.e. *qua* member) and not in some other capacity,[8] but the court adopts a fairly flexible approach to this test.[9]

(7) The phrase "unfairly prejudicial to the interests of its members generally" was introduced by sch. 19, para. 11 of the Companies Act 1989, and was designed to make it clear that a petitioner can obtain redress under the section even though the conduct complained of affects all the members equally, e.g. the failure to declare a dividend.[10]

3. *Re Ringtower Holdings plc* (1989) 5 BCC 82 at 90.
4. *Re a Company (No. 001761 of 1986)* [1987] BCLC 141 at 143g.
5. *Re Bovey Hotel Ventures Ltd* 31 July 1981, Slade J., unreported; cited in *Re RA Noble & Sons (Clothing) Ltd* [1983] BCLC at 290–291.
6. *Re Saul Harrison & Sons plc* [1994] BCC 475, [1995] 1 BCLC 14 (CA).
7. *Re a Company* [1983] Ch. 178 at 189 D–F, *Re a Company* [1986] BCLC 376 at 379d.
8. *Re a Company* [1986] BCLC 382.
9. *Re a Company (No. 003843 of 1986)* [1987] BCLC 562 at 572.
10. Prior to the amendment, which came into force on 4 February 1991, the position was confused: see *Re a Company (No. 00370 of 1987) ex parte Glossop* [1988] 1 WLR 1068 and *Re Sam Weller & Sons Ltd* [1990] Ch. 682.

(8) "Unfairly prejudiced" is, in short, deliberately imprecise language. The starting point of the court's inquiry is whether the conduct complained of was in accordance with the company's articles of association. However, such a finding does not necessarily mean that it was unfair, still less that the court will exercise its discretion to grant relief. Trivial or technical infringements are not intended to give rise to s. 459 petitions. The minimum required to make out a case of unfair prejudice is that the powers of management have been used for an unlawful purpose, or the company's articles have otherwise been infringed, or that there has been a breach of the petitioner's legitimate expectations, on the basis of which the company was formed.[11]

(9) The section covers acts or omissions which are isolated or in the past, continuing or proposed. However, where future conduct is concerned, there must be evidence of a proposed act or omission which would qualify as unfairly prejudicial conduct and not just a fear of future acts that might potentially prejudice the petitioners.[12]

(10) The past acts of the company are capable of being regarded as unfairly prejudicial within the meaning of s. 459, even though, at the date of the petition or the hearing, the unfairness has been remedied.[13]

6.3.1 Who may present a petition?

The applicant must be either a member of the company[14] or a person to whom shares in the company have been transferred or transmitted by operation of law.[15] The category of members is divided between persons who were subscribers to the company's memorandum of association[16] and every other person who agreed to become a member of a company and whose name is entered on its register of members.[17] The section does not require a contractual agreement; the mere assent to registration as a member is sufficient to satisfy the word "agrees" in s. 22(2).[18] One share only will suffice.[19] Where shares are held in the name of a nominee, the nominee is the member and must be the petitioner.

6.3.2 Where reliance is sought to be placed on s. 459(2), the Companies Court has held that the words "transferred by operation of law" require at least that a proper instrument of transfer should have been executed and delivered to the transferee or the company, in respect of the shares in question. It is not sufficient that there should be an agreement for transfer[20] or that the transfer should have been left blank.[21]

The reference in s. 459(2) to a member including a person to whom shares have been transmitted by operation of law, covers the case where, by some legal act, the legal estate

11. *Re Saul Harrison & Sons plc* [1994] BCC 475 at 488–491, [1995] 1 BCLC 14 at 17–20 per Hoffmann L.J. (CA). *Re BSB Holdings Ltd (No. 2)* [1996] 1 BCLC 155 at 234–243.
12. *Re Gorwyn Holdings Ltd* (1985) 1 BCC 99, 479 (CA).
13. *Re Kenyon Swansea Ltd* [1987] BCLC 514 at 521; *Re a Company (No. 00314 of 1989) ex parte Estate Acquisition and Development Ltd* [1990] BCC 221 at 226, [1991] BCLC 154 at 160–161.
14. S. 459(1).
15. S. 459(2).
16. S. 22(1).
17. S. 22(2).
18. *Re Nuneaton Borough Association Football Club Ltd* (1989) 5 BCC 377 (CA).
19. *Re Garage Door Associates Ltd* (1983) 1 BCC 98, 966.
20. *Re a Company (No. 003160 of 1986)* [1986] BCLC 391 at 393h, (1986) 2 BCC 99, 276.
21. *Re Quickdome Ltd* (1984) 4 BCC 296.

has passed, even though there may be some further act, such as registration, to be carried out.[22] Accordingly, personal representatives of a deceased member and a trustee in bankruptcy are entitled to petition in an appropriate case.

6.4 Section 460: Application by the Secretary of State

Mention should be made, in passing, of the right of the Secretary of State to present a petition under s. 460 if, in the case of any company, he has received a report from inspectors appointed by him under s. 437, or has exercised his powers under s. 447 or 448 or under s. 43(A) or 44(2)–(6) of the Insurance Companies Act 1982, and it appears to him that the company's affairs are being or have been conducted in a manner which is unfairly prejudicial to the interests of its members generally or of some part of its members, or that any actual or proposed act or omission of the company (including an act or omission on its behalf) is or would be so prejudicial. Section 460 adopts similar wording to s. 459 except that the words "(including at least himself)" are omitted after "or of some part of its members". The section provides that the Secretary of State may petition under the section "in addition to or instead of presenting a petition for the winding up of the company". So far as the author is aware, no application has yet been made by the Secretary of State under s. 460 and it has therefore not been the subject of judicial consideration. The procedural requirements are the same as those for any other petition. In effect, the section may provide a member with an indirect remedy. He may apply formally for the appointment of inspectors under s. 431, who may produce a report under s. 437, which would give the Secretary of State grounds to petition.

6.5 Who are the respondents?

The language of ss. 459 and 461 confer the widest jurisdiction on the court as regards the parties against whom relief can be sought. Section 459 does not require that the respondents to the petition should be limited to members of the company, or to its directors, or to those conducting its affairs. However, the company should be made a respondent to every petition even though its role will usually be a minor one. This will be discussed in the following sections.

In the case of a small private company, *all* the members ought to be made respondents. The practice of the Companies Court is to require that all members of the company whose interests would have been affected by the misconduct alleged, or would be affected by an order made by the court under the very wide powers conferred by s. 461 (see para. 6.7.5, *infra*), are to be made respondents to the petition and served with it. On the other hand, there may be occasions where it is unnecessary to join all the members of a company, for instance if the articles contain no pre-emption provisions and if some of the members are mere investors who have taken no part in the formation or management of the company.[23]

In the case of a public listed company, it is usually neither necessary nor desirable (on grounds of cost) to join all the members as respondents. Only the alleged wrongdoers should be joined initially, leaving the other members to be given notice of the petition and

22. *Re a Company* (1986) 2 BCC 98, 951.
23. *Re a Company (No. 007281 of 1986)* [1987] BCLC 593 at 598–599.

to apply to be joined at a later stage. At the first hearing of the petition (see below) the court is required to give directions as to the service of the petition on any person who has not been made a respondent. Accordingly, a member against whom no allegation is made and against whom no relief is sought need not take an active part in the proceedings, unless it is sought to amend the petition to raise an allegation against him or to seek relief which might affect him.

6.5.1 The petitioner should add as a respondent to the petition any other person against whom any relief is sought, even when that person is no longer a member,[24] or who might be affected by any relief granted under s. 461, such as another company to which the business of the company has been hived down. The court has power under O. 15, r. 6(2) of the Rules of the Supreme Court to add, as a respondent, any person not initially made a respondent, on the ground that its presence is necessary to ensure that all matters in dispute are determined, or where there is an issue between that person and the petitioner relating to the relief sought in the petition.[25]

However, notwithstanding the width of the court's jurisdiction to order a person who was not a member of the company to be joined as a respondent, the court will not do so where the facts are such that no court would ever grant the relief sought against that person. This would include a person who has never been a shareholder, a director or manager of the company or otherwise responsible for its affairs, and who is not accused of any wrongdoing.[26]

6.6 The role of the company

As mentioned above, the company is a necessary party to every petition but its role is usually only a formal one. It must be borne in mind that s. 459 petitions generally involve disputes between the shareholders, and the courts are very reluctant to permit the misuse of company funds by those in control in defending a petition. Indeed it is a general principle of company law that the company's money should not be expended on disputes between shareholders.[27] Directors are not entitled to take part in such a dispute at the expense of the company and, if they do so, they will commit a misfeasance and be at risk as to the costs incurred.[28] In an appropriate case, the court will grant an injunction to prohibit the expenditure of costs by the company or to prohibit it from being represented and taking an active part in the proceedings.[29]

6.6.1 At the same time, the courts have recognised the impact of s. 459 proceedings on a company. It has been expressly held that it would be proper for the company's funds to be used with respect to an application under s. 127 of the Insolvency Act 1986 (where a s. 459 petition is coupled with a claim for a winding-up order on the just and equitable ground, under s. 122(1)(g) of the Insolvency Act 1986: see Chapter 7), with respect to the giving of discovery (see below) or when judgment is being delivered if a re-purchase of the petitioner's shares by the company is one of the remedies contemplated. The company

24. *Re a Company (No. 005287 of 1985)* [1986] 1 WLR 281; but see *Re Baltic Real Estate Ltd* [1992] BCC 629.
25. *Re BSB Holdings Ltd* [1993] BCLC 246, [1992] BCC 915.
26. *Supreme Travels Ltd* v. *Little Olympian Each-Ways Ltd* [1994] BCC 947, [1994] 2 BCLC 420.
27. *Re Crossmore Electrical and Civil Engineering Ltd* [1989] BCLC 137 at 138e–f.
28. *Re Kenyon Swansea Ltd* [1987] BCLC 514 at 521; *Re a Company (No. 004502 of 1988) ex parte Johnson* [1992] BCLC 701.
29. *Re Milgate Developments Ltd* [1993] BCLC 291.

may have a legitimate interest in the judgment and there may be a need for the interests of the company as a whole to be considered and the board advised about representations to the court about consequential orders.[30]

All in all, the test of whether participation by the company itself in a s. 459 petition and the incurring of expenditure in the form of legal costs is proper, is whether it is necessary or expedient in the interests of the company as a whole. The court's starting point has been said to be "a sort of rebuttable distaste for such participation and expenditure".[31] There is a heavy onus on a company which has actively participated or has incurred costs to satisfy the court with evidence of the necessity or expedience of having done so in any particular case. If a company seeks approval by the court of such participation or expenditure in advance, such approval is very unlikely in the absence of the most compelling circumstances proven by cogent evidence. Such applications for advance approval are likely to be rare.

6.7 Form and contents of the petition

6.7.1 General

The procedural aspects of a s. 459 petition are governed by the Companies (Unfair Prejudice Applications) Proceedings Rules 1986 ("the Rules")[32] which came into force on 29 December 1986. Except in so far as they are inconsistent with the Rules and the Companies Act 1985, the Rules of the Supreme Court and the practice of the High Court apply to s. 459 petitions in the Companies Court.[33] (Equally, the Rules and practice of the County Court apply to such proceedings in a County Court, with any necessary modifications. County Court proceedings are beyond the scope of this work.)

Rule 3(1) provides that a petition should be in the form set out in the schedule to the Rules, "with such variations, if any, as the circumstances may require". Rule 3(2) states that the petition must specify the grounds on which it is presented and the nature of the relief which is sought by the petitioner. As can be seen from the Form set out in the schedule to the Rules (in Appendix 1) the first four paragraphs of a petition are purely formal and require the insertion of: (i) the company's name; (ii) the address of its registered office; (iii) the amount of its authorised and issued share capital and a statement of the petitioner's holding or other capacity for the purposes of s. 459(2); and (iv) the principal objects of the company. This information can usually be obtained from a search of the company's file at the Companies Registry.

6.7.2 It is important to note that there must be a separate petition in respect of each company which is the subject-matter of the proceedings. Accordingly, where a shareholder holds shares in a number of companies which are treated in substance as a single entity, he must issue a separate petition in respect of each of them and then seek directions from the court that the petitions be heard concurrently or consecutively so that they proceed as though they had been consolidated into one document.[34]

30. *Re a Company (No. 004502 of 1988), ex parte Johnson, supra*, at 705–706.
31. *Re a Company (No. 001126 of 1992)* [1993] BCC 325 at 333c, [1994] 2 BCLC 146 at 156b.
32. S.I. 1986 No. 2000.
33. R. 2(2).
34. *Re a Company* [1984] BCLC 307.

Paragraph 5 of the draft form of petition in the schedule to the Rules attempts to meet the requirement of r. 3(2) that the petition sets out the grounds upon which it is presented to the court. The primary function of the petition is to allege the facts on which the claim to exercise the court's jurisdiction is based. It has been held that, provided that facts which can arguably found such a claim are pleaded, it is not fatal that the petition does not specifically identify them as such.[35] The petition has recently been described as intended to be a more discursive and free-running document than an ordinary pleading—in more ordinary daily language rather than the precise averments of bare facts which a pleading proper ought to contain.[36]

6.7.3 However, this part of the petition must be framed with particular care because it must indicate with precision the grounds upon which the petition is presented and the allegations being relied upon.[37] Despite the width of s. 459, the court does not travel outside the allegations that have been pleaded.[38] Draftsmen are therefore advised to particularise their allegations as, in the absence of a detailed statement of the grounds upon which the petition is based, there is a risk that, notwithstanding the procedural rules relating to pleadings, it will be contended by the respondents that there is insufficient information for them to know the precise nature of the case against them, that the petition is embarrassing and that it should therefore be struck out under O. 18, r. 19 of the Rules of the Supreme Court or, alternatively, under the inherent jurisdiction of the court.[39]

6.7.4 The Court of Appeal has recently reviewed the jurisdiction of the court under s. 459, referring once again to s. 459 proceedings as being "notoriously burdensome". A respondent who applies to have a petition struck out must satisfy the court that the petitioner's case is plainly and obviously unsustainable. However, the consequences for the company are such that the court will scrutinise with care the allegations in the petition and, if necessary, the evidence proposed to be adduced in support, in order to see whether the petitioner really does have an arguable case. This is particularly so when the petition rests on allegations of bad faith akin to fraud.[40] Accordingly, petitions must be drafted in detail in order to satisfy the court that the petitioner's case is a substantial one, worthy of proceeding to trial.

6.7.5 It is the normal practice of the Companies Court to order that a pleading in the form of points of claim be delivered by the petitioner (although occasionally, in straightforward cases, the court may still permit the use of supporting affidavits) (see below). However, in order to save time and to avoid arguments that the petition lacks sufficient particulars of the petitioner's case to enable the respondent to understand the grounds upon which it is based, the petitioner's advisers may choose to present a very detailed petition which may then stand as points of claim. This practice avoids a delay in the proceedings whilst points of claim in support of the petition are drafted and served, enabling the petitioner to make maximum impact on the respondents at an early stage and resulting in the respondents having to plead to the detailed allegations in the petition. However, the practice of having the petition stand as a points of claim is one which requires the consent of the respondent or the approval of the court. Moreover, the course

35. *Re a Company* [1986] BCLC 382 at 390d.
36. *Re Unisoft Group Ltd (No. 3)* [1994] BCLC 609 at 613c.
37. *Re Tecnion Investments Ltd* [1985] BCLC 434 at 441 (CA).
38. *Re BSB Holdings Ltd (No. 2)* [1996] 1 BCLC 155 at 160.
39. *Re WR Willcocks & Co. Ltd* [1974] Ch. 163.
40. *Re Saul D. Harrison & Sons plc* [1994] BCC 475 at 492, [1995] 1 BCLC 14 at 22f–h.

of drafting a detailed petition is one which normally cannot be adopted where speed is necessary and an application for interlocutory relief, such as an injunction, is required. In such cases, the petition is likely to be in shorter form, merely summarising the grounds upon which it is based and, as such, is somewhat analogous to a generally endorsed writ of summons. It can usually be amended later, pursuant to O. 20, rr. 5 and 7 of the Rules of the Supreme Court. It will be accompanied by a detailed affidavit explaining the petitioner's case and exhibiting the essential documents. This affidavit must fairly reflect the matters in issue and provide full and frank disclosure if the application is to be made on an *ex parte* basis.

The remainder of para. 5 of the draft petition in the schedule to the Rules requires an express averment of unfair prejudice to the petitioner. This is an absolute requirement and is the foundation for the exercise of the court's jurisdiction. This is the conclusion to be drawn from the factual allegations set out in the petition.

6.8 The relief sought under section 461

Rule 3(2) of the Rules requires the petition to specify the nature of the relief which is sought by the petitioner. The prayer need not contain as much detail as the court would require on the drawing-up of the order or as much as is requisite in a draft minute. It must, however, contain enough to leave no doubt as to what the petitioner desires the court to do.[41] He must take the responsibility of stating specifically what he wants. Moreover, the relief prayed for must be appropriate to the unfairly prejudicial conduct of which the petitioner complains, although it is proper for the petitioner to add, as indeed the draft form of petition set out in the schedule to the Rules envisages, a prayer "that such other order may be made as the Court thinks fit".

6.8.1 The court has a very wide discretion under s. 461 as to the type of order that it may make, once it is satisfied that the petition is well founded and that there has been unfair prejudice within the meaning of s. 459. The court lacks jurisdiction in the absence of such a finding and cannot offer its services as an arbitrator outside the jurisdiction conferred by the section.[42] The essential provisions of s. 461 are as follows:

"(1) If the court is satisfied that a petition under this Part is well founded, it may make such order as it thinks fit for giving relief in respect of the matters complained of.
(2) Without prejudice to the generality of subsection (1), the court's order may—
- (a) regulate the conduct of the company's affairs in the future,
- (b) require the company to refrain from doing or continuing an act complained of by the petitioner or to do an act which the petitioner has complained it has omitted to do,
- (c) authorise civil proceedings to be brought in the name and on behalf of the company by such person or persons and on such terms as the court may direct,
- (d) provide for the purchase of the shares of any members of the company by other members or by the company itself and, in the case of a purchase by the company itself, the reduction of the company's capital accordingly."

The section thereby confers on the court a discretion to do what is considered fair and equitable in all the circumstances of the case.[43]

41. *Re Antigen Laboratories Ltd* [1951] 1 All ER 110.
42. *Re a Company* [1986] BCLC 362 at 368.
43. *Re Bird Precision Bellows Ltd* [1986] Ch. 658 at 669E (CA).

6.8.2 The court is empowered to make such order as it thinks fit in order to remedy or provide relief in respect of the unfair prejudice. However, the relief need not be directed solely towards remedying the particular things that have happened. Section 461(1) enables the court to make orders such as will enable the company, for the future, to be properly run. The time for determining the appropriateness of the order is the date of the hearing and not the date of presentation of the petition. Accordingly, it has been held that, if by that stage events have taken place which render the making of an order unnecessary, (e.g. the appointment of an administrative receiver over the assets of the company, thereby displacing the board of directors and bringing to an end the possibility of further unfair prejudice towards the petitioner) the court will make no order.[44]

Section 461(2) provides, without prejudice to the generality of the wording of subs. (1), for four specific forms of relief, each of which should be considered.

6.8.3 "(a) regulate the conduct of the company's affairs in the future"

The section empowers the court to make an order regulating the company's future affairs and for this purpose it can order that its affairs be under the conduct of somebody in whom the shareholders generally can have confidence that the company will be properly managed.[45] In a decision under the old s. 210 of the Companies Act 1948, the court restrained the respondent chairman and managing director from interfering with the affairs of the company but ordered that instead he be appointed president of the company for life with no powers, rights or duties, thereby reflecting his past contributions to the company.[46]

The court can order the alteration of the memorandum or articles of association of the company. If it does so, such an alteration has the same effect as if it was duly made by a special resolution of the company.[47] An office copy of the order must therefore be delivered by the company to the registrar of companies for registration within 14 days of the making of the order or such longer period as the court may allow.[48]

6.8.4 "(b) require the company to refrain from doing or continuing an act complained of by the petitioner or to do an act which the petitioner has complained it has omitted to do"

The court has power to order a prohibitory or mandatory injunction. It can restrain the company from proceeding with an action that is unfairly prejudicial to the petitioner or it can require the company to carry out an act of which the petitioner has complained it has failed to do. This may include an order restraining the company from altering its memorandum or articles of association in a particular way. If such an order is made, the company thereafter has no power to make any such alteration in breach of the requirement without leave of the court.[49]

44. *Re Hailey Group Ltd* [1993] BCLC 459.
45. *Re a Company (No. 00789 of 1987) ex parte Shooter* [1990] BCLC 384 at 394–395.
46. *Re HR Harmer Ltd* [1959] 1 WLR 62.
47. S. 461(4).
48. S. 461(5).
49. S. 461(3).

6.8.5 "(c) authorise civil proceedings to be brought in the name and on behalf of the company by such person or persons and on such terms as the court may direct"

This form of order avoids all the technical problems associated with minority shareholders' actions by writ as a result of the rule in *Foss* v. *Harbottle*.[50] The court can authorise proceedings to be brought in the company's name and on terms that provide for the legal costs to be paid by the company. Such an order would be analogous to that which can sometimes be obtained in respect of a minority shareholder's action by writ, pursuant to which a plaintiff can obtain an indemnity for the costs of legal proceedings to be conducted for the benefit of the company.[51] However, it should be noted that this provision is at present deprived of much effect because the court can only include such an authority as part of its final order at the end of the proceedings which, like most High Court litigation, can be of considerable duration and cost. It has been held that the court can only exercise its discretion under s. 461 after it has made a finding of unfair prejudice and is satisfied that the petition is well founded.[52]

6.8.6 "(d) provide for the purchase of the shares of any members of the company by other members or by the company itself and, in the case of a purchase by the company itself, the reduction of the company's capital accordingly"

This is the most common form of order sought in s. 459 petitions because it enables a parting of the ways between the shareholders, and facilitates the realisation by one party of his investment in the company. There has been considerable reported authority on this topic, a review of which is beyond the scope of this work. Readers are referred to the leading textbooks on company law. It will suffice to mention that the overriding principle operated by the court is that the price to be fixed must be a fair one, having regard to all the circumstances of the case.[53] In the case of a company which is a quasi-partnership, the court can order that a minority shareholding should be purchased at a price which takes no account of any discount for the minority but is determined on a pro-rata basis.[54] However, where the shares were originally purchased on a discounted basis or a shareholder has elected to remain as a minority shareholder after the company ceased to be a quasi-partnership, the court can order that they be valued on a discounted basis in order to produce a fair result.[55]

6.8.7 Petitions can be drafted so as to include in the prayer a form of order for the purchase by the respondents or the company of the petitioner's shareholding at a price to be determined by the court. Alternatively, but more rarely, they can seek an order that the respondents be obliged to sell their shares at a price so determined.[56] For this purpose the

50. (1843) 2 Hare 461. See para. 6.9.23, *infra*.

51. *Wallersteiner* v. *Moir (No. 2)* [1975] QB 373; *Smith* v. *Croft* [1986] 1 WLR 580; *Jaybird Group Ltd* v. *Greenwood* [1986] BCLC 319.

52. *Re a Company (No. 004175 of 1986)* (1987) 3 BCC 41.

53. *Re Bird Precision Bellows Ltd* [1986] Ch. 658 (CA).

54. *Re Bird Precision Bellows Ltd* [1984] Ch. 419 at 431 per Nourse J.

55. *Re a Company (No. 005134 of 1986) ex parte Harries* [1989] BCLC 383.

56. See e.g. *Re a Company (No. 00789 of 1987) (Nuneaton Borough A.F.C. Ltd)* (1989) 5 BCC 792 and *Re Nuneaton Borough A.F.C. Ltd* [1991] BCC 44 (where the court insisted as a condition of the order for purchase of the respondent's majority holding that the petitioner arrange for the repayment of amounts advanced by the respondent to the company).

court will be involved in fixing the price, which can be a laborious and expensive exercise, involving expert evidence of valuation on both sides. An alternative form of prayer that would avoid the incurring of such substantial professional costs, at least at the stage prior to the trial (when it is often by no means certain that the petitioner will succeed), is to ask the court to order that the petitioner's shares be purchased at a price fixed by an independent valuation to be carried out by an expert Chartered Accountant to be appointed by the court. The prayer can then ask the court to give directions as to the basis and method of valuation, the making and timing of any representations by the parties to the independent valuer and the payment of his costs.

6.8.8 An important factor is often the date as at which the shares should be valued. Generally, the court will order that this is the date of its order. However, there is no overriding rule save that the concept of fairness is paramount.[57] If the fortunes of a company have declined after the exclusion of the petitioner, he may be entitled to a valuation of his shareholding as at an historic date, perhaps even prior to the date of presentation of the petition.[58] On the other hand, the fixing of the price will take into account the petitioner's own conduct and this may be such that he will be held not to be entitled to share in the company's success after his departure.[59] On occasion the court has chosen the date of the petition[60] or even the financial year end closest to the date of the order.[61] It is advisable for the petition to specify the date as at which the valuation is sought if it is to be argued that this should be other than the date of the court's order.

6.9 Procedural steps

6.9.1 Presentation of the petition

The petitioner's solicitors are required by r. 3(2) to deliver to the Companies Court for filing sufficient copies of the petition as drafted by Counsel for service under r. 4 and must pay the fee required on presentation of the petition.[62] Upon delivery of these documents to the court, they are stamped with the date and time of issue and the court then fixes a hearing date, known as the return day, on which the petitioner and the respondents should attend before the registrar of the Companies Court in chambers for directions to be given in relation to the procedure on the petition. On fixing the return day, the court official will return to the petitioner's solicitors sealed copies of the petition for service, each endorsed with the return day and the time of the hearing. The normal period between the date of presentation and the return day is about three to four weeks, thereby enabling the petitioner to complete the service of the petition, and the respondents to obtain legal advice. This period varies, however, when a petition is presented close to a court vacation. No affidavit is required from the petitioner or his solicitor at this stage.

57. *Re London School of Electronics* [1986] Ch. 211; *Re DR Chemicals Ltd* [1989] BCLC 383.
58. *Re OC (Transport) Services Ltd* [1984] BCLC 251 at 258.
59. *Re London School of Electronics*, *supra*, at 224–225.
60. *Re Cumana Ltd* [1986] BCLC 430.
61. *Re Macro (Ipswich) Ltd* [1994] 2 BCLC 354.
62. The current fee is £80 from 15 January 1997: see Supreme Court Fees (Amendment) Order 1993 (S.I. 1996 No. 3191).

6.9.2 Service

The petitioner is required to serve a sealed copy of the petition on the company at least 14 days before the return day.[63] This enables the company to obtain legal advice as to the stance it must adopt at the first hearing for directions. The company ought to be served at the registered office address stated in the petition. By virtue of s. 725 of the Companies Act 1985, service may be effected by leaving the petition at or sending it to the registered office. In addition, the petitioner must serve a sealed copy of the petition on every respondent named in the petition, again at least 14 days prior to the return day.[64]

6.9.3 A petitioner who desires to serve his s. 459 petition on a respondent who is outside the jurisdiction must obtain leave from the court to do so, where necessary, under O. 11 of the Rules of the Supreme Court, the terms of which apply to s. 459 petitions.[65] Compliance with O. 11 is required, notwithstanding that the petition may be combined with an application for winding-up on the just and equitable ground, in respect of which r. 12.12 of the Insolvency Rules 1986 expressly provides that O. 11 does not apply to insolvency proceedings (see para. 8.8.1 below). The burden of showing that England is the more appropriate forum for the trial of the issues in the petition rests on the petitioner.[66]

The application for leave must be supported by an affidavit of the petitioner or his solicitor in accordance with O. 11, r. 4, stating the grounds upon which it is made, the deponent's belief that the petitioner has a good cause of action, the place or country in which the respondent is to be found and (where O. 11, r. 1(1)(c) is relied upon i.e. where the petition is brought against a person duly served within or out of the jurisdiction and a person out of the jurisdiction is a necessary or proper party thereto) the grounds for the deponent's belief that there is, between the petitioner and the respondent on whom the petition has been served, a real issue which the petitioner may reasonably ask the court to try. Moreover, no leave will be given by the court unless it is made sufficiently clear that the case is a proper one for service out of the jurisdiction under O. 11.[67] The petitioner must, for this purpose, show that he has a good arguable case on the merits.

6.9.4 As with any other application for leave to serve proceedings out of the jurisdiction, the application for leave is made to the court on an *ex parte* basis. With s. 459 petitions, the application is made initially to the registrar of the Companies Court. The affidavit in support must make clear which sub-rule of O. 11, r. 1(1) is relied upon. Where an order for the purchase of the petitioner's shares is sought, reliance may be placed on O. 11, r. 1(1)(b) as the respondent is obliged to do something within the jurisdiction.[68] The affidavit must be full and frank. If any material fact is omitted, the court may later decide to discharge the order in accordance with the normal principles of such applications.[69]

63. R. 4(1).
64. R. 4(2).
65. It appears that service of the petition may be permissible without leave where the respondents are domiciled in another "Convention territory" to which the Brussels or the Lugano Convention applies by virtue of the Civil Jurisdiction and Judgments Acts 1982 and 1991, but this has yet to be tested.
66. *Re Harrods (Buenos Aires) Ltd* [1992] Ch. 72 at 114C–117E (CA).
67. RSC O. 11, r. 4(2).
68. *Re Baltic Real Estate Ltd* [1992] BCC 629 at 635.
69. RSC O. 12, r. 8. *The Hagen* [1908] P. 189 at 201.

6.9.5 Hearing for directions

On the stated return date, the petitioner and those respondents who have been served and choose to appear, attend either in person or by solicitor or by solicitor and counsel, before the registrar of the Companies Court in chambers for directions. This is a most important hearing at which the registrar will determine the procedural steps to be taken in the petition. The parties, through their solicitors, are well advised to attempt to agree the directions before the hearing. These should include an agreed timetable for the various steps in the proceedings. Amongst the questions which will be dealt with are the following:

6.9.6 Service of the petition on any other persons. The reader is referred to para. 6.5, *supra*, in which the question of who are the proper respondents to the petition is discussed. The return date for the petition is an appropriate time at which to address this question.

6.9.7 Whether pleadings or affidavits are to be served. The current practice is for the registrar to order that points of claim, points of defence and points of reply (if so advised) be served by the parties. (Although the Rules refer to "particulars" of claim etc. the terminology of the Commercial Court has been adopted in practice.) It is considered by the court that pleadings help to clarify the matters at issue between the parties in a way which is superior to affidavit evidence. The old practice of serving a substantial volume of affidavit evidence in support of and in answer to the petition, with further affidavits in reply, has been the subject of judicial criticism.[70] It is perhaps the case that reliance upon affidavit should be confined, in practice, to cases where there have already been extensive interlocutory proceedings and much time has been spent on the preparation of affidavit evidence, or where the case is a relatively simple one in which the issues are few. Such cases will be rare.

Adequate time must be provided for the service of pleadings and the normal procedural rules for seeking extensions of time will apply.[71] In the absence of an agreed extension, an application should be made to the registrar for an extension of the period in which the pleadings must be served. This application is equivalent to a time summons. Mention was made earlier of the possibility of serving a petition in long form, thereby alleviating the necessity to serve separate points of claim. In such cases a direction is sought from the registrar that the petition stand as points of claim and the respondents are directed to file points of defence. Points of reply will normally follow.

6.9.8 Points of claim and subsequent pleadings must be prepared with skill and care as the normal rules relating to pleadings will apply to them. No averment can be made in the points of claim which does not appear in the petition.[72] Parties can apply for further and better particulars of the allegations made under RSC O. 18, r. 12. While pleadings can be amended in accordance with RSC O. 20, it is the invariable practice of the court to require

70. *Re a Company (No. 005134 of 1986) ex parte Harries* [1989] BCLC 383 at 390g.
71. RSC O. 3, r. 5.
72. *Re Lundie Bros Ltd* [1965] 1 WLR 1051 at 1058, [1965] 2 All ER 692 at 699; *Re Unisoft Group Ltd (No. 3)* [1994] 1 BCLC 609 at 624e, (*sub nom. Re Unisoft Group Ltd (No. 2)* [1994] BCC 766 at 778D).

late amendments (in particular those sought at trial) to be completely and fully particularised. Statements of the petitioner's belief should not appear in the points of claim which should allege facts and not matters of belief.[73]

Any pleading which does not meet these requirements is capable of being struck out, in whole or in part, under RSC O. 18, r. 19 or under the inherent jurisdiction of the court. The Companies Court seeks to ensure that oppression is not caused to the parties, in particular to the respondents, by allowing a trawl through facts which, although they have given rise to grievances, do not constitute relevant conduct of the affairs of the company within the very wide words of s. 459. Pleadings which fail to disclose a cause of action (because, for instance, the conduct alleged was not conduct of the affairs of the respondent company or did not affect the petitioner *qua* member) will be struck out.

6.9.9 Discovery and inspection. The process of discovery on a s. 459 petition is important, and is one of the aspects of the proceedings that will often involve the company in seeking separate and independent legal advice. The normal principles and procedures enshrined in O. 24 of the Rules of the Supreme Court apply, and readers are referred to the relevant section of the Supreme Court Practice. The parties must include in their lists of documents all documents which are, or have been in their possession, custody or power relating to any matter in question in the proceedings. Discovery is limited to the allegations in the petition.[74]

In general, all documents obtained by the company in the course of the administration of the company, such as advice by solicitors to the company about its affairs, are the proper subject of discovery where they relate to any question in the petition. However, this rule will not apply where there is hostile litigation between a shareholder and the company. A s. 459 petition is not usually to be regarded as hostile litigation between a shareholder and the company for this purpose, any more than in the case of a contributory's winding-up petition.[75] Discovery is usually directed to be made by lists unsupported by affidavits, unless there is a serious question in issue as to the retention or destruction of vital documents or the honesty of certain parties, when an affidavit will be required verifying the list.

6.9.10 The timetable for directions must allow adequate time for inspection of documents referred to in the lists of documents served by the parties and for the parties to take copies thereof. When serving his list, a party's solicitor must serve a notice in accordance with RSC O. 24, r. 9 stating a time within seven days after service at which the documents may be inspected at a place specified in the notice. The other procedural rules relating to inspection of documents in High Court proceedings (O. 24, rr. 10, 11, 11A, 12 and 13) apply to s. 459 petitions.

6.9.11 Interrogatories. The parties are entitled to serve interrogatories on each other in accordance with the normal practice and procedure set down in O. 26 of the Rules of the Supreme Court. Readers are referred to the relevant section of the Supreme Court Practice. Applications for interrogatories (under O. 26, r. 1) or for an order that interrogatories served without Order (under O. 26, r. 3) be withdrawn or varied, are made to the registrar

73. *Re Unisoft Group Ltd (No. 3)* [1994] 1 BCLC 609 at 626f, (*sub nom. Re Unisoft Group Ltd (No. 2)* [1994] BCC 766 at 780C.
74. *Re Tecnion Investments* [1985] BCLC 434.
75. *Re Hydrosan Ltd* [1991] BCLC 418.

at later hearings for directions. The procedure is the same as that for writ actions. Interrogatories will be permitted where they constitute an attempt to ascertain facts which are not within the knowledge of the petitioner but are within the knowledge of the respondents or where they seek to obtain admissions. The court has adopted the approach that both purposes are legitimate if they could save costs in shortening the trial or lead to a settlement of some of the issues in dispute. As such, they will be regarded as necessary in order fairly to dispose of the cause or matter as between the petitioner and the respondents. Interrogatories will not be improper merely because the answers to the questions raised might emerge in cross-examination at trial.[76]

6.9.12 Advertisement of the petition. Rule 5(c) of the Rules expressly provides that, on the return date, the court shall give directions as to whether, and if so by what means, the petition is to be advertised. Section 459 petitions, being disputes between the shareholders of a company, do not concern the creditors of the company and are seldom advertised before a late stage in the proceedings in order to avoid unnecessary damage being done to the business and commercial reputation of the company. This will only serve to reduce the value of the petitioner's shareholding. Accordingly, no attempt should be made to advertise a s. 459 petition, whether in the *London Gazette* or anywhere else, before the return date and the hearing for directions.

At the hearing for directions a direction should be sought from the registrar that the petition be not advertised until further order. Where such an order is made, the petition is thereafter referred to by number only. Such a direction will prohibit notice of the existence of the petition being given to the company's bankers or third parties such as suppliers and customers. Breach of the prohibition, if carried out with a view to putting pressure on the respondents, may result in the petition being struck out as an abuse of process.[77] Indeed, in a very recent case, the court has held that the implication of r. 5(c) is that unless the court directs advertisement, there should be none. Where the court has not yet made any direction it constitutes a breach of the spirit of the Rules as well as *prima facie* abuse of the process of the Companies Court to bring to the attention of any person not already a party to the proceedings the fact that the petition exists. As a general rule, the court is very ready to strike out a petition where the breach amounts to a serious abuse.[78]

6.9.13 Other procedural matters. At the hearing for directions on the return date, the registrar, having set out a timetable for the procedure on the petition, will adjourn the further hearing of the petition to a suitable future date, by which stage the steps described in the directions can be expected to have been carried out. At this later hearing for directions it will then be open to the parties to apply for further directions, including orders for further and better particulars of the pleadings, orders for specific discovery, orders relating to interrogatories, and directions as to the service and exchange of expert evidence (if any). Appeals from orders made by the registrar are to the judge, in open court. Once the registrar is convinced that all outstanding procedural matters have been dealt with, he will order that the petition be set down for trial. In due course, counsel will

76. *Neal* v. *December Commercial Properties (No. 1) Ltd* [1996] BCC 577.
77. *Re a Company (No. 00687 of 1991)* [1991] BCC 210.
78. *Re a Company (No. 002015 of 1996)*, *New Law Digest* 20 December 1996.

be required to supply the Companies Court with a signed estimate of the length of trial.

6.9.14 Interlocutory applications

With the growing popularity of s. 459 petitions have come numerous applications to the Companies Court for interlocutory relief in order to preserve the *status quo* pending the trial of the petition. Readers are referred to the standard textbooks on company law for details of such applications. Many applications have sought a wider range of relief than that usually granted by way of final orders under s. 461 and have included applications for:

(i) an injunction restraining voting at a company meeting[79];
(ii) an injunction restraining the holding of a requisitioned meeting[80];
(iii) an injunction ordering the convening of a requisitioned meeting[81];
(iv) an injunction restraining the disposal of assets without shareholder approval[82];
(v) the appointment of a receiver[83];
(vi) an injunction restraining a company from summarily determining the petitioner's service contract.[84]

6.9.15 Interlocutory relief involving injunctions or receivership is sought by notice of motion in the petition, and the application is made to a judge of the Companies Court. Interim relief is granted by analogy with ordinary *American Cyanamid* principles.[85] The basis of the court's jurisdiction is s. 37 of the Supreme Court Act 1981 which empowers the court to make interlocutory orders by way of injunction or the appointment of a receiver in all cases in which it appears to the court to be just and convenient to do so. The burden is on the petitioner to demonstrate on affidavit that the petition raises a triable issue of unfair prejudice. The only question will then be that of the balance of convenience in the preservation of the *status quo* pending the trial of the petition.[86] The court has held that it is most desirable that the position of the company be not altered or disturbed more than is absolutely essential between the presentation and the hearing of the petition, since the *status quo* must affect the remedy which may be available.[87] On the other hand, it is submitted that, where a petition seeks the purchase of the petitioner's shares, the balance of convenience will often be against the grant of an injunction, since the purchase price can be fixed to take into account the depreciation in the value of the petitioner's shares brought about by the unfair prejudice. It should be noted that a petitioner who obtains interlocutory relief will be obliged, in accordance with normal principles, to give an undertaking in damages to the respondents, including the company. This is a factor which must be taken into account by his advisers.

79. *Re Carrington Viyella plc* (1983) 1 BCC 98, 951.
80. *Re Whyte (Petitioner)* (1984) 1 BCC 99, 044 (Ct of Session).
81. *Re McGuiness* (1988) 4 BCC 161 (Ct of Session).
82. *Re Posgate & Denby (Agencies) Ltd* [1987] BCLC 8.
83. *Re a Company (No. 00596 of 1986)* [1987] BCLC 133.
84. *Re Tottenham Hotspur plc* [1994] 1 BCLC 655.
85. *American Cyanamid Co.* v. *Ethicon Ltd* [1975] AC 496.
86. *Re Posgate & Denby (Agencies) Ltd* [1987] BCLC 8 at 15d–16b.
87. *Re a Company* [1985] BCLC 80.

6.9.16 Interlocutory relief does not normally extend to a payment on account of the purchase price for the petitioner's shares. It has been expressly held that the provisions for an interim payment on account of any damages, debt or other sum which a party may be liable to pay under O. 29, r. 10 of the Rules of the Supreme Court do not apply to s. 459 petitions.[88] However, the Court of Session has made an interim order for a payment on account of the share price, pending a final determination of the amount to be paid where there was an admission by the respondents that the company's affairs had been conducted in a manner which was unfairly prejudicial to the interests of the petitioners and the parties had agreed that the court should order the company or other respondents to purchase the petitioners' shares at such price and upon such terms as the court should direct.[89]

6.9.17 Trial

The trial of a s. 459 petition proceeds in the normal manner of a trial of an action in the Chancery Division of the High Court. The parties must accordingly comply with the procedural requirements of the *Chancery Guide* which apply as much to the Companies Court as to any other part of the Chancery Division. In cases which are estimated to take more than 10 days, an application should be made for a pre-trial review before a judge.[90] The hearing is in open court. If affidavit evidence has been filed by the parties, the deponents are cross-examined by the opposing counsel on their affidavits. Invariably a direction is made that deponents must be given a minimum period of notice prior to the trial that they should attend for cross-examination, subject to the proviso that, if they do not attend, their affidavits cannot be read in evidence. Where pleadings have been served, the case proceeds in a similar way to an ordinary writ action. Witness statements will be required under O. 38, r. 2A of the Rules of the Supreme Court. Parties may obtain evidence by writs of subpoena under O. 38, r. 14. No expert evidence will be admissible in the absence of a direction to that effect, pursuant to O. 38, rr. 35–44.

Judges have occasionally expressed strong views about the length of the trial of s. 459 petitions, the unpredictability of their management, and the enormous costs which can be incurred by reason of the number of separate issues which often arise on the pleadings and the volume of documents liable to be produced.[91] The prospect of a lengthy contested petition, sometimes brought by a legally aided petitioner, is a strong inducement to the respondents to settle the dispute on terms favourable to the petitioner. It is likely in the future that the court will insist upon a strict adherence to the normal procedural rules of the High Court, in particular with regard to the requirement for precise and fully particularised pleadings related only to the matters which are properly in issue under s. 459, as a means of restraining the procedure from getting out of hand.

6.9.18 Expert evidence

As mentioned above, no expert evidence will be admissible at trial without the formal leave of the court. An appropriate direction for leave to introduce expert evidence and for

88. *Re a Company (No. 004175 of 1986)* (1987) 3 BCC 41.
89. *Ferguson* v. *Maclennan Salmon Co. Ltd* [1990] BCC 702.
90. See *Chancery Guide*, para. 3.10.
91. *Re a Company (No. 004377 of 1985)* [1987] 1 WLR 102; *Re Unisoft Group Ltd* (No. 3) [1994] BCLC 609.

the exchange of reports should be sought when the matter comes before the registrar in chambers for directions. Expert evidence is by its nature a costly exercise. Parties are well advised, where the petitioner is seeking an order for the purchase of his shares, to take professional accountancy advice at any early stage, preferably from an accountant who is willing to appear in court as an expert witness to stand by his valuation if required. The vast majority of s. 459 petitions are settled, often on the basis of the expert accountancy advice obtained by the parties. Where parties are anxious to reduce expense they may seek an order that the petitioner's shares be purchased by an independent valuer appointed by the court, thereby deferring the need for expert evidence until the issue of liability has been resolved at trial.[92] The use of expert evidence in future trials is likely to be restricted.

6.9.19 Costs

Unlike a minority shareholders' action, where it is possible in an appropriate case to obtain an order for an indemnity from the company as to the costs of the proceedings, a s. 459 petition is concerned with the infringement of the rights of an individual shareholder and the unfair prejudice caused to his interests as a member of the company. He is not, in substance, asserting a right which belongs to the company alone. A petitioner under s. 459 is therefore not entitled to an advance order requiring the company to indemnify him as to his costs. He will always be at risk as to his costs of the petition.[93] An unsuccessful petitioner may even end up losing his shares if an order for costs is made against him which can be enforced by way of a charging order on the shares.[94]

6.9.20 By their very nature, s. 459 petitions frequently raise many separate grievances, some of which may be held to be justified and others not. The Court of Appeal has recently held[95] that the costs of such proceedings are in the discretion of the court and should follow the event, except when it appears to the court that, in the circumstances, some other order should be made. The general rule will not cease to apply simply because the petitioner, who has successfully obtained the relief sought in the petition, has failed on some issues, but he may be deprived of his costs in whole or in part where he has caused a significant increase in the length or cost of the proceedings, or where he has made allegations improperly or unreasonably. In that case, the court may not only deprive him of his costs but may order him to pay the whole or part of the unsuccessful party's costs. (In the particular case under review, the petitioners were deprived of one half of their costs. This decision is a warning to the legal advisers of petitioners not to include in s. 459 petitions material which cannot be justified or is unsubstantiated and will unduly lengthen the trial.)

Where a limited company is the petitioner, it is a "plaintiff in an action or other legal proceeding" within the meaning of s. 726(1) of the Companies Act 1985. It may therefore face an application from the respondents for security for costs under that section, where it appears by credible testimony that there is reason to believe that the petitioner will be unable to pay the respondents' costs if they are successful in their defence. An order for

92. See para. 6.8.7, *supra*.
93. *Re Sherborne Park Residents Co. Ltd* (1986) 2 BCC 99, 528.
94. *Re Estate Acquisition & Developments Ltd* [1995] BCC 338.
95. *Re Elgindata Ltd (No. 2)* [1993] BCLC 119 (CA).

security for costs is discretionary, and will not be made if the court concludes that it would be unfair to make it.[96]

6.9.21 Applications for security for costs against individual petitioners can be made by the respondents under the provision of O. 23 of the Rules of the Supreme Court. Reference should be made to the Supreme Court Practice for the standard procedures under the rule, which apply equally in this area.[97] The provision most commonly relied upon is O. 23, r. 1(1)(a), which provides that the respondent may apply for security where it appears to the court that the petitioner is ordinarily resident outside the jurisdiction. The Court of Appeal has recently held that the court should never exercise its discretion under this rule to order security to be given by an individual plaintiff or petitioner who is a national of and resident in another member state which is a party to the Brussels Convention on Jurisdiction and Enforcement of Judgments in Civil and Commercial Matters, at any rate in the absence of very cogent evidence of substantial difficulty in enforcing a judgment in that other member state. However, the Court of Appeal emphasised that nothing it said had any bearing on the case in which security is sought against a foreign insolvent company, whether resident in a member state or not, nor where the plaintiff is ordinarily resident in a country which is not a member state of the Convention.[98]

6.9.22 Alternative proceedings

Petitions under s. 459 often contain an alternative plan for the winding-up of a company under s. 122(1)(g) of the Insolvency Act 1986, the "just and equitable" ground.[99] When petitions are drafted in this manner they become subject to a different code of procedure contained in the Insolvency Rules 1986. This will be examined in detail in the next chapter.

6.9.23 A minority shareholder sometimes seeks to bring proceedings by writ in order to enforce a personal right or to obtain redress on behalf of his company. The latter proceedings, known as a derivative action, are restricted by the application of the well-known rule in *Foss* v. *Harbottle*[100] to which there are a number of limited exceptions. The body of case law in this area is both obscure and complex. Derivative actions are beyond the scope of this work as they constitute actions at common law, brought in the Chancery Division of the High Court and not the Companies Court. Derivative actions are the subject of a new procedural rule in RSC O. 15, r. 12A which requires the plaintiff minority shareholder to apply to a Master for leave to continue with the action if the defendant has given notice of intention to defend. The application must be supported by an affidavit verifying the facts on which the claim and the entitlement to sue on behalf of the company are based. The new rule follows on from the decision of the Court of Appeal in *Prudential Assurance Co. Ltd* v. *Newman Industries (No. 2)*[101] that minority shareholders must

96. *Re Unisoft Group Ltd (No. 1)* [1993] BCLC 1292, [1994] BCC 11 (CA).

97. See e.g. *Re Little Olympian Each-Ways Ltd (No. 2)* [1995] 1 BCLC 48.

98. *Fitzgerald* v. *Williams* [1996] QB 657 at 671–675 (CA), applying *Mund & Fester* v. *Haltrex International Transport* [1994] ECR 1–467.

99. In its report "Shareholder Remedies", Law Commission Consultation Paper No. 142 (1996), the Law Commission states that of 156 petitions under s. 459 presented at the High Court in 1994 and 1995, just under 40% pleaded s. 122(1)(g) in the alternative.

100. (1843) 2 Hare 461; 67 ER 189.

101. [1982] 2 Ch. 204 at 202.

establish a *prima facie* case (i) that the company is entitled to the relief claimed, and (ii) that the action falls within the proper boundaries of the exception to the rule in *Foss* v. *Harbottle*.

6.9.24 This matter is of relevance in the area of s. 459 petitions because, on occasion, the plaintiff in a derivative action or in some other form of minority shareholder's action decides to petition the court at the same time under s. 459. In a recent case, where a plaintiff chose to join in one action a claim for relief in his personal capacity and a claim as a representative for all the shareholders in the company, and subsequently issued a s. 459 petition, the court held that consideration ought to be given to the question as to whether the derivative action should be allowed to proceed under O. 15, r. 12A in circumstances where there was a pending petition raising substantially the same issues. The court held that all the issues between the parties should be decided on one set of pleadings at a single trial. The proceedings in the writ action would be stayed with the statement of claim in that action standing as points of claim in the petition.[102]

6.9.25 Practitioners who decide to utilise alternative proceedings in this way must therefore expect the court to adopt a vigorous approach to case management. Indeed, where the only substantive relief being sought on a s. 459 petition is a claim on behalf of the company against a third party, the court may not necessarily allow the claimant to proceed by petition instead of by derivative action.[103] The use of alternative procedures to pursue what is in substance the same cause of action has still to be resolved by the courts.

102. *Cooke* v. *Cooke* [1997] BCC 17.
103. *Lowe* v. *Fahey* [1996] 1 BCLC 252.

CHAPTER 7

PETITION FOR WINDING-UP ON THE "JUST AND EQUITABLE" GROUND

7.0 Section 122(1)(g) of the Insolvency Act 1986

The right of a contributory to petition for the winding-up of a company on the "just and equitable" ground has been a part of English company law since the passing of the Companies Act 1862.[1] As the concept has developed, it has become an important and useful remedy for minority shareholders, albeit that the introduction of the right to petition for relief in respect of unfairly prejudicial conduct in s. 75 of the Companies Act 1980 (now s. 459 of the Companies Act 1985) has resulted in fewer petitions being presented in which this drastic form of remedy alone is sought.

The jurisdiction of the Companies Court to wind up a company on this ground is now contained in s. 122(1)(g) of the Insolvency Act 1986 which is in the following terms:

> "(1) A company may be wound up by the court if:
>
> . . . .
>
> (g) the court is of the opinion that it is just and equitable that the company should be wound up."

Important statutory restrictions on the right to petition are thereafter contained in s. 124 of the Insolvency Act 1986, which will be considered in detail below. (In this section of this chapter all references to statutory provisions are to the Insolvency Act 1986 except where the contrary appears.)

7.1 Petition for winding-up combined with petition under s. 459, Companies Act 1985

It is important to note that a winding-up petition on the just and equitable ground is often combined with a petition for alternative relief under s. 459 of the Companies Act 1985. Such a petition invites the court to select the more appropriate remedy in the circumstances of the case but the relief sought under s. 461 of that Act (invariably an order for the purchase of the petitioner's shares) is usually sought as the preferred alternative. However, for the reasons explained below, the presentation of a winding-up petition can cause considerable commercial damage and inconvenience to the company, with the result that it has sometimes been used as a means of bringing improper pressure on respondents to settle a dispute. The court is now alert to the dangers and, in 1990, issued a Practice Direction[2] which drew the attention of practitioners to the undesirability of including in

1. CA 1862, s. 79(5).
2. Practice Direction (Companies Court: Contributory's Petition) [1990] 1 WLR 490; [1990] BCLC 452.

petitions as a matter of course a prayer for winding-up as an alternative to an order for relief under s. 459. The court noted that a prayer for winding-up should only be included if that is the relief which the petitioner prefers, or if it is considered that it may be the only relief to which he is entitled.

Parliament has long recognised that the making of a winding-up order on a contributory's petition invoking the just and equitable ground is to be viewed as a remedy of last resort. Section 125(2) of the Insolvency Act 1986 provides that, in the case of such a petition, if the court thinks that the petitioner is entitled to relief either by winding up the company or by some other means and that in the absence of some other remedy it would be just and equitable that the company should be wound up, it should make a winding-up order. However, an order should not be made if the court is also of the opinion that some other remedy is available to the petitioner and that he is acting unreasonably in seeking to have the company wound up instead of pursuing that other remedy. This statutory injunction is now backed up by the 1990 Practice Direction.

It is likely that breaches of the Practice Direction may result in a severe cost penalty for the petitioner or, alternatively, in an application to strike out that part of the prayer to the petition which seeks the winding-up order.[3] It is apparent from a very recent decision on a striking-out application[4] that the court will have regard to the prospect of a winding-up order being made at trial when assessing whether to strike out the prayer for winding-up contained in such a combined petition. The court recognises that the very existence of such a prayer is a source of potential damage to the company and to its trading prospects. If there is no real possibility of the trial judge making a winding-up order on the facts alleged in the petition and related pleadings, the court in reliance upon s. 125(2) and the 1990 Practice Direction will order that the prayer for winding-up be struck out. The petition will then proceed merely for relief under s. 461.

7.2 Who may petition?

The persons who may present a petition to wind up a company are listed in s. 124(1). Shareholders or members are not mentioned (in contrast to s. 459 of the Companies Act 1985). The right of a shareholder to petition to wind up a solvent company on the just and equitable ground is confined to those persons who come within the statutory definition of a "contributory" contained in s. 79—hence the use of the phrase "contributory's petition" to describe this type of application. Section 79(1) provides that in the Insolvency Act and the Companies Act the expression "contributory" means every person liable to contribute to the assets of a company in the event of its being wound up. A person who is alleged to be a contributory may also present a petition. However, s. 79(2) states that the reference in s. 79(1) to persons liable to contribute to the assets does not include a person so liable by virtue of a declaration by the court under s. 213 (fraudulent trading) or s. 214 (wrongful trading). Reference should also be made to s. 74 which sets out the liability of present and past members to contribute to its assets on a winding-up, and to the leading company law textbooks in this area.

3. The Practice Direction has been cited in the Supreme Court of Hong Kong as a useful guideline: *Re Jan Nam Hong Ltd*: *Chan Chung Wai & Others* v. *Jan Nam Hong Ltd*, 8 May 1991, *H.K. Law Digest*, 1991 May Edn (E19), unreported CW–U No. 228 of 1991. See also *Re Whitchurch Insurance Consultants Ltd* [1994] BCC 51 at 52G–H.

4. *Re a Company (No. 004415 of 1996)* [1997] 1 BCLC 479.

The courts have held that, for the purposes of presenting a petition, the holder of fully paid shares in a company is a "contributory" and may present a petition for the winding-up of the company on the just and equitable ground, provided that he can allege and prove, at least to the extent of a *prima facie* case, that he will have a tangible interest in having the company wound up.[5] Usually this means that he must show that the company is solvent and that, on a winding-up, there will be a surplus of assets available for distribution to the shareholders. However, the courts have upheld an exception to this rule where the petition is based, at least in part, on the failure of the company to supply accounts and information, and the petitioner therefore lacks the information to tell whether or not there will be a surplus of assets available for the contributories.[6] It has also been held that the tangible interest of a fully paid shareholder is not necessarily restricted to the existence or prospective existence of a surplus of assets. In order to establish his *locus standi* to petition, the fully paid shareholder must show that he will, as a member of the company, achieve some advantage or avoid or minimise some disadvantage, which would accrue to him by virtue of his membership of the company.[7]

7.2.1 Nevertheless, s. 124(2) imposes an important restriction on the right of a contributory to petition on the just and equitable ground. This section provides that a contributory is not entitled to present a winding-up petition unless either the number of members is reduced below two, or the shares in respect of which he is a contributory, or some of them, either were originally allotted to him, or have been held by him, and registered in his name, for at least six months during the 18 months before the commencement of the winding-up, or have devolved on him through the death of a former holder. Where a petition is presented by a person who does not meet the requirements of s. 124(2), he will be held to have no *locus standi* and the petition will be struck out.[8] These restrictions do not apply to a person who is liable as a contributory under s. 76 (see s. 124(3)).[9]

Notwithstanding the reference in s. 79 to "any person alleged to be a contributory" being within the statutory definition of a contributory, the rules as to *locus standi* were, until very recently, strictly enforced by the court. If there was a substantial dispute as to the status of a person as a contributory, he would be prevented from petitioning unless and until that dispute had been resolved in his favour.[10] However, in a very recent decision, *Alipour* v. *Ary*,[11] the Court of Appeal has held that it is hard to see why the Companies Court should normally refuse to determine a dispute, even if it does relate to the petitioner's *locus standi*, if the existence of the petition is not likely to cause substantial damage or inconvenience to the company. On a contributory's petition where the *locus standi* of the petitioner is disputed, the court will consider all the circumstances including the likelihood of damage to the company if the petition is not dismissed, in determining whether to require the petitioner to seek the determination of the dispute outside the

5. *Re Rica Gold Washing Co.* (1879) 11 Ch. D. 36; *Re Chesterfield Catering Co. Ltd* [1977] Ch. 373.
6. *Re Newman & Howard Ltd* [1962] Ch. 257 at 261–262; *Re Wessex Computer Stationers Ltd* [1992] BCLC 366.
7. *Re Chesterfield Catering Co. Ltd* [1977] Ch. 373 at 380C–E.
8. *Re a Company (No. 003160 of 1986)* (1986) 2 BCC 99, 276.
9. The persons liable under s. 76 are: (a) former shareholders whose shares have been redeemed or purchased out of capital by a company which is subsequently wound up as insolvent within a year; and (b) directors made jointly and severally liable with such former shareholders.
10. *Re JN2 Ltd* [1978] 1 WLR 183, [1977] 3 All ER 1104 at 1107j–1108a.
11. [1997] 1 WLR 534, [1997] 1 BCLC 557, [1997] BCC 377 reversing the decision of Knox J, reported in *Re a Company (No. 002180 of 1996)* [1996] 2 BCLC 409.

petition. Since establishing the earlier authorities, procedural changes under the Insolvency Act 1986 and the Insolvency Rules 1986 have meant that other safeguards for the company are now in place. In the circumstances, the Court of Appeal held that the old rule of practice that a petitioner should first establish his *locus standi* outside the petition, had to yield to the interests of justice. (The petitioner, who held a share certificate but whose name was omitted from the company's share register, would be left without an effective remedy if the petition were struck out.) This is an important new development in the practice of the Companies Court. It indicates a willingness on the part of the court to weigh up the effect on the respective parties either of dismissing the petition or of allowing it to proceed to trial.

7.2.2 For a petitioner to show that shares were originally allotted to him within the meaning of s. 124(2)(b), he must be able to prove the acceptance by the company of his offer to take the shares. An allotment of a share involves a transaction between a company and an intending shareholder.[12] A person entitled to a transfer of a subscriber share is not within the statutory definition.[13]

A trustee in bankruptcy who has not obtained registration of the bankrupt's shares in his own name has no *locus standi* as a contributory to present a petition.[14] The right of a personal representative of a deceased shareholder to present a petition is expressly given by s. 124(2)(b).

7.3 What is "just and equitable"?

It is beyond the scope of this work to consider in any depth the vast body of case law that has developed in this jurisdiction and throughout the Commonwealth in relation to petitions to wind up on the just and equitable ground. Readers are referred to the leading textbooks on company law for this analysis. The modern English law and practice stems from the decision of the House of Lords in *Re Westbourne Galleries*,[15] to which particular reference should be made. Lord Wilberforce reviewed the various authorities and deplored the tendency to create categories or headings under which cases had to be brought if the section is to apply. Illustrations may be used, but the general words of the statute should remain general and not be reduced to the sum of particular instances. Lord Wilberforce considered that, if there was any criticism of the reported authorities, it was that the courts might sometimes have been too timorous in giving the words "just and equitable" their full force. He held that the provision enabled the court to subject the exercise of legal rights to equitable considerations, i.e. considerations of a personal character arising between one individual and another, which might make it unjust, or inequitable, to insist on legal rights, or to exercise them in a particular way.

Re Westbourne Galleries itself was an exclusion case, in which a former partner, later a director in the company, had been excluded from the board and had thereby been deprived of his right to participate in the rewards of the company, which were shared as directors' remuneration, but was unable to sell his shares without the consent of the other

12. *Re Florence Land and Public Works Co. Ltd* (1885) 29 Ch. D. 421 at 426.
13. *Re Quickdome Ltd* [1988] BCLC 370.
14. Re *HL Bolton Engineering Co. Ltd* [1956] Ch. 577 at 582–583 Wynn-Parry J. In Scotland the position is different by reason of the Bankruptcy (Scotland) Act 1985, s. 31 and such a trustee can petition: *Taylor* v. *Glenrinnes Farms Ltd* [1994] 2 BCLC 522 (Ct of Session).
15. [1973] AC 360.

members. The unexpected impact of the decision, at least until the enactment of s. 75 of the Companies Act 1980 (now s. 459 of the Companies Act 1985), was that it became easier for petitioners with substantial grievances over the conduct of the company's affairs to obtain a winding-up order on the just and equitable ground than it was to obtain alternative, and less drastic relief, under what was then s. 210 of the Companies Act 1948.

7.3.1 Illustrations of the type of case in which a winding-up might be ordered on the just and equitable ground include the following:

(i) exclusion or expulsion of a shareholder from participation in management and remuneration where the company was formed on the basis of an agreement that the petitioner would participate or be consulted on important decisions[16];
(ii) a proven lack of probity on the part of those managing the company in relation to the conduct of its affairs[17];
(iii) where the affairs of the company are totally deadlocked as a result of the refusal of the shareholders to co-operate with each other[18];
(iv) the refusal of a company to pay reasonable dividends to shareholders not involved in management whilst the directors enjoy excessive remuneration[19];
(v) where the principal objects of the company as set out in its memorandum can no longer be achieved.[20]

7.3.2 It has been held, in a case concerning a petition which sought relief under ss. 459 and 461 of the Companies Act 1985, or the winding-up of the company under s. 122(1)(g), that a shareholder cannot seek a just and equitable winding-up order to protect a wider range of interests than he could seek to protect under s. 459. Accordingly, where the petition sought a winding-up in order to protect the petitioner's interests as a freeholder of land occupied by a farming company rather than *qua* member, the court struck out the petition.[21]

7.4 Who are the respondents?

By definition, every petition to wind up a company under s. 122(1)(g) must include the company as a respondent. The Insolvency Rules themselves do not, in fact, require service of a copy of the petition on the named respondents other than the company (see para. 7.8.6, *infra*). However, as in the case of s. 459 petitions, these petitions are in substance usually disputes between the shareholders rather than between the petitioner and the company. It is therefore the position that all the shareholders, in the case of a private company, should be joined as respondents to the petition. In the case of a public company (where such petitions are in any event rare), the petitioner should join as respondents the alleged wrongdoers, leaving other members to apply to be joined at a later stage in

16. *Re Westbourne Galleries* [1973] AC 360; *Re A & BC Chewing Gum* [1975] 1 WLR 579; *RA Noble (Clothing) Ltd* [1983] BCLC 273.
17. *Loch* v. *John Blackwood Ltd* [1924] AC 783; *Re Larchquell Ltd* 6 June 1980, Slade J., unreported.
18. *Re Yenidje Tobacco Co. Ltd* [1916] 2 Ch. 426.
19. *Re a Company (No. 00370 of 1987) ex parte Glossop* [1988] 1 WLR 1068.
20. *Re Perfectair Holdings Ltd* [1990] BCLC 423.
21. *Re JE Cade & Son Ltd* [1991] BCC 360 at 376H.

accordance with the principles applicable under O. 15, r. 6(2) of the Rules of the Supreme Court. A person who is joined as a respondent is served with a copy of the petition.[22]

7.5 The role of the company

The company is a necessary respondent to the petition. However, as the substantial dispute which is the subject of the petition is between the shareholders, the role of the company in respect of a contributory's petition is limited. The courts are very reluctant to permit those in control of the company to utilise its funds to defend their position. It is a general principle of company law that the company's money should not be expended on disputes between shareholders.[23] Directors are not entitled to take part in such a dispute at the expense of the company and, if they do so, they will commit a misfeasance and be at risk as to the costs incurred.[24] In an appropriate case, the court will grant an injunction prohibiting the expenditure of costs by the company, or to prohibit it from being represented and taking an active part in the proceedings.[25]

At the same time, the courts have recognised that the company may have an interest in the matter, separate from its shareholders. It has been expressly held that it would be proper for the company's funds to be used with respect to an application under s. 127 of the Insolvency Act 1986 (see paras 7.7–7.7.4, *infra*), with respect to the giving of discovery (see below) or when judgment is being delivered. The company may have a legitimate interest in the judgment and there may be a need for the interests of the company as a whole to be considered, with the board being advised about the representations to be made to the court about consequential orders.[26]

7.6 Form and contents of the petition

The Insolvency Rules 1986 (as amended) contain the procedural rules relating to contributories' petitions. Rule 12.7 prescribes the forms contained in sch. 4 to the Insolvency Rules, for use in connection with insolvency proceedings, whether in the High Court or County Court. Rule 12.7(2) states that the forms shall be used with such variations, if any, as the circumstances may require. Form 4.14 is a draft form of contributory's petition.[27] Chapter 4 of the Insolvency Rules, which deals specifically with petitions by contributories, is set out in Appendix 1, and a copy of the current Form 4.14 is in Appendix 4.

Rule 4(1) provides that the petition shall specify the grounds on which it is presented. As can be seen from Form 4.14, the first four paragraphs of the petition are formal and require the insertion of:

(i) the name and address of the petitioner;
(ii) the name of the company and its date of incorporation (para. 1);

22. See para. 7.8.3, *et seq.*
23. *Re Crosmore Electrical and Civil Engineering Ltd* [1989] BCLC 137 at 138e–f.
24. *Re Kenyon Swansea Ltd* [1987] BCLC 514 at 521; *Re a Company (No. 004502 of 1988) ex parte Johnson* [1992] BCLC 701.
25. *Re Milgate Developments Ltd* [1993] BCLC 291.
26. *Re a Company (No. 004502 of 1988) ex parte Johnson* [1992] BCLC 701.
27. Form 4.14 in its current version was introduced by the Insolvency (Amendment) Rules 1987 (S.I. 1987 No. 1919) r. 3(1), sch., pt 5, s. 1.

(iii) the address of the company's registered office (para. 2);

(iv) the amount of its authorised and issued share capital and a statement of the petitioner's share holding (para. 3). This must be accompanied by a statement as to the capacity of the petitioner as a contributory for the purposes of s. 124(2). The petition must refer to him either:

(a) as an original allottee of his shares; or

(b) as the registered holder of such shares for more than six months in the last 18 months; or

(c) as someone on whom the shares have devolved through the death of the former holder.

Much of the above information can usually be obtained from a search of the company's file at the Companies Registry.

7.6.1 There must be a separate petition in respect of each company which is the subject-matter of the proceedings. Accordingly, where a shareholder holds shares in a number of companies which are treated in substance as a single entity, he must issue a separate petition in respect of each of them and then seek directions from the court that the petitions be heard concurrently or consecutively so that they proceed as though they had been consolidated into one document.[28]

The draft form of petition then provides, in para. 5, for the petitioner to set out the grounds on which the petition is presented. This is to meet the requirements of r. 4.22(1) of the Insolvency Rules. This part of the petition must be drafted with particular care and should present a detailed factual account of the petitioner's case and the allegations upon which the petition is based. The petition must contain sufficient particulars to enable the petitioner to resist any application to strike it out on the grounds that it is embarrassing in that it fails to disclose to the respondents the precise nature of the petitioner's case against them.[29] An application to strike out can be made by the respondents at any time under O. 18, r. 19 of the Rules of the Supreme Court, or under the inherent jurisdiction of the court.

7.6.2 The practice of the Companies Court is to order that a pleading in the form of points of claim is served by the petitioner in support of the petition (see below) (although occasionally, in straightforward cases, the court may still permit the use of supporting affidavits). However, in order to avoid arguments that the petition lacks sufficient particulars of the petitioner's case to enable the respondent to understand the grounds upon which it is based, the petitioner's advisers may choose to present a very detailed petition which may then stand as points of claim. This practice avoids a delay in the proceedings whilst points of claim in support of the petition are drafted and served, enabling the petitioner to make a maximum impact on the respondents at an early stage and resulting in the respondents having to plead to the detailed allegations in the petition. However, for the petition to stand as points of claim requires the consent of the respondent or the approval of the court, and normally this approach cannot be adopted where speed is necessary and an application for interlocutory relief, such as an injunction, is required. In such cases, the petition is likely to be in shorter form, merely summarising the grounds upon which it is based and as such is somewhat analogous to a generally endorsed writ of summons. It can usually be amended later, pursuant to O. 20, rr. 5 and 7 of the Rules of

28. *Re a Company* [1984] BCLC 307.
29. *Re WR Willcocks & Co. Ltd* [1974] Ch. 163.

the Supreme Court. It will be accompanied by an affidavit explaining, in detail, the petitioner's case and exhibiting the essential documents. This affidavit must fairly reflect the matters in issue and provide full and frank disclosure if the application is to be made on an *ex parte* basis.

Paragraph 6 of Form 4.14 contains an express averment that it is just and equitable that the company should be wound up. However, this alone is not sufficient to meet the jurisdictional requirements for a contributory's petition. As stated in para. 7.2, *supra*, it is essential that a petitioner who is a fully paid shareholder allege and prove, at least to the extent of a *prima facie* case, that there will be a surplus of assets in existence which give him a tangible interest in the winding-up, or that he will achieve some advantage or avoid or minimise some disadvantage accruing to him by virtue of his membership of the company.[30] The only exception to this rule is where the company is in default of supplying him with accounts and information and this is one of the grounds upon which the petition is based.[31]

7.6.3 Although it is by no means an absolute requirement, it is customary in contributory's petitioners concerning quasi-partnership companies, since the decision of the House of Lords in *Re Westbourne Galleries*, for the petition to contain an averment that the conduct of the respondents has caused the petitioner to lose all trust and confidence in the respondents.

The petition must contain a statement as to whether the petitioner consents or objects to an order under s. 127 in the standard form set out in the 1990 Practice Direction (Companies Court: Contributory's Petition).[32] This is an important topic which is considered in detail below.

Finally after setting out the prayer for relief, namely an order that the company be wound up under the provisions of the Insolvency Act 1986 or that such other order be made as the court thinks fit, the petition should list the names of the respondents.

7.7 The impact of section 127

Section 127 invalidates any disposition of the company's property, and any transfer of shares or alteration in the status of members made after the commencement of the winding-up. By virtue of s. 129(2), the winding-up of a company by the court is deemed to commence at the time of presentation of the petition for winding-up (except where a company has, before presentation, passed a resolution for voluntary winding-up, when the relevant time will be the passing of the resolution). These provisions apply to both a creditor's petition in respect of an insolvent company and to a contributory's petition, which almost always concerns a solvent and valuable commercial entity. In the case of creditors' petitions, s. 127 serves the important purpose of preserving the company's assets for its creditors. But in the area of a contributory's petition, where the petitioner is required to allege that the company is solvent, it is often a source of great embarrassment and inconvenience.

30. *Re Rica Gold Washing Co.* (1879) 11 Ch. D. 36; *Re Chesterfield Catering Co. Ltd* [1977] Ch. 373.
31. *Re Newman & Howard Ltd* [1962] Ch. 257 at 261–262; *Re Wessex Computer Stationers Ltd* [1992] BCLC 366.
32. [1990] 1 WLR 490, [1990] BCLC 452.

As a result of a series of decisions taken by the courts in relation to creditors' petitions,[33] culminating in that of the Court of Appeal in *Re Gray's Inn Construction Co. Ltd*,[34] the practice of banks on learning of the presentation of any winding-up petition, including a contributory's petition in respect of a solvent company, is to freeze the company's bank account pending an application to the court by the company for relief under s. 127 validating transactions and transfers into and out of that account in the ordinary course of business. If it does not do this, the bank may be at risk if assets are dissipated or losses incurred. Thus, the presentation of a contributory's petition has very serious consequences for a trading company and can cause substantial damage to its commercial reputation.

7.7.1 This has now been recognised by the Companies Court in the 1990 Practice Direction.[35] This provides that, whenever a prayer for winding-up is included in a contributory's petition, the petition shall include a statement as to whether the petitioner consents or objects to an order under s. 127 in "the standard form" and, if he objects, the affidavit in support of the petition (see below) must contain a short statement of his reasons. The standard form of order is in the following terms:

"ORDER that notwithstanding the presentation of the said petition

(1) payments made into or out of the bank accounts of the company in the ordinary course of the business of the company and
(2) dispositions of the property of the company made in the ordinary course of its business for proper value between the date of presentation of the petition and the date of judgment on the petition or further order in the meantime shall not be void by virtue of the provisions of section 127 of the Insolvency Act 1986 in the event of an order for the winding up of the company being made on the said petition."

7.7.2 The standard form of order thus validates payments in the ordinary course of business and dispositions of company property made in the ordinary course of its business for proper (i.e. full) value. If the petitioner objects to a s. 127 order in the standard form but consents to such an order in a modified form, the petition must set out the form of order to which he consents, and the affidavit in support (as to which see para. 7.8.2, *infra*) must contain a short statement of his reasons for seeking the modification. If the petition contains a statement that the petitioner consents to a s. 127 order, whether in the standard or a modified form, but the petitioner changes his mind before the first hearing of the petition, he is required to notify the respondents and may apply, on notice, to a judge for an order directing that no s. 127 order or a modified order only (as the case may be) shall be made by the registrar, but validating dispositions made without notice of the order made by the judge.

If the petition contains a statement that the petitioner consents to a s. 127 order, whether in the standard or a modified form, the registrar is required, without further inquiry, to make an order in such form at the first hearing of the petition unless an order to the contrary has been made by the judge in the meantime. If the petition contains a statement

33. *Re Al Levy (Holdings) Ltd* [1964] Ch. 19; *Re Operator Control Cabs Ltd* [1970] 3 All ER 657.
34. [1980] 1 WLR 711 (CA).
35. [1990] 1 WLR 490, [1990] BCLC 452. See also *Re a Company (No. 004415 of 1996)* [1997] 1 BCLC 479.

that the petitioner objects to a s. 127 order in the standard form, the company may apply (in cases of urgency *ex parte*) to the judge for an order. Such an application is made by an ordinary application in the petition, supported by an affidavit detailing the company's current financial position and exhibiting its latest audited accounts.

7.7.3 Banks occasionally encounter particular difficulties when dealing with s. 127 orders even in the standard form. To avoid such problems, a proviso to the standard form has been suggested by one experienced judge of the Companies Court. This reads as follows:

> "Provided that [the relevant bank] should be under no obligation to verify for itself whether any transaction through the company's bank accounts is in the ordinary course of business or that it represents full market value for the relevant transaction."[36]

The proviso leaves the obligation upon those who make payments from the company's accounts only to make payments in the ordinary course of business, and any payment not in the ordinary course of business will not be covered by the order and will be recoverable from those who caused it. The bank, however, which is unable to police the payments, will be protected.

An order in the standard form only protects payments and dispositions made in the ordinary course of the company's business. For exceptional transactions, a special application to the court is still required to be made by the company. The supporting affidavit should exhibit copies of the company's most recent audited accounts and details of its up-to-date financial position, so as to assure the court of its solvency. If the application relates to a specific transaction, it must be justified by evidence from one of the directors as being "necessary or expedient in the interests of the company". If the court considers that the reasons given are such as an intelligent and honest man could reasonably hold, it will normally grant the relief sought, and sanction the disposition notwithstanding the opposition of the petitioner, unless he adduces compelling evidence proving that the disposition is in fact likely to injure the company.[37] Great weight is given to the wishes of the directors, because the court considers that the mere presentation of a petition should not enable a shareholder to interfere with the directors' management of the company's business.

7.7.4 However, if the evidence presented to the court is considered to be inadequate, an order will be refused. The more exceptional the transaction sought to be approved, the greater is the duty on the applicant to furnish the court with detailed evidence justifying what is proposed.[38] Moreover, where there is any serious doubt as to the solvency of the company, the court will adopt a much more cautious approach to the application. Even where the petitioner himself alleges a substantial surplus of assets on winding-up, the court will consider whether the continued trading of the company and the operation of its bank account is likely to be in the interests of its creditors and shareholders or will lead to a further depletion in its assets. Relief under s. 127 may be refused.[39]

36. *Re a Company (No. 00687 of 1991)* [1991] BCC 210 per Harman J. at 212.
37. *Re Burton & Deakin Ltd* [1977] 1 WLR 390.
38. *Re Mountforest Ltd* [1993] BCC 565.
39. *Re a Company (No. 007523 of 1986)* [1987] BCLC 200.

7.8 Procedural steps

7.8.1 Presentation of the petition

The petition, appropriately drafted in the proper form, should be presented to the Companies Court office for filing. The Companies Court has jurisdiction to wind up any company registered in England and Wales.[40] To wind up a company registered in Scotland, the petition should be presented to the Court of Session.[41] A fee is payable on presentation and a small additional fee may be paid for a search of the register of pending winding-up petitions, as there can only be one petition in existence against a company at any time.[42] In addition, before the petition can be presented, a deposit must be paid to the court.[43] No petition can be filed unless there is produced with it the receipt for the deposit payable on presentation.[44] The deposit is security for the administration fees of the official receiver incurred in the performance of his general duties on the making of a winding-up order. Where a petition is dismissed or withdrawn, the deposit is repayable in full, unless a winding-up order has been made.[45] If the assets of the company being wound up are sufficient to pay the administration fee, then the deposit is returnable to the extent that it is not required for the payment of that fee.[46]

When the petition is filed with the court (usually by the petitioner's solicitors) it must be accompanied by a copy for service on the company under r. 4.22. Upon delivery of these documents, they are stamped by the court with the date and time of issue, and the court then fixes a hearing date, known as the return day, on which, unless the court otherwise directs, the petitioner and the company and any other respondents who have been served by this stage should attend before the registrar of the Companies Court in chambers for directions to be given in relation to the procedure on the petition. On fixing the return day, the court returns to the petitioner's solicitors a sealed copy of the petition for service, endorsed with the return day and the time of hearing (r. 4.22(3)). The normal period between the date of presentation and the return day is about five to seven weeks, thereby enabling the petitioner to complete the service of the petition and the respondents to obtain legal advice. This period varies, however, when a petition is presented close to a court vacation period.

7.8.2 Chapter 4 of part 4 of the Insolvency Rules does not expressly require the verification of the petition by an affidavit to the effect that the statements in the petition are true, or are true to the best of the deponent's knowledge, information and belief. This is because r. 4.12, which applies to creditors' petitions, is not made applicable to petitions by contributories. However, the 1990 Practice Direction[47] states, in connection with any opposition to the granting of s. 127 relief, that "the affidavit in support" of the petition should contain a short statement by the petitioner of the grounds on which he objects to

40. Insolvency Act 1986, s. 117(1).
41. *Ibid.*, s. 120(1).
42. The current fee is £80 from 15 January 1997: see Supreme Court Fees (Amendments) Order 1996 (S.I. 1996 No. 3191). The current search fee is £5.
43. Insolvency Fees Order 1986 (S.I. 1986 No. 2030) arts 8(1) and 9(a). The deposit is currently £500: S.I. 1994 No. 2541, art. 3(d).
44. Insolvency Rules 1986, r. 4.22 (Insolvency Act).
45. Insolvency Fees Order 1986 (S.I. 1986 No. 2030) art. 11(2).
46. *Ibid.*, art. 11(3).
47. [1990] 1 WLR 490, [1990] BCLC 452.

an order under s. 127 in the standard form. The Practice Direction therefore presupposes the filing of an affidavit in support. If the petitioner consents only to an order under s. 127 in a modified form, "the affidavit in support" must contain a short statement of his reasons for seeking the modification. In the circumstances, it would seem that the correct practice is not to file an affidavit in support of the petition prior to the return day and the hearing for directions before the registrar, save in the exceptional case where the petitioner objects to the making of a s. 127 order in the standard form or consents only to a modified order.

7.8.3 Service

The petitioner is required to serve a sealed copy of the petition on the company at least 14 days before the return day (r. 4.22(4)). The petition must be served at the company's registered office. Chapter 4 of part 4 of the Insolvency Rules does not expressly incorporate the provisions for the service of a creditor's petition set out in rr. 4.8 and 4.9 but, in practice, the court will adopt a similar approach to the service of a contributory's petition. The Rules provide that the registered office for the purposes of service is the place specified in the statement of the intended situation of the registered office delivered by the company under s. 10 of the Companies Act 1985 or the place specified in the last such notice of change of registered office delivered by the company to the registrar of companies under s. 287 of that Act (r. 4.8(2)). If, for any reason, service at the registered office is not practicable, or the company has no registered office, the petition may be served on the company by leaving it at the company's last known principal place of business in such a way that it is likely to come to the attention of the person attending there, or by delivering it to the secretary, or some director, manager or principal officer of the company, wherever that person may be found (r. 4.8(4)). If for any reason service is impracticable, the petition may be served in such manner as the court may direct (r. 4.8(6)). Rule 4.8(3) deals with the means by which service may be effected.

If a petitioner desires to serve his petition on a respondent out of the jurisdiction he must obtain leave from the court under r. 12.12. That rule expressly provides that O. 11 of the Rules of the Supreme Court (and the corresponding County Court Rules) do not apply in insolvency proceedings. "Insolvency proceedings" are defined in r. 13.7 as meaning any proceedings under the Insolvency Act 1986 or the Insolvency Rules. In lieu it is provided by r. 12.12(3) as follows:

> "Where for the purposes of insolvency proceedings any process or order of the Court, or other document, is required to be served on a person who is not in England and Wales, the Court may order service to be effected within such time, on such person, at such place and in such manner as it thinks fit, and may also require such proof of service as it thinks fit."

7.8.4 Any application for leave under r. 12.12 must be supported by an affidavit stating the grounds on which the application is made and the place or country in which the person to be served is to be found or may probably be found (r. 12.12(4)). Applications for leave under r. 12.12 for service out of the jurisdiction are made to the registrar of the Companies Court on an *ex parte* basis.

It should be noted that O. 11 continues to apply to petitions seeking relief under s. 459 of the Companies Act 1985 on grounds of unfair prejudice. Thus, where a winding-up petition seeks, in the alternative, relief under s. 461, leave to serve the proceedings on a respondent outside the jurisdiction must be obtained if required under O. 11.[48]

7.8.5 Hearing for directions

On the return day, the petitioner and those respondents who have been served and who choose to appear, attend in person or by solicitor or by solicitor and counsel before the registrar of the Companies Court in chambers for directions. This is a most important hearing at which the court will determine the procedural steps to be taken on the petition. By virtue of a practice direction introduced in December 1986[49] the Chief Clerk of the Companies Court is authorised to hear applications for directions where the petition is a contributory's petition. However, he is not authorised to hear applications for directions on s. 459 petitions. Accordingly, where alternative relief is sought under s. 459, the application for directions on the contributory's petition must be heard by the registrar. The parties are always well advised to attempt to agree a timetable for the directions to be sought on the petition before the hearing.

It should be noted that, by virtue of r. 4.24, certain provisions of ch. 3 of part 4 of the Insolvency Rules do apply to contributory's petitions. These include r. 4.16 (Notices of appearance) and r. 4.17 (Lists of appearances). Every person who intends to appear at the hearing of the petition should give notice to the petitioner in accordance with r. 4.16. The notice should specify that person's name and address, any telephone number and reference for communication, and whether it is his intention to support or oppose the petition. The petitioner must also prepare for the court a list of the persons who have given notice to him under r. 4.16, specifying their names and addresses and (if known to him) their respective solicitors.

Rule 4.23 lists the matters which must be dealt with by the court on the hearing for directions. They include the following:

7.8.6 Service of the petition. As previously mentioned (in para. 7.4, *supra*) the Rules do not expressly provide for the service of a contributory's petition on anyone other than the company. However, the practice of the Companies Court is to require service of a copy of the petition on all the named respondents. The reader is referred to para. 7.4, *supra*, in which the question of who are the proper respondents is considered. When giving directions, the court must have regard to whether any of the persons specified in r. 4.10 should be served with the petition. These persons include any liquidator (where the company is in voluntary liquidation), any administrative receiver, any administrator (where the company is in administration), any supervisor (where a voluntary arrangement under part I of the Insolvency Act is in force) or the Bank of England (where the company is an authorised institution or former authorised institution under the Banking Act 1987).

7.8.7 Whether pleadings or affidavits are to be served. The current practice is for the registrar invariably to order that points of claim, points of defence and points of reply (if

48. *Re Harrods (Buenos Aires) Ltd* [1992] Ch. 72 (CA) and RSC O. 11, r. 1(2) and see para. 6.93, *supra*, and Note 62.

49. Practice Direction (Companies Court: Insolvency) [1987] 1 WLR 53.

so advised) be served by the parties. It is considered by the court that pleadings help to clarify the matters at issue between the parties in a way which is superior to affidavit evidence. The old practice of serving a substantial volume of affidavit evidence in support of and in answer to the petition, with further affidavits in reply, has been the subject of judicial criticism.[50] It is perhaps the case that reliance upon affidavits should be confined, in practice, to cases where there have already been extensive interlocutory proceedings and much time spent on the preparation of affidavits.

Adequate time must be provided for the service of pleadings, and the normal procedural rules for seeking extensions of time in O. 3 of the Rules of the Supreme Court (with the exception of rr. 3 and 6) will apply (r. 12.9). In the absence of an agreed extension, an application should be made to the registrar by what is, in effect, a time summons for an extension of the period in which the pleadings must be served. Mention has been made earlier of the possibility of serving a petition in long form, thereby alleviating the necessity to serve separate points of claim. In such cases a direction is sought from the registrar that the petition stand as points of claim, and the respondents are directed to file points of defence. Points of reply will normally follow.

Points of claim and subsequent pleadings must be prepared with skill and care, as the normal rules relating to pleadings will apply to them. No averment can be made in the points of claim which does not appear in the petition.[51] Parties can apply for further and better particulars of the allegations made under RSC O. 18, r. 12. While pleadings can be amended in accordance with RSC O. 20, it is the invariable practice of the court to require late amendments (in particular those sought at trial) to be completely and fully particularised. Statements of the petitioner's belief should not appear in the points of claim which should allege facts and not matters of belief.[52] Any pleading which does not meet these requirements is capable of being struck out, in whole or in part, under RSC O. 18, r. 19 or under the inherent jurisdiction of the court.

7.8.8 Section 127. In accordance with the 1990 Practice Direction,[53] the registrar will make a s. 127 order in respect of the company, whether in the standard or a modified form, unless an order to the contrary has been made by the judge in the meantime (see paras 7.7–7.7.4, *supra*).

7.8.9 Discovery and inspection. The process of discovery on a contributory's petition is an important one and is one of the aspects of the proceedings that will usually involve the company in seeking separate and independent legal advice. By virtue of r. 7.51, the normal principles and procedures enshrined in O. 24 of the Rules of the Supreme Court apply, and readers are referred to the relevant section of the Supreme Court Practice. The parties must include in their lists of documents all documents which are or have been in their possession, custody or power relating to any matter in question in the proceedings. Discovery is limited to the allegations in the petition.[54]

50. *Re a Company (No. 005134 of 1986) ex parte Harries* [1989] BCLC 383 at 390g.
51. *Re Lundie Bros Ltd* [1965] 1 WLR 1051 at 1058, [1965] 2 All ER 692 at 699; *Re Unisoft Group Ltd (No. 3)* [1994] BCLC 609 at 624e.
52. *Re Unisoft Group Ltd (No. 3)* [1994] BCLC 609 at 626f.
53. [1990] 1 WLR 490.
54. *Re Tecnion Investments Ltd* [1985] BCLC 434 at 441 (CA).

In general, all documents obtained by the company in the course of the administration of the company, such as advice by solicitors to the company about its affairs, are the proper subject of discovery where they relate to any question in the petition. However, this rule will not apply where there is hostile litigation between a shareholder and the company. A contributory's petition, like that under s. 459 of the Companies Act, is not usually to be regarded as hostile litigation between a shareholder and the company for this purpose.[55] Discovery is usually directed to be made by lists unsupported by affidavits unless there is a serious question in issue as to the retention or destruction of vital documents, or the honesty of certain parties, when an affidavit will be required verifying the list.

The timetable for directions must allow adequate time for inspection of documents referred to in the lists or documents served by the parties, and for the parties to take copies thereof. When serving his list, a party's solicitor must serve a notice in accordance with O. 24, r. 9 stating a time within seven days after service at which the documents may be inspected at a place specified in the notice. The other procedural rules relating to inspection of documents in High Court proceedings (O. 24, rr. 10, 11, 11A, 12 and 13) apply to contributory's petitions.[56]

7.8.10 Interrogatories. The parties are entitled to serve interrogatories on each other in accordance with the normal practice and procedure set down in O. 26 of the Rules of the Supreme Court. Applications for interrogatories (under O. 26, r. 1) or for an order that interrogatories served without order (under O. 26, r. 3) be withdrawn or varied are made to the registrar at later hearings for directions. The procedure is the same as that for writ actions. Interrogatories will be permitted where they constitute an attempt to ascertain facts which are not within the knowledge of the petitioner but are within the knowledge of the respondents or where they seek to obtain admissions. Both purposes will be regarded as legitimate if they can save costs in shortening the trial or lead to a settlement of some of the issues in dispute. As such, they will be regarded as necessary in order fairly to dispose of the cause or matter as between the petitioner and the respondents. Interrogatories will not be improper merely because the answers to the questions raised might emerge in cross-examination at trial.[57]

7.8.11 Advertisement of the petition. Rule 4.23(1)(c) expressly provides that, on the return day, the court shall give directions as to whether, and if so by what means, the petition is to be advertised. Contributories petitions, being disputes between the shareholders of a solvent company, do not concern the creditors of the company and are seldom ordered to be advertised before a late stage in the proceedings, in order to avoid unnecessary damage being done to the business and commercial reputation of the company and severe inconvenience of the type that will require additional applications under s. 127. Advertisement will only serve to reduce the value of the petitioner's shareholding. Accordingly, no attempt should be made to advertise a contributory's petition whether in the *London Gazette* or anywhere else before the return date and the hearing for directions.

55. *Re Hydrosan Ltd* [1991] BCLC 418.
56. By virtue of the Insolvency Rules 1986, r. 7.51.
57. See *Neal* v. *December Commercial Properties (No. 1) Ltd* [1996] BCC 577, a case concerning a s. 459 petition.

If the petition is prematurely advertised, it may be struck out as an abuse of process.[58] The Rules in fact bestow on the court the power to order that the petition should be determined without prior advertisement.[59]

At the hearing for directions, a direction should be sought from the registrar that the petition be not advertised until further order. Where such an order is made, the petition is thereafter referred to by number only. "Advertisement" in this context has a very wide meaning and covers any communication of the existence of the petition to a third party. Such a direction will therefore prohibit notice of the existence of the petition being given to the company's bankers or third parties such as suppliers and customers, even in a solicitor's letter. Once again, it must be emphasised that breach of the prohibition, if carried out with a view to putting pressure on the respondents, may result in the petition being struck out as an abuse of process.[60]

7.8.12 Other procedural matters. At the hearing for directions on the return date, the registrar, having set out a timetable for the procedure on the petition, will adjourn the further hearing of the petition to a suitable future date, by which stage the steps described in the directions can be expected to have been carried out. At this later hearing for directions, it will be open to the parties to apply for further directions, including orders for further and better particulars of the pleadings, orders for specific discovery, orders relating to interrogatories and directions as to the service and exchange of expert evidence (if any). Once the registrar is convinced that all outstanding procedural matters have been dealt with, he will order that the petition be set down for trial. In due course, Counsel will be required to supply the Companies Court with a signed estimate of the length of trial.

7.8.13 Interlocutory applications

The Companies Court has jurisdiction under s. 37 of the Supreme Court Act 1981, to make interlocutory orders in a petition, by way of injunction or the appointment of a receiver, in all cases in which it appears to the court to be just and convenient to do so. Applications frequently seek to restrain the directors from embarking on share issues or otherwise jeopardising the company's assets. Relief is granted by the court in accordance with ordinary *American Cyanamid* principles.[61] A petitioner who obtains such relief is obliged, in accordance with normal principles, to give an undertaking in damages to the respondents. This is a factor which must be taken into account by his advisers. Applications for injunctive relief are made by ordinary application supported by affidavit. Such applications are heard by the judge in open court.

7.8.14 Receiver or provisional liquidator

Under s. 135, the court has power to appoint a provisional liquidator of a company after the presentation of a winding-up petition and before the making of a winding-up order. Rule 4.25 provides that the application for such an appointment may be made by the

58. *Re Doreen Boards Ltd* [1996] 1 BCLC 501.
59. *Ibid.* at 505f, per Laddie J.
60. *Re a Company (No. 00687 of 1991)* [1991] BCC 210; *Re a Company (No. 001127 of 1992)* [1992] BCC 477; *Re a Company (No. 0013925 of 1991)* [1992] BCLC 562.
61. *American Cyanamid* v. *Ethicon Ltd* [1975] AC 496.

petitioner, or any creditor or contributory, or by the company itself, or by the Secretary of State, or by any person who would be entitled to petition for the winding-up of the company. The application must be made direct to the Companies Court Judge[62] and must be accompanied by an affidavit stating:

(a) the grounds on which it is proposed that a provisional liquidator should be appointed;
(b) if some person other than the official receiver is proposed to be appointed, that the person has consented to act and, to the best of the applicant's belief, is qualified to act as an insolvency practitioner in relation to the company;
(c) whether or not the official receiver has been informed of the application and, if so, has been furnished with a copy of it;
(d) whether, to the applicant's knowledge:
    (i) there has been proposed or is in force for the company a voluntary arrangement under part I of the Act; or
    (ii) an administrator or administrative receiver is acting in relation to the company; or
    (iii) a liquidator has been appointed for its voluntary winding-up; and
(e) the applicant's estimate of the value of the assets in respect of which the provisional liquidator is to be appointed.

7.8.15 The appointment is usually only made by the court in respect of a contributory's petition where there are special circumstances such as evidence that the assets of the company are in jeopardy. The provisional liquidator will seek to preserve the assets, pending the effective hearing of the petition. The order appointing the provisional liquidator will specify his functions.

Owing to the far-reaching implications for the company of the appointment of a provisional liquidator, the judge may direct that the application be heard in camera rather than in open court. An appointment is only made in rare cases. The person appointed is invariably the official receiver, but the court has power to appoint someone else.[63] That person must be a qualified insolvency practitioner. The applicant must give an undertaking to the court as to the damages which the company may sustain as a result of the application. Such damages will be payable if the court later determines that the company should not be wound up and that the appointment was inappropriate.

In addition, before an order is made appointing the official receiver as provisional liquidator, the applicant must deposit with him or otherwise secure to his satisfaction such sum as the court directs, to cover the official receiver's remuneration and expenses. The deposit is repayable, if a winding-up order is made, out of the company's assets, provided that they are sufficient to pay the remuneration and expenses of the provisional liquidator. The remuneration of the provisional liquidator other than the official receiver is fixed by the court under r. 4.30. His appointment will terminate if the petition is dismissed.

7.8.16 The provisional liquidator can himself apply to the court for the appointment of a special manager under s. 177, where the nature of the business or property of the company, or the interests of its creditors, contributories or members generally, require the

62. Practice Direction No. 3 of 1996 (Chancery Division: Application to appoint provisional liquidator) [1997] 1 BCLC 130.
63. IA 1986, s. 135(2).

appointment of another person to manage the business or property. This section enables the provisional liquidator to obtain the assistance of someone with particular expertise or experience of the company's business. The provisional liquidator's application must be supported by a report under r. 4.206 setting out the reasons for the application.

Accordingly, in order to obtain the appointment of a provisional liquidator, the petitioner must be able to show that the petition at least raises a triable issue for the winding-up of the company and there are special circumstances of the type referred to above. In view of the drastic consequences for the company, a strong case is in fact usually required. As an alternative to such an appointment, the court has power under s. 37 of the Supreme Court Act 1981, to appoint a receiver of the company pending the outcome of the petition. This may cause less damage to the company's business, but is recognised to cast a slur upon the solvency of the company and its business.[64] A receiver will, for instance, be appointed where there is such a degree of dispute between the shareholders that the composition of the board of directors is in doubt.[65] For further information on such an appointment, the reader is referred to the leading textbooks on the law of receivers. An application can be made for the appointment of either a provisional liquidator or a receiver, leaving it to the court to decide which is the more appropriate. In cases of great urgency, applications can be made *ex parte* in accordance with general principles, but the affidavit evidence in support must be full and frank. The applicant must therefore disclose to the court any fact known to him which might affect the judge's decision on whether to grant relief or on what relief to grant.[66] If the court is minded to make an order, it will then do so for a limited period, over to an *inter partes* hearing when the respondents will be able to appear and, if so ordered, oppose the renewal of the order.

7.8.17 Trial

The trial of a contributory's petition proceeds in the normal manner of a trial of an action in the High Court and is similar to that of a s. 459 petition with which it is often combined, relief being sought in the alternative. The parties must accordingly comply with the procedural requirements of the *Chancery Guide* which apply as much to the Companies Court as to any other part of the Chancery Division. In cases which are estimated to take more than 10 days, an application should be made for a pre-trial review before a judge.[67] The hearing is in open court. If affidavit evidence has been filed by the parties, they are cross-examined by the opposing counsel on their affidavits. Invariably, a direction is made that deponents must be given a minimum period of notice prior to the trial if they must attend for cross-examination, subject to the proviso that if they do not attend, their affidavits cannot be read in evidence. Where pleadings have been served, the case proceeds in a similar way to an ordinary writ action. Witness statements will be required under O. 38, r. 2A of the Rules of the Supreme Court. Parties may obtain evidence by writs of subpoena under O. 38, rr. 35–44.

64. *Re Mountforest Ltd* [1993] BCC 565 at 571–572.
65. *Stanfield* v. *Gibbon* [1925] WN 11.
66. *Fitzgerald* v. *Williams* [1996] 2 WLR 447 at 454E–H (CA).
67. See *Chancery Guide*, para. 3.10.

7.8.18 Costs

The costs of a petition follow the event unless it appears to the court that, in the circumstances, some other order shall be made. If the petitioner is successful in his petition, it is likely that the court will order that the unsuccessful opposing contributories, or some of them, pay his costs and any costs incurred by the company. The court will usually ensure that none of the costs falls on the company, as otherwise there will be a depletion in the assets available for distribution on the winding-up. If the petitioner is unsuccessful, he is likely to be faced with paying not only his own costs but those of the respondents (including any costs incurred by the company).

If a petitioner fails to appear on the return day, at the hearing for directions, and indicates his intention not to proceed with the petition, the petition will be dismissed and he will be liable to pay the costs.[68]

7.8.19 Where a limited company is the petitioner it is a "plaintiff in an action or other legal proceedings" within the meaning of s. 726(1) of the Companies Act 1985. It may therefore be faced with an application from the respondents for security for costs under that section, where it appears by credible testimony that there is reason to believe that the petitioner will be unable to pay the respondents' costs if they are successful in their defence. An order for security for costs is discretionary and will not be made if the court concludes that it would be unfair to make it.[69]

Applications for security for costs against individual petitioners can be made by the respondents under the provisions of O. 23 of the Rules of the Supreme Court. Reference should be made to the Supreme Court Practice for the standard procedures under the rule which apply equally in this area.[70] The provision most commonly relied upon is O. 23, r. 1(1)(a), which provides that the respondent may apply for security where it appears to the court that the petitioner is ordinarily resident outside the jurisdiction. The Court of Appeal has recently held that the court should never exercise its discretion under this rule to order security to be given by an individual plaintiff or petitioner who is a national of and resident in another member state which is a party to the Brussels Convention on Jurisdiction and Enforcement of Judgments in Civil and Commercial Matters, at any rate in the absence of very cogent evidence of substantial difficulty in enforcing a judgment in that other member state. However, the Court of Appeal emphasised that nothing it said had any bearing on the case in which security is sought against a foreign insolvent company, whether resident in a member state or not, nor where the plaintiff is ordinarily resident in a country which is not a member state of the Convention.[71]

7.9 Notice and settling of the winding-up order

When a winding-up order is made, the petitioner and every other person who appeared at the hearing of the petition is required, not later than the business day following that on which the order was made, to leave at the court all the documents required by the court officials to enable the order to be completed forthwith.[72] The order is drafted by the court.

68. *Re Royal Mutual Benefit Building Society* [1960] 1 WLR 1143.
69. *Re Unisoft Group Ltd (No. 1)* [1993] BCLC 1292, [1994] BCC 11 (CA).
70. See e.g. *Re Little Olympian Each-Ways Ltd (No. 2)* [1995] 1 BCLC 48.
71. *Fitzgerald* v. *Williams* [1996] QB 657 at 671–675 (CA), applying *Mund & Fester* v. *Haltrex International Transport* [1994] ECR 1–467.
72. R. 4.20(2).

The court will normally not fix a special appointment for the settling of the order but particular circumstances may make an appointment necessary. The order must be served on the official receiver and the company and on the registrar of companies.[73] Thereafter, the official receiver will advertise the order in the *London Gazette* and in a local newspaper.[74]

73. R. 4.21.
74. Rr. 4.21(4) and 12.20.

CHAPTER 8

COMPANY INVESTIGATIONS

8.1 Introduction

The Companies Court is concerned with investigative powers falling into two broad categories: (1) investigations conducted by or involving the Secretary of State for Trade and Industry; and (2) investigations or examinations carried out by the official receiver or other office holders regarding a company in receivership, administration or liquidation. The former category is considered below. The latter category is considered in Chapter 15.

There are other investigations involving companies, but these do not generally involve the Companies Court. Thus, for example, various investigative powers arise under the Financial Services Act 1986 in relation to suspected insider dealing and in relation to the affairs of companies carrying on investment business. Additionally, under the Criminal Justice Act 1987, the Serious Fraud Office has been established with various investigative duties and powers. Further powers of investigation arise in relation to insurance companies under the Insurance Companies Act 1982. In each of these cases the investigation will be conducted independently, without the need for any application to be made to the Companies Court. Where there is obstruction to or interference with the course of the investigation normally an offence would arise which can be prosecuted as appropriate.

8.2 Investigations by the Secretary of State for Trade and Industry

The Secretary of State has had powers to appoint inspectors to carry out an investigation and to report on a company's affairs since at least the middle of the last century. The object of the investigation has expanded significantly over time. Under part XIV of the Companies Act 1985[1] the powers of the Department of Trade and Industry to appoint inspectors to investigate the affairs of a company are preserved.[2] Following the recommendations of the Jenkins Committee in 1962,[3] however, which criticised the harm caused by the adverse publicity resulting from investigations where a full inquiry was not required, the Secretary of State now also has the ability to carry out an investigation by more informal methods. These are provided for under ss. 447–451 of the Act, which

1. As amended by part III of CA 1989 (brought into force on 21 February 1990 by CA 1989 (Commencement No. 2) Order 1990, S.I. 1990 No. 142). All references in the text are to sections of CA 1985 unless otherwise stated.

2. The powers contained in part XIV are extended to overseas companies by s. 453 (as amended by s. 70 of the 1989 Act) and to unregistered companies by sch. 22 of the 1985 Act, as amended by s. 71 of the 1989 Act.

3. Report of the Company Law Committee (Cmnd 1749/1962).

broadly permit the Secretary of State to require the production of documents. In addition to this form of investigation into the company's affairs, the Secretary of State may also investigate the ownership of a company[4] and may also appoint inspectors to investigate share dealings which are in contravention of the Act.[5]

Company investigations coming within part XIV of the Act do not inevitably involve the Companies Court. Application will be made to the court only in certain specific circumstances. Thus, for example, an application might be made to the court for an order declaring that the affairs of a company ought to be investigated, so forcing the Secretary of State to appoint one or more competent inspectors to commence an investigation.[6] In other cases, the court may be approached in order to deal with the obstruction of inspectors who have been appointed.[7] In the case of investigations into company ownership which have resulted in the imposition of restrictions on shares under part XV of the Act, the court may deal with applications to relax or remove those restrictions.

8.3 Investigation of a company's affairs

An investigation of a company's affairs may be commenced either as a result of the exercise of a discretionary power by the Secretary of State or as a result of an application to the court. The discretionary powers of the Secretary of State arise under ss. 431(1) and (2) and 432(2). Under s. 431(1), the Secretary of State is empowered to appoint one or more competent inspectors to investigate the affairs of a company and to report on them in such manner as he may direct. Under s. 431(2), the appointment may be made in one of three cases: (i) where the company has a share capital and the application is by not less than 200 members or members holding not less than one-tenth of the shares issued; (ii) where the company does not have a share capital, on the application of not less than one-fifth of the persons registered as members; and (iii) in any case, on the application of the company. The application will have to be supported by such evidence as the Secretary of State requires for the purpose of showing that the applicant or applicants have a good reason for requiring the investigation.[8] The Secretary of State is also empowered, before appointing inspectors, to require that the applicant or applicants give security to an amount not exceeding £5,000, for payment of the costs of the investigation.[9]

Under s. 432(2), the Secretary of State may also appoint one or more competent inspectors if it appears to him that there are circumstances suggesting that one of four categories of event have occurred, namely:

(i) that the company's affairs are being or have been conducted with intent to defraud its creditors or the creditors of any other person, or otherwise for a fraudulent or unlawful purpose, or in a manner which is unfairly prejudicial to some part of its members;

(ii) that any actual or proposed act or omission of the company (including an act or omission on its behalf) is or would be so prejudicial, or that the company was formed for any fraudulent or unlawful purpose;

4. See ss. 442–444 of the 1985 Act.
5. S. 446 of the 1985 Act.
6. S. 432.
7. S. 436.
8. S. 431(3).
9. S. 431(4).

(iii) that persons concerned with the company's formation or the management of its affairs have in that connection been guilty of fraud, misfeasance or other misconduct towards it or its members; or

(iv) that the company's members have not been given all the information with respect to its affairs which they might reasonably expect.

8.3.1 Where inspectors are appointed under this section, they may be appointed on terms that any report they may make is not for publication.[10] Additionally these powers may be exercised in respect of a company irrespective of the fact that it is being voluntarily wound up.[11]

The Secretary of State is not required to disclose the information on the basis of which he has appointed inspectors.[12] As long as he acts within his powers and in good faith, his decision cannot be challenged.[13] The fact that the affairs of the company are the subject of civil proceedings alleging fraud does not mean that an appointment has been made improperly.[14]

The Secretary of State's powers to investigate, however, are not limited to the appointment of an inspector under ss. 431 and 432. He may at any time, if he thinks there is good reason to do so, give directions to a company requiring it to produce documents. The documents would be those which he specifies and they would be required to be produced at such a time and such a place as is set out in the directions.[15] Additionally, the Secretary of State may at any time, when he thinks there is good reason to do so, authorise one of his officers or any other competent person to require a company to produce to that officer or other person forthwith, any documents which that officer or other person specifies.[16] These powers to demand the production of documents include a power to require production of such documents from any person who appears to be in possesion of them.[17] They also include a power to take copies of the documents or extracts of them and to require the person who produces them or any other person who is a present or past officer of the company or who was at any time employed by the company in question to provide an explanation of any them.[18] Where documents are not produced, there is a power to require the person who is required to produce them, to state, to the best of his knowledge and belief, where they are.[19] Failure to comply with these demands will result in an offence which is punishable with a fine.[20] Additional provisions are also made for a warrant to be issued for the entry and search of premises, when documents have not been produced as required among other circumstances.[21]

8.3.2 Where the Secretary of State has authorised one of his officers or another competent person to require the production of documents under s. 447(2), that officer or

10. S. 432(2A).
11. S. 432(3).
12. *Norwest Holst* v. *Secretary of State for Trade* [1978] Ch. 201.
13. *Ibid.*, at 225C–E, per Lord Denning M.R., and 230B–E, per Geoffrey Lane L.J.
14. *Re London United Investments plc* [1992] Ch. 578, at 592–594. The judgment of Dillon L.J. (at 593F–594A), with whom the other members of the Court of Appeal agreed, also suggests that the fact that a criminal investigation is imminent or ongoing will not prevent the appointment of inspectors.
15. S. 447(2).
16. S. 447(3).
17. S. 447(4).
18. S. 447(5)(a).
19. S. 447(5)(b).
20. S. 447(6).
21. S. 448.

person must not exceed or abuse the discretion granted to them or use it for some ulterior purpose such as to punish someone.[22] It is also a defence for a person charged with an offence in respect of a requirement to produce documents, that the documents were not within his power or control and that it is not reasonably practicable for him to comply with the requirement. Where a requirement is made for a statement regarding documents, the privilege against self-incrimination would appear to afford no ground of objection.[23]

The provisions of s. 447 for the Secretary of State to obtain documentation are the most commonly used form of investigation. They follow upon the recommendations of the Jenkins Committee, that formal investigations should be avoided if possible, given the considerable public interest which arises as a result of them which in many cases harms the company and its shareholders.

8.4 Application to the court

In addition to the extensive powers of the Secretary of State for the appointment of inspectors and for the production of documents, the court may make a declaration that the affairs of a company ought to be investigated. Where such an order is made, under s. 432(1) the Secretary of State is required to appoint one or more competent inspectors to investigate the affairs of the company and to report on them in such manner as he directs. It has been held that the section extends to all bodies corporate incorporated outside Great Britain but which carry on or have carried on business in Great Britain.[24]

The application is made by way of originating motion.[25] There is no specific rule identifying which persons are entitled to make the application and it appears that it may be made by any person interested.[26] Such an applicant should prepare an appropriate originating notice of motion together with an affidavit in support setting out the facts relied on as justifying the appointment of an inspector.[27] A specific practice direction exists in relation to service of such a notice of motion.[28] This specifies that the notice of motion need not be served on the Secretary of State but rather notice of the intended application should be sent to the solicitor at the Department of Trade together with copies of any affidavits intended to be used at the hearing. Evidence should be filed showing that the practice direction has been complied with.[29] There is no limit to the matters the court can take into account in considering whether to make an order, but the court will have available to it the analogy of the various grounds arising for appointment by the Secretary of State under s. 432(2) described above.

No other special procedures are required to be complied with in relation to an application of this type and, accordingly, the general procedures relevant to all originating notices of motion in the Companies Court are applicable.[30]

22. *R.* v. *Secretary of State for Trade ex parte Perestrello* [1981] QB 19. This case also suggests that the court might set aside a notice under s. 447 requiring the production of documents which is in unreasonably wide terms.
23. S. 447(8) and para. 8.6.1, *infra*.
24. *R.* v. *Secretary of State for Trade ex parte Perestrello, supra*.
25. RSC O. 102, r. 3(1)(b).
26. *Supreme Court Practice 1997*, Vol. 1, p. 1546, para. 102/3/3.
27. *Ibid.*
28. Practice Direction (Companies Court) [1954] 1 WLR 563.
29. *Ibid.* See also *Re Miles Aircraft Ltd (No. 2)* [1948] WN 178.
30. As to which see para. 2.13 *et seq.*, *supra*.

8.5 Conduct of investigation

Where inspectors are appointed by the Secretary of State under ss. 431 and 432, they are commonly appointed in pairs, one inspector being a senior chartered accountant and the other being a senior barrister or solicitor.[31] The company's affairs which they are empowered to investigate under these sections have been held to mean the business affairs, including the goodwill, profit and loss, contracts and investments and assets of the company as well as its shareholding in or ability to control a subsidiary or sub-subsidiary. Furthermore, for these purposes, the affairs of a company do not cease to be its affairs following the appointment of a receiver and manager.[32]

Where the inspectors think it necessary, for the purposes of investigation of the affairs of the company (as so defined), to investigate the affairs of another body corporate, which is or has been in the same group, then the inspectors may carry out such an investigation and report on the affairs of the other body corporate insofar as they think that the results of that investigation are relevant to the affairs of the original company which they were appointed to investigate.[33]

8.5.1 In conducting their investigation under ss. 431 and 432, inspectors have wide powers for the purposes of obtaining documents and evidence. Thus, it is the duty of all officers and agents[34] of the company investigated, as well as any other holding or subsidiary company whose affairs are being investigated under s. 433(1), to produce to the inspectors all documents relating to the company or other subsidiary or holding company which are in their custody or power.[35] Such persons are also under a duty to attend before the inspectors when required to do so and otherwise to give the inspectors all assistance which they are reasonably able to give in connection with the investigation.[36]

Additionally, if the inspectors consider that an officer or an agent of the company or any other person is or may be in possession of information relating to a matter which they believe to be relevant to the investigation, they may require him to produce to them any documents in his possession or power relating to that matter.[37] They may also require such person to attend before them and otherwise to give them all assistance in connection with the investigation which he is reasonably able to give, and in these circumstances it is that person's duty to comply with that requirement.[38]

8.5.2 Documents for the purposes of the above provisions include information recorded in any form and, where that information is recorded otherwise than in legible form, the inspectors have power to require to be produced a copy of the information in legible

31. See, for example, the Parliamentary Answer dated 5 July 1994 of the Corporate Affairs Minister, Neil Hamilton identifying inspectors appointed in the course of explaining the costs of investigations (published in *British Company Law and Practice*, Vol. 2, pp. 97, 416–97, 417).

32. *R.* v. *Board of Trade, ex parte St Martin's Preserving Co. Ltd* [1965] 1 QB 603.

33. S. 433.

34. Including past as well as present officers or agents. "Agents" includes the company's bankers and solicitors and persons employed by it as auditors, whether these persons are or are not officers of the company (s. 434(4)). Also a receiver who is appointed out of court under a debenture providing that he is the company's agent will be treated as agent for the purposes of s. 434 (see *R.* v. *Board of Trade ex parte St Martin's Preserving Co. Ltd* [1965] 1 QB 603, at 622, per Winn J. and s. 44(1)(a) of the IA 1986 which provides that an administrative receiver is deemed to be the company's agent unless and until the company goes into liquidation).

35. S. 434(1)(a).

36. S. 434(1)(b) and (c).

37. S. 434(2)(a).

38. S. 434(2)(b) and (c).

form.[39] Also, when persons attend before the inspectors, the inspectors may for the purpose of the investigation examine such persons on oath and may administer an oath accordingly.[40] In addition, an answer given by a person to a question put to him in exercise of the above powers may be used in evidence against him.[41] All attendances before the inspectors will be in private. They are not entitled to admit the public[42] although it is possible that other persons with statutory inquisitorial powers, such as insolvency office holders, may subsequently gain access to the evidence given.[43] The inspectors may, however, have in attendance anyone whose presence is reasonably necessary such as a shorthand writer to take a note.[44] Counsel may attend to represent parties involved in the investigation.[45]

In exercising their powers of investigation, the proceedings of the inspectors are not judicial or quasi judicial but are administrative in nature. It has been held, however, that despite this, the character of the proceedings requires that the inspectors act fairly.[46] Accordingly, where the inspectors are disposed to condemn or criticise someone in their report, they must give that person a fair opportunity to correct or contradict the allegation made against them and for this purpose an outline charge would usually be sufficient.[47] Directors will not be entitled to refuse to answer questions until they are shown transcripts of evidence or documents used against them or until they have been allowed to cross-examine witnesses.[48] Inspectors will avoid criticism where they have undertaken that directors will not be criticised in the report without first being told in general terms of the allegation against them and where the inspectors are also prepared to make known the purport of the relevant evidence and documents. If directors refuse to give evidence in these circumstances it will be treated as an unjustified refusal.[49]

All of the above matters will be relevant when the Companies Court has before it an obstruction application as described below.

8.6 Obstruction of inspectors

Where the inspectors are obstructed in the course of an investigation under ss. 431 and 432, procedures are available whereby the obstructive conduct may lead to a finding of contempt of court. This is the second type of proceeding in which the Companies Court deals with matters connected with company investigations.

Under s. 436(1), if a person fails to comply with the provisions of s. 434(1) and (2) above, or refuses to answer any question put to him by inspectors for the purposes of their investigation, the inspectors have power to certify that fact in writing to the court. For these purposes a certificate should be lodged with the registrar of the Companies Court.[50]

39. S. 434(6).
40. S. 434(3).
41. S. 434(5).
42. *Hearts of Oak Assurance Co. Ltd* v. *A-G* [1932] AC 392; *Re Pergamon Press* [1971] Ch. 388.
43. See *Soden v. Burns* [1996] 1 WLR 1512 (administrators using powers under s. 236 of the IA 1986 to gain access to transcripts of evidence obtained by inspectors).
44. *Re Gaumont-British Picture Corp. Ltd* [1940] Ch. 506.
45. *McClelland, Pope and Langley Ltd* v. *Howard (1966)* [1968] 1 All ER 569n.
46. *Re Pergamon Press Ltd, supra.*
47. *Ibid.* and see also *Maxwell* v. *Department of Trade and Industry* [1974] QB 523.
48. *Ibid.*
49. *Ibid.*
50. For a sample form of certificate see *Atkin's Court Forms*, Vol. 9, 1995 Edn, Form 142.

Where such a certificate has been filed, under s. 436(3) of the Act, the court may thereupon inquire into the case and, after hearing any witnesses who may be produced against or on behalf of the alleged offender, and after hearing any statement which may be offered in his defence, may punish him in like manner as if he had been guilty of a contempt of court.

8.6.1 An application for an inquiry under s. 436 must be made by way of originating motion.[51] The notice of motion will be issued by the inspectors requesting that an inquiry be made into the refusal of the named individual, describing his office, to produce specified documents or to reply to questions as the case may be.[52] It has been suggested that the motion should be entitled in the matter of the company concerned and in the matter of the relevant offender and in the matter of the Act.[53] The notice of motion will then be served on the person in default, supported by an affidavit. From the terms of s. 436 the motion ought to be dealt with at a hearing with oral evidence and, if the finding of contempt is made, the appropriate order may be for committal. If there is a genuine dispute, however, and the officer or agent, in his evidence or by his counsel, apologises for his contempt in the event of his being held to be wrong he may avoid committal with only an order for costs being made against him.[54]

In this context, it is notable that the House of Lords has held that an officer or agent of a company who is examined by inspectors will be entitled to refuse to answer questions on the ground that the answers would incriminate him but if he does so the matter can then be referred to the court under s. 436. The issue of self-incrimination will then be one for the court rather than the inspectors themselves to decide.[55] If the inspectors assume the power to decide the issue of self-incrimination and induce a person to provide answers under protest, this will not necessarily lead to a successful judicial review at least where the party's legal adviser was present throughout and intervened in the cross-examination.[56] In any event, the Court of Appeal has now established that the privilege against self-incrimination is not a basis for refusing to answer questions put by inspectors.[57] The only issue which may arise is whether, in the circumstances and at the stage which the case has reached, further questioning by the inspectors would be oppressive and therefore unfair. In these circumstances the court might not compel a person to answer under the provisions of s. 436(2).[58] It was accepted by leading counsel appearing on behalf of the inspectors that, in general, a line should be drawn when a person has been charged with a criminal offence. In those circumstances a person would not thereafter be questioned by inspectors on matters relevant to that offence.[59]

51. RSC O. 102, r. 3(1)(c).
52. *Supreme Court Practice 1997*, Vol. 1, p.1546, para. 102/3/4.
53. *Ibid.*
54. See, for example, *Re Gaumont-British Picture Corp. Ltd, supra.*
55. *McClelland, Pope and Langley Ltd* v. *Howard (1966), supra.*
56. *Ibid.*
57. *Re London United Investments plc, supra*; *R.* v. *Seelig* [1991] BCLC 869 and *R* v. *Harris* [1970] 1 WLR 1252.
58. *Re London United Investments, supra.*
59. *Ibid.*, at 600. See also *R* v. *Seelig, supra* at 882b–c (Henry J. considered that the evidence given to inspectors after a defendant is charged would normally be dealt with differently from evidence obtained when he is not charged—a view approved by the Court of Appeal). Note also that the subsequent use of answers obtained compulsorily by inspectors for the purpose of a prosecution has been held to infringe art. 6 of the European Convention on Human Rights (*Saunders* v. *United Kingdom*, *Times*, 18 December 1996).

8.6.2 Other grounds justifying a refusal to disclose information are provided for in the Act. Thus, s. 452 preserves legal professional privilege and certain banking confidences. A person is entitled to refuse to disclose details which would be protected by legal professional privilege in a High Court action except, in the case of a lawyer, the name and address of his client.[60] Disclosure of information or documents in respect of which a person owes a duty of confidence "by virtue of carrying on the business of banking" can also be refused. This will not apply if consent is given by the person to whom the obligation is owed or that person is the company under investigation or the Secretary of States authorises disclosure.[61]

8.7 Consequences of investigation

An investigation of a company's affairs may lead the inspectors involved or the Secretary of State to take various further steps. These can include any one or more of the following.

8.7.1 Report

Inspectors may make interim reports to the Secretary of State during the course of their investigation. This becomes a mandatory obligation if he directs them to do so. In any event, at the conclusion of their investigation there is a further mandatory obligation to provide a final report to the Secretary of State.[62]

Any report produced by inspectors may be published by the Secretary of State and copies provided to certain specified persons.[63] Where the inspectors were appointed following an order of the court under s. 432, the Secretary of State is obliged to furnish a copy of each of their reports to the court.[64]

If matters come to light in the course of an investigation suggesting to the Secretary of State that an offence has been committed, and those matters have been referred to the prosecuting authority, then the Secretary of State may direct that the inspectors are to take no further steps in their investigation or only to take certain further steps as he directs. Where such a direction is made, a final report will only be produced where the appointment of the inspectors was made pursuant to the order of the court or if the Secretary of State specifically so directs.[65]

Any report which is produced will be admissible in any legal proceedings as evidence of the opinion of the inspectors. In relation to proceedings under s. 8 of the Company Directors Disqualification Act 1986, the report will also be evidence of any facts stated in it.[66]

Reports will not be produced in relation to investigations under s. 447 since these do not involve the appointment of inspectors. Instead, specific provision is made for confidentiality. This follows from one of the main reasons for using this form of investigation, namely

60. S. 452(1)–(2).
61. S. 452(1A).
62. S. 437(1).
63. S. 437(3).
64. S. 437(2).
65. S. 437(1B) and (1C).
66. S. 441.

the prevention of adverse publicity causing irreparable harm to the company. Thus, information or documents obtained may not be disclosed without the consent of the company concerned.[67] Exceptions arise, however, where the documents are to be disclosed for certain purposes or to certain "competent authorities".[68] For example, disclosure is permitted for the purposes of certain proceedings under the Company Directors Disqualification Act 1986.[69]

8.7.2 Criminal Proceedings

Inspectors may or, if so directed by the Secretary of State, must inform him of any matters coming to their knowledge as a result of their investigations.[70] Such information could include information suggesting the commission of a criminal offence.[71] Thereafter the Secretary of State could disclose such information or require the inspectors to disclose it to the police or the Director of Public Prosecutions.[72]

Information or documents obtained following investigation without inspectors under s. 447 may also be disclosed for the purposes of criminal prosecution and to the same prosecuting authorities.[73]

Answers given to inspectors in the course of the exercise of their powers in conducting an investigation, or statements made following a requirement to do so under s. 447 could be used in criminal proceedings against the person who provided those answers or statement.[74] As mentioned above, the privilege against self-incrimination is abrogated in such cases.[75] The European Court of Human Rights, however, has held that this would be in breach of art. 6 of the European Convention on Human Rights.[76]

Inspectors, however, may not be forced to produce witness statements supplied to them during the course of their investigation, for the purposes of subsequent criminal proceedings. Thus, a defendant in a criminal trial will not obtain the issue of a witness summons addressed to an inspector requiring his attendance to produce witness statements made to him where such witness statements are to be used purely for cross-examination.[77] Production of such statements may also be refused where to do so would be contrary to the public interest in the confidentiality of such documents.[78]

As mentioned above, where the Secretary of State takes the view that matters have come to light in the course of the investigation suggesting that a criminal offence has been committed, and those matters have been referred to the appropriate prosecuting authority,

67. S. 449(1).
68. Defined in s. 449(3).
69. S. 449(1)(ba).
70. S. 437(1A).
71. See *R* v. *Seelig, supra,* at 872d–e for an example of a direction to inspectors to disclose information concerning possible criminal offences to the Secretary of State.
72. S. 451A(2).
73. Ss. 449(1)(a) and 449(3)(h) and (l).
74. Ss. 434(5) and 447(8); *R* v. *Harris, supra.*
75. *R.* v. *Harris, supra*; *R* v. *Seelig, supra*; and *Re London United Investments plc, supra.*
76. *Saunders* v. *United Kingdom, supra.*
77. *R* v. *Cheltenham Justices ex parte Secretary of State for Trade* [1977] 1 WLR 95.
78. *Ibid.* The importance of the public interest in confidentiality may be discounted where the statements are to be used as important primary evidence and not just material for cross-examination (see *London & County Securities Ltd* v. *Nicholson* [1980] 1 WLR 948 at 957F, per Browne-Wilkinson J.). See also *Soden* v. *Burns, supra.*

the Secretary of State has a discretion whether to direct the inspectors to take no further steps in the investigation or to take only certain further steps as he directs.[79]

8.7.3 Civil Proceedings

Where, from information in an inspector's report, obtained either by inspectors or under s. 447, it appears to the Secretary of State that civil proceedings ought to be brought in the public interest on behalf of the company then the Secretary of State may himself bring those proceedings in the name of and on behalf of that company.[80]

Where civil proceedings are brought in this way on the basis of a report of inspectors, the report itself will generally not be admissible in evidence. This may be on the basis that it contains evidence of opinion on matters on which opinion evidence is not admissible.[81] This is certainly so where the report is proposed to be used at trial. Where it is to be used for an interlocutory application and the report contains hearsay there may be further difficulties in admissibility unless the source and grounds of any hearsay statements are identified.[82] Answers given to inspectors, or statements made under a requirement pursuant to s. 447 by persons who are themselves defendants, will be admissible against them.[83] As mentioned previously, the privilege against self-incrimination is abrogated.

8.7.4 Winding-up proceedings

Following an investigation, the Secretary of State may conclude that it is expedient in the public interest that a company be wound up and may present a winding-up petition on this basis.[84] Such petitions will be considered later.[85] It is notable that, where the accuracy of an inspector's report is not disputed in such winding-up proceedings, the court may elect to act on the basis of the report supported only by an affidavit of a Department of Trade and Industry official.[86] Where allegations made in the report concerning the company and its officers are contested, however, then the petition must be supported by other evidence of "true evidential value".[87] For these purposes, a challenge to the report involves a challenge by a person with direct knowledge of the facts, who is willing to put forward an affidavit and be cross-examined on his evidence in contradiction of the inspectors' report.[88] Even if the report is challenged in this way, it will nevertheless be treated as *prima facie* evidence.[89]

It is also notable that a contributory of the company who wishes to petition for its winding-up may, in some circumstances be able to rely upon an inspector's report.[90] Thus,

79. S. 437(1B).
80. S. 438(1).
81. *Savings and Investment Bank Ltd* v. *Gasco Investments (Netherlands) BV* [1984] 1 WLR 271.
82. RSC O.41, r. 5(2). See also *Savings & Investment Bank* v. *Gasco Investments, supra* which was not followed in *Deutsche Ruckversichering* v. *Walbrook Insurance* [1995] 1 WLR 1017.
83. Ss. 434(5) and 447(8); *London & County Securities Ltd* v. *Nicholson, supra.*
84. Ss. 124(4)(b) and 124A of the IA 1986.
85. See Chapter 9, *infra*.
86. *Re Allied Produce Co.* [1967] 1 WLR 1469; *Re Travel and Holiday Clubs* [1967] 1 WLR 711; and *Re SBA Properties* [1967] 1 WLR 799.
87. *Re ABC Coupler Engineering Co.* [1962] 1 WLR 1236; *Re Koscot Interplanetary (UK) Ltd* [1972] 3 All ER 829.
88. *Re Armvent Ltd* [1975] 1 WLR 1679.
89. *Ibid.*
90. *Re St Piran* [1981] 1 WLR 1300.

where one of the grounds for the appointment of the inspectors is the withholding of information from shareholders, the court has permitted reliance on a report by petitioning contributories since the object of the inspection might be defeated if no reliance could be placed upon the contents of the report in such circumstances.

8.7.5 Unfair prejudice petitions

After a report has been produced by inspectors, or where information and documentation have been obtained under s. 447, the Secretary of State retains the right to petition on the basis that it appears to him that the company's affairs are being or have been conducted in a manner which is unfairly prejudicial to the interests of its members generally, or of some part of its members, or that some actual proposed act or omission of the company is or would be so prejudicial.[91] Such a petition may be combined with an application to wind up the company.[92]

The provisions for petitions by the Secretary of State, for unfairly prejudicial conduct, have remained largely unused in practice. They are governed by the same procedural requirements as any other petition presented under part XVII of the Act.[93] The procedural requirements of these petitions are generally considered in Chapter 6. Presumably, in the case of a petition presented by the Secretary of State following a report, the court would adopt a similar attitude to the evidential value of the contents of that report to that adopted in the context of winding-up petitions. Furthermore, if a report of inspectors can be relied upon by a contributory, where inspectors have been appointed on the basis of the withholding of relevant information from shareholders, there would appear to be no reason why, on similar principles, the report could not be relied upon by members petitioning under part XVII of the Act.[94]

8.8 Investigations of company ownership

An investigation of the ownership of shares in a company may be commenced by the Secretary of State either on his own initiative or, on the satisfaction of certain conditions, following an application by members of the company concerned. Under s. 442(1), if the Secretary of State concludes that there is good reason to do so, he may appoint one or more competent inspectors to investigate and report on the membership of any company and otherwise with respect to the company. The purpose of the investigation will be to determine the true persons who are or have been financially interested in its success or failure (real or apparent) or who are able to control or materially influence its policy. An appointment must be made by the Secretary of State where an application is made by members of a company with respect to particular shares or debentures under s. 442(3). The number of the applicants or the amount of the shares which must be held by them in order for this to occur must be not less than that required for an application for the

91. S. 460(1).
92. *Ibid.*
93. Companies (Unfair Prejudice Applications) Proceedings Rules 1986 (SI 1986 No. 2000), para. 2.
94. Compare *Re St Piran, supra.*

appointment of inspectors by members under s. 431(2).[95] Even if such conditions are satisfied, however, the Secretary of State is not required to appoint inspectors if he is satisfied that the application is vexatious and may exclude any matter from the investigation if he is satisfied that it is unreasonable for it to be investigated.[96] Moreover, the Secretary of State may require the applicants to give security to an amount not exceeding £5,000 for the payment of the costs of an investigation involving inspectors.[97]

Rather than appointing inspectors, the Secretary of State may investigate by simply requiring the production of information.[98] The Secretary of State retains the power to do this if he considers it sufficient in cases where an application in proper form has been made by members for an investigation into share ownership.[99]

8.9 Investigations involving inspectors

Where the Secretary of State appoints inspectors under s. 442, he may define the scope of their investigation. In particular, he may specify the matter or the period to which it is to extend and may limit the investigation to matters connected with particular shares or debentures.[100] Subject to the terms of their appointment, the inspectors powers will extend to the investigation of any circumstances suggesting the existence of an arrangement or understanding which, although not legally binding, is or was observed or likely to be observed in practice, and is relevant to the purposes of the investigation.[101]

Sections 433(1), 434, 436 and 437, which provide for the conduct of investigations into a company's affairs, also apply to investigations under s. 442, with necessary modifications of references to the affairs of a company.[102] Moreover, in their application to s. 442 investigations, they affect various other persons in the same way as they affect officers and agents of the company.[103]

Investigations under s. 442 are subject to the same protection under s. 452 in respect of legal professional privilege and banking secrecy as that which applies to investigations into a company's affairs.[104]

8.10 Other Investigations of company ownership

If the Secretary of State considers there is good reason to investigate the ownership of shares or debentures of a company but that it is unnecessary to appoint inspectors to do so, he may instead require certain persons to provide information to him. Thus, for

95. In other words, in the cases of a company having a share capital, not less than 200 members or members holding not less than one-tenth of the shares issued. Alternatively in the case of a company not having a share capital, on the application of not less than one-fifth of the persons on the company's register of members (s. 431(2)(a) and (b)).

96. S. 442(3A).

97. S. 442(3B).

98. S. 444.

99. S. 442(3C).

100. S. 442(2).

101. S. 442(4).

102. For discussion of these sections see paras 8.5 to 8.7.2, *supra*.

103. S. 443(2). The persons affected include all persons who are or have been, or whom the inspector has reasonable cause to believe to be or have been (a) financially interested in the success or failure of the company, or (b) able to control or materially influence its policy. It also includes any other person whom the inspector has reasonable cause to believe possesses information relevant to the investigation.

104. S. 452(1).

example, he may require any person whom he has reasonable cause to believe to have or to be able to obtain any information as to the present and past interests in the shares or debentures concerned, to give that information to him.[105] These provisions are enforceable by criminal sanctions.[106]

As in the case of investigations under s. 442, investigations of this type are subject to the provisions contained in s. 452 concerning legal professional privilege and banking secrecy.

8.11 Restrictions on shares or debentures

The Companies Court can become involved in investigations into the ownership of a company where such an investigation results in restrictions being imposed on shares or debentures.

If the Secretary of State considers that there is a difficulty in finding out the relevant facts about any shares in an investigation under ss. 442 or 444, he can direct that the shares will be subject to certain restrictions until further order.[107] The Secretary of State, however, may qualify the restrictions imposed if he is satisfied that they might unfairly affect the rights of third parties in respect of shares.[108]

The restrictions which may apply are as follows:

(a) any transfer of the shares or, in the case of unissued shares, any transfer of the right to be issued with them and any issue of them, will be void;
(b) no voting rights will be exercisable in respect of the shares;
(c) no further shares can be issued in right of those which are the subject of the order or direction or in pursuance of any offer made to their holder; and
(d) except in a liquidation, no payment may be made of any sums due from the company on the shares, whether in respect of capital or otherwise.[109]

8.11.1 Additionally, any agreement to transfer the shares or, in the case of unissued shares, the right to be issued with them, will also be void (unless it is an agreement to transfer the shares of which the court or the Secretary of State (as appropriate) approves and orders the removal of restrictions).[110] An agreement to transfer any right to be issued with other shares in right of those which are the subject of restrictions, or to receive any payment on them (otherwise than in a liquidation) will also be void. This is subject to an exception in respect of an agreement transferring any such right, where there is a transfer of shares of which the court or the Secretary of State (as appropriate) approves and orders restrictions to be removed.[111]

Where the Secretary of State has imposed restrictions, application may be made to him for an order disapplying them. Alternatively, instead of applying to the Secretary of State, application may be made to the court by any person aggrieved.[112] This can also be done

105. S. 444(1).
106. S. 444(3).
107. S. 445(1).
108. S. 445(1A) (inserted by the Companies (Disclosure of Interests in Shares) (Orders imposing restrictions on shares) Regulations 1991 (SI 1991 No. 1646), para. 5.
109. S. 454(1).
110. See ss. 454(2) and 456(3)(b).
111. Ss. 454(3) and 456(3)(b).
112. S. 456(1) and (2).

if the Secretary of State refuses to remove the restrictions. Pursuant to s. 456(3), the Secretary of State and the court may only remove the restrictions if satisfied that the relevant facts about the shares have been disclosed to the company and that no unfair advantage has accrued to any person as a result of an earlier failure to make disclosure or if the shares are to be transferred and the Secretary of State or the court approves of the transfer.[113] The court, however, has additional powers to direct that acts by specified persons for specified purposes are not to be treated as a breach of restrictions. These powers may be exercised where the court is satisfied that the order imposing restrictions unfairly affects the rights of third parties in respect of shares.[114]

8.11.2 Separate from the above procedure, a further form of application may be made to the court under s. 456(4), where shares are subject to restrictions, seeking an order that the shares are be sold subject to the court's approval as to the sale. In the course of making such an order, the court may also direct that the shares are to cease to be the subject of restrictions.[115] Where the restrictions were imposed following investigation by the Secretary of State this form of application may be made to the court by the Secretary of State or by the company involved.[116]

If the court makes an order for the sale of shares under s. 456(4), it can also make such further order in respect of the sale or transfer of the shares as it thinks fit.[117] Where the restrictions were imposed by the Secretary of State following investigation, the application for such further orders can be made by the Secretary of State, the company, by the person appointed by or pursuant to the order to effect the sale, or by any person interested in the shares.[118]

8.11.3 Any order, whether made by the court or by the Secretary of State, directing that shares are to cease to be the subject of restrictions so as to permit a transfer of shares or their sale may continue some of the restrictions.[119] Those which can be continued, either wholly or in part, concern the issue of further shares in right of the shares in question or pursuant to an offer made to their holder, and the payment of sums due from the company on shares except on a liquidation. These can be continued, however, only so far as they relate to any right acquired or offer made before transfer. Moreover the Secretary of State or court will be able to remove these remaining restrictions without being satisfied of the matters set out in s. 456(3) described above.[120]

Any application to the court of the type described above must be made by an originating notice of motion.[121] The respondents to the application should include the Secretary of State and the registered holder of the shares, if they are not the applicants.[122] The application will need to be supported by an affidavit. It should set out the circumstances in which the order imposing the restrictions was made, together with the applicant's

113. Prior to amendments introduced by CA 1989, s. 145 and sch. 19, para. 10, the word "sale" as to transfer was adopted in s. 456(3). The old wording did not cover an acquisition of shares by an exchange of other shares (*Re Westminster Property Group plc* [1985] 1 WLR 676).

114. S. 456(1A) inserted by the Companies (Disclosure of Interests in Shares)(Orders imposing restrictions on shares) Regulations 1991, *supra*, para. 8.

115. S. 456(4).

116. *Ibid.*

117. S. 456(5).

118. *Ibid.*

119. S. 456(6).

120. See para. 8.11.1, *supra*.

121. RSC O. 102, rr. 3(1)(d) and (e).

122. *Supreme Court Practice 1995*, Vol. 1, p.1520, para. 102/3/5.

interest in the matter. The affidavit should go on to show the grounds on which the restrictions should be removed. Where the requirements of s. 456(3) must be met, it will be appropriate to state that the required information has now been supplied and that no unfair advantage has been obtained as a result of an earlier failure to make disclosure, even where transfer under court approval is proposed.[123]

8.11.4 Where shares which are the subject of restrictions have been sold pursuant to an order of the court under s. 456(4), the proceeds of sale, less the costs of sale, must be paid into court for the benefit of the persons who are beneficially interested in the shares. Such persons may then apply to the court for the whole or part of those proceeds to be paid to them.[124] On such an application, the court must order payment to the applicant of the whole of the proceeds of sale, together with any accrued interest, or, if any other person has a beneficial interest in the shares at the time of their sale, a proportion of the proceeds and interest equal to the the applicant's beneficial entitlement.[125] An application of this type might be made as an interlocutory application in proceedings commenced by originating motion for an order permitting sale, subject to the court's approval, either where liberty to apply has been granted or at least where such proceedings are still on foot after the date of sale. If this is not possible, the application could be made by way of originating summons, since it is not one of those under the 1985 Act specifically listed as being required to be commenced by originating motion or petition.[126]

Where a court makes an order for shares to be sold subject to the court's approval as to the sale under s. 456(4), and makes further orders relating to the sale or transfer of shares, it may order that the applicant's costs are to be paid out of the proceeds of sale. If this happens, the applicant will be entitled to payment of his costs out of those proceeds, before any person interested in the shares in question receives any part of those proceeds.[127]

8.12 Investigation of share dealings

The final form of investigation in which the Companies Court may become involved is in respect of investigations as to share dealings. In such investigations, applications under s. 436 concerning the obstruction of inspectors may arise for consideration.

Pursuant to s. 446(1), if circumstances arise which appear to the Secretary of State to suggest that contraventions have occurred of ss. 323 or 324 or 328(3)–(5) (dealing with share dealings by directors or their families and the obligation of a director to disclose a shareholding in his own company), the Secretary of State may appoint one or more competent inspectors to carry out an investigation. The investigation will be such as is requisite to establish whether or not such contraventions have occurred and to report the result of the investigation to him. The appointment may limit the period to which the investigation is to extend and, alternatively or additionally, confine it to shares or debentures of a particular class.[128]

123. Compare *Re Geers Gross plc* [1987] 1 WLR 1649 where the Court of Appeal concluded that the court retained the power to refuse to remove restrictions where it was intended to sell the shares concerned. In exercising its discretion the court took into account a failure to disclose the relevant facts.
124. S. 457(1).
125. S. 457(2).
126. RSC O. 102, r. 2(1).
127. S. 457(3).
128. S. 446(2).

In an investigation under s. 446, ss. 434–437 apply with the substitution, for references to any other body corporate whose affairs are investigated under s. 433(1), of a reference to any other body corporate which is, or has at any relevant time been, the company's subsidiary or holding company, or a subsidiary of its holding company.[129] Sections 434–436 will apply to various persons as they apply to officers of the company. For example they will apply to any individual who is an authorised person within the Financial Services Act 1986.[130]

The provisions of s. 452 which preserve legal professional privilege and provide protection of banking secrecy also apply in respect of investigations under s. 446.[131]

Where an application is made to the court for obstruction of inspectors under s. 436 in respect of an investigation under s. 446, the same procedure will apply as that described in respect of investigations into the affairs of a company.[132]

8.13 Costs and expenses

The expenses of any investigation are to be defrayed in the first instance by the Secretary of State. He, however, may recover those expenses from various persons found to be liable. When so recovering his expenses, any reasonable sums which the Secretary of State may determine as being in respect of general staff costs and overheads would be treated as part of the expenses of the investigation.[133] The persons liable will include:

(a) a person who is convicted on a prosecution instituted as a result of an investigation or ordered to pay the costs of civil proceedings brought in the company's name by the Secretary of State[134];
(b) the company in whose name civil proceedings are brought by the Secretary of State is liable to the amount or value of any sums or property recovered by it as a result of those proceedings[135];
(c) a company which is dealt with in an inspector's report where the inspectors are appointed "otherwise than of the Secretary of State's own motion".[136] This would cover a case where the court ordered an investigation under s. 432. This provision, is subject to exceptions, firstly in the case where the company itself applied for the investigation to take place, and secondly, where the Secretary of State himself directs otherwise[137];
(d) the applicant for an investigation under ss. 431 or 442(3) will be liable for the expenses of an investigation to such extent as the Secretary of State directs.[138]

Any report produced by inspectors appointed following a court order may include a recommendation as to the directions which the inspectors think appropriate in relation to

129. S. 446(3).
130. S. 446(4).
131. S. 452(1).
132. See paras. 8.6 to 8.6.2, *supra*.
133. S. 439(1).
134. S. 439(2).
135. S. 439(3).
136. S. 439(3).
137. *Ibid.*
138. S. 439(5).

the categories of liability described in (c) and (d) above. This can be a mandatory element of a report if the Secretary of State so directs.[139]

Costs and expenses incurred by the Secretary of State in connection with civil proceedings are to be treated as expenses of the investigation giving rise to the proceedings.[140]

There are further provisions as to rights of indemnity and contribution between persons who have liabilities imposed upon them to meet the expenses of an investigation.[141] Any expenses not met by persons liable will be paid out of public funds.[142]

139. S. 439(6).
140. S. 439(7).
141. S. 439(8) and (9).
142. S. 439(10).

PART 3

INSOLVENCY PROCEEDINGS

CHAPTER 9

CREDITORS' WINDING-UP PETITIONS

9.1 Introduction

This Chapter deals principally with the procedure for creditors' winding-up petitions against companies registered under the Companies Acts. Creditors' winding-up petitions are governed by part IV (chapter 6) of the Insolvency Act 1986 (as amended), in particular ss. 117 to 130 inclusive, and by part 4 of the Insolvency Rules 1986 (as amended), in particular rr. 4.1 to 4.21A inclusive.[1] This Chapter also deals with the special considerations which apply where the winding-up proceedings are brought by the Secretary of State in the public interest, where the company or association sought to be wound up is already subject to some form of insolvency proceedings or where it is not registered under the Companies Acts. The final part of this Chapter describes the procedure for winding-up insolvent partnerships. This Chapter does not deal with the winding-up of a company by one of its contributories, which is discussed in Chapter 7, *supra*.

SCOPE OF THE WINDING-UP JURISDICTION

COURTS HAVING JURISDICTION TO WIND UP

9.2 High Court

Any company registered in England and Wales under the Companies Acts may be wound up in the High Court.[2] In London, petitions are listed for hearing in the High Court Chancery Division, Companies Court,[3] and are heard in the first instance by the Companies Court Registrar sitting in open court[4] on Wednesdays in term[5] (or on alternate Wednesdays when there is a fall in the number of petitions awaiting hearing). In Chancery district registries of the High Court, petitions are listed for hearing in the first instance by

1. Special rules apply to the winding-up of insurance companies: see the Insurance Companies (Winding-Up) Rules 1985 (S.I. 1985 No. 95) (as amended by S.I. 1986 No. 2002 and S.I. 1991 No. 1997).
2. IA 1986, s. 117(1).
3. The "Companies Court" is not a separate and distinct court, but is a way of describing the High Court when hearing company matters: *Re Shilena Hosiery Co. Ltd* [1980] Ch. 219; *Fabric Sales Ltd* v. *Eratex Ltd* [1984] 1 WLR 863; *Re Tasbian Ltd (No.2)* [1990] BCC 322 at 324G–325B. Accordingly, every High Court Judge has jurisdiction to hear winding-up petitions, but as a matter of practice such proceedings are only issued to be heard by the Companies Court Registrar or the Companies Court Judge.
4. Practice Direction (No. 33 of 1986) [1987] 1 All ER 107, paras (2) and (3).
5. Practice Direction (No. 2 of 1986) [1986] 1 WLR 1428.

a district judge sitting in open court. Petitions may not be presented in district registries which are not Chancery district registries.[6]

9.3 County Court

Provided that the company sought to be wound up has a share capital which is not paid up or credited as paid up in excess of £120,000, the company may alternatively be wound up in the County Court.[7] A company which does not have a share capital (e.g. a company limited by guarantee or an unlimited company) may not be wound up in the County Court.[8]

9.4 Which County Court?

The relevant County Court is the County Court of the district in which the company has its registered office.[9] However, not all County Courts exercise jurisdiction to wind up companies. If a creditor wishes to proceed in a County Court, he should first ascertain by means of a company search that the debtor company's paid up share capital does not exceed £120,000, and secondly identify the relevant County Court. The Appendix to the County Court Practice[10] contains a directory of County Courts and their jurisdictions, and a reference therein to bankruptcy jurisdiction includes jurisdiction to wind up companies. If the County Court for the district of the company's registered office does not have bankruptcy (i.e. winding-up) jurisdiction, the directory states the relevant County Court having that jurisdiction in which the petition should be presented. If the registered office of the company is within central London, only the High Court has jurisdiction to wind up the company.[11]

9.5 Choice of County Court or High Court

As explained in the preceding paragraphs, where the company has its registered office outside the London area and its paid up capital is not more than £120,000, a creditor may choose whether to petition for winding-up in the High Court in London, in a district registry of the High Court, or in the relevant County Court. It has been suggested that the Companies Court in London is particularly well equipped to deal with winding-up petitions and related applications; and that its familiarity with winding-up proceedings and its ability to deal with applications at short notice will often justify presenting a petition

6. Company insolvency proceedings are heard in the Chancery district registries of the High Court in Birmingham, Bristol, Cardiff, Leeds, Liverpool, Manchester, Newcastle upon Tyne and Preston: see RSC O. 1, r. 4(1) and IR 1986, r. 13.2(4)(b).

7. IA 1986, s. 117(2).

8. *Re North of England Iron Steamship Insurance Association* [1900] 1 Ch. 481; *Re Iron Founders (Bradford Branch) Social Club and Institute* [1923] WN 127.

9. IA 1986, s. 117(2).

10. See *County Court Practice 1997*, pp. 2117–2147.

11. *Re Southsea Garage Ltd* (1911) 55 SJ 314.

in the Companies Court in London rather than in the local district registry or County Court.[12]

9.6 Transfer of winding-up proceedings

Winding-up proceedings begun in the High Court can be transferred to the County Court,[13] and such a transfer is possible notwithstanding that the company's paid up share capital is greater than £120,000,[14] provided that the County Court in question has winding-up jurisdiction.[15] Winding-up proceedings begun in a County Court can be transferred to another County Court or to the High Court.[16] Winding-up proceedings can be transferred either before[17] or after a winding-up order has been made and whether or not the winding-up proceedings began before the Insolvency Rules 1986 came into force.[18] A transfer can be made by a court of its own motion,[19] on the application of the official receiver,[20] or on the application of any other person appearing to the court to have an interest in the proceedings.[21] An application for a transfer should be made by ordinary application, preferably supported by affidavit explaining why a transfer is sought.

9.7 Case stated

If a question arises in winding-up proceedings in a County Court which all the parties to the proceedings (or one party and the County Court Judge) wish to have determined by the High Court, the County Court has power to state the facts as a special case for the opinion of the High Court.[22] However, this power is seldom used.

9.8 Proceedings in the wrong court

If winding-up proceedings are inadvertently taken in the wrong court (for example, in a County Court when the company's paid up share capital exceeds £120,000 or in a County Court which is not the court for the district in which the company has its registered office), the proceedings are not a nullity[23]: the court can nevertheless retain the proceedings[24] and may make a winding-up order, although the court may at the same time transfer the further conduct of the winding-up to the proper court.[25] However, if the proceedings have deliberately been taken in the wrong court (for example, in order to suit the petitioner's convenience or to inconvenience the company), the proceedings may be dismissed.[26]

12. See the comments of Harman J. in *Re Pleatfine Ltd* [1983] BCLC 102.
13. IR 1986, r. 7.11(1).
14. *Re Vernon Heaton Co. Ltd* [1936] Ch. 289.
15. IR 1986, r. 7.11(3).
16. IR 1986, r. 7.11(2).
17. *Re Laxon & Co.* [1892] 3 Ch. 31.
18. IR 1986, r. 7.11(6).
19. IR 1986, r. 7.11(5)(a).
20. IR 1986, r. 7.11(5)(b).
21. IR 1986, r. 7.11(5)(c).
22. IA 1986, s. 119(1).
23. IA 1986, s. 118(1).
24. IA 1986, s. 118(2).
25. *Re Milford Haven Shipping Co.* [1895] WN 16.
26. *Re Brightmore, ex parte May* (1884) 14 QBD 37.

9.9 Concurrent High Court and County Court petitions

If concurrent petitions are presented in the High Court and in the County Court against the same company and neither petition is opposed by the company, the County Court petition should be transferred to the High Court: the High Court is then able to resolve the difficulty either by making a winding-up order on both petitions[27] or by making an order on the High Court petition, staying the County Court petition, and directing that the costs of the petitioner in the County Court be paid out of the assets of the company in the High Court winding-up.[28] A High Court judge has power to order the transfer to the High Court of winding-up proceedings pending in a County Court.[29]

9.10 Avoiding concurrent petitions

The High Court in London, each Chancery district registry of the High Court and each County Court having insolvency jurisdiction, maintains a list of the winding-up petitions presented in that court. In addition, a central computerised database has been established at the Companies Court in London which contains details of all companies against which a petition is pending or a winding-up order has been made in all courts which have winding-up jurisdiction (i.e. the High Court in London, Chancery district registries and the County Court). Details of companies on the database can be obtained by telephone, free of charge.[30] This facility should prevent more than one petition being presented in respect of a single company, and should be checked before a petition is presented. Multiple searches of the register to obtain information to be disseminated for commercial gain are not permitted under the Insolvency Rules as presently drafted.[31]

9.11 Bodies which may be wound up by the court

The following entities may be wound up by the court under the Insolvency Act 1986:

(1) a company formed and registered under part I (sections 1 to 42 inclusive) of the Companies Act 1985: this is the type of company most frequently encountered and to which this Chapter principally relates;

(2) a company registered (but not formed) under part XXII (ss. 675–690B inclusive) of the Companies Act 1985;

(3) an "existing company" within the meaning of s. 735(1)(b) of the Companies Act 1985—i.e. a company formed and registered under the former Companies

27. *Re Filby Bros (Provender) Ltd* [1958] 1 WLR 683.
28. *Re Audio Systems Ltd* [1965] 1 WLR 1096.
29. IR 1986, r. 7.11(4).
30. On 0171 936 7328 (correct at the time of writing).
31. *Ex parte Creditnet Ltd & Others* [1996] 1 WLR 1291. On appeal, the Court of Appeal concluded that it did not have jurisdiction to review the first instance decision owing to IR 1986, r. 7.28(3), but expressed concern about the implications of the first instance decision and indicated that the issue should be reviewed by the Insolvency Rules Committee: see *Re Austintel Ltd* [1997] 1 WLR 616. See also *Re an Application pursuant to r. 7.28 of the Insolvency Rules 1986* [1994] BCC 369.

Acts[32] (but not companies registered under the Joint Stock Companies Acts[33] or Ireland's companies legislation as applicable prior to 1922)[34];

(4) a company registered (but not formed) under the Joint Stock Companies Acts or the former Companies Acts: Companies Act 1985, s. 676;

(5) an unlimited company which has re-registered as limited under the Companies Acts 1879, 1908, 1929, 1948 or 1967: Companies Act 1985, s. 677;

(6) an "unregistered company" within the meaning of s. 220(1) of the Insolvency Act 1986—i.e. any association and any company except a registered company.[35] Entities which may be wound up as unregistered companies include:
   (a) a company formed outside Great Britain which has assets and liabilities in Great Britain, or which has carried on business in Great Britain, or which has some other sufficient connection with the jurisdiction[36];
   (b) a company incorporated by a special or private Act of Parliament[37];
   (c) a company incorporated by Royal Charter which carries on some business[38];
   (d) a building society[39];
   (e) a friendly society,[40] including one which has not been registered under the Friendly Societies Acts[41] which carries on some business;
   (f) an insurance or life assurance company carrying on insurance business in the United Kingdom but which is not incorporated or registered in the United Kingdom[42];
   (g) a partnership authorised under the Financial Services Act 1986[43] or the Banking Act 1987[44];
   (h) a partnership[45];

32. Namely, the Joint Stock Companies Acts, CA 1862, the Companies (Consolidation Act) 1908, CA 1929, and CAs 1948 to 1983: CA 1985, s. 735(1)(c).

33. Namely, the Joint Stock Companies Act 1856, the Joint Stock Companies Acts 1856, 1857, the Joint Stock Banking Companies Act 1857, and the Act to enable Joint Stock Banking Companies to be formed on the principle of limited liability, or any one or more of those Acts: CA 1985, s. 735(3).

34. CA 1985, s. 735(1)(b).

35. IA 1986, s. 220(1)(b).

36. *Re a Company (No. 00359 of 1987)* [1988] 1 Ch. 210. A company registered in Northern Ireland may be wound up as an unregistered company if it has a principal place of business in England and Wales: *Re a Company (No. 007946 of 1993)* [1994] Ch. 198.

37. *Re South London Fish Market* (1888) 39 Ch.D. 324; *Re Barton-upon-Humber Water Co.* (1889) 42 Ch.D. 585 (where the company was registered under the Companies Acts but was subsequently granted powers for the public benefit by special Act of Parliament).

38. *Re Oriental Bank Corp.* (1884) 54 LJ Ch. 481; *Re Bank of South Australia* [1895] 1 Ch. 578 (where the bank was incorporated by Royal Charter and had registered itself as a limited company by the date of presentation of the petition for winding-up).

39. Building Societies Act 1986, ss. 37 and 89; *Re Queen's Building Society* (1871) LR 6 Ch. 815.

40. Friendly Societies Act 1974, s. 87(2) (as amended); Friendly Societies Act 1992, s. 52.

41. *Re Victoria Society, Knottingley* (1913) 1 Ch. 167; *Re Sick and Funeral Society of St John's Sunday School, Golcar* [1973] Ch. 51.

42. Insurance Companies Act 1982, ss. 53–55 (as amended); *Re Great Britain Mutual* (1880) 16 Ch.D. 246 at 251.

43. Financial Services Act 1986, s. 72(4).

44. Banking Act 1987, s. 92(2).

45. See IA 1986, s. 420 and the Insolvent Partnerships Order 1994 (S.I. 1994 No. 2421) (as amended by the Insolvent Partnerships (Amendment) Order 1996 (S.I. 1996 No. 1308)).

(7) an industrial and provident society.[46]

9.12 Entities which cannot be wound up by the court

The following entities cannot be wound up by the court:

(1) companies which have been struck off the register of companies and dissolved.[47] Such companies must first be restored to the register and then wound up by the court. In practice, a creditor can combine an application for restoration of the company to the register with an application to wind up in a single petition[48];

(2) a company incorporated outside Great Britain which has no (or no sufficient) connection with Great Britain, or where there is no real possibility that the winding-up in Great Britain of the foreign company would benefit the company's creditors[49];

(3) a society or association which is not authorised, permitted or recognised by law—for example, a partnership which when formed has more members than permitted by statute[50];

(4) municipal or ecclesiastical corporations, literary or scientific institutions[51] or societies, which have been incorporated by Royal Charter, or ordinary clubs,[52] which do not carry on any business: although the High Court has power under its general equitable jurisdiction to order the winding-up of an incorporated association,[53] it does not have jurisdiction to wind up such an association as an unregistered company under the Companies Act 1985, s. 220 where there is no element of trading[54];

(5) an international organisation established by independent sovereign states including the United Kingdom.[55]

46. Industrial and Provident Societies Act 1965, s. 55. In *Re Norse Self Build Association Ltd* [1985] BCLC 219 Harman J. held that by virtue of s. 55 of the Industrial Provident Societies Act 1965, an industrial and provident society could be wound up as a company registered under the CA 1948 and did not have to be wound up as an "unregistered company", which was defined by CA 1948, s. 398 to exclude companies with fewer than eight members. The present definition of an "unregistered company" in IA 1986, s. 220(1) does not contain such a restriction and the difficulty would not now arise.

47. I.e., under CA 1985, s. 653(3).

48. I.e., a petition seeking a so-called "double-barrelled order", discussed later in this Chapter.

49. See *Re a Company (No. 00359 of 1987)* [1988] 1 Ch. 210.

50. CA 1985, s. 716(1); *Re Padstow Total Loss and Collision Assurance Association* (1882) 20 Ch.D. 137 at 143, 148; *Re Ilfracombe Permanent Mutual Benefit Building Society* [1901] 1 Ch. 102.

51. *Re Bristol Athenaeum* (1889) 43 Ch.D. 236; *Re Russell Institution* [1818] 2 Ch. 72 at 79. A literary or scientific institution may be dissolved under the Literary and Scientific Institutions Act 1854, s. 29.

52. *Re St James' Club* (1852) 2 De GM&G 383.

53. *Re Lead Company's Workman's Fund Society* [1904] 2 Ch. 196.

54. *Re Bristol Athenaeum* and *Re Russell Institution, supra*. Note, however, that in those cases the court found that an element of trading was required to wind up the unincorporated association as an unregistered company under CA 1862, s. 199 owing to the reference in s. 199 to the association's "principal place of *business*". It appears that such a restriction does not apply to winding-up as an unregistered company under IA 1986, s. 220 which contains no similar provision.

55. *Re International Tin Council* [1989] 1 Ch. 309. Clearly, such entities are rarely encountered in practice.

9.13 Grounds for a compulsory winding-up

A company may be wound up by order of the court on one or more of seven grounds set out in the Insolvency Act 1986, s. 122(1), namely:

"(a) the company has by special resolution resolved that the company be wound up by the court,
(b) being a public company which was registered as such on its original incorporation, the company has not been issued with a certificate under section 117 of the Companies Act 1985 (public company share capital requirements) and more than one year has expired since it was so registered,
(c) it is an old public company, within the meaning of the Consequential Provisions Act,
(d) the company does not commence its business within a year from its incorporation or suspends its business for a whole year,
(e) except in the case of a private company limited by shares or guarantee, the number of members is reduced below 2,
(f) the company is unable to pay its debts,
(g) the court is of the opinion that it is just and equitable that the company should be wound up."

In addition, a company may be compulsorily wound up on the petition of the Secretary of State for Trade and Industry where it appears to the Secretary of State, as a result of information received from enquiries made, that it is expedient in the public interest to wind up the company.[56]

In the following paragraphs each of the grounds set out in s. 122(2) of the Insolvency Act 1986 is considered in turn. It should be borne in mind that, where one of the grounds is established, the introductory words of s. 122(1)[57] give the court a discretion whether or not to make a winding-up order.[58]

9.14 Special resolution for winding-up by the court

A compulsory winding-up following a special resolution is comparatively rare in practice, because it will usually be quicker and cheaper for the company to proceed by way of a voluntary winding-up. If a petition is presented following a special resolution, it should be expressed to be the petition of the company in question. The petition need not be served[59] and accordingly no affidavit of service is required.

9.15 Failure to obtain a certificate under the Companies Act 1985, s. 17

This ground relates only to public limited companies. It enables a public limited company to be compulsorily wound up if it fails, within one year of its registration as a public limited company, to obtain a certificate from the registrar of companies confirming that the company's allotted share capital is not less than the authorised minimum.[60] A petition on this ground may be presented by the Secretary of State for Trade and Industry,[61] but is rarely encountered in practice.

56. IA 1986, s. 124A, discussed later in this Chapter.
57. I.e., "a company *may* be wound up if . . . " (emphasis added).
58. See *Re Walter L Jacob & Co. Ltd* (1989) 5 BCC 244 at 249G.
59. IR 1986, r. 4.8(1).
60. Presently £50,000, but that sum can be increased by statutory instrument: CA 1985, s. 118(1).
61. IA 1986, s. 124(4)(a).

9.16 Old public company

Again, this ground relates only to public companies. It provides for the compulsory winding-up of a public company which has failed to comply with the requirements of re-registration following the re-definition of "public company" in the Companies Act 1980. An "old public company" is defined as a company incorporated before 22 December 1980 which was not on incorporation a private company (as defined in the Companies Act 1948, s. 28), but which has not re-registered as a public company or become a private company[62]; this ground therefore excludes all companies incorporated after 22 December 1980, all private companies and companies which have re-registered as public or private companies. A petition on this ground may be presented by the Secretary of State for Trade and Industry,[63] but the ground is rarely encountered in practice.

9.17 Failure to commence, or suspension of, business for one year

Where a company fails to commence business within one year of its incorporation or suspends its business for one year, a creditor or contributory may petition for the compulsory winding-up of the company. This ground (like the other grounds in s. 122(1)) gives the court an unfettered discretion: even if a petitioner can prove the fact that the company failed to commence business within a year of incorporation or suspended its business for a whole year, the court can nevertheless refuse to make an order.[64] The court may refuse to make a winding-up order where the evidence establishes that the business will be commenced or resumed within the foreseeable future, and/or where there are good reasons for the delay, and/or most members oppose a winding-up of the company.[65] However, in exercising its discretion, the court will consider the *bona fides* of the members[66] and directors[67]: the fact the majority members are opposed to a winding-up of the company does not preclude the court from making an order if the court finds that the majority is acting unreasonably.[68]

9.17.1 Winding-up within a year of incorporation

The court will make a winding-up order on this ground within a year of incorporation where the substratum of the company has disappeared or where it is impossible for the company to pursue the objects for which it was formed, notwithstanding that the company is solvent.[69] Examples of such cases are where a company fails to locate the mine which

62. Set out in the Companies Consolidation (Consequential Provisions) Act 1985, s. 1.
63. IA 1986, s. 124(4)(a).
64. *Re Metropolitan Railway Warehousing Co. (Ltd)* (1867) 36 LJ Ch. 827.
65. *Ibid.*
66. *Ibid.* at p. 830 per Cairns L.J.
67. *Re Capital Fire Insurance Association* (1882) 21 Ch.D. 209 at 222; *Re Heatons Steel Co.* [1870] WN 85.
68. *Re Tumacacori Mining Co.* (1874) LR 17 Eq 534 (where the court questioned the *bona fides* of the shareholder directors (at p. 539), and where the company had no creditors and no monetary assets, with the consequence that winding-up was the only way to get in the company's property).
69. *Re Suburban Hotel Co.* (1867) 2 Ch. App. 737.

it was formed to work,[70] fails to acquire the patent which it was formed to develop[71] or is not granted the contract which it was formed to carry out.[72]

9.17.2 Meaning of "suspension of business"

The following do not amount to a suspension of business to found a petition on this ground: abandoning part of a business or one of several objects unless that part is in reality "substantially the whole" of the business or its abandonment alters "the fundamental principle of the company"[73]; ceasing to pursue its objects (i.e. ceasing trading) in order to acquire shares in a company or companies which actively pursue the holding company's objects[74]; suspending business where the evidence does not establish an intention to abandon the business or an inability to continue it[75]; or the sale by a company of its principal business, if the principal objects in its memorandum of association give the company power to recommence that business or carry on some other principal business.[76]

9.18 Number of members reduced below two

Prior to the Companies Act 1980,[77] public companies required a minimum of seven members and a private company a minimum of two. Between 1980 and 1992 all companies required a statutory minimum of two members[78]: failure to maintain two members rendered a sole member potentially personally liable for the company's debts[79] and was a ground for the compulsory winding-up of the company.[80] However, since 15 July 1992, a private company limited by shares or by guarantee is permitted to have only one member,[81] and therefore, only a public company or an unlimited company whose members are reduced below two may be wound up on this ground.

9.18.1 Meaning of "member"

A "member" in this context includes not only a subscriber to the company's memorandum and a person who agrees to become a member and is entered on the company's register of members,[82] but also someone to whom shares in the company have been transferred or transmitted by operation of law.[83] Thus, "member" in this context includes

70. *Re Haven Gold Mining Co.* (1882) 20 Ch.D. 151.
71. *Re German Date Coffee Co.* (1882) 20 Ch.D. 169.
72. *Re Blériot Manufacturing Aircraft Co.* (1916) 32 TLR 253.
73. *Re Norwegian Titanic Iron Co. Ltd.* 35 Beav. 223; 55 ER 881; *Re Patent Bread Machinery Co.* (1866) 14 LT 582; *Re Kronand Metal Co.* [1899] WN 14.
74. *Re Eastern Telegraph Co.* [1947] 2 All ER 104.
75. *Re Tomlin Patent Horse Shoe Co.* (1887) 55 LT 314.
76. *Re Kitson & Co.* [1946] 1 All ER 435.
77. See CA 1980, s. 2(1).
78. CA 1985, ss. 1(1) and 24.
79. CA 1985, s. 24.
80. IA 1986, s. 122(1)(e).
81. See the Companies (Single Member Private Ltd Companies) Regulations 1992 (S.I. 1992 No. 1699), reg. 2 and Schedule, para. 8, made pursuant to the European Communities Act 1972, sch. 2, para. 2(2).
82. I.e., the definition of "member" in CA 1985, s. 22.
83. IA 1986, s. 250.

the personal representatives of a deceased member,[84] and a two-member public company or unlimited company cannot be wound up on this ground if one member should die.[85] The decision in *Re Bowling & Welly's Contract*[86] should no longer be regarded as good law in light of the amendment to the Insolvency Act 1986, s. 122(1)(e).

9.19 The company is unable to pay its debts

This is the ground for winding-up most commonly relied upon in practice and is the basis for the vast majority of creditors' petitions (although creditors' petitions generally aver both that "the company is insolvent and unable to pay its debts"[87] and that "it is just and equitable for the company to be wound up"[88]).

9.19.1 Deemed inability to pay debts

A company is deemed to be unable to pay its debts in any one or more of the five cases listed in s. 123(1) of the Insolvency Act 1986, namely:

> "(a) if a creditor (by assignment or otherwise) to whom the company is indebted in a sum exceeding £750 then due has served on the company, by leaving it at the company's registered office, a written demand (in the prescribed form) requiring the company to pay the sum so due and the company has for 3 weeks thereafter neglected to pay the sum or to secure or compound for it to the reasonable satisfaction of the creditor, or
> (b) if, in England and Wales, execution or other process issued on a judgment, decree or order of any court in favour of a creditor of the company is returned unsatisfied in whole or in part, or
> (c) if, in Scotland, the induciae of a charge for payment on an extract decree, or an extract registered bond, or an extract registered protest, have expired without payment being made, or
> (d) if, in Northern Ireland, a certificate of unenforceability has been granted in respect of a judgment against the company, or
> (e) if it is proved to the satisfaction of the court that the company is unable to pay its debts as they fall due."

Only cases (a), (b) and (e) are considered in more detail below.

9.19.2 "Balance sheet" insolvency

In addition to deemed insolvency on the above grounds, under s. 123(2) of the Insolvency Act 1986 a company is also deemed to be unable to pay its debts if it is proved to the satisfaction of the court that the value of the company's assets is less than the amount of

84. See *Roberts* v. *Letter T. Estates Ltd* [1961] AC 795.

85. Unless, of course, the personal representatives transfer the deceased's shares to the sole surviving member.

86. [1895] 1 Ch. 663, where the Court of Appeal held that the statutory requirement of seven members in CA 1862, s. 199 was not satisfied if there were four living and three deceased members. However, CA 1862 did not contain a provision analogous to IA 1986, s. 250.

87. IA 1986, s. 122(1)(f).

88. IA 1986, s. 122(1)(g).

its liabilities, taking into account its contingent and prospective liabilities (i.e. the company has negative net worth on a balance sheet test).

9.19.3 Case (a): Unsatisfied statutory demand

A company is deemed to be unable to pay its debts under this head if a creditor (by assignment[89] or otherwise) who claims a debt in excess of £750 which is then due and not disputed serves on the company a written demand for payment in the prescribed form[90] which is not satisfied by the company within three weeks thereafter. Such a default gives not only that creditor, but also any other creditor or contributory, the right to petition, unless the debt is disputed.[91] The debt must be presently payable and absolutely due[92]—the statutory demand cannot be based on a contingent or prospective debt, although a contingent or prospective debt could found a petition based upon a company's deemed inability to pay its debts under ss. 123(1)(e) or 123(2) of the Insolvency Act 1986. In calculating the three-week period, the day on which the statutory demand is served on the company is disregarded,[93] as is any fraction of a day.[94] Accordingly, a petition based on a statutory demand should not be presented until the 21st full day after service of the demand.

9.19.4 "Neglected to pay"

The statutory demand must be for a liquidated sum in excess of £750—it cannot, for example, be for a specified sum less the amount of an unliquidated claim made by the company against the creditor.[95] If the debt is disputed by the company, either in whole or in part, the company has not "neglected to pay" by failing to satisfy the demand, and the company can resist a petition based upon the demand.[96] However, if only part of the debt is disputed and more than £750 is undisputed, a creditor can obtain a winding-up order based upon the demand[97]: a company may then only resist an order based upon s. 123(1)(a) of the Insolvency Act 1986 if it can show that it did not "neglect to pay" but failed to pay for some other reason, such as non-receipt of the demand.

9.19.5 Form of the statutory demand

The statutory demand must be in the "prescribed form"[98]; an informal demand is not sufficient for the purposes of s. 123(1)(a). The requirements of the "prescribed form" are

89. The assignee of part of a debt cannot serve a demand under IA 1986, s. 123(1)(a) (because the assignment is not absolute and passes only an equitable, not a legal title, to the debt): *Re Steel Wing Co. Ltd* [1921] 1 Ch. 349 at 356. Such an assignee is, however, a creditor within the meaning of IA 1986, s. 124(1) and may petition on any other ground (*ibid.* at 355).

90. As to the form and content of the statutory demand, see para. 9.19.5, *infra*.

91. *Re Anglesea Island Coal and Coke Co. Ltd ex parte Owen* (1861) 4 LT 684.

92. *Re European Life Assurance Society* (1869) LR 9 Eq 122 at 127; *The New Travellers' Chambers Ltd* v. *Messrs Cheese & Green* (1894) 70 LT 271 at 272.

93. *Re Lympne Investments Ltd* [1972] 1 WLR 523.

94. *Trow* v. *Ind Coope (West Midlands) Ltd* [1967] 2 QB 899.

95. *Re Humberstone Jersey Ltd* (1977) Law Soc. Gaz. 711.

96. *Stonegate Securities Ltd* v. *Gregory* [1980] Ch. 576.

97. *Cardiff Coal* v. *Norton* (1867) 2 Ch. 405.

98. IA 1986, s 123(1)(a).

set out in rr. 4.4 to 4.6 inclusive of the Insolvency Rules 1986. The following detail must be set out in the demand:

(a) the date of the demand[99];
(b) the signature of the creditor personally or of a person who states that he is authorised to make the demand on the creditor's behalf[100];
(c) the amount of the debt[101];
(d) the consideration for the debt (or if there is no consideration, the way in which it arose)[102];
(e) if the demand includes any charge for interest not previously notified to the company or any other periodic charge due at the date of the demand, the amount or rate of the charge must be separately identified and the grounds on which the charge is claimed must be stated[103];
(f) an explanation of (i) the purpose of the demand and the fact that non-compliance with the demand may lead to proceedings for winding-up; (ii) the time within which the demand must be complied with to avoid winding up proceedings; and (iii) how the company may comply with the demand[104];
(g) information as to how an officer or representative of the company can contact the creditor or its representative with a view to securing or compounding for the debt to the creditor's satisfaction—the information must include the name, address and telephone number (if any) of the person whom the company should contact.[105]

The statutory demand should follow Form 4.1, with such variations, if any, as the case may require.[106]

9.19.6 Service of a statutory demand

There are conflicting authorities whether the statutory demand must, like a winding-up petition, be left at the company's registered office (personally by the intended petitioner or his agent for that purpose, or whether it may be validly served by post) in a way in which receipt at the company's registered office can be proved. The better view is that it is sufficient that the creditor can prove that the demand was received at the company's registered office (as opposed to merely having been put in the post): once it is accepted that the demand was received at the registered office (e.g. by the use of "recorded delivery" post), service is valid even though it was not left there personally by the creditor or his agent appointed for that purpose.[107] To avoid any dispute as to the validity of the service of the statutory demand, personal service of the demand at the registered office of

99. IR 1986, r. 4.4(3).
100. *Ibid.*
101. IR 1986, r. 4.5(1).
102. *Ibid.*
103. IR 1986, r. 4.5(2).
104. IR 1986, r. 4.6(1).
105. IR 1986, r. 4.6(2).
106. This form is reproduced in Appendix 4, *infra*. See IR 1986, r. 12.7 and sch. 4, part 4 (as amended).
107. *Re a Company (No. 008790 of 1990)* [1992] BCC 11 at 13C–E (where Morritt J. refused to follow the earlier first instance decision in *Re a Company* [1985] BCLC 37, in which Nourse J. held that the service of the demand by telex was invalid).

the company is advisable; recorded delivery is acceptable but ordinary first class post should not be used.

9.19.7 Case (b): Unsatisfied execution on a judgment

A company is deemed to be unable to pay its debts if a judgment creditor causes a writ of execution (e.g. a writ of *fieri facias*) to be issued against the company which does not realise sufficient sums to discharge the petition debt.

9.19.8 Judgment appealed

The mere fact that a judgment is under appeal does not preclude the judgment creditor from petitioning for a winding-up order under s. 123(1)(b) or (c), nor does it require the court to refuse to make a winding-up order or to stay the petition. Provided that a stay of execution has not been obtained by the judgment debtor, the judgment creditor may present a winding-up petition: the court then has a discretion whether to make a winding-up order despite the appeal, or to stay the petition or to dismiss it.[108] In exercising its discretion, the court will consider the nature of the judgment (for example, whether it was a judgment in default or based on the merits of the case) and whether it appears on the evidence filed in the winding-up proceedings that the appeal is *bona fide* and has a prospect of success. The court may stay the petition pending appeal on condition that the company gives security for the amount of the judgment debt and costs. The court may make a winding up order notwithstanding that the judgment is under appeal *and* the company has a counterclaim against the judgment creditor which exceeds the judgment debt.[109]

9.19.9 Case (e): Inability to pay debts as they fall due proved to the satisfaction of the court

A creditor may base his petition on the company's inability to pay its debts under s. 122(1)(e) of the Insolvency Act 1986 even though he cannot bring the case within one of the grounds in subs. 123(1)(a)–(d) inclusive, if he can establish the company's inability to pay its debts in some other way (e.g. by showing that the company is in administrative receivership and the receivers have confirmed that there are insufficient funds to pay unsecured creditors). In particular, the failure to pay an undisputed debt which is presently due and for which demand has been made (e.g. by letter) is evidence of the company's inability to pay its debts within s. 123(1)(e).[110] The failure to pay such a debt can be the basis of a petition under s. 122(1)(e), notwithstanding that the demand for payment made by the creditor does not satisfy the requirements of a statutory demand discussed above. The demand should be made in writing, so as to be capable of being exhibited in evidence if the making of the demand is disputed by the company.

The "informal" demand for payment under s. 123(1)(e) should specify a date by which payment should be made, but this need not be three weeks as in the case of a statutory

108. *Re Amalgamated Properties of Rhodesia (1913) Ltd* [1917] 2 Ch. 115.
109. *Re Douglas (Griggs) Engineering Ltd* [1963] Ch. 19 at 23.
110. *Taylors Industrial Flooring Ltd* v. *M&H Plant Hire (Manchester) Ltd* [1990] BCLC 217.

demand. Similarly, the demand can be made by fax or post, and personal service is not necessary: however, to avoid any dispute about its receipt, the use of recorded delivery may be advisable. The fact that a creditor who relies on a company's failure to satisfy an informal demand as evidence of its inability to pay its debts under s. 123(1)(e) need not wait three weeks before petitioning, may render the use of a statutory demand unattractive in many cases. One advantage of the use of a statutory demand is that the formal wording (and in particular the express reference to the possibility of winding-up proceedings in the event of non-compliance) may encourage payment by the company; a creditor relying on an informal written demand ought to state expressly in the demand that non-compliance may result in winding-up proceedings being brought against the company.

9.19.10 Currency of the debt

For the purpose of proving a debt, a debt or part of a debt incurred in a currency other than sterling must be converted into sterling at the official exchange rate prevailing at the date when the company went into liquidation.[111] In contrast, a winding-up petition can be based on a foreign currency debt, although the better practice is to state in the petition the foreign currency amount of the debt, together with its sterling equivalent at the official exchange rate[112] prevailing at the date of presentation of the petition.

9.19.11 Amount of the debt

The requirement that the debt should exceed £750 is expressed to apply only to a petition based on non-compliance with a statutory demand (i.e. subs. 123(1)(a) of the Insolvency Act 1986) and not to petitions based on subs. 123(1)(b)–(e). However, the court would be likely to refuse to make a winding-up order where the debt claimed was *de minimis*.

9.19.12 Disputed debt

If the debt claimed by the alleged creditor is disputed by the company in good faith on substantial grounds, as a rule of practice the claimant will not usually be regarded as a creditor within the meaning of s. 124(1) of the Insolvency Act 1986 and he will not usually have *locus standi* to serve a statutory demand or to petition for the winding-up of the company until he has established his debt by agreement or judgment.[113] If a statutory demand is served in respect of a debt which is disputed in good faith on substantial grounds, the company will usually be entitled to seek an injunction restraining the claimant from presenting a winding-up petition.

9.20 Just and equitable that the company be wound up

This ground for winding-up is discussed in more detail in Chapter 7 in the context of petitions presented by contributories. In practice, creditors' petitions usually state both

111. See IR 1986, r. 4.91(1).
112. Defined in IR 1986, r. 4.91(2).
113. See *Alipour* v. *Ary* [1997] 1 WLR 534 at 541F–G and 546A; *Re a Company (No. 00212 of 1995)*, *Times*, 7 April 1995; *Mann* v. *Goldstein* [1968] 1 WLR 1091 at 1098H–1099B; *Re Lympne Investments Ltd* [1972] 1 WLR 523 at 527G; *Stonegate Securities Ltd* v. *Gregory* [1980] Ch. 576 at 579F–580C. Disputed debts are discussed in more detail later in this Chapter.

that the company is insolvent and unable to pay its debts as they fall due, and that it is just and equitable that the company be wound up.

WHO MAY PETITION?

9.21 S. 124(1) of the Insolvency Act 1986

Section 124(1) provides that a winding-up petition may be presented in respect of a company:

(a) by the company itself;
(b) by its directors;
(c) by one or more of the company's creditors (including actual, contingent or prospective creditors);
(d) by one or more of the company's contributories;
(e) by the clerk of a Magistrate's Court exercising the power under s. 87A of the Magistrates' Court Act 1980 to enforce fines made against a company;
(f) by any combination of the above.

In addition, a number of statutes relating to particular types of companies confer standing to petition on the relevant governing or regulatory authority, such as the Secretary of State for Trade and Industry.[114] The official receiver may also petition where a company is in voluntary liquidation.[115]

9.22 Restrictions on the standing to petition

The following restrictions apply to the standing to petition conferred by s. 124(1).

9.22.1 Petition by directors

Where a formal board resolution for winding-up has not been passed, the petition must be unanimous (i.e. presented by *all* the directors).[116] The petition should be in the name of the directors and should not be expressed to be the petition of the company. Where a formal board resolution has been validly passed at a properly convened board meeting, any director may present a petition on behalf of all the directors.[117]

9.22.2 Petition by a creditor

This is the category of petitioner most frequently encountered in practice.

(a) The following persons are regarded as "creditors" for the purposes of s. 124(1) and may petition: contingent or prospective creditors[118]; secured creditors[119]; an

114. See, for example, IA 1986, ss. 124(4) and 124A; Financial Services Act 1986, s. 72(1); Insurance Companies Act 1982, ss. 53 and 54; see also Charities Act 1960, s. 30(1) (petition by Attorney General); Building Societies Act 1986, s. 37 (petition by Building Societies Commission); Banking Act 1987, s. 92 (petition by Bank of England).
115. IA 1986, s. 124(5).
116. *Re Instrumentation Electrical Services Ltd* (1988) 4 BCC 301 at 303.
117. *Re Equiticorp International plc* (1989) 5 BCC 599 at 600G–H.
118. IA 1986, s. 124(1).
119. *Moor* v. *Anglo Italian Bank* (1879) 10 Ch.D. 681.

assignee[120] (in law or equity[121]) of all or part of a debt originally due from the company to the assignor; a local authority in respect of unpaid rates[122]; and a surety who has paid the principal debtor's debt, giving rise to a claim by way of subrogation.[123]

(b) The following are not "creditors" within the meaning of s. 124(1) and may not petition: a person whose debt was statute-barred at the date of presentation of the petition (although a person may validly petition if the debt is not time-barred at the date of presentation and only becomes time-barred by the date of the hearing)[124]; a judgment creditor who has a garnishee order against the company to secure payment to the judgment creditor of a debt owed by the company to the judgment debtor; and a plaintiff who claims unliquidated damages and has not obtained judgment.[125]

9.23 Petition by insolvency practitioners

A petition may also be presented by the supervisor of a company's voluntary arrangement,[126] or by the company's administrators,[127] administrative receivers[128] or voluntary liquidators.[129] In the latter three cases, the petition should be expressed to be the petition of the company acting by its administrators,[130] administrative receivers,[131] or voluntary liquidators.

PROCEDURE ON A PETITION FOR WINDING-UP

9.24 Form of petition

The petition must follow Form 4.2 with such variations, if any, as the case may require.[132] Where a creditor wishes to wind up more than one company, he should present a separate petition in respect of each company: in the case of related companies, directions can then be given for the petitions to be heard concurrently or consecutively, effectively consolidating the petitions.[133] The petition should contain the following information:

120. See *Re Paris Skating Rink Co.* (1877) 5 Ch.D. 959 at 962–963 (per Bramwell L.J.).

121. *Re Montgomery Moore Ship Collision Doors Syndicate* [1903] WN 121; (1903) 72 LJ Ch. 624.

122. *Re North Bucks Furniture Depositories* [1939] Ch. 690.

123. See *Re National Permanent Benefit Building Society* (1869) 5 Ch. App. 309 at 313. Even where the debt has not been paid, the surety would be a contingent creditor within IA 1986, s. 124(1); and see IR 1986, rr. 12.3(1) and 13.12(3).

124. *Re Karnos Property Co. Ltd* (1989) 5 BCC 14 at 17G; *Master Terms (Pty) Ltd* (1967) 116 CLR 177.

125. *Re Combined Weighing Machine Co.* (1889) 43 Ch.D. 99 at 104 per Cotton LJ; *Chatterton* v. *Watney* (1881) 17 Ch.D. 259 at 262; cf. *Re European Banking Co., ex parte Bayliss* (1866) 2 Eq. 521 at 522–523.

126. IA 1986, s. 7(4)(b).

127. IA 1986, s. 14(1)(b) and sch. 1, para. 21.

128. IA 1986, s. 42(1) and sch. 1, para. 21.

129. IA 1986, s. 165(3) and sch. 4, part II, para. 4: it is, however, difficult to discern the purpose of such a petition.

130. IR 1986, r. 4.7(7).

131. See *Re Television Parlour plc* (1980) 4 BCC 95 at 98 (l/h col).

132. This form is reproduced in Appendix 4. See IR 1986, r. 12.7 and sch. 4, part 4 (as amended).

133. *Re a Company* [1984] BCLC 307; contrast *Re William Pickles plc* [1996] 1 BCLC 681 (the issue of a single originating application in respect of several companies).

(a) the name and address of the petitioner;
(b) in para. 1, the name of the company and details of its incorporation;
(c) in para. 2, the registered office address of the company;
(d) in para. 3, details of the capital of the company, including the total nominal capital of the company, the number of shares into which the nominal capital is divided and the amount of capital paid up or credited as paid up;
(e) in para. 4, the principal objects of the company as appearing from its memorandum of association;
(f) in para. 5, full particulars of the debt said to be due from the company to the petitioner—including, where applicable, the date of any judgment for the petition debt, or the date of any contract or order giving rise to the petition debt and the contract or order number;
(g) para. 5, should also expressly aver that "the company is insolvent and unable to pay its debts"; and
(h) para. 6, should aver that "in the circumstances it is just and equitable that the company should be wound up".

Where the petition is based on a prospective debt which is not presently due, the petitioner cannot rely on the mere fact of non-payment of the debt to justify the assertion of insolvency: in such a case, the petition ought to set out the facts relied upon by the petitioner in asserting that the company is presently insolvent.[134]

9.25 Prayer

The petition should conclude with a Prayer:

1. that the company, referred to by name, may be wound up by the court under the provisions of the Insolvency Act 1986; or
2. that such other order may be made as the court thinks fit.

It is important to ensure that para. 1 of the Prayer to the petition correctly states the name of the company to be wound up, since the name stated in the order for winding-up (generally referred to as the "usual compulsory order") will be taken from para. 1 of the Prayer. There should appear at the end of the petition an endorsement giving details of the date, time and venue of the hearing of the petition, which will be completed by the appropriate court office when the petition is presented.

9.26 Misstatements in the petition

If it transpires that there are mistakes in the petition, whether by misstatement or omission, the petition will have to be amended with the leave of the court, unless the court can be persuaded that the mistake is trivial and that the defect in the petition ought to be waived. Examples of trivial misstatements which the court should be prepared to waive are: minor discrepancies in the statement of the petitioner's registered office; minor misstatements in the details of the company's capital; and minor misstatements in the description of the

134. *Securum Finance Ltd* v. *Camswell Ltd* [1994] BCC 434 at 436B–G.

company's principal objects. More fundamental mistakes which will require amendment include: errors in the name of the company to be wound up, particularly in the Prayer[135]; material errors in the description of the registered office of the company to be wound up; and errors in the description of the petition debt and how that debt arose.

9.27 Amendment of the petition

If a defect, which is other than trivial, is noticed in the petition, the petitioner should apply to the court for leave to amend the petition.[136] The application may either be made *ex parte* to the registrar in chambers on a date prior to the hearing of the petition, or may be made in open court on the hearing of the petition. If the required amendment is not one which would require the petition to be re-served on the company (for example, an amendment to the name of the company stated in the Prayer to the petition), the application for leave to amend can be left to the hearing of the petition; the registrar will then be able to give leave to amend, and on the petitioner's undertaking to effect the amendment forthwith, the registrar may make the winding-up order without further delay. However, if the amendment is of a kind which requires the petition to be re-served on the company (for example, the petition misstates the debt which is due from the company or does not set out the correct address for the company's registered office),[137] the application to amend should be made prior to the hearing of the petition, so that the petition may be amended and re-served in advance of the hearing. If the application for leave to amend such a defect is left to the hearing of the petition, there will necessarily be an adjournment. Once leave to amend has been obtained, the amendment is made in the conventional way.[138]

9.28 Form of petition by administrator

If the petition is presented at the instance of the company's administrator, the petition should be expressed to be the petition of the company by its administrator,[139] and should contain the following details: the name of the administrator, the number of the petition on which the administration order was made and the date of the administration order[140]; and an application under s. 18 of the Insolvency Act 1986 seeking the discharge of the administration order and such other consequential order upon the discharge as the court thinks fit.[141] If the administrator seeks appointment as the liquidator of the company,[142] the Prayer to the petition should expressly include a request for an order that the administrator be appointed liquidator of the company.

135. See the preceding paragraph.
136. Pursuant to RSC O. 20, rr. 5 and 7.
137. Discrepancies between the registered office of the company as stated in the petition and in the affidavit of service are discussed in para. 9.49, *infra*.
138. See RSC O. 20, r. 10.
139. IR 1986, r. 4.7(7)(a).
140. IR 1986, r. 4.7(7)(b).
141. IR 1986, r 4.7(7)(c).
142. Pursuant to IA 1986, s. 140 and IR 1986, rr. 4.7(10) and 4.102.

VERIFICATION

9.29 Affidavit of verification

The petition must be verified by an affidavit filed in court at the same time as the petition is presented.[143] The affidavit of verification must follow Form 4.3 with such variations, if any, as the case may require.[144] The affidavit must state that the contents of the petition are true, or are true to the best of the deponent's knowledge, information and belief.[145] The affidavit of verification is *prima facie* evidence of the statements made in the petition to which it relates,[146] and the averments made in the affidavit may be based upon hearsay.[147] If there is more than one petitioner, or if the petition relates to debts due to two or more different creditors, the debt due to each creditor must be separately verified.[148] A copy of the petition must be exhibited to the affidavit of verification.[149]

9.30 Who should be the deponent?

The affidavit should be made: (a) by the petitioner, or if there is more than one petitioner, by any one petitioner; or (b) by an officer of the company, such as a director or the company secretary, or by a solicitor who has been concerned in the matters giving rise to the presentation of the petition (i.e. a person who can state how the petition debt came to be incurred and can assert that it remains unpaid); or (c) by some responsible person duly authorised to make the affidavit on behalf of the company who has a requisite knowledge of those matters.[150] If the deponent is not the petitioner himself or one of the petitioners stated in the petition, the deponent must in the affidavit identify himself and state: (a) the capacity in which and the authority by which he makes the affidavit; and (b) the means of his knowledge of the matters deposed to in the affidavit.[151] If the petitioner's solicitor swears the affidavit of verification in circumstances where he knows or ought to know that the petition debt is disputed in good faith on substantial grounds and that the petition is therefore an abuse of process, a wasted costs order[152] may be made against him.[153]

9.31 Verification of simultaneous petitions

If a creditor wishes to present petitions against a number of different debtors, the rules permit the use of a single affidavit of verification.[154] In such a case, the affidavit of

143. IR 1986, r. 4.7(1).
144. This form is reproduced in Appendix 4. See IR 1986, r. 12.7 and sch. 4, part 4 (as amended).
145. IR 1986, r. 4.12(1).
146. IR 1986, r. 4.12(6).
147. Civil Evidence Act 1995, s. 1 (in force on 31 January 1997). Prior to the Civil Evidence Act 1995 coming into force, hearsay statements in the affidavit of verification were nevertheless admissible owing to the wording of IR 1986, r. 4.12(6): see *Re Koscot Interplanetary (UK) Ltd* [1972] 3 All ER 829 at 831J–833G.
148. IR 1986, r. 4.12(2).
149. IR 1986, r. 4.12(3).
150. IR 1986, r. 4.12(4).
151. IR 1986, r 4.12(5).
152. Under the Supreme Court Act 1981, s. 51(6) and RSC O. 62, r. 11(1): see the *Supreme Court Practice 1997*, Vol 1, para. 62/11/2, pp. 1075–1078.
153. *Re a Company (No. 006798 of 1995)* [1996] 1 WLR 491; cf *Ridehalgh* v. *Horsefield*; *Philex plc* v. *Golban (Company No. 0022 of 1993)* [1994] BCC 390.
154. IR 1986, r. 4.12(7). However, a single composite petition should not be used.

verification should state in its title the name of each company to which it relates and should set out in relation to each company the statements relied upon by the petitioner. A legible photocopy of the affidavit should then be filed with each petition to which it relates.

9.32 Delay between verification and presentation

The affidavit of verification should be sworn contemporaneously with (i.e. very shortly before) the presentation of the petition. If there is a delay of more than a few days between verification and presentation, at the hearing of the petition the court will require to be told on instructions that there was no change in circumstances between verification and presentation (i.e. that the petition debt has not been paid). If the delay between verification and presentation is considerable (say, many weeks or months), the court may require an up-to-date affidavit of verification to be filed before making a winding-up order or, alternatively, may insist upon an undertaking to file an up-to-date affidavit of verification as a condition of making the winding-up order.

PRESENTATION OF THE PETITION

9.33 Filing of the petition

Once the petition has been verified by affidavit, the petition must be filed in court.[155] If the company itself is the petitioner, only one copy of the petition need be filed. However, where the petitioner is other than the company itself, three copies of the petition must be delivered for sealing, one of which will be retained on the court file, one will be served on the company and one copy will be exhibited to the affidavit of service.[156]

9.34 Fee and deposit payable on presentation

The petitioner must pay the appropriate fee on presenting the petition,[157] and must also produce a receipt for the deposit payable on presentation.[158] If the company is wound up on the petition, the deposit will be passed to the official receiver and used to defray the initial costs of the winding-up. If the petition is dismissed, the deposit will be returned to the petitioner via the official receiver. The fee payable on presentation is always non-returnable. If the debt of the original petitioning creditor is paid by the company, another creditor is substituted as petitioner and the petition is dismissed, the deposit will be returned to the original petitioner in the usual way. However, if the company is wound up on the application of the substituted petitioner, the deposit will be retained by the official receiver.

155. IR 1986, r. 4.7(1).

156. IR 1986, r. 4.7(3) and (5). The affidavit of service is discussed further below.

157. At the time of writing, the fee for the presentation of a winding-up petition was £80.

158. IR 1986, r. 4.7(2). As at the time of writing, the deposit payable on the presentation of a winding-up petition was £500. A search to ensure that no other petition is pending against the company will also be required before the petition is presented, for which an additional fee of £5 is payable.

9.35 Companies already subject to insolvency proceedings

The petitioner will need to provide additional copies of the petition for sealing if the company sought to be compulsorily wound up is already subject to some other form of insolvency proceedings. If the company is in voluntary liquidation and a liquidator has been appointed, is in administration, is in administrative receivership, or is subject to a corporate voluntary arrangement, the petitioner must send a sealed copy of the petition respectively to the liquidator, the administrator, the administrative receiver or the supervisor of the voluntary arrangement.[159] If the company sought to be wound up is an authorised institution or former authorised institution within the meaning of the Banking Act 1987, the petitioner must send a copy of the petition to the Bank of England.[160] Each copy of the petition delivered pursuant to r. 4.7(4) must have been sealed by the court.[161] A winding-up petition filed in respect of a company in administration or subject to a corporate voluntary arrangement must be presented to the court in which the administration order was made or the court to which the nominee of the voluntary arrangement submitted his report.[162]

9.36 Petition by an administrator

Where the petition is presented by an administrator who seeks appointment as liquidator of the company,[163] the administrator must complete the following additional procedural steps: (i) he must inform the company's creditors, either in writing or at a meeting of creditors, of his intention to seek appointment as liquidator; and (ii) not less than two days before the return day for the petition, he must file in court a report which includes details of the date on which he informed creditors of his intention to seek appointment as liquidator, any responses received from creditors to that notification, and any objections to his appointment.[164] If the administrator is appointed liquidator of the company, he must also file in court a statement that he is an insolvency practitioner, duly qualified under the Insolvency Act 1986 to be the liquidator, and that he consents so to act[165]; and he must give notice of his appointment to all creditors and contributories of the company within 28 days of the appointment.[166]

SERVICE OF THE PETITION

9.37 Service

If the petition is presented by the company, or by the company acting by its administrator or administrative receiver, the petition need not be served and no affidavit of service is required.[167] However, in all other cases the petition must be served in accordance with

159. IR 1986, r. 4.7(4).
160. IR 1986, r. 4.7(4).
161. IR 1986, r. 4.7(5).
162. IR 1986, r. 4.7(8).
163. Pursuant to IA 1986, s. 140.
164. IR 1986, r. 4.7(10).
165. IR 1986, r. 4.102(2).
166. IR 1986, r. 4.102(5) and (6).
167. See IR 1986, r. 4.8(1).

r. 4.8. The petition should be served at the company's registered office—namely, the address provided to the registrar of companies prior to incorporation as the intended location of the company's registered office on incorporation,[168] or the address stated in any notification of change of registered office delivered to the registrar of companies under the Companies Act 1985, s. 287.[169]

9.38 Manner of service

Rule 4.8(3) provides that the petition may be served at the registered office in three specified ways:

(a) the petition may be handed to a person who acknowledges himself to be a director, or other officer, or employee, of the company, or to a person who to the best of the knowledge, information or belief of the server is a director, other officer, or employee, of the company;
(b) the petition may be handed to a person who at the time of service acknowledges himself to be authorised to accept service of documents on behalf of the company; or
(c) in the absence of any such person mentioned in (a) or (b) above, the petition may be deposited at or about the registered office in such a way that it is likely to come to the notice of a person attending at the office.

9.39 No officer present at the registered office

The opening words of r. 4.8(3)(c) make it clear that service by deposit of the petition at or about the registered office should occur only when there is at such office no officer of the company or person authorised to accept service. Rule 4.8(3)(c) does not, however, require the petition to be left at the registered office in such a way as to come to the notice of an officer of the company, but merely in such a way as to come to the attention of *any* person attending the office. It follows that the petition will be validly and effectively served if it is left in a prominent position at the registered office, notwithstanding that the company has ceased to occupy the office and no officer of the company is likely to attend thereat. The most common forms of acceptable service where there is no officer of the company or person authorised to accept service at the registered office, are for the petition to be left in a prominent position (for example, on the reception desk) in the registered office where the office is occupied, or to be posted through the letter-box of the registered office when it is unoccupied. If no access into the registered office can be obtained and the registered office has no postbox or if the postbox is sealed, the petition should be affixed securely to the front door of the registered office in a prominent position. The affidavit of service should not merely state where the petition was served (for example, merely "at the registered office"), but should also state in detail the manner of service (for example, "by leaving it on the reception desk in the registered office", or "by posting it through the letter-box at the registered office", or "by fixing it securely to the front door at the registered office with drawing pins").

168. See CA 1985, s. 10(6).
169. IR 1986, r. 4.8(2).

9.40 Irregular service

Care should be taken to avoid serving the petition in a way which makes it unlikely that the petition would come to the attention of any person. The court will not ordinarily permit service by "pushing the petition under the locked door at the registered office", which involves the danger, for example, that the petition may be hidden by a doormat. If the petition is served in this way, the court would be likely to require the petition to be re-served and a new affidavit of service to be filed, for which purpose the hearing of the petition would need to be adjourned; but if the petition was advertised after the first (defective) service, the court would be likely to dispense with re-advertisement.

9.41 Service at registered office not practicable

If, for any reason, it is not practicable to serve the company at its registered office, (for example, because the registered office premises are behind a locked perimeter fence or have been demolished), or the company has no registered office or is an unregistered company, the petition may be served on the company by leaving it at the company's last known principal place of business in such a way as it is likely to come to the attention of a person attending there (see para. 9.39 *supra*), avoiding irregular means of service (see para. 9.40 *supra*).[170] Alternatively, the petition may be served on the company by delivering it to the company secretary or some director, manager or principal officer of that company, wherever that person may be found.[171] In such a case, the affidavit of service ought to state: (i) that service at the registered office is not practicable, describing the attempts made (if any) to effect service at the registered office; (ii) the reasons why such service is not practicable; and (iii) particulars of how the petition was in fact served under r. 4.8(4), including the name of the officer of the company to whom the petition was delivered and the evidence which shows that he is an officer of the company. If the company is an overseas company without a registered office in England or Wales, service should be effected as provided for in ss. 694A or 695 of the Companies Act 1985[172]—i.e. the petition should be served on the person resident in Great Britain who is named in the overseas company's return to the registrar of companies (delivered pursuant to s. 691) as authorised to accept service on the company's behalf, by leaving the petition at or posting it to the address given for that person in the return[173]; and where the overseas company has failed to make the appropriate return to the registrar of companies or the person named in the return as authorised to accept service cannot be served for any reason (for example, where he has died or has refused to accept service), the petition may be served on the overseas company by leaving it at, or posting it to, any place of business established by the company in Great Britain.[174]

9.42 Substituted service

If the petitioner is unable to serve the petition in any of the ways mentioned in the preceding paragraph—for example, because the registered office is inaccessible or has

170. IR 1986, r. 4.8(4).
171. *Ibid.*
172. IR 1986, r. 4.8(5).
173. CA 1985, ss. 694A(2) and 695(1).
174. CA 1985, ss. 694A(3) and 695(2).

been demolished, the company has no other place of business and the whereabouts of the officers of the company are unknown—the petitioner must apply to the court for leave to serve the petition in some other way approved by the court.[175] This is known as an order for substituted service. The most common form of substituted service is for the court to order that the petition be served on the company by advertising details of the petition in the *London Gazette*.

9.43 Application for substituted service

If difficulties are encountered in serving the petition in the normal way, an application should promptly be made for an order for substituted service, in order to avoid an adjournment on the return day of the petition. A petitioner who requires an order for substituted service should issue an ordinary application[176] to be heard *ex parte*, supported by an affidavit describing his attempts (if any) to serve the petition in the usual way under r. 4.8(2)–(5) and the reasons why it was impracticable to effect regular service. Two copies of the application will be required on issue. The application will be heard by the Court Manager[177] of the Companies Court,[178] at 11.00am on any weekday. On the day before the day fixed for the hearing of the application, the petitioner should bespeak the court file (i.e. arrange for the file to be available for the hearing), which can be done by telephoning the Companies Court.[179] The court will draw up the Court Manager's order which will be sent to the petitioner. The petitioner should effect service as provided for in the order, and file an affidavit of the substituted service of the petition. If, as is usual, the substituted service of the petition is by advertisement in the *London Gazette*, a copy of the *London Gazette* should be lodged in Chambers and the relevant page should be exhibited to the affidavit of substituted service.

PROOF OF SERVICE

9.44 Affidavit of service

Where the rules require the petition to be served (i.e. where the petitioner is not the company itself or the company acting by its administrators or administrative receivers), the petitioner or his process server must file in court an affidavit proving service of the petition.[180] Where the petition has been served at the company's registered office (i.e. service in accordance with r. 4.8(2)), the affidavit must follow Form 4.4 with such variations, if any, as the case may require.[181] Where service has been effected on the company at a place other than its registered office (i.e. service under r. 4.8(4) or substituted

175. IR 1986, r. 4.8(6).
176. See IR 1986, rr. 7.2 and 12.7, and sch. 4 part 4 (as amended).
177. Formerly known as the Chief Clerk of the Companies Court.
178. Practice Direction (Companies Court: Insolvency) (No. 3 of 1986) [1987] 1 WLR 53, para. 4(b).
179. On 0171 936 6294 (correct at the time of writing).
180. IR 1986, r. 4.9(1).
181. This form is reproduced in Appendix 4, *infra*. See IR 1986, r. 12.7 and sch. 4, part 4 (as amended).

service under r. 4.8(6)), the affidavit must follow Form 4.5 with such variations, if any, as the case may require.[182]

9.45 Description of manner of service

The affidavit must expressly state the manner of service.[183] It is insufficient for the affidavit merely to state that the petition was "served on the company by leaving it at the registered office". The affidavit should give more detail as to the *manner* of service—for example, by stating that the petition was served on the company "by leaving it on the reception desk at the registered office of the company" or "by posting it through the letter-box at the registered office of the company" or "by fixing it securely to the locked front door at the registered office of the company"; and the registered office address should be set out in full. If the affidavit merely states that the petition was left at the registered office without explicitly stating the manner of service, and the company does not appear or is not represented at the hearing of the petition, the court will require a better affidavit of service to be sworn describing the manner of service; and the court will refuse to make a winding-up order until the better affidavit is filed. If the defect in the affidavit is only noticed at the hearing of the petition, it will be necessary to adjourn the petition for a short period—say, seven days—in order for a better affidavit of service to be filed. If it transpires that the manner of service was irregular (for example, the petition was pushed under the door at the registered office of the company), the petition must be re-served and a new affidavit of service sworn and filed. This may require a longer adjournment of the petition if the defect is noticed only at the hearing of the petition.

9.46 Exhibits

The affidavit of service filed in court must have exhibited to it a sealed copy of the petition; and if the court has ordered substituted service, a sealed copy of the court's order for substituted service must also be exhibited.[184] The affidavit of service and the exhibits must be filed in court immediately after service.[185]

9.47 Discrepancy between petition and affidavit of service

Care should be taken to ensure that the address for the company's registered office stated in the petition and in the affidavit are correct and correspond exactly. The court will require an explanation of any discrepancy between the two. The possible consequences of a discrepancy are as follows:

(1) *There is a minor error in the petition—such as an error in the postcode of the registered office of the company—but the affidavit of service correctly states the address of the registered office where service was effected.* In such a case, the court would be likely to waive the minor defect in the petition and make a winding-up order.

182. This form is reproduced in Appendix 4, *infra*. See IR 1986, r. 12.7 and sch. 4, part 4 (as amended).
183. IR 1986, r. 4.9(1).
184. IR 1986, r. 4.9(2).
185. *Ibid.*

(2) *There is a major defect in the registered office address stated in the petition—for example, the company moved to a new registered office prior to the presentation of the petition (which was prepared using an out-of-date company search)—but the affidavit of service correctly states the present registered office address at which service was effected.* In such a case, the court would be likely to require the petition to be amended prior to making a winding-up order; but the court would be unlikely to require re-service of the petition, unless it appeared that the petition had not come to the attention of the company. The court may be prepared to make a winding-up order on the undertaking of the petitioner to amend the petition forthwith.

(3) *The petition correctly states the registered office of the company, but the affidavit of service contains a minor misstatement as to the registered office address.* In such a case, the court would be likely to waive the defect in the affidavit of service and make the usual compulsory order.

(4) *The petition correctly states the registered office address of the company, but the affidavit of service contains a major misstatement as to the registered office address.* If the petition was in fact served at the proper registered office and the mistake is merely in the drafting of the affidavit, the court would require a better affidavit of service to be sworn and filed prior to making a winding-up order; however, if the petition was in fact served at an incorrect address as stated in the affidavit of service, before making the usual compulsory order the court would require the petition to be re-served and a new affidavit of service to be sworn and filed.

9.48 Other persons who must receive a copy of the petition

Where the company sought to be wound up is already subject to some other form of insolvency proceedings (i.e. voluntary liquidation, administration, administrative receivership, or a voluntary arrangement), the petitioner must obtain additional sealed copies of the petition at the time of presentation, to be sent to the voluntary liquidator, administrator, administrative receiver, or supervisor of the voluntary arrangement.[186] In addition, if the company is an authorised institution or former authorised institution within the meaning of the Banking Act 1987, a sealed copy of the petition must be sent by the petitioner to the Bank of England.[187] The copy of the petition must be sent to the relevant insolvency practitioner or the Bank of England on the next business day following the day on which the petition is served on the company.[188]

9.49 Other persons entitled to a copy of the petition

Any director, contributory or creditor of the company sought to be wound up is entitled to be provided by the solicitor for the petitioner (or, where the petitioner is acting in person, by the petitioner himself) with a copy of the petition within two days after

186. IR 1986, rr. 4.7(4), (5) and 4.10(1)–(3).
187. IR 1986, rr. 4.7(4), (5) and 4.10(4).
188. IR 1986, r. 4.10(5).

requiring it, on payment of the appropriate fee.[189] If the petitioner or his solicitor fails to comply with this obligation, the director, contributory or creditor of the company seeking to obtain a copy of the petition should apply to the registrar in Chambers by an *inter partes* ordinary application for an order that the petitioner or his solicitor should furnish a copy of the petition to the applicant.

ADVERTISEMENT OF THE PETITION

9.50 Advertisement

Unless the court otherwise directs, the petitioner must advertise the petition once in the *London Gazette*.[190] The advertisement must follow Form 4.6 with such variations, if any, as the case may require.[191] The court has recently stressed that the requirement for advertisement is mandatory, and that a failure to advertise the petition may result in the summary dismissal of the petition.[192] The purpose of the advertisement is two-fold: its primary purpose is to give notice of the petition to those who are entitled to appear at the hearing of the petition (i.e. creditors, whether actual, contingent or prospective); its secondary (but important) purpose is to give notice of the petition to those who might deal with the company in the period between the presentation of the petition and its final determination and who might therefore be adversely affected by the provisions of s. 127 of the Insolvency Act 1986.[193] The court has a general discretion under r. 4.11(1) to direct that the petition should not be advertised, or should not be advertised in the *London Gazette*. In addition, r. 4.11(3) confers on the court an express power to direct that advertisement of the petition appear in a specified newspaper, instead of the *Gazette*, if it is not reasonably practicable to comply with the rules regarding the time at which the advertisement should appear. This would enable the court to direct advertisement in some other newspaper if publication of the *Gazette* were suspended. However, in the vast majority of cases, a creditor's petition will be advertised in the *London Gazette* in the usual way without the need for any direction from the court.

9.51 Time of advertisement

If the petitioner is the company itself or the company acting by its voluntary liquidator, administrator or administrative receiver, the advertisement of the petition must be made to appear in the *London Gazette* not less than seven business days before the day appointed for the hearing.[194] In all other cases, the advertisement must appear not less than seven business days after service of the petition on the company, and not less than seven business days before the day appointed for the hearing.[195] The purpose of r. 4.11(2)(b) is

189. IR 1986, r. 4.13. At the time of writing, the appropriate fee was 15p per A4 or A5 page, and 30p per A3 page: IR 1986, r. 13.11(b).
190. IR 1986, r. 4.11(1).
191. This form is reproduced in Appendix 4, *infra*. See IR 1986, r. 12.7 and sch. 4, part 4 (as amended).
192. Practice Direction (Companies Court: winding-up) [1996] 1 WLR 1255.
193. *Re a Company (No. 007923 of 1994)* [1995] 1 WLR 953 at 958F–H; *Applied Data Base Ltd* v. *Secretary of State for Trade and Industry* [1995] 1 BCLC 272 at 274f–h.
194. IR 1986, r. 4.11(2)(a).
195. IR 1986, r. 4.11(2)(b).

to give the company seven days' opportunity after service of the petition on it, either to pay the petition debt or to apply to the court to restrain advertisement of the petition if the company disputes the debt—in either case avoiding the damage to its business and goodwill which may flow from the advertisement of the petition. In calculating each of the seven-day periods, Saturdays, Sundays, Bank Holidays, Christmas Day and Good Friday are excluded.[196] Given that r. 12.9 of the Insolvency Rules 1986 applies the provisions of RSC O. 3, r. 2 to the computation of periods of time under the Rules, it should follow that, in calculating the period of not less than seven business days before the hearing of the petition, the day of advertisement is excluded but the day of the hearing is included.[197] However, the court has construed r. 4.11(2) as if it provided for seven *clear* business days.[198] It follows that, if the petition is due to be heard on, say, Wednesday the 14th of the month, the advertisement should be made to appear in the *London Gazette* on or before Friday the 2nd of the month in order to give seven clear business days between the date of the advertisement and the date of the hearing. The court has power to abridge the periods stipulated in r. 4.11(2).[199]

9.52 Late service or advertisement

If there are only five or six clear business days between service and advertisement of the petition, and not the seven business days required by r. 4.11(2)(b), or if there are only five or six clear business days between the date of advertisement and the date of the hearing of the petition and not the seven business days required by r. 4.11(2)(a) or (b), the breach of r. 4.11 is not a bar to a winding-up order: the court will ordinarily waive those defects and permit the petition to proceed without re-service or re-advertisement. However, if the advertisement appears three or more days late, thus leaving only four clear business days or fewer between advertisement and the hearing of the petition, the court will not waive the defect but will require the petition to be re-advertised in order to give creditors a proper opportunity to appear at the hearing of the petition.

9.53 Contents of advertisement

The advertisement of the petition must contain the following information[200]:

(a) the name of the company and its registered office address, or in the case of an unregistered company the address of its principal place of business, and in the case of an oversea company the address at which service of the petition was effected;
(b) the name and address of the petitioner;
(c) if the petitioner is the company itself, the address of its registered office or, in the case of an unregistered company, of its principal place of business;

196. This follows from the reference to "business" days, but weekends and Bank Holidays would in any event be excluded in the calculation of the seven-day period under RSC O. 3, r. 2(5) which applies to the calculation of time under IR 1986: see r. 12.9. See also *Re Display Multiples Ltd* [1967] 1 WLR 571.

197. See RSC O. 3, r. 2(3) and *Supreme Court Practice 1997*, Vol. 1, para. 3/2/7, p. 14.

198. This is perhaps a throw-back to r. 28 of the Companies (Winding-Up) Rules 1949 which provided that the petition should be advertised not less than seven *clear* days before the day fixed for the hearing.

199. See, for example, *Applied Data Base Ltd* v. *Secretary of State for Trade and Industry* [1995] 1 BCLC 272 at 274d–e.

200. IR 1986, r. 4.11(4).

(d) the date on which the petition was presented;
(e) the venue fixed for the hearing of the petition;
(f) the name and address of the petitioner's solicitors (if any); and
(g) a statement that any person intending to appear at the hearing (whether to support or oppose the petition) must give notice of his intention to appear in accordance with r. 4.16.

9.54 Misstatements in the advertisement

If the advertisement contains trivial errors or omissions—such as an error in or omission from the petitioner's registered office address—the court is likely to waive that defect and make the usual compulsory order without requiring re-advertisement of the petition. However, any defect in the advertisement which goes to the identity of the company sought to be wound-up and which is other than trivial—such as a significant error in the company's name or a significant error in, or omission from, the company's registered office address—would not be waived and the court would require the petition to be re-advertised. If such a defect comes to light at or shortly before the hearing of the petition, it is likely that the petition would have to be adjourned for 14 or 21 days to enable re-advertisement to take place.

9.55 Dismissal of the petition for breach of r. 4.11

Rule 4.11(5) provides that, if the petition is not duly advertised in accordance with r. 4.11, the court may dismiss the petition. The power of dismissal is discretionary and disciplinary. The court has exercised its power of dismissal according to the following principles.

(1) *Where a petitioner advertised*[201] *the petition prematurely in breach of r. 4.11, or failed to advertise the petition by the date of the hearing, or advertised the petition too late for the hearing, the practice of the court was not to dismiss the petition if the company did not oppose the petition and did not appear to take the point of non-compliance with r. 4.11*. In the case of premature advertisement, the court would make a winding-up order notwithstanding the premature advertisement, and in the case of a failure to advertise the petition prior to the hearing date or a very late advertisement, the court would usually grant an adjournment for the purpose of advertisement or re-advertisement.
(2) *Where the petition was advertised prematurely in breach of r. 4.11, and the company appeared at the hearing of the petition to take the point*:
   (a) if the breach of the rule appeared to be culpable or an abuse of process, the practice of the court was to dismiss the petition with an order for costs against the petitioning creditor, unless there was a supporting creditor appearing on the petition who wished to take over the petition.[202] If, for

201. There are conflicting authorities whether "advertised" in IR 1986, r. 4.11 means formally advertised in the *London Gazette* (as suggested in *SN Group plc* v. *Barclays Bank plc* [1993] BCC 506 at 509C–F and *Re a Company (No. 0013925 of 1991), ex parte Rousell* [1992] BCLC 562 at 563g–h) or whether it includes less formal publication of the petition, such as orally informing the company's bankers (as suggested in *Re a Company (No. 001127 of 1992)* [1992] BCC 477 at 478C–D).
202. See *Re Signland Ltd* [1982] 2 All ER 609.

example, the purpose of the premature advertisement was to bring improper pressure to bear on the company, that would constitute an abuse of the process of the court, and the petition would be dismissed under r. 4.11(5)[203];

(b) if the court was satisfied that the breach of r. 4.11 was inadvertent (i.e. where the breach of the rule did not arise from some fault of the petitioner) and did not amount to an abuse of process, the court would refuse to strike out the petition and would allow it to proceed to a hearing.[204]

(3) *Where premature publicity was given to the existence of the petition (for example, by sending a copy of the petition to the company's bankers) in order to bring improper pressure to bear on the company.* Irrespective of the question whether the petition could be dismissed under r. 4.11(5),[205] the court could dismiss the petition under its inherent jurisdiction as an abuse of process.[206]

However, the court has recently stressed that the requirement of advertisement is mandatory, that a breach of r. 4.11(2)(b) may result in the summary dismissal of the petition under r. 4.11(5), and that, if the court in its discretion adjourns the petition, it will only do so on condition that the petition is advertised in due time for the adjourned hearing.[207] It remains to be seen whether the court will now exercise its power of dismissal under r. 4.11(5) more readily. In order to avoid the risk of dismissal of the petition, a petitioner should ensure that his petition is duly advertised in accordance with r. 4.11(2), that any breach of the rule can be adequately explained to the court at the hearing of the petition, and that if an adjournment is obtained, the petition is duly advertised for the adjourned hearing.

9.56 Direction for no advertisement

Rule 4.11(1) provides that the court may direct that a petition should not be advertised, but the Rules do not give any guidance on the exercise of that discretionary power. Where the petition is presented by a creditor, a direction for no advertisement will seldom be appropriate: where the petition debt is disputed in good faith on substantial grounds and the petition is therefore an abuse of process, the company will generally apply to restrain the advertisement of the petition and to have the petition struck out[208]; conversely, where the petition debt is not disputed in good faith on substantial grounds and the petition

203. See *Re Signland Ltd, supra*; and see *Re Doreen Boards Ltd* [1996] 1 BCLC 501 at 505f–h and 506b–e (a contributory's petition).

204. See *Re Corbenstoke Ltd* (1989) 5 BCC 197 (in which the advertisement was premature because service was invalid as a result of the Registrar of Companies having failed to record a notice of change of registered office) and *Re Garton (Western) Ltd* (1989) 5 BCC 198 (in which the petitioner permitted a delay to occur between making a search against the company and presenting its petition; in the interim, the company's registered office changed; the court refused to strike out the petition as the petitioner's conduct could not be characterised as an abuse of the process of the court).

205. I.e., depending upon whether the publicity could be said to be an "advertisement": see Note 202 above.

206. *Re a Company (No. 0013925 of 1991), ex parte Roussell, supra.*

207. Practice Direction (Companies Court: winding-up), *supra*.

208. *Applied Data Base Ltd* v. *Secretary of State for Trade and Industry, supra*, at 274h. Applications to restrain advertisement are discussed later in this Chapter.

is not an abuse of process, the petitioner is entitled *ex debito justitiae* to a winding-up order[209] and the court will usually allow advertisement to proceed in order to inform the class of creditors which the petitioner represents, of the existence of the petition.[210] Where the petition does not amount to an abuse of process but the company can exceptionally point to some good reason why the petition should not be advertised prior to the hearing, the company may apply for a direction that petition should not be advertised. The power to make a direction dispensing with advertisement is discretionary and will only be exercised in exceptional circumstances[211]: the direction is most likely to be made on a "public interest" petition under s. 124A of the Insolvency Act 1986 where the company is not alleged to be insolvent and opposes the petition, no third parties would be prejudiced by the direction, there is no compelling reason why the public should be told of the existence of the petition, and advertisement would cause serious damage to the reputation and financial stability of the company (for example, where the company is actively trading).[212] The court may also make a direction dispensing with advertisement in order to facilitate the presentation of a petition for an administration order.[213] In deciding whether to exercise its discretion to direct that the petition should not be advertised, the court balances the need to bring the proceedings to the attention of all those who may have an interest in resisting or supporting them, with the serious consequences for the stability of the company which may result from advertisement.[214] The application for such a direction should be made by ordinary application returnable before the Companies Court Judge and should be supported by an affidavit.

CERTIFICATE OF COMPLIANCE

9.57 Filing of certificate

Once the petition has been duly served and advertised, the petitioner must file in court a certificate stating that the rules relating to service and advertisement[215] have been complied with.[216] The certificate must follow Form 4.7 with such variations, if any, as the case may require.[217] The certificate must state: (a) the date of presentation of the petition; (b) the date fixed for the hearing of the petition; and (c) the date or dates on which the petition was served and advertised in accordance with the Rules.[218] Where the petition does not need to be served (for example, a petition presented by the company itself or by its

209. See *Coulon Sanderson & Ward Ltd* v. *Ward* (1986) 2 BCC 99, 207 at 99, 215 (l/h col) and *Bryanston Finance Ltd* v. *de Vries (No. 2)* [1976] Ch. 63 at 78C–E: in both of these cases the court refused to restrain the presentation of a contributory's winding-up petition, where the presentation would not have been an abuse of process.

210. *Re a Company (No. 001448 of 1989)* [1989] BCLC 715 at 716h–717a.

211. *Applied Data Base Ltd* v. *Secretary of State for Trade and Industry, supra*, at 274e.

212. *Re a Company (No. 007923 of 1994)* [1995] 1 WLR 953; *Re Golden Chemical Products Ltd* [1976] Ch. 300 at 309; contrast *Applied Data Base Ltd* v. *Secretary of State for Trade and Industry, supra*, where an application that advertisement be dispensed with was refused.

213. *Re a Company (No. 001448 of 1989)* [1989] BCLC 715.

214. *Re a Company (No. 007923 of 1994)*, *supra*, at 960B–D.

215. I.e., IR 1986, rr. 4.8 and 4.11 respectively.

216. IR 1986, r. 4.14(1).

217. This form is reproduced in Appendix 4, *infra*. See IR 1986, r. 12.7 and sch. 4, part 4 (as amended).

218. IR 1986, r. 4.14(2).

voluntary liquidator, administrator or administrative receiver), the certificate will state only the date of its presentation, the date fixed for the hearing and the date of advertisement.

9.58 Filing of the advertisement

A copy of the advertisement of the petition should be attached to the certificate of compliance and filed in court with the certificate.[219] Only the relevant page of the *London Gazette* (or such other newspaper in which the court has directed that the advertisement should appear),[220] rather than the entire publication, need be filed in court. Care should be taken to ensure that the date of the advertisement (appearing at the top of the page in the *London Gazette*) is legibly shown on the copy advertisement filed with the certificate and not omitted when photocopying the advertisement, so that compliance with r. 4.11(2) can be proved. Where the advertisement appears over two pages of the *London Gazette,* both pages should be filed with the certificate. A copy of *every* advertisement of the petition should be filed in court as soon as possible after publication, even if the petitioner does not intend to pursue the petition or the advertisement is defective.[221] If a petitioner advertises a petition but subsequently decides not to pursue the petition, the filing of a valid advertisement will enable the court to dispense with re-advertisement should a different creditor apply to be substituted as petitioner under r. 4.19.

9.59 Time for filing the certificate

A Practice Direction[222] in relation to the predecessor of r. 4.14[223] states that *every* advertisement should be filed in court as soon as possible after publication, even where the advertisement is defective or the petitioner has decided not to pursue his petition. Rule 4.14(1) states that the certificate of compliance should be filed in court at least five days before the hearing of the petition—i.e. a certificate relating to a petition to be heard on a Wednesday would have to be filed by the preceding Wednesday.[224] However, in practice the Companies Court allows the certificate to be filed as late as the Friday preceding the Wednesday on which the petition is due to be heard.

9.60 Failure to file the certificate on time

A failure to file the certificate of compliance in accordance with r. 4.14 (subject to the practice referred to in the preceding paragraph) gives the court power to dismiss the petition.[225] However, the court would rarely dismiss the petition on this ground. If the certificate has not been filed on time (whether owing to an oversight or a delay in receiving a copy of the *London Gazette*), when the petition is called on for hearing, the petitioner should seek leave to file the certificate out of time, which will generally be granted; and

219. *Ibid.*
220. See IR 1986, r. 4.11(3).
221. Practice Direction (Companies: Advertisement of Petition) [1986] 1 WLR 286 (referring to the Companies (Winding-up) Rules 1949, r. 33).
222. *Ibid.*
223. I.e., Companies (Winding-up) Rules 1949, r. 33.
224. See IR 1986, r. 12.9, which applies the computation of time rules in RSC O. 3, r. 2.
225. IR 1986, r. 4.14(3).

the petition will then be adjourned. If the registrar intends to hear the list of petitions for a second time later that day (i.e. if petitions are to be "taken second time around"), the petition will be adjourned to later in the day: in the interim, the certificate and advertisement will be checked by the Companies Court staff, and if they are in order, the usual compulsory order will be made second time around. However, recently the court has been more reluctant to take petitions "second time around", and a failure to file the certificate on time has resulted in the adjournment of the petition to the next available Wednesday.

If the certificate is not available but a copy of the advertisement is available when the petition is first called on for hearing, the registrar may grant leave to file the advertisement alone, and, if it is in order, may make the usual compulsory order second time around (i.e. if the list of petitions is heard for the second time that day); alternatively, he may adjourn the petition to the next available Wednesday to enable the certificate to be filed and grant leave for it to be filed out of time. If neither the certificate nor the advertisement is available when the petition is called on for hearing, the petitioner should seek an adjournment to file the certificate and advertisement, or to advertise the petition where it has yet to be advertised. If the petitioner repeatedly fails to file the certificate of compliance, the court may dismiss the petition,[226] and if the petitioner fails to advertise the petition, the court may dismiss the petition[227] or may substitute as petitioner any creditor or contributory who wishes to pursue the petition.[228]

WITHDRAWAL OF PETITION

9.61 When a petition can be withdrawn

A petition may be withdrawn prior to the date fixed for its hearing on the application of the petitioner if (and only if) the following criteria are satisfied[229]:

(a) the application is made at least five business days before the date fixed for the hearing of the petition[230];
(b) the petition has not been advertised;
(c) no notices (whether in support of, or in opposition to, the petition)[231] have been received by the petitioner or its solicitor in relation to the petition;
(d) the company which is the subject of the petition consents to the proposed order for withdrawal under r. 4.15[232]; and
(e) the petitioner and the company have agreed the order for costs (if any) to be made upon withdrawal.

226. IR 1986, r. 4.14(3).
227. Under IR 1986, r. 4.11(5).
228. Under IR 1986, r. 4.19.
229. IR 1986, r. 4.15.
230. I.e., where the petition is due to be heard on a Wednesday, the application to withdraw must be made by the preceding Wednesday at the latest: see IR 1986, r. 12.9 applying the computation of time rules in RSC O. 3, r. 2.
231. An informal indication of a creditor's intention to support the petition and to seek substitution, which does not comply with IR 1986, r. 4.16, precludes the withdrawal of the petition: see *Re Wavern Engineering Co. Ltd* (1987) 3 BCC 3.
232. The wording of IR 1986, r. 4.15 appears to require the consent of the company for withdrawal even where the petition has not been served.

If the above criteria are not satisfied (for example, where the petition debt has been paid but the parties have been unable to agree terms as to costs) the petition may not be withdrawn and must proceed to a hearing in open court before the registrar: this will be a powerful incentive for the company to agree costs, because if the petition proceeds to a hearing, another creditor who has learnt of the petition may appear on the hearing and seek to be substituted as the petitioner under r. 4.19. If the petitioner wrongly obtains the withdrawal of the petition when the above criteria are not satisfied (for example, where a notice of intention to support the petition has been given to the petitioner or his solicitors), the court may restore the petition and substitute another creditor as petitioner.[233]

9.62 Form of application to withdraw

The application for leave to withdraw a petition[234] should be made *ex parte* by ordinary application under r. 7.2 to the Court Manager[235] of the Companies Court in Chambers.[236] The Court Manager hears such applications at 11.00am each weekday. A petitioner wishing to withdraw its petition should telephone the Companies Court[237] at least a day before the day on which the application is to be made, and arrange for the relevant file to be available for the application. The petitioner should issue the *ex parte* ordinary application by 10.45am on the day of the hearing before the Court Manager. No fee is payable on issuing the application and no affidavit in support is required. The petitioner should produce at the hearing a letter of consent from the company or its solicitors, or a duly signed consent order, agreeing to the withdrawal of the petition and to the costs order (if any) to be made upon dismissal.

NOTICE OF APPEARANCE AND EVIDENCE IN OPPOSITION

9.63 Requirement of notice

Any person who wishes to appear on the hearing of the petition, whether to support or oppose the petition, must give written notice of his intention to appear to the petitioner or his solicitor.[238] The notice must follow Form 4.9 with such variations, if any, as the case may require.[239] The notice must contain the following information[240]:

(a) the name and address of the person giving notice, and his telephone number and reference (if any);

(b) the name and address of any person authorised to speak or act on behalf of the person giving notice, including his telephone number and reference (if any);

233. *Re Wavern Engineering Co. Ltd, supra.*
234. Under IR 1986, r. 4.15.
235. Formerly known as the Chief Clerk of the Companies Court.
236. See IR 1986, r. 13.2(2) and Practice Direction (No. 3 of 1986) [1987] 1 WLR 53 (a copy of which is reproduced in Appendix 3, *infra*).
237. On 0171 936 6294 (correct at time of writing).
238. IR 1986, r. 4.16(1).
239. This form is reproduced in Appendix 4, *infra*. See IR 1986, r. 12.7 and sch. 4, part 4 (as amended).
240. IR 1986, r. 4.16(2).

(c) whether the person giving notice intends to support or oppose the petition; and

(d) the amount and nature of his debt.

9.64 Where and when notice should be sent

The notice must be sent to the petitioner at the address shown for him in the court records (i.e. in the petition or in the Companies Court database) or in the advertisement of the petition, or it may be sent to his solicitor.[241] In practice, the notice is generally sent to the petitioner's solicitor. The notice should be sent in sufficient time to be received by the petitioner or his solicitor not later than 4.00pm on the business day before the day of the hearing or adjourned hearing.[242] If the court makes a winding-up order, it usually allows only one set of costs to be shared amongst all supporting creditors who have given notice under r. 4.16, and accordingly, those who give notice of an intention to appear on the petition under r. 4.16 should consider being represented by the same solicitor or counsel at the hearing. Where a person fails to give notice under r. 4.16 (or gives notice too late) of his intention to appear on the hearing of the petition (whether to support or oppose it), he requires the leave of the court to appear at the hearing.[243] Such a person may be represented at the hearing and may seek leave to be added to the list of persons appearing out of time. The registrar will generally grant leave to a creditor or contributory to be added to the list out of time as a matter of course, but only if the applicant undertakes not to seek an order for the payment of his costs of appearing on the petition to seek leave to be added to the list out of time (often referred to as "the usual undertaking").[244] When the petition is finally disposed of, a person added to the list out of time can apply to be released from the usual undertaking. In appropriate cases (for example, where the failure to give notice was not the fault of the applicant for leave to be added to the list out of time,) the applicant will be released from the undertaking. The court will not usually refuse leave to be added to the list out of time merely because the company contends that the applicant's alleged debt is disputed.

9.65 List of appearances

Shortly before the hearing, the petitioner must prepare a list of the persons (if any) who have given notice under r. 4.16, of their intention to appear on the hearing of the petition.[245] The list should follow Form 4.10 with such variations, if any, as the case may require.[246] The list must state:

(1) the names and addresses of the persons who have given notice under r. 4.16, and (if known to the petitioner) the names and addresses of their respective solicitors[247]; and

241. IR 1986, r. 4.16(3).
242. IR 1986, r. 4.16(4).
243. IR 1986, r. 4.16(5).
244. Practice Note (Winding-up: Appearance) [1976] 1 WLR 515.
245. IR 1986, r. 4.17(1).
246. This form is reproduced in Appendix 4, *infra*. See IR 1986, r. 12.7 and sch. 4, part 4 (as amended).
247. IR 1986, r. 4.17(1).

(2) whether each of the persons appearing on the list intends to support or oppose the petition.[248]

The petitioner should hand a copy of the list to the court staff before the commencement of the hearing,[249] and the list is then placed on the court file. Where no notices under r. 4.16 have been received by the petitioner (usually referred to as a case where "the list is negative"), a blank list is commonly filed in court but the Rules do not require this. The Rules do not prescribe any sanction for a failure to file a list in court. If the court grants leave to be added to the list out of time to a creditor or contributory who has not given proper notice under r. 4.16, the petitioner should add the details of that person to the list.[250]

9.66 Evidence in opposition

Rule 4.18(1) provides that, if the company intends to oppose the petition, an affidavit in opposition should be filed in court not less than seven days before the date fixed for the hearing. A copy of the affidavit should be sent by the company to the petitioner immediately after filing.[251] However, the seven-day rule is often not observed: if an affidavit in opposition is produced shortly before, or at, the hearing of the petition and the petitioner wishes to pursue the petition, the registrar will usually adjourn the petition and give directions for the petitioner to file evidence in answer and for the company to file evidence in reply. On the adjourned hearing, the registrar will usually adjourn the petition to the judge for determination. Where the company fails to produce any affidavit evidence prior to the first hearing of the petition but is represented at the hearing and contends that the petition debt is disputed, the registrar will generally give directions for the filing of evidence. Before doing so, the registrar is likely to require an explanation why an affidavit has not been filed before the hearing. The Rules do not impose any time limit for evidence filed by opposing creditors or contributories (but any such evidence should, if possible, be filed at least seven days prior to the date fixed for the hearing by analogy with r. 4.18(1)).

SUBSTITUTION

9.67 Court's power to order substitution

The court may order that a creditor or contributory, who in the opinion of the court would be entitled to present a petition against the company and who wishes to pursue an existing petition against the company, be substituted as the petitioner on the existing petition.[252] The court's power to order substitution arises in four specified circumstances[253]:

(1) where a person petitions and is subsequently found not entitled to do so (for example, because the petition debt is disputed in good faith on substantial

248. IR 1986, r. 4.17(2).
249. IR 1986, r. 4.17(3).
250. IR 1986, r. 4.17(4).
251. IR 1986, r. 4.18(2).
252. IR 1986, r. 4.19(2).
253. IR 1986, r. 4.19(1).

grounds): the court therefore could order substitution following a successful application to restrain advertisement or after a contested hearing of the petition itself[254];

(2) where the petitioner fails to advertise the petition within the time allowed by r. 4.11 or such further time allowed by the court;

(3) where the petitioner consents to the withdrawal or dismissal of his petition,[255] or to an adjournment, or fails to appear when the petition is called on for its first hearing or at any subsequent adjournment; or

(4) where the petitioner appears on the hearing of the petition but does not seek the usual compulsory order.

The most common reasons for orders for substitution are that the petitioning creditor has been paid and is therefore not pursuing his petition, or is in protracted negotiations with the company and seeks several adjournments of the petition. The court can order a succession of substitutions on a petition where there are a number of supporting creditors and the company pays the debt of each substituted petitioner in turn. Where a petitioner has been paid the amount of the petition debt but not his costs, and a supporting creditor applies for and obtains leave to be substituted as petitioner, the original petitioner may apply for leave to be added to the list of supporting creditors in respect of his costs.

9.68 Application for substitution

In the vast majority of cases, a supporting creditor or contributory will make his application for an order for substitution orally in open court on the hearing or adjourned hearing of the petition when it becomes clear that the present petitioner does not appear or is not pursuing his petition, has failed to advertise the petition or seeks an adjournment. No formal application need be issued. Where more than one supporting creditor appears and seeks substitution, the court will usually substitute as petitioner the creditor claiming the largest undisputed debt. Where there is only one supporting creditor and the petitioner does not pursue the petition, the court will not refuse substitution merely because the company contends that the alleged debt of the applicant for substitution is disputed: in such cases, the court will usually order substitution and give directions for the filing of evidence.

9.69 Earlier application for substitution

Where the application for substitution is based on the petitioner's failure to advertise the petition or consent to the withdrawal of the petition, an order for substitution may be made at any time.[256] In such cases a supporting creditor who wishes to be substituted will often wait until the first hearing of the petition to apply, but (less commonly) may issue an ordinary application for leave to be substituted. Two copies of the application are required

254. For a case where the court ordered substitution after a winding-up order had been made irregularly and then set aside, see *Re Goldthorpe & Lacey Ltd* (1987) 3 BCC 595.

255. Note that in *Re Xyllyx plc (No. 1)* [1992] BCLC 376 (at 377e) the court refused an application by contributories of the company for substitution as petitioners in place of the Secretary of State for Trade and Industry who had decided not to pursue a "public interest" petition presented by him under IA 1986, s. 124A.

256. IR 1986, r. 4.19(3).

for issue. The application is heard by the Court Manager[257] of the Companies Court in Chambers.[258] The petitioner should be made the Respondent to the application so that he can confirm to the court that the petition has not been advertised and that he does not wish to pursue it; if the petitioner is not a party, a letter should be obtained from the petitioner giving that confirmation. If it transpires that the petition has been advertised, the Court Manager will refuse to order substitution. Substitution may also be refused if there are thought to be other supporting creditors who might have larger claims and might seek substitution at the hearing of the petition, unless those creditors are joined as Respondents to the application for substitution or consent in writing to the substitution of the applicant as petitioner.

9.70 Directions on substitution

When making an order for substitution, the court may impose such terms as it thinks fit.[259] The court will usually direct that:

(a) the petition be amended in the conventional way[260] to show the name and address of the new petitioner and particulars of his debt;
(b) the petition be re-verified;
(c) the petition be re-served on the company at its registered office and an affidavit of service be sworn and filed, unless the company is represented at the hearing when the order for substitution is made, in which case re-service may be dispensed with and a copy of the amended petition may merely be sent to the company by the new petitioner; and
(d) the amended petition be advertised in the *London Gazette*; but if the petition has already been duly advertised by an earlier petitioner in accordance with r. 4.11, the court will usually dispense with re-advertisement.

APPLICATION FOR THE APPOINTMENT OF A PROVISIONAL LIQUIDATOR

9.71 Jurisdiction

The court has a discretionary power to appoint a provisional liquidator of a company at any time after the presentation of a winding-up petition against the company[261] and before the making of the winding-up order,[262] provided that the court is satisfied that sufficient grounds are shown for the appointment.[263] The court will be slow to appoint a provisional liquidator unless there is at least a good *prima facie* case for saying that a winding-up order will be made.[264] The principal reason for the appointment is usually that the

257. Formerly known as the Chief Clerk of the Companies Court.
258. See IR 1986, r. 13.2(2) and Practice Direction (No. 3 of 1986) [1987] 1 WLR 53, para. 4(d) (a copy of which is reproduced in Appendix 3, *infra*).
259. IR 1986, r. 4.19(2).
260. I.e. in accordance with RSC O. 20, r. 10.
261. IA 1986, s. 135(1).
262. IA 1986, s. 135(2). In other words, a winding-up petition must be extant for the court to be able to appoint a provisional liquidator: *Re a Company* [1973] 1 WLR 1566 at 1572D.
263. IR 1986, r. 4.25(4).
264. *Re Highfield Commodities Ltd* [1985] 1 WLR 149 at 158D.

company's assets are in jeopardy and need to be preserved pending the hearing of the petition, but the section is expressed in general terms, and other reasons may be relied upon.[265] The appointment is a temporary measure.[266] The appointment may be made in respect of a company registered under the Companies Acts or an unregistered company.[267] The application for the appointment of a provisional liquidator may be made by the petitioner, by any other creditor of the company, by a contributory, by the company itself, by the Secretary of State for Trade and Industry, or by any person who is entitled under any Act to present a petition for the winding-up of the company.[268] A provisional liquidator is commonly appointed on the application of the Secretary of State for Trade and Industry in "public interest" petitions under s. 124A of the Insolvency Act 1986, where the grounds of the petition often include an allegation that the company's assets are in jeopardy.[269] The court also has power under s. 177 of the Act to appoint a special manager to the company where it appears to the liquidator or provisional liquidator that the nature of the business or property of the company, or the interests of the company's creditors or contributories or members generally, require the appointment of another person to manage the company's business or property.[270] The special manager may be given similar powers to those of a provisional liquidator.[271]

9.72 Who may be the provisional liquidator

The court may appoint as provisional liquidator either the official receiver or any other "fit person".[272] The person appointed must be qualified to act as an insolvency practitioner and must have consented to act as provisional liquidator.[273] Two or more insolvency practitioners may be appointed as joint provisional liquidators,[274] which may be convenient where the case is particularly complex or where, for example, the provisional liquidators may have to take steps to preserve the company's assets in more than one jurisdiction. If joint provisional liquidators are to be appointed, care should be taken to ensure that the order appointing them states whether they must only act jointly or can exercise their powers and functions jointly and severally.[275] If the order fails to state this, it should be amended under the "slip rule"[276] or clarified by a further application to the court.

265. *Ibid.* at 159D.
266. *Re ABC Coupler & Engineering Co. Ltd (No. 3)* [1970] 1 WLR 702 at 715G.
267. See, for example, *Re a Company (No. 00359 of 1987)* [1988] Ch. 210.
268. IR 1986, r. 4.25(1).
269. See, for example, the comments of Millett L.J. in *Re SHV Senator Hanseatische Verwaltungs Gesellschaft mbH* [1997] 1 WLR 515 at 526G–H. "Public interest" petitions are discussed in more detail later in this Chapter.
270. IA 1986, s. 177(1). The procedure for the appointment of a special manager is governed by IR 1986, rr. 4.206–4.210 and is discussed later in this Chapter.
271. IA 1986, s. 177(3), (4).
272. IA 1986, s. 135(2).
273. See IR 1986, r. 4.25(2)(b).
274. Although IA 1986, s. 135(1) refers to the appointment of "a liquidator provisionally" (i.e. in the singular) words in the singular include the plural: Interpretation Act 1978, s. 6. See also IA 1986, s. 231(1).
275. See IA 1986, s. 231(2).
276. See RSC O. 20, r. 11.

9.73 Form of application

The application is made by ordinary application returnable before the Companies Court Judge.[277] The application need not state the grounds on which the application is made nor the proposed functions nor powers of the provisional liquidator. The company should be joined as the respondent to the application, although, in exceptional cases (for example, where the case is extremely urgent or where giving the company prior notice of the application would be likely to further jeopardise the company's assets), the application may be made *ex parte*[278]; but the court has stated that *ex parte* applications should be made only where absolutely necessary.[279] Rule 4.25(4) empowers the court to impose whatever terms it thinks fit when making an appointment. If a provisional liquidator is appointed on an *ex parte* application, the court is likely to require the applicant (unless the applicant is the Secretary of State for Trade and Industry) to give an undertaking in damages (i.e. an undertaking to abide by any order which the court may subsequently make regarding damages sustained by the company as a result of the appointment of the provisional liquidator).[280] No undertaking in damages will be required if the appointment of the provisional liquidator is made following an *inter partes* hearing; nor where the appointment is made on the *ex parte* application of the Secretary of State for Trade and Industry in a "public interest" petition under s. 124A of the Insolvency Act 1986, unless the company can establish special circumstances justifying the requirement of an undertaking.[281] The affidavit in support of the application should show that the applicant has assets to support his undertaking in damages. Where the appointment is made following an *ex parte* application, the court is also likely to grant the company liberty to apply on notice[282] to the applicant's solicitors to discharge the appointment of the provisional liquidator. Notwithstanding the appointment of a provisional liquidator, the board of directors of the company retains a residuary power to instruct solicitors and counsel to oppose the petition, appeal against the winding-up order, and make interlocutory applications, including an application to discharge the appointment of the provisional liquidator.[283]

9.74 Affidavit in support

The application must be supported by an affidavit which states[284]:

(a) the grounds upon which the applicant relies in seeking the appointment of a provisional liquidator: this should include cogent evidence that the company is

277. Practice Direction (Companies Court: Provisional Liquidator) [1997] 1 WLR 3; *Supreme Court Practice 1997*, Vol. 2, para. 838, p. 183 (as amended by the Practice Direction).

278. See, for example, *Re WF Fearman Ltd (No. 2)* (1988) 4 BCC 139 at 141 (r/h col).

279. See the comments of Hoffmann J. in *Re Secure & Provide plc* [1992] BCC 405 at 414H–415B and *Re First Express Ltd* [1991] BCC 782 at 785D–G.

280. *Re Highfield Commodities Ltd, supra*, at 155C–D.

281. *Ibid.* at 155H–156A.

282. For example, on 48 hours written notice: see *Re Highfield Commodities Ltd, supra*, at 153F.

283. *Re Union Accident Insurance Co. Ltd* [1972] 1 WLR 640; see also *Re Gosscott (Groundworks) Ltd* (1988) 4 BCC 372 at 374 (r/h col).

284. IR 1986, r. 4.25(2).

insolvent[285] and, for example, that its assets are in jeopardy prior to the hearing of the petition without such appointment;

(b) if the proposed provisional liquidator is a person other than the official receiver, that he has consented to act and is to the best of the applicant's belief qualified to act as an insolvency practitioner: ideally the proposed appointee's consent to act and his certificate of qualification as an insolvency practitioner should be exhibited to the affidavit;

(c) whether or not the official receiver has been informed of the application or been furnished with a copy of it: the official receiver should be sent a copy of the application and affidavit in support in every case[286]; if the official receiver has not been informed of the application prior to the affidavit in support being sworn, the affidavit should explain why this has not been done and state the applicant's intention to serve a copy of the application and affidavit on the official receiver;

(d) whether, to the applicant's knowledge:
   (i) a voluntary arrangement for the company under part I of the Insolvency Act 1986 has been proposed or is in force;
   (ii) an administrator or administrative receiver is acting in relation to the company; or
   (iii) whether a voluntary liquidator has been appointed to the company;

   if any of the appointments mentioned in (i)–(iii) has been made, the affidavit should explain why a provisional liquidator is necessary (for example, why the assets remain in jeopardy) notwithstanding the intervention of the supervisor of the voluntary arrangement, the administrator, administrative receiver or voluntary liquidator, as the case may be;

(e) the applicant's estimate of the value of the company's assets in respect of which the provisional liquidator is to be appointed: the applicant may be able to give only a vague estimate, particularly where the assets in question are not readily realisable.[287]

The affidavit in support should also explain the applicant's *locus standi* to make the application: for example, where the applicant is a creditor of the company, the affidavit should state the amount of the applicant's debt and explain how the debt arose. The affidavit should also state and give reasons for the functions which it is proposed that the provisional liquidator should carry out[288] (for example, preservation of the company's assets by taking them into his possession, or the preservation of goodwill by continued trading pending the sale of the business, or the sale of perishing assets) and the powers which it is proposed he should have[289] (for example, the power to borrow money for the purpose of continuing the company's business). The affidavit should make full and frank disclosure of all relevant facts.

285. Documentary evidence of the company's insolvency (such as audited accounts) should be exhibited if available.

286. IR 1986, r. 4.25(3).

287. The actual value of the assets with which the provisional liquidator has had to deal is one of the factors taken into account by the court when fixing the provisional liquidator's remuneration: IR 1986, r. 4.30(2)(e).

288. See IA 1986, s. 135(4).

289. See IA 1986, s. 135(5).

9.75 Service and notification to the official receiver

The application and the evidence in support should be served on the company, except in cases where it is necessary to apply *ex parte*.[290] The applicant must send a copy of the application and affidavit in support to the official receiver in all cases,[291] irrespective of whether the application is to be made *ex parte*, or the proposed provisional liquidator is an insolvency practitioner other than the official receiver. If it is not practicable to supply copies of the application and affidavit in support to the official receiver (for example, owing to the urgency of the application), the applicant must nevertheless inform the official receiver about the application in sufficient time to enable him to attend the hearing.[292] The official receiver is entitled to attend any hearing of the application and make representations.[293]

9.76 The hearing

The hearing will be before the Companies Court Judge, in the first instance sitting in open court.[294] The judge may, if he thinks fit, direct that the application be heard in camera.[295]

9.77 Notice of appointment

When the court appoints a provisional liquidator, it must forthwith give notice of the appointment to the official receiver, irrespective of whether the official receiver is the appointee.[296] Where the appointee is not the official receiver, the court must at the same time also send a copy of the notice to the appointee.[297] The notice should follow Form 4.14A with such variations, if any, as the case may require.[298]

9.78 Order for appointment

The order appointing the provisional liquidator should follow Form 4.15 with such variations, if any, as the case may require.[299] The order may be made on such terms as the court thinks fit,[300] may limit the provisional liquidator's powers,[301] and must specify the functions to be carried out by him in relation to the company's affairs.[302] The functions will usually include the provisional liquidator taking into his physical possession all or

290. See para. 9.73, *supra*.
291. IR 1986, r. 4.25(3).
292. *Ibid.*
293. *Ibid.*
294. Practice Direction (Companies Court: Provisional Liquidator) [1997] 1 WLR 3: *Supreme Court Practice 1997*, Vol. 2, para. 838, p. 183 (as amended by the Practice Direction).
295. *Ibid.* at para. 3.
296. IR 1986, r. 4.25A(1).
297. IR 1986, r. 4.25A(2).
298. This form is reproduced in Appendix 4, *infra*. See IR 1986, r. 12.7 and sch. 4, part 4 (as amended).
299. The form is reproduced in Appendix 4, *infra*. See IR 1986, r. 12.7 and sch. 4, part 4 (as amended).
300. IR 1986, r. 4.25(4).
301. IA 1986, s. 135(5).
302. IR 1986, r. 4.26(1).

some part of the assets of the company (which, if only part, may conveniently be identified by a list scheduled to the order). Less commonly, the functions may include the sale of assets (especially perishing assets) and the deposit of the net proceeds of sale pending the hearing of the petition. The affidavit in support of the application must satisfy the court that such functions are necessary. Where two or more persons are appointed as joint provisional liquidators, the order must state whether they may exercise their functions individually or must act unanimously.[303] If the order is silent as to the provisional liquidator's powers, he will enjoy all the powers which are necessarily incidental to the functions conferred upon him by the order. However, the order may expressly limit the powers of the provisional liquidator.[304] Examples of the limitations which the court may impose are the power to borrow money only to a stated level, the power to sell assets only for a minimum amount, and a bar on using the proceeds of sale in the company's business without the leave of the court.

9.79 Despatch of copy orders

Sealed copies of the order appointing a provisional liquidator are sent out by the court forthwith upon the order being made, as follows[305]:

(a) two copies are sent to the official receiver where the official receiver is the appointee, one copy of which must be sent by the official receiver to the company or its voluntary liquidator (if any)[306];
(b) where the appointee is a person other than the official receiver, one copy is sent to the official receiver and two copies are sent to the appointee who must send one to the company or its voluntary liquidator (if any)[307];
(c) one copy is sent to any administrative receiver of the company.[308]

9.80 Deposit with the official receiver

If the court is persuaded that the official receiver should be appointed as provisional liquidator, the court will not issue its sealed order to the applicant pursuant to r. 4.26(2) until the applicant deposits with the official receiver (or otherwise secures to the reasonable satisfaction of the official receiver) such sum as the court directs to cover the official receiver's remuneration and expenses.[309] The amount of the sum to be deposited or secured should be stated in the order appointing the official receiver as provisional liquidator. The court has power to order that additional sums be deposited or secured, on the application of the official receiver, if the amount originally ordered to be secured or deposited is subsequently found to be insufficient.[310] If the person to whom the order for security is directed fails to comply with the order for additional sums to be deposited or secured within two days after service of the order on him, the court has power to discharge

303. IA 1986, s. 231(2).
304. IA 1986, s. 135(5).
305. IR 1986, r. 4.26(2).
306. IR 1986, r. 4.26(2)(a) and (3).
307. IR 1986, r. 4.26(2)(b) and (3).
308. IR 1986, r. 4.26(2)(c).
309. IR 1986, r. 4.27(1).
310. IR 1986, r. 4.27(2).

the order appointing the provisional liquidator on an application by the official receiver for such an order.[311] If the company's assets are insufficient to meet the official receiver's costs following discharge of the order, the official receiver may deduct them from the monies deposited by the applicant under r. 4.27.[312]

9.81 Security for the provisional liquidator

A person (other than the official receiver) may not act as an insolvency practitioner in relation to a company (including acting as its provisional liquidator[313]) unless there is in force for the duration of his appointment, security for the proper performance of his functions which meets the prescribed statutory requirements relating to his so acting.[314] A provisional liquidator (other than the official receiver) must himself pay the cost of providing that security, subject to the possibility of reimbursement when the petition is finally determined.[315] If the provisional liquidator (other than the official receiver) fails to put in place or maintain his security, the court may remove him with whatever order for costs it thinks fit,[316] may discharge the order appointing him and may give directions as to the steps (if any) to be taken for the appointment of another qualified insolvency practitioner in his place.[317] Although the rules are silent as to who may apply for an order for the removal, discharge or replacement of the provisional liquidator for a failure to maintain his security, it appears that the order may be made by the court of its own motion, or by analogy with r. 4.25(1), on the application of the official receiver, the petitioner, any creditor or contributory, or by the company itself acting by its board of directors under their residuary powers. The application should be by an ordinary application, supported by an affidavit giving the reasons for seeking the removal of the provisional liquidator. The application and affidavit in support should be served on the provisional liquidator and, as a matter of good practice, copies should be sent to the official receiver and the petitioner (if the petitioner is not the applicant).

9.82 Cost of providing security

The cost of providing the security must in the first instance be paid by the provisional liquidator, but he may be reimbursed that cost according to the outcome of the winding-up proceedings: where a winding-up petition has been presented but a winding-up order is not ultimately made, the provisional liquidator is entitled to reimbursement of the costs of providing security out of the property of the company, and the court may make an order requiring the company to pay those costs or permitting the provisional liquidator to retain monies or assets to cover his costs[318]; where a winding-up order is made on the petition, the costs of providing security are payable out of the assets of the company in liquidation

311. *Ibid.*
312. The rules governing the return of the deposit are set out in IR 1986, rr. 4.27(3) and 4.30(3).
313. IA 1986, s. 388(1)(a).
314. IA 1986, s. 390(3). The prescribed requirements are set out in the Insolvency Practitioners Regulations 1990 (S.I. 1990 No. 439), as amended by the Insolvency Practitioners (Amendment) Regulations 1993 (S.I. 1993 No. 221).
315. IR 1986, rr. 4.28(2) and 4.30(3). See para. 9.82, *infra*.
316. IR 1986, r. 4.29(1).
317. IR 1986, r. 4.29(2).
318. IR 1986, r. 4.28(2)(a).

in the prescribed order of priority.[319] The above rules determine how the provisional liquidator recoups his costs of providing security in the absence of any other order, but those rules do not prevent the court from ordering any party to the proceedings to bear the ultimate liability for those costs: where the court dismisses a winding-up petition, and the provisional liquidator recovers the costs of providing security out of the assets of the company,[320] the court may order the petitioning creditor to reimburse the company for the amount of those costs; alternatively, the court may direct the provisional liquidator not to deduct his costs of providing security from the company's assets, and may order the petitioning creditor to pay those costs directly to the provisional liquidator.

9.83 Termination of appointment

The appointment of the provisional liquidator terminates on the dismissal of the winding-up petition or on the making of a winding-up order. In addition, the court has power to discharge the appointment of a provisional liquidator owing to the applicant's failure to provide a deposit or security for the official receiver's remuneration and expenses, or owing to the provisional liquidator (other than the official receiver) failing to give or maintain his security. The court may also terminate the appointment on the application of the provisional liquidator or on the application of the persons specified in r. 4.25(1).[321] Rule 4.31 does not entitle the court to terminate the appointment of its own motion. An application for the termination of the provisional liquidator's appointment should follow the procedure set out in para. 9.81, *supra,* in relation to an application for the removal of a provisional liquidator who fails to give or maintain his security. On the termination of the appointment of the provisional liquidator for whatever reason, the court may give such directions as it thinks fit, including directions for the filing of accounts by the former provisional liquidator of his administration of the company.[322] Where the provisional liquidator's appointment is terminated on the making of a winding-up order which appoints the official receiver as liquidator, the official receiver may apply to the court for the appointment of the former provisional liquidator as a special manager to assist him until the first creditors' meeting.[323]

9.84 Effect of appointment

Once a provisional liquidator has been appointed no proceedings may be commenced or continued against the company or its property, except with the leave of the court and subject to such conditions as the court imposes.[324]

9.85 Applications to discharge the appointment

An *ex parte* order appointing a provisional liquidator will usually provide that the company may apply to discharge the appointment on, say, 48 hours' written notice to the

319. IR 1986, r. 4.28(2)(b). For the prescribed order of priority, see IR 1986, r. 4.218(1) (in particular sub-para. (e)).
320. I.e., pursuant to IR 1986, r. 4.28(2)(a).
321. IR 1986, r. 4.31(1).
322. IR 1986, r. 4.31(2).
323. *Re WF Fearman Ltd (No. 2)* (1988) 4 BCC 141.
324. IA 1986, s. 130(2).

applicant. If an order is silent as regards applications to discharge the appointment, the company ought to issue an ordinary application seeking the discharge of the appointment. The provisional liquidator and the applicant for his appointment should be the respondents to the application. In cases of extreme urgency, the company may make an immediate *ex parte* application for discharge to the judge, notice of which should be given to the provisional liquidator and the applicant. The court is unlikely to order a discharge of the provisional liquidator on an *ex parte* application, except in the plainest of cases.

9.86 Evidence

The application to discharge the appointment should be supported by an affidavit sworn on behalf of the company which answers the evidence relied upon by the applicant in obtaining the appointment of the provisional liquidator. The affidavit should deal, *inter alia*, with any allegation that the company's assets are in jeopardy or that it is insolvent. On the return day the judge may determine the application for discharge or may give directions for further evidence, if required.

9.87 Remuneration and costs

A provisional liquidator (other than the official receiver) is entitled to remuneration which is fixed by the court on the application of the provisional liquidator.[325] The official receiver's remuneration for acting as a provisional liquidator is paid on a standard scale.[326] The factors which the court must take into account in fixing the remuneration of a provisional liquidator (other than the official receiver) are set out in r. 4.30(2) of the Insolvency Rules 1986. Rule 4.30(3) provides that, without prejudice to any order the court may make as to costs, the provisional liquidator's remuneration (whether he is the official receiver or some other person), and the amount of any expenses incurred by him (including the remuneration and expenses of any special manager appointed under s. 177 of the Insolvency Act 1986), will be paid and reimbursed as follows:

(1) if a winding-up order is not made (i.e. if the winding-up petition is dismissed), it will be paid/reimbursed out of the property of the company;
(2) if a winding-up order is made, it will be paid/reimbursed out of the assets of the company in the prescribed order of priority[327]; and
(3) if, in either of the above cases, the assets of the company are insufficient to pay/reimburse the remuneration and expenses of the provisional liquidator and special manager, their remuneration and expenses will be paid/reimbursed out of any sum deposited under r. 4.27 as security for the official receiver's remuneration and expenses as provisional liquidator.[328]

9.88 Costs on dismissal of the winding-up petition

It does not follow automatically from the dismissal of the winding-up petition that the unsuccessful petitioner should be ordered to pay the costs of the provisional liquidator and

325. IR 1986, r. 4.30(1).
326. I.e., under the Insolvency Regulations 1994 (S.I. 1994 No. 2507).
327. I.e., according to the order of priority set out in IR 1986, r. 4.218(1).
328. IR 1986, r. 4.30(3).

the special manager, although such an order will often be made on dismissal.[329] It has been suggested that, having regard to r. 4.30(3), the ordinary order on the dismissal of a winding-up petition should be that the costs of the provisional liquidator and special manager are paid out of the property of the company, and that although the court retains a discretion to make whatever order it thinks fit in respect of costs, the court should depart from that rule and order the unsuccessful petitioner to pay those costs only where it is convinced that it ought to do so.[330] However, that suggestion was made in the context of a public interest winding-up petition presented by the Secretary of State at a time when it was the practice of some courts not to make orders for costs against the Secretary of State when litigating in the public interest. That practice has now been rejected by the Court of Appeal,[331] and the court may now be more willing to order an unsuccessful petitioner to reimburse the company for the amount of any money or property retained by the provisional liquidator or special manager in satisfaction of his costs and remuneration. Alternatively, the court may order that the remuneration and expenses of the provisional liquidator and special manager on the dismissal of the winding-up petition should be paid directly by the petitioner and should not be retained out of the company's assets: such an order may be appropriate, for example, where the court concludes that it was inappropriate for the application for the appointment of the provisional liquidator to have been made *ex parte*.[332]

APPLICATION FOR THE APPOINTMENT OF A SPECIAL MANAGER

9.89 Jurisdiction

Prior to the coming into force of the Insolvency Act 1986, the court had power to order the appointment of a special manager only in a compulsory winding-up where the liquidator or provisional liquidator was the official receiver.[333] Under the Insolvency Act 1986, the court now has a discretionary power to appoint a person to be a special manager of the business or property of a company at any time after the appointment of a liquidator or provisional liquidator to the company[334]—i.e. whether the person appointed as liquidator or provisional liquidator is the official receiver or a licensed insolvency practitioner. Thus, in a compulsory liquidation, a special manager may be appointed after the making of the winding-up order, or before the making of the winding-up order if a provisional liquidator has been appointed; but in a voluntary liquidation, a special manager may only be appointed once the liquidator has been appointed. Two or more persons may be appointed as joint special managers.[335] The application for the appointment of a special manager may be made by the liquidator or provisional liquidator of a company where it

329. See, for example, *Re European Banking Co., ex parte Baylis* (1866) LR 2 Eq. 521 at 524.

330. *Re Walter L Jacob & Co. Ltd* (1987) 3 BCC 532 at 534 (r/h col) per Harman J.; reversed on appeal on another point: (1989) 5 BCC 244.

331. See *Re Southbourne Sheet Metal Co. Ltd (No. 2)* [1993] BCLC 135.

332. See the order made in *Re Secure & Provide plc* [1992] BCC 405 at 415B.

333. See CA 1985, s. 556(1) (now repealed).

334. IA 1986, s. 177(1). The relevant rules governing the appointment of a special manager are IR 1986, rr. 4.206–4.210.

335. As in *Re WF Fearman Ltd (No. 2)* (1988) 4 BCC 141. Although the Act makes no reference to the appointment of more than one special manager (contrast s. 231(1)), the reference to "any person" in s. 177(1) should be construed as including the plural: Interpretation Act 1978, s. 6(c).

appears to him that the nature of the business or property of the company, or the interests of the company's creditors or contributories or members generally, require the appointment of another person to manage the company's business or property.[336] Section 177 enables the court to appoint a specially skilled person to manage a business where such management requires particular skills which the liquidator does not possess.[337] Common grounds for the appointment of a special manager are that a provisional liquidator proposes to continue a business pending the final hearing of the winding-up petition, or a liquidator proposes to continue a business with a view to its disposal or proposes to realise its assets,[338] and the business and/or its assets are unusual or complex, or special commercial expertise is required. Examples of businesses in respect of which a special manager has been appointed are dealers in strategic metal commodities,[339] an ostrich farm[340] and an importer of clothing.[341]

9.90 Qualification of the special manager

Although a special manager may in certain cases be qualified to act as an insolvency practitioner,[342] there is no requirement that he should be so qualified. The court may appoint "any person" as special manager.[343] In most cases the special manager will be appointed because of his particular skill and experience in relation to the company's business and/or assets which the liquidator or provisional liquidator lacks, and his ability to assist the liquidator or provisional liquidator in managing the business or in realising the assets. The report of the liquidator or provisional liquidator filed in support of the application for the appointment of a special manager should explain the nature of the company's business and assets, the proposed functions of the special manager and his particular skills and expertise which render him a suitable appointee.

9.91 Form of application

The application for the appointment of a special manager is by ordinary application, supported by a report setting out the grounds relied upon by the applicant, and is returnable before the Companies Court Register in Chambers in the first instance.[344] The applicant will be the liquidator or provisional liquidator who seeks the assistance of a special manager. Where the liquidator is the applicant, the application should be made *ex parte*; where a provisional liquidator is the applicant, the company should usually be

336. IA 1986, s. 177(2).
337. *Re North Wales Gunpowder Co.* [1892] 2 QB 220 at 224.
338. As in *Re US Ltd* (1984) 1 BCC 98, 985.
339. *Re Highfield Commodities Ltd* [1985] 1 WLR 149.
340. *Re Pinstripe Farming Co. Ltd* [1996] BCC 913.
341. *Re US Ltd, supra.*
342. See *Re WF Fearman Ltd (No. 2)* (1988) 4 BCC 141 where the court appointed the former provisional liquidators as special managers to assist the Official Receiver as liquidator, pending the appointment of liquidators by a creditors' meeting.
343. IA 1986, s. 177(1).
344. IR 1986, r. 7.6(1) and (2).

joined as the respondent,[345] unless the provisional liquidator's need for the assistance of a special manager is so urgent that an *inter partes* hearing is impractical[346]: if the special manager is appointed on an *ex parte* application, the court may limit the appointment to a short period of time or may specify that the duration of the appointment is to be subject to a further order of the court,[347] in order to give the company an opportunity to argue at an *inter partes* hearing that the appointment should be set aside. In cases of exceptional urgency, a provisional liquidator may apply for the appointment of a special manager immediately following his appointment as provisional liquidator, giving an undertaking to the court to file a report setting out the grounds for the appointment of the special manager as explained to the court. Where the application for the appointment of a special manager is made *ex parte*, two copies of the application will be required on issue; where the company is joined as a respondent, three copies will be required.[348]

9.92 Report and service

The application for the appointment of a special manager must be supported by a report to the court made by the applicant liquidator or provisional liquidator setting out the reasons for the application,[349] which should be filed in court. The report should explain the nature of the company's business and assets and the reasons why the applicant liquidator or provisional liquidator requires the assistance of a special manager: this will usually require an explanation of how the liquidator or provisional liquidator proposes to deal with the business or assets of the company and the functions which he proposes to delegate to the special manager. Any special powers sought for the special manager should be justified in the report.[350] The report should identify the proposed appointee, and describe his particular skills, experience and expertise which render him an appropriate person to be appointed as the special manager. The written consent of the proposed appointee to act as special manager should be annexed to the report. The report must state the applicant's estimate of the value of the company's assets in respect of which the special manager is to be appointed.[351] Where the application is made by a provisional liquidator *inter partes*, a copy of the ordinary application and the report should be served on the respondent company by leaving them at, or sending them by post to, the company's registered office[352] at least 14 days before the date fixed for the hearing.[353]

345. Despite the appointment of a provisional liquidator, the board of directors of a company retains a residuary power (*inter alia*) to oppose the winding-up petition and to make interlocutory applications, including (*semble*) an application to discharge the appointment of a special manager (*Re Union Accident Insurance Co. Ltd* [1972] 1 WLR 640 at 642B), and to incur liabilities for the Company in so doing: see *Legal Protection Group Ltd* v. *Secretary of State for Trade and Industry*, New Law Digest, 1 March 1996, Rimer J.

346. But note the comments of Hoffmann J. in *Re First Express Ltd* [1991] BCC 782 at 785D–G and *Re Secure & Provide plc* [1992] BCC 405 at 414H–415B about the undesirability of making applications *ex parte* where not absolutely essential.

347. See IR 1986, rr. 4.206(3) and 7.4(6).

348. IR 1986, r. 7.4(1).

349. IR 1986, r. 4.206(1). As to the use of reports generally, see IR 1986, r. 7.9.

350. See IA 1986, s. 177(3) and (4).

351. IR 1986, r. 4.206(1).

352. CA 1985, s. 725(1).

353. IR 1986, r. 7.4(5).

9.93 The hearing

The hearing in the first instance will be before the Companies Court Registrar sitting in Chambers.[354] Where an *inter partes* application by a provisional liquidator for the appointment of a special manager is opposed, or will take some time to determine owing to its complexity, the registrar may adjourn the application to the Companies Court Judge for determination,[355] giving such directions as he thinks appropriate. Where the application is extremely urgent and a prompt hearing before the registrar cannot be obtained, the application may be made directly to the Companies Court Judge.[356]

9.94 The order, and powers of the special manager

The special manager enjoys only such powers as the court entrusts to him by its order.[357] Once appointed, the special manager is an officer of the court[358] and is subject to the control of the court. When fixing the powers of the special manager, the court may direct that any provision of the Insolvency Act 1986 which applies to a liquidator or provisional liquidator should equally apply to the special manager for the purposes of the special manager carrying out any of the functions of the liquidator or provisional liquidator.[359] Thus, the court may grant the special manager certain of the powers of a liquidator set out in sch. 1 to the Insolvency Act 1986, and may require him to obtain appropriate sanction before exercising certain powers.[360] The applicant's report should set out those powers which are sought for the special manager, and the applicant and special manager should carefully check the order as drawn up by the court to ensure that it accurately records the special manager's powers. Where two or more persons are appointed as joint special managers, the order appointing them should state whether their powers may be exercised only jointly or whether they may be exercised individually.[361] Any error in the order should be corrected under the "slip rule"[362] or clarified by a further application to the court. The order should also specify the duration of the special manager's appointment, in one of three ways: the order may appoint him for a fixed period of time, or may appoint him until the occurrence of a specified event (for example, the conclusion of the first meeting of creditors, or the final disposal of the winding-up petition where the applicant is the provisional liquidator), or may state that the duration of the appointment is to be subject to a further order of the court.[363] The court may renew the appointment of the special manager from time to time,[364] but any order renewing the appointment should similarly state the duration of the renewed appointment. The order appointing a special

354. IR 1986, r. 7.6(1) and (2).
355. IR 1986, r. 7.6(3).
356. IR 1986, r. 7.6(4).
357. IA 1986, s. 177(3). For the form of the order, see IR 1986, sch. 4, part 4 (as amended), Form 4.60.
358. See *Re Walter L Jacob & Co. Ltd* (1989) 5 BCC 244 at 255A.
359. IA 1986, s. 177(4).
360. For example, the sanction required by IA 1986, ss. 165(2) or 167(1).
361. By analogy with IA 1986, s. 231(2) (which does not apply expressly to special managers).
362. I.e., under RSC O. 20, r. 11.
363. IR 1986, r. 4.206(3).
364. IR 1986, r. 4.206(4).

manager will also usually require the special manager to provide security for his appointment within a stipulated period,[365] and may fix his remuneration,[366] although in practice it will often be more convenient for the special manager's remuneration to be fixed at a later date by the Companies Court Registrar in Chambers once the extent of his duties have become clearer: in many cases, his remuneration is not fixed until he has completed his duties.[367] Evidence may be required, giving details of the work undertaken by the special manager before the court will fix his remuneration.[368]

9.95 Security

The appointment of a special manager is not effective until the appointee gives security to the person who applied for his appointment (i.e. the liquidator or provisional liquidator), although the court may permit the appointee to give an undertaking to provide security[369] (for example, in cases where the need for the appointment is urgent). The security may be given by the appointee specially for a particular liquidation, or may be given by the appointee generally for any liquidation in respect of which he might be appointed as a special manager.[370] The amount of the security provided must be not less than the value of assets in respect of which he is appointed, as estimated by the applicant liquidator or provisional liquidator in his report filed in support of the application.[371] Once the special manager has provided security to the applicant, the applicant must file in court a certificate stating that the security is adequate.[372] The cost of providing the security must in the first instance be paid by the special manager, but the special manager will be reimbursed that cost according to the type of liquidation[373]: where a winding-up petition has been presented but a winding-up order is not ultimately made, the special manager is entitled to reimbursement of the cost of providing security out of the property of the company, and the court may make an order requiring the company to pay those costs or permitting the special manager to retain monies to cover his costs[374]; where a winding-up order is made on the petition[375] or where the liquidation is voluntary,[376] the costs of providing security are payable out of the assets of the company in liquidation in the prescribed order of priority.[377] The above rules determine how the special manager recoups his costs of providing security, but do not prevent the court from ordering any party to the proceedings to bear the ultimate liability for those costs: where the court dismisses a winding-up petition and the special manager recovers his costs of providing security out of the property of the company,[378] the court may order the petitioning creditor to reimburse the company for the amount of those costs.

365. See IA 1986, s. 177(5) and IR 1986, r. 4.207.
366. See IR 1986, r. 4.206(5).
367. As in *Re US Ltd* (1984) 1 BCC 98, 985.
368. *Ibid.*
369. IA 1986, s. 177(5)(a) and IR 1986, r. 4.207(1).
370. IR 1986, r. 4.207(2).
371. IR 1986, rr. 4.206(1) and 4.207(3).
372. IR 1986, r. 4.207(4).
373. IR 1986, r. 4.207(5) and (6).
374. IR 1986, r. 4.207(5)(a).
375. IR 1986, r. 4.207(5)(b).
376. IR 1986, r. 4.207(6).
377. For the prescribed order of priority, see IR 1986, r. 4.218(1) (especially sub-para. (e)).
378. I.e., pursuant to IR 1986, r. 4.207(5)(a).

9.96 Failure to give or maintain security

If the special manager fails to give security in the amount and within the period required by the order appointing him, or within any extension of time granted by the court, the liquidator or provisional liquidator who applied for his appointment must report the special manager's failure to the court: the court may then discharge the order appointing the special manager.[379] The liquidator or provisional liquidator must similarly report to the court any failure by the special manager to maintain his security during the currency of his appointment: the court may then remove the special manager and make such order as it thinks fit as to costs.[380] In each case, the report by the liquidator or provisional liquidator should be in writing filed in court, and should describe the order made for security and the special manager's non-compliance with the order. If the court makes an order discharging the appointment of a special manager or removes him for a failure to provide or maintain his security, the court will give directions as to the steps (if any) to be taken for the appointment of a new special manager in his place.[381]

9.97 Termination of appointment

The appointment of the special manager will terminate on the expiry of the duration of the appointment stated in the order appointing him, unless renewed by order of the court.[382] In a compulsory winding-up, the special manager's appointment also terminates if the winding-up petition is dismissed or, where a provisional liquidator has been appointed, the provisional liquidator is discharged without a winding-up order having been made.[383] If the liquidator in a compulsory or voluntary winding-up, or the provisional liquidator, is of the opinion that the employment of the special manager is no longer necessary or profitable for the company, he must apply to the court for directions: the court may then order the appointment of the special manager to be terminated.[384] The liquidator or provisional liquidator must also apply to the court for directions if the company's creditors pass a resolution requesting the termination of the appointment of the special manager.[385] In each of the above cases the application is made by ordinary application returnable before the Companies Court Registrar sitting in chambers, and should be supported by a report from the liquidator or provisional liquidator setting out the facts giving rise to the possibility of termination of the appointment. The special manager should be served with the application and report, and should be given the opportunity to make representations at the hearing at which the termination of his appointment is under consideration. Where a provisional liquidator has been appointed but a winding-up order has not yet been made, copies of the application and report should also be sent to the petitioner. If the company seeks the discharge of the appointment of the special manager prior to the making of a winding-up order,[386] it should do so by ordinary application supported by an affidavit

379. IR 1986, r. 4.208(1).
380. IR 1986, r. 4.208(2).
381. IR 1986, r. 4.208(3).
382. See IR 1986, r. 4.206(3).
383. IR 1986, r. 4.210(1).
384. IR 1986, rr. 4.206(2) and 4.210(2).
385. IR 1986, rr. 4.206(2) and 4.210(3).
386. I.e., under the residuary powers of the board of directors: see *Re Union Accident Insurance Co. Ltd* [1972] 1 WLR 640 at 642B.

setting out the grounds relied upon for the termination of the appointment. The special manager and liquidator or provisional liquidator who applied for his appointment should be joined as respondents to the application. Notice of the application should also be given to the petitioner.

9.98 Costs of the special manager

The Insolvency Rules 1986 contain specific provisions governing the incidence of the special manager's costs of providing security,[387] discussed above. Different provisions govern his costs generally. Where the special manager is appointed on the application of a liquidator, the special manager's remuneration is payable as an expense of the liquidation according to the prescribed order of priority.[388] Where the special manager is appointed on the application of a provisional liquidator, the special manager's remuneration and expenses are reimbursed in the same way as the provisional liquidator's remuneration and expenses.[389]

THE HEARING OF THE PETITION

9.99 Venue

In London, winding-up petitions are listed for hearing in the first instance before the Companies Court Registrar sitting in open court[390] on each Wednesday during term-time (or on alternate Wednesdays when there is a fall in the number of petitions awaiting hearing). Outside London, petitions are heard in the first instance by the district judge. Where the petition debt is disputed by the company or where there are opposing creditors, the registrar will not himself determine the petition: the registrar will give directions for the filing of evidence, and once the evidence is complete, will adjourn the petition to the Companies Court Judge sitting in open court for determination.[391]

9.100 Rights of audience and representation

Solicitors, properly robed,[392] and counsel have rights of audience before the registrar. Where the petitioner (or a supporting or opposing creditor) is an individual, he or she may appear in person.[393] Where the petitioner (or supporting or opposing creditor) is a company, it must be represented by a solicitor or counsel, and may not appear by a director[394]: although the court has a discretion, under its inherent power to regulate its own proceedings, to permit a director of a company to appear as an advocate on its behalf, it

387. See IR 1986, r. 4.207(5) and (6). See para. 9.95, *supra*.
388. I.e., according to IR 1986, r. 4.218(1) (see in particular sub-para. (j)).
389. As to the remuneration of a provisional liquidator, see para. 9.87, *supra*.
390. Practice Direction (No. 3 of 1986) [1987] 1 WLR 53 at 54 (paras 2 and 3) (a copy of which is in Appendix 3, *infra*).
391. Practice Direction (No. 2 of 1986) [1986] 1 WLR 1428.
392. *Ibid.*
393. See RSC O. 5, r. 6(1).
394. RSC O. 5, r. 6(2). The Woolf Report on "*Access to Justice*" proposes that companies should no longer be required to appear only through solicitors (Recommendation 152).

should only do so in exceptional circumstances.[395] Where the company subject to the petition is represented at the first hearing by a director, the registrar may as a matter of discretion allow the director to make representations, but the director has no right to do so[396]: if the director indicates that the debt is disputed, the registrar will usually adjourn the petition for a short period (say, seven days) to enable the company to instruct a solicitor, and counsel if so advised, and may at the same time direct that evidence in opposition to the petition be filed and served prior to the adjourned hearing. If the director merely requests further time in which to pay an undisputed petition debt, the registrar may hear representations from the director why an adjournment is required (although he is not obliged to do so): in that event, the director should explain why the debt has not yet been paid, when it will be paid and indicate the source and certainty of any anticipated funds; the registrar will then hear representations from the petitioner and any supporting creditor why a winding-up order should be made immediately, which should include details of the age of the debt and any previous broken promises of payment. Only in exceptional cases will the registrar grant an adjournment requested by the company to give further time for payment, because a petitioner who has an undisputed debt and who has complied with the relevant rules, as between himself and the company is entitled to a winding-up order as of right.[397] Where, prior to the hearing of the petition, a provisional liquidator or special manager has been appointed to the company, the court should admit in evidence on the hearing of the petition any report prepared by the provisional liquidator or special manager (particularly where the petition is based on "public interest" grounds under s. 124A of the Insolvency Act 1986) and should permit the provisional liquidator or special manager to appear by counsel and make representations.[398] A person who is interested in the property of the company but is not a creditor or contributory of the company, may be permitted to appear at the hearing of the petition, in the court's discretion; but such a person has no right to be heard on the petition and does not have *locus standi* to appeal against a winding-up order.[399]

9.101 Right to a winding-up order

A petitioner whose debt is undisputed and who has complied with the procedural requirements of the Insolvency Rules 1986 as between himself and the company is entitled *ex debito justitiae* to a winding-up order.[400] The petitioner cannot be required to give the

395. See *Supreme Court Practice 1997*, Vol. 1, para 5/6/2, p. 31. Where a director is permitted to represent a company, the costs of his time will not be recoverable, nor will the company be able to recover costs as a litigant in person: *Jonathan Alexander Ltd* v. *Proctor* [1996] 1 WLR 518.

396. See *Radford* v. *Freeway Classics Ltd* [1994] 1 BCLC 445 and *Arbuthnot Leasing International Ltd* v. *Havelet Leasing Ltd* [1990] BCLC 802 at 811. The company's failure to instruct a solicitor is not the sort of irregularity which the court should waive: *Re a Company (No. 001029 of 1990), ex parte F Ltd* [1991] BCLC 567 at 568.

397. See *Re London Suburban Bank* (1871) 6 Ch. App. 641 at 643.

398. See *Re Walter L Jacob & Co. Ltd* (1989) 5 BCC 245 at 254F–255A.

399. *Re Bradford Navigation Company* (1870) LR 5 Ch.App.Cas. 600 at 603 per James LJ.

400. *Re London Suburban Bank* (1871) 6 Ch. App. 641 at 643; *Re Western of Canada Oil, Lands and Works Co.* (1873) LR 17 Eq. 1 at 7; *Re Krasnapolsky Restaurant and Winter Garden Co.* [1892] 3 Ch. 174 at 177; *Re Crigglestone Coal Co. Ltd* [1906] 2 Ch. 327 at 330–331, 337; *Re Globe Trust* [1915] WN 221. See also *Bowes* v. *Hope Life Insurance and Guarantee Co.* (1865) 11 HL Cas. 389 at 402; *Re General Company for the Promotion of Land Credit* (1870) 5 Ch. App. 363 at 380–381; *Re Camburn Petroleum Products Ltd* [1980] 1 WLR 86 at 93F–94E.

company further time for payment.[401] A creditor who has agreed to accept deferred payment or payment by instalments of a due debt may nevertheless be able to petition in respect of the entire debt if the agreement is not supported by consideration moving to the creditor.[402] The petitioner remains entitled (as between himself and the company) *ex debito justitiae* to a winding-up order, even where the company has gone into voluntary liquidation, if the petition debt remains unpaid.[403] The court may make a winding-up order where the company does not have any realisable assets if its creditors might benefit in some way from a winding-up, such as by an investigation into the affairs of the company[404]; and the court may make a compulsory winding-up order to facilitate an independent investigation into the company, notwithstanding that the company is at an advanced stage of a voluntary liquidation, if there are grounds for concluding that such an investigation is required or for doubting the independence of the voluntary liquidator.[405]

9.102 Opposition by other creditors

The right of a petitioner to a winding-up order where the debt is undisputed and the procedural requirements have been complied with is a class right to be exercised by the petitioner on behalf of the general body of creditors of the company.[406] It follows that the court will have regard to the wishes of the majority of creditors.[407] Where the majority in value of creditors appear on the hearing of the petition and oppose a winding-up order, the court may in its discretion[408] dismiss the petition,[409] but it is not bound to do so.[410] The Court of Appeal will be slow to interfere with the exercise of the unfettered discretion of the Companies Court Judge, and will only overturn a decision whether or not to grant a compulsory winding-up order if the decision was wrong in principle or if the judge left any relevant matter out of account.[411] Where opposing creditors wish to appear at the hearing of the petition, they should file affidavit evidence at least seven days prior to the hearing,[412] setting out the grounds for their opposition.[413] The petitioner (and any supporting creditor who wishes to do so) should file affidavit evidence in answer, showing why a compulsory winding-up order should be made. The role of the court is then to carry out a balancing exercise, between those matters which constitute the reasons why the company should be wound up compulsorily, and those which constitute reasons why it should

401. See *Re Home Assurance Association (No. 2)* (1871) LR 12 Eq. 112 at 114.
402. See *Re Selectmove Ltd* [1994] BCC 349 at 354D–F.
403. IA 1986, s. 116; *Re James Millward & Co.* [1940] Ch. 333 at 334.
404. *Bell Group Finance (Pty) Ltd (in liquidation)* v. *Bell Group (UK) Holdings Ltd* [1996] 1 BCLC 304; *Re Crigglestone Coal Co. Ltd, supra*, at 332.
405. *Re Gordon & Breach Science Publishers Ltd* [1995] BCC 261 at 269C–270A.
406. *Re Leigh Estates (UK) Ltd* [1994] BCC 292 at 294F; *Re Crigglestone Coal Co. Ltd, supra*, at 331–332; *Re Lines Bros Ltd* [1983] Ch. 1 at 20E.
407. *Re Crigglestone Coal Co. Ltd, supra*, at 332; *Re Home Remedies Ltd* [1943] Ch. 1 at 2.
408. See IA 1986, s. 125(1).
409. *Re Krasnapolsky Restaurant and Winter Garden Co.* [1892] 3 Ch. 174 at 177; *Re Home Remedies Ltd, supra*, at 2–3; *Re Southard & Co. Ltd* [1979] 1 WLR 546; affirmed on appeal [1979] 1 WLR 1198; *Re Medisco Equipment Ltd* (1983) 1 BCC 98, 944 at 98, 948.
410. See, for example, *Re Hewitt Brannan (Tools) Co. Ltd* [1990] BCC 354 at 360F–G; and see *Re Southard & Co. Ltd, supra*, at 1208C–D.
411. *Re Southard & Co. Ltd, supra*, at 1203H and 1207B–D.
412. IR 1986, r. 4.18 (although in practice the seven-day rule is often breached—see para. 9.66, *supra*).
413. *Re Television Parlour plc* (1988) 4 BCC 95 at 99 (l/h col); *Re JD Swain Ltd* [1965] 1 WLR 909 at 913.

not, giving such weight to each factor as it thinks fit.[414] In assessing whether a winding-up order should be made, the court will give less weight to the views of opposing creditors who are also directors or contributories of the company subject of the petition and who might accordingly have reasons for wishing a particular course which are distinct from the considerations which are common to the general body of creditors.[415] The court will not have regard to the opposition of a secured creditor if its purpose in opposing the winding-up petition is to prevent a liquidator challenging its security.[416] Where it appears that a secured creditor has a shortfall as regards its security, the court may treat that creditor as falling within the class of unsecured creditors to the extent of the shortfall.[417]

9.103 Company in voluntary liquidation

Where the company is in voluntary liquidation, the court has an unfettered discretion whether to make a winding-up order or to dismiss the petition.[418] In deciding whether a compulsory liquidation should supersede a voluntary liquidation, considerable weight is given to the views of the majority in value of the independent creditors.[419] Where the majority in value of creditors wish the voluntary liquidation to continue, the court will usually dismiss the petition unless the petitioner can establish a good reason why the voluntary winding-up should not continue[420]: for example, where the evidence filed by the petitioner shows that the directors of a company who are also creditors have procured the appointment of a sympathetic liquidator who refuses properly to investigate their conduct as directors, the court is likely to make a compulsory winding-up order. A voluntary liquidator is entitled to, and perhaps should, appear on the hearing of the petition represented by a solicitor or counsel to assist the court, to report on the progress of the liquidation and of his investigations, and to answer any allegations of misconduct made against him.[421] The voluntary liquidator must not, however, assert a view as to whether or not a compulsory winding-up order should be made but should remain neutral in that respect.[422] Where a compulsory winding-up order is opposed by creditors who are not a majority in value of the creditors, on the grounds that a voluntary winding-up would be more desirable but has not yet commenced, an adjournment of the petition may result in other creditors (in the majority) voting against a voluntary liquidation, in which case the liquidation will have been unnecessarily delayed; in those circumstances, the court may refuse an adjournment for the necessary meetings to be convened and may order a compulsory winding-up.[423] If a licensed insolvency practitioner has been appointed and a

414. *Re Walter L Jacob & Co. Ltd* (1989) 5 BCC 244 at 250C–D (a "public interest" petition by the Secretary of State under IA 1986, s. 124A).

415. *Re Medisco Equipment Ltd* (1983) 1 BCC 98, 944 at 98, 947; *Re Southard & Co. Ltd, supra*, at 1205C–E; *Re Camburn Petroleum Products Ltd, supra*, at 93H–94A.

416. *Bell Group Finance (Pty) Ltd (in liquidation)* v. *Bell Group (UK) Holdings Ltd, supra.*

417. *Re Leigh Estates (UK) Ltd, supra*, at 295A.

418. *Re Southard & Co. Ltd, supra*, at 1208C–E.

419. *Re William Thorpe & Son Ltd* (1989) 5 BCC 156; *Re Falcon RJ Developments Ltd* [1987] BCLC 437 at 442; *Re HJ Tomkins & Son Ltd* [1990] BCLC 76 at 78C; and see IA 1986, s. 195.

420. *Re JD Swain Ltd* [1965] 1 WLR 909 at 915C–D; *Re Homes Remedies Ltd, supra*, at 2; *Re Medisco Equipment Ltd, supra*, at 98, 948; *Re Hewitt Brannan (Tools) Ltd, supra*, at 360A–C; *Re Falcon RJ Developments Ltd, supra*, at 442a–b; *Re MCH Services Ltd* (1987) 3 BCC 179 at 182.

421. *Re Medisco Equipment Ltd, supra*, at 98, 947 (l/h col).

422. *Ibid.; Re Hewitt Brannan (Tools) Ltd, supra*, at 360H–361A.

423. *Re Television Parlour plc, supra*, at 99 (r/h col).

meeting of creditors convened to consider proposals for a voluntary arrangement, the court may be asked to adjourn the petition to the next available date after the proposed meeting of creditors.

9.104 Adjournments of the petition

The court has an inherent power to adjourn the hearing of any matter before it, to do justice between the parties.[424] It has long been recognised that it is inappropriate for a winding-up petition to be outstanding for a long period of time, since a winding-up order relates back to the date of presentation of the petition,[425] with the result that when a liquidator is appointed he may have to investigate a large number of post-presentation transactions to assess whether they should be set aside.[426] The court will not therefore usually permit lengthy adjournments of winding-up petitions, even where the petitioner and the company agree to a lengthy adjournment, for example, for payments to be made by instalments.[427] The court may permit a petition to be adjourned for a short period to comply with any outstanding procedural requirements—for example, to enable the petition to be advertised, or be re-advertised where the first advertisement is defective.[428] An adjournment may also be granted where proposals for a voluntary arrangement or some other form of reconstruction are being formulated.[429]

9.105 Short adjournments for settlement/*Tomlin* orders

The registrar is often prepared to grant a short adjournment for the petition debt to be paid if the petitioner consents to the adjournment; and the registrar may be prepared to grant more than one adjournment for that purpose (although any supporting creditor would be entitled to seek to be substituted as petitioner[430] if the original petitioner does not seek a winding-up order when the petition is called on for hearing). However, where the petition debt is to be repaid by instalments over a long period of time, the court is unlikely to agree to repeated adjournments—the petitioner will then have to elect whether to seek the usual compulsory order (in which case any sums paid to him by the company after the presentation of the petition would be recoverable by the liquidator),[431] or dismiss the petition (in which case, the creditor would have to petition again if the company does not adhere to the agreed payment schedule). Similarly, the court will not permit a winding-up petition to be compromised on the basis of a *Tomlin* order—i.e. an order staying all further proceedings on the petition except for the purpose of carrying into effect the terms agreed between the parties—because if a winding-up order were subsequently to be made, the commencement of the liquidation would relate back to the date of presentation of the

424. See *Hinckley and South Leicestershire PBS* v. *Freeman* [1941] Ch. 32, and *Supreme Court Practice 1997*, Vol. 1, para. 35/3/1, p. 617.
425. IA 1986, s. 129(2).
426. Under IA 1986, s. 127.
427. Practice Note (Companies: winding-up) [1977] 1 WLR 1066.
428. But see Practice Direction (Companies Court: winding-up) [1996] 1 WLR 1255.
429. See, for example, *Re Bank of Credit and Commerce International SA* [1992] BCC 83 (a "public interest" winding-up petition under IA 1986, s. 124A).
430. Under IR 1986, r. 4.19.
431. Under IA 1986, s. 127.

petition.[432] The court will adjourn the petition on the application of a contributory only in exceptional circumstances, since a creditor whose debt is not disputed is *prima facie* entitled to a winding-up order.[433] Where the petition debt is not disputed, and the registrar refuses an application for an adjournment and makes a winding-up order, on appeal the Companies Court Judge will not interfere with the registrar's exercise of discretion unless there are grounds for holding that the registrar misdirected himself.[434]

9.106 Concurrent petitions for winding-up and for an administration order

Where a company which is the subject of a winding-up petition or its directors or one of its creditors presents a petition for an administration order[435] which has not been adjudicated upon by the hearing of the winding-up petition, the court cannot make a winding-up order.[436] The winding-up petition will be adjourned, often to come on for hearing immediately following the hearing of the administration petition: if the administration petition is then dismissed, the court will usually make a winding-up order; if an administration order is made, the winding-up petition must be dismissed. If the directors of a company which is the subject of a winding-up petition cause an administration petition to be presented without good reason in order to secure an adjournment of the winding-up petition, they would be guilty of an abuse of process[437] and could be made personally liable for costs, whether the administration petition is in the name of the company or its directors.[438] Where the administration petition is not an abuse of process but is unsuccessful, the court has a discretion whether to order that the costs of the administration petition be costs in the winding-up[439] or to make no order for costs which will then be borne by the directors.[440] Where an administration petition has been presented in respect of a company, a creditor may nevertheless present a winding-up petition pending the hearing of the administration petition, but the creditor should take no further steps to progress his petition (such as advertisement).[441] The court may restrain advertisement of a winding-up petition where an administration petition has been presented but not yet heard[442] or where the company gives an undertaking to present an administration petition forthwith,[443] but not where an administration petition is merely contemplated and no undertaking to present a petition forthwith is given.[444]

432. Practice Note: Re a Company (No. 003324 of 1979) [1981] 1 WLR 1059 at 1060C.
433. *Re Camburn Petroleum Products Ltd*, *supra*, at 93H–94A.
434. See *Re Dollar Land (Feltham) Ltd* [1995] BCC 740 at 745H–746C.
435. Under IA 1986, s. 9.
436. IA 1986, s. 10(1)(a). Where the administration petition has not yet been presented but the proposed petitioner undertakes to present it forthwith, the court may restrain advertisement of the winding-up petition pending the hearing of the administration petition: *Re a Company (No. 001448 of 1989)* [1989] BCLC 715 and *Re a Company (No. 001992 of 1989)* [1989] BCLC 9.
437. Compare *Re Pinstripe Farming Co. Ltd* [1996] BCC 913 at 916E.
438. Such orders are exceptional, and applications for such orders must be treated with considerable caution: see *Re Land & Property Trust Co. plc (No. 4)* [1994] 1 BCLC 232 and *Re Tajik Air Ltd* [1996] 1 BCLC 317 at 324f–h.
439. As in *Re Gosscott (Groundworks) Ltd* (1988) 4 BCC 372 at 375–376.
440. As in *Re WF Fearman Ltd* (1988) 4 BCC 141 at 143 (r/h col).
441. *Re a Company (No. 001992 of 1988)* [1989] BCLC 9 at 11f–h.
442. *Re a Company (No. 001992 of 1988)*, *supra*, at 11h.
443. *Re a Company (No. 001448 of 1989)* [1989] BCLC 715.
444. *Re Manlon Trading Ltd* (1988) 4 BCC 455 at 456 (l/h col).

9.107 The usual compulsory order

An order of the court winding-up a company is known as the "usual compulsory order" and should follow Form 4.11 with such variations, if any, as the case may require.[445] The order should state that the company, referred to by its full name, "be wound up by this court under the provisions of the Insolvency Act 1986". The order will also state which parties' costs of appearing on the hearing of the petition are to be paid out of the assets of the company. The order will give notice that the official receiver attached to that court is by virtue of the order appointed the liquidator of the company.

9.108 Drawing up the order

The usual compulsory order is drafted in the chambers of the registrar, and one copy is sent to the person having carriage of the order (usually the petitioner's solicitors). The order is usually drafted without any reference to the parties' solicitors, and it is not necessary for any appointment to be made to settle the order, unless the case is unusually complicated.[446] The petitioner and every other person who has appeared on the hearing of the petition must lodge in court not later than the business day following the day on which the usual compulsory order is made, any documentation required to enable the order to be drawn[447]: this includes, for example, the amended petition where the usual compulsory order is made on the petitioner's undertaking to amend a minor inaccuracy in the petition. In the High Court the usual compulsory order is not sealed until eight days after the order is made, since the Insolvency Rules provide that an application to rescind the winding-up order may be made within seven days after the date on which the order was made.[448]

9.109 Notification of the usual compulsory order

When a usual compulsory order is made, the court forthwith notifies the official receiver of that fact.[449] When the order has been drafted and sealed, three sealed copies are sent by the court to the official receiver.[450] The official receiver will serve one copy on the company by posting to its registered office (or principal or last known principal business if there is no registered office),[451] and will send one copy to the registrar of companies.[452] The official receiver will also forthwith advertise the making of the order in the *London Gazette*.[453]

9.110 Orders dismissing the petition

An order dismissing a petition will generally not be drawn up at all, unless it includes a costs order (i.e. an order for taxation or payment of costs) or one of the parties requests

445. IR 1986, r. 12.7 and sch. 4, part 4 (as amended). This form is reproduced in Appendix 4, *infra*.
446. IR 1986, r. 4.20(3).
447. IR 1986, r. 4.20(2).
448. IR 1986, r. 7.47(4).
449. IR 1986, r. 4.20(1).
450. IR 1986, r. 4.21(1).
451. IR 1986, r. 4.21(2).
452. IA 1986, s. 130(1) and IR 1986, r. 4.21(3).
453. IR 1986, r. 4.21(4).

the order to be drawn.[454] Where the advertisement of a petition has caused a company's bank to "freeze" its bank account, the bank may require sight of a sealed order dismissing the petition before allowing the company to operate its account again.

COSTS

9.111 Discretionary

The incidence of costs is always a matter of discretion for the court.[455] The following paragraphs set out the usual practice of the Companies Court in relation to the costs of winding-up proceedings. It should be noted that these are not rigid rules and the court may depart from its usual practice in appropriate cases.

9.112 Costs before a winding-up order is made

The registrar does not generally hear argument about, or make orders in relation to, costs prior to the final disposal of the petition (for example, in relation to an adjournment of the petition). Where a petition is adjourned, the costs of the adjournment are usually reserved to be dealt with at the final hearing of the petition.

9.113 Costs where a winding-up order is made

The general practice[456] when the usual compulsory order is made is to award costs to the petitioner and the company, and to allow one set of costs to be shared amongst the contributories who appear on the petition to support it and one set to be shared amongst the supporting creditors, provided they have given notice of their intention to appear under r. 4.16[457] or have been given leave to appear out of time.[458] The costs are an expense of the liquidation[459] and are payable out of the assets of the company (if any) subject to the payment of other expenses which have priority under r. 4.218(1) of the Insolvency Rules 1986.

9.114 Costs on a dismissal of a petition by consent

Where a petition is dismissed by consent because the company pays the debt after presentation of the petition, the usual practice is for the court in its discretion to order the company to pay the petitioner's costs of the petition, even if the company does not appear at the hearing, as the petitioner is then regarded as having succeeded, in which case the

454. Practice Direction (Companies Court: Orders) [1984] 1 WLR 1046, para. 2.
455. RSC O. 62, r. 3(3).
456. See, for example, *Re William Thorpe & Son Ltd*, *supra*, at 159E; *Re European Banking Co., ex parte Baylis* (1866) LR 2 Eq. 521 at 523–524; *Re Anglo-Egyptian Navigation Co.* (1869) LR 8 Eq. 660 at 661; *Re Marlborough Club Co.* (1865) LR 1 Eq. 216; *Re Anglo-Greek Steam Co.* (1866) LR 2 Eq. 1 at 11; *Re Humber Ironworks Co.* (1866) LR 2 Eq. 15; *Re European Life Assurance Society* (1870) LR 10 Eq. 403; and see IR 1986, r. 4.218(1)(h).
457. See para. 9.63, *supra*.
458. See para. 9.64, *supra*.
459. IR 1986, r. 4.218(1)(h).

costs should follow the event.[460] The company will also usually be ordered to pay the petitioner's costs where the petition is dismissed following payment by the company of the undisputed part of the petition debt (which is not *de minimis*), the balance of which is disputed.[461] The onus is therefore on the company to place before the court any material on which it relies for contending that the usual practice as to the costs on dismissal of the petition after payment of the petition debt should not be followed: the material need not necessarily be formal affidavit evidence, but may be, for example, an undisputed letter from a director of the company.[462] However, the court will only make an order that the company pay the petitioner's costs where the petition debt has been paid, if all the procedural steps have been complied with or the company agrees to that order. Where the procedural steps have not been fully complied with (for example, the petition has not been advertised), the registrar will not usually make any order for costs against the company unless the company appears on the hearing of the petition and consents to the order being made, or agrees by letter to pay the petitioner's costs. If the petitioner is paid the petition debt but not his costs, the petition has not been advertised and the company will not agree to pay the petitioner's costs, the registrar will adjourn the petition to enable advertisement to take place; at the adjourned hearing an order for costs will then be made. The risk of an advertisement and consequent damage to the company's goodwill and business will generally be enough to persuade the company to agree to an order for costs. If the company subsequently fails to pay the petitioner's costs, the petitioner will have to present another petition based on the unpaid costs order.[463]

9.115 Dismissal not by consent

If the petition is contested by the company and is dismissed (for example, because the petition is disputed in good faith on substantial grounds),[464] the petitioner will usually be ordered to pay the company's costs (although in exceptional cases the petitioner may avoid liability for the company's costs—for example, if it can be shown that the company is in some way in default[465] or is to blame for the presentation of the petition).[466] The petitioner will usually also be ordered to pay one set of costs to be shared amongst the contributories, and one set to be shared amongst the creditors, who have given notice under r. 4.16 and appeared on the petition to oppose it.[467] Where it appears that the petition was presented by the petitioner to compel the company to pay a debt which was disputed, the court may show its disapproval of the abuse of process by ordering the petitioner to

460. *Re Nowmost Co. Ltd* [1996] BCLC 492 at 496d–e; *Re Flagstaff Silver Mining Co. of Utah* (1875) LR 10 Eq. 268.

461. *Re Pendigo Ltd* [1996] BCC 608 at 611F.

462. *Re Nowmost Co. Ltd, supra*, at 496f–497a.

463. A costs order may be the basis of a winding-up petition before the costs are taxed and the precise liability established: see *Tottenham Hotspur plc* v. *Edennote plc* [1994] BCC 681 at 684E–F and *Re Portedge Ltd* [1997] BCC 23 at 25E, H.

464. Disputed debts are considered in more detail below.

465. See *Re Newman and Howard Ltd* [1962] Ch. 257 (a case concerning a contibutory's winding-up petition).

466. *Re M. McCarthy & Co. (Builders) Ltd (No. 2)* [1976] 2 All ER 339. If the petition is based on a default judgment which is subsequently set aside, the company may be ordered to pay the petitioner's costs on dismissal of the petition: *Re Lanaghan Bros Ltd* [1977] 1 All ER 265.

467. *Re European Banking Co., ex parte Baylis* (1866) LR 2 Eq. 521 at 523–524.

pay the company's costs on the indemnity basis,[468] even where the question of the company's insolvency has not been investigated by the court.[469]

9.116 Dismissal at behest of opposing creditors

Where the petitioner is entitled to a winding-up order and the company is not already in voluntary liquidation, the court will make a winding-up order unless the opposing creditors establish good reason why the order should not be made.[470] If the opposing creditors succeed in showing such a good reason that the petition is dismissed, the court may make no order for costs. This is so whether the petitioner is a judgment creditor,[471] an ordinary trade creditor[472] or a contributory.[473] If, before presenting his petition, the petitioner was aware that the petition would be opposed by the majority of creditors (and was aware of their reasons), the court may regard the presentation of the petition as unreasonable and may order the petitioner to pay the costs of the company and one set of costs to the opposing creditors[474] who have given notice under r. 4.16.[475]

9.117 Dismissal where company is in voluntary liquidation

Where a company is in voluntary liquidation and the petition is opposed by the majority of its creditors, the petitioner must establish a good reason why the winding-up order should be made.[476] If the petitioner fails to establish any such reason, the court may regard the presentation of the petition as unreasonable, dismiss the petition and order the petitioner to pay the costs of the company and one set of costs to the opposing creditors[477] who have given notice under r. 4.16.[478]

9.118 Costs of unreasonable opposition to a petition

Where the company's opposition to a petition was found to be unreasonable and a winding-up order was made, it was formerly the practice of the court to order that the company's costs should not be paid out of its assets[479] or that the payment of the company's costs be deferred until all unsecured creditors had been paid in full.[480] The latter order became known as a "*Bathampton* order". The effect of a *Bathampton* order where the company was insolvent was that the company's solicitors did not receive their costs. Given the court's power to disallow costs as between the company and its solicitors

468. *Re a Company (No. 0012209 of 1991)* [1992] 1 WLR 351.
469. *Re a Company (No. 00751 of 1992), ex parte Avocet Aviation Ltd* [1992] BCLC 869 at 871d–g.
470. *Re P&J Macrae Ltd* [1961] 1 WLR 229. See para. 9.102, *supra*.
471. *Re RW Sharman Ltd* [1957] 1 WLR 774; *Re ABC Coupler and Engineering Co. Ltd* [1961] 1 WLR 243.
472. *Re Sklan Ltd* [1961] 1 WLR 1013.
473. *Re Great Northern Copper Mining Co.* (1866) 14 WR 705; *Re London Suburban Bank* (1872) LR 15 Eq. 274; *Re Tyneside Permanent Benefit Building Society* [1885] WN 148.
474. *Re AE Hayter & Sons (Portchester) Ltd* [1961] 1 WLR 1008.
475. See para. 9.63, *supra*.
476. See para. 9.103, *supra*.
477. *Re Riviera Pearls* [1962] 1 WLR 722; *Re AN Thermo Products Ltd* [1963] 1 WLR 1341; *Re Medisco Equipment Ltd* (1983) 1 BCC 98, 944 at 98, 947–998, 948.
478. *Re Blériot Manufacturing Aircraft Co. Ltd* (1916) 32 TLR 253.
479. *Re Blériot Manufacturing Aircraft Co. Ltd* (1916) 32 TLR 253.
480. *Re Bathampton Properties Ltd* [1976] 1 WLR 168.

where they have been unreasonably or improperly incurred,[481] and to make orders for costs against a person who is not a party to the proceedings,[482] it will now rarely (if ever) be appropriate to make a "*Bathampton* order".[483] Where it is held that the company's opposition to the petition was unreasonable, it may be appropriate to seek an order for costs against the directors who promoted the opposition; but the directors should be given a proper opportunity to be represented, to file evidence (where appropriate) and make representations why they should not bear the costs.[484] Where the petition is unreasonably opposed by some of the company's creditors or its contributories, those opposing creditors or contributories may be ordered to pay the petitioner's costs.[485]

9.119 One set of costs for contributories and creditors

The rule that one set of costs is shared between the creditors, and one set shared between the contributories, who have given notice under r. 4.16 and support the successful party (i.e. the petitioner, where a winding-up order is made, or the company where the petition is dismissed),[486] means that care should be taken in arranging representation for such persons. If the creditors and contributories have the same solicitor as the successful party, their names should be added to the brief for that party and they may not be entitled to share in any costs.[487] If the creditors and contributories have the same solicitor but different counsel, only one set of costs will be allowed.[488]

9.120 Costs of other insolvency proceedings

Where a winding-up order is made in respect of a company which is already in voluntary liquidation, the court may order that the remuneration of the voluntary liquidator and the costs and expenses of the voluntary liquidation rank as an expense of the compulsory liquidation in priority to other expenses.[489] An application for such an order should be made by the (former) voluntary liquidator by ordinary application to the registrar in chambers. The application should be supported by an affidavit, explaining the steps which the voluntary liquidator has taken to get in and administer the company's assets and giving a breakdown of the time spent, the hourly rates of remuneration charged and the disbursements made. The application should be served on the liquidator in the compulsory liquidation. Where the winding-up order is made on the petition of the company acting by its administrative receivers or administrators, the court will generally direct that the costs and expenses of the administrative receivership or administration (as the case may be) should rank as an expense of the liquidation.

481. RSC O. 62, r. 11.

482. Supreme Court Act 1981, s. 51; *Aiden Shipping Co. Ltd* v. *Interbulk Ltd* [1986] AC 965.

483. *Re a Company, ex parte Doe Sport Ltd* [1991] BCLC 865 at 867.

484. *Re Land & Property Trust Co. plc (No. 4)* [1994] 1 BCLC 232. The court has power to order costs against a person who is not party to the proceedings under the Supreme Court Act 1981, s. 51, but such orders are exceptional and applications for such orders are treated with considerable caution: *Re Tajik Air Ltd* [1996] 1 BCLC 317 at 324f-h.

485. *Re A and BC Chewing Gum Ltd* [1975] 1 WLR 579.

486. *Re European Banking Co., ex parte Baylis* (1866) LR 2 Eq. 521 at 523–524.

487. *Re Brighton Marine Palace and Pier Co.* [1897] WN 12; *Re Ibo Investment Trust* [1904] 1 Ch. 26 at 29.

488. *Re Silberhuilte Supply Co.* [1910] WN 81.

489. IR 1986, r. 4.219.

WINDING-UP DEFUNCT COMPANIES

9.121 Introduction

A creditor may wish to wind up a company which has been struck off the Register of Companies by the registrar of companies as a result of its failure to file accounts or returns.[490] Prior to its striking off and dissolution, the company may have had assets which would be available for distribution pro rata to its creditors, or the creditors may want a liquidator to investigate the conduct of the company's directors. The procedure described in the preceding paragraphs is generally applicable to winding-up companies which have been struck off the Register of Companies, but special rules apply governing the form of the petition, the parties entitled to notice of the petition, the evidence to be filed in support of the petition and the form of order to be made thereon. These special rules are considered below.

9.122 Form of petition

The petition should follow the usual form of a creditor's petition,[491] but should include a paragraph stating that "the name of the Company has been struck off the register of companies pursuant to section 652 of the Companies Act 1985 on [date] and dissolved by notice published in the *London Gazette*". The petition should conclude with a Prayer[492]:

> "1. that [the company, referred to by name] be restored to the register of companies;
> 2. that [the company, referred to by name] be wound up by the court under the provisions of the Insolvency Act 1986[493];
> 3. that such other order may be made as the court thinks fit."

Such an order is generally referred to as "the usual double-barrelled order".

9.123 Ignorance of the striking-off

If the petition is presented in ignorance of the fact that the company has been struck off and dissolved, the petitioner will have to seek leave to amend the petition[494] to include the detail set out in the preceding para. An adjournment will be necessary for the amendments to be made, for notice to be given to the Treasury Solicitor[495] and for further evidence to be filed. If the fact that the company has been struck off is not discovered until after a winding-up order has been made,[496] the petitioner must apply to rescind[497] the winding-up

490. I.e., under CA 1985, s. 652. The procedure for restoring companies to the register under CA 1985, s. 653 without winding-up is discussed in Chapter 5, *supra*.
491. See para. 9.24, *supra*.
492. See para. 9.25, *supra*.
493. *Re Cambridge Coffee Room Association Ltd* [1952] 1 All ER 112.
494. See para. 9.27, *supra*.
495. See the next para.
496. The fact that the company has been struck off is often only discovered by the Official Receiver as liquidator when he sends a copy of the winding-up order to the registrar of companies pursuant to IA 1986, s. 130(1).
497. Rescission applications are dealt with later in this Chapter.

order and seek leave to amend the petition. The petition will then be adjourned, and the "usual double-barrelled order" will be made on the return day, provided that the appropriate amendments to the petition have been made and the requirements of the next two paragraphs have been satisfied.

9.124 Notification to the Treasury Solicitor

Prior to restoration, any assets of a company which has been struck off the register are vested in the Crown as *bona vacantia*.[498] Notice of the application to restore the name of the company to the Register of Companies must be given to the Treasury Solicitor as the representative of the Crown.[499] There is no need to give any notice of the application to the registrar of companies.

9.125 Affidavit of service

Once the Treasury Solicitor has been given notice of and considered the application for restoration, he will send to the petitioner's solicitors a standard form letter which refers to the company by name and states that, insofar as the Crown has any interest in the assets of the company as *bona vacantia*, it does not oppose the application for restoration. This letter is known as "the *bona vacantia* waiver letter". The *bona vacantia* waiver letter must be exhibited to an affidavit which states that notice of the application has been given to the Treasury Solicitor, and which refers to the *bona vacantia* waiver letter as evidencing that the Treasury Solicitor does not oppose the relief sought. If an affidavit of service is not filed, the court will refuse to make the "usual double-barrelled order" and will adjourn the petition for the affidavit to be filed. If the *bona vacantia* waiver letter is only received shortly before the hearing and is available in court but no affidavit of service has been sworn, the registrar will usually accept a copy of the *bona vacantia* waiver letter and make the "usual double-barrelled order", subject to the petitioner undertaking forthwith to swear an affidavit exhibiting the letter.

WINDING UP UNREGISTERED COMPANIES

9.126 Jurisdiction

The Insolvency Act 1986 gives the court power to wind up an "unregistered company",[500] which is defined as any association and any company except a company registered in any part of the United Kingdom under the Joint Stock Companies Acts or the past or present legislation relating to companies in Great Britain.[501] Despite the width of the definition, the reference to "any association" has been restrictively construed. The jurisdiction is, in practice, now commonly invoked only in respect of two types of association: namely:

498. CA 1985, s. 654(1).
499. Practice Note [1928] WN 218; Practice Note [1931] WN 199.
500. IA 1986, s. 221(1).
501. IA 1986, s. 220(1).

(1) a company incorporated outside Great Britain which establishes a place of business in Great Britain or has some other sufficient connection with the English jurisdiction[502]; or
(2) an insolvent partnership, which is deemed to be an unregistered company for the purposes of its winding-up under the Insolvent Partnerships Order 1994.[503]

The jurisdiction may also be invoked to wind up a statutory company formed under a private Act of Parliament which is not registered under the Companies Acts, but such companies are infrequently encountered today. All of the provisions of the Insolvency Act 1986 concerning winding-up apply to an unregistered company, subject to the exceptions and additions set out in part V of the Act[504] (i.e. ss. 220 to 229). An unregistered company may not be wound up voluntarily under the Act.[505] The following paragraphs discuss the rules generally applicable to the winding-up of unregistered companies, and the particular rules for the winding-up of foreign companies. The winding-up of insolvent partnerships is discussed later in this Chapter.[506]

9.127 Meaning of "association"

Not every unincorporated association is susceptible to winding-up as an unregistered company under part V of the Act. Despite the generality of the reference to "any association" in s. 220, the section has been construed so as to exclude many types of club and association from the winding-up jurisdiction.[507] The word "association" in s. 220 does not include an association which Parliament could not reasonably have intended to be subject to the statutory winding-up procedure.[508] That question is determined by analysing the rules and constitution of the association, rather than by the activities of the association.[509] Where the constitution of the association does not give a member any transferable interest but merely confers a right of enjoyment of the association's facilities whilst it continues, the association is likely to be excluded from the winding-up jurisdiction in s. 220.[510] Applying that approach, the court has refused to wind up as an unregistered company a members' social club[511] and a football club.[512]

9.128 Winding-up foreign companies

A company incorporated outside Great Britain may be wound up as an unregistered company under part V of the Act if the petitioner can establish that the company has a sufficiently close connection with the English jurisdiction to entitle the English court to

502. *Re a Company (No. 00359 of 1987)* [1988] Ch. 210.
503. S.I. 1994 No. 2421 (as amended by the Insolvent Partnerships (Amendment) Order 1996 (S.I. 1996 No. 1308)).
504. IA 1986, s. 221(1).
505. IA 1986, s. 221(4).
506. See paras 9.220–9.248, *infra*.
507. See *Re St James's Club* (1852) 2 De GM&G 383 at 389; 42 ER 920 at 923.
508. *Re International Tin Council* [1989] Ch. 309 at 330C–D.
509. *Re Witney Town Football and Social Club* [1994] 2 BCLC 487.
510. *Re St James's Club* (1852) 2 De GM&G 383 at 387–389; 42 ER 920 at 922–923.
511. *Ibid.*
512. *Re Witney Town Football and Social Club, supra*. See also *Re International Tin Council, supra* (refusal to wind up as an unregistered company an international organisation established by independent sovereign states, including the United Kingdom).

assert jurisdiction. The fact that a foreign company has or had a place of business[513] or has assets within the jurisdiction will usually be a sufficient connection to permit the making of a winding-up order against it, but the presence of assets within the jurisdiction is not essential.[514] A sufficiently close connection may arise in some other way—for example, where a contract giving rise to the petitioning creditor's claim was negotiated, executed and performed in England, the directors of the foreign company were resident in England, the unregistered company's bank accounts were in England, and there was no evidence that the unregistered company had carried on business outside England.[515]

9.128.1 In deciding whether to assume jurisdiction, the court will consider whether there is any more appropriate jurisdiction for the winding-up of the company, and whether there is any reasonable possibility of a benefit accruing to those who seek the winding-up order (usually the creditors of the company) from the making of a winding-up order by the English court.[516] Before making a winding-up order against a foreign company, the court will also require there to be one or more persons interested in the distribution of the company's assets over whom the court is able to exercise jurisdiction[517] or who submit to the jurisdiction of the court.[518] The fact that a company incorporated outside Great Britain has ceased to carry on business in Great Britain, and has been dissolved or has otherwise ceased to exist under the laws of its country of incorporation, is not a bar to its winding-up as an unregistered company under the Insolvency Act 1986.[519] However, a sufficient connection with the jurisdiction and a reasonable possibility of a benefit to creditors from the making of a winding-up order must still be shown by the petitioning creditor. The English court has been satisfied that there was a sufficiently close connection with the jurisdiction and a sufficient prospect of a benefit to creditors to permit a winding-up of a foreign company as an unregistered company, where its creditors would be able to recover sums in England from a third party which would not be recoverable in a winding-up in another jurisdiction (for example, statutory redundancy payments,[520] or a claim under an insurance policy[521]). On the other hand, the court may refuse to wind up an unregistered company, and may stay a winding-up petition on *forum non conveniens* grounds, where it considers that the winding-up would be more appropriately pursued in some other jurisdiction.[522]

9.129 England, Scotland and Northern Ireland companies

Where an unregistered company has a place of business in England and Wales or in Scotland, it is deemed to be registered in England and Wales or in Scotland respectively, for the purpose of determining the court's winding-up jurisdiction, and should be wound

513. See IA 1986, s. 225.
514. *Re a Company (No. 003102 of 1991), ex parte Nyckeln Finance Co. Ltd* [1991] BCLC 539 at 540h.
515. *Re a Company (No. 00359 of 1987)* [1988] 1 Ch. 210.
516. *Ibid.* at 224H–225A and 225H–226A.
517. *Re Real Estate Development Co.* [1991] BCLC 210.
518. *Banque des Marchands de Moscou (Koupetschesky)* v. *Kindersley* [1951] Ch. 112 at 125.
519. IA 1986, s. 225.
520. *Re Eloc Electro-Optieck and Communicatie BV* [1982] Ch. 43.
521. Pursuant to the Third Parties (Rights Against Insurers) Act 1930: see *Re Compania Merabello San Nicholas SA* [1973] Ch. 75 and *Re Allobrogia Steamship Corp.* [1978] 3 All ER 423, [1979] 1 Lloyd's Rep 190.
522. See *Re Wallace Smith & Co. Ltd* [1992] BCLC 970 at 985d–h.

up in England and Wales or in Scotland accordingly; if the unregistered company has a principal place of business in England and Scotland, it is deemed to be registered in both countries and may be wound up in either country.[523] A company registered in Northern Ireland may be wound up by the English courts as an unregistered company provided that it has a principal place of business in England or Wales.[524] Where an unregistered company has a principal place of business situated in Northern Ireland, it may not be wound up in the English or Scottish courts unless it also has a principal place of business in England and Wales or in Scotland.[525]

9.130 Circumstances for winding-up

An unregistered company may only be wound up under part V of the Insolvency Act 1986 in the following circumstances:

(a) where the unregistered company has been dissolved, or has ceased to carry on business, or is carrying on business only for the purpose of winding-up its affairs;
(b) where the unregistered company is unable to pay its debts; or
(c) where the court is of the opinion that it is just and equitable that the unregistered company should be wound up.[526]

The grounds for winding-up an unregistered company are therefore narrower than for winding-up a company registered under the Companies Acts.[527] Even if one of the grounds in s. 221(5) is established, the court retains a discretion whether to wind up the unregistered company. The ground most commonly relied upon in practice is the unregistered company's inability to pay its debts. The unregistered company is deemed to be unable to pay its debts in one or more of five ways.[528]

9.130.1 Unsatisfied statutory demand

An unregistered company is deemed to be unable to pay its debts where a creditor, to whom the unregistered company is indebted for a sum in excess of £750, has served on the unregistered company a written demand in the prescribed form[529] requiring the unregistered company to pay the sum due, and the unregistered company has, for three weeks thereafter, failed to pay the sum demanded or to secure or compound it to the creditor's satisfaction.[530] The demand must be served[531] on the unregistered company by leaving it at its principal place of business, or by delivering it to the secretary, or a director, manager or principal officer of the company, or by serving it in some other way approved

523. IA 1986, s. 221(3).
524. *Re Normandy Marketing Ltd* [1993] BCC 879 at 883G.
525. IA 1986, s. 221(2).
526. IA 1986, s. 221(5).
527. I.e., the grounds in IA 1986, s. 122(1), discussed earlier in this Chapter.
528. See IA 1986, ss. 222–224. These are similar to the deeming provisions applicable to a registered company (i.e. s. 123(1)), discussed earlier in this Chapter.
529. For the contents of the demand, see IR 1986, rr. 4.4–4.6, r. 12.7, and sch. 4, part 4 (as amended); Form 4.1, discussed earlier in this Chapter, which is reproduced in Appendix 4, *infra*.
530. IA 1986, s. 222(1).
531. See further, para. 9.19.6, *supra*.

or directed by the court.[532] Where the creditor has encountered difficulty in serving the demand on the unregistered company, the court may direct substituted service by advertisement of the demand in an appropriate newspaper.

9.130.2 Unpaid debt after action brought

An unregistered company is also deemed to be unable to pay its debts where a creditor has brought an action against any member of the unregistered company claiming a debt due from the company, or due from the defendant as a member of the unregistered company, and written notice of the action has been served on the unregistered company, but the unregistered company has not, within three weeks after service of the notice paid, secured or compounded the debt, nor obtained a stay of the proceedings, nor indemnified the defendant to his reasonable satisfaction against the claim and all costs, damages and expenses arising therefrom.[533] The written notice of the action must be served on the unregistered company in the same way as a statutory demand (see 9.130.1, *supra*).[534] An unregistered company's deemed inability to pay its debts under s. 223 does not require the creditor to have obtained a judgment against the member defendant, merely to have instituted the proceedings. Where the plaintiff's claim is disputed, an application to restrain the presentation of a winding-up petition against the unregistered company should be made promptly after service of the notice of the action, in which case it will be necessary to show a good arguable defence to the plaintiff's claim.

9.130.3 Unsatisfied execution

Where, in England and Wales, execution on a judgment in favour of a creditor against the unregistered company, or against any member of it in his capacity as a member, or against any person sued as a nominal defendant on behalf of the unregistered company, is returned unsatisfied, the company is deemed to be unable to pay its debts.[535] Similar provision is made for unsatisfied judgments obtained in Scotland or Northern Ireland.[536] Where the judgment in question is under appeal, the court may in its discretion refuse to make a winding-up order and may adjourn the petition pending the outcome of the appeal.[537]

9.130.4 Otherwise proved

Inability to pay debts is also deemed where it is otherwise proved to the satisfaction of the court that the unregistered company is unable to pay its debts as they fall due[538]—for example, where the unregistered company has failed to pay an undisputed debt following receipt of a demand which does not satisfy the requirements of a statutory demand. This general provision corresponds with s. 123(1)(e) for a registered company, and is discussed further in para. 9.19.9, *supra*.

532. IA 1986, s. 222(1)(a).
533. IA 1986, s. 223. There is no equivalent provision for a registered company.
534. IA 1986, s. 223(a).
535. IA 1986, s. 224(1)(a). For the corresponding provision for a registered company, see para. 9.19.7, *supra*.
536. IA 1986, s. 224(1)(b) and (c).
537. See further, para. 9.19.8, *supra*.
538. IA 1986, s. 224(1)(d).

9.130.5 "Balance sheet" insolvency

Inability to pay debts is also deemed where it is proved to the satisfaction of the court that the value of the unregistered company's assets is less than the value of its liabilities, taking into account contingent and prospective liabilities.[539]

9.131 Procedure

Subject to the matters discussed above, the procedure for winding-up an unregistered company under part V of the Act is virtually identical to the procedure under part IV of the Act for winding-up of a company registered under the Companies Acts.[540] The provisions of part IV of the Act also apply to the winding-up of an unregistered company and are not to be restricted by the provisions in part V; and the court may exercise any power in respect of an unregistered company which may be exercised in respect of a registered company.[541] However, special provision is made for service of a winding-up petition against, and staying proceedings against, an unregistered company.

9.131.1 Service[542]

As an unregistered company does not have a registered office, the winding-up petition should be served by leaving it at the unregistered company's last known principal place of business in such a way that it is likely to come to the attention of a person attending there, or by delivering it to the secretary or some director, manager or principal officer of the unregistered company, wherever he may be found.[543] If for any reason the petition cannot be served on the unregistered company in that way, the petitioner will need to apply for an order for substituted service.[544] Where the unregistered company is an "oversea company"—i.e. a company incorporated outside Great Britain which establishes a place of business in Great Britain[545]—and has delivered to the registrar of companies for registration the name and address of one or more persons resident in Great Britain authorised to accept service of proceedings on the company's behalf,[546] the petition is validly served if it is addressed to such a person and left at, or sent by post to, the address notified to the registrar of companies for service.[547] Where an oversea company fails to deliver to the registrar of companies the name and address of a person resident in Great Britain who is authorised to accept service on its behalf, or service on those persons is for any reason impracticable (for example, because they have died, or have ceased to reside in Great Britain or have refused to accept service on the oversea company's behalf), the

539. IA 1986, s. 224(2), which corresponds with s. 123(2) for a registered company. For an example of a case in which the balance sheet test was applied in the winding-up of an unregistered company, see *Re a Company (No. 00359 of 1987), supra.*

540. See paras 9.24–9.119, *supra.*

541. IA 1986, s. 229(1).

542. See generally paras 9.37–9.49, *supra,* in respect of registered companies.

543. IR 1986, r. 4.8(4).

544. See IR 1986, r. 4.8(6) and (7).

545. CA 1985, s. 744.

546. As required by CA 1985, s. 691(1)(b)(ii).

547. CA 1985, s. 695(1) and IR 1986, r. 4.8(5).

petition may be served by leaving it at, or posting it to, any place of business established by the unregistered company in Great Britain.[548]

9.131.2 Stay

Where an application is made by a creditor to stay, sist or restrain proceedings against an unregistered company after the presentation of a winding-up petition against it but before a winding-up order is made, the court also has power to stay, sist or restrain proceedings against any deemed contributory of the company.[549] Where a winding-up order is made against an unregistered company, no proceedings may be commenced or continued against any contributory of the unregistered company in respect of a debt of the unregistered company, unless the court grants the plaintiff leave to do so on whatever terms it thinks fit.[550]

"PUBLIC INTEREST" PETITIONS BY THE SECRETARY OF STATE

9.132 Jurisdiction

Where it appears to the Secretary of State[551] from information obtained under certain of his investigative powers that it is expedient in the public interest that a company[552] should be wound up, he may petition for an order that the company be wound up if the court thinks it just and equitable so to order.[553] This is often referred to as a "public interest petition". An oversea company may be wound up in the public interest if the court is satisfied that it has a sufficient connection with the jurisdiction to make the winding-up just and equitable.[554] Section 124A has two distinct limbs[555]: first, as a prerequisite of his standing to petition, the Secretary of State must decide that it is expedient in the public interest that the company should be wound up[556]; second, if a petition is presented following such a decision, the court then has to decide whether it is just and equitable that the company should be wound up.[557] The Secretary of State's decision that a winding-up would be expedient in the public interest must be based on information derived from one (or more) of the following sources[558]:

548. CA 1985, s. 695(2). For the court's power to order service out of the jurisdiction, see IR 1986, r. 12.12.

549. IA 1986, s. 227. As to when a person is deemed to be a contributory of an unregistered company, and his liability as a deemed contributory, see IA 1986, s. 226.

550. IA 1986, s. 228.

551. I.e., the Secretary of State for Trade and Industry.

552. For the extended meaning of "company" in this context, see para. 9.11, *supra*.

553. IA 1986, s. 124A(1) (inserted by CA 1989, s. 60(3) as from 21 February 1990). The predecessor of s. 124A was CA 1985, s. 440 which was omitted when the winding-up provisions of CA 1985 were re-enacted in IA 1986.

554. *Re Companies (No. 004088 and 004089 of 1996)*, 9 August 1996, per Blackburne J., unreported. A company incorporated elsewhere than in Great Britain (e.g., in Northern Ireland) but having a principal place of business in England and Wales may be wound up under IA 1986, s. 124A: *Re a Company (No. 007946 of 1993)* [1994] Ch. 198.

555. See *Re Golden Chemical Products Ltd* [1976] 1 Ch. 300 at 303H; *Re Walter L Jacob & Co. Ltd* (1989) 5 BCC 244 at 250H–251G.

556. As to this phrase, see further para. 9.133, *infra*.

557. *Re SHV Senator Hanseatische Verwaltungs Gesellschaft mbH* [1997] 1 WLR 515 at 522H–523B.

558. See IA 1986, s. 124A(1)(a)–(d).

(a) a report made or information obtained under part XIV of the Companies Act 1985[559] following investigations by inspectors appointed by the Secretary of State at the request of members of the company,[560] investigations by inspectors into company ownership,[561] and the requisition and seizure of documents[562];
(b) any report made following investigations by inspectors appointed by the Secretary of State into unit trust schemes or collective investment schemes[563] or into suspected insider dealing,[564] or any information obtained following investigation[565] of the affairs of a person who is or was carrying on investment business[566];
(c) any information obtained following investigation by the Serious Fraud Office (or, in Scotland, by a person nominated by the Lord Advocate) of the affairs of any person in connection with a suspected offence involving serious or complex fraud[567];
(d) any information obtained for the purpose of assisting an overseas regulatory authority.[568]

9.132.1 The Secretary of State may not present a petition on public interest grounds if the company in question is already being wound up by the court[569] (for example, on the petition of an unpaid creditor); but the commencement of a creditors' voluntary liquidation is not a bar to winding-up on public interest grounds, and the Secretary of State's petition for winding-up may prevail over the wishes of opposing creditors.[570] The decision that it would be expedient in the public interest for a winding-up order to be made need not be (and in practice, is not) made by the Secretary of State personally, but may be made by one of his officers within the Department of Trade and Industry.[571] Where the decision is made by such an officer, that officer should depose to the affidavit of verification,[572] describing his position in the Department of Trade and Industry, and explaining that he was the person to whom the Secretary of State's powers under s. 124A were delegated and the person to whom it appeared expedient in the public interest that the company should be wound up.[573]

9.133 Expedient in the public interest

The expression "expedient in the public interest" in s. 124A(1) is of the widest import: the Secretary of State may petition whenever he considers that members of the public who deal with the company should be protected from indivisible loss whether the company's

559. I.e., CA 1985, ss. 431–453.
560. CA 1985, ss. 431–441.
561. CA 1985, ss. 442–446.
562. CA 1985, ss. 447–451A.
563. I.e., under the Financial Services Act 1986 ("FSA 1986"), s. 94.
564. I.e., under FSA 1986, s. 177.
565. I.e., under FSA 1986, s. 105.
566. As defined in FSA 1986, s. 1 and sch. 1, parts II and III.
567. I.e., under the Criminal Justice Act 1987, s. 2 and the Criminal Justice (Scotland) Act 1987, s. 2.
568. I.e., under the Companies Act 1989, s. 83.
569. IA 1986, s. 124A(2).
570. See, for example, *Re Lubin, Rosen and Associates Ltd* [1975] 1 WLR 122.
571. *Re Golden Chemical Products Ltd*, *supra*, at 304H–305B and 310F–H.
572. For the affidavit of verification, see para. 9.138, *infra*.
573. *Re Golden Chemical Products Ltd*, *supra*, at 311E.

activities are legal or not.[574] However, there has been little detailed judicial analysis of the phrase "expedient in the public interest" in s. 124A(1) or its predecessor sections.[575] This is probably because the court hearing the petition does not usually focus its consideration on the Secretary of State's decision: ordinarily the court is not concerned with the decision-making process of the Secretary of State at the earlier stage which resulted in the presentation of the petition, nor with the question what was the material then before the Secretary of State. The court forms its own opinion as to what the public interest requires as at the date of the hearing.[576] The principal legal effect of the first limb of s. 124A is that the forming and holding of the relevant opinion by the Secretary of State is a prerequisite which gives the Secretary of State his standing to petition. If the formation of the Secretary of State's opinion were to be challenged, it should be challenged not before the court hearing the winding-up petition but in judicial review proceedings. Such a challenge would usually be pointless: if no reasonable Secretary of State could have formed the necessary opinion as to the requisite public interest, the petition would be bound to fail on its merits in any event.[577]

9.134 The function of the court

The proper function of the court when hearing a public interest petition by the Secretary of State under s. 124A was analysed by the Court of Appeal in *Re Walter L Jacob Ltd.*[578] The function of the court is to carry out a balancing exercise between those matters relied upon by the Secretary of State which constitute reasons why the company should be wound up compulsorily, and those matters relied upon by the company which constitute reasons why it should not, giving such weight to each matter as it thinks appropriate in light of all the evidence before the court and the submissions made thereon.[579] In conducting its balancing exercise, the court will have regard to the considerations of public interest relied upon, but rather than examining the Secretary of State's decision, the court will evaluate for itself whether those reasons (and the evidence in support thereof) afford sufficient cause for making a winding-up order in the particular case. In so doing, the court will have regard to the submissions of the Secretary of State, and the fact that he and his officers can be expected to exercise the power to petition under s. 124A with a proper sense of responsibility, but the submissions made on behalf of the Secretary of State are to be tested for cogency or weight in the same way as any other submission. The objective of the court is to identify for itself the aspect or aspects of public interest which, in the view of the court, would be promoted by making a winding-up order in the particular case.[580] If the court is not satisfied that a winding-up order would be in the public interest, it could not conclude that it was just and equitable that the company should be wound up, because the reasons relied upon by the petitioner for a winding-up order in the public interest would then not have been made out.[581] The question whether something

574. See *Re Senator Hanseatische Verwaltungsgesellschaft mbH*, *supra*, at 526B–C per Millett LJ.
575. Nor in other enactments in which the same phrase is used—for example, ss. 7(1) and 8(1) of the Company Directors Disqualification Act 1986.
576. See the next paragraph.
577. *Re Walter L Jacob & Co. Ltd*, *supra*, at 251A.
578. *Supra*. See also *Re SHV Senator Hanseatische Verwaltungs Gesellschaft mbH*, *supra*, at 522H–523B.
579. *Re Walter L Jacob & Co. Ltd*, *supra*, at 250C–D and 251C–D.
580. *Ibid.* at 251E–G; *Re Secure & Provide plc* [1992] BCC 405 at 405G–H and 413E.
581. *Re Walter L Jacob & Co. Ltd*, *supra*, at 252B.

is in the public interest is a question of fact to be decided in the circumstances as they exist when the question falls to be determined by the court,[582] even if the circumstances then prevailing would probably not have been in the contemplation of the legislature when the enactment was passed.[583] It is impractical and beyond the scope of a book of this nature to attempt to set out exhaustively every circumstance or consideration which might lead a court to conclude that a winding-up order is required in the public interest, but some guidance can be derived from the grounds commonly relied on by the Secretary of State in public interest petitions (discussed in para. 9.135, *infra*).

9.135 Grounds for the petition

The Secretary of State's petition under s. 124A will aver that it appears to the petitioner expedient in the public interest that the company in question should be wound up compulsorily. The petition will usually go on to set out the grounds on which the Secretary of State has come to that conclusion. The jurisdiction is not limited to cases where the company subject to the petition has acted unlawfully because its business or business methods are illegal.[584] The grounds set out in the petition may typically include one or more of the following:

- (i) that the company has carried on, or has aided and abetted the carrying on, of unauthorised insurance business[585] or unauthorised investment business[586];
- (ii) that the company (whether or not authorised to conduct investment business) has maintained inadequate records for the purposes of its business to the prejudice of investors or the public, and/or that the records fail properly to disclose the company's true financial position[587];
- (iii) that the company has misled the public in attracting investment business or has otherwise breached the rules of the self-regulating organisation of which it is a member[588];
- (iv) that gross mismanagement of the company's investment business has jeopardised investors' monies[589];
- (v) that the company's marketing practices constitute "pyramid selling"[590] or a lottery[591];

582. See *Re Amalgamated Anthracite Collieries Ltd's Application* (1927) 43 TLR 672 at 673 (col 2) (a case concerning the phrase "national interest").

583. See *Cartwright* v. *Post Office* [1968] 2 All ER 646 at 651G (construing a reference to "the public interest" in s. 1 of the Telegraph (Construction) Act 1916).

584. *Re SHV Senator Hanseatische Verwaltungs Gesellschaft mbH*, at 522H–523A.

585. See, for example, *Re a Company (No. 007923 of 1994)* [1995] 1 WLR 953 at 955D–E; contrast *Re a Company (No. 007816 of 1994)* [1995] 2 BCLC 539 (upheld on appeal *sub nom Re Great Western Assurance Co.*, Lord Woolf M.R., Hobhouse L.J. and Morritt L.J., unreported, 31 July 1996).

586. See, for example, *Re Pinstripe Farming Co. Ltd* [1996] 2 BCLC 295 (in which one of the grounds relied upon was that the company's business constituted an unauthorised collective investment scheme contrary to FSA 1986, ss. 3 and 75).

587. See, for example, *Re Walter L Jacob & Co. Ltd*, *supra*, at 248B and 256E.

588. *Ibid.* at 248C.

589. *Ibid.* at 248E–F and 256E–F.

590. See, for example, *Re Secure & Provide plc*, *supra*, at 406A–D (a case in which the petition was dismissed).

591. See, for example, *Applied Data Base Ltd* v. *Secretary of State for Trade and Industry* [1995] 1 BCLC 272 at 273i–274a.

(vi) that the company's business is fundamentally unsound and the company is bound to fail or could ultimately only result in loss to the public[592];

(vii) that unjustified payments have been made from company funds to third parties with no benefit to the company, in breach of the directors' fiduciary duties[593]; and

(viii) that the company is insolvent.[594]

The fact that the company in question has ceased the activities to which objection was taken by the Secretary of State is not a bar to a winding-up order in the public interest—the public interest may be served by the court publicly expressing its disapproval of the company's past misconduct by the making of a winding-up order.[595]

9.136 Procedure

The procedure on a petition by the Secretary of State based on public interest grounds is in most respects identical to the procedure on a creditor's petition discussed above. Reference should be made to the earlier paragraphs of this Chapter for the procedure generally applicable to winding-up petitions.[596] The following paragraphs discuss the special procedural rules applicable to public interest petitions.

9.137 Form of petition[597]

Whereas a creditor's petition will set out particulars of the company's debt due to the petitioner, a "public interest" petition will aver that it appears to the petitioner (i.e. the Secretary of State) expedient in the public interest that the company should be wound up. The petition should then set out succinctly[598] in numbered paragraphs the grounds on which the Secretary of State bases his opinion that it is expedient in the public interest that the company should be wound up.[599]

9.138 Affidavit of verification[600]

The decision that a winding-up order would be expedient in the public interest will not normally be taken by the Secretary of State personally, but will be taken by one of his officers within the Department of Trade and Industry. In such a case, the affidavit of verification ought to be more detailed than on a creditor's petition. To wind up an active company compulsorily is a serious step, and a person who asserts that it is just and equitable for the court to do so must put forward reasons and evidence in support which have a weight justifying that order.[601] The officer within the Department of Trade and

592. *Ibid.*
593. See, for example, *Re Ostrich Farming Corp. Ltd*, 3 April 1996, Rattee J., unreported.
594. See, for example, *Re Pinstripe Farming Co. Ltd, supra*; *Re A Company (No. 007923 of 1994), supra*, at 957E–F.
595. *Re Walter L Jacob & Co. Ltd, supra*, at 257G–258C; *Re Secure & Provide plc, supra*, at 413E–F.
596. See, generally, paras 9.24–9.120, *supra*.
597. See, generally, paras 9.24–9.27, *supra*.
598. See RSC O. 9, r. 2(1).
599. See, for example, *Re Golden Chemical Products Ltd, supra*, at 304D.
600. See, generally, paras 9.29–9.30, *supra*.
601. See *Re Walter L Jacob & Co. Ltd, supra*, at 252D.

Industry who took the decision that a winding-up order would be expedient in the public interest should be the deponent of the affidavit: he should describe his position within the Department, and explain that he is the person to whom the Secretary of State's powers under s. 124A have been delegated and that he was the person to whom it appeared expedient in the public interest that the company should be wound up.[602]

9.139 Evidence in support

"Public interest" petitions, unlike uncontested creditors' petitions, will generally be supported by more detailed affidavit evidence than a simple affidavit of verification. Evidence filed in support of the petition will ordinarily explain in more detail the grounds for seeking a winding-up order in the public interest as set out in the petition. Typically, the affidavit will describe: the enquiries which have been made into the company's affairs and which resulted in the Secretary of State forming his opinion that a winding-up order would be expedient in the public interest; whether inspectors were appointed by the Secretary of State to inquire into the company's affairs[603]; the outcome of the enquiries—i.e. the information obtained or the report made by inspectors, and the conclusions to be drawn therefrom; and those aspects of the company's business to which objection is taken and the dangers which they pose for the public. Where the officer within the Department of Trade and Industry who took the decision to present the petition was also responsible for conducting the enquiries into the company's affairs, he may swear a single affidavit verifying the petition and setting out in detail the evidence relied upon. Where that officer was not responsible for the enquiries into the company's affairs on which he based his decision to petition, he may nevertheless give hearsay evidence of the information and material obtained on behalf of the Secretary of State under his statutory powers, which was taken into account in deciding whether to present a petition under s. 124A: formerly, such evidence was admissible under an implied exception to the hearsay rule,[604] but now hearsay evidence is generally admissible.[605] However, the court retains a discretion as to the weight which should be given to hearsay evidence, and if the company opposes the petition and contests the information on which the decision to petition was based, it may be necessary for the Secretary of State to adduce first-hand evidence from the person who conducted the enquiries and to tender him for cross-examination.[606]

9.140 Advertisement[607]

Rule 4.11(1) of the Insolvency Rules 1986 provides that unless the court otherwise directs, the petition should be advertised once in the *London Gazette*. As the requirement of advertisement in r. 4.11(1) is mandatory in the absence of a direction that advertisement be dispensed with, the burden is upon the company to establish a sufficient reason to

602. *Re Golden Chemical Products Ltd*, *supra*, at 311E.
603. See para. 9.132(a)–(d), *supra*.
604. *Re Rex Williams Leisure plc* [1994] 2 BCLC 555 at 566a–567h, where the relevant authorities are reviewed. See also *Secretary of State for Trade and Industry* v. *Ashcroft*, *The Times*, 4 March 1997.
605. Civil Evidence Act 1995, s. 1 (in force 31 January 1997).
606. Civil Evidence Act 1995, ss. 3 and 4; and see *Re Rex Williams Leisure plc*, *supra*, at 568c–d (note that this was a disqualification case, not a public interest winding-up petition, but the principle should apply equally to such petitions).
607. See, generally, paras 9.50–9.56, *supra*.

depart from the normal practice of requiring advertisement.[608] Rule 4.11(1) applies both to creditors' winding-up petitions and to public interest winding-up petitions by the Secretary of State, but different considerations apply to each category of petition. Although the power to make a direction against advertisement under r. 4.11(1) does not depend on a finding of abuse of process,[609] in respect of a creditor's petition alleging insolvency it is difficult to envisage circumstances in which the court would make such a direction where the facts do not justify a finding of abuse of process (i.e. where the petition debt is not disputed in good faith on substantial grounds): the facts would have to be exceptional, and the burden on the company would be an onerous one.

9.140.1 Different considerations apply to advertisement of a public interest petition presented by the Secretary of State which does not allege insolvency and which is opposed on grounds other than abuse of process[610]: a public interest petition to wind up a company which is actively trading and is not insolvent is more akin to a contributory's petition (where the question whether the petition should be advertised is left to the court to direct on the first return day or thereafter under r. 4.23(1)(c)).[611] The primary purpose of the advertisement is to give notice of the petition to those who would be entitled to be heard on it (i.e., creditors and contributories), and its secondary purpose is to give notice of the petition to those who might deal with the company before its determination and who might be adversely affected by s. 127 of the Insolvency Act 1986.[612] Whether those purposes remain a compelling reason for requiring advertisement will depend on the facts of each case. The advertisement of a winding-up petition is capable of causing significant harm to the company's business (although this danger is often exaggerated).[613] Thus, if the company can show that a direction against advertisement of a public interest petition would not deprive creditors of the company of any significant advantage which they would otherwise have had, that the contributories have had effective notice of the petition, that those who might trade with the company after presentation of the petition are protected by an order under s. 127 of the Insolvency Act 1986, *and* that advertisement may cause serious damage to the reputation and financial stability of the company, the court may in its discretion direct that there be no advertisement; but proof of likely damage is essential, and in the absence of evidence of such damage, the court will require advertisement.[614] In *Re a Company (No. 007923 of 1994)* the court made a direction that the petition should not be advertised[615]: in making that direction the court was influenced by the fact that there was no allegation of insolvency; there was no substantial ground for believing that the company's customers would be prejudiced if the allegations in the petition were proved; the contributories were all directors of the company or other companies controlled by the same directors; undertakings had been given to the court to prevent the conduct of further unlawful business as alleged in the petition; third parties

608. *Re a Company (No. 007923 of 1994), supra*, at 958D, approving *Re a Company (No. 007946 of 1993)* [1994] Ch. 198.

609. *Re a Company (No. 007923 of 1994), supra*, at 957B and 960A–C.

610. *Ibid.* at 957E–F and 960A–C. Where a public interest petition alleges insolvency, it appears that the normal practice of requiring advertisement under r. 4.11(1) will usually apply, as in a creditor's petition.

611. *Ibid.* at 957G.

612. *Ibid.* at 958F–H.

613. *Ibid.* at 959G.

614. *Ibid.* at 959B–D; contrast *Applied Data Base Ltd* v. *Secretary of State for Trade and Industry, supra*, where such a direction was refused in a public interest petition by the Secretary of State under IA 1986, s. 124A.

615. *Supra*, at 959H.

were protected by an order which had been made under s. 127 of the Insolvency Act 1986[616]; advertisement could cause serious damage to the reputation and financial stability of the company; and the direction was to be in force for only a short period of time pending the hearing of an application for the appointment of a provisional liquidator.[617]

9.141 Substitution[618]

Where a creditor presents a winding-up petition but does not pursue it, the court will readily order substitution of another creditor as petitioner. However, where the Secretary of State presents a petition under s. 124A on the grounds that it appears expedient in the public interest that the company should be wound up, but then does not proceed with the petition, the court may be more reluctant to substitute as petitioner some other person claiming to be interested. The court has refused to substitute contributories as petitioners in place of the Secretary of State where voluminous evidence had been filed on the Secretary of State's petition, none of which would have been relevant to an amended petition after substitution, and where the effect of an order for substitution would have been to convert a public interest petition into a contributories' petition based on unknown grounds.[619] The authorities leave open the question whether the court would be prepared to order substitution of a creditor as petitioner where the ground (or one of the grounds) initially relied on by the Secretary of State was that the company was insolvent and where the creditor can produce a straightforward creditor's petition by amending the petition to delete any other ground previously relied upon by the Secretary of State: in a case where there has been an allegation of insolvency from an early date, it would seem that the court should be prepared to contemplate such a substitution in order to preserve the date of presentation of the public interest petition by the Secretary of State as the date of commencement of the winding-up.

9.142 Appointment of provisional liquidator[620]

Public interest winding-up petitions by the Secretary of State under s. 124A are frequently based on grounds that the company's business is being (or has been) conducted unlawfully, or that its business practices are inappropriate and place the public at risk of loss, or that the assets of investors are in jeopardy.[621] The very nature of those grounds is likely to make the appointment of a provisional liquidator desirable, and the Secretary of State will often apply to the court shortly after the presentation of the petition for such an appointment.[622] The procedure on an application by the Secretary of State for the appointment of a provisional liquidator is precisely the same as on an application by a petitioning creditor,[623] save that the Secretary of State, unlike a petitioning creditor, may not be required to provide an undertaking in damages if he applies *ex parte* for the

616. *Ibid.* at 958H–959B.
617. *Ibid.* at 959G–H.
618. See, generally, paras 9.67–9.70, *supra.*
619. *Re Xyllyx plc (No. 1)* [1992] BCLC 376 at 377e.
620. See, generally, paras 9.71–9.88, *supra.*
621. For the common grounds of such petitions, see para. 9.135, *supra.*
622. *Re Highfield Commodities Ltd* [1985] 1 WLR 149 at 157H and 159D.
623. See paras 9.71–9.88, *supra.*

appointment of the provisional liquidator.[624] Once appointed, the provisional liquidator may apply to the court for the appointment of a special manager if it appears to him that the nature of the company's business or property, or the interests of the company's creditors, contributories or members generally, require the appointment of another person to manage the company's business or property.[625]

9.143 The hearing

The same principles generally apply to the hearing of a public interest petition by the Secretary of State as apply to the hearing of a creditor's petition.[626] Where the Secretary of State has applied for and obtained the appointment of a provisional liquidator or a special manager has been appointed, the court should admit in evidence any report made by him,[627] and should allow him to appear and make relevant representations.

9.144 Costs

The general principles applicable to the costs of public interest petitions by the Secretary of State under s. 124A are the same as for a creditor's petition.[628] In *Re Xyllyx plc (No. 2)*[629] it was suggested by Harman J. that, where a public interest petition by the Secretary of State is dismissed, the Secretary of State should not automatically be ordered to pay the company's costs: it was said that the proper approach was to ask whether the petition was properly presented on the basis of the information then available to the Secretary of State; applying that approach, the company was ordered to pay the costs of the Secretary of State from presentation until such date as it ceased to be proper to pursue the petition, and the Secretary of State was ordered to pay the costs of the company caused by the pursuit of the petition thereafter, each being netted off against the other. That approach has not been adopted in other unsuccessful petitions by the Secretary of State under s. 124A[630] and it is to be doubted if it would now be followed: the approach was influenced by the fact that the Secretary of State was not bringing ordinary hostile litigation, but bringing proceedings for the protection of the public.[631] Similar arguments on behalf of the Secretary of State were successful in early cases under the Company Directors Disqualification Act 1986, in which the application of the Secretary of State failed and the originating summons was dismissed, but no order for costs was made.[632] However, in *Re Southbourne Sheet Metal Co. Ltd (No. 2)*, the Court of Appeal emphatically rejected that practice in disqualification proceedings.[633]

624. *Re Highfield Commodities Ltd*, *supra*, at 155H–156H; *Re Secure & Provide plc* [1992] BCC 405 at 415.

625. See, generally, paras 9.89–9.98, *supra*.

626. See, generally, paras 9.99–9.110, *supra*.

627. *Re Walter L Jacob & Co. Ltd*, *supra*, at 254F–H.

628. See, generally, paras 9.111–9.120, *supra*.

629. [1992] BCLC 378.

630. See, for example, *Re Secure & Provide plc* [1992] 405 at 415B, where the Secretary of State was ordered to pay the costs of the company and of the provisional liquidator on the dismissal of his public interest petition.

631. *Re Xyllyx plc (No. 2)*, *supra*, at 379i–380e.

632. See the cases summarised in *Re Southbourne Sheet Metal Co. Ltd (No. 2)* [1993] BCLC 135 at 140h–141a.

633. *Ibid.* at 136c–e.

Although the Court of Appeal did not express any final view[634] on the correctness of the approach to the costs of an unsuccessful public interest petition adopted in *Re Xyllyx plc (No. 2)*,[635] it rejected the contention that special rules applied to the costs of proceedings brought in the public interest, holding that the Crown must take its chance on costs just like any other litigant[636]; and that in the absence of special circumstances, a successful respondent is entitled to order that the Secretary of State should pay the respondent's costs of the proceedings. It appears likely that a similar approach would now be adopted by the court in respect of an unsuccessful public interest petition by the Secretary of State.[637]

REVIEW AND RESCISSION OF A WINDING-UP ORDER

9.145 Jurisdiction to review or rescind

Every court which has jurisdiction under the Insolvency Act 1986 to wind up companies[638] is given power by the Insolvency Rules 1986 to review, rescind or vary any order made by it in the exercise of that jurisdiction,[639] but the power is to be exercised with caution.[640] A winding-up order may be reviewed because, for example, new evidence has become available.[641] An order of the registrar should ordinarily be reviewed, if at all, by the registrar and not by the Companies Court Judge; if the registrar's order is to be challenged before the Companies Court Judge, the application should be by an appeal under r. 7.47(2).[642] Although no time limit is stipulated in which the court may review an order, any application to rescind a winding-up order ought to be made within seven days after the date on which the order was made: a winding-up order is not drawn up and sealed until eight days after the order was made, to enable a rescission application to be made in the interim (although the court has jurisdiction to rescind the winding-up order after the order has been perfected).[643] Thus, if the registrar makes a winding-up order on a Wednesday, the application to rescind should be made on or before the following Wednesday. Inexcusable delay in applying for rescission is likely to result in the refusal of the application.[644] The registrar hears application for rescission at the end of the list of

634. *Ibid.* at 142a–d.

635. *Supra.*

636. *Re Southbourne Steel Metal Co. Ltd (No. 2)*, *supra*, at 140d–h per Nourse L.J.; and at 142i–143a per McCowan L.J.

637. As in *Re Secure & Provide plc*, *supra.*

638. For the meaning of this term, see paras 9.2–9.4, *supra*.

639. IR 1986, r. 7.47(1).

640. *Re Dollar Land (Feltham) Ltd* [1995] BCC 740 at 748D; Practice Note (Winding-up order: rescission) [1974] 1 WLR 4.

641. Fresh evidence would appear to be admissible on a review: see *Re Portedge Ltd* [1997] BCC 23 at 27B and the cases there cited; and see *Lehmann Bros* v. *Phillips*, New Law Digest, 21 April 1996, Evans-Lombe J, (where it was held that in order to succeed, the applicant must produce new material, which was not before the court on the making of the winding-up order, tending to show that the original order ought not to have been made).

642. *Re SN Group plc* [1993] BCC 808 at 810C–D.

643. *Re Virgo Systems Ltd* (1989) 5 BCC 833 at 834D–E; *Re Calmex Ltd* (1988) BCC 761. Prior to the IR 1986, the court did not have power to rescind a perfected winding-up order (i.e. under CA 1985, s. 549): see *Re Intermain Properties Ltd* (1985) 1 BCC 99, 555.

644. See *Lehmann Bros* v. *Phillips*, *supra*, (where there was a delay of 14 months between the winding-up order and the application for rescission).

winding-up petitions on Wednesdays in term time. Outside term time, the application for rescission should be made to the vacation judge. The jurisdiction under r. 7.47(1) is most commonly invoked to rescind a winding-up order where the company has subsequently made arrangements to pay the petitioning creditor.

9.146 Extension of time

The court has power to extend time for applying for rescission of a winding-up order[645] in appropriate circumstances—for example, where the company was not aware that a winding-up order had been made until after the expiry of the seven-day period but applied for rescission within seven days of becoming aware that the order had been made.[646]

9.147 Form of application

No formal application for rescission need be issued[647] (although the court ought to be informed in advance of the intended application, to enable the relevant file to be brought to court). Where the making of the winding-up order has not been opposed owing to an oversight or error (for example, an error or misunderstanding when instructing counsel), an affidavit may not be necessary and the circumstances which led to the winding-up order being made may be explained to the court by counsel.[648] In all other cases, the application must be supported by affidavit.[649] The application should be by a creditor of the company, or by a contributory, or by the company jointly with a creditor or a contributory, but not by the company alone[650]: this rule ensures that if the application for rescission fails, the costs of the application will be payable by the creditor or contributory who joins in the application rather than out of the assets of the company, which would prejudice the general body of creditors. A stranger to the liquidation (i.e. someone who is not a creditor nor a contributory and who did not appear at the hearing of the winding-up petition) does not have *locus standi* to apply to rescind the winding-up order.[651]

9.148 Notice of application

Notice of the application to rescind should be given to the petitioning creditor, to any supporting or opposing creditors of whom the applicant is aware, and the official receiver. The court has a discretion under r. 4.16(5) to give leave to opposing creditors to appear and be heard on the application to rescind the winding-up order.[652]

9.149 Content of affidavit

The affidavit in support of the application for rescission should identify the applicant, stating whether the applicant is a creditor or contributory and whether the application is

645. IR 1986, r. 12.9 and RSC O. 3, r. 5.
646. *Re Virgo Systems Ltd, supra*, at 834F–G; *Re Calmex Ltd, supra*, at 762–763.
647. Chancery Division Practice Direction No. 10 B.(ix): *Supreme Court Practice 1997*, Vol. 2, para. 841, p. 184.
648. Practice Note (Winding-up order: rescission), *supra*.
649. *Ibid.*
650. Practice Note (Winding-up order: rescission) (No. 2) [1971] 1 WLR 757.
651. *Lehmann Bros* v. *Phillips, supra*; see also *Re Bradford Navigation Company* (1870) LR 5 Ch.App. Cas. 600 at 603.
652. *Re Dollar Land (Feltham) Ltd, supra*, at 747F.

made by that person alone or jointly with the company. The affidavit should explain how the winding-up order came to be made and why any previous demands for payment or statutory demands were not complied with (for example, because the company had moved offices without informing the petitioner or the registrar of companies, as a result of which the demands and the petition never came to its notice[653]). Unless the debt is disputed or the applicant contends that for some other reason the order should not have been made, the affidavit should record that arrangements have been made to satisfy the petition debt and the debts of any supporting creditors, or should state that the petitioner and supporting creditors (although not yet paid) consent to the rescission. Where the petition debt is disputed or the applicant contends that for some other reason the winding-up order should not have been made, the affidavit should set out the grounds for the dispute or for that contention. Where the application is based on arrangements made to pay the undisputed petition debt, the affidavit should also exhibit the assets and liabilities of the company, ideally supported by exhibits such as recent audited accounts, management accounts or a written confirmation from the company's auditors, showing that the company is solvent.[654] If there has been any delay in applying for rescission, this should also be explained.[655]

9.150 Failure to swear affidavit in time

If the company learns of the winding-up order only shortly before the expiry of the seven-day period in which the application must be made, and no affidavit evidence is available in time, the company ought to apply to the registrar, in open court on a Wednesday at the end of the winding-up list, for a direction that the winding-up order should not be sealed for a further seven days and the application for rescission should be adjourned for seven days: the company will then be able to file evidence in the meantime and proceed with the application the following Wednesday.

9.151 Grounds for rescission

Where the petition debt is disputed and the company files evidence showing (i) why the winding-up order came to be made, and (ii) a *prima facie* case that there is a dispute, the court will rescind the order and give directions for further evidence in relation to the alleged dispute.[656] Where it is clear that the petition is misconceived (for example, it is accepted that the petition was presented against the wrong company) the court will rescind the winding-up order and dismiss the petition. The court may also direct that the winding-up order be removed from the company's file maintained by the registrar of companies as it is a nullity, but the registrar of companies may leave a note on the file recording that the order was filed by mistake.[657] Where the application for rescission is based on the same grounds as were relied upon before the Companies Court Registrar in unsuccessfully opposing the making of a winding-up order (for example, opposition on the ground that the company in question is a foreign company with an insufficient connection with the

653. See, for example, *Re Virgo Systems Ltd*, *supra*, at 834A–B.
654. Practice Note (Winding-up order: rescission), *supra*.
655. *Ibid.*
656. If the petitioner has been guilty of a gross breach of the rules (for example, a failure to serve the company at its registered office), the court may strike out the petition.
657. *Re Calmex Ltd*, *supra*.

jurisdiction to justify a winding-up order), the application for rescission will be discussed unless the applicant produces new material, which was not before the court when the original winding-up order was made, and which tends to show that the original order ought not to have been made.[658] Where the petition debt is not disputed and the object of the rescission application is to secure the dismissal of the winding-up petition, the winding-up order will usually only be rescinded if: (i) the petition debt and the sums owed to all supporting creditors have been paid or arrangements are made to pay them immediately the petition is dismissed; (ii) it is established that the company is solvent; *and* (iii) the official receiver does not consider that the affairs of the company require investigation and his costs are paid.[659] In such a case, if the company's assets are exceeded by its liabilities, the court is likely to refuse to rescind the winding-up order unless further funds are introduced to meet the deficit; where the company's assets exceed its liabilities only if sums owed to the directors are left out of account, the court may rescind the order on an undertaking by the directors to postpone their claims to those of all other creditors. Where the object of the rescission application is not to have the winding-up petition dismissed (for example, where the object is to adjourn the petitions for a short period to enable proposals for a voluntary arrangement to be formulated), the court may rescind the winding-up orders notwithstanding that the company is insolvent and the creditors appearing on the petition will not be paid in full.[660]

9.152 Costs of the rescission application

Where the application for rescission fails, the creditor or contributory making the application will usually be ordered to pay the costs of the petitioner, of any supporting creditor appearing on the application, and of the official receiver.[661] Where the winding-up order was made owing to the fault of the company (for example, because it failed to notify the registrar of companies of a change in its registered office), the applicant(s) will usually be ordered to pay the costs of the petition and of the application for rescission of the petitioner, any supporting creditor and the official receiver. Where the winding-up order was made owing to the fault of the petitioner (for example, the petitioner relied on an out-of-date company search with the result that the petition stated, and service was effected at, a former registered office of the company), the petitioner might be ordered to pay the costs of the applicants and of the official receiver. When a winding-up order is rescinded and the petition dismissed, the official receiver may seek a direction that he be at liberty to retain on account of his costs the deposit paid by the petitioner at the time of presentation.

APPEALS IN WINDING-UP PROCEEDINGS

9.153 Appeal to which court?

An appeal against the grant or refusal of a winding-up order made by a County Court district judge, a County Court judge or a registrar of the High Court is made to a single

658. *Lehmann Bros* v. *Phillips*, *supra*.

659. *Re Dollar Land (Feltham) Ltd*, *supra*, at 747H–748D; *Re SN Group plc*, *supra*, at 812E–813G; *Re Virgo Systems Ltd*, *supra*, at 835A.

660. *Re Dollar Land (Feltham) Ltd*, *supra*, at 748D–G.

661. Practice Note (Winding-up order: rescission) (No. 2), *supra*, applied in *Re SN Group plc*, *supra*, at 815G.

judge of the High Court.[662] An appeal from a decision of a High Court judge lies to the Court of Appeal, but only with the leave of that judge or of the Court of Appeal.[663] A County Court exercising its jurisdiction to wind up may not be restrained in the exercise of that jurisdiction by an order of any other court, and the only avenue of appeal is to the single judge of the High Court.[664]

9.154 Nature of appeal

An appeal against the grant or refusal of a winding-up order by the County Court, or by the registrar of the High Court, to a single High Court judge under r. 7.47(2) is a true appeal—i.e. it is a rehearing and not a hearing *de novo*.[665] The jurisdiction under s. 122 to make a winding-up order is discretionary. Consequently, the single High Court judge may not intervene and set aside the decision of the County Court district judge or judge or of the High Court registrar unless he is satisfied that, when exercising the discretion conferred by s. 122, the County Court judge or High Court registrar misdirected himself on the law or the evidence, or that his decision is so plainly wrong that he must have exercised his discretion wrongly, or that there has been an error of law or disregard of principle.[666] The same restriction applies to the power of the Court of Appeal to set aside an order made by the single High Court judge in the exercise of his discretion under s. 122.[667]

9.155 Procedure on appeal

An appeal from the County Court or High Court registrar to the single High Court judge in relation to winding-up proceedings is not governed by RSC O. 58 as might be expected, but is governed by the procedure and practice of the Supreme Court for appeals to the Court of Appeal (i.e. RSC O. 59).[668] Where O. 59 refers to the Court of Appeal, that should be read as a reference to the single High Court judge, and any reference to the Registrar of Civil Appeals should be read as a reference to the Companies Court Registrar.[669]

9.156 Form of appeal

An appeal from a County Court or High Court registrar to the single High Court judge, or from a decision of that judge hearing such an appeal to the Court of Appeal with leave, is made by ordinary application under r. 7.2 of the Insolvency Rules 1986. An application

662. IR 1986, r. 7.47(2); and see *Re Calahurst Ltd* (1989) 5 BCC 318 at 319E–F; *Re Tasbian Ltd (No. 2)* [1990] BCC 322; *Re Industrial & Commercial Securities plc* (1989) 5 BCC 320.
663. IR 1986, r. 7.47(2).
664. IR 1986, r. 7.47(3).
665. IR 1986, r. 7.49(1) and RSC O. 59, r. 3(1); *Re Industrial and Commercial Securities plc, supra*, at 323A–B.
666. *Re Probe Data Systems Ltd (No. 3)* [1991] BCC 428; *Re Tasbian Ltd (No. 3)* [1991] BCC 435; *Re Industrial and Commercial Securities plc, supra*, at 325A–C. For the correct approach of the appellate court in a rehearing, see the cases summarised in *Supreme Court Practice 1997*, Vol. 1, paras 59/1/58 and 59/1/59, pp. 947–948.
667. *Re Walter L Jacob & Co. Ltd* (1989) 5 BCC 244 at 249F–H.
668. IR 1986, r. 7.49(1).
669. IR 1986, r. 7.49(2).

to the Court of Appeal for leave to appeal should also be made by ordinary application.[670] The Insolvency Rules 1986 do not prescribe what an appellant should include in his ordinary application when appealing: by analogy with the procedure on an appeal to the Court of Appeal under RSC O. 59, the ordinary application should specify the grounds of the appeal and the precise form of the order which the appellant proposes to ask the court hearing the appeal to make.[671]

9.157 Time for appealing

An ordinary application appealing against the grant or refusal of a winding-up order by the County Court or High Court registrar must be issued *and served* not later than four weeks after the date on which the order appealed against is sealed or otherwise perfected.[672] An application to the Court of Appeal for leave to appeal must be issued and served within the same period.[673] The court may extend these time limits in appropriate cases.[674]

9.158 Service of the ordinary application

The ordinary application must be served on all parties directly affected by the appeal.[675] Where the petitioner appeals against the refusal of a winding-up order, the application should be served on the company and any opposing creditors or contributories who appeared below and were awarded their costs. Where the appeal is against the making of a winding-up order, the application should be served on the petitioner and the official receiver[676]: the official receiver need not appear at the hearing of the appeal unless there are matters which he believes ought to be brought to the attention of the court; if the official receiver appears on the appeal without proper reason, his costs may be disallowed. The application need not be served on any supporting creditors and contributories who appeared on the hearing of the petition, unless they were awarded costs and the appeal seeks to overturn or vary those costs orders. The supporting creditors or contributories should, however, be informed of the appeal and that it is not intended to interfere with the costs order in their favour. If the application is served on the supporting creditors or contributories and they appear on the appeal, they may be allowed separate sets of costs.[677]

9.159 Identity of appellant

An application appealing against a winding-up order may be issued by a creditor or contributory who had given notice under r. 4.16 of his intention to appear at the hearing of the petition (or was given leave to be added to the list out of time) and who appeared when the winding-up order was made,[678] or it may be issued by the company itself. The

670. IR 1986, r. 7.49(3).
671. IR 1986, r. 7.49(1) and RSC O. 59, r. 3(2); and see *Re Calahurst Ltd*, *supra*, at 320A.
672. RSC O. 59, r. 4(1).
673. RSC O. 59, r. 4(3).
674. RSC O. 3, r. 5 and O. 59, r. 15.
675. RSC O. 59, r. 3(5).
676. *Re Webber, ex parte Webber* (1889) 24 QBD 313.
677. *Re Ibo Investments Co.* [1903] 2 Ch. 373 at 376–377.
678. *Re New Gas Co.* (1877) 5 Ch.D. 703; *Re JD Swain Ltd* [1965] 1 WLR 909.

directors of the company retain a residual discretion to appeal the winding-up order in the name of the company, notwithstanding the cesser of their usual powers. Creditors or contributories who did not appear in the court below require leave to appeal.[679] The court may in its discretion hear any other person who appears to have a sufficient interest in the appeal,[680] but such a person has no right to appeal.[681]

9.160 Costs

Where the company is the sole named appellant but the appeal is in fact promoted by its directors or contributories, security for the petitioner's costs of the appeal must be provided.[682] If security for costs is not sought and the appeal is dismissed, the court may order that the petitioner should have his costs out of the assets of the company, but that there should be no order as to the costs of the appellants.[683] Where an appeal against a winding-up order succeeds, and the winding-up order is set aside, the petitioner may be ordered to pay the company's costs of the petition, the appellant's costs of the appeal, both on the standard basis, together with the costs of the official receiver of the appeal taxed on the indemnity basis, and the costs and disbursements of the official receiver incurred in the winding-up: the assessment of his costs and disbursements may be adjourned to the registrar for determination. The official receiver may be permitted to deduct his proper costs and disbursements fixed by the registrar from the company's assets in his hands before accounting to the company for the balance.[684] Where directors have incurred costs in petitioning to wind-up the company or appealing against the dismissal of their petition, they may be restrained by injunction from paying those costs out of the company's assets, notwithstanding a provision in the articles of association of the company granting the directors an indemnity out of the company's assets.[685]

9.161 Security for costs of appeal

If the company is the sole appellant, security for the costs of the appeal must be given.[686] The security must not be provided from the company's own assets, but should be provided

679. *Re Securities Insurance Co.* [1894] 2 Ch. 410. (*Semble*, leave should be sought from the High Court Registrar or the Companies Court Judge).

680. See, for example, *Re Austintel Ltd* [1977] 1 WLR 616 at 619H (where the Court of Appeal, *de bene esse*, heard submissions made on behalf of the Society of Practitioners of Insolvency, which had not appeared in the Court below).

681. *Re Bradford Navigation Co.* (1870) 5 Ch. App. 600 at 603 per James LJ.

682. See paras 9.161–9.164, *infra*.

683. *Re National Savings Bank Association* (1866) 1 Ch. App. 547; *Re Diamond Fuel Co.* (1879) 13 Ch.D. 400. But it is questionable whether the court would now grant such an order, the effect of which is that the appellant company's solicitors may be unable to recover their costs. In *Re a Company (No. 004055 of 1991), ex parte Doe Sport Ltd* [1991] BCLC 865, Hoffmann J. suggested that a costs order having such a consequence (known as a "*Bathampton* order"; see para. 9.118, *supra*), was inappropriate in light of the court's powers under RSC O. 62, r. 11 to disallow solicitors' costs, or under the Supreme Court Act 1981, s. 51 to order third parties to pay the costs.

684. *Re Joseph Phillips Ltd* [1964] 1 WLR 369.

685. *Smith* v. *Duke of Manchester* (1883) 24 Ch.D. 611 at 615–616.

686. RSC O. 59, r. 10(5); *Supreme Court Practice 1997*, Vol. 1, paras 59/10/19–26, pp. 1005–1008; *Re Photographic Artists' Co-operative Supply Association* (1883) 23 Ch.D. 370; *Re Diamond Fuel Co.* (1879) 13 Ch.D. 400; *Northampton Coal, Iron and Waggon Co.* v. *Midland Waggon Co.* (1878) 7 Ch.D. 500; *Re Amalgamated Properties of Rhodesia (1913) Ltd* [1917] 2 Ch. 115.

by the contributories or directors who promote the appeal. The security must be substantial.[687]

9.162 Application for security

A petitioner who is respondent to an appeal by the company alone should in the first instance write to the company's solicitors requesting that security be provided, otherwise than from the company's assets, in a sum sufficient to cover the petitioner's anticipated costs of the appeal.[688] If substantial security is not provided, the petitioner should apply to the Companies Court Registrar for an order that the appeal be stayed until the directors or contributories who promote the appeal provide security for costs, and that in default of security being provided within a particular period, the appeal should be dismissed. The request for security should be made promptly after the appeal has been served and in default an application for security should be properly issued. The application for security for costs is made by ordinary application supported by affidavit, both of which should be served on the appellant company. The affidavit should set out or exhibit a detailed and itemised bill of the petitioner's anticipated costs of the appeal.[689]

9.163 Form of order for security

The order should provide:

(i) that those who provide the appeal should provide security within a fixed period (usually 14 to 28 days);
(ii) that the appeal be stayed in the meantime; and
(iii) that in default of providing security within the time stipulated, the appeal should be dismissed with costs.[690]

The security is usually to be provided by payment of money into court, although a guarantee of a first class bank might in some cases be ordered.

9.164 Stay pending appeal

An appeal does not stay proceedings unless it is so ordered by the judge or the Court of Appeal.[691] As a matter of practice the court will not order a stay of the winding-up proceedings pending determination of the appeal,[692] but may order a stay of the advertisement of the winding-up order[693] pending appeal. The High Court single judge and the Court of Appeal will not order a stay whilst the appellant is in default of an order for security for costs.[694]

687. *Re Consolidated South Rand Mines Deep Ltd* [1909] WN 66; *Re EK Wilson & Sons Ltd* [1972] 1 WLR 791.
688. *Supreme Court Practice 1997*, Vol. 1, para. 59/10/26, p. 1008.
689. *Supreme Court Practice 1997*, Vol. 1, para. 59/10/26, p. 1008.
690. *Ibid.*
691. RSC O. 59, r. 13(1).
692. *Re A and BC Chewing Gum Ltd* [1975] 1 WLR 579 at 592; *Re Amalgamated Properties of Rhodesia Ltd* [1917] 2 Ch. 115.
693. Pursuant to IR 1986, r. 4.21(4).
694. *Re Corporation of British Investors* (1897) 41 Sol. J 384.

9.165 When leave to appeal is required

Leave to appeal is not required for an appeal to the single judge of the High Court against the grant or refusal of a winding-up order by the district judge or judge of the County Court, or by the High Court registrar.[695] Leave to appeal is required for an appeal against the decision of the single High Court judge sitting in an appellate capacity hearing such an appeal from the County Court or High Court registrar.[696] Where the single High Court judge is not sitting in an appellate capacity but determines the matter as a court of first instance (for example, where the registrar adjourns a disputed petition to the judge for determination), the usual rules[697] for determining whether leave is required apply: the notice of appeal in such a case is by way of an ordinary application under r. 7.2.[698] Leave is not required for an appeal against the making of, or a refusal to make, a winding-up order by a High Court judge since both orders are final and not interlocutory.[699] Leave will be required to appeal against an order of the single High Court judge striking out a petition as an abuse of process or because the debt is disputed,[700] since such orders are interlocutory.[701]

STAY OF WINDING-UP PROCEEDINGS

9.166 Jurisdiction

The court has power to stay all the proceedings in a winding-up at any time after an order for winding-up has been made, if the court is satisfied that all proceedings in the winding-up ought to be stayed.[702] The power to stay proceedings in the winding-up is discretionary. The order staying the proceedings may be absolute (i.e. without any limit in time and without any conditions), or it may be made for a limited time and subject to such conditions as the court thinks fit.[703] Before granting a stay of the winding-up proceedings, the court *may* require the official receiver to provide a report to the court dealing with any matters which the official receiver considers to be relevant to the application.[704] The court also has power to stay all proceedings in a voluntary liquidation at any time after the resolution has been passed and the liquidator has been appointed.[705]

9.167 Who may apply for a stay

The application may be made by the liquidator, the official receiver or any creditor or contributory of the company.[706]

695. IR 1986, r. 7.47(2); *Re Busytoday Ltd* [1992] 1 WLR 683.
696. *Ibid*; *Midrome Ltd* v. *Shaw* [1993] BCC 659.
697. I.e., under RSC O. 59.
698. IR 1986, r. 7.49(3).
699. RSC O. 59, r. 1A(5)(d); *Supreme Court Practice 1997*, Vol. 1, para. 59/1A/25, p. 959.
700. Disputed debts are dealt with in more detail below.
701. Supreme Court Act 1981, s. 18(1)(h); RSC O. 59, r. 1A(6)(k); *Supreme Court Practice 1997*, Vol. 1, para. 59/1A/14, p. 957.
702. IA 1986, s. 147(1).
703. *Ibid.*
704. IA 1986, s. 147(2).
705. IA 1986, s. 112(1); *Re South Barrule State Quarry Co.* (1869) LR 8 Eq. 688.
706. IA 1986, s. 147(1).

9.168 Form of application

In a compulsory liquidation, the application for a stay should be by way of ordinary application. In a voluntary liquidation, the application should be by way of originating application (unless there has been an earlier originating application in relation to the voluntary winding-up in which liberty to apply has expressly been given, in which case an ordinary application should be used). In each case, the application should be supported by an affidavit setting out the grounds for a stay.[707] The application should in the first instance be returnable before the registrar in chambers,[708] but the registrar may adjourn the application to the judge if it is opposed.[709]

9.169 Respondents to the application

Where the applicant is a creditor or contributory of the company, the respondents should be the official receiver (where he is the liquidator of the company) or the official receiver and the liquidator (where the official receiver is not the liquidator). In a compulsory liquidation, the petitioner should also be joined as a respondent unless the petitioner has consented to the stay: if the petitioner is not joined as a respondent but is given notice of the application, he may apply to be joined as a respondent as a person interested in the matter.[710] Where the applicant is the official receiver or the liquidator, the application may be made *ex parte*. However, if the petitioning creditor has not been paid and has not consented to the stay, he ought to be joined as a respondent to the application: if he is not joined but is given notice of the application, he may apply to be joined as respondent.[711]

9.170 Service of the application

Where the application is to be made *ex parte* (i.e. an application by the official receiver or liquidator with the consent of the petitioner), two copies of the application will be required when it is issued,[712] and the application need not be served on any person. Where the application is to be made *inter partes* (i.e. an application by a creditor or contributory, or by the official receiver or liquidator where the petitioner is a respondent), two copies of the application plus a copy for service on each respondent will be required.[713] The applicant should serve a copy of the application on each respondent at least 14 days prior to the date fixed for the hearing (unless the court otherwise directs).[714]

9.171 Affidavit in support

The application should be supported by an affidavit setting out the grounds for a stay, which should be filed in court and served on each respondent to the application.[715] Where

707. See paras 9.171–9.172, *infra*.
708. IR 1986, r. 7.6(1),(2).
709. IR 1986, r. 7.6(3).
710. I.e., under RSC O. 15, r. 6(2)(b); *Re Lowston Ltd* [1991] BCLC 570 at 571a.
711. *Ibid.*
712. IR 1986, r. 7.4(1).
713. *Ibid.*
714. IR 1986, r. 7.4(3),(5).
715. IR 1986, r. 7.8(1).

the applicant is the official receiver, or the liquidator on an *ex parte* application (and the court has not ordered otherwise), a report may be used instead of an affidavit.[716] The affidavit (or report) should contain the following information:

(1) details of all creditors of the company at the date of liquidation, including the amount of their debts, whether they have been paid or whether they consent to the stay[717];
(2) that there are no partly paid shares, or where there are, that the holders of those shares consent to the stay;
(3) where there are surplus assets (i.e. there would be a return to the members in the liquidation), that the members all consent or arrangements have been made to ensure that dissentient members receive what they would have received in the liquidation;
(4) that there has been no return to the members of the company which would have been an unlawful return or reduction of capital[718] had the company not been in liquidation[719];
(5) that the company has or will have sufficient capital with which to continue its business (if that is intended) should the stay be granted.

9.172 Grounds for a stay

The power of the court to grant a stay is discretionary.[720] The court must be satisfied on the evidence filed that all proceedings in the winding-up ought to be stayed.[721] The burden is on the applicants to make out a sufficient case for a stay.[722] The court will not grant a stay merely because the winding-up order is under appeal.[723] The court has to be satisfied that it is right to stay the winding-up proceedings, and if there are matters in respect of which the court has doubts, it should not grant a stay.[724] In appropriate cases the stay may be ordered to enable the company to resume business, but the court has to be satisfied that it is proper to allow the company (in light of its previous trading history) "to re-emerge back as an unencumbered company able to trade and carry on business".[725] Winding-up proceedings may be stayed where all creditors who have proved in the liquidation have been paid or consent to the stay, and the fact that there is a creditor whose debt has not been paid because it is disputed is not a bar to a stay.[726] However, if it appears that the applicant directors have misconducted themselves or been guilty of improper dealings

716. IR 1986, r. 7.9(1).
717. *Re Calgary & Edmonton Land Co. Ltd* [1975] 1 WLR 355.
718. I.e., contrary to CA 1985, part VIII.
719. If there has been such a return, the court is likely to require the members in question to reinsure the company for the capital received, prior to granting a stay.
720. *Re Calgary & Edmonton Land Co. Ltd*, *supra*, at 358H.
721. IA 1986, s. 147(1).
722. *Re Calgary & Edmonton Land Co. Ltd*, *supra*, at 358H–359A.
723. *Re A and BC Chewing Gum Ltd* [1975] 1 WLR 579 at 592.
724. *Re Telescriptor Syndicate Ltd* [1903] 2 Ch. 177.
725. *Re Lowston Ltd* [1991] BCLC 570 at 572h, per Harman J.
726. *Re Lowston Ltd*, *supra*, at 571h and 572i–573a, where the case for a stay was strengthened because the judgment on which the petition had been based had been set aside. Contrast *Re Empire Builders* [1919] WN 178 (which suggests that a stay is not the correct means of challenging the validity of a winding-up order).

prior to the litigation, the court may refuse a stay which would have the effect of restoring the company to the directors' hands.[727]

9.173 Imposing terms for a stay

Where there has been no misconduct by the applicants for a stay (in the sense of improper dealings) but the company has not been properly administered (for example, it was at the date of liquidation in default in filing accounts and returns with the registrar of companies), the court can impose terms as a condition of granting the stay.[728] Thus, the court may require the applicants to undertake to complete and file, or procure the completion and filing of, all outstanding returns and accounts within a stipulated period.[729] Where the evidence discloses that the company is in fact insolvent, the court is likely to refuse a stay. However, where the members and directors have claims against the company, the court may be prepared to order a stay on terms that the members and directors undertake to postpone their claims until the other creditors have been paid.[730] The court will also require the costs of the official receiver, and of the liquidator (if not the official receiver), to be paid if a stay is to be ordered.[731] If the official receiver or liquidator is the applicant, then costs will be payable out of the company's assets in his hands, before he accounts for the balance to the directors or contributories; if the application is brought by a creditor or contributory, the applicant will be ordered to pay the costs of the official receiver and liquidator. The court may impose terms designed to bring the stay to the notice of creditors or contributories (for example, by requiring that a notice be advertised in the *Gazette* or a circular be sent)[732]; or the court may grant a stay on terms that any dissentient creditor or the official receiver shall have liberty to apply within three months to remove the stay.[733]

9.174 Official receiver's report

Where a stay of all winding-up proceedings in a compulsory liquidation is sought, the court may (but is not obliged to) seek a report from the official receiver concerning any matter which he considers to be relevant to the application.[734] The official receiver may not have anything to report, and if that is the case, the official receiver will appear on the application and so inform the court.[735] The official receiver's report may deal with matters such as the estimated deficiency of the company (particularly where he disagrees with the applicant's estimate), any evidence of improper dealings or maladministration by the directors prior to liquidation,[736] and any proceedings which are pending or contemplated

727. *Re Telescriptor Syndicate Ltd, supra*; *Re Lowston Ltd, supra*, at 573b.
728. IA 1986, s. 147(1).
729. *Re Lowston Ltd, supra*, at 573c–e.
730. *Ibid.* at 573e–574a (where the contributory was required to postpone part of his claim for one year).
731. *Ibid.* at 574a.
732. IR 1986, r. 4.48(2).
733. *Re Baxters Ltd* [1898] WN 60.
734. IA 1986, s. 147(2).
735. The official receiver and his deputies have rights of audience in insolvency proceedings: IR 1986, r. 7.52(1).
736. In which case, terms may be imposed: see the preceding para.

against the directors such as misfeasance[737] or disqualification proceedings.[738] The court has no jurisdiction to require a report in relation to an application to stay proceedings in a voluntary winding-up.[739]

9.175 Effect of a stay

Where the order "altogether"[740] stays all proceedings in the winding-up, the liquidation is for all practical purposes at an end, the liquidator may be discharged and control reverts to the directors.[741] Where the order does not stay "altogether" all proceedings in the winding-up, but only operates for a limited time, the liquidation is in effect suspended, and control reverts to the directors for that period only and the liquidator is not discharged from office: at the expiry of the period, the directors cease once again to have any control and the liquidator resumes his duties, unless some other order is made in the meantime.

9.176 The order

A copy of the order staying all proceedings in the winding-up must be sent forthwith by the company to the registrar of companies whether the winding-up is compulsory,[742] or voluntary,[743] and details of the stay will be entered in the company's file maintained by the registrar of companies.

DISPUTED DEBTS

9.177 Scope of the winding-up jurisdiction

A creditor who has an undisputed claim against a company is entitled to petition to wind up that company, and the presentation of the petition cannot be restrained by injunction if there are no grounds for saying that the petition would be an abuse of process.[744] Although the court has an unfettered discretion when hearing petitions,[745] that discretion is exercised in accordance with well-established principles: thus a creditor with an undisputed claim is generally entitled (as against the company) *ex debito justitiae* to a winding-up order. Conversely, where an alleged debt is disputed by the company in good faith on substantial grounds, the claimant cannot claim to be a creditor within the meaning of s. 124(1) of the Insolvency Act 1986, and has usually no *locus standi* to present a

737. I.e., under IA 1986, s. 212.
738. I.e., under the Company Directors Disqualification Act 1986.
739. *Re Serene Shoes Ltd* [1958] 1 WLR 1087.
740. IA 1986, s. 147(1).
741. See *Re Lowston Ltd, supra*, at 573b.
742. IA 1986, s. 147(3).
743. IA 1986, s. 112(3).
744. *Re a Company (No. 007923 of 1994)* [1995] 1 WLR 953; and see *Coulon Sanderson & Ward Ltd* v. *Ward* (1986) 2 BCC 99, 207 at 99, 215 (l/h col) and *Bryanston Finance Ltd* v. *de Vries (No. 2)* [1976] Ch. 63 at 75C–F, in which the court refused to restrain the presentation of contributories' winding-up petitions.
745. Under IA 1986, s. 125(1); *Re P&J Macrae Ltd* [1961] 1 WLR 229 at 231, 237–240; *Re Southard & Co. Ltd* [1979] 1 WLR 1198.

petition.[746] The petition should therefore be dismissed or struck out with costs,[747] even if the petitioner was not aware at the time of presentation of all the matters giving rise to the dispute about the indebtedness[748]; but the court will not dismiss the petition if the petitioner has a good arguable case that he is a creditor and the effect of dismissal would be to deprive him of a remedy, or otherwise injustice would result, or for some other sufficient reason the petition should proceed.[749] If the Companies Court Judge concludes that a debt is *bona fide* disputed on substantial grounds and dismisses the petition, the Court of Appeal will be slow to interfere with that finding.[750]

9.178 Abuse of process

It is frequently stated that the Companies Court is not to be regarded or used as a debt collecting court. Although a petitioner may present a petition with the motive of compelling the company to pay its debt,[751] it has been stated on numerous occasions that it is an abuse of the process of the court for a creditor to present a petition in respect of a debt which is disputed in good faith on substantial grounds in order to enforce payment of that debt.[752] Such a petition is liable to be dismissed[753] or struck out[754] with costs, and the abuse of process may be reflected in an order for indemnity costs[755]; a wasted costs order[756] may also be made against a petitioner's solicitor who ought to have realised that the petition debt is *bona fide* disputed and fails to advise his client that the petition is an abuse of process[757] or who improperly swears the affidavit of verification where he ought to have known that the petition debt was *bona fide* disputed.[758] On the other hand, if the debt is undisputed, the mere fact that the petitioner, in presenting his petition, is motivated by personal hostility or has some ulterior motive, is not without more an abuse of process[759]; but if the petitioner's reason for seeking to have the company wound up is to

746. See, for example, *Mann* v. *Goldstein* [1968] 1 WLR 1091 at 1095; *Stonegate Securities Ltd* v. *Gregory* [1980] 1 Ch. 575 at 579f.

747. *Re a Company (No. 00212 of 1995)*, *Times*, 7 April 1995; *Re a Company (No. 003079 of 1990)* [1991] BCC 683 at 685C–E.

748. *Re a Company (No. 003079 of 1990)*, *supra*, at 686C; *Re Fernforest Ltd* [1991] BCC 680 at 681H–682B; and see *Re Cannon Screen Entertainment Ltd* [1989] BCLC 660; contrast *Re Trinity Insurance Co. Ltd* [1990] BCC 235.

749. *Alipour* v. *Ary* [1997] 1 WLR 534 at 546A B; *Re Claybridge Shipping Co. SA* [1997] 1 BCLC 572.

750. *Pentagin Technologies International Ltd* v. *Express Company Securities*, *Times*, 7 April 1995.

751. *Re St Thomas's Dock Co.* (1876) 2 Ch.D. 116; *Mann* v. *Goldstein* [1968] 1 WLR 1091; *Holt Southey Ltd* v. *Catric Components Ltd* [1978] 1 WLR 630.

752. See, for example, *Re Catholic Publishing & Bookselling Co.* (1864) 2 De GJ & Son 116; *Re London and Paris Banking Corp.* (1875) LR 19 Eq. 444; *Re a Company* [1894] 2 Ch. 349.

753. *Alipour* v. *Ary*, *supra*, at 541F–G and 546A.

754. Under the inherent jurisdiction of the court: *Re Gold Hill Mines* (1883) 23 Ch.D. 210 at 211. (Since a petition is not a pleading (see RSC O. 1, r. 4(1)), it may not be struck out under RSC O. 18, r. 19).

755. *Re a Company (No. 0012209 of 1991)* [1992] BCLC 865; *Re a Company (No. 00751 of 1992), ex parte Avocet Aviation Ltd* [1992] BCLC 869 at 871d–f. For a useful review of the court's power to award indemnity costs, see *Munkenbeck & Marshall* v. *McAlpine* 44 Con. LR 30; see also *Supreme Court Practice 1997*, Vol. 1, para. 62/3/3, p. 1057.

756. Under the Supreme Court Act 1981, s. 51(6) and RSC O. 62, r. 11: see *Supreme Court Practice 1997*, Vol. 1, para. 62/11/2, pp. 1075–1078.

757. *Ridehalgh* v. *Horsefield*, and *Philex* v. *Golban (Company No. 0022 of 1993)* [1994] BCC 390.

758. *Re a Company (No. 006798 of 1995)* [1996] 1 WLR 491.

759. *Mann* v. *Goldstein*, *supra*, at 1095; *Bryanston Finance Ltd* v. *de Vries (No. 2)* [1976] Ch. 63 at 75D–F (a contributory's winding-up petition); but contrast *Barrett* v. *Duckett* [1995] BCC 362 (also a contributory's winding-up petition).

gain a benefit for himself (such as a preference over other creditors of the company), and a winding-up order would not improve the position of other creditors who oppose the petition, the court may dismiss the petition.[760]

9.179 Burden on the company

The burden is on the company to show that the alleged debt is disputed in good faith on substantial grounds. It is not sufficient that the company honestly believes that the debt is disputed on substantial grounds (i.e. the test is not subjective): the evidence adduced by the company should indicate objectively that there is an issue whether the debt is due and owing which has substance, is not frivolous, and which ought to be tried.[761] An analysis of the numerous authorities in this area[762] suggests that the court applies the following general principles in determining whether a debt can be said to be disputed in good faith on substantial grounds and whether the alleged creditor has *locus standi* to petition.

9.179.1 Part of debt disputed

The mere fact that some part of the debt is disputed is not sufficient to remove the creditor's right to petition: provided that a quantified part of the alleged debt can be shown to be undoubtedly due for payment which is not *de minimis* and which could be the subject of a demand, the court can infer that the company is insolvent owing to its failure to pay the undisputed part.[763]

9.179.2 Admitted debts and cross-claims

Where the creditor's claim is admitted, but the company asserts that it has an unrelated counterclaim which equals or exceeds the creditor's claim and which it has not been able to litigate, the court has an unfettered discretion on the hearing of the petition[764] whether to dismiss the petition or make a winding-up order.[765] In exercising the discretion, the court will have regard to factors such as the extent of the connection (if any) between the admitted debt and the cross-claim, whether proceedings in relation to the cross-claim are pending or are merely contemplated, whether the company has been guilty of any delay in seeking to have the cross-claim determined, the age of the admitted debt and the age of the cross-claim, and the nature and extent of any dispute in relation to the cross-claim.

760. *Re Leigh Estates (UK) Ltd* [1994] BCC 292 at 295E–H.

761. *Mann* v. *Goldstein, supra*, at 1096; *Re Great Britain Mutual Life Assurance Society* (1880) 16 Ch.D. 246 at 253; *Re General Exchange Bank Ltd* (1866) 14 LT 582 at 583.

762. A detailed analysis is outside the scope of this work.

763. *Re Pendigo Ltd* [1996] BCC 608 at 610A–D; *Re Tweeds Garages Ltd* [1962] Ch. 406; *Re Steel Wing Co.* [1921] 1 Ch. 349.

764. But, it seems, not on the hearing of an application to restrain the presentation or advertisement of a petition, when an injunction will not be granted merely owing to the existence of a cross-claim: see *Re Leasing & Finance Services Ltd* [1991] BCC 29 at 31F–H and *Re a Company (No. 006273 of 1992)* [1993] BCLC 131 at 133 g–i; but contrast *Re a Company (No. 009080 of 1992)* [1993] BCLC 269 and *Re Pendigo Ltd, supra*, at 611C–E.

765. *Re Pendigo Ltd, supra*, at 611D–E; *Re FSA Business Software Ltd* [1990] BCLC 825 at 831a; *Re Leasing & Finance Services Ltd* [1991] BCC 29.

9.179.3 Set-off

In contrast, where the company files evidence to show that the petition debt is equalled or exceeded by a true set-off available to the company (i.e. arising out of the same transaction), the court will dismiss the petition, since a true set-off extinguishes the debt and is thus a defence to the alleged creditor's claim.[766]

9.179.4 Leave to defend under RSC O. 14

The fact that the debt on which the petition is based has also been claimed in a specially endorsed writ and the company has been given unconditional leave to defend the action pursuant to RSC O. 14, will be taken into consideration by the court, but the fact that leave has been given does not preclude the court, on considering a petition and the evidence filed thereon, from finding that the debt is due and owing and that a winding-up order should be made.[767] By analogy, it would appear that the court could make a winding-up order notwithstanding that a judgment in default in relation to the petition debt has been set aside, if the evidence filed on the petition clearly shows that the debt is due and owing[768] (see 9.179.6, *infra*).

9.179.5 Judgment debts

Where the petition is based on a default judgment and the evidence filed by the company indicates that there is a *bona fide* substantial dispute in relation to the debt, on an undertaking by the company to apply to set aside the judgment, the court may direct the petition to be adjourned pending the outcome of the application to set aside, or it may dismiss the petition in a clear case of dispute. Where the company complains that a default judgment was obtained by fraud, the court may, on an undertaking by the company to apply to set aside the judgment, adjourn the petition pending the outcome of the application.[769] Where, by the date of the first hearing of the petition before the registrar, an application to set aside a default judgment on which the petition is based has been issued but not determined, the registrar is likely to adjourn the petition to await the outcome of that application: if by the date of the adjourned hearing of the petition the judgment stands, a winding-up order may be made; if the judgment has been set aside, the petition will be dismissed unless the petitioner wishes to file evidence and to seek to persuade the judge that a winding-up order should be made notwithstanding the setting aside of the judgment.[770]

9.179.6 Judgment under appeal

The fact that the petition is based on a judgment which is under appeal but not subject to a stay of execution is not in itself justification for refusing a winding-up order: the court may consider on the evidence filed on the petition that a winding-up order should be made.

766. *Hanak* v. *Green* [1958] 2 QB 9 at 29.
767. *Re Welsh Brick Industries Ltd* [1946] 2 All ER 197.
768. But see *Re Anglo Bavarian Steel Ball Co.* [1899] WN 80.
769. *Bowes* v. *Hope Life Insurance and Guarantee Co.* (1865) 11 HL Cas. 389.
770. By analogy with *Re Welsh Brick Industries Ltd, supra.*

On the other hand, the court may refuse to make an order if the company has obtained a stay of execution on the judgment under appeal.[771] Where the first instance judgment on which the petition is based is set aside on appeal, the court may dismiss the petition notwithstanding that the setting aside of the judgment is itself subject to appeal.[772]

9.179.7 Costs orders

An order for costs made against the company in earlier proceedings or on an earlier application is a debt on which a winding-up petition can be based, notwithstanding that the costs have not yet been taxed or agreed, and the precise liability has therefore not been ascertained.[773]

9.180 Determining disputes on a petition

Where the dispute between the parties is one which depends solely on the interpretation of documentary evidence (such as the construction of a contract), the court may be prepared to determine that issue in the winding-up proceedings if the relevant documents are in evidence.[774] Where, however, the dispute requires the court to resolve disputes of fact (for example, to choose between two conflicting versions of events), winding-up proceedings are inappropriate. The Companies Court is ill-equipped to deal with disputes of fact[775]: in winding-up proceedings, there is generally no discovery and no cross-examination[776] of deponents, and thus the Companies Court Judge is not in a position to assess credibility. Where the evidence filed by the company would, if true, provide a defence to the petitioner's claim and is not manifestly incredible on its face, the Companies Court Judge will usually dismiss the petition, leaving the dispute to be resolved in a writ action: the court need not be satisfied that the company will succeed at trial, merely that there is a dispute in good faith on substantial grounds. However, the court will not dismiss the petition if the petitioner has a good arguable case that he is a creditor and the effect of dismissal would be to deprive him of a remedy, or otherwise injustice would result, or for some other sufficient reason the petition should proceed.[777]

9.181 Powers of the court where the debt is disputed

Where a debt is disputed in good faith on substantial grounds, the court may restrain the presentation of a winding-up petition based on the debt, may restrain the advertisement of the petition and strike out the petition, or may dismiss the petition or adjourn it (either

771. *Re Amalgamated Properties of Rhodesia (1913) Ltd* [1917] 2 Ch. 115; *Re Douglas Griggs Engineering Ltd* [1963] Ch. 19; cf *Re LHF Wools Ltd* [1970] Ch. 27.

772. Re *Anglo Bavarian Steel Ball Co.* [1899] WN 80.

773. *Tottenham Hotspur plc* v. *Edennote plc* [1994] BCC 681 at 684E–F; *Re Portedge Ltd* [1997] BCC 23 at 25E, H; and *Securum Finance Ltd* v. *Camswell Ltd* [1994] BCC 434 at 434H–435A. To the extent that *Re a Company (No. 001573 of 1983)* (1983) 1 BCC 98, 937 and *Re Laceward Ltd* [1980] 1 WLR 133 suggest that untaxed costs can *never* be the basis of a winding-up petition, they are no longer good law.

774. See, for example, *Re Janeash Ltd* [1990] BCC 250 at 252B–G (where the court concluded on the documents that there was no genuine dispute and made a winding-up order).

775. *Alipour* v. *Ary, supra* at 541F–G.

776. In *Re Janeash Ltd, supra,* at 251E Browne-Wilkinson V-C criticised a direction made by the Registrar for the cross-examination of deponents at the hearing of the petition.

777. *Alipour* v. *Ary, supra,* at 546A–B; *Tottenham Hotspur plc* v. *Edennote plc* [1994] BCC 681.

conditionally or unconditionally) at the hearing. The court retains a wide discretion,[778] and in extremely rare cases the court may make a winding-up order even where the petitioner's debt is disputed: orders have been made in relation to Russian banks which had branches in England, notwithstanding that the debt was disputed, since this was the only remedy available to the creditor.[779]

9.182 Relevance of solvency

The fact the company can establish in evidence that it is solvent (i.e. that its assets exceed its liabilities and that it is profitable), is not sufficient in itself to defeat the petition. If the court finds that the company has failed to comply with a valid demand to pay a debt which is not disputed in good faith on substantial grounds, the court may infer that the company is insolvent and make a winding-up order, notwithstanding that the company's evidence indicates that it is solvent.[780] This is the case whether the demand is made by formal statutory demand or by letter.[781] Conversely, where the petition debt is shown to be disputed in good faith on substantial grounds, the petitioner has no *locus standi* to petition, and the petition must be dismissed[782] notwithstanding that the evidence indicates that the company is insolvent; and if the court finds that the debt is *bona fide* disputed, it may dismiss the petition without considering the question of the company's solvency.[783] The evidence filed by the company[784] and the petitioner will nevertheless usually deal with the company's apparent solvency or insolvency, since this may be relevant to the court's assessment of the *bona fides* of the dispute.

9.183 What should the company do?

A company which *bona fide* disputes a debt claimed by an alleged creditor may challenge the alleged creditor's *locus standi* at one of three stages of the winding-up proceedings:

(1) Following receipt of a demand (either by formal statutory demand or letter[785]) for payment of a disputed debt which threatens the presentation of a winding-up petition in default of payment, the company may make an immediate application

778. IA 1986, s. 125(1).

779. *Re Russian and English Bank* [1932] 1 Ch. 663; *Re Russian Bank for Foreign Trade* [1933] Ch. 745; *Re Tovarishestro Manufactur, Luidvig-Rabenck* [1944] Ch. 409; and see *Alipour* v. *Ary, supra*, at 546A–B; and *Tottenham Hotspur plc* v. *Edennote plc, supra*.

780. *Cornhill Insurance plc* v. *Improvement Services Ltd* [1986] 1 WLR 114.

781. IA 1986, s. 123(1)(e) and see *Taylors Industrial Flooring Ltd* v. *M&H Plant Hire (Manchester) Ltd* [1990] BCLC 217 and *Cornhill Insurance plc* v. *Improvement Services Ltd* [1986] 1 WLR 114. In exceptional circumstances, a winding-up order may be obtained although no demand has been served on the company, but the court will be slow to infer insolvency from non-payment of a due debt which has never been demanded of the company: *Re a Company (No. 006798 of 1995)* [1996] 1 WLR 491 at 502C–E.

782. *Mann* v. *Goldstein* [1968] 1 WLR 1091 at 1095–1096; cf *Niger Merchants Co.* v. *Capper* (1877) 18 Ch.D. 557n at 559 which suggests that it is inappropriate for a creditor to petition to wind-up a solvent company, but is criticised in *Mann* v. *Goldstein, supra*, at 1095.

783. *Re a Company (No. 00212 of 1995), Times*, 7 April 1995; and see, for example, *Re a Company (No. 00751 of 1992)* [1992] BCLC 869.

784. See *Re Portedge Ltd* [1997] BCC 23 at 25B–C where it is suggested that the company should be frank about its financial position on an *ex parte* application to restrain presentation or advertisement.

785. *Taylors Industrial Flooring Ltd* v. *M&H Plant Hire (Manchester) Ltd, supra*.

for an injunction to restrain the presentation of a winding-up petition based on the debt until the debt is established by a judgment.[786]

(2) Once a winding-up petition has been presented for a debt in respect of which there is a *bona fide* dispute, the company may apply for an injunction to restrain the advertisement of the petition and for an order that the petition be struck out as an abuse of process on the basis of the dispute.[787] The company may combine this with an application for a validation order to preserve its ability to trade in the interim.[788]

(3) Where the company fails to seek injunctive relief and the petition is presented and advertised, the company may file evidence to oppose the petition on the hearing thereof.[789]

9.183.1 The point at which the company launches its challenge will often be dictated by the speed with which it instructs solicitors in relation to the demand, but it will generally be in the best interests of the company to challenge the demand at the earliest opportunity and before a petition is presented: the presentation may cause the company difficulty in relation to its creditors and bankers (for example, if enquiries are made of the company regarding its solvency or creditworthiness), and advertisement of the petition may cause considerable damage to its goodwill. If the court refuses a motion by the company to restrain presentation of a petition because it is not satisfied that the debt is *bona fide* disputed on substantial grounds, the company may not apply to restrain advertisement on the same grounds based on evidence which was, or with reasonable diligence had been, adduced in the earlier application[790]; but the same grounds may be raised on the hearing of the petition when the court has to decide whether to exercise its discretion to make a winding-up order.[791] Each of the stages at which the company may challenge the creditor's standing is discussed in more detail in the following paragraphs.

APPLICATIONS TO RESTRAIN PRESENTATION OF A PETITION

9.184 Undertaking not to petition

If a company receives a demand for payment of a debt which it disputes in good faith on substantial grounds, it (or its solicitors) should immediately write to the alleged creditor (or its solicitors): (i) setting out in detail why the company disputes the debt; (ii) stating that the threat of winding-up proceedings is therefore inappropriate (and that such proceedings would be an abuse of process); and (iii) requiring that an undertaking be given within a stated period that a winding-up petition will not be presented, or alternatively requiring that a particular period of notice will be given prior to presentation (say, 48 hours) to enable an *ex parte* application to restrain the presentation of the petition to be made. The deadline for the undertaking stipulated by the company should expire in

786. See paras 9.184 *et seq.*, *infra.*
787. See paras 9.192 *et seq.*, *infra.*
788. Under IA 1986, s. 127.
789. See IR 1986, r. 4.18, and para. 9.199, *infra.*
790. *Re Portedge Ltd* [1997] BCC 23.
791. *Ibid.* at 28A–B.

sufficient time before the deadline for payment imposed by the creditor. Where the creditor has served a statutory demand, the company should be able to calculate the date on which the three weeks for payment[792] will expire and make an application for an injunction before that date if no undertaking is given. Where the creditor makes a demand by letter which stipulates a much shorter period for payment (say five or seven days),[793] the company will have to react promptly to prevent presentation of a petition: the company will have to stipulate a short period in which the creditor must undertake not to petition, and must promptly apply for an injunction if the undertaking is not given. If the company's request for an undertaking is refused, or the creditor does not respond to the request, the company should apply for an order restraining the creditor from presenting a winding-up petition based on the disputed debt. The court has power to make such an order in the exercise of its inherent jurisdiction to prevent an abuse of its process.[794]

9.185 Form of application to restrain presentation

The application to restrain the presentation of a petition is made by a notice of originating motion[795] returnable before the Companies Court Judge sitting in open court.[796] Three copies of the notice of originating motion will be required for issue. The notice of originating motion need not identify the judge by name (nor the court number): it is sufficient if the notice of originating motion merely refers to an application to be made on a particular date before the Companies Court Judge.[797] The alleged creditor should be named as the respondent in the originating motion, which should be supported by an affidavit. The notice of originating motion will usually seek an order restraining the alleged creditor named in a statutory demand or letter of demand, whether by itself, its servants or agents, or otherwise howsoever, from presenting a winding-up petition against the company, based on the debt referred to in the demand or any part thereof, on the grounds that the debt is disputed and the petition would be an abuse of the process of the court.

9.186 Service

The notice of originating motion must be addressed to and served on the alleged creditor who has served the demand, in the same way a writ would be served,[798] on the alleged creditor who has served the demand, at least two clear days[799] before the date fixed for the hearing (i.e. two working days must intervene between the day of service and the day of the hearing[800]), unless the court orders to the contrary. The creditor does not have to

792. IA 1986, s. 123(1)(a).

793. See, for example, *Taylors Industrial Flooring Ltd* v. *M&H Plant Hire (Manchester) Ltd, supra.*

794. *Re Portedge Ltd* [1997] BCC 23 at 27C–D; *Bryanston Finance Ltd* v. *de Vries (No. 2)* [1976] Ch. 63 at 76 and 79; *Mann* v. *Goldstein* [1968] 1 WLR 1092 at 1094.

795. Practice Direction (Company: Restraint on Petition) [1988] 1 WLR 988. This form is reproduced in Appendix 3, *infra*.

796. Practice Direction (No. 3 of 1986) [1987] 1 WLR 53 (paras (i), (iii)) (a copy of which is at Appendix 3, *infra*).

797. Practice Direction (Chancery Division: Forms) [1992] 1 WLR 791.

798. *Supreme Court Practice 1997*, Vol. 1, para. 8/1–5/11, p. 67.

799. RSC O. 8, r. 2(2).

800. RSC O. 3, r. 2(4.)

acknowledge service.[801] The notice of originating motion and the affidavit in support should be served on the alleged creditor on the same day as it is issued,[802] if necessary by fax[803]: the alleged creditor should again be asked to give an undertaking not to petition pending the hearing of the originating motion, and if this is refused, an urgent *ex parte* application to the court may be required.

9.187 Urgent applications

Where the alleged creditor has indicated that the presentation of the petition is imminent, (or has failed to confirm that presentation is not imminent), there may not be sufficient time to issue and await the hearing of the notice of originating motion. In that case, the company should make an immediate application to the Companies Court Judge for an order restraining the presentation of the petition pending an *inter partes* hearing of the notice of originating motion.[804] Although the application can be made *ex parte* without notice to the alleged creditor,[805] the better and usual practice is to give the alleged creditor notice (by telephone or fax) of the time and place of the *ex parte* hearing (i.e. a hearing *ex parte* on notice): on receiving such notice the creditor will often give an undertaking not to present a petition until the effective hearing of the notice of originating motion.

9.187.1 It is not necessary for the company to have issued a notice of originating motion prior to making its *ex parte* application: where no notice of originating motion has been issued, the court may grant an interim injunction restraining presentation pending a full *inter partes* hearing, on the company's undertaking to issue an originating motion. Where a notice of originating motion has been issued but two clear days have not intervened, the court may abridge time for service[806] and may grant the interim injunction pending a full *inter partes* hearing. In either case, the company's application should be supported by affidavit evidence: where the affidavit has been drafted but there has not been time to swear it, the court may make an order on the company's undertaking to swear an affidavit in the form, or substantially in the form, of the draft placed before the court. Where an *ex parte* application for an injunction is made, all relevant facts must be put before the court, whether or not they assist the company's case,[807] including details of the company's financial position[808]; if full and frank disclosure of all relevant facts is not made by the company, the injunction may be set aside irrespective of the merits.[809] If an order is made on the *ex parte* application, the court will give directions for the service of the company's evidence and of the order and service of further evidence, and will fix a return day for the *inter partes* hearing. The court is likely to require the company to give an undertaking as to damages as a condition of granting the interlocutory injunction,[810] although it may be of limited value if the company is insolvent.

801. *Supreme Court Practice 1997*, Vol. 1, para. 8/1–5/6, p. 66.
802. I.e., on the day on which it is sealed by an officer of the court: RSC O. 8, r. 3(6).
803. But note the requirements of RSC O. 65, r. 5(2B).
804. Such an application is properly regarded as vacation business, given its urgency; but note the comments of the judge in *Re Secure & Provide plc* [1992] BCC 405 at 414H–415B and *Re First Express Ltd* [1991] BCC 782 at 785D–G about the undesirability of *ex parte* applications except where absolutely necessary.
805. RSC O. 8, r. 2(1).
806. RSC O. 8, r. 2(2).
807. *R* v. *Kensington Income Tax Commissioners* [1917] 1 KB 486 at 504.
808. *Re Portedge Ltd, supra*, at 25B–C.
809. *Boyce* v. *Gill* (1891) 64 LT 824.
810. See *Supreme Court Practice 1991*, Vol. 1, para. 29/1/12, pp. 508–510.

9.188 Affidavit in support

The affidavit filed by the company should explain:

(i) the relationship between the company and the alleged creditor giving rise to the dispute between them—for example, where the claim arises out of a contract, the terms and nature of the contract should be explained;
(ii) full and detailed particulars of the dispute relating to that claim, including particulars of any alleged set-off[811];
(iv) the stage reached in any related litigation regarding the alleged debt[812];
(v) the attempts made by the company to persuade the creditor that the debt is disputed and that a petition is an inappropriate way to proceed; and
(vi) evidence of the solvency of the company.

The affidavit may contain hearsay evidence, although direct evidence should be given where possible.

9.189 Exhibits

The exhibits should include:

(i) the demand in which the creditor threatens to petition;
(ii) all relevant documents relating to the alleged debt, such as the contract documents, invoices and credit notes;
(iii) any documentation evidencing a set-off in favour of the company;
(iv) documents showing the progress of any related litigation in relation to the claim;
(v) any *inter partes* correspondence in which the creditor's claims are refuted by the company;
(vi) any correspondence between the parties' solicitors with regard to the threatened petition; and
(vii) documentary evidence of solvency, such as recent audited accounts, recent management accounts (including a balance sheet and a profit and loss account), bank statements showing credit balances at the bank and, ideally, confirmation by the company's auditors that it is, or appears to be, solvent.

9.190 The *inter partes* hearing

The hearing of the motion will be in open court before the Companies Court Judge. Consequently, it may be made only by counsel or by solicitors holding a High Court advocacy certificate. Care should be taken to refer to the company in court by the application number and not by name, to avoid damage to its goodwill or reputation. If the court grants an injunction restraining presentation of a petition or continues indefinitely an *ex parte* injunction, the alleged creditor must establish his debt by a judgment before

811. See para. 9.179, *supra*. An unrelated counterclaim of equivalent value is not a good ground for an injunction to restrain presentation or advertisement: *Re a Company (No. 006273 of 1992)* [1993] BCLC 131 at 133g–i.

812. See para. 9.179, *supra*.

seeking to wind up the company. If the injunction is refused or an *ex parte* injunction is set aside, the creditor may present his petition.

9.191 Costs

Where the injunction is granted, the alleged creditor will generally be ordered to pay the company's costs of the application to restrain presentation. This is so even where the creditor had no reason to believe, at the time it served its demand (i.e. prior to the injunction proceedings), that the debt was disputed: a creditor serves a demand at his own risk, and if it transpires that the debt is disputed, he must pay the costs of the injunction proceedings.[813] Where the creditor has persisted in the threat of a petition in relation to a debt which is clearly disputed, the court may reflect the abuse of process in an order for indemnity costs.[814] Where the injunction is refused, the company will be ordered to pay the creditor's costs. In exceptional cases, the creditor may persuade the court to make an order for costs against a non-party,[815] such as the directors who have promoted the company's application for an injunction, to avoid the costs falling on the general body of creditors when the company is wound up.

APPLICATION TO RESTRAIN ADVERTISEMENT

9.192 Undertaking not to advertise

If a petition is served based on a debt which the company disputes in good faith on substantial grounds, the company's solicitors should immediately write to the petitioner:

(i) giving full details why the debt is disputed;
(ii) stating that the winding-up proceedings are accordingly inappropriate and an abuse of process; and
(iii) seeking an undertaking that the petition will not be advertised and will be withdrawn.

If the undertaking is refused or there is no response, the company should apply promptly to restrain advertisement. However, if the court has previously refused a motion to restrain presentation of the petition because the debt was not *bona fide* disputed on substantial grounds, the company may not apply to restrain advertisement on the same ground based on evidence which was, or with reasonable diligence could have been, available to the court on the earlier application[816]; but the same grounds may be raised at the hearing of the petition when the court has to decide whether in its discretion to make a winding-up order.[817]

813. *Re Cannon Screen Entertainment Ltd* [1990] BCLC 660 at 662h–663b.
814. *Re a Company (No. 0012209 of 1991)* [1992] BCLC 865.
815. See *Taylor* v. *Pace Developments Ltd* [1991] BCC 406 at 409C–E and *Re Land & Property Trust Co. plc (No. 4)* [1994] 1 BCLC 232. Such orders are exceptional, and the court must treat applications for such orders with considerable caution: *Re Tajik Air Ltd* [1996] 1 BCLC 317 at 324f–h.
816. *Re Portedge Ltd*, *supra*, at 28A–B.
817. *Ibid.*

9.193 Form of application

The application to restrain advertisement is by ordinary application returnable before the Companies Court Judge sitting in open court.[818] Three copies of the application will be required, unless there is more than one petitioner, in which case an additional copy will be required for service on each additional petitioner.[819] The ordinary application need not identify the judge by name nor the court number: it is sufficient if the application states that it will be heard by the Companies Court Judge[820] on a specified date. The petitioner(s) should be named as respondent(s) to the application, which should be supported by an affidavit.[821] The application will usually seek an order (i) restraining the petitioner, whether by itself, its servants or agents or otherwise howsoever, from advertising or proceeding further on the petition, and (ii) directing that the petition be removed from the file of proceedings (i.e. struck out). It is also common to include an application under the Insolvency Act 1986, s. 127 to validate the operation of the company's bank accounts and dispositions of the company's property in the ordinary course of business for full value,[822] pending the determination of the application.

9.194 Timing

The ordinary application must be served on the respondent(s) at least 14 days before the date fixed for its hearing.[823] However, the petitioner is entitled to advertise the petition seven clear business days after service.[824] It follows that, even if the company were to apply to restrain advertisement on the day on which the petition was served, the petitioner would be entitled to advertise before the hearing of the application to restrain advertisement, unless an undertaking is given not to advertise prior to the hearing date, or the company obtains an *ex parte* order restraining advertisement.

9.195 Urgent applications

The position is similar to that described above in relation to urgent applications to restrain presentation of a petition. If it appears that the advertisement is or might be imminent, the court can hear the application to restrain advertisement *ex parte* before any application is issued,[825] whether or not the petitioner has been given notice of the application. Alternatively, if the application to restrain advertisement has been issued but not yet heard, the court may abridge time and make an order on the application pending an *inter partes* hearing[826]: in the former case, an undertaking must be given to issue *pro forma* application. In either case, notice of the time and place of the intended *ex parte* application should

818. Practice Direction (No. 3 of 1986) [1987] 1 WLR 53 at 54A (para. (1)(iii) (a copy of which is at Appendix 3, *infra*.

819. IR 1986, r. 7.4(1).

820. Practice Direction (Chancery Division: Forms) [1992] 1 WLR 791.

821. See paras 9.188, *supra*, and 9.196, *infra*.

822. See para. 9.202, *infra*.

823. IR 1986, r. 7.4(3), (5). In calculating the 14-day period, weekends and bank holidays are included (IR 1986, r. 12.9 and RSC O. 3, r. 2(5)) and the day of service is included but not the date of the hearing: RSC O. 3, r. 2(3).

824. IR 1986, r. 4.11(2)(b). In calculating the seven-day period weekends and bank holidays are excluded: RSC O. 3, r. 2(5).

825. IR 1986, r. 7.4(6)(a).

826. IR 1986, r. 7.4(6)(b).

be given to the petitioner or his solicitors, and the application should be supported by an affidavit (although in appropriate cases an undertaking to swear an affidavit in the form of a draft affidavit produced to the court may be acceptable). Where an *ex parte* application for an injunction is made, all relevant facts must be put before the court whether or not they assist the company's case,[827] including details of the company's financial position[828]; if full and frank disclosure of all relevant facts is not made by the company, the injunction may be set aside irrespective of the merits.[829] If the court grants an *ex parte* injunction pending the *inter partes* hearing, the court may give directions regarding the filing and service of the company's evidence, service of the order, service of further evidence and the fixing of a return date for an *inter partes* hearing. The court is likely to require the company to give an undertaking in damages as a condition of granting the interlocutory injunction[830] although this will be of little value if the company is insolvent. The court may at the same time make an *ex parte* order under s. 127 of the Insolvency Act 1986 to enable the company to continue to trade prior to the *inter partes* hearing of the application to have the petition struck out.[831]

9.196 Affidavit and exhibits in support

The affidavit should contain the same information as set out in para. 9.88, *supra*, in relation to an application to restrain presentation. The affidavit should in addition contain any particulars why an application to restrain presentation was not made—for example, because the relevant pre-petition demand was not received by the company. Hearsay evidence is admissible, but direct evidence should be given where possible. The exhibits should contain the same documents as described in para. 9.189, *supra*. Where the company seeks relief under s. 127 of the Insolvency Act 1986, the affidavit should go into considerable detail about the company's financial position, trading performance and the need for a validation order.[832]

9.197 The *inter partes* hearing

The hearing of the application will be as described in para. 9.190, *supra*. If the court grants an injunction restraining advertisement or continues indefinitely an *ex parte* injunction, it will dismiss or strike out the petition. If the court refuses to grant an injunction restraining advertisement or discharges an earlier *ex parte* injunction, the petitioner will be entitled to advertise and pursue his petition.

9.198 Costs

For the costs consequence of the grant or refusal of an injunction, see para. 9.191, *supra*.

827. *R* v. *Kensington Income Tax Commissioners* [1917] 1 KB 486 at 504.
828. *Re Portedge Ltd*, *supra*, at 25B–C.
829. *Boyce* v. *Gill* (1891) 64 LT 824.
830. See *Supreme Court Practice 1997*, Vol. 1, para. 29/1/12, pp. 508–510.
831. See *infra*.
832. The evidence required on a s. 127 application is dealt with *infra*.

CONTESTING THE PETITION ITSELF

9.199 If the company disputes the petition debt (but does not apply to restrain presentation or advertisement of the petition), or contends that the court in the exercise of its discretion should not make a winding-up order on the petition,[833] the company may file evidence in opposition and contest the petition. The company may also apply for relief under s. 127 of the Insolvency Act 1986 pending the hearing of the petition.[834]

9.200 Evidence in opposition

The affidavit in opposition to the petition should be filed in court and served on the petitioner, not less than seven days before the date fixed for the hearing thereof[835] (although this rule is often breached in practice, and affidavits are produced as late as at the hearing itself). Where the company files an affidavit in opposition, the registrar will give directions for the petitioner to file evidence in answer and for the company to file evidence in reply, and when the evidence is complete, the registrar will adjourn the petition to the judge for determination. In rare cases, the petitioner may be content for the company's affidavit to remain unanswered (for example, where the petitioner regards the alleged dispute raised to be a hopeless claim). If the hearing before the judge will take more than two hours, the petition will be adjourned by order for a date to be fixed; if the parties are agreed that the hearing will take less than two hours, the registrar may adjourn the petition directly into the list of the Companies Court Judge for the following Monday.

9.201 Contents of affidavit and exhibits

The affidavit should contain the same details as set out in para. 9.188, *supra*, in relation to applications to restrain presentation, and may contain hearsay evidence.[836] In addition, the affidavit should explain why no application was made to restrain presentation or advertisement if such an application could have been made. In contrast to applications to restrain presentation or advertisement of the petition, at the hearing of the petition the company may rely on a counterclaim which is not related to the petition debt and is therefore not a set-off, in asking the court to exercise its discretion to dismiss the petition[837]: in that case, the affidavit in opposition to the petition should set out full particulars of the counterclaim. The exhibits should contain the same categories of documents as set out in para. 9.189, *supra.*

833. For example, because the company has a counterclaim against the petitioner which exceeds the petition debt: see *Re a Company (No. 006273 of 1992)* [1993] BCLC 131 at 133g–i.

834. S. 127 applications are discussed *infra.*

835. IR 1986, r. 4.18.

836. Civil Evidence Act 1995, s. 1 (in force 31 January 1997). Decisions such as *Re Koscot Interplanetary (UK) Ltd* [1972] 3 All ER 829 and *Re FSA Business Software Ltd* [1990] BCLC 825 at 829d, which held that hearsay was admissible in the affidavit of verification but not in the evidence filed for the contested hearing of the petition, are no longer good law.

837. *Re a Company (No. 006273 of 1992)* [1993] BCLC 131 at 133g–i; but contrast *Re Pendigo Ltd* [1996] BCC 608 at 611C–E and *Re a Company (No. 009080 of 1992)* [1993] BCLC 269.

VALIDATION ORDERS UNDER S. 127 OF THE INSOLVENCY ACT 1986[838]

9.202 Effect of winding-up order

The effect of a winding-up order in relation to a company is that all dispositions of the property of that company since the presentation of the petition are, unless the court otherwise orders, void. Section 127 thus has a retrospective effect once the winding-up order is made, and the applicability of the section does not depend upon the company being insolvent. The purpose of the section is to ensure that the assets of the company at the commencement of the liquidation (i.e. the date of presentation of the petition[839]) are preserved and are available for *pari passu* distribution amongst all creditors: once an order has been made, a person who has received property from the company after the date of presentation of the petition can be required to restore that property to the company if that would be for the benefit of creditors generally (although obviously a liquidator would not seek to reverse any post-presentation transactions which were clearly beneficial to the company). There is therefore a danger that persons who deal with a company after a petition has been presented will find that their transaction is void when the company is wound up. In particular, the company's bankers may discover that they have permitted drawings on the company's bank account which are void and the bank may then be obliged to make good the resulting deficit. For this reason, the bank will usually "freeze" the company's accounts as soon as it learns that a petition has been presented.[840]

9.203 What transactions may be validated

Applications for a validation order generally fall into two categories[841]: first, the court may effectively validate the continuation of the company's trading, by validating (a) dispositions of the property of the company made in the ordinary course of business for full value, and (b) payments made into and out of the company's bank accounts in the ordinary course of business; second, the court may validate an isolated transaction or disposition which is beneficial to the company and hence its creditors, either before or after the transaction has taken place.[842]

9.204 Requirements for validation

The overriding requirement is that in validating the disposition of property, the court must "do its best to ensure that the interests of the unsecured creditors will not be prejudiced".[843] The jurisdiction is exercised with caution.[844] The court will make a validation order where the company is clearly solvent, has net assets, and is able to pay its debts as

838. IA 1986, ss. 127 and 129.

839. IA 1986, s. 129(2).

840. Payments into (where the account is overdrawn) and out of the bank accounts of the company are "dispositions of property" for the purpose of IA 1986, s. 127: *Re Gray's Inn Construction Co. Ltd* [1980] 1 WLR 711 at 715H–716B; *Re McGuinness Bros (UK) Ltd* (1989) 3 BCC 571 at 574; but payment into the company's bank account is not a disposition of the company's property in favour of the bank if the account is in credit: *Re Barn Crown Ltd* [1994] BCC 381 at 388H–389A.

841. *Re Fairway Graphics Ltd* [1991] BCLC 468 at 468h–469a.

842. See, for example, *Re Webb Electrical Ltd* (1988) 4 BCC 230 at 233–234.

843. *Re Gray's Inn Construction Co. Ltd, supra*, at 717 per Buckley J.

844. *Re a Company (No. 007523 of 1986)* (1987) 3 BCC 57 at 61 (a contributory's winding-up petition).

they fall due.[845] The court must be "satisfied by credible evidence"[846] that the validation order is likely to benefit all creditors as a class,[847] not merely the petitioner and supporting creditors.[848] Where the validation order is sought to enable the company to continue to trade and operate its bank accounts, the court must be satisfied by credible evidence that the trading is likely to be profitable[849] and therefore for the benefit of all creditors: such trading during the life of the petition will increase the assets of the company available for the unsecured creditors, even if (as a consequence of the company's historic accrued liabilities) a winding-up order is likely to be made on the petition. However, the court would not validate the operation of the bank account in the absence of profitable trading merely to enable the petitioner and supporting creditors to be paid. Where the validation application relates to a specific disposition, the court must be satisfied that that disposition is beneficial to all creditors—for example, a sale of an asset at an attractive price.[850] The proper approach on an application for a validation order is not to ask whether the transaction in question would damage the company and to make an order where it would not damage the company; the proper approach is to ask whether the transaction would benefit the company and only to make the order where it would benefit the company: applying that test, the court will not sanction a transaction which confers no benefit on the company and merely substitutes one creditor of the company for another.[851]

9.205 Who may apply?

The application may be made by any person interested in the transaction to be validated.[852] In the vast majority of cases, the application is made by the company and only the company would have the detailed financial information to satisfy the court that the transaction (or continued trading) would be beneficial to creditors. In appropriate cases, a shareholder in the company, or the person to whom the property is to be or has been transferred, or a person claiming a proprietary right in the asset disposed of, may be the applicant.[853]

9.206 Who should be respondent?

Where the company is the applicant, the petitioner should be joined as respondent; where the applicant is a shareholder or the person to whom the property is to be or has been transferred, the petitioner and the company should be joined as respondents (unless the company is a joint applicant). If the application for validation is made after a winding-up order has been made, the company will be represented by its liquidator.

845. *Re Fairway Graphics Ltd*, *supra*, at 468h.
846. *Ibid.* at 468h.
847. *Ibid.* at 469a.
848. *Ibid.* at 469c.
849. *Ibid.* at 468i–469a; *Re a Company (No. 007523 of 1986)*, *supra*, at 61.
850. See, for example, *Re Sugar Properties (Derisley Wood) Ltd* (1987) 3 BCC 88; *Re French's (Wine Bar) Ltd*; [1987] BCLC 499 at 504i–505b, g; *Re Tramway Building & Construction Co. Ltd* [1988] Ch. 293.
851. *Re Webb Electrical Ltd*, *supra*, at 233–234.
852. See, for example, *Re Tramway Building & Construction Co. Ltd*, *supra*, at 294G–H.
853. *Re Argentum Reductions (UK) Ltd* [1975] 1 WLR 186 at 189H–191A; *Re Tramway Building & Construction Co. Ltd* [1988] Ch. 293.

9.207 Form of application

Applications for a validation order to enable continued trading often form part of an ordinary application to the Companies Court Judge seeking an injunction restraining the petitioner from advertising the petition. Where this is not the case, the application should be made by ordinary application supported by affidavit. If the application is made prior to any winding-up order being made, the application should be made to the Companies Court Judge[854] sitting in open court, not the registrar; if the application is made after the winding-up order, it may be made to the registrar in the first instance.[855] Where the petitioner is the only respondent, three copies of the application are required on issue, and an additional copy is required for each additional respondent.[856] The application should be served on the respondent(s) at least 14 days before the hearing of the application,[857] but the court has power to grant interim s. 127 relief (for example, to enable trading to continue and bank accounts to be operated) on an *ex parte* application pending the *inter partes* hearing.[858] The court may also abridge time for service of the application.[859]

9.208 When should the application be made?

The application may be made either before[860] or after[861] completion of the transaction sought to be validated. Where the validation order is to facilitate further trading, the application should be made promptly after service of the petition, and should be made as a matter of urgency if the petition has been advertised, in order to "un-freeze" the company's bank accounts. Where the application is made to validate *ex post facto* a transaction which has taken place, the court will consider two questions: (i) whether the court would have validated the proposed transfer had a prior application been made; and (ii) whether the transaction has had the effect of reducing the assets available in the winding-up for unsecured creditors.[862]

9.209 Evidence in support

The affidavit in support of the s. 127 application should explain any dispute in relation to petition debt, and should also set out in detail the facts which illustrate that the transaction(s) sought to be validated would be to the benefit of all creditors. Thus, where a single disposition of property is to be validated, the evidence must show, for example, that the sale price is equal to or in excess of its value, or that the asset is of no use to the company and is diminishing in value. Where the validation order is sought to enable continued trading, the evidence should deal with the company's financial position in detail (i.e. its assets and liabilities), and in particular should show that the company's trading is

854. Practice Direction (Companies Court: Insolvency) (No. 3 of 1986) [1987] 1 WLR 53 at 54A (para. (1)(ii)) (a copy of which is in Appendix 3, *infra*).
855. *Ibid.* at 54B (para. 2).
856. IR 1986, r. 7.4(1).
857. IR 1986, r. 7.4(3), (5).
858. IR 1986, r. 7.4(6)(a).
859. IR 1986, r. 7.4(6)(b).
860. *Re AI Levy (Holdings) Ltd* [1964] Ch. 19.
861. *Re Tramway Building & Construction Co. Ltd, supra*; *Re French's (Wine Bar) Ltd, supra.*
862. *Re Tramway Building & Construction Co. Ltd, supra*, at 303C–D.

profitable.[863] The exhibits should confirm profitable trading, i.e. recent audited or management accounts; ideally, the company's auditors may be prepared to confirm in writing that they believe the company to be trading profitably; any bank statements showing credit balances at the bank may also be exhibited.

9.210 The hearing

As the hearing is usually before the judge sitting in open court, only counsel and solicitors having a High Court advocacy certificate have rights of audience. If the validation order is granted, the usual order is that the costs are to be costs in the petition (or in the winding-up if the application is made after the making of the winding-up order); if the order is refused, the costs of the application will be payable by the applicant (i.e. usually the company).

SECURITY FOR COSTS

9.211 When security may be ordered

A petitioner may be ordered to give security for the costs of a contested petition if he falls within one of the established categories of litigant against whom security can be ordered under RSC O. 23, r. 1(1) or the Companies Act 1985, s. 726(1).[864] In practice, the most common grounds for an order for security for costs on a winding-up petition are that the petitioner is ordinarily resident out of the jurisdiction,[865] or that it is a limited company and it appears that it would be unlikely to be able to pay the company's costs if the petition is unsuccessful.[866] The court has an unfettered discretion in deciding whether or not to order security to be provided.[867]

9.212 When should the company apply

If the company (or opposing creditor or contributory) intends to contest the petition and considers that security for costs should be provided, it should in the first instance request security by letter to the petitioner or its solicitors, if time permits, setting out the grounds on which security is sought.[868] If time does not permit, or security is refused, the company should apply to the court for an order for security as soon as possible after service of the petition. This should enable security to be ordered and provided, or the proceedings stayed before costs are incurred in preparing evidence in opposition to the petition. Where the hearing of the application for security is fixed for a date after the first hearing of the petition, the registrar should be asked to adjourn the petition pending the outcome of the security for costs application. Whilst the company will not want to prepare and file its

863. *Re a Company (No. 007523 of 1986)* [1987] 3 BCC 57.
864. For a detailed discussion of the circumstances in which security might be ordered, see RSC O. 23 and the notes thereunder.
865. RSC O. 23, r. 1(1)(a).
866. CA 1985, s. 726(1); *Supreme Court Practice 1997*, Vol. 1, para. 23/1–3/14, p. 412.
867. *Sir Lindsay Parkinson & Co. Ltd* v. *Triplan Ltd* [1973] QB 609 at 626–627; *Supreme Court Practice 1997*, Vol. 1, para. 23/1–3/2, p. 407.
868. *Supreme Court Practice 1997*, Vol. 1, para. 23/1–3/18, p. 415.

detailed evidence in opposition prior to the first hearing,[869] it should outline in its evidence in support of the security for costs application the intended grounds of opposition: this can then be shown to the registrar at the first hearing of the petition in support of the application for an adjournment.

9.213 Form of application

The application for security is by ordinary application supported by affidavit,[870] returnable before the registrar in chambers,[871] although the application may be adjourned to the judge sitting in open court.[872] The petitioner(s) should be named as respondent(s) to the application. Three copies of the application will be required on issue, unless there is more than one petitioner from whom security is sought, in which case an additional copy of the application will be required for service on each additional petitioner.[873] The application should seek an order:

(i) that the respondent(s) provide security for the costs of the company in a specific sum by payment into court,[874] or less commonly by the guarantee of a first class bank or by bond,[875] within a stated period;
(ii) that all proceedings on the petition be stayed pending the provision of security; and
(iii) that the petition be dismissed in default of the petitioner giving security in the prescribed period without further order.[876]

As an alternative to (iii), the court may grant the company liberty to apply, which may be invoked in the event that security is not provided (although such orders are less common). A general liberty to apply should in any event be granted, in case, for example, the original order for security proves to be inadequate and the applicant wishes to seek an increase.[877]

9.214 Service

The application should be served on the respondent(s) at least 14 days before the date fixed for the hearing of the application.[878] In cases of urgency, the time for service may be abridged,[879] although there will often be no urgency if the petition has been adjourned to await the outcome of the security for costs application.

869. In accordance with IR 1986, r. 4.18(1).
870. See para. 9.215, *infra* for the form of the affidavit.
871. IR 1986, r. 7.6(2); Practice Direction (No. 3 of 1986) [1987] 1 WLR 57 (para. 2) (a copy of which is at Appendix 3, *infra*).
872. IR 1986, r. 7.6(3); Practice Direction (No. 3 of 1986), *supra*, para. 3(iii).
873. IR 1986, r. 7.4(1).
874. *Supreme Court Practice 1997*, Vol. 1, para. 23/1–3/26. This is generally the more usual and convenient order.
875. *Ibid.* at para. 23/1–3/27, p. 417.
876. *Ibid.* at para. 23/1–3/30, p. 418; *La Grange* v. *McAndrew* (1879) 4 QBD 210.
877. *Sturla* v. *Freccia* [1877] WN 166 at 188, and [1876] WN 161; *Republic of Costa Rica* v. *Erlanger* (1876) 3 Ch.D. 62; see also *Supreme Court Practice 1997*, para. 23/1–3/29, pp. 417–418.
878. IR 1986, r. 7.4(3) and (5).
879. IR 1986, r. 7.4(6)(b).

9.215 Affidavit in support

The application should be supported by an affidavit setting out:

(i) the grounds on which the petition is opposed;
(ii) details of the grounds on which security is sought—for example, evidence that the petitioner is ordinarily resident out of the jurisdiction[880] or is a limited company which appears to be insolvent[881];
(iii) an estimate of the applicants' anticipated costs of the petition by reference to an itemised and detailed bill of costs.[882]

The grounds on which the petition is to be disputed need not be exhaustively set out: if security is ordered and provided, or the application is refused, directions will be given for filing a detailed affidavit in opposition to the petition.

9.216 Exhibits

The exhibits should include documentary evidence to support the grounds on which security is sought—for example, documents showing that the petitioner is ordinarily resident out of the jurisdiction, or is an insolvent limited company, according to its audited accounts showing a net deficiency on the balance sheet. The exhibits should also include an itemised and detailed bill of costs.

9.217 Once security is ordered

If an order for security is made, the petition will be stayed pending provision of the security, and will be dismissed in the event of default in giving security. If security is provided (for example, by payment into court) the petitioner must notify the company of that fact before the petitioner can proceed with the petition. If directions for the filing of evidence on the petition have not previously been given and are not agreed between the parties, the question should be referred to the registrar for further directions.

WINDING UP AN INSOLVENT PARTNERSHIP[883]

9.218 Jurisdiction

Section 420 of the Insolvency Act 1986 empowers the Lord Chancellor to make regulations applying the provisions of the Act to insolvent partnerships. That power was originally exercised to make the Insolvent Partnerships Order 1986[884] ("the 1986 Order")

880. RSC O. 23, r. 1(1)(a).
881. CA 1985, s. 726(1).
882. See *Bennett* v. *Digby*, *Times*, 21 November 1982 (security for costs on appeal), and *Supreme Court Practice 1997*, Vol. 1, paras 23/1–3/29, p. 417.
883. This part of the Chapter deals with the winding-up of a conventional partnership as an unregistered company. If the Department of Trade and Industry's proposals for the creation of limited liability partnerships (see the consultation paper *Limited Liability Partnership—A New Form of Business Association for Professions*, published on 20 February 1997) are enacted, such a partnership is likely to be wound up as a registered company and not as an unregistered company under the Insolvent Partnerships Order 1994.
884. S.I. 1986 No. 2142.

which provided for the winding-up of an insolvent partnership as an unregistered company under Part V of the Insolvency Act 1986.[885] The 1986 Order has been replaced and revoked with effect from 1 December 1994 by the Insolvent Partnerships Order 1994[886] ("the 1994 Order") (as amended by the Insolvent Partnerships (Amendment) Order 1996[887]), which contains modified provisions for the winding-up of an insolvent partnership by the court as an unregistered company.[888] The 1994 Order applies, in a modified form, the provisions of the Insolvency Act 1986, in particular the provisions for winding-up an unregistered company under Part V of the Act, to the winding-up of an insolvent partnership.[889] The relevant provisions of the Act as modified by the 1994 Order are set out in full in the schedules to the 1994 Order for ease of reference.[890] In the modified provisions of the Act, references to "the company" have been replaced by references to "the insolvent partnership".[891] The Insolvency Rules 1986 apply, with such modifications as the context requires, for the winding-up of an insolvent partnership as an unregistered company,[892] but no modified Rules are set out in the schedules to the 1994 Order. In the case of any conflict between the 1994 Order and the Insolvency Rules 1986, the 1994 Order prevails.[893] The schedules to the 1994 Order also contain copies of the various forms which must be used, with such variations as are necessary, in any proceedings under the 1994 Order, whether brought in the High Court or in a County Court.[894] Where the 1994 Order does not contain a particular form required for the winding-up of an insolvent partnership, the form prescribed for the winding-up of a company[895] applies with such modification as is necessary to make it appropriate for the winding-up of an insolvent partnership.

9.219 Categories of winding-up petitions

The 1994 Order provides for four different types of winding-up petition in respect of an insolvent partnership:

(1) a winding-up petition presented against the partnership by a creditor, a responsible insolvency practitioner, the Secretary of State for Trade and Industry *or any other person other than a member,*[896] where no concurrent insolvency petition is presented against a member of the partnership (art. 7 of, and sch. 3 to, the 1994 Order);

885. I.e., ss. 220–229.
886. S.I. 1994 No. 2421.
887. S.I. 1996 No. 1308 (in force on 14 June 1996).
888. An insolvent partnership may not be wound up under the IA 1986 voluntarily: IA 1986, s. 221(4) (as modified by arts 7(2), 8(2), 9 and 10(1) of, and sch. 3–6 to, the 1994 Order).
889. See, for example, IA 1986, s. 221(5) (as modified by art. 7(2) of, and para. 3 of sch. 3 to, the 1994 Order).
890. In contrast to the 1986 Order, where the modified provisions were not set out *in extenso*.
891. See art. 3(2) and (4) of the 1994 Order for the interpretation, in relation to insolvent partnerships, of references which are in IA 1986 appropriate to companies.
892. Art. 18(1) of, and sch. 10 to, the 1994 Order.
893. Art. 18(2).
894. Art. 17 and sch. 9.
895. I.e., prescribed by IR 1986, r. 12.7 and sch. 4.
896. The words in italics were introduced by the Insolvent Partnerships (Amendment) Order 1996 (S.I. 1996 No. 1308).

(2) a winding-up petition presented against the partnership by a creditor, where concurrent insolvency petitions are presented against one or more members of the partnership (art. 8 and sch. 4);
(3) a winding-up petition presented against the partnership by a member of the partnership, where no concurrent insolvency petition is presented against a member of the partnership (art. 9 and sch. 5);
(4) a winding-up petition presented against the partnership by a member, where concurrent insolvency petitions are presented against all members of the partnership in their capacity as members (art. 10 and sch. 6).

The 1994 Order also provides for the presentation of a joint bankruptcy petition by the members of an insolvent partnership, which does not involve the winding-up of the insolvent partnership as an unregistered company[897] and which, accordingly, is outside the scope of this book. The procedure for winding-up an insolvent partnership as an unregistered company in the four categories set out above follows in many respects the procedure for winding-up a company registered under the Companies Acts on the petition of a creditor. The following paragraphs discuss the special rules applicable to the winding-up of an insolvent partnership in each of the above four categories: reference should be made to the earlier paragraphs of this Chapter for the procedure generally applicable to creditors' winding up petitions.

WINDING UP AN INSOLVENT PARTNERSHIP AS AN UNREGISTERED COMPANY, WITHOUT A CONCURRENT PETITION AGAINST ANY MEMBER

9.220 Jurisdiction

An insolvent partnership may be wound up as an unregistered company on the petition of a creditor, a "responsible insolvency practitioner", the Secretary of State or any person other than a member, without any concurrent insolvency petition against a member of the insolvent partnership.[898] A "responsible insolvency petitioner" is defined as: (a) in winding-up, the liquidator of an insolvent partnership or of a corporate member (i.e. of an insolvent member which is a company); or (b) in bankruptcy, the trustee of the estate of an individual member (i.e. of an insolvent member who is an individual),[899] including the official receiver acting in either capacity. The 1994 Order thus allows a creditor to petition to wind up an insolvent partnership without seeking a bankruptcy order against any member of the partnership, and also allows the liquidator or trustee in bankruptcy of an insolvent member of the partnership, to petition to wind up the partnership in order that the partnership's assets can be applied in part in paying off the creditors of the insolvent member. Although art. 7(1) of the 1994 Order refers to the winding-up of an insolvent partnership on the petition of a creditor, a "responsible insolvency practitioner" or the Secretary of State where there are no concurrent petitions against members of the

897. See art. 11 and sch. 7.

898. IA 1986, ss. 220 and 221 (as modified by art. 7 of, and paras 1–3 to, the 1994 Order and the Insolvent Partnerships (Amendment) Order 1996 (S.I. 1996 No. 1308)), which deem the insolvent partnership to be an unregistered company.

899. See definitions in art. 2(1).

partnership, the modified provisions of the Insolvency Act 1986 set out in sch. 3 to the 1994 Order provide for a wider range of petitioner. A petition may also be presented by: an administrator of a corporate member, or a liquidator or administrator of a former corporate member, of the insolvent partnership[900]; the administrator of the insolvent partnership[901]; the trustee of the estate of a former member of the insolvent partnership[902]; or the supervisor of a voluntary arrangement approved under Part I of the Insolvency Act 1986 in relation to a corporate member or the insolvent partnership, or under Part VIII of the Act in relation to an individual member of the insolvent partnership.[903] Each of the above persons is referred to as a "petitioning insolvency practitioner".[904]

9.221 Location of the partnership and choice of court

The modified provisions of the Insolvency Act 1986 set out in sch. 3 to the 1994 Order[905] contain additional jurisdictional requirements which depend on the place of business of the insolvent partnership and which extend the jurisdiction beyond the limits laid down in the 1986 Order. The insolvent partnership may, subject to two limitations, be wound up as an unregistered company on the petition of a creditor if it has, at the date of presentation of the winding-up petition, or at any time had (a) a principal place of business in England or Wales, or (b) a place of business in England or Wales at which business is being or has been carried on in the course of which business the petition debt (or part of the petition debt) arose.[906] In those cases, the insolvent partnership may be wound up by the High Court[907] (i.e. by the Companies Court in London or by any Chancery district registry of the High Court[908]) or in the County Court which exercises winding-up jurisdiction for the district in which the insolvent partnership has or had a principal place of business, or in which it has or had a place of business whose activities gave rise to some or all of the petition debt.[909]

9.221.1 There are two limitations on the jurisdiction conferred by ss. 117 and 221(1) (as modified by the 1994 Order). First, the insolvent partnership may not be wound up as an unregistered company if it has not carried on business in England and Wales at any time in the three years ending on the date on which the winding-up petition is presented.[910] Second, where an insolvent partnership presently has a principal place of business situated (a) in Scotland or (b) in Northern Ireland, the court in England and Wales may not wind up the partnership unless the partnership had a principal place of business in England or Wales within the period of (a) one year, or (b) three years respectively, ending on the date

900. IA 1986, s. 221A(1)(a) (as modified by the 1994 Order, art. 7(2) and sch. 3, para. 3).
901. IA 1986, s. 221A(1)(b) (*ibid.*).
902. IA 1986, s. 221A(1)(c) (*ibid.*).
903. IA 1986, s. 221A(1)(d) (*ibid.*).
904. IA 1986, s. 221A(2) (*ibid.*).
905. I.e., IA 1986, ss. 117(1)–(4) and 221(1)–(3) (as modified by art. 7(2) of, and paras 6 and 3 respectively of sch. 3 to, the 1994 Order).
906. IA 1986, s. 221(1) (*ibid.*). Contrast the 1986 Order, under which the courts in England and Wales only had jurisdiction if the partnership had a *principal* place of business in England and Wales. That restriction continues to apply to a member's petition: IA 1986, s. 221(1) (as modified by para. 2 of sch. 5 and para. 4 of sch. 6 to the 1994 Order).
907. IA 1986, s. 117(1) (as modified by art. 7(2) of, and para. 6 of sch. 3 to, the 1994 Order).
908. For a list of the Chancery District Registries of the High Court, see para. 9.2, Note 6, *supra*.
909. IA 1986, s. 117(2) (as modified by art. 7(2) of, and para. 6 of sch. 3 to, the 1994 Order).
910. IA 1986, ss. 117(3) and 221(2) (as modified by the 1994 Order, art. 7(2) and sch. 3, paras 3 and 6 respectively).

of presentation of the winding-up petition.[911] The effect of these jurisdictional rules will often be to give the proposed petitioner a wide choice of court in which to present his winding-up petition against an insolvent partnership: he will generally be able to choose between the Companies Court in London, any Chancery district registry of the High Court, or any County Court(s) exercising winding-up jurisdiction for the district(s) in which the insolvent partnership has a principal place of business or in which the insolvent partnership has a place of business from which the petition debt arose in whole or in part.

9.222 Grounds for the petition[912]

An insolvent partnership may be wound up as an unregistered company if: (a) the partnership is dissolved, or has ceased to carry on business, or is carrying on business only for the purpose of winding-up its affairs; (b) the partnership is unable to pay its debts; or (c) the court is of the opinion that it is just and equitable that the partnership should be wound up.[913] The ground most commonly relied upon by the petitioner will be the partnership's inability to pay its debts.[914] An insolvent partnership may be deemed to be unable to pay its debts in one or more of five ways:

(1) where the insolvent partnership has been duly served by a creditor with a written demand for payment of a debt exceeding £750 and has failed to comply with the demand for three weeks after service of the demand[915];
(2) where proceedings have been brought against a member of an insolvent partnership for a debt due or claimed to be due from the partnership, or from the defendant in his capacity as a member of the partnership, and notice of the proceedings have been duly served on the partnership, but the partnership has failed (a) to pay or secure the debt, (b) to obtain a stay of the proceedings or (c) to indemnify the defendant to his reasonable satisfaction against the claim and all related costs and expenses[916];
(3) where execution on a judgment or court order in favour of a creditor against the insolvent partnership or against a member of the partnership in that capacity is returned unsatisfied[917];
(4) where it is otherwise proved to the satisfaction of the court that the unregistered partnership is unable to pay its debts as they fall due[918];
(5) where it is proved to the satisfaction of the court that the value of the partnership's assets is less than the value of its liabilities, taking into account its

911. IA 1986, ss. 117(4) and 221(3) (*ibid.*).
912. Contrast paras 9.13–9.20, *supra*.
913. IA 1986, s. 221(7) (as modified by art. 7(2) of, and para. 3 of sch. 3 to, the 1994 Order).
914. See further, para. 9.19, *supra*.
915. IA 1986, s. 222 (as modified by art. 7(2) of, and para. 4 of sch. 3 to, the 1994 Order).
916. IA 1986, s. 223 (as modified by art. 7(2) of, and para. 5 of sch. 3 to, the 1994 Order).
917. IA 1986, s. 224(1)(a). S. 224, as modified to apply to insolvent partnerships, is not set out *in extenso* in sch. 3 to the 1994 Order, but all references in s. 224 to "a company" or "an unregistered company" should be read as a reference to an insolvent partnership: art. 3(2) of the 1994 Order, and IA 1986, s. 221(5) (as modified by art. 7(2) of, and para. 3 of sch. 3 to, the 1994 Order).
918. IA 1986, s. 224(1)(d). See further para. 9.19, *supra*.

contingent and prospective liabilities.[919] Where the winding-up petition is presented by a "petitioning insolvency practitioner"[920] on the grounds that the partnership is unable to pay its debts, the partnership's inability to pay its debts will be established if the petitioning insolvency practitioner can show that an insolvency order has been made against the member whose liquidator or trustee he is, because of the member's inability to pay a joint debt.[921]

9.223 Procedure

The procedure on a petition presented by a creditor against an insolvent partnership without concurrent petitions against any member of the partnership closely follows the procedure on a creditor's petition against a company registered under the Companies Acts discussed in the earlier part of this Chapter, to which reference should be made. The following paragraphs deal only with the particular rules applicable to a winding-up petition against an insolvent partnership where there are no concurrent petitions against its members.

9.224 Form of petition

Schedule 9 to the 1994 Order does not contain a form for a creditor's petition against an insolvent partnership where there are no concurrent petitions against its members. The petition should follow the usual form of a creditor's petition,[922] substituting for each reference to "the company" a reference to "the partnership". Where the petition is presented by a liquidator, administrator, trustee or supervisor of an insolvent member of the partnership, the petition should follow Form 3 in sch. 9 to the 1994 Order. The petition should set out the grounds relied upon in seeking to wind up the partnership as an unregistered company.[923]

9.225 Affidavit of verification[924]

Any petition against an insolvent partnership must be verified by an affidavit following Form 2 in sch. 9 to the 1994 Order.[925]

9.226 Service[926]

The winding-up petition should be served on the insolvent partnership by leaving it at the partnership's last known principal place of business in such a way as it is likely to come to the attention of a person attending there.[927] Where a voluntary arrangement has been

919. IA 1986, s. 224(2).
920. See IA 1986, s. 221A(1) and (2) (as modified by art. 7(2) of, and para. 3 of sch. 3 to, the 1994 Order).
921. IA 1986, s. 221A(3) (*ibid.*).
922. I.e., Form 4.2: IR 1986, r. 12.7 and sch. 4, part 4. See further para. 9.24, *supra*.
923. See para. 9.222, *supra*.
924. See generally paras 9.29–9.32, *supra*.
925. IA 1986, s. 221(8) (as modified by art. 7(2) of, and para. 3 of sch. 3 to, the 1994 Order).
926. See, generally paras 9.37–9.49, *supra*.
927. IR 1986, r. 4.8(4) (as modified by Insolvency (Amendment) Rules, S.I. 1987 No. 1919, r. 3(1), sch., pt 1, para. 37(1)).

approved or an administration order has been made in respect of the insolvent partnership,[928] copies of the petition should be served on the supervisor of the voluntary arrangement or the administrator.[929]

9.227 Advertisement[930]

The advertisement of a winding-up petition against an insolvent partnership must follow Form 8 in sch. 9 to the 1994 Order. The advertisement must appear in the *Gazette* not less than seven business days before the day fixed for the hearing if the winding-up petition is presented by the partnership itself acting by its administrator[931] or by the supervisor of a voluntary arrangement approved in respect of the partnership[932]; in any other case, the advertisement must appear not less than seven business days after service of the petition on the partnership at its last known principal place of business, and not less than seven days before the day fixed for the hearing.[933]

9.228 The order[934]

The usual compulsory order made in respect of an insolvent partnership will ordinarily appoint the official receiver as liquidator of the partnership, but the court has power[935] to appoint any of the insolvency practitioners mentioned in s. 221A(1) of the Insolvency Act 1986[936] as liquidator of the partnership. The usual compulsory order against the partnership does not affect the status of the members of the partnership.

A CREDITOR'S PETITION TO WIND UP AN INSOLVENT PARTNERSHIP AS AN UNREGISTERED COMPANY, WITH CONCURRENT PETITIONS AGAINST ONE OR MORE MEMBERS

9.229 Jurisdiction

The court has jurisdiction to wind up an insolvent partnership as an unregistered company on the petition of a creditor[937] where there are concurrent petitions against one[938] or more members of the insolvent partnership (whether corporate or individual members of the partnership).[939] This procedure enables a creditor to have recourse to the assets of the member(s) as well as of the partnership in satisfaction of his claim.

928. Pursuant to arts 14 and 16 respectively of the 1994 Order.
929. By analogy with IR 1986, r. 4.10(2) and (3).
930. See, generally paras 9.50–9.56, *supra*.
931. I.e., pursuant to IA 1986, s. 221A(1)(b) (as modified by art. 7(2) of, and para. 3 of sch. 3 to, the 1994 Order).
932. I.e. pursuant to IA 1986, s. 221A(1)(d) (*ibid.*).
933. IR 1986, r. 4.11(2).
934. See paras 9.107–9.110, *supra*.
935. Under IA 1986, s. 221A(5) (as modified by art. 7(2) of, and para. 3 of sch. 3 to, the 1994 Order).
936. As modified by the 1994 Order.
937. Contrast the wider range of possible petitioners where there is no concurrent petition against any member of the insolvent partnership, discussed in para. 9.220, *supra*.
938. In contrast to the 1986 Order, which required concurrent petitions against the insolvent partnership and at least two members of the partnership.
939. Art. 8 of, and sch. 4 to, the 1994 Order.

9.230 Location of the partnership and choice of court

A petition by a creditor to wind up an insolvent partnership presented concurrently with petitions against one or more members of the partnership is subject to the same jurisdictional requirements concerning the location of the insolvent partnership's place of business as a winding-up petition presented against the partnership alone, without concurrent petitions against any of its members.[940] A petition to wind up an insolvent partnership presented concurrently with petitions against one or more members is also subject to the same rules regarding the court having jurisdiction to wind up the partnership,[941] subject to the following qualifications: the court which has jurisdiction to wind up the insolvent partnership on a petition presented under art. 8 of the 1994 Order[942] also has jurisdiction concurrently to wind up a corporate member or former corporate member of the partnership, or to make a bankruptcy order against an individual member or former individual member of the partnership[943]; but where the petition under art. 8 to wind up the insolvent partnership is presented in the High Court[944] concurrently with a petition for the bankruptcy of one or more individual members or former individual members of the partnership, it must be presented in London and not in a Chancery district registry of the High Court,[945] which do not have any bankruptcy jurisdiction. Where the petition to wind up an insolvent partnership under art. 8 is presented concurrently with a petition to wind up one or more *corporate* members or former *corporate* members of the partnership, there would appear to be no jurisdictional bar to proceeding in a Chancery district registry of the High Court; but if it subsequently became desirable to join an *individual* member or former member of the insolvent partnership as a party to the proceedings,[946] it would first be necessary for the petitioner to apply to transfer the winding-up proceedings to a court having bankruptcy jurisdiction.[947]

9.231 Grounds for the petition[948]

A creditor's petition to wind up an insolvent partnership under art. 8 in conjunction with a petition against one or more of its members may only be based on the inability of the partnership to pay its debts.[949] Under Art. 8, an insolvent partnership is deemed to be unable to pay its debts if a creditor of the partnership, for a sum exceeding £750, serves a written demand for payment[950] on the partnership, and also serves on one or more members or former members of the partnership liable to pay the sums due, a written

940. I.e., the jurisdictional requirements of IA 1986, ss. 117(1)–(4) and 221(1)–(3) (as modified by arts 7 and 8 of, and schs 3 and 4 to, the 1994 Order). These are discussed in para. 9.221, *supra*.

941. I.e., IA 1986, s. 117(1) and (2) (as modified by the 1994 Order), discussed in para. 9.221, *supra*.

942. I.e., the High Court, or the County Court having insolvency jurisdiction for the partnership's principal place of business or its place of business at which the petition debt (or part thereof) arose: see IA 1986, ss. 117(1) and (2) (as modified by the 1994 Order).

943. IA 1986, s. 117(5) (as modified by art. 8(3) of, and para. 5 of sch. 4 to, the 1994 Order).

944. I.e., under IA 1986, s. 117(1) (modified as aforesaid).

945. IA 1986, s. 117(6) (modified as aforesaid).

946. Pursuant to the power contained in IA 1986, s. 124(4) (modified as aforesaid).

947. For example, the relevant County Court enjoying insolvency jurisdiction. For the court's power of transfer, see IR 1986, r. 7.11.

948. Contrast para. 9.222, *supra*.

949. IA 1986, s. 221(8) (as modified by art. 8 of, and para. 3 of sch. 4 to, the 1994 Order).

950. The demand must follow Form 4 in sch. 9 to the 1994 Order.

demand[951] requiring the member or members to pay the sum due, and the partnership and its members fail to pay, secure or compound the sum due, for three weeks after the service of the last of the demands.[952] The demand served on the partnership may be served by leaving it at the principal place of business of the partnership, by leaving it at a place of business of the partnership at which the debt (or part of the debt) arose, by delivering it to an officer of the partnership, or by serving it in such other manner as the court may direct.[953] The demand served on a corporate member of the partnership must be left at the corporate member's registered office, and the demand served on an individual member must be served in accordance with the Insolvency Rules 1986.[954]

9.232 Grounds for the petition against the corporate member

A corporate member or former corporate member of an insolvent partnership may be wound up concurrently with the winding-up of the partnership if it is unable to pay its debts.[955] The corporate member or former corporate member will be deemed to be unable to pay its debts if a creditor, for a sum exceeding £750, for which the member or former member is liable, has served a written demand for payment[956] on the corporate member or former corporate member and on the partnership, and the debt has not been paid, secured or compounded, for three weeks after service of the last of the demands.[957] The demands are served on the corporate member or former corporate member and on the partnership as described in the preceding paragraph.[958]

9.233 Procedure

The procedure on a petition presented by a creditor against an insolvent partnership concurrently with petitions against one or more corporate members or former corporate members closely follows the procedure on a creditor's petition against a company registered under the Companies Acts, discussed in the earlier part of this Chapter, to which reference should be made. The following paragraphs deal only with the special rules applicable to concurrent winding-up petitions against an insolvent partnership and one or more of its corporate members or former corporate members.

9.234 Form of petition

The petition to wind up the insolvent partnership should follow Form 5 in sch. 9 to the 1994 Order. The petition to wind up a corporate member or former corporate member of the partnership should follow Form 6 in sch. 9.[959] The petitions must be in respect of a liquidated sum payable immediately, for which the partnership and corporate member or

951. *Ibid.*
952. IA 1986, s. 222(1) (as modified by art. 8(2) of, and para. 4 of sch. 4 to, the 1994 Order).
953. IA 1986, s. 222(2) (*ibid.*).
954. IA 1986, s. 222(1)(b) (*ibid.*). For service of the demand on an individual member, see IR 1986, r. 6(3) and (11).
955. IA 1986, s. 122 (as modified by art. 8(3) of, and para. 6(a) of sch. 4 to, the 1994 Order).
956. The demand should follow Form 4 in sch. 9 to the 1994 Order.
957. IA 1986, s. 123(1) (as modified by art. 8(3) of, and para. 7(a) of sch. 4 to, the 1994 Order).
958. IA 1986, s. 123(2) (*ibid.*).
959. IA 1986, s. 124(1)(a) and (b) (as modified by art. 8(3) of, and para. 8 of sch. 4 to, the 1994 Order).

former corporate member is indebted.[960] Each petition should contain details of any other petition which is being presented concurrently, in relation to the partnership, identifying in each case the partnership in question and the corporate members or former corporate members concerned.[961]

9.235 Presentation, advertisement[962] and joinder

The petitions against the partnership and the corporate member or former corporate member must be presented in the same court, and unless the court otherwise permits, must be presented on the same day.[963] Only one deposit is payable, as the deposit in respect of the petition against the partnership is treated as the deposit for all the concurrent petitions.[964] The petitions must be advertised in the *Gazette*, the form of the advertisement following Form 8 in sch. 9 to the 1994 Order.[965] The advertisement must appear not less than seven business days after service of the petitions on the partnership and on the corporate member or former corporate member, and not less than seven days before the day fixed for the hearing.[966] At any time after the presentation of concurrent petitions against the partnership and one or more of its corporate members or former corporate members, the court may grant the petitioning creditor leave to add further corporate members or former corporate members to the proceedings on such terms as the court thinks just.[967] An application for leave to join a new party to the proceedings should be made by ordinary application returnable before the Companies Court Registrar in Chambers. The application should be supported by an affidavit setting out the grounds relied upon for joinder and an explanation as to why the new party was not joined at the outset.

9.236 Withdrawal of the petition[968] and substitution[969]

The petitioning creditor may withdraw a concurrent petition presented in relation to a partnership if (a) he withdraws at the same time all other petitions presented in relation to the partnership, and (b) he gives notice to the court at least three days before the date fixed for the hearing of the relevant petition of his intention to withdraw the petition.[970] If the court is satisfied on the application of the petitioner that the continuance of a petition against an insolvent member of the partnership would be likely for any reason to prejudice or delay the petition presented against the partnership or against any other insolvent member of the partnership (for example, because of difficulty in serving a member of the partnership), the court may permit the petitioner to withdraw the petition against the insolvent member without requiring the withdrawal of the petitions against the partnership

960. IA 1986, s. 124(2) (*ibid.*).
961. IA 1986, s. 124(5) (*ibid.*).
962. See generally paras 9.50–9.56, *supra*.
963. IA 1986, s. 124(3)(a) (as modified as aforesaid).
964. Art. 13 of the 1994 Order.
965. IA 1986, s. 124(3)(b) (as modified as aforesaid).
966. IR 1986, r. 4.11(2).
967. IA 1986, s. 124(4) (as modified by art. 8(3) of, and para. 8 of sch. 4 to, the 1994 Order).
968. See generally paras 9.61–9.62, *supra*.
969. See generally paras 9.67–9.70, *supra*.
970. IA 1986, s. 124(9) (as modified by art. 9(3) of, and para. 8 of sch. 4 to, the 1994 Order).

or any other insolvent members.[971] Where the petitioning creditor gives notice to the court of his intention to withdraw the petitions, the court may substitute as petitioner on the petition against the partnership and on each of the petitions against any insolvent members of the partnership, any other creditor of the partnership who in the opinion of the court would have the right to present the petitions; if the court orders substitution, the petitions will not be withdrawn, and the court may impose such terms as it thinks fit[972] (for example, it may direct the amendment, re-verification and re-service of the petitions).

9.237 The hearing of the petition against the partnership[973]

The hearing date of the petition against the insolvent partnership, fixed by the court, must be before the hearing of the petition against the corporate member or former corporate member.[974] On the day fixed for the hearing of the petition against the partnership, the petitioner must hand to the court a notice of the progress of the various petitions presented in respect of the partnership, before the petition against the partnership is called on for hearing.[975] Any member of the partnership, and any person against whom a concurrent bankruptcy or winding-up petition has been presented in relation to the insolvent partnership, is entitled to appear and make representations on the hearing of the petition against the partnership.[976] Where a concurrent petition is presented against a corporate member or former corporate member of the partnership, the corporate member may only appear by a solicitor or counsel and may not be represented by a director or other officer of the corporate member, unless the court, in exceptional circumstances, grants leave for it to do so.[977]

9.238 Hearing of the petition against a corporate member

In most cases, the outcome of the hearing of a concurrent winding-up petition against a corporate member of an insolvent partnership will follow the outcome of the earlier hearing of the petition against the insolvent partnership. The court nevertheless retains a wide discretion as to the orders it may make on the petition against the corporate member. The petitioner must draw to the attention of the court hearing the petition against the corporate member the outcome of the earlier hearing of the petition against the partnership.[978] If the court has not yet made an order winding-up the partnership, nor an order dismissing the petition against the partnership (i.e. where the petition against the partnership was adjourned on its first hearing), the court may in its discretion adjourn the hearing of the petition against the corporate member until the petition against the partnership is finally determined either by the making of a winding-up order against the partnership or the dismissal of the petition.[979] If a winding-up order has been made against the partnership, the court may make a winding-up order against the corporate member.[980] If,

971. IA 1986, s. 124(10) (*ibid.*).
972. IA 1986, s. 124(11) (as modified by art. 8(3) of, and para. 8 of sch. 4 to, the 1994 Order).
973. See paras 9.99–9.110, *supra*.
974. IA 1986, s. 124(6) (as modified as aforesaid).
975. See Form 9 in sch. 9 to the 1994 Order.
976. IA 1986, s. 124(8) (as modified as aforesaid).
977. RSC O. 5, r. 6(2); *Supreme Court Practice 1997*, Vol. 1, para. 5/6/2, p. 31.
978. IA 1986, s. 125A(1) (as modified as aforesaid).
979. IA 1986, s. 125A(2) (*ibid.*).
980. IA 1986, s. 125A(3) (*ibid.*).

however, a winding-up order is not made against the corporate member within 28 days after the making of the winding-up order against the partnership, the petition against the partnership and the petitions against the corporate member cease to be dependent on each other[981]: after the expiry of the 28 days, the petition against the partnership proceeds as if it were a petition presented alone under art. 7 of the 1994 Order without any concurrent petition against its members[982]; and the petition against any corporate member proceeds as an ordinary creditor's petition. Where the court has dismissed the winding-up petition against the partnership, it may dismiss a petition against the corporate member.[983] If, however, the court makes a winding-up order against the corporate member notwithstanding the dismissal of the petition against the partnership, the corporate member must be wound up according to the provisions of the Insolvency Act 1986, without regard to the modifications made to the Act by the 1994 Order (i.e. a conventional creditor's winding-up).[984] Where a winding-up order has been made against the partnership, but there has been a change in circumstances by the time the petition against the corporate member comes on for hearing, the court may in its discretion dismiss the winding-up petition against the corporate member.[985] Where the member is a limited partner, the court may dismiss the petition against it if that member (a) lodges in court for the benefit of the creditors of the partnership sufficient money or security to meet the limited partner's liability for the debts and obligations of the partnership, or (b) the limited partner satisfies the court that he is no longer under any liability in respect of the debts and obligations of the partnership.[986]

A MEMBER'S PETITION TO WIND UP AN INSOLVENT PARTNERSHIP AS AN UNREGISTERED COMPANY, WITHOUT CONCURRENT PETITIONS AGAINST ITS MEMBERS

9.239 Jurisdiction

A member of an insolvent partnership may petition to wind up the partnership as an unregistered company under Part V of the Insolvency Act 1986, without issuing concurrent petitions against other members of the partnership,[987] if the partnership consists of not less than eight members.[988]

Where the partnership consists of less than eight members, three alternatives are available. Firstly, a member may apply for leave of the court to present a petition against the partnership alone if he can show that he has duly served on the partnership at a principal place of business a written demand in the proper form[989] for a joint debt exceeding £750 which was due from the partnership but paid by the member; that the partnership has failed to pay, secure or compound that sum for three weeks thereafter; and

981. IA 1986, s. 125A(4) (*ibid.*).
982. See paras 9.220–9.228, *supra*.
983. IA 1986, s. 125A(5) (*ibid.*).
984. *Ibid.*
985. IA 1986, s. 125A(6).
986. IA 1986, s. 125A(7).
987. See art. 9 of, and sch. 5 to, the 1994 Order.
988. IA 1986, s. 221A(1) (as modified by art. 9(a) of, and para. 2 of sch. 5 to, the 1994 Order).
989. I.e., Form 10 in sch. 9 to the 1994 Order.

that the member has obtained judgment against the partnership for that sum and taken all reasonable steps to enforce the judgment.[990] Secondly, where all the members are individuals and are prepared to be made bankrupt, the appropriate procedure is a joint bankruptcy petition presented by all the individual members of the partnership without winding-up the partnership as an unregistered company.[991] Thirdly, where the partnership consists of less than eight members, a member of the partnership may petition to wind up the partnership concurrently with insolvency petitions against all its members.[992]

9.240 Location of the partnership and choice of court

The rules regarding the location of the place of business of the partnership and choice of court on a member's winding-up petition under art. 9 against the partnership alone, are similar but not identical to those which apply to a creditor's petition under art. 7 against the partnership alone where there are no concurrent petitions.[993] The partnership may be wound up on the petition of one of its members under art. 9 if it has, or at any time had, a principal place of business in England or Wales[994] and the business of the partnership has been carried on in England and Wales at any time during the period of three years ending with the day on which the winding-up petition is presented.[995] If those requirements are satisfied, the partnership may be wound up by the High Court or by a County Court having insolvency jurisdiction for the district in which the partnership has, or at any time had, a principal place of business.[996] Where the partnership has a principal place of business in Scotland or Northern Ireland, the jurisdiction of the court in England and Wales is subject to the same restrictions as apply to a petition under art. 7 by a creditor against the partnership alone.[997]

9.241 Grounds for the petition

An insolvent partnership may be wound up under art. 9 on the petition of a member without concurrent petitions against any other member, on the same grounds as a partnership may be wound up under art. 7 on the petition of a creditor without concurrent petitions against its members[998]—namely, dissolution, cessation of business, informal winding-up of its affairs, inability to pay its debts, or where it appears to the court that it is just and equitable that the partnership be wound up. On a member's petition under art. 9, the partnership will be deemed to be unable to pay its debts in the same five ways[999] as

990. IA 1986, s. 221A(2) (as modified as aforesaid).
991. See art. 11 of, and sch. 7 to, the 1994 Order.
992. See art. 10 of, and sch. 6 to, the 1994 Order.
993. See para. 9.221, *supra*.
994. IA 1986, s. 221(1) (as modified by art. 9(a) of, and para. 2 of sch. 5 to, the 1994 Order). Contrast petitions under art. 7, which may be presented if the partnership did not have a *principal* place of business in England or Wales, but had a place of business in England or Wales at which the petition debt (or part thereof) arose.
995. IA 1986, s. 221(2) (*ibid.*).
996. IA 1986, s. 117(1)–(3) (*ibid.*).
997. IA 1986, ss. 117(4) and 221(3) (*ibid.*). See para. 9.221, *supra*.
998. IA 1986, s. 221(7) (*ibid.*). See para. 9.222, *supra*.
999. See IA 1986, ss. 222, 223, 224(1)(a), 224(1)(d) and 224(2) (as applied and modified by art. 9 of, and part I of sch. 3 to, the 1994 Order).

a partnership may be deemed to be unable to pay its debts on a creditor's petition against the partnership alone under art. 7, discussed in paragraph 9.222, *supra*.

9.242 Procedure

The procedure on a member's winding-up petition under art. 9 against the partnership alone, where there are no concurrent petitions against its other members, is very similar to the procedure on a creditor's petition against the partnership alone under art. 7.[1000] No standard form for the petition is included in sch. 9 to the 1994 Order: where the ground for the member's petition is that the partnership is insolvent and unable to pay its debts, the usual form of a creditor's winding-up petition should be adapted as necessary; where some other ground is relied upon, that ground should be set out in the petition in place of the averment of insolvency. Where the petition is presented by a member's liquidator or administrator (in the case of an individual member) or his supervisor or trustee (in the case of a corporate member), Form 3 in sch. 9 to the 1994 Order should be adapted as necessary.

A MEMBER'S PETITION TO WIND UP AN INSOLVENT PARTNERSHIP AS AN UNREGISTERED COMPANY, WITH CONCURRENT PETITIONS AGAINST ALL ITS OTHER MEMBERS

9.243 Jurisdiction

The court has jurisdiction to wind up an insolvent partnership as an unregistered company on the petition of a member, where concurrent insolvency petitions are presented against all the other members of the partnership.[1001] The 1994 Order does not stipulate any minimum number of partners for the jurisdiction under art. 10 to be invoked[1002]—in other words, a partnership between two or more members may be wound up under art. 10 on the petition of one of the members, if a concurrent petition is also presented against the other member or members, as the case may be. Where it is not practicable to present petitions against the partnership and every member of it, the intended petitioner may apply to the court for leave to present the petition against the partnership and only such member or members as the court directs.[1003] The application should be made to the Companies Court Registrar sitting in Chambers. All the members of the partnership must be willing for an insolvency order to be made against them,[1004] but the court may grant leave to present petitions against the partnership and all the willing members, without requiring petitions to be presented against unwilling members. A member may decide to petition to wind up the partnership under art. 10 with concurrent petitions against all its willing members in order to have recourse to the assets of the partnership and of all its members to satisfy the partnership debts for which they are jointly liable. The rules governing a petition to wind

1000. See paras 9.221–9.228, *supra*.
1001. See art. 10 of, part I of sch. 3 to, and sch. 6 to, the 1994 Order.
1002. Contrast the requirement of a minimum of eight partners where a member seeks to wind up the partnership under art. 9 without presenting concurrent petitions against any of its members: see para. 9.239, *supra*.
1003. IA 1986, s. 124(3) (as modified by art. 10(1)(a) to, and para. 2 of sch. 6 to, the 1994 Order).
1004. IA 1986, s. 124(2) (*ibid.*).

up a partnership under art. 10 where there are concurrent petitions against all of its members are a hybrid of the rules governing a creditor's petition to wind up the partnership under art. 8 where there are concurrent petitions against one or more of its members,[1005] and the rules governing a member's petition to wind up the partnership under art. 9 where there are no concurrent petitions against its other members: the grounds for a member's petition under art. 10 mirror those for a creditor's petition under art. 8, whereas the requirements concerning the location of the partnership's place of business and the choice of court mirror those for a member's petition under art. 9.

9.244 Location of partnership and choice of court

The rules concerning the partnership's place of business are set out in s. 221(1) to (3) of the Insolvency Act 1986 as modified by the 1994 Order.[1006] The rules regarding the choice of court are set out in s. 117(1) to (4).[1007] In each case, the rules are precisely the same as the rules governing a member's petition to wind up the partnership under art. 9 where there are no concurrent petitions against its other members,[1008] discussed in para. 9.240, *supra.*[1009]

9.245 Grounds for the petitions against the partnership and its members

A petition by a member to wind up a partnership under art. 10 may only be presented on the ground that the partnership is unable to pay its debts.[1010] The grounds for the member's concurrent petitions under art. 10 against all the members are also the same as the grounds which apply to a creditor's concurrent petitions under art. 8 against one or more members, discussed in para. 9.232, *supra*—namely, that the members are unable to pay their debts[1011]: both art. 8 and art. 10 apply the modified provisions of the Insolvency Act 1986 set out in Part II of sch. 4 to the 1994 Order to insolvency petitions presented against the members of an insolvent partnership.[1012] A corporate member of the partnership will be deemed to be unable to pay its debts in the ways discussed in para. 9.232, *supra.*

9.246 Procedure

The procedure on a member's petition to wind up the partnership under art. 10 concurrently with petitions against all its members, closely follows the procedure on a creditor's petition to wind up the partnership under art. 8 with concurrent petitions against one or more of its members.[1013] The following paragraphs deal only with those aspects of the procedure under art. 10 which differ from the procedure under art. 8.

1005. See paras 9.229–9.238, *supra.*
1006. See art. 10(1)(a) of, and para. 4 of sch. 6 to, the 1994 Order.
1007. See art. 10(1)(a) of, and para. 1 of sch. 6 to, the 1994 Order.
1008. I.e., art. 9(a) of, and paras 1 and 2 of sch. 5 to, the 1994 Order.
1009. See para. 9.230, *supra* as to the bar to insolvency proceedings against an individual member in a Chancery District Registry of the High Court.
1010. IA 1986, ss. 124(2) and 221(8) (as modified by art. 10(1)(a) of, and paras 2 and 4 of sch. 6 to, the 1994 Order).
1011. IA 1986, s. 122 (as modified by art. 10(6) of, and para. 6(a) of part II of sch. 4 to, the 1994 Order).
1012. See arts 8(3) and 10(6) of the 1994 Order.
1013. See paras 9.233–9.238, *supra.*

9.247 Form of petition,[1014] parties and joinder[1015]

The member's petition to wind up the insolvent partnership should follow Form 11 in sch. 9 to the 1994 Order, and a petition to wind up a corporate member or former corporate member of the partnership should follow Form 12 in sch. 9.[1016] The petition against the partnership must state that each member is willing for an insolvency order to be made against him or it,[1017] unless the court has granted the petitioner leave to present the petitions against the partnership and only some of its members[1018]: in that case, the petition should refer to the grant of leave and should state that every member against whom a petition has been presented in accordance with the court's order is willing for an insolvency order to be made against him or it. As all the members of the partnership are either joined as parties to the proceedings from the outset, or are excluded from the proceedings by the leave of the court given prior to presentation of the petitions, the 1994 Order does not make provision for joinder of a party to the proceedings under art. 10 after presentation of the petitions.[1019]

9.248 The hearing of the petition against the partnership[1020]

Any member against whom a winding-up or bankruptcy petition has been presented in relation to the insolvent partnership may appear and be heard on the petition against the partnership.[1021]

1014. See para. 9.234, *supra*.
1015. See para. 9.235, *supra*.
1016. IA 1986, s. 124(1) (as modified by art. 10(1)(a) of, and para. 2 of sch. 6 to, the 1994 Order).
1017. IA 1986, s. 124(2)(b) (*ibid*.).
1018. See IA 1986, s. 124(3) (*ibid*.).
1019. Contrast IA 1986, s. 124(4) (as modified by art. 8(3) of, and para. 8 of part II of sch. 4 to, the 1994 Order) in respect of a creditor's concurrent petitions.
1020. See para. 9.237, *supra*.
1021. IA 1986, s. 124(8) (as modified as aforesaid).

CHAPTER 10

PART 7 OF THE INSOLVENCY RULES 1986: THE ORIGINATING AND ORDINARY APPLICATION PROCEDURE

INTRODUCTION

10.1 The new procedure

Chapter 1 of part 7 of the Insolvency Rules 1986 introduced a new procedure for applying to the court for relief or other orders under the Insolvency Act or the Insolvency Rules, namely, the "originating application" and the "ordinary application". All applications made under the Insolvency Act or the Insolvency Rules, except a petition for an administration order or a winding-up order, must now follow the procedure and practice set out in chapter 1 of part 7 of the Insolvency Rules[1] and, except so far as inconsistent therewith, the Rules of the Supreme Court and the practice of the High Court, or the County Court Rules and the practice of the County Court – in either case with any necessary modifications.[2] This Chapter aims to set out, in a logical form, the practice and procedure that appertains to originating and ordinary applications in the Companies Court. As this book is confined to the practice and procedure of the Companies Court,[3] any supplementary requirements necessitated by the County Court Rules and the practice of the County Court in respect of originating or ordinary applications in the County Court will not be considered. In substance, the additional requirements are of little significance.

10.2 Writs and other originating processes

If relief is sought in respect of any jurisdiction granted to or exercised by the High Court other than by virtue of the Insolvency Act or the Insolvency Rules, such relief must usually be applied for by writ or other process in one or other of the Divisions of the High Court, but not in the Companies Court. This can raise problems in practice which, in the case of a company in liquidation, are considered in more detail in the next Chapter.[4]

1. IR 1986, r. 7.1. An exception would appear to be an application under IA 1986, s. 423 which is not made in existing proceedings in the Companies Court or Bankruptcy Court or which is brought otherwise than by virtue of a right to apply to those courts by some other provision of parts I to XI of the Insolvency Act 1986: such an application might be commenced by writ in any part of the High Court: *TSB Bank plc* v. *Katz*, *Times*, 2 May 1994.

2. IR 1986, r. 7.51. The "practice" of the Supreme Court now includes Practice Direction (Civil Litigation: Case Management) [1995] 1 WLR 262 and the *Chancery Guide 1995*: Practice Direction (Chancery Division: Procedure and Case Management), [1995] 1 WLR 785.

3. For an explanation of what comprises "the Companies Court" see Chapter 1.

4. See Chapter 11.

ORIGINATING AND ORDINARY APPLICATIONS

10.3 The appropriate court

The courts having jurisdiction to make orders under the Insolvency Act and the Insolvency Rules in respect of companies are courts which would have jurisdiction to wind up the company in respect of which the application relates.[5] The High Court has jurisdiction to wind up all companies registered in England and Wales, as well as jurisdiction to wind up many other companies.[6] All causes and matters involving the exercise of the High Court's jurisdiction under enactments relating to companies are assigned to the Chancery Division,[7] but only certain district registries have a winding-up jurisdiction.[8] In all company insolvency proceedings, in the High Court, "the registrar" means a registrar in bankruptcy of the High Court[9] or, where the proceedings are in a district registry having winding-up jurisdiction, a district judge of that registry.[10] A county court only has jurisdiction to wind up companies where the amount of the company's share capital paid up or credited as paid up does not exceed £120,000[11] and where the company has a registered office in the district of the county court.[12]

10.4 Should an application be made by way of originating or ordinary application?

Originating applications are applications to the court which are not applications in pending proceedings before the court; all other applications must be by way of ordinary application.[13] Confusion often arises in practice as to whether an application should be originating or ordinary. The test is not whether there are already pending proceedings relating to the particular company before the court but whether the application desired to be made can properly be described as an application *in* those pending proceedings.[14] It does not follow, because a company has been wound up by the court in winding-up proceedings, that all applications thereafter should be ordinary application within those proceedings: for instance, an application to remove a liquidator of a company being wound up by the court is not an application in the petition, which is no longer pending, and must be commenced

5. See the definition of court in CA 1985, s. 744 as applied by IA 1986, s. 251.

6. See Chapter 9 for a more detailed exposition of this jurisdiction.

7. S. 61(1) Supreme Court Act 1981, sch. 1, para. 1.

8. IR 1986, r. 13.2(4): the District Registries are Birmingham, Bistol, Cardiff, Leeds, Liverpool, Manchester, Newcastle-upon-Tyne and Preston.

9. IR 1986, r. 13.2(4)a.

10. IR 1986, r. 13.2(4)b and s. 74 Courts and Legal Services Act 1990.

11. S. 117(2) Insolvency Act 1986; the figure may be increased or reduced: Insolvency Act 1986 ss. 117(3), 416.

12. S. 117(4) Insolvency Act 1986 provides that the Lord Chancellor may by order in a statutory instrument exclude a county court from having winding-up jurisdiction, and for the puroses of that jurisdiction may attach its district, or any part thereof, to any other county court, and may by statutory instrument revoke or vary any such order provided that a county court is not to have winding-up jurisdiction unless it has for the time being jurisdiction for the purposes of parts VIII to XI of the Insolvency Act 1986 (individual insolvency).

13. IR 1986, r. 7.2.

14. An "ordinary application" is an application which in a writ action, would be commenced by summons or by motion, whereas an "originating application" is an application which, other than in insolvency proceedings, would be commenced by writ or originating summons or originating motion: *Port* v. *Auger* [1994] 1 WLR 862.

by an originating and not an ordinary application.[15] Indeed, once a final order has been made on a petition, whether for a winding-up order or an administration order, then, unless a general liberty to apply has been given, those proceedings are no longer "pending" and any relief sought thereafter should be by way of originating application, unless the application amounts to an application to vary, modify or discharge any orders made on the substantive hearing of the petition.

10.5 The title to applications

The title should clearly indicate, in the top left hand corner, that the application is being issued out of the Chancery Division of the High Court. If issued out of a district registry, the name of the district registry should appear under "Chancery Division". If issued at the Companies Court in the Royal Courts of Justice, and not out of a district registry, there should be inserted under "Chancery Division" the words "Companies Court". Underneath either "Companies Court" or the name of the relevant district registry, the application must state that it is "In the matter of . . . [naming the company to which the proceedings relate]" "And in the matter of the Insolvency Act 1986".[16] Where a liquidator is a party to any application he must not be described by his individual name but, where the official receiver is liquidator, by the style of "the official receiver and Liquidator" of the particular company in liquidation and, where a person other than the official receiver is liquidator, by the style of "the Liquidator" of the particular company in liquidation.[17] Where the application is brought by a liquidator in the name of a company, the applicant's name should appear in the title simply as "The A.B. Company Limited"[18]: there is no requirement to state in the title that the company is in liquidation. The same applies if a company in liquidation is a respondent to an application. However, if the company is in liquidation, or is a foreign company, it is the usual practice to record this fact after setting out the address of the parties to the application.

10.6 Form and contents of applications

Every application must be in the form appropriate to the application concerned as the circumstances require[19]: originating applications must be in Form 7.1,[20] ordinary applications must be in Form 7.2.[21] Both originating and ordinary applications must state the names of the parties,[22] the nature of the relief or order applied for or the directions sought,[23] the names and addresses of the persons (if any) on whom it is intended to serve the application or that no person is intended to be served,[24] the names and addresses of those persons to whom notice of the application is to be given[25] and the applicant's

15. *Re Corbenstoke (No. 2)* (1989) 5 BCC 767.
16. IR 1986, r. 7.26.
17. S. 163 Insolvency Act 1986.
18. IR 1986, r. 7.51, *Supreme Court Practice 1997*, p. 33, para. 6/1/7.
19. IR 1986, rr. 7.2(2) and 12.7(1)(2).
20. Sch. 4 to the Rules.
21. Sch. 4 to the Rules.
22. IR 1986, r. 7.3(1)(a).
23. IR 1986, r. 7.3(1)(b).
24. IR 1986, r. 7.3(1)(c).
25. IR 1986, r. 7.3(1)(d).

address for service.[26] The application must be signed by the applicant if he is acting in person or, where he is not so acting, by or on behalf of his solicitor.[27] Originating applications must set out the grounds on which the applicant claims to be entitled to the relief or order sought,[28] although as a matter of practice, reference can be made to an affidavit sworn on behalf of the applicant in which the grounds are set out. An ordinary application need not set out the grounds relied upon for the relief or order sought.

10.7 Filing of applications

The application must be presented to the court for filing, together with enough copies for service on the respondents, and with one additional copy. If presented at the Royal Courts of Justice, it must be presented at the Chambers of the Registrar, Companies Court, 2nd Floor, Thomas More Building, Royal Courts of Justice, Strand, London WC2A 2LL (Room TM 209): if not, it must be presented to one of the district registries having jurisdiction to wind up companies.[29] Upon filing, the court fixes a time, date and place for the hearing.[30]

10.8 Service of applications

Unless the relevant provisions of the Insolvency Act or the Insolvency Rules do not require service of the application on, or notice of it to be given to, any person,[31] or unless the court otherwise directs, sealed copies of the application with the time, date and place for the hearing endorsed thereon must be served on the respondents named in the application.[32] Subject to certain modifications,[33] Order 65 of the Rules of the Supreme Court applies as regards any matter relating to the service of applications.[34] Personal service of an application on a respondent is not expressly required and, therefore, the applicant is entitled to serve the application in one of the following ways:

(a) by leaving the document:
   (i) at the business address of the solicitor (if any) who is acting in the proceedings[35] for the person to be served in the proceedings in connection with which service of the document in question is to be effected[36];
   (ii) in the case of an individual, his usual or last known address[37];
   (iii) where the application is brought against individuals in the name of a firm, the principal or last known place of business of the firm within the jurisdiction[38];

26. IR 1986, r. 7.3(1)(e).
27. IR 1986, r. 7.3(3).
28. IR 1986, r. 7.3(2).
29. See para. 11.3, *supra*.
30. IR 1986, rr. 7.4(2), 13.6.
31. IR 1986, r. 7.5(1).
32. IR 1986, r. 7.4(3).
33. Set out in rr. 12.10 and 12.11.
34. IR 1986, r. 12.11(1).
35. There is no form for acknowledgement of service and there is no formal document requiring a solicitor to state whether he is acting for a respondent: the question is whether, using ordinary language, it can be said that the solicitor is *already* acting *in* the proceedings for a respondent.
36. IR 1986, r. 12.11(1); RSC O. 65, r. 5(2)(a).
37. IR 1986, r. 12.11(1); RSC O. 65, r. 5(2)(b).
38. IR 1986, r. 12.11(1); RSC O. 65, r. 5(2)(c).

(iv) in the case of a body corporate, the registered or principal office of the body[39];

(b) by posting the application to the respondent in an envelope addressed to the respondent at his last known address[40] and prepaid for either first or second class post[41] or, if a solicitor has stated in correspondence or otherwise that he is authorised to accept service, by posting the application to the respondent's solicitors; where first class post is used, the document is treated as served on the second business day after the date of posting, unless the contrary is shown[42]; where second class post is used, the document is treated as served on the fourth business day after the date of posting, unless the contrary is shown[43]; the date of posting is presumed, unless the contrary is shown, to be the date shown in the post-mark on the envelope in which the document is contained.[44]

(c) through a document exchange[45];

(d) by fax[46];

(e) in such other manner as the court may direct.[47]

Service of an application which is effected by leaving it at the address of the respondent between 12 noon on a Saturday and midnight on the following day or after 4.00pm on any other weekday is, for the purpose of computing any period of time after service of the application, deemed to have been served on the Monday following that Saturday or on the day following that other weekday, as the case may be.[48] An application can only be served within the jurisdiction on a Sunday with the leave of the court and then only in cases of urgency.[49]

10.9 Service out of the jurisdiction

Leave is required to serve an application out of the jurisdiction. The Court may order service on a person who is not in England and Wales to be effected within such time and at such place and in such manner as the court thinks fit.[50] Any application for leave must be supported by an affidavit stating the grounds on which the application is made and in what place or country the person to be served is to, or probably may, be found.[51] The court has a much wider discretion to order a method of service out of the jurisdiction than is provided in Orders 10, 11 or 65 of the Rules of the Supreme Court, and there is no obligation to require service to be in accordance with the law of the country where service is to be effected.[52] In deciding whether the case is a proper one for service out of the jurisdiction, one of the factors the court will take into account is the strength or weakness

39. IR 1986, rr. 12.11(1); RSC O. 65, r. 5(2)(d).
40. IR 1986, r. 12.10(IA).
41. IR 1986, r. 12.10(1).
42. IR 1986, r. 12.10(2).
43. IR 1986, r. 12.10(3).
44. IR 1986, r. 12.10(4).
45. IR 1986, r. 12.11(1); RSC O. 65, r. 5(c).
46. IR 1986, r. 12.11(1); RSC O. 65, r. 5(ca).
47. IR 1986, r. 12.11(1); RSC O. 65, r. 5(1)(d).
48. IR 1986, r. 12.11(1) and (2); RSC O. 65, r. 7.
49. IR 1986, r. 12.11(1) and (4); RSC O. 65, r. 10.
50. IR 1986, r. 12.12(1) and (3).
51. IR 1986, r. 12.12(4).
52. *Re Busytoday* [1992] BCC 480.

of the applicant's claim: there must be a real issue which the applicant may reasonably ask the court to hear.[53]

10.10 Time for service

Unless provided for otherwise, the application must be served at least 14 days before the date fixed for the hearing of the application.[54] However, if the application is urgent, the court has power to hear the application immediately, either with or without notice to, or the attendance of, other parties. Alternatively, the court may authorise a shorter period of service. Any such application may be heard on terms providing for the filing or service of documents, or the carrying out of other formalities, as the court thinks fit.[55] It is only in exceptional cases that the court will make an order against a person without giving that person an opportunity to be heard. Two conditions must be satisfied: first, that giving the person such an opportunity will be likely to cause injustice to the applicant, by reason either of the delay involved or the action which it appears likely that the respondent or others will take before the order can be made; and second, that the court is satisfied either that any damage which the respondent may suffer through having to comply with the order is compensatable under a cross-undertaking in damages, or that the risk of uncompensatable loss is clearly outweighed by the risk of injustice to the applicant if the order is not made.[56] Any applicant who applies for an order without serving the application on the person against whom relief is sought, and without giving that person notice of the application, is under a duty to the court to make full and accurate disclosure of all relevant facts.[57] Where there is no requirement for service of the application on, or notice of it to be given to any person, the court can hear the application *ex parte* either forthwith,[58] or by fixing a time, date and place for the hearing of the application.[59]

10.11 The hearing of the application

Except where a general or special direction has been given to the contrary[60] or the registrar is expressly excluded from making the order required, the jurisdiction of the court to hear and determine the application may be exercised by the registrar and in the first instance the application must be made to the registrar.[61] The following directions have been given[62] as to applications which must be made direct to the judge:

(a) applications to commit to prison;
(b) applications for urgent interlocutory relief;

53. *Re Paramount Airways Ltd (No. 2)* [1992] BCC 416 at 426; *Re Tucker* [1988] 1 WLR 497 at 502; re *Howard Holdings Ltd*, 6 June 1997, unreported (Chadwick J).
54. IR 1986, r. 7.4(5).
55. IR 1986, r. 7.4(6).
56. *Re First Express Ltd* [1991] BCC 782.
57. *Re First Express Ltd* [1991] BCC 782 at 786.
58. IR 1986, r. 7.5(2).
59. IR 1986, r. 7.5(3).
60. See Practice Direction (Companies Court: Insolvency), [1987] 1 WLR 53; *Supreme Court Practice 1997*, para. 838 for such directions to the contrary.
61. IR 1986, r. 7.6(2).
62. See Practice Direction (Companies Court: Insolvency), *supra*.

(c) applications to restrain the presentation or advertisement of a petition to wind up;
(d) applications after an administration order has been made for directions, or to vary or discharge the order;
(e) applications to stay a winding-up or discharge an administration order, or for directions where a voluntary arrangement has been approved; and
(f) appeals from a decision made by a County Court or a registrar of the High Court.

In addition, the registrar may refer to the judge any matter which he thinks should properly be decided by the judge, and the judge may either dispose of the matter or refer it back to the registrar with such directions as he thinks fit.[63] As a matter of practice, the registrar will refer to the judge matters which involve substantial disputes of fact that require cross-examination or where an important point of law or principle is involved.

10.12 In open court or in chambers

Unless allowed or authorised to be made otherwise, every application before the registrar shall, and every application before the judge may, be heard in chambers.[64] In practice, applications for directions are heard by a judge in chambers but all other applications will be heard by a judge in open court.

10.13 Adjournments

The court may adjourn the hearing of an application on such terms as it thinks fit.[65]

10.14 Directions

The court may at any time give such directions as it thinks fit as to:

(a) service or notice of the application on or to any person, whether in connection with the date time and place of a resumed hearing or for any other purpose[66];
(b) whether particulars of claim and reference are to be delivered and generally as to the procedure on the application[67];
(c) the manner in which any evidence is to be adduced at a resumed hearing and in particular as to:
  (i) the taking of evidence wholly or in part by affidavit or orally[68];
  (ii) the cross-examination either before the judge or registrar on the hearing in court or in chambers of any deponents to affidavits[69];
  (iii) any report to be given by the official receiver or any person mentioned in r. 7.9(1)(b);

63. IR 1986, r. 7.6(3).
64. IR 1986, r. 7.6(1).
65. IR 1986, r. 7.10(1).
66. IR 1986, r. 7.10(a).
67. IR 1986, r. 7.10(b).
68. IR 1986, r. 7.10(c)(i).
69. IR 1986, r. 7.10(c)(ii).

(d) the matters to be dealt with in evidence.[70]

10.15 The first hearing

The first hearing of an application, especially an originating application which seeks substantive relief, will usually be treated as an opportunity for the court to give directions as to the further conduct of the application. There is no requirement to support an application with affidavit evidence: indeed, if the application will involve substantial disputes of fact and it is a case in which it is likely that particulars of claim and defence will be ordered, it is both unusual and unnecessary to file affidavit evidence. If, however, the applicant intends to rely at the first hearing on affidavit evidence, he must file such evidence in court and serve copies thereof on the respondents not less than 14 days before the date fixed for hearing.[71] Where a respondent to an application intends to oppose it and rely for that purpose on affidavit evidence, such evidence must be filed in court and copies thereof served on the applicants not less than 7 days before the date fixed for the hearing. The respondent is entitled to file evidence in opposition even if the applicant has not filed evidence in support, as might be the case if on the first hearing the respondent was to apply to strike out the application.[72]

10.16 Counterclaims

No express provision is made for the service by a respondent of a counterclaim. If a respondent wishes to make a claim against the applicant and that claim can be said to arise *in* the pending proceedings commenced by the applicant, the claim can be brought by ordinary application in those proceedings: if not, the claim must be made by way of originating application. On the first hearing of such an originating application it is likely that the court will either consolidate the proceedings or order that the applications be heard together.[73] The claims to be brought by counterclaim must be claims which can properly be brought by way of originating or ordinary application. If it is necessary for a respondent to issue separate writ proceedings against the insolvent company, the proceedings can be transferred to the Companies Court, but only in limited circumstances and only if an order for the winding-up of the company has been made by the High Court or a provisional liquidator has been appointed or winding-up proceedings have been transferred to the High Court from a county court.[74]

10.17 Third party proceedings

It is clearly desirable in many instances that a respondent should be permitted to issue third party proceedings if:

(a) he wishes to claim as against a person not a party to the action a contribution or indemnity; or

70. IR 1986, r. 7.10(d).
71. IR 1986, r. 7.8(1)(a).
72. See para. 10.22, *infra*.
73. IR 1986, r. 7.51; RSC O. 4, r. 9.
74. IR 1986, r. 7.15.

(b) he wishes to claim any relief or remedy relating to or connected with the original subject-matter of the application and substantially the same relief or remedy is claimed by the applicant; or
(c) he wishes that any question or issue relating to or connected with the original subject-matter of the application should be determined not only as between the applicant and the respondent but also as between either or both of them and a person not already a party to the action.

At first sight, it would appear that a respondent is entitled to issue such proceedings, since by r. 7.51 the practice and procedure of the High Court apply where no provision is made otherwise, and this would bring in the provisions of RSC O. 16. However, *re A Singer and Co. (Hat Manufacturers) Ltd*[75] is authority for the proposition that the Companies Court has no jurisdiction to permit third party proceedings to be issued if the third party proceedings will not decide anything material to the winding-up of the company itself. In that case, a liquidator brought proceedings seeking a declaration that a payment to a bank was a fraudulent preference of the bank and/or of those who stood surety for the company and sought repayment from the bank. Only the bank was made a respondent. The relevant rules, the Companies (Winding-Up) Rules 1929, provided[76] that the practice and procedure of the Rules of the Supreme Court should apply where no provision was made otherwise, and the bank applied to issue third party proceedings against the sureties and to join them in as respondents. The Court of Appeal held there was no jurisdiction. It was stated that the winding-up procedure was a summary jurisdiction and that the judge would not be deciding anything material to the winding-up in the third party proceedings in that whether the bank had a right over against third persons had nothing to do with winding-up, so that there was no jurisdiction to hear such matters.[77] It therefore appears that a respondent who wishes to bring third party proceedings will instead be obliged to commence separate High Court proceedings. In a district registry, the same district judge can hear all interlocutory matters in both sets of proceedings together, since he has conferred on him all the jurisdiction conferred on both a master and a registrar in bankruptcy. However, when the proceedings are not in a district registry, the interlocutory stage does cause a problem, since the jurisdiction of the registrar is limited to the jurisdiction conferred by the Insolvency Act and Rules. One solution is to ensure that interlocutory matters in both proceedings are heard by a judge. Alternatively the master or registrar will have to be informed what the other is being asked to order, so that timetables and orders can be synchronised. If the claim being brought in the Companies Court is one which could also be commenced by writ or other originating process, the Companies Court may, if the matter is one of discretion, decline to hear it, on the basis that

75. [1943] Ch. 121.
76. As in r. 7.51.
77. It has since been recognised that the Companies Court is not a court separate and distinct from the High Court with its own peculiar jurisdiction and that the Companies Court is merely a way of describing the High Court when dealing with matters originating in the chambers of the bankruptcy registrar. However, whilst a judge of the High Court clearly does have jurisdiction to hear all matters that can properly be heard by the High Court, the jurisdiction of the registrar is still limited to the jurisdiction conferred by the Insolvency Act and the Insolvency Rules, and *Re A. Singer and Company (Hat Manufacturer) Ltd* would appear still good authority for the proposition that third party proceedings raising issues not material to the winding-up itself cannot be taken in the Companies Court. See, generally, *Re Rolls Razor Ltd (No. 2)* [1970] Ch. 576 at 588; *Re Shilena Hosiery Co. Ltd* [1980] 1 Ch. 219; *Fabric Sales Ltd* v. *Eratex Ltd* [1984] 1 WLR 863; *Re Brampton Securities Ltd (No. 2)* (1988) 4 BCC 436 and, in respect of IA 1986, s. 35, re *Therm-a-Stor Ltd* [1997] BCC 301.

justice would be better served by the commencement of the proceedings by writ or other originating process so as to enable the respondent to commence third party proceedings.

10.18 Indemnities and contribution claims between co-respondents

It was held in *Re Morecombe Bowling Ltd*[78] that, where proceedings are brought against more than one respondent and the court has power either expressly or impliedly to apportion their liability and determine the priority of their liability as between themselves, one respondent can take third party proceedings in the Companies Court against another respondent claiming an indemnity or contribution, and that nothing in the Court of Appeal's decision in *Re A Singer and Co. (Hat Manufacturer) Ltd*[79] prevented the court from permitting the issue of such proceedings.

10.19 Particulars of claim and defence

The court has a discretion on the first (or any subsequent) hearing of an application to give directions as to whether particulars of claim and defence are to be delivered.[80] Where the application is not interlocutory in nature and involves any substantial dispute of fact, such particulars are now frequently ordered, especially where, as is common, no affidavits in support have been filed and served at the first hearing. If an originating application sets out in the body of the application the grounds on which the application is made, in a form which in effect amounts to particulars of the claim, rather than by reference to an affidavit served with the application, an order is usually made that the grounds set out in the originating application stand as the applicant's particulars of claim.

10.20 Particulars of reply

Unlike the practice set out in the Rules of the Supreme Court, the applicant has no automatic right to serve a reply but the court has a discretion to permit such a reply and any other subsequent pleadings to be served by either party.[81] If there are matters which the applicant wishes to reply to, it is usual practice to permit such a reply; indeed, the court may order the applicant to serve a reply so as to enable the respondent to know what the applicant's case is in response to the defence.

10.21 Further or better particulars

Any party can request from any other party further or better particulars of any particulars of claim or defence served. The general discretion in the court to give directions on the hearing of an application[82] entitles the court to order any party to give further or better particulars of their particulars of claim or defence, or any other pleading as the case may be, on such terms as the court thinks fit.

78. [1969] 1 WLR 133.
79. *Supra*.
80. IR 1986, r. 7.10(2)(b).
81. IR 1986, r. 7.10(2).
82. IR 1986, r. 7.10(2).

10.22 Summary determination

The court has all the powers of the High Court to determine summarily[83] an application, or to dispose of it on a point of law.[84] The court also has the same inherent jurisdiction as the High Court to strike out any part of an application or any particulars of claim or defence served pursuant to it, if it discloses no reasonable cause of action or defence, or is scandalous, frivolous or vexatious or may prejudice, embarrass or delay the fair trial of the action or is otherwise an abuse of the process of the court.[85] The applications must be made by way of ordinary application and supported by affidavit.

10.23 Interim payments

An applicant is entitled to make an application to the court for an interim payment.[86] For the purpose of obtaining an interim payment, the applicant must show a case of a strength which would justify judgment under an application for summary judgment under RSC O. 14,[87] not, of course, in respect of the whole amount claimed in the application but in respect of the amount for which payment is sought on an interim basis. The amount of any interim payment ordered to be paid must be paid to the applicant unless the order provides for it to be paid into court and, where the amount is paid into court, the court may on the application of the applicant order the whole or any party of it to be paid out to him at such time or times as the court thinks fit.[88] The fact that an interim order has been made must not be referred to in any pleadings and, unless the respondent consents or the court so directs, no communication of that fact or of the fact that an interim payment has been made must be made to the court at the hearing of any question or issue as to liability or damages until all questions of liability and amount have been determined.[89]

10.24 Discovery

There is no provision for automatic discovery but any party may, with the leave of the court, obtain discovery from any other party to an application.[90] An order for discovery can only be made in respect of documents which are or have been in the possession, custody or power of the party against whom discovery is sought.[91]

10.25 Inspection

In many applications an "office holder" will have a large amount of documentation which might be relevant to the issue in the case. The task of enumerating the documents by

83. IR 1986, r. 7.51; RSC O. 14.
84. IR 1986, r. 7.51; RSC O. 14A.
85. *Port* v. *Auger* [1994] 1 WLR 862 where Harman J. held that r. 7.51; RSC O. 18, r. 19 of itself did not give the court jurisdiction to strike out an originating or ordinary application as neither was a "pleading" and neither was expressly referred to in RSC O. 18, r. 19(3). Query whether particulars of claim and defence are "pleadings".
86. IR 1986, r. 7.51; RSC O. 29, r. 10; *Re Shoe Lace Ltd* [1993] BCC 609 (C.A.).
87. See Hoffmann J. at first instance in *Re Shoe Lace Ltd* [1992] BCC 367 at 371 (upheld by the Court of Appeal [1993] BCC 609).
88. IR 1986, r. 7.51; RSC O. 29, r. 13.
89. IR 1986, r. 7.51; RSC O. 29, r. 15.
90. IR 1986, r. 7.60; *Re Primlaks (UK) Ltd (No. 2)* [1900] BCLC 234; *Re BCCI (No. 6)* [1994] 1 BCLC 450.
91. IR 1986, r. 12.11(1); RSC O. 24.

describing each of them or, in the cases of bundles of documents of the same nature, each bundle, to enable them to be identified[92] will be time-consuming and expensive. Where it is considered that those against whom an application is made will have sufficient familiarity with the documents so as to enable them to search for documents they require without the documents being listed, an order is frequently made permitting inspection of documents without requiring a list of documents to be served or verified.

10.26 What documents are within the "power" of a liquidator?

Questions often arise as to whether documents in the custody of an administrative receiver are within the "power" of a liquidator subsequently appointed to that company. The expression "power" means a presently enforceable legal right to obtain, from whomsoever actually holds the document, inspection of it without the need to obtain the consent of anyone else.[93] If an administrative receiver refuses to comply with a request by the liquidator for documents (which he might do, on the grounds, amongst others, that to comply with the request would require undue expenditure of time and money in searching through the company's records to identify documents within the ambit of the request) the only remedy of the liquidator is to apply to the court for an order directing compliance.[94] The court has a discretion whether to make such an order and although a court might normally make an order at the request of the liquidator if satisfied that compliance with it would not place an unreasonable burden on the administrative receivers, it cannot be said that the court would be bound to do so. It is, therefore, doubtful whether documents in the custody of administrative receivers are within the power of the liquidator.[95]

10.27 *Ex parte* applications for discovery

Normally an application for discovery will be made *inter partes*, but there is jurisdiction for the application to be made *ex parte*.[96]

10.28 Pre-action discovery

No provision is made for pre-action discovery. However, the Court of Appeal has stated[97] that there is jurisdiction under what is now s. 112 of the Insolvency Act to permit creditors to inspect the records and documents generated by the liquidation in order to enable them to inquire whether the company had a cause of action against the liquidator for misfeasance. The view was expressed that liquidators should not oppose inspection of documents by a creditor as their resistance is "either unnecessary, if there is nothing the documents can reveal, or, an unpleasant alternative, involves the use by the liquidators of

92. IR 1986, r. 12.11(1); RSC O. 24, r. 5(1).
93. *Lonrho Ltd* v. *Shell Petroleum Co. Ltd* [1980] 1 WLR 627 at 635G per Lord Diplock.
94. Pursuant to IA 1986, s. 234(2).
95. See also *Re Lombard Shipping and Forwarding Ltd* [1992] BCC 700, in which it was held that the Secretary of State, in bringing an application for the disqualification of a director under the Company Directors Disqualification Act 1986, did not have in his power documents in the custody of former administrative receivers even though he was entitled to apply to the court under r. 5 of the Insolvent Companies (Reports on Conduct of Directors) No. 2 Rules 1986 (S.I. 1986 No. 2134).
96. IR 1986, r. 7.60(2).
97. *Re Movitex* [1992] 1 WLR 303.

their control over the company and its documents for their own protection".[98] A similar jurisdiction will exist in respect of companies being wound up by the court.[99]

10.29 Interrogatories

Any party to insolvency proceedings may, with the leave of the court, administer interrogatories to any other party to those proceedings.[100]

10.30 The manner in which evidence is to be given

At the first or any subsequent hearing of an application, the court can give directions as to the manner in which any evidence is to be adduced at a resumed hearing and, in particular, as to the taking of evidence wholly or in part by affidavit or orally, the cross-examination of any deponents to affidavits, and any reports[101] which are to be given instead of affidavits.[102] Affidavits can be ordered in any proceedings commenced by way of application unless by any provision of the Rules it is otherwise provided, but the court may, on the application of any party, order the attendance for cross-examination of the person making the affidavit.[103] If the person ordered to attend for cross-examination does not do so, the affidavit cannot be used in evidence without the leave of the court.[104] The rules and practice of the High Court with regard to affidavits apply in all insolvency proceedings in any court[105] save where they are inconsistent with or necessarily excluded by provisions in the Rules.[106]

10.31 When will a deponent be ordered to attend for cross-examination?

Prima facie, parties who have sworn affidavits are liable to be cross-examined on those affidavits where any facts contained therein are disputed and when the proceedings in question are of a final and not an interlocutory nature: a court is reluctant to disbelieve a deponent where that deponent has not been cross-examined.[107] Where there is a conflict of evidence and the resolution of that conflict is necessary for the determination of an issue in dispute, the court will almost order a party to produce its deponents for cross-examination, on pain of such evidence not being read if such deponent is not produced. There is no universal rule, however, that in the absence of some contrary sworn evidence, cross-examination of a deponent will not be ordered: the test is what is necessary for fairly disposing of the case.[108]

98. *Ibid.*, at 312.
99. See Chapter 11, of this book, para. 11.7.3.
100. IR 1986, r. 7.60(1).
101. IR 1986, r. 7.9.
102. IR 1986, r. 7.10(2)(c).
103. IR 1986, r. 7.7(1).
104. IR 1986, r. 7.7(2).
105. IR 1986, r. 7.57.
106. IR 1986, r. 7.57(2).
107. *Re Smith and Fawcett Ltd* [1942] Ch. 304; *Comet Products UK Ltd* v. *Hawkex Plastics Ltd* [1971] 2 QB 67; *Re Lifecare International plc* (1989) 5 BCC 749 at 757.
108. *Re BCCI (No. 6)* [1994] 1 BCLC 450.

10.32 Reports

In certain instances reports can be filed instead of affidavits[109] and the report is treated for the purposes of any hearing as if it were an affidavit.[110] An official receiver or a deputy official receiver is always entitled to file a report instead of an affidavit.[111] Any report filed by an official receiver (but not a deputy official receiver[112]) is *prima facie* evidence of any matter contained in it.[113] This renders admissible matters contained in both the report and the documents annexed to it, even though such matter might otherwise be inadmissible as hearsay evidence if contained in an affidavit; but they are *prima face* evidence only and the court will, in assessing the weight to be given to such statements, consider the source of the official receiver's information as well as any other evidence and all the circumstances.[114] Where an application does not involve any other parties, or where the court otherwise orders, reports may also be filed instead of affidavits by an administrator, a liquidator, a trustee in bankruptcy, a provisional liquidator, an interim receiver, a special manager or an insolvency practitioner appointed under s. 273(2) of the Insolvency Act 1986.[115] However, the report is treated as if it were an affidavit[116] and is *prima facie* evidence of any matters contained therein.

10.33 Oral evidence

The court can direct that any evidence to be given at a hearing shall be given orally either in whole or in part.[117] If it considers it appropriate for the purpose of disposing fairly and expeditiously with the cause or matter and saving costs, the court can direct any party to serve on the other parties, on such terms as it thinks just, written statements of the oral evidence which the party intends to lead on any issues of fact to be decided at the trial, or if a party is unable to obtain a written statement from an intended witness, the court may direct that party to provide the other parties with the name of the witness and a statement of the nature of the evidence intended to be adduced.[118] It is now the usual practice of the Companies Court to order the exchange of witness statements where evidence is not to be given by way of affidavit and for such evidence to stand as evidence in chief.[119]

10.34 Hearsay evidence

The procedure for adducing hearsay statements is now set out in RSC O. 38, rr. 20 to 34 as amended and this procedure must be followed in the Companies Court.[120]

109. IR 1986, r. 7.9.
110. IR 1986, r. 7.9(2).
111. IR 1986, r. 7.9(1)(a).
112. IR 1986, r. 7.9 makes express reference to deputy official receivers filing reports but only refers to the reports of official receivers as being *prima facie* evidence of any matters contained: contrast r. 3(2) of the Insolvent Companies (Disqualification of Unfit Directors) Proceedings Rules 1987 and *Re Homes Assured Corp. plc* [1993] BCC 573.
113. IR 1986, r. 7.9(3).
114. *Re City Investment Centres Ltd* [1992] BCLC 956; *Re Moonbeam Cards* [1993] BCLC 1099.
115. IR 1986, r. 7.9(1)(b).
116. IR 1986, r. 7.9(2).
117. IR 1986, r. 7.10(2)(c)(i).
118. IR 1986, r. 7.51; RSC O. 38, r. 2A.
119. Practice Direction (Civil Litigation: Case Management), [1995] 1 WLR 262, para. 3.
120. IR 1986, r. 7.51.

10.35 Admissions adverse to a party

An admission adverse to a party to the proceedings, whether made by that party or by another person, may be given in evidence against that party for the purpose of proving any facts stated in the admission.[121] Additionally, a statement of affairs prepared for the purposes of any provision of the Insolvency Act 1986 which is derived from the Insolvency Act 1985 and any other statement made in pursuance of a requirement imposed by or under any such provision or by or under the Insolvency Rules 1986 may be used in evidence against any person making or concurring in making such statement.[122] Such statements include:

(a) statements made by officers of a company in a public examination[123];
(b) information provided to an administrator, administrative receiver, liquidator or provisional liquidator pursuant to the duty to co-operate with the relevant office-holder[124];
(c) information provided to the court upon the court's inquiry into the company's dealings[125];
(d) information by a person proposing a company voluntary arrangement provided to the nominee[126];
(e) the statement of affairs submitted to an administrator[127];
(f) the statement of affairs submitted to an administrative receiver[128];
(g) the liquidator's statement of affairs laid before a creditor's meeting[129];
(h) the company's statement of affairs in a compulsory liquidation[130];
(i) a bankrupt's statement of affairs.[131]

10.36 Evidence of proceedings at meetings

A minute of proceedings at a meeting held under the Act or the Rules of creditors or members of a company or of the contributories in a company's liquidation, signed by a person describing himself as, or appearing to be, the chairman of that meeting is admissible without further proof and is *prima facie* evidence that the meeting was duly convened and held, that all resolutions passed at the meeting were duly passed, and that all proceedings of the meeting duly took place.[132]

10.37 Documents issuing from the Secretary of State

Any document purporting to be, or to contain, any order, directions or certificate issued by the Secretary of State must be received in evidence and deemed to be or contain that order

121. S. 9(2)(a), Civil Evidence Act 1968.
122. IA 1986, s. 433.
123. IA 1986, s. 133.
124. IA 1986, s. 235.
125. IA 1986, ss. 236 and 237; IR 1986, r. 9.4(7).
126. IA 1986, s. 2(3).
127. IA 1986, s. 22(1).
128. IA 1986, s. 47(1).
129. IA 1986, s. 95(3).
130. IA 1986, s. 131.
131. IA 1986, ss. 272 and 288.
132. IR 1986, r. 12.5.

or certificate, or those directions, without further proof, unless the contrary is shown, and this applies where the document is signed by the Secretary of State himself or any officer on his behalf.[133] A certificate signed by the Secretary of State or an officer on his behalf which confirms the making of any order, or the issuing of any document, or the exercise of any discretion, power or obligation arising or imposed under the Act or the Rules is conclusive evidence of the matters dealt with in the certificate.[134]

10.38 Judicial notice of court documents

All courts, judges and persons judicially acting, and all officers, judicial or ministerial, of any court or employed in enforcing the process of any court must take judicial notice:

(a) of the signature of any officer of the High Court or of a County Court in England and Wales, or of the Court of Session or a sheriff court in Scotland, or of the High Court in Northern Ireland[135]; and also

(b) of the official seal or stamp of the several officers of the High Court in England and Wales or Northern Ireland, or of the Court of Session, appended to or impressed on any document made, issued or signed under the provisions of the Insolvency Act 1986 or the Companies Act 1985, or any official copy of such a document.[136]

10.39 Company's books to be evidence

Where a company is being wound up, all books and papers of the company and of the liquidators are, as between the contributories of the company, *prima facie* evidence of the truth of all matters purporting to be recorded in them.[137]

10.40 Evidence on commission

Where a company is wound up in England and Wales, the court may refer the whole or any part of the examination of witnesses on any matter to a specified county court in England and Wales[138] or to the sheriff principal for a specified sheriffdom in Scotland[139] or to the High Court in Northern Ireland or a specified Northern Ireland County Court.[140] The person exercising jurisdiction as the judge of the court to which reference is made is a commissioner for the purpose of taking the evidence of those witnesses[141] and has the same power of summoning and examining witnesses, or requiring the production and delivery of documents, or punishing defaults by witnesses, and of allowing costs and expenses to witnesses as the court which made the winding-up order.[142] The examination

133. IR 1986, r. 12.6(1),(2).
134. IR 1986, r. 12.6(3).
135. IA 1986, s. 196(a).
136. IA 1986, s. 196(b).
137. IA 1986, s. 191.
138. IA 1986, s. 197(1)(a).
139. IA 1986, s. 197(1)(b).
140. IA 1986, s. 197(1)(c).
141. IA 1986, s. 197(2).
142. IA 1986, s. 197(3).

taken must then be returned or reported to the court which made the order in such manner as that court requests.[143]

10.41 Examinations in Scotland

The court in England, in winding-up a company, may direct the examination in Scotland of any person for the time being in Scotland, whether a contributory of the company or not, in regard to the trade, dealings, affairs or property of any company in the course of being wound up, or of any person being a contributory of the company, so far as the company may be interested by reason of his being a contributory[144] and provision is made for the taking of the examination and powers and entitlement of fees of the sheriff principal who is to take the examination.[145]

10.42 Evidence by deposition

If it is considered necessary for the purpose of justice, an order may be made for the examination on oath—before a judge, an officer or examiner of the court or some other person—at any place of any person as in normal proceedings in the High Court.[146] Such order may be made on such terms (including, in particular, terms as to the giving of discovery before the examination takes place) as the court thinks fit and may contain an order for the production of any document which appears to the court to be necessary for the purposes of the examination.[147] Where the person to be examined is outside the jurisdiction, an application must be made for the issue of a letter of request to the judicial authorities of the country in which the evidence of that person is to be taken,[148] if the government of the country in question allows a person to be examined there or before a person appointed by the English courts, application may be made for an order appointing a special examiner to take the evidence in that country.[149]

10.43 Expert evidence

If the court directs that evidence at the hearing is to be given by way of affidavit, then a party is entitled to adduce expert evidence without the leave of the court. Where the evidence is not to be given by way of affidavit, no expert evidence may be adduced at the hearing unless the party wishing to adduce expert evidence has applied to the court to determine whether a direction should be given under RSC O. 37, r. 37 or r. 41 and has complied with any direction given on the application.[150]

143. IA 1986, s. 197(4).
144. IA 1986, s. 198(1).
145. IA 1986, s. 198(2)–(6).
146. IR 1986, r. 7.51; RSC O. 39, r. 1(1).
147. IR 1986, r. 7.51; RSC O. 39, r. 1(2).
148. IR 1986, r. 7.51; RSC O. 39, r. 2(1).
149. IR 1986, r. 7.51; RSC O. 39, r. 2(2).
150. IR 1986, r. 7.51; RSC O. 38, r. 36(1)(a).

10.44 Representation orders

If the proceedings concern property subject to a trust or the construction of a written instrument or statute then such an order can be made if the court is satisfied that a person, class or member of a class:

(a) cannot be ascertained;
(b) cannot readily be ascertained;
(c) although ascertainable cannot be found; or
(d) although ascertainable, it appears to the court expedient, having regard to all the circumstances, including the amount at stake and the degree of difficulty of the point to be determined.[151]

Further, even where the proceedings do not concern property subject to a trust or the construction of a written instrument or statute, the court can appoint any one or more respondents to represent others who have the same interest.[152] The issue of representation orders should be brought to the attention of the court, if at all possible, at the first hearing, so that the court can make the representation orders either immediately or direct that notice be given to those who might be concerned or interested.

10.45 Representation orders in practice

Where all the unsecured creditors have the same interest and the company is in liquidation, the practice is for the liquidator to argue the case of the unsecured creditors and not to join in one of the unsecured creditors as a representative of that class. For instance, if a liquidator requires the determination of the court as to whether a charge created over the assets of the company is valid or not and, if valid, whether it is fixed or floating, the liquidator can argue the case of the unsecured creditors. He may, however, not be able to have recourse to assets, other than those available purely for the general unsecured creditors, in respect of the costs of the proceedings and any costs ordered to be paid by him,[153] and adequate arrangements must be made. Where there are a number of preferential creditors it is usual to join, at least initially, only one or more with large claims as respondents and then seek an order on the first hearing that that creditor or those creditors represent the other preferential creditors. It is not uncommon for the Commissioners of Inland Revenue or the Commissioners of Customs and Excise to be appointed to represent all preferential creditors, including employees. Where the unsecured creditors do not have a common interest but have a number of different interests, it is not appropriate for the liquidator to represent the interest of any one particular class of unsecured creditor and, in this instance, it is appropriate to join as respondents the largest unsecured creditors and to seek an order that they represent creditors with similar interests. Although less frequent, an application may be begun by one party as representing all persons having the same interest[154]: this might be the case where one unsecured creditor brings proceedings representing all the unsecured creditors.

151. IR 1986, r. 7.51; RSC O. 15, r. 13.
152. IR 1986, r. 7.51; RSC O. 15, r. 12; for examples of the court exercising such jurisdiction in insolvency proceedings see *Re Westdock Realisations Ltd* (1988) 4 BCC 192 and *Re Exchange Securities & Commodities Ltd (No. 3)* (1987) 3 BCC 48, as explained in *Re Stetzel Thomson & Co. Ltd* (1988) 4 BCC 74.
153. See Chapter 11, para. 11.23.3.
154. IR 1986, r. 7.51; RSC O. 15, r. 12(1).

10.46 Judgments in representation proceedings

A judgment or order given in proceedings where representation orders have been made is binding on all the persons represented, even though not parties, but it cannot be enforced against any person not a party to the proceedings except with the leave of the court.[155]

10.47 Costs in representation proceedings

These are dealt with below.[156]

10.48 Injunctions and receivers

The High Court has power to grant an injunction or appoint a receiver in all cases in which it appears to the court to be just and convenient to do so, either unconditionally, or on such terms and conditions as the court thinks fit.[157] The power includes the power to grant interlocutory injunctions and the appointment of receivers pending the hearing of any application. Such applications for injunctions or receivers are not applications which arise under the Insolvency Act 1986 or the Insolvency Rules 1986 and cannot be made by way of ordinary application in proceedings already commenced.[158] As the proceedings already commenced, or intended to be commenced, will be in the Companies Court, which is part of the Chancery Division, the application for an interlocutory injunction, or the appointment of a receiver, as with all such applications in the Chancery Division, must be made by way of motion. The application must be heard in open court and not in chambers[159] and must be made direct to a judge of the Chancery Division of the High Court.[160] The judge will normally be the judge hearing Companies Court business but the application can be made to any judge of the Chancery Division if the Companies Court Judge is unavailable.

10.49 Cross-undertaking in damages

A cross-undertaking in damages ought to be given on every occasion where such interlocutory relief is granted. However, it is not the case that a liquidator is always required to give an unlimited cross-undertaking. In a case where proceedings were brought by the liquidators of a company against former directors to recover sums derived from the company's assets, liquidators were permitted to give a limited undertaking commensurate with the size of the company's assets and were not required to provide an unlimited guarantee that the respondents would suffer no loss.[161] However, no order was made at that stage that the liquidators would be entitled to indemnify themselves out of the assets of the company should they be called upon in respect of their undertaking.

155. IR 1986, r. 7.51; RSC O. 15, r. 12(4).
156. See paras. 10.55–10.56.
157. S. 37(1) and (2), Supreme Court Act 1981.
158. IR 1986, r. 7.1.
159. But the hearing can be heard in camera.
160. See Practice Direction (Companies Court: Insolvency), [1987] 1 WLR 53; *Supreme Court Practice 1997*, para. 838.
161. *Re DPR Futures Ltd* [1989] 1 WLR 778.

10.50 Rights of attendance

In any company insolvency proceedings[162] any person who has stated in writing, in records kept by the court for that purpose, to be a creditor or contributory of the company is entitled at his own cost to attend in court or in chambers at any stage of any such proceedings[163] either by himself in person or by his solicitor.[164] Any such creditor or contributory can also request the court in writing to give him notice of any step in the proceedings and, subject to his paying the costs involved and keeping the court informed as to his address, the court must comply with such request.[165] However, if the court is satisfied that the exercise by a person of any such rights has given rise to costs being incurred on behalf of the insolvent company which would not otherwise have been incurred and which ought not to fall on the company or its assets, the court may direct that the costs be paid by the person concerned, to an amount specified.[166] So long as the costs are not paid, the person's rights of attendance and notification are in abeyance. The court may at any time appoint one or more persons to represent the creditors or the contributories, or any class of them, to have the rights of attendance and notification set out above instead of the rights being exercisable by any or all of them individually. Two or more persons are so appointed under this paragraph to represent the same interest, and they must if at all instruct the same solicitor.[167]

10.51 Incapacitated persons

Where it appears to the court that a person affected by proceedings is one who is incapable of managing and administering his property and affairs either by reason of mental disorder within the meaning of the Mental Health Act 1983 or due to physical affliction or disability,[168] the court may appoint such person as it thinks fit to appear for, represent or act for the incapacitated person.[169] The appointment may be made either generally or for the purpose of any particular application or proceeding or for the exercise of particular rights or powers which such incapacitated person might have exercised but for his incapacity.[170] The appointment may be made either by the court of its own motion[171] or on application by a person who has been appointed by a court in the United Kingdom or elsewhere to manage the affairs of, and to represent, the incapacitated person,[172] or any relative or friend of the incapacitated person who appears to the court to be a proper person to make the application,[173] or the official receiver,[174] or the person who, in relation to the proceedings, is the responsible insolvency practitioner.[175] The application may be

162. Defined in IR 1986, r. 13.7 as meaning proceedings under the Act or the Rules.
163. IR 1986, r. 7.53(1).
164. IR 1986, r. 7.53(2).
165. IR 1986, r. 7.53(3).
166. IR 1986, r. 7.53(3).
167. IR 1986, r. 7.51(5).
168. IR 1986, r. 7.43(1).
169. IR 1986, r. 7.44(1).
170. IR 1986, r. 7.44(2).
171. IR 1986, r. 7.44(3).
172. IR 1986, r. 7.44(3)(a).
173. IR 1986, r. 7.44(3)(b).
174. IR 1986, r. 7.44(3)(c).
175. IR 1986, r. 7.44(3)(d).

made *ex parte*[176] but the court may require notice to be given to the person alleged to be incapacitated or any other person and may adjourn the hearing of the application to enable the notice to be given.[177] All applications, other than where made by the official receiver, must be supported by an affidavit of a registered medical practitioner as to the mental or physical condition of the incapacitated person.[178] Where the application is made by the official receiver, he may support his application by a report only.[179] Any notice served on, or sent to, a person appointed under this jurisdiction has the same effect as if it had been served on, or given to the incapacitated person.[180]

10.52 Rights of audience

Official receivers and deputy official receivers have rights of audience in insolvency proceedings whether in the High Court or a County Court.[181] A company can only appear by counsel or a solicitor and not a director or any other person, other than in exceptional circumstances.[182] Otherwise those who have rights of audience before a judge and master in the High Court have rights of audience respectively before a judge and registrar in the Companies Court.

10.53 Costs and taxation

Except as provided otherwise and with any necessary modifications, O.62 of the Rules of the Supreme Court applies to insolvency proceedings in the High Court.[183] No party to any proceedings under the Act or the Rules is entitled to recover any of the costs of those proceedings except under an order of the court.[184] If the court, in the exercise of its discretion, sees fit to make any order as to the costs of any proceedings, the court must order the costs to follow the event except when it appears to the court that in the circumstances of the case some other order should be made as to the whole or any part of the costs.[185] The amount of the costs which any party is entitled to recover is the amount allowed after taxation on the standard basis unless it appears to the court to be appropriate to order costs to be taxed on the indemnity basis.[186] Where costs are taxed on the standard basis there is allowed a reasonable amount in respect of all costs reasonably incurred and any doubts as to whether the costs were reasonably incurred or were a reasonable amount are resolved in favour of the paying party.[187] On a taxation on the indemnity basis all costs are allowed except insofar as they are of an unreasonable amount or have been unreasonably incurred and any doubts as to whether the costs were reasonably incurred or were a

176. IR 1986, r. 7.44(4).
177. IR 1986, r. 7.44(4).
178. IR 1986, r. 7.45(1).
179. IR 1986, r. 7.45(2).
180. IR 1986, r. 7.46.
181. IR 1986, r. 7.52(1).
182. *Radford* v. *Samuel* [1993] BCC 870; *Arbuthnot Leasing International Ltd* v. *Havelot Leasing Ltd* [1992] 1 WLR 455.
183. IR 1986, r. 7.33.
184. IR 1986, r. 7.33; RSC O. 62, r. 3(2).
185. IR 1986, r. 7.33; RSC O. 62, r. 3(3).
186. IR 1986, r. 7.33; RSC O. 62, r. 3(4). A liquidator is in no different position: costs are only allowed on the standard basis unless the court otherwise directs or authorises: r. 7.34(5).
187. IR 1986, r. 7.33; RSC O. 62, r. 12(1).

reasonable amount are resolved in favour of the receiving party.[188] As in normal proceedings, the costs are generally limited to the costs of employing solicitors, counsel and expert witnesses: no sums are usually allowable to compensate the litigant for the time he has spent in dealing with the proceedings. A liquidator or other insolvency practitioner should not confuse his entitlement under an order for costs to have his costs taxed with his right to receive remuneration.[189]

10.54 Time of application for costs

All applications for costs should be made during or at the conclusion of the relevant proceedings. If a party wishes to apply for an order for costs after the proceedings have concluded, he must issue an ordinary application, a sealed copy of which must be served on the appropriate insolvency practitioner and, in a winding-up by the court, on the official receiver.[190] No costs of or incidental to this application will be allowed to the applicant unless the court is satisfied that the application could not have been made at the time of the proceedings.[191]

10.55 Payment of the costs of an unsuccessful party out of the assets of the company

The general rule is that costs follow the event. However, there are many cases in which it is essential for the due performance of his duties as a liquidator, administrator or receiver that a decision from the court is made concerning costs. This is equally so where there are large classes of creditors, contributories or other claimants, the exact membership of which class is not easily established or even known, who will be affected by the decision but where the sum at stake for an individual respondent who may be joined does not justify him in incurring the costs involved in litigating the matter. In such cases, in order to ensure that the matter is properly determined, the costs of such representative respondents may be ordered to be paid out of the assets of the company, even though they were unsuccessful.[192]

10.56 Anticipatory costs orders

In rare cases, such a respondent may be able, before the substantive hearing of the proceedings, to obtain an order that his costs be paid out of assets of the company. Without the protection of such an order, some respondents would not take part in proceedings. At one time it was thought that a court did not have jurisdiction to make such an order,[193] but it is now clear that the court does have jurisdiction to make an order as to the ultimate incidence of costs at any stage of the proceedings.[194] Such orders, however, are only made

188. IR 1986, r. 7.33; RSC O. 62, r. 12(2).
189. For the various orders that can be made in respect of applications in a liquidation see Chapter 11, para. 11.22.
190. IR 1986, r. 7.40(1),(2).
191. IR 1986, r. 7.40(4).
192. *Re Westdock Realisations Ltd* (1988) 4 BCC 192.
193. *Wallersteiner* v. *Moir (No. 2)* [1975] QB 373; *Re Chargecard Services Ltd* (1986) 2 BCC 99, 371.
194. *Re Westdock Realisations Ltd* (1988) 4 BCC 192.

in very exceptional circumstances,[195] where, for example, it is necessary for the proper execution of the duties of the liquidator or receiver or administrator to have the matter determined, and a pre-emptive order is a necessary prerequisite to that determination being obtained, because without one there would be no person to put the opposite case. Such an order will not be made where there is a limited class of persons who are interested, all of whom are capable of meeting costs.[196]

10.57 Security for costs

If proceedings are being brought by a limited company, the court has power under s.726 of the Companies Act 1985[197] to order the company to provide security for costs if it appears that there is reason to believe that the company will be unable to pay the respondent's costs should he succeed. The fact that a company is in liquidation or administration or receivership is *prima facie* evidence that it is unable to pay the respondent's costs should he succeed.[198] In deciding whether to order security for costs under s.726 of the Companies Act 1985, the court will take into account similar factors to that which it takes into account in respect of an application made under RSC O.23, r.3.[199] The power is discretionary. It is the usual practice to order an insolvent company to provide full security for costs, but where such an order might result in oppression in that the company would be forced to abandon a claim which had a reasonable prospect of success, the court is entitled to refuse to make such an order notwithstanding that, if unsuccessful, the company would be unable to pay the respondent's costs.[200] The applicant need only show that there is a probability that it would be unable to pursue the action if the order was granted, not that with certainty it would be unable to do so.[201] Where a liquidator has sufficient assets to pay both his own and his opponent's costs it will be usual to order security for costs to be given. Even where there are no assets, but there are one or maybe two large creditors who are in effect funding the action and who will benefit from its success, the fact that there are no assets available to the liquidator will not prevent a court from ordering security to be paid: the court will adopt the attitude that the large creditors for whom the benefit of the action is being brought should not be put in a better position than other litigants by not having to face the risk of being ordered to pay costs if unsuccessful. The situation most frequently encountered where it is not possible for the liquidator to provide security for costs is where there are no or insufficient assets and a very large body of unsecured creditors with small claims from whom it would be impracticable or unlikely that a fighting fund would be available. If the court is satisfied that no funds would be made available and it is a claim which ought to be pursued, the

195. *Re Biddencare Ltd* [1993] BCC 757.

196. *Re Westdock Realisations Ltd* (1988) 4 BCC 192 at 198.

197. See the wide definition given to "proceeding" and "plaintiff" in *Re Unisoft Group Ltd* [1994] BCC 11.

198. *Northampton Coal, Iron & Waggon Co.* v. *Midland Waggon Co.* (1878) 7 Ch.D. 500; *Pure Spirit Company* v. *Fowler* (1890) 25 QBD 235.

199. The principles of which are set out in *Sir Lindsay Parkinson and Co. Ltd* v. *Triplan* [1973] QB 609.

200. *Aquila Design (GRB) Products Ltd* v. *Cornhill Insurance plc* [1988] BCLC 134.

201. *Trident International Freight Services Ltd* v. *Manchester Ship Canal Co.* [1990] BCLC 263.

court may in the exercise of its discretion permit it to continue without ordering security.

10.58 Security for costs: where an insolvency practitioner is applicant

Section 726 of the Companies Act 1985 does not apply where the liquidator or administrator or receiver is personally the applicant, since the applicant will not be "a limited company" within the meaning of the section.[202] Although RSC O.23 applies to applications under the Insolvency Act 1986 and the Insolvency Rules 1986, it appears that a liquidator or administrator or receiver who is entitled to bring an application in his own name is not a nominal plaintiff within RSC O.23, r.1(1)(b)[203] and the Court of Appeal has held that a misfeasance summons brought in the name of the liquidator, (under a predecessor of what is now s.212 of the Insolvency Act 1986) is not an action by the company and that the poverty of the liquidator is not a sufficient ground for ordering him to provide security for costs.[204] However, where an application is made by a liquidator, or administrator or receiver in his own name, he will be liable if costs are ordered to be paid to a respondent.[205] It is unlikely in practice that a liquidator, administrator or receiver will commence such proceedings without making arrangements for an indemnity out of the assets of the company or from the creditors directly.

10.59 Enforcement of court orders

Orders of the court are enforced in the same manner as a judgment to the same effect.[206]

APPEALS

10.60 Appeals from registrars, district judges and county court judges

An appeal from a decision made in the exercise of the jurisdiction under the Act to wind up companies by a County Court, whether it be a decision of a judge or a district judge in the County Court, or by a registrar or district judge of the High Court lies to a single judge of the High Court.[207] The reference to the exercise of the jurisdiction to wind up companies is not limited to the making of a winding-up order but embraces all the jurisdiction conferred on the court under the Act for the purpose of winding-up the affairs of a company after the commencement of the winding-up. No leave is necessary in the case of an initial appeal to a single judge.[208] An appeal from a decision of a district judge of the County Court is to a single judge of the High Court and not the judge of the County

202. In *Re Strand Wood Co. Ltd* [1904] 2 Ch. 1.
203. *Pooley's Trustee* v. *Whetham* (1884) 28 Ch.D. 38, where it was held that the fact of a trustee in bankruptcy suing in his official name was no ground for ordering him to give security for costs.
204. *Re Strand Wood Ltd* [1904] 2 Ch. 1.
205. *Metalloy Supplies Ltd* v. *MA(UK) Ltd* [1997] BCC 165.
206. IR 1986, r. 7.19.
207. IR 1986, r. 7.47(2).
208. *Re Busytoday Ltd* [1992] 1 WLR 683.

Court.[209] All appeals from a registrar or district judge are of right and do not require leave. The practice and procedure of the Supreme Court relating to appeals to the Court of Appeal apply to appeals to a single judge of the High Court[210] and in relation to any such appeal any reference in the Rules of the Supreme Court to the Court of Appeal is replaced by a reference to the judge of the High Court and any reference to the registrar of civil appeals is replaced by a reference to the registrar of the High Court who deals with insolvency proceedings of the kind involved.[211]

10.61 Appeal made by ordinary application

The appeal to a single judge is made by way of ordinary application.[212] It may be in respect of the whole or in respect of any specified part of any judgment or order but must specify the grounds of the appeal and the precise form of the order which the appellant proposes to ask the judge to make.[213] Every such application must be issued and served on all parties to the proceedings who are directly affected by the appeal not later than four weeks after the date on which the judgment or order appealed against was sealed or otherwise perfected.[214] Both a registrar and a judge of the High Court have jurisdiction to extend the time for issue and service of such an application,[215] but the application must in the first instance be made to the registrar of the High Court. In determining whether an extension should be given, the court will take into account the length of the delay, the reasons for the delay, the chances of the appeal succeeding if time for appealing is extended and the degree of prejudice to the potential respondent if the application is granted. Where the delay in serving such an application is short and there is an acceptable excuse for it, an extension of time will not be refused on the basis of the merits of the intended appeal, unless the appeal is hopeless.[216] A registrar or district judge or judge in the court from which the decision appealed was made has jurisdiction to extend the time for issuing or serving an application of appeal provided the application for extension is issued before the expiration of four weeks from the date on which the order appealed against was sealed or otherwise perfected.[217]

10.62 Setting down

Within seven days after the later of either the date on which service of the application was effected or the date on which the judgment or order of the court appealed against was sealed or otherwise perfected, the applicant must set down his appeal by lodging with the registrar of the High Court a copy of the judgment or order and two copies of the application, one of them being endorsed with the amount of the fee paid, and the other being endorsed with a certificate of the date of service of the notice.[218]

209. *Re Langley Marketing Ltd* [1992] BCC 585; *Re Tasbian (No. 2)* [1990] BCC 322.
210. IR 1986, r. 7.49(1).
211. IR 1986, r. 7.49(2).
212. IR 1986, r. 7.1.
213. IR 1986, r. 7.49(1); RSC O. 59, r. 3(2).
214. IR 1986, r. 7.49(1); RSC O. 59, r. 4(1).
215. IR 1986, r. 7.49(1); RSC O. 3, r. 5(4).
216. IR 1986, r. 7.49(1); *Palata Investments Ltd* v. *Birt & Sinfield Ltd* [1985] 1 WLR 942.
217. IR 1986, r. 7.49(1); RSC O. 59, r. 15.
218. IR 1986, r. 7.49(1); RSC O. 59, r. 5.

10.63 Respondent's notice

A respondent who, having been served with an application of appeal, desires either:

(a) to contend on the appeal that the decision appealed against should be varied, either in any event or in the event of the appeal being allowed in whole or in part; or
(b) to contend that the decision should be affirmed on grounds other than those relied upon by the person giving the judgment or making the order; or
(c) to contend by way of cross-appeal that the decision of the court below was wrong in whole or in part;

must give notice to that effect, specifying the grounds of his contention and, in a case to which paragraph (a) or (c) relates, the precise form of the order which he proposes to ask the court to make.[219] An application or a respondent's notice may be amended by or with the leave of a judge or registrar of the High Court at any time.[220] The practice of providing skeleton arguments for appeals to the Court of Appeal applies equally to appeals to a judge.

On an appeal, the judge of the High Court can:

(a) affirm, vary or discharge the order of the judge, district judge or registrar against which an appeal has been made and can make any order which could have been made by the district judge, judge or registrar[221];
(b) order that a new hearing takes place[222];
(c) draw any inferences of fact and give any judgment or make any order which ought to have been made and make such further or other order as the case may require[223];
(d) make any order, on such terms as he thinks just, to ensure the determination on the merits of the real question of controversy between the parties, notwithstanding that no notice of such grounds has been given by either party in respect of any particular point of the decision below nor that any ground for allowing the appeal or affirming that decision has been specified by either party to the appeal.[224]

10.64 Appeal by way of rehearing

The appeal to the judge of the High Court is by way of rehearing.[225] The relevant principles are those applicable to appeals to the Court of Appeal generally and require only brief mention here. Witnesses are not heard afresh but the court will consider the documentary evidence and transcripts of any oral evidence given. The burden of showing that the trial judge was wrong in his decision as to the facts lies on the appellant and, if the judge is not satisfied that the decision of the district judge, judge or registrar was wrong, the appeal will be dismissed. Where there was conflicting testimony, weight will

219. IR 1986, r. 7.49(1); RSC O. 59, r. 6.
220. IR 1986, r. 7.49(1); RSC O. 59, r. 7(1)(a).
221. IR 1986, r. 7.49(1); RSC O. 59, r. 10(1).
222. IR 1986, r. 7.49(1); RSC O. 59, rr. 2 and 11.
223. IR 1986, r. 7.49(1); RSC O. 59, r. 10(3).
224. IR 1986, r. 7.49(1); RSC O. 59, r. 10(4).
225. IR 1986, r. 7.49(1); RSC O. 59, r. 3(1); *Re Hitco 2000* [1995] BCC 161.

be given to the decision of the judge who saw and heard the witnesses. Where the decision appealed against was one in respect of which the district judge, judge or registrar was given a discretion as to the order to be made, the decision will not be overturned unless it be shown that the discretion was exercised under a mistake of law or in disregard of principle or under a misapprehension as to the facts, or that irrelevant matters were taken into account, or the discretion was not exercised, or the conclusion which was reached was outside the ambit within which a reasonable disagreement was possible.

10.65 Further evidence on appeal

The judge of the High Court has power to receive further evidence on questions of fact, either by oral examination in court, by affidavit, or by deposition taken before an examiner, but, in the case of an appeal from a judgment or order after trial or hearing of any cause or matter on the merits, no such further evidence other than evidence as to matters which have occurred after the date of the trial or hearing shall be admitted except on special grounds.[226] For this purpose, it must be shown that the evidence could not have been obtained with reasonable diligence for use at the trial or the hearing, that the evidence is such that, if given, would probably have had an importance influence on the result of the case although it need not be decisive, and that the evidence must be such as is presumably to be believed, or, in other words, it must be apparently credible though it need not be incontrovertible.[227]

10.66 Appeals from judges of the High Court exercising an appellate jurisdiction

An appeal from a decision of a judge of the High Court on the hearing of an appeal lies, with the leave of that judge or of the Court of Appeal, to the Court of Appeal.[228] The procedure under RSC O.59 applies but is by application and not summons.[229]

10.67 Court records

The court must keep records of all insolvency proceedings and must enter in those records the taking of any steps in the proceedings and such decisions of the court in relation thereto as the court thinks fit.[230] In order to inspect such records a person must satisfy the registrar as to the propriety of the purpose for which inspection is required.[231] The registrar must be satisfied that inspection is required for a legitimate purpose, having regard to the purpose for which records are made available for inspection, namely, to enable persons who have a legitimate interest in a particular insolvency proceeding to discover what had taken place: creditors have a legitimate purpose to inspect the record of insolvency proceedings and, in cases of wide public interest, the press will also have a legitimate interest in the proceedings but insolvency consultants seeking potential clients

226. IR 1986, r. 7.49(1); RSC O. 59, r. 10(2).
227. IR 1986, r. 7.49(1); *Ladd* v. *Marshall* [1954] 1 WLR 1489.
228. IR 1986, r. 7.49(2); *Midrome Ltd* v. *Shaw* [1993] BCC 659.
229. IR 1986, r. 7.49(3).
230. IR 1986, r. 7.27.
231. IR 1986, r. 7.28(1),(2).

or business do not have the requisite legitimate interest.[232] If inspection is refused by the registrar, the person may then apply forthwith *ex parte* to a judge who may refuse the inspection or allow it on such terms as he thinks fit.[233] The judge's decision is final.[234]

10.68 Confidentiality of documents

If in insolvency proceedings the responsible insolvency practitioner considers that a document (other than a proof of debt or a proxy[235]) should be treated as confidential or that it is of such a nature that its disclosure would be calculated to be injurious to the interests of the company's creditors or its members or the contributories in this winding-up, he may decline to allow it to be inspected even by the members of a liquidation committee or a creditors committee,[236] subject to the right of the person refused inspection applying to the court for the refusal to be overruled.[237]

232. Re *Austintel Ltd* [1997] BCC 362.
233. IR 1986, r. 7.28(2).
234. IR 1986, r. 7.28(3).
235. IR 1986, r. 12.13(4).
236. IR 1986, r. 12.13(1),(2).
237. IR 1986, r. 12.13(3).

CHAPTER 11

APPLICATIONS IN LIQUIDATIONS

11.1 The voluntary liquidation of a company

Where a company is being wound up voluntarily, it is the duty of the liquidator as agent for the company to collect in and realise its property and assets and, save where those assets are charged to third parties, and subject to the payment of the preferential creditors and the expenses of the liquidation, to apply the proceeds in satisfaction of the company's liabilities *pari passu* and to distribute any surplus among the members according to their rights and interests in the company.[1] In carrying out these functions on behalf of the company, a liquidator of a company in voluntary liquidation is not an officer of the court.

11.2 The compulsory liquidation of a company

Where a company is being wound up by the court, the collection and realisation of its assets and their application in discharge of the company's liabilities[2] is carried out by the court, but the court's duty is discharged by the liquidator as an officer of the court and subject to its control.[3]

11.3 Dissolution

Upon completion of the winding-up, both in compulsory and voluntary liquidations, the company is dissolved and ceases to exist.

11.4 The aim of this Chapter

The purpose of this Chapter is to describe the practice and procedure of the Companies Court in respect of applications made following the liquidation of a company. The purpose is not to set out the substantive law that governs the success or failure of the applications

1. IA 1986, s. 107.
2. IA 1986, s. 148(1).
3. IR 1986, r. 4.179(1).

but the practice and procedure that the court applies in dealing with and disposing of those applications.

11.5 Originating and ordinary application procedure

As seen in Chapter 10, all applications made in a liquidation under the Insolvency Act or the Insolvency Rules must be made by originating or ordinary application and must follow the procedure and practice set out in chapter 1 of part 7 of the Insolvency Rules.[4] All references to applications in this Chapter are references to either originating or ordinary applications. This present Chapter of the book assumes familiarity with Chapter 10 and deals in detail only with the extent to which those applications require modification.

11.6 Scope of Chapter 11

This Chapter considers applications to the court in respect of:

(a) directions[5];
(b) proofs of debt[6];
(c) stays and transfers of proceedings[7];
(d) control and collection of assets[8];
(e) collection of debts[9];
(f) claims (other than debts) against other parties[10];
(g) fraudulent and wrongful trading[11];
(h) adjustment of prior transactions[12];
(i) disclaimers of onerous property[13];
(j) rescission of contracts[14];
(k) contributories[15];
(l) removal of liquidators[16];
(m) the expenses of the liquidation[17];
(n) the cost of applications in liquidations[18];
(o) the remuneration of the liquidator[19];
(p) dissolution of the company.[20]

4. Chapter 10, para. 10.1.
5. See para. 11.7.
6. See para. 11.8.
7. See para. 11.9.
8. See para. 11.10.
9. See para. 11.11.
10. See para. 11.12.
11. See paras 11.13–14.
12. See para.. 11.15.
13. See paras 11.16–17.
14. See para. 11.17.
15. See para. 11.19.
16. See para. 11.20.
17. See para. 11.21.
18. See para. 11.22.
19. See para. 11.23.
20. See para. 11.24.

11.7 Applications for directions

11.7.1 Voluntary liquidations

The liquidator of any contributory or creditor[21] can apply to the court to determine any question arising in the winding-up of a company, or to exercise, as respects the enforcing of calls or any other matter, all or any of the powers which the court might exercise if the company were being wound up by the court.[22] If the court is satisfied that the determination of the question or the required exercise of the power will be just and beneficial, it may accede wholly or partly to the application on such terms and conditions as it thinks fit or may make such other order on the application as it thinks just.[23]

11.7.2 Compulsory liquidations: applications by the liquidator

The liquidator may apply to the court for directions in relation to any particular matter arising in the winding-up.[24] Although no express power is given to the court, as in voluntary liquidations, "to determine any question arising in the liquidation" nor to accede to such application "on such terms as it thinks fit" nor to make "such other order... as it thinks just', the court nevertheless possesses such power: since the liquidator is an officer of the court subject to the court's control[25] with the same powers as a receiver appointed by the court,[26] and since it is the court itself[27] which is winding-up the company through its own officer, there is an inherent jurisdiction in the court to determine any question arising in a compulsory liquidation relating to the realisation of the company's assets and their distribution.

11.7.3 Compulsory liquidations: applications other than by the liquidator

The Insolvency Act 1986 does not expressly give creditors or contributories any right to apply to the court to determine any question arising in the winding-up of a company by the court[28] but provision is made for any person[29] "aggrieved" by an act or decision of the liquidator to apply to the court and on such an application the court may confirm, reverse or modify the act or decision complained of and make such order in the case as it thinks just.[30] As one might expect where it is the court which is winding-up the company,

21. It is considered that "creditor" includes a post-liquidation creditor, but the issue was left undecided in *Re Movitex Ltd* [1992] 1 WLR 303; it does, however, include a secured creditor: *Re Alfred Priestman* [1936] 2 All ER 1340.

22. IA 1986, s. 112(1).

23. IA 1986, s. 112(2). The provisions are not wide enough to enable a creditor to apply for the private examination of a director: *Re James McHale Automobiles Ltd* [1997] BCC 202.

24. IA 1986, s. 168(3).

25. IR 1986, r. 4.179(1).

26. IR 1986, r. 4.179(2).

27. IA 1986, s. 148(1).

28. As it does in respect of companies being voluntarily wound up: s. 112.

29. Which includes a creditor: *Re Edennote* [1996] BCC 718.

30. IA 1986, s. 168(5). However, where the decision complained of is one which was taken by the liquidator in exercising his discretionary powers to manage and distribute the assets in the liquidation pursuant to s. 168(4), the court will only interfere with such a decision if the applicant can establish *mala fides* or perversity (*Re Hans Place* [1992] BCC 737 or that the liquidator did something so utterly unreasonable and absurd that no reasonable man would have done it (*Re Edennote* [1996] BCC 718 where the Court of Appeal held that selling an asset of the company, without taking into account the possibility that a third party might well have made a better offer for it than he to whom it was sold, satisfied the test).

through one of its officers, rather than the company winding itself up, as in the case of a voluntary liquidation, a decision on any matter arising in the winding-up must first be sought from the liquidator and only then can an application be made to the court in respect of that matter if the applicant is dissatisfied with the liquidator's response.

11.7.4 Directions

The advantage to the liquidator of seeking a direction from the court is that he cannot thereafter be sued for negligence in respect of that matter,[31] provided a full and frank disclosure has been made to the court. In respect of most issues the liquidator can seek the approval of the liquidation committee or the creditors, but where there is vociferous opposition from a minority of creditors or others interested, the direction of the court gives added protection, as well as a forum for the opposite views to be put forward.

11.7.5 Width of the jurisdiction

The Companies Court has adopted an increasingly wide jurisdiction as to the disputes and issues that can be resolved before it. In *Re Shilena Hosiery Co. Ltd*[32] the liquidator issued in the Companies Court a summons seeking a declaration that a contract previously entered into by the company was void under what was then s. 172 of the Law of Property Act 1925.[33] Proceedings in respect of such relief were normally commenced by writ. Brightman J. held that the Companies Court was not a separate court with its own peculiar jurisdiction: the Companies Court was merely a way of describing the High Court when dealing with matters originating in the Chambers of the Bankruptcy Registrar dealing with company matters, and the Companies judge was merely a way of describing a High Court judge when trying such matters.[34] It was argued in that case that the court had no jurisdiction on hearing an application in a liquidation to decide the merits of an issue between the company and a stranger unless the claim fell within the four corners of the relevant Companies Act legislation. This argument was rejected. Brightman J. held that the court could entertain an application by a liquidator claiming relief against strangers if that claim needed to be decided in order to complete the collection and distribution of the assets of the company, although whether the court *should* entertain such an application was a matter of discretion.[35] In *Re Brompton Securities Ltd (No. 2),*[36] Vinelott J. considered that a liquidator could apply in the liquidation for relief against the forfeiture of a lease as it was a matter arising in the liquidation, but again considered that, in each case, the Companies Court should consider whether there were disadvantages for it being heard in the liquidation and whether proceedings could more conveniently be commenced

31. *Highland Engineering and Another* v. *Anderson and Others* (1970) SLT 122.
32. [1980] Ch. 219.
33. The predecessor to ss. 423 to 425 of the Insolvency Act 1986 (transactions defrauding creditors).
34. Citing in support Megarry V.C.'s analysis in *Re Rolls Razor Ltd (No. 2)* [1970] Ch. 576 at 588 *et seq.*
35. Brightman J. considered that *Re Centrifugal Butter Co. Ltd* [1913] 1 Ch. 188 (voluntary liquidator not entitled to apply in the liquidation for the setting aside of a sale agreement and cancellation of an allotment of shares) and *Re Vimbos Ltd* [1900] 1 Ch. 470 (where it was held application by liquidator in the liquidation to fix the remuneration of receiver should have been brought by way of an ordinary action) should be viewed as cases of discretion and not jurisdiction.
36. (1988) 4 BCC 436.

elsewhere.[37] In *Re Clasper Group Services Ltd*,[38] Warner J. permitted a liquidator to amend an application in a liquidation to claim that recipients of payments held the same on constructive trust for the company.[39]

11.7.6 The present practice

The cases referred to above were concerned with summonses under the Companies (Winding-Up) Rules 1949 or its predecessor. However, the reasoning is equally applicable to originating and ordinary applications under the Insolvency Rules. As will be seen later in this Chapter, there are many instances under the Insolvency Act and the Insolvency Rules where applications for relief under the Act or the Rules may need to be coupled with applications for relief available only to the company at common law or in equity. In practice, increasingly the court permits such applications to be brought by way of originating or ordinary application. However, the perceived view that the Companies Court cannot entertain third party proceedings[40] is often cited as a reason why proceedings should proceed by writ rather than in the liquidation and why, as a matter of discretion, the Companies Court should decline to hear the matter. Each case, however, turns on its own facts.

11.7.7 Procedure

The procedure on all applications is that contained in chapter 1 of part 7 of the Insolvency Rules.[41] The particular costs orders that can be made are discussed below.[42]

11.8 Applications concerning proofs of debt

11.8.1 Admitting proofs of debt

In order to ascertain the liabilities of the company, the liquidator will need to ascertain who claims to be a creditor and the amount claimed to be owed by each such creditor. Chapter 9 of the Insolvency Rules sets out how creditors must prove in the liquidation for amounts outstanding to them. If, on receipt of a proof of debt, the liquidator is in doubt as to whether a proof should be admitted or rejected, or as to whether it is preferential or otherwise, an application can be made to the court for directions.[43] Alternatively, the liquidator can reject the proof and leave the onus on the purported creditor to make an application to the court. If the liquidator does reject a proof in whole or in part, he must prepare a written statement of his reasons for so doing and send it forthwith to the creditor concerned.[44] If a creditor is dissatisfied with the liquidator's decision with respect to his proof, including any decision on the question of preference, he must apply, within 21 days

37. As was the case in *Re Blue Jeans Sales Ltd* [1979] 1 WLR 362.
38. (1988) 4 BCC 673.
39. See, also, in respect of IA 1986, s. 35, *Re Therm-a-Star Limited* [1997] BCC 301.
40. See Chapter 10, para. 10.17.
41. See Chapter 10.
42. See para. 11.22.
43. IA 1986, s. 112 (voluntary winding-up); IA 1986, s. 168(3) (compulsory winding-up); see para. 11.17, *supra*.
44. IR 1986, r. 4.82(2).

of his receiving the statement of reasons for rejection, to the court for the decision to be reversed or varied.[45] The application will be by way of originating or ordinary application and will follow the procedure set out in Chapter 10 of this book. Additionally, a contributory or any other creditor may, if dissatisfied with a liquidator's decision admitting or rejecting the whole or any part of a proof, make an application for the decision to be reversed or varied.[46] This application must be made within 21 days of the contributory or creditor becoming aware of the liquidator's decision.[47] Notice of all such applications regarding proofs of debt must be given to the liquidator, and to the creditor who lodged the proof if the applicant is not that creditor.[48] On receipt of the notice, the liquidator must file with the court the proof against which the appeal is brought, together with a copy of his statement of reasons for rejection, if appropriate.[49] The procedure is that contained in chapter 1 of part 7 of the Insolvency Rules.[50] On the hearing of the application the court may make such order as it considers fit. After the application has been heard and determined the proof is returned by the court to the liquidator unless it has been wholly disallowed.[51]

11.8.2 Admitting proofs of debt for voting purposes

A creditors' voting power at any meeting is determined by the amount owed to that creditor. If the amount of the claim has not been determined as set out in the previous paragraph, as would be the case at the first meeting of creditors, and the chairman of the meeting is in doubt whether a proof should be admitted or rejected, he must mark it as objected to and allow the creditor to vote, subject to his vote being subsequently declared invalid if the objection to the proof is sustained.[52] Any creditor or contributory can appeal to the court in respect of the chairman's decision.[53] An appeal is commenced by way of originating application. The court considers any admissible evidence the parties put before it and the determination is not limited to matters that were put to the chairman.[54]

11.8.3 Costs

The official receiver is not personally liable for costs incurred on any such applications. The liquidator, if other than the official receiver, is only so liable if the court makes an order to that effect.[55]

11.8.4 Applications in respect of proofs after they have been admitted

Where a proof has already been admitted the court may expunge such a proof or reduce the amount claimed on an application by the liquidator where he thinks that the proof has

45. IR 1986, r. 4.83(1).
46. IR 1986, r. 4.83(2).
47. IR 1986, r. 4.83(2).
48. IR 1986, r. 4.83(3).
49. IR 1986, r. 4.83(4).
50. See Chapter 10.
51. IR 1986, r. 4.83(5).
52. IR 1986, r. 4.70(3).
53. IR 1986, r. 4.70(2).
54. *Re a Company (No. 004539 of 1993)* [1993] BCC 116.
55. IR 1986, r. 4.84(6).

been improperly admitted or ought to be reduced,[56] or on the application of a creditor, if the liquidator declines to interfere in the matter.[57] The application is made in accordance with the procedure set out in chapter 1 of part 7 of the Insolvency Rules.[58] Notice of the application must be sent by the applicant, in the case of an application by the liquidator, to the creditor who made the proof[59] and, in the case of an application by a creditor, to the liquidator and to the creditor who made the proof.[60]

11.8.5 Proofs of debt by secured creditors

A secured creditor is a creditor of the company who holds, in respect of his debt, any mortgage, charge, lien or other security over the property of the company.[61] A secured creditor is entitled to lodge a proof of debt, but must state thereon the value of his security. He will then receive a dividend in respect of that amount of the proof which is admitted, less the value of his security. If the secured creditor omits to disclose his security in his proof of debt, he will surrender his security for the general benefit of the other creditors unless the court, on an application by him, determines that the omission was inadvertent or the result of an honest mistake.[62] The application will be by way of either originating or ordinary application and must follow the procedure in chapter 1 of part 7 of the Insolvency Rules.[63] If the court grants relief on such an application, it may require or allow the creditor's proof of debt to be amended on such terms as may be just.[64] A secured creditor may, either with the agreement of the liquidator, or the leave of the court, at any time alter the value which he has put upon his security in his proof of debt.[65] However, if the secured creditor, being a petitioner, has put a value on his security in the petition, or has voted in respect of the unsecured balance of his debt then, in respect of a company being wound up by the court, he may revalue his security only with the leave of the court.[66] If the company is being wound up voluntarily, he may in all cases revalue his security with the agreement of the liquidator. If the liquidator is dissatisfied with the value which a secured creditor puts on his security, whether in his proof or by way of revaluation, the liquidator may require any property comprised in the security to be offered for sale.[67] If the terms of the sale cannot be agreed between the secured creditor and the liquidator, an application may be made to the court for directions as to the terms of the sale by either the secured creditor or the liquidator.[68] If the sale is by auction, the liquidator (on behalf of the company), and the secured creditor (on his own behalf), may appear and bid.[69] If a creditor who has valued his security subsequently realises it, the net amount realised must be substituted for the value previously put by the secured creditor

56. IR 1986, r. 4.85(1)(a).
57. IR 1986, r. 4.85(1)(b).
58. See Chapter 10.
59. IR 1986, r. 4.85(2)(a).
60. IR 1986, r. 4.84(2)(b).
61. IA 1986, s. 248.
62. IR 1986, r. 4.96(1).
63. See Chapter 10.
64. IR 1986, r. 4.96(2).
65. IR 1986, r. 4.95(1).
66. IR 1986, r. 4.95(2).
67. IR 1986, r. 4.98(1).
68. IR 1986, r. 4.98(2).
69. IR 1986, r. 4.98(2).

on the security, and that amount will then be treated as an amended valuation made by him.[70] The liquidator is entitled at any time to give notice to the secured creditor that he proposes, at the expiration of 28 days from the date of the notice, to redeem the security at the value put upon it by the creditor.[71] The secured creditor then has 21 days, or as long as the liquidator may allow, in which, with the agreement of the liquidator or of the court, he may revalue his security.[72] If the creditor revalues his security, the liquidator can only redeem at the new value.[73] A secured creditor is entitled at any time by notice in writing to call on the liquidator to elect whether he will or will not exercise his power to redeem the security at the value then placed upon it and the liquidator then has six months in which to exercise the power or determine not to exercise it.[74]

11.9 Stays and transfers of proceedings

11.9.1 Compulsory liquidation

Prior to the making of the winding-up order, the court has power on the application of the company or a creditor or a contributory, to restrain any action or proceeding against the company at any time between the presentation of the petition and the making of the order.[75] Where the action or proceeding is pending in the High Court or the Court of Appeal in England and Wales or Northern Ireland, the application for a stay must be made to the court in which the action or proceeding is pending.[76] This will normally be by way of summons, but may be made on motion if sufficient urgency can be demonstrated. Where any other action or proceeding is pending against the company, an application must be made to the court having jurisdiction to wind up the company to restrain those further proceedings.[77] This will be by way of originating application.

11.9.2 After the making of a winding-up order

Upon the making of a winding-up order by the court, no action or proceeding can be proceeded with or commenced against the company or its property except with the leave of the court and subject to such terms as the court may impose.[78]

11.9.3 Voluntary liquidation

A voluntary winding-up does not result in an automatic stay of proceedings against the company, but the liquidator or any contributory or creditor may apply to the court to exercise its discretion under s. 112 of the Insolvency Act, and the court may restrain or stay proceedings against the company as if the company was being wound up by the court.

70. IR 1986, r. 4.99.
71. IR 1986, r. 4.97(1).
72. IR 1986, r. 4.97(2); but see r. 4.95(2), *supra*.
73. IR 1986, r. 4.97(2).
74. IR 1986, r. 4.97(4).
75. IA 1986, s. 126(1).
76. IA 1986, s. 126(1)(a).
77. IA 1986, s. 126(1)(b).
78. IA 1986, s. 130(2).

11.9.4 Proceedings

Proceedings have been held to include a counterclaim in excess of the company's claim,[79] an inter-pleader summons,[80] criminal proceedings,[81] executions,[82] or distraint by a landlord or the Crown.[83]

11.9.5 The principles upon which the court acts

Where a company is being compulsorily wound up, it is for the party wishing actions or proceedings to be commenced or continued, to apply to the court, whereas where the company is being wound up voluntarily, it is for the liquidator or any creditor or contributory to apply for proceedings which have been commenced to be stayed. The principles upon which the court acts are the same in each case.

The object of winding-up a company is to put all unsecured creditors on an equal footing and to distribute the surplus assets to them *pari passu*.[84] The winding-up procedure is designed to stop creditors racing to be the first to obtain judgment and execution and it is this principle which guides the exercise by the court of its discretion.[85] If the claim is for a monetary sum which is undisputed, the court will not permit proceedings to be commenced or continued against the company in liquidation, as such proceedings serve no purpose: the creditor can prove in the liquidation and obtain an appropriate dividend. On the other hand, where the debt is substantially disputed and there is likely to be a dividend for unsecured creditors, the issue in dispute will need to be resolved. If an action has been commenced prior to the commencement of the liquidation, the court will usually permit it to be continued, since this will be more convenient than a new application in the liquidation when the liquidator disputes the proof of debt.[86] However, a condition will usually be attached that any judgment obtained be not enforced without the leave of the court. If no action has been started prior to the commencement of the winding-up, the most convenient course is for the creditor to lodge a proof of debt and for the procedure set out above for disputed proofs to be followed.[87] Proceedings by secured creditors for the purpose of realising or enforcing their rights of security over the company's property are permitted as a matter of course,[88] as are actions by landlords for forfeiture. A claim for specific performance of an agreement to sell property entered into prior to the commencement of the liquidation will also be allowed to proceed.[89] The plaintiff in this case will already be the beneficial owner of the property and is merely seeking a transfer of the legal title. If the company is a necessary party to any other proceedings then the court will not

79. *Langley Construction* v. *Wells* [1969] 1 WLR 503.
80. *Eastern Holdings* v. *Singer & Friedlander* [1967] 1 WLR 1017.
81. *R* v. *Dickson* [1991] BCC 719.
82. *Re Artistic Colour Printing Co.*, (1880) 14 Ch.D. 502 at 505.
83. *Herbert Berry Associates Ltd* v. *IRC* [1977] 1 WLR 1437; *Re Memco Engineering* [1986] Ch. 86.
84. *Re Oak Pitts Colliery Co.* (1882) 21 Ch.D. 322 at 329 per Lindley L.J.
85. *Re International Pulp Co.* (1876) 3 Ch.D. 594; *Re Dynamics Corp. of America* [1973] 1 WLR 63.
86. *Currie* v. *Consolidated Kent Collieries Corp.* [1906] 1 KB 134; *Cook* v. *"X" Chain Patents Co.* [1960] 1 WLR 68.
87. See para. 11.8.
88. *Lloyd* v. *Lloyd* [1877] 6 Ch.D. 339; *Re Pound* (1889) 42 Ch.D. 402.
89. *Thames Plate Glass Co.* v. *Land and Sea Construction Telegraph Co.* [1870] LR 11 Eq. 248.

usually prevent the company from being joined as a necessary party to those proceedings.

11.9.6 Service of order

Where in insolvency proceedings the court makes an order staying any action, execution or other legal process against the company, the order can be served by sending a sealed copy to whatever is the address for service of the plaintiff or other party having the carriage of the proceedings to be stayed.[90]

11.9.7 Execution or attachment not completed before commencement of winding-up

Where a creditor has issued execution against the goods or land of a company or has attached any debt to it and the company is subsequently wound up, that creditor is not entitled without the leave of the court[91] to retain the benefit[92] of the execution or attachment against the liquidator unless he completed the execution or attachment before the commencement of the winding-up.[93] A voluntary winding-up is deemed to commence at the time the resolution under s. 84 of the Insolvency Act is passed by the members in general meeting.[94] Where a company is wound up by the court, the commencement of the winding-up is deemed to have taken place at the time of the presentation of the petition for winding-up[95] unless, before the presentation of the petition, a resolution had been passed by the members for a voluntary winding-up, in which case upon the court ordering the company to be wound up it is deemed to have commenced at the time of the passing of the resolution.[96] If a creditor has had notice of a meeting at which a resolution for a voluntary winding-up is to be proposed, the date on which he had such notice is the date for determining whether that creditor is entitled to retain the benefit of the execution or attachment and not the date of commencement of the winding-up.[97]

11.9.8 Completion of execution or attachment

An execution against goods is completed by seizure and sale or by the making of a charging order under s. 1 of the Charging Orders Act 1979.[98] An attachment of a debt is completed by receipt of the debt.[99] An execution against land is completed by seizure, by the appointment of a receiver, or by the making of a charging order under s. 1 of the Charging Orders Act 1979.[100] However, a person who purchases in good faith, under a sale by the sheriff, any goods of a company on which execution has been levied, acquires

90. IR 1986, r. 7.56.
91. IA 1986, s. 183(1).
92. IA 1986, s. 86.
93. IA 1986, s. 183(1).
94. IA 1986, s. 86.
95. IA 1986, s. 129(2).
96. IA 1986, s. 129(1).
97. IA 1986, s. 183(2)(a).
98. IA 1986, s. 183(3)(a).
99. IA 1986, s. 183(3)(b).
100. IA 1986, s. 183(3)(c).

a good title to them as against the liquidator.[101] Distress by a landlord is not affected by s. 183 of the Insolvency Act.[102]

11.9.9 Duties of the sheriff

Where goods are taken by the sheriff in execution and before their sale or the completion of the execution by the receipt or recovery of the full amount of the levy, notice is served on the sheriff that a provisional liquidator has been appointed, that a winding-up order has been made, or that a resolution for voluntary winding-up has been passed.[103] The sheriff must then deliver the goods and any money seized or received in part satisfaction of the execution to the liquidator, but the costs of the execution are a first charge on goods or money so delivered and the liquidator may sell the goods for the purpose of satisfying that charge.[104] Money paid to avoid a sale is not money received in part satisfaction of the execution. If, under an execution in respect of a judgment for a sum exceeding £500, a company's goods are sold or money is paid in order to avoid a sale, the sheriff must deduct the costs of the execution from the proceeds of sale or the money paid, and retain the balance for 14 days.[105] If, within the 14 days, notice is served on the sheriff of a petition for the winding-up of the company having been presented, or of a meeting having been called at which there is to be proposed a resolution for the voluntary winding-up and an order is made or a resolution is passed, the sheriff must pay the balance to the liquidator, who is entitled to retain it as against the execution creditor.[106] Any creditor, however, may apply to the court to retain any benefits conferred on the liquidator, and on such an application the court can make such an order as it thinks fit.[107]

11.9.10 Execution creditors: principles on which the court permits them to retain the benefit

The principles of winding-up require that all unsecured creditors are paid *pari passu*. Strong reasons are needed for the court to permit one creditor to complete execution or attachment and to obtain an advantage over other unsecured creditors.[108] However, the courts have permitted execution or attachment to be completed where the postponement of execution was caused by a trick on the part of the company,[109] where the execution creditor postponed completing execution as a result of undue pressure and persuasion by the company,[110] and where the action which led to the execution had been delayed as a result of the company obtaining leave to defend the action based on an affidavit, denying the existence of the debt sworn only some three months after the company had admitted the debt.[111]

101. IA 1986, s. 183(2)(b).
102. *Re Bellaglade* [1977] 1 All ER 319.
103. IA 1986, s. 184(1).
104. IA 1986, s. 184(2).
105. IA 1986, s. 184(3).
106. IA 1986, s. 184(4).
107. IA 1986, s. 184(5).
108. *Re Caribbean Products (Yam Importers) Ltd* [1966] Ch. 331.
109. *Armorduct Manufacturing Co. Ltd* v. *General Incandescent Co. Ltd* [1911] 2 KB 143.
110. *Re Grosvenor Metal Co. Ltd* [1950] 1 Ch. 63.
111. *Re Suidair International Airways Ltd* [1951] Ch. 165; but see *Re Redman (Builders) Ltd* [1964] 1 WLR 541 where it was distinguished.

11.9.11 Where execution or attachment has been put in force after the commencement of the winding-up

Section 128(1) of the Insolvency Act provides that, where a company is being wound up by the court, any attachment, sequestration, distress or execution put in force against the estate or effects of the company after the commencement of the winding-up is void. Although this section confers no express discretion on the court, it is well established that the court may give leave to issue execution or to levy distress on the application of the creditor.[112] The court will exercise its discretion according to the same principles conferred by s. 183 and 184.[113]

11.9.12 Transfer of proceedings

Where various proceedings have been commenced in different courts against the company, it is often convenient for such proceedings to be transferred to the Companies Court so that directions can be given by the court that has control of the winding-up. Where an order for the winding-up of a company has been made by the High Court, or a provisional liquidator has been appointed or winding-up proceedings have been transferred to that court from a county court, a judge of any Division of the High Court has power of his own motion to order the transfer to that Division of any proceedings brought against the company for the purpose of enforcing any claims against the company which are pending, either in another Division of the High Court or in a court in England and Wales other than the High Court.[114] Where proceedings are transferred, the registrar has power to dispose of any matter arising in the proceedings which would, but for the transfer, have been disposed of in chambers or, in the case of proceedings transferred from a county court, by the district judge of that court.[115]

11.10 Control and collection of assets

11.10.1 By action commenced by writ

If the company's title to, or its right of possession of any property is disputed or challenged, the liquidator can bring proceedings in the company's name by writ seeking possession or recovery of the company's property. However, the defendant will be able to seek and ordinarily obtain, an order for security for costs.[116] To avoid this, the liquidator may pursue one of the courses set out below[117] which are, in many cases, wider in scope than the company would otherwise possess. However, it is probable that there is jurisdiction for the Companies Court to permit all claims to be brought before it by a liquidator, that would otherwise be commenced only by writ if these applications are necessary for the collection, realisation and distribution of its assets.[118]

112. *Re Exhall Coal Mining Co.* (1864) 4 De GJ & S 377; *Re Lancashire Cotton Spinning Co.* (1877) 35 Ch.D. 656; *Higginshaw Mills and Spinning Co.* [1896] 2 Ch. 544; *The Constellation* [1966] 1 WLR 272.
113. See para 11.9.10.
114. IR 1986, r. 7.15(1), (2) and (3).
115. IR 1986, r. 7.15(4).
116. See Chapter 10, para. 10.57.
117. See paras 11.10.2–6, *infra*.
118. *Re Shilena Hosiery Co. Ltd* [1980] Ch. 219; see para. 11.7.5, *supra*.

11.10.2 Compulsory liquidations

In a compulsory liquidation, it is the duty of the court to cause the company's assets to be collected and applied in discharge of its liabilities.[119] The duties imposed on the court with regard to the collection of the company's assets and their application in discharge of its liabilities are discharged by the liquidator as an officer of the court and subject to its control.[120] In the discharge of his duties, the liquidator, for the purposes of acquiring and retaining possession of the company's property, has the same powers as a receiver appointed by the High Court, and the court may on his application enforce such acquisition or retention accordingly.[121] Thus, once a liquidator has taken possession of property, any interference with his possession without the leave of the court will constitute a contempt of court and be punishable by committal.[122] Further, as with a court-appointed receiver, the liquidator can apply for orders seeking delivery up and possession of property belonging to the company and injunctions restraining further interference. Except for applications for committal, which are commenced by originating motion, other applications by the liquidator must be commenced either by originating or ordinary application. Alternatively, the liquidator may apply pursuant to s. 234 of the Insolvency Act.[123]

11.10.3 Voluntary liquidations

A liquidator of a company in voluntary liquidation is not an officer of the court and any interference with his possession is not a contempt of court. Nevertheless, under s. 112 of the Insolvency Act, such a liquidator may apply to the court for orders seeking delivery up of property and injunctions restraining interference as if the company were being wound up by the court. However, having regard to the powers contained in s. 234 of the Insolvency Act, it is likely that any application for delivery up of possession will be made pursuant to that section.

11.10.4 S. 234 of the Insolvency Act

Section 234 provides that, where any person has in his possession or control any property, books, papers or records to which the company appears to be entitled, the court may require that person forthwith or within such period as the court may direct, to pay, deliver, convey, surrender or transfer the property, books, papers or records to the liquidator.[124] Unlike the predecessor of the section,[125] it was held in *Re London Iron and Steel Co. Ltd*[126] that the court had jurisdiction to determine in such an application whether the company was or was not entitled to the property in question. The practice and procedure for such application is that set out in chapter 1 of part 7 to the Insolvency Rules.[127]

119. IA 1986, s. 148.
120. IR 1986, r. 4.179(1).
121. IR 1986, r. 4.179(2).
122. *Ames* v. *Birkenhead Docks Trustees* (1855) 20 Beav. 332 at 353.
123. See para. 11.10.4.
124. IA 1986, s. 234(2).
125. IA 1986, s. 551.
126. [1990] BCC 159.
127. See Chapter 10 of this book.

11.10.5 Ss. 236 and 237 of the Insolvency Act

Under s. 236 of the Insolvency Act, the court may on the application of the liquidator summon various persons to appear before it. These are: any officer of the company[128]; any person known or suspected to have in his possession any property of the company or supposed to be indebted to the company[129]; or any person whom the court thinks capable of giving information concerning the promotion, formation, business dealings, affairs or property of the company.[130] The court may require any such person to submit an affidavit to the court[131] or be examined on oath either orally or by interrogatories[132] in respect of his dealings with the company or to produce any books, papers or other records in his possession or under his control relating to the company or to its promotion, formation, business dealings, affairs or property.[133] If it appears to the court on consideration of any evidence thus obtained that any person has in his possession any property of the company, the court may on the application of the liquidator order that person to deliver the whole or any part of the property to the liquidator in such manner and on such terms as the court thinks fit.[134] If it appears to the court from evidence so obtained that any person is indebted to the company, the court may on the application of the liquidator order that person to pay to the liquidator, at such time and in such manner as the court may direct, the whole or any part of the amount due, whether in full discharge of the debt or otherwise as the court thinks fit.[135]

11.10.6 S. 212 of the Insolvency Act

If in the course of a winding-up of a company it appears that a person, who is or has been an officer of the company, has acted as liquidator, administrator or administrative receiver of the company, or is or has been concerned or has taken part in the promotion, formation or management of the company, has retained any property of the company, the court may on the application of the official receiver or the liquidator or any creditor or, with the leave of the court, any contributory, examine into the conduct of that person and compel him to restore the property to the company.[136] Applications must follow the procedure set out in chapter 1 of part 7 of the Insolvency Rules.[137]

11.10.7 Vesting of company property in liquidator

Where a company is being wound up by the court, the court has power on the application of the liquidator to vest in the liquidator by his official name[138] all or any part of the

128. IA 1986, s. 236(2)(a).
129. IA 1986, s. 236(2)(b).
130. IA 1986, s. 236(2)(c).
131. IA 1986, s. 236(3).
132. IA 1986, s. 237(4).
133. These powers and the relevant procedure are considered in detail in Chapter 15.
134. IA 1986, s. 237(1).
135. IA 1986, s. 237(2).
136. See paras 11.12 where the section is considered in more detail.
137. See Chapter 10 of this book and para 11.5 of this Chapter.
138. IA 1986, s. 163 provides that the liquidator must not be described by the name of the individual who occupies the office but, where the official receiver is liquidator, by the style of "the official receiver and liquidator" of the particular company and, where a person other than the official receiver is liquidator, by the style of "the liquidator" of the particular company.

property of whatsoever description belonging to the company or held by trustees, on its behalf.[139] The liquidator may then, after giving such indemnity if any as the court might direct, bring or defend in his official name any action or other legal proceeding which relates to that property or which it is necessary to bring or defend for the purpose of effectually winding-up the company and recovering its property.[140] In practice, the court commonly makes vesting orders in the following situations:

(1) in the case of a winding-up under part V of the Insolvency Act of an unregistered company which cannot sue or be sued in a common name;
(2) where the company is an overseas company and the liquidator needs to take proceedings in another jurisdiction where there is doubt as to whether he will be considered by that jurisdiction to have the authority of the company to bring proceedings in its name; and
(3) where a group of companies has been wound up and there is a single liquidator but it is unclear which company owns which property.

If action is needed to be taken urgently to preserve or protect that property, the property can be vested in the liquidator who has been appointed to all the companies if there is only one liquidator, or in one of the liquidators if different liquidators have been appointed to different companies, the liquidators agreeing amongst themselves that the vesting of the property in one of them shall not prejudice the rights of any of the other liquidators to make claims at a later stage. This procedure avoids any dispute as to the title of the party seeking to recover or protect the property. If the application is not made in pending proceedings, it is made by way of originating application and must follow the procedure set out in chapter 1 of part 7 of the Insolvency Rules.[141] All parties who claim ownership of the property in question must be made parties to the application. If there are no other parties who claim ownership, the application should be made *ex parte*, with no party named as respondent.

11.10.8 Liens

A lien or other right to retain possession of any of the books, papers or other records of the company is unenforceable to the extent that its enforcement would deny possession of any books, papers or other records of the liquidator.[142] This does not, however, apply to a lien on documents which give a title to property and are held as such (for example, documents of title held by a bank as security for a loan[143]).

11.11 Collection of debts

11.11.1 By action commenced by writ

It is usual for the liquidator to commence debt recovery proceedings by writ, but there is no reason why the Companies Court should not entertain such an application by the

139. IA 1986, s. 145(1).
140. IA 1986, s. 145(2).
141. See Chapter 10.
142. IA 1986, s. 246(2).
143. IA 1986, s. 246(3).

liquidator if, as will be the case, it is necessary for the collection, realisation and distribution of the company's assets.[144]

11.11.2 Ss. 236 and 237 of the Insolvency Act

As has been seen above,[145] under s. 236, the liquidator may, in addition, apply to the court to summon to appear before it *inter alia* any person supposed to be indebted to the company[146] and may require any such person to submit an affidavit to the court or be examined on oath, either orally or by interrogatories, in respect of his dealings with the company. If it appears from such evidence that the person is indebted to the company, the court may direct that person to pay to the liquidator at such time and in such manner as the court may direct the whole or any part of the amount due, whether in full discharge of the debt or otherwise as the court thinks fit.[147]

11.12 Realisation of claims (other than debts) against other parties

11.12.1 Introduction

All claims that the company has in its own name against other parties may be realised by the liquidator bringing claims by way of writ action commenced in the name of the company. Section 212 of the Insolvency Act provides an alternative procedure for realising certain claims against certain individuals, which procedure can be used not only by the liquidator, but also by creditors and contributories.

11.12.2 S. 212 of the Insolvency Act

Section 212 enables the court to examine the conduct of any person who is or has been an officer[148] of the company, has acted as liquidator, administrator or administrative receiver of the company, or is or has been concerned, or has taken part in the promotion, formation or management of the company. The section was designed to obviate the necessity of bringing an action by way of writ and to enable complete justice to be done between the parties.[149] However, proceedings can only be brought under s. 212 against those set out above if it is alleged that the person has misapplied or retained, or become accountable for, any money or other property of the company, or been guilty of any misfeasance or breach of any fiduciary or other duty in relation to the company.[150] This includes, in the case of a person who has acted as liquidator or administrator of the

144. *Re Shilena Hosiery Co. Ltd*; see para. 11.7.5, *supra*.
145. See para. 11.10.5, *supra*.
146. IA 1986, s. 236(2)(b).
147. See Chapter 15 for the detailed procedure on such application.
148. As defined by s. 744, Companies Act 1985 as applied by s. 251 of the Insolvency Act 1986, which has been held to include *de facto* officers who have been irregularly appointed: *Gibson* v. *Barton* (1875) LR 10 QB 329; *Coventry and Dixon's Case* (1880) 14 Ch.D. 660; *Re Western Counties Steam Bakeries Co.* [1897] 1 Ch. 617; it has also been held that the auditors of a bank (*Re London General Bank* [1895] 2 Ch. 166) and of a company with audit regulations such as those contained in Table A (*Re Kingston Cotton Mill Co. (No. 1)* [1896] 1 Ch. 6; *R.* v. *Schacter* [1960] 2 QB 252; *Re Thomas Gerrard & Co.* [1968] Ch. 455) are officers for the purposes of this procedure; bankers and solicitors are not, *per se*, officers of the company; *Re Imperial Land Co. of Marseilles* (1870) LR 10 Eq. 298; *Carter's Case* (1886) 31 Ch.D. 496.
149. *Re Royal Hotel Co. of Great Yarmouth* (1867) LR 4 Eq. 244; *Stringer's Case* (1869) 4 Ch. App. 475.
150. IA 1986, s. 212(1).

company, any misfeasance or breach of any fiduciary or other duty in connection with the carrying out of his functions as such.[151] Examples of misfeasance include the payment of dividends out of capital,[152] the sale of the company's assets at an undervalue,[153] the making of fraudulent preferences,[154] the making of secret profits by promoters,[155] improper payments by directors to promoters,[156] and the application by directors of the company's assets for an *ultra vires* or illegal[157] object.

11.12.3 Who can apply?

An application can be made without the leave of the court by the official receiver, the liquidator or any creditor or contributory.[158] The power of a contributory to make an application, however, is not exercisable except with the leave of the court[159] which leave must be obtained by way of separate application. The court can exercise its powers on an application made by a contributory notwithstanding that the contributory will not benefit from any order the court may make on the application.[160] The power to make an application in relation to a person who has acted as liquidator or administrator of the company is not exercisable, except with the leave of the court, after that person has had his release.[161] The application for leave must be by way of separate application.

11.12.4 No claim against personal representatives

It has been held that misfeasance proceedings, under a predecessor of s. 212 of the Insolvency Act 1986, will not lie against the personal representative of a deceased director.[162] Although, following the Law Reform (Miscellaneous Provisions) Act 1934, all causes of action subsisting against any person survive against that person's estate, it is doubtful if this permits proceedings to be commenced or continued under s. 212 of the Insolvency Act 1986 against any personnel representatives. Proceedings can, of course, be commenced or continued in a writ action.

11.12.5 Orders the court can make

In its discretion, the court may compel the respondent to repay, restore or account for misapplied property or to contribute compensation in such sum as it thinks just in respect of the misfeasance or breach of fiduciary or other duty.[163] The court has power to take into

151. IA 1986, s. 212(2).
152. *Re National Funds Assurance Co.* (1872) 10 Ch.D. 118; *Flitcroft's Case* (1882) 21 Ch.D. 519; *Re Sharp* [1892] 1 Ch. 154; *Moxhan* v. *Grant* [1900] 1 QB 88.
153. *Re Travellers' Chambers* (1892) 12 TLR 529.
154. *Re Washington Diamond Mining Co.* [1893] 3 Ch. 95; *Gluckstein* v. *Barnes* [1900] AC 240.
155. *Re J. Franklin & Son Ltd* (1937) 157 LT 188.
156. *Collerne* v. *London and Surburban Building Society* (1890) 25 QBD 485; *Re Liverpool Household Stores* (1890) 59 L.J. Ch. 616; *Joint Stock Discount Co.* v. *Brown* (1869) LR 8 Eq. 376.
157. *Re Faure Electric Accumulator Co.* (1889) 40 Ch.D. 141.
158. IA 1986, s. 212(3).
159. IA 1986, s. 212(5).
160. IA 1986, s. 212(5).
161. IA 1986, s. 212(4).
162. *Re British Guardian Assurance Co.* (1880) 14 Ch.D. 335.
163. IA 1986, s. 212(3).

account factors which it might have no discretion to do if an action for damages had been brought in the company's name by writ. For instance, the court might order only such contribution to be made as would enable the creditors to be paid in full[164] although in such a situation a court may well wish to be informed of the wishes of the contributories.[165] It has been said that there is no jurisdiction under this section to set aside a contract entered into between the company and a person mentioned in s. 212(1).[166]

11.12.6 "Summary remedy"

Although the heading to s. 212 of the Insolvency Act 1986 describes the remedy provided by the section as "summary", and the procedure is frequently referred to as providing a "summary remedy", the power given by the section to the court is not restricted to cases where there is no arguable defence to the claim or claims which do not involve the determination of any questions of law. The purpose of the section has been described as a remedy provided by the legislature to prevent double sets of proceedings.[167]

11.12.7 Shilena Hosiery Co. Ltd[168]

It was at one time considered that the only claims that could be made against third parties by the Companies Court in the liquidation were those that came within what is now s. 212. *Re Shilena Hosiery Co. Ltd* would appear to be authority, however, for the proposition that all claims against third parties can be heard by the Companies Court if the determination is incidental to the collection and distribution of the company's assets.[169] If this is right, the boundaries of the s. 212 jurisdiction will decrease in importance and significance.

11.12.8 Absence of procedure for third party notices

Although one co-respondent to a s. 212 application may serve a notice on another claiming an indemnity or contribution in the normal way,[170] third party proceedings are not normally available.[171] This can cause substantial injustice to a respondent and is a factor the court takes into account in deciding whether to undertake an examination pursuant to s. 212. If a party against whom one of the respondents wishes to take third party proceedings is also a party against whom the liquidator can bring proceedings by way of originating or ordinary application in the liquidation, either pursuant to s. 212 or otherwise, that respondent could make an application for directions seeking an order that the liquidator bring proceedings against the other party, so as to enable an indemnity or contribution notice to be served. Such an application would, in practice, only be acceded to upon a suitable indemnity being provided to the liquidator for his costs.

164. *Re Home and Colonial Insurance Co.* [1930] 1 Ch. 102.
165. See *Re Sunlight Incandescent Gas Lamp Co.* (1900) 16 TLR 535.
166. *Re Centrifugal Butter Co.* [1913] 1 Ch. 188; see however *Re Shilena Hosiery Co. Ltd* [1980] Ch. 219 and para. 11.7.5.
167. Per Giffard L.J. in *Stringer's Case* (1869) 4 Ch. App. 475 at 493.
168. [1980] Ch. 219.
169. See para. 11.7.5 for a more detailed discussion.
170. *Re Morecombe Bowling* [1969] 1 WLR 133; see Chapter 10, para. 10.18.
171. See Chapter 10, para. 10.17.

11.13 Fraudulent and wrongful trading: adjustment of prior transactions

11.13.1 Introduction

Provision is provided in the Insolvency Act for applications to be made in respect of prior trading carried on fraudulently[172] or wrongfully[173] and for the adjustment of the following transactions entered into prior to liquidation:

(a) transactions at an undervalue[174];
(b) preferences[175];
(c) extortionate credit transactions[176];
(d) certain floating charges.[177]

In all cases the procedure is that set out in chapter 1 of part 7 of the Insolvency Rules.[178] The jurisdiction to make such orders is set out below. As the purpose of this book is not to deal with the substantive law, the scope of the jurisdiction will be dealt with only briefly. However, there are a number of issues which are common and can be dealt with before consideration is given to each separate jurisdiction. These are:

(a) who benefits from the proceeds of such proceedings;
(b) costs orders;
(c) the overlap with similar common law or equitable causes of action vested in the company;
(d) procedural problems where there are fixed and/or floating charges over the assets of the company.

11.13.2 Who benefits from the proceeds of such proceedings?

Millett J. had to consider this issue in *Re MC Bacon Ltd (No. 2)*.[179] The case concerned an application under s. 239 of the Insolvency Act 1986 to set aside a voidable preference. The judge held that the powers in that section were not intended to be exercised so as to enable a debenture holder to obtain the benefit of the proceedings brought by the liquidator. He stated that a payment or other transaction in the course of business bound the debenture holder even if its effect was to prefer another creditor,[180] and it was for this reason that an application to set aside a voidable preference could only be made by a liquidator or administrator and, in the absence of a liquidation or administration order, could not be made at all. The judge held that any sum recovered from a creditor who has been wrongfully preferred enures for the benefit of the general body of creditors and not for the benefit of the company or the holder of a floating charge: it does not become part

172. IA 1986, s. 213.
173. IA 1986, s. 214.
174. IA 1986, ss. 238 and 423.
175. IA 1986, s. 239.
176. IA 1986, s. 244.
177. IA 1986, s. 245.
178. See Chapter 10 of this book.
179. [1990] BCLC 607. The reasoning was followed in *Re Oasis Merchandising Services Ltd* [1997] BCC 282 at 290.
180. Relying on *Willmott* v. *London Celluloid Co.* (1886) 34 Ch. 147 where Cotton L.J. pointed out that the preference section (then CA 1862, s. 164), was "only intended to apply in the case of a winding-up and for the benefit of the general creditors".

of the company's assets but is received by the liquidator, in effect impressed with a trust in favour of those creditors amongst whom he has to distribute the assets of the company, relying on *Re Yagerphone Ltd.*[181] The position prior to 1986 was still thought by Millett J. to be good law, notwithstanding either s. 239(3) of the Insolvency Act 1986, (which empowers the court, on finding a voidable preference proved, to make such order as it thought fit for restoring the position to what it would have been if the company had not given a preference), or s. 241(1)(c), (which empowers the court to release or discharge any security given by the company). The judge stated that those powers were intended not to be exercised so as to enable a debenture holder to obtain the benefit of the proceedings brought by the liquidator. Thus, if a disposition of property which was subject to a fixed charge to set aside as being a preference and an order made for restoring the property to the company, it follows from *MC Bacon (No. 2)* that, upon restoration, the property is not subject to any charge in favour of the debenture holder.

11.13.3 How wide is the application of MC Bacon (No. 2)?

It would appear that its reasoning is equally applicable to all those applications which may be brought only by a liquidator or administrator, namely those applications under s. 238 (transactions at an undervalue), s. 239 (preferences), s. 244 (extortionate credit transactions), and s. 245 (avoidance of certain floating charges), or those which are given exclusively to a liquidator, namely, applications under s. 213 (fraudulent trading), and s. 214 (wrongful trading).

11.13.4 Costs

If the liquidator is the applicant, he will be a party to the litigation and any order "that the applicant do pay the respondent(s) costs" will be payable by him in the absence of any order to the contrary.[182] The proceedings are for the benefit only of the general body of unsecured creditors,[183] and any order the court makes entitling the liquidator to recoup such costs payable from the assets of the company will be recoupable out of the assets available for distribution to the general body of creditors and are not "expenses of the liquidation" within r. 4.218(1) so as to make them payable out of floating charge assets.[184]

11.13.5 Right of recoupment

A liquidator is entitled to an order permitting him to recoup all costs incurred from the assets available to the general body of unsecured creditors unless he has been guilty of misconduct.[185] In order to satisfy himself that the proceedings are properly brought and that he will be entitled to recoup his costs from the assets available to the general body of creditors, the liquidator can seek the directions of the court as to whether the proceedings should be commenced and/or continued and that he will be indemnified in respect of

181. [1935] Ch. 392.
182. See para. 11.22.2.
183. See para. 11.13.2.
184. *Re MC Bacon (No. 2)* [1990] BCLC 607 at 615.
185. *Re Wilson Lovatt & Sons Ltd* [1971] 1 All ER 274.

all costs to be incurred as and when they are incurred from the assets available for the general unsecured creditors. The court exercises its jurisdiction in the same way that it does when giving directions to trustees.

11.13.6 Overlap with common law and equitable remedies available to the company

All directors and other agents of a company owe to the company the common law and equitable duties of such directors and agents. Further, in respect of breaches of fiduciary duties, third parties are liable to account to the company as constructive trustees if they either receive property beneficially belonging to the company with knowledge that it was transferred in breach of fiduciary duty, or assist in a dishonest and fraudulent breach of fiduciary duty with knowledge of the dishonest and fraudulent design.

Remedies in respect of such breaches are those of the company and not the liquidator, although it will be the liquidator who instigates or continues proceedings in the name of the company. Such proceedings will normally be commenced by writ. However, it is frequently the case that the circumstances leading to fraudulent and wrongful trading applications and applications to set aside transactions at an undervalue and preferences will also provide the company with a cause of action itself for breach of common law and equitable duties and that as part of a "belt and braces" approach, the liquidator will want to commence concurrent proceedings. There is little doubt that such concurrent proceedings can be commenced in the Companies Court by way of application if the case comes within s. 212 of the Insolvency Act.[186] It also appears to be the case that any application can be commenced by the liquidator in the Companies Court if it involves an issue connected with the collection, realisation and distribution of the company's assets.[187] The liquidator would be the applicant and would seek declarations, for example, that the respondents hold certain property on constructive trust for the company.[188]

11.13.7 Debenture holders

If sums owing from the company to third parties are secured by fixed and/or floating charges over the assets of the company, it is likely that such charges will be drafted so as to include any causes of action the company has at common law or in equity. Any administrative receiver appointed over the charged assets will have power to bring proceedings in the name of the company, and any proceeds from the litigation will be payable in the same manner as the proceeds from the realisation of other assets subject to charges. If an administrative receiver has been appointed and has commenced proceedings in the name of the company, seeking relief similar to that under consideration, the liquidator should give notice of the proceedings to the administrative receiver as it will be necessary to ensure that both matters are heard at the same time: each of the remedies given to the liquidator by the Insolvency Act is discretionary and the court will need to ensure that the respondents are not ordered to pay compensation twice in respect of the same or similar matters.

186. See para. 11.12.

187. *Re Shilena Hosiery Co. Ltd* [1970] Ch. 219.

188. See *Re Clasper Group Services Ltd* (1988) 4 BCC 673 where Warner J. permitted a liquidator to amend an application to claim that recipients of payments held the same on constructive trust for the company.

11.14 Fraudulent and wrongful trading

11.14.1 Fraudulent trading

On the application of a liquidator, the court may declare that any persons who were knowingly parties to the carrying on of the business of the company being wound up, with intent to defraud creditors of the company or creditors of any other person or for any other fraudulent purpose, are liable to make such contributions to the company's assets as the court thinks proper.[189] The marginal note to s. 213 of the Insolvency Act 1986, but not the section itself, calls this "fraudulent trading". To make out a claim of fraudulent trading requires proof of actual dishonesty on the part of those accused of knowingly participating in the carrying on of the business with intent to defraud creditors or for any other fraudulent purpose.

11.14.2 Wrongful trading

The court also has power to make such a declaration, but only in respect of a director or shadow director[190] of a company which has gone into insolvent liquidation if, at the time that the person was a director or shadow director, that person knew or ought to have concluded that there was no reasonable prospect that the company would avoid going into insolvent liquidation.[191] It is a defence to such a claim if the director or shadow director can establish that, at the time when he knew or ought to have concluded that there was no reasonable prospect that the company would avoid going into insolvent liquidation, he took every step with a view to minimising the potential loss to the company's creditors as he ought to have taken.[192] The director or shadow director will be judged by the standards of a reasonably diligent person having both the general knowledge, skill and experience that may reasonably be expected of a person carrying out the same functions as were carried out by the director concerned or which were entrusted to him, and the general knowledge, skill and experience that the director or shadow director had.[193] The marginal note to s. 214 of the Insolvency Act 1986, but not the section itself, calls this "wrongful trading".

11.14.3 Orders the court may make

Where the court makes a declaration that any person is liable to contribute to the company's assets for fraudulent or wrongful trading, it may give further directions for giving effect to the declaration. In particular, the court may provide for the liability of that person to be a charge on any debt or obligation due from the company to him, or on any mortgage or charge or any interest in a mortgage or charge on assets of the company held

189. IA 1986, s. 213.
190. IA 1986, s. 214(2), (7).
191. IA 1986, s. 214(1), (2).
192. IA 1986, s. 214(3).
193. IA 1986, s. 214(4), (5); CA 1985 s. 727, has no application: *Re Produce Marketing Consortium Ltd* (1989) 5 BCC 399.

by or vested in him or any person on his behalf, or any person claiming as assignee from or through the person liable or any person acting on his behalf, and can give any further directions from time to time as may be necessary for enforcing any charge so imposed.[194] The term "assignee" includes a person to whom or in whose favour, by the directions of the person made liable, the debt, obligation, mortgage or charge was created, issued or transferred or the interest created, but does not include an assignee for valuable consideration given in good faith and without notice of any of the matters on the ground of which the declaration is made.[195] The court also has power to direct that the whole or any part of any debt owed by the company to a person liable to contribute to the assets of the company, and any interest thereon, shall rank in priority after all other debts owed by the company and after any interest on those debts.[196] The liquidator will need to consider at the outset whether he wishes to ask the court to make any orders that affect persons other than those accused of fraudulent or wrongful trading as they will need to be made respondents to the application. Unless they are made respondents, it will be open to them to argue that the findings of the court do not bind them. In many cases that person may not wish to take any substantive part in the proceedings but limit his role to making submissions in respect of the order to be made. However, that person is entitled to call evidence and make submissions in respect of the allegations of fraudulent and wrongful trading. If he does so, however, and if fraudulent or wrongful trading is proved, an order for costs may be made against him.

11.14.4 Basis of compensation

It has been held that a predecessor to s. 213 of the Insolvency Act 1986 was in the nature of a punitive provision and that the court had a discretion to make an order without limiting the order to the amount of the debts of those creditors proved to have been defrauded.[197] It is the creditors in general who are entitled to the sum ordered to be paid, and not the particular defrauded creditors,[198] and the sum must be dealt with by the liquidator as part of the general assets of the company.[199] Similarly, the purpose of orders under s. 214 is to recoup the loss to the company so as to benefit the creditors as a whole, and there is no jurisdiction to direct payment to creditors or to direct that moneys paid to the company should be applied in payment of one class of creditors in preference to another.[200] *Prima facie*, the appropriate amount under s. 214 that a director is declared to be liable to contribute is the amount by which the company's assets can be discerned to have been depleted by the director's conduct, but the inclusion of a penal element has not been ruled out.[201] Where proceedings are commenced under s. 212, at the same time

194. IA 1986, s. 215(2).
195. IA 1986, s. 215(3).
196. IA 1986, s. 215(4).
197. *Re William C. Leitch Bros* [1932] 2 Ch. 71 per Maughan J.
198. *Re William C. Leitch Bros. (No. 2)* [1933] Ch. 261.
199. But see *Re Cyona Distributors Ltd* [1967] Ch. 889 where Lord Denning M.R. and Danckwerts L.J. thought that the court could direct payment to a particular creditor or class of creditor.
200. *Re Purpoint Ltd* [1991] BCC 121.
201. *Re Produce Marketing Consortium Ltd* (1989) 5 BCC 569.

the court must ensure that there is no element of double counting.[202] The same must apply where the claim is brought at the same time as claims to adjust prior transactions.

11.15 Adjustment of prior transactions

11.15.1 Transactions at an undervalue

There are two different, albeit similar, powers to set aside transactions at an undervalue:

(a) Under s. 238, the court has power if a company has entered into such a transaction to make such order as it thinks fit for restoring the position to what it would have been if the transaction had not been entered into.[203] For this purpose to be exercisable, the company must either have gone into liquidation or administration[204] and the transaction must have been entered into at a relevant time, ordinarily the period of two years ending with the onset of insolvency.[205] A transaction is at an undervalue if:
  (i) the company makes a gift to a person: or
  (ii) the company enters into a transaction with the person on terms that provide for the company to receive no consideration; or
  (iii) the company enters into a transaction for a consideration the value of which is significantly less than the value of the consideration provided by the company.[206]

  No order can be made if the court is satisfied that the company entered into the transaction in good faith and for the purpose of carrying on its business, and that at the time it did so there were reasonable grounds for believing that the transaction would benefit the company.[207]

(b) Under s. 423, the court has power to make any such order as it thinks fit for restoring the position to what it would have been if the transaction had not been entered into, and for protecting the interests of persons who are victims of the transaction.[208] For this power to be exercisable, the court has to be satisfied that it was entered into for the purpose:
  (i) of putting assets beyond the reach of a person who is making or may at some time make a claim against the company; or
  (ii) of otherwise prejudicing the interests of such a person in relation to the claim which he is making or may make.[209]

  The definition of a transaction at an undervalue is similar to that under s. 238.[210] It is not a requirement that the company should have gone into liquidation or administration, nor is there any time limit.

202. *Re Purpoint Ltd, supra.*
203. IA 1986, s. 238(3).
204. IA 1986, s. 238(1).
205. IA 1986, s. 240(1). The onset of insolvency is the commencement of the winding-up or the date of presentation of the petition for an administrator order: see IA 1986, s. 240(3).
206. IA 1986, s. 238(4).
207. IA 1986, s. 238(5).
208. IA 1986, s. 423(2).
209. IA 1986, s. 423(3).
210. IA 1986, s. 423(1).

11.15.2 Who can apply

Under s. 238, the application must be made either by the liquidator or administrator.[211] Under s. 423, it may be made either by the liquidator or administrator or, with the leave of the court, by a victim of the transaction.[212] In a case where a victim of the transaction is bound by a voluntary arrangement, the application may be made by the supervisor of the voluntary arrangement, or by any person who (whether or not so bound) is such a victim.[213]

11.15.3 How is the application to be brought?

Applications must be commenced by originating application.[214] The only exception is an application under s. 423 Insolvency Act 1986 which is not made in existing proceedings in the Companies Court or Bankruptcy Court or which is brought otherwise than by virtue of a right to apply to those courts by some other provision of parts I to XI of the Insolvency Act 1986. Such an application can be commenced by writ in any part of the High Court.[215]

11.15.4 Orders that can be made

The Insolvency Act 1986 provides examples of a number of specific orders which the court might make to restore the position to what it would have been if the company had not entered into the transaction at an undervalue and, in the case only of s. 423 Insolvency Act 1986, to protect the interest of persons who are victims of the transaction. The "and" between paragraph (a) and (b) in s. 423(2) must be read conjunctively and not disjunctively; any order made under that sub-section must seek, so far as practicable, both to restore the position to what it would have been if the transaction had not been entered into, and to protect the interests of the victim of it: it is not a power to restore the position generally, but in such a way as to protect the victims' interests by restoring assets to the debtor to make them available for execution by the victims.[216] The court may[217]:

(a) require any property transferred as part of the transaction to be vested in the company;
(b) require any property to be so vested if it represents, in any person's hands, the application either of the proceeds of sale of property so transferred or of money so transferred;
(c) release or discharge (in whole or in part) any security given by the company;
(d) require any person to pay, in respect of benefits received by him from the company, such sums as the court may direct;
(e) provide for any surety or guarantor whose obligations to any person were released or discharged (in whole or in part) under the transaction to be under

211. IA 1986, s. 238(2).
212. IA 1986, s. 424(1)(a).
213. IA 1986, s. 424(1)(b).
214. IR 1986, r. 7.1.
215. *TSB Bank plc* v. *Katz*, *Times*, 2 May 1994.
216. *Arbuthnot Leasing International Ltd* v. *Havelet Leasing Ltd (No. 2)* [1990] BCC 636; *Chohan* v. *Saggar* [1994] BCC 134.
217. IA 1986, ss. 240 and 425.

such new or revived obligations to that person as the court thinks appropriate;

(f) provide for security to be provided for the discharge of any obligation imposed by or arising out of the order, for such an obligation to be charged on any property and for the security or charge to have the same priority as a security or charge released or discharged (in whole or in part) under the transaction; and

(g) (in the case of s. 238 Insolvency Act 1986 only) provide for the extent to which any person whose property is vested by the order of the court, or on whom obligations are imposed by the order, is to be able to prove in the winding-up of the company for debts or other liabilities which arose from, or were released or discharged (in whole or in part) under or by, the transaction or the giving of the preference.

11.15.5 Outside parties to the transactions

Any such order may affect the property of, or impose an obligation on any person whether or not he is the person with whom the company entered into the transaction[218] but such an order must not prejudice any interest in property which was acquired from a person other than the company and was acquired in good faith, for value and without notice of the relevant circumstances, or prejudice any interest deriving from such an interest[219] and must not require a person who received a benefit from the transaction in good faith, for value and without notice of the relevant circumstances to pay a sum, except where that person was a party to the transaction.[220]

11.15.6 Preferences

Where a company has, at a relevant time, given a preference to any person, the court may[221] make such order as it thinks fit for restoring the position to what it would have been if the company had not given that preference.[222] The examples of specific orders which the court may make when setting aside transactions at an undervalue are equally applicable to preferences with necessary modifications.[223] A company gives a preference to a person if, at a relevant time,[224] that person is one of the company's creditors or a surety or guarantor for any of the company's debts or other liabilities and the company does anything or suffers anything to be done which has the effect of putting that person into a position which, in the event of the company going into insolvent liquidation, would be better than the position he would have been in if that thing had not been done.[225] An order cannot be made unless the company which gave the preference was influenced in

218. IA 1986, ss. 241(2) and 425(2).
219. IA 1986, ss. 241(2)(a) and 425(2)(a).
220. IA 1986, ss. 244(2)(b) and 425(2)(b).
221. On the application of the liquidator or administrator: IA 1986, s. 239(2). The application is brought by originating application: see Chapter 10.
222. IA 1986, s. 239(3).
223. IA 1986, s. 241; see para. 11.15.4.
224. IA 1986, s. 240.
225. IA 1986, s. 239(4), (5).

deciding to give it by a desire[226] to produce the preferential effect.[227] A company which has given a preference to a person connected[228] with the company (otherwise than by reason only of being its employee) at the time the preference was given is presumed, unless the contrary is shown, to have been influenced in deciding to give it by such desire.[229] The fact that something has been done pursuant to an order of court does not, without more, prevent the doing or suffering of that thing from constituting the giving of a preference.[230]

11.15.7 Overlapping transactions

It is expressly provided that the provisions of ss. 238 to 241 apply without prejudice to the availability of any other remedy, even in relation to a transaction or preference which the company had no power to enter into or give.[231] The court will endeavour to ensure that there is no element of double counting. It is also expressly provided that the powers exercisable by the court in respect of an extortionate credit transaction[232] are exercisable concurrently with the powers exercisable in relation to that transaction as a transaction at an undervalue.[233]

11.15.8 Extortionate credit transactions

Where a company is in liquidation or administration and is or has been a party to a transaction for, or involving, the provision of credit to the company which is or was extortionate and was entered into in the period of three years ending with the day on which an administration order was made or the company went into liquidation, the administrator or liquidator may apply[234] to the court in respect of that credit transaction for the credit transaction to be set aside or otherwise altered.[235] The court may make one or more of the following orders:

(a) setting aside the whole or part of any obligation created by the transaction[236];
(b) otherwise varying the terms of the transaction or varying the terms on which any security for the purpose of the transaction is held[237];
(c) requiring any person who is or was a party to the transaction to pay to the administrator or liquidator any sums paid to him by the company by virtue of the transaction[238];

226. *Re MC Bacon Ltd* [1990] BCC 78; *Re Beacon Leisure Ltd* [1991] BCC 213; *Re Fairway Magazines Ltd* [1992] BCC 924.
227. IA 1986, s. 239(5).
228. See IA 1986, s. 249.
229. IA 1986, s. 239(6).
230. IA 1986, s. 239(7).
231. IA 1986, s. 241(4).
232. IA 1986, s. 244.
233. IA 1986, s. 244(5).
234. By originating application: see Chapter 10.
235. IA 1986, s. 244(1), (2), (3).
236. IA 1986, s. 244(4)(a).
237. IA 1986, s. 244(4)(b).
238. IA 1986, s. 244(4)(c).

(d) requiring any person to surrender to the liquidator or administrator any property held by him as security for the purposes of the transaction[239]; and
(e) directing accounts to be taken between any persons.[240]

It is expressly provided that the powers conferred are exercisable in relation to any transaction concurrently with any powers in relation to that transaction as a transaction at an undervalue.[241]

11.15.9 Avoidance of certain floating charges

The Act makes certain floating charges[242] invalid. These are charges created within one year prior to the onset of insolvency.[243] For the section to apply, the charge must either have been created at a time when the company was unable to pay its debts,[244] or the company must have become unable to pay its debts in consequence of the transaction under which the charge is created.[245] Such a charge is invalid except to the extent of the aggregate of;

(a) the value of so much of the consideration for the creation of the charge as consists of money paid, or goods or services supplied, to the company at the same time as, or after, the creation of the charge;
(b) the value of so much of that consideration as consists of the discharge or reduction, at the same time as, or after, the creation of the charge, of any debt of the company; and
(c) the amount of any agreed interest on such amounts.[246]

If the charge is created in favour of a connected person,[247] the period is two years rather than one and it is irrelevant whether or not the company is unable to pay its debts or became unable to do so in consequence of the transaction under which the charge was created.[248]

11.15.10 Method of application

The application must be brought by the liquidator or administrator,[249] by originating application.[250]

239. IA 1986, s. 244(4)(d).
240. IA 1986, s. 244(4)(e).
241. IA 1986, s. 244(5).
242. See IA 1986, s. 251 for the definition of a floating charge.
243. IA 1986, s. 245(2)(b). The onset of insolvency in case of an administration order is the date of presentation of the petition on which the administration order was made, and in the case of liquidation the date of commencement of the winding-up: see IA 1986, s. 245(5).
244. Within the meaning of IA 1986, s. 124; see IA 1986, s. 254(4)(b).
245. IA 1986, s. 245(4).
246. IA 1986, s. 245(2); see *Re Shoe Lace Ltd* [1993] BCC 609.
247. See the definition in IA 1986, s. 249.
248. IA 1986, ss. 245(3)(a) and 245(4).
249. IA 1986, s. 245(1).
250. See Chapter 10.

11.16 Disclaimer of onerous property

11.16.1 Introduction

Where a company goes into liquidation it is frequently the case that the company:

(a) is subject to continuing liabilities to pay money or perform other onerous acts either pursuant to contracts or as an incident to the ownership of any property; and/or

(b) has assets which are unsaleable or not readily saleable.

The liquidator must, as soon as practicable, decide whether the property and contracts to which the company is entitled, or by which it is bound, are beneficial to the creditors and likely to realise proceeds which can be distributed. If they are not beneficial because they are unrealisable or subject to onerous liabilities, the liquidator can disclaim the company's interest. If he does not disclaim immediately then further debts may arise in respect of the continuing liabilities, which will be provable in the liquidation to the detriment of unsecured creditors generally. Perhaps more importantly, it may also be argued that he is continuing to "preserve" the asset or contract for the convenience or benefit of the liquidation and that the liabilities accruing thereunder after the commencement of the liquidation are therefore "expenses" of the liquidation[251] and payable out of the assets of the company in priority to all other expenses and all other creditors, including holders of floating charges, and that if he does not treat those liabilities as such, the creditor to whom they are owed can apply for them to be treated as such in the liquidation.[252]

11.16.2 Onerous Property

The liquidator is entitled to disclaim any onerous[253] property, defined to mean any unprofitable contract, or any other property[254] which is unsaleable, not readily saleable, or such that it may give rise to a liability to pay money or perform any other onerous act.[255]

11.16.3 Effect

The effect of disclaimer is to determine any rights or liabilities of the company in respect of the property from the date of the disclaimer.[256] Thus, a claim for rent under a lease for the period between the commencement of the winding-up and the date upon which the lease is disclaimed, is not affected by the disclaimer. Disclaimer does not affect, except so far as is necessary for the purpose of releasing the company from any liability, the rights or liabilities of any other person.[257]

251. *Re Oak Pitts Colliery* (1882) 21 Ch.D. 322; *Re ABC Coupler (No. 3)* [1970] 1 WLR 702; *Re Downer Enterprises* [1974] 1 WLR 1460; *Re Atlantic Computer Systems plc* [1990] BCC 859; *Re Kentish Homes* [1993] BCC 212.
252. See para. 11.21.
253. IA 1986, s. 178(2).
254. "Property" being defined by s. 436 to include money, goods, things in action, etc.
255. IA 1986, s. 178(3)(a) and (b).
256. IA 1986, s. 178(4)(a); the date of disclaimer being the date endorsed on the notice, see r. 4.187(2) and (4).
257. IA 1986, s. 178(4)(b).

11.16.4 When to disclaim

The liquidator is not barred from disclaiming property simply because he has attempted to sell it, taken possession of it or otherwise exercised the rights of ownership in relation to it[258]; nor is there now any time limit within which he must disclaim.[259] To that extent, a liquidator does not automatically "elect" whether or not to disclaim an item of property at the outset of the liquidation. However, since disclaimer does not have a retrospective effect, a liquidator will wish to disclaim property at the earliest possible stage to prevent accruing liabilities from becoming "expenses" in the liquidation.[260]

11.16.5 Forcing the liquidator to elect

A person interested in any property may force the liquidator's hand by applying to him in writing and requiring him to decide whether he will disclaim or not.[261] The liquidator then has 28 days from the date of that application, or such longer period as the court may allow, to give a notice of disclaimer under the section, otherwise he may not do so at all.[262] It is a strong possibility that the liabilities accruing thereafter will be treated as "expenses" in the liquidation and be payable accordingly.[263]

11.16.6 Ascertaining persons interested

If it appears to the liquidator that there is some person who is claiming or may claim some interest in the property, he may give notice[264] to that person, calling on him to declare whether he claims any such interest and, if so, the nature and extent of it. If that person fails to comply with that notice within 14 days of it, the liquidator is entitled to assume that that person has no such interest in the property as to prevent or impede its disclaimer.[265]

11.16.7 Persons sustaining loss or damage by reason of a disclaimer

Any person who suffers loss or damage as a consequence of disclaimer is deemed to be a creditor of the company to the extent of that loss or damage, and may therefore prove for that loss in the winding-up.[266] However, the decision as to whether to disclaim or not is only challengeable by any person aggrieved if made *mala fides* or perversely.[267]

258. IA 1986, s. 178(2).
259. As was previously the case under CA 1985, s 617.
260. See para. 11.21.5, *infra*.
261. See IR 1986, r. 4.191, requiring the application to be made on Form 4.54 (sch. 4 to the Rules) or a substantially similar form, and delivered to the liquidator personally or by registered post.
262. IA 1986, s. 178(5).
263. See para. 11.21.5, *infra*.
264. In Form 4.55 (sch. 4 to the Rules).
265. IR 1986, r. 4.192.
266. IA 1986, s. 178(6); as to how such losses should be calculated in respect of a disclaimer of a lease see *Re Park Air Services plc*, 1 May 1997, unreported, Court of Appeal.
267. *Re Hans Place* [1992] BCC 737.

11.17 Procedure

11.17.1 The prescribed notice

A liquidator disclaims property by serving the prescribed notice,[268] which must contain sufficient particulars of the property to enable it to be easily identified.

11.17.2 Filing notice

The notice must be signed by the liquidator and, filed in court together with a copy. Both original and copy are sealed and dated by the court, before the copy is handed to the liquidator or his agent, or posted to him.[269]

11.17.3 Giving notice

Within seven days of the day on which the copy was returned by the court to him, the liquidator must send or give copies of the notice to each of the following persons[270]:

(a) where the property is leasehold, every person whom he knows to claim under the company as underlessee or mortgagee[271];
(b) where the property is an unprofitable contract, any person whom he knows to be a party to the contract or to have any interest under it; and
(c) in any case, any person who to his knowledge claims an interest in the property, or is under any liability in respect of the property, not being a liability discharged by the disclaimer.

If the liquidator subsequently comes to know of other persons who would have been entitled to such notice, he must also give notice to them,[272] unless he is satisfied that they have already been made aware of the disclaimer and its date, or unless the court so orders. The liquidator may also give notice of the disclaimer to any other person who, in his opinion, ought in the public interest or otherwise to be informed of it.[273] The court should be kept notified of the names, addresses and interests, of each of the persons to whom he has given notice of the disclaimer.[274]

11.17.4 Applications for vesting/delivery orders

Where property has been disclaimed by a liquidator, any person who claims an interest in the disclaimed property may apply to the court, which may make an order vesting the property in, or for the delivery of the property to, that person or a trustee for him, on such terms as it thinks fit.[275] The vesting order need not be completed by conveyance, assignment or transfer and is, in practice, effected simply as a matter of court order.[276]

268. Form 4.53, in compliance with the conditions set out in IR 1986, r. 4.187.
269. IR 1986, r. 4.187(2) and (3).
270. As set out in IR 1986, r. 4.188(2)–(4).
271. IR 1986, r. 4.188(2); IA 1986, s. 179(1).
272. IR 1986, r. 4.188(5).
273. IR 1986, r. 4.189, Form 4.53.
274. IR 1986, r. 4.190.
275. IA 1986, s. 181.
276. IA 1986, s. 181(6).

Such an application may equally be made by a person who is under such a liability in respect of the property that will not be discharged by the disclaimer,[277] although in that case the court may only make an order in his favour if it considers it just to do so for the purpose of compensating him in respect of the disclaimer.[278] Special rules apply in respect of leasehold property.[279]

11.17.5 Procedure for such applications

Where a person makes an application for a vesting or delivery order, the following procedures applies:

(a) except as set out below, the application follows the procedure in chapter 1 of part 7 of the Insolvency Rules[280];
(b) the application must be made within three months of the earlier of the applicant becoming aware of the disclaimer or receiving notice of it[281];
(c) the application should be filed in court with a supporting affidavit stating whether the applicant is applying in respect of a claim for an interest in the property, or of a liability in respect of it, specifying the date on which the applicant received notice or became aware of the disclaimer, and specifying the grounds of his application and the order which he seeks[282];
(d) the court will then fix a time, date and place for the application to be heard, of which the applicant should give the liquidator notice, together with copies of the application and supporting affidavit, at least seven days before the date fixed for the hearing[283];
(e) at the first (or any subsequent) hearing, the court may give directions as to which other persons, if any, should likewise be given notice of the application[284];
(f) sealed copies of any order made will be sent by the court to the applicant and the liquidator.[285]

11.17.6 Disclaimer of leaseholds

Where it is leasehold property which is being disclaimed, the following extra rules apply:

(a) By s. 179, provision is made to suspend the disclaimer to enable underlessees or mortgagees to apply for a vesting order under s. 181. By that section the disclaimer will not take effect unless either:
    (i) 14 days has elapsed, from the day on which the last of the requisite notices to underlessees and mortgagees has been served and no application has been made under s. 181 of the Act; or

277. It does not in respect of part liabilities or liabilities discharged by the disclaimer: *Re Yarmarine (IW) Ltd* [1992] BCC 28; *Re No. 1 London Ltd* [1991] BCC 118.
278. IA 1986, s. 181(2)(b) and (4).
279. See para. 11.17.6, *infra*.
280. See Chapter 10.
281. IR 1986, r. 4.194(2).
282. IR 1986, r. 4.194(3).
283. IR 1986, r. 4.194(4).
284. IR 1986, r. 4.194(5).
285. IR 1986, r. 4.194(6).

(ii) the court directs that the disclaimer shall take effect despite such an application having been made.[286]

This section operates to suspend the effect of the disclaimer, not to delay it, so that once the necessary conditions have been met, the disclaimer will be deemed to have taken effect from its date of filing in the normal way.

(b) In cases where s. 179 applies, the court is obliged to lift this suspension and give effect to the disclaimer if it makes a vesting/delivery order under s. 181 of the Act,[287] unless other applications under s. 181 are pending.

(c) If the court refuses to make an order under s. 181 it retains a discretion as to whether or not to give effect to the disclaimer, and thus in these limited circumstances the court may prevent the disclaimer from taking effect at all.[288] It might do this, for example, where disclaimer for the lease would put an end to a guarantor's liability for breach of the tenant's covenants in the lease, and thus leave the landlord without any redress.[289]

(d) Where the court lifts the suspension and gives effect to the disclaimer, and whether or not it is also making a vesting/delivery order under s. 181, it may make such an order as it thinks fit regarding fixtures, tenant's improvements and other matters arising out of the lease.[290]

(e) Vesting property in underlessees or mortgagees: no order will be made under s. 181 vesting leasehold property in any person claiming under the company as underlessee or mortgagee, except on terms that he takes the property subject, either to the same liabilities and obligations as those to which the company was subject at the commencement of the winding-up[291] or, if the court thinks fit, to the same liabilities and obligations as he would have been subject if the lease had been assigned to him at the commencement of the winding-up.[292] If an underlessee or mortgagee refuses to accept an order on these terms, he is excluded from all interest in the property.[293] If there is no underlessee or mortgagee willing to accept an order on such terms, then the court may order that the property be vested in any person who is liable to perform the lessee's covenants in the lease,[294] and may so vest it free from all estates, incumbrances or interests created by the company. In all cases, therefore, where there is an underlessee or mortgagee the court should insist on notice being given to them

286. IA 1986, s. 179(1).
287. IR 1986, r. 4.194(7).
288. IR 1986, r. 4.194(7) appears to be mandatory ("there shall be included in the court's order a direction giving effect to the disclaimer . . . "), but subr. (6) ("any order"), and s. 179(2) of the Act, ("instead of or in addition to any order it makes under section 181 . . . ") presuppose that it must be possible for the court to refuse to make any order at all under s. 181, thus avoiding any obligation to remove the suspension on the effect of the disclaimer imposed by s. 179.
289. See, albeit under the previous regime where leave to disclaim was required, *Re Katherine et Cie* [1932] 1 Ch. 70, contrasting with *Re Distributors & Warehousing Ltd* [1986] BCLC 129. See also, *Re Hans Place* [1992] BCC 737.
290. IA 1986, s. 179(2).
291. IA 1986, s. 182(1)(a).
292. IA 1986, s. 182(1)(b).
293. IA 1986, s. 182(4).
294. IA 1986, s. 182(3); see also *Re AE Realisations (1985) Ltd* [1987] 3 All ER 83.

to give them an opportunity to apply for a vesting order if it is some other person that is applying for a vesting order.

11.17.7 Disclaimer of property subject to rent charge

Property which is disclaimed will often vest automatically in some other person, usually in the Crown as *bona vacantia*. If property subject to a rent charge vests in a person in this way, he will only be liable in respect of any sums becoming due after he, or someone claiming under or through him, has taken possession or control or entered into occupation of the property.[295]

11.18 Rescission of contracts

11.18.1 Introduction

On the application of a person who is, as against the liquidator, entitled to the benefit or subject to the burden of a contract made with the company in liquidation, the court has discretion to rescind the contract on such terms as to the payment by or to either party of damages for the non-performance of the contract or otherwise as the court thinks just.[296] Any damages payable under the order to such a person may be proved by him as a debt in the winding-up.[297]

11.18.2 Procedure and practice

The procedure is that set out in chapter 1 of part 7 to the Insolvency Rules[298]; there are no specific provisions in the Rules dealing with such applications. All applications should be made *inter partes* and the applicant should join as respondents not only the liquidator but any other party who has an interest in the contract. Applications will usually be made where the contract is one of long term supply by the applicant of a company in liquidation and where there is no provision for the automatic termination of such contract upon the insolvency of the company in liquidation. The liquidation of a company will not automatically terminate such a contract in the absence of any express provision. Although the failure by the liquidator to pay any monies outstanding or perform any other acts under the contract will usually amount to a repudiatory breach, there may well be a period of time after the commencement of the liquidation where the party to the contract would be uncertain as to whether the liquidator will or will not repudiate the contract. In these circumstances, the solvent party can apply to the court immediately for a rescission of the contract: in practice, the court will order rescission unless the liquidator undertakes to perform the contract. Although such applications must be made *inter partes*, the court will abridge time for the hearing of the application where, as will be usual, the applicant will need to know as a matter of urgency whether or not the contract will be rescinded.

295. IA 1986, s. 180.
296. IA 1986, s. 186(1).
297. IA 1986, s. 186(2).
298. See Chapter 10.

Applications can also be made for the rescission of contracts capable of specific performance.

11.19 Contributories

11.19.1 Introduction

This section is concerned with applications to the court in connection with the list of contributories which the liquidator of a company in compulsory liquidation is obliged to prepare on behalf of the court and in connection with calls on and payment of debts due from the contributories.

11.19.2 Settlement of contributories

The following provisions apply to a company being wound up by the court. However, in a voluntary liquidation, application can be made to the court to exercise exactly the same powers.[299] After a winding-up order has been made by the court, the court must settle a list of contributories.[300] The court may dispense with the list if it appears that it will not be necessary to make calls on or adjust the rights of contributories.[301] These duties of the court are delegated to the liquidator.[302] The liquidator must, as soon as practical after his appointment, exercise the court's power to settle a list of the company's contributories and may, with the court's approval, rectify the register of members.[303]

If the liquidator decides to postpone or to dispense with settlement of list of contributories then an application must be made to the court. It is usual for such an application to be made *ex parte*.

If the duty to draw up a list of contributories is not dispensed with or postponed, the liquidator must draw up a list which identifies the several classes of the company's shares if more than one,[304] and the several classes of contributories, distinguishing between those who are contributories in their own right and those who are so as representatives of, or liable for the debts of, others.[305] In the case of each contributory there must be stated in the list his address,[306] the number and class of shares, the extent of any other interest to be attributed to him,[307] and if the shares are not fully paid up, the amounts which have been called up and paid in respect of them and the equivalent if any where his interest is other than the shares.[308] The liquidator must then give notice to all those included on the list that the list has been settled.[309] The notice must contain the prescribed particulars[310] and must inform any person to whom it is given that if he objects to any entry in or omission from the list he should so inform the liquidator in writing within 21 days from

299. IA 1986, s. 112.
300. IA 1986, s. 148(1).
301. IA 1986, s. 148(2).
302. IR 1986, r. 4.195.
303. IR 1986, r. 4.196(1).
304. IR 1986, r. 4.197(1)(a).
305. IR 1986, r. 4.197(1)(b).
306. IR 1986, r. 4.197(2)(a).
307. IR 1986, r. 4.197(2)(b).
308. IR 1986, r. 4.197(2)(c).
309. IR 1986, r. 4.198(1).
310. IR 1986, r. 4.198(2).

the date of the notice.[311] On receipt of any such objection the liquidator must, within 14 days, give notice to the objector either that he has amended the list or that he considers the objection not to be well founded and declines to amend the list.[312]

11.19.3 Persons objecting to the list

If any person objects to any entry in or exclusion from the list of contributories and the liquidator maintains his objection, the objector may apply to the court for an order removing the entry to which he objects or, as the case may be, otherwise amending the list.[313] This application must be made within 21 days of the service on the applicant of the liquidator's notice.[314] On any such application to the court all books and papers of the company and of the liquidator are as between the contributories of the company *prima facie* evidence of the truth of all matters purporting to be recorded in them.[315]

11.19.4 Costs orders

A liquidator is only personally liable for any costs incurred by a person in respect of an application to set aside or vary his act or decision in settling the list of contributories or varying or adding to the list if the court makes an order to that effect.[316] An order will often be made against a liquidator if the liquidator's objection is not well founded and he failed to seek the directions of the court. If the directions of the court were sought then it is likely that no such order would be made against the liquidator. If the liquidator is the official receiver then he is not personally liable for any costs in any event.[317]

11.19.5 Calls

The following applies to companies being wound up by the court; in a voluntary liquidation, application can be made for the court to exercise in the voluntary liquidation all the powers that it can exercise in a compulsory liquidation.[318] The liquidator of a company in compulsory liquidation cannot make any call without the special leave of the court or the sanction of the liquidation committee.[319] Leave of the court may be applied for *ex parte* supported by affidavit.[320] The application must state the amount of the proposed call and the contributories on whom it is proposed to be made.[321] The court may direct that notice of any order made by the court in respect of a call be given to the contributories concerned, or to other contributories, or may direct that the notice be publicly advertised.[322] If the liquidator wishes to have payment of the amount due from any contributory enforced by order of the court, notice of the call must be given to each

311. IR 1986, r. 4.198(3).
312. IR 1986, r. 4.198(4).
313. IR 1986, r. 4.199.
314. IR 1986, r. 4.199(2).
315. IA 1986, s. 191.
316. IR 1986, r. 4.201.
317. IR 1986, r. 4.201.
318. IA 1986, s. 112.
319. IA 1986, s. 160(2).
320. IR 1986, r. 4.204(1).
321. IR 1986, r. 4.201(2).
322. IR 1986, r. 4.204(3).

of the contributories concerned, specifying the amount or balance due from him in respect of it and whether the call is made with the sanction of the court or the liquidation committee.[323] The application follows the practice and procedure set out in chapter 1 of part 7 of the Insolvency Rules.[324] After the hearing of the application, the court may order payment of the amount due from any contributory.[325] An order made by the court against a contributory is, subject to any right of appeal, conclusive evidence that the money appearing to be due or order to be paid is due.[326] The court also has power to arrest a contributory and seize his books, papers and moveable personal property if he is about to leave the United Kingdom, otherwise abscond or remove or conceal any of his property for the purpose of evading payment of calls.[327]

11.19.6 Other debts due from contributories

At any time after the making of a winding-up order, the court can order a contributory on the list of contributories to pay in such manner as the court may direct any money due from him or from the estate of the person he represents, to the company, exclusive of any money payable by virtue of any call.[328] In a voluntary liquidation, application may be made to the court for the court to exercise the same powers as it has in a compulsory liquidation.[329]

11.20 Removal of liquidators

11.20.1 Where the company is being wound up by the court

A liquidator may be removed from office only by a court order or by a general meeting of the company's creditors summoned specially for that purpose under the rules.[330] There are restrictions on the convening of a meeting of creditors for this purpose in certain cases.[331] The restrictions are that the meeting can only be summoned if:

(i) the liquidator thinks fit; or
(ii) the court so directs; or
(iii) the meeting is requested in accordance with the rules by not less than one-quarter in value of the creditors.

These restrictions apply:

(a) where the official receiver is the liquidator otherwise than in succession under s. 136(3) to a person who held office as a result of a nomination by a meeting of the company's creditors or contributories; or
(b) the liquidator was appointed by the court otherwise than under s. 139(4)(a) or s. 140(1) or was appointed by the Secretary of State.

323. IR 1986, r. 4.205(1); Form 4.58.
324. See Chapter 10.
325. See form 4.59 for the form of order.
326. IA 1986, s. 152(1).
327. IA 1986, s. 158.
328. IA 1986, s. 149(1).
329. IA 1986, s. 112.
330. IA 1986, s. 172(2).
331. IA 1986, s. 172(3).

It follows that there are no restrictions where:

(i) the liquidator was originally appointed by a meeting of the company's creditors or contributories[332]; or
(ii) the official receiver is liquidator in succession to a person so appointed[333]; or
(iii) the liquidator was a nominee of the contributories whom the court appointed liquidator either jointly with or instead of a nominee of the creditors[334]; or
(iv) the liquidator was formerly the administrator of the company who was appointed by the court when the winding-up order was made immediately upon the discharge of the administration order.[335]

A provisional liquidator can only be removed by order of the court.[336]

As a matter of practice, the court will be reluctant to entertain an application for the removal of a liquidator where the grounds relied upon can more conveniently be put to a creditors' meeting and the wish of the majority of the creditors thereby ascertained. On the hearing of any application, the court has power to convene a creditors' meeting to consider a revolution for the liquidator's removal, directing when and where it should be held.[337] Alternatively, the court may convene a creditors' meeting simply to obtain their views, without any formal resolution being put to them. As the replacement of a liquidator will increase the costs of the liquidation, the court will require good reasons before it is satisfied that a liquidator should be replaced but it is only necessary to show that the removal would be for the advantage of the creditors or members generally and not that there has been any misconduct or that the liquidator is personally unfit.[338]

11.20.2 Application to the court

The application will invariably be by way of originating application and must set out the grounds on which the application is made. It is subject to initial court scrutiny and will be placed before the registrar for him to consider. He may dismiss the application if no sufficient cause is shown, but he must not do so unless the applicant has had an opportunity to attend the court for an *ex parte* hearing of which he shall have been given at least seven days' notice.[339] If the application is not dismissed, the court must fix a date, time and place for the hearing of the application.[340] A deposit or security for the costs to

332. IA 1986, s. 172(2).
333. IA 1986, s. 172(3)(a).
334. IA 1986, s. 139(4)(a).
335. IA 1986, s. 140(1).
336. IA 1986, s. 172(2).
337. IA 1986, s. 195(1).
338. *Re Keypak Homecare Ltd* (1987) 3 BCC 558 (liquidator's attitude to investigating claims against former directors too complacent); *Re Sir John Moore Gold Mining Co.* (1879) 12 Ch.D. 325 (liquidator refused to take action against directors with whom he was intimate); *Re Charterland Goldfields* (1909) 26 TLR 132 (liquidator had close business connections with directors of the company who were also directors of other companies which had had dealings with the company of which he was liquidator); *Re Corbenstoke Ltd (No. 2)* (1989) 5 BCC 767 (liquidator was trustee in bankruptcy of the main shareholder and had been a director of the company in liquidation); *Re Edennote* [1996] BCC 718 (liquidator who was honest and whose integrity and good faith was accepted was not removed even though he had made a serious mistake, as there were no adequate grounds for a reasonable loss of creditors' confidence).
339. IR 1986, r. 4.119(2).
340. IR 1986, r. 4.119(2).

be incurred by the liquidator may be required on any such application[341] because unless otherwise ordered, the costs of the application are not payable out of the assets.[342] The applicant must, at least 14 days before the hearing, send to the liquidator and the official receiver a notice stating the time and place of the hearing and accompanying it with a copy of the application and any evidence which he intends to adduce in support of it.[343] At the first *inter partes* hearing, the registrar will give directions for the further conduct of the application. If the liquidator is removed by the court, the order can include any provision the court thinks fit with respect to his removal.[344] Copies of the order will be sent to the liquidator who has been removed and to the official receiver.

11.20.3 Voluntary liquidation

A liquidator in a voluntary winding-up can only be removed by an order of the court or, in the case of a members' voluntary winding-up, by a resolution of the court in general meeting passed at a meeting summoned for that purpose or, in the case of a creditors' voluntary winding-up, by a resolution of the company's creditors passed at a meeting summoned for that purpose.[345] On an application to the court, cause must be shown for the removal of the liquidator.[346] Where the liquidator has been appointed by the court under s. 108 of the Act, the respective meetings of the members or creditors may only be called if the liquidator agrees, the court directs or one half of the members or creditors, respectively, require it.[347]

11.20.4 Application to the court

The procedure[348] for applying for the removal of a liquidator or for a direction that the liquidator be ordered to summon a creditors' meeting for that purpose, is the same as that in respect of a company being wound up by the court[349] with one exception: namely, two copies of the order removing him will be sent to him, one of which must be sent by him forthwith to the registrar of companies with notice of his ceasing to act. No copy will be sent to the official receiver.

11.20.5 Members' application to remove the creditors' nominee as liquidator in a voluntary liquidation

In a creditors' voluntary liquidation, the liquidator is initially the person nominated to be liquidator by the members. If, subsequently, at their first meeting, the creditors nominate somebody other than the members' appointee to be liquidator, their wishes prevail and their nominee immediately takes office as liquidator.[350] However, any director, member or

341. IR 1986, r. 4.119(3).
342. IR 1986, r. 4.119(5).
343. IR 1986, r. 4.119(4).
344. IR 1986, r. 4.119(6)(b).
345. IA 1986, s. 171.
346. IA 1986, s. 108(2).
347. IA 1986, s. 171(3).
348. IR 1986, r. 4.120.
349. See para. 11.20.2, *supra*.
350. IA 1986, s. 100(2).

creditor may, within seven days after the date on which the nomination was made by the creditors, apply to the court for an order either directing that the person nominated as liquidator by the members shall be liquidator instead of or jointly with the person nominated by the creditors or appointing some other person to be liquidator instead of the person nominated by the creditors.[351] The application will be by way of originating application.[352] The respondent to the application should be the liquidator appointed by the creditors. At the first hearing, the court will as a matter of practice determine how notice of the application is to be given to the creditors and members and what order, if any, should be made in respect of any one or more creditors or members representing the interests of other creditors or members.

11.20.6 Release of liquidator

The release of a liquidator discharges the liquidator from all liability both in respect of acts or omissions of his in the winding-up and otherwise in relation to his conduct as liquidator but does not prevent the court from subsequently exercising its powers under s. 212 of the Act.[353] Except in the case of a provisional liquidator, the court plays no role in the release of a liquidator, the release taking place either in accordance with the prescribed rules or by the order of the Secretary of State. A provisional liquidator must apply to the court for his release.

11.21 Expenses of the liquidation

11.21.1 Compulsory liquidations

The court may, in the event of the assets being insufficient to satisfy the liabilities, make an order as to the payment out of the assets of the expenses incurred in the winding-up in such order of priority as the court thinks just.[354]

11.21.2 Voluntary liquidations

All expenses properly incurred in the winding-up, including the remuneration of the liquidator, are payable out of the company's assets in priority to all other claims.[355] In a voluntary liquidation the liquidator or any contributory or creditor may apply to the court for it to exercise any of the powers which the court might exercise if the company were being wound up by the court.[356] Thus, the liquidator or any contributory or creditor may apply to the court for an order that all or any of the expenses incurred in the winding-up be paid otherwise than in priority to all other claims.

11.21.3 What are "the company's assets"?

Under the predecessor of the Insolvency Act it was clearly established that "assets" from which expenses were payable did not include assets held on trust or subject to a fixed

351. IA 1986, s. 100(3).
352. IR 1986, r. 7.1; Chapter 10.
353. IA 1986, ss. 173(4) and 174(6).
354. IA 1986, s. 156.
355. IA 1986, s. 115.
356. IA 1986, s. 112(1).

charge but did include all other assets including assets subject to a floating charge at the commencement of the liquidation and that the expenses were payable out of such assets in priority to all other claims unless the court ordered otherwise.[357] The position is the same under the Insolvency Act 1986[358] with one difference: a floating charge is now defined[359] as a charge which *as created* was a floating charge, so that expenses are payable now out of an asset which was subject to fixed charges at the commencement of the liquidation if, when that charge was first created over that asset, it was a floating charge.[360]

11.21.4 What are "the expenses"?

The expenses which are payable out of *such* assets are *only*[361] those expenses listed in r. 4.218.

11.21.5 R. 4.218(1)(a): "expenses properly chargeable or incurred . . . in preserving, realising or getting in any of the assets of the company"

A payment of rent can be an expense incurred in preserving an asset of the company if made by the liquidator to avoid forfeiture of a lease.[362] If the liquidator refuses to pay rent, the landlord can apply for the rent to be paid as an expense in the liquidation.[363]

11.21.6 Applications: compulsory liquidation

If there is a dispute as to:

(a) whether any post-liquidation debt incurred by the liquidator or on behalf of the company in the course of the winding-up of the company is properly owing; and/or
(b) whether it is an "expense" in the liquidation and payable out of the "assets"; and/or
(c) in what priority it should be paid;

then the liquidator can apply for directions[364] and an order as to the priority of payment. Any person aggrieved with an act or decision of the liquidator, including his failure to apply for such directions or orders, can apply to the court and the court can make such order as it considers just.[365] The application must follow the practice and procedure set out

357. *Re Barleycorn Ltd* [1970] Ch. 465. In exceptional circumstances, costs incurred by a liquidator can be paid from trust assets: *Re Berkeley Applegate (Investment Consultants) Ltd (No. 2)* [1989] 1 Ch. 32; *Re Telesure Ltd* [1997] BCC 580.
358. *Re MC Bacon Ltd (No. 2)* [1990] BCLC 607.
359. IA 1986, s. 251.
360. *Re Portbase (Clothing) Ltd* [1993] BCC 96.
361. *Re MC Bacon Ltd (No. 2)* [1990] BCLC 607; but see *Re Kentish Homes Ltd* [1993] BCC 212 where it was assumed that there was a wider discretion.
362. *Re Linda Marie Ltd* (1988) 4 BCC 463.
363. *Re Oak Pits Colliery Co.* (1882) 21 Ch.D. 322; *Re Downer Enterprises Ltd* [1974] 1 WLR 1460; *Re Atlantic Computer Systems plc* [1990] BCC 859; *Re Kentish Homes Ltd* [1993] BCC 212. In respect of non-domestic rates, see *Re Nolton Business Centres* [1996] BCC 500.
364. IA 1986, s. 168(3).
365. IA 1986, s. 168(5).

in chapter 1 of part 7 of the Insolvency Rules[366] and directions should be sought from the court on the first hearing as to which other interested parties should be given notice of the application.

11.21.7 Applications: voluntary liquidations

Similar applications can be made by the liquidator or any creditor or contributory. It is considered that "creditor" includes a post-liquidation creditor.[367]

11.22 The costs of applications in liquidation

11.22.1 Introduction

Para. 11.22 supplements the discussion of costs in Chapter 10.[368]

11.22.2 Where the liquidator is a party

If the liquidator personally is the applicant but is unsuccessful, the normal rule is that costs follow the event[369] and the liquidator is personally liable to pay any costs so ordered[370]; however, unless the liquidator has been guilty of misconduct, he is entitled to ask the court for an order that he recoup such costs from the assets of the insolvent estate.[371]

> "A company in winding-up ought to be dealt with as a matter of course like any other litigant, and if an action be brought or resisted for the benefit of the estate, and that action be brought fruitlessly or defended fruitlessly, then the estate, that is to say, the other creditors, ought, like everybody else, to be fixed with the costs to which they have improperly and unnecessarily put their opponent."[372]

11.22.3 From which assets are such costs payable?

The costs are payable only out of the assets available for distribution to the general body of creditors and are not "expenses of the liquidation" within r. 4.218(1) so as to make them payable out of floating charge assets.[373]

11.22.4 Where the company in liquidation is a party

Where it is the company and not the liquidator that is party to the proceedings and ordered to pay the costs of the litigation, the successful litigant is *prima facie* entitled to be paid in full (at least in respect of the costs incurred after the liquidation) from the assets, in priority to pre-liquidation creditors and ahead of the general expenses of the liquidation,[374]

366. See Chapter 10.
367. However, the point was expressly left open in *Re Movitex* [1992] 1 WLR 303.
368. See Chapter 10, paras 10.53–4.
369. IR 1986, r. 7.33(a); RSC O. 62, r. 3(3).
370. *Metalloy Supplies Ltd* v. *MA (UK) Ltd* [1997] BCC 165.
371. *Re Silver Valley Mines* (1882) 21 Ch.D. 381; *Re Wilson Lovatt & Sons Ltd* [1977] 1 All ER 274; *Re MC Bacon (No. 2)* [1990] BCLC 607.
372. Per James V.C. in *Bailey and Leetham's Case* (1869) LR 8 Eq. 94 at 97.
373. *Re MC Bacon (No. 2)* [1990] BCLC 607 at 615.
374. *Re Home Investment Society* (1880) 14 Ch.D. 167; *Re Dominion of Canada Plumbago Co.* (1884) 27 Ch.D. 33; *Re London Metallurgical Co.* [1895] 1 Ch. 758; *Re Movitex Ltd* [1990] BCC 491 (Mervyn Davies J. at first instance).

but not out of any assets subject to a trust or charge, including assets subject to a floating charge.[375] *Prima facie*, the costs are immediately payable by the liquidator.[376] The onus is on the liquidator at the time the order is made to show that the condition and value of the assets from which payment is to be made are such that, taken together with such other creditors who are to be paid in priority or *pari passu*,[377] the other payment should be postponed until a later date.[378] Where it is the liquidator who is personally a party, the court also has a discretion to order the costs of the successful party to be paid out of the assets of the company and not by the liquidator personally,[379] in which case the position is exactly the same as above.

11.23 The liquidator's remuneration

11.23.1 Official receiver as liquidator

Where the official receiver is liquidator, the official receiver's fees are in accordance with a fixed scale.[380] Unlike the situation where the liquidator is not the official receiver, there is no jurisdiction in the court to order the remuneration of the official receiver to be determined on any other basis or for any other sum than that laid down in the fixed scales. If any creditor or contributory or other liquidator of the same company is of the opinion that the official receiver has failed to exercise the due care, skill and diligence to be expected of a liquidator, the court can examine the conduct of the official receiver and compel him to contribute such sum to the company's assets by way of compensation in respect of such breach of duty to the company as the court thinks just.[381]

11.23.2 Liquidators other than the official receiver

Applications to the court in respect of the remuneration of a liquidator who is not the official receiver are not common. The liquidator's remuneration is a matter to be determined by the liquidation committee or, if there is none or it fails to make any determination, by a resolution of the creditors or, if not fixed by resolution of the liquidation committee or the creditors, by the scale laid down for the official receiver.[382] It is only if the liquidator or the creditors are unsatisfied with the remuneration as so determined or fixed, that applications are made to the court.

11.23.3 Basis of a liquidator's remuneration

A liquidator is entitled to receive remuneration for his services.[383] This is to be fixed either as a percentage of the value of the assets which are realised or distributed, or of the one

375. *Re MC Bacon (No. 2)* [1990] BCLC 607.
376. Except in exceptional circumstances, the costs are not payable by him personally as he is a non-party: *Metalloy Supplies Ltd* [1997] BCC 165.
377. *Re London Metallurgical Co.* [1895] 1 Ch. 758.
378. *Ibid.*
379. I.e., other post-liquidation creditors.
380. See the Insolvency Fees Order 1986 and the Insolvency Regulations 1986, as amended.
381. IA 1986, s. 212; see para. 11.12.
382. IR 1986, r. 4.127(3), (5) and (6).
383. IR 1986, r. 4.127.

value and the other in combination,[384] or by reference to the time properly given by the insolvency practitioner and his staff in attending to matters arising in the winding-up.[385] Where the liquidator is not the official receiver, the basis and the amount of the remuneration of the liquidator is determined by the liquidation committee.[386] The committee must have regard to the complexity or otherwise of the case,[387] any respects in which, in connection with the winding-up, there falls on the insolvency practitioner as liquidator any responsibility of an exceptional kind or degree,[388] the effectiveness with which the insolvency practitioner appears to be carrying out, or to have carried out, his duties as liquidator,[389] and the value and nature of the assets with which the liquidator has to deal.[390] If there is no liquidation committee or the committee does not make the requisite determination, the remuneration may be fixed by resolution of a meeting of creditors who must take into account the same matters as a liquidation committee.[391] If the liquidator considers the rate or amount of the remuneration fixed by the liquidation committee to be insufficient, he may request that it be increased by resolution of the creditors.[392] If not fixed by the liquidation committee or the creditors, the remuneration is in accordance with the scale laid down for the official receiver.[393]

11.23.4 Liquidator dissatisfied with remuneration

If the liquidator is dissatisfied with his remuneration, howsoever determined, he may apply to the court for an order increasing its amount or rate.[394] The liquidator must give at least 14 days' notice of his application to the members of the liquidation committee and the committee may nominate one or more members to appear or be represented, and to be heard, on the application.[395] If there is no liquidation committee, then on the first hearing of the application the court will determine which creditor or creditors should be given notice of the application who may then nominate one or more of their number to appear or be represented at an adjourned hearing.[396] The court will be anxious to avoid costs being unnecessarily incurred and will normally order that one creditor or member of the liquidation committee, represents all other creditors or member if they all have the same interest. Where the dispute is between the liquidator and the liquidation committee, the court may well order a meeting of creditors to be held under s. 195 of the Insolvency Act to ascertain the wishes of the creditors or contributories.

11.23.5 Creditors dissatisfied with liquidator's remuneration

The Insolvency Rules provide that any creditor of the company may, with the concurrence of at least 25% in value of the creditors including himself, apply to the court for an order

384. IR 1986, r. 4.127(2)(a).
385. IR 1986, r. 4.127(2)(b).
386. IR 1986, r. 4.127(3).
387. IR 1986, r. 4.127(4)(a).
388. IR 1986, r. 4.127(4)(b).
389. IR 1986, r. 4.127(4)(c).
390. IR 1986, r. 4.127(4)(d).
391. IR 1986, r. 4.127(5).
392. IR 1986, r. 4.129.
393. IR 1986, r. 4.127(6); see note 391, *infra*.
394. IR 1986, r. 4.130(1).
395. IR 1986, r. 4.130(2).
396. IR 1986, r. 4.130(3).

that the liquidator's remuneration be reduced on the grounds that it is in all the circumstances excessive.[397] The procedure on such applications is unusual in that, upon filing of such an application, the court subjects it to scrutiny to see if it can be said that it shows no sufficient cause for a reduction in the remuneration. If such a view is formed then seven days notice must be given to the applicant to attend an *ex parte* hearing to justify such a reduction as is claimed in the application.[398] If the application is to go forward, the court will fix a time, date and place for the hearing of the application as in the case of any other application.[399] The applicant must then give 14 days notice of the hearing to the liquidator, accompanied by a copy of the application and any evidence which the applicant intends to adduce in support of it.[400] The application then proceeds as it would on an application by the liquidator to increase his remuneration.

11.23.6 Dissatisfied debenture holders and preferential creditors

It is not infrequently the case that the remuneration comes out of assets which would otherwise not be available for distribution to the unsecured creditors, but which would be paid either to the preferential creditors or the holders of debentures over assets which as created were subject to floating charges.[401] No express provision is made in the Rules for such creditors to be able to challenge the remuneration of the liquidator. This could result in injustice to such creditors and it is considered that the court would be willing to entertain applications by such creditors under the court's jurisdiction to give directions.[402]

11.23.7 Evidence on application

Evidence is almost invariably given by affidavit. Although the registrars have built up considerable experience in determining questions of reasonableness of remuneration, expert evidence should also be considered.

11.23.8 Costs

If, on a liquidator's application, the court considers it to be a proper case, the costs of the application including the costs of any member of the liquidation committee appearing or being represented on it or any creditor so appearing or being represented may be ordered to be paid out of the assets.[403] However, on an application by a creditor, unless the court otherwise orders, the costs of the application shall be paid by the applicant and not payable out of the assets.[404] Although "assets" are not defined, it is considered that it is a reference to those assets from which the remuneration is normally payable.[405]

397. IR 1986, r. 4.131(1).
398. IR 1986, r. 4.131(2).
399. IR 1986, r. 4.131(2).
400. IR 1986, r. 4.131(3).
401. IA 1986, s. 175.
402. IA 1986, s. 112, in the case of liquidators of companies in voluntary liquidation, and under the inherent jurisdiction of the court to control its own officers in the case of a liquidator of a company being compulsorily wound up by the court.
403. IR 1986, r. 4.130(4).
404. IR 1986, r. 4.131(5).
405. See para. 11.21.3, *supra*.

11.23.9 Remuneration for selling assets on behalf of a secured creditor

Where the liquidator sells assets on behalf of a secured creditor, he is entitled to take for himself, out of the proceeds of sale, a sum by way of remuneration equivalent to that which is chargeable in corresponding circumstances by the official receiver under general regulations.[406] The sale must be in circumstances in which the secured creditor was entitled himself to sell the asset but requested the liquidator to sell it on his behalf.

11.23.10 Trust assets

Liquidators are not automatically entitled to remuneration as liquidators for work done in respect of assets held by the company on trust, but the court has jurisdiction to allow remuneration to be paid out of the trust assets if it thinks it appropriate.[407]

11.23.11 Joint liquidators' remuneration

Where there are joint liquidators, it is for them to agree between themselves as to how the remuneration payable should be apportioned. Any dispute arising between them may be referred to the court for settlement by order or to the liquidation committee or a meeting of creditors for settlement by resolution.[408] The referral to the court for settlement by order takes place by way of application following the normal procedure.[409]

11.24 Dissolution of a company

11.24.1 Introduction

A company ceases to exist at the point when it is dissolved. "Unlike a natural person, however, a company which has ceased to exist may be restored to life."[410] A company can only be restored to life as a result of a court order. Before considering the practice and procedure of the court in restoring such companies, it is necessary to consider the different ways in which a company may be dissolved.

11.24.2 Dissolution: voluntary liquidation

In a voluntary liquidation, the company is deemed to be dissolved three months after the final account and return[411] has been sent by the liquidator to the registrar of companies and registered.[412] However, any person who appears to be interested may apply to the court for an order deferring the date on which such dissolution is to take effect.[413] Such an

406. IR 1986, r. 4.128(1).
407. *Re Berkeley Applegate (Investment Consultants) (No. 2)* [1989] Ch. 32; *Re Berkeley Applegate (Investment Consultants) (No. 3)* (1989) 5 BCC 803; *Re Eastern Capital Futures Ltd* (1989) 5 BCC 223.
408. IR 1986, r. 4.128(2).
409. See Chapter 10.
410. Hoffmann L.J. in *Re Forte's (Manufacturing) Ltd* [1994] BCC 84 at 85.
411. Produced pursuant to IA 1986, ss. 94(1) or 106(1).
412. IA 1986, s. 201(1) and (2).
413. IA 1986, s. 201(3).

application follows the practice and procedure set out in chapter 1 of part 7 of the Insolvency Rules.[414] The successful applicant must deliver a copy of such order to the registrar of companies for registration, within seven days.[415]

11.24.3 Dissolution: compulsory liquidation

In a compulsory liquidation, the company will be dissolved three months after the registration with the registrar of companies of a notice from the liquidator that a final meeting of creditors has been held, or of a notice from the official receiver that the winding-up is complete.[416] The official receiver or any person who appears to be interested may apply to the Secretary of State for Trade and Industry, who may give a direction deferring, for such period as he thinks fit, the date on which the dissolution will take effect.[417] It is the duty of the successful applicant to deliver a copy of any such direction obtained to the registrar of companies for registration.[418]

11.24.4 Procedure for early dissolution

Where the official receiver is the liquidator, a procedure exists for dissolving a company which is hopelessly insolvent without incurring the expense of a winding-up.[419] Under this procedure, the official receiver may apply to the registrar of companies for the early dissolution of the company,[420] which will then occur automatically three months later,[421] unless the Secretary of State intervenes by exercising his power to give directions.[422] The application will be registered on receipt by the registrar.[423] Before invoking this procedure, the official receiver must conclude both that the realisable assets of the company are insufficient to cover the expenses of the winding-up and that the affairs of the company do not require further investigation.[424] Before making the application, the official receiver must give the creditors and contributories, and any administrative receiver, 28 days' notice of his intention to make the application,[425] and they then have the opportunity to apply to the Secretary of State for directions. The service of the notice on the creditors, contributories and any administrative receiver exonerates the official receiver from performing any duties imposed on him in relation to the company, its creditors or contributories by virtue of any provision of the Act, and his only duty is then to make application to the registrar for early dissolution.[426]

414. See Chapter 10.
415. IA 1986, s. 201(4).
416. IA 1986, s. 205(1)(a), (b) and (2).
417. IA 1986, s. 205(3).
418. IA 1986, s. 205(6) and (7).
419. IA 1986, ss. 202 and 203.
420. IA 1986, s. 202(2).
421. IA 1986, s. 202(5).
422. IA 1986, s. 202(5).
423. IA 1986, s. 202(4).
424. IA 1986, s. 202(2)(b).
425. IA 1986, s. 202(3).
426. IA 1986, s. 202(4).

11.24.5 Grounds

The grounds on which the application for directions may be made are[427]:

(a) that the realisable assets of the company are sufficient to cover the expenses of the winding-up;
(b) that the affairs of the company do require further investigation; or
(c) that for any other reason the early dissolution of the company is inappropriate.

Where one of these grounds is established, the Secretary of State may give a direction making such provision as he thinks fit for enabling the winding-up of the company to proceed as if no notice had been given.[428] He may also give a direction deferring the date on which the dissolution is to take effect for such period as he thinks fit.[429] An application for directions may be made by a person other than a creditor, contributory or administrative receiver, if that person appears to the Secretary of State to be "interested".[430] It is not clear whether directions must be given by the Secretary of State before the end of the three-month period in all cases, or only in those cases where the application for directions is made by the official receiver or an interested person under s. 202(5). Where the Secretary of State gives a direction under s. 203, he must send two copies of the direction to the applicant, and the applicant must, in turn, send one copy to the registrar of companies within seven days.[431]

11.24.6 Appeal

An appeal lies to the court from any decision of the Secretary of State on any application for directions made under s. 203.[432] The application must be made in accordance with the procedure set out in chapter 1 of part 7 of the Insolvency Rules.[433] The Secretary of State should be made the respondent. Following an appeal, the court sends two sealed copies of its order to the person in whose favour the appeal was determined, and that party must send one of the copies to the registrar of companies within seven days.[434]

11.24.7 Dissolution by the registrar of companies

The registrar of companies has power to dissolve companies in three cases:

(1) The first is where the registrar of companies has reasonable cause to believe that the company is not carrying on business or in operation.[435] This might occur, for example, where a company has failed to file its annual returns. The registrar of

427. IA 1986, s. 203(2).
428. IA 1986, s. 203(3)(a).
429. IA 1986, s. 203(3)(b).
430. IA 1986, s. 202(5).
431. IR 1986, r. 4.224 and IA 1986, s. 203(5).
432. IA 1986, s. 203(4).
433. See Chapter 10.
434. IR 1986, r. 4.225 and IA 1986, s. 203(5).
435. CA 1985, s. 652(1).

companies in such a case may post a letter to the company[436] inquiring whether or not it is carrying on business or in operation. If he receives no reply to that letter within a month of sending it, he will, within 14 days from the expiry of that month, send a follow up letter, this time by registered post.[437] If no answer is received to this letter within a month from its date, or if an answer is received to the effect that the company is not carrying on a business or in operation, a notice may be published in the *Gazette* stating that after three months from the notice, and unless the contrary is shown, the company's name will be struck off the register and the company will be dissolved.[438]

(2) The second case is where the company is being wound up, and the registrar of companies has reasonable cause to believe either that no liquidator is acting, or that the affairs of the company have been fully wound up, and the appropriate returns have not been made by the liquidator for a period of six months. In such a case, the registrar of companies will publish in the *Gazette* and send to the company[439] or the liquidator[440] (if there is one), a notice stating that, after three months, and unless the contrary is shown, the company's name will be struck off the register and the company will be wound up.[441]

(3) The third applies where a private company itself applies for the company's name to be struck off the register of companies[442] on the grounds that the company has not traded or engaged in any other activity (except paying its debts) for three months. In such a case, the registrar of companies will publish in the *Gazette* a notice stating that he may exercise his power to strike the company's name off the register and will invite any person to show cause why he should not do so.[443]

11.24.8 Striking off

In any of the above cases, after the expiry of the three-month period, if cause to the contrary is not shown, the registrar of companies may strike the company's name off the register and publish notice to that effect in the *Gazette*, on which publication the company is dissolved. Where the registrar of companies has dissolved a company in this way, any liability of directors, managing officers and members of the company remains intact and may be enforced as if the company had not been dissolved,[444] and the power of the court to wind up the company remains unaffected.[445]

436. At its registered office if one has been registered, failing which the letter may be sent to the care of some officer of the company, or if no such address is known, to the address set out in the memorandum of each of its subscribers: CA 1985, s. 652(7).

437. CA 1985, s. 652(2).

438. CA 1985, s. 652(3).

439. See note 436, *supra*.

440. At his last known place of business, CA 1985, s. 652(7); the last known place of business within the jurisdiction is not suitable if a later address abroad is known: *R.* v. *Farmer* [1892] 1 QB 637, [1891–4] All ER 921, C.A.

441. CA 1985, s. 652(4).

442. CA 1985, s. 652A(1), inserted by the Deregulation and Contracting Out Act 1994, s. 13(1), sch. 5, paras 1 and 2, as from 1 July 1995.

443. CA 1986, s. 652A(3).

444. CA 1985, ss. 652(6)(a) and 652A(6).

445. CA 1985, ss. 652(6)(b) and 652A(7).

11.24.9 Re-opening a dissolution

Each mode of dissolution, set out above, prescribes its own procedure under which certain persons may object to the dissolution of the company. Even after dissolution, limited avenues of challenge remain.

11.24.10 Declaring the dissolution to have been void

The main such avenue of challenge is provided for by s. 651 of the Companies Act 1985, under which the court may make an order, on such terms as it thinks fit, declaring the dissolution to be void. An application may be made under this section even in respect of companies dissolved by the registrar of companies pursuant to ss. 652 and 652A of the Act and is an additional remedy to that provided by virtue of s. 653.[446]

An application for such an order should be made by originating motion if the company has not been wound up but by originating summons if it has.[447] It may be made by the erstwhile liquidator of the company, or any other person appearing to the court to be interested.[448] A person who has an unsatisfied claim against the dissolved company, for example, is entitled to apply.[449]

11.24.11 Notice to Crown

Notice of the application must also be given to the Crown, in whom the property of the company will have vested as *bona vacantia* on dissolution.[450] Such notice should be given through the Treasury Solicitor, who will usually confirm by letter that the Crown has no objection to the restoration. The application should be supported by an affidavit stating that the Treasury Solicitor consents to the restoration, a matter which can usually be established by exhibiting a copy of the Treasury Solicitor's letter to the affidavit.[451] Notice should also be given to the registrar of companies.

The court will not automatically grant relief to an applicant who shows he is entitled to apply,[452] although there will naturally be a considerable overlap between showing oneself to be an interested person, and explaining why the dissolution needs to be avoided. A liquidator might wish to apply, for example, in order to distribute assets which have been realised since the dissolution and which would otherwise vest in the Crown as *bona vacantia*.[453] Equally, a person might wish to pursue a claim against the dissolved company, particularly one in respect of which the company was insured.[454] In a recent case,

446. Where application is made for restoration under that section, the applicant may apply in the alternative for an order under s. 651—see *Re Thompson & Riches Ltd* [1981] 1 WLR 682.

447. RSC O. 102, r. 3(1)(f); *Re Scicon Consultancy International Ltd* [1992] BCC 385.

448. CA 1985, s. 651(1).

449. *Re Spottiswood, Dixon and Hunting Ltd* [1912] 1 Ch. 410, [1911–13] All ER 526.

450. See *Practice Note* [1952] WN 170; *Re Home and Colonial Insurance Co. Ltd* (1928) 44 TLR 718.

451. *Re Belmont & Co. Ltd* [1952] Ch. 10 at 15.

452. *Re Thompson & Riches Ltd* [1981] 2 All ER 477, [1981] 1 WLR 682.

453. CA 1985, s. 654.

454. See Third Parties (Rights Against Insurers) Act 1930, and *Bradley* v. *Eagle Star Insurance Co. Ltd* [1989] AC 957.

Re Forte's (Manufacturing) Ltd,[455] the Court of Appeal restored a company to the register in order that a landlord could claim against an original tenant on its liabilities for the default of the eventual tenant, which was in insolvent liquidation. In many cases, the rule that prior distributions on insolvency cannot be disturbed will stand in the way of a party receiving any benefit from the restoration of the company. However, in that case there was a chance that the company could itself claim an indemnity in respect of the landlord's claim from intervening assignees of the term, and that chance was held sufficient to grant the landlord an interest and justify the restoration of the company.

11.24.12 Time limits

The time limits are the main practical restriction on this jurisdiction to declare the dissolution void. The standard limitation period expires after two years from the date of the dissolution of the company.[456] Where the application is made for the purpose of bringing proceedings against the company for damages, either in respect of personal injuries[457] or under the Fatal Accidents Act 1976, a different period applies. Such an application may be made at any time, but no order will be granted if it appears to the court that the proceedings would fail by virtue of the expiry of the limitation periods governing that cause of action.[458] However, as one of the terms on which it makes the order, the court may direct that the period between the dissolution of the company and the making of the order shall not count for the purposes of such limitation periods.[459] It has recently been held that, by contrast with the equivalent power in s. 653,[460] s. 651 does not confer a general jurisdiction to make such a "limitation override order" where the application is brought for purposes other than those set out in subs. (5).[461] In most cases this will make little difference, since periods of limitation generally cease to run at the point when a winding-up is commenced, whether voluntary or compulsory.[462]

If the court makes the order the dissolution is declared to have been void for all purposes, not for a limited purpose only,[463] such proceedings may be taken as might have been taken if the company had not been dissolved[464] but the validity of proceedings brought between dissolution and avoidance is not affected,[465] so to that extent the declaration is not retrospective.

455. [1994] BCC 84.
456. CA 1985, s. 651(4).
457. As defined by CA 1985, s. 651(7) to include any disease and any impairment of a person's physical or mental condition, and including any sum claimed by virtue of the Law Reform (Miscellaneous Provisions) Act 1934 (funeral expenses)—CA 1985, s. 651(5)(a).
458. CA 1985, s. 651(5).
459. CA 1985, s. 651(6).
460. See para. 11.24.14, *infra*.
461. *Re Mixhurst Ltd* [1993] BCC 748.
462. *Re General Rolling Stock Co.* (1872) LR 7 Ch. App. 646; *Re Mixhurst Ltd* [1993] BCC 748 at 751 B–C.
463. *Re Champdany Jute Co. Ltd* [1924] SC 209.
464. CA 1985, s. 651(2).
465. *Morris* v. *Harris* [1927] AC 252, [1926] All ER 15, H.L.; *Re Lewis and Smart Ltd* [1954] 2 All ER 19, [1954] 1 WLR 755; *Re Mixhurst Ltd* [1993] BCC 748; *Re Philip Powis Ltd*, unreported, 25 April 1997 (Sir John Knox).

11.24.13 Notice to registrar

As with challenges to dissolution before it occurs, the successful applicant must, within seven days of the order (or under this section, such further period as the court shall allow), deliver a copy of the order to the registrar of companies.[466]

11.24.14 Restoration to the register of companies

Where a company has been dissolved by the registrar pursuant to s. 652 Companies Act 1985, the dissolved company, or any person who was a member or creditor of it when it was dissolved,[467] may apply to have the company restored to the register.[468] Clearly there is an element of fiction in an application by the company, since notionally it no longer exists. In practice, this fiction may not be as apparent, since it is relatively common for a functioning company which has, for example, failed to file returns and moved from its registered office without updating the register, to be dissolved by the registrar without being aware of the fact. Indeed it may only be future litigation, or an attempt to wind up the company, which brings the dissolution to light. Moreover, the fiction is equally applicable to creditors and members: there can be no creditors or members of a company which does not exist.

An application under this section should be made by petition,[469] and must be made before the expiry of a 20-year period from the time of dissolution. Notice should be given to the Treasury Solicitor and confirmation sought to the effect that the Crown has no objection to the restoration of the company. The registrar of companies must also be joined as a respondent.

11.14.15 Restoration to register

The court may order that the company's name be restored to the register if it is satisfied that, at the time when it was struck off, the company was carrying on business or in operation, or that it is for any other reason just that the company be restored to the register.[470]

Where a company has been dissolved by the registrar pursuant to an application by the company under s. 652A Companies Act 1985, any person to whom a copy of the company's application was required to be given under ss. 652B or 652C may apply before the expiration of 20 years from publication in the *Gazette* of notice under s. 652A(4) for the company's name to be restored to the register.[471] On such an application the court may, if satisfied that any duty under ss. 625B or 652C with respect to the giving to that person of a copy of the company's application under s. 652A was not performed or that the making of the company's application under s. 652A involved a breach of duty under s. 652B(1) or (3) or that it is for some other reason just to do so, order the company's name

466. CA 1985, s. 651(3).

467. See *Re New Timbiqui Gold Mines Ltd* [1961] Ch. 319, [1961] 1 All ER 865, but note that a "creditor" for these purposes can include a person who has only an unquantified claim against the company, see *Re Harvest Lane Motor Bodies Ltd* [1969] 1 Ch. 457, [1968] 2 All ER 1012.

468. CA 1985, s. 653.

469. See RSC O. 102, r. 4(1)(g).

470. See *Re Priceland* [1997] BCC 207.

471. CA 1985, s. 653(2B).

to be restored to the register. An application under this section should be made by petition. Notice should be given to the Treasury Solicitor and confirmation sought, to the effect that the Crown has no objection to the restoration of the company. The registrar of companies must also be joined as a respondent.

11.24.16 Ancillary directions

The court may include in an order restoring the name of the company to the register such directions and provisions as seem just for placing the company and others as nearly as possible in the position in which they would have been if the company's name had not been struck off.[472] This might include, for instance, an order that, in respect of persons who had outstanding claims against the company when it was dissolved, the period between dissolution and restoration should not be counted for the purposes of the Limitation Acts.[473]

Where there is a business or property to be dealt with, the court will usually make the order, but only on the terms that all property accounts and returns are made and filed.[474] For that reason, if a member is petitioning, it will generally be appropriate to join the company as co-petitioner in order that it may undertake to file the appropriate returns.[475] The practice of the registrar of companies, however, is now to oppose application to restore the name of the company to the register unless the paperwork is up-to-date and has already been sent to him. Where a creditor is petitioning this is not required. Usually the creditor also seeks an order that the company be wound up immediately afterwards.

11.24.17 Retrospective effect

Where an order is made under this section, it will have restrospective effect so that the company will be deemed to have continued in existence as if its name had not been struck off.[476] Any business which the company has transacted in the meantime will therefore be undisturbed, and the directors may not by reason of the dissolution be sued for breach of any warranty of authority.[477]

When a company is dissolved, any property which was vested in it immediately before dissolution will be deemed to be *bona vacantia*,[478] and accordingly becomes the property of the Crown, the Duchy of Lancaster or the Duke of Cornwall for the time being.

As a result of the restrospective effect of challenges to dissolution, the Crown's[479] rights in *bona vacantia* are defeasible, and although it would be rare for it to have any objection, it is for this reason the Crown has an interest in the proceedings and should be notified of them through the Treasury Solicitor. Nevertheless, the Crown may dispose of the property while it is *bona vacantia*, and that disposition will not be upset by the restoration of the company.[480] Instead, if the company is restored, the Crown becomes liable to compensate

472. CA 1985, s. 653(3).
473. See *Re Donald Kenyon Ltd* [1965] 3 All ER 596, [1956] 1 WLR 1397.
474. *Re Johannesburg Mining and General Syndicate Ltd* (1901) 45 Sol.Jo. 343.
475. *Re Walter Wright Ltd* [1923] WN 128, (1923) 67 Sol.Jo. 577.
476. CA 1985, s. 653(3).
477. *Re Lindsay Bowman Ltd* [1969] 1 WLR 1443.
478. CA 1985, s. 654.
479. Or those of the Duchy of Lancaster or Duke of Cornwall, as the case may be.
480. CA 1985, s. 655(1).

the company to the extent of the consideration received for the property, the value of such consideration at the time of the disposition, or if no consideration was received, the value of the property sold at the time when it was sold.[481]

11.25 Disclaimer

11.25.1 Introduction

When a company is dissolved, any property which was vested in the company immediately before dissolution will be deemed to be *bona vacantia*[482] and will become the property of the Crown.[483] Clearly, where the property thus vesting in the Crown carries with it liabilities, the Crown may not wish to take on those liabilities, and may choose to disclaim it.[484]

11.25.2 Procedure

The procedure by which the Crown may disclaim property is different from that which applies in respect of disclaimer by a liquidator, and is as follows:

(a) the Crown may expressly or impliedly waive its right to disclaim property[485];
(b) notice of disclaimer is given by the Treasury Solicitor representing the Crown[486];
(c) such notice will only be effective if made within 12 months of the date on which the vesting of the property first came to the notice of the Crown representative[487];
(d) any person interested in the property may force the Crown to decide whether it will disclaim it, by applying in writing to the Treasury Solicitor, in which case the disclaimer will only be effective if made within three months from the receipt of that application; this period may be extended by the court which would have had jurisdiction to wind up the company if it had not been dissolved[488];
(e) the notice of disclaimer should state the date on which vesting the property first came to the notice of the Crown representative, and that no application requiring the Crown to decide has been made before a specified date,[489] and the notice itself will be sufficient evidence of each of those facts until the contrary is proved[490];

481. CA 1985, s. 655(2).
482. CA 1985, s. 654—see para. 11.24.17, *supra*.
483. Or the Duchy of Lancaster, or the Duke of Cornwall, as the case may be. References in the text to the Crown or the Treasury Solicitor should be read also to refer respectively to the Duchy of Lancaster or the Duke of Cornwall, or each of their solicitors.
484. CA 1985, s. 656.
485. CA 1985, s. 656(2).
486. CA 1985, s. 656(1) and (6).
487. CA 1985, s. 656(3)(a).
488. CA 1985, s. 656(3)(b).
489. Namely the date before which the notice of disclaimer would now be out of time.
490. CA 1985, s. 656(4).

(f) the notice should be delivered to the registrar of companies, who will register it, and copies should be published in the *Gazette* and sent to any persons who have given the Treasury Solicitor notice that they claim to be interested in the property.[491]

11.25.3 Effect of Crown disclaimer

Disclaimer by the Crown results in the property being deemed never to have vested in the Crown at all,[492] and must be treated as if disclaimed by the liquidator immediately before the dissolution of the company, and therefore subject to the provisions governing dissolution by the liquidator.[493] When a company is restored to the register, the property is treated as though it never vested in the Crown, subject to the provisions leaving undisturbed any intervening disposition by the Crown[494]; disclaimer is distinct from a disposition, and on restoration of the company, will be deemed never to have occurred.[495]

491. CA 1985, s. 656(5).
492. CA 1985, s. 657(1) and (2) as amended.
493. Namely IA 1986, ss. 178(4), and 179 to 182; see paras 11.16–11.17, *supra*.
494. CA 1985, s. 655(2)(a).
495. *Allied Dunbar Assurance plc* v. *Fowle* [1994] BCC 422.

CHAPTER 12

ADMINISTRATION PROCEDURE

INTRODUCTION

12.1 Administration

Administration procedure is an innovation in English law introduced for the first time by the Insolvency Act 1986. Its purpose is to facilitate rescue operations for companies in financial difficulties. It does this by permitting an application to be made to the court for the appointment of a qualified professional to act as the administrator of the company. Before making the order, the court has to be satisfied that making the order would be likely to achieve one of the statutory purposes. These are:

(a) the survival of the company or the whole or part of its undertaking as a going concern;
(b) the approval of a voluntary arrangement under part I of the Insolvency Act 1986;
(c) the sanctioning under s. 425 of the Companies Act 1985 of a compromise or arrangement; and
(d) a more advantageous realisation of the company's assets than would be effected on a winding-up.[1]

The aim is that the administrator should carry on the business as a going concern with a view to achieving one or more of the statutory objectives.[2] For this purpose, the administrator is obliged to draw up proposals for the future management of the company's affairs for approval by the creditors.[3] If the proposals are approved, they will be implemented. If not, the court may discharge the administration order.[4] While the order is in force, a statutory moratorium protects the company from claims by creditors: the company cannot be wound up, an administrative receiver cannot be appointed, no steps may be taken to enforce security over the company's property except with the consent of the administrator or the leave of the court, and no proceedings may be taken or execution levied against the company or its property without such consent or leave.[5]

1. IA 1986, s. 8(3).
2. *Bristol Airport plc* v. *Powdrill* [1990] Ch. 744, at 758 per Browne-Wikinson V-C. The case is also reported as *Re Paramount Airways* [1990] BCC 130.
3. IA 1986, s. 23.
4. IA 1986, s. 24(5).
5. IA 1986, s. 11(3).

The administration procedure implements recommendations made in the Report of the Cork Committee.[6] The Committee concluded that such a procedure was needed in cases where a company was in financial difficulties but an administrative receiver could not be appointed because of the absence of a floating charge, or where the holder of a floating charge did not want to appoint an administrative receiver. This is reflected in the provision giving the holder of such a charge a statutory right to veto the making of an administration order.[7] In practice, an administration order is unlikely to be made in a case in which a floating charge exists, since the holder is likely to prefer the cheaper and quicker alternative of appointing an administrative receiver.

The chief advantage of the administration procedure is that it provides a shelter for the company from its creditors whilst a reorganisation of its affairs is undertaken under the control of an independent professional. There may often be cases in which most creditors are ready to agree to a moratorium to enable a rescue to be mounted, but an obdurate creditor refuses to co-operate and insists on presenting a winding-up petition. Such a creditor will be prevented from taking such action by the making of an administration order.

Since the Act came into force, the administration procedure has proved remarkably popular. Orders have been made in respect of companies in businesses as diverse as property development, building, financial services, and football.

This chapter deals with matters of practice and procedure. For a thorough treatment of the substantive law, see Lightman and Moss, *The Law of Receivers and Administrators*, 2nd edition.

APPLICATION FOR ADMINISTRATION ORDER

12.2 Petitioner

The application for an administration order must be made by petition.[8] It may be presented by any of the following[9]:

(a) the company;
(b) the directors;
(c) a creditor or creditors (including contingent or prospective creditors);
(d) the supervisor of a voluntary arrangement under part 1 of the Act[10];
(e) the clerk of a magistrates' court in exercise of the powers conferred by s. 87A of the Magistrates' Court Act 1980, being powers conferred for the enforcement of fines imposed on companies[11];
(f) in relation to a company which is an "authorised person" under the Financial Services Act 1986, by the self-regulating organisation of which the company is a member or, in the absence of such an organisation, by the Secretary of State[12]; and

6. Cmnd 8558, chapter 9.
7. IA 1986, s. 9(3).
8. IA 1986, s. 9(1).
9. IA 1986, s. 9(1).
10. IA 1986, s. 7(4)(b).
11. Criminal Justice Act 1988, s.62(2)(a).
12. FSA 1986, s. 74.

(g) in relation to a company which is the water undertaker or sewerage undertaker appointed under part II of the Water Industry Act 1991, by the Secretary of State or by the Director General of Water Services.[13]

12.3 Company's petition

A petition by the company may be presented if an ordinary resolution to that effect is passed by the company in general meeting. The company has an interest in having its affairs properly conducted and adequately wound up; this gives it a sufficient interest to petition for winding-up under s. 124, and the same principle gives it a sufficient interest to present an administration petition.[14] The members of the company, as such, are not entitled to present a petition.

12.4 Directors' petition

An application by the directors must be made by all the directors.[15] However, where a resolution has been passed by the directors for the presentation of an administration petition, it is the duty of all the directors to implement it, including directors who voted against the resolution or took no part in it.[16] A petition presented by the directors must state that it is so presented, but from and after presentation it is to be treated for all purposes as the petition of the company.[17]

12.5 Creditors' petition

As regards petitions by creditors, a contingent creditor is a creditor in respect of a debt which will only become due in an event which may or may not occur; a prospective creditor is a creditor in respect of a debt which will certainly become due in the future.[18]

12.6 Supervisor's petition

Although the supervisor of a voluntary arrangement under part I of the Act is not specifically mentioned in s. 9(1) as one of the persons entitled to present a petition, the language of s. 7(4) is sufficiently clear to enable him to do so.

12.7 Petition under Financial Services Act

Section 74 of the Financial Services Act 1986 applies in a case in which the company is (a) an authorised person,[19] or (b) a person whose authorisation is suspended under s. 28

13. Water Industry Act 1991, ss. 23 to 25 and sch. 3, which provide for the making of a "special administration order" and apply thereto many of the provisions of part II of IA 1986.
14. *Re Land and Property Trust Co. plc* [1991] BCC 446.
15. *Re Instrumentation Electrical Services Ltd* (1988) 4 BCC 301.
16. *Re Equiticorp International plc* [1989] 1 WLR 1010; (1989) 5 BCC 599.
17. IR 1986, r. 2.4(3).
18. *Stonegate Securities Ltd* v. *Gregory* [1980] Ch. 576.
19. An authorised person is a member of a recognised self-regulating organisation: see FSA 1986, s. 7.

of that Act,[20] or (c) a person who is subject to a direction under s. 33(1)(b),[21] or (d) an appointed representative.[22] The section permits an administration petition to be presented by:

(a) in the case of an authorised person who is an authorised person by virtue of membership of a recognised self-regulating organisation or certification by a recognised professional body, by that organisation or body; and
(b) in the case of an appointed representative or an authorised person who is not authorised as mentioned in (a) above, or is so authorised but is not subject to the rules of that organisation or body in the carrying on of all investment business carried on by him, by the Secretary of State.

12.8 Form of petition

The petition must follow Form 2.1 with such variations, if any, as the case may require.[23] It must specify the name and address of the person proposed to be appointed as administrator; and it must be stated that, to the best of the petitioner's knowledge and belief, that person is qualified to act as an insolvency practitioner in relation to the company.[24]

12.9 Withdrawal of petition

The petition once presented cannot be withdrawn without the leave of the court.[25] This provision is designed to discourage frivolous applications, an important consideration in view of the impact which the mere presentation of the petition has on the affairs of the company.[26]

12.10 Filing of petition

The petition, together with the supporting affidavit (see below), must be filed in court, with a sufficient number of copies for service and use as provided in r. 2.6.[27] Each of the copies of the petition and affidavit delivered to the court will have the seal of the court applied to it and be issued to the petitioner. Each copy is endorsed with the date and time of filing.[28] The court will fix a venue for the hearing of the petition, which is also endorsed on each copy of the petition.[29] Once the petition is filed, it is the duty of the petitioner to notify the court in writing of any winding-up petition presented against the company, as soon as he becomes aware of it.[30]

20. FSA 1986, s. 28 gives the Secretary of State power to withdraw or suspend any authorisation granted by him if it appears to him that the holder of the authorisation is not a fit and proper person to carry on investment business.
21. FSA 1986, s. 33 gives the Secretary of State power to direct that an authorised person shall cease to be one where that person has contravened that Act or the regulations made under it.
22. An appointed representative is an exempted person who is employed by an authorised person under a contract for services requiring or permitting him to carry on investment business: see FSA 1986, s. 44.
23. This form is reproduced in Appendix 4. See IR 1986, r. 12.7 and sch. 4.
24. IR 1986, r. 2.4(5).
25. IA 1986, s. 9(3). *Re a Company (No. 00175 of 1987)* [1987] BCLC 467.
26. See paras 12.13–12.17, *infra*.
27. IR 1986, r. 2.5(1).
28. IR 1986, r. 2.5(2).
29. IR 1986, r. 2.5(3).
30. IR 1986, r. 2.5(4).

12.11 Companies in respect of which application may be made

Section 8 confers jurisdiction on the court to make an administration order in relation to a "company". A company is defined for these purposes by s. 735 of the Companies Act 1985, which is incorporated, by reference, into the Insolvency Act 1986 by s. 251. The definition makes it clear that a company, except where otherwise expressly defined, means a company formed and registered under the Companies Act 1985 or earlier Companies Acts, and does not include a company established overseas.[31] However, there is an exception which is discussed in the next paragraph.

12.12 Foreign companies and letters of request under s. 426

Section 426(4) provides that the courts having jurisdiction in relation to insolvency law in any part of the United Kingdom shall assist the courts having the corresponding jurisdiction in any relevant country or territory.[32] Such assistance is given pursuant to a letter of request from the foreign court. The request is authority for the English court to apply, in relation to any matters specified in the request, the insolvency law which is applicable by either court in relation to comparable matters falling within its jurisdiction.[33] In exercising its discretion, the court must have regard in particular to the rules of private international law.[34] For this purpose, "insolvency law" means in relation to England and Wales, provision made under the Insolvency Act 1986 or various sections of the Directors Disqualification Act 1986.[35] In relation to any relevant country or territory, "insolvency law" means so much of the law of that country or territory as corresponds to the relevant provisions of English law.[36] These provisions give the English court, as the requested court, a jurisdiction which it will not otherwise possess to make an administration order in relation to a company established in one of the designated countries, even where the foreign court does not have a procedure equivalent to administration procedure.[37] It has been held that, where the conditions for the exercise of this jurisdiction are satisfied, the English court does not have a discretion whether or not to make an administration order, because s. 426(4) contains mandatory language ("the courts . . . shall assist the courts having the corresponding jurisdiction in . . . any relevant country or territory").[38] However, it has been held that the concluding words of s. 426(5) confer a discretion on the requested court whether to apply its own law or the law of the requesting court to the matters specified in the request.[39] Section 426(5) applies to enable the requested court to apply not only procedural but also substantive provisions of English insolvency law.[40]

31. *Re Dallhold Estates (UK) Pty Ltd* [1992] BCC 394.
32. Relevant country or territory means the Channel Islands, the Isle of Man and any country or territory designated by the Secretary of State by statutory instrument: see IA 1986, s. 426(11). The Secretary of State has made an order designating various commonwealth countries and former protectorates, including Australia, New Zealand and Canada: see the Co-operation of Insolvency Courts (Designation of Relevant Countries and Territories) Order 1986, S.I. 1986 No. 2123.
33. IA 1986, s. 426(5).
34. IA 1986, s. 426(5).
35. IA 1986, s. 426(10)(a).
36. IA 1986, s. 426(10)(d).
37. *Re Dallhold Estates (UK) Pty Ltd* [1992] BCC 394.
38. *Ibid.*
39. *Re Bank of Credit and Commerce International SA* [1993] BCC 787.
40. *Ibid.*

EFFECT OF APPLICATION

12.13 Winding-up

During the period beginning with the presentation of a petition for an administration order and ending with the making of such an order or the dismissal of the petition, no resolution or order for winding-up the company can be passed or made.[41] This does not prevent a petition for winding-up from being *presented*,[42] but no further step may be taken, such as advertisement of such petition.[43]

12.14 Security

No steps may be taken to enforce any security over the company's property, nor to repossess goods in the company's possession under any hire-purchase agreement, except with the leave of the court and subject to such terms as the court may impose.[44] The language in s. 10(1)(c) is similar to that in s. 11(3)(c) (which lays down the effect of the making of an administration order on the enforcement of security over the company's property), and the relevant case law is noted in the section of the text dealing with that section.[45] By s. 10(4), a hire purchase agreement includes conditional sale agreements,[46] chattel leasing agreements[47] and retention of title agreements.[48] An application for leave to enforce a security or re-possess goods is an ordinary application under part 7 of the Insolvency Rules, and follows the procedure laid down in that part.[49]

12.15 Execution

No other proceedings and no execution or other legal process may be commenced or continued, and no distress may be levied, against the company or its property except with the leave of the court and subject to such terms as the court may impose.[50] The language in s. 10(1)(d) is similar to that in s. 11(3)(d) (which lays down the effect of the making of an administration order on execution against the company's property), and the relevant case law is noted in the section of the text dealing with that section.[51] An application for leave is an ordinary application under part 7 of the Insolvency Rules, and follows the procedure laid down in that part.[52]

41. IA 1986, s. 10(1).
42. IA 1986, s. 10(2)(a).
43. IA 1986, s. 10(1)(c); *Re a Company (No. 001992 of 1988)* (1988) 4 BCC 451; *Re Manlon Trading Ltd* (1988) 4 BCC 455; *Re a Company (No. 001448 of 1989)* (1989) 5 BCC 706.
44. IA 1986, s. 10(1)(c).
45. See para. 12.50, *infra*.
46. A term which has the same meaning as in the Consumer Credit Act 1974: see IA 1986, s. 436.
47. An agreement for the bailment of goods which is capable of subsisting for more than three months: see s. 251.
48. An agreement for the sale of goods to a company, being an agreement which does not constitute a charge on the goods, but under which, if the seller is not paid and the company is wound up, the seller will have priority over all other creditors of the company as respects the goods or any property representing the goods: see s. 251.
49. See Chapter 10.
50. IA 1986, s. 10(1)(c).
51. See para. 12.51, *infra*.
52. See Chapter 10.

12.16 Exceptions

Notwithstanding the limitations on enforcement of security and execution in s. 10(1), the leave of the court is not required for the appointment of an administrative receiver or for the carrying out by such receiver (whenever appointed) of any of his functions.[53] The position is of course different once an administration order has been made.[54]

12.17 Absence of administrative receiver's consent

The restrictions discussed above do not come into operation if the petition was presented at a time when there was an administrative receiver and the person by whom he was appointed has not consented to the making of the administration order; the restrictions do commence to operate as and when the person who appointed the administrative receiver consents.[55]

AFFIDAVIT IN SUPPORT

12.18 Deponent

An affidavit complying with r. 2.3 must be prepared and sworn, with a view to it being filed in court in support of the petition.[56] The deponent will vary according to the identity of the petitioner. In the case of a petition presented by the company or the directors, the affidavit must be sworn by one of the directors or by the secretary.[57] In the case of a petition presented by creditors, the affidavit must be sworn by a person acting under the authority of them all, whether or not one of their number himself.[58] In all cases, the deponent must state the nature of his authority and the means of his knowledge of the matters to which the affidavit relates.[59] If the petition is presented by the supervisor of a voluntary arrangement under part I of the Act, it is to be treated as if it were a petition by the company.[60]

12.19 Contents of affidavit

The affidavit must state the deponent's belief that the company is, or is likely to become, unable to pay its debts and the grounds of that belief.[61] It must also state which of the purposes specified in s. 8(3) of the Act is expected to be achieved by the making of an administration order.[62] The affidavit must include a statement of the company's financial position, specifying (to the best of the deponent's knowledge and belief) assets and

53. IA 1986, s. 10(2)(b) and (c).
54. See IA 1986, ss. 11(1)(b) and 11(2).
55. IA 1986, s. 10(3).
56. IR 1986, r. 2.1(1).
57. IR 1986, r. 2.1(2).
58. IR 1986, r. 2.1(3).
59. IR 1986, r. 2.1(3).
60. IR 1986, r. 2.1(4).
61. IR 1986, r. 2.3(1).
62. IR 1986, r. 2.3(1)(a).

liabilities, including contingent and prospective liabilities.[63] Details must be given of any security known or believed to be held by creditors of the company, and whether in any case the security is such as to confer power on the holder to appoint an administrative receiver.[64] If an administrative receiver has been appointed, that fact must be stated.[65] If a petition has been presented for the winding-up of the company, details of it must be given in the affidavit, so far as within the immediate knowledge of the deponent.[66] If there are other matters which, in the opinion of those intending to present the petition, will assist the court in deciding whether to make an order, those matters must be stated so far as they lie within the knowledge or belief of the deponent.[67] The courts have stressed that all facts relevant to the exercise of discretion to appoint an administrator must be revealed, even though to do so may be embarrassing to the applicant.[68] This rule is important because in many cases the only information available to the court will emanate from the company and its officers, together with the independent report (if any). If an independent report has been prepared for the company under r. 2.2,[69] that fact must be stated. If no such report has been prepared, the omission to do so must be explained.[70]

12.20 Exhibits

The following must be exhibited to the affidavit[71]:

(a) a copy of the petition;
(b) a written consent by the proposed administrator to accept appointment, if an administration order is made; this must be in Form 2.2[72];
(c) if an independent report has been prepared under r. 2.2, a copy of that report.[73]

12.21 Form of affidavit

The prescribed forms do not include a form of affidavit. Provided that the Rules summarised above are complied with, the affidavit will be acceptable.

12.22 Filing of affidavit

The affidavit (together with the petition) must be filed in court, with a sufficient number of copies for service and use as provided in Rule 2.6.[74]

63. IR 1986, r. 2.3(2).
64. IR 1986, r. 2.3(3).
65. IR 1986, r. 2.3(3).
66. IR 1986, r. 2.3(4).
67. IR 1986, r. 2.3(5).
68. *Re Sharps of Truro Ltd* (1990) BCC 94; *Astor Chemicals Ltd* v. *Synthetic Technology Ltd* (1990) BCC 97 at 107–108; *Cornhill Insurance plc* v. *Cornhill Financial Services Ltd* (1992) BCC 818 at 856 per Dillon L.J.
69. See paras 12.23 to 12.25, *infra*.
70. IR 1986, r. 2.3(6).
71. IR 1986, r. 2.4(6).
72. IR 1986, r. 12.7 and sch. 4, part 2.
73. See paras 12.23 to 12.25, *infra*.
74. See para. 12.27, *infra*.

INDEPENDENT REPORT

12.23 Requirements

There may be prepared, with a view to its being exhibited to an affidavit in support of the petition, a report by an independent person to the effect that the appointment of an administrator for the company is expedient.[75] The report may be by the person proposed to be administrator, or by any other person having adequate knowledge of the company's affairs, not being a director, secretary, manager, member, or employee of the company.[76] The report must specify the purposes which, in the opinion of the person preparing it, may be achieved for the company by the making of the administration order, being the purposes specified in s. 8(3) of the Act.[77] It is not obligatory to prepare an independent report, but if no such report is exhibited to the affidavit in support of the petition, the deponent must explain the reason for its absence.

12.24 Purpose

An independent report carries considerable weight with the court because it is an objective assessment of the company's position and whether the making of an order would be likely to achieve one or more of the statutory purposes set out in s. 8(3).[78] The absence of such a report may induce the court to refuse the order sought.[79] However, a recent Practice Note states that such reports should not be unduly detailed, thereby adding unnecessarily to the expense of obtaining an order.[80] The aim of administration orders is the rescue and rehabilitation of insolvent but potentially viable businesses. The Practice Note states that it is of the greatest importance that this aim should not be frustrated by expense, and that the costs of obtaining an administration order should not operate as a disincentive or put the process out of the reach of smaller companies. The court has found that independent reports are sometimes unnecessarily elaborate and detailed. What the court requires is a concise assessment of the company's situation and of the prospects of an administration order achieving one or more of the statutory purposes. This would normally include an explanation of any finance required during the administration. Every endeavour should be made to avoid disproportionate investigation and expense. The court accepts that in some cases a brief investigation and report is all that is required. This is essentially a matter of judgement for the professional advisers concerned in the preparation of the application, and the length and complexity of the investigation and report will clearly vary from case to case. The Practice Note also suggests a number of methods by which any deficiencies in the initial independent report could be cured. These include:

(a) permitting oral evidence to be given at the hearing of the application by the proposed administrator, in which case a supplemental report should later be prepared covering the matters on which oral evidence was given for placing on the court file;

75. IR 1986, r. 2.2(1).
76. IR 1986, r. 2.2(2).
77. IR 1986, r. 2.2(3).
78. See *Re Newport County Association Football Club Ltd* (1987) 3 BCC 635 and para. 12.35, *infra*.
79. See *Re WF Fearman Ltd* (1988) 4 BCC 139.
80. Practice Statement (Administration orders: reports) [1994] 1 WLR 160, reproduced in Appendix 3.

(b) making an order coupled with a requirement that the administrator should report back to the court within a short period so that the court could consider whether to allow the administration to continue or to discharge the order;
(c) making an order coupled with a requirement that the administrator should hold a meeting of creditors and then report back to the court within a short period.

Generally, the Practice Note states that the independent report is valuable as a safeguard in assisting the court to see whether the application has a sound basis, whilst acknowledging that there might be straightforward cases in which such a report is not necessary because it provides little assistance. The Practice Note reminds practitioners that the Rules do not require that an independent report be provided in every case.

12.25 Form of independent report

The prescribed forms do not include a form of independent report. It is suggested that the report should include the following, whilst recognising that the content will vary from case to case:

(a) the qualifications of the independent person[81];
(b) the sources of his knowledge of the company's affairs[82];
(c) the facts relating to and reasons for the company's insolvency[83];
(d) the statutory purpose or purposes which may be achieved for the company by the making of the administration order, and why the maker of the report holds the opinion that such purpose or purposes may be achieved[84];
(e) the reasons why the maker of the report considers that it is expedient to appoint an administrator.[85]

NOTICE AND SERVICE OF PETITION

12.26 Notice

Notice and service are distinct operations. Notice of the petition must be given forthwith to anyone who has or is entitled to appoint an administrative receiver of the company.[86] The purpose of this provision is to enable the holder of a floating charge to exercise his veto over the appointment of an administrative receiver.[87] Notice of presentation of the petition must also be given forthwith after filing, to any sheriff or other officer who to the knowledge of the petitioner is charged with an execution or other legal process against the company or its property, and to any person who to the knowledge of the petitioner has

81. IR 1986, r. 2.2(1).
82. IR 1986, r. 2.2(2).
83. IA 1986, s. 8(1).
84. IR 1986, r. 2.2(3).
85. IR 1986, r. 2.2(1).
86. IA 1986, s. 9(2). Notice must also be given to the Bank of England in the case of authorised institutions or former authorised institutions within the meaning of the Banking Act 1987, unless the Bank of England is itself the petitioner: see the Banks (Administration Proceedings) Order 1989, SI 1989 No. 1276, art. 2, sch., para. 4.
87. See IA 1986, s. 9(3).

distrained against the company or its property.[88] The purpose of this provision is to prevent execution against the property of the company from being continued in contravention of s. 10(1)(c).

12.27 Who to serve

The petition issued by the court, together with the affidavit in support and its exhibits (other than the copy petition) must be served:

(a) on any person who has appointed, or is or may be entitled to appoint, an administrative receiver for the company;
(b) if an administrative receiver has been appointed, on him;
(c) if there is a pending petition for the winding-up of the company, on the petitioner (and also on the provisional liquidator, if any); and
(d) on the person proposed as administrator.[89]

In addition, if the petition is presented by creditors of the company, the petition shall be served on the company.[90]

12.28 When to serve

Service is to be effected not less than five days before the date fixed for the hearing.[91] The court has power to abridge this period.[92] In cases of urgency, the court is willing to make an order *ex parte*, and has even done so before presentation of the petition against an undertaking, to present a petition immediately.[93] However, the practice of hearing applications *ex parte* has been described as undesirable and one which should not continue.[94] An order made *ex parte* may be rescinded by the judge who made it in exercise of the power contained in r. 7.47 of the Insolvency Rules 1986.[95]

12.29 Manner of service

Service on the company is effected by delivering the documents to its registered office. If delivery to the company's registered office is not practicable, service may be effected by delivery to its last known principal place of business in England and Wales.[96] Service on

88. IR 1986, r. 2.6A, inserted by Insolvency (Amendment) Rules 1987, S.I. 1987 No. 1919, r. 3(1), sch., part I, para. 7.
89. IR 1986, r. 2.6(2).
90. IR 1986, r. 2.6(3).
91. IR 1986, r. 2.7(1).
92. *Re a Company (No. 00175 of 1987)* (1987) 3 BCC 124; *Re Gallidoro Trawlers Ltd* [1991] BCC 691.
93. *Re Rowbotham Baxter Ltd* [1990] BCC 113; *Re Cavco Floors Ltd* [1990] BCC 589; *Re Shearing & Loader Ltd* [1991] BCC 249; *Re Chancery plc* [1991] BCC 171.
94. *Re Rowbotham Baxter Ltd* [1990] BCC 113 at 114 per Harman J., approved in *Cornhill Insurance plc* v. *Cornhill Financial Services Ltd* [1992] BCC 818 at 856 per Dillon L.J. However, *ex parte* orders may still be made in appropriate circumstances, and have been in some notable cases, such as *Atlantic Computers plc* and *British and Commonwealth Holdings plc*. See also the remarks of Harman J in *re Cavco Floors Ltd* [1990] BCC 589, *Re Shearing & Loader Ltd* [1991] BCC 232 and *Re Chancery plc* [1991] BCC 171.
95. *Cornhill Insurance plc* v. *Cornhill Financial Services Ltd* [1992] BCC 818, following *Re Tasbian Ltd (No. 2)* [1990] BCC 322.
96. IR 1986, r. 2.7(2) and (3).

the company may also be effected in such other manner as the court may direct.[97] Service on any other person is effected by delivering the documents to his proper address, which is any address which he has previously notified as his address for service, or, if he has not notified any such address, his usual or last known address.[98] There is a special rule for service on a bank which has appointed or is entitled to appoint an administrative receiver of the company and which has not notified an address for service: in such a case, the proper address for service is the address of an office of the bank where, to the knowledge of the petitioner, the company maintains a bank account. Where no such office is known to the petitioner, service may be effected at the registered office, or, if there is no such office, the bank's usual or last known address.[99] For the purposes of these rules, delivery of documents to any place or address may be made by leaving them there, or sending them by first class post.

12.30 Proof of service

Service of the petition must be verified by affidavit, specifying the date on which, and the manner in which, service was effected.[100] The affidavit of service must be in Form 2.3.[101] The affidavit, with a sealed copy of the petition exhibited to it, must be filed in court forthwith after service, and in any event not less than one day before the hearing of the petition.[102]

12.31 Advertisement

There is no requirement that the petition for an administration order should be advertised, whether in the *Gazette* or elsewhere. Where a winding-up petition has also been presented, the court will restrain its advertisement by injunction pending the hearing of the administration petition, since such advertisement would be to continue proceedings against the company in breach of s. 10(1)(c).[103] The court also has jurisdiction to restrain advertisement of a winding-up petition where a petition for an administration order is going to be but has not yet been presented.[104]

THE HEARING

12.32 Appearance

At the hearing, any of the following may appear to be represented:

(a) the petitioner;

97. IR 1986, r. 2.7(2)(c).
98. IR 1986, r. 2.7(2) and (4).
99. IR 1986, r. 2.7(4).
100. IR 1986, r. 2.8(1).
101. Reproduced in Appendix 4.
102. IR 1986, r. 2.8(2).
103. *Re a Company (No. 001992 of 1988)* (1988) 4 BCC 451; *Re a Company (No. 001448 of 1989)* (1989) 5 BCC 706.
104. *Re a Company (No. 001448 of 1989)* (1989) 5 BCC 706 (Hoffmann J.), not following *Re Manlon Trading Ltd* (1988) 4 BCC 455 (Harman J.). (Manlon Trading Ltd was the company concerned in the previously noted case, *Re a Company (No. 001992 of 1988)* 4 BCC 451).

(b) the company;
(c) any person who has appointed, or is or may be entitled to appoint, an administrative receiver of the company;
(d) the administrative receiver if one has been appointed;
(e) any person who has presented a petition for the winding-up of the company;
(f) the person proposed for appointment as administrator; and
(g) with the leave of the court, any other person who appears to have an interest justifying his appearance.[105]

Members of the company have no right to be heard. A member of the company who wishes the court to exercise its discretion under para. (g) must show that he has a "sufficient interest" in the outcome.[106] Since the company will either be insolvent or likely to become insolvent, it is unlikely that this test will be satisfied, even though the evidence may show that if the administration order achieves its purpose the members may have an interest in the outcome.[107] Creditors may be given leave to be heard[108] and the hearing of the petition may be adjourned to enable them to give evidence.

12.33 Grounds for order

The conditions which have to be satisfied before an order can be made are:

(a) that the company is or is likely to be unable to pay its debts (within the meaning of that expression in s. 123); and
(b) that the making of the order would be likely to achieve one or more of the statutory purposes.[109]

12.34 Inability to pay debts

A company is unable to pay its debts for the purposes of s. 123 if it fails to meet a statutory demand, fails to satisfy execution on a judgment, or is unable to pay its debts as they fall due.[110] A company is also deemed unable to pay its debts if it is proved to the satisfaction of the court that the value of the company's assets is less than the amount of its liabilities, taking into account contingent and prospective liabilities.[111] Even though the assets may exceed the liabilities, the company is still unable to pay its debts if the requirements of s. 123(1) are satisfied.[112] The test for the making of an administration order is wider than that for winding-up, because the former can be made upon proof that the company is *likely to be* unable to pay its debts. Application can therefore be made in anticipation of insolvency.

105. IR 1986, r. 2.9(1).
106. See *Re Rica Gold Washing Co.* (1879) 11 Ch.D. 36 at 43 per Sir George Jessel M.R., applied in *Re Chelmsford City Football Club (1980) Ltd* [1991] BCC 133.
107. *Re Chelmsford City Football Club (1980) Ltd* [1991] BCC 133.
108. See *Re Rowbotham Baxter plc* [1990] BCC 113; *Re Maxwell Communications Corp. Ltd* (1992) BCC 372.
109. IA 1986, s. 8(1).
110. IA 1986, s. 123(1).
111. IA 1986, s. 123(2).
112. *Re Business Properties Ltd* (1988) 4 BCC 684; *Re Imperial Motors (UK) Ltd* (1989) 5 BCC 214.

12.35 Statutory purposes

The statutory purposes are:

(a) the survival of the company as a going concern;
(b) the approval of a voluntary arrangement under part 1 of the Insolvency Act 1986;
(c) the sanctioning under s. 425 of the Companies Act 1985 of a compromise or arrangement;
(d) a more advantageous realisation of the company's assets than would be effected on a winding-up.[113]

Before an order can be made, it has to be shown that an order would be likely to achieve one or more of these purposes.[114] The better view appears to be that this requires the court to be satisfied that there is "a real prospect" that one or more of these purposes will be achieved, rather than the stricter test of "likely on the balance of probabilities".[115]

12.36 Discretion

If the statutory requirements are satisfied, the court has a discretion whether to make an order.[116] There are no words in s. 8(1) limiting the considerations to which the court is to have regard in exercising such discretion, and it has to take account of all relevant circumstances, but in order to further and not frustrate the purposes of the Act.[117] In considering whether to make an order, the interests of secured creditors weigh lighter in the scales than the interests of other creditors, because they do not stand to lose so much.[118] It is the duty of the judge hearing the petition to look critically at what is proposed.[119] If a majority in value of the creditors oppose an administration order, this can be taken into account by the court in the exercise of its discretion because it would be unlikely that the administrator could put forward proposals which would be approved by the creditors.[120] The administration procedure is designed for a short-term intensive care operation, and may not be suitable where the company is deadlocked and where, albeit that it is unable to pay its debts as they fall due, there is likely to be a substantial

113. IA 1986, s. 8(3).

114. *Re Consumer and Industrial Press Ltd* (1988) 4 BCC 68; *Re SCL Building Services Ltd* (1989) 5 BCC 746.

115. See *Re Consumer and Industrial Press Ltd* (1988) 4 BCC 68 (Peter Gibson J.: balance of probabilities); *Re Manlon Trading Ltd* (1988) 4 BCC 455 (Harman J.: balance of probabilities); *Re Harris Simons Construction Ltd* [1989] 1 WLR 368, (1989) 5 BCC 11 (Hoffmann J.: real prospect); *Re Primlaks (UK) Ltd* (1989) 5 BCC 710 (Vinelott J.: real prospect); *Re SCL Building Services Ltd* (1989) 5 BCC 746 (Peter Gibson J.: real prospect); *Re Rowbotham Baxter Ltd* [1990] BCC 113 (Harman J.: real prospect); *Re Land and Property Trust Co. plc* [1991] BCC 446 (Harman J.: real prospect); *Re Maxwell Communications Corp Ltd* [1992] BCC 372 (Hoffmann J.: real prospect); *Re Arrows Ltd (No. 3)* [1992] BCC 131 (Hoffmann J.: real prospect); *Re Dallhold Estates (UK) Pty Ltd* [1992] BCC 394 (Chadwick J.: real prospect).

116. *Re Business Properties Ltd* (1988) 4 BCC 684; *Re Consumer and Industrial Press Ltd* (1988) 4 BCC 68; *Re Imperial Motors (UK) Ltd* (1989) 5 BCC 214.

117. *Re Consumer and Industrial Press Ltd* (1988) 4 BCC 68.

118. *Re Consumer and Industrial Press Ltd* (1988) 4 BCC 68; *Re Imperial Motors (UK) Ltd* (1989) 5 BCC 214.

119. *Cornhill Insurance plc* v. *Cornhill Financial Services Ltd* [1992] BCC 818 at 856 per Dillon L.J.

120. *Re Land and Property Trust Co. plc* [1991] BCC 446 at 453 per Harman J.; *Re Arrows Ltd (No. 3)* [1992] BCC 131.

distribution to shareholders because the assets exceed the liabilities: in such a case the appropriate course is a winding-up.[121] Where the court is considering a letter of request under s. 436(5), there is no discretion to refuse an order.[122]

12.37 Cases in which no order can be made

Normally, the prior appointment of an administrative receiver is a bar to the appointment of an administrator, and the court is compelled to dismiss the petition unless it is satisfied that the person by whom or on whose behalf the administrative receiver was appointed has consented to the making of the order.[123] This rule also applies where the administrative receiver is appointed after the administration petition has been presented, since s. 9(3) is mandatory.[124] There are, however, three exceptions to this rule:

(a) where, if an administration order was made, any security by virtue of which the administrative receiver was appointed would be liable to be released or discharged under ss. 238 to 240 in part VI (transactions at an undervalue or preferences);
(b) where, if an administration order were made, such security would be avoided under s. 245 in part VI (avoidance of floating charges); and
(c) where, if an administration order were made, such security would be challengeable under s. 242 in part VI (gratuitous alienation) or 243 in that part (unfair preferences).[125]

By an amendment to s. 9(3) yet to be brought into force, there will be a further exception in a case where the security would be void against the administrator to any extent by virtue of part XII of the Companies Act 1985 (registration of company charges).[126]

Moreover, no order can be made if the company is in liquidation,[127] nor if the company is an insurance company within the Insurance Companies Act 1982 or an authorised institution or former authorised institution under the Banking Act 1987.[128] However, part II of the Insolvency Act 1986 (i.e. the part dealing with administration procedure) has now been extended, with modifications, to those banks which are companies within s. 735 of the Companies Act 1985.[129] The Bank of England may petition for an order in respect of such a company.[130] Where a petition is presented in relation to such a company, there are

121. *Re Business Properties Ltd* (1988) 4 BCC 684.
122. *Re Dallhold Estates (UK) Pty Ltd* [1992] BCC 394, but see also *Re Bank of Credit and Commerce International SA* [1993] BCC 787.
123. IA 1986, s. 9(3). See also *Re Croftbell Ltd* [1990] BCC 781.
124. *Re a Company (No. 00175 of 1987)* (1987) 3 BCC 124.
125. IA 1986, s. 9(3).
126. CA 1989, s. 107 and sch. 6 para. 3.
127. IA 1986, s. 8(4).
128. IA 1986, s. 8(4). Paragraph (b) was substituted by the Banking Act 1987, s. 108(1) and sch. 6, para. 25(1).
129. Banks (Administration Proceedings) Order 1989, S.I. 1989 No. 1276, para. 2. An administration order was made in respect of an authorised institution under the Banking Act 1987 in *Re Chancery plc* [1991] BCC 171.
130. Para. 3, Schedule to the Banks (Administration Proceedings) Order 1989, S.I. 1989 No. 1276.

various modifications to the procedure which, broadly speaking, provide for the involvement of the Bank of England.[131]

12.38 Powers of court

On hearing a petition, the court may dismiss it, or adjourn the hearing conditionally or unconditionally, or make an interim order, or make any other order that it thinks fit.[132] Although there is no power to appoint an interim administrator, the court can, if satisfied that the assets or business of a company are in jeopardy, and that there exists a *prima facie* case for the making of an administration order, make an order that the proposed administrator should take control of the property of the company and manage its affairs pending the hearing of the administration petition.[133] If the court makes an interim order, it can restrict the powers of the directors or of the company (whether by reference to the consent of the court or of a person qualified to act as an insolvency practitioner in relation to the company, or otherwise).[134] An interim order under s. 9(4) is not an administration order for the purposes of s. 6(2)(b) of the Company Directors Disqualification Act 1986.[135] The court can resolve a dispute as to who should be the administrator[136] and in doing so will have regard to the best interests of the creditors, and in particular the likely cost involved. The language of s. 9(4), wide though it is, does not permit the court to appoint provisional liquidators.[137]

12.39 Form of order

An administration order is an order directing that, during the period for which the order is in force, the affairs, business and property of the company shall be managed by a person (i.e. the administrator) appointed for the purpose by the court.[138] The order will identify the administrator.[139] The order must specify the purpose for which it is made,[140] and must be in Form 2.4.[141]

12.40 Variation of order

The administrator may apply to the court for the order to be varied so as to specify an additional purpose.[142] For example, where an administration order has been made specifying purposes (a) and (d) in s. 8(3), and the company's assets have been realised, the court may add purpose (b) (approval of voluntary arrangement) so as to enable the administrator to produce a voluntary arrangement for approval by the creditors.[143]

131. See Schedule to the Banks (Administration Proceedings) Order 1989, S.I. 1989 No. 1276.
132. IA 1986, s. 9(4).
133. *Re a Company (No. 00175 of 1987)* (1987) 3 BCC 124; *Re Gallidoro Trawlers Ltd* [1991] BCC 691.
134. IA 1986, s. 9(5).
135. *Secretary of State for Trade and Industry* v. *Palmer* [1993] BCC 650, affirmed on appeal [1994] BCC 990.
136. *Re Maxwell Communications Corp. Ltd* [1992] BCC 372.
137. *Re WF Fearman* (1988) 4 BCC 139.
138. IA 1986, s. 8(2).
139. IA 1986, s. 13(1).
140. IA 1986, s. 8(3).
141. Reproduced in Appendix 4.
142. IA 1986, s. 18(1).
143. *Re St Ives Windings Ltd* (1987) 3 BCC 634.

12.41 Costs

If the court makes an administration order, the costs of the petitioner, and of any person appearing whose costs are allowed by the court, are payable as an expense of the administration.[144] If the petition of a company is dismissed, the court has jurisdiction to order the directors to pay costs personally, but should not do so without giving the directors a proper opportunity to prepare evidence on the question and be properly represented.[145] Where the decision of the directors to seek an administration petition has been taken in good faith, reasonably and on professional advice, the court ought not to visit the costs on them personally if the court refuses an administration order and instead orders a winding-up.[146] Where petitions for an administration order and for a winding-up order are before the court, and the court orders a winding-up, the court can order the company's costs on the administration petition to be paid in the winding-up, together with the company's costs of the winding-up petition.[147] Where the directors of a company cause a petition for an administration order to be presented, but the company is subsequently wound up, the directors will not normally be ordered to pay the costs personally, but such an order may be appropriate if the evidence shows that they petitioned for an administration order for the purpose of concealing their own wrongdoings.[148]

12.42 Inspection of court file

The provisions dealing with the right to inspect the court's file are considered in Chapter 10.[149] It should be noted that the court can order that the documents filed in support of the application for an administration order should not be open to inspection without the court's leave.[150] Where such an order has been made, a person whose right of inspection has thereby been removed can apply under r. 7.31(4) for leave.[151]

NOTICE AND ADVERTISEMENT OF ORDER

12.43 Notice to administrator

If the court makes an administration order, it must forthwith give notice to the person appointed as administrator,[152] and send to him two sealed copies of the order. The notice must be in Form 2.4A.[153]

12.44 Notice by administrator

Where an administration order has been made, it is the duty of the administrator forthwith to send to the company a notice of the order.[154] He must also send such a notice to all

144. IR 1986, r. 2.9(2).
145. *Re Land and Property Trust Co. plc* [1993] BCC 462 (CA), reversing Harman J., [1991] BCC 446, who had refused the directors an adjournment.
146. *Re Gosscott (Groundworks) Ltd* (1988) 4 BCC 372.
147. *Ibid.*
148. *Re Tajik Air Ltd* [1996] BCC 368.
149. Para. 10.67, *supra.*
150. IR 1986, r. 7.31(5).
151. *Astor Chemicals Ltd* v. *Synthetic Technology Ltd* (1990) BCC 97.
152. IR 1986, r. 2.10(1).
153. Reproduced in Appendix 4, as modified by Insolvency Amendment Rules 1987, S.I. 1987 No. 1919, r. 3(1), schedule, part 5, para. 1.
154. IA 1986, s. 21(1).

creditors of the company (so far as he is aware of their addresses) within 28 days after the making of the order.[155] The administrator must also forthwith give notice of the making of the order:

(a) to any person who has appointed, or is or may be entitled to appoint, an administrative receiver of the company;
(b) to the administrative receiver, if one has been appointed;
(c) if there is pending a petition for the winding-up of the company, to the petitioner (and also to the provisional liquidator, if any); and
(d) to the registrar of companies.[156]

These notices must be in Form 2.6.[157]

12.45 Advertisement

Forthwith after the order is made, the administrator must advertise its making once in the *Gazette*, and once in such newspaper as he thinks most appropriate for ensuring that the order comes to the notice of the company's creditors.[158] The advertisement must be in Form 2.5.[159]

12.46 Notice in business documents

While a company is in administration, every invoice, order for goods or business letter issued by the company or the administrator, being a document on or in which the company's name appears, must also contain the administrator's name and a statement that the affairs, business and property of the company are being managed by the administrator.[160]

EFFECT OF ORDER

12.47 Winding-up

Upon the making of an administration order, any petition to wind up the company must be dismissed.[161] Since administration is an alternative to winding-up, dismissal of any petition to wind up is necessary. It is because of this effect of an administration order that the petitioner under any pending petition for winding-up must be served with the petition for an administration order,[162] and that any person who has presented a petition for the winding-up of the company has the right to appear or be represented at the hearing of the administration petition.[163] Moreover, during the period for which an administration order is in force, no resolution may be passed or order made for the winding-up of the company.[164]

155. IA 1986, s. 21(1).
156. By sending one of the sealed copies to him within 14 days: see IA 1986, s. 21(2), IR 1986, r. 2.10(3) and Form 2.7, reproduced in Appendix 4.
157. Reproduced in Appendix 4.
158. IR 1986, r. 2.10(2).
159. Reproduced in Appendix 4, as modified by Insolvency Amendment Rules 1987, S.I. 1987 No. 1919, r. 3(1), schedule, part 5, para. 1.
160. IA 1986, s. 12.
161. IA 1986, s. 11(1)(a).
162. IR 1986, r. 2.6(2)(c).
163. IR 1986, r. 2.9(1)(e).
164. IA 1986, s. 11(3)(a).

12.48 Administrative receiver

Upon the making of an administration order, any administrative receiver of the company must vacate office,[165] and during the period for which an administration order is in force, no administrative receiver of the company may be appointed.[166] However, the order could not have been made in the first place unless either the person by whom or on whose behalf the administrative receiver was appointed consented,[167] or the court found that the security by virtue of which the receiver was appointed was liable to be invalidated under s. 9(3)(b). An administrative receiver who has vacated office under these provisions has a charge for his remuneration on the property of the company in his custody or under his control in priority to the security of the person appointing him.[168] An administrative receiver who vacates office is also absolved thereafter from his duty to pay preferential creditors under ss. 40 and 59.[169]

12.49 Receiver of part of company's property

Where an administration order has been made, any receiver of part of the company's property shall vacate office on being required to do so by the administrator.[170] A receiver who has vacated office under these provisions has a charge for his remuneration on the property of the company in his custody or under his control in priority to the security of the person appointing him.[171] A receiver who vacates office is also absolved thereafter from his duty to pay preferential creditors under ss. 40 and 59.[172]

12.50 S. 11(3)(c): Enforcement of security or repossession of goods under hire-purchase agreement

No steps may be taken to enforce any security[173] over the company's property,[174] or to re-possess goods in the company's possession[175] under any hire-purchase agreement,

165. IA 1986, s. 11(1)(b).
166. IA 1986, s. 11(3)(b).
167. IA 1986, s. 9(3).
168. IA 1986, s. 11(4).
169. IA 1986, s. 11(5).
170. IA 1986, s. 11(2).
171. IA 1986, s. 11(4).
172. IA 1986, s. 11(5).
173. This term is defined in s. 248 as "any mortgage, charge, lien or other security". It has been held to include the rights of a landlord under a proviso for re-entry for non-payment of rent: *Exchange Travel Agency Ltd* v. *Triton Property Trust plc* [1991] BCC 341, cf *Re Olympia & York Canary Wharf Ltd* [1993] BCC 154. However, although *Exchange Travel Agency Ltd* v. *Triton Property Trust plc* has been accepted or assumed to be correct in *Doorbar* v. *Alltime Securities* [1995] 1 WLR 456 and in *Gunmark* v. *March Estates* [1996] 2 BCC 1, it has now been held to have been wrongly decided in another first instance case: see *Razzaq* v. *Pala* (1997) unreported, Lightman J. who pointed out that the scheme of the Act is to use the word "security" in its strict legal sense, and who referred to the decision of the Court of Appeal in *Ezekiel* v. *Orakpo* [1997] 1 QB 260. It also includes a statutory right to detain an aircraft: *Bristol Airport plc* v. *Powdrill* [1990] 1 Ch. 744, also reported as *Re Paramount Airways* [1990] BCC 130.
174. The expression "property" is defined in s. 436. It includes the interest of a company under a lease of a chattel: *Bristol Airport plc* v. *Powdrill* [1990] 1 Ch. 744, also reported as *Re Paramount Airways* [1990] BCC 130.
175. The meaning of this expression was considered in *Re Atlantic Computer Systems plc* [1990] BCC 454 (Ferris J.) [1992] Ch. 505; [1990] BCC 859 (CA), where it was held that goods in the possession of the company under a hire purchase agreement were protected by IA 1986, s. 11(3)(c) not only where they remained on the company's premises, but also where they were entrusted by the company to others for repair, or sublet by the company as part of its trade to others.

except with the consent of the administrator or the leave of the court and subject to such terms as the court may impose.[176] By s. 10(4), a hire-purchase agreement includes conditional sale agreements,[177] chattel leasing agreements[178] and retention of title agreements.[179] If the administrator gives his consent, an application to the court is unnecessary. However, if consent is refused, application may be made to the court. The onus is on the applicant to show that the case is a proper one for leave to be given to enforce the security.[180] The application is an ordinary application under part 7 of the Insolvency Rules, and follows the procedure laid down in that Part[181] The principles on which the court acts in deciding whether to grant leave have been discussed in a number of cases.[182] The question whether s. 11(3)(c) precludes the owner of goods from demanding their return so as to constitute a cause of action in conversion was left open in a recent case.[183] However, the assertion of a possessory lien over goods belonging to the company constitutes the taking of a step to enforce his security within s. 11(3)(c) and this therefore requires the leave of the court in the absence of the administrator's consent.[184] Section 11(3)(c) applies to goods which were the subject of a hire-purchase agreement, whether or not that hire-purchase agreement has been terminated before the presentation of the petition for administration or on that event, provided that they remain in the company's possession.[185]

12.51 S. 11(3)(d): Other proceedings, execution, other legal process or distress

No other proceedings[186] and no execution or other legal process[187] may be commenced or

176. IA 1986, s. 11(3)(c).

177. A term which has the same meaning as in the Consumer Credit Act 1974: see s. 436.

178. An agreement for the bailment of goods which is capable of subsisting for more than three months: see s. 251.

179. An agreement for the sale of goods to a company, being an agreement which does not constitute a charge on the goods, but under which, if the seller is not paid and the company is wound up, the seller will have priority over all other creditors of the company as respects the goods or any property representing the goods: see s. 251.

180. *Re Meesan Investments Ltd* (1988) 4 BCC 788.

181. See Chapter 10, para. 10.3 *et seq.*

182. See especially *Re Atlantic Computer Systems plc* [1992] Ch. 505, [1990] BCC 859 (CA) at 541–544. See also *Royal Trust Bank* v. *Buchler* (1989) BCLC 130; *Re Meesan Investments Ltd* (1988) 4 BCC 788; *Bristol Airport plc* v. *Powdrill* [1990] Ch. 744 (reported also as *Re Paramount Airways* [1990] BCC 130); *Re David Meek Access Ltd* [1993] BCC 175; *Scottish Exhibition Centre Ltd, Noters* [1993] BCC 529; and *Euro Commercial Leasing Ltd* v. *Cartwright & Lewis* [1995] BCC 830.

183. *Re Sibec Developments Ltd* [1993] BCC 148.

184. *Bristol Airport plc* v. *Powdrill* [1990] 1 Ch. 744, also reported as *Re Paramount Airways* (1990) BCC 130; *Re Sabre International Products Ltd* (1991) BCC 694.

185. *Re David Meek Access Ltd* (1993) BCC 175.

186. This means judicial or quasi-judicial proceedings: *Bristol Airport plc* v. *Powdrill* [1990] Ch. 744, also reported as *Re Paramount Airways* (1990) BCC 130. See also *Air Ecosse* v. *Civil Aviation Authority* (1987) 3 BCC 492. It includes an application to an industrial tribunal for unfair dismissal: *Carr* v. *British International Helicopters Ltd* (1993) BCC 855. An application for an extension of time for the registration of a charge cannot be described as "proceedings against the company or its property" within IA 1986, s. 11(3)(d): *Re Barrow Borough Transport Ltd* [1990] Ch. 227; (1989) 5 BCC 646. Service of a notice to determine a lease by reason of the appointment of a receiver or administrator of the tenant does not fall within the term "proceedings" nor is it legal process: *Scottish Exhibition Centre Ltd* v. *Mirestop* (1994) BCC 845 (Ct of Session).

187. The meaning of this expression was considered in *Re Olympia & York Canary Wharf Ltd* (1993) BCC 154, in which Millett J. held that "proceedings" and "legal process" do not cover the taking of non-judicial steps such as the service of a contractual notice in order to crystallise the liability of the party on whom the notice is served, not following *Exchange Travel Agency Ltd* v. *Triton Property Trust plc* (1991) BCC 341, in which Harman J. held that a landlord's peaceable re-entry amounts to the commencement or continuation of a legal process.

continued, and no distress[188] may be levied, against the company or its property except with the consent of the administrator or the leave of the court and subject to such terms as the court may impose.[189] If the administrator gives his consent, an application to the court is unnecessary. However, if consent is refused, application may be made to the court. The application is an ordinary application under part 7 of the Insolvency Rules, and follows the procedure laid down in that part.[190] A party who wishes to bring a claim against the company cannot get round the bar in s. 11(3)(d) by making an ordinary application in the administration for the determination of the substantive rights of the parties.[191]

APPOINTMENT AND REMOVAL OF ADMINISTRATOR

12.52 Appointment

This is effected by the order for administration.[192]

12.53 Removal or resignation

The administrator may at any time be removed from office by order of the court and may, in the prescribed circumstances, resign his office by giving notice of his resignation to the court.[193] The prescribed circumstances are ill health, cessation of practice as an insolvency practitioner, or conflict of interest or change of personal circumstances which precludes or makes impractical the further discharge by the administrator of his duties.[194] The notice of resignation must be in Form 2.16.[195] The administrator may, with the leave of the court, give notice of his resignation on some other ground.[196] In such a case, the notice must be in Form 2.17.[197] The administrator must give seven days' notice of his intention to resign, or to apply for the court's leave to do so to any continuing administrator, or if none, to the creditors' committee, and if there is no such administrator or committee, to the company and its creditors.[198]

12.54 Death

Where the administrator has died, it is the duty of his personal representatives to give notice of the fact to the court, specifying the date of the death.[199] However, if the deceased administrator was a partner in a firm, notice may given by a partner in the firm who is

188. The meaning of this expression was considered in *Bristol Airport plc* v. *Powdrill* [1990] 1 Ch. 744, also reported as *Re Paramount Airways* (1990) BCC 130.
189. IA 1986, s. 11(3)(d).
190. See Chapter 10, paras 10.3 *et seq.*
191. *Re Olympia & York Canary Wharf Ltd (No. 2)* (1993) BCC 159.
192. IA 1986, ss. 8(2) and 13(1).
193. IA 1986, s. 19(1).
194. IR 1986, r. 2.53.
195. Reproduced in Appendix 4.
196. IR 1986, r. 2.53(2).
197. Reproduced in Appendix 4.
198. IR 1986, r. 2.53(3).
199. IR 1986, r. 2.54(1).

qualified to act as an insolvency practitioner, or who is a member of any body recognised by the Secretary of State for the authorisation of insolvency practitioners.[200]

12.55 Ceasing to be administrator

Where a person ceases to be administrator, his remuneration and any expenses properly incurred by him are charged on and paid out of any property of the company which is in his custody or under his control at that time in priority to any security to which s. 15(1) then applies.[201] Also, any sums payable in respect of debts or liabilities incurred while he was administrator, under contracts entered into or contracts of employment adopted by him or a predecessor of his in the carrying out of his or the predecessor's functions, stand charged on and are to paid out of the property of the company in his custody or under his control at the time that he ceases to be the administrator.[202] This charge takes priority over that arising under s. 19(4) in respect of the administrator's remuneration and expenses.[203] For this purpose, the administrator is not to be taken to have adopted a contract of employment by reason of anything done or omitted to be done within 14 days after his appointment.[204] However, if the administrator causes the company to continue an employee's employment for more than 14 days, he adopts the contract of employment.[205]

12.56 Release of administrator

A person who has ceased to be the administrator has his release from such date as the court may determine, save in the case of death, in which case the release dates from the time at which notice is given to the court in accordance with the rules.[206] The normal order provides for the release of the administrator on the expiration of a specified period after he has filed his receipts and payments account.[207] From the date of his release, the administrator is discharged from all liability in respect of his acts or omissions as administrator.[208] The court will not grant a release if it appears that there is a proper claim against the administrator which ought to be tried.[209] Nor will the court grant a release if it appears that the administrator may have expended time and money in pursuing purposes not mentioned in the administration order.[210]

200. IR 1986, r. 2.54(2).
201. IA 1986, s. 19(3) and (4).
202. IA 1986, s. 19(3) and (5).
203. IA 1986, s. 19(5).
204. IA 1986, s. 19(5). *Re Paramount Airways Ltd (No. 3)* [1993] BCC 662; *Re Atlantic Computer Systems* [1990] BCC 859.
205. *Powdrill* v. *Watson* [1995] BCC 319. In respect of contracts adopted on or after 15 March 1994 the liability of the administrator is restricted to payment of wages, salary and contributions to a pension scheme in respect of services rendered after the adoption of the contract: see IA 1994, s. 1.
206. IA 1986, s. 20(1).
207. *Re Sibec Developments Ltd* [1993] BCC 148. However, in an appropriate case, the court may be granted in a form saving and excepting one or more claims: *Re Powerstore (Trading) Limited* (1997) unreported, Lightman J.
208. IA 1986, s. 20(2).
209. *Re Sibec Developments Ltd* [1993] BCC 148.
210. *Re Sheridan Securities Ltd* (1988) 4 BCC 200.

12.57 Filling a vacancy

If a vacancy occurs by death, resignation or otherwise in the office of administrator, the court may by order fill the vacancy.[211] Such an application may be made by any continuing administrator, or where there is no such administrator, by a creditors' committee established under s. 26,[212] or where there is no such administrator and no such committee, by the company or the directors, or by any creditor or creditors of the company.[213] Where the court makes an order filling a vacancy, the same provisions apply in respect of giving notice of, and advertising, the order as in the case of an administration order. The application is an ordinary application under part 7 of the Insolvency Rules, and follows the procedure laid down in that Part.[214] However, the court's powers under s. 212 (which provides a summary remedy against an administrator who has been guilty of misfeasance) are preserved.[215]

POWERS AND DUTIES OF ADMINISTRATOR

12.58 General powers

The administrator (a) may do all things as may be necessary for the management of the affairs, business and property of the company, and (b) has the powers specified in sch. 1 to the Act.[216] They are the same powers as those accorded to an administrative receiver.[217] Anyone dealing with the administrator thus knows precisely the power which he has to bind the company. In any event, a person dealing with the administrator in good faith and for value is not concerned to inquire whether the administrator is acting within his powers.[218] The administrator also has power to remove any director of the company and to appoint any person to be a director of it, whether to fill a vacancy or otherwise.[219] He may also call any meeting of the members or creditors of the company.[220] These powers take precedence over any powers conferred on the company or its officers whether by statute or by the memorandum and articles, the exercise of the latter powers requiring the administrator's consent.[221] In exercising his powers, the administrator is deemed to act as the company's agent.[222]

12.59 Directions from the court

Notwithstanding the wide powers given to the administrator, he may apply to the court for directions in relation to any particular matter arising in connection with the carrying out

211. IA 1986, s. 13(2).
212. See para. 12.83, *infra*.
213. IA 1986, s. 13(3). Application may also be made by the Bank of England in the case of authorised institutions or former authorised institutions within the meaning of the Banking Act 1987: see the Banks (Administration Proceedings) Order 1989, S.I. 1989 No. 1276, art. 2, schedule, para. 5.
214. See Chapter 10, paras 10.3 *et seq.*
215. IA 1986, s. 20(3).
216. IA 1986, s. 14(1).
217. IA 1986, s. 42.
218. IA 1986, s. 14(6).
219. IA 1986, s. 14(2)(a).
220. IA 1986, s. 14(2)(b).
221. IA 1986, s. 14(4).
222. IA 1986, s. 14(5); *Re Hartlebury Printers* [1992] BCC 428.

of his functions.[223] This power has been used to permit administrators to call a meeting of creditors to the exclusion of subordinated creditors,[224] to obtain the court's guidance as to whether the company was entitled to exclude from a scheme of arrangement under s. 425 of the Companies Act 1985 the holders of convertible subordinated bonds,[225] as to how the administrator should deal with claims for unfair dismissal,[226] to obtain approval for a scheme to reconstruct a property company[227] and to seek directions as to the trusts upon which the takings of a department store occupied by concessionaires were held.[228] Exceptionally, the court has allowed the use of this power to permit an administrator to implement revised proposals which had not been approved by the creditors, in circumstances where substantial loss would be occasioned by waiting the 14 days required by s. 25(2)(b) to elapse.[229] The application is an ordinary application under part 7 of the Insolvency Rules, and follows the procedure laid down in that part.[230]

12.60 Limitations on administrator's powers

An administrator has no power to disclaim onerous property or contracts.[231] The administration order does not relieve a company of its contractual obligations or deprive others of their proprietary rights, save to the extent that a moratorium against suit or against enforcement of security is provided.[232] Moreover, he does not have power to do acts which are *ultra vires* the company.[233]

12.61 Power to deal with charged property: floating charges

The administrator is given important powers to override charges over the company's property.[234] For this purpose, a distinction is drawn between a security which, as created, was a floating charge, and any other security.[235] In the case of a floating charge, the administrator is given power without the need for any application to the court, to dispose of or otherwise exercise his powers in relation to the property as if it were not subject to the floating charge.[236] Where property is disposed of under this power, the holder of the security has the same priority in respect of any property of the company directly or

223. IA 1986, s. 14(3).
224. *Re British and Commonwealth Holdings plc* [1992] 1 WLR 672.
225. *Re Maxwell Communications Corp. plc* [1993] BCC 369.
226. *Re Paramount Airways Ltd (No. 3)* [1993] BCC 662.
227. *Re Olympia & York Canary Wharf Holdings Ltd* [1993] BCC 866.
228. *Re Lewis's of Leicester Ltd* [1995] BCC 514.
229. *Re Smallman Construction Ltd* (1988) 4 BCC 784. For the procedure for obtaining creditors' approval of the administrator's proposals and any revisions to those proposals, see paras 12.77–12.82, *infra*.
230. See Chapter 10, paras 10.3 *et seq.*
231. *Astor Chemicals Ltd* v. *Synthetic Technology Ltd* [1990] BCC 97 at 105–106. See also *Re P & C and R & T (Stockport) Ltd* [1991] BCC 98.
232. *Re P & C and R & T (Stockport) Ltd* [1991] BCC 98.
233. *Re Home Treat Ltd* [1991] BCC 165.
234. IA 1986, s. 15.
235. IA 1986, s. 15(3).
236. IA 1986, s. 15(1).

indirectly representing the property disposed of as he would have had in respect of the property subject to the security.[237]

12.62 Power to deal with charged property: other charges

In the case of a security other than a floating charge, the administrator may apply to the court. If the court is satisfied that the disposal of the property would be likely to promote the purpose, or one or more of the purposes, specified in the administration order, the court may by order authorise the administrator to dispose of the property as if it were not subject to the security.[238] Such an application may also be made in respect of goods in the possession of the company under a hire-purchase agreement, in which case the order authorises the administrator to dispose of the goods as if all the rights of the owner under the hire-purchase agreement were vested in the company.[239] By s. 15(9), hire-purchase agreements include conditional sale agreements,[240] chattel leasing agreements[241] and retention of title agreements.[242]

12.63 Conditions of order under s. 15(2)

It must be a condition of an order under s. 15(2) that the net proceeds of the disposal shall be applied towards discharging the sums secured by the security or payable under the hire-purchase agreement.[243] Where the proceeds of the disposal are less than the amount which would be realised on a sale of the property or goods in the open market by a willing vendor, it must be a condition of an order under s. 15(2) that a sum equal to the deficiency shall be applied towards discharging sums secured by the security or payable under the hire-purchase agreement.[244] The expression "the sums secured by the security" in s. 15(5) includes not only the capital sum but all interest properly payable under the security and any costs which the proprietor of the security is entitled to add to his security in accordance with the general law and the terms of the instrument in question.[245] Where there are two or more securities, the sums referred to in s. 15(5) are applied towards discharging the sums secured by those securities in order of their priorities.[246] There is no power to make an interim order, but the court can deal with the matter in two stages, first making an order authorising the administrator to dispose of the property, and at a later stage assess the amount, if any, payable under s. 15(2)(b).[247] Where this course is taken,

237. IA 1986, s. 15(4). This subsection is obscure and gives rise to many difficulties outside the scope of this work.
238. IA 1986, s. 15(2).
239. IA 1986, s. 15(2).
240. A term which has the same meaning as in the Consumer Credit Act 1974: see s. 436.
241. An agreement for the bailment of goods which is capable of subsisting for more than three months: see s. 251.
242. An agreement for the sale of goods to a company, being an agreement which does not constitute a charge on the goods, but under which, if the seller is not paid and the company is wound up, the seller will have priority over all other creditors of the company as respects the goods or any property representing the goods: see s. 251.
243. IA 1986, s. 15(5)(a).
244. IA 1986, s. 15(5)(b).
245. *Re ARV Aviation Ltd* (1988) 4 BCC 708.
246. IA 1986, s. 15(6).
247. *Re ARV Aviation Ltd* (1988) 4 BCC 708.

the administrators will be required to undertake to prosecute the necessary inquiry with all reasonable dispatch.

12.64 Exercise of discretion under s. 15(2)

It is not a requirement for the court to have jurisdiction that there should be a *bona fide* dispute between qualified valuers as to the value of the charged property.[248] The court has to balance the prejudice to the secured creditor if the order is made, against the prejudice to those interested in the promotion of the purposes specified in the administration order.[249] The power to allow the disposal of the charged property should not be exercised in such a manner as to circumvent the requirement that the administrator put a statement of his proposals for achievement of the relevant statutory purpose before a meeting of creditors.[250]

12.65 Mode of application under s. 15(2)

Where the administrator makes an application under s. 15(2), the court must fix a venue for the hearing of the application, and the administrator must forthwith give notice of the venue to the person who is the holder of the security or, as the case may be, the owner under the hire-purchase agreement.[251] If an order is made under s. 15(2), the administrator must forthwith give notice of it to the holder of the security or the owner under that agreement.[252] The court must send two sealed copies of the order to the administrator, who must send one of them to the holder or owner.[253] The application is an ordinary application under part 7 of the Insolvency Rules and, subject to the foregoing, the procedure follows that laid down in that part.[254] Where an order is made under s. 15(2), the administrator must send an office copy to the registrar of companies within 14 days after the making of the order.[255]

12.66 General duties

On his appointment, the administrator is under a duty to take into his custody or under his control all the property to which the company is or appears to be entitled.[256] Until proposals have been approved in accordance with the statutory procedure,[257] the administrator must manage the affairs, business and property of the company in accordance with any directions given by the court.[258] After proposals have been approved, it is his duty to manage the company in accordance with those proposals.[259] The administrator must

248. *Ibid.*
249. *Ibid.*
250. See paras 12.77–12.82, *infra.*
251. IR 1986, r. 2.51(2).
252. IR 1986, r. 2.51(3).
253. IR 1986, r. 2.51(4).
254. See Chapter 10, paras 10.3 *et seq.*
255. IA 1986, s. 15(7).
256. IA 1986, s. 17(1).
257. See para. 12.79, *infra.*
258. IA 1986, s. 17(2)(a).
259. IA 1986, s. 17(2)(b).

summon a meeting of the creditors of the company if he is requested to do so by one-tenth in value of the company's creditors, or if he is directed to do so by the court.[260]

12.67 Officer of the court

An administrator is an officer of the court and acts under its directions.[261] Where, therefore, an administrator wrongfully retains goods belonging to another, otherwise than for the proper purposes of the administration—for example, to use them as a bargaining counter—the owner can apply to the court to direct the administrators to hand over the goods without the need for action, and to pay compensation for having retained them in the meantime.[262] Such a claim will lie, whether or not the administrator has committed or procured the commission of the tort of conversion. It appears that the court would have a discretion in such a case to decide whether the administrator is personally liable, whether he should have a right of recoupment against the company's assets, or be released from liability. Where the owner of the goods wishes to claim both in conversion and against the administrator as an officer of the court, the appropriate course is for the issues to be determined by the court having control of the administration (i.e. the companies court).[263]

12.68 Liability on contracts

The administrator is not personally liable on contracts entered into by him in carrying out his functions.[264]

STATEMENT OF AFFAIRS

12.69 Notice requiring statement of affairs

The administrator's first task is to assemble information about the position of the company. For this purpose, the Act imposes a mandatory requirement that the administrator require the officers of the company to make out and submit to him a statement as to the affairs of the company.[265] The notice sent by the administrator must be in Form 2.8.[266] It must inform each of the deponents:

(a) of the names and addresses of all others (if any) to whom the same notice has been sent;
(b) of the time within which the statement must be delivered;
(c) of the effect of s. 22(6) (penalty for non-compliance); and
(d) of the application to him, and to each of the other deponents, of s. 235 (duty to provide information, and to attend on the administrator if required).[267]

260. IA 1986, s. 17(3).
261. *Re Sabre International Products Ltd* [1991] BCC 694.
262. *Re Sibec Developments Ltd* [1993] BCC 148.
263. *Ibid.*
264. *Re Atlantic Computer Systems plc* [1990] BCC 859.
265. IA 1986, s. 22(1).
266. See IR 1986, r. 2.11. Form 2.8 is reproduced in Appendix 4.
267. IR 1986, r. 2.11(3).

The administrator must, on request, furnish each deponent with the forms required for the preparation of the statement of affairs.[268]

12.70 Who can be required to make a statement of affairs

The persons from whom the administrator may require such a statement are:

(a) those who have been officers[269] of the company;
(b) those who have taken part in the company's formation at any time within one year before the date of the administration order;
(c) those who are in the company's employment[270] or have been in its employment within that year, and are, in the administrator's opinion, capable of giving the information required;
(d) those who are or have been within that year officers of or in the employment of a company which is, or within that year was, an officer of the company.[271]

12.71 Form of statement of affairs

The statement must be verified by affidavit and show:

(a) particulars of the company's assets, debts and liabilities;
(b) the names and addresses of its creditors;
(c) the securities held by the creditors;
(d) the dates when the securities were given; and
(e) such further or other information as may be prescribed.[272]

The statement of affairs must be in Form 2.9, must contain all the particulars required by that form and must be verified by affidavit by the deponents using that form.[273] The administrator may require any of the persons mentioned in s. 22(3)[274] to submit an affidavit of concurrence, stating that he concurs in the statement of affairs.[275] An affidavit of concurrence may be qualified in respect of matters dealt with in the statement of affairs, where the maker of the affidavit is not in agreement with the deponent, or he considers the statement of affairs to be erroneous or misleading, or he is without the direct knowledge necessary for concurring with it.[276]

12.72 Time for submitting statement of affairs

Where any persons are required to submit a statement of affairs, they must do so before the end of the period of 21 days beginning with the day after that on which the prescribed

268. IR 1986, r. 2.11(4).
269. The term "officer" in relation to a company includes a director, manager or secretary: see CA 1985, s. 744.
270. The term "employment" includes employment under a contract for services: see the concluding words of IA 1986, s. 22(3).
271. IA 1986, s. 22(3).
272. IA 1986, s. 22(2).
273. IR 1986, r. 2.12(1). Form 2.9 is reproduced in Appendix 4.
274. See para. 12.70, *supra*.
275. IR 1986, r. 2.12(2).
276. IR 1986, r. 2.12(3).

notice of the requirement is given to them by the administrator.[277] The statement of affairs must be delivered to the administrator by the deponent making the affidavit of verification (or by one of them, if more than one), together with a copy of the verified statement.[278] Every affidavit of concurrence must be delivered by the person who makes it, together with a copy.[279]

12.73 Filing of statement of affairs

The administrator must file the verified copy of the statement of affairs, and the affidavits of concurrence (if any) in court.[280] However, the court has power to order limited disclosure of the statement of affairs.[281]

12.74 Limited disclosure of statement of affairs

Where the administrator thinks that it would prejudice the conduct of the administration for the whole or part of the statement of affairs to be disclosed, he may apply to the court for an order of limited disclosure in respect of the statement, or any specified part of it.[282] The application is an ordinary application under part 7 of the Insolvency Rules, and follows that laid down in that part.[283] The court may, on the application, order that the statement or, as the case may be, the specified part of it, be not filed in court, or that it is to be filed separately and not be open to inspection otherwise than with the leave of the court.[284] The court's order may include directions as to the delivery of documents to the registrar of companies and the disclosure of relevant information to other persons.[285]

12.75 Release from duty to submit statement of affairs

The administrator, if he thinks fit, may at any time release a person from an obligation imposed on him to make out and submit a statement of affairs.[286] The administrator may also extend the period for submitting the statement of affairs.[287] If the administrator refuses to exercise this power, the court may, if it thinks fit, exercise it.[288] The powers mentioned may be exercised at the administrator's discretion, or at the request of any deponent.[289] A deponent who has requested a release or an extension of time and been refused by the administrator may apply to the court for such release or extension.[290] The application is an ordinary application under part 7 of the Insolvency Rules and, subject to

277. IA 1986, s. 22(4).
278. IR 1986, r. 2.12(4).
279. IR 1986, r. 2.12(5).
280. IR 1986, r. 2.12(6).
281. See para. 12.76, *infra*.
282. IR 1986, r. 2.13(1).
283. See Chapter 10, paras 10.3 *et seq.*
284. IR 1986, r. 2.13(2).
285. IR 1986, r. 2.13(3).
286. IA 1986, s. 22(5)(a).
287. IA 1986, s. 22(5)(b).
288. IA 1986, s. 22(5).
289. IR 1986, r. 2.14(1).
290. IR 1986, r. 2.14(2).

the specific requirements set out below, follows the procedure laid down in that part.[291] The court may, if it thinks that no sufficient cause is shown for the application, dismiss it; but it must not do so unless the applicant has had an opportunity to attend the court for an *ex parte* hearing, of which he has been given at least seven days' notice.[292] If the application is not dismissed, the court must fix a venue for it to be heard, and give notice to the deponent accordingly.[293] In such case, the deponent must, at least 14 days before the hearing, send to the administrator a notice stating the venue and accompanied by a copy of the application, and of any evidence which he (the deponent) intends to adduce in support of it.[294] The administrator may appear and be heard on the application; and whether or not he appears, he may file a written report of any matters which he considers ought to be drawn to the court's attention. If such a report is filed, a copy of it must be sent by the administrator to the deponent, not later than five days before the hearing.[295] Sealed copies of any order made on the application must be sent by the court to the deponent and the administrator.[296] On any application under these provisions, the applicant's costs must be paid in any event by him, and, unless the court otherwise orders, no allowance towards them shall be made out of the assets of the company.[297]

12.76 Expenses of statement of affairs

A deponent making a statement of affairs and affidavit shall be allowed, and paid by the administrator out of his receipts, any expenses incurred by the deponent in so doing which the administrator considers reasonable.[298] Any decision by the administrator about such expenses is subject to appeal to the court.[299] Such an appeal is made by ordinary application under part 7 of the Insolvency Rules, and follows the procedure laid down in that part.[300]

ADMINISTRATOR'S PROPOSALS

12.77 Statement of proposals

Armed with the information provided in the statement of affairs, the administrator is required to formulate proposals for achieving the purpose or purposes specified in the administration order. Within three months after the making of the order appointing him, he must send to the registrar of companies and to all creditors a statement of these proposals, and lay a copy of the statement before a meeting of the company's creditors

291. See Chapter 10, paras 10.3 *et seq.*
292. IR 1986, r. 2.14(3).
293. IR 1986, r. 2.14(3).
294. IR 1986, r. 2.14(4).
295. IR 1986, r. 2.14(5).
296. IR 1986, r. 2.14(6).
297. IR 1986, r. 2.14(7).
298. IR 1986, r. 2.15(1).
299. IR 1986, r. 2.15(2).
300. See Chapter 10, paras 10.3 *et seq.*

summoned for the purpose on not less than 14 days' notice.[301] The meeting of creditors has to have been *held*, not merely summoned, within the period of three months. The administrator must, also within the same period of three months, send a copy of the statement to all members of the company, or publish in the prescribed manner[302] a notice stating an address to which members of the company may write for copies of the statement to be sent to them free of charge.[303] The three-month period for taking the foregoing steps may be extended by the court. Although the company has *locus standi* to make an application for such extension, it is preferable for it to be made by the administrator.[304] It is made by ordinary application under part 7 of the Insolvency Rules, and follows the procedure laid down in that part.[305] Where the administration order specifies two purposes and the administrator forms the view that one of them is incapable of achievement but that he should implement the other, he should put a statement of proposals before the creditors relating to the latter.[306] Only the administrator's proposals can be considered by the creditors' meeting so summoned: it cannot, for example, consider whether the company should petition for its own winding-up.[307]

12.78 Form and content of statement of proposals

There must be, annexed to the administrator's proposals when sent to the registrar of companies under s. 23 and laid before the creditors' meeting summoned under that section, a statement by him showing:

(a) details relating to his appointment as administrator, the purposes for which an administration order was applied for and made, and any subsequent variation of those purposes;
(b) the names of the directors and secretary of the company;
(c) an account of the circumstances giving rise to the application for an administration order;
(d) if a statement of affairs has been submitted, a copy or summary of it, with the administrator's comments, if any;
(e) if no statement of affairs has been submitted, details of the financial position of the company at the latest practicable date (which must, unless the court otherwise orders, be a date not earlier than that of the administration order);
(f) the manner in which the affairs and business of the company:
    (i) have, since the date of the administrator's appointment, been managed and financed; and
    (ii) will, if the administrator's proposals are approved, continue to be managed and financed; and

301. IA 1986, s. 23(1). The proposals must also be sent to the Bank of England in the case of authorised institutions or former authorised institutions within the meaning of the Banking Act 1987: see the Banks (Administration Proceedings) Order 1989, S.I. 1989 No. 1276, art. 2, schedule, para. 6.
302. This is by gazetting and advertisement once in the newspaper in which the administration order was advertised: r. 2.17.
303. IA 1986, s. 23(2).
304. *Re Newport County Association Football Club Ltd* (1987) 3 BCC 634; [1987] BCLC 582.
305. See Chapter 10, paras 10.3 *et seq*.
306. *Re Charnley Davies Business Services Ltd & Others* (1987) 3 BCC 408.
307. *Ibid.*

(g) such other information (if any) as the administrator thinks necessary to enable creditors to decide whether or not to vote for the adoption of the proposals.[308]

12.79 Consideration of proposals by creditors' meeting

The meeting of creditors summoned under s. 23 must decide whether to accept the administrator's proposals.[309] The proposals may be approved with modifications, but these must be consented to by the administrator.[310] It seems that the meeting does not have power to approve a scheme of distribution of the proceeds of sale of the company's assets.[311] Notice of the meeting must be given to all creditors who are identified in the statement of affairs, or are known to the administrator and had claims against the company at the date of the administration order.[312] Notice of the meeting must also be given by advertisement in the newspaper in which the administration order was advertised, unless the court otherwise directs.[313] Notice must also be given to any directors or officers of the company (including those who have been directors or officers in the past) whose presence at the meeting is, in the administrator's opinion, required.[314] The procedure and voting at the meeting are dealt with in detail in the Rules.[315]

12.80 Report to the court

After the creditor's meeting has been held, the administrator must report the result of the meeting to the court.[316] If the creditors have approved the proposals, they will be implemented, subject to the requirement that the administrator report to the creditors at six-monthly intervals on the progress of the administration.[317] If the creditors have declined to approve the administrator's proposals, the court may discharge the order for administration and make such consequential provision as it thinks fit, or it may adjourn the hearing conditionally or unconditionally, or make an interim order or any other order that it thinks fit.[318]

12.81 Notice to creditors

After the creditors' meeting, the administrator must also give notice of the result (including, where appropriate, details of the proposals approved) to every creditor who received

308. IR 1986, r. 2.16.
309. IA 1986, s. 24(1).
310. IA 1986, s. 24(2).
311. *Re St Ives Windings Ltd* (1987) 3 BCC 634. However, the administrator does have power, if the assets of the company permit him to do so, to pay off the pre-administration creditors in full: see *Re John Slack Ltd* [1995] BCC 1116. Further, in special circumstances, the court can permit a distribution to preferential creditors on the basis of a notional winding-up at the date of the administration order and to the unsecured creditors *pari passu*: see *Re WBSL Realisations 1992 Ltd* [1995] BCC 1118.
312. IR 1986, r. 2.18(1).
313. IR 1986, r. 2.18(2).
314. IR 1986, r. 2.18(3).
315. IR 1986, rr. 2.19–2.28.
316. IA 1986, s. 24(4).
317. IR 1986, r. 2.30(2).
318. IA 1986, s. 24(5).

notice of the meeting, and to any other creditor of whom the administrator has since become aware.[319] This notice must be in Form 2.12.[320] He must do this within 14 days of the conclusion of the meeting. The notice must have annexed to it details of the proposals which were considered by the meeting and of the revisions and modifications to the proposals which were so considered.[321]

12.82 Revision of administrator's proposals

After his proposals have been approved, the administrator may wish to revise them. If he considers the revisions to be substantial, he must send to all creditors a statement of his proposed revisions, and lay a copy of the statement before a meeting of the creditors summoned for the purpose on not less than 14 days' notice.[322] He must not make the proposed revisions unless they are approved by the meeting.[323] In exceptional circumstances, the court may authorise the administrator to depart from an approved scheme without the revisions being approved by the creditors under s. 14(3).[324] The proposals may be approved with modifications, but each modification must be consented to by the administrator.[325] The administrator must also either send a copy of the statement of proposed revisions to all members of the company, or publish a notice stating an address to which members of the company should write for copies of the statement to be sent to them free of charge.[326] The procedure and voting at the meeting are dealt with in detail in the Rules.[327] It is not necessary for the administrator to report on the outcome of the meeting to the court, but he must give notice of the result to the registrar of companies.[328] He must also give notice of the result (including, where appropriate, details of the proposals approved) to every creditor who received notice of the meeting, and to any other creditor of whom the administrator has since become aware.[329] This notice must be in Form 2.12.[330] He must do this within 14 days of the conclusion of the meeting. The notice must have, annexed to it, details of the proposals which were considered by the meeting and of the revisions and modifications to the proposals which were so considered.[331] If the creditors approve the revisions to the proposals, the administrator may implement them, subject to the requirement that he report to the creditors at six-monthly intervals on the progress of the administration.[332] If the creditors decline to approve the revised proposals, the administrator may continue to act under the previous proposals. Alternatively, he may formulate a new set of revised proposals and seek further approval from the creditors. In the further alternative, he may apply to the court under s. 18(1) to vary the purpose

319. IA 1986, s. 24(4) and IR 1986, r. 2.30.
320. Reproduced in Appendix 4.
321. IR 1986, r. 2.29.
322. IA 1986, s. 25(2). The revised prosposals must also be sent to the Bank of England in the case of authorised institutions or former authorised institutions within the meaning of the Banking Act 1987: see the Banks (Administration Proceedings) Order 1989, S.I. 1989 No. 1276, art. 2, schedule, para. 7.
323. IA 1986, s. 25(2).
324. *Re Smallman Construction Ltd* (1988) 4 BCC 784.
325. IA 1986, s. 25(4).
326. IA 1986, s. 25(3).
327. IR 1986, rr. 2.19–2.28.
328. IA 1986, s. 25(6).
329. IA 1986, s. 25(6) and IR 1986, r. 2.30(1).
330. Reproduced in Appendix 4.
331. IR 1986, r. 2.29.
332. IR 1986, r. 2.30(2).

specified in the administration order. In the last resort, he may apply to the court under s. 18(2) for the discharge of the order for administration.

CREDITORS' COMMITTEE

12.83 Nature and purpose

The creditors' committee is a committee established by the creditors at the meeting summoned under s. 23 for the purpose of keeping the creditors informed about the progress of the administration.[333] The creditors can only decide to establish such a committee where the administrator's proposals have been approved (with or without modifications).[334] The committee is intended to operate as a channel for the communication of information about the administration to the creditors, and it is charged with the duty of assisting the administrator in carrying out his functions.[335] The committee's principal weapon is the power conferred on it to require the administrator, on not less than seven days' notice, to attend before it at any reasonable time, and furnish it with such information relating to the carrying out of his functions as it may reasonably require.[336] This power is exercised by notice in writing signed by the majority of the members of the committee.[337] If the creditors are dissatisfied, they have two main remedies available to them. They can apply under s. 27 alleging that the administrator has managed the affairs of the company in a manner which is unfairly prejudicial to the creditors.[338] Alternatively, they can require the administrator to convene a creditors' meeting under s. 17(3)(a) (which he must do if so requested by one-tenth in value of the creditors). The creditors' meeting can in turn call on the administrator to make an application under s. 18 for the discharge or variation of the administration order.[339] The administrator is obliged to make an application under that section if required to do so by a meeting of the company's creditors summoned for the purpose in accordance with the Rules.[340] The court may discharge or vary the administration order, and make such consequential provision as it thinks fit.[341]

12.84 Composition and procedure

The creditors' committee consists of at least three and not more than five creditors of the company elected at the creditors' meeting.[342] The committee does not come into being, and cannot act, until the administrator issues a certificate of its due constitution.[343] The procedure to be followed by the committee is set out in detail in the rules.[344]

333. IA 1986, s. 26(1).
334. IA 1986, s. 26(1).
335. IR 1986, r. 2.34(1).
336. IA 1986, s. 26(2).
337. IR 1986, r. 2.44(1).
338. See para. 12.86, *infra*.
339. See para. 12.85, *infra*.
340. IA 1986, s. 18(2)(a).
341. IA 1986, s. 18(3).
342. IR 1986, r. 2.32(1).
343. IR 1986, r. 2.31(1).
344. See IR 1986, rr. 2.32–2.46A.

DISCHARGE OR VARIATION OF ADMINISTRATION ORDER

12.85 Application by administrator

The administrator may at any time apply to the court for the administration order to be discharged, or to be varied so as to specify an additional purpose.[345] The administrator has a duty to make such an application in two cases:

(1) if it appears to him that the purpose of each of the purposes specified in the order either has been achieved or is incapable of achievement; and
(2) if he is required to do so by a meeting of the company's creditors summoned for the purpose in accordance with the Rules.[346]

On the hearing of such an application, the court may by order discharge or vary the administration order and make such consequential provision as it thinks fit, or adjourn the hearing conditionally or unconditionally or make an interim order or any other order it thinks fit.[347] Where the discharge of the administrator is sought, coupled with approval of a scheme for restructuring of the company, the court does not have to be satisfied that the success of the scheme is assured, and such approval may be given where the scheme stands a fair chance of success and provides the best hope for the company and its creditors.[348]

Where the purposes of the administration order have been achieved, and it is proposed that the company should go into voluntary liquidation, it is essential that the discharge of the administration orders and the resolutions to go into voluntary liquidation are contemporaneous, if the onset of insolvency for the purposes of ss. 238 and 239 of the Insolvency Act 1986 (transactions at an undervalue and preferences) is to be deemed to be the date of presentation of the petition for the making of the administration order, and not the date of the resolutions to wind-up. The usual practice is to make the order for discharge conditional on the passing of the resolutions to go into voluntary liquidation.[349] The alternative is to direct (a) that the orders for discharge shall not be drawn up until copies of the resolutions have been lodged at the Court Office with letters from the administrators' solicitors certifying the resolutions were duly passed; and (b) that those documents be lodged either on the same or the following day.[350]

There may be cases in which it makes a difference to the creditors whether the company goes into voluntary or compulsory liquidation, for in the case of a compulsory liquidation the preferential creditors are to be ascertained as at the date of the administration order, whereas in the case of voluntary liquidation, they are to be ascertained as at the date of the resolution to wind-up. However, the court does not have jurisdiction under either ss. 14(3) or 18 to order that the creditors who would be preferential creditors if the company went into compulsory liquidation shall enjoy a like preference if the companies go into a voluntary liquidation.[351] This means that the costs of a compulsory liquidation will have to be incurred in such cases.

345. IA 1986, s. 18(1).
346. IA 1986, s. 18(2).
347. IA 1986, s. 18(3). This does not enable the court to make a winding-up order: see *Re Brooke Marine Ltd* [1988] BCLC 546.
348. *Re Olympia & York Canary Wharf Holdings Ltd* [1993] BCC 866.
349. *Re Powerstore (Trading) Limited* (1997) unreported, Lightman J.
350. *Ibid.*
351. *Ibid.*

Where the administration order is discharged or varied, the administrator must, within 14 days after the making of the order effecting the discharge or variation, send an office copy of the order to the registrar of companies.[352] Where the administrator intends to apply to the court under s. 18 for the administration order to be discharged at a time before he has sent a statement of proposals to creditors in accordance with s. 23(1), he must, at least 10 days before he makes such an application, send to all creditors of the company (so far as he is aware of their addresses) a report containing the information required by paras (1)(a) to (f)(i) of r.2.16(1).[353]

PROTECTION FOR CREDITORS AND MEMBERS

12.86 Unfair prejudice

A creditor or member may apply to the court if they believe that the administrator is managing the affairs of the company in a way which is prejudicial to their interests.[354] Such an application may be made by a creditor or member on the ground:

(a) that the company's affairs, business or property are being or have been managed by the administrator in a manner which is unfairly prejudicial to the interests of its creditors or members generally, or some part of its creditors or members (including at least himself); or
(b) that any actual or proposed act or omission of the administrator is or would be so prejudicial.[355]

It will be seen that this jurisdiction is very similar to that which exists under s. 459 of the Companies Act 1985.[356] The section is specifically concerned with the administrator's conduct during the time that the administration order is in force. It is wider in scope than s. 459 in that it enables a creditor as well as a member to petition. Where the administrator negligently sells the company's assets at an undervalue, this is insufficient to establish a claim for relief.[357] The proper course in such a case is to have the administration order discharged and a liquidator appointed who would then bring a claim against the administrator under s. 212 of the Insolvency Act 1986. An allegation that the acts complained of are unlawful or infringe the petitioner's legal rights is not a necessary averment in a s. 27 petition, nor is it a sufficient averment.[358] The petitioner must allege and prove that the matters complained of are evidence or instances of mismanagement of the company's affairs by the administrator in a manner which is unfairly prejudicial to the petitioner's interests; the court will not put a gloss on the statutory language.[359] An order may only be made whilst the administration order remains in force.

352. IA 1986, s. 18(4).
353. IR 1986, r. 2.16(2). See para. 12.78, *supra*.
354. IA 1986, s. 27.
355. IA 1986, s. 27.
356. See Chapter 6 for a discussion of that jurisdiction.
357. *Re Charnley Davies Ltd* [1990] BCC 605.
358. *Ibid.*
359. *Ibid.*

12.87 Application

The application is made by petition.[360] The Bank of England may also apply in the case of authorised institutions or former authorised institutions within the meaning of the Banking Act 1987.[361]

12.88 Order

The order may:

(a) regulate the future management by the administrator of the company's affairs, business and property;
(b) require the administrator to refrain from doing or continuing an act complained of by the petitioner, or to do an act which the petitioner has complained he has omitted to do;
(c) require the summoning of a meeting of creditors or members for the purpose of considering such matters as the court may direct;
(d) discharge the administration order and make such consequential provision as the court thinks fit.[362]

12.89 Limits of order

There are two limitations on the power of the court to make an order. First, an order is not to prejudice or prevent the implementation of a voluntary arrangement approved under s. 4 of part I, or any compromise or arrangement sanctioned under s. 425 of the Companies Act.[363] The rationale for this limitation is that a member or creditor who objects to a voluntary arrangement under s. 4 or a compromise or arrangement under s. 425 of the Companies Act has statutory rights to object thereto.[364] If the member or creditor has not exercised those rights, or has done so but without success, the arrangement or compromise should stand, and not be capable of being upset by a petition under s. 27. Second, where the application for an order was made more than 28 days after the approval of any proposals or revised proposals under ss. 24 or 25, the order under s. 27 shall not prejudice or prevent the implementation of those proposals or revised proposals.[365] Thus, a creditor who opposes the administrator's proposals (or any revised proposals) may object at the creditors' meeting called for the purpose of considering those proposals under s. 24, but if his objections are overridden at that meeting, he can apply to the court by petition under s. 27 within 28 days. If he waits longer than the 28 days, the implementation of the proposals or revised proposals cannot be prevented by an order under s. 27.

360. IA 1986, s. 27.
361. See the Banks (Administration Proceedings) Order 1989, SI 1989 No. 1276, art. 2, schedule, para. 8.
362. IA 1986, s. 27(4).
363. IA 1986, s. 27(3)(a).
364. In respect of a voluntary arrangement, under ss. 6 and 7(3), and in respect of a scheme of compromise or arrangement, under CA 1985, s. 425(2).
365. IA 1986, s. 27(3)(a).

12.90 Discharge of administration order

Where the administration order is discharged, the administrator must within 14 days after the making of the order send an office copy to the registrar of companies.[366]

366. IA 1986, s. 27(6).

CHAPTER 13

APPLICATIONS IN ADMINISTRATIVE RECEIVERSHIPS

INTRODUCTION

13.1 Status of receiver appointed under a floating charge

The idea of a receiver or manager appointed under a floating charge is well established in English law. The concept encourages lending as the properly secured creditor will be able rapidly to appoint a receiver to take control of a company, facilitating the speedy and advantageous enforcement and realisation of security. Although the concept was well established prior to the insolvency legislation of 1985 and 1986, the law relating to such appointments suffered from uncertainty. The Cork Committee recommended that the law be clarified by statute. IA 1985, chapter IV introduced for the first time the concept of the administrative receiver (consolidated with part of CA 1985 in part III of IA 1986).

13.2 Definition

IA 1986, s. 29 defines an "administrative receiver" as:

> "(i) a receiver or manager of the whole (or substantially the whole) of a company's property appointed by or on behalf of the holders of any debentures of the company secured by a charge which, as created, was a floating charge, or by such a charge and one or more other securities;
>
> or
>
> (ii) a person who would be such a receiver or manager but for the appointment of some other person as the receiver of part of the company's property."

13.2.1 Looking at the definition in greater detail, the administrative receiver must be:

(1) "*A receiver or manager*".

(2) "*Of the whole (or substantially the whole) of a company's property*": The issue of what constitutes substantially the whole of a company's property must be determined as a question of fact in the light of the purpose of the legislation which is to allow a receiver having substantive control of the company to deal with those assets as a going concern. The question should be answered as at the date of appointment.

(3) "*The company*": Despite the definition of "the company" as a company formed and registered under CA 1985 or predecessor legislation,[1] it has been held that

1. CA 1985, s. 735.

the jurisdiction includes companies incorporated overseas but capable of being wound up as unregistered companies under Part V, IA 1986.[2]

(4) "*Appointed by or on behalf of the holders of any debentures of the company*": This excludes a court appointed receiver.

(5) "*Secured by a charge which, as created, was a floating charge or by such a charge and one or more other securities*": Given the purpose of the legislation as discussed in (2) above, the receiver must be appointed under a floating as opposed to a fixed charge. An appointee under a fixed charge by a person holding the benefit of both fixed and floating charges has been held not to be an administrative receiver.[3]

13.3 Comparison with other forms of receiver

There are two other main types of receiver: a court appointed receiver or manager and a receiver appointed pursuant to the Law of Property Act 1925, s. 101. The most important distinctions are as follows:

(a) Neither of these types of receiver need be a licenced insolvency practitioner as is the case with administrative receivers.[4]

(b) They can be displaced by an administrator. In the case of an administrative receiver, the automatic moratorium which is essential to the administration procedure[5] will not operate while an administrative receiver remains in office without the consent of the debenture-holder on whose behalf the administrative receiver was appointed.[6]

(c) Unlike the administrative receiver, neither is an office-holder. As a result, he does not have the right to manage the supply of utilities,[7] the right to examine company officers and others and to require the production of company property and documents.[8] Nor does he have a duty to require a statement of affairs and to report to all secured creditors and to the registrar of companies.

(d) Their powers are entirely defined by the debenture or, in the case of a court appointed receiver, are implied by statute. The administrative receiver may apply for an order allowing him to dispose of property subject to a prior ranking charge as if it were not subject to such security.[9] The charge will attach to the proceeds of sale.[10]

(e) Persons dealing with this type of receiver should be concerned to inquire if he is acting within the scope of his powers[11] and as to whether there are any defects in his appointment, nomination or qualifications.[12] In the case of an admini-

2. *Re International Bulk Commodities* [1993] Ch. 77 per Mummery J. But see *Re Devon and Somerset Farmers Ltd* [1993] BCC 410 for a contrary decision.

3. *Meadrealm Ltd* v. *Transcontinental Golf Construction* (29 November 1991, Vinelott J, unreported); see (1993) 6 *Insolvency Intelligence* 41.

4. IA 1986, s. 388(1).

5. IA 1986, s. 10.

6. IA 1986, s. 10(3).

7. IA 1986, s. 233.

8. IA 1986, ss. 234–236; see Chapter 15.

9. IA 1986, s. 43.

10. IA 1986, s. 43(1) and (7).

11. IA 1986, s. 42(3).

12. IA 1986, s. 232.

strative receiver, no such defects (at least those relating to form or procedure) will affect his acts.

(f) There are no statutory provisions barring the removal or replacement of a non-administrative receiver.[13]

APPLICATIONS RELATING TO APPOINTMENT

13.4 Challenge to appointment

The appointment of an administrative receiver, unlike the position in liquidation, does not terminate the director's office, although, dependent upon the contractual terms of the debenture under which the receiver is appointed, the powers of the directors will be minimal. The purpose of appointing an administrative receiver is to allow the realisation and management of the company's property without interference from the directors.[14]

The directors' residual powers would include bringing an action on behalf of the company to challenge the appointment of an administrative receiver.[15]

13.4.1 Where a debenture holder appoints a receiver before prior ranking creditors, the creditors with priority may wish to challenge the appointment. IA 1986, s. 29 clearly provides that only one receiver (or jointly appointed receivers) may hold office at any one time. Apart from the company itself, persons with a potential interest in challenging an appointment with *locus standi* might include a subsequently appointed liquidator, other debenture holders[16] and judgment creditors.[17]

13.5 Procedure for application

Any challenge to the validity of an appointment would not be made under IA 1986, since the inevitable inference to be drawn where it is alleged that there was no valid appointment under the debenture, is that no jurisdiction under the IA 1986 has arisen. Such actions are not strictly within the scope of this book and might encompass a wide range of parties and possible causes of action. Challenges might centre upon the validity of the instrument under which the receiver was purportedly appointed: for example, alleging that it was invalid by reason of non-registration,[18] that the instrument was a forgery or was procured by misrepresentation. Alternatively, it might be said that one of the events triggering a right of appointment had not yet taken place, for example by reason of a failure to make a valid demand for payment[19] or to give a reasonable time to effect payment.[20] A third

13. IA 1986, s. 45(1).

14. *Gomba Holdings Ltd* v. *Homan* [1986] 1 WLR 1301 at 1306 per Hoffmann J.

15. *Cripps (Pharmaceuticals) Ltd* v. *Wickenden and Others* [1973] 2 All ER 606; *Hawkesbury Development Co. Ltd* v. *Landmark Finance Pty Ltd* [1969] 92 WN (NSW) 199; *Paramount Acceptance Co. Ltd* v. *Souster* [1981] 2 NZLR 38.

16. *Re Metropolitan Amalgamated Estates Ltd* [1912] 2 Ch. 497; *Re Slogger Automatic Feeder Co. Ltd* [1915] 1 Ch. 478.

17. *Kasofsky* v. *Kreegers* [1937] 4 All ER 374.

18. Charges which require registration must be registered within 21 days of creation: CA 1985, s. 404. Failure to register such a charge renders it void against a liquidator, administrator or any creditor of the company: CA 1985, s. 395.

19. See, for example: *Elwich Bay Shipping Co.* v. *Royal Bank of Scotland* (1982) SLT 62; *Cripps* v. *Wickenden* [1973] 1 WLR 944.

20. See, for example: *Bank of Baroda* v. *Panessar* [1987] Ch. 335; *Re Toynar Ltd (in receivership)* [1988] 4 BCC 6; *Macleod* v. *Jones* (1883) 24 Ch.D. 289, C.A.; *Duke* v. *Robson* [1973] 1 WLR 267.

possibility might be to challenge the ability of the receiver himself to act, perhaps because he was not a licensed insolvency practitioner. The action brought might be against the receiver and/or the person appointing him, based upon trespass or constructive trust. Such actions would be commenced by writ or originating summons and might seek declaratory and/or injunctive relief, together with damages or equitable compensation.

13.6 Application by receiver for indemnity

If the floating charge under which a receiver is appointed is invalid, it follows that his appointment will also be invalid. The receiver will therefore be exposed to liability for any actions he has taken after his appointment, typically as a trespasser or constructive trustee of the assets he holds belonging to the company.[21] The potential for such claims was sufficiently worrying to prompt the Jenkins Report to propose that an appointee be relieved from any such liability. Unfortunately, the proposals were not implemented. The prudent receiver will therefore seek to ensure that the contract relating to his appointment from the debenture-holder includes a contractual right of indemnity.

If for some reason, the appointment of a person as a receiver is discovered to be invalid (whether by virtue of the invalidity of the instrument or otherwise), the court may order the person by whom or on whose behalf the appointment was made, to indemnify the appointee against any liability which arises solely by reason of the invalidity of the appointment.[22] The word "solely" suggests that the power to order an indemnity will only apply where the appointment is void or avoided, for example where it is discovered that the debenture was not registered or it is subsequently successfully challenged by a liquidator. Other circumstances which might give rise to this situation might be where the debenture was found to amount to unlawful financial assistance for the purchase of shares or where an invalid demand was made. The power to make such an order is discretionary. It is unlikely that the court would grant relief where the facts giving rise to the invalidity of the appointment were or could reasonably have been established at the time of appointment by the appointee. In those circumstances, the receiver would be wise to seek to ensure that he is not exposed to any risk. Whilst IA 1986, s. 232 provides that the acts of an individual as administrative receiver are valid despite any defect in his appointment, this will not validate the acts of an appointee where there was no power to appoint him in the first place.[23]

13.7 Procedure

The application is made by *inter partes* originating application.[24] The respondent should be the person by whom or on whose behalf the appointment was made. The application should be filed at court accompanied by one additional copy and a number of copies equal to the number of persons who are to be served with the application.[25] The sealed copy of

21. *Re Goldberg (No. 2)* [1912] 1 KB 606; *Ford & Carter* v. *Midland Bank* (1979) 129 N.L.J. 543, H.L.; for an article on the subject see *Doyleu* [1995] 11 IL & P 5.
22. IA 1986, s. 34.
23. See *Morris* v. *Canzone & Others* [1946] AC 459 for the analogous position regarding defects in the appointment of directors.
24. IR 1986, r. 7.2(1).
25. IR 1986, r. 7.4(1).

the originating application is then served upon the respondent. If the matter is straightforward and could be dealt with at the first hearing, the applicant then files affidavit(s) in support and serves the respondent not less than 14 days before the date fixed for the hearing.[26] The respondent may file affidavits in response which should be filed not less than seven days before the date fixed for the hearing.[27] The hearing will be before the Registrar. If the applicant is successful, the court will usually order the respondent to indemnify the applicant against all damages, costs liabilities and expenses occasioned by the invalidity of the instrument of appointment.

APPLICATIONS FOLLOWING APPOINTMENT

13.8 Directions under s. 35

A receiver, or the persons by whom or on whose behalf he has been appointed, may apply to the court for directions in relation to any particular matter arising in connection with the performance of the receiver's functions.[28] The court may give such directions, or make such order declaring the rights of persons before the court or otherwise, as it thinks fit.[29] This is a useful and wide-ranging provision of which, in cases of uncertainty, the receiver should be prepared to make use. The purpose of the section is to allow the receiver or appointor easy access to the court to sort out any difficulty in connection with the performance of the receiver's duties.[30] However, although the power to give directions should be interpreted liberally, directions should not be sought on matters which are properly matters of commercial judgment.[31] The following are some of the most common areas where applications are made, although the list is far from exhaustive.

13.9 Validity of appointment

Where the validity of a receiver's appointment is at issue, usually because of issues concerning the debenture, there is some doubt as to whether the receiver himself can apply for directions, since the section appears to envisage applications by the receiver, only when he is "so appointed".[32] In such circumstances, it might be more appropriate for the debenture holder to make the application. Where there is some doubt, the proposed receiver might require the debenture holder to seek a declaration that the charge is valid. In reality, the appointment of a receiver usually has to be made quickly in order to safeguard the assets of the company and such a course would therefore be impractical. On balance, there is little reason why an application should not be made by the receiver himself pursuant to the section, as he has an interest in establishing the position and the section affords an easy method of clarifying such issues. The court could declare whether

26. IR 1986, rr. 7.7(1), 7.8(1).
27. IR 1986, r. 7.8(1)(b).
28. IA 1986, s. 35(1).
29. IA 1986, s. 35(2).
30. *Re Therm-a-Stor Ltd* [1996] 2 BCLC 400 at 407.
31. *Deputy Commissioner of Taxation* v. *Best & Less* (1992) 10 ACLC 520.
32. See by analogy the decision of *Re Wood and Martin Ltd* [1971] 1 WLR 293 where it was held in relation to an application to declare the dissolution of a company void, that a liquidator not properly appointed was not "a person interested".

the appointment was valid or not and, if not, direct that such steps be taken as might be required to remedy any defect.

13.10 Priorities

Questions often arise as to priorities and order of distribution of assets, especially relating to the status of other charges. The issue of floating charges over book debts in particular, has caused uncertainty in recent years.[33]

13.11 Sale of assets to interested party

There is nothing wrong *per se* with a receiver disposing of charged assets to anyone who is connected with his appointee. Indeed, there may be very good commercial reasons for doing so.[34] In such a case, however, the receiver, being bound to seek the best price reasonably obtainable, will wish to ensure that he could not subsequently be criticised. An application pursuant to IA 1986, s. 35 will often be the most appropriate method of ensuring this.

Where the receiver himself wishes to purchase assets on his own account, he will *prima facie* be liable to account for any profit made by him based on the usual principles applicable to fiduciaries.[35] This principle applies whether the receiver is directly interested or whether there is a trustee acting for him.[36] Court consent for the sale can be sought by application pursuant to IA 1986, s. 35. The receiver will have to show that the price he is offering is the best that could reasonably be obtained.

13.12 Scheme of arrangement

This may be a suitable alternative to a sale of the business of the company. However, a receiver is not within the class of persons entitled to apply to the court for sanction of such a scheme.[37] If he wished to be involved in the promotion of such a scheme, the receiver would be well advised to consider seeking directions pursuant to IA 1986, s. 35.

13.13 Procedure

The application is usually made by *ex parte* originating application, save where an order for general liberty to apply has previously been made, where an ordinary application is appropriate. The applicant should file an affidavit in support. On the first hearing before the registrar, in other than straightforward cases, directions may be given as to service on other parties of notice of the application (where necessary) together with further directions as to evidence. On the adjourned hearing, the registrar will deal with the substantive application.

33. *Re Woodroffes (Musical Instruments) Ltd* [1986] Ch. 366; *Re Brightlife Ltd* [1987] Ch. 200; *Re New Bullas Trading Ltd* [1994] BCC 36, [1994] 1 BCLC 485; *Re Pearl Maintenance Services Ltd* [1995] 1 BCLC 449; *Royal Trust Bank* v. *National Westminster Bank plc* [1996] 2 BCLC 682.

34. See for example *Farrar* v. *Farrars Ltd* (1888) 40 Ch.D. 395; *Tse Kwong La* v. *Wong Chit Sen* [1983] 3 All ER 54.

35. See *Nugent* v. *Nugent* [1908] 1 Ch. 546.

36. *Alven* v. *Bond* (1841) Fl&K 196.

37. CA 1985, s. 425(1).

13.14 Costs

If the issue involves parties in dispute, the usual rule that costs follow the event will be applied. In many cases, the application will be *ex parte*, with no other parties being involved. The court has a discretion to order the costs to be paid out of the company's assets covered by the receivership. In cases where it is necessary for the receiver to obtain a decision from the court in order properly to carry out his functions, there may often be large classes of creditors, contributories or other claimants, the exact membership of which class is often not easily established or even known, who will be affected by such a decision. In such a case, the receiver may join a representative respondent to argue the point on behalf of the class. Frequently the sum at stake for the individual respondent joined does not justify him incurring the costs involved in litigating the matter. In order to ensure that the matter is properly determined, the costs of the representative respondents are frequently paid out of the fund. An agreement to that effect is often made before the proceedings are heard and the receiver would be wise to seek the sanction of the court if he wishes to adopt this course.[38]

13.15 Remuneration

Where a receiver and the liquidator cannot reach agreement over the level of fees incurred by the receiver during his term in office, the liquidator is empowered to apply to the court to fix the receiver's remuneration.[39] Section 36(2) provides that the court may order remuneration for any period before the making of the order or the application or where the receiver has died or ceased to act prior to the order or application. The court may also order a receiver or his personal representatives to repay excessive remuneration paid prior to the making of the order. An order requiring a receiver to repay remuneration already paid will only be made where such remuneration can clearly be seen to have been excessive.[40]

13.16 Procedure

If the liquidator and the receiver reach this level of impasse, it is possible that the receiver may refuse to pay over the residue of the company's property held by him. In such circumstances, the appropriate course for the liquidator to adopt is to combine the application under IA 1986, s. 36 with applications for an account of receipts and payments and payment over to the liquidator of the amount properly payable to him pursuant to IA 1986, s. 41.[41] In addition, the liquidator may request that the receiver lodge a statement of remuneration taken, including details of the work done and the charging rate for that work. The application is again made by originating application by the liquidator supported by affidavit evidence.

38. *Re Westdock Realisations Ltd* [1988] BCLC 354; *Re Biddencare Ltd* [1994] 2 BCLC 146.
39. IA 1986, s. 36.
40. *Re Potters Oils Ltd* [1986] 1 WLR 201.
41. See para. 13.17, *infra*.

13.17 Returns and accounts

A receiver has important obligations with regard to giving notice of his appointment, reporting to the registrar of companies and delivering to the registrar accounts of his receipts and payments as receiver. If he defaults, a creditor or member of the company, or the registrar of companies may apply to the court under IA 1986, s. 41 for an order directing the receiver to make good his default. The most important of these obligations are as follows;

(a) To send to the company and creditors and to publish a notice of his appointment.[42] The notice should state:
   (i) the registered name of the company, as at the date of the appointment, and its registered number;
   (ii) any other name with which the company has been registered in the 12 months preceding that date;
   (iii) any other name with which the company has traded at any time in those 12 months, if substantially different from its then registered name;
   (iv) the name and address of the administrative receiver, and the date of his appointment;
   (v) the name of the person by whom the appointment was made;
   (vi) the date of the instrument conferring the power under which the appointment was made, and a brief description of the instrument;
   (vii) a brief description of the assets of the company (if any) in respect of which the person appointed is not made the receiver.

   He should advertise notice of his appointment once in the *Gazette* and once in such newspaper as he thinks most appropriate for ensuring that it comes to the notice of the company's creditors.[43] The advertisement should be in Form 3.1A and state matters in sub-paras (i) to (v) above.
(b) To give notice of his appointment in statutory Form 405 to the registrar of companies within seven days of appointment.[44]
(c) Within three months of appointment (or longer if sanctioned by the court) to send a report to the registrar of companies, trustees for secured creditors and all other secured creditors of which he is aware.[45]
(d) To deliver to the registrar of companies accounts of receipts and payments as receiver within two months (or such longer period as the registrar may allow) after the expiration of 12 months from the date of his appointment and of every subsequent period of 12 months.[46] The accounts should be in the form of an abstract, showing receipts and payments during the period, or where the receiver has ceased to act, receipts and payments during the period from the end of the last 12-month period to the time when he ceased to act.[47]

13.17.1 Section 41 provides that if a receiver, having made default in filing, delivering or making any return, account or other document, or in giving any notice, which a receiver

42. IA 1986, s. 46(1).
43. IR 1986, r. 3.2(3).
44. CA 1985, s. 405(1).
45. IA 1986, s. 48.
46. IA 1986, s. 38.
47. IR 1986, r. 3.2(3).

is by law required to file, deliver, make or give, fails to make good the default within 14 days after the service on him of a notice requiring him to do so, any creditor or member of the company, or the registrar of companies, may apply to the court for an order directing the receiver to make good the default within such time as is specified in the order.

In addition, where the receiver has been appointed under powers in an instrument, if after being required at any time by the liquidator of the company he fails to render proper accounts of his receipts and payments and to vouch for them and pay over to the liquidator the amount properly payable to him, the liquidator may apply for an order directing the receiver to do so on similar terms as stated above.[48]

In either case, the court may order that all costs incidental to the application be borne by the receiver.[49]

13.18 Application for extension of time

The court may, on an application by the receiver, extend the period of two months. The application is by way of originating application supported by affidavit evidence. The registrar of companies, the company, the person by whom he was appointed and the members of the creditors' committee (if there is one) should be joined as respondents.

13.19 Powers of the administrative receiver

Whilst a debenture appointing a receiver may set out various powers which he may exercise, in the case of administrative receivership the powers conferred by the debenture are deemed to include (except in so far as they are inconsistent with any of the provisions of the debenture) the powers specified in IA 1986, schedule 1.[50] These include:

(a) power to take possession of, collect and get in the property of the company and, for that purpose, to take such proceedings as may seem to him expedient;
(b) power to sell or otherwise dispose of the property of the company by public auction or private auction or private contract or, in Scotland, to sell, feu, hire out or otherwise dispose of the property of the company by public roup or private bargain;
(c) power to raise or borrow money and grant security therefor over the property of the company;
(d) power to appoint a solicitor or accountant or other professionally qualified person to assist him in the performance of his functions;
(e) power to bring or defend any action or other legal proceedings in the name and on behalf of the company;
(f) power to refer to arbitration any question affecting the company;
(g) power to effect and maintain insurances in respect of the business and property of the company;
(h) power to appoint any agent to do any business which he is unable to do himself or which can more conveniently be done by an agent, and power to employ and dismiss employees;

48. IA 1986, s. 41(1)(b).
49. IA 1986, s. 41(2).
50. IA 1986, s. 42(1).

(i) power to do all things (including the carrying out of works) as may be necessary for the realisation of the property of the company;
(j) power to carry on the business of the company;
(k) power to transfer to subsidiaries of the company the whole or any part of the business and property of the company;
(l) power to present or defend a petition for the winding-up of the company;
(m) power to do all things incidental to the exercise of the forgoing powers.[51]

13.20 Power to dispose of charged property

Where, on an application by the receiver, the court is satisfied that the disposal of any relevant property which is subject to a security would be likely to promote a more advantageous realisation of the company's assets than would otherwise be effected, the court may, by order, authorise the receiver to dispose of the property as if it were not subject to the security.[52]

"Relevant property" for these purposes is defined as that property of which the receiver is, or, but for the appointment of some other person as receiver of part of the company's property would be, the receiver or manager.[53]

The power does not include security held by the person by or on whose behalf the receiver was appointed, or any security to which a security so held has priority.[54]

Any order made is conditional upon the net proceeds of the disposal and (where the proceeds are less than such amount as may be determined by the court to be the net amount which would be realised on the sale of the property in the open market by a willing seller) such sum as may be required to make good the deficiency, being applied towards discharging the sums secured by the security.[55]

13.21 Procedure

The application is by way of *inter partes* originating application. The holder of the security in question is the respondent. The court will fix a venue for the hearing of the application and the receiver should forthwith give notice of the venue to the person who is holder of the security.[56] Unless the court orders otherwise, this is done by way of serving a sealed copy of the application. The applicant files and serves on the respondent an affidavit in support, not less than 14 days before the date fixed for the hearing.[57] The respondent may file affidavits in response which should be filed not less than seven days before the date fixed for the hearing.[58] The parties will then attend before the registrar on the hearing. If an order is made, the court will send two sealed copies to the receiver. He should send one of these to the holder of the security to which the property in question relates.[59] An office copy of the order must also be sent by the receiver to the registrar of

51. See IA 1986, sch. 1, for the full list.
52. IA 1986, s. 43(1).
53. IA 1986, s. 43(7).
54. IA 1986, s. 43(2).
55. IA 1986, s. 43(3).
56. IR 1986, r. 3.31(1) and (2) and r. 13.6.
57. IR 1986, r. 7.8(1)(a).
58. IR 1986, r. 7.8(1)(b).
59. IR 1986, r. 3.31(3).

companies within 14 days of the making of the order.[60] Failure to send a copy to the registrar of companies renders the applicant liable to a default fine.[61]

POWERS OF RECOVERY AND INVESTIGATION

13.22 Position as office holder

As discussed above,[62] IA 1985 introduced the idea of the "office holder" having particular rights and obligations. The receiver, as an office holder, in addition to his obligations to realise the assets for the benefit of the debenture holder who appoints him, must also act in the interests of creditors generally[63] and indeed the wider public. The following are his most important obligations.

13.23 Notice to submit statement of affairs

The receiver is obliged forthwith upon his appointment, to require some or all of a defined group of persons[64] to make out and submit to him a statement in the prescribed form[65] as to the affairs of the company.[66] The requirements relating to statements of affairs are more fully explored in Chapter 15.

13.24 Getting in the company's property

The receiver can apply for an order that any person who has in his possession any property, books, papers or records to which the company appears to be entitled should give those items up to the receiver.[67]

13.25 Procedure

Such applications are usually made *inter partes*, save where two conditions are satisfied. First, that to give the respondent an opportunity to be heard is likely to cause injustice to the applicant, either by reason of the delay involved or the action which it appears likely that the respondent or others could take before the order could be made. Secondly, when any damage which the respondent might suffer through having to comply with the order is compensatable under the cross-undertaking or that the risk of uncompensatable loss is clearly outweighed by the risk of injustice to the applicant if the order was not made.[68] This area is more fully explored in Chapter 15.

60. IA 1986, s. 43(5).
61. IA 1986, s. 43(6).
62. Para. 13.3, *supra*.
63. *Re Aveling Barford Ltd* [1989] 1 WLR 360 at 365 per Hoffmann J.
64. Defined by IA 1986, s. 47(3) as those who have been officers of the company; those who have taken part in the company's formation at any time within one year before the date of the receiver's appointment; those in the company's employment or who were employed within that year who in the receiver's opinion are capable of giving the information required; those who are or have been officers of or in the employment of a company which is, or was within that year, an officer of the company.
65. Form 3.1B.
66. IA 1986, s. 47.
67. IA 1986, s. 234.
68. *Re First Express Ltd* [1991] BCC 782.

13.26 Duty to co-operate with receiver

Directors and other persons defined in s. 235(3) must give to the receiver such information concerning the company and its promotion, formation, business, dealings, affairs or property as the receiver may at any time after the date of his appointment[69] require, and attend on the receiver at such times as he may reasonably require. A person who without reasonable excuse fails to comply with any obligation imposed by this section is liable to a fine and, in the event of continued default, to a daily default fine.[70] This obligation is more fully discussed in Chapter 15.

13.27 Inquiry into company dealings

On an application by a receiver, the court may summon to appear before it any officer of the company or any person known or suspected to have in his possession any property of the company or supposed to be indebted to the company or any person whom the court thinks capable of giving information concerning the promotion, formation, business, dealings, affairs or property of the company.[71] That person may be ordered to submit an affidavit to the court containing an account of his dealings with the company or to produce any books, papers or other records in his possession or under his control relating to the company.[72] The person may be examined on oath, either orally or on interrogatories.[73] Where a person without reasonable excuse fails to appear before the court when summoned to do so, or there are reasonable grounds to believe the person has absconded or is about to abscond with a view to avoiding his appearance before the court, the court may cause a warrant to be issued for the arrest of that person and for the seizure of any books, papers, records, money or goods in that person's possession.[74] These wide-ranging powers are more fully discussed in Chapter 15.

13.28 Notice to submit statement of affairs

The receiver is obliged forthwith upon his appointment to require some, all, or a defined group of persons[75] to make out and submit to him a statement in the prescribed form[76] as to the affairs of the company.[77] The requirements relating to statements of affairs are more fully explored in Chapter 15.

13.29 Duty to investigate conduct of directors

The receiver is under a duty to report to the Secretary of State if he finds conduct defined in CDDA 1986, s. 6(1) in relation to a person who is or has been a director of the

69. IA 1986, s. 235(4)(b).
70. IA 1986, s. 235(5).
71. IA 1986, s. 236(2).
72. IA 1986, s. 236(4).
73. IA 1986, s. 237(4).
74. IA 1986, s. 236(4) and (5).
75. Defined by s. 47(3) as those who have been officers of the company; those who have taken part in the company's formation at any time within one year before the date of the receiver's appointment; those in the company's employment or who were employed within that year who in the receiver's opinion are capable of giving the information required; those who are or have been officers of or in the employment of a company which is, or was within that year, an officer of the company.
76. Form 3.1B.
77. IA 1986, s. 47.

company.[78] The company for these purposes is deemed to have become insolvent as at the date of the receiver's appointment.[79] The report is made in the statutory form.[80] The procedure for the disqualification of directors is more fully explored in Chapter 16.

REPORTING

13.30 Report

The receiver must within three months (or such longer period as the court may allow) after his appointment, send a report to the registrar of companies, to any trustees of secured creditors of the company and (so far as he is aware of their addresses) to all such creditors.[81]

The report must state:

(a) the events leading up to his appointment, so far as he is aware of them[82];
(b) the disposal or proposed disposal by him of any property of the company and the carrying on or proposed carrying on by him of any business of the company[83];
(c) the amounts of principal and interest payable to the debenture holders by whom or on whose behalf he was appointed, and the amounts payable to preferential creditors[84];
(d) the amount (if any) likely to be available for the payment of other creditors[85];
(e) a summary of the statement of affairs made out and submitted to the administrative receiver under s. 47 and of his comments (if any) upon it.[86]

13.30.1 The receiver is not required to include in the report any information the disclosure of which would seriously prejudice the carrying out by the receiver of his functions.[87] Whilst the receiver owes duties to the company, his primary obligations relate to the realisation of assets on behalf of the debenture holder.[88] On the basis that the receiver is the best judge of the commercial consequences of disclosing information about his activities, the test in relation to CA 1985, s. 497 was stated to be whether the decision was taken in bad faith or whether it was a decision which no reasonable receiver could have made.[89] There is no reason to believe that this would not be followed in relation to the current provisions.

78. CDDA 1986, s. 7(3)(c).
79. CDDA 1986, s. 6(2)(c).
80. Form D6 or 6A or 6B.
81. IA 1986, s. 48(1).
82. IA 1986, s. 48(1)(a).
83. IA 1986, s. 48(1)(b).
84. IA 1986, s. 48(1)(c).
85. IA 1986, s. 48(1)(d).
86. IA 1986, s. 48(5).
87. *Ibid.*
88. See, for example, *Downsview* v. *First City Corp.* [1993] AC 295.
89. *Gomba Holdings UK Ltd and Others* v. *Homan and Another* [1986] 1 WLR 1301 at 1307, per Hoffmann J.

13.31 Application by receiver to limit disclosure of the statement of affairs

Where the administrative receiver thinks that it would prejudice the conduct of the receivership for the whole or part of the statement of affairs to be disclosed, he may apply to the court for an order of limited disclosure in respect of the statement or a specified part of it.[90]

13.32 Procedure

The application would be made by the receiver *ex parte* to the court by way of originating application. The court may on the application order that the statement, or the specified part of it, be not open to inspection otherwise than with leave of the court.[91] The order may also include directions as to the delivery of documents to the registrar of companies and the disclosure of relevant information to other persons.[92] Given the context of this latter provision, the documents and relevant information referred to are only those which would otherwise be disclosed in the statement of affairs.

13.33 Application to dispense with laying of report

The receiver may form the view that a meeting of the unsecured creditors would not serve any useful purpose. Such circumstances might arise where he formed the view that the cost of summoning such a meeting outweighed the benefits that might accrue to the unsecured creditors. In such circumstances, the receiver may apply to the court for a direction that no report be laid before a meeting of the unsecured creditors.[93] No such direction will be given unless the report to the unsecured creditors states that the receiver intends to apply for such a direction and a copy of the report is sent to all unsecured creditors of the company (so far as the receiver is aware of their addresses)[94] or a notice is published in the newspaper in which his appointment was originally published,[95] not less than 14 days before the hearing of the application.[96]

13.34 Creditors' meeting

Unless the court otherwise directs in accordance with para. 13.33 above, the receiver must lay a copy of the report before a meeting of the unsecured creditors summoned for the purpose.

13.35 Venue and notice

The receiver must have regard to the convenience of the persons invited to attend in fixing the venue.[97] It should be summoned to commence between 10.00 am and 4 pm on a

90. IR 1986, r. 3.5(1).
91. IR 1986, r. 3.5(2).
92. IR 1986, r. 3.5(3).
93. IA 1986, s. 48(2).
94. IA 1986, s. 48(3).
95. IR 1986, rr. 3.8(1), 3.2(3).
96. IA 1986, s. 48(3).
97. IR 1986, r. 3.9(1).

business day, unless the court otherwise directs.[98] At least 14 days' notice should be given to all creditors identified in the statement of affairs or known to the receiver and who had claims against the company at the date of his appointment.[99] Proxy forms[100] should be sent out with the notice summoning the meeting.[101] The notice should state that creditors whose claims are wholly secured are not entitled to attend or be represented at the meeting.[102] The notice of the venue should also be published in the same newspaper as the receiver's appointment was advertised.[103]

13.36 Chairman

The receiver or a person nominated (who must be qualified to act as an insolvency practitioner in relation to the company or an employee of the receiver or his firm experienced in insolvency matters) must be chairman at the meeting.[104]

13.37 Voting

A person may only vote if he has given to the receiver, not later than 12.00 noon, on the business day before the meeting, details in writing of the debt he claims is due to him and the claim has been duly admitted and he has lodged any proxy he intends to be used on his behalf.[105] The receiver retains a discretion to admit a vote if satisfied that the failure to comply with these requirements was due to circumstances beyond the creditor's control.[106] Voting is permitted only with regard to the amount of ascertained unsecured debt as at the date of the receiver's appointment, after deducting any amounts paid in respect of the debt after that date.[107] A creditor may not vote in respect of a debt for an unliquidated amount, or any debt whose value is not ascertained, except where the chairman agrees to put upon the debt an estimated minimum value for the purpose of determining entitlement to vote and admits the claim for that purpose.[108] "Agrees" has been subject to judicial consideration in the context of voluntary arrangements where it has been held that it does not require some element of bilateral concurrence between the chairman of the creditors' meeting and the creditor, merely that the chairman should be willing to place a value on the unliquidated claim by the creditor. It was held that all that the sub-rule required was that the chairman put an estimated minimum value on the unliquidated or unascertained claim.[109]

98. IR 1986, r. 3.9(2).
99. IR 1986, r. 3.9(3).
100. Form 8.3.
101. IR 1986, r. 3.9(4).
102. IR 1986, r. 3.9(5).
103. IR 1986, r. 3.9(6).
104. IR 1986, r. 3.10.
105. IR 1986, r. 3.11(1).
106. IR 1986, r. 3.11(2).
107. IR 1986, r. 3.11(4).
108. IR 1986, r. 3.11(5).
109. See *Doorbar* v. *Alltime Securities (Nos 1 & 2)* [1996] 1 BCLC 487, CA, doubting *Re Cranley Mansions Ltd* [1994] BCC 576; [1995] 1 BCLC 290; [1995] 1 WLR 1610.

13.38 Admission and rejection of claims

At a creditors' meeting the chairman has power to admit or reject a creditor's claim for the purpose of his entitlement to vote. If the chairman is in doubt as to whether a claim should be admitted or rejected, he should mark it as objected to and allow the creditor to vote, subject to his vote being subsequently declared invalid if the objection to the claim is sustained.[110]

13.39 Appeal from decision of chairman

The chairman's decision to admit or reject a claim or his decision to admit an estimated minimum sum on a claim is subject to appeal to the court by any creditor.

13.40 Procedure

The application is by way of originating application by the aggrieved creditor. The respondent should be the chairman of the meeting. The usual procedure regarding evidence applies.[111] On the hearing before the registrar, the court may order that the chairman's decision be reversed or varied, that a creditor's vote be declared invalid, another meeting be summoned, or it may make such other order as it thinks fit.[112] Neither the receiver nor any person nominated by him to be chairman is personally liable for costs incurred by any person in respect of an appeal to the court unless the court makes an order to that effect.[113] The inference is that the court will be extremely reluctant to order the receiver to bear the costs of such an application unless he can be shown to have acted improperly.

13.41 Creditors' committee

Where a creditors' meeting is summoned pursuant to s. 48, the meeting may establish a creditors' committee to exercise the functions conferred on it by or under IA 1986.[114] The committee should consist of not less than three and not more than five creditors elected at the meeting.[115]

The committee is required to assist the receiver in discharging his functions and to act in relation to him in such manner as may be agreed.[116] Pursuant to that function, the committee may, on giving not less than seven days' notice, require the receiver to attend before it at any reasonable time and furnish it with such information relating to the carrying out by him of his functions as it may reasonably require.[117]

Details of the procedure to be adopted by the committee are set out in IR 1986, rr. 3.16 to 3.30A.

110. IR 1986, r. 3.12(3).
111. See para. 13.7, *supra*.
112. IR 1986, r. 3.12(4).
113. IR 1986, r. 3.12(5).
114. IA 1986, s. 49(1).
115. IR 1986, r. 3.16.
116. IR 1986, r. 3.18.
117. IA 1986, s. 49(2).

13.42 Members of the committee dealing with the company

Membership of the committee does not prevent a person from dealing with the company while the receiver is acting, provided that any transaction in the course of such dealings is entered into in good faith and for value.[118] It is not uncommon for creditors of the company to contract with the receiver following his appointment, in order to keep the company operating as a going concern or to ensure that existing contracts are completed.

13.43 Application to set aside transaction

The court may, on the application of any person interested,[119] set aside a transaction which appears to it to be contrary to the requirements set out above and may give such directions as it thinks fit, for compensating the company for any loss which it may have incurred in consequence of the transaction.[120] The terms of the rule are very wide and would appear to include an order that the receiver himself compensate the company for any loss suffered.

13.44 Procedure

The application would be made by way of *inter partes* originating application. The parties to the transaction (including the company) should be joined as respondents. The applicant files and serves on the respondent an affidavit in support not less than 14 days before the date fixed for the hearing.[121] The respondent may file affidavits in response which should be filed not less than seven days before the date fixed for the hearing.[122] The parties will then attend before the registrar on the hearing.

VACATION OF OFFICE

13.45 Situations in which the receiver may vacate office

An administrative receiver may only vacate office in the following circumstances:

(a) *Resignation by giving notice of his resignation in the prescribed manner*[123]: He must give at least seven days' notice of his intention to resign to his appointer, the company (or if it is in liquidation, the liquidator) and any creditors' committee.[124] The notice must specify the date on which the receiver intends his resignation to take effect.[125]

118. IR 1986, r. 3.30(1).
119. See *Re Roehampton Swimming Pool Ltd* [1968] 3 All ER 661 where, in relation to an application to declare the dissolution of a company void, it was held that a "person interested" was someone with a proprietary or pecuniary interest. This would include creditors or, if there was a prospect of a surplus being available to contributories, members.
120. IR 1986, r. 3.30(2).
121. IR 1986, r. 7.8(1)(a).
122. IR 1986, r. 7.8(1)(b).
123. IA 1986, s. 45(1).
124. IR 1986, r. 3.33(1).
125. IR 1986, r. 3.33(2).

(b) *The receiver dying whilst in office*: The appointor must forthwith upon becoming aware of the death give notice to the registrar of companies in statutory Form 3.7, the company (or if it is in liquidation, its liquidator) and to the members of any creditors' committee.[126]

(c) *Ceasing to be qualified to act as an insolvency practitioner*[127] in relation to the company.[128]

(d) *Being removed from office by order of the court*: (but not otherwise)[129] as to which, see below.

13.46 Removal by order of the court

Unlike other forms of receiver, the administrative receiver may not be removed from office by his appointor. This distinction seeks to ensure that he is able to carry out his statutory obligations without interference.

The debenture holder who appointed the receiver may seek his removal where he is dissatisfied with the manner in which the appointee has conducted the receivership. There is no English authority directly on the point. In Australia it has been held that the debenture holder must show sufficient cause for removing the appointee and the court will not lightly intervene.[130] By analogy, the case law relating to the removal of liquidators in the case of a voluntary liquidation, may apply. If that is the case, the applicant will have to show cause.[131]

13.46.1 Another security holder entitled to appoint an administrative receiver in priority to the present appointee may seek to ensure that their interests are safeguarded by having their own appointee in place. It is not sufficient for such a party merely to exercise their right of appointment as provided for in their security instrument, as s. 45(1) makes it clear that only one administrative receiver (or joint appointees) may hold office at one time. If the original appointee was validly appointed, the party seeking to enforce a prior security right must secure his removal, before appointing their own appointee.

Where a company is also in liquidation, the liquidator may seek to intervene if it appears that the receivership is being conducted improperly, or that the interests of the unsecured creditors are otherwise being prejudiced. This is subject to the caveat that the court will have regard to the priority afforded by the security.

13.47 Procedure

There is no specific procedure laid down by IR 1986 for making such an application. The application is made by *inter partes* originating application, the respondent being the receiver. The usual rules relating to such procedure apply. The applicant files an affidavit(s) in support and serves the respondent not less than 14 days before the date fixed for the hearing.[132] The respondent may file affidavits in response which should be filed not

126. IR 1986, r. 3.34.
127. As defined by IA 1986, s. 388(1).
128. IA 1986, s. 45(2).
129. IA 1986, s. 45(1).
130. *Re Neon Signs (Australasia) Ltd* [1965] VR 125.
131. IA 1986, s. 108; *Re Rubber and Produce Investment Trust* [1915] 1 Ch. 382; *Re Charterland Goldfields Ltd* (1909) 26 TLR 132; *Re Keypak Homecare Ltd* (1987) 3 BCC 558.
132. IR 1986, rr. 7.7(1), 7.8(1).

less than seven days before the date fixed for the hearing.[133] The parties attend before the registrar on the hearing date.

The first hearing date may, in cases which are not straightforward, be treated as a hearing for directions. It is possible that a receiver may seek to apply the procedure relating to the removal of a liquidator[134] by analogy. This allows for an initial hearing for directions at which the receiver may apply to show sufficient cause to reject the application, although the court will not do this unless the applicant has had an opportunity to attend before the court for an *ex parte* hearing, of which the applicant has been given at least seven days' notice.[135] The court may require the applicant to make a deposit or give security for costs to be incurred by the receiver on the application.[136] Although there may be comparisons between the jurisdictions and in either case the burden of proof will be on the applicant, there must be some doubt as to whether this procedure is necessarily applicable, given that Parliament only saw fit to provide for it in the case of liquidation.

133. IR 1986, r. 7.8(1)(b).
134. IA 1986, s. 108; IR 1986, r. 4.413.
135. IR 1986, r. 4.413(2).
136. IR 1986, r. 4.413(3).

CHAPTER 14

APPLICATIONS IN VOLUNTARY ARRANGEMENTS

14.1 Introduction

Company voluntary arrangements are provided for by ss. 1 to 7 of the Insolvency Act 1986, and part 1 of the Insolvency Rules 1986 (as amended). The intention behind the creation of this procedure was to provide a simple means[1] by which a company might enter into a binding arrangement with its creditors, akin to a composition, but without the necessity for the consent of every creditor. Company voluntary arrangements may be appropriate, in certain circumstances, to solvent companies as well as to insolvent ones.

Such an arrangement lays down the terms of a composition in satisfaction of a company's debts, or a scheme of arrangement of its affairs.[2] Its implementation is supervised by someone who is qualified to act as an insolvency practitioner in relation to the company.[3] There is no provision for the making of a protective interim order in respect of a proposal for a company voluntary arrangement.[4] In practice, the nearest equivalent is a petition for an administration order with the approval of the voluntary arrangement as one of its purposes. The arrangement may be approved by a majority of anything over 75%, by value, of the company's creditors.[5] Once in force, it binds every person with notice in accordance with the rules and entitled to vote at the creditors' meetings as if he were a party to it.[6]

The voluntary arrangement procedure is essentially an out-of-court one. The role of applications in voluntary arrangements is to police or assist their genesis and implementation. In order to deal intelligibly with the practice peculiar to these applications, it is necessary to explain some of the main features of voluntary arrangements.

14.2 Summary of voluntary arrangement procedure

By way of a brief overview:

(1) A voluntary arrangement starts with a proposal. This may be made by the directors (when no administration order is in force and the company is not being

1. At any rate relative to the statutory procedures regulating schemes of arrangement under s. 425, CA 1985.
2. IA 1986, s. 1(1).
3. IA 1986, s. 1(2).
4. See the position in respect of a proposal for an individual voluntary arrangement under IA 1986, s. 252.
5. IR 1986, r. 1.9(1). The details of this and requirements relating to the members' meeting are summarised at para. 14.2(4) and (5), *infra*.
6. IA 1986, s. 5(2)(b).

wound up[7] an administrator (when an administration order is in force), or a liquidator (when the company is being wound up).[8] The proposal details the company's assets and liabilities, and the way in which it is proposed they should be dealt with.[9] It provides for a licensed insolvency practitioner, called the nominee,[10] to supervise the arrangement.

(2) If the directors propose the arrangement, they are required to submit the proposal, and a statement of affairs,[11] to the scrutiny of the nominee, so that he can prepare a report on it.[12] The report either recommends the calling of creditors' and members' meetings to consider approving the arrangement,[13] and annexes his comments on the proposal, or gives reasons why no meeting should be called.[14] If the proposer of the arrangement is an administrator or liquidator, he may himself be the nominee, in which case none of this is necessary.[15]

(3) If the report recommends that meetings be called, these are then summoned by the nominee.[16] At least 14 days notice is given to members and creditors of whom the nominee is aware. Copies of the proposal, a statement of affairs or summary thereof, any nominee's report, and a proxy voting form accompany each notice.[17]

(4) The creditors' and members' meetings must be held on the same day and in the same place, with the creditors' meeting in advance of the members' meeting, both being between 10.00am and 4.00pm on a business day.[18] Within these constraints, the venue should be fixed having regard primarily to the convenience of the creditors.[19] The nominee or his representative acts as chairman.[20] The meetings may approve the proposal (or a modification) which does not offend against the Insolvency Act 1986, s. 4(2), 4(3) or 4(4). These provisions ensure that any modification meets the requirements applied to an initial proposal; that any proposal or modification does not affect the rights of a secured creditor without his consent; and that the priority of preferential debts is not disturbed. The proposal must be approved by a majority of more than 75% in the case of the creditors' meeting,[21] and by more than 50% in the case of the members' meeting.[22] Alternatively, both meetings may be adjourned to another date, so long as it is not more than 14 days after the date of the first meetings. Failure to reach agreement within that timescale is deemed to be rejection.[23]

7. IA 1986, s. 1(1).
8. IA 1986, s. 1(3)(a) and (b).
9. IR 1986, r. 1.3.
10. IA 1986, s. 1(2).
11. IA 1986, s. 2(3)(a) and (b).
12. IA 1986, s. 2(2).
13. The date specified in the nominee's report must be not less than 14 and not more than 28 days from the date on which the report is filed in court: IR 1986, r. 1.9(1).
14. IR 1986, r. 1.7(2).
15. IA 1986, s. 2(1); IR 1986, r. 1.12.
16. Redefined in IR 1986, r. 1.13(1) as the "convener".
17. IR 1986, rr. 1.9(3), 1.11(2) and 1.13(4).
18. IR 1986, r. 1.13(2) and (3).
19. IR 1986, r. 1.13(1).
20. IR 1986, r. 1.14.
21. IR 1986, r. 1.19(1) subject to the safeguard for unconnected creditors provided by IR 1986, r. 1.19(4).
22. IR 1986, r. 1.20(1).
23. IR 1986, r. 1.21.

There is no jurisdiction in the court to order new meetings thereafter.[24] After the conclusion of the meetings the chairman prepares a report of them, which must be filed in court within four days of the meetings, and the chairman must immediately give notice of the result of each meeting to all those notified beforehand.[25]

(5) Members' votes are counted according to the weightings attached by the articles. Creditors' votes are counted, broadly, according to the value of claim.[26] Some creditors, however, are not entitled to vote.[27] Some other creditors' votes are left out of account for all purposes (those in respect of claims not notified to the chairman or nominee in writing,[28] wholly secured claims,[29] the secured part of partly secured claims,[30] and, in certain circumstances, claims wholly or partly on, or secured by, a bill of exchange or promissory note[31]). Connected creditors are not counted against any majority.[32] Decisions on all these matters are made by the chairman of the meeting.[33]

(6) If approved, the arrangement takes effect from the time of the creditors' meeting,[34] and should be implemented according to its terms, under the supervision of the supervisor (ordinarily the person who was formerly the nominee).[35]

(7) The supervisor has a duty to report on the progress of the arrangement, and his receipts and payments, at least once every 12 months. He reports to the court, the registrar of companies, the company, the creditors and members bound by the arrangement, and, if the company is not in liquidation, its auditors.[36] In addition, a final report is sent out after completion of the arrangement.

14.3 Points of general application

14.3.1 Form of application

Because company voluntary arrangements are essentially an out-of-court procedure, the proper vehicle for an application made in such an arrangement is an originating application under part 7 of the Insolvency Rules.[37] Such applications should accordingly follow the procedure laid down in that part.[38] This is so even where the arrangement has been

24. *Kent Carpets* v. *James William Sykes* [1986] BCC 137 at 152 e–f.
25. IA 1986, s. 4(6); IR 1986, r. 1.24(1) and (4).
26. IR 1986, rr. 1.17(2) and 1.18(1). The quorums are provided for by IR 1986, r. 12.4A(2)(a) and (b).
27. See para. 14.7.4, *infra*.
28. IR 1986, r. 1.19(3)(a).
29. IR 1986, r. 1.19(3)(b).
30. *Calor Gas Ltd* v. *Piercy* [1994] BCC 69 at 78 a–b.
31. IR 1986, r. 1.19(3)(c).
32. IR 1986, r. 1.19(4)(c).
33. The chairman's decision may be challenged on an application to the court: see para. 14.6.1, *infra*. There is, in addition, provision for proxy voting rights and conflicts of interest in that regard: IR 1986, rr. 1.15 and 1.19(6).
34. IA 1986, s. 5(2)(a).
35. IA 1986, s. 7(2).
36. IR 1986, r. 1.26(2) and (4).
37. Save, obviously, for petitions by the supervisor for adminstration or liquidation.
38. See paras 10.2 *et seq.*, *supra* for a description of this procedure.

proposed by an administrator or liquidator in the course of the administration or liquidation.[39]

14.3.2 Hearing

All applications in voluntary arrangements[40] should be made in the first instance to the registrar who may give any necessary directions, may hear the matter himself, or may refer it to the judge, usually in chambers.[41]

14.3.3 Costs

The court has a general discretion as to costs,[42] which has been exercised by the courts notwithstanding express provisions in the Insolvency Rules.[43] Thus, where there has been some personal conduct on the part of the chairman falling short of the standard which can be expected of a reasonable licensed insolvency practitioner, he may be ordered to pay all or part of the costs incurred as a result of his actions or omissions.[44] In many cases, the costs of applications in voluntary arrangements should be paid out of the company's assets.[45] If an arrangement has been approved, those assets will be subject to the terms of the arrangement.[46] If an arrangement has not yet been approved, the possibility of approval should be catered for. Accordingly, the court, in exercising its discretion, may take account of any relevant terms of the arrangement, and the Insolvency Rules 1986, r. 1.28, dealing with fees, costs, charges and expenses that may be incurred for any of the purposes of the voluntary arrangement.

14.4 The nominee's report

14.4.1 Extension of time for nominee's report

Written notice of the proposal,[47] and a copy of it, must be delivered to the nominee or someone authorised to take delivery for him.[48] An intended nominee who agrees to act causes a copy of the notice to be endorsed with a statement that it was received by him on a specified date,[49] and returns it forthwith to the proposer.[50] Within 28 days after the

39. *Re Primlaks (UK) Ltd (No. 2)* [1990] BCLC 234 e–f. See the position in individual voluntary arrangements, where an interim order is already on foot: *Re a Debtor (No. 222 of 1990) ex parte Bank of Ireland* [1992] BCLC 137 at 138f–139f.

40. Save for applications pursuant to IA 1986, s. 5(3), administration and winding-up petitions: see paras 14.8.1, 14.8.3 and 14.8.9, *infra*.

41. Chancery Division (Companies Court) Practice Direction No. 3 of 1986, para. (2); *Re a Debtor (No. 222 of 1990) ex parte Bank of Ireland* [1992] BCLC 137 at 141b–e.

42. Supreme Court Act 1981, s. 51(1).

43. *Re a Debtor (No. 222 of 1990) ex parte Bank of Ireland (No. 2)* [1993] BCLC 233 at 235c–236a; IR 1986, rr. 1.17(9) and 1.19(7). The conflict was further considered in *Re Cranley Mansions Ltd* [1994] BCC 576 at 596a–597b.

44. *Re Naeem* [1990] 1 WLR 48 at 51b; *Re a Debtor (No. 222 of 1990) ex parte Bank of Ireland (No. 2)* [1993] BCLC 233 at 235c–236a.

45. By analogy with *Re Naeem* [1990] 1 WLR 48 at 51b.

46. A petition by the supervisor for administration or liquidation may give rise to an exception, but the costs of such proceedings can be provided for in those proceedings.

47. IR 1986, r. 1.4(1).

48. IA 1986, s. 2(3)(a); IR 1986, r. 1.4(2).

49. IR 1986, r. 1.4(3).

50. IR 1986, r. 1.4(4) and 1.12(2).

date there stated, the nominee is required to submit his report to the court. But the court may allow a longer period,[51] presumably on the application of the nominee before or after the expiry of the 28-day period.

14.4.2 Nominee's removal

If the nominee fails to submit a report, the proposer of the arrangement may apply to the court for a direction that the nominee be replaced as such by another person qualified to act as an insolvency practitioner in relation to the company.[52] The proposer must first give the nominee at least seven days' notice of the application.[53] The application may be made after the expiry of the 28-day time limit referred to above, or any extended time limit granted by the court under the Insolvency Act 1986, s. 2(2). Of course, if the nominee consents, the proposal may be abandoned (perhaps to be relaunched with another nominee) without the court's assistance, since neither the court nor the members or creditors will have become formally involved at this stage.

14.5 Summoning meetings

14.5.1 Directions as to meetings

Where there is a nominee's report which states that members' and creditors' meetings should be summoned to consider the proposal, the nominee must summon the meetings as proposed unless the court otherwise directs.[54] The application may be made at any time after the report is filed with the court. Evidently, a nominee may make an application under this section, but it is unclear whether any other person is so entitled. Creditors and members do not have formal notice at this stage, and may challenge any violation, e.g. of the Insolvency Rules 1986, r. 1.13(1), by way of application under the Insolvency Act 1986, s. 6.[55] The proposer of the arrangement loses the power to replace the nominee once his report is filed, and a power to replace the supervisor only operates after the arrangement has been approved. It may be, however, that the proposer must simply abandon the proposal, to renew it with a different nominee.[56]

14.6 Conduct of meetings

14.6.1 Challenge to the chairman's decisions on voting

Any creditor or member[57] may apply to the court by way of appeal against the chairman's decision on a creditor's entitlement to vote,[58] or the chairman's decision on votes to be left out of account at a creditors' meeting, or the chairman's decision on whether a creditor is

51. IA 1986, s. 2(2).
52. IA 1986, s. 2(4).
53. IR 1986, rr. 1.8 and 1.12.
54. IA 1986, s. 3(1).
55. See para. 14.7.1 *et seq.*, *infra*.
56. In company voluntary arrangements there is no prohibition comparable with the 12-month moratorium on interim order applications imposed in respect of individual voluntary arrangements by IA 1986, s. 255(1)(c).
57. This is to be contrasted with IA 1986, s. 6 (dealt with at para. 14.7.1 *et seq.*, *infra*) which adds the qualification "entitled, in accordance with the rules, to vote at either of the meetings".
58. IR 1986, r. 1.17(5).

a connected person for voting purposes.[59] Although not expressly stated to be a matter for the chairman to decide,[60] any question as to who was sent notice of the meeting for the purposes of the Insolvency Rules 1986, r. 1.19(4)(a) is one which the chairman must answer in deciding whether, at the creditors' meeting, non-connected creditors to whom notice of the meeting was sent, may override the wishes of an overall majority in excess of 75% of the purposes of the Insolvency Rules 1986, r. 1.19(4). Accordingly, the position which he adopts on the issue of notice is arguably a decision which can be challenged like the chairman's other decisions on voting rights.

14.6.2 When to apply

The application must be made during the 28 days beginning with the first day on which each of the reports of the outcome of the meetings has been filed with the court.[61] But the court, either before or after the expiry of any time limit, may extend time on such terms as it thinks just, by virtue of the Insolvency Rules 1986, r. 12.9, which imports RSC O. 3 (save for rr. 3 and 6) as regards computation and extensions of time in respect of anything required or authorised by the Insolvency Rules to be done. The relevant factors to be considered by the court on an application, after the expiry of the 28-day time limit, to allow a challenge out of time are the length of the delay, the reasons for the delay, the apparent merits of the underlying application and the prejudice to each side, other than the inevitable prejudice in reopening the matter.[62]

14.6.3 Erroneous decision

If the chairman's decision is reversed or varied or a creditor's vote is declared invalid, the court may order another meeting to be summoned or make such other order as it thinks just.[63] The test to be applied in deciding whether a chairman's decision should be reversed or varied is not specified in the Act or Rules. In the context of voting at a creditors' meeting in a liquidation, where the chairman's decision may similarly be challenged,[64] the court is entitled to consider whatever admissible evidence on the issue the parties to the appeal choose to place before the court, rather than confining itself to the evidence before the chairman at the time. The onus of demonstrating that the chairman's decision was wrong and should be reversed or varied lies on the creditor mounting the appeal, who has to satisfy the court that, on balance, for example, the claim against the company is established, and, if so, in what amount.[65] It is suggested that the same approach would be followed by the court in the context of voluntary arrangements.

14.6.4 Discretion

The power to make an order is exercisable only if the court considers that the matter is such as gives rise to unfair prejudice or material irregularity.[66] Under the Insolvency Rules

59. IR 1986, r. 1.19(7).
60. IR 1986, r. 1.19(5)(b).
61. IR 1986, rr. 1.17(8) and 1.19(7).
62. *Tager* v. *Westpac Banking Corp.* [1997] 1 BCLC 313 at 325d.
63. IR 1986, r. 1.17(7). But see para. 14.7.12, *infra*.
64. IR 1986, r. 4.70(2).
65. *Re a Company (No. 004539 of 1993)* [1995] BCC 116 at 120c–d, f–g.
66. IR 1986, r. 1.17(7) and 1.19(7). This meaning of these phrases is considered at paras 14.7.6 and 14.7.7, *infra*.

1986, r. 1.17(6), if the chairman doubts a claim, he is directed to mark it as objected to, but to allow the creditor to vote, subject to his vote being subsequently declared invalid if the objection to the claim is sustained. It is clear that challenges to such claims are envisaged within the Insolvency Rules 1986, r. 1.17(5). It therefore seems that counting such a vote, when the claim is in fact unfounded, will be treated as a material irregularity, notwithstanding compliance with the Insolvency Rules 1986, r 1.17(6).[67]

14.6.5 Costs

The chairman is not personally liable for any costs incurred by any person in respect of such an appeal,[68] except where his conduct falls short of the standard which can be expected of a reasonable licensed insolvency practitioner: see para. 14.3.3, above.

14.7 Unfair prejudice and material irregularity

14.7.1 General challenge

The regularity of the procedure at or in relation to the members' or creditors' meetings, and the fairness of any voluntary arrangement approved by them, are open to challenge by an application to the court under the Insolvency Act 1986, s. 6.

14.7.2 Who may apply

The persons who may make such an application are:

(a) any person entitled, in accordance with the rules, to vote at either of the meetings,[69]
(b) the nominee (or any person who has replaced him under the Insolvency Act 1986, ss. 2(4) or 4(2))[70]; and
(c) the liquidator or administrator, if there is one.[71]

14.7.3 Members entitled to vote

Any member is entitled, in accordance with the rules, to vote at the members' meeting. This is so even where the articles attach no voting rights to a member's shares.[72]

14.7.4 Creditors entitled to vote

The class of creditors entitled to vote, in accordance with the rules, requires further definition. Subject to a number of qualifications, each creditor who was given notice of the creditors' meeting is so entitled.[73] Formal notice should be sent at least 14 days in advance

67. *Re a Debtor (No. 222 of 1990) ex parte Bank of Ireland* [1992] BCLC 137 at 145f.
68. IR 1986, rr. 1.17(9) and 1.19(7).
69. IA 1986, s. 6(2)(a). This is similar to the definition of those bound by the arrangement: IA 1986, s. 5(2)(b).
70. IA 1986, s. 6(2)(b).
71. IA 1986, s. 6(2)(c).
72. IR 1986, r. 1.18(2). Such a member would, however, have difficulty in establishing that an irregularity affecting his vote alone was material: IR 1986, r. 1.20(2).
73. IR 1986, r. 1.17(1). It appears this statement is not exhaustive however: *Re Debtors (Nos 400 and 401 of 1996), Times*, 27 February 1997.

of the meeting.[74] Where the creditor does not receive the notice, it will suffice if the creditor was nevertheless aware in advance of the meeting and the proposals to be made at it.[75] Indeed, actual notice, howsoever obtained, entitles the creditor to vote even if the nominee has deliberately failed to serve him with notice, if the creditor attends the meeting (in person or by proxy) and attempts to vote.[76] Votes are calculated according to the amount of the creditor's debt as at the date of the meeting or, where the company is being wound up or is subject to an administration order, the date of its going into liquidation or the date of the administration order, as the case may be.[77] The following points deserve mention:

(a) A person who is entitled to a future or contingent debt, such as future payment of rent to fall due under an existing lease, is a creditor for these purposes.[78] A claim for costs which is not yet the subject of a court order is not a contingent claim,[79] and no such claimant will be entitled to vote.
(b) By virtue of the Insolvency Rules 1986, r. 1.17(3), a creditor is only entitled to vote in respect of a debt for an unliquidated amount, or a debt whose value is not ascertained, if the chairman agrees to put an estimated minimum value on the debt for the purposes of entitlement to vote. For these purposes there need not be agreement as to the minimum value: the chairman need only express a willingness to put an estimated minimum value on the debt.[80]
(c) A creditor with a claim for an unliquidated or unascertained sum may not disentitle himself from voting merely by being neither present nor represented at the meeting. the Insolvency Rules 1986, r. 1.17(3) only applies to persons who are present or represented at the meeting.[81]

14.7.5 When to apply

The application must be made during the 28 days beginning with the first day on which each of the reports of the meetings has been filed with the court.[82] There is no provision for this time limit to be extended.[83]

14.7.6 Unfair prejudice as a ground

The application may be made on the ground that the voluntary arrangement approved, unfairly prejudices the interest of a creditor, member or contributory of the company.[84]

74. IR 1986, rr. 1.9(2) and 1.11(1)(b).
75. *Beverley Group plc* v. *McClue* [1995] BCC 751 at 758h–759a.
76. *Re Debtors (Nos 400 and 401 of 1996)*, *Times*, 27 February 1997.
77. IR 1986, r. 1.17(2).
78. *Re Cancol Ltd* [1996] 1 All ER 37 at 46e–f.
79. *Re Wisepark Ltd* [1994] BCC 221 at 224h–225a.
80. *Doorbar* v. *Alltime Securities* [1996] 1 WLR 456 at 464e, 466c.
81. *Beverley Group plc* v. *McClue* [1995] BCC 751 at 759f–g.
82. IA 1986, s. 6(3).
83. The power to extend time limits under RSC O. 3, r. 5 is only imported by IR 1986, r. 12.9 so far as things required or authorised to be done by the Rules are concerned. IA 1986, s. 376 provides for extensions of time only in cases of individual insolvency and bankruptcy. See also para. 14.7.12, *infra*.
84. IA 1986, s. 6(1)(a).

This means unfairness brought about by the terms of the arrangement.[85] If the creditor is put in exactly the same position as every other creditor bound he cannot succeed.[86] The issue is whether, by reason of the arrangement, there is some differential treatment of a creditor, some restriction on a creditor, or special favour or advantage to another creditor[87] which cannot be justified.[88]

14.7.7 Material irregularity as a ground

Alternatively, the application may be made on the ground that there has been some material irregularity at or in relation to either of the meetings.[89] "Irregularity" comprehends breaches of the relevant rules, e.g. a wrong decision to exclude a vote,[90] or a failure to comply with the rules governing the content of the proposal or statement of affairs.[91] To be material, the irregularity must be such as could affect the outcome of the meetings.[92]

14.7.8 Discovery

It has been held that the court may order discovery under the Insolvency Rules 1986, r. 7.60 and, where necessary, cross-examination at the hearing in support of an unfair prejudice application, on the basis that it is necessary for the applicant to know the details of the facts of the transactions which he alleges to be unfair.[93]

14.7.9 Orders

If the court is satisfied as to either ground it may:

(a) revoke or suspend the approval given by both meetings (or, where appropriate,[94] the meeting in question)[95]; and/or

(b) give a direction to any person for the summoning of further meetings[96] (or, where appropriate, a further meeting of the type in question[97]) to reconsider the original proposal.[98]

85. *Re Primlaks (UK) Ltd (No. 2)* [1990] BCLC 234 at 239i–240a; *Re a Debtor (No. 259 of 1990)* [1992] 1 WLR 226 at 228h–229a; *Re a Debtor (No. 222 of 1990) ex parte Bank of Ireland* [1992] BCLC 137 at 145d.
86. *Re a Debtor (No. 259 of 1990)* [1992] 1 WLR 226 at 229e–f.
87. *Re a Debtor (No. 222 of 1990) ex parte Bank of Ireland* [1992] BCLC 137 at 145d–f.
88. *Re Cancol Ltd* [1996] 1 All ER 37 at 54a–b.
89. IA 1986, s. 6(1)(b).
90. *Re a Debtor (No. 222 of 1990) ex parte Bank of Ireland* [1992] BCLC 137 at 145f–g.
91. *Re a Debtor (No. 87 of 1993) (No. 2)* [1996] BCC 80 at 108e.
92. *Re a Debtor (No. 259 of 1990)* [1992] 1 WLR 226 at 229g–h.
93. *Re Primlaks (UK) Ltd (No. 2)* [1990] BCLC 234 at 240a–241d; *Re a Debtor (No. 87 of 1993) (No. 2)* [1996] BCC 80 at 89f.
94. Isolation of one meeting is not possible where the court proceeds on the basis of a finding of unfair prejudice: IA 1986, s. 6(4)(a) and (b).
95. IA 1986, s. 6(4)(a).
96. If the order directs any person to summon a further meeting, then this person must be served by the applicant: IR 1986, r. 1.25(3).
97. See Note 94, *supra*.
98. IA 1986, s. 6(4)(b).

14.7.10 Doomed proposals

The court will not make an order directing the summoning of a further meeting if it is clear that the proposal cannot be passed, e.g. because creditors have indicated that they will not support it.[99] If the court is subsequently satisfied that the person who made the original proposal does not intend to submit a revised proposal, it must revoke any direction to summon a further meeting, and simply revoke or suspend the approvals given at the previous meetings.[100] The Insolvency Rules provide for the applicant to serve on the proposer a sealed copy of any revocation or suspension order made, and require the proposer to give notice to the court whether it is intended to make a revised proposal, or to invite re-consideration of the original proposal.[101]

14.7.11 Supplemental powers

Whenever the court makes an order under the Insolvency Act 1986, s. 6(4)(a), 6(4)(b) or 6(5), it may give such supplemental directions as it think fit, in particular with respect to things done since the meeting, under any voluntary arrangement which has been approved.[102] The making of an application under the Insolvency Act 1986, s. 6 does not, in itself, operate as a stay on the implementation of the arrangement.

14.7.12 Validity of approval

No other irregularity at or in relation to a meeting invalidates any approval given at that meeting.[103] This means that, once the 28-day time limit referred to in para. 14.7.5, above has expired, the approval is irrebuttably deemed valid. The subsection is unequivocal in its terms, notwithstanding the power to challenge the chairman's decisions on voting,[104] which is subject to no strict time limit.

14.8 Implementation

14.8.1 Stay of administration or liquidation

If 28 days beginning with the first day on which each of the reports of meetings has been filed with the court have elapsed,[105] and there is no pending challenge for unfair prejudice or material irregularity, or, if there has been one, the period during which an appeal in respect of any such challenge has expired,[106] the court may stay all proceedings in the winding-up or discharge the administration order.[107] The stay may be for a limited time or altogether, in which case the order for liquidation is in effect terminated, the liquidator is entitled to a discharge and the directors reinstated in control of the company.

99. *Re a Debtor (No. 222 of 1990) ex parte Bank of Ireland* [1992] BCLC 137 at 146d–f; *Re a Debtor (No. 83 of 1988)* [1990] 1 WLR 708 at 717b–718a.
100. IA 1986, s. 6(5).
101. IR 1986, r. 1.25(2) and 1.25(4)(b).
102. IA 1986, s. 6(6).
103. IA 1986, s. 6(7).
104. See paras 14.6.1 to 14.6.4, *supra*.
105. IA 1986, s. 5(4)(a); again, the time limit is a strict one and cannot be abridged; see Note 83, *supra*.
106. IA 1986, s. 5(4)(b).
107. IA 1986, s. 5(3)(a).

14.8.2 Discretion

Proceeding by way of analogy, the court is likely to exercise its discretion against making an order where an application is pending, or where the time limit provided for an appeal in respect of an Insolvency Rules 1986, r. 1.17(5) challenge has yet to expire. Otherwise, the court has to be satisfied that it is right to stay the winding-up. If there are matters as to which the court has doubts (e.g. adverse effects on the liquidator, members or creditors) it will be reluctant to order a stay.[108]

14.8.3 Directions in the administration or liquidation

If the company is being wound up or an administration order is in force, the court may give such other directions with respect to the conduct of the winding-up or the adminstration as it thinks appropriate for facilitating the implementation of the approved voluntary arrangement.[109] The application may be made at any time after approval.

14.8.4 Hearing

In the case of applications for a stay, and applications for directions, the application is made direct to the judge and, unless otherwise ordered, shall be heard in open court.[110]

14.8.5 Policing the supervisor

If any of the company's creditors or any other person is dissatisfied by any act, omission or decision of the supervisor, he may apply to the court[111]; and on the application the court may confirm, reverse or modify any act or decision of the supervisor[112]; give him directions[113]; or make such other order as it thinks fit.[114]

14.8.6 Who may apply

The category of "any person who is dissatisfied" is a broad one. "Dissatisfied" may require that the applicant has some substantial interest that has been adversely affected.[115]

14.8.7 Directions for the supervisor

The supervisor may apply to the court for directions in relation to any particular matter arising under the voluntary arrangement.[116] In *Re FMS Financial Management Services*

108. *Re Lowston Ltd* [1991] BCLC 570 at 572h. See also *Re Calgary and Edmonton Land Co. Ltd* [1975] 1 WLR 355 at 360b–363f.
109. IA 1986, s. 5(3)(b).
110. Chancery Division (Companies Court) Practice Direction No. 3 of 1986, para. (1)(vi).
111. IA 1986, s. 7(3).
112. IA 1986, s. 7(3)(a).
113. IA 1986, s. 7(3)(b).
114. IA 1986, s. 7(3)(c).
115. *Port* v. *Auger* [1994] 1 WLR 862 at 874a, on the similarly worded IA 1986, s. 303(1) regarding trustees in bankruptcy.
116. IA 1986, s. 7(4)(a).

Ltd[117] the court directed that a group of people with good claims against the company, who were excluded from the benefit of the arrangement, be admitted to prove as creditors. The dividend of the existing creditors was thereby significantly reduced. The order was made in somewhat exceptional circumstances.[118] The Court of Appeal has since stressed that no amendment of an arrangement can be ordered in an application for directions.[119]

14.8.8 Transactions defrauding creditors

The supervisor has power to apply to the court under the Insolvency Act 1986, s. 423 in respect of transactions defrauding creditors, where a victim of the transactions is bound by the voluntary arrangement.[120]

14.8.9 Petitions by the supervisor for winding-up or administration

The supervisor may apply to the court for the winding-up of the company or for an administration order to be made in relation to it.[121] Any winding-up petition is presented to the court to which the nominee's report was submitted. The petition is treated as if it were a petition filed by contributories of the company, and the Insolvency Rules 1986, rr. 4.22 to 4.24 apply accordingly.[122] A winding-up order made on the petition brings the voluntary arrangement to an end.[123] The supervisor may be appointed liquidator,[124] and if a petition proposes the supervisor as liquidator, then a report must be filed in court at least two days before the hearing. The report should include particulars of a date on which he notified the company's creditors, in writing or at a meeting, of the intention to seek his appointment as a liquidator, together with details of any objections or other responses from creditors.[125] The date on which he notified creditors must be at least 10 days before the date on which the report is filed. A petition for an administration is treated for all purposes as the petition of the company,[126] and should be brought in the name of the company.

14.8.10 Appointment of supervisors

The court may appoint a person qualified to act as an insolvency practitioner in relation to the company, either in substitution for the existing supervisor or to fill a vacancy, if it is expedient to appoint a person to carry out the supervisor's functions and inexpedient, difficult or impracticable for an appointment to be made without the assistance of the court.[127] The reference to the possibility of an appointment without the assistance of the

117. (1989) 5 BCC 191.

118. The state of affairs was unfair, and unforseen at the time the arrangement was approved. Legal action by the members of the unfortunate group was impracticable or unlikely. Moreover, the arrangement had already been implemented to a very significant degree, dividends having been paid out.

119. *Mills* v. *Samuels*, 21 December 1995, unreported.

120. IA 1986, s. 424(1)(b).

121. IA 1986, s. 7(4)(b).

122. IR 1986, r. 4.7(8) and (9).

123. *Davis* v. *Martin-Sklan* [1995] BCC 1,122 at 1,125a–f.

124. IA 1986, s. 140(2).

125. IR 1986, r. 4.7(10).

126. IR 1986, r. 2.1(4).

127. IA 1986, s. 7(5).

court is odd, since there is no provision for out-of-court appointment after approval. This power is exercisable so as to increase the number of persons exercising the functions of supervisor or, where there is more than one person exercising those functions, so as to replace one or more of those persons.[128]

14.8.11 Who may apply

As well as the creditors and, perhaps, the members of the company, the recognised professional body for a licensed insolvency practitioner has standing to apply for the appointment of a fresh supervisor in appropriate cases.[129]

14.9 Reporting

14.9.1 Varying the reporting duties

In respect of his annual reporting duties,[130] the supervisor may apply to the court for an order:

(a) dispensing altogether with the sending of abstracts and reports to members[131]; or
(b) that the supervisor simply advertise the availability of the abstract or report to members in a specified manner[132]; or
(c) varying the dates on which the obligation to send abstracts or reports arises.[133]

14.10 Completion

14.10.1 Final report

Within 28 days after completion of the arrangement, the supervisor must send to all the creditors and members bound by it, to the Registrar of Companies, and to the court, a notice that the arrangement has been fully implemented, and a report summarising receipts and payments and explaining any difference between the original proposal and its implementation.[134] The court may, on application by the supervisor, extend the period of 28 days.[135]

128. IA 1986, s. 7(6).
129. *Re Stella Metals Ltd* [1997] BPIR 293 at 297b–e, a case where the insolvency practitioner had ceased to be qualified, and he was replaced in respect of a number of his professional appointments.
130. See para. 14.2(7), *supra*.
131. IR 1986, r. 1.26(5)(a).
132. IR 1986, r. 1.26(5)(a).
133. IR 1986, r. 1.26(5)(b).
134. IR 1986, r. 1.29(1), (2) and (3).
135. IR 1986, r. 1.29(4).

CHAPTER 15

INSOLVENCY INVESTIGATIONS

15.1 Introduction

When a liquidator or other "office holder"[1] is appointed he will have the important duties of gathering in and preserving the assets of the insolvent company. Most office holders also have the task of realising these assets and distributing the proceeds. These duties are potentially onerous and difficult to fulfil since the office holder will usually have little previous knowledge of the company's affairs when he is first appointed. In cases of suspected fraud, there can be additional difficulties since documentation held by the company may be seriously deficient or unreliable. The office holder will often therefore be dependent on information from the officers of the company or from third parties who have been involved with it, information which he will need to obtain speedily and economically.[2]

Additionally, as a matter of public policy, the circumstances of insolvency should be open to full investigation. This is seen as a necessary step towards maintaining business standards and confidence in UK insolvency law.[3]

15.1.1 To meet these requirements, the Insolvency Act 1986 contains a broad range of inquisitorial measures ranging from requirements for the preparation of statements of affairs to private or public examination of witnesses in court for the purposes of eliciting information concerning the insolvent company. Each of the powers can involve applications to the Companies Court which will deal with them as part of its jurisdiction in insolvency matters.[4]

Additionally, the 1986 Act places a specific duty upon the official receiver to investigate in cases of compulsory liquidation.[5] He must investigate, if the company has failed, the causes of failure and generally the promotion, formation, business, dealings and affairs of the company.[6] He must then submit a report to the court.[7] He is also given various powers including special inquisitorial powers, such as those concerning public examination, to enable him to fulfil these duties.

1. The term "office holder" has been given a statutory definition in IA 1986, s. 234(1) so as to encompass an administrator, an administrative receiver, liquidator or provisional liquidator.

2. See the comments of Lord Browne-Wilkinson in *Re Arrows (No. 4)* [1995] 2 AC 75 at 101D–E and see also *Cloverbay Ltd* v. *BCCI* [1991] Ch. 90 at 102D and *Bishopsgate Investment Management Ltd* v. *Maxwell* [1993] Ch. 1 at 31C–D, per Dillon L.J.

3. See "Insolvency Law & Practice", Report of the Review Committee, June 1982, Cmnd. 8558, para. 238.

4. See Chapter 1, *supra*.

5. IA 1986, s. 132. All references to sections are to IA 1986 unless otherwise stated.

6. S. 132(1).

7. S. 132(2).

INQUISITORIAL PROCEDURES

15.2 Statement of Affairs

15.2.1 Powers

A basic requirement for most office holders in carrying out their duties is a statement of affairs setting out the company's assets and liabilities. The Insolvency Act 1986 contains provisions for such a document to be prepared by the company's officers at the request of an administrator or administrative receiver.[8] The official receiver is also given specific power to require officers to prepare a statement of affairs where a company is in compulsory liquidation or where a provisional liquidator has been appointed.[9] In both cases, persons other than officers, such as recent employees, can also be required to provide a statement of affairs.[10]

Various detailed provisions are contained in the Insolvency Act 1986 and the Insolvency Rules 1986 as to the giving of notice[11] to the person required to prepare these documents and the form which they must take.[12] There is also provision for the preparation of affidavits of concurrence in the statement of affairs by persons who have not prepared it but who could have been required to do so.[13] Although different rules apply, depending on the type of insolvency and whether the official receiver is the person exercising the power, their substantive effect is largely the same in each case.

15.2.2 Applications

The Companies Court may have to deal with four forms of application in relation to a statement of affairs (although it would appear that such applications are extremely rare with few reported cases on the subject):

(1) applications to enforce the duty to submit a statement of affairs;
(2) applications to be released from the obligation of preparing a statement of affairs or for more time to prepare such a document;
(3) applications relating to the filing and disclosure of a statement of affairs; and
(4) applications relating to the expenses of preparing a statement of affairs.

8. S. 22 (administrators) and s. 47 (administrative receivers).

9. S. 131(1).

10. The persons other than officers who may be required to produce a statement of affairs are: persons involved in the formation of the company within one year prior to "the relevant date"; persons who are or were employees of the company in that period and considered by the relevant office holder or official receiver to be capable of providing the information; or persons who are, or within that year were, officers or employees of a person who is or was within that year an officer of the company (this covers cases where another company is the officer of the insolvent company): see s. 22(3) (administrator), s. 47(3) (administrative receiver) and s. 131(3) (official receiver). The "relevant date" is the date of the winding-up order in compulsory liquidation (s. 131(6)), the date of his appointment in the case of a provisional liquidator (s. 131(6)), the date of the administration order in administration (s. 22(3)) and the date of their appointment in cases of administrative receivers (s. 47(3)).

11. See s. 22(4) and r. 2.11 (administrator); s. 47(4) and r. 3.3 (administrative receiver); and s. 131(4) and r. 4.32 (official receiver).

12. See s. 22(2) and r. 2.12 (administrator); s. 47(2) and r. 3.4 (administrative receiver); and s. 131(2) and r. 4.33 (official receiver).

13. *Ibid.*

15.2.3 ENFORCEMENT

Under r. 7.20, the "competent person" may apply to court to enforce the obligation to submit a statement of affairs. The term "competent person" is the administrator where the obligation arises in administration,[14] the administrative receiver in the context of receivership[15] and the official receiver in the context of compulsory liquidation.[16] On such an application, the court can make such order as it thinks necessary for the purposes of enforcement of the obligation in question.[17]

The application will be made by an originating application supported by an affidavit or by a report, if he so wishes, in the case of the official receiver.[18] The proceedings will have to comply with the standard requirements for such applications as outlined in Chapter 10 above. The respondent will be the person against whom the order is sought.

15.2.4 The affidavit or report in support of the application ought to set out the material facts relied on. It should establish that the respondent is a person who can be required to prepare a statement of affairs, that the formalities regarding the giving of notice have been complied with and that there has been a refusal or failure to comply.

At the hearing of the application, in addition to making orders enforcing the obligation to provide a statement of affairs, the court can make special provision for the costs of the application. It can order that all costs of and incidental to the application shall be borne by the person against whom an order is made.[19]

15.2.5 RELEASE OR FURTHER TIME

The Insolvency Act 1986 and the Insolvency Rules 1986 permit the relevant office holder or official receiver to release persons from their obligations to prepare a statement of affairs or to verify that document on affidavit.[20] They also provide for a standard 21-day period for submission of the statement of affairs, beginning on the day following that of the giving of notice in the prescribed manner, but they permit the office holder concerned, or official receiver, to extend that period.[21] The powers to release or to grant further time are discretionary and may be exercised at the office holder's or official receiver's own discretion or at the request of the person required to prepare the statement of affairs.

Where a request has been made for a release or further time, and this has been refused, an application may be made to the court.[22] The form of application will normally be an originating application supported by an affidavit complying with the standard formalities in insolvency applications (discussed in Chapter 10 above). The affidavit ought to contain details of the applicant's position and relationship with the company concerned, and a detailed explanation of the reasons for seeking a release or more time. For example, a release might be sought where the office holder already has the information and it would

14. Under s. 22.
15. Where the obligation to provide a statement arises under s. 47.
16. Where the obligation to provide a statement arises under s. 131.
17. IR 1986, r. 7.20(1). All references to rules are to the IR 1986.
18. R. 7.9(1). The report will then be *prima facie* evidence of its contents: r. 7.9(3).
19. R. 7.20(3).
20. See s. 22(5) and r. 2.14(1) (administrator); s. 47(5) and r. 3.6(1) (administrative receiver); and s. 131(5) and r. 4.36(1) (official receiver). Strangely, these provisions do not appear to extend to affidavits of concurrence.
21. *Ibid.*
22. See s. 22(5) and r. 2.14(2) (administrators); s. 47(5) and r. 3.6(2) (administrative receivers); and s. 131(5) and r. 4.36(2) (official receiver).

be expensive and time consuming for the applicant to go through the exercise again. More time might be sought so as to obtain further information or documents with which to prepare the statement or to obtain professional assistance in its preparation, or simply because of the complexity of the affairs of the company.

15.2.6 The court (being a Companies Court Registrar in most cases) will consider the matter first on paper. If it comes to the conclusion that no sufficient cause is shown for the application, it will invite the applicant to attend *ex parte* to make submissions. He will receive at least seven days' notice of the hearing. If, at the conclusion of that hearing, the court's view remains unchanged, it may dismiss the application.[23]

If the court does not dismiss the application summarily in this way it will fix a venue for the hearing and give the applicant notice accordingly.[24] The applicant then comes under a duty to send the office holder or the official receiver a notice stating the venue, a copy of the application and a copy of any evidence on which he relies.[25]

15.2.7 The office holder or official receiver may file a written report of any matters which he considers ought to be drawn to the court's attention. If he does so, he must send a copy to the applicant not later than five days before the hearing.[26] The office holder or the official receiver may also appear and be heard on the hearing of the application.[27]

If any order is made by the court, a sealed copy will be sent to the office holder or official receiver and to the applicant.[28] Whatever the outcome, the applicant's costs must be paid by him and, unless the court orders otherwise, no allowance is to be made in respect of them out of the assets of the company or the assets in the administrative receiver's control (as the case may be).[29]

15.2.8 FILING AND DISCLOSURE

The statement of affairs and any affidavits verifying or concurring in it must be filed in court in the case of an administrator or the official receiver.[30] In the case of administrative receivers, these documents are retained as part of the records of the receivership.[31] Each of the above office holders and the official receiver may apply to the court for an order of limited disclosure in respect of the statement[32] or any specified part of it.[33] The application must be made on the ground that it would prejudice the conduct of the administration, receivership or liquidation (as the case may be) for the whole or part of the statement of affairs to be disclosed.[34] The application may be specifically designed to restrict rights of inspection of the court file which otherwise arise,[35] or the duty to provide copies of the statement and affidavits to creditors in the case of administrative receivers,[36] or the similar

23. See r. 2.14(3) (administrators); r. 3.6(3) (administrative receivers); and r. 4.36(3) (official receiver).
24. *Ibid.*
25. See r. 2.14(4) (administrators); r. 3.6(4) (administrative receivers); and r. 4.36(4) (official receiver).
26. See r. 2.14(5) (administrators); r. 3.6(5) (administrative receivers); and r. 4.36(5) (official receiver).
27. *Ibid.*
28. See r. 2.14(6) (administrators); r. 3.6(6) (administrative receivers); and r. 4.36(6) (official receiver).
29. See r. 2.14(7) (administrators); r. 3.6(7) (administrative receivers); and r. 4.36(7) (official receiver).
30. See r. 2.12(6) (administrators) and r. 4.33(6) (official receiver).
31. R. 3.4(6).
32. But not, it would seem, the affidavits verifying or concurring in it.
33. R. 2.13(1) (administrators); r. 3.5(1) (administrative receivers); and r. 4.35(1) (official receiver).
34. *Ibid.*
35. See rr. 7.28 and 7.31 and in particular r. 7.31(5) and see *Ex parte Austintel* [1996] 1 WLR 1291 (Jonathan Parker J.) and [1997] 1 WLR 616, C.A.
36. R. 3.8(3) and (4).

duties to report on details of the statement of affairs in the case of the administrators and the official receiver.[37]

The application will normally be made by an originating application following the standard requirements for such proceedings which have been discussed in detail in Chapter 10. It should be noted that the official receiver can support the application with a report instead of an affidavit which will then be treated as *prima facie* evidence of its contents.[38] Since the application will not normally involve other parties, a report may also be filed by administrators, unless the court orders otherwise.[39] The report or affidavit should set out in detail the reasons for restricting disclosure. For example, it may be that certain assets have been disclosed which are held by parties who, if they became aware of the office holder's or official receiver's interest in them might seek to dissipate them or conceal them and prevent their recovery.

15.2.9 The court has wide powers on hearing the application. In the case of administrators and the official receiver it can order that the statement or a specified part of it is not to be filed or that it is to be filed separately. In any case, including those involving administrative receivers, it can order that the statement, or a specified part of it, is not to be open to inspection without the leave of the court.[40] Where administrators or administrative receivers are involved, the court can also give directions which alter obligations to deliver documents to the registrar of companies or to disclose relevant information to other persons.[41] This reflects the fact that these office holders have duties to file the statement of affairs with the registrar of companies.[42]

15.2.10 EXPENSES

The person required to make a statement of affairs is to be allowed and paid by the office holder out of his receipts, any expenses incurred by him in carrying out that task which the office holder considers to be reasonable.[43] In the case of the official receiver the provisions are different. The official receiver is permitted, at the expense of the assets of the company in liquidation, to employ some person or persons to assist in the preparation of the statement of affairs. He can do this where the person whom he has required to prepare that statement cannot prepare it properly himself.[44] Additionally, the official receiver may receive a request from the person who has been required to prepare the statement seeking an allowance payable out of the assets of the company in liquidation towards the expenses of employing some person or persons to assist him in doing so. Such a request must be made on the ground that the person making the request cannot himself prepare a proper statement.[45] When such a request is made it must be accompanied by an estimate of the expenses involved.[46] The Insolvency Rules provide details as to the manner in which authorisation may then be provided by the official receiver.[47]

37. R. 2.16(1)(d) (administrators) and r. 4.45 (official receiver).
38. R. 7.9(1) and (3).
39. R. 7.9(2).
40. R. 2.13(2) (administrators); r. 3.5(2) (administrative receivers); and r. 4.35(2) (official receiver).
41. R. 2.13(3) (administrators) and r. 3.5(3) (administrative receivers).
42. See s. 23 and r. 2.16 (administrators); and s. 48 and r. 3.8(3) (administrative receivers).
43. R. 2.15(1) (administrators) and r. 3.7(1) (administrative receivers).
44. R. 4.37(1).
45. R. 4.32(2).
46. R. 4.37(3).
47. R. 4.37(3), *et seq.*

15.2.11 In the case of administrators and administrative receivers, their decision as to the allowance to be made in respect of expenses incurred in the preparation of the statement of affairs may be the subject of appeal to the court.[48] If such an appeal is made, then this will normally be by way of originating application following the standard form of procedure which applies in such applications as set out in Chapter 10 above. The affidavit supporting the application ought to include details of the nature of the work involved in preparing the statement, and the expenses which are likely to be incurred, including details of the fees of any professionals assisting.

It should be noted that, pending the appeal, a person required to make the statement of affairs remains under that obligation.[49]

15.3 Recovery of company documents

15.3.1 Powers

Under s. 234 of the 1986 Act, an administrator, an administrative receiver, liquidator or provisional liquidator[50] may seek an order from the court requiring "any person" who has in his possession or control any books, papers or records to which the company "appears to be entitled" to deliver them up to that office holder.[51] This section also contains equivalent provisions for the recovery of property.[52] In addition it contains protections for the office holder who seizes or disposes of property, believing on reasonable grounds that he is entitled to seize or dispose of it (with or without an order of the court), where it transpires that the property was not the property of the company.[53]

The provisions of the Act are supplemented by the Insolvency Rules in the case of liquidators appointed in a compulsory winding-up, and provisional liquidators. Under r. 4.185, the powers conferred on the court are exercisable by the liquidator or provisional liquidator in the first instance. Without first making application to the court, such an office holder may require the delivery up of the documentation which is in issue.[54] Any person on whom such a requirement is imposed must comply with it without avoidable delay.[55] If there is a failure to comply, then the liquidator or provisional liquidator may apply to the court for enforcement.[56]

15.3.2 Application

An application under s. 234 can be commenced by an originating application complying with the standard requirements in connection with such applications (discussed earlier in

48. R. 2.15(2) (administrators) and r. 3.7(2) (administrative receivers).
49. R. 2.15(3) (administrators) and r. 3.7(3) (administrative receivers).
50. S. 234(1).
51. S. 234(2).
52. *Ibid.* Property in this context means tangible property, with intangible property being excluded (see *Welsh Development Agency* v. *Export Finance* (1992) BCC 270).
53. S. 234(3) and (4). In such cases the office holder will not be liable in respect of loss or damage resulting from the seizure or disposal unless it was caused by his own negligence. In some cases he will even have a lien over the property or its proceeds of sale for any expenses incurred in the seizure or disposal.
54. R. 4.185(1).
55. R. 4.185(2).
56. The need for a court application in cases of dispute appears to have been recognised in *Re London Iron & Steel Co. Ltd* [1990] BCLC 372, at 376.

Chapter 10). The application will be supported by an affidavit rather than a detailed pleading. This procedure allows for an immediate hearing which may result in a summary determination and the swift delivery up of the documents sought (or property, as the case may be). It avoids the need for an acknowledgment of service and delivery of a statement of claim before applying for summary judgment, as would be the case if proceedings were commenced by way of writ action. Accordingly, the procedure has considerable advantages from the office holder's perspective.

Under the predecessor provision to s. 234, delivery could only be ordered up where it appeared that the company was "*prima facie* entitled" and this was thought to create a bar on proceedings under the Insolvency Act (as opposed to a writ action) where there was a genuine dispute in connection with the liquidator or other office holder's claim. However, in *Re London Iron & Steel Co. Ltd*,[57] Warner J., held that the provisions of s. 234(2) operated differently. The change in the wording of the section to "appears to be entitled" permitted proceedings to be commenced under s. 234, even where there was a dispute as to the true ownership of the property in question. The judge also took into account the fact that the respondent to such an application could be adequately protected procedurally, in so far as there were disputes of fact, by virtue of the court's power under the Insolvency Rules to direct the service of pleadings, discovery or other procedural steps as and when necessary.[58]

15.3.3 Interlocutory relief

In the light of the Court of Appeal decision in *Morris* v. *Murjani*[59] (a case concerning equivalent powers in bankruptcy), it would appear that s. 234 creates a statutory power which is enforceable by the office holder, sufficient to entitle him to appropriate interlocutory relief including, if necessary, interlocutory injunctions. Accordingly, the office holder may seek orders requiring the preservation of documents pending the final hearing of the proceedings or even an Anton Piller order in appropriate circumstances.[60] In circumstances such as these, the proceedings might be begun at the same time as an application for such interlocutory relief *ex parte*.

15.3.4 Liens

It should be noted that, in the context of administration, liquidation or provisional liquidation, the powers of the office holder to apply under s. 234 are supplemented by s. 246. This latter section provides that a lien or other right to retain possession of any of the books, papers or other records of the company is unenforceable to the extent that its enforcement would deny possession of any books, papers or other records to the office holder concerned.[61] The only exception is in the context of a lien on documents which

57. *Supra*.
58. See rr. 7.7, 7.10, 7.51 and 7.60 and the detailed review of these provisions contained in Chapter 10, *supra*.
59. [1996] 1 WLR 848.
60. In the case of *Re First Express Ltd* [1991] BCC 782, it appears to have been recognised that, if there were some danger that assets or books would be wrongfully disposed of, an application under s. 234(2) could be begun *ex parte* with appropriate interlocutory orders being obtained.
61. S. 246(2).

give title to property and which are held as such.[62] Even where such a special form of lien arises, however, it may still be possible to obtain inspection of the documents concerned, exercising other inquisitorial powers such as the power of private examination.[63] The power of private examination may also allow office holders who do not have the benefit of s. 246, such as administrative receivers, to gain access to the documents concerned.[64]

15.4 Powers under s. 235

15.4.1 Scope

Section 235 contains powers which were introduced for the first time under the 1986 Act and which constitute a powerful addition to an office holder's investigative armoury. It can be used by the same persons who can apply under s. 234 with the addition of the official receiver in the context of compulsory liquidation (irrespective of whether he is the liquidator or not[65]).

The section imposes a duty on specified persons to give to the office holder such information concerning the company and its promotion, formation, business, dealings, affairs or property, as the office holder may at any time after "the effective date" reasonably require. Such persons may also be required to attend on the office holder at such times as he reasonably requires.[66] The persons upon whom these duties are imposed are principally those who are or have at any time been officers of the company.[67] The obligations also arise in respect of those who have taken part in the formation of the company at any time within one year before "the effective date" or who have been employed by the company within that year and who are, in the office holder's opinion, capable of giving the information which he requires.[68] Additionally, persons who are or have been, within that year, officers or employees of another company which, within that year, was an officer of the insolvent company, are covered.[69] This in effect covers officers or employees of a corporate officer of the insolvent company. Finally, where the company is in compulsory winding-up, any person who acted as an administrator, administrative receiver or liquidator is covered.[70]

"The effective date" varies, depending upon the type of insolvency. In the case of administration, it is the date of the administration order; in the case of administrative receivership, it is the date of the appointment of the administrative receivers (or the first of the administrative receivers if there has been a succession of them); in the case of a provisional liquidator it is the date of appointment; and in the case of liquidation, it is the date the company went into liquidation.

62. S. 246(3). The words "as such" refer to the circumstances, manner or capacity in which documents are held which give rise to a lien so as to differentiate from the situation where documents are held by a person who could sometimes be entitled to assert a lien but does not in the circumstances, manner and capacity in the case in question (see *Re SEIL Trade Finance* [1992] BCC 538).

63. Discussed *infra*.

64. See *Re Aveling Barford* [1989] BCLC 122.

65. S. 235(1).

66. S. 235(2).

67. S. 235(3)(a).

68. S. 235(3)(b) and (c).

69. S. 235(3)(d).

70. S. 235(3)(e).

15.4.2 Applications

Section 235 can be enforced by criminal sanctions.[71] Civil procedures for enforcement, however, also exist under the Insolvency Rules 1986, r. 7.20.[72] This provision allows the court, on an application made by "the competent person", to make "such orders as it thinks necessary" for the enforcement of obligations under s. 235.[73] The "competent person" for these purposes is the office holders and the official receiver who are entitled to exercise powers under s. 235.[74] Recognition has been given to the official receiver's right to proceed under this rule where there has been non-compliance with obligations under s. 235.[75]

15.4.3 Where application is made under r. 7.20, the application will normally be made by originating application following the standard procedure for proceedings of this kind.[76] The application in the case of an office holder such as a liquidator or administrator will be supported by an affidavit but, in the case of the official receiver, it may be supported by a report which will be treated as *prima facie* evidence of its contents.[77]

The affidavit or report ought to set out details of the information or assistance requested under the provisions of s. 235 and details of the person to whom the request was made, so as to establish that they fall within the categories of persons who can be required to provide information or assist. The affidavit should then set out details of their refusal and details of the requirements of the office holder or official receiver in relation to the information sought. This latter aspect of the affidavit or report may have to be drafted with care since too specific an explanation of the need for the information may have a prejudicial effect on other aspects of the insolvency. The relevant office holder or official receiver may prefer such matters to remain confidential. In such circumstances, the court may adopt a similar procedure to that adopted in the context of applications under s. 236, where confidential reports are often submitted by the relevant office holder and in relation to which special arrangements may have to be made, as discussed in detail below.[78]

15.4.4 Analogy with s. 236

In drafting the affidavit it should also be noted that s. 235 only permits the office holder to obtain such information as he "reasonably requires". This qualification may bring into play the possibility of a contest as to whether there is a legitimate requirement on the part of the office holder to obtain the information requested in an application under r. 7.20. This may give rise to a similar balancing exercise to that which the court often has to

71. S. 235(5).
72. In light of the decision of Harman J. in *Re Oriental Credit* [1988] Ch. 204, the existence of a specific rule giving rise to a civil remedy is significant. If only a criminal sanction were imposed it would suggest that the section created no private legal or equitable right which was capable of enforcement by civil process on the part of the office holder but only to a public right enforceable by the Attorney-General. Harman J. so held in connection with earlier legislation contained in ss. 528 *et seq.* and s. 561 of the Companies Act 1985 which created duties to provide information or to produce documentation which were enforceable purely by criminal sanctions.
73. R. 7.20(1)(c).
74. R. 7.20(2)(d).
75. *Re Wallace Smith Trust Co.* [1992] BCC 707.
76. See Chapter 10, *supra.*
77. R. 7.9(1) and (3).
78. See paras 15.5.5–15.5.6, *infra.*

conduct in the context of s. 236 applications. This is discussed below in connection with the s. 236 procedure.[79]

Where r. 7.20 is used, many other principles which have emerged in connection with applications under s. 236 may also be applicable. In particular, in determining whether the proceedings should be commenced *ex parte* and which persons should be notified of the proceedings, equivalent principles to those which apply under s. 236 may well be relevant. These matters are discussed further below in the context of s. 236 proceedings.[80]

15.4.5 It will not be a defence to an application under r. 7.20 that the person who is required to provide information wishes to exercise the privilege against self-incrimination. Following the Court of Appeal decision in *Bishopsgate Investment Management* v. *Maxwell*, it is now clear that the privilege is abrogated in this context.[81] The threat or existence of criminal proceedings, however, may still be a matter to be considered by the court as part of the exercise of its discretion. Decisions relating to these matters under s. 236 may also be relevant in this context.[82]

Where the court makes an order enforcing obligations under s. 235 it may provide that the costs of and incidental to the application be borne by the person against whom the order is made.[83]

15.4.6 Interlocutory applications

Since r. 7.20 creates a civil cause of action which can be brought by an office holder or the official receiver, it would appear that interlocutory relief can be sought to ensure that those rights remain enforceable.[84] For example, where appropriate, the office holder might seek to prevent a person who is under a duty to comply with obligations under s. 235 from leaving the jurisdiction or, alternatively, injunctions might be sought requiring such a person to preserve documentation.[85]

15.4.7 Confidentiality

Certain difficulties can arise under s. 235, given that interviews are often conducted in an atmosphere of informality and confidentiality. The informality and confidentiality may result in a greater flow of information to the relevant office holder or the official receiver.[86] However, the confidentiality associated with the interview cannot prevent the office holder from complying with statutory duties to report crime[87] and it may not prevent the prosecuting authorities from seeking the delivery up of transcripts or notes of examinations conducted under s. 235. Where this occurs, the court may be reluctant to prevent the

79. See paras 15.5.12–15.5.14, *infra*.
80. See paras 15.5.4 and 15.5.7–15.5.10, *infra*.
81. [1993] Ch. 1.
82. As to which see para. 15.5.14, *infra*.
83. R. 7.20(3).
84. *Morris* v. *Murjani*, *supra*.
85. Prior to the current legislation it was necessary to seek an order under the predecessor to s. 236, for a private examination, before an order could be made restraining a person who was under an obligation to provide information from departing from the jurisdiction (see *Re Oriental Credit*, *supra*).
86. See the comments of Millett J. in *Re Barlow Clowes* [1992] Ch. 208 at 222E–F and see also *Re Arrows (No. 4)*, *supra*, at 82D–F.
87. See, for example, s. 218 and see also *Re Arrows (No. 4)*, *supra*.

office holder or the official receiver from disclosing the information so obtained, leaving the matter to be considered by the judge conducting the criminal proceedings.[88]

15.5 Powers under s. 236

15.5.1 Scope

Section 236 contains the most wide ranging investigative provisions available to company office holders. It provides that the court may, on the application of the office holder, summon to appear before it:

(i) any officer of the company,
(ii) any person known or suspected to have in his possession any property of the company or supposed to be indebted to the company, or
(iii) any person whom the court thinks capable of giving information concerning the promotion, formation, business, dealings, affairs or property of the company.[89]

Clearly the latter of these categories is wide ranging, going well beyond the category of person who may be the subject of requirements to provide a statement of affairs or to provide information pursuant to a requirement under s. 235,[90] and can include the Crown.[91]

The section can be used by the same office holders as applicable under s. 234, with the addition of the official receiver in the case of compulsory winding-up (irrespective of whether he is also the liquidator of the company concerned).[92]

15.5.2 Rather than summon the above persons to appear before it, the court may instead require them to prepare and submit an affidavit to the court containing an account of the relevant person's dealings with the company. Alternatively, the court can make an order requiring that person to produce any books, papers or other records in its possession or under its control relating to the company or its promotion, formation, business, dealings, affairs or property.[93] Moreover the court has the power to order persons who are summoned to appear before it to answer interrogatories concerning the above matters.[94]

In addition to the above inquisitorial orders which the court may make, the court also has a summary jurisdiction when dealing with s. 236 hearings. Accordingly, if it appears to the court, on consideration of any evidence obtained under s. 236, that a person has in his possession any property of the company, the court may, on the application of the office holder, order that person to deliver the whole or any part of that property to the office holder at such time and in such manner and on such terms as the court thinks fit.[95] Similarly, if it appears to the court, on consideration of the evidence so obtained, that any person is indebted to the company, the court may, on the application of the office holder,

88. See *Re Arrows (No. 4), supra*; *Re Barlow Clowes, supra*; and *R* v. *Clowes* [1992] BCLC 1158 (a case in which the criminal trial judge ordered that transcripts of voluntary interviews be disclosed to defendants in criminal proceedings).
89. S. 236(2).
90. For a historical review of the types of person who have been summoned under the predecessors to this section see *Buckley on the Companies Acts (14th Edn)*, Vol. 1, pp. 647–650.
91. See *Soden* v. *Burns* [1996] 1 WLR 1512.
92. A creditor or contributory cannot use this position; see *Re James McHale Automobiles* [1997] BCC 202.
93. S. 236(3).
94. S. 237(4).
95. S. 237(1).

order that person to pay the office holder, at such a time and in such manner as the court directs, the whole or any part of the amount due, whether in full discharge of the debt or otherwise, as the court thinks fit.[96]

15.5.3 Application

Specific provision is made under the Insolvency Rules for applications under s. 236.[97] Rule 9.2 provides that the application must be in writing and be accompanied by a brief statement of the grounds on which it is made.[98] Additionally, the application must sufficiently identify the respondent[99] and it must state the form of the relief which is sought, namely whether the respondent is to be ordered to appear before the court or to answer interrogatories, submit affidavits or to produce books, papers or other records or any two or more of such orders. Particulars are required to be given where interrogatories, affidavits or documentation are sought. In the case of interrogatories, particulars are required of the matters in respect of which answers are sought.[100] In the case of affidavits, particulars are required to be given of the matters to which the respondent is required to swear.[101] In the case of documentation, the items in issue are required to be specified.[102]

The application may be made on the basis that there is a *prima facie* probability that the respondent is capable of providing the information sought.[103]

The application will be made to the registrar[104] in the first instance, but may be adjourned to the judge, for example, where there is likely to be a contest over whether an order should be made raising difficult issues.

15.5.4 Ex parte or *inter partes*

Rule 9.2(4) provides that the application for an order under s. 236 may be made *ex parte*. It was the long established practice of the Companies Court, for applications under s. 236 to be made *ex parte*.[105] Within the last few years a substantial change in this practice has occurred. This began with the decision of Vinelott J. in *Re Maxwell Communications Corp.*[106] where the learned judge stated that an *ex parte* application for a s. 236 order might only be justified where documents which fell clearly within s. 236 would not be produced voluntarily and there were good reasons for insisting on confidentiality of the statement of the office holder in support of the application. Vinelott J. also concluded that an *ex parte* application might be justified if production of documentation or an examination was urgently required, and delay in obtaining an *inter partes* hearing, on giving notice to the person affected, would unduly hamper the office holder's task.

96. S. 237(2).
97. See IR 1986, part 9.
98. R. 9.2(1).
99. R. 9.2(2).
100. R. 9.2(3)(b).
101. R. 9.2(3)(c).
102. R. 9.2(3)(d).
103. See *Re Financial Insurance Co.* (1867) 36 LJ (Ch.) 687; *Clement's Case* (1868) LR 13 Eq. 179n; *Re Gold Co.* (1879) 12 Ch. 77 and *Re A Debtor (No. 12 of 1958)* [1968] 1 WLR 788.
104. See r. 7.6(2) and *Re Nowgong Tea Co.* (1867) 16 LT 47.
105. See, for example, *Re British & Commonwealth (Nos 1 and 2)* [1992] Ch. 342.
106. [1994] BCC 741.

However, in *Re Murjani*,[107] Lightman J., when dealing with applications under the equivalent provisions in bankruptcy, concluded that *ex parte* applications would generally only be justifiable in cases of urgency or where there was a real risk that property or documentation might be disposed of if notice was given of the application. The fact that material would not be provided voluntarily or that a confidential statement was intended to be relied upon, could not justify, on their own, an *ex parte* application. Lightman J. went on to emphasise that where an *ex parte* application was made, it would normally have to be made with all due diligence by the relevant office holder. If he had not demonstrated due urgency in the period up to the making of the application he could not "catch up time" by adopting an *ex parte* procedure. In the light of the above decision, it would now appear that *ex parte* applications will be rare.[108]

15.5.5 The confidential statement

The brief statement which is required to be prepared in support of an application under s. 236 is a document which will require careful preparation. In the past, the court has treated such "brief statements" as confidential so that they were not to be supplied at any stage to the respondent.[109] This was on the basis that the statements often contained material which was of a sensitive nature in the context of the insolvency and because it was thought that the office holder should be able to be entirely candid.

The above approach is no longer applicable. In *Re British & Commonwealth (Nos 1 and 2)*,[110] the Court of Appeal held that it will no longer be automatically the case that an office holder's "confidential statement" remains confidential to him. In appropriate cases it may be made available to the respondent should he wish to challenge the application for a s. 236 order. The Court of Appeal concluded that inspection of the confidential statement would *prima facie* be allowed where the court was of the opinion that it would or might be unable fairly and properly to dispose of the application for an order if part of the evidence was withheld from the person against whom that order was sought. It would then be for the office holder to satisfy the court that confidentiality in whole or in part was nevertheless appropriate. In effect, this decision means that the judge hearing the matter will have to read the confidential statement and weigh the arguments for each side after hearing the submissions of the office holder as to confidentiality. The submissions of the office holder regarding the reasons for confidentiality may have to be disposed of without the other side being present or, in the event that they are legally represented, on the basis that their legal advisers do not communicate what is said, to their clients. Such arrangements had to be made in the case of *Re Murjani*,[111] where Lightman J. concluded that there were sustainable grounds for maintaining confidentiality in relation to the office holder's statement following an *in camera* hearing where an explanation of the sustainable grounds was given in the absence of the representatives of the examinee. This followed upon an *inter partes* hearing at which the examinee had put forward his submissions.

15.5.6 In the light of this practice, when preparing his statement to support the application under s. 236, the office holder or the official receiver will need to consider

107. [1996] 1 WLR 1498.
108. See also *Re PFTZM Ltd* [1995] BCC 280.
109. See, for example, in *Re Gold Company, supra*, at 82–83 and *Re Aveling Barford Ltd, supra*, at 36.
110. *Supra.*
111. [1996] BCC 278.

carefully whether or not it is necessary to include confidential matters. The Court of Appeal in *Re British & Commonwealth (Nos 1 and 2)*[112] provided the following guidance where confidential matters do have to be included. The applicant should identify any material for which he could argue that confidentiality ought to be maintained and to embody it in an annexure or annexures to the statement. The ground or grounds for maintaining confidentiality should then be stated in the statement itself. Where the application is made *inter partes*, the statement and any non-confidential annexures can be served upon the respondent. It ought then to be possible for any disputed question of inspection to be dealt with at the start of any contested hearing and, at any rate where the judge decides that confidentiality should be maintained, it ought often to be possible to avoid an adjournment.

15.5.7 Notification to third parties

When making an application for an order under s. 236, the office holder or official receiver will not only have to consider whether it is appropriate to make the application *ex parte* or *inter partes*, but he will also have to consider whether it is right that persons other than the proposed examinee should be notified of the application and given an opportunity to be heard in relation to it. In *Morris* v. *Serious Fraud Office*,[113] the Vice Chancellor, Sir Donald Nichols was faced with an application by liquidators of an insolvent bank who were seeking disclosure of documents held by the bank's auditors relating to the bank's financial dealings. The auditors were unwilling to provide the documentation to the liquidators but it transpired that the Serious Fraud Office had obtained many of the documents from the auditors pursuant to their investigative powers. The liquidators made an application under s. 236 for an order that the Serious Fraud Office produce certain categories of these documents. The Vice Chancellor held, confining his remarks to cases of production of documents,[114] that where the documents whose production was sought belonged to or related to the affairs of a third party, it was right in principle that the court should also take into account any prejudice to that third party if production was ordered. By "third party", the Vice Chancellor referred to a person other than the person who had possession or control of the documents, otherwise, the liquidator would be in a better position by bringing an application under s. 236 against an agent of a third party, than if he had made the application directly against the third party. The Vice Chancellor concluded that this could not be right and there was nothing in the legislative scheme of which s. 236 was a part which could lead to that conclusion. He accordingly provided the following guidance:

(1) Where documents are sought under s. 236, the person to whom those documents belong (or to whose affairs they relate)[115] is entitled to an opportunity to present to the court any ground of objection that they may have to the production of the documents and should be notified therefore of the application or proposed application.
(2) There may, however, be exceptional cases, where for example:

112. *Supra*, at 356.
113. [1993] Ch. 372.
114. *Supra*, at 382F.
115. *Supra*, at 382G and 384C.

(a) notice to the third party of the office holder's application might seriously prejudice the object the office holder is seeking to achieve in the existing or proposed proceedings;
(b) the third party may not be traceable; or
(c) the documents may be needed as a matter of dire emergency.

(The above list is not intended to be comprehensive.)[116] In such exceptional cases the court might make an order under s. 236, even though the third party who would normally have the right to be heard could not be notified.

15.5.8 The above principles were applied in *Re Murjani*.[117] Lightman J. concluded that, where the solicitors or other agents were the subject of a s. 236 type application, in the normal course their clients would be parties with the solicitors or agents effectively taking a neutral stance or "interpleading". However, in the circumstances of the particular case before him, the clients of the solicitors could not be traced, and this justified the making of an application for a s. 236 type order, without joining those clients in the proceedings. It should be noted that the *Murjani* case appears to extend the decision in *Morris* v. *Serious Fraud Office* to some extent, since the Vice Chancellor's comments in the latter case were confined to an application concerning documentation, whereas the decision of Lightman J. in *Murjani* related to an application for both oral examination and for the production of documentation.

15.5.9 The position in relation to notification to third parties has been considered again recently in the case of *Soden* v. *Burns*.[118] In this case the joint administrators of Atlantic Computers plc sought the production of certain transcripts of evidence of witnesses given to Department of Trade & Industry inspectors under the Companies Act 1985, s. 432. The question arose as to whether the relevant witnesses should be notified of the application and allowed to participate before an order was made. The transcripts which were sought included the evidence of witnesses who were involved in proceedings which the administrators had commenced arising out of the collapse of Atlantic Computers. Robert Walker J. concluded that this case raised some distinct considerations from those which arose in the *Morris* and *Murjani* cases since neither of those decisions concerned transcripts of witnesses. He took into account the possible oppression to individual witnesses who gave evidence to inspectors with the Department of Trade & Industry, where those witnesses were involved in civil litigation and where the administrators might obtain, by virtue of s. 236, transcripts which might not otherwise come to them until a much later stage, if indeed at all. He concluded that he should apply the practice set out in the *Morris* and *Murjani* cases.

Robert Walker J. went on to review the procedure which should be used in giving notification to the third party witnesses. He reviewed the cases of *London & Counties Securities Ltd* v. *Nicholson*[119] and *Re Kingcroft Insurance Co. Ltd*.[120] The procedure in *London & County Securities* involved giving the witnesses 14 days' notice to enable them to object to disclosure of the transcripts of their evidence and included an undertaking from the office holder not to disclose the contents of the transcripts other than to professional advisers except to the extent that the disclosure was necessary for the

116. *Supra*, at 385B–C.
117. *Supra*.
118. *Supra*.
119. [1980] 1 WLR 948.
120. 14 July 1993, unreported.

performance of the office holder's duty in conducting litigation. In the *Kingscroft Insurance* case, an order for disclosure without prior notification to the witnesses was ordered, but only to a strictly limited class (in general terms, the office holders themselves and their professional advisers) and only on undertakings not to use the transcripts or information contained in them for litigation in Liechtenstein or elsewhere, without returning to the Companies Court for a further hearing. Harman J. in that case had intended the first stage to be purely an exercise in which the office holders and their advisers informed themselves about the contents of the transcripts, and any consequent use of the information, or action based on it, was prohibited unless or until sanctioned by the Companies Court at the second stage (which was never in the event reached). Until the second stage there was to be a Chinese Wall between knowledge and action.

15.5.10 In *Soden* v. *Burns*, Robert Walker J. stated that he had considerable doubts about the feasibility of the procedure used by Harman J. in *Kingscroft Insurance* and considered that the order was made in circumstances which were exceptional (in the case before Harman J. there was great urgency in trying to trace and recover assets which were overseas and there was no immediate prospect of civil proceedings against those whose transcripts were sought under s. 236). Accordingly, he concluded that he would not apply the two-stage procedure used by Harman J. and instead ordered disclosure of all the transcripts of evidence sought, but only after prior notification to each of the witnesses whose evidence was covered by the order and subject to any application by them to set it aside. He required a period of 21 days' notice (rather than the 14 days adopted in the *London & County Securities* case) to each witness.

15.5.11 Corporate Respondents

In *Re Highgrade Traders*[121] it was held that the word "person", in s. 236, included a company, and that a company could be required to produce documents through its proper officer. Moreover, suggestion was made during the course of argument by Lightman J. in *Re Murjani*[122] that a company could also be orally examined by its proper officer. Clearly a procedure which allows for an examination of a corporate director or officer of a company by its proper officer would be convenient and would be in line with other inquisitorial procedures, such as those concerning statements of affairs and examinations under s. 235, which envisage individuals who are officers or employees of a corporate officer of a company in insolvency being the subject of investigation.[123]

15.5.12 Contested applications

On contested s. 236 applications, the court will normally have before it the confidential statement of the office holder and affidavit evidence filed by the respondent or any interested third party who objects. When preparing these items of evidence, careful consideration needs to be given to the manner in which the court exercises its discretion under the section in contested applications. Historically the court has tended to view s. 236 as a provision which was particularly useful in enabling office holders to determine

121. [1984] BCLC 151.
122. *Supra.*
123. See para. 15.4.1, *infra.*

whether or not to make a claim for the recovery of property or compensation.[124] However, this was always treated as simply an instance of the wider purpose of the provision, namely to enable the officer holder to discover the truth of the circumstances in connection with the affairs of the company so that he might, as effectively as possible and with as little expense as possible, complete his function to put the affairs of the company in order and complete his various tasks.[125] At one stage, following the decision of the Court of Appeal in *Cloverbay* v. *BCCI*[126] it appeared that this wide purpose of proceeding under s. 236 might be restricted. Sir Nicolas Browne-Wilkinson V.C. concluded that the purpose of s. 236 was to enable an office holder only to obtain sufficient information to reconstitute the state of knowledge that the insolvent company should possess. In the House of Lords' decision in *Re British and Commonwealth (Nos 1 & 2)*,[127] however, it was held that the power of the court to make an order under s. 236 was not limited to such purposes. The key issue in any application under s. 236 was whether it was a proper case for making an order, balancing the reasonable requirements of the office holder to carry out his task and the need to avoid making an order which worked wholly unreasonably or unnecessarily or oppressively to the person concerned.

15.5.13 The House of Lords went on to consider particular matters which might affect the court's balancing exercise. It was stated that an application was not necessarily unreasonable simply because it was inconvenient to the respondent to the application or caused him a lot of work or might make him vulnerable to future claims or was addressed to a person who was not an officer or employee or a contractor of the company which was in insolvency. In addition, guidance given by the Court of Appeal in the *Cloverbay* case, appears to remain good law on this balancing exercise. The Court of Appeal held that the case for making an order under s. 236 would usually be stronger in the case of an officer or former officer of the company as opposed to that of a third party. Since the third party is under no general duty to give information to the office holder (apart from an order under s. 236), if by giving information he risks exposing himself to liability, the court would consider that this involved an element of oppression. This would not prevent an order being made against a third party but it would be borne in mind that there was a degree of possible oppression which was greater than in the case of an officer of the company. The court would also generally treat the production of documents as less oppressive than oral examination of witnesses. Finally, the court concluded that, whether or not the liquidator reached a firm decision to sue or not, or indeed had commenced proceedings or not, against the examinee, did not prevent an application being made under s. 236 (as it had under previous practice).[128] It would merely be a factor to be considered by the court in weighing the reasonable requirements of the office holder as against the possible oppression of the examinee. Nevertheless, it still appears that the existence of proceedings against the examinee, or his possible exposure to liability, does continue to arise regularly. Its continuing importance as a factor was emphasised by Robert Walker J. in *Soden* v. *Burns*.[129]

124. See *Re Gold Company, supra*, at 85.
125. See *Re Rolls Razor* [1968] 3 All ER 698 at 700; and *Re Esal (Commodities) Ltd* [1989] BCLC 59 at 64.
126. [1991] Ch. 90.
127. [1993] AC 426.
128. See *Re Castle New Homes Ltd* [1979] 1 WLR 1075, at 1089–1090 and *Cloverbay* v. *BCCI, supra* at 99H.
129. *Supra*, at 1532–1533 and see also *Re James McHale Automobiles, supra*.

15.5.14 The existence of possible or actual criminal charges has also been raised as a basis of objection from time to time, but with mixed success. Thus in *Bishopsgate Investment Management Ltd* v. *Maxwell*,[130] at first instance, the existence of possible criminal charges was raised as an argument on behalf of Kevin Maxwell. Hoffmann J. refused to set aside an order for a s. 236 examination as a matter of discretion on this basis. Similarly, in *Re Arrows Ltd (No. 2)*[131] Vinelott J. came to the conclusion that, where a criminal charge had actually been preferred but where the criminal proceedings lay some months ahead, there was insufficient risk of oppression to prevent a s. 236 examination proceeding. The possibility of the examinee having to fight on two fronts was reduced. He also came to the view that, given the scale of the insolvency, the need for information as a matter of urgency and the amount of funds which remained to be traced in that case, the reasonable requirements of the office holder outweighed any possible oppression to the examinee of providing information which might incriminate him after a criminal charge had already been made. The judge did comment, however, that the balance might be different if the examination did not take place before the examinee was committed for trial and before further charges were brought. To avoid any delays which might result in this, however, he considered that the parties might consider holding the examination before a judge so that any possible disputes regarding particular questions could be dealt with immediately rather than by referral or appeal from a registrar who would normally hear the examination. These two authorities are in line with *Re Wallace Smith Trust Co. Ltd*,[132] a case dealing with applications under r. 7.20 in connection with s. 235.

Finally, the importance attached to the nature of the insolvency in considering whether to make an order under s. 236 has been emphasised recently in the case of *Re Bank of Credit and Commerce International SA (No. 12)*.[133] Robert Walker J. held that any honest person who found themselves to have been involved, however innocently, in a major fraud must be expected to co-operate with those whose duty it was to investigate the fraud. In the context of the s. 236 application in that case, this meant providing various categories of books and correspondence and other documents relating to the BCCI liquidation and related liquidations.

15.5.15 Order under s. 236

Rule 9.3 of the Insolvency Rules provides detailed provisions as to the form of order which the court must make on a s. 236 application.[134] The rule provides that whatever order is sought by the office holder, the court may make any order which it has power to make under the section.[135] Where the court makes an order for affidavits to be submitted, then the order must specify what matters are to be dealt with in the affidavits and the time in which they are to be submitted to the court.[136] If the order is made to produce books, papers or other records, the time and manner of compliance must also be specified.[137] Where the respondent has been ordered to answer interrogatories, the court will direct him

130. 23 December 1991, unreported.
131. [1992] BCLC 1176.
132. *Supra.*
133. [1997] BCLC 526.
134. See also the prescribed Form 9.1.
135. R. 9.3(1).
136. R. 9.3(3).
137. R. 9.3(4).

as to the questions he is required to answer and as to whether his answers (if any) are to be made on affidavit.[138] Where the order is for an oral examination then it must specify a venue for the appearance of the respondent which must be no less than 14 days from the date of the order.[139] Whatever order is made it must be served forthwith on the respondent, personally, unless the court otherwise orders.[140]

When directions are given for an oral examination to take place, the respondent may seek directions for advance notice to be given of the topics which are to be covered or the key questions which are to be asked. The process of providing a note of the topics which are to be pursued, together with copies of the documents to which reference is to be made was a course suggested by Vinelott J. in *Re Norton Warburg Holdings*.[141] Applications for detailed questionnaires have also been made in *Re Bishopsgate Investment Management Ltd (No. 2)*[142] and in *Re Maxwell Communications Corp. plc*.[143] In both cases the court was loathe to require the office holder to provide a detailed questionnaire. In the former case, Hoffmann J. rejected suggestions that answers given in the course of an oral examination without prior questionnaire might result in an over-hasty reaction or responses which might be a product of confusion or poor recollection. In the latter case Vinelott J. accepted a submission that written questionnaires might lead to tailored answers and the need for further written questionnaires, thus increasing the time and expense involved. Although he suggested that a list of topics might be advantageous, this was not insisted upon by the judge and no written questionnaire was ordered. The objective, where a list of topics is provided, is to assist the respondent in answering the questions put to him, thus avoiding the necessity for adjournments of the examination for points to be researched from documentation.

15.5.16 The Examination

Any oral examination will normally take place before a registrar. In some cases, for example, where a respondent has criminal proceedings pending against him, it may be appropriate for the examination to take place before the judge rather than the registrar. This will avoid delays caused by the need for questions to be referred to the judge or for appeals to take place (which might result in the examination continuing beyond the committal stage with additional oppression to the respondent).[144] At the examination, the office holder or official receiver may attend in person, or he may be represented by a solicitor, with or without counsel, and put such questions to the respondent as the court allows.[145] In addition, any other person who could have applied for an order under this section in respect of the insolvent company's affairs may, with leave of the court, and if the applicant office holder or official receiver does not object, attend the examination and put questions to the respondent (but only through the applicant).[146] Where the application

138. R. 9.4(3).
139. R. 9.3(2).
140. R. 9.3(5). The word "forthwith" has been interpreted as meaning as soon as practicable (see *Re Seagull Manufacturing Co. Ltd* [1993] Ch. 345).
141. (1983) 1 BCC 98, 907, at 98, 913.
142. [1994] BCC 732.
143. *Supra.*
144. As suggested by Vinelott J. in *Re Arrows Ltd (No. 2), supra.*
145. R. 9.4(1).
146. R. 9.4(2).

has been made under s. 236, on information provided by a creditor, that creditor may, with leave of the court and if the applicant does not object, attend the examination and put questions to the respondent (again, however, such questions can only be put through the applicant).[147]

The respondent is also permitted at his own expense to employ a solicitor, with or without counsel, to put questions to him as the court allows, for the purposes of enabling him to explain or qualify any answers given by him and to make representations on his behalf.[148] For example, the respondent's representatives might wish to make representations about matters which are the subject of professional privilege, which operates in favour of some other party or in favour of the respondent.[149] In such circumstances, the registrar may have to make a direction or refer the matter to the judge for resolution.[150]

15.5.17 The Insolvency Rules specifically provide for a written record of the examination in such form as the court thinks proper. Normally it takes the form of a transcript. They also provide for that record to be read over either to or by the respondent, and signed by him at a venue fixed by the court at the conclusion of the examination.[151] The written record may then be used in any proceedings (whether under the Insolvency Act or otherwise) as evidence against the respondent of any statement made by him in the course of his examination.[152] These provisions, in combination with the statutory scheme of which s. 236 forms a part, have been held by the Court of Appeal to abrogate any privilege against self-incrimination on the part of the respondent.[153]

The examination is conducted in chambers[154] and is not open to the public generally.[155] The special provisions as to the attendance of other persons who could have made an application under s. 236 or of creditors who supplied information to facilitate the application indicates the highly confidential nature of the process. This is emphasised by IR 1986, r. 9.5(1) which requires that, unless the court directs otherwise, the written record of the examination or any answer given to interrogatories or any affidavit submitted in compliance with an order of the court will not be filed in court. Additionally, under r. 9.5(2), the written record, answers and affidavits are not to be open to inspection without an order of the court, by any person other than the applicant for the order under s. 236 or any person who could have applied for such an order in respect of the affairs of the same insolvent company. These restrictions also apply to the part of the court file that shows the grounds of the application and to any copy of any proposed interrogatories.[156] Additionally, the court may from time to time give directions as to the custody and inspection of

147. R. 9.4(4).

148. R. 9.4(5). For the purposes of such re-examination, the respondent's legal advisers may take a note of the proceedings but the notes are not to be used for any other purpose (see *Re Cambrian Mining Co.* (1881) 20 Ch.D. 376 and *Re Heseltine & Son* [1891] WN 25).

149. See *Re Compass Airlines* (1992) ACLC 1380 and *Price Waterhouse* v. *BCCI* [1992] BCLC 583 regarding claims to legal professional privilege in s. 236 cases.

150. See the comments as to this practice in *Morris* v. *Serious Fraud Office*, Note 112, *supra* at 384F–G.

151. R. 9.4(6).

152. R. 9.4(7).

153. *Bishopsgate Investment Management* v. *Maxwell*, *supra*.

154. But it may nevertheless be conducted on oath (and usually is) (see s. 237(4)).

155. See *Re Western of Canada Oil, Lands & Works Co.* (1877) 6 Ch.D. 109; *Re Grey's Brewery Co.* (1883) 25 Ch.D. 400: *Re Heseltine & Son*, *supra*; *Re Empire Assurance Corp.* (1868) 17 LT 488; and *Re Norwich Equitable Fire Insurance Co.* (1884) 27 Ch.D. 515).

156. R. 9.5(3).

any documents to which these rules apply and as to the provision of copies of, or extracts from, such documents.[157]

15.5.18 Costs

Where there is a contested hearing as to whether or not a s. 236 order should be made at all, the court will have its usual discretion as to what form of order as to costs should be made. Normally, costs will follow the event. It should be noted, however, that where the person who is the subject of the s. 236 examination has no personal interest in the information sought to be disclosed, such as a solicitor whose client is the person truly interested in the confidential information, the court will not look favourably on steps being taken by that respondent in contesting the application. Instead, their stance should be that of a neutral party or of "interpleading". It should be for the client to take any positive steps to contest the application. Consequently where solicitors did not adopt a neutral stance in *Re Murjani*[158] Lightman J. made an indemnity costs order against them.

Rule 9.6 also provides specifically for the costs of the proceedings. In particular, r. 9.6(1) states that, where the court has ordered an examination and it appears that the examination was made necessary because information had been unjustifiably refused by the respondent, it may order that the costs of the examination are to be paid for by him. Where such an order is not made, the costs of the office holder or the official receiver will, unless the court otherwise orders, be paid out of the insolvent estate.[159] As far as the respondent is concerned, he is to be tendered a reasonable sum in respect of his travelling expenses in connection with his attendance. The other costs falling on him are to be at the court's discretion.[160] In the case of the official receiver, where he makes the application otherwise than in the capacity of liquidator, no order is to be made for the payment of costs by him.[161] In *Re Aveling Barford*[162] Hoffmann J. came to the view that there was no automatic rule that an examinee would be indemnified in respect of its costs. Since the examination was conducted on the basis of a public duty, the applicable principles would be analogous to those in cases of a subpoena in an ordinary action. Costs would therefore normally be dealt with at the end of the examination after a review of the overall conduct of the proceedings.

15.5.19 Appeals/referrals

Where the examination takes place before the registrar, the normal appeal procedures in connection with appeals to the judge will apply.[163] In addition, the registrar may refer particular issues to the judge during the course of the examination for determination under

157. R. 9.5(4).
158. *Supra.*
159. R. 9.6(3).
160. R. 9.6(4).
161. R. 9.6(5).
162. *Supra*, at 366.
163. See Chapter 10 and in particular the review of rr. 7.47 and 7.49.

the Insolvency Rules 1986, r. 7.6(3). Once those issues have been determined, the judge may refer the matter back to the registrar for continuation of the examination.

15.5.20 Location of examination

Section 237(3) provides that the court may, if it thinks fit, order that any person shall be examined in any part of the United Kingdom where he is for the time being, or in a place outside the United Kingdom if he is a person who could have been summoned to appear before the court if he had been within the jurisdiction. However, by reason of the decision of the Court of Appeal in *Re Tucker*,[164] a decision in bankruptcy concerning an equivalent provision to s. 236 of the Bankruptcy Act 1914, it appears that the court will not make an order for the examination of a person abroad if he cannot be compelled to attend. The Court of Appeal held that the provisions allowing the examination to occur outside the jurisdiction did not actually create any extra-territorial jurisdiction but merely provided machinery whereby an examination which has already been properly founded jurisdictionally, could take place. The case has been subsequently distinguished in *Re Seagull Manufacturing*,[165] a case concerning public examinations, where it was emphasised that public examinations were concerned with a much narrower class of persons than private examinations under s. 236 and equivalent provisions.

It seems therefore that, notwithstanding comments concerning the harmonisation of public and private examinations in *Bishopsgate Investment Management* v. *Maxwell*,[166] this harmonisation does not extend to the question of extra-territorial effect. In order to conduct private examinations relating to persons who are located abroad, it will therefore be necessary to use some form of international assistance. One possibility is requesting assistance in relation to jurisdictions which are covered by the provisions enacted in or under s. 426 of the 1986 Act. The jurisdictions covered by these reciprocal assistance provisions, however, are relatively limited. They cover other parts of the United Kingdom, the Channel Islands and the Isle of Man. Some other countries have been designated.[167] Besides these provisions, the obvious other method by which to obtain assistance would be under the Hague Convention concerning the taking of evidence abroad. Serious doubts, however, arise, as to whether this Convention can be used in relation to insolvency, following the decision in *Re International Power Industries*.[168] Another possibility is to apply using assistance provisions which exist under a foreign jurisdiction's domestic law. One example may arise in connection with the United States where ancillary bankruptcy procedures are available and recognition is given to office holders appointed within the United Kingdom. It might also be possible in some cases to use 28 United States Code, s. 1782 which has wide ranging measures for the gathering of evidence in connection with proceedings abroad and which does not appear to be limited in the same way as the Hague Convention.[169]

164. [1988] 1 All ER 603.
165. [1993] Ch. 345.
166. *Supra.*
167. Those designated include Anguilla, Australia, the Bahamas, Bermuda, Botswana, Canada, Cayman Islands, Falkland Islands, Gibraltar, Republic of Ireland, Monserrat, New Zealand, St. Helena, Turks and Caicos Islands, Tuvalu, Hong Kong and Virgin Islands (see the Co-operation of Insolvency Courts (Designation of relevant countries and territories) Order 1986, S.I. 1986 No. 2123.
168. [1985] BCLC 128.
169. In relation to the operation of 28 USC s. 1782 see *South Carolina* v. *Assurantie* [1987] AC 24.

15.5.21 Warrants for enforcement

Section 236(4) provides for cases where there is a failure to comply with the court's orders under this section. Where a person, without reasonable excuse, fails to appear before the court when he is summoned to do so, or where there are reasonable grounds for believing that he has absconded or is about to abscond with a view to avoiding his appearance before the court, then the court may cause a warrant to be issued to a constable or prescribed officer of the court for his arrest or for the seizure of any books, papers, records, money or goods in his possession.[170] The court may then authorise the person arrested under the warrant to be kept in custody and anything seized under that warrant to be held, in accordance with the rules, until that person is brought before the court under the warrant or until such time as the court orders.[171]

Detailed provision is made under rr. 7.23 and 7.24 in connection with the issue and execution of warrants under these provisions. They provide that, when a person is arrested under a warrant issued under this section, the officer arresting him must forthwith bring him before the court issuing the warrant in order that he may be examined.[172] If he cannot immediately be brought up for examination, the officer is to deliver him into the custody of the governor of a prison named in the warrant who is to keep him in custody and produce him before the court as the court may from time to time direct.[173] After arresting the person named in the warrant, the officer is to report the matter to the court and apply to the court to fix a venue for the person's examination.[174] The court is then to appoint the earliest possible time for the examination and is to direct the governor of the prison to produce the person for examination at the time and place appointed and to forthwith give notice of the venue to the person who applied for the warrant.[175] Any property in the arrested person's possession which is seized is to be lodged with or otherwise dealt with as instructed by the person specified in the warrant as authorised to receive, or is to be kept by the officer seizing it pending receipt of written orders from the court as to its disposal.[176] Various forms are specified for use in conjunction with these matters.[177]

15.5.22 The issue of warrants under s. 236 is an extremely rare event. On occasion, the court has had to deal with applications to restrain persons from leaving the jurisdiction who were the subject of s. 236 orders. In such circumstances, an application for a warrant has not been made and instead there has been an application for an injunction. This occurred in the case of *Re Oriental Credit*.[178] Following the decision of the Court of Appeal in *Morris* v. *Murjani*,[179] applications for interlocutory orders of this kind appear to be fully justified, given the statutory powers which arise under the section in favour of the office holder or official receiver.

170. S. 236(4) and (5).
171. S. 236(6).
172. R. 7.23(1).
173. R. 7.23(2).
174. R. 7.23(3).
175. R. 7.23(4).
176. R. 7.23(5).
177. See Forms 7.8 and 7.9 provided for under IR 1986.
178. *Supra*, and see also *Morris* v. *Murjani*, *supra*, a bankruptcy case which arose in similar circumstances.
179. *Supra*.

15.6 Special inquisitorial powers of the official receiver

15.6.1 Accounts

Certain special powers are granted to the official receiver under the Insolvency Rules. Under r. 4.39 he is given the power to request persons who could be examined under s. 235, to furnish him with accounts of the company of such nature, as at such date and for such period as he may specify.[180] The period specified may begin from a date up to three years preceding the date of the presentation of a winding-up petition, or from an earlier date to which the audited accounts of the company were last prepared.[181]

The official receiver can apply to the court to require accounts for an earlier period. Any such application would normally be an originating application following the standard forms for such applications as set out in Chapter 10 above. The application may be supported by an affidavit or, if the official receiver so wishes, a report which will constitute *prima facie* evidence of its contents.[182]

15.6.2 The official receiver may require the accounts to be verified by affidavit and to be delivered to him within 21 days of the request or such longer period as he allows. Two copies of the accounts, together with any affidavit are to be delivered to the official receiver by the person required to furnish them, and the official receiver is then required to file one copy in court with the affidavit if any.[183] Similar provisions arise in connection with the expenses of preparing such accounts as arise in the context of preparing a statement of affairs for the benefit of the official receiver.

If the person requested to supply the official receiver with accounts fails to do so, an application can be made under r. 7.20 to enforce compliance. This is on the basis that there would have been a breach of the obligations arising under s. 235. The procedure for such applications, as outlined above, would apply in this context also.[184]

15.6.3 Further disclosure

In addition to the above powers to obtain accounts, the official receiver is given specific power under r. 4.42 to require persons who have prepared a statement of affairs or any accounts at his request, to submit (in writing) further information amplifying, modifying or explaining any matter contained in the statement of affairs or accounts which they have submitted.[185] The official receiver can direct that the information be verified by affidavit and it must be delivered to him within 21 days of the requirement or such longer period as he allows.[186] The rules then provide for two copies of the documents containing the information and any affidavit to be delivered by the relevant person to the official receiver who is then to file one copy in court together with any affidavit.[187]

It would appear that such further disclosure is encompassed by the official receiver's general powers under s. 235. Accordingly, if there is a failure by the relevant respondent to comply with the official receiver's reasonable requirements then an application might

180. R. 4.39(1).
181. R. 4.39(2).
182. R. 7.9(1) and (3).
183. R. 4.39(5) and (6).
184. See paras 15.4.2–15.4.3, *infra*.
185. R. 4.42(1).
186. R. 4.42(2).
187. R. 4.42(3).

be made under r. 7.20. In such circumstances the practice and procedure outlined above in connection with applications under that rule will apply.[188]

15.6.4 Public examination

POWERS

Under s. 133, the official receiver has special powers to apply for the public examination of persons who have been officers of the company, who have acted as liquidators or administrators or as receivers or managers of the company, or persons who have been concerned in or taken part in the promotion, formation or management of the company.[189] This power was introduced by the Insolvency Act in the expectation that it would be used more frequently,[190] among other things, to give publicity to the salient facts and unusual features associated with a company's failure.[191] The use of the provision in the context of bankruptcy prior to the 1986 Act had been reasonably widespread. The practice in company insolvency was that such applications were very rarely made.[192]

15.6.5 Notwithstanding the objective of the legislation, the provision is still very rarely used. The official receiver normally takes the view that information can be obtained more economically and expeditiously and more fully if interviews are conducted informally under s. 235. As set out below, however, the powers of public examination do have a particular importance where the relevant person who is sought to be examined is not within the jurisdiction. The court has wider extra-territorial powers under this provision than under s. 236.

15.6.6 Where an application is made for a public examination it must be carried out in the context of a compulsory liquidation and it must be made prior to the dissolution of the company concerned.[193] The application may be made by the official receiver and he must make the application if he is requested to do so by one half in value of the company's creditors or three quarters in value of the company's contributories.[194] A request by creditors or contributories forcing the official receiver to take action must be made in writing and must be accompanied by a list of the creditors concurring in the request and the amounts of their respective claims in liquidation or (in the case of contributories) the details of their respective values and from each creditor or contributory concurring, a written confirmation of his concurrence. These provisions, however, will not apply where the requisitioning creditors' debt or the requisitioning contributories' shareholding is by itself, sufficient without the concurrence of others.[195] Additionally, the request must specify the name of the proposed examinee, the relationship which he has or has had with the company and the reasons why the examination is requested.[196] Before an application to the court is made on the request, the requisitionists must deposit with the official

188. See paras 15.4.2–15.4.3, *infra*.
189. S. 133(1).
190. Earlier provisions such as s. 270, Companies Act 1948 required a report of fraud before an application could be made, and were little used.
191. "Insolvency Law and Practice", Report of the Review Committee, *supra*, paras 653–657.
192. Prior to IA 1986, no public examination in company insolvency had occurred since 1935.
193. S. 133(1).
194. S. 133(2).
195. R. 4.213(1).
196. R. 4.213(2).

receiver a sum by way of security for the expenses of the hearing of a public examination if ordered.[197]

After receiving the request, the official receiver must, within 28 days, make the application to the court for an order under s. 133, but if he is of the opinion that the request is unreasonable, he can apply to the court for an order relieving him from the obligation to make the application.[198] This would normally be by way or originating application supported by an affidavit or report[199] (complying with the usual procedures for such applications as set out in Chapter 10). The rules envisage that such an application may be made *ex parte*[200] but it would appear that the same considerations which arise in s. 236 examinations concerning the making of orders *ex parte*, ought to apply in this context. In other words, the application ought not to be *ex parte* unless there is some good reason for doing so, for example because the matter is one of dire urgency or no notice can be given or there is some risk of harm if notification was given.[201] Where an application is made *ex parte*, then notice of any order which the court has made must be given forthwith by the official receiver to the requisitionists.[202] It would then appear that the requisitionists could apply to set that order aside in the same way as a respondent could apply to set aside an order which had been made *ex parte* against him under s. 236.

15.6.7 APPLICATION

The application under s. 133 would normally be an originating application and, in the case of a person who is to be examined on the basis of his being concerned or taking part in the promotion, formation or management of the company, must be accompanied by a report by the official receiver. That report must indicate the grounds on which the person is supposed to fall within such a category and whether, in the official receiver's opinion, it is likely that service of the order on that person can be effected by post to a known address.[203] If, in the report, the official receiver gives as his opinion that there is no reasonable certainty that service by post will be effective, the court can direct that the order be served by some other means in addition to post service.[204] It would appear that the application ought to be made *inter partes* in the same way as in a s. 236 application, unless there is good reason for it to be made *ex parte*.[205] The court, on the hearing of the application, if it is objected to, may then consider whether or not the application is properly constituted and in particular whether the person sought to be examined falls within the categories of person who can be examined. It can also consider whether such an examination is reasonably required, applying by analogy the principles adopted in s. 236 cases.[206]

Any order which the court makes for a public examination must specify a venue for the examination and must also direct the respondent's attendance at that examination.[207]

197. R. 4.213(3).
198. R. 4.213(4) and (5).
199. See r. 7.9(1) and (3).
200. R. 4.213(6).
201. See para 15.5.4, *infra*.
202. R. 4.213(6).
203. R. 4.211(2).
204. R. 4.211(3).
205. See paras 15.5.12–15.5.14, *supra*.
206. See paras 15.5.12–15.5.14, *supra*.
207. R. 4.212(1).

The court order must then be served forthwith on the person who is to be examined.[208] The order will direct that the person to be examined attends, on the date specified, to be publically examined as to the promotion, formation or management of the company, or as to the conduct of its business and affairs, or his conduct or dealings in relation to the company.[209]

15.6.8 The Rules provide that the official receiver must give at least 14 days' notice of the hearing to any liquidator who has been appointed, to any special manager who has been appointed and, subject to any contrary direction of the court, to every creditor and contributory of the company who is known to the official receiver or who is identified in the company's statement of affairs.[210] Additionally, the official receiver may, if he thinks fit, cause notice of the order to be given, by advertisement in one or more newspapers, at least 14 days before the day fixed for the hearing.[211] The Rules provide that, unless the court directs otherwise, there shall be no such advertisement before at least seven days have elapsed since the examinee was served with the order.[212] This appears to allow for the possibility, where the order is obtained *ex parte*, that the examinee may wish to apply to set it aside before he is subject to the adverse publicity which may arise from advertisement of the fact that a public examination order has been made against him.

15.6.9 WITNESS UNFIT FOR EXAMINATION

Specific provision is made for an examinee who is suffering from any mental disorder or physical affliction or disability rendering him unfit to undergo or attend a public examination. The Insolvency Rules provide that an application may be made by the examinee to either stay the order for his public examination or direct that it should be conducted in such manner and at such place as it thinks fit on such grounds.[213] The application must be made by the person who has been appointed by a court in the United Kingdom or elsewhere to manage the affairs of or to represent the examinee, or by a relative or friend of the examinee whom the court considers to be a proper person to make the application, or by the official receiver.[214]

Additionally, where the application is made by a person other than the official receiver, unless the examinee is a patient within the meaning of the Mental Health Act 1983, it must be supported by an affidavit of a registered medical practitioner as to the examinee's mental and physical condition. Moreover, seven days' notice for the application must be given to the official receiver and the liquidator (if that is a person other than the official receiver).[215] Finally, before any order is made on the application, the applicant is required to deposit with the official receiver such sum as the latter certifies to be necessary for the additional expenses of any examination which may be ordered on the application.[216] This covers the possibility of the examination being conducted otherwise than before a court.

208. R. 4.211(1).
209. S. 133(3).
210. R. 4.212(2).
211. R. 4.212(3).
212. *Ibid.*
213. R. 4.214(1).
214. R. 4.214(2).
215. R. 4.214(3)(b).
216. R. 4.214(3)(c).

15.6.10 The application may be made by ordinary application since it is made in the context of proceedings for a public examination. Rule 4.214(4) provides for it to be made by the official receiver *ex parte*, supported by evidence in the form of a report by the official receiver to the court. This may be appropriate where no opposition is anticipated to the application. Where there is any possibility of a contest, however, it would appear that the application ought to be *inter partes* in the usual way unless special reasons arise to make this inappropriate.[217] Where an order is made on such an application it may provide for the expenses of the examination to be payable as to a specified proportion, out of the deposit made by the applicant in respect of the additional expenses caused by the application.[218]

15.6.11 HEARING

At the hearing of the public examination, the examinee must be examined on oath and is required to answer all questions the court puts or allows to be put to him.[219] Various persons are allowed to take part in the public examination. According to s. 133(4), these are the official receiver, the liquidator of the company, any person who has been appointed as a special manager of the company's property or business, any creditor of the company who has tendered a proof, and any contributory of the company. Such persons may question the examinee concerning matters relating to the promotion, formation or management of the company or as to the conduct of its business and affairs, or may ask the examinee concerning his conduct or dealings in relation to the company.[220] Any of the persons permitted to appear and ask questions may, with the approval of the court, (made known either at the hearing or in advance of it), appear by solicitor or counsel or alternatively they may in writing, authorise another person to question the examinee on their behalf.[221] Additionally, the examinee himself may, at his own expense, employ a solicitor, with or without counsel, who can put questions if the court allows for the purpose of enabling him to explain or qualify answers given by him and also to make representations on his behalf.[222]

A record in writing of the examination, in a form that the court thinks proper, is required to be made.[223] This would normally be in the form of a transcript. The record is to be read over either to or by the examinee and signed by him and verified by affidavit at a venue fixed by the court.[224]

15.6.12 The rules provide that the written record may be used in evidence against the examinee in any proceedings under the Insolvency Act or otherwise as a statement made by him in the course of his examination.[225] In *Bishopsgate Investment Management* v. *Maxwell*[226] it was noted that under s. 133, no privilege against self-incrimination arose in

217. Compare the guidance given on *ex parte* and *inter partes* applications in the s. 236 context as set out in paras 15.5.4 *et seq., supra*.
218. R. 4.214(3).
219. R. 4.215(1).
220. S. 133(4).
221. R. 4.215(2).
222. R. 4.215(3).
223. R. 4.215(4).
224. *Ibid.*
225. R. 4.215(5).
226. *Supra.*

favour of the examinee, the privilege having been abrogated by the statutory provisions.

The rules specifically provide that if criminal proceedings have been instituted against the examinee, and the court is of the opinion that the continuance of the hearing would be calculated to prejudice a fair trial of those proceedings, the hearing may be adjourned.[227]

15.6.13 The Insolvency Rules also make provisions for an adjournment of the public examination either to a fixed date or generally.[228] Where the examination is adjourned generally, the court may at any time, on the application of the official receiver or of the examinee, fix a venue for the resumption of the examination and give directions as to the manner in which and the time within which notice of the resumed public examination is to be given to persons entitled to take part in it.[229] Where the application is made by the examinee, the court may grant it on terms that the expenses of giving these notices are to be paid for by him and that, before a venue for the resumed public examination is fixed, he is to deposit with the official receiver such a sum as the latter considers necessary to cover those expenses.[230]

15.6.14 EXPENSES

Where the public examination is ordered by the court on a creditor's or contributor's requisition under r. 4.213, the court has power to order the expenses of the examination to be paid as to a specified proportion, out of the deposit made by such creditors or contributories instead of out of the assets of the insolvent company.[231] The rules also provide that in no case are the costs and expenses of the public examination to fall on the official receiver personally.[232] Subject to these provisions it would appear that the costs and expenses of the public examination are at the discretion of the court, which may order the costs of the examinee to be paid out of the insolvent estate in an appropriate case, or for the examinee to pay his own costs and expenses and those of the official receiver as considered appropriate, having regard to the basis upon which the public examination is conducted and how it has progressed.[233]

15.6.15 ENFORCEMENT

Section 134 provides for the enforcement of a court order for a public examination under s. 133. In particular, if a person, without reasonable excuse, fails at any time to attend his public examination, he will be guilty of contempt of court and liable to be punished accordingly.[234] Additionally, if there are reasonable grounds for believing that he has absconded or is about to abscond with a view to avoiding or delaying his examination, the court may cause a warrant to be issued to a constable or a prescribed officer of the court for his arrest or for the seizure of any books, papers, records, money or goods in his

227. R. 4.215(6).
228. R. 4.216(1).
229. R. 4.216(2).
230. R. 4.216(3).
231. R. 4.217(1).
232. R. 4.217(2).
233. Compare the position in s. 236 applications and, in particular, the case of *Re Aveling Barford, supra*.
234. S. 134(1).

possession.[235] In such a case, the court may authorise the person arrested under the warrant to be kept in custody, and anything seized under the warrant to be held until such time as the court orders.[236] Special provision is made under the rules for such warrants, in similar form to warrants for the enforcement of orders made under s. 236.[237]

15.6.16 EXTRA-TERRITORIAL EFFECT

Unlike s. 236, it would appear that the provisions of s. 133 are not limited by any territoriality principles. Accordingly, an order may be made for a person's public examination whether or not they are British subjects and whether or not they are within the jurisdiction of the court at the relevant time.[238] Where a person is outside the jurisdiction, an order may be made for their public examination under s. 133 with the order then being served on them when they return to the jurisdiction with public examination occurring thereafter.[239] Additionally, it may be possible to use the provisions for co-operation between jurisdictions made in connection with s. 426 of the Insolvency Act 1986 referred to above.[240]

235. S. 134(2).
236. S. 134(3).
237. See rr. 7.22–7.24 and paras 15.5.21–15.5.22, *supra*.
238. See *Re Seagull Manufacturing Ltd* [1993] Ch. 345.
239. This would appear to comply with the requirement that the order for public examination be served forthwith, since "forthwith" means as soon as reasonably practicable (see *Re Seagull Manufacturing*, *supra*, at 359).
240. See para. 15.5.20, *supra*.

PART 4

DISQUALIFICATION PROCEEDINGS

CHAPTER 16

COMPANY DIRECTOR DISQUALIFICATION PROCEEDINGS

16.1 Scope

The Company Directors Disqualification Act 1986 ("the CDDA 1986") gives courts the jurisdiction to disqualify persons from acting as directors of companies, or from acting in certain other capacities in relation to companies or their property.[1] Orders to that effect are referred to as "disqualification orders".[2]

The Insolvent Companies (Disqualification of Unfit Directors) Proceedings Rules 1987 ("the Rules") set out the general rules and procedures to be followed in cases where the application is made under s. 7(1) of the CDDA 1986 (unfitness to be concerned in the management of a company) or s. 8 (expedient in the public interest). Such applications are the most common, and this Chapter will concentrate on applications made under the Rules. Reference should also be made to Practice Direction No. 2 of 1995[3] and to the provisions of the *Chancery Guide* as to the general procedure to be adopted in the Companies Court.

16.1.1 The Companies (Disqualification Orders) Regulations 1986 ("the Regulations") set out regulations made under s. 18 of the CDDA 1986 by which the clerks of various courts with jurisdiction to make disqualification orders are to furnish the Secretary of State with particulars of orders for disqualification, for leave to act, for variation, or for cessation of an order made under the CDDA 1986. This information enables the Secretary of State to maintain a register of orders and of cases in which leave has been granted.

The CDDA 1986 applies to companies[4] and to building societies[5] and its scope is extended to partners or persons having control or management of partnerships which are wound up as unregistered companies.[6]

16.2 Context of the Act

Prior to 1985 the disqualification regime was contained in the Companies Acts.[7] The Insolvency Act 1985 enacted but did not bring into force the new law relating to insolvency which was consolidated into the Insolvency Act 1986 and the CDDA 1986.

1. See para. 16.3.1, *infra*.
2. CDDA 1986, s. 1(1).
3. [1996] 1 WLR 170, reproduced at Appendix 3.
4. See the extended definition in s. 22(2).
5. CDDA 1986, s. 22A.
6. Insolvent Partnerships Order 1994, art. 16.
7. See, for example, s. 188, CA 1948, s. 28(1), CA 1976, s. 3, CA 1981 and s. 300, CA 1985.

The Insolvency Act 1985 and hence the CDDA 1986 arose out of the wholesale review of the regime governing personal and corporate insolvency and owes much to the Cork Committee which was established in 1977 for this purpose. The Cork Report was published in June 1982.[8]

The CDDA 1986 must be considered in the context of the Companies Act 1985 and the Insolvency Act 1986. Indeed, it has been said that the Insolvency Act 1986 and the CDDA 1986 should be seen as part of a single statutory scheme.[9] Both civil and criminal courts may make disqualification orders in the context of other proceedings in respect of defaults or offences committed under, or in relation to such Acts. The relevant circumstances are summarised briefly below, but it is not the function of this Chapter to deal with the procedure by which a disqualification order may be made other than by the Companies Court.

16.3 Disqualification

Section 1 of the CDDA 1986 sets out the general jurisdiction. Critically—but often overlooked—a disqualification order is not an absolute bar on a person acting as a director of a company, merely a bar on a person acting as a director without leave. This should be considered in the context of the proposals (which were abandoned by the government and which had not been recommended by the Cork Committee) for *automatic* disqualification in cases of multiple insolvency.

In particular, the Act is not designed to punish the individual, but to protect the public. A disqualification order is not of itself penal, although it has been said to be "clearly restrictive of the liberty of the person against whom it is made".[10] While this is true in general terms, the "liberty" being restricted is—in respect of the prohibition against acting as a director of a company—very often the counterpart of what is referred to as the "privilege" of trading with limited liability.[11] Companies are creatures of statute, and the liberty to be a director of a company, if a true liberty, is one given only by statute. The CDDA 1986 does not encroach on what would ordinarily be regarded as a fundamental freedom, and the consequences of an order under the CDDA 1986 are not truly restrictive of the freedom of the individual in the sense of a criminal penalty.

16.3.1 The mandatory disqualification under s. 6 of the Act (unfitness)[12] has come under considerable criticism, not least from the judges who do not like their discretion to be fettered in this way,[13] but no individual need actually suffer prejudice if the public can be adequately protected in the context of an application for leave to act.

Section 1 of the CDDA 1986 provides that, where an order is made under the Act, a person shall not, without leave:

(a) be a director of a company;

8. 1982, Cmnd. 8558.
9. *Re Jeffrey S. Levitt* [1992] BCLC 250 at 236 per Vinelott J.—both Acts having their origins in the IA 1985.
10. *Secretary of State* v. *Langridge* [1991] BCLC 543 at 548e. See also *Re Living Images Ltd* [1996] 1 BCLC 348 at 355 in the context of a discussion as to the standard of proof in disqualification proceedings.
11. See for example in *Re Pamstock Ltd* [1994] 1 BCLC 716 at 736 per Vinelott J., approved by Hoffmann L.J. in *Re Grayan Building Services Ltd* [1995] Ch. 241 (See also Henry and Neil L.JJ.).
12. The application for an order under CDDA 1986, s. 6 is actually made under s. 7.
13. See, for example, the reluctance with which Vinelott J. disqualified a director in *Pamstock, supra.*

(b) be a liquidator or administrator of a company;
(c) be a receiver or manager of a company's property;
(d) in any way, whether directly or indirectly, be concerned or take part in the promotion, formation or management of a company[14];

for a specified period (which may range under the Act from two to 15 years) from the date of the order. The width of the prohibition is apparent; the prohibition at (d) in particular is easily overlooked and can given rise to difficulty in the grey areas of "junior management" or consultancy and an application for leave must be made in case of doubt.[15]

A disqualification order can be made against any person; that is, an individual or a corporation. Separate forms are provided by the Regulations for a court clerk to notify the Secretary of State of an order made in respect of an individual: reg. 5(a) and Form DO1; or a corporation: reg. 5(b) and Form DO2.

16.4 Criminal procedure

Sections 2 and 5 of the CDDA 1986 provide for courts of criminal jurisdiction to make disqualification orders in the context of criminal proceedings brought against a person. Criminal procedure is beyond the scope of this Chapter, and it is sufficient to note that such proceedings are brought not for the purpose of obtaining a disqualification order, but because it appears that a person has committed a criminal offence.

The powers under ss. 2 and 5 of the CDDA 1986 are available to the criminal court when sentencing, and no procedural questions arise beyond the requirement, under the Regulations, that the clerk of the court furnish the relevant particulars to the Secretary of State.

16.5 Jurisdiction

16.5.1 To whom does the CDDA 1986 apply?

By s. 24, the CDDA 1986 extends to England and Wales and to Scotland, but not to Northern Ireland.[16]

Section 6 of the CDDA 1986 gives the court power to make orders against any person, whether or not they are present in the jurisdiction, and whether or not the acts complained of took place in relation to a company incorporated in the jurisdiction.[17] Further, s. 6 applies to a person irrespective of where the conduct occurred.[18]

The very wide jurisdiction is limited in practice by the control exercised by the Secretary of State in deciding to institute proceedings under the section, and the discretion given to the court under r. 5(2) of the Rules to decline to order service on a person out of the jurisdiction.[19]

14. See para. 16.20, *infra*, as to the form of the order.
15. See *R.* v. *Campbell* [1984] BCLC 83, a case on s. 188(1), CA 1948 but relevant as to the meaning of the phrase "be concerned in". A management consultant advising on the financial management and restructuring of a company was "concerned in" its management. Beldam J., at p. 88d–e emphasised the wisdom of applying to the court in a case of doubt.
16. A similar regime operates in Northern Ireland under part II, Companies (Northern Ireland) Order 1989 and ancillary rules.
17. *Re Aldermanbury Trust plc* [1993] BCC 598 at 601D–E.
18. *Re Seagull Manufacturing Ltd (No. 2)* [1994] Ch. 91.
19. *Seagull Manufacturing, supra*, at 284a–d.

16.5.2 To which court is the application made?

The jurisdiction of a court to make a disqualification order arises only from the CDDA 1986. The expression "the court" means different things in different contexts.

An order under s. 2 of the CDDA 1986 (disqualification on conviction of indictable offence) may be made[20] by:

(a) any court having jurisdiction to wind up the company in relation to which the offence was committed; or
(b) the court by or before which the person is convicted of the offence; or
(c) in the case of a summary conviction in England and Wales, any other magistrates' court acting for the same petty sessions area.

16.5.3 Under s. 3 of the CDDA 1986 (disqualification for persistent breaches of companies legislation), "the court" is any court having jurisdiction to wind up any of the companies in relation to which the offence or other default has been or is alleged to have been committed.[21] This definition also applies under s. 4 of the CDDA 1986 (Disqualification for fraud, etc., in winding-up).[22]

Under s. 5 of the CDDA 1986 (disqualification on summary conviction) only the court by which a person is convicted, or in England and Wales any other magistrates' court acting for the same petty sessions area, may make a disqualification order.

16.5.4 Section 6 of the CDDA 1986 (unfit directors of insolvent companies) is, for the purpose of this Chapter, the most important section. It applies only to a person who has been a director of an insolvent company and the meaning of "the court" depends upon the nature of the insolvency. It means[23]:

(a) in the case of a person who is or has been a director of a company which is being wound up by the court, the court by which the company is being wound up;
(b) in the case of a person who is or has been a director of a company which is being wound up voluntarily, any court having jurisdiction to wind up the company;
(c) in the case of a person who is or has been a director of a company in relation to which an administration order is made, the court by which that order was made; and
(d) in any other case, the High Court or, in Scotland, the Court of Session.[24]

Under s. 8 of the CDDA 1986 (disqualification after investigation of company) "the court" means the High Court or, in Scotland, the Court of Session.

16.5.5 Finally, under s. 10 of the CDDA 1986 (participation in wrongful trading), the court is not defined but must (given that the jurisdiction only arises when the court makes a declaration under s. 213 or 214 of the Insolvency Act 1986) be the court winding-up, or having jurisdiction to wind up, the relevant company.[25]

20. CDDA 1986, s. 2(2).
21. CDDA 1986, s. 3(4).
22. CDDA 1986, s. 4(2).
23. CDDA 1986, s. 6(3).
24. This will include a company which has been dissolved, see *Re NP Engineering and Security Products Ltd* [1995] 2 BCLC 585.
25. *Secretary of State* v. *Langridge* [1991] BCLC 543 per Balcombe J. at 549c.

It will be apparent that there may, in any one case, be a number of courts having concurrent jurisdiction to make a disqualification order. This may well be the case where a person has been a director of a number of companies, or where a person is convicted of an offence in a criminal court and a company is wound up (as it must be) in another court, or where a county court has, with the High Court, jurisdiction to wind up a company.[26]

The courts to which application is made for leave to act are considered at para. 16.23, *infra*.

16.5.6 When does a court have jurisdiction

Under s. 6(3)(a) of the CDDA 1986, jurisdiction is conferred on the court in which a company "is being wound up". Under s. 6(3)(b), where a company "is being wound up voluntarily" any court which has jurisdiction to wind up the company is "the court". Section 6(3)(c) applies where "an administration order is in force". Note the use of the present tense; the matter is tested at the date the disqualification proceedings are brought.[27]

The use of the present tense in s. 6(3) subsections (a) to (c) gives rise to no difficulties so long as the winding-up, or administration order as the case may be, is still in force. It is now clear that the jurisdiction of the relevant court will continue *after* the winding-up (and presumably after discharge of an administration order), provided that, at the time proceedings were commenced, that court had jurisdiction. The words "for the purpose of the commencement of proceedings" must be implied into s. 6(3).[28] A winding-up ceases on dissolution of the company and not before.[29]

16.5.7 If a company has been wound up *and* dissolved, or the winding-up has been stayed, or an administration order made and discharged prior to an application for disqualification being brought under s. 6, this will be "any other case" under s. 6(4) and the High Court—or in Scotland, the Court of Session—will have jurisdiction. In this case, only the Secretary of State may bring the proceedings.[30]

Under ss. 2(2)(a), 3(4) and 4(2), a court may be "the court" because it has jurisdiction to wind up the relevant company. When this jurisdictional basis applies it is not clear whether it would continue even after a company has been wound up and dissolved, or struck off the Register.

16.5.8 Under s. 10 of the CDDA 1986 (participation in wrongful trading) it appears from the use of the word "also"—not present in the similar provisions of ss. 2(1) or 5(2)—that the court can only make a disqualification order in the same proceedings as it makes the relevant declaration under ss. 213 or 214 of the Insolvency Act 1986.

26. See IA 1986, ss. 117–121.
27. *Re Lichfield Freight Terminal Ltd* [1997] BCC 11.
28. *Re Working Project Ltd, Re Fosterdown Ltd, Re Davies Flooring Ltd* [1995] BCC 197. This is relevant only where a county court is given jurisdiction under subs. (a)–(c)—the High Court has jurisdiction under subs. (d) even where proceedings are commenced after the relevant company has been dissolved.
29. *Re Working Project Ltd, supra*, per Carnworth J. at p. 202A.
30. See *NP Engineering Ltd* [1995] 2 BCLC 585 at 590g.

16.6 The 10-day letter

Section 16(1) of the CDDA 1986 requires that a person intending to apply for the making of a disqualification order[31] shall give not less than 10 days' notice of his intention to do so to the person against whom the order is sought. The notice is not required to set out any grounds justifying an order.

The requirement is that 10 clear days are given, not counting the day on which notice is given and the day on which proceedings are issued.[32]

16.6.1 Neither the Act nor the Rules makes express provision for how the 10-days' notice is to be given, but the Rules incorporate (to the extent that there is no inconsistent provision in the Rules) the Rules of the Supreme Court 1965 or (as the case may be) the County Court Rules 1981.[33] Order 65, r. 5(1)(b) would appear to allow such notice to be given by post and the notice would (in the absence of evidence to the contrary) be deemed served, if served by first class post, on the second working day after posting, and if by second class post on the fourth working day after posting.[34]

However, the requirement for 10 days' notice has been held to be directory not mandatory.[35] Accordingly, the failure to give the requisite notice is an irregularity which may be waived by the court. It should not be thought that in every case such an irregularity will be waived, nevertheless, unless the respondent can show that he has suffered prejudice by the failure (or possibly that the applicant had deliberately ignored the requirement) the subsequent proceedings should stand.[36] Note also that only s. 6 prescribes a time limit within which proceedings must be commenced; in all other cases an applicant could re-start proceedings after a fresh 10-days' notice.

16.7 Where notice is not required

The requirement for 10 days' notice applies to all persons *intending to apply* for the making of a disqualification order.[37] It is, however, open to the courts to make disqualification orders of their own motion under ss. 2, 5 and 10 of the CDDA 1986. In these cases it has been suggested that the rules of natural justice require that the person concerned should be given some notice that the court is contemplating making a disqualification order.[38]

Certainly it is to be expected that an order under s. 10, in purely civil proceedings, would not be made unless the respondent had been given the opportunity to address the court on the question of disqualification. It would be a matter for the court itself to consider the procedure in this regard, but as proceedings under ss. 213 or 214 of the

31. This will include any person who applies, for which see CDDA 1986, s. 16(2).
32. *Re Jaymar Management Ltd* [1990] BCLC 617.
33. Rules, r. 2(b).
34. Interpretation Act 1978, s. 7. *Supreme Court Practice 1995*, Vol. 1, para. 65/5/5.
35. *Secretary of State* v. *Langridge* [1991] BCLC 541. The purpose of the 10-day letter is obscure. It gives no opportunity to the proposed respondent to seek to dissuade the applicant from commencing proceedings, nor is there very much that the respondent can usefully do in the meantime.
36. In *Secretary of State* v. *Langridge* it was conceded by Counsel for the Secretary of State, and accepted by Leggatt L.J. that the failure of the Secretary of State to give due notice "will enable the respondent to apply for, and if the court think fit obtain, an order striking out the proceedings".
37. CDDA 1986, s. 16(1).
38. *Secretary of State* v. *Langridge*, per Balcombe L.J. at 550c.

Insolvency Act 1986 will be brought by a liquidator for the purpose of recovering assets, the court will be reluctant to extend the length of the trial so that "public interest" can be determined at the expense of the creditors of the company.

16.7.1 It is likely that an order under s. 10 would be made only in the plainest of cases, where the facts sufficient to establish liability under ss. 213 or 214 of the Insolvency Act 1986 were clearly sufficient to justify an order under s. 10 of the CDDA 1986.

In the case of criminal proceedings, the orders open to the court under ss. 2 and 5 of the CDDA 1986 may properly be regarded as an extension of their sentencing powers.[39]

16.8 Who may apply?

The answer to this question also depends on which section of the CDDA 1986 it is proposed to rely on.

Under ss. 2 to 5 of the CDDA 1986 the application may be made[40] by:

(a) the Secretary of State;
(b) the official receiver[41]; or
(c) the liquidator or any past or present member or creditor of a company in respect of which the person against whom the order is sought has committed or is alleged to have committed an offence or default.

An application under s. 7 of the CDDA 1986 for an order under s. 6 is made[42] by:

(a) the Secretary of State or,
(b) if the Secretary of State so directs in the case of a person who has been a director of a company which is being wound up in England and Wales, the official receiver.[43]

An application under s. 8 of the CDDA 1986 is made by the Secretary of State.

16.8.1 It appears that "any person" may make an application to the court under s. 10 of the CDDA 1986. Only the liquidator of a company can bring proceedings under ss. 213 or 214 of the Insolvency Act 1986. If the liquidator thought it expedient to do so, no doubt he could give 10 days notice of his intention to apply for a disqualification order.

In the light of Harman J.'s decision in *Jaymar Management Ltd* that "application" in s. 16 of the CDDA 1986 means the originating application, it appears that the liquidator

39. *Secretary of State* v. *Langridge*, per Nourse L.J. at 558f. The reference to a disqualification order being a "mode of punishment" may be apt in criminal proceedings and does not detract from the general principle that the purpose of such an order in civil proceedings is to protect the public rather than punish the offender.

40. CDDA 1986, s. 16(2).

41. Defined in CDDA 1986, s. 21.

42. CDDA 1986, s. 7(1).

43. Note also that the Secretary of State can, under IA 1986, s. 400, confer on the official receiver the function of making an application under CDDA 1986, s. 6, even in a case where the company is not being wound up by the court. In such a case, the application must be made in the name of the Secretary of State and not the official receiver and a mistake in this regard cannot be cured by amendment: *Re Probe Data Systems Ltd* [1989] BCLC 561. See also *Re NP Engineering and Security Products Ltd* [1995] 2 BCLC 585 where a company had been dissolved and proceedings were wrongly brought by the official receiver, a mistake which could not be cured.

would have to give 10 day's notice of his intention to issue the s. 213 or s. 214 proceedings if he intended to apply therein for a disqualification order.

16.8.2 In practice, a liquidator would be most unlikely (in an ordinary case) to make such an application; the creditors would have little or no financial interest in the disqualification of a director, and the liquidator would not wish to put himself at risk as to costs. A reminder to the court—perhaps at the outset of the proceedings—that it has the power to disqualify under s. 10 should it think fit, would be as far as most prudent liquidators would go.

It is hard to see how any other person (save perhaps the Secretary of State or the official receiver) would have standing to appear before the court on such an application, and the meaning of the words "any person" in s. 10 must be subject to some doubt.

16.9 Information provided to the Secretary of State

Apart from the requirement for the 10-day notice discussed above, there are no formal procedures which must take place prior to applications under ss. 2 to 6 of the CDDA 1986. However, an application under s. 8 of the CDDA 1986 can only be made by the Secretary of State where it appears to him expedient in the public interest in consequence of information received by him from certain sources. Each of the sources mentioned[44] arises under statute and the procedures by which such information will come into the hands of the Secretary of State should be considered from texts covering those statutes.

No formal limits are placed on the information which may be considered by the Secretary of State under s. 6 of the CDDA 1986. In practice, the relevant information will usually come from the official receiver or an insolvency practitioner who is, under s. 7(3), obliged to report to the Secretary of State where it appears to him that the conditions for disqualification under s. 6(1) of the CDDA 1986 are satisfied in relation to a person who is or was a director of the relevant company.

16.9.1 In a winding-up by the court in England and Wales, the official receiver is obliged to submit the relevant report.[45] In any other case, under rules made for the purpose ("the Reporting Rules")[46] the relevant insolvency practitioner is the "office holder responsible".[47]

In the case of an insolvent company, the insolvency practitioner must, within six months of the "relevant date" (usually the date of the resolution to wind up),[48] make a return in the appropriate form to the Secretary of State in respect of every person who was a

44. CDDA 1986, s. 8(1).

45. In the usual case in England and Wales, the official receiver will automatically become liquidator of a company which is wound up by the court. Under IA 1986, s. 140, an administrator, or the supervisor of a voluntary arrangement, may be appointed liquidator. In the former case there may be no difficulty as s. 7(3)(c) will apply and the "relevant date" will be six months from the appointment of the administrator. It is assumed that, even if the administration order were discharged within six months, the duty under s. 7(3) and the Reporting Rules would continue. Where the supervisor of a voluntary arrangement is appointed liquidator, there would appear to be no mechanism for reporting to the Secretary of State. However, the official receiver will have been notified of the appointment under IR 1986, r. 4.102(3).

46. See Insolvent Companies (Reports on Conduct of Directors) No. 2 Rules 1986 and Insolvent Companies (Reports on Conduct of Directors) (No. 2) (Scotland) Rules 1986.

47. CDDA 1986, s. 7(3).

48. Reporting Rules, r. 4(4).

director or a shadow director on, or in the three years previous to that date.[49] The return requires the insolvency practitioner to state why they have not submitted a report (or a report on every relevant director) under s. 7(3) of the CDDA 1986.

16.9.2 Furnished with a report under s. 7(3), the Secretary of State can determine whether or not it appears to him to be expedient in the public interest that a disqualification order should be made. Further information from the relevant insolvency practitioner can be obtained under s. 7(4) of the CDDA 1986 for the purpose of determining whether to exercise, or of exercising, any function under the section.[50]

Information provided to the Secretary of State under s. 7(3) (and necessarily s. 7(4)) are privileged from production to the respondent on discovery.[51]

16.10 Time limits for applications

There is no time limit within which an application must be made under ss. 2, 4, 5 or 8 of the CDDA 1986.[52]

Section 3 of the Act (persistent breaches of companies legislation, for example the failure to prepare and file statutory returns and accounts) does not impose a time limit as such, but to take advantage of the "conclusive proof" provisions of s. 3(2), a person must have been adjudged guilty of three or more defaults (on one or more occasions) within the five years preceding the application. The power of the court to make an order under this section is discretionary and it is unlikely that stale breaches (in this context more than five years old) would, of themselves, ever persuade a court to make an order under this section.

16.10.1 Section 10 of the CDDA 1986 does not prescribe a time limit, but it would appear that an order would not be made under that section save in proceedings which were extant under ss. 213 or 214 of the Insolvency Act 1986.

No action shall, without the leave of the court, be brought[53] against any person, under s. 6 of the CDDA 1986, more than two years after the day on which the company of which that person was a director, became insolvent.[54] A company becomes insolvent on the happening of any of the events set out in s. 6(2) of the CDDA 1986, namely:

49. Reporting Rules, r. 4(2) and 4(5).

50. The relationship between the insolvency practitioner's duties in this regard, and any indications or undertakings of confidentiality which he may give to persuade a person to provide him with information, were considered by Vinelott J. in *Re Polly Peck International plc, ex parte joint administrators* [1994] BCC 15.

51. *Secretary of State for Trade and Industry* v. *Sananas* [1994] BCC 375.

52. See, however, *Secretary of State for Trade and Industry* v. *Ashman*, in *Re Atlantic Computers plc*, Jacob J., 26 June 1997 unreported. In a case brought under s. 8 of the Act it was plainly desirable that any proceedings based upon an inspectors' report were commenced with expedition.

53. The date on which the summons (or in Scotland petition) is presented to the court: see *Secretary of State for Trade and Industry* v. *Normand* [1995] BCC 158.

54. CDDA 1986, s. 7(2). The day on which the insolvency occurred is treated as the first day of the period. If a company were wound up on 1 April 1996, the summons would have to be presented on or before 31 March 1998. If the court office is closed on the last day, the period is extended to the next day the court office is open. *Re Philipp and Lion Ltd* [1994] BCC 261.

(a) it goes into (insolvent) liquidation[55];
(b) an administration order is made in respect of it; or
(c) an administrative receiver is appointed over it.

16.10.2 The jurisdiction under s. 6 of the CDDA 1986 only arises in respect of a person who is or was a director of a company which has become insolvent[56] within the meaning of s. 6(2) of the CDDA 1986. Subsections (b) and (c) brook little room for argument,[57] but a winding-up may give rise to problems. If the company was able to pay its debts and the expenses of the liquidation at the time of the winding-up (whether a members' or creditors' voluntary or a compulsory winding-up) then no proceedings may be brought under this head in respect of that company.

This will be so even if the company has *subsequently* become insolvent. This does give scope for a director to argue that the subsequent insolvency was due to the poor performance of the liquidator, or even (in the case of property or other assets) the market falling between the date of the winding-up and the date of disposal of an asset. The courts would treat such a claim with care but, where the liquidation has been brought about by an inability to pay debts, rather than a want of assets, the point may be open.

16.10.3 A more practical problem will arise where a members' voluntary winding-up (in respect of a company which was not "solvent" when it went into liquidation) appears to the liquidator to become insolvent. The liquidator is obliged to call a creditors' meeting under s. 95 of the Insolvency Act 1986. The effect of this is that the winding-up becomes a creditors' voluntary winding-up (backdated to the date of the original meetings to wind up).[58] In consequence, the two-year period under s. 7(2) will run from the date of the members' voluntary winding-up.

The provisions of the Reporting Rules require a return within six months from the date on which, in a members' voluntary winding-up, it appears to the liquidator that *at the time* the company went into liquidation[59] it was unable to pay its debts and the expenses of the liquidation in full.[60] Thus, time which passed between the members' voluntary winding-up and it appearing to the liquidator that the winding-up was insolvent from the outset, will be "lost". This may, particularly in the case of a director who swore the statutory declaration under s. 89 of the Insolvency Act 1986, be a good ground for the court to give leave under s. 7(2) of the CDDA 1986 to proceed out of time.[61] On the other hand, where the insolvency was due to the expenses of the winding-up being unexpectedly high, this may not be persuasive.

16.10.4 Where a number of events occur in relation to a company, each of which amounts to the company becoming insolvent, it is the first of those dates which is relevant

55. The expression "goes into liquidation" is taken from IA 1986, s. 247, applied by CDDA 1986, s. 22(3). The relevant date in a winding-up by the court is the date of the order, not the date of the petition: *Re Walter Jacob & Co. Ltd* [1993] BCC 512.

56. CDDA 1986, s. 6(1)(a).

57. Although note that an interim order under IA 1986, s. 9(4), is not an administration order for the purposes of CDDA 1986, s. 6(2)(b): *Secretary of State for Trade and Industry* v. *Palmer* [1993] BCC 650. The two-year period will run from the date on which the final order is made under IA 1986, s. 8. Where the relevant company wishes to challenge the validity of the appointment of an administrative receiver, the appropriate course is to stay or adjourn disqualification proceedings to allow that challenge to proceed. Such a challenge must be prompt. See *Secretary of State for Trade and Industry* v. *Jabble*, *The Times*, 5 August 1997, CA.

58. IA 1986, s. 96.

59. Contrast this with IA 1986, s. 95(1).

60. Reporting Rules, r. 4(4)(b).

61. *Secretary of State for Trade and Industry* v. *McTighe, Re Copecrest* [1994] 2 BCLC 284.

for the purpose of s. 7(2). Thus, where an administrative receiver is appointed over a company which subsequently goes into liquidation, it is the earlier date which will start the two-year period running.[62] The same would apply where a winding-up order is made on the discharge of an administrative order and, presumably, where a company follows the popular route of a creditors' voluntary winding-up following the discharge of an administration order. There is still room for argument as to the extent to which a company must "become solvent" between two events of insolvency before the second can start time running anew.[63]

An application under s. 7(1) of the CDDA 1986 may be struck out for want of prosecution[64] and the same principles will apply in relation to an application under s. 8.[65] The court has approached the matter on the usual principles applicable to civil litigation[66] and has admitted evidence of prejudice both as to the fair conduct of the trial, and the commercial prejudice caused to directors by the continuation of the proceedings.[67] However, the fact that the proceedings are brought in the public interest is an additional matter to be taken into account; the protection of the public is a factor which militates against striking out the proceedings. The public interest does not reduce as time passes, but the private prejudice will increase.[68]

The delay in an application coming on for trial has been held to be a factor to be taken into account in determining the appropriate period of disqualification.[69]

16.11 Leave to apply out of time

Neither the CDDA 1986 nor the Rules sets out any procedure for making an application for leave to apply for a disqualification order under s. 6 out of time,[70] and the courts have approved two procedures:

(1) an *ex parte* application to the registrar who should then (if satisfied that there is a *prima facie* case) give directions for the *inter partes* hearing of the leave application[71]; and,
(2) an application by way of *inter partes* originating summons made to the registrar or judge.[72]

The latter procedure is that presently adopted by the Secretary of State.

62. *Re Tasbian Ltd (No. 1)* [1991] BCLC 54.
63. In *Re Tasbian Ltd (No. 1)*, *supra*, this was considered by Dillon L.J. at 56d h and by Woolf L.J. at 57g–h.
64. *Re Noble Trees Ltd* [1993] BCLC 1185.
65. *Secretary of State for Trade and Industry* v. *Ashman*, in *Re Atlantic Computers plc*, 26 June 1997, Jacob J., unreported, applying in relation to s. 8 what was said about s. 6 by Hoffmann L.J. in *Re Grayan Ltd* [1995] Ch. 241 at 257.
66. See *Birkett* v. *James* [1978] AC 297 and *Department of Transport* v. *Chris Smaller (Transport) Ltd* [1989] AC 1197. It follows that applications to strike out within the two-year period will fail, as fresh proceedings could be recommenced. As the limitation period is flexible, the court would not strike out for want of prosecution if it would thereafter give leave to commence proceedings out of time. This suggests that (unusually for civil litigation) the gravity of the case may be relevant.
67. *Official Receiver* v. *B Ltd* [1994] 1 BCLC 1.
68. *Re Manlon Trading Ltd* [1995] 1 BCLC 578.
69. *Re Aldermanbury Trust plc* [1993] BCC 598; *Re Grayan Building Services Ltd* [1995] Ch. 241 at 247. See, to the contrary, *Secretary of State for the Trade and Industry* v. *Arif* [1997] 1 BCLC 34 where Chadwick J. held that such an approach would be contrary to the scheme of the Act. However, the period of *de facto* disqualification may be relevant on an application for leave to act under s. 17.
70. CDDA 1986, s. 7(2).
71. *Probe Data Systems Ltd (No. 2)* [1990] BCLC 574, per Millet J.
72. *Crestjoy Products Ltd* [1990] BCLC 677, per Harman J.

Once the two-year period has expired, delinquent directors are not immune from disqualification proceedings; but they are immune from such proceedings brought without the leave of the court. It is therefore inappropriate to characterise the time limit as a "limitation period".[73]

16.11.1 On the hearing of the application, it is for the applicant to satisfy the court that an order should be made. The court will conduct a balancing exercise taking into account the following considerations[74]:

(a) the length of the delay[75];
(b) the reasons for the delay[76];
(c) the strength of the case against the director[77];
(d) any prejudice caused to the director by the delay.[78]

These factors are not exhaustive, although they conveniently summarise the considerations which should ordinarily enable a judge to balance the public interest and the interest of the director.[79]

It is important that the application for leave does not turn into a mini-trial, particularly on the question of the strength of the case against the director.[80] The respondent should direct his case to whether the allegations are sufficiently grave to require the court to hear them, notwithstanding the expiry of the two-year period, and not to whether the allegations are well-founded.[81]

16.11.2 The application for leave will be tried on affidavit, and the court will be reluctant to order cross-examination or discovery which go to the issues of "strength of case",[82] although the full reasons for delay must properly be put before the court and, in a case of doubt, this may involve cross-examination. The better the explanation, the easier it will be to get leave, but the explanation is not necessarily determinative of the application. It must be remembered that the applicant must show good reason for an extension of time, which is not the same thing as good reason for any delay.[83]

73. *Secretary of State for Trade and Industry* v. *Davies* [1997] BCC 235 at 234G and 246H–247A.

74. *Secretary of State for Trade and Industry* v. *Desai* [1992] BCLC 405 at 416, per Scott L.J. *Re Copecrest Ltd* [1994] 2 BCLC 284. These are not statutory requirements, but will guide the court in the exercise of its discretion.

75. Including the delay prior to the expiry of the two-year period: *Re Cedar Developments Ltd* [1994] 2 BCLC 714. *Secretary of State for Trade and Industry* v. *Cleland* [1997] 1 BCLC 437 at 444f.

76. Where the application for leave to commence proceedings out of time is itself made after the expiry of the two-year limit, an extra burden is placed on the applicant: *Re Crestjoy Products Ltd* [1990] BCLC 677.

77. The case must be at least arguable: *Re Tasbian Ltd (No. 3)*, *supra*, but the applicant will usually have to show more than that: *Re Packaging Direct Ltd* [1994] BCC 214, and *Re Polly Peck International plc (No. 2)* [1994] 1 BCLC 574 (where Lindsay J. at p. 601a, shied away from the phrases "an arguable case" or a "*prima facie* case"). In *Secretary of State for Trade and Industry* v. *Cleland*, *supra*, the applicant was to show as a minimum "that there is a fairly arguable case".

78. In *Polly Peck International plc (No. 2)*, *supra*, at p. 602e–f, Lindsay J. considered delay in the fourth test as having a different meaning from that in the first three tests. He looked to see what prejudice would be caused by the trial of the action being heard one year later than would otherwise be the case. See also *Re Blackspur Group plc* [1995] BCC 835.

79. Per Hobhouse L.J. in *Secretary of State for Trade and Industry* v. *Davies* [1997] BCC 235 at 248A–B.

80. See, in particular, *Re Packaging Direct Ltd*, *supra*, per Jacob J. at 215G–216B.

81. *Probe Data Systems Ltd (No. 2)*, per Millet J. There is a difference of approach between Millet (now L.J.) in *Davies*, *supra*, at 242A: "strength of the case" referring to gravity of the charges, and Lloyd J. in *Secretary of State for Trade and Industry* v. *Cleland*, *supra*, at 447g, where he considered whether the charges were "fairly raised on the evidence", which required him to look also at the respondent's evidence.

82. *Polly Peck International plc* v. *Nadir (No. 3)* [1994] BCLC 661.

83. *Secretary of State for Trade and Industry* v. *Davies*, *supra*.

Where proceedings have been commenced in time against certain respondents, it is inappropriate for an application to be made under O. 15, r. 6 of the Rules of the Supreme Court to join an additional director out of time.[84] Such an application should be made by a separate originating summons seeking leave to commence new proceedings out of time.

16.12 The originating summons

Except where the court is given jurisdiction to make a disqualification order of its own motion, an application to the court will be necessary. In all cases other than s. 10 (wrongful trading), the application will be by whatever originating process is appropriate to the relevant court.[85] The procedure will, save in the case of applications under ss. 7(1) or 8 of the CDDA 1986, be governed by that court's own procedure.

An application made by the Secretary of State or official receiver under s. 7(1) of the CDDA 1986, or by the Secretary of State under s. 8 of the CDDA 1986, is governed by the Rules. These provide[86] that an application in the High Court is by originating summons[87] and in a county court by way of originating application (referred to in the Rules and this Chapter as a summons). Save to the extent provided for by the Rules, the Rules of the Supreme Court 1965 or, as the case may be, the County Court Rules 1981 apply.

16.12.1 Specific provision is made for the endorsement of certain information on the summons,[88] the most important of which (from a procedural point of view) is that:

(a) the application may be heard summarily without further notice to the respondent (in which case the court may impose a period of disqualification of up to five years)[89];
(b) if it appears on the hearing of the application that, on the evidence then before it, the court would be minded to impose a period longer than five years, the court will not make a disqualification order but will adjourn the application to be heard at a later date (with the possibility of further evidence)[90]; and
(c) any evidence which the respondent wishes the court to take into account must be filed within the time limits set out in r. 6—that is 28 days after service of the summons.[91] The consequence of this requirement is considered below.[92]

The usual practice in the case of more than one respondent is to issue one summons against all persons involved in the relevant company or companies.[93]

84. Or it seems at all: *Re Westmid Packaging Services Ltd* [1995] BCC 203.
85. As to which, see para. 16.5.2, *supra*.
86. Rules, r. 2.
87. Form 10 in Appendix A to RSC 1965, with such adaptation as appropriate.
88. Rules, r. 4.
89. Rules, r. 4(c).
90. Rules, r. 4(d).
91. *Ibid.* The evidence is filed in the court out of which the summons was issued: O. 28, r. 1A(1) and (4), RSC 1965, and implicit in O. 2, r. 4, County Court Rules 1981.
92. See para. 16.15.1, *infra*.
93. See the comments of Harman J. in *Re Cladrose* [1990] BCLC 204 at 205g.

16.13 Service

The Rules contain specific provision for service of the summons. By r. 5(1), the summons is required to be served by first class post to the respondent's last known address and is deemed to be served on the seventh day next following that on which the summons was posted unless a different date of service is shown.[94] The provisions of this sub-rule do not affect service of any other document, which will be governed by O. 65 of the Rules of the Supreme Court or O. 7 of the County Court Rules as the case may be.

The wide power of the court to allow service out of the jurisdiction under r. 5(2) is tempered by a judicial discretion not to order such service, unless the applicant has shown a good arguable case that the conditions in ss. 6(1) or 8 of the CDDA 1986 are satisfied.[95]

The summons must be served, together with a form of acknowledgement of service,[96] which requires the respondent to state whether he intends to contest:

(a) that he is a person against whom an order might be made under ss. 6 or 8 of the CDDA 1986; and
(b) that his conduct renders him unfit to be concerned in the management of a company; or
(c) whether he intends not to resist the application, but intends to adduce mitigating factors.[97]

16.14 Evidence in support of the application

Evidence in support of the application is to be filed on issue of the summons, and served on the respondent with the summons.[98] The evidence served in support is by affidavit, except that the official receiver[99] may submit a report, which is treated as an affidavit by him and is *prima facie* evidence of any matter stated in it.[100] This latter provision is less

94. Rules, r. 5(1). There is no provision for personal service. Neither is there the requirement of O. 10, r. 1, RSC for an affidavit of service to contain a statement of belief that posting will bring the proceedings to the attention of the respondent, or that the summons has not been returned to the applicant undelivered. The last known address of a director will usually be taken from the company's own records and may well be out of date. There must be some doubt as to whether O. 10, r. 1 "applies" to an originating summons issued under ss. 7(1) or 8, CDDA 1986 (r. 5(1) being inconsistent with that Order) and hence some doubt as to whether the provisions of O. 65, r. 4 (substituted service) are applicable. It is not clear what action should be taken when the summons is returned "not known at this address". In the County Court, the wider provisions of O. 7, r. 8 of the County Court Rules 1981 would appear to allow an order for substituted service.

95. *Re Seagull Manufacturing (No. 2) Ltd* [1994] 1 BCLC 273.

96. Rules, r. 5(4).

97. "With a view to justifying only a short period of disqualification"; a phrase which may require some thought. Perhaps five years (the limit for summary determination) is considered to be "short" in this context. In practice, any person intending to adduce evidence in mitigation should tick this box.

98. Rules, r. 3(1), but this has been held to be directory only and a failure is an irregularity which may be waived by the court: *Copecrest Ltd* [1993] BCC 844 at 851 and *Re Jazzgold Ltd* [1994] 1 BCLC 38. Where the Secretary of State seeks leave to file evidence out of time, the court will look for "a reason for delay which may reasonably be accepted as sufficient to justify an extension of time in all the circumstances of the particular case", per Millet L.J. in *Secretary of State for Trade and Industry* v. *Davies* [1997] BCC 235 at 244F–H. There is no threshold test which must be satisfied and the application will be easier to justify than an application for leave to commence proceedings out of time, although the court will take similar considerations into account.

99. Or a deputy official receiver: *Re Holmes Assured Corp. Ltd* [1994] 2 BCLC 71.

100. Rules, r. 3(2).

important following the Civil Evidence Act 1995, since hearsay is now admissible in affidavit evidence.[101]

In the High Court, hearsay contained in affidavit evidence in support of the application was, even prior to the Civil Evidence Act 1995, admissible.[102] Information in the form of statements to the Secretary of State under s. 447 of the Companies Act 1985 is admissible in disqualification proceedings.[103] By s. 9(1) of the Civil Evidence Act 1995, the records of a business are admissible in evidence, which may be of considerable importance in disqualification proceedings.

16.14.1 The status of affidavits in county court proceedings has been held to be governed by the County Court Rules 1981.[104] The consequence is that hearsay evidence contained in an affidavit (in accordance with O. 20, r. 10 of the County Court Rules 1981) will be admissible in county court proceedings. Reference should also be made to the Civil Evidence Act 1995.

A statement of affairs prepared by, or statement made by, a respondent pursuant to any requirement of the Insolvency Act 1986 is admissible against that person[105] in disqualification proceedings. In practice, the applicant is likely to rely extensively on the statement of affairs and on any further statements made to the liquidator or other insolvency practitioner.

16.14.2 The evidence in support of the application must state the matters by reference to which the respondent is alleged to be unfit.[106] Further grounds may, at the discretion of the court, be added at a later date, even at the trial itself (where they may emerge only in the course of cross-examination) but proper notice to the respondent must be given and leave will not be given if injustice will be caused to the respondent.[107] If necessary, a respondent will be granted an adjournment to deal with such new matters, the paramount requirement being that he should have notice of the case he has to meet. It is unnecessary for the evidence in support of the application to deal with every matter which could possibly be a source of complaint,[108] although on the principles referred to above, all material averments upon which reliance will be placed must be set out clearly. If not, the respondent's remedy is to apply to strike out the application, or the parts of it which are embarrassing.[109]

16.15 The respondent's evidence

Section 16(1) of the CDDA 1986 provides that the respondent may appear at the hearing of an application to disqualify him, and may himself give evidence or call witnesses. The apparently wide nature of this provision, which would appear to give the respondent the

101. Without the need for a hearsay notice: see RSC O. 38, r. 21(3)(a).
102. *Secretary of State for Trade and Industry* v. *Ashcroft* [1997] BCC 634.
103. *Re Rex Williams Leisure plc* [1994] 2 BCLC 555.
104. *Re Circle Holidays International plc* [1994] BCC 226.
105. IA 1986, s. 433; see the equivalent provision at CDDA 1986, s. 20.
106. Rules, r. 3(3). Failure to comply is an irregularity which may be cured: *Re Jazzgold Ltd* [1994] 1 BCLC 38.
107. *Re Sevenoaks Stationers (Retail) Ltd* [1991] BCLC 325, per Dillon L.J. at 330e–331c. For an example of a case where the allegation was extended from one of actual to constructive knowledge of trading while insolvent, see *Re City Investment Centres Ltd* [1992] BCLC 956 at 967b.
108. *Re Pamstock Ltd* [1994] BCC 264.
109. *Re Sutton Glassworks Ltd* [1996] BCC 174 at 178A.

right to give oral evidence at the trial, has been held to be cut down by rr. 4 and 6 of the Rules.[110]

The respondent is obliged by r. 6 to file in court any affidavit evidence in opposition to the summons within 28 days of the date of service of the summons on him. He must forthwith serve a copy of the evidence on the applicant[111] who has 14 days to file evidence in answer.[112]

16.15.1 This apparently innocuous rule has been held by the court to limit the manner in which evidence may be given by the respondent under s. 16(1) of the CDDA 1986. In *Rex Williams Leisure Ltd* the Court of Appeal agreed with Nicholls V.C.[113] holding that a respondent did not have the right to give oral evidence at the hearing of the originating summons.[114]

The consequence of this ruling is that if a respondent wishes to be able to give evidence, he is obliged to file affidavit evidence before the hearing.[115] If he wishes to submit no case to answer at the close of the applicant's case, he will not be allowed to lead any evidence should the application fail.[116]

16.15.2 The respondent's affidavit will be governed by the Rules of the Supreme Court 1965[117] or, in the County Court, the County Court Rules 1981. The provisions of the Civil Evidence Act 1995 will govern the admissibility of statements made in the affidavit or exhibits, although, if information given to the Secretary of State under s. 447 has come into the hands of a respondent (perhaps on the publication of an Inspector's Report) then the respondent could rely on such evidence to the same extent as the applicant.

The respondent's evidence should not contain advocacy or submission and may be struck out if it is irrelevant.[118] The court will not receive "expert" evidence as to a respondent's fitness as a director (that is a matter for the court to determine), nor evidence as to character.[119]

The Rules make no provision for discovery, subpoenas, interrogatories and so forth. All such matters will be governed by the Rules of the Supreme Court 1965 or the County Court Rules 1981 as the case may be. Orders for discovery against the applicant may be

110. *Re Rex Williams Leisure plc* [1994] 2 BCLC 555.

111. Rules, r. 6(1).

112. Which evidence must also be served forthwith on the respondent. In practice these limits can be, and are, extended by agreement or by order of the court. In any but the simplest case these limits will be quite inadequate. The respondent will need time not only to instruct any legal advisor but also to make any necessary legal aid application, to gather evidence—much of which may be in the hands of the relevant insolvency practitioner or other third parties—and so forth. In the case of the applicant's reply, neither the applicant, nor the insolvency practitioner will have first-hand knowledge of any matters prior to the insolvency and it may take some considerable time to gather evidence in reply to new issues raised by the respondent.

113. [1993] BCLC 568; affirmed at [1994] 2 BCLC 555.

114. Such evidence might be given with the leave of the court (which has an inherent power to regulate its own procedure) in particular where it is convenient to allow the respondent to supplement his affidavit evidence by oral evidence in chief prior to being cross-examined.

115. And, strictly, in accordance with the time limit set by r. 6(1) of the Rules or such other time as may be allowed.

116. *Rex Williams Leisure Ltd, supra*, per Hoffmann L.J. at 564g–565d.

117. Notwithstanding the admissibility of hearsay evidence contained in affidavit evidence under O. 38, r. 21(3)(a), an affidavit must still contain only such facts as the deponent is able of his own knowledge to prove. The affidavit must therefore make clear that which is the deponent's own knowledge, and that which the deponent has been told.

118. *Re Oakframe Construction Ltd* [1996] BCC 67.

119. *Re Dawes & Henderson (Agencies) Ltd*, Blackburne J. [1997] 1 BCLC 329. Not only can a third party not give evidence of the respondent's good character or apparent "fitness", but the respondent's own evidence to such effect is inadmissible. Such evidence may be relevant on an application for leave under s. 17.

of little use, given that reports under s. 7(3) of the CDDA 1986 are privileged[120] and material held by the relevant insolvency practitioner is not within his power, within the meaning of O. 24 of the Rules of the Supreme Court 1965, notwithstanding the provisions of s. 7(4) of the CDDA 1986.[121] If the respondent requires further assistance, extensive use of subpoenas may be necessary.

16.15.3 In *Re Sutton Glassworks Ltd*,[122] Chadwick J. considered the relationship between RSC O. 26, r. 1(1) and disqualification proceedings. His remarks, that the respondent should file evidence before seeking interrogatories, are of general application to interlocutory applications; only once the respondent has filed evidence will the issues be defined. If the applicant's evidence is obscure or embarrassing, the respondent should try to resolve the matter in correspondence or, as a last resort, apply to strike it out.

In practice, the applicant will endeavour to make available to the respondent any relevant material which is the subject of a reasonable request. The applicant will of course have to rely upon the insolvency practitioner to provide the bulk of such material.[123]

16.16 The return date of the application

The return date of the application must be not less than eight weeks from the date of the issue of the summons.[124] This would indicate that the summons should be served not more than two weeks after issue, to give time for evidence to be served in accordance with the Rules. Given the seven-day deemed service provision of r. 5(1), a summons must be posted promptly after issue.

The hearing in the first instance is in open court before the registrar[125] who has power either to determine the case or to adjourn it with appropriate directions for the filing of further evidence, or other consequential matters.[126] All interlocutory directions should be sought at the first hearing of the summons.[127]

16.16.1 The case must be adjourned for further consideration if it appears to the registrar (on a provisional view) that an order in excess of five years disqualification is appropriate.[128] It must also be adjourned if the registrar is of the opinion that questions of law or fact arise which are not suitable for summary determination.[129] The most common example of such a case will be where cross-examination of deponents is required, although any case which is likely to require a detailed analysis of fact or law is unlikely to be dealt with on a summary basis, if only because time will not so permit.

If disputes of fact are likely to arise, then the registrar may give directions for cross-examination of deponents. Such a direction may be given on the first return date or—as frequently happens—in the light of an extended period of time given to the respondent to

120. *Secretary of State for Trade and Industry* v. *Sananas* [1994] BCC 375.
121. *Re Lombard Shipping and Forwarding* [1993] BCLC 238.
122. [1996] BCC 174 at 177B–H.
123. See *Re Dexmaster Ltd* [1995] BCC 186 where an application to strike out the proceedings on the grounds of prejudice failed. Documents taken from the company and the respondent had been lost by the liquidator.
124. Rules, r. 7(1).
125. Rules, r. 7(2).
126. Rules, r. 7(3) and 7(4).
127. Practice Direction, para. 3.
128. Rules, r. 7(4)(a), reflecting the statement to this effect required to be endorsed on the summons under r. 4(c). Note that five years has been adopted as a rule of thumb by the courts (see *Re Sevenoaks Stationers Ltd* [1991] BCLC 325 at 328d) as the top of the category of cases which are "relatively, not very serious".
129. Rules, r. 7(4)(b).

put in evidence, at a later interlocutory application. The form of such a direction can usually be agreed between the parties, but is likely to be to the effect that all deponents attend for cross-examination at the trial, failing which their affidavit shall not be read, save with the leave of the court.[130]

16.16.2 A useful additional stipulation is that only those persons on whom a notice has been served not less than 14 days prior to the trial need attend for cross-examination. Some deponents may swear to formal matters only or, in the case of the applicant's witnesses, merely speak from the documents with no personal knowledge of the relevant events. By giving notice that such persons are not required to attend, substantial costs may be saved.

The registrar may adjourn the matter to the judge, or for a further registrar's appointment.[131] Adjournments to the judge will generally be made only in cases where there appear to be substantial questions of law or principle to be decided, or where the case is likely to take a substantial amount of court time for which a registrar would not be available. If the registrar does adjourn the case, he will, so far as possible, give all directions for trial, including a direction whether the matter is to be heard by a registrar or judge.[132]

16.16.3 The registrar must give his reasons for the adjournment[133] which reasons must be given to the respondent (if not present).[134]

If the case is suitable for summary determination, the registrar may deal with it on the first return date. An order may be made (on the first return date or on any adjournment) in the absence of the respondent, or any evidence from the respondent.[135] If no acknowledgement of service has been filed, an affidavit of service[136] will be required.

Where an order is made in the absence of the respondent, it may be set aside or varied by the court on such terms as the court thinks just.[137] This provision appears to mirror O. 13, r. 9 of the Rules of the Supreme Court, but an order made in disqualification proceedings will always be "on the merits"; there is no equivalent to a default judgment.

16.16.4 If the respondent can show that the proceedings did not come to his attention, it would be relatively simply to set aside an order. If service is proven, that task will be difficult and some good reason why the proceedings were undefended (and a good likelihood of establishing a defence) will have to be shown. The respondent might, in any event, be required to pay any costs thrown away.

At the appropriate stage, the registrar will direct the applicant to set the matter down for trial within a specified period (usually five days). In an attempt to ensure that disqualification matters are heard expeditiously, this time cannot be extended without the leave of the

130. The court has jurisdiction to make an order requiring the deponent to attend for cross-examination under O. 38, r. 2(3) and this power is not excluded by the CDDA 1986 or the Rules, see *Re Dominion Group plc* [1995] 1 WLR 649.

131. Rules, r. 7(5)(a).

132. Practice Direction, para. 9.

133. Rules, r. 7(5)(b).

134. A requirement inherent in r. 7(5)(i) of the Rules.

135. Rules, r. 8(1).

136. Showing service in accordance with r. 5(1) or 5(2) as the case may be.

137. Rules, r. 8(2).

court. The court will be astute to ensure that proceedings, brought in the public interest, are not unduly delayed.[138]

16.16.5 In line with general Chancery procedure, where it is estimated that a case will last 10 days or more, a pre-trial review should be obtained, between eight and four weeks prior to the trial. This is the case whether the hearing is to be before a registrar or a judge. The relevant provisions of the Chancery Guide govern the pre-trial review.[139]

The modifications imposed where disqualification proceedings are brought in a District Registry of the Chancery Division are set down in para. 17 of the Practice Direction.

16.17 Interlocutory matters and inspection of the file

Any applications for further directions after the first return date should be made, in the first instance, to the registrar.

Such applications may cover any matters usually dealt with by a master, district judge or registrar in civil litigation. All the provisions of the Rules of the Supreme Court 1965 or the County Court Rules 1981 will apply to an extent not inconsistent with the Rules.[140] Accordingly, the parties have full access to orders for discovery, subpoenas of documents,[141] applications under the Bankers Books Evidence Act 1879 and so forth.

16.17.1 Matters for the court's discretion, such as questions of adjournment,[142] will be dealt with on usual principles, always bearing in mind that the proceedings are brought in the public interest. This is illustrated by the failure of the respondent in *Re Rex Williams Leisure Ltd*,[143] to obtain a stay of the disqualification proceedings pending the outcome of an action brought against him by the administrator of the company.

Applications by third parties interested in disqualification proceedings will be rare.[144] However, applications are occasionally made for leave to inspect the court file on which the reports or affidavits of the applicant, and the affidavits of the respondent, will have been placed. Such an application is made pursuant to O. 63, r. 4 of the Rules of the Supreme Court 1965,[145] or O. 50, r. 10(2) of the County Court Rules 1981 as the case may be, and the question of leave will be at the general discretion of the court. Any person can, on payment of the prescribed fee, search for and take a copy of the originating summons, but this will not set out the grounds on which the application is sought.

16.17.2 There has been considerable doubt as to whether disqualification proceedings are subject to the Insolvency Rules or (where inconsistent) the Rules of the Supreme Court. These doubts have not yet been resolved. Analysis suggests that the Insolvency Rules do not apply to disqualification proceedings, and first instance decisions support this

138. The consequential steps are set out in Practice Direction, paras 5–7.

139. Practice Direction, paras 8–9.

140. Rules, r. 2.

141. Notwithstanding r. 6 of the Rules and the interpretation placed on it in *Rex Williams*, witnesses might be subpoenaed. The court would have to give leave for the evidence of such witnesses to be admitted and a party would have to show that it had not proved possible to obtain an affidavit from such witnesses.

142. See *Re Firedart Ltd* [1994] 1 BCLC 340 at 343b–344f.

143. [1993] BCLC 569, [1994] 2 BCLC 555, C.A. Note, however, the procedure suggested in *Secretary of State for Trade and Industry* v. *Jabble*, *The Times*, 5 August 1997, C.A.

144. In *Re Westmid Packaging Services Ltd* [1995] BCC 203 at 207F–208C, Micklem J. considered that O. 15, r. 6 has no application to disqualification proceedings.

145. Such an application may be made *ex parte*: *Dobson* v. *Hastings* [1992] Ch. 394 at 401E.

view.[146] The Court of Appeal has decided otherwise in the case of the procedure to be adopted on an appeal.[147] The pragmatic answer is to assume that the Insolvency Rules have no application to disqualification proceedings unless there is clear authority, in any particular instance, that they do. At present such authority is limited to appeals—there is no reason to suppose that it will be extended.

16.18 The effective hearing

Official receivers and deputy official receivers have full rights of audience in any court, in proceedings brought under ss. 7(1) or 8 of the CDDA 1986.[148] Otherwise, the usual rules applicable in the relevant court will govern rights of audience. The respondent, if an individual, always has a right to appear and represent himself in person. A corporate respondent would, in the county court, generally be given leave to appear by a director, but in the High Court would have to show "exceptional circumstances".

The procedure to be adopted at the hearing will be a matter for the court itself, but the usual rules applicable to civil proceedings tried on affidavit will apply. The Practice Direction (following the *Chancery Guide*) requires that skeleton arguments, a chronology and *dramatis personae* should, in all but the simplest cases, be lodged not less than two days prior to the hearing. This is so, whether the trial is before a registrar or a judge. Bundles should be lodged with the court, again complying with the *Chancery Guide*. An additional requirement is that the advocate for the applicant should, in respect of each respondent, lodge a list of the references to the relevant evidence for each matter relied on as constituting unfitness.

16.18.1 The applicant bears the burden of proving that each of the requirements in s. 6(1) of the CDDA 1986 is satisfied. Accordingly, the applicant will open the case, and will have a right to reply. The standard of proof required is the usual civil standard of a balance of probabilities. In *Re Living Images Ltd*,[149] Laddie J. considered the question of burden of proof and the standard of evidence which might be required in any case.[150]

Before making the order, the court must be satisfied that a person has been shown to be unfit. It follows that an order can be made neither by default nor by consent.[151]

16.18.2 It is not the practice of the applicant to suggest an appropriate period of disqualification. The applicant may, however, indicate how serious the case is alleged to be, and this will usually be done by reference to the divisions adopted by Dillon L.J. in *Re Sevenoaks Stationers (Retail) Ltd.*[152]

The respondent may put forward matters to be taken into account in mitigation whether or not he has defended the proceedings.[153]

146. *Dobson* v. *Hastings*, *supra*, and (in the County Court) a decision of Micklem J.: *Re Circle Holidays International plc* [1994] BCC 226.

147. See *Re Tasbian Ltd (No. 2)* and *Re Probe Data Systems Ltd (No. 3)* both of which are discussed at para. 16.22, *infra*.

148. Rules, r. 10.

149. [1996] 1 BCLC 348 at 355(f).

150. In *Secretary of State for Trade and Industry* v. *Fine*, 13 June 1997, Neuberger J., unreported, adopted the approach in *Hornal* v. *Neuberger Products Ltd* [1957] 1 QB 247 that the graver the allegations, the harder it would be to satisfy the court (on the balance of probabilities) that the allegations were true.

151. *Re Carecraft Construction Co. Ltd* [1993] BCLC 1259 at 1627b. See, however, the procedure actually adopted in that case, considered at para. 16.19.1, *infra*.

152. [1991] Ch. 164.

153. Rules, r. 5(4)(c).

16.19 The *Carecraft* procedure

Disqualification proceedings may be subject, in general terms, to civil procedure, but there are some fundamental differences. In the first place, the applicant is not bringing proceedings under ss. 7(1) or 8 of the CDDA 1986 for any private purpose. Proceedings are in the public interest and cannot be withdrawn by the applicant unless it appears that it is no longer in the public interest that they be pursued.[154] In the second, the respondent cannot, by consenting to an order, prevent the court from having to consider the case on the merits.

It is not, therefore, possible to settle disqualification proceedings in the way of ordinary civil litigation; that is, by each side agreeing to compromise the extent of its claim, or defence. In this respect, disqualification proceedings have more in common with criminal rather than civil procedure.

16.19.1 In *Re Carecraft Construction Co. Ltd*,[155] Ferris J. considered the jurisdiction of the court to allow the parties to adopt a summary procedure to dispose of disqualification proceedings. He considered that the court could adopt a procedure whereby the parties would agree:

(i) a statement of agreed or non-disputed facts;
(ii) that such facts showed unfitness;
(iii) that a disqualification order was appropriate; and
(iv) the range in which the order should be made.

Ferris J. set out[156] four observations on the question of summary procedure:

(1) The court had to be satisfied as to unfitness, therefore must have before it some evidence (beyond mere assertion or admission) sufficient to establish unfitness.
(2) The court must consider the scope not only of the unchallenged evidence (i.e. the agreed facts) but the evidence which remained not agreed. It is not open to the applicant to "choose" which evidence should and should not be relied on by the court; if it appeared that the evidence still in dispute would, if proven, make the case one of a different degree of seriousness[157] then the summary procedure would not be appropriate. In the light of *Secretary of State for Trade and Industry* v. *Rogers*,[158] this requirement is no longer necessary.
(3) If the agreed facts are not sufficient to persuade the court that the respondent has been shown to be unfit (an unlikely event in the light of the respondent's own admission) then the court should not adopt the summary procedure. If there are unagreed facts which would, if proved, justify a disqualification order, the court will adjourn the application for a full trial. If even these facts do not satisfy the court, then the application would be dismissed.

154. In which case they must be withdrawn at once, and in such a case the applicant will ordinarily pay the respondent's costs. See also *Re Carecraft Construction Co. Ltd* [1993] BCLC 1259 at 1266h–i. Note that the Secretary of State will not attempt to agree a *Carecraft* disposal in such circumstances.

155. [1993] BCLC 1259.

156. At 1269e–1270d.

157. I.e., moving the case into a different *Sevenoaks* band, or taking the case from the lower end of a band to the higher. Ferris J. himself had to consider this question in *Re Aldermanbury Trust plc* [1993] BCC 598 at 600F–601D.

158. [1996] 1 WLR 1569.

(4) If the court is not prepared to deal with the application on a summary footing, and adjourns to a full trial, then it is open to the parties to ensure that any admissions made for the purposes of the summary procedure are without prejudice to the position at trial.[159]

16.19.2 The Court of Appeal has reviewed the *Carecraft* procedure in *Secretary of State for Trade and Industry* v. *Rogers*, above. It is no longer necessary to put before the court those facts which are "not agreed", even if they might take the case into a different bracket of seriousness. The conduct of the case is, as with all civil proceedings, in the hands of the parties and it is for the applicant, albeit acting in the public interest, to decide which allegations to pursue.

Where the *Carecraft* procedure is adopted, the Practice Direction provides for the statement of agreed (or not opposed) facts to be lodged with the court not less than two days before the hearing.[160] The statement should also set out the period of disqualification, or the range, agreed by the parties to be appropriate.

If the court is satisfied that the summary procedure is appropriate, it will hear the respondent on mitigation before determining the appropriate period of disqualification.

16.19.3 The judge is not bound by any aspect of the *Carecraft* agreement, but he cannot go outside it without the consent of the parties; in the absence of consent—or if he doubts whether an order should be made, he should notify the parties at the earliest possible moment, so that consideration can be given to directing a full trial. The judge is not, however, entitled to look beyond the statement of facts and cannot rely upon the totality of the (non-agreed) evidence to justify his refusal to make an order within the agreed bracket.[161]

The agreed statement of facts should be clear and unambiguous. In particular, it should be made clear which allegations are admitted. There should be no room for the judge to draw inferences from secondary facts and the statement should not "mince its words".[162]

16.19.4 The agreed statement of facts may be couched in terms which keep it confidential as between the parties. However, the Secretary of State is unlikely to agree to any statement which does not permit him to make reference to the statement for the purpose of any further disqualification proceedings against the respondent (or the existing proceedings against any co-respondent who has not agreed a *Carecraft* disposal. The Secretary of State will also reserve the right to refer to the agreed statement for the purpose of any s. 17 application for leave made by the respondent, and for the purpose of any press announcement.

The statement should make it clear that any admissions made by the respondent are for the purpose of the disqualification proceedings only. This will be of some importance to a director who is being pursued by a third party (for example a liquidator) in an action

159. It will be sensible for a party to set out in writing the terms on which any admissions are made.

160. In *Secretary of State for Trade and Industry* v. *Rogers*, Scott V.C. emphasised that it is important for the judge to have an opportunity to read the papers in advance.

161. *Official Receiver* v. *Bond*, 10 June 1997, Evans-Lombe J., unreported.

162. *Re PB Barnarse & Co. (Products) Ltd* [1997] BCC 425. In practice it can be difficult for a respondent who does not wish to contest the proceedings on pragmatic—usually cost—grounds (but who has been advised that he has a reasonable prospect of success) to admit sufficient facts to justify the period of disqualification needed to satisfy the Secretary of State. There is something of a pantomime quality about certain statements as a result.

arising out of the same facts as the disqualification. Further, the court may direct that the statement should not become part of the record of the case,[163] although the Secretary of State is, in principle, unlikely to consent to such a course.

16.19.5 Consideration has been given to whether the court should sanction a procedure whereby undertakings are accepted from the respondent in consideration of which the proceedings will be stayed.[164] Such undertakings have been accepted by the court in two cases where there was a severe risk to the health of the respondents by the continuation of the proceedings.[165] Further, on the basis of such an undertaking, leave to commence proceedings out of time has been refused.[166] The cases were reviewed by Rattee J. in *Re Blackspur Group plc*[167] where he made clear that, absent exceptional circumstances, the Secretary of State could not be required to agree to a stay of properly constituted disqualification proceedings on the basis of undertakings offered by a respondent.

16.20 The order

An order made by the court in proceedings brought under s. 7(1) or 8 of the CDDA 1986 will not commence until the 21st day after it is made, unless the court otherwise orders.[168] The court can abridge or extend the time, and will usually consider this in the context of any application for leave to act. (For the question of whether the court will grant a stay of the disqualification order pending an appeal, see para. 16.2.4, *infra*.)

The court clerk is responsible for registration of the order[169] within 14 days of the date on which it is made (not the date on which it is to commence).[170]

When an order is made under s. 6 of the CDDA 1986, the order should follow the terms of s. 1(1) (see para. 16.3.1, *supra*). The court has no power to limit the restriction to three or fewer of the heads of disqualification. The former practice of making an order in the terms of subs (a) and (d) only (it being assumed that the prohibition would then extend to subs (b) and (c)) was incorrect, but an order made in the "old" form may if necessary be amended under the slip rule.[171]

163. *Re Brombard Securities plc*, 14 December 1994, Harman J., unreported.

164. In *Secretary of State for Trade and Industry* v. *Rogers* [1996] 1 WLR 1569 at 1574H, Scott V.C. reiterated his view, expressed in his introduction to the Practice Direction [1996] 1 WLR 170 that a formal procedure whereby a respondent could enter undertakings not to act as a director without the need for a court order would be beneficial. He recognised that such a procedure would need a statutory amendment.

165. *Re Holmes Assured Corp. plc* [1996] BCC 297 and *Re X Co. Ltd*, 1 February 1996, unreported.

166. *Secretary of State for Trade and Industry* v. *Cleland, supra.*

167. [1997] 1 WLR 710.

168. Rules, r. 9. There is a doubt as to whether or not this rule is *ultra vires*, given the mandatory terms of CDDA 1986, s.1. The point was touched upon, but did not arise for decision, in *Secretary of State for Trade and Industry* v. *Bannister* [1996] 1 WLR 118 at 123H–124A. In *Secretary of State for Trade and Industry* v. *Edwards* [1997] BCC 222, Evans-Lombe J. held that the rule did not conflict with the Act; the effect of the rule was to suspend the operation of the order (which had commenced on the date on which it was pronounced) for 21 days. In *Official Receiver* v. *Hannon, Re Cannonquest Ltd* [1997] BCC 644 Harman J. came to the same conclusion.

169. Reg. 4(1).

170. Reg. 6.

171. See *Re Gower Enterprises Ltd* [1995] 2 BCLC 201; *Re Seagull Manufacturing Co. Ltd (No. 3)* [1996] BCLC 51; and *Re Brian Sheridan Cars Ltd* [1996] 1 BCLC 327, approved by the Court of Appeal in *Official Receiver* v. *Hannon, Re Cannonquest Ltd* [1997] BCC 644 at 649.

16.21 Costs

Costs are at the discretion of the court, and are to be awarded on the principles usually applicable to civil litigation.[172] The old practice of automatically awarding the applicant (if successful) costs on an indemnity basis on the grounds that the proceedings were brought in the public interest has been disapproved.[173] Indemnity costs will only be awarded against the respondent in special circumstances; where, for example, a wholly false or futile defence has been put forward, or a claim has been defended where there is no conceivable basis for the defence.

A further consequence of this approach is that, if the proceedings are withdrawn at any stage, the usual order will be that the applicant pays the respondent's costs. This will be so even where the proceedings were, *prima facie*, properly brought on the information then available to the Secretary of State.[174]

A successful applicant may be deprived of some of his costs if the application is overlooked with unjustified complaints. It is not, however, wrong in principle for the respondent's history as a director of other insolvent companies to be put before the court.[175]

16.22 Appeals

The question of appeals has caused some difficulty. In *Re Tasbian Ltd (No. 2)*,[176] an appeal was brought from the Companies Court Registrar directly to the Court of Appeal. The Court of Appeal held that they had no jurisdiction to hear the appeal which lay instead to a single judge of the High Court, pursuant to r. 7.47(2) of the Insolvency Rules 1986.

In *Re Probe Data Systems Ltd (No. 3)*,[177] the court had to consider an appeal from the registrar (in the Companies Court) granting leave to the Secretary of State to commence disqualification proceedings out of time. Both parties agreed that the Insolvency Rules 1986 governed such procedure, the question was whether the appeal was by way of review[178] or true appeal.[179] Harman J. held that the appeal was a true appeal which could only succeed if the registrar had made an error of law or exercised his discretion on wrong principles.[180]

172. See *Re Southbourne Sheet Metal (No. 2)* [1994] BCLC 135 and *Re Godwin Warren Control Systems plc* [1993] BCLC 80 at 94.

173. *Re Dicetrade* [1994] BCC 371 per Dillon L.J. at 373c–d.

174. *Re Southbourne Sheet Metal Co. Ltd (No. 2)* [1993] BCLC 135.

175. *Re Pamstock Ltd* [1996] BCC 341. See also *Secretary of State for Trade and Industry* v. *Ivens*, C.A. 25 July 1997, unreported.

176. [1991] BCLC 59.

177. [1991] BCLC 586.

178. IR 1986, r. 7.47(1), the usual position on an appeal from the registrar to a single judge: *Rolls Razor Ltd (No. 2)* [1970] 1 Ch. 576.

179. IR 1986, r. 7.47(2).

180. Note the consequence of the appeal to the single judge being of the nature of a "true" appeal. The appellant must set out in his "notice of appeal" the reasons why the tribunal was wrong. If the respondent to the appeal wishes to support the decision of the registrar or district judge on alternative grounds to those stated in the judgment, a respondent's notice should be served. *Re Time Utilising Business Systems Ltd* [1990] BCLC 568, but note that the wrong (per *Tasbian (No. 2)* appeals procedure was adopted in this case.

16.22.1 The decision of Harman J. was upheld on appeal.[181] The appellant argued that *Re Tasbian (No. 2)* was wrong, and should therefore not be followed. The Court of Appeal held itself bound by its previous decision. The Court of Appeal delivered judgment on 21 November 1991. On 8 November 1991, Nicholls V.C. had given judgment in *Dobson v. Hastings*.[182] He held that proceedings under s. 7(1) of the CDDA 1986 were not "insolvency proceedings" for the purposes of r. 13.7 (and hence, rr. 7.30 and 7.31) of the Insolvency Rules 1986.

Dobson v. *Hastings* had not been decided at the time of argument in the Court of Appeal in *Probe Data (No. 3)*. Given that the Court of Appeal in *Probe Data (No. 3)* held that *Re Tasbian (No. 2)* was binding upon them, it may be that even if they had been referred to the decision in *Dobson* v. *Hastings*, the outcome would have been the same.

16.22.2 Accordingly, in disqualification proceedings an appeal from the registrar of the Companies Court lies to a single judge of the High Court. This is the case for both interlocutory and final decisions. The procedure on appeal is governed by r. 7.49 of the Insolvency Rules 1986 which provides that the practice and procedure of the Supreme Court relating to appeals to the Court and Appeal governs appeals to the single judge, as if the references (generally in O. 59 of the Rules of the Supreme Court 1965) to the Court of Appeal were references to the single judge.[183] Because disqualification proceedings are not "insolvency proceedings"[184] the appeal will be by way of summons, not application.[185]

An appeal from a district judge in a county court is also made to a single judge of the High Court under r. 7.47(2) of the Insolvency Rules 1986 and not by way of appeal to a circuit judge under the County Court Rules 1981.[186] An appeal from a decision of a circuit judge (which can only be an original decision) will also go to the single judge.[187]

16.22.3 Where a matter is heard by a single judge of the High Court on appeal from a registrar or county court, an appeal only lies to the Court of Appeal with leave.[188]

An original decision of a single judge of the High Court (i.e. where a case has been adjourned by the registrar under r. 7(5) of the Rules) will be governed by the provisions of O. 59 of the Rules of the Supreme Court 1965.[189] Thus, an appeal from an interlocutory decision (or a decision on costs) will lie with leave, an appeal from a final decision being as of right.

181. [1992] BCLC 405.
182. [1992] Ch. 394.
183. IR 1986, r. 7.49(2).
184. *Dobson* v. *Hastings* [1992] Ch. 394 at 401A–B.
185. See IR 1986, r. 7.49(3).
186. *Secretary of State for Trade and Industry* v. *Langley* [1993] BCLC 1340, Hoffmann J. at 1341i–1342a considered that the thrust of r. 2 of the Rules was to apply county court (and by analogy High Court) procedure to the originating application "rather than other forms of court court process". Notwithstanding this decision, it is suggested that, as stated at para. 16.17.2, *supra*, the Insolvency Rules 1986 will not generally govern procedure in disqualification proceedings; the language of the specific rule must be considered to see whether it has any application. To date, only appeals have been held to be governed by the Insolvency Rules.

It is not clear, in the light of *Dobson* v. *Hastings* and *Re Probe Data (No. 3)* whether Practice Direction No. 3 of 1992 applies to such appeals. This Practice Direction allows appeals to be heard either in London, or by a circuit judge who exercises the powers of a judge of the Chancery Division at the larger commercial centres. The heading uses the words "insolvency matters"; para. (1) of the Direction refers to appeals from district judges in the High Court or the county court "exercising insolvency jurisdiction over companies or individuals".
187. See, for example, *Re Dexmaster Ltd* [1995] BCC 186.
188. IR 1986, r. 4.47(2); the leave of the judge or of the Court of Appeal.
189. SCA 1981, s. 16.

16.22.4 An appeal may be brought by either the applicant or the respondent and may concern whether an order should have been granted or refused[190] or against the length of the disqualification as being too short[191] or too long.[192]

The High Court (but not necessarily the County Court) has an inherent jurisdiction to grant a stay of the disqualification order pending an appeal, but would do so only in exceptional circumstances and in particular where an application under s. 17 for leave to act would be an inadequate remedy.[193]

16.23 Applications for leave to act

Applications for leave to act under s. 1(1) of the CDDA 1986 are made not only where a disqualification order has been made, but where a person is disqualified by virtue of an undischarged bankruptcy.[194]

Section 17 of the CDDA 1986 specifies the court to which an application for leave shall be made[195]:

(a) Where the application is for leave to promote or form a company it may be made to any court with jurisdiction to wind up companies.[196] This will include both the High Court, and county courts.[197]
(b) An application for leave to act as a liquidator, administrator or director, or otherwise to take part in the management of a company, or to be a receiver or manager of a company's property is made to any court having jurisdiction to wind up that company.[198]
(c) The High Court will always have jurisdiction to wind up any company, and a county court will have jurisdiction if it is the court of the district in which the company has its registered office, and the paid up capital of the company does not exceed £120,000.[199]

16.23.1 The application for leave need not be made to the court which itself made the disqualification order. Indeed, in the case of an order made by a court of criminal jurisdiction, that court will not have power to grant leave and the respondent will, if he wishes to continue in any present position in relation to a company, have to apply to an appropriate court of civil jurisdiction forthwith. The 21-day period of grace under the Rules (as to which see para. 16.20, above) applies only to orders made under s. 6 or s. 8 of the CDDA 1986.[200]

Section 17(2) of the CDDA 1986 provides that, where the order was made on the application of the Secretary of State, official receiver or liquidator, such person shall appear on the application for leave and call the attention of the court to any matters which

190. See for example *Re Hitco* [1995] BCC 161; *Re Grayan Building Services* [1995] Ch. 241.
191. *Secretary of State for Trade and Industry* v. *Ettinger, Re Swift 736 Ltd* [1993] BCLC 896.
192. *Re Sevenoaks Stationers (Retail) Ltd* [1991] BCLC 325.
193. *Secretary of State for Trade & Industry* v. *Bannister* [1996] 1 WLR 119.
194. CDDA 1986, s. 11.
195. Applications for leave in the case of revocation of an administration order under part VI of the County Courts Act 1984 (individual debtor) are made to the court which made the order.
196. CDDA 1986, s. 17(1)(a).
197. IA 1986, s. 117(1) and (2).
198. CDDA 1986, s. 17(1)(b).
199. CA 1985, s. 117(1) and (2).
200. Rules, r. 9.

seem to him to be relevant, and may give evidence or call witnesses.[201] An application for leave must in such a case be served on the person who obtained the original disqualification order.

16.23.2 Where the application for leave is in respect of a company with which the respondent is presently involved (or anticipates being involved) at the time the order is made, the convenient course is for the application to be made as soon as the court makes the disqualification order. Although no formal notice need be served on the Secretary of State, notice of the intention to make the application should be given, and any relevant evidence served, in time for the Secretary of State to consider whether there are matters to be drawn to the court's attention and whether any further evidence needs to be advanced.

It is not the function of the Secretary of State either to consent to, or to oppose an application for leave[202]; but there is a statutory duty to draw relevant matters to the attention of the court. What is relevant will be any matter which might indicate that, in the public interest, the person should or should not be granted leave.

16.23.3 The procedural questions involved in an application for leave were considered to some extent by the Court of Appeal in *Re Dicetrade*.[203] The real question before the court was one of costs, but Dillon L.J. made some observations which are of interest and from which the following principles may be advanced:

(i) It was plainly desirable that the application for leave should, where possible, be heard at the time the original order is made. In this case it may be that no special order for costs will be necessary.

(ii) A person who is not ready to make the application[204] at the time the order is made—with the result that extra costs are incurred in respect of an adjourned hearing—will usually bear the costs of that further hearing.

(iii) Where an application is made which was not anticipated at the time of the order, then there is no general rule as to costs. No order for costs might be appropriate where the Secretary of State stated that the application would not be opposed, but intimated that certain matters would be drawn to the attention of the court.

16.23.4 The person wishing to obtain leave will bear a burden to show that:

(i) there is some need for him to have leave (beyond his own convenience); and

(ii) the public will be adequately protected.[205]

In this latter regard, it is common for the order granting leave to impose conditions on the person applying.[206] By way of example, a schedule of such conditions appears in *Re*

201. Note the power of the court to call on the liquidator for assistance on an application for leave to act as a director of a company with a prohibited name under IA 1986, s. 216(3), IR 1986, r. 4.227.

202. But see the comments of Dillon L.J. in *Re Dicetrade Ltd* [1994] BCC 371.

203. [1994] BCC 371.

204. Or perhaps one who has served their application or evidence so late as to require the Secretary of State to seek an adjournment to consider it.

205. See, for example, *Re Cargo Agency Ltd* [1992] BCC 388, and *Re Gibson Davies Ltd* [1995] BCC 11.

206. A jurisdiction adopted by the courts in England and Wales and followed out of comity in Scotland: *Secretary of State for Trade and Industry* v. *Palfreyman* [1995] BCC 193 at 195E–G.

Gibson Davies Ltd.[207] Where the court makes an order under s. 17 on terms which have to be complied with by a certain time, it is desirable for the court to require an affidavit to be lodged (with a copy to the applicant) within a specified time, certifying that the various requirements have been satisfied.[208]

In accordance with *Re Tasbian (No. 2)*, appeals from a refusal of leave will be governed by r. 7.47(2) of the Insolvency Rules, as to which see para. 16.22.2, above. It is difficult to see that the Secretary of State would be in a position to appeal from a grant of leave, unless perhaps the order was perverse.

207. [1995] BCC 11 at 17–18.
208. *Re Brian Sheridan Cars Ltd* [1996] 1 BCLC 327.

STATUTORY INSTRUMENTS

1.1 INSOLVENCY RULES 1986, SI 1986 No. 1925

. . .

PART 2: ADMINISTRATION PROCEDURE

CHAPTER 1: APPLICATION FOR, AND MAKING OF, THE ORDER

Affidavit to support petition

2.1.—(1) Where it is proposed to apply to the court by petition for an administration order to be made in relation to a company, an affidavit complying with Rule 2.3 below must be prepared and sworn, with a view to its being filed in court in support of the petition. **[FORM 2.1]**

(2) If the petition is to be presented by the company or by the directors, the affidavit must be made by one of the directors, or the secretary of the company, stating himself to make it on behalf of the company or, as the case may be, on behalf of the directors.

(3) If the petition is to be presented by creditors, the affidavit must be made by a person acting under the authority of them all, whether or not himself one of their number. In any case there must be stated in the affidavit the nature of his authority and the means of his knowledge of the matters to which the affidavit relates.

(4) If the petition is to be presented by the supervisor of a voluntary arrangement under Part I of the Act, it is to be treated as if it were a petition by the company.

Independent report on company's affairs

2.2.—(1) There may be prepared, with a view to its being exhibited to the affidavit in support of the petition, a report by an independent person to the effect that the appointment of an administrator for the company is expedient.

(2) The report may be by the person proposed as administrator, or by any other person having adequate knowledge of the company's affairs, not being a director, secretary, manager, member, or employee of the company.

(3) The report shall specify the purposes which, in the opinion of the person preparing it, may be achieved for the company by the making of an administration order, being purposes particularly specified in section 8(3).

Contents of affidavit

2.3.—(1) The affidavit shall state—

(a) the deponent's belief that the company is, or is likely to become, unable to pay its debts and the grounds of that belief; and

(b) which of the purposes specified in section 8(3) is expected to be achieved by the making of an administration order.

(2) There shall in the affidavit be provided a statement of the company's financial position, specifying (to the best of the deponent's knowledge and belief) assets and liabilities, including contingent and prospective liabilities.

(3) Details shall be given of any security known or believed to be held by creditors of the company, and whether in any case the security is such as to confer power on the holder to appoint an administrative receiver. If an administrative receiver has been appointed, that fact shall be stated.

(4) If any petition has been presented for the winding up of the company, details of it shall be given in the affidavit, so far as within the immediate knowledge of the deponent.

(5) If there are other matters which, in the opinion of those intending to present the petition for an administration order, will assist the court in deciding whether to make such an order, those matters (so far as lying within the knowledge or belief of the deponent) shall also be stated.

(6) If a report has been prepared for the company under Rule 2.2, that fact shall be stated. If not, an explanation shall be provided why not.

Form of petition

2.4.—(1) If presented by the company or by the directors, the petition shall state the name of the company and its address for service, which (in the absence of special reasons to the contrary) is that of the company's registered office.

(2) If presented by a single creditor, the petition shall state his name and address for service.

(3) If the petition is presented by the directors, it shall state that it is so presented under section 9; but from and after presentation it is to be treated for all purposes as the petition of the company.

(4) If the petition is presented by two or more creditors, it shall state that it is so presented (naming them); but from and after presentation it is to be treated for all purposes as the petition of one only of them, named in the petition as petitioning on behalf of himself and other creditors. An address for service for that one shall be specified.

(5) The petition shall specify the name and address of the person proposed to be appointed as administrator; and it shall be stated that, to the best of the petitioner's knowledge and belief, the person is qualified to act as an insolvency practitioner in relation to the company.

(6) There shall be exhibited to the affidavit in support of the petition—

(a) a copy of the petition;
(b) a written consent by the proposed administrator to accept appointment, if an administration order is made **[FORM 2.2]**; and
(c) if a report has been prepared under Rule 2.2, a copy of it.

Filing of petition

2.5.—(1) The petition and affidavit shall be filed in court, with a sufficient number of copies for service and use as provided by Rule 2.6.

(2) Each of the copies delivered shall have applied to it the seal of the court and be issued to the petitioner; and on each copy there shall be endorsed the date and time of filing.

(3) The court shall fix a venue for the hearing of the petition and this also shall be endorsed on each copy of the petition issued under paragraph (2).

(4) After the petition is filed, it is the duty of the petitioner to notify the court in writing of any winding-up petition presented against the company, as soon as he becomes aware of it.

Service of petition

2.6.—(1) In the following paragraphs of this Rule, references to the petition are to a copy of the petition issued by the court under Rule 2.5(2) together with the affidavit in support of it and the documents (other than the copy petition) exhibited to the affidavit.

(2) The petition shall be served—

(a) on any person who has appointed, or is or may be entitled to appoint, an administrative receiver of the company;
(b) if an administrative receiver has been appointed, on him;

(c) if there is pending a petition for the winding up of the company, on the petitioner (and also on the provisional liquidator, if any); and
(d) on the person proposed as administrator.

(3) If the petition for the making of an administration order is presented by creditors of the company, the petition shall be served on the company.

Notice to sheriff, etc

2.6A. The petitioner shall forthwith after filing the petition give notice of its presentation to—
(a) any sheriff or other officer who to his knowledge is charged with an execution or other legal process against the company or its property, and
(b) any person who to his knowledge has distrained against the company or its property.

Manner in which service to be effected

2.7.—(1) Service of the petition in accordance with Rule 2.6 shall be effected by the petitioner, or his solicitor, or by a person instructed by him or his solicitor, not less than 5 days before the date fixed for the hearing.

(2) Service shall be effected as follows—
(a) on the company (subject to paragraph (3) below), by delivering the documents to its registered office;
(b) on any other person (subject to paragraph (4)), by delivering the documents to his proper address;
(c) in either case, in such other manner as the court may direct.

(3) If delivery to the company's registered office is not practicable, service may be effected by delivery to its last known principal place of business in England and Wales.

(4) Subject to paragraph (4A), for the purposes of paragraph (2)(b), a person's proper address is any which he has previously notified as his address for service; but if he has not notified any such address, service may be effected by delivery to his usual or last known address.

(4A) In the case of a person who—
(a) is an authorised institution or former authorised institution within the meaning of the Banking Act 1987,
(b) has appointed, or is or may be entitled to appoint, an administrative receiver of the company, and
(c) has not notified an address for service,

the proper address is the address of an office of that person where, to the knowledge of the petitioner, the company maintains a bank account or, where no such office is known to the petitioner, the registered office of that person, or, if there is no such office, his usual or last known address.

(5) Delivery of documents to any place or address may be made by leaving them there, or sending them by first class post.

Proof of service

2.8.—(1) Service of the petition shall be verified by affidavit, specifying the date on which, and the manner in which, service was effected. **[FORM 2.3]**

(2) The affidavit, with a sealed copy of the petition exhibited to it, shall be filed in court forthwith after service, and in any event not less than one day before the hearing of the petition.

The hearing

2.9.—(1) At the hearing of the petition, any of the following may appear or be represented—
(a) the petitioner;
(b) the company;
(c) any person who has appointed, or is or may be entitled to appoint, an administrative receiver of the company;
(d) if an administrative receiver has been appointed, he;
(e) any person who has presented a petition for the winding up of the company;

(f) the person proposed for appointment as administrator; and
(g) with the leave of the court, any other person who appears to have an interest justifying his appearance.

(2) If the court makes an administration order, the costs of the petitioner, and of any person appearing whose costs are allowed by the court, are payable as an expense of the administration. **[FORM 2.4]**

Notice and advertisement of administration order

2.10.—(1) If the court makes an administration order, it shall forthwith give notice to the person appointed as administrator.

(2) Forthwith after the order is made, the administrator shall advertise its making once in the Gazette, and once in such newspaper as he thinks most appropriate for ensuring that the order comes to the notice of the company's creditors. **[FORM 2.5]**

(3) The administrator shall also forthwith give notice of the making of the order—
(a) to any person who has appointed, or is or may be entitled to appoint, an administrative receiver of the company;
(b) if an administrative receiver has been appointed, to him;
(c) if there is pending a petition for the winding up of the company, to the petitioner (and also to the provisional liquidator, if any); and
(d) to the registrar of companies. **[FORM 2.6]**

(4) Two sealed copies of the order shall be sent by the court to the administrator, one of which shall be sent by him to the registrar of companies in accordance with section 21(2). **[FORM 2.7]**

(5) If under section 9(4) the court makes any other order, it shall give directions as to the persons to whom, and how, notice of it is to be given.

CHAPTER 2: STATEMENT OF AFFAIRS AND PROPOSALS TO CREDITORS

Notice requiring statement of affairs

2.11.—(1) Where the administrator determines to require a statement of the company's affairs to be made out and submitted to him in accordance with section 22, he shall send notice to each of the persons whom he considers should be made responsible under that section, requiring them to prepare and submit the statement. **[FORM 2.8]**

(2) The persons to whom the notice is sent are referred to in this Chapter as "the deponents".

(3) The notice shall inform each of the deponents—
(a) of the names and addresses of all others (if any) to whom the same notice has been sent;
(b) of the time within which the statement must be delivered;
(c) of the effect of section 22(6) (penalty for non-compliance); and
(d) of the application to him, and to each of the other deponents, of section 235 (duty to provide information, and to attend on the administrator if required).

(4) The administrator shall, on request, furnish each deponent with the forms required for the preparation of the statement of affairs.

Verification and filing

2.12.—(1) The statement of affairs shall be in Form 2.9, shall contain all the particulars required by that form and shall be verified by affidavit by the deponents (using the same form). **[FORM 2.9]**

(2) The administrator may require any of the persons mentioned in section 22(3) to submit an affidavit of concurrence, stating that he concurs in the statement of affairs.

(3) An affidavit of concurrence may be qualified in respect of matters dealt with in the statement of affairs, where the maker of the affidavit is not in agreement with the deponents, or he considers

the statement to be erroneous or misleading, or he is without the direct knowledge necessary for concurring with it.

(4) The statement of affairs shall be delivered to the administrator by the deponent making the affidavit of verification (or by one of them, if more than one), together with a copy of the verified statement.

(5) Every affidavit of concurrence shall be delivered by the person who makes it, together with a copy.

(6) The administrator shall file the verified copy of the statement, and the affidavits of concurrence (if any) in court.

Limited disclosure

2.13.—(1) Where the administrator thinks that it would prejudice the conduct of the administration for the whole or part of the statement of affairs to be disclosed, he may apply to the court for an order of limited disclosure in respect of the statement, or any specified part of it.

(2) The court may on the application order that the statement or, as the case may be, the specified part of it, be not filed in court, or that it is to be filed separately and not be open to inspection otherwise than with leave of the court.

(3) The court's order may include directions as to the delivery of documents to the registrar of companies and the disclosure of relevant information to other persons.

Release from duty to submit statement of affairs; extension of time

2.14.—(1) The power of the administrator under section 22(5) to give a release from the obligation imposed by that section, or to grant an extension of time, may be exercised at the administrator's own discretion, or at the request of any deponent.

(2) A deponent may, if he requests a release or extension of time and it is refused by the administrator, apply to the court for it.

(3) The court may, if it thinks that no sufficient cause is shown for the application, dismiss it; but it shall not do so unless the applicant has had an opportunity to attend the court for an *ex parte* hearing, of which he has been given at least 7 days' notice.

If the application is not dismissed under this paragraph, the court shall fix a venue for it to be heard, and give notice to the deponent accordingly.

(4) The deponent shall, at least 14 days before the hearing, send to the administrator a notice stating the venue and accompanied by a copy of the application, and of any evidence which he (the deponent) intends to adduce in support of it.

(5) The administrator may appear and be heard on the application; and, whether or not he appears, he may file a written report of any matters which he considers ought to be drawn to the court's attention.

If such a report is filed, a copy of it shall be sent by the administrator to the deponent, not later than 5 days before the hearing.

(6) Sealed copies of any order made on the application shall be sent by the court to the deponent and the administrator.

(7) On any application under this Rule the applicant's costs shall be paid in any event by him and, unless the court otherwise orders, no allowance towards them shall be made out of the assets.

Expenses of statement of affairs

2.15.—(1) A deponent making the statement of affairs and affidavit shall be allowed, and paid by the administrator out of his receipts, any expenses incurred by the deponent in so doing which the administrator considers reasonable.

(2) Any decision by the administrator under this Rule is subject to appeal to the court.

(3) Nothing in this Rule relieves a deponent from any obligation with respect to the preparation, verification and submission of the statement of affairs, or to the provision of information to the administrator.

Statement to be annexed to proposals

2.16.—(1) There shall be annexed to the administrator's proposals, when sent to the registrar of companies under section 23 and laid before the creditors' meeting to be summoned under that section, a statement by him showing—

(a) details relating to his appointment as administrator, the purposes for which an administration order was applied for and made, and any subsequent variation of those purposes;
(b) the names of the directors and secretary of the company;
(c) an account of the circumstances giving rise to the application for an administration order;
(d) if a statement of affairs has been submitted, a copy or summary of it, with the administrator's comments, if any;
(e) if no statement of affairs has been submitted, details of the financial position of the company at the latest practicable date (which must, unless the court otherwise orders, be a date not earlier than that of the administration order);
(f) the manner in which the affairs and business of the company—
 (i) have, since the date of the administrator's appointment, been managed and financed, and
 (ii) will, if the administrator's proposals are approved, continue to be managed and financed; and
(g) such other information (if any) as the administrator thinks necessary to enable creditors to decide whether or not to vote for the adoption of the proposals.

(2) Where the administrator intends to apply to the court under section 18 for the administration order to be discharged at a time before he has sent a statement of his proposals to creditors in accordance with section 23(1), he shall, at least 10 days before he makes such an application, send to all creditors of the company (so far as he is aware of their addresses) a report containing the information required by paragraph (1)(a)–(f)(i) of this Rule.

Notice to members of proposals to creditors

2.17. The manner of publishing—

(a) under section 23(2)(b), notice to members of the administrator's proposals to creditors, and
(b) under section 25(3)(b), notice to members of substantial revisions of the proposals,

shall be by gazetting; and the notice shall also in either case be advertised once in the newspaper in which the administration order was advertised.

CHAPTER 3: CREDITORS' AND COMPANY MEETINGS

SECTION A: CREDITORS' MEETINGS

Meeting to consider administrator's proposals

2.18.—(1) Notice of the creditors' meeting to be summoned under section 23(1) shall be given to all the creditors of the company who are identified in the statement of affairs, or are known to the administrator and had claims against the company at the date of the administration order.

(2) Notice of the meeting shall also (unless the court otherwise directs) be given by advertisement in the newspaper in which the administration order was advertised.

(3) Notice to attend the meeting shall be sent out at the same time to any directors or officers of the company (including persons who have been directors or officers in the past) whose presence at the meeting is, in the administrator's opinion, required. **[FORM 2.10]**

(4) If at the meeting there is not the requisite majority for approval of the administrator's proposals (with modifications, if any), the chairman may, and shall if a resolution is passed to that effect, adjourn the meeting for not more than 14 days.

Creditors' meetings generally

2.19.—(1) This rule applies to creditors' meetings summoned by the administrator under—

(a) section 14(2)(b) (general power to summon meetings of creditors);

(b) section 17(3) (requisition by creditors; direction by the court);

(c) section 23(1) (to consider administrator's proposals); or

(d) section 25(2)(b) (to consider substantial revisions).

(2) In fixing the venue for the meeting, the administrator shall have regard to the convenience of creditors.

(3) The meeting shall be summoned for commencement between 10.00 and 16.00 hours on a business day, unless the court otherwise directs.

(4) Notice of the meeting shall be given to all creditors who are known to the administrator and had claims against the company at the date of the administration order; and the notice shall specify the purpose of the meeting and contain a statement of the effect of Rule 2.22(1) (entitlement to vote). **[FORM 2.11]**

(4A) Except in relation to a meeting summoned under section 23(1) or 25(2), at least 21 days' notice of the meeting shall be given.

(5) With the notice summoning the meeting there shall be sent out forms of proxy. **[FORM 8.2]**

(6) If within 30 minutes from the time fixed for commencement of the meeting there is no person present to act as chairman, the meeting stands adjourned to the same time and place in the following week or, if that is not a business day, to the business day immediately following.

(7) The meeting may from time to time be adjourned, if the chairman thinks fit, but not for more than 14 days from the date on which it was fixed to commence.

The chairman at meetings

2.20.—(1) At any meeting of creditors summoned by the administrator, either he shall be chairman, or a person nominated by him in writing to act in his place.

(2) A person so nominated must be either—

(a) one who is qualified to act as an insolvency practitioner in relation to the company, or

(b) an employee of the administrator or his firm who is experienced in insolvency matters.

Meeting requisitioned by creditors

2.21.—(1) Any request by creditors to the administrator for a meeting of creditors to be summoned shall be accompanied by—

(a) a list of the creditors concurring with the request, showing the amounts of their respective claims in the administration;

(b) from each creditor concurring, written confirmation of his concurrence; and

(c) a statement of the purpose of the proposed meeting.

This paragraph does not apply if the requisitioning creditor's debt is alone sufficient, without the concurrence of other creditors.

(2) The administrator shall, if he considers the request to be properly made in accordance with section 17(3), fix a venue for the meeting, not more than 35 days from his receipt of the request, and give at least 21 days' notice of the meeting to creditors.

(3) The expenses of summoning and holding a meeting at the instance of any person other than the administrator shall be paid by that person, who shall deposit with the administrator security for their payment.

(4) The sum to be deposited shall be such as the administrator may determine, and he shall not act without the deposit having been made.

(5) The meeting may resolve that the expenses of summoning and holding it are to be payable out of the assets of the company, as an expense of the administration.

(6) To the extent that any deposit made under this Rule is not required for the payment of expenses of summoning and holding the meeting, it shall be repaid to the person who made it.

Entitlement to vote

2.22.—(1) Subject as follows, at a meeting of creditors in administration proceedings a person is entitled to vote only if—

(a) he has given to the administrator, not later than 12.00 hours on the business day before the day fixed for the meeting, details in writing of the debt which he claims to be due to him from the company, and the claim has been duly admitted under the following provisions of this Rule, and

(b) there has been lodged with the administrator any proxy which he intends to be used on his behalf.

Details of the debt must include any calculation for the purposes of Rules 2.24 to 2.27.

(2) The chairman of the meeting may allow a creditor to vote, notwithstanding that he has failed to comply with paragraph (1)(a), if satisfied that the failure was due to circumstances beyond the creditor's control.

(3) The administrator or, if other, the chairman of the meeting may call for any document or other evidence to be produced to him, where he thinks it necessary for the purpose of substantiating the whole or any part of the claim.

(4) Votes are calculated according to the amount of a creditor's debt as at the date of the administration order, deducting any amounts paid in respect of the debt after that date.

(5) A creditor shall not vote in respect of a debt for an unliquidated amount, or any debt whose value is not ascertained, except where the chairman agrees to put upon the debt an estimated minimum value for the purpose of entitlement to vote and admits the claim for that purpose.

Admission and rejection of claims

2.23.—(1) At any creditors' meeting the chairman has power to admit or reject a creditor's claim for the purpose of his entitlement to vote; and the power is exercisable with respect to the whole or any part of the claim.

(2) The chairman's decision under this Rule, or in respect of any matter arising under Rule 2.22, is subject to appeal to the court by any creditor.

(3) If the chairman is in doubt whether a claim should be admitted or rejected, he shall mark it as objected to and allow the creditor to vote, subject to his vote being subsequently declared invalid if the objection to the claim is sustained.

(4) If on an appeal the chairman's decision is reversed or varied, or a creditor's vote is declared invalid, the court may order that another meeting be summoned, or make such other order as it thinks just.

(5) In the case of the meeting summoned under section 23 to consider the administrator's proposals, an application to the court by way of appeal under this Rule against a decision of the chairman shall not be made later than 28 days after the delivery of the administrator's report in accordance with section 24(4).

(6) Neither the administrator nor any person nominated by him to be chairman is personally liable for costs incurred by any person in respect of an appeal to the court under this Rule, unless the court makes an order to that effect.

Secured creditors

2.24. At a meeting of creditors a secured creditor is entitled to vote only in respect of the balance (if any) of his debt after deducting the value of his security as estimated by him.

Holders of negotiable instruments

2.25. A creditor shall not vote in respect of a debt on, or secured by, a current bill of exchange or promissory note, unless he is willing—

(a) to treat the liability to him on the bill or note of every person who is liable on it antecedently to the company, and against whom a bankruptcy order has not been made (or, in the case of a company, which has not gone into liquidation), as a security in his hands, and

(b) to estimate the value of the security and, for the purpose of his entitlement to vote, to deduct it from his claim.

Retention of title creditors

2.26. For the purpose of entitlement to vote at a creditors' meeting in administration proceedings, a seller of goods to the company under a retention of title agreement shall deduct from his claim the value, as estimated by him, of any rights arising under that agreement in respect of goods in possession of the company.

Hire-purchase, conditional sale and chattel leasing agreements

2.27.—(1) Subject as follows, an owner of goods under a hire-purchase or chattel leasing agreement, or a seller of goods under a conditional sale agreement, is entitled to vote in respect of the amount of the debt due and payable to him by the company as at the date of the administration order.

(2) In calculating the amount of any debt for this purpose, no account shall be taken of any amount attributable to the exercise of any right under the relevant agreement, so far as the right has become exercisable solely by virtue of the presentation of the petition for an administration order or any matter arising in consequence of that, or of the making of the order.

Resolutions and minutes

2.28.—(1) Subject to paragraph (1A), at a creditors' meeting in administration proceedings, a resolution is passed when a majority (in value) of those present and voting, in person or by proxy, have voted in favour of it.

(1A) Any resolution is invalid if those voting against it include more than half in value of the creditors to whom notice of the meeting was sent and who are not, to the best of the chairman's belief, persons connected with the company.

(2) The chairman of the meeting shall cause minutes of its proceedings to be entered in the company's minute book.

(3) The minutes shall include a list of the creditors who attended (personally or by proxy) and, if a creditors' committee has been established, the names and addresses of those elected to be members of the committee.

Reports and notices under sections 23 and 25

2.29. Any report or notice by the administrator of the result of a creditors' meeting held under section 23 or 25 shall have annexed to it details of the proposals which were considered by the meeting and of the revisions and modifications to the proposals which were so considered.

Notices to creditors

2.30.—(1) Within 14 days of the conclusion of a meeting of creditors to consider the administrator's proposals or revised proposals, the administrator shall send notice of the result of the meeting (including, where appropriate, details of the proposals as approved) to every creditor who received notice of the meeting under the Rules, and to any other creditor of whom the administrator has since become aware. **[FORM 2.12]**

(2) Within 14 days of the end of every period of 6 months beginning with the date of approval of the administrator's proposals or revised proposals, the administrator shall send to all creditors of the company a report on the progress of the administration.

(3) On vacating office the administrator shall send to creditors a report on the administration up to that time.

This does not apply where the administration is immediately followed by the company going into liquidation, nor when the administrator is removed from office by the court or ceases to be qualified as an insolvency practitioner.

SECTION B: COMPANY MEETINGS

Venue and conduct of company meeting

2.31.—(1) Where the administrator summons a meeting of members of the company, he shall fix a venue for it having regard to their convenience.

(2) The chairman of the meeting shall be the administrator or a person nominated by him in writing to act in his place.

(3) A person so nominated must be either—

(a) one who is qualified to act as an insolvency practitioner in relation to the company, or

(b) an employee of the administrator or his firm who is experienced in insolvency matters.

(4) If within 30 minutes from the time fixed for commencement of the meeting there is no person present to act as chairman, the meeting stands adjourned to the same time and place in the following week or, if that is not a business day, to the business day immediately following.

(5) Subject as above, the meeting shall be summoned and conducted as if it were a general meeting of the company summoned under the company's articles of association, and in accordance with the applicable provisions of the Companies Act.

(6) The chairman of the meeting shall cause minutes of its proceedings to be entered in the company's minute book.

CHAPTER 4: THE CREDITORS' COMMITTEE

Constitution of committee

2.32.—(1) Where it is resolved by a creditors' meeting to establish a creditors' committee for the purposes of the administration, the committee shall consist of at least 3 and not more than 5 creditors of the company elected at the meeting.

(2) Any creditor of the company is eligible to be a member of the committee, so long as his claim has not been rejected for the purpose of his entitlement to vote.

(3) A body corporate may be a member of the committee, but it cannot act as such otherwise than by a representative appointed under Rule 2.37 below.

Formalities of establishment

2.33.—(1) The creditors' committee does not come into being, and accordingly cannot act, until the administrator has issued a certificate of its due constitution.

(2) No person may act as a member of the committee unless and until he has agreed to do so and, unless the relevant proxy or authorisation contains a statement to the contrary, such agreement may be given by his proxy-holder or representative under section 375 of the Companies Act present at the meeting establishing the committee.

(2A) The administrator's certificate of the committee's due constitution shall not issue unless and until at least 3 of the persons who are to be members of the committee have agreed to act.

(3) As and when the others (if any) agree to act, the administrator shall issue an amended certificate.

(4) The certificate, and any amended certificate, shall be filed in court by the administrator. **[FORM 2.13]**

(5) If after the first establishment of the committee there is any change in its membership, the administrator shall report the change to the court. **[FORM 2.14]**

Functions and meetings of the committee

2.34.—(1) The creditors' committee shall assist the administrator in discharging his functions, and act in relation to him in such manner as may be agreed from time to time.

(2) Subject as follows, meetings of the committee shall be held when and where determined by the administrator.

(3) The administrator shall call a first meeting of the committee not later than 3 months after its first establishment; and thereafter he shall call a meeting—

(a) if so requested by a member of the committee or his representative (the meeting then to be held within 21 days of the request being received by the administrator), and

(b) for a specified date, if the committee has previously resolved that a meeting be held on that date.

(4) The administrator shall give 7 days' written notice of the venue of any meeting to every member of the committee (or his representative designated for that purpose), unless in any case the requirement of notice has been waived by or on behalf of any member.

Waiver may be signified either at or before the meeting.

The chairman at meetings

2.35.—(1) Subject to Rule 2.44(3), the chairman at any meeting of the creditors' committee shall be the administrator or a person nominated by him in writing to act.

(2) A person so nominated must be either—

(a) one who is qualified to act as an insolvency practitioner in relation to the company, or

(b) an employee of the administrator or his firm who is experienced in insolvency matters.

Quorum

2.36. A meeting of the committee is duly constituted if due notice of it has been given to all the members, and at least 2 members are present or represented.

Committee-members' representatives

2.37.—(1) A member of the committee may, in relation to the business of the committee, be represented by another person duly authorised by him for that purpose.

(2) A person acting as a committee-member's representative must hold a letter of authority entitling him so to act (either generally or specially) and signed by or on behalf of the committee-member, and for this purpose any proxy or any authorisation under section 375 of the Companies Act in relation to any meeting of creditors of the company shall, unless it contains a statement to the contrary, be treated as a letter of authority to act generally signed by or on behalf of the committee-member.

(3) The chairman at any meeting of the committee may call on a person claiming to act as a committee-member's representative to produce his letter of authority, and may exclude him if it appears that his authority is deficient.

(4) No member may be represented by a body corporate, or by a person who is an undischarged bankrupt, or is subject to a composition or arrangement with his creditors.

(5) No person shall—

(a) on the same committee, act at one and the same time as representative of more than one committee-member, or

(b) act both as a member of the committee and as representative of another member.

(6) Where a member's representative signs any document on the member's behalf, the fact that he so signs must be stated below his signature.

Resignation

2.38. A member of the committee may resign by notice in writing delivered to the administrator.

Termination of membership

2.39.—(1) Membership of the creditors' committee is automatically terminated if the member—

(a) becomes bankrupt, or compounds or arranges with his creditors, or

(b) at 3 consecutive meetings of the committee is neither present nor represented (unless at the third of those meetings it is resolved that this Rule is not to apply in his case), or

(c) ceases to be, or is found never to have been, a creditor.

(2) However, if the cause of termination is the member's bankruptcy, his trustee in bankruptcy replaces him as a member of the committee.

Removal

2.40. A member of the committee may be removed by resolution at a meeting of creditors, at least 14 days' notice having been given of the intention to move that resolution.

Vacancies

2.41.—(1) The following applies if there is a vacancy in the membership of the creditors' committee.

(2) The vacancy need not be filled if the administrator and a majority of the remaining members of the committee so agree, provided that the total number of members does not fall below the minimum required under Rule 2.32.

(3) The administrator may appoint any creditor (being qualified under the Rules to be a member of the committee) to fill the vacancy, if a majority of the other members of the committee agree to the appointment, and the creditor concerned consents to act.

Procedure at meetings

2.42.—(1) At any meeting of the creditors' committee, each member of it (whether present himself, or by his representative) has one vote; and a resolution is passed when a majority of the members present or represented have voted in favour of it.

(2) Every resolution passed shall be recorded in writing, either separately or as part of the minutes of the meeting.

(3) A record of each resolution shall be signed by the chairman and placed in the company's minute book.

Resolutions by post

2.43.—(1) In accordance with this Rule, the administrator may seek to obtain the agreement of members of the creditors' committee to a resolution by sending to every member (or his representative designated for the purpose) a copy of the proposed resolution.

(2) Where the administrator makes use of the procedure allowed by this Rule, he shall send out to members of the committee or their representatives (as the case may be) a copy of any proposed resolution on which a decision is sought, which shall be set out in such a way that agreement with or dissent from each separate resolution may be indicated by the recipient on the copy so sent.

(3) Any member of the committee may, within 7 business days from the date of the administrator sending out a resolution, require him to summon a meeting of the committee to consider the matters raised by the resolution.

(4) In the absence of such a request, the resolution is deemed to have been passed by the committee if and when the administrator is notified in writing by a majority of the members that they concur with it.

(5) A copy of every resolution passed under this Rule, and a note that the committee's concurrence was obtained, shall be placed in the company's minute book.

Information from administrator

2.44.—(1) Where the committee resolves to require the attendance of the administrator under section 26(2), the notice to him shall be in writing signed by the majority of the members of the committee for the time being. A member's representative may sign for him.

(2) The meeting at which the administrator's attendance is required shall be fixed by the committee for a business day, and shall be held at such time and place as he determines.

(3) Where the administrator so attends, the members of the committee may elect any one of their number to be chairman of the meeting, in place of the administrator or a nominee of his.

Expenses of members

2.45.—(1) Subject as follows, the administrator shall out of the assets of the company defray any reasonable travelling expenses directly incurred by members of the creditors' committee or their representatives in relation to their attendance at the committee's meetings, or otherwise on the committee's business, as an expense of the administration.

(2) Paragraph (1) does not apply to any meeting of the committee held within 3 months of a previous meeting, unless the meeting in question is summoned at the instance of the administrator.

Members' dealings with the company

2.46.—(1) Membership of the committee does not prevent a person from dealing with the company while the administration order is in force, provided that any transactions in the course of such dealings are in good faith and for value.

(2) The court may, on the application of any person interested, set aside any transaction which appears to it to be contrary to the requirements of this Rule, and may give such consequential directions as it thinks fit for compensating the company for any loss which it may have incurred in consequence of the transaction.

Formal defects

2.46A. The acts of the creditors' committee established for any administration are valid notwithstanding any defect in the appointment, election or qualifications of any member of the committee or any committee-member's representative or in the formalities of its establishment.

CHAPTER 5: THE ADMINISTRATOR

Fixing of remuneration

2.47.—(1) The administrator is entitled to receive remuneration for his services as such.

(2) The remuneration shall be fixed either—

(a) as a percentage of the value of the property with which he has to deal, or

(b) by reference to the time properly given by the insolvency practitioner (as administrator) and his staff in attending to matters arising in the administration.

(3) It is for the creditors' committee (if there is one) to determine whether the remuneration is to be fixed under paragraph (2)(a) or (b) and, if under paragraph (2)(a), to determine any percentage to be applied as there mentioned.

(4) In arriving at that determination, the committee shall have regard to the following matters—

(a) the complexity (or otherwise) of the case,

(b) any respects in which, in connection with the company's affairs, there falls on the administrator any responsibility of an exceptional kind or degree,

(c) the effectiveness with which the administrator appears to be carrying out, or to have carried out, his duties as such, and

(d) the value and nature of the property with which he has to deal.

(5) If there is no creditors' committee, or the committee does not make the requisite determination, the administrator's remuneration may be fixed (in accordance with paragraph (2)) by a resolution of a meeting of creditors; and paragraph (4) applies to them as it does to the creditors' committee.

(6) If not fixed as above, the administrator's remuneration shall, on his application, be fixed by the court.

(7) Where there are joint administrators, it is for them to agree between themselves as to how the remuneration payable should be apportioned. Any dispute arising between them may be referred—

(a) to the court, for settlement by order, or

(b) to the creditors' committee or a meeting of creditors, for settlement by resolution.

(8) If the administrator is a solicitor and employs his own firm, or any partner in it, to act on behalf of the company, profit costs shall not be paid unless this is authorised by the creditors' committee, the creditors or the court.

Recourse to meeting of creditors

2.48. If the administrator's remuneration has been fixed by the creditors' committee, and he considers the rate or amount to be insufficient, he may request that it be increased by resolution of the creditors.

Recourse to the court

2.49.—(1) If the administrator considers that the remuneration fixed for him by the creditors' committee, or by resolution of the creditors, is insufficient, he may apply to the court for an order increasing its amount or rate.

(2) The administrator shall give at least 14 days' notice of his application to the members of the creditors' committee; and the committee may nominate one or more members to appear or be represented, and to be heard, on the application.

(3) If there is no creditors' committee, the administrator's notice of his application shall be sent to such one or more of the company's creditors as the court may direct, which creditors may nominate one or more of their number to appear or be represented.

(4) The court may, if it appears to be a proper case, order the costs of the administrator's application, including the costs of any member of the creditors' committee appearing or being represented on it, or any creditor so appearing or being represented, to be paid as an expense of the administration.

Creditors' claim that remuneration is excessive

2.50.—(1) Any creditor of the company may, with the concurrence of at least 25 per cent. in value of the creditors (including himself), apply to the court for an order that the administrator's remuneration be reduced, on the grounds that it is, in all the circumstances, excessive.

(2) The court may, if it thinks that no sufficient cause is shown for a reduction, dismiss the application; but it shall not do so unless the applicant has had an opportunity to attend the court for an *ex parte* hearing, of which he has been given at least 7 days' notice.

If the application is not dismissed under this paragraph, the court shall fix a venue for it to be heard, and give notice to the applicant accordingly.

(3) The applicant shall, at least 14 days before the hearing, send to the administrator a notice stating the venue and accompanied by a copy of the application, and of any evidence which the applicant intends to adduce in support of it.

(4) If the court considers the application to be well-founded, it shall make an order fixing the remuneration at a reduced amount or rate.

(5) Unless the court orders otherwise, the costs of the application shall be paid by the applicant, and are not payable as an expense of the administration.

Disposal of charged property, etc.

2.51.—(1) The following applies where the administrator applies to the court under section 15(2) for authority to dispose of property of the company which is subject to a security, or goods in the possession of the company under an agreement, to which that subsection relates.

(2) The court shall fix a venue for the hearing of the application, and the administrator shall forthwith give notice of the venue to the person who is the holder of the security or, as the case may be, the owner under the agreement.

(3) If an order is made under section 15(2), the administrator shall forthwith give notice of it to that person or owner.

(4) The court shall send 2 sealed copies of the order to the administrator, who shall send one of them to that person or owner.

Abstract of receipts and payments

2.52.—(1) The administrator shall—

(a) within 2 months after the end of 6 months from the date of his appointment, and of every subsequent period of 6 months, and

(b) within 2 months after he ceases to act as administrator,

send to the court, and to the registrar of companies, and to each member of the creditors' committee, the requisite accounts of the receipts and payments of the company. **[FORM 2.15]**

(2) The court may, on the administrator's application, extend the period of 2 months mentioned above.

(3) The accounts are to be in the form of an abstract showing—

(a) receipts and payments during the relevant period of 6 months, or

(b) where the administrator has ceased to act, receipts and payments during the period from the end of the last 6-month period to the time when he so ceased (alternatively, if there has been no previous abstract, receipts and payments in the period since his appointment as administrator).

(4) If the administrator makes default in complying with this Rule, he is liable to a fine and, for continued contravention, to a daily default fine.

Resignation

2.53.—(1) The administrator may give notice of his resignation on grounds of ill health or because **[FORM 2.16]**—

(a) he intends ceasing to be in practice as an insolvency practitioner, or

(b) there is some conflict of interest, or change of personal circumstances, which precludes or makes impracticable the further discharge by him of the duties of administrator.

(2) The administrator may, with the leave of the court, give notice of his resignation on grounds other than those specified in paragraph (1). **[FORM 2.17]**

(3) The administrator must give to the persons specified below at least 7 days' notice of his intention to resign, or to apply for the court's leave to do so—

(a) if there is a continuing administrator of the company, to him;

(b) if there is no such administrator, to the creditors' committee; and

(c) if there is no such administrator and no creditors' committee, to the company and its creditors.

Administrator deceased

2.54.—(1) Subject as follows, where the administrator has died, it is the duty of his personal representatives to give notice of the fact to the court, specifying the date of the death.

This does not apply if notice has been given under any of the following paragraphs of this Rule.

(2) If the deceased administrator was a partner in a firm, notice may be given by a partner in the firm who is qualified to act as an insolvency practitioner, or is a member of any body recognised by the Secretary of State for the authorisation of insolvency practitioners.

(3) Notice of the death may be given by any person producing to the court the relevant death certificate or a copy of it.

Order filling vacancy

2.55. Where the court makes an order filling a vacancy in the office of administrator, the same provisions apply in respect of giving notice of, and advertising, the order as in the case of the administration order.

CHAPTER 6: VAT BAD DEBT RELIEF

Issue of certificate of insolvency

2.56.—(1) In accordance with this Rule, it is the duty of the administrator to issue a certificate in the terms of paragraph (b) of section 22(3) of the Value Added Tax Act 1983 (which specifies the circumstances in which a company is deemed insolvent for the purposes of that section) forthwith upon his forming the opinion described in that paragraph.

(2) There shall in the certificate be specified—

(a) the name of the company and its registered number;

(b) the name of the administrator and the date of his appointment;

(c) the date on which the certificate is issued.

(3) The certificate shall be intituled "CERTIFICATE OF INSOLVENCY FOR THE PURPOSES OF SECTION 22(3)(b) OF THE VALUE ADDED TAX ACT 1983".

Notice to creditors

2.57.—(1) Notice of the issue of the certificate shall be given by the administrator within 3 months of his appointment or within 2 months of issuing the certificate, whichever is the later, to all of the company's unsecured creditors of whose address he is then aware and who have, to his knowledge, made supplies to the company, with a charge to value added tax, at any time before his appointment.

(2) Thereafter, he shall give the notice to any such creditor of whose address and supplies to the company he becomes aware.

(3) He is not under obligation to provide any creditor with a copy of the certificate.

Preservation of certificate with company's records

2.58.—(1) The certificate shall be retained with the company's accounting records, and section 222 of the Companies Act (where and for how long records are to be kept) shall apply to the certificate as it applies to those records.

(2) It is the duty of the administrator, on vacating office, to bring this Rule to the attention of the directors or (as the case may be) any successor of his as administrator.

. . .

PART 4: COMPANIES WINDING UP

. . .

CHAPTER 2: THE STATUTORY DEMAND (NO CVL APPLICATION)

Preliminary

4.4.—(1) This Chapter does not apply where a petition for the winding up of a company is presented under section 124 on or after the date on which the Rules come into force and the petition is based on failure to comply with a written demand served on the company before that date.

(2) A written demand served by a creditor on a company under section 123(1)(a) (registered companies) or 222(1)(a) (unregistered companies) is known in winding-up proceedings as "the statutory demand".

(3) The statutory demand must be dated, and be signed either by the creditor himself or by a person stating himself to be authorised to make the demand on the creditor's behalf.

Form and content of statutory demand

4.5.—(1) The statutory demand must state the amount of the debt and the consideration for it (or, if there is no consideration, the way in which it arises). **[FORM 4.1]**

(2) If the amount claimed in the demand includes—

(a) any charge by way of interest not previously notified to the company as included in its liability, or

(b) any other charge accruing from time to time,

the amount or rate of the charge must be separately identified, and the grounds on which payment of it is claimed must be stated.

In either case the amount claimed must be limited to that which has accrued due at the date of the demand.

Information to be given in statutory demand

4.6.—(1) The statutory demand must include an explanation to the company of the following matters—

(a) the purpose of the demand, and the fact that, if the demand is not complied with, proceedings may be instituted for the winding up of the company;

(b) the time within which it must be complied with, if that consequence is to be avoided; and

(c) the methods of compliance which are open to the company.

(2) Information must be provided for the company as to how an officer or representative of it may enter into communication with one or more named individuals, with a view to securing or compounding for the debt to the creditor's satisfaction.

In the case of any individual so named in the demand, his address and telephone number (if any) must be given.

CHAPTER 3: PETITION TO WINDING-UP ORDER (NO CVL APPLICATION) (NO APPLICATION TO PETITION BY CONTRIBUTORIES)

Presentation and filing of petition

4.7.—(1) The petition, verified by affidavit in accordance with Rule 4.12 below, shall be filed in court. **[FORM 4.2] [FORM 4.3]**

(2) No petition shall be filed unless there is produced with it the receipt for the deposit payable on presentation.

(3) If the petitioner is other than the company itself, there shall be delivered with the petition—

(a) one copy for service on the company, and

(b) one copy to be exhibited to the affidavit verifying service.

(4) There shall in any case be delivered with the petition—

(a) if the company is in course of being wound up voluntarily, and a liquidator has been appointed, one copy of the petition to be sent to him;

(b) if an administration order is in force in relation to the company, one copy to be sent to the administrator;

(c) if an administrative receiver has been appointed in relation to the company, one copy to be sent to him;

(d) if there is in force for the company a voluntary arrangement under Part I of the Act, one copy for the supervisor of the arrangement; and

(e) if the company is an authorised institution or former authorised institution within the meaning of the Banking Act 1987 and the petitioner is not the Bank of England, one copy to be sent to the Bank.

(5) Each of the copies delivered shall have applied to it the seal of the court, and shall be issued to the petitioner.

(6) The court shall fix a venue for the hearing of the petition; and this shall be endorsed on any copy issued to the petitioner under paragraph (5).

(7) Where a petition is filed at the instance of a company's administrator the petition shall—

(a) be expressed to be the petition of the company by its administrator,

(b) state the name of the administrator, the number of the petition on which the administration order was made and the date of that order, and

(c) contain an application under section 18 requesting that the administration order be discharged and that the court make any such order consequential upon that discharge as it thinks fit.

(8) Any petition filed in relation to a company in respect of which there is in force an administration order or a voluntary arrangement under Part I of the Act shall be presented to the court which made the administration order or, as the case may be, to which the nominee's report under section 2 was submitted.

(9) Any petition such as is mentioned in paragraph (7) above or presented by the supervisor of a voluntary arrangement under Part I of the Act in force for the company shall be treated as if it were a petition filed by contributories, and Chapter 4 in this Part of the Rules shall apply accordingly.

(10) Where a petition contains a request for the appointment of a person as liquidator in accordance with section 140 (appointment of former administrator or supervisor as liquidator) the person whose appointment is sought shall, not less than 2 days before the return day for the petition, file in court a report including particulars of—

(a) a date on which he notified creditors of the company, either in writing or at a meeting of creditors, of the intention to seek his appointment as liquidator, such date to be at least 10 days before the day on which the report under this paragraph is filed, and

(b) details of any response from creditors to that notification, including any objections to his appointment.

Service of petition

4.8.—(1) The following paragraphs apply as regards service of the petition on the company (where the petitioner is other than the company itself); and references to the petition are to a copy of the petition bearing the seal of the court in which it is presented.

(2) Subject as follows, the petition shall be served at the company's registered office, that is to say—

(a) the place which is specified, in the company's statement delivered under section 10 of the Companies Act as the intended situation of its registered office on incorporation, or

(b) if notice has been given by the company to the registrar of companies under section 287 of that Act (change of registered office), the place specified in that notice or, as the case may be, in the last such notice.

(3) Service of the petition at the registered office may be effected in any of the following ways—

(a) it may be handed to a person who there and then acknowledges himself to be, or to the best of the server's knowledge, information and belief is, a director or other officer, or employee, of the company; or

(b) it may be handed to a person who there and then acknowledges himself to be authorised to accept service of documents on the company's behalf; or

(c) in the absence of any such person as is mentioned in sub-paragraph (a) or (b), it may be deposited at or about the registered office in such a way that it is likely to come to the notice of a person attending at the office.

(4) If for any reason service at the registered office is not practicable, or the company has no registered office or is an unregistered company, the petition may be served on the company by leaving it at the company's last known principal place of business in such a way that it is likely to come to the attention of a person attending there, or by delivering it to the secretary or some director, manager or principal officer of the company, wherever that person may be found.

(5) In the case of an oversea company, service may be effected in any manner provided for by section 695 of the Companies Act.

(6) If for any reason it is impracticable to effect service as provided by paragraphs (2) to (5), the petition may be served in such other manner as the court may approve or direct.

(7) Application for leave of the court under paragraph (6) may be made *ex parte*, on affidavit stating what steps have been taken to comply with paragraphs (2) to (5), and the reasons why it is impracticable to effect service as there provided.

Proof of service

4.9.—(1) Service of the petition shall be proved by affidavit, specifying the manner of service. **[FORM 4.4] [FORM 4.5]**

(2) The affidavit shall have exhibited to it—

(a) a sealed copy of the petition, and

(b) if substituted service has been ordered, a sealed copy of the order;

and it shall be filed in court immediately after service.

Other persons to receive copies of petition

4.10.—(1) If to the petitioner's knowledge the company is in course of being wound up voluntarily, a copy of the petition shall be sent by him to the liquidator.

(2) If to the petitioner's knowledge an administrative receiver has been appointed in relation to the company, or an administration order is in force in relation to it, a copy of the petition shall be sent by him to the receiver or, as the case may be, the administrator.

(3) If to the petitioner's knowledge there is in force for the company a voluntary arrangement under Part I of the Act, a copy of the petition shall be sent by him to the supervisor of the voluntary arrangement.

(4) If the company is an authorised institution or former authorised institution within the meaning of the Banking Act 1987, a copy of the petition shall be sent by the petitioner to the Bank of England.

This does not apply if the petitioner is the Bank of England itself.

(5) A copy of the petition which is required by this Rule to be sent shall be despatched on the next business day after the day on which the petition is served on the company.

Advertisement of petition

4.11.—(1) Unless the court otherwise directs, the petition shall be advertised once in the Gazette. **[FORM 4.6]**

(2) The advertisement must be made to appear—

(a) if the petitioner is the company itself, not less than 7 business days before the day appointed for the hearing, and

(b) otherwise, not less than 7 business days after service of the petition on the company, nor less than 7 business days before the day so appointed.

(3) The court may, if compliance with paragraph (2) is not reasonably practicable, direct that advertisement of the petition be made to appear in a specified London morning newspaper, or other newspaper, instead of in the Gazette.

(4) The advertisement of the petition must state—

(a) the name of the company and the address of its registered office, or—

(i) in the case of an unregistered company, the address of its principal place of business;

(ii) in the case of an oversea company, the address at which service of the petition was effected;

(b) the name and address of the petitioner;

(c) where the petitioner is the company itself, the address of its registered office or, in the case of an unregistered company, of its principal place of business;

(d) the date on which the petition was presented;

(e) the venue fixed for the hearing of the petition;

(f) the name and address of the petitioner's solicitor (if any); and

(g) that any person intending to appear at the hearing (whether to support or oppose the petition) must give notice of his intention in accordance with Rule 4.16.

(5) If the petition is not duly advertised in accordance with this Rule, the court may dismiss it.

Verification of petition

4.12.—(1) The petition shall be verified by an affidavit that the statements in the petition are true, or are true to the best of the deponent's knowledge, information and belief. **[FORM 4.2] [FORM 4.3]**

(2) If the petition is in respect of debts due to different creditors, the debts to each creditor must be separately verified.

(3) The petition shall be exhibited to the affidavit verifying it.

(4) The affidavit shall be made—

(a) by the petitioner (or if there are two or more petitioners, any one of them), or

(b) by some person such as a director, company secretary or similar company officer, or a solicitor, who has been concerned in the matters giving rise to the presentation of the petition, or

(c) by some responsible person who is duly authorised to make the affidavit and has the requisite knowledge of those matters.

(5) Where the deponent is not the petitioner himself, or one of the petitioners, he must in the affidavit identify himself and state—

(a) the capacity in which, and the authority by which, he makes it, and

(b) the means of his knowledge of the matters sworn to in the affidavit.

(6) The affidavit is prima facie evidence of the statements in the petition to which it relates.

(7) An affidavit verifying more than one petition shall include in its title the names of the companies to which it relates and shall set out, in respect of each company, the statements relied on by the petitioner; and a clear and legible photocopy of the affidavit shall be filed with each petition which it verifies.

Persons entitled to copy of petition

4.13. Every director, contributory or creditor of the company is entitled to be furnished by the solicitor for the petitioner (or by the petitioner himself, if acting in person) with a copy of the petition within 2 days after requiring it, on payment of the appropriate fee.

Certificate of compliance

4.14.—(1) The petitioner or his solicitor shall, at least 5 days before the hearing of the petition, file in court a certificate of compliance with the Rules relating to service and advertisement. **[FORM 4.7]**

(2) The certificate shall show—

(a) the date of presentation of the petition,

(b) the date fixed for the hearing, and

(c) the date or dates on which the petition was served and advertised in compliance with the Rules.

A copy of the advertisement of the petition shall be filed in court with the certificate.

(3) Non-compliance with this Rule is a ground on which the court may, if it thinks fit, dismiss the petition.

Leave for petitioner to withdraw

4.15. If at least 5 days before the hearing the petitioner, on an *ex parte* application, satisfies the court that—

(a) the petition has not been advertised, and

(b) no notices (whether in support or in opposition) have been received by him with reference to the petition, and

(c) the company consents to an order being made under this Rule,

the court may order that the petitioner has leave to withdraw the petition on such terms as to costs as the parties may agree. **[FORM 4.8]**

Notice of appearance

4.16.—(1) Every person who attends to appear on the hearing of the petition shall give to the petitioner notice of his intention in accordance with this Rule. **[FORM 4.9]**

(2) The notice shall specify—

(a) the name and address of the person giving it, and any telephone number and reference which may be required for communication with him or with any other person (to be also specified in the notice) authorised to speak or act on his behalf;

(b) whether his intention is to support or oppose the petition; and

(c) the amount and nature of his debt.

(3) The notice shall be sent to the petitioner at the address shown for him in the court records, or in the advertisement of the petition required by Rule 4.11; or it may be sent to his solicitor.

(4) The notice shall be sent so as to reach the addressee not later than 16.00 hours on the business day before that which is appointed for the hearing (or, where the hearing has been adjourned, for the adjourned hearing).

(5) A person failing to comply with this Rule may appear on the hearing of the petition only with the leave of the court.

List of appearances

4.17.—(1) The petitioner shall prepare for the court a list of the persons (if any) who have given notice under Rule 4.16, specifying their names and addresses and (if known to him) their respective solicitors. **[FORM 4.10]**

(2) Against the name of each creditor in the list it shall be stated whether his intention is to support the petition, or to oppose it.

(3) On the day appointed for the hearing of the petition, a copy of the list shall be handed to the court before the commencement of the hearing.

(4) If any leave is given under Rule 4.16(5), the petitioner shall add to the list the same particulars in respect of the person to whom leave has been given.

Affidavit in opposition

4.18.—(1) If the company intends to oppose the petition, its affidavit in opposition shall be filed in court not less than 7 days before the date fixed for the hearing.

(2) A copy of the affidavit shall be sent by the company to the petitioner, forthwith after filing.

Substitution of creditor or contributory for petitioner

4.19.—(1) This Rule applies where a person petitions and is subsequently found not entitled to do so, or where the petitioner—

(a) fails to advertise his petition within the time prescribed by the Rules or such extended time as the court may allow, or

(b) consents to withdraw his petition, or to allow it to be dismissed, consents to an adjournment, or fails to appear in support of his petition when it is called on in court on the day originally fixed for the hearing, or on a day to which it is adjourned, or

(c) appears, but does not apply for an order in the terms of the prayer of his petition.

(2) The court may, on such terms as it thinks just, substitute as petitioner any creditor or contributory who in its opinion would have a right to present a petition, and who is desirous of prosecuting it.

(3) An order of the court under this Rule may, where a petitioner fails to advertise his petition within the time prescribed by these Rules, or consents to withdraw his petition, be made at any time.

Notice and settling of winding-up order

4.20.—(1) When a winding-up order has been made, the court shall forthwith give notice of the fact to the official receiver. **[FORM 4.11] [FORM 4.12] [FORM 4.13]**

(2) The petitioner and every other person who has appeared on the hearing of the petition shall, not later than the business day following that on which the order is made, leave at the court all the documents required for enabling the order to be completed forthwith.

(3) It is not necessary for the court to appoint a venue for any person to attend to settle the order, unless in any particular case the special circumstances make an appointment necessary.

Transmission and advertisement of order

4.21.—(1) When the winding-up order has been made, 3 copies of it, sealed with the seal of the court, shall be sent forthwith by the court to the official receiver.

(2) The official receiver shall cause a sealed copy of the order to be served on the company by prepaid letter addressed to it at its registered office (if any) or, if there is no registered office, at its principal or last known principal place of business.

Alternatively, the order may be served on such other person or persons, or in such other manner, as the court directs.

(3) The official receiver shall forward to the registrar of companies the copy of the order which by section 130(1) is directed to be so forwarded by the company.

(4) The official receiver shall forthwith—

(a) cause the order to be gazetted, and

(b) advertise the order in such local newspaper as the official receiver may select.

Expenses of voluntary arrangement

4.21A. Where a winding-up order is made and there is at the time of the presentation of the petition in force for the company a voluntary arrangement under Part I of the Act, any expenses properly incurred as expenses of the administration of the arrangement in question shall be a first charge on the company's assets.

CHAPTER 4: PETITION BY CONTRIBUTORIES (NO CVL APPLICATION)

Presentation and service of petition

4.22.—(1) The petition shall specify the grounds on which it is presented and shall be filed in court with one copy for service under this Rule. **[FORM 4.14]**

(1A) No petition shall be filed unless there is produced with it the receipt for the deposit payable on presentation.

(2) The court shall fix a hearing for a day ("the return day") on which, unless the court otherwise directs, the petitioner and the company shall attend before the registrar in chambers for directions to be given in relation to the procedure on the petition.

(3) On fixing the return day, the court shall return to the petitioner a sealed copy of the petition for service, endorsed with the return day and time of hearing.

(4) The petitioner shall, at least 14 days before the return day, serve a sealed copy of the petition on the company.

NOTE: See Form 4.14 in Appendix 4.

Return of petition

4.23.—(1) On the return day, or at any time after it, the court shall give such directions as it thinks appropriate with respect to the following matters—

(a) service of the petition, whether in connection with the venue for a further hearing, or for any other purpose;

(b) whether particulars of claim and defence are to be delivered, and generally as to the procedure on the petition;

(c) whether, and if so by what means, the petition is to be advertised;

(d) the manner in which any evidence is to be adduced at any hearing before the judge and in particular (but without prejudice to the generality of the above) as to—

(i) the taking of evidence wholly or in part by affidavit or orally;
(ii) the cross-examination of any deponents to affidavits;
(iii) the matters to be dealt with in evidence;
(e) any other matter affecting the procedure on the petition or in connection with the hearing and disposal of the petition.

(2) In giving directions under paragraph (1)(a), the court shall have regard to whether any of the persons specified in Rule 4.10 should be served with a copy of the petition.

Application of Rules in Chapter 3

4.24. The following Rules in Chapter 3 apply, with the necessary modifications—
Rule 4.16 (notice of appearance);
Rule 4.17 (list of appearances);
Rule 4.20 (notice and settling of winding-up order);
Rule 4.21 (transmission and advertisement of order); and
Rule 4.21A (expenses of voluntary arrangement).

...

PART 7: COURT PROCEDURE AND PRACTICE

CHAPTER 1: APPLICATIONS

Preliminary

7.1. This Chapter applies to any application made to the court under the Act or Rules except a petition for—
(a) an administration order under Part II,
(b) a winding-up order under Part IV, or
(c) a bankruptcy order under Part IX
of the Act.

Interpretation

7.2.—(1) In this Chapter, except in so far as the context otherwise requires—
"originating application" means an application to the court which is not an application in pending proceedings before the court; and **[FORM 7.1]**
"ordinary application" means any other application to the court. **[FORM 7.2]**

(2) Every application shall be in the form appropriate to the application concerned.

Form and contents of application

7.3.—(1) Each application shall be in writing and shall state—
(a) the names of the parties;
(b) the nature of the relief or order applied for or the directions sought from the court;
(c) the names and addresses of the persons (if any) on whom it is intended to serve the application or that no person is intended to be served;
(d) where the Act or Rules require that notice of the application is to be given to specified persons, the names and addresses of all those persons (so far as known to the applicant); and
(e) the applicant's address for service.

(2) An originating application shall set out the grounds on which the applicant claims to be entitled to the relief or order sought.

(3) The application must be signed by the applicant if he is acting in person or, when he is not so acting, by or on behalf of his solicitor.

Filing and service of application

7.4.—(1) The application shall be filed in court, accompanied by one copy and a number of additional copies equal to the number of persons who are to be served with the application.

(2) Subject as follows in this Rule and the next, or unless the Rule under which the application is brought provides otherwise, or the court otherwise orders, upon the presentation of the documents mentioned in paragraph (1) above, the court shall fix a venue for the application to be heard.

(3) Unless the court otherwise directs, the applicant shall serve a sealed copy of the application, endorsed with the venue for the hearing, on the respondent named in the application (or on each respondent if more than one).

(4) The court may give any of the following directions—

(a) that the application be served upon persons other than those specified by the relevant provision of the Act or Rules;

(b) that the giving of notice to any person may be dispensed with;

(c) that notice be given in some way other than that specified in paragraph (3).

(5) Unless the provision of the Act or Rules under which the application is made provides otherwise, and subject to the next paragraph, the application must be served at least 14 days before the date fixed for the hearing.

(6) Where the case is one of urgency, the court may (without prejudice to its general power to extend or abridge time limits)—

(a) hear the application immediately, either with or without notice to, or the attendance of, other parties, or

(b) authorise a shorter period of service than that provided for by paragraph (5);

and any such application may be heard on terms providing for the filing or service of documents, or the carrying out of other formalities, as the court thinks fit.

Other hearings ex parte

7.5.—(1) Where the relevant provisions of the Act or Rules do not require service of the application on, or notice of it to be given to, any person, the court may hear the application *ex parte*.

(2) Where the application is properly made *ex parte*, the court may hear it forthwith, without fixing a venue as required by Rule 7.4(2).

(3) Alternatively, the court may fix a venue for the application to be heard, in which case Rule 7.4 applies (so far as relevant).

Hearing of application

7.6.—(1) Unless allowed or authorised to be made otherwise, every application before the registrar shall, and every application before the judge may, be heard in chambers.

(2) Unless either—

(a) the judge has given a general or special direction to the contrary, or

(b) it is not within the registrar's power to make the order required,

the jurisdiction of the court to hear and determine the application may be exercised by the registrar, and the application shall be made to the registrar in the first instance.

(3) Where the application is made to the registrar he may refer to the judge any matter which he thinks should properly be decided by the judge, and the judge may either dispose of the matter or refer it back to the registrar with such directions as he thinks fit.

(4) Nothing in this Rule precludes an application being made directly to the judge in a proper case.

Use of affidavit evidence

7.7.—(1) In any proceedings evidence may be given by affidavit unless by any provision of the Rules it is otherwise provided or the court otherwise directs; but the court may, on the application of any party, order the attendance for cross-examination of the person making the affidavit.

(2) Where, after such an order has been made, the person in question does not attend, his affidavit shall not be used in evidence without the leave of the court.

Filing and service of affidavits

7.8.—(1) Unless the provision of the Act or Rules under which the application is made provides otherwise, or the court otherwise allows—

(a) if the applicant intends to rely at the first hearing on affidavit evidence, he shall file the affidavit or affidavits (if more than one) in court and serve a copy or copies on the respondent, not less than 14 days before the date fixed for the hearing, and

(b) where a respondent to an application intends to oppose it and to rely for that purpose on affidavit evidence, he shall file the affidavit or affidavits (if more than one) in court and serve a copy or copies on the applicant, not less than 7 days before the date fixed for the hearing.

(2) Any affidavit may be sworn by the applicant or by the respondent or by some other person possessing direct knowledge of the subject matter of the application.

Use of reports

7.9.—(1) A report may be filed in court instead of an affidavit—

(a) in any case, by the official receiver (whether or not he is acting in any capacity mentioned in sub-paragraph (b)), or a deputy official receiver, or

(b) unless the application involves other parties or the court otherwise orders, by—

(i) an administrator, a liquidator or a trustee in bankruptcy,

(ii) a provisional liquidator or an interim receiver,

(iii) a special manager, or

(iv) an insolvency practitioner appointed under section 273(2).

(2) In any case where a report is filed instead of an affidavit, the report shall be treated for the purposes of Rule 7.8(1) and any hearing before the court as if it were an affidavit.

(3) Any report filed by the official receiver in accordance with the Act or the Rules is prima facie evidence of any matter contained in it.

Adjournment of hearing; directions

7.10.—(1) The court may adjourn the hearing of an application on such terms (if any) as it thinks fit.

(2) The court may at any time give such directions as it thinks fit as to—

(a) service or notice of the application on or to any person, whether in connection with the venue of a resumed hearing or for any other purpose;

(b) whether particulars of claim and defence are to be delivered and generally as to the procedure on the application;

(c) the manner in which any evidence is to be adduced at a resumed hearing and in particular (but without prejudice to the generality of this sub-paragraph) as to—

(i) the taking of evidence wholly or in part by affidavit or orally;

(ii) the cross-examination either before the judge or registrar on the hearing in court or in chambers, of any deponents to affidavits;

(iii) any report to be given by the official receiver or any person mentioned in Rule 7.9(1)(b);

(d) the matters to be dealt with in evidence.

CHAPTER 2: TRANSFER OF PROCEEDINGS BETWEEN COURTS

General power of transfer

7.11.—(1) Where winding-up or bankruptcy proceedings are pending in the High Court, the court may order them to be transferred to a specified county court.

(2) Where winding-up or bankruptcy proceedings are pending in a county court, the court may order them to be transferred either to the High Court or to another county court.

(3) In any case where proceedings are transferred to a county court, the transfer must be to a court which has jurisdiction to wind up companies or, as the case may be, jurisdiction in bankruptcy.

(4) Where winding-up or bankruptcy proceedings are pending in a county court, a judge of the High Court may order them to be transferred to that Court.

(5) A transfer of proceedings under this Rule may be ordered—

(a) by the court of its own motion, or

(b) on the application of the official receiver, or

(c) on the application of a person appearing to the court to have an interest in the proceedings.

(6) A transfer of proceedings under this Rule may be ordered notwithstanding that the proceedings commenced before the coming into force of the Rules.

Proceedings commenced in wrong court

7.12. Where winding-up or bankruptcy proceedings are commenced in a court which is, in relation to those proceedings, the wrong court, that court may—

(a) order the transfer of the proceedings to the court in which they ought to have been commenced;

(b) order that the proceedings be continued in the court in which they have been commenced; or

(c) order the proceedings to be struck out.

Applications for transfer

7.13.—(1) An application by the official receiver for proceedings to be transferred shall be made with a report by him—

(a) setting out the reasons for the transfer, and

(b) including a statement either that the petitioner consents to the transfer, or that he has been given at least 14 days' notice of the official receiver's application.

(2) If the court is satisfied from the official receiver's report that the proceedings can be conducted more conveniently in another court, the proceedings shall be transferred to that court.

(3) Where an application for the transfer of proceedings is made otherwise than by the official receiver, at least 14 days' notice of the application shall be given by the applicant—

(a) to the official receiver attached to the court in which the proceedings are pending, and

(b) to the official receiver attached to the court to which it is proposed that they should be transferred.

Procedure following order for transfer

7.14.—(1) Subject as follows, the court making an order under Rule 7.11 shall forthwith send to the transferee court a sealed copy of the order, and the file of the proceedings.

(2) On receipt of these, the transferee court shall forthwith send notice of the transfer to the official receivers attached to that court and the transferor court respectively.

(3) Paragraph (1) does not apply where the order is made by the High Court under Rule 7.11(4). In that case—

(a) the High Court shall send sealed copies of the order to the county court from which the proceedings are to be transferred, and to the official receivers attached to that court and the High Court respectively, and

(b) that county court shall send the file of the proceedings to the High Court.

(4) Following compliance with this Rule, if the official receiver attached to the court to which the proceedings are ordered to be transferred is not already, by virtue of directions given by the Secretary of State under section 399(6)(a), the official receiver in relation to those proceedings, he becomes, in relation to those proceedings, the official receiver in place of the official receiver attached to the other court concerned.

Consequential transfer of other proceedings

7.15.—(1) This Rule applies where—

(a) an order for the winding up of a company, or a bankruptcy order in the case of an individual has been made by the High Court, or

(b) in either such case, a provisional liquidator or (as the case may be) an interim receiver has been appointed, or

(c) winding-up or bankruptcy proceedings have been transferred to that Court from a county court.

(2) A judge of any Division of the High Court may, of his own motion, order the transfer to that Division of any such proceedings as are mentioned below and are pending against the company or individual concerned ("the insolvent") either in another Division of the High Court or in a court in England and Wales other than the High Court.

(3) Proceedings which may be so transferred are those brought by or against the insolvent for the purpose of enforcing a claim against the insolvent estate, or brought by a person other than the insolvent for the purpose of enforcing any such claim (including in either case proceedings of any description by a debenture-holder or mortgagee).

(4) Where proceedings are transferred under this Rule, the registrar may (subject to general or special directions of the judge) dispose of any matter arising in the proceedings which would, but for the transfer, have been disposed of in chambers or, in the case of proceedings transferred from a county court, by the registrar of that court.

CHAPTER 3: SHORTHAND WRITERS

Nomination and appointment of shorthand writers

7.16.—(1) In the High Court the judge and, in a county court, the registrar may in writing nominate one or more persons to be official shorthand writers to the court. **[FORM 7.3]**

(2) The court may, at any time in the course of insolvency proceedings, appoint a shorthand writer to take down the evidence of a person examined under section 133, 236, 290 or 366. **[FORM 7.4]**

(3) Where the official receiver applies to the court for an order appointing a shorthand writer, he shall name the person he proposes for appointment; and that appointment shall be made, unless the court otherwise orders.

Remuneration

7.17.—(1) The remuneration of a shorthand writer appointed in insolvency proceedings shall be paid by the party at whose instance the appointment was made, or out of the insolvent estate, or otherwise, as the court may direct.

(2) The remuneration payable shall be calculated in accordance with Schedule 3 to the Rules.

Cost of shorthand note

7.18 Where in insolvency proceedings the court appoints a shorthand writer on the application of the official receiver, in order that a written record may be taken of the evidence of a person to be examined, the cost of the written record is deemed an expense of the official receiver in the proceedings.

CHAPTER 4: ENFORCEMENT PROCEDURES

Enforcement of court orders

7.19.—(1) In any insolvency proceedings, orders of the court may be enforced in the same manner as a judgment to the same effect.

(2) Where an order in insolvency proceedings is made, or any process is issued, by a county court ("the primary court"), the order or process may be enforced, executed and dealt with by any other

county court ("the secondary court"), as if it had been made or issued for the enforcement of a judgment or order to the same effect made by the secondary court.

This applies whether or not the secondary court has jurisdiction to take insolvency proceedings.

Orders enforcing compliance with the Rules

7.20.—(1) The court may, on application by the competent person, make sure orders as it thinks necessary for the enforcement of obligations falling on any person in accordance with—

(a) section 22, 47 or 131 (duty to submit statement of affairs in administration, administrative receivership or winding up),

(b) section 143(2) (liquidator to furnish information, books, papers, etc.), or

(c) section 235 (duty of various persons to co-operate with office-holder).

(2) The competent person for this purpose is—

(a) under section 22, the administrator,

(b) under section 47, the administrative receiver,

(c) under section 131 or 143(2), the official receiver, and

(d) under section 235, the official receiver, the administrator, the administrative receiver, the liquidator or the provisional liquidator, as the case may be.

(3) An order of the court under this Rule may provide that all costs of and incidental to the application for it shall be borne by the person against whom the order is made.

Warrants (general provisions)

7.21.—(1) A warrant issued by the court under any provision of the Act shall be addressed to such officer of the High Court or of a county court (whether or not having jurisdiction in insolvency proceedings) as the warrant specifies, or to any constable.

(2) The persons referred to in sections 134(2), 236(5), 364(1), 365(3) and 366(3) (court's powers of enforcement) as the prescribed officer of the court are—

(a) in the case of the High Court, the tipstaff and his assistants of the court, and

(b) in the case of a county court, the registrar and the bailiffs.

(3) In this Chapter references to property include books, papers and records.

Warrants under ss.134, 364

7.22. When a person is arrested under a warrant issued by the court under section 134 (officer of company failing to attend for public examination), or section 364 (arrest of debtor or bankrupt) **[FORM 7.6] [FORM 7.7]**

(a) the officer apprehending him shall give him into the custody of the governor of the prison named in the warrant, who shall keep him in custody until such time as the court otherwise orders and shall produce him before the court as it may from time to time direct; and

(b) any property in the arrested person's possession which may be seized shall be—

(i) lodged with, or otherwise dealt with as instructed by, whoever is specified in the warrant as authorised to receive it, or

(ii) kept by the officer seizing it pending the receipt of written orders from the court as to its disposal,

as may be directed by the court in the warrant.

Warrants under ss.236, 366

7.23.—(1) When a person is arrested under a warrant issued under section 236 (inquiry into insolvent company's dealings) or 366 (the equivalent in bankruptcy), the officer arresting him shall forthwith bring him before the court issuing the warrant in order that he may be examined. **[FORM 7.8]**

(2) If he cannot immediately be brought up for examination, the officer shall deliver him into the custody of the governor of the prison named in the warrant, who shall keep him in custody and produce him before the court as it may from time to time direct. **[FORM 7.9]**

(3) After arresting the person named in the warrant, the officer shall forthwith report to the court the arrest or delivery into custody (as the case may be) and apply to the court to fix a venue for the person's examination.

(4) The court shall appoint the earliest practicable time for the examination, and shall—

(a) direct the governor of the prison to produce the person for examination at the time and place appointed, and **[FORM 7.9]**

(b) forthwith give notice of the venue to the person who applied for the warrant.

(5) Any property in the arrested person's possession which may be seized shall be—

(a) lodged with, or otherwise dealt with as instructed by, whoever is specified in the warrant as authorised to receive it, or

(b) kept by the officer seizing it pending the receipt of written orders from the court as to its disposal,

as may be directed by the court.

Execution of warrants outside court's district

7.24.—(1) This Rule applies where a warrant for a person's arrest has been issued in insolvency proceedings by a county court ("the primary court") and is addressed to another county court ("the secondary court") for execution in its district. **[FORM 7.10]**

(2) The secondary court may send the warrant to the registrar of any other county court (whether or not having jurisdiction to take insolvency proceedings) in whose district the person to be arrested is or is believed to be, with a notice to the effect that the warrant is transmitted to that court under this Rule for execution in its district at the request of the primary court.

(3) The court receiving a warrant transmitted by the secondary court under this Rule shall apply its seal to the warrant, and secure that all such steps are taken for its execution as would be appropriate in the case of a warrant issued by itself.

Warrants under s.365

7.25.—(1) A warrant issued under section 365(3) (search of premises not belonging to the bankrupt) shall authorise any person executing it to seize any property of the bankrupt found as a result of the execution of the warrant.

(2) Any property seized under a warrant issued under section 365(2) or (3) shall be **[FORM 7.12] [FORM 7.13]**—

(a) lodged with, or otherwise dealt with as instructed by, whoever is specified in the warrant as authorised to receive it, or

(b) kept by the officer seizing it pending the receipt of written orders from the court as to its disposal,

as may be directed by the warrant.

CHAPTER 5: COURT RECORDS AND RETURNS

Title of proceedings

7.26.—(1) Every proceeding under Parts I to VII of the Act shall, with any necessary additions, be intituled "IN THE MATTER OF . . . (naming the company to which the proceedings relate) AND IN THE MATTER OF THE INSOLVENCY ACT 1986".

(2) Every proceeding under Parts IX to XI of the Act shall be intituled "IN BANKRUPTCY".

Court records

7.27. The court shall keep records of all insolvency proceedings, and shall cause to be entered in the records the taking of any step in the proceedings, and such decisions of the court in relation thereto, as the court thinks fit.

Inspection of records

7.28.—(1) Subject as follows, the court's records of insolvency proceedings shall be open to inspection by any person.

(2) If in the case of a person applying to inspect the records the registrar is not satisfied as to the propriety of the purpose for which inspection is required, he may refuse to allow it. The person may then apply forthwith and *ex parte* to the judge, who may refuse the inspection, or allow it on such terms as he thinks fit.

(3) The judge's decision under paragraph (2) is final.

Returns to Secretary of State

7.29.—(1) The court shall from time to time send to the Secretary of State the following particulars relating to winding-up and bankruptcy proceedings—

(a) the full title of the proceedings, including the number assigned to each case;

(b) where a winding-up or bankruptcy order has been made, the date of the order.

(2) The Secretary of State may, on the request of any person, furnish him with particulars sent by the court under this Rule.

File of court proceedings

7.30.—(1) In respect of all insolvency proceedings, the court shall open and maintain a file for each case; and (subject to directions of the registrar) all documents relating to such proceedings shall be placed on the relevant file.

(2) No proceedings shall be filed in the Central Office of the High Court.

Right to inspect the file

7.31.—(1) In the case of any insolvency proceedings, the following have the right, at all reasonable times, to inspect the court's file of the proceedings—

(a) the person who, in relation to those proceedings, is the responsible insolvency practitioner;

(b) any duly authorised officer of the Department; and

(c) any person stating himself in writing to be a creditor of the company to which, or the individual to whom, the proceedings relate.

(2) The same right of inspection is exercisable—

(a) in proceedings under Parts I to VII of the Act, by every person who is, or at any time has been, a director or officer of the company to which the proceedings relate, or who is a member of the company or a contributory in its winding up;

(b) in proceedings with respect to a voluntary arrangement proposed by a debtor under Part VIII of the Act, by the debtor;

(c) in bankruptcy proceedings, by—

(i) the bankrupt,

(ii) any person against whom, or by whom, a bankruptcy petition has been presented, and

(iii) any person who has been served, in accordance with Chapter 1 of Part 6 of the Rules, with a statutory demand.

(3) The right of inspection conferred as above on any person may be exercised on his behalf by a person properly authorised by him.

(4) Any person may, by special leave of the court, inspect the file.

(5) The right of inspection conferred by this Rule is not exercisable in the case of documents, or parts of documents, as to which the court directs (either generally or specially) that they are not to be made open to inspection without the court's leave.

An application for a direction of the court under this paragraph may be made by the official receiver, by the person who in relation to any proceedings is the responsible insolvency practitioner, or by any party appearing to the court to have an interest.

(6) If, for the purpose of powers conferred by the Act or the Rules, the Secretary of State, the Department or the official receiver requires to inspect the file of any insolvency proceedings, and requests the transmission of the file, the court shall comply with the request (unless the file is for the time being in use for the court's own purposes).

(7) Paragraphs (2) and (3) of Rule 7.28 apply in respect of the court's file of any proceedings as they apply in respect of court records.

Filing of Gazette notices and advertisements

7.32.—(1) In any court in which insolvency proceedings are pending, an officer of the court shall file a copy of every issue of the Gazette which contains an advertisement relating to those proceedings.

(2) Where there appears in a newspaper an advertisement relating to insolvency proceedings pending in any court, the person inserting the advertisement shall file a copy of it in that court.

The copy of the advertisement shall be accompanied by, or have endorsed on it, such particulars as are necessary to identify the proceedings and the date of the advertisement's appearance.

(3) An officer of any court in which insolvency proceedings are pending shall from time to time file a memorandum giving the dates of, and other particulars relating to, any notice published in the Gazette, and any newspaper advertisements, which relate to proceedings so pending.

The officer's memorandum is prima facie evidence that any notice or advertisement mentioned in it was duly inserted in the issue of the newspaper or the Gazette which is specified in the memorandum.

CHAPTER 6: COSTS AND TAXATION

Application of Rules of Supreme Court and County Court Rules

7.33. Subject to provision to inconsistent effect made as follows in this Chapter—

(a) Order 62 of the Rules of the Supreme Court applies to insolvency proceedings in the High Court, and

(b) Order 38 of the County Court Rules applies to such proceedings in a county court,

in either case, with any necessary modifications.

Requirement to tax costs

7.34.—(1) Subject as follows, where the costs, charges or expenses of any person are payable out of the insolvent estate, those costs, charges or expenses shall be taxed unless agreed between the responsible insolvency practitioner and the person entitled to payment, and in the absence of such agreement the responsible insolvency practitioner may require taxation by notice in writing requiring that person to deliver his bill of costs to the appropriate taxing officer for taxation; the appropriate taxing officer is that in relation to the court to which the insolvency proceedings are allocated or, where in relation to a company there is no such court, that in relation to any court having jurisdiction to wind up the company.

(2) If a liquidation or creditors' committee established in insolvency proceedings (except administrative receivership) resolves that any such costs, charges or expenses be taxed, the insolvency practitioner shall require taxation.

(3) Where the costs, charges or expenses of any person employed by an insolvency practitioner in insolvency proceedings are required to be taxed or fixed by order of the court, this does not preclude the insolvency practitioner from making payments on account to such person on the basis of an undertaking by that person to repay immediately any money which may, on taxation, prove to have been overpaid, with interest at the rate specified in section 17 of the Judgments Act 1838 on the date payment was made and for the period from the date of payment to that of repayment.

(4) In any proceedings before the court, including proceedings on a petition, the court may order costs to be taxed.

(5) Unless otherwise directed or authorised, the costs of a trustee in bankruptcy or a liquidator are to be allowed on the standard basis specified in Rule 12 of Order 62 of the Rules of the Supreme Court.

(6) This Rule applies additionally (with any necessary modifications) to winding-up and bankruptcy proceedings commenced before the coming into force of the Rules.

Procedure where taxation required

7.35.—(1) Before taxing the costs of any person employed in insolvency proceedings by a responsible insolvency practitioner, the taxing officer shall require a certificate of employment, which shall be endorsed on the bill and signed by the insolvency practitioner.

(2) The certificate shall include—

(a) the name and address of the person employed,

(b) details of the functions to be carried out under the employment, and

(c) a note of any special terms of remuneration which have been agreed.

(3) Every person whose costs are required to be taxed in insolvency proceedings shall, on being required in writing to do so by the insolvency practitioner, deliver his bill of costs to the taxing officer for taxation.

(4) If that person does not so deliver his bill within 3 months of the requirement under paragraph (3), or within such further time as the court, on application, may grant, the insolvency practitioner may deal with the insolvent estate without regard to any claim by that person, whose claim is forfeited.

(5) Where in any such case such a claim lies additionally against an insolvency practitioner in his personal capacity, that claim is also forfeited.

(6) Where costs have been incurred in insolvency proceedings in the High Court and those proceedings are subsequently transferred to a county court, all costs of those proceedings directed by the court or otherwise required to be taxed may nevertheless, on the application of the person who incurred the costs, be ordered to be taxed in the High Court.

Costs of sheriff

7.36.—(1) Where a sheriff—

(a) is required under section 184(2) or 346(2) to deliver up goods or money, or

(b) has under section 184(3) or 346(3) deducted costs from the proceeds of an execution or money paid to him,

the responsible insolvency practitioner may require in writing that the sheriff's bill of costs be taxed.

(2) Where such a requirement is made, Rule 7.35(4) applies.

(3) Where, in the case of a deduction under paragraph (1)(b), any amount is disallowed on taxation, the sheriff shall forthwith pay a sum equal to that amount to the insolvency practitioner for the benefit of the insolvent estate.

Petitions presented by insolvents

7.37.—(1) In any case where a petition is presented by a company or individual ("the insolvent") against himself, any solicitor acting for the insolvent shall in his bill of costs give credit for any sum or security received from the insolvent as a deposit on account of the costs and expenses to be incurred in respect of the filing and prosecution of the petition; and the deposit shall be noted by the taxing officer on the taxing certificate.

(2) Paragraph (3) applies where a petition is presented by a person other than the insolvent to whom the petition relates and before it is heard the insolvent presents a petition for the same order, and that order is made.

(3) Unless the court considers that the insolvent estate has benefitted by the insolvent's conduct, or that there are otherwise special circumstances justifying the allowance of costs, no costs shall be allowed to the insolvent or his solicitor out of the insolvent estate.

Costs paid otherwise than out of the insolvent estate

7.38. Where a bill of costs is taxed under an order of the court directing that the costs are to be paid otherwise than out of the insolvent estate, the taxing officer shall note on the certificate of taxation by whom, or the manner in which, the costs are to be paid.

Award of costs against official receiver or responsible insolvency practitioner

7.39. Without prejudice to any provision of the Act or Rules by virtue of which the official receiver is not in any event to be liable for costs and expenses, where the official receiver or a responsible insolvency practitioner is made a party to any proceedings on the application of another party to the proceedings, he shall not be personally liable for costs unless the court otherwise directs.

Applications for costs

7.40.—(1) This Rule applies where a party to, or person affected by, any proceedings in an insolvency—

(a) applies to the court for an order allowing his costs, or part of them, incidental to the proceedings, and

(b) that application is not made at the time of the proceedings.

(2) The person concerned shall serve a sealed copy of his application on the responsible insolvency practitioner, and, in a winding up by the court or bankruptcy, on the official receiver.

(3) The insolvency practitioner and, where appropriate, the official receiver may appear on the application.

(4) No costs of or incidental to the application shall be allowed to the applicant unless the court is satisfied that the application could not have been made at the time of the proceedings.

Costs and expenses of witnesses

7.41.—(1) Except as directed by the court, no allowance as a witness in any examination or other proceedings before the court shall be made to the bankrupt or an officer of the insolvent company to which the proceedings relate.

(2) A person presenting any petition in insolvency proceedings shall not be regarded as a witness on the hearing of the petition, but the taxing officer may allow his expenses of travelling and subsistence.

Certificate of taxation

7.42.—(1) A certificate of taxation of the taxing officer is final and conclusive as to all matters which have not been objected to in the manner provided for under the rules of the court.

(2) Where it is proved to the satisfaction of a taxing officer that a certificate of taxation has been lost or destroyed, he may issue a duplicate.

(3) "Certificate of taxation" includes, for the purposes of the Rules, an order of the registrar in a county court.

CHAPTER 7: PERSONS INCAPABLE OF MANAGING THEIR AFFAIRS

Introductory

7.43.—(1) The Rules in this Chapter apply where in insolvency proceedings it appears to the court that a person affected by the proceedings is one who is incapable of managing and administering his property and affairs either—

(a) by reason of mental disorder within the meaning of the Mental Health Act 1983, or

(b) due to physical affliction or disability.

(2) The person concerned is referred to as "the incapacitated person".

Appointment of another person to act

7.44.—(1) The court may appoint such person as it thinks fit to appear for, represent or act for the incapacitated person. **[FORM 7.19]**

(2) The appointment may be made either generally or for the purpose of any particular application or proceeding, or for the exercise of particular rights or powers which the incapacitated person might have exercised but for his incapacity.

(3) The court may make the appointment either of its own motion or on application by—

(a) a person who has been appointed by a court in the United Kingdom or elsewhere to manage the affairs of, or to represent, the incapacitated person, or

(b) any relative or friend of the incapacitated person who appears to the court to be a proper person to make the application, or

(c) the official receiver, or

(d) the person who, in relation to the proceedings, is the responsible insolvency practitioner.

(4) Application under paragraph (3) may be made *ex parte*; but the court may require such notice of the application as it thinks necessary to be given to the person alleged to be incapacitated, or any other person, and may adjourn the hearing of the application to enable the notice to be given.

Affidavit in support of application

7.45.—(1) Except where made by the official receiver, an application under Rule 7.44(3) shall be supported by an affidavit of a registered medical practitioner as to the mental or physical condition of the incapacitated person.

(2) In the excepted case, a report made by the official receiver is sufficient.

Service of notices following appointment

7.46. Any notice served on, or sent to, a person appointed under Rule 7.44 has the same effect as if it had been served on, or given to, the incapacitated person.

CHAPTER 8: APPEALS IN INSOLVENCY PROCEEDINGS

Appeals and reviews of court orders (winding up)

7.47.—(1) Every court having jurisdiction under the Act to wind up companies may review, rescind or vary any order made by it in the exercise of that jurisdiction.

(2) An appeal from a decision made in the exercise of that jurisdiction by a county court or by a registrar of the High Court lies to a single judge of the High Court; and an appeal from a decision of that judge on such an appeal lies, with the leave of that judge or the Court of Appeal, to the Court of Appeal.

(3) A county court is not, in the exercise of its jurisdiction to wind up companies, subject to be restrained by the order of any other court, and no appeal lies from its decision in the exercise of that jurisdiction except as provided by this Rule.

(4) Any application for the rescission of a winding-up order shall be made within 7 days after the date on which the order was made.

Appeals in bankruptcy

7.48.—(1) In bankruptcy proceedings, an appeal lies at the instance of the Secretary of State from any order of the court made on an application for the rescission or annulment of a bankruptcy order, or for a bankrupt's discharge.

(2) In the case of an order made by a county court or by a registrar of the High Court, the appeal lies to a single judge of the High Court; and an appeal from a decision of that judge on such an appeal lies, with the leave of that judge or the Court of Appeal, to the Court of Appeal.

Procedure on appeal

7.49.—(1) Subject as follows, the procedure and practice of the Supreme Court relating to appeals to the Court of Appeal apply to appeals in insolvency proceedings.

(2) In relation to any appeal to a single judge of the High Court under section 375(2) (individual insolvency) or Rule 7.47(2) above (company insolvency), any reference in the Rules of the Supreme Court to the Court of Appeal is replaced by a reference to that judge and any reference to the registrar of civil appeals is replaced by a reference to the registrar of the High Court who deals with insolvency proceedings of the kind involved.

(3) In insolvency proceedings, the procedure under Order 59 of the Rules of the Supreme Court (appeal to the Court of Appeal) is by application, and not by summons.

Appeal against decision of Secretary of State or official receiver

7.50. An appeal under the Act or the Rules against a decision of the Secretary of State or the official receiver shall be brought within 28 days of the notification of the decision.

CHAPTER 9: GENERAL

Principal court rules and practice to apply

7.51. Except so far as inconsistent with the Insolvency Rules, the Rules of the Supreme Court and the practice of the High Court apply to insolvency proceedings in the High Court, and the County Court Rules and the practice of the county court apply to insolvency proceedings in a county court, in either case with any necessary modifications.

Right of audience

7.52.—(1) Official receivers and deputy official receivers have right of audience in insolvency proceedings, whether in the High Court or a county court.

(2) Subject as above, rights of audience in insolvency proceedings are the same as obtained before the coming into force of the Rules.

Right of attendance (company insolvency)

7.53.—(1) Subject as follows, in company insolvency proceedings any person stating himself in writing, in records kept by the court for that purpose, to be a creditor or member of the company or, where the company is being wound up, a contributory, is entitled, at his own cost, to attend in court or in chambers at any stage of the proceedings.

(2) Attendance may be by the person himself, or his solicitor.

(3) A person so entitled may request the court in writing to give him notice of any step in the proceedings; and, subject to his paving the costs involved and keeping the court informed as to his address, the court shall comply with the request.

(4) If the court is satisfied that the exercise by a person of his rights under this Rule has given rise to costs for the insolvent estate which would not otherwise have been incurred and ought not, in the circumstances, to fall on that estate, it may direct that the costs be paid by the person concerned, to an amount specified.

The person's rights under this Rule are in abeyance so long as those costs are not paid.

(5) The court may appoint one or more persons to represent the creditors, the members or the contributories of an insolvent company, or any class of them, to have the rights conferred by this Rule, instead of the rights being exercisable by any or all of them individually.

If two or more persons are appointed under this paragraph to represent the same interest, they must (if at all) instruct the same solicitor.

Insolvency practitioner's solicitor

7.54. Where in any proceedings the attendance of the responsible insolvency practitioner's solicitor is required, whether in court or in chambers, the insolvency practitioner himself need not attend, unless directed by the court.

Formal defects

7.55. No insolvency proceedings shall be invalidated by any formal defect or by any irregularity, unless the court before which objection is made considers that substantial injustice has been caused by the defect or irregularity, and that the injustice cannot be remedied by any order of the court.

Restriction on concurrent proceedings and remedies

7.56. Where in insolvency proceedings the court makes an order staying any action, execution or other legal process against the property of a company, or against the property or person of an individual debtor or bankrupt, service of the order may be effected by sending a sealed copy of the order to whatever is the address for service of the plaintiff or other party having the carriage of the proceedings to be stayed.

Affidavits

7.57.—(1) Subject as follows, the rules and practice obtaining in the High Court with regard to affidavits, their form and contents, and the procedure governing their use, are to be taken as applicable in all insolvency proceedings in any court.

(2) In applying RSC Order 41 (which relates to affidavits generally), there are to be disregarded provisions which are inconsistent with, or necessarily excluded by, the following paragraphs of this Rule.

(3) Where in insolvency proceedings an affidavit is made by the official receiver or the responsible insolvency practitioner, the deponent shall state the capacity in which he makes it, the position which he holds, and the address at which he works.

(4) Notwithstanding RSC Order 41 Rule 8 (affidavit not to be sworn before party's own solicitor), a creditor's affidavit of debt may be sworn before his own solicitor.

(5) The official receiver, any deputy officer receiver, or any officer of the court duly authorised in that behalf, may take affidavits and declarations.

Security in court

7.58.—(1) Where security has to be given to the court (otherwise than in relation to costs), it may be given by guarantee, bond or the payment of money into court.

(2) A person proposing to give a bond as security shall give notice to the party in whose favour the security is required, and to the court, naming those who are to be sureties to the bond.

(3) The court shall forthwith give notice to both the parties concerned of a venue for the execution of the bond and the making of any objection to the sureties.

(4) The sureties shall make an affidavit of their sufficiency (unless dispensed with by the party in whose favour the security is required) and shall, if required by the court, attend the court to be cross-examined.

Payment into court

7.59. The Rules of the Supreme Court and the County Court Rules relating to payment into and out of court of money lodged in court as security for costs apply, in the High Court and a county court respectively, to money lodged in court under the Rules.

Discovery

7.60.—(1) Any party to insolvency proceedings may, with the leave of the court, administer interrogatories to, or obtain discovery from, any other party to those proceedings.

(2) Application under this Rule may be made *ex parte*.

Office copies of documents

7.61.—(1) Any person who has under the Rules the right to inspect the court file of insolvency proceedings may require the court to provide him with an office copy of any document from the file.

(2) A person's rights under this Rule may be exercised on his behalf by his solicitor.

(3) An office copy provided by the court under this Rule shall be in such form as the registrar thinks appropriate, and shall bear the court's seal.

. . .

PART 9: EXAMINATION OF PERSONS CONCERNED IN COMPANY AND INDIVIDUAL INSOLVENCY

Preliminary

9.1.—(1) The Rules in this Part relate to applications to the court for an order under—

(a) section 236 (inquiry into company's dealings when it is, or is alleged to be, insolvent), or **[FORM 9.1]**

(b) section 366 (inquiry in bankruptcy, with respect to the bankrupt's dealings). **[FORM 9.1]**

(2) The following definitions apply—

(a) the person in respect of whom an order is applied for is "the respondent";

(b) "the applicable section" is section 236 or section 366, according to whether the affairs of a company or those of a bankrupt or (where the application under section 366 is made by virtue of section 368) a debtor are in question;

(c) the company or, as the case may be, the bankrupt or debtor concerned is "the insolvent".

Form and contents of application

9.2.—(1) The application shall be in writing, and be accompanied by a brief statement of the grounds on which it is made.

(2) The respondent must be sufficiently identified in the application.

(3) It shall be stated whether the application is for the respondent—

(a) to be ordered to appear before the court, or

(b) to answer interrogatories (if so, particulars to be given of the matters in respect of which answers are required), or

(c) to submit affidavits (if so, particulars to be given of the matters to which he is required to swear), or

(d) to produce books, papers or other records (if so, the items in question to be specified),

or for any two or more of those purposes.

(4) The application may be made *ex parte*.

Order for examination, etc.

9.3.—(1) The court may, whatever the purpose of the application, make any order which it has power to make under the applicable section.

(2) The court, if it orders the respondent to appear before it, shall specify a venue for his appearance, which shall be not less than 14 days from the date of the order.

(3) If he is ordered to submit affidavits, the order shall specify—

(a) the matters which are to be dealt with in his affidavits, and

(b) the time within which they are to be submitted to the court.

(4) If the order is to produce books, papers or other records, the time and manner of compliance shall be specified.

(5) The order must be served forthwith on the respondent; and it must be served personally, unless the court otherwise orders.

Procedure for examination

9.4.—(1) At any examination of the respondent, the applicant may attend in person, or be represented by a solicitor with or without counsel, and may put such questions to the respondent as the court may allow.

(2) Any other person who could have applied for an order under the applicable section in respect of the insolvent's affairs may, with the leave of the court and if the applicant does not object, attend the examination and put questions to the respondent (but only through the applicant).

(3) If the respondent is ordered to answer interrogatories, the court shall direct him as to the questions which he is required to answer, and as to whether his answers (if any) are to be made on affidavit.

(4) Where application has been made under the applicable section on information provided by a creditor of the insolvent, that creditor may, with the leave of the court and if the applicant does not object, attend the examination and put questions to the respondent (but only through the applicant).

(5) The respondent may at his own expense employ a solicitor with or without counsel, who may put to him such questions as the court may allow for the purpose of enabling him to explain or qualify any answers given by him, and may make representations on his behalf.

(6) There shall be made in writing such record of the examination as the court thinks proper. The record shall be read over either to or by the respondent and signed by him at a venue fixed by the court.

(7) The written record may, in any proceedings (whether under the Act or otherwise) be used as evidence against the respondent of any statement made by him in the course of his examination.

Record of examination

9.5.—(1) Unless the court otherwise directs, the written record of the respondent's examination, and any answer given by him to interrogatories, and any affidavits submitted by him in compliance with an order of the court under the applicable section, shall not be filed in court.

(2) The written record, answers and affidavits shall not be open to inspection, without an order of the court, by any person other than—

(a) the applicant for an order under the applicable section, or

(b) any person who could have applied for such an order in respect of the affairs of the same insolvent.

(3) Paragraph (2) applies also to so much of the court file as shows the grounds of the application for an order under the applicable section and to any copy of proposed interrogatories.

(4) The court may from time to time give directions as to the custody and inspection of any documents to which this Rule applies, and as to the furnishing of copies of, or extracts from, such documents.

Costs of proceedings under ss.236, 366

9.6.—(1) Where the court has ordered an examination of any person under the applicable section, and it appears to it that the examination was made necessary because information had been unjustifiably refused by the respondent, it may order that the costs of the examination be paid by him.

(2) Where the court makes an order against a person under—

(a) section 237(1) or 367(1) (to deliver up property in his possession which belongs to the insolvent), or

(b) section 237(2) or 367(2) (to pay any amount in discharge of a debt due to the insolvent),

the costs of the application for the order may be ordered by the court to be paid by the respondent.

(3) Subject to paragraphs (1) and (2) above, the applicant's costs shall, unless the court otherwise orders, be paid out of the insolvent estate.

(4) A person summoned to attend for examination under this Chapter shall be tendered a reasonable sum in respect of travelling expenses incurred in connection with his attendance. Other costs falling on him are at the court's discretion.

(5) Where the examination is on the application of the official receiver otherwise than in the capacity of liquidator or trustee, no order shall be made for the payment of costs by him.

PART 12: MISCELLANEOUS AND GENERAL

. . .

Forms for use in insolvency proceedings

12.7.—(1) The forms contained in Schedule 4 to the Rules shall be used in and in connection with, insolvency proceedings, whether in the High Court or a county court.

(2) The forms shall be used with such variations, if any, as the circumstances may require.

(3) Where any form contained in Schedule 4 is substantially the same as one used for a corresponding purpose under either—

(a) the law and practice obtaining before the coming into force of the Rules; or

(b) if the form was first required to be used after the coming into force of the Rules, the law and practice obtaining before the making of the requirement,

whichever shall be appropriate in any case, the matter may continue to be used (with the necessary modifications) until 1 March 1988.

1.2 COMPANIES (UNFAIR PREJUDICE APPLICATIONS) PROCEEDINGS RULES 1986, SI 1986 No. 2000

Made	*21 November 1986*
Laid before Parliament	*8 December 1986*
Coming into Force	*29 December 1986*

The Lord Chancellor, in the exercise of his powers under section 411 of the Insolvency Act 1986,[a] with the concurrence of the Secretary of State, and after consulting the committee existing for that purpose under section 413 of that Act, hereby makes the following Rules:—

Citation, commencement and interpretation

1.—(1) These Rules may be cited as the Companies (Unfair Prejudice Applications) Proceedings Rules 1986 and shall come into force on 29th December 1986.

(2) In these Rules "the Act" means the Companies Act 1985.[b]

Preliminary

2.—(1) These Rules apply in relation to petitions presented to the court on or after 29th December 1986 under Part XVII of the Act (protection of company's members against unfair prejudice) by a member of a company under section 459(1), by a person treated as a member under section 459(2) or by the Secretary of State under section 460.

(2) Except so far as inconsistent with the Act and these Rules, the Rules of the Supreme Court and the practice of the High Court apply to proceedings under Part XVII of the Act in the High

a. 1986 c.45.
b. 1985 c.6.

Court, and the Rules and practice of the County Court apply to such proceedings in a county court, with any necessary modifications.

Presentation of petition

3.—(1) The petition shall be in the form set out in Schedule to these Rules, with such variations, if any, as the circumstances may require.

(2) The petition shall specify the grounds on which it is presented and the nature of the relief which is sought by the petitioner, and shall be delivered to the court for filing with sufficient copies for service under Rule 4.

(3) The court shall fix a hearing for a day ("the return day") on which, unless the court otherwise directs, the petitioner and any respondent (including the company) shall attend before the registrar in chambers for directions to be given in relation to the procedure on the petition.

(4) On fixing the return day, the court shall return to the petitioner sealed copies of the petition for service, each endorsed with the return day and the time of hearing.

Service of petition

4.—(1) The petitioner shall, at least 14 days before the return day, serve a sealed copy of the petition on the company.

(2) In the case of a petition based upon section 459 of the Act, the petitioner shall also, at least 14 days before the return day, serve a sealed copy of the petition on every respondent named in the petition.

Return of petition

5. On the return day, or at any time after it, the court shall give such directions as it thinks appropriate with respect to the following matters—

(a) service of the petition on any person, whether in connection with the time, date and place of a further hearing, or for any other purpose;

(b) whether particulars of claim and defence are to be delivered, and generally as to the procedure on the petition;

(c) whether, and if so by what means, the petition is to be advertised;

(d) the manner in which any evidence is to be adduced at any hearing before the judge and in particular (but without prejudice to the generality of the above) as to—

  (i) the taking of evidence wholly or in part by affidavit or orally;

  (ii) the cross-examination of any deponents to affidavits;

  (iii) the matters to be dealt with in evidence;

(e) any other matter affecting the procedure on the petition or in connection with the hearing and disposal of the petition.

Settlement and advertisement of the order

6.—(1) When an order has been made by the court under Part XVII of the Act, the petitioner and every other person who has appeared on the hearing of the petition shall, not later than the business day following that on which the order is made, leave at the court all the documents required for enabling the order to be completed forthwith.

(2) It is not necessary for the court to appoint a time, date and place for any person to attend to settle the order, unless in any particular case the special circumstances make an appointment necessary.

(3) If the court considers that the order should be advertised, it shall give directions as to the manner and time of advertisement.

HAILSHAM OF ST MARYLEBONE C.

20 November 1986

I concur,

MICHAEL HOWARD
Parliamentary Under-Secretary of State
Department of Trade and Industry

21 November 1986

SCHEDULE

RULE 3: PETITION ON GROUND THAT MEMBERS UNFAIRLY PREJUDICED

(a) Insert title of court	To (a) The petition of (b)
(b) Insert full name(s) and address(es) of petitioner	
(c) Insert full name of company	1. (c) (hereinafter called "the company" was incorporated on (d) under the Companies Act(s) 19
(d) Insert date	2. The registered office of the company is at (e)
(e) Insert address of registered office	3. The nominal capital of the company is £ divided into shares of £ each. The amount of the capital paid up or credited as paid up is £ The petitioner(s) is/are the holders of shares of £ each.
(f) Delete as applicable	Such shares at the date of this petition (f) [are registered in the name(s) of the petitioner(s)] [have been transferred or transmitted to the petitioner(s) by operation of law].
	4. The principal objects for which the company was established are as follows: and other objects stated in the memorandum of association of the company.
(g) Set out the grounds on which the petition is presented	5. (g)

In these circumstances your petitioner submits that the affairs of the company are being conducted in a manner which is unfairly prejudicial to the interests of (f) [some part of the members (including your petitioner)] [your petitioner]
or
(f) [The act or omission] [the proposed act or omission] referred to in part 5 above (f) [is] [would be] unfairly prejudicial to the interests of (f) [some part of the members (including your petitioner)] [your petitioner].

(h) Here set out the nature of relief sought

The petitioner therefore prays as follows (h)
or

that such other order may be made as the court thinks fit.

Note
It is intended to serve this petition on:

Endorsement

This petition having been presented to the court on let all parties attend before the Registrar in Chambers on:
Date ....
Time ....
Place ....
for directions to be given
The Solicitor(s) for the petitioner is/are:
Name ....
Address ....
....
Tel. No. ....
Reference ....

(j) Delete if London Agents not instructed

(j) Whose London Agents are:
Name ....
Address ....
....
Tel. No. ....
Reference ....

EXPLANATORY NOTE

(This Note does not form part of the Rules.)

These Rules set out a new procedure governing petitions presented to the court in England and Wales under Part XVII of the Companies Act 1985 (which provides for applications to the court to grant relief against a company whose members are unfairly prejudiced). The Rules apply where the petition is presented on or after 29th December 1986. For petitions presented before that date the procedure under Part XVII will continue to be governed by the Companies (Winding-up) Rules 1949 (S.I. 1949/330).

The Rules contain a new form of petition in the Schedule. They also provide for a hearing before the registrar at an early stage in the proceedings. The registrar is given wide powers to direct that the petition proceed in the manner best suited to the particular petition, including powers to direct the service and advertisement of the petition and the manner in which any evidence is to be adduced at subsequent hearings.

APPENDIX 2

RULES OF THE SUPREME COURT, ORDER 102

Definitions

1. In this Order—

"the Act" means the Companies Act 1985;

"the companies court registrar" means any officer of the High Court who is a registrar within the meaning of any rules for the time being in force relating to the winding up of companies;

"the Court," without prejudice to Order 1, rule 4(2), includes the companies court registrar.

Applications to be made by originating summons

2.—(1) Except in the case of the application mentioned in rules 3 and 4 every application under the Act must, in accordance with Order 5, rule 3, be made by originating summons.

(2) An originating summons under this rule shall be in Form No. 10 in Appendix A, unless the application made by summons is—

(a) an application under section 427 of the Act for an order to make provision for all or any of the matters mentioned in subsection (3) of that section where an order sanctioning the compromise or arrangement to which the application relates has previously been made, or

(b) an application under section 713 of the Act for an order directing a company and any officer thereof to make good any such default as is mentioned in that section, or

(c) an application under section 242(3) of the Act for an order directing the directors of a company or any of them to make good any such default as is therein mentioned or,

(d) an application under section 216 of the Act for an order directing that any shares in a company shall be subject to the restrictions imposed by Part XV of the Act.

(3) An application under section 721 of the Act may be made by ex parte originating summons.

(4) An originating summons under this rule may be issued out of the office of the companies court registrar or any Chancery district registry, and Order 7, rule 5(2), shall not apply in relation to such a summons.

Applications to be made by originating motion

3.—(1) The following applications under the Act must be made by originating motion, namely, applications—

(a) under section 88(6) for an order extending the time for delivery to the registrar of companies of any documents required by that section to be delivered,

(b) under section 432 for an order declaring that the affairs of a company ought to be investigated by an inspector appointed by the Secretary of State,

(c) under section 436 for an inquiry into any such case as is therein mentioned,

(d) under section 456(1) for an order directing that any shares in or debentures of a company shall cease to be subject to restrictions imposed by Part XV,

(e) under section 456(4) for an order directing that any shares in or debentures of a company shall, on a sale, cease to be subject to restrictions imposed by Part XV,

(f) [*revoked by S.I. 1995 No. 2206, r. 46*],
(g) under section 359(1) for rectification of the register of members of a company and
(h) under section 217(5) for amendment of the register of interests in shares of a company,
(i) under section 245B(1) for an order declaring that the annual accounts of a company do not comply with the requirements of the Act and requiring the directors of the company to prepare revised accounts.

(2) The notice of the motion by which any such application is made may be issued out of the office of the companies court registrar or any Chancery district registry.

Applications to be made by petition

4.—(1) The following applications under the Act must be made by petition, namely, applications—

(a) under section 5 to cancel the alteration of a company's objects,
(b) under section 17 to cancel the alteration of a condition contained in a company's memorandum,
(c) under section 130 to confirm a reduction of the share premium account of a company,
(d) under section 136 to confirm a reduction of the share capital of a company,
(e) under section 127 to cancel any variation or abrogation of the rights attached to any class of shares in a company,
(f) under section 425 to sanction a compromise or arrangement between a company and its creditors or any class of them or between a company and its members or any class of them,
(g) under section 653 for an order restoring the name of a company to the register, where the application is made in conjunction with an application for the winding up of the company,
(h) under section 690 to cancel the alteration of the form of a company's constitution,
(i) under section 727 for relief from liability of an officer of a company or a person employed by a company as auditor,
(j) under section 54(1) to cancel a special resolution to which that section applies,
(k) under sections 157(2) or 176(1) to cancel a special resolution to which either of those sections applies, and
(l) under section 170 in relation to the reduction of capital redemption reserve.

(2) A petition by which any such application is made may be presented in the office of the companies court registrar or any Chancery district registry and Order 9, rule 3, shall not apply in relation to such a petition.

Assignment and entitlement of proceedings

5.—(1) All proceedings to which this Order relates shall be assigned to the Chancery Division.

(2) Every originating summons, notice of originating motion and petition by which any such proceedings are begun and all affidavits, notices and other documents in those proceedings must be entitled in the matter of the company in question and in the matter of the Companies Act 1985.

Summons for directions

6.—(1) After presentation of a petition by which any such application as is mentioned in rule 4 is made, the petitioner, except where his application is one of those mentioned in paragraph (2) must take out a summons for directions under this rule.

(2) The applications referred to in paragraph (1) are—

(a) an application under section 425 of the Act to sanction a compromise or arrangement unless there is included in the petition for such sanction an application for an order under section 427 of the Act;
(b) an application under section 653 of the Act for an order restoring the name of a company to the register;

(c) an application under section 54(1) of the Act for an order cancelling a special resolution to which that section applies; and

(d) an application under section 157(2) or 176(1) of the Act for an order cancelling a special resolution to which those sections apply.

(3) On the hearing of the summons the Court may by order give such directions as to the proceedings to be taken before the hearing of the petition as it thinks fit including, in particular, directions for the publication of notices and the making of any inquiry.

(4) Where the application made by the petition is to confirm a reduction of the share capital, the share premium account, or the capital redemption reserve, of a company, then, without prejudice to the generality of paragraph (3) the Court may give directions—

(a) for an inquiry to be made as to the debts of, and claims against, the company or as to any class or classes of such debts or claims;

(b) as to the proceedings to be taken for settling the list of creditors entitled to object to the reduction and fixing the date by reference to which the list is to be made;

and the power of the Court under section 136(6) of the Act to direct that section 136(3) to (5) thereof shall not apply as regards any class of creditors may be exercised on any hearing of the summons.

(5) Rules 7 to 12 shall have effect subject to any directions given by the Court under this rule.

Inquiry as to debts: company to make list of creditors

7.—(1) Where under rule 6 the Court orders such an inquiry as is mentioned in paragraph (4) thereof, the company in question must, within 7 days after the making of the order, file on the office of the companies court registrar an affidavit made by an officer of the company competent to make it verifying a list containing—

(a) the name and address of every creditor entitled to any debt or claim to which the inquiry extends,

(b) the amount due to each creditor in respect of such debt or claim or, in the case of a debt or claim which is subject to any contingency or sounds only in damages or for some other reason does not bear a certain value, a just estimate of the value thereof, and

(c) the total of those amounts and values.

(2) The deponent must state in the affidavit his belief that at the date fixed by the Court as the date by reference to which the list is to be made there is no debt or claim which, if that date were the commencement of the winding up of the company, would be admissible in proof against the company, other than the debts or claims set out in the list and any debts or claims to which the inquiry does not extend, and must also state his means of knowledge of the matters deposed to.

(3) The list must be left at the office mentioned in paragraph (1) not later than one day after the affidavit is filed.

Inspection of list of creditors

8.—(1) Copies of the list made under rule 7 with the omission, unless the Court otherwise directs, of the amount due to each creditor and the estimated value of any debt or claim to which any creditor is entitled, shall be kept at the registered office of the company and at the office of that company's solicitor and of that solicitor's London agent, if any.

(2) Any person shall be entitled during ordinary business hours, on payment of a fee of 5p to inspect the said list at any such office and to take extracts therefrom.

Notice to creditors

9. Within 7 days after filing the affidavit required by rule 7 the company must send by post to each creditor named in the list exhibited to the affidavit, at his last known address, a notice stating—

(a) the amount of the reduction sought to be confirmed,

(b) the effect of the order directing an inquiry as to debts and claims,

(c) the amount or value specified in the list as due or estimated to be due to that creditor, and

(d) the time fixed by the Court within which, if he claims to be entitled to a larger amount, he must send particulars of his debt or claim and the name and address of his solicitor, if any, to the company's solicitor.

Advertisement of petition and list of creditors

10. After filing the affidavit required by rule 7 the company must insert, in such newspapers and at such times as the Court directs, a notice stating—

(a) the date of presentation of the petition and the amount of the reduction thereby sought to be confirmed,

(b) the inquiry ordered by the Court under rule 6,

(c) the places where the list of creditors may be inspected in accordance with rule 9, and

(d) the time within which any creditor not named in the list who claims to be entitled to any debt or claim to which the inquiry extends must send his name and address, the name and address of his solicitor, if any, and particulars of his debt or claim to the company's solicitor.

Affidavit as to claims made by creditors

11. Within such time as the Court directs the company must file in the office of the companies court registrar an affidavit made by the company's solicitor and an officer of the company competent to make it—

(a) proving service of the notices mentioned in rule 9 and advertisement of the notice mentioned in rule 10,

(b) verifying a list containing the names and addresses of the persons (if any) who in pursuance of such notices sent in particulars of debts or claims, specifying the amount of each debt or claim,

(c) distinguishing in such list those debts or claims which are wholly, or as to any and what part thereof, admitted by the company, disputed by the company or alleged by the company to be outside the scope of the inquiry, and

(d) stating which of the persons named in the list made under rule 7, and which of the persons named in the list made under this rule, have been paid or consent to the reduction sought to be confirmed.

Adjudication of disputed claims

12. If the company contends that a person is not entitled to be entered in the list of creditors in respect of any debt or claim or in respect of the full amount claimed by him in respect of any debt or claim, then, unless the company is willing to secure payment of that debt or claim by appropriating the full amount of the debt or claim, the company must, if the Court so directs, send to that person by post at his last known address a notice requiring him—

(a) within such time as may be specified in the notice, being not less than 4 clear days after service thereof, to file an affidavit proving his debt or claim or, as the case may be, so much thereof as is not admitted by the company, and

(b) to attend the adjudication of his debt or claim at the place and time specified in the notice, being the time appointed by the Court for the adjudication of debts and claims.

Certifying lists of creditors entitled to object to reduction

13. The list of creditors entitled to object to such reduction as is mentioned in rule 6(4) as settled by the Court under section 136(4) of the Act, shall be certified and filed by the companies court registrar and his certificate shall—

(a) specify the debts or claims (if any) disallowed by the Court,

(b) distinguish the debts or claims (if any) the full amount of which is admitted by the company, the debts or claims (if any) the full amount of which, though not admitted by the company, the company is willing to appropriate, the debts or claims (if any) the amount of which has been fixed by adjudication of the Court under section 136(4) of the Act and other debts or claims;

(c) specify the total amount of the debts or claims payment of which has been secured by appropriation under the said section 136(4);

(d) show which creditors consent to the reduction and the total amount of their debts or claims;

(e) specify the creditors who sought to prove their debts or claims under rule 12 and state which of such debts or claims were allowed.

Evidence of consent of creditor

14. The consent of a creditor to such reduction as is mentioned in rule 6(4) may be proved in such manner as the Court thinks sufficient.

Time, etc., of hearing of petition for confirmation of reduction

15.—(1) A petition for the confirmation of any such reduction as is mentioned in rule 6(4) shall not, where the Court has directed an inquiry pursuant to that rule, be heard before the expiration of at least 8 clear days after the filing of the certificate mentioned in rule 13.

(2) Before the hearing of such a petition, a notice specifying the day appointed for the hearing must be published at such times and in such newspapers as the Court may direct.

Affidavits to be filed in district registry

16. Where an application to which this Order relates is proceeding in any Chancery district registry, all affidavits made in connection with the application must be filed in that registry.

APPENDIX 3

PRACTICE DIRECTIONS

3.1 CHANCERY DIVISION PRACTICE DIRECTIONS, NO. 6 COMPANIES (OTHER THAN INSOLVENCY)

Postal issue

The Court will issue any process by post subject to the following directions being complied with:

(i) The use of postal facilities is at the risk of the solicitor or party concerned who should have regard to any material time limits prescribed and should enclose all necessary papers.

(ii) Applications for the conduct of business by post must be made by a letter signed by or on behalf of the solicitor for a party or by the party if he is acting in person:

(a) specifying precisely what the court is being asked to do including whether or not Counsel's appointment is required;

(b) enclosing any requisite documents and fee. Cheques and postal orders must be made payable to HM Paymaster General;

(c) enclosing a DX or stamped addressed envelope for the return of any relevant documents.

(iii) The letter of application together with any requisite documents must be posted in a pre-paid envelope properly addressed to The Companies Court, Room TM2.09, Thomas More Building, Royal Courts of Justice, Strand, London, WC2A 2LL.

(iv) Applications will be treated as having been made at the date and time of the actual receipt of the requisite documents in the registrar's chambers.

(v) If an acknowledgment of the receipt of papers is required they must be accompanied by a list setting out the papers in question, sent with a stamped or DX addressed envelope. The Court will not accept responsibility for papers which are alleged to have been sent to it unless an acknowledgment is produced.

(vi) The documents required for the conduct of any business by post will include all those documents which would have been required had the business been conducted by personal attendance.

(vii) Any application by post which does not comply with the relevant rules or with this discretion will be rejected and, in any other case, the court may exercise its power to decline to deal with a postal application.

(viii) It is emphasised that any party applying for the issue of proceedings by post will be responsible for the service of all documents requiring to be served under the Rules in the same way as if the proceedings had been issued on personal attendance and that the costs of any adjournment occasioned by non-service of any necessary documents are likely to be awarded against the party responsible.

3.2 CHANCERY DIVISION PRACTICE DIRECTIONS, NO. 8 (EVIDENCE), PART A (AFFIDAVITS), PARA (III)

(iii) Swearing before commencement of proceedings

Affidavits will not be rejected because they have been sworn shortly before the proceedings started. The Court may nevertheless at any time direct the re-swearing of such an affidavit and will do so if the affidavit seeks to prove facts which have to be shown to be existing at the date of the commencement of the proceedings, for example that money is owing at that date, and the cause of action would not otherwise be established. In cases where the date of commencement is of no particular significance, for example in most applications for construction of documents or under the Trustee Act 1925 or the Variation of Trusts Act 1958, the Court will assume that state of affairs set out in the affidavit has continued until the date of commencement but it will be the duty of solicitors and litigants to draw the Court's attention to any relevant changes in the interim.

3.3 CHANCERY DIVISION PRACTICE DIRECTIONS, NO. 10 (INSOLVENCY), PART B (COMPANIES)

B. COMPANIES

(i) Advertisement of winding up petition

Copies of every advertisement published in connection with a winding up petition must be lodged with the Companies Court as soon as possible after publication and in any event not later than the day appointed by the registrar pursuant to r. 4.14 of the Insolvency Rules 1986. This direction applies even if the advertisement is defective in any way (*e.g.* is published at a date not in accordance with the Insolvency Rules, or omits or misprints some important words) or if the petitioner decides not to pursue the petition (*e.g.* on receiving payment).

(ii) Appearance out of time on a winding up petition

Rule 4.16(4) of the Insolvency Rules 1986 requires a person who intends to appear on the hearing of a winding up petition to send the prescribed notice so as to reach the petitioner of his solicitors not later than 4.00 p.m. on the business day before the hearing or the adjourned hearing, failing which he cannot appear without the leave of the Court. An application by a creditor or contributory to be added to the list out of time will in normal circumstances be granted as a matter of course, provided that the applicant undertakes not to seek an order for the payment of his costs appearing on the petition. When the petition is ultimately granted or dismissed, an applicant so added to the list may apply to be discharged from his undertaking.

(iii) Certificate of compliance—time for filing

In order to assist practitioners and the Court the time laid down by r. 4.14 of the Insolvency Rules 1986, for filing a certificate of compliance and a copy of the advertisement, is hereby extended to not later than 4.30 p.m. on the Friday preceding the day on which the petition is to be heard. Applications to file the certificate and the copy advertisement after 16.30 hours on the Friday will only be allowed if some good reason is shown for the delay.

(iv) Contributory's petitions and section 127 of the Insolvency Act 1986

(i) Practitioners' attention is drawn to the undesirability of including as a matter of course a prayer for winding up as an alternative to a s. 459 order. It should be included only if that is the relief which the practitioner prefers or if it is considered that it may be the only relief to which he is entitled.

(ii) Whenever a prayer for winding up is included in a contributory's petition, the petition shall include a statement whether the petitioner consents or objects to a s. 127 order in the standard form, and if he objects the affidavit in support shall contain a short statement of his reasons.

(iii) If the petitioner objects to a s. 127 order in the standard form but consents to such an order in a modified form, the petition shall set out the form of order to which he consents, and the affidavit in support shall contain a short statement of his reasons for seeking the modification.

(iv) If the petition contains a statement that the petitioner consents to a s. 127 order, whether in the standard or a modified form, but the petitioner changes his mind before the first hearing of the petition, he shall notify the respondents and may apply on notice to a Judge for an order directing that no s. 127 order or a modified order only (as the case may be) shall be made by the registrar, but validating dispositions made without notice of the order made by the Judge.

(v) If the petition contains a statement that the petitioner consents to a s. 127 order, whether in the standard or a modified form, the registrar shall without further enquiry make an order in such form at the first hearing unless an order to the contrary has been made by the Judge in the meantime.

(vi) If the petition contains a statement that the petitioner objects to a s. 127 order in the standard form, the company may apply (in the case of urgency *ex parte*) to the Judge for an order.

Section 127 Order: Standard Form

ORDER that notwithstanding the presentation of the said Petition

(1) payments made into or out of the bank accounts of the Company in the ordinary course of the business of the Company and

(2) dispositions of the property of the Company made in the ordinary course of its business for proper value between the date of presentation of the Petition and the date of judgement on the Petition or further order in the meantime shall not be void by virtue of the provisions of section 127 of the Insolvency Act 1986 in the event of an Order for the winding up of the Company being made on the said Petition.

(v) Errors in petitions

Applications should be made to the Chief Clerk for leave to amend errors in petitions which are discovered subsequent to a winding up order being made.

Where the error appears in the name of the company, the Chief Clerk, upon application, is authorised to make any necessary amendments to ensure that the winding up order is drawn with the correct name of the company inserted. If he is in any doubt, *e.g.* where he thinks there might be another company in existence which could be confused with the company to be wound up, he will refer the application to the registrar.

Where an error appears in the registered office of the company, the Official Receiver should proceed to wind up the company as if the correct registered office had appeared in the petition. If any director or member of the company claims that the company was unaware of the petition by reason of it having been served at the wrong registered office it will be open to them to apply to rescind the winding up order in the usual way. In such a case, the Official Receiver should not press on with the winding up until the matter is resolved.

Where it is discovered that the company had been struck off the Register of Companies prior to the winding up order being made, the matter must be restored to the list before the order is entered to enable an order for the restoration of the name to be made as well as the order to wind up.

(vi) Applications to the Judge, Registrar and Chief Clerk

(i) The following applications shall be made direct to the Judge and, unless otherwise ordered, shall be heard in open court:—

(a) Applications to commit any person to prison for contempt.
(b) Applications for urgent interlocutory relief (*e.g.* applications pursuant to s. 127 of the Insolvency Act 1996 prior to any winding up order being made).
(c) Applications to restrain the presentation or advertisement of a petition to wind up.
(d) Petitions for administration orders or an interim order upon such a Petition.
(e) Applications after an administration order has been made pursuant to s. 14(3) of the Insolvency Act 1986 (for directions) of s. 18(3) of the Insolvency Act 1986 (to vary or discharge the order).
(f) Petitions to discharge administration orders and to wind up.
(g) Applications pursuant to s. 5(3) of the Insolvency Act 1986 (to stay a winding up or discharge an administration order or for directions) where a voluntary arrangement has been approved.
(h) Appeals from a decision made by a county court or by a registrar of the High Court.
(i) Motions.

(ii) Subject to paragraph (iv) below all other applications shall be made to the registrar in the first instance who may give any necessary directions and may, in the exercise of his discretion, either hear and determine it himself or refer it to the Judge.

(iii) The following matters will also be heard in open court:—

(a) Petitions to wind up (whether opposed or unopposed). The registrar will sit in Court on a Wednesday each week of the term when he will hear all unopposed petitions and related applications. Solicitors properly robed have the right of audience before the registrar.

(aa) Petitions to confirm reduction of capital and/or share premium account and petitions to sanction schemes of arrangements. These petitions will be heard in court on a Wednesday each week after completion of the list of winding up petitions. The arrangements for the hearing of such petitions in the long vacation remains unchanged.

(b) Public examinations.

(c) All matters and applications heard by the Judge except those referred by the registrar to be heard in chambers or so directed by the Judge to be heard.

(iv) In accordance with directions given by the Lord Chancellor the registrar has authorised certain applications to be dealt with by the Chief Clerk of the Companies Court pursuant to r. 13.2(2) of the Insolvency Rules 1986. The applications are:—

(a) To extend or abridge time prescribed by the rules in connection with winding up (r. 4.3).

(b) For substituted service of winding up petitions (r. 4.8(6)).

(c) To withdraw petitions (r. 4.15).

(d) For the substitution of a petitioner (r. 4.19).

(e) For directions on a petition presented by a contributory (r. 4.22(2)).

(f) By the Official Receiver for limited disclosure of a statement of affairs (r. 4.35).

(g) By the Official Receiver for relief from duties imposed upon him by the rules (r. 4.47).

(h) By the Official Receiver for leave to give notice of a meeting by advertisement only (r. 4.59).

(j) By a liquidator for relief from the requirement to send out forms of proof of debt (r. 4.84).

(k) To expunge or reduce a proof of debt (r. 4.85).

(l) To appoint a liquidator in either a compulsory or a voluntary winding up (rr. 4.102 and 4.103).

(m) For leave to a liquidator to resign (r. 4.111).

(n) By a liquidator for leave to make a return of capital (r. 4.221).

(o) To transfer proceedings from the High Court to the county courts (r. 7.11).

(p) For leave to amend any originating application.

[*N.B.* In District Registries all such applications must be made to the District Judge.]

(vii) Orders, drawing up of

The Court will draft and engross all orders with the following exceptions:—

(a) orders by the registrar on the application of the Official Receiver or for which the Treasury Solicitor is responsible under the existing practice,

(b) orders by the registrar in relation to reductions of capital, share premium account or capital redemption reserve fund or in relation to schemes of arrangement and

(c) orders dismissing winding up petitions unless the order contains a direction for the taxation or payment of costs or unless any party requests that a particular order be drawn.

(viii) Postal issue

[*See App. 3.1, above.*]

(ix) Rescission of a winding up order

Any application for the rescission of a winding up order shall be made within seven days after the date on which the order was made (r. 747(4) of the Insolvency Rules 1986).

Applications will only be entertained if made (a) by a creditor, or (b) by a contributory, or (c) by the company jointly with a creditor or with a contributory. The application must be supported by an affidavit of assets and liabilities.

In the case of an unsuccessful application the costs of the petitioning creditor and of the supporting creditors will normally be ordered to be paid by the creditor or the contributory making or joining in the application. The reason for this is that if the costs of an unsuccessful application are made payable by the company, they fall unfairly on the general body of creditors.

Cases in which the making of the winding up order has not been opposed owing to some matter such as an error or misunderstanding in instructing counsel may, if the application is made promptly, still be dealt with on a statement by counsel of the circumstances; but apart from such cases, the Court will normally require any application to be supported by affidavit.

There is no need to issue a formal application as the petition is restored before the Court.

(x) Restraint of presentation of winding up petition

An application to restrain presentation of a winding up petition must be made by originating motion in the Companies Court.

(xi) Directors' disqualification

1. This Practice Direction is to be read in conjunction with the *Insolvent Companies (Disqualification of Unfit Directors) Proceedings Rules 1987* ("the Rules") and the *Chancery Guide*. The definitions in the Rules apply in this Practice Direction.

2. When the summons (which must be an originating summons) is issued, the applicant will be given a date for the first hearing of the summons. The Rules provide that this date is to be not less than 8 weeks from the date of issue of the summons. The Rules further provide that evidence in support of a summons shall be filed when the application is issued and that evidence in answer and in reply shall be filed within 28 days of service of the summons and 14 days from receipt of the evidence in answer respectively. This timetable may only be extended by consent or with the leave of the court. All evidence should be filed before the first hearing of the summons.

The first hearing of the summons

3. All interlocutory directions should be sought at the first hearing of the summons so that the application can be determined at the earliest possible date. The parties should take all such steps as they respectively can to avoid successive directions hearings.

4. If at the first hearing the registrar adjourns the case for further consideration under Rule 7(4), he will so far as possible give all the directions for trial including where Rule 7(4) applies a direction as to whether the matter is to be heard by a Judge or a registrar. This direction may at any time be varied by the Court either on application or of its own motion. If the Court varies the direction in the absence of all the parties, notice will be given to the parties.

Setting down for trial

5. (a) At the appropriate stage the registrar will direct the applicant to set the case down for trial within such period (usually 5 days) as he may order. The parties may not extend this period by agreement. The applicant must give notice to the respondent(s) when he has set the case down.
   (b) If the case is to be heard by a Judge, the case will be entered in the Judges' Companies List.
   (c) If the case is not set down for trial within the period specified by the registrar, it may be listed before the Court to show cause why it should not be struck out.

Fixing a date for trial

6. (a) Within 15 working days of setting down (or such other period as the Court may allow) the parties shall together attend:—

(i) if the case is to be heard by a registrar, at Room 405, Thomas More Building, Royal Courts of Justice

or

(ii) if the case is to be heard by a Judge, before the Chancery Clerk of the Lists

in either case to fix a date for trial. For this purpose they must produce to the Chief Clerk or the Chancery Clerk of the Lists a written estimate of the length of the trial signed by the advocates for all the parties.

(b) The parties may not by agreement extend the period for attendance to fix a trial date. In the event of non-compliance with paragraph (a) above, the Court will fix a date for trial and give notice of the date to the parties.

Estimates of length

7. (a) If a party does not provide an estimate of the length of trial to the Court when required to do so, the Court may act on the estimate of the other party.

(b) As stated in section 5.2 of the *Chancery Guide*, the parties must inform the Court immediately of any material change in an estimate.

Pre-trial review (PTR)

8. In all cases where the hearing is estimated to take 10 days or more and in any other case where the Court so directs a PTR will be held by a registrar or if the case is to be heard by a Judge by a Judge in Chambers. If the PTR is to be heard by a registrar, the date for the hearing of the PTR will be fixed at a hearing of the summons. If the PTR is to be heard by a Judge the applicant must issue a separate summons for a PTR, and it is the responsibility of the applicant to ensure that a hearing date for a PTR is obtained so that the PTR is held between eight and four weeks before the trial date. If (where the PTR is to be heard by a Judge) the applicant fails to issue a summons for a PTR, or to obtain a hearing date for the summons, the case may be listed by the Chancery Clerk of the Lists (on notice to the parties) for a PTR.

9. The provisions of section 3.10(3) to (7) of the *Chancery Guide* apply to PTRs in disqualification cases whether the PTR is to be heard by a Judge or a registrar.

The trial

10. Skeleton arguments should be prepared by all the parties in all but the simplest cases whether the case is to be heard by a registrar or a Judge. They should comply with the guidelines in Appendix 3 to the *Chancery Guide*.

11. The advocate for the applicant should also in all but the simplest cases provide:

(a) a chronology

(b) a *dramatis personae*

(c) in respect of each respondent, a list of the references to the relevant evidence for each matter relied upon as constituting unfitness.

12. The documents mentioned in paragraphs 10 and 11 above must be delivered to the Court not less that two clear days before the day fixed for the hearing. If the case is to be heard by a Judge but the name of the Judge is not known, or the Judge is a deputy judge, these documents must be delivered to the Chancery Clerk of the Lists. If the name of the Judge (other than a deputy judge) is known, these documents must be delivered to the Judge's clerk. If the case is to be heard by a registrar, these documents must be delivered to Room 405, Thomas More Building, Royal Courts of Justice. Copies must be provided to the other party so far as possible when they are delivered to the Court.

13. Section 5.3 of the *Chancery Guide* applies to bundles of documents for use at the trial.

Summary procedure

14. If parties decide to make an application under the procedure adopted in *Re Carecraft Construction Co Ltd* [1994] 1 W.L.R. 172 ("a *Carecraft*" application), they should inform the Court immediately and obtain a date for the hearing of the application.

15. Whenever a *Carecraft* application is made, the applicant must:
   (a) except in simple cases where the circumstances do not merit it or when the Court otherwise directs, submit a written statement containing in respect of each respondent any material facts which (for the purposes of the application) are either agreed or not opposed (by either party); and
   (b) specify in the written statement (or, if none, a separate document) the period of disqualification which the parties will invite the Court to order or the bracket (*i.e.* 2–5 years; 6–10 years; 11–15 years) into which they will submit that the case falls.

16. Paragraph 12 of the above applies to the documents mentioned in paragraph 15 above unless the Court otherwise directs.

Hearings outside London

17. Where application for a disqualification order is made by summons issued in the Chancery District Registries in Birmingham, Bristol, Cardiff, Leeds, Liverpool, Manchester or Newcastle this Practice Direction shall apply with the following modifications:
   (a) Upon the issue of the summons the Court shall endorse it with the date and time for the first hearing before a District Judge. The powers exercisable by a registrar under this Practice Direction shall be exercisable by a District Judge.
   (b) If the District Judge (either at the first hearing or at any adjourned hearing before him) directs that the summons is to be heard by a High Court Judge or by an authorised Circuit Judge he will direct that the case be entered forthwith in the list for hearing by that Judge and the Court will allocate (i) a date for the hearing of the trial by that Judge and (ii) unless the District Judge directs otherwise a date for the hearing of a PTR by the trial Judge.

18. The documents mentioned in paragraphs 10, 11, and 15 above must be delivered to the appropriate Court (at the address given below) not less than two clear days before the day fixed for the hearing. Copies must be provided to the other party so far as possible when they are delivered to the Court. Addresses for the delivery of documents are as follows:

Birmingham:
The Chancery Listing Officer, The District Registry of the Chancery Division of the High Court, 33 Bull Street, Birmingham B4 6DS.

Bristol:
The Chancery Listing Officer, The District Registry of the Chancery Division of the High Court, 3rd Floor, Greyfriars, Lewins Mead, Bristol BS1 2NR.

Cardiff:
The Chancery Listing Officer, The District Registry of the Chancery Division of the High Court, 1st Floor, 2 Park Street, Cardiff CF1 1NR.

Leeds:
The Chancery Listing Officer, The District Registry of the Chancery Division of the High Court, Leeds Combined Court Centre, The Court House, 1 Oxford Row Leeds LS1 3BG.

Liverpool and Manchester:
The Chancery Listing Officer, The District Registry of the Chancery Division of the High Court, Manchester Courts of Justice, Crown Square, Manchester M60 9DJ.

Newcastle:
The Chancery Listing Officer, The District Registry of the Chancery Division of the High Court, The Law Courts, Quayside, Newcastle upon Tyne NE1 3LA.

3.4 CHANCERY DIVISION PRACTICE DIRECTIONS, NO. 12 (LISTING), PART B (LISTING OF PARTICULAR BUSINESS), PARA. (III)

(iii) Companies Court

Applications and petitions adjourned by the registrar and motions which are presently heard by the Companies Judge on each Monday of a term shall continue to be listed by the Companies Court.

Any such applications, petitions, and motions which are estimated to exceed two hours shall be liable to be stood over to a date to be fixed by the Chancery Clerk of the Lists. Adjourned applications estimated to last at least three days shall be listed in like manner to actions set down in the Witness List part 1.

3.5 PRACTICE NOTE [1934] WN 142

Company—Compromise with creditors—Meetings of class of creditors—Companies Act, 1929 (19 & 20 Geo, c. 23), s. 153

In proceedings under s. 153 of the Companies Act 1929, for the sanction by the Court of a compromise or arrangement between a company and its creditors, or any class of them, his Lordship said that the responsibility for determining what creditors are to be summoned to any meeting, as constituting a class, is the applicant's and if the meetings are incorrectly convened or constituted, or an objection is taken to the presence of any particular creditors as having interests competing with the others, the objection must be taken on the hearing of the petition for sanction, and the applicant must take the risk of having it dismissed.

3.6 PRACTICE DIRECTION [1947] WN 116

Practice—Company—Reduction of capital—Writing off—Valuation of assets—Evidence—Affidavit by valuer

In any case of a reduction of capital, involving the writing off of share capital as lost or unrepresented by available assets, in which reliance is placed upon a valuation to prove the value of any particular asset, an affidavit by the valuer himself should, as a rule, be filed in which he deposes to the effect that the value shown by the valuation (which should be exhibited) is in his opinion fair and proper.

3.7 PRACTICE DIRECTION (COMPANIES COURT: INSOLVENCY) (NO. 3 OF 1986) [1987] 1 WLR 53

Company—Companies Court—Insolvency—Applications for hearing in open court—Directions for certain applications to be heard by Chief Clerk—Insolvency Act 1986 (c. 45), ss. 5(3), 14(3), 18(3), 127—Insolvency Rules 1986 (S.I. 1986 No. 1925)

1. As from 29 December 1986 the following applications shall be made direct to the judge and, unless otherwise ordered, shall be heard in open court: (i) applications to commit any person to prison for contempt; (ii) applications for urgent interlocutory relief (e.g. applications pursuant to section 127 of the Insolvency Act 1986 prior to any winding up order being made); (iii) applications to restrain the presentation or advertisement of a petition to wind up; (iv) petitions for administration orders or an interim order upon such a petition; (v) applications after an administration order had been made pursuant to section 14(3) of the Act (for directions) or section 18(3) of the Act (to vary or discharge the order); (vi) applications pursuant to section 5(3) of the Act (to stay a winding up or discharge an administration order or for directions) where a voluntary arrangement has been approved; (vii) appeals from a decision made by a county court or by a registrar of the High Court.

2. Subject to 4 below all other applications shall be made to the registrar in the first instance who may give any necessary directions and may, in the exercise of his discretion, either hear and determine it himself or refer it to the judge.

3. The following matters will also be heard in open court: (i) petitions to wind up (whether opposed or unopposed); (ii) public examinations; (iii) all matters and applications heard by the judge except those referred by the registrar to be heard in chambers or so directed by the judge to be heard.

4. In accordance with directions given by the Lord Chancellor the registrar has authorised certain applications to be dealt with by the Chief Clerk of the Companies Court pursuant to rule 13.2(2) of the Insolvency Rules 1986 (S.I. 1986 No. 1925). The applications are (a) to extend or abridge time prescribed by the Rules in connection with winding up (rule 4.3); (b) for substituted service of winding up petitions (rule 4.8(6)); (c) to withdraw petitions (rule 4.15); (d) for the substitution of a petitioner (rule 4.19); (e) for directions on a petition presented by a contributory (rule 4.22(2)); (f) by the official receiver for limited disclosure of a statement of affairs (rule 4.35); (g) by the official receiver for relief from duties imposed upon him by the Rules (rule 4.47); (h) by the official receiver for leave to give notice of a meeting by advertisement only (rule 4.59); (i) by a liquidator for relief from the requirement to send out forms or proof of debt (rule 4.74(4)); (j) to expunge or reduce a proof of debt (rule 4.85); (k) to appoint a liquidator in either a compulsory or a voluntary winding up (rules 4.102 and 4.103); (l) for leave to a liquidator to resign (rule 4.111); (m) by a liquidator for leave to make a return of capital (rule 4.221); (n) to transfer proceedings from the High Court to the county courts (rule 7.11); (o) for leave to amend any originating application.

5. The practice directions dated 15 October 1979, *Practice Direction (Companies Court: Chief Clerk)* [1979] 1 W.L.R. 1416; and 3 March 1982, *Practice Direction (Companies Court: Chief Clerk) (No. 2)* [1982] 1 W.L.R. 389 are hereby revoked.

By direction of the Vice-Chancellor.

10 December 1986

3.8 PRACTICE DIRECTION (COMPANIES COURT: CONTRIBUTORY'S PETITION) (NO. 1 OF 1990) [1990] 1 WLR 490

Company—Winding up—Petition—Prayer for relief—Petitioner to state whether or not he consents to order prohibiting disposition of company's assets—Alternative to winding up order not to be included as matter of practice—Companies Act 1985 (c. 6), s. 459—Insolvency Act 1986 (c. 45), s. 127

1. Practitioners' attention is drawn to the undesirability of including as a matter of course a prayer for winding up as an alternative to an order under section 459 of the Companies Act 1985. It should be included only if that is the relief which the petitioner prefers or if it is considered that it may be the only relief to which he is entitled.

2. Whenever a prayer for winding up is included in a contributory's petition, the petition shall include a statement whether the petitioner consents or objects to an order under section 127 of the Insolvency Act 1986 in the standard form, and if he objects the affidavit in support shall contain a short statement of his reasons.

3. If the petitioner objects to a section 127 order in the standard form but consents to such an order in a modified form, the petition shall set out the form of order to which he consents, and the affidavit in support shall contain a short statement of his reasons for seeking the modification.

4. If the petition contains a statement that the petitioner consents to a section 127 order, whether in the standard or a modified form, but the petitioner changes his mind before the first hearing of the petition, he shall notify the respondents and may apply on notice to a judge for an order directing that no section 127 order or a modified order only (as the case may be) shall be made by the registrar, but validating dispositions made without notice of the order made by the judge.

5. If the petition contains a statement that the petitioner consents to a section 127 order, whether in the standard or a modified form, the registrar shall without further inquiry make an order in such form at the first hearing unless an order to the contrary has been made by the judge in the meantime.

6. If the petition contains a statement that the petitioner objects to a section 127 order in the standard form, the company may apply (in cases of urgency ex parte) to the judge for an order.

Section 127 order: Standard form

"ORDER that notwithstanding the presentation of the said petition
(1) payments made into or out of the bank accounts of the company in the ordinary course of the business of the company and
(2) dispositions of the property of the company made in the ordinary course of its business for proper value
between the date of presentation of the petition and the date of judgment on the petition or further order in the meantime shall not be void by virtue of the provisions of section 127 of the Insolvency Act 1986 in the event of an order for the winding up of the company being made on the said petition."

By direction of the Vice-Chancellor.

22 February 1990

3.9 PRACTICE DIRECTION (CHANCERY DIVISION: FORMS) (NO. 2 OF 1992) [1992] 1 WLR 791

Practice—Chancery Division—Forms—Notices of motion and Companies Court summonses—No need to name judge—Chancery Division Practice Direction (14)(B)(i)

1. In future notices of motion (other than in the Patents Court) need not state the name of the judge before whom the motion will be moved. It will be sufficient for the notice to state "the Chancery motions judge." Similarly, it will be sufficient for Companies Court summonses returnable before a judge to state "the Companies Court judge." The names of those judges will appear in the daily cause list and also in the Chancery Division term list.

2. The following direction will now supersede practice direction (14)(B)(i) of the Chancery Division Practice Directions (see *The Supreme Court Practice 1991, Fourth Cumulative Supplement*, p. 215) relating to motions judges: "(i) A judge ('the motions judge') will be assigned to hear motions on each motion day."

By direction of the Vice-Chancellor.

R. D. Munrow
Chief Master

20 July 1992

3.10 PRACTICE STATEMENT (ADMINISTRATION ORDERS: REPORTS) [1994] 1 WLR 160

Practice Chancery Division—Insolvency—Application for administration order—Independent report in support—Disproportionate investigation and expense to be avoided—No report necessary in some straightforward cases—Insolvency Rules 1986 (S.I. 1986 No. 1925), r. 2.2

Sir Donald Nicholls, at the sitting of the court, handed down the following practice statement. Administration orders under Part 2 of the Insolvency Act 1986 are intended primarily to facilitate the rescue and rehabilitation of insolvent but potentially viable businesses. It is of the greatest importance that this aim should not be frustrated by expense, and that the costs of obtaining an administration order should not operate as a disincentive or put the process out of the reach of smaller companies.

Rule 2.2 of the Insolvency Rules 1986 provides that an application for an administration order may be supported by a report by an independent person to the effect that the appointment of an administrator for the company is expedient. It is the experience of the court that the contents of the rule 2.2 report are sometimes unnecessarily elaborate and detailed. Because a report of this character is thought to be necessary, the preliminary investigation will often have been unduly protracted and extensive and, hence, expensive.

The extent of the necessary investigation and the amount of material to be provided to the court must be a matter for the judgment of the person who prepares the report and will vary from case to case. However, in the normal case, what the court needs is a concise assessment of the company's situation and of the prospects of an administration order achieving one or more of the statutory purposes. The latter will normally include an explanation of the availability of any finance required during the administration.

Every endeavour should be made to avoid disproportionate investigation and expense. In some cases a brief investigation and report will be all that is required. Where the court has insufficient material on which to base its decision, but the proposed administrator is in court, he may offer to supplement the material by giving oral evidence. In such a case he should subsequently provide a supplemental report covering the matters on which oral evidence was given so that this can be placed on the court file.

In suitable cases the court may appoint an administrator but require him to report back to the court within a short period so that the court can consider whether to allow the administration to continue or to discharge the order. In some cases the court may require the administrator to hold a meeting of creditors before reporting back to the court, both within a relatively short period.

It is the experience of the judges who sit in the Companies Court that, in general, a rule 2.2 report is valuable as a safeguard in assisting the court to see whether the application has a sound basis. However, there may be straightforward cases in which such a report is not necessary because it would provide little assistance. Practitioners are reminded that the Rules do not require that a rule 2.2 report must be provided in every case.

This statement is made after consultation with the other judges of the Chancery Division.

3.11 PRACTICE DIRECTION (CHANCERY DIVISION: PROCEDURE AND CASE MANAGEMENT) [1995] 1 WLR 785

Practice—Chancery Division—Case management—Procedure—Chancery Guide to apply to litigation in Chancery Division

1. The provisions of the Chancery Guide shall apply to litigation in the Chancery Division of the High Court of Justice.

2. In the case of any inconsistency between the provisions of the Chancery Guide and the provisions of any previous direction (including *Practice Direction (Civil Litigation: Case Management)* [1995] 1 W.L.R. 508) the provisions of the Chancery Guide shall prevail.

3. The provisions of the Chancery Guide are subject to any subsequent practice direction that may be made.

SIR RICHARD SCOTT V.-C.

25 April 1995

Note. Copies of the Chancery Guide may be obtained from Room E01, Royal Courts of Justice, Strand, London, WC2A 2LL at a cost of £3 per copy.

3.12 PRACTICE DIRECTION (COMPANIES COURT: DIRECTORS DISQUALIFICATION) (NO. 2 OF 1995) [1996] 1 WLR 170

Company—Director—Disqualification—Procedure for disqualification application—Insolvent Companies (Disqualification of Unfit Directors) Proceedings Rules 1987 (S.I. 1987 No. 2023), r. 7(4)

1. This practice direction is to be read in conjunction with the Insolvent Companies (Disqualification of Unfit Directors) Proceedings Rules 1987 ("the Rules") and the *Chancery Guide*: see the *Third Cumulative Supplement to The Supreme Court Practice 1995*, pp. 143–176, paras. 874–899. The definitions in the Rules apply in this practice direction.

2. When the summons (which must be an originating summons) is issued, the applicant will be given a date for the first hearing of the summons. The Rules provide that this date is to be not less than eight weeks from the date of issue of the summons. The Rules further provide that evidence in support of a summons shall be filed when the application is issued and that evidence in answer and in reply shall be filed within 28 days of service of the summons and 14 days from receipt of the evidence in answer respectively. This timetable may only be extended by consent or with the leave of the court. All evidence should be filed before the first hearing of the summons.

The first hearing of the summons

3. All interlocutory directions should be sought at the first hearing of the summons so that the application can be determined at the earliest possible date. The parties should take all such steps as they respectively can to avoid successive directions hearings.

4. If at the first hearing the registrar adjourns the case for further consideration under rule 7(4), he will so far as possible give all the directions for trial including where rule 7(4) applies a direction as to whether the matter is to be heard by a judge or a registrar. This direction may at any time be varied by the court either on application or of its own motion. If the court varies the direction in the absence of all the parties, notice will be given to the parties.

Setting down for trial

5. (a) At the appropriate stage the registrar will direct the applicant to set the case down for trial within such period (usually five days) as he may order. The parties may not extend this period by agreement. The applicant must give notice to the respondent(s) when he has set the case down. (b) If the case is to be heard by a judge, the case will be entered in the judge's Companies List. (c) If the case is not set down for trial within the period specified by the registrar, it may be listed before the court to show cause why it should not be struck out.

Fixing a date for trial

6. (a) Within 15 working days of setting down (or such other period as the court may allow) the parties shall together attend: (i) if the case is to be heard by a registrar, at Room 405, Thomas More Building, Royal Courts of Justice or (ii) if the case is to be heard by a judge, before the Chancery Clerk of the Lists, in either case to fix a date for trial. For this purpose they must produce to the Chief Clerk or the Chancery Clerk of the Lists a written estimate of the length of the trial signed by the advocates for all the parties. (b) The parties may not by agreement extend the period for attendance to fix a trial date. In the event of non-compliance with paragraph (a) above, the court will fix a date for trial and give notice of the date to the parties.

Estimates of length

7. (a) If a party does not provide an estimate of the length of trial to the court when required to do so, the court may act on the estimate of the other party. (b) As stated in section 5.2 of the *Chancery Guide*, the parties must inform the court immediately of any material change in an estimate.

Pre-trial review ("P.T.R.")

8. In all cases where the hearing is estimated to take 10 days or more and in any other case where the court so directs a P.T.R. will be held by a registrar or, if the case is to be heard by a judge, by a judge in chambers. If the P.T.R. is to be heard by a registrar, the date for the hearing of the P.T.R. will be fixed at a hearing of the summons. If the P.T.R. is to be heard by a judge the applicant must issue a separate summons for a P.T.R., and it is the responsibility of the applicant to ensure that a hearing date for a P.T.R. is obtained so that the P.T.R. is held between eight and four weeks before the trial date. If (where the P.T.R. is to be heard by a judge) the applicant fails to issue a summons for a P.T.R., or to obtain a hearing date for the summons, the case may be listed by the Chancery Clerk of the Lists (on notice to the parties) for a P.T.R.

9. The provisions of section 3.10(3) to (7) of the *Chancery Guide* apply to P.T.R.s in disqualification cases whether the P.T.R. is to be heard by a judge or a registrar.

The trial

10. Skeleton arguments should be prepared by all the parties in all but the simplest cases whether the case is to be heard by a registrar or a judge. They should comply with the guidelines in Appendix 3 to the *Chancery Guide*.

11. The advocate for the applicant should also in all but the simplest cases provide: (a) a chronology, (b) a dramatis personae, (c) in respect of each respondent, a list of the references to the relevant evidence for each matter relied upon as constituting unfitness.

12. The documents mentioned in paragraphs 10 and 11 above must be delivered to the court not less than two clear days before the day fixed for the hearing. If the case is to be heard by a judge but the name of the judge is not known, or the judge is a deputy judge, these documents must be delivered to the Chancery Clerk of the Lists. If the name of the judge (other than a deputy judge) is known, these documents must be delivered to the judge's clerk. If the case is to be heard by a registrar, these documents must be delivered to Room 40, Thomas More Building, Royal Courts of Justice. Copies must be provided to the other party so far as possible when they are delivered to the court.

13. Section 5.3 of the *Chancery Guide* applies to bundles of documents for use at the trial.

Summary procedure

14. If parties decide to make an application under the procedure adopted in *In re Carecraft Construction Co. Ltd* [1994] 1 W.L.R. 172 ("a *Carecraft* application"), they should inform the court immediately and obtain a date for the hearing of the application.

15. Whenever a *Carecraft* application is made, the applicant must: (a) except in simple cases where the circumstances do not merit it or when the court otherwise directs, submit a written statement containing in respect of each respondent any material facts which (for the purposes of the application) are either agreed or not opposed (by either party); and (b) specify in the written statement (or, if none, a separate document) the period of disqualification which the parties will invite the court to order or the bracket (i.e. two to five years; six to ten years; 11 to 15 years) into which they will submit that case falls.

16. Paragraph 12 of the above applies to the documents mentioned in paragraph 15 above unless the court otherwise directs.

Hearings outside London

17. Where application for a disqualification order is made by summons issued in the Chancery district registries in Birmingham, Bristol, Cardiff, Leeds, Liverpool, Manchester or Newcastle this practice direction shall apply with the following modifications. (a) Upon the issue of the summons the court shall endorse it with the date and time for the first hearing before a district judge. The powers exercisable by a registrar under this practice direction shall be exercised by a district judge. (b) If the district judge (either at the first hearing or at any adjourned hearing before him) directs that the summons is to be heard by a High Court judge or by an authorised circuit judge he will direct that the case be entered forthwith in the list for hearing by that judge and the court will allocate (i)

a date for the hearing of the trial by that judge and (ii) unless the district judge directs otherwise a date for the hearing of a P.T.R. by the trial judge.

18. The documents mentioned in paragraphs 10, 11 and 15 above must be delivered to the appropriate court (at the address given below) not less than two clear days before the day fixed for the hearing. Copies must be provided to the other party so far as possible when they are delivered to the court. Addresses for the delivery of documents are as follows:

Birmingham: The Chancery Listing Officer, The District Registry of the Chancery Division of the High Court, 33, Bull Street, Birmingham B4 6DS.

Bristol: The Chancery Listing Officer, The District Registry of the Chancery Division of the High Court, 3rd Floor, Greyfriars, Lewins Mead, Bristol BS1 2NR.

Cardiff: The Chancery Listing Officer, The District Registry of the Chancery Division of the High Court, 1st Floor, 2, Park Street, Cardiff CF1 1NR.

Leeds: The Chancery Listing Officer, The District Registry of the Chancery Division of the High Court, Leeds Combined Court Centre, The Court House, 1, Oxford Row, Leeds LS1 3BG.

Liverpool and Manchester: The Chancery Listing Officer, The District Registry of the Chancery Division of the High Court, Manchester Courts of Justice, Crown Square, Manchester M60 9DJ.

Newcastle: The Chancery Listing Officer, The District Registry of the Chancery Division of the High Court, The Law Courts, Quayside, Newcastle upon Tyne NE1 3LA.

Commencement

19. This practice direction shall come into force on 1 January 1996.

SIR RICHARD SCOTT V.-C.

14 December 1995

3.13 PRACTICE DIRECTION (COMPANIES COURT: SCHEMES AND REDUCTIONS) (NO. 2 OF 1996) [1997] 1 WLR 1

Company—Companies Court—Schemes and reductions—Petitions to sanction schemes of arrangement to be heard by judge—Petitions to confirm reductions of capital to be heard by registrar—Practice in Long Vacation—Chancery Division Practice Directions, dirs. 6E, 10B(vi)(iii)(aa)

1. *Practice Direction (Chancery Division: 6) (Companies (Other than Insolvency))* is amended by deleting paragraph E (as amended) (see *The Supreme Court Practice 1997*, vol. 2, p. 173, para. 816) and substituting the following:

"*E Schemes of arrangement and reductions of capital: hearing*

(i) This paragraph E applies to (a) schemes of arrangement under sections 425 to 427A of the Companies Act 1985, whether made with creditors or members; (b) schemes for the transfer of the whole or part of the long-term business of an insurance company to which Schedule 2C to the Insurance Companies Act 1982 (as amended) applies, and (c) reductions of capital, share premium account and capital redemption reserve.

References in this paragraph E to 'schemes' are to schemes falling within (a) or (b) above, and references in this paragraph E to reductions are to reductions falling within (c) above.

(ii) Petitions to sanction schemes of arrangement will be heard by the Companies Court Judge.

(iii) Petitions to confirm reductions will be heard by the Companies Court Registrar unless otherwise ordered. The registrar will hear petitions to confirm reductions in open court on a Wednesday each week after completion of the list of winding up petitions.

(iv) Schemes and reductions in the Long Vacation.

The following requirements must be satisfied for a hearing to be fixed to sanction a scheme and/or confirm a reduction in the Long Vacation: (a) The application is one in which for financial, commercial or economic reasons a hearing before the end of the Long Vacation is desirable. This category will include cases of mergers and takeovers which arise in the summer and are likely to be affected by market fluctuations. (b) The application is one which could not with reasonable diligence have been made and prosecuted in time to be heard before the Long Vacation begins.

An informal application in chambers, to the court manager, accompanied by an advocate's certificate that requirements (a) and (b) are satisfied, must be made as soon as possible so that a suitable timetable may be settled, including a date for hearing.

In the case of reductions to be heard by the registrar, certain applications which do not fall within the above categories will be heard provided (i) that there is an urgent need for a hearing or (ii) that there is sufficient time available after the registrar has disposed of the urgent applications.

Applications to the registrar in chambers for orders convening meetings to consider schemes and for directions on reduction applications will continue to be heard during the Long Vacation. Provided notice is given to the court before the Long Vacation begins, a timetable will be fixed which will enable any necessary documents to be settled in chambers and enable the registrar to hear the application.

The vacation judge will be available to hear petitions to sanction schemes and any petitions to confirm reductions which require to be heard by a judge on one Wednesday in August and two Wednesdays in September on dates to be arranged and subsequently notified in the Long Vacation Notice which is printed in the Daily Cause List.

The vacation judge may also hear petitions to sanction schemes or confirm reductions on other days if he thinks fit."

2. *Practice Direction (Chancery Division: 10B) (Insolvency: Companies)*, set out in *The Supreme Court Practice 1997*, vol. 2, p. 183, para. 838, is amended by deleting paragraph (vi)(iii)(aa).

SIR RICHARD SCOTT V.-C.

27 November 1996

Explanatory Note. The principal effect of this practice direction is that petitions to sanction schemes will in future be heard by a judge. The Chancery judges consider that this change of practice is desirable. Among the considerations which they have taken into account is the fact that schemes often bind numerous persons who are not before the court. Arrangements have been made so that in term time petitions to sanction schemes will be listed on Mondays.

APPENDIX 4

INSOLVENCY RULES 1986 FORMS

Form 2.1

Rule 2.1

Petition for Administration Order

(TITLE)

(a) Insert title of court

To (a) ______________________________

____

(b) Insert full name(s) and address(es) of petitioner(s)

The petition of (b) ______________________________

____

____

(c) Delete if petition not presented by the company's directors

(c) [presented by the directors under section 9 of the Insolvency Act 1986].

(d) Insert full name of company subject to petition

(e) Insert date of incorporation

1. (d)______________________________

(hereinafter called "the company") was incorporated on (e) ____________ under the Companies Act 19 ____

(f) Insert address of registered office

2. The registered office of the company is at (f) ______________________________

____

____

(g) Insert amount of nominal capital and how it is divided

(h) Insert amount of capital paid up or credited as paid up

3. The nominal capital of the company is (g) £_____ divided into _____ shares of £_____ each. The mount of the capital paid up or credited as paid up is (h) £_____

4. The principal objects for which the company was established are as follows ______________________________

____

and other objects set forth in the memorandum of association thereof.

5. The petitioner(s) believe(s) that the company is or is likely to become unable to pay its debts and that an administration order would be likely to achieve

(j) Delete such as are inapplicable

(j)
(i) the survival of the company and the whole or some part of its undertaking as a going concern
(ii) the approval of a voluntary arrangement with its creditors under Part 1 of the Insolvency Act 1986
(iii) the sanctioning of a compromise or arrangement between the company and such persons as are mentioned in section 425 of the Companies Act 1985
(iv) a more advantageous realisation of the company's assets than would be effected on a winding up

for the reasons stated in the affidavit of   filed in support hereof.

Form 2.1 continued

Form 2.1 contd.

6. The petitioner(s) propose(s) that during the period for which the order is in force the affairs, business and property of the company be managed by

(k) Insert full name(s) and address(es) of proposed administrator(s)

(k) ____________________

____

____

who is (are) to the best of the petitioner's knowledge and belief qualified to act as (an) insolvency practitioner(s) in relation to the company. The petitioner(s) therefore pray(s) as follows:—

(i) Insert full name of company

(1) that the court make an administration order in relation to (l) ____________________

____

(m) Insert name(s) of proposed administrator(s)

(2) that (m) ____________________

be appointed to be the administrator(s) of the said company

(n) Insert details of any ancilliary orders sought

(3) (n)

or

(4) that such other order may be made in the premises as shall be just.

Note:
It is intended to serve this petition on ____________________

____

____

____

(o) Insert here name, address, telephone number and reference (if any) of a solicitor acting for the petitioner

This petition was issued by (o) ____________________

____

____

____________________ (solicitor for)

the petitioner(s) whose address for service is:

____

____

____

Rule 2.8 Form 2.3

Affidavit of Service of Petition for Administration Order

(TITLE)

(a) Insert full name, address and description of deponent

I (a) ______________________________

of ______________________________

____

Make oath and say as follows

1. That I did on ________ day the __________ day of ___________ 19 serve the above-named company with a copy of the petition duly sealed with the seal of the court and its supporting documents by leaving the same at the registered office of the said company at (b) ______________________________

(b) Insert the address stated in the petition to be the company's registered office

____

OR by posting the same on __________ day the ___________ day of ________________ 19 , by ordinary post first class mail in an envelope duly pre-paid and properly addressed to the said company at its registered office at (b)

____

____

2. That I did on _______ day the _____________ day of ________ 19 , serve (c) ________________ a person who has appointed or is [or may be] entitled to appoint an administrative receiver of the said company with a copy of the petition duly sealed with the seal of the court and its supporting documents by leaving the same at his proper address at (d) ______________________________

(c) Insert name

(d) Insert address where served

____

OR by posting the same on ___________ day the __________ day of ________________ 19 , by ordinary post first class mail in an envelope duly pre-paid and properly addressed to the said (c) ______________________________
at (d) ______________________________

____

____

3. That I did on _____________ day the ________________ day of 19 , serve (c) ____________________ the administrative receiver of the said company with a copy of the petition duly sealed with the seal of the court and its supporting documents by leaving the same at his proper address at (d) ______________________________

____

OR by posting the same on ____________ day the __________ day of ______________________ 19 , by ordinary post first class mail in an envelope duly pre-paid and properly addressed to the said (c) ______________________________
at (d) ______________________________

____

____

Form 2.3 continued

4. That I did on ______ day the ______________ day of ______________ 19 __, service (c) __________________ who has presented a petition to wind up the said company with a copy of the petition duly sealed with the seal of the court and its supporting documents by leaving the same at his proper address at (d) __________

____

____

OR by posting the same on ______________ day, the ____________ day of ____________________ 19___, by ordinary post first class mail in an envelope duly pre-paid and properly addressed to the said (c) __________________ at (d) ____

____

____

5. That I did on ______ day the ______________ day of ______________ 19 __, serve (c) ___________________ the provisional liquidator of the said company with a copy of the petition duly sealed with the seal of the court and its supporting documents by leaving the same at his proper address at (d) ________________

____

____

OR by posting the same on ______________ day the ____________ day of ____________________ 19___, by ordinary post first class mail in an envelope duly pre-paid and properly addressed to the said (c) __________________ at (d) ____

____

6. That I did on ______ day the ______________ day of ______________ 19 __, serve (c) __________________________ the person proposed to be the administrator of the said company with a copy of the petition duly sealed with the seal of the court and its supporting documents by leaving the same at his proper address at (d) ____

____

____

OR by posting the same on ______________ day the ____________ day of ____________________ 19___, by ordinary post first class mail in an envelope duly pre-paid and properly addressed to the said (c) __________________ at (d) ____

____

____

A sealed copy of the petition and its supporting documents are now produced and shown to me marked "A"

SWORN

Rule 2.9 Form 2.4

Administration Order

(TITLE)

(a) Insert name, and address of petitioner

UPON THE PETITION OF (a) ____________________

____

____

(b) Delete where company itself is petitioner OR insert status of petitioner ie director, creditor etc

(c) Insert details of any other parties (including the company) appearing and by whom represented

(b) (a   of the above named company hereinafter called "the company") presented to the court on ____________________ 19 ____
And upon hearing counsel for the petitioner
and for (c) ____________________

____

____

____

and upon reading the evidence

____

____

____

____

____

____

(d) Set out the purpose(s) which the order is likely to achieve

IT IS ORDERED that during the period for which this order is in force the affairs, business and property of the company be managed by the administrator hereinafter appointed pursuant to the provisions of section 8 of the Insolvency Act 1986 for the following purpose(s) (d) ____________________

____

____

____

____

(e) Insert full name(s) and address(es) of administrator(s)

AND it is ordered that (e) ____________________

____

____

be appointed administrator(s) of the company

Form 2.4 continued

AND it is ordered that

(f) Insert particulars of any further order made by the court

(f) ______________________________

____

____

And it is ordered that the costs of the said petition

(i) Insert terms of order for costs

(g) ______________________________

____

____

Dated

Form 2.4A

Rule 2.10

Notice to Administrator of Administration Order

(TITLE)

(a) Insert name and address of administrator

To: (a)

Order pronounced this ________________ day of ____________ 19 ____ by Mr

for an administration order against the under-named company under section 8 of the Insolvency Act 1986.

Name of company:

Registered office of company:

(b) Insert full name, address, telephone number and reference (if any)

Petitioner: (b)

Petitioner's solicitors: (b)

Date of presentation of petition:

Form 2.5

Rule 2.10

Notice of Administration Order (for newspaper or London Gazette)

(TITLE)

Registered number ____________________

Nature of business ____________________

(a) Insert the number of the trade classification listed overleaf which most closely relates to the business of the company

Trade classification (a) ____________________

(b) Insert date

Administration order made (b) ____________________ 19___

____

Administrator/Joint administrators (office holder no(s))

Form 2.5 continued

TRADE CLASSIFICATION

NOTE: This page is *not* part of the advertisement

DIVISION 0

01 AGRICULTURE
02 FORESTRY AND FISHING

DIVISION 1

03 MINING AND ENERGY INDUSTRIES

DIVISION 2

MANUFACTURING INDUSTRIES:—
04 MANUFACTURE OF FOOD, DRINK AND TOBACCO
05 MANUFACTURE OF CHEMICALS
06 METAL MANUFACTURE
07 ENGINEERING AND ALLIED INDUSTRIES
08 TEXTILES AND CLOTHING MANUFACTURE
09 MANUFACTURE OF TIMBER AND FURNITURE
10 PAPER, PRINTING AND PUBLISHING
11 OTHER MANUFACTURE

DIVISION 3

WHOLESALE DISTRIBUTION:—
12 WHOLESALE OF FOOD AND DRINK
13 WHOLESALE OF TEXTILES AND CLOTHING
14 MOTOR VEHICLE WHOLESALERS
15 OTHER WHOLESALE

DIVISION 4

RETAILING:—
16 RETAIL OF FOOD, DRINK AND TOBACCO
17 RETAIL OF TEXTILES AND CLOTHING
18 RETAIL OF BOOKS, PAPERS ETC.
19 MOTOR VEHICLES AND PETROL SALES
20 RETAIL OF FURNITURE
21 RETAIL OF ELECTRICAL GOODS
22 OTHER RETAIL

DIVISION 5

CONSTRUCTION:—
(SIC Division 5)
23 GENERAL CONSTRUCTION AND DEMOLITION
24 HOME IMPROVEMENTS
25 DECORATING AND SMALLWORKS
26 BUILDING REPAIRS
27 ELECTRICAL AND PLUMBING

DIVISION 6

TRANSPORT AND COMMUNICATIONS:—
28 ROAD TRANSPORT
29 AIR TRANSPORT
30 SHIPPING
31 TRAVEL AGENTS
32 OTHER TRANSPORT AND COMMUNICATIONS

DIVISION 7

FINANCE AND BUSINESS SERVICES:—
33 INSURANCE
34 ACCOUNTANTS AND LEGAL SERVICES
35 REAL ESTATE
36 COMPUTER SERVICES
37 MANAGEMENT SERVICES
38 OTHER BUSINESS SERVICES

DIVISION 8

OTHER SERVICES:—
39 RECREATIONAL SERVICES
40 MEDICAL SERVICES
41 EDUCATIONAL SERVICES
42 REPAIRS OF CONSUMER GOODS
43 LAUNDRY
44 HAIRDRESSING AND BEAUTY PARLOURS
45 SCRAP METAL DEALERS
46 OTHER SERVICES

DIVISION 9

HOTELS AND CATERING:—
47 RESIDENTIAL ACCOMMODATION
48 LICENSED PREMISES
49 RESTAURANTS
50 OTHER CATERING

Rule 2.10

Form 2.6

The Insolvency Act 1986

Notice of Administration Order

R.2.10

Pursuant to Rule 2.10(3) of the Insolvency Rules 1986

For official use

To the Registrar of Companies

Company Number

Name of Company

Insert full name of company

Limited

I/We ______________________________

of ______________________________

give notice that an administration order was made against the above company on:

Insert date

Signed ______________ Dated ______________

Joint/Administrator(s)

Presenter's name, address and reference (if any): ______________

For Official Use

Insolvency Section | Post Room

Rule 2.10

Form 2.7

S.21(2)

The Insolvency Act 1986

Administration Order

Pursuant to Section 21(2) of the Insolvency Act 1986

For official use

To the Registrar of Companies

Company Number

Name of Company

Insert full name of company

Limited

I/We ______________________________

of ______________________________

____

____

administrator(s) of the company attach a copy of the administration order.

Signed ________________ Dated ________________

Presenter's name, address and reference (if any): ________________

For Official Use

Insolvency Section | Post Room

Form 2.8

Rule 2.11

Notice Requiring Preparation and Submission of Administration Statement of Affairs

(TITLE)

(a) Insert name of company

Take notice that you are required to prepare and submit to me a statement as to the affairs of (a)

(b) Insert date by which statement must be submitted

by (b)

(c) Insert names and addresses of other persons concerned

A similar notice has been sent to each of the following persons (c)

(d) Delete words in brackets if not applicable

Section 235 of the Insolvency Act 1986 places a duty on you (d) (as an officer of the company) to provide the administrator with information and attend upon him if required; I have to warn you that failure to submit the statement of affairs as required by this notice, or to co-operate with the administrator under section 235 of the Insolvency Act 1986, may make you liable to a fine and, for continued contravention, to a daily default fine.

Under paragraph 10 of Schedule 1 to the Company Directors Disqualification Act 1986 failure to submit a statement of affairs or to co-operate with the administrator under section 235 of the Insolvency Act 1986 are matters which may be taken into account by the court in determining whether a person is unfit to be an officer of or to be involved in the management of a company. Unfit conduct may result in a disqualification order being made by the court.

Dated ______________________________

Administrator (name and address)

Note:
Forms for the preparation of the statement of affairs
(a) may be obtained from the administrator on request; or
(b) are enclosed.

Rule 2.12 Form 2.9

Statement of Affairs

In the No. of 19
Statement as to the Affairs of

On the 19 The date of the administration order

Affidavit

This affidavit must be sworn before a solicitor or commissioner of oaths or an officer of the court duly authorised to administer oaths when you have completed the rest of this form

(a) Insert name and occupation

I (a) ____________________

____

(b) Insert full address

of (b) ____________________

____

(c) Insert date of administration order

make oath and say that the several pages exhibited hereto and attached marked __________ are to the best of my knowledge and belief a full, true and complete statement as to the affairs of the above named company as at (c) __________ the date of the administration order and that the said company carried on business as

____

____

____

Sworn at ____________________

Dated ____________________

Signature(s) ____________________

Before me ____________________

____

A solicitor or Commissioner of Oaths or duly authorised officer

The Solicitor or Commissioner is particularly requested, before swearing the affidavit, to make sure that the full name, address and description of the Deponent are stated, and to initial any crossings out or other alterations in the printed form. A deficiency in the affidavit in any of the above respects will mean that it is refused by the court, and will necessitate its being re-sworn.

Form 2.9 continued

A—Summary of Assets

ASSETS	Book Value £	Estimated to Realise £
Assets specifically pledged:—		
	£	
Assets not specifically pledged:—		
Estimated total assets available for preferential creditors	£	

Signature ____________________ Date ______________

Form 2.9 continued

A1—Summary of Liabilities

			Estimated to realise £
Estimated total assets available for preferential creditors (carried from page A)		£	
Liabilities Preferential creditors:—	£		
Estimated deficiency/surplus as regards preferential creditors		£	
Debts secured by a floating charge:—	£		
Estimated deficiency/surplus of assets available for non-preferential creditors		£	
Non-preferential claims:—	£		
Estimated deficiency/surplus as regards creditors		£	
Issued and called up capital:—	£		
Estimated total deficiency/surplus as regards members		£	

Signature ________________________ Date ____________

Form 2.9 continued

COMPANY CREDITORS

Note. You must identify creditors under hire-purchase, chattel leasing or conditional sale agreements *and* customers claiming amounts paid in advance of the supply of goods or services *and* creditors claiming retention of title over property in the company's possession.

Name of creditor or Claimant	Address (with postcode)	Amount of debt £	Details of any security held by creditor	Date security given	Value of security £

Signature ______________________ Date __________

Form 2.12

Rule 2.30

Report of Meeting of Creditors

(TITLE)

I ____

administrator of the company hereby report that [a] [an adjourned] meeting of creditors in the above matter was held at ________________________

____

____

on the ________ day of __________ 19____

at which:

(1) Proposals [Revised proposals] in the form hereto annexed were approved

(2) ____

____

____

____

were nominated to act as members of the creditors' committee

(3) The meeting declined to approve the proposals [revised proposals]

Dated this ________ day of __________ 19____

The Administrator

Form 2.16

Rule 2.53

Notice to Court of Resignation by Administrator Under Rule 2.53(1) of the Insolvency Rules 1986

(TITLE)

(a) Insert full name and address of administrator	I, (a)________________________________ ________________________________ ________________________________
(b) Insert date	the administrator of the above company give notice that I am resigning from the said office of administrator with effect from (b) ________________________________
(c) See Rule 2.53(1)	for the following reason(s): (c) ____________________ ________________________________ ________________________________ ________________________________
(d) the date must be at least 7 days before that stated at (b) above	I confirm that on (d) ________________ I gave notice to: (i) ____________________ (ii) ____________________ (iii) ____________________

being persons who under section 13(3) of the Insolvency Act 1986 are entitled to apply for a vacancy in the office of administrator to be filled, of my intention to resign as administrator.

Signed ____________________________

Dated ____________________________

Form 2.17

Rule 2.53

Notice to Court of Resignation by Administrator Under Rule 2.53(2) of the Insolvency Rules 1986

(TITLE)

(a) Insert full name and address of administrator	I, (a)____________________________ ____________________________
(b) Insert date	the administrator of the above company give notice that on (b) ____________, the court gave me leave to resign from the said office of administrator with effect from (b) ____________
(c) See Rule 2.53(2)	for the following reason(s): (c) ____________________ ____________________________ ____________________________ ____________________________ ____________________________
	and I hereby resign.
(d) The date must be at least 7 days before application was made to the court for leave to resign.	I confirm that on (d) ________________ I gave notice to: (i) ____________________ (ii) ____________________ (iii) ____________________
	being persons who under section 13(3) of the Insolvency Act 1986 are entitled to apply for a vacancy in the office of administrator to be filled, of my intention to apply to the court for leave to resign as administrator.

Signed ____________________

Dated ____________________

Form 2.18

The Insolvency Act 1986

Notice of Order to Deal with Charged Property

S.15(7)

Pursuant to Section 15(7) of the Insolvency Act 1986

To the Registrar of Companies

For official use

Company Number

Name of Company

Insert full name of company

Limited

I/We ____________________

of ____________________

____

____

*delete whichever is not applicable

administrator(s) of the company obtained an order for the disposal of charged property*/goods in possession of the company under a hire-purchase agreement on

insert date

An office copy of the said Court order is attached.

Signed ____________________ Dated ____________________

Presenter's name, address and reference (if any)

____

____

____

____

For Official Use

Insolvency Section | Post Room

Form 4.1

Rule 4.5

Statutory Demand under section 123(1)(a) or 222(1)(a) of the Insolvency Act 1986

Warning

- This is an **important** document. This demand must be dealt with **within 21 days** after its service upon the company or a winding-up order could be made in respect of the company.
- Please read the demand and notes carefully.

Notes for Creditor

- If the creditor is entitled to the debt by way of assignment, details of the original creditor and any intermediary assignees should be given in part B on page 3.
- If the amount of debt includes interest not previously notified to the company as included in its liability, details should be given, including the grounds upon which interest is charged. The amount of interest must be shown separately.
- Any other charge accruing due from time to time may be claimed. The amount or rate of the charge must be identified and the grounds on which it is claimed must be stated.
- In either case the amount claimed must be limited to that which has accrued due at the date of the demand.
- If signatory of the demand is a solicitor or other agent of the creditor the name of his/her firm should be given.

Demand

To ____

Address ____

____

This demand is served on you by the creditor:

Name __________________________

Address __________________________

____

The creditor claims that the company owes the sum of £______, full particulars of which are set out on page 2.

The creditor demands that the company do pay the above debt or secure or compound for it to the creditor's satisfaction.

Signature of individual ____________________

Name __________________________
(BLOCK LETTERS)

Date __________________________

*Position with or relationship to creditor ____________________

____

*Delete if signed by the creditor himself

* I am authorised to make this demand on the creditor's behalf.

Address ____________________________________

____

Tel. No. ____________________ Ref.______________

N.B. The person making this demand must complete the whole of this page, page 2 and parts A and B (as applicable) on page 3.

Form 4.1 continued

Form 4.1 contd.

Particulars of Debt.
(These particulars must include (a) when the debt was incurred, (b) the consideration for the debt (or if there is no consideration the way in which it arose) and (c) the amount due as at the date of this demand.)

Notes for Creditor
Please make sure that you have read the notes on page 1 before completing this page.

Note:
If space is insufficient continue on reverse of page 3 and clearly indicate on this page that you are doing so.

Form 4.1 continued

Form 4.1 contd.

PART A

The individual or individuals to whom any communication regarding this demand may be addressed is/are:—

Name ______________ (BLOCK LETTERS)	
Address ______________	
______________	
Telephone Number ______________	
Reference ______________	

PART B

For completion if the creditor is entitled to the debt by way of assignment

	Name	Date(s) of Assignment
Original creditor		
Assignees		

How to comply with a statutory demand
If the company wishes to avoid a winding-up petition being presented it must pay the debt shown on page 1, particulars of which are set out on page 2 of this notice, within the period of **21 days after** its service upon the company. Alternatively, the company can attempt to come to a settlement with the creditor. To do this the company should:

- inform the individual (or one of the individuals) named in part A above immediately that it is willing and able to offer security for the debt to the creditor's satisfaction; or
- inform the individual (or one of the individuals) named in Part A immediately that it is willing and able to compound for the debt to the creditor's satisfaction.

If the company disputes the demand in whole or in part it should:

- contact the individual (or one of the individuals) named in part A immediately.

REMEMBER! The company has only 21 days after the date of service on it of this document before the creditor may present a winding-up petition.

Form 4.3

Rule 4.7, 4.12 Affidavit Verifying Winding-up Petition

(TITLE)

(a) Insert name and address of person making oath	I (a)
	Make oath and say as follows:—
(b) Delete if affidavit not made by Petitioner in person	1. (b) I am the Petitioner. The statements in the Petition now produced and shown to me marked "A" are (c) [true] [true to the best of my knowledge, information and belief].
(c) Delete as applicable	1. (d) I am (e) of the Petitioner.
(d) Delete if affidavit is made by Petitioner in person	2. (d) I am duly authorised by the Petitioner to make this affidavit on (c) [its] [his] behalf.
(e) State capacity eg. director, secretary, solicitor etc	3. (d) I have been concerned in the matters giving rise to the Petition and have the requisite knowledge of the matters referred to in the Petition because (f)
(f) State means of knowledge of matters sworn to in affidavit	4. (d) The statements in the Petition now produced and shown to me marked "A" are (c) [true] [true to the best of my knowledge, information and belief].

Sworn at

Form 4.4

Rule 4.9

Affidavit of Service of Winding-Up Petition at Registered Office

(TITLE)

Note: If the petition was served on an officer or an employee of the company use Part A of this form. If it was served on a person authorised to accept service on behalf of the company use Part B. If it was served by depositing it at the registered office use Part C.

I (a)

make oath and say as follows:—

(a) Insert name, address and description of person making oath
(b) Insert date
(c) Delete as applicable

Part A.
That I did on (b)
serve the above-named company with a sealed copy of the petition now produced and shown to me marked "A" by handing the same to ______________ (c) [who acknowledged himself to be] [who is to the best of my knowledge, information and belief] (c) [a director] [an officer] [an employee] of the company at (d)

the registered office of the said company.

OR
Part B.
That I did on (b)
serve the above-named company with a sealed copy of the petition now produced and shown to me marked "A" by handing the same to __________________ who acknowledged to me that he was authorised to accept service of documents on behalf of the company at (d)

(d) Insert address of registered office

the registered office of the said company.

OR
Part C.
That I did on (b)
having failed to find any officer, employee or other person authorised to accept service of documents on behalf of the company, deposit a sealed copy of the petition now produced and shown to me marked "A" at (d)

(e) Insert where the petition was left in such a way that it was likely to come to the attention of a person attending the registered office e.g. on a desk, through the letter box, affixed to the above, etc.

the registered office of the said company by leaving it (e)

Sworn at

Form 4.5

Rule 4.9

Affidavit of Service of Winding-Up Petition other than at Registered Office or on an Oversea Company

Note: If the petition was served on an officer or on an employee of the company use Part A of this form. If it was served on a person authorised to accept service on behalf of the company use Part B. If the petition was served on an oversea company use Part C only

(a) Insert name, address and description of person making oath

(b) State reason why petition has been served at an address other than a registered office

(c) Insert date

(d) Delete as applicable

(e) Insert address at which service effected

(f) Insert class of postage

(g) Insert name

(TITLE)

I (a)

make oath and say as follows

1. (b)

Part A

2. That I did on (c) serve the above named company with a sealed copy of the petition now produced and shown to me marked "A" by handing the same to (d) [who acknowledged himself to be] [who is to the best of my knowledge, information and belief] (d) [a director] [an officer] [an employee] of the company at (e)

(d) [the company's last known principal place of business in England and Wales] [a place where the company carried on business in England and Wales]

or

Part B

2. That I did on (c) serve, the above-named company with a sealed copy of the petition now produced and shown to me marked "A" by handing the same to who acknowledged to me that he was authorised to accept service of documents on behalf of the company at (e)

(d) [the company's last known principal place of business in England and Wales] [a place where the company carried on business in England and Wales].

or

Part C

That I did on (c) serve the above-named company with a sealed copy of the petition now produced and shown to me marked "A" by (d) [leaving it] [sending it by (f) post] to (e)

(d) [the address of (g)
whose name has been delivered to the Registrar of Companies as a person authorised to accept on the said company's behalf service of process and any notices required to be served on it] [a place of business established by the said company in Great Britain].

Sworn at

Form 4.6

Rule 4.11 Advertisement of Winding-Up Petition

(TITLE)

(a) Insert registered office address of company, or (if an unregistered company) the address of its principal place of business, or (if an oversea company) the address at which service of the petition was effected.

(b) Insert date

(c) Insert name and address of petitioner.

(d) Delete where the petition is presented by the company itself, or by a person who is not a creditor or contributory.

(e) Delete as applicable

(f) Insert date, which should be the business day before that appointed for the hearing

(g) Where applicable insert name and address of solicitor

A Petition to wind up the above-named company of (a)

presented on (b)

by (c)

(d) [Claiming to be a (e) [creditor] [contributory] of the company] will be heard at (e) [The Royal Courts of Justice, Strand, London WC2A 2LL] [________________ County Court at ________________] [________________ District Registry at ________________]

Date ____

Time ____ hours
(or as soon thereafter as the petition can be heard)

Any person intending to appear on the hearing of the petition (whether to support or oppose it) must give notice of intention to do so to the petitioner or his/its solicitor in accordance with Rule 4.16 by 16.00 hours on (f)

The petitioner's solicitor is (g)

Dated ____

Form 4.9

Rule 4.16 Notice of Intention to Appear on Petition

(TITLE)

(a) Insert date — Winding-up petition presented on (a) ______________________

to be heard on (a) ______________________

(b) Insert full name and address, or if a firm, the name of the firm and address — Take notice that (b) ______________________

____

____

(c) Delete as applicable — (c) [a creditor of the above-named company for £ ________] [a contributory of the above-named company holding ________ shares in the company] intends to appear on the hearing of the above-mentioned petition to (c) [support] [oppose] it.

Signed ______________________

Dated ______________________

Position with or relationship to (c) [creditor] [contributory]

(d) If creditor or contributory's solicitor or other agent please give name and address of firm and insert name(s) and address(es) of petitioner(s) or petitioner(s) solicitor — (d) ______________________

____

____

____

To (d) ______________________

____

____

____

Telephone No ______________________

Reference No ______________________

Form 4.10

Rule 4.17

List of Persons Intending to Appear on the Hearing of the Petition

(TITLE)

Winding-up petition presented on
The following persons have given notice that they intend to appear on the hearing of the above-mentioned petition on ______________________

Name and Address	Name and Address of Solicitors if any	Amount owed to creditor £	Number of shares held by contributory	Whether supporting or opposing the petition

Form 4.11

Rule 4.20 Order for Winding Up by the Court

(TITLE)

(a) Insert name and address of petitioner (as appropriate) "the company" or "... a creditor of the company" or "... a contributory of the company"

Upon the petition of (a)

presented to this court on

And upon hearing

And upon reading the evidence

(b) Insert full name of the company

It is ordered that (b)
be wound up by this court under the provisions of the Insolvency Act 1986

(c) Insert names of all parties to be awarded their costs

(d) Insert any terms concerning costs

And it is ordered that the costs of (c) ______________________
of the said petition be paid out of the assets of the company (d)

Dated ______________________

*Delete as appropriate

Note: [The] [One of the]* official receiver(s)* attached to the court is by virtue of this order liquidator of the company.

Form 4.14

Rule 4.22

Petition by Contributory

(TITLE)

(a) Insert title of court	To (a)
(b) Insert full name(s) and address(es) of petitioner(s)	The petition of (b)
(c) Insert full name of company subject to petition	1. (c)
(d) Insert date of incorporation	(hereinafter called "the company") was incorporated on (d) under the Companies Act 19
(e) Insert address of registered office	2. The registered office of the company is at (e)
	3. The nominal capital of the company is £ divided into shares of £ each. The amount of the capital paid up or credited as paid up is £
(f) Delete as applicable	The petitioner(s) is/are the holder(s) of shares of £ each. Such shares (f) [were allotted to him/them on the incorporation of the company] [have been registered in his/their name(s) for more than 6 months in the last 18 months] [devolved upon him/them through the death of the former holder of the shares].
	4. The principal objects for which the company was established are as follows:—
	and other objects stated in the memorandum of association of the company.
(g) Set out the grounds on which the petition is presented	5. (g)

6. In the circumstances it is just and equitable that the company should be wound up.

The petitioner(s) therefore pray(s) as follows:—

(1) that (c)

may be wound up by the court under the provisions of the Insolvency Act 1986

OR

(2) that such other order may be made as the court thinks fit.

Form 4.14 continued

Note:
It is intended to serve this petition on:—

ENDORSEMENT

This petition having been presented to the court on____________________
let all parties attend before the Registrar in Chambers on

Date ____

Time ____________________________________ hours

Place ____
for directions to be given.

The solicitor(s) for the petitioner is/are:

Name ____

Address ______________________________________

____

Telephone No. __________________________________

Reference ______________________________________

(h) Delete if London agents not instructed

(h) [Whose London agents are:—

Name ____

Address ______________________________________

____

Telephone No. __________________________________

Reference ____________________________________]

Form 4.14A

Rule 4.25A

Notice to Official Receiver of appointment of Provisional Liquidator

(TITLE)

(a) Insert address

To the Official Receiver of the Court (a)

Order pronounced this ______________ day of _______________ 19 _____ by Mr

(b) Insert "the official receiver" or, if an insolvency practitioner is to be appointed, his full name and address (including name of firm if appropriate)

for the appointment of (b)

as provisional liquidator of the under-named company prior to any winding-up order being made.

Name of company:

Registered office of company:

(c) Insert full name, address, telephone number and reference (if any)

Petitioner: (c)

Petitioner's solicitors: (c)

Rule 4.26 **Form 4.15**

Order of Appointment of Provisional Liquidator

(TITLE)

Mr Registrar in Chambers

(a) Give full name and address of applicants

Upon the application of (a)

And upon hearing

And upon reading the petition to wind up the above named company and the evidence

(b) If a person other than the official receiver is to be appointed delete the words in [ ] otherwise insert the amount to be deposited

It is ordered that (b) [upon the sum of £ _________ being deposited by the applicant with the official receiver] the following person is appointed provisional liquidator of the above-named company.

(c) Insert either "the official receiver" or if an insolvency practitioner is to be appointed, his full name and address

Name of provisional liquidator (c)____________________

Address (if applicable)____

____

____

And it is ordered that:—

(d) Insert details of the functions to be carried out by the provisional liquidator in relation to the company's affairs

(d)

Dated____

NOTICE TO OFFICERS OF COMPANY

You are required by Section 235 of the Insolvency Act 1986 to give the provisional liquidator all the information as he may reasonably require relating to the company's property and affairs and to attend upon him at such times as he may reasonably require.

Date ____

Form 7.1

Rule 7.2

Originating Application

(TITLE)

Between
Applicant ______________________________
and
Respondent ______________________________

(a) Insert name and address of respondent

Let (a)

attend

before the Judge/Registrar on:—

Date ______________________________

Time ______________ hours

Place ______________________________

(b) Insert name of applicant

On the hearing of an application by (b)
the applicant for an order in the following terms:—

(c) State the terms of the order to which the applicant claims to be entitled

(c)

The grounds on which the applicant claims to be entitled to the order are:—

(d) Set out grounds or refer to an affidavit in support

(d)

The names and addresses of the persons upon whom it is intended to serve this application are:—

(e) State the names and addresses of the persons intended to be served

(e)

OR

It is not intended to serve any person with this application.

(f) State the applicant's address for service

The applicant's address for service is: (f)

Dated ______________________________

Signed: ______________________________
(SOLICITOR FOR THE) APPLICANT

If you do not attend, the court may make such order as it thinks fit.

Form 7.2

Rule 7.2

Ordinary Application

(TITLE)

Between

Applicant ____________________

and

Respondent ____________________

Take notice that I intend to apply to the Judge/Registrar on:

Date ____________________

Time ____________________ hours

Place ____________________

(a) State nature and grounds of application

for (a)

Signed: ____________________

(SOLICITOR FOR THE) APPLICANT

My/Our address for service is:—

(b) Give the name(s) and address(es) of the person(s) (including the respondent) on whom it is intended to serve the application

To: (b)

OR

It is not intended to serve any person with this application

If you do not attend, the court will make such order as it thinks fit

INDEX